COMPLEX LITIGATION

CASES AND MATERIALS ON ADVANCED CIVIL PROCEDURE

Fourth Edition

By

Richard L. Marcus

Horace O. Coil ('57) Chair in Litigation,
University of California
Hastings College of the Law

Edward F. Sherman

Professor of Law,
Tulane Law School

AMERICAN CASEBOOK SERIES®

THOMSON
™
WEST

Mat #40156522

American Casebook Series and West Group are trademarks
registered in the U.S. Patent and Trademark Office.

COPYRIGHT © 1985, 1992 WEST PUBLISHING CO.
COPYRIGHT © 1998 WEST GROUP
© 2004 West, a Thomson business
   610 Opperman Drive
   P.O. Box 64526
   St. Paul, MN 55164–0526
   1–800–328–9352

Printed in the United States of America

ISBN 0–314–14734–9

*TEXT IS PRINTED ON 10% POST
CONSUMER RECYCLED PAPER*

Preface

In the nearly 20 years since the first edition of this book was published, complex litigation has proliferated and evolved. Large-scale related litigation, sometimes coordinated by the Judicial Panel on Multidistrict Litigation, has become more commonplace. Class actions have achieved a higher profile; they are said to constitute bread-and-butter activities for many lawyers. Class actions have also achieved a political prominence that prompted numerous legislative proposals in Congress and in state legislatures.

These changes have contributed to the inclusion of a course on complex litigation in the curricula of most law schools, which has confirmed that complex litigation is a subject worthy of serious study. We attempt in this fourth edition to provide 21st century materials for continuing this study.

Over the past 20 years much has changed, and so has this edition. More pertinently, since the third edition appeared in 1998 there have been a number of important developments—several in the last year or so—that are featured in this new edition. They include many new principal cases, as well as coverage of a number of other developments. For example, in 2003, the first substantive amendments to Rule 23 went into effect, as did a comprehensive reworking of Rule 53 on special masters. In 2004, a new and expanded fourth edition of the Manual for Complex Litigation appeared. During the current Congress the Class Action Fairness Act has come close to passage, and it may become law in the relatively near future.

Materials in this edition support thorough consideration of these developments. The class action chapter, in particular, has been substantially revised. Among other things, it now includes a new section on overlapping class actions to address the phenomenon of "dueling class actions" in both state and federal courts. Coverage of consumer class actions and choice of law issues has been added. Throughout the chapter, materials have been updated. Elsewhere in the book, additions reflect developments since the third edition. A new section in Chapter III addresses federal courts' use of the All Writs Act to enjoin overlapping suits in state court. A new section in Chapter V examines the increasingly important topic of discovery of electronically stored information. A new "exploding tire" litigation confidentiality case offers this important topic in an important contemporary context. Chapter VIII on preclusion has been augmented by addition of the *Stephenson v. Dow* decision of the Second Circuit, which the Supreme Court affirmed by a 4–4 vote. Chapter IX addresses the still uncertain course of class arbitrations after the Supreme Court's 2003 *Bazzle* decision.

Despite these significant additions, users will find that the book has not ballooned. To the contrary, the fourth edition is actually shorter than the third edition. We have also removed coverage of some topics that seemed no longer of comparable importance to the ones we have added, and in other places have compressed coverage of topics that formerly warranted full sections into much briefer note material.

Altogether, we believe that this book will serve the needs of students and teachers grappling with 21st century complex litigation challenges. Indeed, because this casebook attempts a comprehensive view of complex litigation, we hope it will provide a useful resource for students after they enter practice.

As in prior editions, we have principally focused on litigation in the federal courts, and have edited cases substantially to improve their readability. Ellipses are used when any portion of text is deleted, but not when case or source citations are omitted. We have taken out footnotes unless the seem to add something significant, and left in the original number of the ones that remain.

We have attempted, subject to the constraints of our publication schedule, to be as current as possible. As a general matter, we have tried to include developments through March, 2004.

We are indebted to many people for help and guidance. Over the years, many other teachers have been good enough to share with us their thoughts about these topics, and provide very helpful pointers on related developments that we have incorporated into this edition. We hope that this assistance will continue. We are grateful to our colleagues, who have offered background information about unfamiliar areas of the law that as well as insights and suggestions that we have employed. We are also indebted to our students, who have over the years raised many interesting and challenging points. We owe a special debt to Corey Parson of Hastings for invaluable research assistance on this edition. Finally, we want to thank our spouses, Andrea Saltzman and Alice Sherman, for their advice, help, and patience.

We are also indebted to the copyright holders identified below for permission to reprint excerpts from the following copyrighted materials (listed in the order they appear in the book), in addition to the copyright holders of the cartoons we reprint, which are identified where the cartoons appear. Except for granting us permission to reprint in this book, the following copyright holders have retained all rights:

Chayes, The Role of the Judge in Public Law Litigation, 89 Harv. L. Rev. 1143 (1976), copyright © 1976, by Abram Chayes.

RAND Institute for Civil Justice, Class Action Dilemmas: Pursuing Public Goals for Private Gain, copyright © 2000, RAND Corp.

Sherman, Aggregate Disposition of Related Cases: The Policy Issues, 10 Review of Litigation 231 (1991), copyright © 1991, The Review of Litigation.

Rheingold, The MER/29 Story—An Instance of Successful Mass Disaster Litigation, 56 Calif. L. Rev. 116 (1968), copyright © 1968, California Law Review, Inc.

Hansel, Extreme Litigation: An Interview with Judge Wm. Terrell Hodges, Chairman of the Judicial Panel on Multidistrict Litigation, 2 Me. Bar J. 16 (2004), copyright © 2004, Gregory P. Hansel.

Weigel, The Judicial Panel on Multidistrict Litigation, Transferor Courts and Transferee Courts, 78 F.R.D. 575 (1978), copyright © 1978, West Publishing Co.

Resnik, Managerial Judges, 96 Harv. L. Rev. 374 (1982), copyright © 1982, Harvard Law Review Association.

Peckham, A Judicial Response to the Cost of Litigation: Case Management, Two-Stage Discovery Planning and Alternative Dispute Resolution, 37 Rutgers L. Rev. 253 (1985), copyright © 1985, Hon. Robert F. Peckham.

Schwarzer, Reforming Jury Trials, 132 F.R.D. 575 (1991), copyright © 1991, The University of Chicago.

Buxton & Glover, Managing a Big Case Down to Size, 15 Litigation 22 (1989), copyright © 1989, Section of Litigation, American Bar Assocation.

Parker, Streamlining Complex Cases, 10 Review of Litigation 547 (1991), copyright © 1991, The Review of Litigation.

McCrystal & Muschari, Will Electronic Technology Take the Witness Stand?, 11 U. Tol. L. Rev. 239 (1980), copyright © 1980, University of Toledo Law Review.

Murray, Rau & Sherman, Materials on Dispute Resolution (1992), copyright © by the authors.

Mnookin, Beyond Litigation, 23 Stanford Lawyer 5 (Spring/Summer 1989), copyright © 1989, The Stanford Lawyer.

Green, Growth of the Mini-Trial, 9 Litigation 12 (Fall 1982), copyright © 1982, Section of Litigation, American Bar Association.

Fitzpatrick, The Center for Claims Resolution, 53 Law & Contemp. Probs. 13 (1990), copyright © 1990, Duke University School of Law.

RICHARD L. MARCUS
EDWARD F. SHERMAN

June 2004

*

Summary of Contents

	Page
PREFACE	iii
TABLE OF CASES	xvii
TABLE OF AUTHORITIES	xxxvii

Chapter I. The Nature of Complex Litigation — **1**

A. The Metamorphosis of Litigation — 2
B. The Aggregation Debate — 9
C. Evaluating Innovation in Litigation — 15

Chapter II. Joinder and Structure of Suit in a Unitary Federal Forum — **24**

A. Permissive Party Joinder — 24
B. Compulsory Party Joinder — 45
C. Intervention — 62
D. Consequences of Failure to Join — 86

Chapter III. Disposition of Duplicative or Related Litigation — **103**

A. Multiple Proceedings in Federal Court — 104
B. Dual State–Federal Proceedings — 164
C. Bankruptcy Proceedings — 209

Chapter IV. Class Actions — **218**

A. Ethical Considerations in Class Action Practice — 223
B. Prerequisites to a Class Action — 230
C. Types of Class Actions Maintainable — 298
D. Settlement Class Actions — 372
E. Overlapping Class Actions — 391
F. Class Action Remedies — 405
G. Problems of Jurisdiction and Choice of Law — 412
H. Prejudgment Notice to Class Members — 440
I. Intervention and Opt–Out — 448
J. Statutes of Limitations — 460
K. Communications With Unnamed Members of Class — 470
L. Mootness — 481
M. Decertification and Modification of Class Definition — 497
N. Judicial Control of Settlement — 509

Chapter V. Discovery — **541**

A. Overview of Large Case Discovery — 542

Page

B. E–Discovery --- 546
C. Document Preservation------------------------------------ 561
D. Discovery Confidentiality and Protective Orders ------------- 571
E. Preserving Privilege Protection ------------------------------ 594

Chapter VI. Judicial Control of Pretrial Litigation ----------- **626**
A. The Case Management Movement ------------------------------- 626
B. Sanctions --- 644
C. Reliance on Judicial Surrogates------------------------------- 653
D. Judicial Selection of Counsel--------------------------------- 664
E. Attorneys' Fees Awards--------------------------------------- 680
F. Recusal -- 717

Chapter VII. Trying Complex Cases-------------------------------- **731**
A. Judicial Management of the Trial ----------------------------- 734
B. Striking Jury Demands --------------------------------------- 737
C. Improved Trial Methods-------------------------------------- 743
D. Bifurcation and Trifurcation --------------------------------- 762
E. Trial by Statistics-- 777

**Chapter VIII. Preclusive Effects of Judgments in Complex
      Litigation** -- **786**
A. Claim Preclusion (Res Judicata) ------------------------------ 786
B. Issue Preclusion in Complex Litigation----------------------- 848

Chapter IX. Alternatives to Litigation---------------------------- **883**
A. Extra–Judicial Mechanisms ---------------------------------- 884
B. Judicial Mechanisms--- 938

INDEX --- 947

Table of Contents

	Page
PREFACE	iii
TABLE OF CASES	xvii
TABLE OF AUTHORITIES	xxxvii

Chapter I. The Nature of Complex Litigation 1

A. The Metamorphosis of Litigation 2

Chayes, The Role of the Judge in Public Law Litigation 3

Rand Institute for Civil Justice, Class Action Dilemmas: Pursuing Public Goals for Private Gain 7

B. The Aggregation Debate 9

Sherman, Aggregate Disposition of Related Cases: The Policy Issues 10

C. Evaluating Innovation in Litigation 15

   1. Judicial Involvement and Management 15

   2. Dispute Resolution as Goal of Civil Litigation 17

   3. Combined or Individual Treatment 18

   4. Broad v. Specific Rules 19

   5. Impact of Procedure on Substance 20

   6. Modeling Procedures on Complex Cases 21

   7. Federalism Concerns 22

Chapter II. Joinder and Structure of Suit in a Unitary Federal Forum 24

A. Permissive Party Joinder 24

Mosley v. General Motors Corp. 24

Brunet, A Study in the Allocation of Scarce Resources: The Efficiency of Federal Intervention Criteria 28

Notes and Questions 32

Stanford v. Tennessee Valley Authority 34

Notes and Questions 37

Hall v. E.I. Du Pont De Nemours & Co., Inc. 39

Chance v. E.I. Du Pont De Nemours & Co., Inc. 39

Notes and Questions 43

B. Compulsory Party Joinder 45

Eldredge v. Carpenters 46 Northern California Counties JATC 45

Notes and Questions 49

The Rule 19(b) Determination 54

Supplemental Jurisdiction for Joinder of Additional Parties 57

Joinder Problems Involving State Governmental Entities 60

Page

C. Intervention ----- 62
    Brunet, A Study in the Allocation of Scarce Resources: The
      Efficiency of Federal Intervention Criteria ----- 63
    Planned Parenthood v. Citizens for Community Action ----- 64
    Notes and Questions ----- 67
    United States v. Reserve Mining Co. ----- 73
    Notes and Questions ----- 82
D. Consequences of Failure to Join ----- 86
    Martin v. Wilks ----- 86
    Notes and Questions ----- 98

Chapter III. Disposition of Duplicative or Related Litigation ----- **103**
A. Multiple Proceedings in Federal Court ----- 104
    1. Stay Orders or Injunctions Against Prosecution of Suits in
       Other Federal Courts ----- 104
       William Gluckin & Co. v. International Playtex Corp. ----- 104
       Notes and Questions ----- 108
       Semmes Motors, Inc. v. Ford Motor Co. ----- 109
       Notes and Questions ----- 114
    2. Pretrial Consolidation ----- 115
       Katz v. Realty Equities Corp. of New York ----- 116
       Rheingold, The Mer/29 Story—An Instance of Successful
         Mass Disaster Litigation ----- 123
       Notes and Questions ----- 125
    3. Transfer to a More Convenient Forum ----- 128
       Ginsey Industries, Inc. v. I.T.K. Plastics, Inc. ----- 128
       Notes and Questions ----- 130
    4. Dismissal for Forum Non Conveniens ----- 132
       De Melo v. Lederle Laboratories ----- 132
       Notes and Questions ----- 140
    5. Transfer Under Multidistrict Litigation Procedures ----- 142
       Hansel, Extreme Litigation: An Interview With Judge Wm.
         Terrell Hodges, Chairman of the Judicial Panel on Multi-
         district Litigation ----- 143
       In re Aviation Products Liability Litigation ----- 146
       Notes and Questions ----- 151
       Weigel, The Judicial Panel on Multidistrict Litigation,
         Transferor Courts and Transferee Courts ----- 154
       In re Factor VIII or IX Concentrate Blood Products Litiga-
         tion ----- 156
       Notes and Questions ----- 158
B. Dual State–Federal Proceedings ----- 164
    1. Federal Court's Decline of Jurisdiction or Grant of Stay
       Order ----- 165
       a. Traditional Abstention (Pullman and Burford) ----- 165
         BT Investment Managers, Inc. v. Lewis ----- 165
         Notes and Questions ----- 168
       b. Equitable Abstention under Younger v. Harris ----- 171
         Pennzoil Co. v. Texaco, Inc. ----- 171
         Notes and Questions ----- 180

Page

B. Dual State–Federal Proceedings—Continued
    c. Stay of Federal Suit in Interests of "Wise Judicial Administration" 184
        Life–Link International, Inc. v. Lalla 184
        Notes and Questions 187
    2. Federal Court's Injunction Against Prosecution of State Proceedings (Anti–Injunction Act) 190
        Standard Microsystems Corp. v. Texas Instruments, Inc. 191
        Notes and Questions 196
    3. All Writs Act as Authority for Federal Court Orders Relating to State–Court Suits 199
        In re Baldwin–United Corp. 199
        Notes and Questions 205
C. Bankruptcy Proceedings 209
    The Gathering Power of Bankruptcy Courts 213

Chapter IV. Class Actions **218**
A. Ethical Considerations in Class Action Practice 223
    Kline v. Coldwell, Banker & Co. 223
    Notes and Questions 226
B. Prerequisites to a Class Action 230
    1. Adequate Definition of the Class 231
        Simer v. Rios 231
        Notes and Questions 237
    2. Numerosity 241
        Board of Education of Township High School v. Climatemp, Inc. 241
        Notes and Questions 243
    3. Commonality 245
        Blackie v. Barrack 246
        Notes and Questions 254
        Smilow v. Southwestern Bell Mobile Systems, Inc. 257
        Notes and Questions 263
    4. Typicality 267
        General Telephone Company of the Southwest v. Falcon 267
        Notes and Questions 274
        La Mar v. H & B Novelty & Loan Co. 278
        Notes and Questions 282
    5. Representativeness 285
        Hansberry v. Lee 285
        Notes and Questions 287
        Peil v. National Semiconductor Corp. 290
        Notes and Questions 292
C. Types of Class Actions Maintainable 298
    1. Rule 23(b)(1)(A)—"Incompatible Standards" Class Actions .. 298
    2. Rule 23(b)(1)(B)—"Limited Fund" Class Actions 302
        Ortiz v. Fibreboard Corp. 302
        Notes and Questions 314
    3. Rule 23(b)(2) Classes 318
        In re Monumental Life Ins. Co. 318
        Notes and Questions 326

Page

C. Types of Class Actions Maintainable—Continued
    4. Rule 23(b)(3) Classes 330
        Jenkins v. Raymark Industries, Inc. 331
        Notes and Questions 336
        Castano v. The American Tobacco Co. 340
        Notes and Questions 353
    5. Defendant Class Actions 359
        Thillens, Inc. v. Community Currency Exchange Association of Illinois 359
        Notes and Questions 366
        Timing of Class Certification Decisions 368
        Timing of Appeals From Class Certification Decisions 370
D. Settlement Class Actions 372
    Amchem Products, Inc. v. Windsor 373
    Notes and Questions 387
E. Overlapping Class Actions 391
    In re Diet Drugs 391
    Notes and Questions 400
F. Class Action Remedies 405
    Simer v. Rios 406
    Notes and Questions 408
G. Problems of Jurisdiction and Choice of Law 412
    Phillips Petroleum Co. v. Shutts 412
    Notes and Questions 425
    Subject Matter Jurisdiction Limitations on State–Law Class Actions 427
    In re Bridgestone/Firestone, Inc. 429
    Notes and Questions 435
H. Prejudgment Notice to Class Members 440
    Eisen v. Carlisle & Jacquelin 440
    Notes and Questions 443
I. Intervention and Opt–Out 448
    Woolen v. Surtran Taxicabs, Inc. 448
    Notes and Questions 455
J. Statutes of Limitations 460
    Crown Cork & Seal Co. v. Parker 462
    Notes and Questions 465
K. Communications With Unnamed Members of Class 470
    Gulf Oil Co. v. Bernard 470
    Kleiner v. First National Bank of Atlanta 473
    Notes and Questions 475
    Discovery From Unnamed Class Members 479
    Notes and Questions 480
L. Mootness 481
    Deposit Guaranty National Bank v. Roper 481
    United States Parole Commission v. Geraghty 484
    Notes and Questions 494
M. Decertification and Modification of Class Definition 497
    Payne v. Travenol Laboratories, Inc. 497
    Notes and Questions 507
N. Judicial Control of Settlement 509

Page

N. Judicial Control of Settlement ---- 509
   Parker v. Anderson ---- 511
   Notes and Questions ---- 514
   In re Prudential Insurance Co. Sales Practices Litigation ---- 519
   Notes and Questions ---- 533
   Distributing the Settlement Funds ---- 539

Chapter V. Discovery ---- **541**
A. Overview of Large Case Discovery ---- 542
B. E–Discovery ---- 546
   Zubulake v. UBS Warburg LLC ---- 546
   Notes and Questions ---- 556
C. Document Preservation ---- 561
   Nation–Wide Check Corp. v. Forest Hills Distributors, Inc. ---- 561
   Notes and Questions ---- 566
D. Discovery Confidentiality and Protective Orders ---- 571
   Seattle Times Co. v. Rhinehart ---- 574
   Notes and Questions ---- 579
   Chicago Tribune Co. v. Bridgestone/Firestone, Inc. ---- 582
   Notes and Questions ---- 590
E. Preserving Privilege Protection ---- 594
   Transamerica Computer Co. v. International Business Machines Corp. ---- 595
   Notes and Questions ---- 602
   United States v. American Telephone & Telegraph Co. ---- 606
   Notes and Questions ---- 610
   Berkey Photo, Inc. v. Eastman Kodak Co. ---- 612
   Notes and Questions ---- 616
   Rhone–Poulenc Rorer, Inc. v. Home Indemnity Co. ---- 619
   Notes and Questions ---- 623

Chapter VI. Judicial Control of Pretrial Litigation ---- **626**
A. The Case Management Movement ---- 626
   Resnik, Managerial Judges ---- 628
   Peckham, A Judicial Response to the Cost of Litigation: Case Management, Two–Stage Discovery Planning and Alternative Dispute Resolution ---- 631
   Notes and Questions ---- 634
   Judicial Settlement Promotion ---- 639
   Notes and Questions ---- 641
B. Sanctions ---- 644
   Chapman v. Pacific Telephone & Telegraph Co. ---- 644
   Notes and Questions ---- 649
C. Reliance on Judicial Surrogates ---- 653
   Cobell v. Norton ---- 654
   Notes and Questions ---- 660
D. Judicial Selection of Counsel ---- 664
   McAllister v. Guterma ---- 664
   Notes and Questions ---- 666
   In re Fine Paper Antitrust Litigation ---- 669
   Notes and Questions ---- 675

	Page
E. Attorneys' Fees Awards	680
1. Authority to Award Attorneys' Fees	681
2. Determining the Amount to Be Awarded	685
a. The Emergence of the Lodestar	686
Hensley v. Eckerhart	687
Notes and Questions	697
b. The Challenge to the Lodestar	703
In re Activision Securities Litigation	703
Matter of Superior Beverage/Glass Container Consolidated Pretrial	706
Notes and Questions	712
F. Recusal	717
United States v. State of Alabama	717
In re International Business Machines Corp.	721
Notes and Questions	726
Chapter VII. Trying Complex Cases	**731**
A. Judicial Management of the Trial	734
Notes and Questions	735
B. Striking Jury Demands	737
Notes and Questions	740
C. Improved Trial Methods	743
Schwarzer, Reforming Jury Trials	743
1. Jury "Empowerment"	745
Notes and Questions	747
2. Use of Technology	748
Notes and Questions	751
3. Alternatives to In–Court Testimony	755
Notes and Questions	756
4. Limiting the Amount of Evidence and Duration of Trial	758
MCI Communications Corp. v. American Telephone and Telegraph Co.	758
Notes and Questions	760
D. Bifurcation and Trifurcation	762
Symbolic Control, Inc. v. International Business Machines Corp.	762
Notes and Questions	765
In re Bendectin Litigation	768
Notes and Questions	773
E. Trial by Statistics	777
Notes and Questions	780
Chapter VIII. Preclusive Effects of Judgments in Complex Litigation	**786**
A. Claim Preclusion (Res Judicata)	786
1. Persons or Entities Bound by Prior Judgment	787
Tyus v. Schoemehl	788
Notes and Questions	797
2. The Effect of Judgments in Class Actions	803
Matsushita Elec. Indus. Co. v. Epstein	803
Notes and Questions	816
Stephenson v. Dow Chemical Co.	819

Page

A. Claim Preclusion (Res Judicata)—Continued
    Notes and Questions ---- 827
    Cooper v. Federal Reserve Bank of Richmond ---- 831
    Notes and Questions ---- 838
    Goff v. Menke ---- 841
    Notes and Questions ---- 844
B. Issue Preclusion in Complex Litigation ---- 848
  1. Persons or Entities Bound ---- 848
    In re Nissan Motor Corp. Antitrust Litigation ---- 848
    Notes and Questions ---- 853
    Hardy v. Johns–Manville Sales Corp. ---- 854
    Notes and Questions ---- 856
  2. Which Issues Were Actually Determined? ---- 857
    Friends for All Children v. Lockheed Aircraft ---- 857
    Notes and Questions ---- 863
    Hardy v. Johns–Manville Sales Corp. ---- 864
    Notes and Questions ---- 873
    Fraley v. American Cyanamid Co. ---- 877
    Notes and Questions ---- 880
    Efforts to Blunt Estoppel by Vacating Judgments ---- 881

Chapter IX. Alternatives to Litigation ---- **883**
A. Extra–Judicial Mechanisms ---- 884
  1. Arbitration ---- 884
    a. Invalidation of Arbitration Clauses under State Contract Law ---- 893
    b. Arbitrable and Non-arbitrable Claims in the Same Suit ---- 895
    c. Consolidation of Arbitration Proceedings ---- 899
    Murray, Rau & Sherman, Materials on Dispute Resolution ---- 899
    Notes and Questions ---- 902
    d. Classwide Arbitration ---- 903
    Blue Cross of California et al. v. The Superior Court of Los Angeles County ---- 903
    Notes and Questions ---- 913
    Green Tree Financial Corp. v. Bazzle ---- 914
    Notes and Questions ---- 921
    e. Innovative Techniques in Arbitration ---- 923
    Mnookin, Beyond Litigation ---- 924
  2. Mini–Trials ---- 927
    Green, Growth of the Mini–Trial ---- 928
    Note and Questions ---- 929
  3. Rent–a–Judge Programs ---- 930
    Notes and Questions ---- 931
  4. Industry–Wide Claims Settlement Through a Subscriber Facility: The Asbestos Claims Agreement ---- 931
    Fitzpatrick, The Center for Claims Resolution ---- 932
    Notes and Questions ---- 937
B. Judicial Mechanisms ---- 938
  1. Summary Jury Trials ---- 939
    Notes and Questions ---- 941

Page

B. Judicial Mechanisms—Continued
  2. Court–Annexed Arbitration -------------------------------- 943
  3. Early Neutral Evaluation (ENE) ---------------------------- 944
  4. Court–Annexed Mediation -------------------------------- 945
  5. Emerging Patterns of ADR Use in Federal Courts ------------- 946

INDEX -- 947

Table of Cases

The principal cases are in bold type. Cases cited or discussed in the text are roman type. References are to pages. Cases cited in principal cases and within other quoted materials are not included.

Abbott Laboratories, In re, 51 F.3d 524 (5th Cir.1995), 429

ABC Industries, United States v., 153 F.R.D. 603 (W.D.Mich.1993), 83

Abdallah v. Coca–Cola Co., 186 F.R.D. 672 (N.D.Ga.1999), 479

Ace Heating & Plumbing Co. v. Crane Co., 453 F.2d 30 (3rd Cir.1971), 372

ACF Industries, Inc. v. Guinn, 384 F.2d 15 (5th Cir.1967), 109

Activision Securities Litigation, In re, 723 F.Supp. 1373 (N.D.Cal.1989), **703**

Activision Securities Litigation, In re, 1986 WL 15339 (N.D.Cal.1986), 469

Acuna v. Brown & Root Inc., 200 F.3d 335 (5th Cir.2000), 636

Adams v. Robertson, 520 U.S. 83, 117 S.Ct. 1028, 137 L.Ed.2d 203 (1997), 458

Adashunas v. Negley, 626 F.2d 600 (7th Cir.1980), 237, 239

Advanced Tissue Sciences Securities Litigation, In re, 184 F.R.D. 346 (S.D.Cal. 1998), 293

Aetna Life Ins. Co. v. Lavoie, 475 U.S. 813, 106 S.Ct. 1580, 89 L.Ed.2d 823 (1986), 726

African American Voting Rights Legal Defense Fund, Inc. v. Villa, 54 F.3d 1345 (8th Cir.1995), 797

'Agent Orange' Product Liability Litigation, In re, 100 F.R.D. 718 (E.D.N.Y.1983), 339

Agent Orange Product Liability Litigation, In re, 506 F.Supp. 762 (E.D.N.Y.1980), 339

Agent Orange Product Liability Litigation MDL No. 381, In re, 818 F.2d 145 (2nd Cir.1987), 445

Aguinda, In re, 241 F.3d 194 (2nd Cir. 2001), 729

A.H. Robins Co., Inc., In re, 880 F.2d 709 (4th Cir.1989), 339

A.H. Robins Co., Inc., In re, 88 B.R. 742 (E.D.Va.1988), 215

Air Communication and Satellite Inc. v. EchoStar Satellite Corp., 38 P.3d 1246 (Colo.2002), 477

Air Crash Disaster at Florida Everglades on December 29, 1972, In re, 549 F.2d 1006 (5th Cir.1977), 683

Air Crash Disaster at Stapleton Intern. Airport, Denver, Colo., on Nov. 15, 1987, In re, 720 F.Supp. 1505 (D.Colo.1989), 876

Air Crash Disaster at Stapleton Intern. Airport, Denver, Colo., On Nov. 15, 1987, In re, 720 F.Supp. 1433 (D.Colo.1988), 641

Air Crash Disaster Near Chicago, Illinois, on May 25, 1979, In re, 644 F.2d 633 (7th Cir.1981), 435

Airline Ticket Com'n Antitrust Litigation, In re, 307 F.3d 679 (8th Cir.2002), 411

A. J. Industries, Inc. v. United States Dist. Court for Central Dist. of California, 503 F.2d 384 (9th Cir.1974), 130

Alabama, State of v. Blue Bird Body Co., Inc., 573 F.2d 309 (5th Cir.1978), 264, 764, 766, 767

Alabama, State of, United States v., 828 F.2d 1532 (11th Cir.1987), **717**

Alcan Aluminum, Inc., United States v., 25 F.3d 1174 (3rd Cir.1994), 83

Aldinger v. Howard, 427 U.S. 1, 96 S.Ct. 2413, 49 L.Ed.2d 276 (1976), 59

Alexander v. Anthony Intern., L.P., 341 F.3d 256 (3rd Cir.2003), 894

Alexander v. Chicago Park Dist., 927 F.2d 1014 (7th Cir.1991), 701

Alexander v. Fulton County, Ga., 207 F.3d 1303 (11th Cir.2000), 32

Alexander v. Gardner–Denver Co., 415 U.S. 36, 94 S.Ct. 1011, 39 L.Ed.2d 147 (1974), 888, 899

Alexander Grant & Co. v. McAlister, 116 F.R.D. 583 (S.D.Ohio 1987), 243, 299, 300

Alexander Grant & Co. Litigation, In re, 110 F.R.D. 528 (S.D.Fla.1986), 243

Alford v. Dean Witter Reynolds, Inc., 939 F.2d 229 (5th Cir.1991), 888

Allapattah Services, Inc. v. Exxon Corp., 333 F.3d 1248 (11th Cir.2003), 429

Allen v. McCurry, 449 U.S. 90, 101 S.Ct. 411, 66 L.Ed.2d 308 (1980), 802

Allen–Bradley Co., LLC v. Kollmorgen Corp., 199 F.R.D. 316 (E.D.Wis.2001), 882

Allen–Myland, Inc. v. International Business Machines Corp., 709 F.Supp. 491 (S.D.N.Y.1989), 729

Allied–Bruce Terminix Companies, Inc. v. Dobson, 513 U.S. 265, 115 S.Ct. 834, 130 L.Ed.2d 753 (1995), 886, 889

Allied Machinery Service, Inc. v. Caterpillar Inc., 841 F.Supp. 406 (S.D.Fla.1993), 187

Allison v. Citgo Petroleum Corp., 151 F.3d 402 (5th Cir.1998), 326, 327, 328

Alyeska Pipeline Service Co. v. Wilderness Society, 421 U.S. 240, 95 S.Ct. 1612, 44 L.Ed.2d 141 (1975), 684

Amarel v. Connell, 102 F.3d 1494 (9th Cir. 1996), 162

Amchem Products, Inc. v. Windsor, 521 U.S. 591, 117 S.Ct. 2231, 138 L.Ed.2d 689 (1997), 159, 207, 337, 338, **373**, 387, 388, 389, 390, 403, 426, 444, 465, 477, 510, 511, 515, 535, 783, 830

American Computer Trust Leasing v. Jack Farrell Implement Co., 136 F.R.D. 160 (D.Minn.1991), 476

American Disposal Services, Inc. v. O'Brien, 839 F.2d 84 (2nd Cir.1988), 188

American Medical Systems, Inc., In re, 75 F.3d 1069 (6th Cir.1996), 353

American Pipe & Const. Co. v. Utah, 414 U.S. 538, 94 S.Ct. 756, 38 L.Ed.2d 713 (1974), 461, 462, 463, 465, 466, 467, 468, 469

American Safety Equipment Corp. v. J. P. Maguire & Co., 391 F.2d 821 (2nd Cir. 1968), 887

American Tel. and Tel. Co., United States v., 642 F.2d 1285, 206 U.S.App. D.C. 317 (D.C.Cir.1980), **606,** 610, 611

Anderson v. Cryovac, Inc., 805 F.2d 1 (1st Cir.1986), 582

Anderson v. Mills, 664 F.2d 600 (6th Cir. 1981), 170

Andrews v. American Tel. & Tel. Co., 95 F.3d 1014 (11th Cir.1996), 264

Angel Music, Inc. v. ABC Sports, Inc., 112 F.R.D. 70 (S.D.N.Y.1986), 284

Antibiotic Antitrust Actions, In re, 333 F.Supp. 267 (S.D.N.Y.1971), 447

Appleton Elec. Co. v. Graves Truck Line, Inc., 635 F.2d 603 (7th Cir.1980), 469

Arabian American Oil Co. v. Scarfone, 119 F.R.D. 448 (M.D.Fla.1988), 942

Ardrey v. Federal Kemper Ins. Co., 142 F.R.D. 105 (E.D.Pa.1992), 330

Arizona, State of v. Motorola, Inc., 139 F.R.D. 141 (D.Ariz.1991), 83

Arkansas Ed. Ass'n v. Board of Ed. of Portland, Ark. School Dist., 446 F.2d 763 (8th Cir.1971), 244

Armendariz v. Foundation Health Psychcare Services, Inc., 99 Cal.Rptr.2d 745, 6 P.3d 669 (Cal.2000), 893, 894

Armstrong v. Martin Marietta Corp., 93 F.3d 1505 (11th Cir.1996), 469

Arthur Young & Co., United States v., 465 U.S. 805, 104 S.Ct. 1495, 79 L.Ed.2d 826 (1984), 612

Asbestos Products Liability Litigation (No. VI), In re, 771 F.Supp. 415 (Jud.Pan. Mult.Lit.1991), 159

Asbestos School Litigation, In re, 594 F.Supp. 178 (E.D.Pa.1984), 336

Atlantic Coast Line R. Co. v. Brotherhood of Locomotive Engineers, 398 U.S. 281, 90 S.Ct. 1739, 26 L.Ed.2d 234 (1970), 196, 199

Austin v. Owens–Brockway Glass Container, Inc., 78 F.3d 875 (4th Cir.1996), 889

Aviation Products Liability Litigation, In re, 347 F.Supp. 1401 (Jud.Pan. Mult.Lit.1972), **146,** 151, 152

Bacon v. Honda of America Mfg., Inc., 205 F.R.D. 466 (S.D.Ohio 2001), 768

Bailey v. Meister Brau, Inc., 57 F.R.D. 11 (N.D.Ill.1972), 616

Baldwin–United Corp. (Single Premium Deferred Annuities Ins. Litigation), In re, 770 F.2d 328 (2nd Cir. 1985), 191, **199,** 205, 206, 207, 208, 209, 400, 403

Ballan v. Upjohn Co., 159 F.R.D. 473 (W.D.Mich.1994), 256

Barrentine v. Arkansas–Best Freight System, Inc., 450 U.S. 728, 101 S.Ct. 1437, 67 L.Ed.2d 641 (1981), 899

Basch v. Ground Round, Inc., 139 F.3d 6 (1st Cir.1998), 467

Basic Inc. v. Levinson, 485 U.S. 224, 108 S.Ct. 978, 99 L.Ed.2d 194 (1988), 254

Bates v. State Bar of Arizona, 433 U.S. 350, 97 S.Ct. 2691, 53 L.Ed.2d 810 (1977), 227

Becherer v. Merrill Lynch, Pierce, Fenner, and Smith, Inc., 193 F.3d 415 (6th Cir. 1999), 819

Beef Industry Antitrust Litigation, In re, 607 F.2d 167 (5th Cir.1979), 372

Belke v. Merrill Lynch, Pierce, Fenner & Smith, 693 F.2d 1023 (11th Cir.1982), 898

Beltran–Tirado v. I.N.S., 213 F.3d 1179 (9th Cir.2000), 752

Bendectin Litigation, In re, 857 F.2d 290 (6th Cir.1988), **768,** 773, 774, 775, 876

Bendectin Products Liability Litigation, In re, 732 F.Supp. 744 (E.D.Mich.1990), 876

Bendectin Products Liability Litigation, In re, 749 F.2d 300 (6th Cir.1984), 437

Bender v. A.G. Edwards & Sons, Inc., 971 F.2d 698 (11th Cir.1992), 888

Benson and Ford, Inc. v. Wanda Petroleum Co., 833 F.2d 1172 (5th Cir.1987), 798

Berger v. Compaq Computer Corp., 257 F.3d 475 (5th Cir.2001), 293

Berger, State ex rel. Dunlap v., 211 W.Va. 549, 567 S.E.2d 265 (W.Va.2002), 894

Berger v. Xerox Corp. Retirement Income Guarantee Plan, 338 F.3d 755 (7th Cir. 2003), 329

Berkey Photo, Inc. v. Eastman Kodak Co., 74 F.R.D. 613 (S.D.N.Y.1977), **612,** 616, 618

Berkowitz, United States v., 328 F.2d 358 (3rd Cir.1964), 131

Bertrand v. Johns–Manville Sales Corp., 529 F.Supp. 539 (D.Minn.1982), 857

Betts v. Reliable Collection Agency, Ltd., 659 F.2d 1000 (9th Cir.1981), 256, 508

Bhatnagar v. Surrendra Overseas Ltd., 52 F.3d 1220 (3rd Cir.1995), 141

Birmingham Reverse Discrimination Employment Litigation, In re, 20 F.3d 1525 (11th Cir.1994), 98

Birmingham Reverse Discrimination Employment Litigation, In re, 833 F.2d 1492 (11th Cir.1987), 100

Birmingham Steel Corp. v. Tennessee Valley Authority, 353 F.3d 1331 (11th Cir. 2003), 278, 507

Blackie v. Barrack, 524 F.2d 891 (9th Cir.1975), **246,** 255, 256

Blair v. Equifax Check Services, Inc., 181 F.3d 832 (7th Cir.1999), 267, 371

Blanchard v. Bergeron, 489 U.S. 87, 109 S.Ct. 939, 103 L.Ed.2d 67 (1989), 701, 713

Block v. First Blood Associates, 763 F.Supp. 746 (S.D.N.Y.1991), 245

Block v. First Blood Associates, 743 F.Supp. 194 (S.D.N.Y.1990), 245

Blonder–Tongue Laboratories, Inc. v. University of Illinois Foundation, 402 U.S. 313, 91 S.Ct. 1434, 28 L.Ed.2d 788 (1971), 848

Bloom v. State of Ill., 391 U.S. 194, 88 S.Ct. 1477, 20 L.Ed.2d 522 (1968), 651

Blue Cross of California v. Superior Court, 78 Cal.Rptr.2d 779 (Cal.App. 2 Dist.1998), **903,** 913

Blum v. Stenson, 465 U.S. 886, 104 S.Ct. 1541, 79 L.Ed.2d 891 (1984), 699

BMW of North America, Inc. v. Gore, 517 U.S. 559, 116 S.Ct. 1589, 134 L.Ed.2d 809 (1996), 436

Boardman Petroleum, Inc. v. Federated Mut. Ins. Co., 135 F.3d 750 (11th Cir. 1998), 435

Board of Educ. of Tp. High School v. Climatemp, Inc., 1981 WL 2033 (N.D.Ill.1981), **241,** 243

Boeing Co. v. Van Gemert, 444 U.S. 472, 100 S.Ct. 745, 62 L.Ed.2d 676 (1980), 681, 682

Bogard v. Cook, 586 F.2d 399 (5th Cir. 1978), 846, 847

Bogosian v. Gulf Oil Corp., 738 F.2d 587 (3rd Cir.1984), 618

Boise Cascade Sec. Litigation, In re, 420 F.Supp. 99 (W.D.Wash.1976), 738

Bolin v. Sears, Roebuck & Co., 231 F.3d 970 (5th Cir.2000), 321, 327

Borel v. Fibreboard Paper Products Corp., 493 F.2d 1076 (5th Cir.1973), 856, 857, 873, 874

Boston's Children First, In re, 244 F.3d 164 (1st Cir.2001), 729

Boyd v. Orkin Exterminating Co., Inc., 191 Ga.App. 38, 381 S.E.2d 295 (Ga.App. 1989), 329

Brand Name Prescription Drugs Antitrust Litigation, In re, 123 F.3d 599 (7th Cir. 1997), 428

Brennan v. Midwestern United Life Ins. Co., 450 F.2d 999 (7th Cir.1971), 479

Bridgeport Music, Inc. v. 11C Music, 202 F.R.D. 229 (M.D.Tenn.2001), 39

Bridgestone/Firestone, Inc., In re, 288 F.3d 1012 (7th Cir.2002), **429,** 435, 436, 437, 438, 439

Bridgestone/Firestone, Inc., Tires Products Liability Litigation, In re, 333 F.3d 763 (7th Cir.2003), 356, 404, 405, 438

Brillhart v. Excess Ins. Co. of America, 316 U.S. 491, 62 S.Ct. 1173, 86 L.Ed. 1620 (1942), 190

Brown v. Superior Court, 245 Cal.Rptr. 412, 751 P.2d 470 (Cal.1988), 45

Brown v. Ticor Title Ins. Co., 982 F.2d 386 (9th Cir.1992), 457, 458

Bruce v. Martin, 680 F.Supp. 616 (S.D.N.Y. 1988), 198, 199

BT Inv. Managers, Inc. v. Lewis, 559 F.2d 950 (5th Cir.1977), **165,** 170

Burford v. Sun Oil Co., 319 U.S. 315, 63 S.Ct. 1098, 87 L.Ed. 1424 (1943), 165, 168, 169, 170

Burger King Corp. v. American Nat. Bank and Trust Co. of Chicago, 119 F.R.D. 672 (N.D.Ill.1988), 55

Burkhalter v. Montgomery Ward and Co., Inc., 92 F.R.D. 361 (E.D.Ark.1981), 496

Burlington, City of v. Dague, 505 U.S. 557, 112 S.Ct. 2638, 120 L.Ed.2d 449 (1992), 697, 701

Burney v. Rheem Mfg. Co., Inc., 196 F.R.D. 659 (M.D.Ala.2000), 838

Burns v. Jaquays Min. Corp., 156 Ariz. 375, 752 P.2d 28 (Ariz.App. Div. 2 1987), 330

Bush v. Viterna, 740 F.2d 350 (5th Cir. 1984), 72

Cable Belt Conveyors, Inc. v. Alumina Partners of Jamaica, 717 F.Supp. 1021 (S.D.N.Y.1989), 896

Cada v. Costa Line, Inc., 93 F.R.D. 95 (N.D.Ill.1981), 478

Calderon v. Presidio Valley Farmers Ass'n, 863 F.2d 384 (5th Cir.1989), 469

California, State of v. Levi Strauss & Co., 224 Cal.Rptr. 605, 715 P.2d 564 (Cal. 1986), 409

Cameron–Grant v. Maxim Healthcare Services, Inc., 347 F.3d 1240 (11th Cir. 2003), 497

Camotex, S.R.L. v. Hunt, 741 F.Supp. 1086 (S.D.N.Y.1990), 466

Campos v. Ticketmaster Corp., 140 F.3d 1166 (8th Cir.1998), 164

Canady v. Allstate Ins. Co., 282 F.3d 1005 (8th Cir.2002), 828

Cape Cod Food Products v. National Cranberry Ass'n, 119 F.Supp. 900 (D.Mass. 1954), 746

Carbon Dioxide Industry Antitrust Litigation, In re, 229 F.3d 1321 (11th Cir. 2000), 161

Caridad v. Metro–North Commuter R.R., 191 F.3d 283 (2nd Cir.1999), 276

Carlough v. Amchem Products, Inc., 10 F.3d 189 (3rd Cir.1993), 191, 403

Carlucci v. Piper Aircraft Corp., 102 F.R.D. 472 (S.D.Fla.1984), 567

Carmichael v. Birmingham Saw Works, 738 F.2d 1126 (11th Cir.1984), 839

Carpenter, United States v., 298 F.3d 1122 (9th Cir.2002), 72

Cascade Natural Gas Corp. v. El Paso Natural Gas Co., 386 U.S. 129, 87 S.Ct. 932, 17 L.Ed.2d 814 (1967), 67

Castano v. American Tobacco Co., 84 F.3d 734 (5th Cir.1996), **340,** 353, 355, 356, 357, 358, 389, 390, 404, 435, 437, 767, 776

Catholic Social Services, Inc. v. I.N.S., 232 F.3d 1139 (9th Cir.2000), 467

Cavanaugh, In re, 306 F.3d 726 (9th Cir. 2002), 293, 678

Cella v. Togum Constructeur Ensembleier en Industrie Alimentaire, 173 F.3d 909 (3rd Cir.1999), 127

Celotex Corp. v. Catrett, 477 U.S. 317, 106 S.Ct. 2548, 91 L.Ed.2d 265 (1986), 16

Cement Antitrust Litigation (MDL No. 296), In re, 673 F.2d 1020 (9th Cir. 1981), 726

Cendant Corp. Litigation, In re, 264 F.3d 201 (3rd Cir.2001), 537

Cendant Corp. Prides Litigation, In re, 311 F.3d 298 (3rd Cir.2002), 540

Cendant Corp. PRIDES Litigation, In re, 243 F.3d 722 (3rd Cir.2001), 681, 714

Central Railroad & Banking Co. v. Pettus, 113 U.S. 116, 5 S.Ct. 387, 28 L.Ed. 915 (1885), 681

Central Wesleyan College v. W.R. Grace & Co., 6 F.3d 177 (4th Cir.1993), 266

Chambers v. NASCO, Inc., 501 U.S. 32, 111 S.Ct. 2123, 115 L.Ed.2d 27 (1991), 653

Chance v. E. I. Du Pont De Nemours & Co., Inc., 371 F.Supp. 439 (E.D.N.Y.1974), 44

Chance v. E.I. Du Pont De Nemours & Co., Inc., 345 F.Supp. 353 (E.D.N.Y. 1972), **39,** 40, 43, 44

Chancery Clerk of Chickasaw County, Miss. v. Wallace, 646 F.2d 151 (5th Cir.1981), 170

Chapman v. Pacific Tel. and Tel. Co., 613 F.2d 193 (9th Cir.1979), **644,** 649, 650, 651, 757

Charchenko v. City of Stillwater, 47 F.3d 981 (8th Cir.1995), 183

Cheeves v. Southern Clays, Inc., 128 F.R.D. 128 (M.D.Ga.1989), 611

Chemetron Corp. v. Business Funds, Inc., 682 F.2d 1149 (5th Cir.1982), 881

Chevalier v. Baird Sav. Ass'n, 72 F.R.D. 140 (E.D.Pa.1976), 469

Chevron U.S.A., Inc., In re, 109 F.3d 1016 (5th Cir.1997), 781

Chicago Flood Litigation, In re, 819 F.Supp. 762 (N.D.Ill.1993), 189

Chicago Tribune Co. v. Bridgestone/Firestone, Inc., 263 F.3d 1304 (11th Cir.2001), **582,** 590, 591, 593

Chicken Antitrust Litigation American Poultry, In re, 669 F.2d 228 (5th Cir. 1982), 535

Chick Kam Choo v. Exxon Corp., 486 U.S. 140, 108 S.Ct. 1684, 100 L.Ed.2d 127 (1988), 197

Chiles v. Thornburgh, 865 F.2d 1197 (11th Cir.1989), 69

China Trade and Development Corp. v. M.V. Choong Yong, 837 F.2d 33 (2nd Cir.1987), 198

Chisholm v. Georgia, 2 U.S. 419, 2 Dall. 419, 1 L.Ed. 440 (1793), 61

Christiana Mortg. Corp. v. Delaware Mortg. Bankers Ass'n, 136 F.R.D. 372 (D.Del. 1991), 244

Cimino v. Raymark Industries, Inc., 151 F.3d 297 (5th Cir.1998), 779, 780

Cimino v. Raymark Industries, Inc., 751 F.Supp. 649 (E.D.Tex.1990), 778, 779, 781, 782, 783

Cimino v. Raymark Industries, Inc., No. B–86–0456–Ca (1989), 126

Cincinnati Gas & Elec. Co. v. General Elec. Co., 117 F.R.D. 597 (S.D.Ohio 1987), 940

Cintech Indus. Coatings, Inc. v. Bennett Industries, Inc., 85 F.3d 1198 (6th Cir. 1996), 643

Ciotti v. Cook County, 712 F.2d 312 (7th Cir.1983), 182

Cipollone v. Liggett Group, Inc., 785 F.2d 1108 (3rd Cir.1986), 572, 590

Cipollone v. Liggett Group, Inc., 113 F.R.D. 86 (D.N.J.1986), 581, 590, 592

Circuit City Stores, Inc. v. Adams, 532 U.S. 105, 121 S.Ct. 1302, 149 L.Ed.2d 234 (2001), 885

Citizen Potawatomi Nation v. Norton, 248 F.3d 993 (10th Cir.2001), 60

City of (see name of city)

Class Plaintiffs v. City of Seattle, 955 F.2d 1268 (9th Cir.1992), 542

Coast Plaza Doctors Hosp. v. Blue Cross of California, 99 Cal.Rptr.2d 809 (Cal.App. 2 Dist.2000), 898

Coates v. Johnson & Johnson, 756 F.2d 524 (7th Cir.1985), 566

Cobell v. Norton, 334 F.3d 1128, 357 U.S.App.D.C. 306 (D.C.Cir.2003), **654,** 661, 662, 663

Coca–Cola Bottling Co. of Shreveport, Inc. v. Coca–Cola Co., 107 F.R.D. 288 (D.Del. 1985), 593

Codex Corp. v. Milgo Electronic Corp., 553 F.2d 735 (1st Cir.1977), 108

Cole v. Wodziak, 169 F.3d 486 (7th Cir. 1999), 701

Coleman v. General Motors Acceptance Corp., 296 F.3d 443 (6th Cir.2002), 329

Coleman v. Kaye, 87 F.3d 1491 (3rd Cir. 1996), 701

Collins, In re, 233 F.3d 809 (3rd Cir.2000), 160

Collins, United States v., 226 F.3d 457 (6th Cir.2000), 748

Colorado River Water Conservation Dist. v. United States, 424 U.S. 800, 96 S.Ct. 1236, 47 L.Ed.2d 483 (1976), 187, 188, 189, 897

Columbus–America Discovery Group v. Atlantic Mut. Ins. Co., 974 F.2d 450 (4th Cir.1992), 85

Compact Disc Minimum Advertised Price Antitrust Litigation, In re, 216 F.R.D. 197 (D.Me.2003), 409, 536

Conner v. Burford, 836 F.2d 1521 (9th Cir. 1988), 53

Consolidated Pac. Engineering, Inc. v. Greater Anchorage Area Borough for and on Behalf of Greater Anchorage Area Borough School Dist., 563 P.2d 252 (Alaska 1977), 896

Consolidated Pretrial Proceedings in Air West Securities Litigation, In re, 73 F.R.D. 12 (N.D.Cal.1976), 370

Consorti v. Armstrong World Industries, Inc., 72 F.3d 1003 (2nd Cir.1995), 127

Continental Illinois Securities Litigation, In re, 572 F.Supp. 931 (N.D.Ill.1983), 702

Continental Illinois Securities Litigation, Matter of, 962 F.2d 566 (7th Cir.1992), 702

Cook v. Niedert, 142 F.3d 1004 (7th Cir. 1998), 230

Cooper v. Federal Reserve Bank of Richmond, 467 U.S. 867, 104 S.Ct. 2794, 81 L.Ed.2d 718 (1984), 330, **831,** 838, 840

Coopers & Lybrand v. Livesay, 437 U.S. 463, 98 S.Ct. 2454, 57 L.Ed.2d 351 (1978), 371

Cordoza v. Pacific States Steel Corp., 320 F.3d 989 (9th Cir.2003), 653

Corrugated Container Antitrust Litigation, In re, 659 F.2d 1332 (5th Cir.1981), 206, 207, 537

Corrugated Container Antitrust Litigation, In re, 643 F.2d 195 (5th Cir.1981), 537, 643

Cotchett v. Avis Rent A Car System, Inc., 56 F.R.D. 549 (S.D.N.Y.1972), 297

County of (see name of county)

Cox v. American Cast Iron Pipe Co., 784 F.2d 1546 (11th Cir.1986), 479

Crasto v. Kaskel's Estate, 63 F.R.D. 18 (S.D.N.Y.1974), 255

Crazy Eddie Securities Litigation, In re, 135 F.R.D. 39 (E.D.N.Y.1991), 294

Crown, Cork & Seal Co., Inc. v. Parker, 462 U.S. 345, 103 S.Ct. 2392, 76 L.Ed.2d 628 (1983), **462,** 465, 466, 467

Crown Life Ins. Premium Litigation, In re, 178 F.Supp.2d 1365 (Jud.Pan. Mult.Lit.2001), 153

Cruz v. PacifiCare Health Systems, Inc., 133 Cal.Rptr.2d 58, 66 P.3d 1157 (Cal. 2003), 898

Curtin v. United Airlines, Inc., 275 F.3d 88, 348 U.S.App.D.C. 309 (D.C.Cir.2001), 369

Dafforn v. Rousseau Associates, Inc., 1976 WL 1358 (N.D.Ind.1976), 240

Daniels v. City of New York, 198 F.R.D. 409 (S.D.N.Y.2001), 328

Darby v. Cisneros, 509 U.S. 137, 113 S.Ct. 2539, 125 L.Ed.2d 113 (1993), 182

Daubert v. Merrell Dow Pharmaceuticals, Inc., 509 U.S. 579, 113 S.Ct. 2786, 125 L.Ed.2d 469 (1993), 784

Davenport v. International Broth. of Teamsters, AFL–CIO, 166 F.3d 356, 334 U.S.App.D.C. 228 (D.C.Cir.1999), 102

Deakins v. Monaghan, 484 U.S. 193, 108 S.Ct. 523, 98 L.Ed.2d 529 (1988), 188

Dean Witter Reynolds, Inc. v. Byrd, 470 U.S. 213, 105 S.Ct. 1238, 84 L.Ed.2d 158 (1985), 898

Deford v. Schmid Products Co., a Div. of Schmid Laboratories, Inc., 120 F.R.D. 648 (D.Md.1987), 592

Dellums v. Powell, 566 F.2d 167, 184 U.S.App.D.C. 275 (D.C.Cir.1977), 480

de Melo v. Lederle Laboratories, Div. of American Cyanamid Corp., 801 F.2d 1058 (8th Cir.1986), **132,** 141

Deposit Guaranty Nat. Bank, Jackson, Miss. v. Roper, 445 U.S. 326, 100 S.Ct. 1166, 63 L.Ed.2d 427 (1980), **481,** 496

Detroit, City of v. Grinnell Corp., 495 F.2d 448 (2nd Cir.1974), 517, 533

Deutschman v. Beneficial Corp., 132 F.R.D. 359 (D.Del.1990), 295

Devlin v. Scardelletti, 536 U.S. 1, 122 S.Ct. 2005, 153 L.Ed.2d 27 (2002), 428, 460, 519

Diamond v. Charles, 476 U.S. 54, 106 S.Ct. 1697, 90 L.Ed.2d 48 (1986), 71

Diaz v. Sheppard, 85 F.3d 1502 (11th Cir. 1996), 847

Dickerson v. United Parcel Service, Inc., 1996 WL 806696 (N.D.Tex.1996), 889

Dickler v. Shearson Lehman Hutton, Inc., 408 Pa.Super. 286, 596 A.2d 860 (Pa.Super.1991), 913

Diet Drugs, In re, 282 F.3d 220 (3rd Cir. 2002), 184, 191, **391,** 401, 403, 404, 428, 460, 540

Discover Bank v. Superior Court, 129 Cal. Rptr.2d 393 (Cal.App. 2 Dist.2003), 913

District of Columbia Court of Appeals v. Feldman, 460 U.S. 462, 103 S.Ct. 1303, 75 L.Ed.2d 206 (1983), 183, 184

Diversified Industries, Inc. v. Meredith, 572 F.2d 596 (8th Cir.1977), 611

Doctor's Associates, Inc. v. Casarotto, 517 U.S. 681, 116 S.Ct. 1652, 134 L.Ed.2d 902 (1996), 889

Doe v. Charleston Area Medical Center, Inc., 529 F.2d 638 (4th Cir.1975), 244

Doe v. Karadzic, 192 F.R.D. 133 (S.D.N.Y. 2000), 315

Doe v. Meachum, 126 F.R.D. 444 (D.Conn. 1989), 480

Doe, 1–13 ex rel. Doe Sr. 1–13 v. Bush, 261 F.3d 1037 (11th Cir.2001), 327

Doi v. Halekulani Corp., 276 F.3d 1131 (9th Cir.2002), 643

Domestic Air Transp. Antitrust Litigation, In re, 148 F.R.D. 297 (N.D.Ga.1993), 715

Domestic Air Transp. Antitrust Litigation, In re, 1992 WL 357433 (N.D.Ga.1992), 479

Domestic Air Transp. Antitrust Litigation, In re, 141 F.R.D. 534 (N.D.Ga.1992), 448

Donaldson v. United States, 400 U.S. 517, 91 S.Ct. 534, 27 L.Ed.2d 580 (1971), 67, 68

Dondore v. NGK Metals Corp., 152 F.Supp.2d 662 (E.D.Pa.2001), 480

Dow Corning Corp., In re, 261 F.3d 280 (2nd Cir.2001), 604

Dow Corning Corp., In re, 255 B.R. 445 (E.D.Mich.2000), 217

Dow Corning Corp., In re, 211 B.R. 545 (Bkrtcy.E.D.Mich.1997), 217, 768, 942

Dubin v. United States, 380 F.2d 813 (5th Cir.1967), 131

Dugas v. Trans Union Corp., 99 F.3d 724 (5th Cir.1996), 497

Duhaime v. John Hancock Mut. Life Ins. Co., 183 F.3d 1 (1st Cir.1999), 518

Duke v. Uniroyal Inc., 928 F.2d 1413 (4th Cir.1991), 32

Dunavant v. Ford Motor Co., Civ.Ac. No. H–80–1159 (U.S.Dist.Ct. S.D.Tex.1980), 33, 151

Dunlap, State ex rel. v. Berger, 211 W.Va. 549, 567 S.E.2d 265 (W.Va.2002), 894

Dunn v. Lederele Laboratories, 121 Mich. App. 73, 328 N.W.2d 576 (Mich.App. 1982), 880

Eckstein v. Balcor Film Investors, 8 F.3d 1121 (7th Cir.1993), 164

Edelman v. Jordan, 415 U.S. 651, 94 S.Ct. 1347, 39 L.Ed.2d 662 (1974), 62

Edwards v. City of Houston, 78 F.3d 983 (5th Cir.1996), 100

Edwards v. Logan, 38 F.Supp.2d 463 (W.D.Va.1999), 752

E.E.O.C. v. Pipefitters, Local No. 120, 235 F.3d 244 (6th Cir.2000), 51

Eisen v. Carlisle and Jacquelin, 417 U.S. 156, 94 S.Ct. 2140, 40 L.Ed.2d 732 (1974), 221, 356, 368, 370, 408, **440,** 443, 444, 445, 447

Eisen v. Carlisle and Jacquelin, 391 F.2d 555 (2nd Cir.1968), 443

Eisen v. Carlisle & Jacquelin, 479 F.2d 1005 (2nd Cir.1973), 409

Eisenberg v. Gagnon, 766 F.2d 770 (3rd Cir.1985), 254

Eldredge v. Carpenters 46 Northern California Counties Joint Apprenticeship and Training Committee, 94 F.3d 1366 (9th Cir.1996), 51

Eldredge v. Carpenters 46 Northern California Counties Joint Apprenticeship and Training Committee, 833 F.2d 1334 (9th Cir.1987), 50

Eldredge v. Carpenters 46 Northern California Counties Joint Apprenticeship and Training Committee, 662 F.2d 534 (9th Cir.1981), **45,** 49, 50, 56, 60, 99

Elkins v. American Showa Inc., 219 F.R.D. 414 (S.D.Ohio 2002), 277

Ellis v. Great Southwestern Corp., 646 F.2d 1099 (5th Cir.1981), 131

England v. Louisiana State Bd. of Medical Examiners, 375 U.S. 411, 84 S.Ct. 461, 11 L.Ed.2d 440 (1964), 169, 183

Ensley Branch, N.A.A.C.P. v. Seibels, 31 F.3d 1548 (11th Cir.1994), 99

Ensley Branch, N.A.A.C.P. v. Seibels, 20 F.3d 1489 (11th Cir.1994), 99

Enterprise Wall Paper Mfg. Co. v. Bodman, 85 F.R.D. 325 (S.D.N.Y.1980), 447

Epstein v. MCA, Inc., 179 F.3d 641 (9th Cir.1999), 817, 828, 829, 830

Erie R. Co. v. Tompkins, 304 U.S. 64, 58 S.Ct. 817, 82 L.Ed. 1188 (1938), 44, 354, 818

ETSI Pipeline Project v. Burlington Northern, Inc., No. B–84–979–CA (E.D.Tex. 1987), 748

Eubanks v. Billington, 110 F.3d 87, 324 U.S.App.D.C. 41 (D.C.Cir.1997), 456

Evans v. Jeff D., 475 U.S. 717, 106 S.Ct. 1531, 89 L.Ed.2d 747 (1986), 702

Everhart v. Bowen, 853 F.2d 1532 (10th Cir.1988), 328

Ex parte (see name of party)

Exxon Corp., United States v., 94 F.R.D. 246 (D.D.C.1981), 624

Exxon Valdez, In re, 270 F.3d 1215 (9th Cir.2001), 316

Factor VIII or IX Concentrate Blood Products Litigation, In re, 169 F.R.D. 632 (N.D.Ill.1996), **156,** 354

Falcon v. General Telephone Co., 815 F.2d 317 (5th Cir.1987), 274

Farmers Ins. Exchange v. Leonard, 125 S.W.3d 55 (Tex.App.-Austin 2003), 438

Federal Deposit Ins. Corp. v. Eckhardt, 691 F.2d 245 (6th Cir.1982), 801

Federal Deposit Ins. Corp. v. Marine Midland Realty Credit Corp., 138 F.R.D. 479 (E.D.Va.1991), 603

Federal Skywalk Cases, In re, 97 F.R.D. 370 (W.D.Mo.1983), 400

Federal Skywalk Cases, In re, 93 F.R.D. 415 (W.D.Mo.1982), 301

Ferens v. John Deere Co., 494 U.S. 516, 110 S.Ct. 1274, 108 L.Ed.2d 443 (1990), 131

Fibreboard Corp., In re, 893 F.2d 706 (5th Cir.1990), 777, 783

Fielder v. Credit Acceptance Corp., 188 F.3d 1031 (8th Cir.1999), 183, 184

Fine Paper Antitrust Litigation, In re, 751 F.2d 562 (3rd Cir.1984), 676

Fine Paper Antitrust Litigation, In re, 98 F.R.D. 48 (E.D.Pa.1983), **669,** 675, 676, 677, 679

Fine Paper Antitrust Litigation, In re, 695 F.2d 494 (3rd Cir.1982), 294, 468

Finley v. United States, 490 U.S. 545, 109 S.Ct. 2003, 104 L.Ed.2d 593 (1989), 59

First Federal of Michigan v. Barrow, 878 F.2d 912 (6th Cir.1989), 299

First Nat. Bank and Trust Co. v. Hollingsworth, 931 F.2d 1295 (8th Cir.1991), 757

First Nat. Bank of Circle, United States v., 652 F.2d 882 (9th Cir.1981), 737

First Options of Chicago, Inc. v. Kaplan, 514 U.S. 938, 115 S.Ct. 1920, 131 L.Ed.2d 985 (1995), 890

Fitzpatrick v. Bitzer, 427 U.S. 445, 96 S.Ct. 2666, 49 L.Ed.2d 614 (1976), 61

Flaminio v. Honda Motor Co., Ltd., 733 F.2d 463 (7th Cir.1984), 761

Flink v. Carlson, 856 F.2d 44 (8th Cir. 1988), 893

Ford v. Philips Electronics Instruments Co., 82 F.R.D. 359 (E.D.Pa.1979), 617

Ford Motor Co., In re, 345 F.3d 1315 (11th Cir.2003), 604

Ford Motor Co. v. Bisanz Bros., Inc., 249 F.2d 22 (8th Cir.1957), 52

Ford Motor Co. v. Department of Treasury of State of Indiana, 323 U.S. 459, 65 S.Ct. 347, 89 L.Ed. 389 (1945), 61

Forehand v. Florida State Hosp. at Chattahoochee, 89 F.3d 1562 (11th Cir.1996), 507

FPI/Agretech Securities Litigation, In re, 105 F.3d 469 (9th Cir.1997), 716

Fraley v. American Cyanamid Co., 570 F.Supp. 497 (D.Colo.1983), **877,** 880

Frank v. United Airlines, Inc., 216 F.3d 845 (9th Cir.2000), 839

Franklin v. Kaypro Corp., 884 F.2d 1222 (9th Cir.1989), 643

Franks v. Kroger Co., 649 F.2d 1216 (6th Cir.1981), 510

Fraser v. Major League Soccer, L.L.C., 180 F.R.D. 178 (D.Mass.1998), 296

Fraser v. Nationwide Mut. Ins. Co., 352 F.3d 107 (3rd Cir.2003), 560

Freehill v. Lewis, 355 F.2d 46 (4th Cir. 1966), 639

Freeman v. Lester Coggins Trucking, Inc., 771 F.2d 860 (5th Cir.1985), 798

Friends for All Children, Inc. v. Lockheed Aircraft Corp., 497 F.Supp. 313 (D.D.C.1980), 853, **857**

F.T.C. v. Swedish Match North America, Inc., 197 F.R.D. 1 (D.D.C.2000), 752

Gap Stores Securities Litigation, In re, 79 F.R.D. 283 (N.D.Cal.1978), 243

Gardiner v. A.H. Robins Co., Inc., 747 F.2d 1180 (8th Cir.1984), 728

Garrity v. Gallen, 697 F.2d 452 (1st Cir. 1983), 85

Garrity v. Lyle Stuart, Inc., 386 N.Y.S.2d 831, 353 N.E.2d 793 (N.Y.1976), 891

Gary Plastic Packaging Corp. v. Merrill Lynch, Pierce, Fenner & Smith, Inc., 903 F.2d 176 (2nd Cir.1990), 257

Gau Shan Co., Ltd. v. Bankers Trust Co., 956 F.2d 1349 (6th Cir.1992), 198

General Motors Class E Stock Buyout Securities Litigation, In re, 696 F.Supp. 1546 (Jud.Pan.Mult.Lit.1988), 164

General Motors Corp. Pick–Up Truck Fuel Tank Products Liability Litigation, In re, 134 F.3d 133 (3rd Cir.1998), 403, 538

General Signal Corp. v. MCI Telecommunications Corp., 66 F.3d 1500 (9th Cir. 1995), 761

General Telephone Co. of Southwest v. Falcon, 457 U.S. 147, 102 S.Ct. 2364, 72 L.Ed.2d 740 (1982), **267,** 274, 276, 277, 278, 337, 353, 368, 507, 838

Georgevich v. Strauss, 772 F.2d 1078 (3rd Cir.1985), 170

Georgine v. Amchem Products, Inc., 160 F.R.D. 478 (E.D.Pa.1995), 477

Georgine v. Amchem Products, Inc., 157 F.R.D. 246 (E.D.Pa.1994), 444

Gerstein v. Pugh, 420 U.S. 103, 95 S.Ct. 854, 43 L.Ed.2d 54 (1975), 494

Gibson Greetings Securities Litigation, In re, 159 F.R.D. 499 (S.D.Ohio 1994), 296

Giles v. Secretary of Army, 627 F.2d 554, 201 U.S.App.D.C. 95 (D.C.Cir.1980), 412

Gilmer v. Interstate/Johnson Lane Corp., 500 U.S. 20, 111 S.Ct. 1647, 114 L.Ed.2d 26 (1991), 887, 888

Ginsey Industries, Inc. v. I. T. K. Plastics, Inc., 545 F.Supp. 78 (E.D.Pa. 1982), **128,** 131, 142

Girsh v. Jepson, 521 F.2d 153 (3rd Cir. 1975), 533

Glenn W. Turner Enterprises Litigation, In re, 521 F.2d 775 (3rd Cir.1975), 459

Globe Newspaper Co. v. Superior Court for Norfolk County, 457 U.S. 596, 102 S.Ct. 2613, 73 L.Ed.2d 248 (1982), 581

Goff v. Menke, 672 F.2d 702 (8th Cir. 1982), **841,** 844, 845

Goldberger v. Integrated Resources, Inc., 209 F.3d 43 (2nd Cir.2000), 715

Goldlawr, Inc. v. Heiman, 369 U.S. 463, 82 S.Ct. 913, 8 L.Ed.2d 39 (1962), 131

Golenia v. Bob Baker Toyota, 915 F.Supp. 201 (S.D.Cal.1996), 888

Gonce v. Veterans Admin., 872 F.2d 995 (Fed.Cir.1989), 899

Gordon v. Boden, 224 Ill.App.3d 195, 166 Ill.Dec. 503, 586 N.E.2d 461 (Ill.App. 1 Dist.1991), 409

Gottlieb v. Barry, 43 F.3d 474 (10th Cir. 1994), 682

Graham v. Wyeth Laboratories, a Div. of American Home Products Corp., 118 F.R.D. 511 (D.Kan.1988), 592

Granfinanciera, S.A. v. Nordberg, 492 U.S. 33, 109 S.Ct. 2782, 106 L.Ed.2d 26 (1989), 212, 213

Grayson v. K–Mart Corp., 849 F.Supp. 785 (N.D.Ga.1994), 33

Great Rivers Co-op. of Southeastern Iowa v. Farmland Industries, Inc., 59 F.3d 764 (8th Cir.1995), 475

Green v. Crapo, 181 Mass. 55, 62 N.E. 956 (Mass.1902), 610

Green v. McKaskle, 788 F.2d 1116 (5th Cir.1986), 846

Green v. McKaskle, 770 F.2d 445 (5th Cir. 1985), 845

Green v. Obledo, 172 Cal.Rptr. 206, 624 P.2d 256 (Cal.1981), 509

Green v. Santa Fe Industries, 82 F.R.D. 688 (S.D.N.Y.1979), 287

Greenspan v. Brassler, 78 F.R.D. 130 (S.D.N.Y.1978), 295

Green Tree Financial Corp. v. Bazzle, 539 U.S. 444, 123 S.Ct. 2402, 156 L.Ed.2d 414 (2003), 891, **914,** 921, 922

Griffin v. Singletary, 17 F.3d 356 (11th Cir.1994), 468

Grill v. United States, 516 F.Supp. 15 (E.D.N.Y.1981), 876

Grimes v. Vitalink Communications Corp., 17 F.3d 1553 (3rd Cir.1994), 439, 818, 828

Grutter v. Bollinger, 188 F.3d 394 (6th Cir. 1999), 68

GTFM, Inc. v. Wal–Mart Stores, Inc., 2000 WL 335558 (S.D.N.Y.2000), 559

Guam Society of Obstetricians and Gynecologists v. Ada, 100 F.3d 691 (9th Cir. 1996), 701

Guidi v. Inter–Continental Hotels Corp., 203 F.3d 180 (2nd Cir.2000), 142

Gulf Oil Co. v. Bernard, 452 U.S. 89, 101 S.Ct. 2193, 68 L.Ed.2d 693 (1981), **470,** 475, 476, 477, 478

Gulf Oil Corp. v. Gilbert, 330 U.S. 501, 67 S.Ct. 839, 91 L.Ed. 1055 (1947), 128

Gulf Oil Corp., United States v., 760 F.2d 292 (Temp.Emer1985), 612

Gunderson v. ADM Investor Services, Inc., 976 F.Supp. 818 (N.D.Iowa 1997), 199

Gusman v. Unisys Corp., 986 F.2d 1146 (7th Cir.1993), 699

Haas v. Pittsburgh Nat. Bank, 60 F.R.D. 604 (W.D.Pa.1973), 282, 283

Hadix v. Johnson, 322 F.3d 895 (6th Cir. 2003), 230

Halkin, In re, 598 F.2d 176, 194 U.S.App. D.C. 257 (D.C.Cir.1979), 579

Hall v. E. I. Du Pont De Nemours & Co., Inc., 345 F.Supp. 353 (E.D.N.Y. 1972), **39,** 43

Handgards, Inc. v. Johnson & Johnson, 413 F.Supp. 926 (N.D.Cal.1976), 623

Hanlon v. Chrysler Corp., 150 F.3d 1011 (9th Cir.1998), 389, 460

Hanon v. Dataproducts Corp., 976 F.2d 497 (9th Cir.1992), 257

Hans v. Louisiana, 134 U.S. 1, 10 S.Ct. 504, 33 L.Ed. 842 (1890), 61

Hansberry v. Lee, 311 U.S. 32, 61 S.Ct. 115, 85 L.Ed. 22 (1940), **285,** 288, 289, 292, 426, 445, 799, 853

Hanson v. Polk County Land, Inc., 608 F.2d 129 (5th Cir.1979), 637

Hardy v. Johns–Manville Sales Corp., 851 F.2d 742 (5th Cir.1988), 877

Hardy v. Johns–Manville Sales Corp., 681 F.2d 334 (5th Cir.1982), 338, **854,** 856, **864,** 874, 875, 876, 877, 880, 881

Harik v. California Teachers Ass'n, 326 F.3d 1042 (9th Cir.2003), 244

Harris v. Forklift Systems, Inc., 510 U.S. 17, 114 S.Ct. 367, 126 L.Ed.2d 295 (1993), 277

Harris v. Pernsley, 755 F.2d 338 (3rd Cir. 1985), 846

Harris County Com'rs Court v. Moore, 420 U.S. 77, 95 S.Ct. 870, 43 L.Ed.2d 32 (1975), 168

Harriss v. Pan American World Airways, Inc., 74 F.R.D. 24 (N.D.Cal.1977), 275

Hartman v. Duffey, 19 F.3d 1459, 305 U.S.App.D.C. 256 (D.C.Cir.1994), 276

Hawaii v. Standard Oil Co. of Cal., 405 U.S. 251, 92 S.Ct. 885, 31 L.Ed.2d 184 (1972), 801

Hawaii, State of v. Gordon, 373 U.S. 57, 83 S.Ct. 1052, 10 L.Ed.2d 191 (1963), 61

Hayes v. Compass Group USA, Inc., 202 F.R.D. 363 (D.Conn.2001), 558

Hearn v. Rhay, 68 F.R.D. 574 (E.D.Wash. 1975), 624

Heckman v. United States, 224 U.S. 413, 32 S.Ct. 424, 56 L.Ed. 820 (1912), 55

Hensley v. Eckerhart, 461 U.S. 424, 103 S.Ct. 1933, 76 L.Ed.2d 40 (1983), 681, **687,** 698, 700, 702, 712, 713

Henson v. East Lincoln Tp., 814 F.2d 410 (7th Cir.1987), 367

Hernandez v. Motor Vessel Skyward, 61 F.R.D. 558 (S.D.Fla.1973), 300

Hernandez, United States v., 176 F.3d 719 (3rd Cir.1999), 748

Hester v. Bayer Corp., 206 F.R.D. 683 (M.D.Ala.2001), 571

Hewlett–Packard Co. v. Bausch & Lomb, Inc., 115 F.R.D. 308 (N.D.Cal.1987), 611

Hilao v. Estate of Marcos, 103 F.3d 767 (9th Cir.1996), 266, 779, 780

Hines v. Widnall, 183 F.R.D. 596 (N.D.Fla. 1998), 544

Hoexter v. Simmons, 140 F.R.D. 416 (D.Ariz.1991), 257

Hoffman v. Blaski, 363 U.S. 335, 80 S.Ct. 1084, 4 L.Ed.2d 1254 (1960), 130

Hoffmann–La Roche Inc. v. Sperling, 493 U.S. 165, 110 S.Ct. 482, 107 L.Ed.2d 480 (1989), 466

Holmes v. Continental Can Co., 706 F.2d 1144 (11th Cir.1983), 456

Holsey v. Armour & Co., 743 F.2d 199 (4th Cir.1984), 276

Hosie v. Chicago & N. W. Ry. Co., 282 F.2d 639 (7th Cir.1960), 766

Hospitality Management Associates, Inc. v. Shell Oil Co., 356 S.C. 644, 591 S.E.2d 611 (S.C.2004), 828

Howsam v. Dean Witter Reynolds, Inc., 537 U.S. 79, 123 S.Ct. 588, 154 L.Ed.2d 491 (2002), 890, 895

ILC Peripherals Leasing Corp. v. International Business Machines Corp., 458 F.Supp. 423 (N.D.Cal.1978), 741, 742

Independent Federation of Flight Attendants v. Zipes, 491 U.S. 754, 109 S.Ct. 2732, 105 L.Ed.2d 639 (1989), 100

Initial Public Offering Securities Litigation, In re, 294 F.3d 297 (2nd Cir.2002), 727

In re (see name of party)

Insolia v. Philip Morris Inc., 186 F.R.D. 547 (W.D.Wis.1999), 37

Insull v. New York World–Telegram Corp., 172 F.Supp. 615 (N.D.Ill.1959), 39

Integra Realty Resources, Inc., In re, 354 F.3d 1246 (10th Cir.2004), 390

Intel Corp. v. Advanced Micro Devices, Inc., 12 F.3d 908 (9th Cir.1993), 187

Intermedics, Inc. v. Ventritex, Inc., 139 F.R.D. 384 (N.D.Cal.1991), 618

Internal Imp. Fund Trustees v. Greenough, 105 U.S. 527, 26 L.Ed. 1157 (1881), 681

International Business Machines Corp., In re, 45 F.3d 641 (2nd Cir.1995), 729

International Business Machines Corp., In re, 618 F.2d 923 (2nd Cir. 1980), **721**

International Business Machines Corp. v. Edelstein, 526 F.2d 37 (2nd Cir.1975), 617

International Business Machines Corp. v. United States, 493 F.2d 112 (2nd Cir. 1973), 606, 650

International Tank Terminals, Ltd. v. M/V Acadia Forest, 579 F.2d 964 (5th Cir. 1978), 72

International Tel. & Tel. Corp. v. United Tel. Co. of Florida, 60 F.R.D. 177 (M.D.Fla.1973), 623

Intern. Business Machines Corp., In re, 687 F.2d 591 (2nd Cir.1982), 728

Ivan F. Boesky Securities Litigation, In re, 948 F.2d 1358 (2nd Cir.1991), 668

Ivy Club v. Edwards, 943 F.2d 270 (3rd Cir.1991), 169

Jack Faucett Associates, Inc. v. American Tel. and Tel. Co., 744 F.2d 118, 240 U.S.App.D.C. 103 (D.C.Cir.1984), 875

Jackson v. Johns–Manville Sales Corp., 750 F.2d 1314 (5th Cir.1985), 44

Jackson v. Motel 6 Multipurpose, Inc., 130 F.3d 999 (11th Cir.1997), 278, 476

Japanese Electronic Products Antitrust Litigation, In re, 631 F.2d 1069 (3rd Cir. 1980), 738, 742

Jaquette v. Black Hawk County, Iowa, 710 F.2d 455 (8th Cir.1983), 701

Jefferson v. Ingersoll Intern. Inc., 195 F.3d 894 (7th Cir.1999), 326, 327

Jenkins v. Raymark Industries, Inc., 782 F.2d 468 (5th Cir.1986), **331,** 336, 338, 356, 390, 776, 777

Jenkins by Jenkins v. State of Mo., 78 F.3d 1270 (8th Cir.1996), 456

Jenson v. Eveleth Taconite Co., 139 F.R.D. 657 (D.Minn.1991), 277

Jimenez v. Weinberger, 523 F.2d 689 (7th Cir.1975), 370

John Doe Corp., In re, 675 F.2d 482 (2nd Cir.1982), 612

Johns–Manville Corp., In re, 27 F.3d 48 (2nd Cir.1994), 403

Johns–Manville Corp., In re, 36 B.R. 727 (Bkrtcy.S.D.N.Y.1984), 214

Johns–Manville Corp., In re, 26 B.R. 420 (Bkrtcy.S.D.N.Y.1983), 214

Johns–Manville Corp., Matter of, 26 B.R. 405 (Bkrtcy.S.D.N.Y.1983), 213

Johnson v. American Credit Co. of Georgia, 581 F.2d 526 (5th Cir.1978), 277, 296, 507

Johnson v. General Motors Corp., 598 F.2d 432 (5th Cir.1979), 445

Johnson v. Georgia Highway Exp., Inc., 488 F.2d 714 (5th Cir.1974), 686

Johnson v. Manhattan Ry. Co., 289 U.S. 479, 53 S.Ct. 721, 77 L.Ed. 1331 (1933), 115, 127

Johnson v. McKaskle, 727 F.2d 498 (5th Cir.1984), 845

Joint Eastern and Southern Dist. Asbestos Litigation, In re, 129 B.R. 710 (E.D.N.Y. 1991), 214

Joint Eastern and Southern Districts Asbestos Litigation, In re, 120 B.R. 648 (E.D.N.Y.1990), 191, 214, 403

Joyce v. City and COunty of San Francisco, 1994 WL 443464 (N.D.Cal.1994), 238

Juidice v. Vail, 430 U.S. 327, 97 S.Ct. 1211, 51 L.Ed.2d 376 (1977), 180

Kaepa, Inc. v. Achilles Corp., 76 F.3d 624 (5th Cir.1996), 198

Kahan v. Rosenstiel, 424 F.2d 161 (3rd Cir. 1970), 254

Kanter v. Warner–Lambert Co., 265 F.3d 853 (9th Cir.2001), 429

Kaplan v. Pomerantz, 132 F.R.D. 504 (N.D.Ill.1990), 295

Kaplan v. Pomerantz, 131 F.R.D. 118 (N.D.Ill.1990), 481

Katchen v. Landy, 382 U.S. 323, 86 S.Ct. 467, 15 L.Ed.2d 391 (1966), 212

Katz v. Realty Equities Corp. of New York, 521 F.2d 1354 (2nd Cir.1975), **116,** 125

Keith v. Daley, 764 F.2d 1265 (7th Cir. 1985), 70

Kennedy, Matthews, Landis, Healy & Pecora, Inc. v. Young, 524 N.W.2d 752 (Minn.App.1994), 891

Kilgo v. Bowman Transp., Inc., 789 F.2d 859 (11th Cir.1986), 508

King v. South Cent. Bell Tel. and Tel. Co., 790 F.2d 524 (6th Cir.1986), 840

King Resources Co. Securities Litigation, In re, 385 F.Supp. 588 (Jud.Pan. Mult.Lit.1974), 153

King Resources Co. Securities Litigation, In re, 342 F.Supp. 1179 (Jud.Pan. Mult.Lit.1972), 152

Kingsepp v. Wesleyan University, 142 F.R.D. 597 (S.D.N.Y.1992), 677

Kirchoff v. Flynn, 786 F.2d 320 (7th Cir. 1986), 702

Kirkpatrick v. J.C. Bradford & Co., 827 F.2d 718 (11th Cir.1987), 295

Kleiner v. First Nat. Bank of Atlanta, 751 F.2d 1193 (11th Cir.1985), **473,** 477, 478, 479

Kleissler v. United States Forest Service, 157 F.3d 964 (3rd Cir.1998), 69

Kline v. Coldwell, Banker & Co., 508 F.2d 226 (9th Cir.1974), **223,** 229

Knapp v. Ernst & Whitney, 90 F.3d 1431 (9th Cir.1996), 255

Kodekey Electronics, Inc. v. Mechanex Corp., 486 F.2d 449 (10th Cir.1973), 593

Korean Air Lines Disaster of Sept. 1, 1983, In re, 829 F.2d 1171, 265 U.S.App.D.C. 39 (D.C.Cir.1987), 164

Korwek v. Hunt, 827 F.2d 874 (2nd Cir. 1987), 467

Koster v. Chase Manhattan Bank, 93 F.R.D. 471 (S.D.N.Y.1982), 581

Kovaleff v. Piano, 142 F.R.D. 406 (S.D.N.Y. 1992), 257

Kremer v. Chemical Const. Corp., 456 U.S. 461, 102 S.Ct. 1883, 72 L.Ed.2d 262 (1982), 802

Kroeger v. United States Postal Service, 865 F.2d 235 (Fed.Cir.1988), 899

Kucala Enterprises, Ltd. v. Auto Wax Co., Inc., 2003 WL 21230605 (N.D.Ill.2003), 568

Kuntz v. Sea Eagle Diving Adventures Corp., 199 F.R.D. 665 (D.Hawai'i 2001), 755

Kyriazi v. Western Elec. Co., 647 F.2d 388 (3rd Cir.1981), 539

La Buy v. Howes Leather Company, 352 U.S. 249, 77 S.Ct. 309, 1 L.Ed.2d 290 (1957), 663

Lake Country Estates, Inc. v. Tahoe Regional Planning Agency, 440 U.S. 391, 99 S.Ct. 1171, 59 L.Ed.2d 401 (1979), 62

Laker Airways Ltd. v. Sabena, Belgian World Airlines, 731 F.2d 909, 235 U.S.App.D.C. 207 (D.C.Cir.1984), 198

La Mar v. H & B Novelty & Loan Co., 489 F.2d 461 (9th Cir.1973), **278,** 282, 283, 284, 299, 828

Lane v. Bethlehem Steel Corp., 93 F.R.D. 611 (D.Md.1982), 469

Larionoff v. United States, 533 F.2d 1167, 175 U.S.App.D.C. 32 (D.C.Cir.1976), 445

Lazy Oil Co. v. Witco Corp., 166 F.3d 581 (3rd Cir.1999), 515, 516

Leach v. Pan American World Airways, 842 F.2d 285 (11th Cir.1988), 743

Lease Oil Antitrust Litigation (No. II), In re, 200 F.3d 317 (5th Cir.2000), 209, 404

Lease Oil Antitrust Litigation No. II, In re, 48 F.Supp.2d 699 (S.D.Tex.1998), 209

Lelsz v. Kavanagh, 710 F.2d 1040 (5th Cir. 1983), 85, 456

Leonhardt v. Western Sugar Co., 160 F.3d 631 (10th Cir.1998), 429

Lewis v. Goldsmith, 95 F.R.D. 15 (D.N.J. 1982), 297

Lewis v. Tully, 99 F.R.D. 632 (N.D.Ill.1983), 496

Lexecon Inc. v. Milberg Weiss Bershad Hynes & Lerach, 523 U.S. 26, 118 S.Ct. 956, 140 L.Ed.2d 62 (1998), 160, 161

Life–Link Intern., Inc. v. Lalla, 902 F.2d 1493 (10th Cir.1990), **184,** 187

Liggett Group Inc. v. Engle, 853 So.2d 434 (Fla.App. 3 Dist.2003), 358

Linder v. Thrifty Oil Co., 97 Cal.Rptr.2d 179, 2 P.3d 27 (Cal.2000), 228

Lindy Bros. Builders, Inc. of Phila. v. American Radiator & Standard Sanitary Corp., 487 F.2d 161 (3rd Cir.1973), 686, 703

Linerboard Antitrust Litigation, In re, 292 F.Supp.2d 644 (E.D.Pa.2003), 683

Link v. Wabash R. Co., 370 U.S. 626, 82 S.Ct. 1386, 8 L.Ed.2d 734 (1962), 652, 668

Liteky v. United States, 510 U.S. 540, 114 S.Ct. 1147, 127 L.Ed.2d 474 (1994), 727, 729

Litton Bionetics, Inc. v. Glen Const. Co., Inc., 292 Md. 34, 437 A.2d 208 (Md. 1981), 895

Litton Industries, Inc. v. Chesapeake & Ohio Ry. Co., 129 F.R.D. 528 (E.D.Wis. 1990), 581

Litton Systems, Inc. v. American Tel. and Tel. Co., 700 F.2d 785 (2nd Cir.1983), 875, 876

Lois Sportswear, U.S.A., Inc. v. Levi Strauss & Co., 104 F.R.D. 103 (S.D.N.Y. 1985), 603

London v. Wal–Mart Stores, Inc., 340 F.3d 1246 (11th Cir.2003), 297

Lore v. Lone Pine Corp., 1986 WL 637507 (N.J.Super.L.1986), 636

Love v. Turlington, 733 F.2d 1562 (11th Cir.1984), 497

Lowery v. Circuit City Stores, Inc., 158 F.3d 742 (4th Cir.1998), 298

Lumen Const., Inc. v. Brant Const. Co., Inc., 780 F.2d 691 (7th Cir.1985), 189

Lynch v. Merrell–National Laboratories Div. of Richardson–Merrell, Inc., 646 F.Supp. 856 (D.Mass.1986), 876

Lynch, Inc. v. SamataMason Inc., 279 F.3d 487 (7th Cir.2002), 643

MacAlister v. Guterma, 263 F.2d 65 (2nd Cir.1958), 664

Macon Prestressed Concrete Co. v. Duke, 46 B.R. 727 (M.D.Ga.1985), 212

Mago v. Shearson Lehman Hutton Inc., 956 F.2d 932 (9th Cir.1992), 888

Makuc v. American Honda Motor Co., Inc., 835 F.2d 389 (1st Cir.1987), 245

Malchman v. Davis, 706 F.2d 426 (2nd Cir. 1983), 297

Malcolm v. National Gypsum Co., 995 F.2d 346 (2nd Cir.1993), 126

Male v. Crossroads Associates, 320 F.Supp. 141 (S.D.N.Y.1970), 244

Manufacturers Hanover Trust Co. v. Yanakas, 11 F.3d 381 (2nd Cir.1993), 882

Marcal Paper Mills, Inc. v. Ewing, 790 F.2d 195 (1st Cir.1986), 182

Marcera v. Chinlund, 595 F.2d 1231 (2nd Cir.1979), 366, 367

Marchetti, United States v., 466 F.2d 1309 (4th Cir.1972), 580

Marrese v. American Academy of Orthopaedic Surgeons, 470 U.S. 373, 105 S.Ct. 1327, 84 L.Ed.2d 274 (1985), 818

Mars Steel Corp. v. Continental Illinois Nat. Bank and Trust Co. of Chicago, 834 F.2d 677 (7th Cir.1987), 372

Martin v. Wilks, 490 U.S. 755, 109 S.Ct. 2180, 104 L.Ed.2d 835 (1989), 52, 86, 98, 99, 100, 101, 102, 80

Martinez–Catala, In re, 129 F.3d 213 (1st Cir.1997), 728

Masonite Corp. Hardboard Siding Products Liability Litigation, In re, 170 F.R.D. 417 (E.D.La.1997), 355

Mastrobuono v. Shearson Lehman Hutton, Inc., 514 U.S. 52, 115 S.Ct. 1212, 131 L.Ed.2d 76 (1995), 891

Matsushita Elec. Indus. Co., Ltd. v. Epstein, 516 U.S. 367, 116 S.Ct. 873, 134 L.Ed.2d 6 (1996), 209, 289, 404, 426, 803, 816, 828, 841

Matsushita Elec. Indus. Co., Ltd. v. Zenith Radio Corp., 475 U.S. 574, 106 S.Ct. 1348, 89 L.Ed.2d 538 (1986), 573

Matter of (see name of party)

Matthews v. Rollins Hudig Hall Co., 72 F.3d 50 (7th Cir.1995), 888

Mausolf v. Babbitt, 85 F.3d 1295 (8th Cir. 1996), 70

Maywalt v. Parker & Parsley Petroleum Co., 67 F.3d 1072 (2nd Cir.1995), 516

McCargo v. Hedrick, 545 F.2d 393 (4th Cir. 1976), 735

McCarthy v. Madigan, 503 U.S. 140, 112 S.Ct. 1081, 117 L.Ed.2d 291 (1992), 182

McConnell, In re, 370 U.S. 230, 82 S.Ct. 1288, 8 L.Ed.2d 434 (1962), 651

McDonald v. City of West Branch, Mich., 466 U.S. 284, 104 S.Ct. 1799, 80 L.Ed.2d 302 (1984), 899

McDonnell Douglas Corp. Securities Litigation, In re, 98 F.R.D. 613 (E.D.Mo.1982), 256

MCI Communications Corp. v. American Tel. and Tel. Co., 708 F.2d 1081 (7th Cir.1983), 758

McKay v. Ashland Oil, Inc., 120 F.R.D. 43 (E.D.Ky.1988), 942

McKowan Lowe & Co., Ltd. v. Jasmine, Ltd., 295 F.3d 380 (3rd Cir.2002), 468

McManus v. Fleetwood Enterprises, Inc., 320 F.3d 545 (5th Cir.2003), 327

McPeek v. Ashcroft, 202 F.R.D. 31 (D.D.C. 2001), 558

Meadows v. Pacific Inland Securities Corp., 36 F.Supp.2d 1240 (S.D.Cal.1999), 469

Mekdeci By and Through Mekdeci v. Merrell Nat. Laboratories, a Div. of Richardson–Merrell, Inc., 711 F.2d 1510 (11th Cir.1983), 880

Menowitz v. Brown, 991 F.2d 36 (2nd Cir. 1993), 164

Mercoid Corp. v. Mid–Continent Inv. Co., 320 U.S. 661, 64 S.Ct. 268, 88 L.Ed. 376 (1944), 188

Meritcare Inc. v. St. Paul Mercury Ins. Co., 166 F.3d 214 (3rd Cir.1999), 429

Mertens v. Abbott Laboratories, 99 F.R.D. 38 (D.N.H.1983), 331

Metz v. Merrill Lynch, Pierce, Fenner & Smith, Inc., 39 F.3d 1482 (10th Cir. 1994), 888

MGM Grand Hotel Fire Litigation, In re, 660 F.Supp. 522 (D.Nev.1987), 676

Microsoft Corp., United States v., 253 F.3d 34, 346 U.S.App.D.C. 330 (D.C.Cir. 2001), 729

Middlesex County Ethics Committee v. Garden State Bar Ass'n, 457 U.S. 423, 102 S.Ct. 2515, 73 L.Ed.2d 116 (1982), 181

Migra v. Warren City School Dist. Bd. of Educ., 465 U.S. 75, 104 S.Ct. 892, 79 L.Ed.2d 56 (1984), 802

Miley v. Oppenheimer & Co., Inc., 637 F.2d 318 (5th Cir.1981), 898

Milks v. Eli Lilly & Co., 97 F.R.D. 467 (S.D.N.Y.1983), 880

Miller v. Hygrade Food Products Corp., 202 F.R.D. 142 (E.D.Pa.2001), 32

Mills v. Electric Auto-Lite Co., 396 U.S. 375, 90 S.Ct. 616, 24 L.Ed.2d 593 (1970), 682

Minnesota, State of v. United States Steel Corp., 44 F.R.D. 559 (D.Minn.1968), 447

Mirkin v. Wasserman, 23 Cal.Rptr.2d 101, 858 P.2d 568 (Cal.1993), 255

Mississippi Protection & Advocacy System, Inc. v. Cotten, 929 F.2d 1054 (5th Cir. 1991), 296

Mitchum v. Foster, 407 U.S. 225, 92 S.Ct. 2151, 32 L.Ed.2d 705 (1972), 190, 191

Mitsubishi Motors Corp. v. Soler Chrysler–Plymouth, Inc., 473 U.S. 614, 105 S.Ct. 3346, 87 L.Ed.2d 444 (1985), 887

Mokhiber v. Davis, 537 A.2d 1100 (D.C. 1988), 582

Molski v. Gleich, 318 F.3d 937 (9th Cir. 2003), 329

Monosodium Glutamate Antitrust Litigation, In re, 205 F.R.D. 229 (D.Minn. 2001), 294

Montana v. United States, 440 U.S. 147, 99 S.Ct. 970, 59 L.Ed.2d 210 (1979), 848

Montgomery Ward & Co. v. Langer, 168 F.2d 182 (8th Cir.1948), 218

Monumental Life Ins. Co., In re, ___ F.3d ___, 2004 WL 718806 (5th Cir. 2004), **318,** 321, 327, 329, 404, 405, 426

Monument Builders of Pennsylvania, Inc. v. American Cemetery Ass'n, 206 F.R.D. 113 (E.D.Pa.2002), 366

Moore v. New York Cotton Exchange, 270 U.S. 593, 46 S.Ct. 367, 70 L.Ed. 750 (1926), 58

Morales v. City of San Rafael, 96 F.3d 359 (9th Cir.1996), 701

Morgan v. Deere Credit, Inc., 889 S.W.2d 360 (Tex.App.-Hous. (14 Dist.) 1994), 301

Morrison v. Circuit City Stores, Inc., 317 F.3d 646 (6th Cir.2003), 894

Moses H. Cone Memorial Hosp. v. Mercury Const. Corp., 460 U.S. 1, 103 S.Ct. 927, 74 L.Ed.2d 765 (1983), 896, 897, 898

Mosley v. General Motors Corp., 497 F.2d 1330 (8th Cir.1974), **24,** 32, 34

Mountain States Tel. and Tel. Co. v. District Court, City and County of Denver, 778 P.2d 667 (Colo.1989), 448

Mt. Healthy City School Dist. Bd. of Educ. v. Doyle, 429 U.S. 274, 97 S.Ct. 568, 50 L.Ed.2d 471 (1977), 62

Mullane v. Central Hanover Bank & Trust Co., 339 U.S. 306, 70 S.Ct. 652, 94 L.Ed. 865 (1950), 444

Mullen v. Treasure Chest Casino, LLC, 186 F.3d 620 (5th Cir.1999), 244, 768

Muniz v. Hoffman, 422 U.S. 454, 95 S.Ct. 2178, 45 L.Ed.2d 319 (1975), 651

Murphy v. F.D.I.C., 208 F.3d 959 (11th Cir.2000), 164

Murphy v. Hunt, 455 U.S. 478, 102 S.Ct. 1181, 71 L.Ed.2d 353 (1982), 496

Nagy v. Jostens, Inc., 91 F.R.D. 431 (D.Minn.1981), 476

Nash County Bd. of Ed. v. Biltmore Co., 640 F.2d 484 (4th Cir.1981), 800, 801

National City Lines, Inc. v. LLC Corp., 687 F.2d 1122 (8th Cir.1982), 197

National Equipment Rental, Limited v. Fowler, 287 F.2d 43 (2nd Cir.1961), 115

National Hockey League v. Metropolitan Hockey Club, Inc., 427 U.S. 639, 96 S.Ct. 2778, 49 L.Ed.2d 747 (1976), 652

Nation–Wide Check Corp., Inc. v. Forest Hills Distributors, Inc., 692 F.2d 214 (1st Cir.1982), **561,** 567, 568, 569, 570

Nelson v. County of Allegheny, 60 F.3d 1010 (3rd Cir.1995), 469

Nestle Co., Inc. v. Chester's Market, Inc., 756 F.2d 280 (2nd Cir.1985), 881

Nevada Dept. of Human Resources v. Hibbs, 538 U.S. 721, 123 S.Ct. 1972, 155 L.Ed.2d 953 (2003), 61

Newby v. Johnston, 681 F.2d 1012 (5th Cir.1982), 509

New England Mut. Life Ins. Co. Sales Practices Litigation, In re, 183 F.R.D. 33 (D.Mass.1998), 162

Newman v. Graddick, 696 F.2d 796 (11th Cir.1983), 590

New Orleans Public Service, Inc. v. Council of City of New Orleans, 491 U.S. 350, 109 S.Ct. 2506, 105 L.Ed.2d 298 (1989), 181

New Orleans Public Service, Inc. v. United Gas Pipe Line Co., 732 F.2d 452 (5th Cir.1984), 70

Newton v. A.C. & S., Inc., 918 F.2d 1121 (3rd Cir.1990), 641

Newton v. Merrill Lynch, Pierce, Fenner & Smith, Inc., 259 F.3d 154 (3rd Cir.2001), 275

Newton v. Thomason, 22 F.3d 1455 (9th Cir.1994), 164

New York State Ass'n for Retarded Children, Inc. v. Carey, 711 F.2d 1136 (2nd Cir.1983), 699

New York Tel. Co., United States v., 434 U.S. 159, 98 S.Ct. 364, 54 L.Ed.2d 376 (1977), 207

New York Times Co. v. United States, 403 U.S. 713, 91 S.Ct. 2140, 29 L.Ed.2d 822 (1971), 580

Nissan Motor Corp. Antitrust Litigation, In re, 471 F.Supp. 754 (S.D.Fla. 1979), **848,** 853

NLO, Inc., In re, 5 F.3d 154 (6th Cir.1993), 942

Noel v. Hall, 341 F.3d 1148 (9th Cir.2003), 184

Norplant Contraceptive Products Liability Litigation, In re, 1996 WL 264729 (E.D.Tex.1996), 357

Northern Dist. of California, Dalkon Shield IUD Products Liability Litigation, In re, 693 F.2d 847 (9th Cir.1982), 284, 354

Northern Dist. of California Dalkon Shield IUD Products Liability Litigation, In re, 526 F.Supp. 887 (N.D.Cal.1981), 6

Northern Pipeline Const. Co. v. Marathon Pipe Line Co., 458 U.S. 50, 102 S.Ct. 2858, 73 L.Ed.2d 598 (1982), 212

Northrop Corp. v. McDonnell Douglas Corp., 705 F.2d 1030 (9th Cir.1983), 56

Northwest Airlines, Inc. v. American Airlines, Inc., 989 F.2d 1002 (8th Cir.1993), 114

Northwestern Nat. Bank of Minneapolis v. Fox & Co., 102 F.R.D. 507 (S.D.N.Y. 1984), 243

Norwalk CORE v. Norwalk Redevelopment Agency, 395 F.2d 920 (2nd Cir.1968), 241

Nottingham Partners v. Trans–Lux Corp., 925 F.2d 29 (1st Cir.1991), 818

Novak, In re, 932 F.2d 1397 (11th Cir. 1991), 640, 650

Ocelot Oil Corp. v. Sparrow Industries, 847 F.2d 1458 (10th Cir.1988), 664

Ohio Bureau of Employment Services v. Hodory, 431 U.S. 471, 97 S.Ct. 1898, 52 L.Ed.2d 513 (1977), 183

Ohralik v. Ohio State Bar Ass'n, 436 U.S. 447, 98 S.Ct. 1912, 56 L.Ed.2d 444 (1978), 618

Olitt v. Murphy, 453 F.Supp. 354 (S.D.N.Y. 1978), 183

On the House Syndication, Inc. v. Federal Exp. Corp., 203 F.R.D. 452 (S.D.Cal. 2001), 479

Oostendorp v. Khanna, 937 F.2d 1177 (7th Cir.1991), 756

Oppenheimer Fund, Inc. v. Sanders, 437 U.S. 340, 98 S.Ct. 2380, 57 L.Ed.2d 253 (1978), 447, 448, 476, 509, 557

Oracle Securities Litigation, In re, 132 F.R.D. 538 (N.D.Cal.1990), 677

Oracle Securities Litigation, In re, 131 F.R.D. 688 (N.D.Cal.1990), 677

Orthopedic Bone Screw Products Liability Litigation, In re, 246 F.3d 315 (3rd Cir. 2001), 540

Orthopedic Bone Screw Products Liability Litigation, Matter of, 79 F.3d 46 (7th Cir.1996), 163

Ortiz v. Fibreboard Corp., 527 U.S. 815, 119 S.Ct. 2295, 144 L.Ed.2d 715 (1999), **302,** 314, 316, 317, 318, 388, 390, 426, 515, 535, 830

Otero v. Buslee, 695 F.2d 1244 (10th Cir. 1982), 639

Owen Equipment & Erection Co. v. Kroger, 437 U.S. 365, 98 S.Ct. 2396, 57 L.Ed.2d 274 (1978), 58, 60, 427

PacifiCare Health Systems, Inc. v. Book, 538 U.S. 401, 123 S.Ct. 1531, 155 L.Ed.2d 578 (2003), 895

Padovani v. Bruchhausen, 293 F.2d 546 (2nd Cir.1961), 736

Paris Air Crash of March 3, 1974, In re, 399 F.Supp. 732 (C.D.Cal.1975), 436

Parker v. Anderson, 667 F.2d 1204 (5th Cir.1982), **511,** 515, 519, 595, 840

Parklane Hosiery Co., Inc. v. Shore, 439 U.S. 322, 99 S.Ct. 645, 58 L.Ed.2d 552 (1979), 848, 853, 864, 874

Parks v. Eastwood Ins. Services, Inc., 235 F.Supp.2d 1082 (C.D.Cal.2002), 478

Parsons Steel, Inc. v. First Alabama Bank, 474 U.S. 518, 106 S.Ct. 768, 88 L.Ed.2d 877 (1986), 198

Patenaude, In re, 210 F.3d 135 (3rd Cir. 2000), 160

Patsy v. Board of Regents of State of Fla., 457 U.S. 496, 102 S.Ct. 2557, 73 L.Ed.2d 172 (1982), 182

Paul, Johnson, Alston & Hunt v. Graulty, 886 F.2d 268 (9th Cir.1989), 714

Payne v. Travenol Laboratories, Inc., 673 F.2d 798 (5th Cir.1982), 467, **497,** 507, 509

Peil v. National Semiconductor Corp., 86 F.R.D. 357 (E.D.Pa.1980), **290,** 292, 295, 680

Pennhurst State School & Hosp. v. Halderman, 465 U.S. 89, 104 S.Ct. 900, 79 L.Ed.2d 67 (1984), 62, 197

Pennsylvania v. Delaware Valley Citizens' Council for Clean Air, 478 U.S. 546, 106 S.Ct. 3088, 92 L.Ed.2d 439 (1986), 700

Pennsylvania Bureau of Correction v. United States Marshals Service, 474 U.S. 34, 106 S.Ct. 355, 88 L.Ed.2d 189 (1985), 207

Pennzoil Co. v. Texaco, Inc., 481 U.S. 1, 107 S.Ct. 1519, 95 L.Ed.2d 1 (1987), **171,** 180, 181, 183, 190, 211

Permian Corp. v. United States, 665 F.2d 1214, 214 U.S.App.D.C. 396 (D.C.Cir. 1981), 610

Perrone v. General Motors Acceptance Corp., 232 F.3d 433 (5th Cir.2000), 263

Perry v. Thomas, 482 U.S. 483, 107 S.Ct. 2520, 96 L.Ed.2d 426 (1987), 886

Pettway v. American Cast Iron Pipe Co., 681 F.2d 1259 (11th Cir.1982), 410

Philadelphia Housing Authority v. American Radiator & Standard Sanitary Corp., 323 F.Supp. 381 (E.D.Pa.1970), 163

Philip Morris Inc. v. National Asbestos Workers Medical Fund, 214 F.3d 132 (2nd Cir.2000), 370

Phillips v. Joint Legislative Committee on Performance and Expenditure Review of State of Miss., 637 F.2d 1014 (5th Cir. 1981), 244

Phillips ex rel. Estates of Byrd v. General Motors Corp., 307 F.3d 1206 (9th Cir. 2002), 593

Phillips Petroleum Co. v. Shutts, 472 U.S. 797, 105 S.Ct. 2965, 86 L.Ed.2d 628 (1985), 141, 337, **412,** 426, 427, 799, 817

Phoceene Sous–Marine, S. A. v. United States Phosmarine, Inc., 682 F.2d 802 (9th Cir.1982), 652

Phoenix Canada Oil Co. Ltd. v. Texaco, Inc., 78 F.R.D. 445 (D.Del.1978), 141

Piper Aircraft Co. v. Reyno, 454 U.S. 235, 102 S.Ct. 252, 70 L.Ed.2d 419 (1981), 141, 142

Piper Aircraft Distribution System Antitrust Litigation, In re, 405 F.Supp. 1402 (Jud.Pan.Mult.Lit.1975), 152

Pitney–Bowes, Inc. v. Mestre, 86 F.R.D. 444 (S.D.Fla.1980), 624

Planned Parenthood of Minnesota, Inc. v. Citizens for Community Action, 558 F.2d 861 (8th Cir.1977), **64,** 67, 69, 70, 71

Playboy Enterprises, Inc. v. Welles, 60 F.Supp.2d 1050 (S.D.Cal.1999), 560, 662

Plumbing Fixtures Litigation, In re, 342 F.Supp. 756 (Jud.Pan.Mult.Lit.1972), 163, 164

Poliquin v. Garden Way, Inc., 154 F.R.D. 29 (D.Me.1994), 592

Pollard v. Cockrell, 578 F.2d 1002 (5th Cir. 1978), 798

Poster v. Central Gulf S. S. Corp., 25 F.R.D. 18 (E.D.Pa.1960), 37

Powell v. Georgia–Pacific Corp., 119 F.3d 703 (8th Cir.1997), 411

Powertel, Inc. v. Bexley, 743 So.2d 570 (Fla. App. 1 Dist.1999), 913

Prado–Steiman ex rel. Prado v. Bush, 221 F.3d 1266 (11th Cir.2000), 371

Pratt v. Chicago Housing Authority, 155 F.R.D. 177 (N.D.Ill.1994), 240

Premier Elec. Const. Co. v. National Elec. Contractors Ass'n, Inc., 814 F.2d 358 (7th Cir.1987), 459, 818

Prezant v. De Angelis, 636 A.2d 915 (Del. Supr.1994), 817

Prima Paint Corp. v. Flood & Conklin Mfg. Co., 388 U.S. 395, 87 S.Ct. 1801, 18 L.Ed.2d 1270 (1967), 885

Primus, In re, 436 U.S. 412, 98 S.Ct. 1893, 56 L.Ed.2d 417 (1978), 227, 618

Procter & Gamble Co. v. Bankers Trust Co., 78 F.3d 219 (6th Cir.1996), 572

Provident Tradesmens Bank & Trust Co. v. Patterson, 390 U.S. 102, 88 S.Ct. 733, 19 L.Ed.2d 936 (1968), 54, 55

Prudential Ins. Co. of America v. Lai, 42 F.3d 1299 (9th Cir.1994), 893

Prudential Ins. Co. of America Sales Practice Litigation, In re, 261 F.3d 355 (3rd Cir.2001), 816

Prudential Ins. Co. of America Sales Practices Litigation, In re, 314 F.3d 99 (3rd Cir.2002), 404

Prudential Ins. Co. of America Sales Practices Litigation, In re, 148 F.3d 283 (3rd Cir.1998), **519,** 533, 534, 535, 539

Prudential Ins. Co. of America Sales Practices Litigation, In re, 962 F.Supp. 450 (D.N.J.1997), 355

Prudential Ins. Co. of America Sales Practices Litigation, In re, 169 F.R.D. 598 (D.N.J.1997), 559, 571

Pulitzer–Polster v. Pulitzer, 784 F.2d 1305 (5th Cir.1986), 52, 56

Puricelli v. CNA Insurance Company, 185 F.R.D. 139 (N.D.N.Y.1999), 32

Pyke v. Cuomo, 209 F.R.D. 33 (N.D.N.Y. 2002), 370

Quackenbush v. Allstate Ins. Co., 517 U.S. 706, 116 S.Ct. 1712, 135 L.Ed.2d 1 (1996), 168

Railroad Commission of Tex. v. Pullman Co., 312 U.S. 496, 61 S.Ct. 643, 85 L.Ed. 971 (1941), 165, 168, 169, 170, 183

Ralston v. Volkswagenwerk, A. G., 61 F.R.D. 427 (W.D.Mo.1973), 481

Rand v. Monsanto Co., 926 F.2d 596 (7th Cir.1991), 297, 443

Randleel v. Pizza Hut of America, Inc., 182 F.R.D. 542 (N.D.Ill.1998), 33

Ravelo Monegro v. Rosa, 211 F.3d 509 (9th Cir.2000), 142

R.B. Matthews, Inc. v. Transamerica Transp. Services, Inc., 945 F.2d 269 (9th Cir.1991), 754

Real Estate Title and Settlement Services Antitrust Litigation, In re, 869 F.2d 760 (3rd Cir.1989), 439

Reaves, United States v., 636 F.Supp. 1575 (E.D.Ky.1986), 760

Rebney v. Wells Fargo Bank, 220 Cal. App.3d 1117, 269 Cal.Rptr. 844 (Cal. App. 1 Dist.1990), 508

Repetitive Stress Injury Litigation, In re, 11 F.3d 368 (2nd Cir.1993), 127

Reserve Mining Co., United States v., 56 F.R.D. 408 (D.Minn.1972), 71, **73,** 85, 101, 102

Residential Funding Corp. v. Degeorge Financial Corp., 306 F.3d 99 (2nd Cir. 2002), 568

Reynolds v. Beneficial Nat. Bank, 288 F.3d 277 (7th Cir.2002), 402, 534

Rhone–Poulenc Rorer Inc., Matter of, 51 F.3d 1293 (7th Cir.1995), 354, 357, 371, 768, 774

Rhone–Poulenc Rorer Inc. v. Home Indem. Co., 32 F.3d 851 (3rd Cir.1994), 480, **619,** 624, 625

Rhone–Poulenc Rorer Pharmaceuticals, Inc., Matter of, 138 F.3d 695 (7th Cir. 1998), 159

Rice v. City of Philadelphia, 66 F.R.D. 17 (E.D.Pa.1974), 330

Richards v. Jefferson County, Ala., 517 U.S. 793, 116 S.Ct. 1761, 135 L.Ed.2d 76 (1996), 798

Richardson, United States v., 233 F.3d 1285 (11th Cir.2000), 748

Rieff v. Evans, 672 N.W.2d 728 (Iowa 2003), 743

Rinehart v. Locke, 454 F.2d 313 (7th Cir. 1971), 787

Riverside, City of v. Rivera, 477 U.S. 561, 106 S.Ct. 2686, 91 L.Ed.2d 466 (1986), 700

Riverside, County of v. McLaughlin, 500 U.S. 44, 111 S.Ct. 1661, 114 L.Ed.2d 49 (1991), 494

Robbin v. Fluor Corp., 835 F.2d 213 (9th Cir.1987), 467

Roberts v. Heim, 130 F.R.D. 416 (N.D.Cal. 1988), 480

Robertson v. National Basketball Ass'n, 389 F.Supp. 867 (S.D.N.Y.1975), 239, 297, 300

Robinson v. Metro–North Commuter R.R. Co., 267 F.3d 147 (2nd Cir.2001), 328, 768

Roby v. St. Louis Southwestern Ry. Co., 775 F.2d 959 (8th Cir.1985), 276

Rochford v. Joyce, 755 F.Supp. 1423 (N.D.Ill.1990), 466

Rodriguez de Quijas v. Shearson/American Exp., Inc., 490 U.S. 477, 109 S.Ct. 1917, 104 L.Ed.2d 526 (1989), 887

Rogers v. Kroger Co., 669 F.2d 317 (5th Cir.1982), 652

Rolex Employees Retirement Trust v. Mentor Graphics Corp., 136 F.R.D. 658 (D.Or.1991), 257

Rooker v. Fidelity Trust Co., 263 U.S. 413, 44 S.Ct. 149, 68 L.Ed. 362 (1923), 183, 184

Rosmer v. Pfizer Inc., 263 F.3d 110 (4th Cir.2001), 429

Ross v. Bernhard, 396 U.S. 531, 90 S.Ct. 733, 24 L.Ed.2d 729 (1970), 737, 738, 743

Rossini v. Ogilvy & Mather, Inc., 798 F.2d 590 (2nd Cir.1986), 276

Rowe Entertainment, Inc. v. William Morris Agency, Inc., 205 F.R.D. 421 (S.D.N.Y. 2002), 558

Ruiz v. Estelle, 161 F.3d 814 (5th Cir.1998), 69

Ruiz v. Estelle, 679 F.2d 1115 (5th Cir. 1982), 661, 662

Russell v. Curtin Matheson Scientific, Inc., 493 F.Supp. 456 (S.D.Tex.1980), 625

Rutherford v. Owens–Illinois, Inc., 67 Cal. Rptr.2d 16, 941 P.2d 1203 (Cal.1997), 45

Rutstein v. Avis Rent–A–Car Systems, Inc., 211 F.3d 1228 (11th Cir.2000), 278

Sackman v. Liggett Group, Inc., 167 F.R.D. 6 (E.D.N.Y.1996), 71

Sanders v. Shell Oil Co., 678 F.2d 614 (5th Cir.1982), 602

San Jose Mercury News, Inc. v. United States Dist. Court–Northern Dist. (San Jose), 187 F.3d 1096 (9th Cir.1999), 591

San Juan Dupont Plaza Hotel Fire Litigation, In re, 859 F.2d 1007 (1st Cir.1988), 637

Sargent v. Genesco, Inc., 492 F.2d 750 (5th Cir.1974), 131

Saturn Distribution Corp. v. Williams, 905 F.2d 719 (4th Cir.1990), 886

Schmidt v. E.N. Maisel and Associates, 105 F.R.D. 157 (N.D.Ill.1985), 56

Schnabel v. Lui, 302 F.3d 1023 (9th Cir. 2002), 127

Schneider v. Lockheed Aircraft Corp., 658 F.2d 835, 212 U.S.App.D.C. 87 (D.C.Cir. 1981), 863

Schomber by Schomber v. Jewel Companies, Inc., 614 F.Supp. 210 (N.D.Ill. 1985), 189

School Asbestos Litigation, In re, 789 F.2d 996 (3rd Cir.1986), 355, 437

Schur v. Friedman & Shaftan, P.C., 123 F.R.D. 611 (N.D.Cal.1988), 467

SCM Corp. v. Xerox Corp., 463 F.Supp. 983 (D.Conn.1978), 941

Scott v. American Tobacco Co., 725 So.2d 10 (La.App. 4 Cir.1998), 358, 776

Scott v. City of Anniston, Ala., 682 F.2d 1353 (11th Cir.1982), 330, 508

Scott v. The American Tobacco Company, Inc., Docket No. 2003–C–1872 (La.Ct. App.4th Cir.2003), 776

Scott v. The American Tobacco Company, Inc., et al., 1997 WL 33635686 (La.Civil D.Ct.1997), 358

Screws Antitrust Litigation, In re, 91 F.R.D. 52 (D.Mass.1981), 265

Sealed Case, In re, 877 F.2d 976, 278 U.S.App.D.C. 188 (D.C.Cir.1989), 603

Seattle Times Co. v. Rhinehart, 467 U.S. 20, 104 S.Ct. 2199, 81 L.Ed.2d 17 (1984), **574,** 580, 581, 582, 590, 591, 593

Seattle Totems Hockey Club, Inc. v. National Hockey League, 652 F.2d 852 (9th Cir.1981), 198, 199

S.E.C. v. TheStreet.Com, 273 F.3d 222 (2nd Cir.2001), 591

Securities Industry Ass'n v. Connolly, 883 F.2d 1114 (1st Cir.1989), 886

Seminole Tribe of Florida v. Florida, 517 U.S. 44, 116 S.Ct. 1114, 134 L.Ed.2d 252 (1996), 61, 62

Semmes Motors, Inc. v. Ford Motor Co., 429 F.2d 1197 (2nd Cir.1970), **109,** 114, 199

Setter v. A.H. Robins Company, Inc., 748 F.2d 1328 (8th Cir.1984), 876

Shaw v. Toshiba America Information Systems, Inc., 91 F.Supp.2d 942 (E.D.Tex. 2000), 517

Shearson/American Exp., Inc. v. McMahon, 482 U.S. 220, 107 S.Ct. 2332, 96 L.Ed.2d 185 (1987), 887

Shelton v. Pargo, Inc., 582 F.2d 1298 (4th Cir.1978), 510

Shimkus v. Gersten Companies, 816 F.2d 1318 (9th Cir.1987), 52

Shipes v. BIC Corp., 154 F.R.D. 301 (M.D.Ga.1994), 544

Shores v. Sklar, 885 F.2d 760 (11th Cir. 1989), 497

Showa Denko K.K. L–Tryptophan Products Liability Litigation–II, In re, 953 F.2d 162 (4th Cir.1992), 683

Shutts v. Phillips Petroleum Co., 240 Kan. 764, 732 P.2d 1286 (Kan.1987), 435, 436, 439, 448, 456, 457, 479

Sierra Club v. City of San Antonio, 112 F.3d 789 (5th Cir.1997), 168

Silberkleit v. Kantrowitz, 713 F.2d 433 (9th Cir.1983), 187

Silvestri v. General Motors Corp., 271 F.3d 583 (4th Cir.2001), 569

Simer v. Rios, 661 F.2d 655 (7th Cir. 1981), **231, 406,** 408, 409

Simon II Litigation, In re, 211 F.R.D. 86 (E.D.N.Y.2002), 316

Sims v. ANR Freight System, Inc., 77 F.3d 846 (5th Cir.1996), 761

Sindell v. Abbott Laboratories, 163 Cal. Rptr. 132, 607 P.2d 924 (Cal.1980), 44, 45

Singer v. City of Waco, Tex., 324 F.3d 813 (5th Cir.2003), 686

Six (6) Mexican Workers v. Arizona Citrus Growers, 904 F.2d 1301 (9th Cir.1990), 410

Smilow v. Southwestern Bell Mobile Systems, Inc., 323 F.3d 32 (1st Cir. 2003), **257,** 263, 265, 266, 267, 404

Smith v. Armour Pharmaceutical Co., 838 F.Supp. 1573 (S.D.Fla.1993), 605

Smith v. Swormstedt, 57 U.S. 288, 16 How. 288, 14 L.Ed. 942 (1853), 218

Smith v. Texaco, Inc., 263 F.3d 394 (5th Cir.2001), 327, 356

Smith Kline & French Laboratories Ltd v. Bloch, 1982 WL 222260 (CA 1982), 140

Smuck v. Hobson, 408 F.2d 175, 132 U.S.App.D.C. 372 (D.C.Cir.1969), 67

Snyder v. Harris, 394 U.S. 332, 89 S.Ct. 1053, 22 L.Ed.2d 319 (1969), 221, 428

Solid Waste Agency of Northern Cook County v. United States Army Corps of Engineers, 101 F.3d 503 (7th Cir.1996), 71

Sonmore v. CheckRite Recovery Services, Inc., 206 F.R.D. 257 (D.Minn.2001), 230

South Central Bell Telephone Co. v. Alabama, 526 U.S. 160, 119 S.Ct. 1180, 143 L.Ed.2d 258 (1999), 798

Southern Const. Co. v. Pickard, 371 U.S. 57, 83 S.Ct. 108, 9 L.Ed.2d 31 (1962), 199

Southern Ute Indian Tribe v. Amoco Production Co., 2 F.3d 1023 (10th Cir.1993), 448

Southland Corp. v. Keating, 465 U.S. 1, 104 S.Ct. 852, 79 L.Ed.2d 1 (1984), 885, 889, 897

Southwest Airlines Co. v. Texas Intern. Airlines, Inc., 546 F.2d 84 (5th Cir.1977), 800

Span–Eng Associates v. Weidner, 771 F.2d 464 (10th Cir.1985), 115

Sparshott v. Feld Entertainment, Inc., 311 F.3d 425, 354 U.S.App.D.C. 63 (D.C.Cir. 2002), 762

Spiller v. Tennessee Trailers, Inc., 97 F.R.D. 347 (N.D.Ga.1982), 56

Sporck v. Peil, 759 F.2d 312 (3rd Cir.1985), 618

Stallworth v. Monsanto Co., 558 F.2d 257 (5th Cir.1977), 84, 85

Standard Microsystems Corp. v. Texas Instruments Inc., 916 F.2d 58 (2nd Cir.1990), 190, **191,** 197

Stanford v. Tennessee Val. Authority, 18 F.R.D. 152 (M.D.Tenn.1955), **34,** 37, 43

State Compensation Ins. Fund v. WPS, Inc., 82 Cal.Rptr.2d 799 (Cal.App. 2 Dist. 1999), 605

State ex rel. v. _____ (see opposing party and relator)

State Farm Fire & Cas. Co. v. Tashire, 386 U.S. 523, 87 S.Ct. 1199, 18 L.Ed.2d 270 (1967), 316

State Farm Mut. Auto. Ins. Co. v. Campbell, 538 U.S. 408, 123 S.Ct. 1513, 155 L.Ed.2d 585 (2003), 317, 436

State of (see name of state)

Stephenson v. Dow Chemical Co., 273 F.3d 249 (2nd Cir.2001), 289, **819,** 827, 828, 829, 830

Sterling v. Velsicol Chemical Corp., 855 F.2d 1188 (6th Cir.1988), 338

Stevenson v. Union Pacific R. Co., 354 F.3d 739 (8th Cir.2004), 567

Stine v. Marathon Oil Co., 976 F.2d 254 (5th Cir.1992), 752

Stoll v. Gottlieb, 305 U.S. 165, 59 S.Ct. 134, 83 L.Ed. 104 (1938), 802

St. Pierre, United States v., 132 F.2d 837 (2nd Cir.1942), 623

Strandell v. Jackson County, Ill., 838 F.2d 884 (7th Cir.1987), 942

Strawbridge v. Curtiss, 7 U.S. 267, 2 L.Ed. 435 (1806), 58, 427

Stringfellow v. Concerned Neighbors in Action, 480 U.S. 370, 107 S.Ct. 1177, 94 L.Ed.2d 389 (1987), 85
Student Public Interest Research Group of New Jersey, Inc. v. AT & T Bell Laboratories, 842 F.2d 1436 (3rd Cir.1988), 699
Suburban Sew 'N Sweep, Inc. v. Swiss–Bernina, Inc., 91 F.R.D. 254 (N.D.Ill. 1981), 602
Sullivan v. Everhart, 494 U.S. 83, 110 S.Ct. 960, 108 L.Ed.2d 72 (1990), 328
Summers v. Tice, 33 Cal.2d 80, 199 P.2d 1 (Cal.1948), 44
Sun Refining & Marketing Co. v. Brennan, 921 F.2d 635 (6th Cir.1990), 181
Superior Beverage/Glass Container Consol. Pretrial, Matter of, 133 F.R.D. 119 (N.D.Ill.1990), **706**
Supreme Tribe of Ben Hur v. Cauble, 255 U.S. 356, 41 S.Ct. 338, 65 L.Ed. 673 (1921), 218, 427, 428, 429
Suson v. Zenith Radio Corp., 763 F.2d 304 (7th Cir.1985), 726
Symbolic Control, Inc. v. International Business Machines Corp., 643 F.2d 1339 (9th Cir.1980), **762,** 765, 773
Syngenta Crop Protection, Inc. v. Henson, 537 U.S. 28, 123 S.Ct. 366, 154 L.Ed.2d 368 (2002), 208, 827, 828
Synthroid Marketing Litigation, In re, 264 F.3d 712 (7th Cir.2001), 715
Szabo v. Bridgeport Machines, Inc., 249 F.3d 672 (7th Cir.2001), 370
Szetela v. Discover Bank, 118 Cal.Rptr.2d 862 (Cal.App. 4 Dist.2002), 913

Taylor v. Hayes, 418 U.S. 488, 94 S.Ct. 2697, 41 L.Ed.2d 897 (1974), 651
Taylor v. Illinois, 484 U.S. 400, 108 S.Ct. 646, 98 L.Ed.2d 798 (1988), 737
TBK Partners, Ltd. v. Western Union Corp., 675 F.2d 456 (2nd Cir.1982), 516
Technitrol, Inc. v. Digital Equipment Corp., 1974 WL 20497 (N.D.Ill.1974), 623
Telectronics Pacing Systems, Inc., In re, 221 F.3d 870 (6th Cir.2000), 314
Telectronics Pacing Systems, Inc., In re, 172 F.R.D. 271 (S.D.Ohio 1997), 301, 357
Tele–Media Co. of Western Connecticut v. Antidormi, 179 F.R.D. 75 (D.Conn. 1998), 38
Tell v. Trustees of Dartmouth College, 145 F.3d 417 (1st Cir.1998), 60
Temple v. Synthes Corp., Ltd., 498 U.S. 5, 111 S.Ct. 315, 112 L.Ed.2d 263 (1990), 54
Tennenbaum v. Deloitte & Touche, 77 F.3d 337 (9th Cir.1996), 605
Terrell v. DeConna, 877 F.2d 1267 (5th Cir.1989), 799
Texas Eastern Transmission Corp., United States v., 923 F.2d 410 (5th Cir.1991), 83

Texas State Teachers Ass'n v. Garland Independent School Dist., 489 U.S. 782, 109 S.Ct. 1486, 103 L.Ed.2d 866 (1989), 698
Thillens, Inc. v. Community Currency Exchange Ass'n of Illinois, Inc., 97 F.R.D. 668 (N.D.Ill.1983), **359,** 366, 426
Thirteen Appeals Arising Out of San Juan Dupont Plaza Hotel Fire Litigation, In re, 56 F.3d 295 (1st Cir.1995), 716
Thomas v. Albright, 139 F.3d 227, 329 U.S.App.D.C. 190 (D.C.Cir.1998), 457
Three Additional Appeals Arising Out of San Juan Dupont Plaza Hotel Fire Litigation, In re, 93 F.3d 1 (1st Cir.1996), 684
Tice v. American Airlines, Inc., 162 F.3d 966 (7th Cir.1998), 799
Ticor Title Ins. Co. v. Brown, 511 U.S. 117, 114 S.Ct. 1359, 128 L.Ed.2d 33 (1994), 457
TIG Ins. Co. v. Reliable Research Co., 334 F.3d 630 (7th Cir.2003), 60
Tiller v. Atlantic Coast Line R. Co., 323 U.S. 574, 65 S.Ct. 421, 89 L.Ed. 465 (1945), 34
Tilley v. TJX Companies, Inc., 345 F.3d 34 (1st Cir.2003), 367, 368, 371
Ting v. AT&T, 319 F.3d 1126 (9th Cir. 2003), 913
TMI Litigation, In re, 193 F.3d 613 (3rd Cir.1999), 127
Tosti v. City of Los Angeles, 754 F.2d 1485 (9th Cir.1985), 468
Toucey v. New York Life Ins. Co., 314 U.S. 118, 62 S.Ct. 139, 86 L.Ed. 100 (1941), 190
Transamerica Computer Co., Inc. v. International Business Machines Corp., 573 F.2d 646 (9th Cir.1978), **595,** 602, 604, 606, 650
TransOcean Tender Offer Securities Litigation, In re, 427 F.Supp. 1211 (N.D.Ill. 1977), 818
Traylor v. Husqvarna Motor, 988 F.2d 729 (7th Cir.1993), 754
Trbovich v. United Mine Workers of America, 404 U.S. 528, 92 S.Ct. 630, 30 L.Ed.2d 686 (1972), 68, 72
Tucker v. United States Dept. of Commerce, 135 F.R.D. 175 (N.D.Ill.1991), 240
Tull v. United States, 481 U.S. 412, 107 S.Ct. 1831, 95 L.Ed.2d 365 (1987), 743
Twelve John Does v. District of Columbia, 117 F.3d 571, 326 U.S.App.D.C. 17 (D.C.Cir.1997), 495
Twentieth Century Fox Film Corp., United States v., 882 F.2d 656 (2nd Cir.1989), 651
Twitty v. Minnesota Mining & Mfg. Co., 1993 WL 540515 (Pa.Com.Pl.1993), 942
Two Appeals Arising Out of San Juan Dupont Plaza Hotel Fire Litigation, In re, 994 F.2d 956 (1st Cir.1993), 684

Tyus v. Schoemehl, 93 F.3d 449 (8th Cir. 1996), **788,** 797, 798, 799, 800

Union Carbide Corp. Gas Plant Disaster at Bhopal, India in Dec., 1984, In re, 809 F.2d 195 (2nd Cir.1987), 140

Union Elec. Co., United States v., 64 F.3d 1152 (8th Cir.1995), 83

Uniroyal Goodrich Tire Co. v. Mutual Trading Corp., 63 F.3d 516 (7th Cir.1995), 702

United Airlines, Inc. v. McDonald, 432 U.S. 385, 97 S.Ct. 2464, 53 L.Ed.2d 423 (1977), 84, 468

United Food & Commercial Workers Union Local No. 115 v. Armour and Co., 106 F.R.D. 345 (N.D.Cal.1985), 637

United Mine Workers of America v. Gibbs, 383 U.S. 715, 86 S.Ct. 1130, 16 L.Ed.2d 218 (1966), 58

United Mine Workers of America Employee Ben. Plans Litigation, In re, 854 F.Supp. 914 (D.D.C.1994), 164

United Nuclear Corp. v. Cranford Ins. Co., 905 F.2d 1424 (10th Cir.1990), 580

United States v. _____ (see opposing party)

United States Bancorp Mortg. Co. v. Bonner Mall Partnership, 513 U.S. 18, 115 S.Ct. 386, 130 L.Ed.2d 233 (1994), 882

United States E.P.A. v. City of Green Forest, Ark., 921 F.2d 1394 (8th Cir.1990), 801

United States Financial Securities Litigation, In re, 609 F.2d 411 (9th Cir.1979), 739

United States Parole Commission v. Geraghty, 445 U.S. 388, 100 S.Ct. 1202, 63 L.Ed.2d 479 (1980), **484,** 494, 495, 496, 497

Upjohn Co. v. United States, 449 U.S. 383, 101 S.Ct. 677, 66 L.Ed.2d 584 (1981), 594, 611

Upjohn Co. Antibiotic Cleocin Products Liability Litigation, In re, 664 F.2d 114 (6th Cir.1981), 162

U.S. Information Systems, Inc. v. International Bhd. of Elec. Workers Local Union No. 3, 2002 WL 31296430 (S.D.N.Y. 2002), 612

Valentino v. Carter–Wallace, Inc., 97 F.3d 1227 (9th Cir.1996), 354

Valley Drug Co. v. Geneva Pharmaceuticals, Inc., 350 F.3d 1181 (11th Cir.2003), 295

Vanderbilt v. Geo–Energy Ltd., 725 F.2d 204 (3rd Cir.1983), 227

Van Dusen v. Barrack, 376 U.S. 612, 84 S.Ct. 805, 11 L.Ed.2d 945 (1964), 131, 163, 164

Van Gemert v. Boeing Co., 739 F.2d 730 (2nd Cir.1984), 412

Van Gemert v. Boeing Co., 259 F.Supp. 125 (S.D.N.Y.1966), 298

Van Gerwen v. Guarantee Mut. Life Co., 214 F.3d 1041 (9th Cir.2000), 700

Vaught v. Showa Denko K.K., 107 F.3d 1137 (5th Cir.1997), 466

Vendo Co. v. Lektro–Vend Corp., 433 U.S. 623, 97 S.Ct. 2881, 53 L.Ed.2d 1009 (1977), 196, 199

Venegas v. Mitchell, 495 U.S. 82, 110 S.Ct. 1679, 109 L.Ed.2d 74 (1990), 701, 703

Vergara v. Hampton, 581 F.2d 1281 (7th Cir.1978), 244

Vimar Seguros y Reaseguros, S.A. v. M/V SKY REEFER, 515 U.S. 528, 115 S.Ct. 2322, 132 L.Ed.2d 462 (1995), 895

Vincent v. Hughes Air West, Inc., 557 F.2d 759 (9th Cir.1977), 668, 683

Vincent v. Thompson, 50 A.D.2d 211, 377 N.Y.S.2d 118 (N.Y.A.D. 2 Dept.1975), 874

Visa Check/MasterMoney Antitrust Litigation, In re, 280 F.3d 124 (2nd Cir.2001), 265, 266, 357

Vitamins Antitrust Class Actions, In re, 215 F.3d 26, 342 U.S.App.D.C. 26 (D.C.Cir. 2000), 459, 534

Vizcaino v. Microsoft Corp., 290 F.3d 1043 (9th Cir.2002), 698

VMS Securities Litigation, Matter of, 103 F.3d 1317 (7th Cir.1996), 828

V. Mueller & Co. v. Corley, 570 S.W.2d 140 (Tex.Civ.App.-Hous. (1 Dist.) 1978), 216

Vollmer v. Publishers Clearing House, 248 F.3d 698 (7th Cir.2001), 518

Volt Information Sciences, Inc. v. Board of Trustees of Leland Stanford Junior University, 489 U.S. 468, 109 S.Ct. 1248, 103 L.Ed.2d 488 (1989), 886, 889, 891, 897, 913

von Bulow, In re, 828 F.2d 94 (2nd Cir. 1987), 603

von Bulow by Auersperg v. von Bulow, 114 F.R.D. 71 (S.D.N.Y.1987), 603

Vuyanich v. Republic Nat. Bank of Dallas, 505 F.Supp. 224 (N.D.Tex.1980), 778

Walker v. City of Birmingham, 388 U.S. 307, 87 S.Ct. 1824, 18 L.Ed.2d 1210 (1967), 650

Walker v. Jim Dandy Co., 747 F.2d 1360 (11th Cir.1984), 276

Walker v. Liggett Group, Inc., 175 F.R.D. 226 (S.D.W.Va.1997), 388

Walters v. Inexco Oil Co., 440 So.2d 268 (Miss.1983), 731

Washington v. Lee, 263 F.Supp. 327 (M.D.Ala.1966), 283

Washington v. Philadelphia County Court of Common Pleas, 89 F.3d 1031 (3rd Cir.1996), 701

Washington Mutual Bank, FA v. Superior Court, 103 Cal.Rptr.2d 320, 15 P.3d 1071 (Cal.2001), 438

Waters v. International Precious Metals Corp., 237 F.3d 1273 (11th Cir.2001), 540

Watson v. Shell Oil Co., 979 F.2d 1014 (5th Cir.1992), 776, 783

Weil v. Investment/Indicators, Research and Management, Inc., 647 F.2d 18 (9th Cir.1981), **602,** 605, 606

Weinberger v. Kendrick, 698 F.2d 61 (2nd Cir.1982), 372

Weiss, In re, 596 F.2d 1185 (4th Cir.1979), 611

Welling v. Alexy, 155 F.R.D. 654 (N.D.Cal. 1994), 296

Western Pac. R. Co., United States v., 352 U.S. 59, 77 S.Ct. 161, 1 L.Ed.2d 126 (1956), 170

Westinghouse Elec. Corp. v. Kerr–McGee Corp., 580 F.2d 1311 (7th Cir.1978), 680

Westinghouse Elec. Corp. v. Republic of Philippines, 951 F.2d 1414 (3rd Cir. 1991), 611

Westinghouse Elec. Corp. v. Rio Algom Ltd., 448 F.Supp. 1284 (N.D.Ill.1978), 680

Westinghouse Elec. Corp. Uranium Contracts Litigation, In re, 405 F.Supp. 316 (Jud.Pan.Mult.Lit.1975), 153

Westinghouse Electric Corp. v. Newman & Holtzinger, 46 Cal.Rptr.2d 151 (Cal.App. 2 Dist.1995), 594

West Virginia Rezulin Litigation, In re, 214 W.Va. 52, 585 S.E.2d 52 (W.Va.2003), 355

Wheeling–Pittsburgh Steel Corp., United States v., 866 F.2d 57 (3rd Cir.1988), 83

White v. Auerbach, 500 F.2d 822 (2nd Cir. 1974), 682

White, United States v., 887 F.2d 267, 281 U.S.App.D.C. 39 (D.C.Cir.1989), 625

Whyham v. Piper Aircraft Corp., 96 F.R.D. 557 (M.D.Pa.1982), 53

Wickard v. Filburn, 317 U.S. 111, 63 S.Ct. 82, 87 L.Ed. 122 (1942), 885

Wicker v. Board of Educ. of Knott County, Ky., 826 F.2d 442 (6th Cir.1987), 169

Wilko v. Swan, 346 U.S. 427, 74 S.Ct. 182, 98 L.Ed. 168 (1953), 886, 887

William Gluckin & Co. v. International Playtex Corp., 407 F.2d 177 (2nd Cir. 1969), **104,** 108

Williams v. Lane, 851 F.2d 867 (7th Cir. 1988), 661

Williams v. Robinson, 1 F.R.D. 211 (D.D.C 1940), 34

Williams v. United States Dist. Court, 658 F.2d 430 (6th Cir.1981), 478

Wilson v. American Motors Corp., 759 F.2d 1568 (11th Cir.1985), 881

Wilson v. Minor, 220 F.3d 1297 (11th Cir. 2000), 100

Wilson Wear, Inc. v. United Merchants and Mfrs., Inc., 713 F.2d 324 (7th Cir.1983), 885

Wilton v. Seven Falls Co., 515 U.S. 277, 115 S.Ct. 2137, 132 L.Ed.2d 214 (1995), 189, 190

Wing v. Asarco Inc., 114 F.3d 986 (9th Cir.1997), 701

Winkler v. Eli Lilly & Co., 101 F.3d 1196 (7th Cir.1996), 191

Wirebound Boxes Antitrust Litigation, In re, 128 F.R.D. 256 (D.Minn.1989), 675

Wisland v. Admiral Beverage Corp., 119 F.3d 733 (8th Cir.1997), 131

Woolen v. Surtran Taxicabs, Inc., 684 F.2d 324 (5th Cir.1982), **448,** 456, 841

WorldCom, Inc. Securities Litigation, In re, 219 F.R.D. 267 (S.D.N.Y.2003), 227

Wright v. AmSouth Bancorporation, 320 F.3d 1198 (11th Cir.2003), 558

Wyandotte Nation v. City of Kansas City, Kansas, 214 F.R.D. 656 (D.Kan.2003), 367

Wyeth Laboratories, a Div. of American Home Products Corp. v. United States Dist. Court for Dist. of Kansas, 851 F.2d 321 (10th Cir.1988), 591

Yaffe v. Detroit Steel Corp., 50 F.R.D. 481 (N.D.Ill.1970), 496

Yaffe v. Powers, 454 F.2d 1362 (1st Cir. 1972), 237

Young, Ex parte, 209 U.S. 123, 28 S.Ct. 441, 52 L.Ed. 714 (1908), 61, 62

Younger v. Harris, 401 U.S. 37, 91 S.Ct. 746, 27 L.Ed.2d 669 (1971), 180, 181, 182, 183

Ysbrand v. DaimlerChrysler Corp., 81 P.3d 618 (Okla.2003), 438

Zahn v. International Paper Co., 414 U.S. 291, 94 S.Ct. 505, 38 L.Ed.2d 511 (1973), 221, 428, 429

Zauderer v. Office of Disciplinary Counsel of Supreme Court of Ohio, 471 U.S. 626, 105 S.Ct. 2265, 85 L.Ed.2d 652 (1985), 476

Zawikowski v. Beneficial Nat. Bank, 1999 WL 35304 (N.D.Ill.1999), 913

Zenith Radio Corp. v. Matsushita Elec. Indus. Co., Ltd., 529 F.Supp. 866 (E.D.Pa. 1981), 572, 573, 593

Zimmer Paper Products, Inc. v. Berger & Montague, P.C., 758 F.2d 86 (3rd Cir. 1985), 540

Zinser v. Accufix Research Institute, Inc., 253 F.3d 1180 (9th Cir.2001), 301, 436

Zubulake v. UBS Warburg LLC, 220 F.R.D. 212 (S.D.N.Y.2003), 567, 569, 570, 604

Zubulake v. UBS Warburg LLC, 217 F.R.D. 309 (S.D.N.Y.2003), **546,** 557, 558, 559, 560, 561

Zubulake v. UBS Warburg LLC, 216 F.R.D. 280 (S.D.N.Y.2003), 556, 604

Zucker v. Occidental Petroleum Corp., 192 F.3d 1323 (9th Cir.1999), 681

*

Table of Authorities

References are to pages.

Abelson & Glater, Tough Questions are Raised on Fen–Phen Compensation, N.Y.Times, Oct. 7, 2003, at C1, p. 540

ALI, Restatement (Third) of the Law Governing Lawyers § 128 comment d(iii) (2000), 515

American Law Institute, Complex Litigation: Statutory Recommendations and Analysis § 5.01 (1994), 153

Andrews, N., English Civil Procedure 337 (2003), 639

Bacigal, R., The Limits of Litigation—The Dalkon Shield Controversy 125–26 (1990), 784

Baker, "Our Federalism" in *Pennzoil Co. v. Texaco, Inc.* or How the *Younger* Doctrine Keeps Getting Older Not Better, 9 Rev.Litig. 303 (1990), 181

Bandes, The Idea of a Case, 42 Stan.L.Rev. 227 (1990), 496

Bartel, Reconceptualizing the Joint Defense Doctrine, 65 Fordham L.Rev. 871 (1996), 610

Bell, Serving Two Masters: Integration Ideals and Client Interests in School Desegregation Litigation, 85 Yale L.J. 470 (1976), 241

Berger, Away From the Courthouse and Into the Field, The Odyssey of a Special Master, 78 Colum.L.Rev. 707 (1978), 661

Berger, Court Awarded Attorneys' Fees: What is Reasonable?, 126 U.Pa.L.Rev. 281 (1977), 687

Bishop, Hard Times for Women in Construction, N.Y. Times, Sept. 27, 1992, at B2, p. 49

Bishop, Scant Success for California Efforts to Put Women in Construction Trades, N.Y. Times, Feb. 14, 1991 at A16 col. 1, p. 49

Blair & Maron, An Evaluation of Retrieval Effectiveness for a Full–Text Document–Retrieval System, 28 Commun. of the A.C.M. 289 (1985), 544

Bone & Evans, Class Certification and the Substantive Merits, 51 Duke L.J. 1251 (2002), 356

Bone, Rethinking the "Day in Court" Ideal and Nonparty Preclusion, 67 N.Y.U. L. Rev. 193 (1992), 802

Bone, Statistical Adjudication: Rights, Justice and Utility in a World of Process Scarcity, 46 Vand. L. Rev. 561 (1993), 781

Bordens & Horowitz, Mass Tort Civil Litigation: The Impact of Procedural Changes on Jury Decisions, 73 Judicature 22 (1989), 775

Brazil, Special Masters in Complex Cases: Extending the Judiciary or Reshaping Adjudication?, 53 U.Chi.L.Rev. 394 (1986), 637, 661, 662

Brazil, What Lawyers Want From Judges in the Settlement Arena, 106 F.R.D. 85 (1985), 642

Brazil, Kahn, Newman & Gold, Early Neutral Evaluation: An Experimental Effort to Expedite Dispute Resolution, 69 Judicature 279 (1986), 944

Brickman, On the Theory Class's Theories of Asbestos Litigation: The Disconnect Between Scholarship and Reality?, 31 Pepp. L. Rev. 33 (2003), 230

Brodeur, P., Outrageous Misconduct 64 (1985), 873

Brookings Institution, Charting a Future for the Civil Jury System 10 (1992), 732

Brunet, A Study in the Allocation of Scarce Resources: The Efficiency of Federal Intervention Criteria, 12 Georgia L.Rev. 701 (1978), 28, 63, 84

Brunet, Class Action Objectors: Extortionist Free Riders or Fairness Guarantors, 2003 U.Chi.Legal F. 403, pp. 518, 519, 679

Brunet, Questioning the Quality of Alternative Dispute Resolution, 62 Tulane L.Rev. 1 (1987), 941

Burbank, Interjurisdictional Preclusion, Full Faith and Credit and Federal Common Law: A General Approach, 71 Cornell L.Rev. 733 (1986), 801

Burbank, The Costs of Complexity, 85 Mich.L.Rev. 1463 (1987), 19

Burke & Kummer, Controlling Discovery Costs, Legal Times, Aug. 18, 2003, at 19, p. 543

Burns, Decorative Figureheads: Eliminating Class Representatives in Class Actions, 42 Hastings L.J. 165 (1990), 295

Buxton & Glover, Managing a Big Case Down to Size, 15 Litigation 22, 22–23 (Summer 1989), 748

Byron, Computer Forensics Sleuths Help Find Fraud, Wall. St. J., March 18, 2003, at B1, p. 543

Cabraser, Life After Amchem: The Class Struggle Continues, 31 Loyola L.A. L. Rev. 373 (1998), 389

Camisa, The Constitutional Right To Solicit Potential Class Members in a Class Action, 25 Gonzaga L.Rev. 95 (1989), 476

Capello & Strenio, Jury Questioning: The Verdict Is In, Trial, June 2000, at 44, p. 748

Carrington, Virtual Civil Litigation: A Visit to John Bunyan's Celestial City, 98 Colum. L. Rev. 1516 (1998), 752

Carrington & Haagen, Contract and Jurisdiction, 1996 S.Ct. Rev. 331, p. 889

Catania & Sullivan, Judging Judgments: The 1991 Civil Rights Act and the Lingering Ghost of Martin v. Wilks, 57 Brooklyn L. Rev. 995 (1992), 99

C. Bingham & L. Gansler, Class Action 181 (2002), 277

Cellini, An Overview of Antitrust Class Actions, 49 Antitrust L.J. 1501, (1980), 666

Chafee, Z., Some Problems of Equity 257 (1950), 219

Chayes, Foreword: Public Law Litigation and the Burger Court, 96 Harv.L.Rev. 4 (1982), 495

Chayes, Public Law Litigation and the Burger Court, 96 Harv. L. Rev. 4 (1982), 69

Chayes, The Role of the Judge in Public Law Litigation, 89 Harv.L.Rev. 1281 (1976), 3, 222

Clermont & Currivan, Improving on the Contingent Fee, 63 Cornell L.Rev. 529 (1978), 716

Coffee, Class Action Accountability: Reconciling Exit, Voice, and Loyalty in Representative Litigation, 100 Colum. L. Rev. 370, 391 (2000), 514

Coffee, Class Wars: The Dilemma of the Mass Tort Class Action, 95 Colum. L. Rev. 1343 (1995), 534

Coffee, The Regulation of Entrepreneurial Litigation: Balancing Fairness and Efficiency in the Large Class Action, 54 U.Chi.L.Rev. 877 (1987), 229, 676

Coffee, The Unfaithful Champion: The Plaintiff as Monitor in Shareholder Litigation, 48 Law & Contemp. Problems 5 (Summer 1985), 229, 617, 714

Coffee, Understanding the Plaintiff's Attorney: The Implications of Economic Theory for Private Enforcement of Law Through Class and Derivative Actions, 86 Colum.L.Rev. 669 (1986), 229

Cohen, A. & D. Lender, Electronic Discovery § 8.04 (2003), 545

Cohen, A. & D. Lender, Electronic Discovery: Law and Practice (2003), 561

Cohn, The New Federal Rules of Civil Procedure, 54 Geo.L.J. 1204 (1966), 455

Cole, The Revised Uniform Arbitration Act: Is It the Wrong Cure?, 8 No. 4 Disp. Resol. Mag. 10 (2002), 884

Comment, Compulsory Joinder of Classes, 58 U.Chi.L.Rev. 1453 (1991), 52

Comment, The First Amendment and Pretrial Discovery Hearings: When Should the Public and Press Have Access?, 36 UCLA L.Rev. 609 (1989), 582

Comment, The Judicial Panel on Multidistrict Litigation: Time for Rethinking, 140 U. Pa. L. Rev. 711 (1991), 152

Connell, The Task–Based Billing Express, Calif. Lawyer, Aug. 1995, at 25, p. 698

Cooper, Interstate Consolidation: A Comparison of the ALI Project with the Uniform Transfer of Litigation Act, 54 La. L. Rev. 897 (1994), 132

Cooter & Rubinfeld, Reforming the New Discovery Rules, 84 Geo. L.J. 61 (1995), 558

Cox, Making Securities Fraud Class Actions Virtuous, 39 Az. L. Rev. 497 (1997), 254

Crampton, Lawyer Ethics and the Lunar Landscape of Asbestos Litigation, 31 Pepp. L. Rev. 175 (2003), 230

Currie, Pendent Parties, 45 U.Chi.L.Rev. 753 (1978), 428

C. Wright & M. Kane, Law of Federal Courts (6th ed. 2002), 165, 191

Dam, Class Actions: Efficiency, Compensation, Deterrence, and Conflict of Interest, 4 J.Legal Studies 47 (1975), 228

Damaska, M., The Faces of Justice and State Authority 62 (1986), 757

Dann & Logan, Jury Reform: The Arizona Experience, 79 Judicature 280 (1996), 745

Dawson, Lawyers and Involuntary Clients in Public Interest Litigation, 88 Harv. L.Rev. 849 (1975), 713, 715

Degnan, Adequacy of Representation in Class Actions, 60 Calif.L.Rev. 705 (1972), 292

Degnan, Federalized Res Judicata, 85 Yale L.J. 733 (1976), 801

Developments in the Law—Class Actions, 89 Harv.L.Rev. 1318 (1976), 256

Developments in the Law, Conflicts of Interest in the Legal Profession, 94 Harv. L.Rev. 1224 (1981), 680

Donohue & Siegelman, The Changing Nature of Employment Discrimination Litigation, 43 Stan.L.Rev. 983 (1991), 221

Dungworth, Statistical Overview of Civil Litigation in the Federal Courts (Rand Corp. 1990), 3

Eisenberg & Miller, Attorney Fees in Class Action Settlements: An Empirical Study, 1 J. Empir. Legal Stud. 27 (2004), 685, 716

Erichson, Beyond the Class Action: Lawyer Loyalty and Client Autonomy in Non–Class Collective Representation, 2003 U.Chi. Legal F. 519, p. 388

Fedders & Guttelplan, Document Retention and Destruction: Practical, Legal and Ethical Considerations, 56 Notre Dame Law. 5 (1980), 567

Feinberg, The Dalkon Shield Claimant's Trust, 53 Law & Contemp. Probs. 79 (Autumn 1990), 215, 783

Fisch, Aggregation, Auctions, and Other Developments in the Selection of Lead Counsel Under the PSLRA, 64 Law & Contemp. Probs. 53 (Spring/Summer 2001), 293, 678

Fisch, Lawyers on the Auction Block: Evaluating the Selection of Class Counsel by Auction, 102 Colum.L.Rev. 649 (2002), 294, 679

Fiss, Against Settlement, 93 Yale L.J. 1073 (1984), 18, 641

Fiss, Foreword—The Forms of Justice, 93 Harv.L.Rev. 1 (1979), 241

Fitzpatrick, The Center for Claims Resolution, 53 Law & Contemp. Probs. 13 (Autumn 1990), 338, **932**

Flamm, R., Judicial Disqualification (1997), 726

Frankel, A Trial Judge's Perspective on Providing Tools for Rational Decisionmaking, 85 Nw.L.Rev. 221 (1990), 754

Frankel, The Search for Truth: An Umpireal View, 123 U.Pa.L.Rev. 1031 (1975), 17

Freer, Avoiding Duplicative Litigation: Rethinking Plaintiff Autonomy and the Court's Role in Defining the Litigative Unit, 50 U.Pitt.L.Rev. 809 (1989), 53

Freer, Rethinking Compulsory Joinder: A Proposal to Restructure Federal Rule 19, 60 N.Y.U.L.Rev. 1061 (1985), 49

Friedenthal, A Divided Supreme Court Adopts Discovery Amendments to the Federal Rules of Civil Procedure, 69 Calif.L.Rev. 806 (1981), 2, 21

Friedenthal, J., M. Kane, A. Miller, Civil Procedure 89 (2d ed. 1993), 132

Friedland, The Competency and Responsibility of Jurors in Deciding Cases, 85 Nw.L.Rev. 190 (1990), 747

Fuller, The Forms and Limits of Adjudication, 92 Harv.L.Rev. 353 (1978), 635

Galanter, Reading the Landscape of Disputes: What We Know and Don't Know (And Think We Know) About Our Allegedly Contentious and Litigious Society, 31 U.C.L.A.L.Rev. 4 (1983), 21

Galanter, The Emergence of the Judge as a Mediator in Civil Cases, 69 Judicature 257 (1986), 640

Galanter, The Life and Times of the Big Six: or, The Federal Courts Since the Good Old Days, 1988 Wis.L.Rev. 921, p. 3

Garth, Conflict and Dissent in Class Actions: A Suggested Perspective, 77 Nw. L.Rev. 492 (1982), 241

Gelfand, "Taking" Informational Property Through Discovery, 66 Wash.U.L.Rev. 703 (1988), 593

Gensler, Bifurcation Unbound, 75 Wash. U.L. Rev. 705 (2000), 768

George, Sweet Uses of Adversity: Parklane Hosiery and the Collateral Class Action, 32 Stan.L.Rev. 655 (1980), 853

Gibson, Jury Trials in Bankruptcy: Obeying the Commands of Article III and the Seventh Amendment, 72 Minn.L.Rev. 967 (1988), 212

Gidi, Class Actions in Brazil—A Model for Civil Law Countries, 51 Amer.J.Comp.L. 311 (2003), 222

Gibeaut, Junior G–Men, ABA J., June 2003, at 46, p. 605

Gnaizda, Secret Justice for the Privileged Few, 66 Judicature 6 (1982), 931

Goldberg, The Influence of Procedural Rules on Federal Jurisdiction, 28 Stan. L.Rev. 397 (1976), 428

Green, Conflicts of Interest in Litigation: The Judicial Role, 65 Fordham L.Rev. 71 (1996), 515

Green, Growth of the Mini–Trial, 9 Litigation No. 1 at 12 (Fall 1982), 928

Green, E., The CPR Legal Program Mini–Trial Handbooks in Corporate Dispute Management 111–14 (1981), 927

Greene, Woody & Winter, Compensating Plaintiffs and Punishing Defendants: Is Bifurcation Necessary?, 24 Law & Human Behav. 187 (2000), 767

Green, M., Bendectin and Birth Defects: The Challenge of Mass Toxic Substances Litigation (1996), 546, 774

Greenstein, Bridging the Mootness Gap in Federal Court Class Actions, 35 Stan. L.Rev. 897 (1983), 495

Gruenberger, Discovery From Class Members: A Fertile Field for Abuse, 4 Litigation No. 1 at 35 (Fall 1977), 480

Halverson, Coping With the Fruits of Discovery in the Complex Case—The Systems Approach to Litigation Support, 44 Antitrust L.J. 39 (1975), 542

Handler, Antitrust—Myth and Reality in an Inflationary Era, 50 N.Y.U.L.Rev. 211 (1975), 409

Hannaford, "Speaking Rights": Evaluating Juror Discussions During Civil Trials, 85 Judicature 237 (2002), 746

Hannaford, Hans & Munsterman, Permitting Jury Discussions During Trial: Impact of the Arizona Reform, 24 Law & Human Behav. 359 (2000), 746

Hannaford & Munsterman, Beyond Note Taking, Innovations in Jury Reform, Trial, July 1997, at 48, p. 748

Hansel, Extreme Litigation: An Interview With Judge Wm. Terrell Hodges, Chairman of the Judicial Panel on Multidistrict Litigation, 2 Me. Bar J. 16–20 (Winter 2004), 143

Hare, Gilbert & Ellenberger, Confidentiality Orders in Products Liability Cases, 13 Am.J.Trial Advocacy 597 (1989), 592

Hazard, Gedid & Sowle, An Historical Analysis of the Binding Effect of Class Suits, 146 U.Pa.L.Rev. 1849 (1998), 314

Hazard & Rice, Judicial Management of the Pretrial Process in Massive Litigation: Special Masters as Case Managers, 1982 A.B.F.Res.J. 375, p. 662

Hazard & Rice, Special Masters as Case Managers, 1982 A.B.F.Res.J. 375, p. 604

Hensler, As Time Goes By: Asbestos Litigation After Amchem and Ortiz, 80 Texas L.Rev. 1899 (2002), 388

Hensler, Resolving Mass Toxic Torts: Myths and Realities, 1989 U.Ill.L.Rev. 89, pp. 634, 784

Hensler, D., W. Felstiner, M. Selvin & P. Ebener, Asbestos in the Courts: The Challenge of Mass Toxic Torts 89–97 (1985), 733, 784

Heuer & Penrod, Juror Notetaking and Question Asking During Trials, 18 Law & Human Behav. 121 (1994), 748

Heuer & Penrod, Trial Complexity, 18 Law & Human Behav. 29 (1994), 740, 748

Heuer & Penrod, Trial Lawyers in the Box, The Docket 4 (Fall 1988), 748

Hines, Challenging the Issue Class Action End–Run, 52 Emory L.J. 758 (2003), 266

Hines, Obstacles to Determining Punitive Damages in Class Actions, 36 Will. & Mary L. Rev. 889 (2001), 317

Hirsch, A., & D. Sheehey, Awarding Attorneys' Fees and Managing Fee Litigation (1994), 685

Hitt, Toxic Dreams: A California Town Finds Meaning in An Acid Pit, Harper's Mag., July 1995, at 57, p. 19

Hooper & Leary, Auctioning the Role of Class Counsel, 209 F.R.D. 519 (2001), 677

Horne, Presenting Direct Testimony in Writing, 3 Litigation 30 (1977), 755

Horrigan, Producing Those Documents, Nat. L.J., March 17, 2003, at C3, p. 543

H & R Block Accord Draws Fire, Wall St.J., Dec. 24, 2002, p. 410

Huber, Junk Science and the Jury, 1990 U.Chi.Legal Forum 273, p. 742

Hufstedler, New Blocks on Old Pyramids: Reshaping the Judicial System, 44 So. Cal.L.Rev. 901 (1971), 3

Issacharoff, "Shocked": Mass Torts and Aggregate Asbestos Litigation after Amchem and Ortiz, 80 Tex. L.Rev. 1926 (2002), 387

Issacharoff, When Substance Mandates Procedure—Martin v. Wilks and the Rights of Vested Incumbents in Consent Decrees, 77 Cornell L. Rev. 189 (1992), 101

Jacoubovitch, M., & C. Moore, Summary Jury Trials in the Northern District of Ohio (Federal Judicial Center 1982), 939

James, Hazard, & Leubsdorf, Civil Procedure 619 (4th ed. 1992), 55

Johnson, Class–Action Suits Let the Aggrieved in China Appeal for Rule of Law, Wall. St.J., 222

Jones, Rough Justice in Mass Future Claims: Should Bankruptcy Courts Direct Tort Reform?, 76 Texas L. Rev. 1695 (1998), 317

Jordan, Allison v. Citgo Petroleum: The Death Knell for the Title VII Class Action?, 51 Ala.L.Rev. 847 (2000), 327

Judicial Conference, Civil Justice Reform Act: Final Report, 175 F.R.D. 62 (1997), 939

Jury Comprehension in Complex Cases 27–28 (Report of Special Committee of the ABA Section of Litigation, Dec. 1989), 760

Kahan & Silberman, Matsushita and Beyond: The Role of State Courts in Class Actions Involving Exclusive Federal Claims, 1996 Sup.Ct. Rev. 219, p. 816

Kakalik, J., et al., An Analysis of Judicial Case Management Under the Civil Justice Reform Act (1997), 635

Kakalik, J., et al., An Evaluation of Judicial Case Management Under the Civil Justice Reform Act (1997), 939

Kakalik, J., et al., An Evaluation of Mediation and Early Neutral Evaluation Under the Civil Justice Reform Act (1997), 939

Kamp, The History Behind Hansberry v. Lee, 20 U.C.Davis L.Rev. 481 (1987), 289

Kaplan, A Prefatory Note, 10 Boston College Ind. & Com.L.Rev. 497 (1969), 220

Kaplan, Continuing Work of the Civil Committee: The 1966 Amendments of the Federal Rules of Civil Procedure, 81 Harv.L.Rev. 356 (1967), 455

Kennedy, The Supreme Court Meets the Bride of Frankenstein: Phillips Petroleum Co. v. Shutts and the State Multistate Class Action, 34 U.Kan.L.Rev. 255 (1985), 426

Kirst, Finding a Role for the Civil Jury in Modern Litigation, 64 Judicature 333 (1986), 760

Kolata, Controversial Drug Makes Comeback, N.Y. Times, Sept. 26, 2000, 776

Kramer, Choice of Law in Complex Litigation, 71 N.Y.U.L. Rev. 547 (1996), 437

Kramer, Consent Decrees and the Rights of Third Parties, 87 Mich.L.Rev. 321, 338–52 (1988), 101

Krause, Frequent Filers, ABAJ, Aug. 2003, at 52, p. 567

Krause, What a Concept!, ABA Journal, Aug. 2003, at 60, p. 542

Lambros, Summary Jury Trial—An Alternative Method of Resolving Disputes, 69 Judicature 286 (1986), 939

Lambros, The Judge's Role in Fostering Voluntary Settlements, 29 Vill. L. Rev. 1363 (1984), 941

Lambros, The Summary Jury Trial and Other Alternative Methods of Dispute Resolution, 103 F.R.D. 461 (1984), 939

Landes, Sequential Versus Unitary Trials: An Economic Analysis, 22 J. Legal Stud. 99 (1993), 767

Larkin, Incentive Awards to Class Representatives in Class Action Settlements, 3 BNA Class Action Rep. 195 (March 22, 2002), 229

Lawyers Get Tips on Using Early Neutral Evaluation, 4 ADR Rep. 124 (April 12, 1990), 945

Laycock, Consent Decrees Without Consent: The Rights of Nonconsenting Third Parties, 1987 U.Chi.Legal F. 103, pp. 101, 102

Lee, Deconstitutionalizing Justiciability: The Example of Mootness, 105 Harv. L.Rev. 603 (1992), 495

Lempert, Civil Juries and Complex Cases: Let's Not Rush to Judgment, 80 Mich. L.Rev. 68 (1981), 740

Lenkowsky, Goal is to Safeguard Confidentiality, Nat.L.J., May 14, 1990, at 23, p. 570

Leubsdorf, The Contingency Factor in Attorney Fee Awards, 90 Yale L.J. 473 (1981), 701

Leubsdorf, The Standard for Preliminary Injunctions, 91 Harv.L.Rev. 525 (1978), 108

Leubsdorf, Theories of Judging and Judge Disqualification, 62 N.Y.U.L.Rev. 237 (1987), 726

Leval, From the Bench, 12 Litigation 7 (Fall 1985), 761

Levine, The Authority for the Appointment of Remedial Special Masters in Federal Institutional Reform Litigation: The History Reconsidered, 17 U.C. Davis L.Rev. 753 (1984), 661

Lind, E., & T. Tyler, The Social Psychology of Procedural Justice (1988), 634

Lowenthal & Feder, The Impropriety of Class Action Tolling for Mass Tort Statutes of Limitations, 64 Geo.Wash.L.Rev. 532 (1996), 465

Lundquist, Trial Lawyer or Litigator, 7 Litigation 3 (Summer 1981), 6

Macey & Miller, The Plaintiffs' Attorneys' Role in Class Action and Derivative Litigation: Economic Analysis and Recommendations for Reform, 58 U.Chi.L.Rev. 1 (1991), 295, 443, 676

Manual for Complex Litigation (4th) (2004), 115, 161, 213, 369, 391, 403, 475, 478, 479, 533, 539, 561, 571, 593, 604, 644, 662, 664, 666, 668, 677, 680, 681, 682, 702, 712, 716, 745, 746, 748, 753, 756

Marcus, Apocalypse Now? (book review), 85 Mich.L.Rev. 1267 (1987), 340

Marcus, Benign Neglect Reconsidered, 148 U.Pa.L.Rev. 2009, 20031–32 n. 113 (2000), 318

Marcus, Completing Equity's Conquest? Reflections on the Future of Trial Under the Federal Rules of Civil Procedure, 50 U.Pitt.L.Rev. 725 (1989), 732, 753

Marcus, Conflicts Among Circuits and Transfers Within the Federal Judicial System, 93 Yale L.J. 677 (1984), 164

Marcus, Confronting the Consolidation Conundrum, 1995 BYU L. Rev. 879, pp. 125, 126

Marcus, Confronting the Future: Coping With Discovery of Electronic Material, 64 Law & Contemp. Probs. 253 (Spring/Summer 2001), 558

Marcus, "Deja Vu All Over Again?" An American Reaction to the Woolf Report, in Reform of Civil Procedure (A. Zuckerman & R. Cranston, eds) 219 (1995), 635

Marcus, Discovery Containment Redux, 39 Bos.Coll.L.Rev. 747 (1998), 21, 558

Marcus, Fraudulent Concealment in Federal Court: Toward a More Disparate Standard?, 71 Geo.L.J. 829 (1983), 767

Marcus, Malaise of the Litigation Superpower, in Civil Justice in Crisis (A. Zuckerman, ed., 1999), at 71, p. 639

Marcus, Myth and Reality in Protective Order Litigation, 69 Cornell L.Rev. 1 (1983), 590

Marcus, Reassessing the Magnetic Pull of Mega-cases on Procedure, 51 De Paul L.Rev. 457 (2001), 358

Marcus, Reexamining the Bendectin Litigation Story, 83 Iowa L.Rev. 231 (1997), 546

Marcus, Reigning in the American Litigator: The New Role of American Judges, 27 Hast. Int'l & Compar.L.Rev. 3 (2003), 626

Marcus, Retooling American Discovery for the Twenty–First Century: Toward a New World Order?, 7 Tulane J. Int'l & Comp. L. Rev. 153 (1999), 542

Marcus, Slouching Toward Discretion, 78 Notre Dame L.Rev. 1561 (2003), 20, 638

Marcus, The Discovery Confidentiality Controversy, 1991 U.Ill.L.Rev. 457, p. 590

Marcus, The Perils of Privilege: Waiver and the Litigator, 84 Mich.L.Rev. 1605 (1986), 595, 604

Marcus, The Puzzling Persistence of Pleading Practice, 76 Texas L.Rev. 1749 (1998), 254

Marcus, They Can't Do That, Can They? Tort Reform Via Rule 23, 80 Cornell L. Rev. 858 (1995), 23, 316

Martin, The Rise and Fall of the Class–Action Lawsuit, N.Y.Times, Jan. 8, 1988, at 10 col. 3, p. 221

Marvel, Netter & Robinson, Price Fixing and Civil Damages, 40 Stan.L.Rev. 561 (1988), 443

McCrystal & Maschari, Will Electronic Technology Take the Witness Stand?, 11 U.Tol.L.Rev. 239 (1980), 750

McElhaney, An Introduction to Direct Examination, 2 Litigation 37 (1976), 755

McGeehan, Wall St. Banks May be Fined for Discarding E–Mail Traffic, N.Y.Times, Aug. 2, 2002, at C1, p. 567

Meador, Inherent Judicial Authority in the Conduct of Civil Litigation, 73 Texas L. Rev. 1805 (1995), 115

Meese, Inadvertent Waiver of the Attorney–Client Privilege by Disclosure of Documents: An Economic Analysis, 23 Creighton L.Rev. 513 (1990), 603

Meierhofer, B., Court–Annexed Arbitration in Ten District Courts (1989), 943

Meites & Aborn, Distributing the Settlement Fund in a Class Action, 7 Litigation No. 4 at 33 (Summer 1981), 526

Mengler, Consent Decree Paradigms: Models Without Meaning, 29 B.C.L.Rev. 291 (1988), 102

Mentschikoff, Commercial Arbitration, 61 Colum.L.Rev. 846 (1961), 884

M. Green, Bendectin and Birth Defects 131 (1996), 159

Miller, Confidentiality, Protective Orders, and Public Access to the Courts, 105 Harv.L.Rev. 427 (1991), 590

Miller, Of Frankenstein Monsters and Shining Knights: Myth, Reality, and the "Class Action Problem," 92 Harv.L.Rev. 664 (1979), 221

Miller, Payment of Expenses in Securities Class Actions: Ethical Dilemmas, Class Counsel, and Congressional Intent, 22 Rev.Lit. 557 (2003), 227

Miller, Problems of Giving Notice in Class Actions, 58 F.R.D. 313 (1972), 446

Miller, The Pretrial Rush to Judgment: Are the "Litigation Explosion," "Liability Crisis," and Efficiency Cliches Eroding Our Day in Court and Jury Trial Commitments?, 78 N.Y.U. L. Rev. 982 (2003), 16, 636

Miller & Crump, Jurisdiction and Choice of Law in Multistate Class Actions After Phillips Petroleum v. Shutts, 96 Yale L.J. 1 (1986), 426

Miller & Singer, Nonpecuniary Class Action Settlements, 60 Law & Contemp. Probs. 97 (Fall 1997), 536

Mills, Taking Chances at Depositions, Litigation, Fall 2001, at 30, p. 619

Minnesota Court Denies Class Certification in Light Cigarette Suit Against Phillip Morris, 5 Class Action Litigation Report 39 (Jan. 23, 2004), 358

Mitchell & Barrett, Novel Effort to Settle Asbestos Claims Fails as Lawsuits Multiply, Wall St.J., June 7, 1988, p. 339

Mnookin, Beyond Litigation, 23 Stanford Lawyer 5 (Spring/Summer 1989), 924

Molot, An Old Judicial Role for a New Judicial Era, 113 Yale L.J. 27 (2003), 5, 640, 734

Morrison, Protective Orders, Plaintiffs, Defendants and the Public Interest in Disclosure: Where Does the Balance Lie?, 24 U.Rich.L.Rev. 109 (1989), 590

Nagareda, Administering Adequacy in Class Representation, 82 Tex.L.Rev. 287, 314 (2003), 289

Nagareda, Punitive Damages Class Actions and the Baseline of Tort, 36 Will. & Mary L. Rev. 943 (2001), 317

Newberg, H. & A. Conte, Newberg on Class Actions § 16.09 (3d ed. 1992), 456

Newberg, H., Attorney Fee Awards (1986), 685

Newberg, H., Newberg on Class Actions § 17.06 at 373 (2d ed. 1985), 336

Note, A More Rational Approach to Complex Civil Litigation in the Federal Courts: The Special Jury, 1990 U.Chi.Legal Forum 575, p. 742

Note, Burford Abstention in Actions for Money, 99 Colum.L.Rev. 1871 (1999), 168

Note, Classwide Arbitration and 10B–5 Claims in the Wake of *Shearson/Ameri-*

can Express, Inc. v. McMahon, 74 Cornell L.Rev. 380 (1989), 922

Note, Conflicts in Class Actions and Protection of Absent Class Members, 91 Yale L.J. 590, 603–14 (1982), 476

Note, Constrained Individualism in Group Litigation: Requiring Class Members to Make a Good Cause Showing Before Opting Out of a Federal Class Action, 100 Yale L.J. 745 (1990), 459

Note, Defendant Class Actions, 91 Harv. L.Rev. 630 (1978), 366

Note, Discovery of Plaintiff's Financial Situation in Federal Class Actions: Heading 'Em Off at the Passbook, 30 Hast. L.J. 449 (1978), 297

Note, Evading Friendly Fire: Achieving Class Certification After the Civil Rights Act of 1991, 100 Colum.L.Rev. 1847 (2000), 327

Note, Federal Court Stays and Dismissals in Deference to Parallel State Court Proceedings, 44 U.Chi.L.Rev. 641 (1977), 103

Note, Interactions Between Memory Refreshment Doctrine and Work Product Protection Under the Federal Rules, 88 Yale L.J. 390 (1978), 616

Note, Mass Products Liability Litigation: A Proposal for Dissemination of Discovered Material Covered by a Protective Order, 60 N.Y.U.L.Rev. 1137 (1985), 593

Note, Multiple Defendant Settlement in 10b–5: Good Faith Contribution Bar, 40 Hast.L.J. 1253 (1989), 643

Note, Offensive Assertion of Collateral Estoppel by Persons Opting Out of a Class Action, 31 Hast.L.J. 1189 (1980), 459

Note, Permian Corporation v. United States and the Attorney–Client Privilege for Corporations: Unjustified Severity on the Issue of Waiver, 77 Nw.L.Rev. 223 (1982), 611

Note, Rule 53, Inherent Powers, and Institutional Reform: The Lack of Limits on Special Masters, 66 N.Y.U.L.Rev. 800 (1991), 661

Note, Seattle Times: What Effect on Discovery Sharing?, 1985 Wis.L.Rev. 1055, pp. 546, 592

Note, Statutes of Limitation and Defendant Class Actions, 82 Mich.L.Rev. 347 (1983), 470

Note, Statutes of Limitations and Opting Out of Class Actions, 81 Mich.L.Rev. 399 (1982), 468

Note, Summary Jury Trials and Mock Trials, 24 Tort & Ins. L.J. 563 (1989), 941

Note, The American Pipe Dream: Class Actions and Statutes of Limitations, 67 Iowa L.Rev. 743 (1982), 468

Note, The California Rent-a-Judge Experiment: Constitutional and Policy Considerations of Pay–As–You–Go Courts, 94 Harv.L.Rev. 1592 (1981), 931

Note, The Importance of Being Adequate: Due Process Requirements Under Rule 23, 123 U.Pa.L.Rev. 1217 (1975), 292

Note, The Judicial Panel and the Conduct of Multidistrict Litigation, 87 Harv. L.Rev. 1001 (1974), 401

Note, The Limited Waiver Rule: Creation of an SEC–Corporation Privilege, 36 Stan. L.Rev. 789 (1984), 611

Note, The Right to a Jury Trial in Complex Civil Litigation, 92 Harv.L.Rev. 898 (1979), 741

Note, The Supreme Court—Leading Cases, 103 Harv.L.Rev. 310 (1989), 101

O'Brien & Kovach, Moderated Settlement Conference, 51 Tex.B.J. 38 (1988), 944

Oesterle, A Private Litigant's Remedies for an Opponent's Inappropriate Destruction of Relevant Documents, 61 Texas L.Rev. 1185 (1983), 570

Orey, Uncle and Nephew Find Legal Ethics Strain Family Ties, Wall St.J., Aug. 7, 2002, at A1, p. 727

Overly, M., Electronic Evidence in California (1999), 561

Parker, Streamlining Complex Cases, 10 Review of Litigation 547 (1991), 737, 750

Peckham, A Judicial Response to the Cost of Litigation: Case Management, Two–Stage Discovery Planning and Alternative Dispute Resolution, 37 Rutgers L.Rev. 253 (1985), 631

Peckham, The Federal Judge as Case Manager: The New Role in Guiding a Case From Filing to Disposition, 69 Calif.L.Rev. 770 (1981), 627, 735

Pennington & Hastie, Evidence Evaluation in Complex Decision Making, 51 J. of Personality and Soc. Psy. 242–58 (1986), 774

Pfander, Supplemental Jurisdiction and Section 1367: The Case for a Sympathetic Textualism, 148 U.Pa.L.Rev. 109 (1999), 429

Plapinger & Stienstra, ADR and Settlement in the Federal District Courts: A Sourcebook for Judges and Lawyers, in Alternative Dispute Resolution: The Litigators' Handbook 406–408 (ABA Section of Litigation 2000), 946

Poirier, Robb & Mosher, Computer–Based Litigation Support Systems: The Discoverability Issue, 54 U.M.K.C.L.Rev. 440 (1986), 545

Pooley & Shaw, Finding What's Out There: Technical and Legal Aspects of Discovery, 4 Tex. Intell. Prop. L.J. 57 (1995), 559

Posner, The Summary Jury Trial and Other Methods of Alternate Dispute Resolution: Some Cautionary Observations, 53 U.Chi.L.Rev. 366 (1986), 941

Post, The Management of Speech, Discretion and Rights, 1984 Sup.Ct.Rev. 169, p. 580

Priest, The Cumulative Sources of the Asbestos Litigation Phenomenon, 31 Pepp. L. Rev. 261, 264 (2004), 390

Rand Institute for Civil Justice, Class Action Dilemmas: Pursuing Public Goals for Private Gain, 9, 49–51 (2000), 7

Rangel & Epstein, Efficiency Analysis Driving the Need for Task–Based Billing, Corp. Legal Times, Feb. 1993, at 33, p. 698

Ratliff, Offensive Collateral Estoppel and the Option Effect, 67 Texas L.Rev. 63 (1988), 864

Redish, Electronic Discovery and the Litigation Matrix, 51 Duke L.J. 561 (2001), 558

Redish, The Anti–Injunction Act Reconsidered, 44 U.Chi.L.Rev. 717 (1977), 205

Reid & Coutroulis, Checkmate in Class Actions: Defensive Strategy in the Initial Moves, 28 Litigation 21, 21 (Winter 2002), 221

Reifenberg, Texaco Settlement in Racial–Bias Case Endorsed by Judge, Wall St.J., March 26, 1997, at B9, p. 230

Report, Procedure in Anti–Trust and Other Protracted Cases, 13 F.R.D. 62 (1951), 731

Resnik, From "Cases" to "Litigation," 54 Law & Contemp. Probs 5 (Summer 1991), 126

Resnik, Managerial Judges, 96 Harv. L.Rev. 374 (1982), 628

Rheingold, P., Mass Tort Litigation § 18.24 (1996), 214

Rheingold, The Mer/29 Story—An Instance of Successful Mass Disaster Litigation, 56 Calif.L.Rev. 116 (1968), 123, 545

Richey, A Modern Management Technique for Trial Courts to Improve the Quality of Justice: Requiring Direct Testimony to be Submitted in Written Form Prior to Trial, 72 Geo.L.J. 73 (1983), 756

Richey, Rule 16 Revisited: Reflections For the Benefit of Bench and Bar, 139 F.R.D. 525 (1992), 751

Rickerson, Law Firm Profits Increase With Strategic Legal Management, 68 Def. Couns.J. 228 (2001), 698

Rooks, Let The Sun Shine In, Trial, June 2003, at 26, p. 591

Rosenberg, The Causal Connection in Mass Exposure Cases: A "Public Law" Vision of the Tort System, 97 Harv.L.Rev. 851 (1984), 44

Rosenberg, The Federal Civil Rules After Half a Century, 36 Me.L.Rev. 243 (1984), 22

Rosenberg, M., The Pretrial Conference and Effective Justice (1964), 737

Roundtable Discussion, The Future of Class Action Mass Torts, 66 Fordham L. Rev. 1657 (1998), 222

Rowe, Predicting the Effects of Attorney Fee Shifting, 47 Law & Contemp.Probs. 139 (Winter 1984), 686

Rowe & Sibley, Beyond Diversity: Federal Multiparty, Multiforum Jurisdiction, 135 U. Pa. L. Rev. 7 (1986), 44

Rubenstein, Divided We Litigate: Addressing Disputes Among Group Members and Lawyers in Civil Rights Campaigns, 106 Yale L.J. 1623 (1997), 241

Rubin, A Paperless Trial, 19 Litigation 5 (Spring 1993), 755

Rutherglen, Title VII Class Actions, 47 U.Chi.L.Rev. 688 (1980), 276

Sabel & Simon, Destabilization Rights: How Public Law Litigation Succeeds, 117 Harv.L.Rev. 1015 (2004), 5

Saks & Blanck, Justice Improved: The Unrecognized Benefits of Sampling and Aggregation in the Trial of Mass Torts, 44 Stan.L.Rev. 815 (1992), 781

Saks & Kidd, Human Information Processing and Adjudication: Trial by Heuristics, 15 Law & Soc'y Rev. 123 (1980), 761

Sand & Reiss, A Report on Seven Experiments Conducted by District Court Judges in the Second Circuit, 60 N.Y.U.L.Rev. 423 (1985), 748

Sanders, The Bendectin Litigation, A Case Study in the Life–Cycle of Mass Torts, 43 Hast.L.J. 301 (1992), 775

Schmitt, Objecting to Class–Action Pacts Can be Lucrative for Attorneys, Wall.St. J., Jan. 10, 1997, at B1, p. 517

Schroeder, Relitigation of Common Issues: The Failure of Nonparty Preclusion and an Alternative Proposal, 67 Iowa L.Rev. 880 (1982), 875

Schuck, The Role of Judges in Settling Complex Cases: The Agent Orange Example, 53 U.Chi.L.Rev. 337 (1986), 642

Schuck, P., Agent Orange on Trial 178–79 (1986), 340, 538

Schwartz, Severance—A Means of Minimizing the Role of Burden and Expense in Determining the Outcome of Litigation, 20 Vand.L.Rev. 1197 (1967), 766

Schwarzer, Reforming Jury Trials, 132 F.R.D. 575 (1991), 736, 743

Schwarzer, Hirsch & Barrans, The Analysis and Decision of Summary Judgment Motions, 139 F.R.D. 441 (1992), 758

Schwarzer, Weiss & Hirsch, Judicial Federalism in Action: Coordination of Litigation in State and Federal Courts, 78 Va.L.Rev. 1689 (1992), 402

Scialli, Bendectin, Science, and the Law, 3 Reproductive Toxicology 157 (1989), 775

Shapiro, Class Actions: The Class as Party and Client, 73 Notre Dame L. Rev. 913 (1998), 495

Shepherd & Cloud, Time and Money: Discovery Leads to Hourly Billing, 1999 U.Ill.L.Rev. 91, p. 685

Sherman, Aggregate Disposition of Related Cases: The Policy Issues, 10 Rev. of Litigation 231 (1991), 10

Sherman, American Class Actions: Significant Features and Developing Alternatives in Foreign Legal Systems, 215 F.R.D. 130 (2003), 7, 337

Sherman, Class Actions and Duplicative Litigation, 62 Ind. L.J. 507, 541–45 (1987), 207

Sherman, Complimentary Devices to Prevent Duplicative Litigation, 1995 B.Y.U. L.Rev. 943, p. 404

Sherman, Consumer Class Actions: Who are the Real Winners?, 56 Maine L. Rev.225 (2004), 536

Sherman, Group Litigation Under Foreign Legal Systems: Variations and Alternatives to American Class Actions, 52 DePaul L. Rev. 401 (2002), 222

Sherman, Reshaping the Lawyer's Skills for Court–Supervised ADR, 51 Tex.Bar J. 47 (1988), 941

Sherman & Kinnard, The Development, Discovery and Use of Computer Support Systems in Achieving Efficiency in Litigation, 79 Colum. L. Rev. 266 (1979), 543

Silberman, Judicial Adjuncts Revisited: The Proliferation of Ad Hoc Procedure, 137 U.Pa.L.Rev. 2131 (1989), 653

Silver, Comparing Class Actions and Consolidations, 10 Rev.Litig. 495 (1991), 126

Silver, Merging Roles: Mass Tort Lawyers as Agents and Trustees, 31 Pepp. L. Rev. 301 (2003), 230

Simon, Fee Sharing Between Lawyers and Public Interest Groups, 98 Yale L.J. 1069 (1989), 713

Simpson, The Problem of Trial, in D.D. Field, Centenary Essays 141 (1949), 731

Sipes, Where Do We Go From Here?, 23 Judges J. 44 (1984), 22

Sobol, R., Bending the Law: The Story of the Dalkon Shield Bankruptcy (1991), 215, 783

Solimine & Hines, Deciding to Decide: Class Action Certification and Interlocutory Review by the United States Courts of Appeals Under Rule 23(f), Will. & Mary L. Rev. 1531 (2000), 371

Solum & Marzen, Destruction of Evidence, 16 Litigation 11 (Fall 1989), 566

Steinman, Law of the Case: A Judicial Puzzle in Consolidated and Transferred Cases and in Multidistrict Litigation, 135 U.Pa.L.Rev. 595 (1987), 163

Steinman, Managing Punitive Damages: A Role for Mandatory "Limited Generosity" Classes and Anti–Suit Injunctions?, 36 Will. & Mary L. Rev. 1043 (2001), 317

Steinman, The Effects of Case Consolidation on the Procedural Rights of Litigants: What They Are, What They Might Be, Part I: Justiciability and Jurisdiction (Original and Appellate), 42 UCLA L. Rev. 717 (1995), 127

Steinman, The Effects of Case Consolidation on the Procedural Rights of Litigants: What They Are, What They Might Be, Part II: Non–Jurisdictional Matters, 42 UCLA L. Rev. 967 (1995), 128

Stempel, Jurisprudential Inconsistency and the Felt Necessities of the Time: The Supreme Court's Functional and Formal Arbitration Jurisprudence, Florida State U. Lawyer 33 (1997), 889

Steuer, A., Max Steuer, Trial Lawyer 89–109 (1950), 617

Strickler, Martin v. Wilks, 64 Tulane L.Rev. 1557 (1990), 101

Subrin, Federal Rules, Local Rules, and State Rules: Uniformity, Divergence, and Emerging Procedural Patterns, 137 U.Pa.L.Rev. 1999 (1989), 638

Subrin: Fishing Expeditions Allowed: The Historical Background of the 1938 Federal Discovery Rules, 39 Bos.Coll.L.Rev. 691 (1998), 541

Subrin, How Equity Conquered Common Law: The Federal Rules of Civil Procedure in Historical Perspective, 135 U.Pa. L.Rev. 909 (1987), 19

S. Yeazell, From Medieval Group Litigation to the Modern Class Action 252–54 (1987), 458

Taylor, Second Class Citizens, American Lawyer, Sept. 1989, at 42, p. 101

Tempel–Raston, Class–Action Lawsuits Gain Strength on the Web, N.Y. Times, July 28, 2002, pp. 221, 444

Third Circuit Task Force Report on the Selection of Class Counsel, 74 Temple L. Rev. 689 (2001), 677

Tidmarsh, The Story of Hansberry: The Foundation for Modern Class Actions, in Civil Procedure Stories. (K. Clermont, ed. 2004), 290

Tobias, Rule 19 and the Public Rights Exception to Party Joinder, 65 N.C.L.Rev. 745 (1987), 53

Tobias, Standing to Intervene, 1991 Wis. L.Rev. 415, p. 69

Trangsrud, Mass Trials in Mass Tort Cases: A Dissent, 1989 U.Ill.L.Rev. 69, pp. 774, 784

T. Willging, L. Hooper, M. Leary, D. Miletich, T. Reagan & J. Shapard, Special Masters' Incidence and Activity (Fed. Jud.Ctr.2000), 663

Varchaver, Dispute Resolution, The American Lawyer 60 (April 1992), 931

Varchaver & Bonamici, The Perils of E-mail, Fortune, Feb. 17, 2003, p. 559

Vestal, Reactive Litigation, 47 Iowa L.Rev. 11 (1961), 104

Vestal, Repetitive Litigation, 45 Iowa L.Rev. 525 (1960), 104

Vidmar, Juror Discussion During Civil Trials: Studying an Arizona Innovation, 45 Az. L. Rev. 1 (2003), 746

Walker, Lind & Thibaut, The Relation Between Procedural and Distributive Justice, 65 Va.L.Rev. 1401 (1979), 634

Walker & Monahan, Sampling Damages, 83 Iowa L.Rev. 545 (1998), 784

Walker & Monahan, Sampling Liability, 85 Va.L.Rev. 329 (1999), 784

Weber, Preclusion and Procedural Due Process in Rule 23(b)(2) Class Actions, 21 U.Mich.J.Law Reform 347 (1988), 445

Weigel, The Judicial Panel on Multidistrict Litigation, Transferor Courts and Transferee Courts, 78 F.R.D. 575 (1978), 154

Weinstein, Ethical Dilemmas in Mass Tort Litigation, 88 Nw. L. Rev. 469 (1994), 227

Weinstein, Routine Bifurcation of Jury Negligence Trials: An Example of the Questionable Use of Rule Making Power, 14 Vand.L.Rev. 831 (1961), 766

Weinstein, The Power and Duty of Federal Judges to Marshall and Comment on the Evidence in Jury Trials and Some Suggestions on Charging Juries, 118 F.R.D. 161 (1988), 747

Weinstein & Hershenov, The Effects of Equity on Mass Torts, 1991 U.Ill.L.Rev. 269, p. 337

Weinstein & Schwartz, Notes From the Cave: Some Problems of Judges in Dealing With Class Action Settlements, 163 F.R.D. 369 (1995), 538

Weiss & Beckerman, Let the Money Do the Monitoring: How Institutional Investors Can Reduce Agency Costs in Securities Class Actions, 104 Yale L.J. 2053 (1995), 292

Wellborn, Demeanor, 76 Cornell L.Rev. 1075 (1991), 753

Wells, Tort Law as Corrective Justice: A Pragmatic Justification for Jury Adjudication, 88 Mich.L.Rev. 2348 (1990), 733

Wheeler, Predismissal Notice and Statutes of Limitation in Federal Class Actions After American Pipe and Construction Co. v. Utah, 48 So.Cal.L.Rev. 771 (1975), 466

White, J. & R. Summers, Uniform Commercial Code 7 (2d ed.1980), 438

Willging, T., Trends in Asbestos Litigation 70–76 (1987), 640

Willging, Hooper & Niemic, An Empirical Analysis of Rule 23 To Address the Rulemaking Challenges, 71 N.Y.U. L. Rev. 74 (1996), 226, 230, 359

Willging, T., J. Shapard, D. Stienstra & D. Miletich, Discovery and Disclosure Practice, Problems, and Proposals for Change 52–55 (1997), 635

Woolley, Mass Tort Litigation and the Seventh Amendment Reexamination Clause, 83 Iowa L. Rev. 499 (1998), 768

Woolley, Rethinking the Adequacy of Adequate Representation, 75 Texas L. Rev. 571 (1997), 456

Woolley, The Availability of Collateral Attack for Inadequate Representation in Class Suits, 79 Texas L. Rev. 383 (2000), 289

Wright, C., A. Miller & E. Cooper, Federal Practice & Procedure Vol. 13B, § 3567, at 117 (2d ed. 1984), 59

Wright, C., A. Miller & M. Kane, Federal Practice and Procedure: Civil 2nd Vol. 7C, § 1908 (1986), 67

Wright, C., A. Miller & M. Kane, Federal Practice & Procedure (2d ed. 1986), 447, 283, 455, 461, 479

Wright, C., A. Miller & R. Marcus, Federal Practice & Procedure (2d ed. 1994), 603, 605

Wright, C., & M. Kane, Law of Federal Courts 120 (6th ed. 2002), 58

Wright, C., & M. Kane, Law of Federal Courts 282 (6th ed. 2002), 131

Wright, C., N. King & S. Klein, Federal Practice & Procedure § 702 at 434 (3d ed. 2004), 650

Yablon, Stupid Lawyer Tricks: An Essay on Discovery Abuse, 96 Colum. L. Rev. 1618 (1996), 566

Yeazell, S., From Medieval Group Litigation to the Modern Class Action 234–54 (1987), 289

Zuckerman, A., Civil Procedure 1 (2003), 639

COMPLEX LITIGATION

CASES AND MATERIALS ON ADVANCED CIVIL PROCEDURE

Fourth Edition

DOONESBURY by GB Trudeau

Chapter I

THE NATURE OF COMPLEX LITIGATION

Despite tales of lawyer burnout, complex litigation need not drive a lawyer to seek socially-useful work as a janitor. Nevertheless, complex cases can impress both the public and the bar as wasteful, inefficient and unnecessary. Many see them as symptoms of a widespread pathology in American civil litigation today, gobbling up resources without providing any accompanying social advantage. Lawyers lament the transformation of the "trial lawyer" of the past into the "litigator" of the present, a change that seems most pronounced in complex litigation. Judges decry the delay and cost of litigation, often blaming both on lawyers, and have begun to take the initiative to curtail both. Even Congress has become involved, prodding the courts into innovation in handling of civil litigation to deal with problems originally attributed to complex litigation.

Complex litigation is central to the present controversy over civil litigation in general. Arguably it is not significantly different from other litigation, only larger. Thus, some of the topics addressed in this book can be important in lawsuits that would not be described as complex; to some extent one is tempted to emphasize "complex litigation" because it has a cachet holding special appeal. Indeed, nobody has devised a litmus test by which one may decide whether a given case is properly labelled complex. The various editions of the Manual for Complex Litigation have not offered a firm definition. As a beginning matter, it may be said that three characteristics serve, individually or together, to distinguish complex cases. First, they may involve difficult legal and factual issues (often scientific) of a sort not encountered often in court until recently. Second, the sheer number of parties involved may make litigation complex where it would not be in a one-on-one litigation format. Third, the amount of money involved may prompt litigation efforts of such dimension that a case that would otherwise not be complex becomes complex.

Whatever the definition, it is clear that complex litigation has become a prime focus of innovation in litigation. Besides the Manual for Complex Litigation, mentioned above, it is also true that when it passed the Civil Justice Reform Act in 1990 Congress directed courts to consider special procedures for "cases that the court or an individual judicial officer determines are complex." 28 U.S.C.A. § 473(a)(3). Additionally, the American Law Institute's Complex Litigation Project has recommended special procedures for litigation characterized by multiple related lawsuits proceeding in many courts. See American Law Institute, Complex Litigation: Statutory Recommendations and Analysis (1994).

The evolution of complex litigation has reached a point where it deserves study as a discrete area of dispute resolution. That is the purpose of this book, but it should be emphasized at the outset that this study provides insights that often apply to the judicial handling of all kinds of civil litigation. At the same time, a prime concern is the extent to which complex litigation should be treated significantly differently from other litigation. To set the scene, this chapter provides a brief overview of issues that will be with us throughout the book.

A. THE METAMORPHOSIS OF LITIGATION

When the Federal Rules of Civil Procedure were adopted in 1938, there was no substantial concern with complex litigation. Indeed, one could argue that there was then no substantial amount of complex litigation. The federal courts handled "simple" litigation that was usually of little interest to anyone except the parties. There were no employment discrimination suits, securities fraud class actions, or product-liability cases. Although hindsight often lapses into nostalgia, it is understandable that some might view this past with fondness.

Certainly the feeling of tranquility is now gone with respect to all litigation. Since the mid–1970s, there have been increasingly frequent assertions that the American judicial system is in a state of crisis. By the 1990s, the concern became a matter of general public debate.

A starting point is the widespread concern about a litigation "boom," often illustrated with statistics on growth in the number of filings (and bolstered by references to the growing number of lawyers in the country). In many ways this growth can be traced to the creation of new rights to sue. Congress, for example, has created a large number of new types of civil claims since 1960. Courts have also created new types of suits, notably constitutional claims and expanded notions of product liability that simply did not exist before. To some, the increase in the number of filings is also a symptom of undue litigiousness on the part of Americans, one that is fueled by large awards in some cases and "plaintiffs who sometimes treat the judicial system as if it were a gigantic slot machine." Friedenthal, A Divided Supreme Court Adopts Discovery Amendments to the Federal Rules of Civil Procedure, 69 Calif.L.Rev. 806, 818 (1981). Thoughtful judges have recoiled from this perception:

> The etiology of judicial distress can be stated briefly: we have poured more into courts than they can digest. The legal profession and the general public have long accepted the premise that any controversy

that can be cast in the form of a lawsuit should have a ticket of admission to the courts.

Hufstedler, New Blocks on Old Pyramids: Reshaping the Judicial System, 44 So.Cal.L.Rev. 901, 906 (1971).

But these attitudes must be scrutinized with care. Although there are widespread concerns about increased delay in disposition of civil cases, a study of civil cases in federal court during the period 1971 to 1989 showed that the median time from filing to disposition had not fluctuated significantly and had actually declined. See T. Dungworth, Statistical Overview of Civil Litigation in the Federal Courts (Rand Corp. 1990). Moreover, Professor Galanter has pointed out that significant growth in filings in federal court can often be traced to conscious governmental policy. Examining the types of cases in which the number of filings has increased most dramatically, he found that one area of great increase in the 1980s was in suits by the government to recover defaulted student loans or overpayments of veterans' benefits, reflecting a governmental policy of pursuing such matters. Similarly, federal court filings challenging denials of claims by the Social Security Administration grew substantially in the early 1980s, but seemingly in response to a policy of strictness in approving claims. Galanter, The Life and Times of the Big Six: or, The Federal Courts Since the Good Old Days, 1988 Wis.L.Rev. 921.

Putting aside raw numbers, it does seem that there has been a significant shift in the type of litigation that is being filed. Indeed, that follows from the fact that an important segment of the docket consists of cases involving claims that were not made a few decades ago. Rather than intersection collisions and breaches of contract, federal courts have found themselves immersed in public law cases that tend to involve a much more complex form of litigation. The paradigms for public law litigation are constitutional cases seeking the reform of various public institutions such as schools, prisons and jails, mental health and hospital facilities, and welfare bureaucracies. Closely related to such constitutional cases is litigation based on rights derived from legislation and administrative regulations that seek to effect systematic changes in government operations and programs. Many environmental cases, and even some business cases, also fit this mold. Professor Chayes described the dramatic changes in the form of litigation brought about by such cases:

CHAYES, THE ROLE OF THE JUDGE
IN PUBLIC LAW LITIGATION
89 Harv.L.Rev. 1281, 1282–84 (1976).

We are witnessing the emergence of a new model of civil litigation and, I believe, our traditional conception of adjudication and the assumptions upon which it is based provide an increasingly unhelpful, indeed misleading, framework for assessing either the workability or the legitimacy of the roles of judge and court within this model.

In our received tradition, the lawsuit is a vehicle for settling disputes between private parties about private rights. The defining features of this conception of civil adjudication are:

(1) The lawsuit is *bipolar*. Litigation is organized as a contest between two individuals or at least two unitary interests, diametrically opposed, to be decided on a winner-takes-all basis.

(2) Litigation is *retrospective*. The controversy is about an identified set of completed events: whether they occurred, and if so, with what consequences for the legal relations of the parties.

(3) *Right and remedy are interdependent.* The scope of the relief is derived more or less logically from the substantive violation under the general theory that the plaintiff will get compensation measured by the harm caused by the defendant's breach of duty—in contract by giving plaintiff the money he would have had absent the breach; in tort by paying the value of the damage caused.

(4) The lawsuit is a *self-contained* episode. The impact of the judgment is confined to the parties. If plaintiff prevails there is a simple compensatory transfer, usually of money, but occasionally the return of a thing or the performance of a definite act. If defendant prevails, a loss lies where it has fallen. In either case, entry of judgment ends the court's involvement.

(5) The process is *party-initiated* and *party-controlled*. The case is organized and the issues defined by exchanges between the parties. Responsibility for fact development is theirs. The trial judge is a neutral arbiter of their interactions who decides questions of law only if they are put in issue by an appropriate move of a party.

This capsule description of what I have called the traditional conception of adjudication is no doubt overdrawn. It was not often, if ever, expressed so severely; indeed, because it was so thoroughly taken for granted, there was little occasion to do so. Although I do not contend that the traditional conception ever conformed fully to what judges were doing in fact, I believe it has been central to our understanding and our analysis of the legal system.

Whatever its historical validity, the traditional model is clearly invalid as a description of much current civil litigation in the federal district courts. Perhaps the dominating characteristic of modern federal litigation is that lawsuits do not arise out of disputes between private parties about private rights. Instead, the object of litigation is the vindication of constitutional or statutory policies. The shift in the legal basis of the lawsuit explains many, but not all, facets of what is going on "in fact" in federal trial courts. For this reason, although the label is not wholly satisfactory, I shall call the emerging model "public law litigation."

The characteristic features of the public law model are very different from those of the traditional model. The party structure is sprawling and amorphous, subject to change over the course of the litigation. The

traditional adversary relationship is suffused and intermixed with negotiating and mediating processes at every point. The judge is the dominant figure in organizing and guiding the case, and he draws for support
not only on the parties and their counsel, but on a wide range of
outsiders—masters, experts, and oversight personnel. Most important,
the trial judge has increasingly become the creator and manager of
complex forms of ongoing relief, which have widespread effects on
persons not before the court and require the judge's continuing involvement in administration and implementation. School desegregation, employment discrimination, and prisoners' or inmates' rights cases come
readily to mind as avatars of this new form of litigation. But it would be
mistaken to suppose that it is confined to these areas. Antitrust, securities fraud and other aspects of the conduct of corporate business,
bankruptcy and reorganizations, union governance, consumer fraud,
housing discrimination, electoral reapportionment, environmental management—cases in all these fields display in varying degrees the features
of public law litigation.

––––––––

Public law remedies, on which Professor Chayes focused, have
remained significant. See Sabel & Simon, Destabilization Rights: How
Public Law Litigation Succeeds, 117 Harv.L.Rev. 1015 (2004). But they
have not been the only source of the complex litigation revolution. To
the contrary, the expansion of liability rules by both legislatures and
courts has also provided new legal avenues for awarding damages for
personal injuries. "By the later 1990s, * * * Professor Chayes's model
itself was outdated. Chayes may have succeeded in addressing the civil
rights class actions of the 1960s and 1970s, but he failed to anticipate
and 'capture the dynamics of modern mass tort litigation,' which came to
dominate the litigation landscape in the 1980s and 1990s." Molot, An
Old Judicial Role for a New Judicial Era, 113 Yale L.J. 27, 29 (2003).
Consider the views of Judge Williams, who was presiding over cases
involving the Dalkon Shield contraceptive device:

> The latter half of the twentieth century has witnessed a virtual
> explosion in the frequency and number of lawsuits filed to redress
> injuries caused by a single product manufactured for use on a
> national level. Indeed, certain products have achieved such national
> notoriety due to their tremendous impact on the consuming public,
> that the mere mention of their names—Agent Orange, Asbestos,
> DES, MER/29, Dalkon Shield—conjure images of massive litigation,
> corporate stonewalling, and infrequent yet prevalent, "big money"
> punitive damage awards.

> In a complex society such as ours, the phenomenon of numerous
> persons suffering the same or similar injuries as a result of a single
> pattern of misconduct on the part of a defendant is becoming
> increasingly frequent.

In re Northern District of California "Dalkon Shield" IUD Products Liability Litigation, 526 F.Supp. 887, 892 (N.D.Cal.1981), rev'd, 693 F.2d 847 (9th Cir.1982), cert. denied, 459 U.S. 1171, 103 S.Ct. 817, 74 L.Ed.2d 1015 (1983).

In part, these changes in litigation resulted from the procedural reforms of 1938. Using the new procedural tools the Federal Rules made available, creative litigants and judges made the federal court system a significant force for social change and new theories of liability. These developments were enhanced by technological advances. In 1938, there were no electric typewriters, long distance telephone calls could not be dialed direct, and jet planes did not exist for passenger travel. Today's litigator simply could not operate without a cell phone, a blackberry, e-mail, a fax machine, word processing capacity, data banks, and a photo-copying machine. Technological changes making possible the collection and synthesis of vast amounts of data were essential to proving the new theories of liability.

Together, these changes have also dramatically altered the work of the lawyer. Where the lawyer of 1938 was a trial lawyer, the lawyer in the 21st century is a litigator engaged in a competitive business of lawyering. This transformation has changed what lawyers do:

> [D]iscovery has replaced trial as the mechanism for resolving disputes. Litigators march forth from law firms flanked by junior partners, associates and paralegals much as fifteenth century Italian armies ventured from warring city-states. These armies left home and lived well off the land as they proceeded to confront the enemy. They avoided direct combat at all costs. The process leading to it was too rewarding, while battle itself was too risky. Thus does litigation proceed today.

Lundquist, Trial Lawyer or Litigator, 7 Litigation 3, 4 (Summer 1981). But discovery can be a nasty business; reports of "Rambo" tactics are frequent.

The 1938 Rules of Civil Procedure permitted the parties and issues in a lawsuit to be expanded by such joinder devices as counterclaims, crossclaims, third-party complaints, intervention, and interpleader. They also provided for aggregation of cases through consolidation and class actions. These were not entirely new devices, and the 1938 Rules largely codified and streamlined what were deemed to be the best practices from the common law and equity courts. However, in the next several decades, as courts and legislatures created new grounds for liability under substantive law, the procedures for expanding the size and scope of lawsuits came into their own. In addition, the complexity of modern society, with increased likelihood that many individuals would be injured by the same or similar conditions or conduct, also provided an impetus for using joinder and aggregation devices to expand the scope of lawsuits.

The class action, a creation of equity that was considerably limited under the 1938 rules, became an important procedure for aggregating claims. Amendments were made to the class action rule in 1966 that allowed class actions for injunctive and declaratory relief (for example, civil rights and institutional reform suits) under Rule 23(b)(2), and for damages when the court finds that "questions of law or fact common to the members of the class predominate over any questions affecting only individual members, and that a class action is superior to other available methods for the fair and efficient adjudication of the controversy" under Rule 23(b)(3). "Today, a very high percentage of American class actions are Rule 23(b)(3) class actions. They have become the vehicle for damage class action suits across a broad spectrum of antitrust, civil rights, securities fraud, consumer, mass tort, environmental, and product liability claims." Sherman, American Class Actions: Significant Features and Developing Alternatives in Foreign Legal Systems, 215 F.R.D. 130, 134–35 (2003). Class actions have become a principal construct of complex litigation and one of the most controversial features of contemporary litigation.

RAND INSTITUTE FOR CIVIL JUSTICE, CLASS ACTION DILEMMAS: PURSUING PUBLIC GOALS FOR PRIVATE GAIN

9, 49–51 (2000).

Whether and when to enable large numbers of individuals to bring claims collectively against a single or a few defendants has long been a subject of debate in the civil law. The language of the debate is the language of civil procedure: the formal rules that govern when and how plaintiffs may bring suits against defendants; how those defendants may contest the plaintiffs' claims; and how the adversaries may bring to bear the facts and law that are relevant to their dispute, so as to ultimately reach a resolution of the case. But underlying disagreements about procedural rules rests the sometimes unspoken but widely shared understanding that procedural rules have important effects on litigation outcomes. Nowhere in the law is this truth more evident than in the battle over the class action rule, which empowers plaintiffs to bring cases that otherwise either would not be possible or would only be possible in a very different form. At times, the protagonists in the class action debate have focused on "big questions," such as securing civil rights and protecting consumers, and at times they have focused on narrow technical issues, such as when the decision to permit a class action can be challenged. But the larger social and political conflicts of the day always echo in the rooms in which the proper uses of class actions are debated.

* * *

After more than 30 years of controversy, the U.S. legal system seems to have reached an uneasy accommodation with class actions seeking affirmation of rights—of children, taxpayers, prisoners, and other groups in society. There is political disagreement about which and whose rights we should honor, and Congress has enacted legislation forbidding the federally funded Legal Services Corporation to assist in bringing rights-based (or any other) class actions. But these actions reflect fundamental arguments about individual and group rights more than disagreement about the appropriateness of providing a vehicle, such as the class action, for collective litigation of these issues.

The history of the debate over Rule 23 shows that we have not reached a similar consensus on the appropriate uses of Rule 23(b)(3) damage class actions. Is the Rule 23(b)(3) class action primarily an administrative efficiency mechanism, a means for courts and parties to manage a large number of similar legal claims, without requiring each litigant to come forward and have his or her claim considered individually? Or is it primarily a means of enabling litigation that could not be brought on an individual basis, in pursuit of larger social goals such as enforcing government regulations and deterring unsafe or unfair business practices? As we have seen, clashing views on the objective of Rule 23(b)(3) are at the heart of past and present controversy over revising the class action rule.

But the distinction in the public debate between the *efficiency* and *enabling* goals of class actions for money damages is illusory. In practice, any change in court processes that provides more efficient means of litigating is likely to enable more litigation. Greater efficiency can lower the costs of bringing lawsuits, making it more attractive for litigants to sue and for lawyers to take their cases. Moreover, because Rule 23(b)(3) requires telling people that they may have a claim of which they were previously unaware, but does not require them to take any initial action to join in the litigation, virtually every damage class action has the potential to expand the pool of litigants beyond what it would have been without class litigation. In other words, whatever efficiencies it may achieve, Rule 23 is inherently an enabling mechanism.

When we take a closer look at the controversy over damage class actions, we can see that it is, in fact, a dispute about what kinds of lawsuits and what kinds of resolutions of lawsuits *the legal system should enable.*

Business representatives from diverse sectors of the economy argue that Rule 23(b)(3), in practice, enables large numbers of lawsuits about trivial or nonexistent violations of statutes and regulations that govern advertising, marketing, pricing and other business practices, and about trivial losses to individual consumers. They claim that such suits, in reality, are vehicles for enriching plaintiff class action attorneys, not mechanisms for ensuring that important legal rules are enforced or for compensating consumers. In the end, they say, consumers pay for this litigation in the form of increased product and service costs without receiving commensurate benefits.

Manufacturers argue, as well, that Rule 23(b)(3) enables massive product defect suits that rest on dubious scientific and technical evidence. Because of the huge financial exposure associated with these mega-lawsuits, manufacturers say they feel forced to settle damage class actions, rather than contest them. The end result, they claim, is to drive good products from the market and to deter investment in developing other beneficial products.

Consumer advocates counter that a prime purpose of Rule 23(b)(3) is to enable just the kind of regulatory enforcement suits—sometimes termed "private attorneys general suits"—that businesses complain about. They say that the public cannot rely on regulatory agencies to adequately enforce consumer protection statutes, because these agencies are often underfunded and sometimes subject to influence by the businesses that they regulate. They also believe that consumers ought to have a vehicle for obtaining compensation for losses that result from corporate wrong-doing, even when these losses are small. In addition, they support mass product defect litigation, which they believe provides a powerful incentive for businesses to invest in designing safer products.

But some consumer advocates and other public interest lawyers worry that, in practice, Rule 23(b)(3) enables otherwise good cases to produce bad *outcomes*—settlements that they say serve plaintiff class action attorneys and business defendants better than they serve consumers and the general public. As a result, these advocates argue, injured consumers get less compensation than they deserve and corporations do not pay enough in damages to deter future misconduct.

All these arguments revolve around questions of what injuries ought to be compensated and what behaviors ought to be deterred. A different argument about the enabling effects of Rule 23(b)(3) concerns the right of individualized consideration of one's legal claims. When class members' claims involve such small losses that they could not realistically be pursued through individual litigation, few people worry that class actions abrogate class members' rights to individual treatment of those claims. But legal scholars and some personal injury lawyers believe that creating a single product liability class action, by combining individual cases claiming significant damages, results in lawyers and courts running roughshod over individual litigants' rights.

B. THE AGGREGATION DEBATE

Aggregation of related cases for unitary pretrial preparation and trial (whether accomplished by joinder, consolidation, or class action) has become one of the central issues in complex litigation. There are significant policies weighing in favor of aggregation and against it. Consider the following discussion of these issues:

SHERMAN, AGGREGATE DISPOSITION OF RELATED CASES: THE POLICY ISSUES

10 Rev. of Litigation 231, 237–54 (1991).

I. POLICIES FAVORING AGGREGATION

A. *Economy and Efficiency*

Aggregation of cases promises savings by eliminating duplication and providing economies of scale. Critics of case aggregation, however, argue that the savings are not nearly so clear. Professor Richard Epstein contends that an aggregate trial can impose greater costs than individual trials and actually involve diseconomies of scale.[22] The amount of time and money expended in resolving an issue in litigation is partly a function of the amount of money at stake. When a consolidated case increases the amount in controversy by perhaps a thousandfold, he says that "we must make some estimate of the increase in costs incurred in response to the higher stakes in this new litigation setting." For example, he points out that we should expect to see both sides in drug-product cases invest far more heavily in independent experiments and in expert witnesses on the issue of causation.

It is certainly true that some litigation expenses will increase when there is more money at stake; an example is greater willingness to expend more resources on expert witnesses and lawyers. On the other hand, other litigation expenses are not likely to vary much with the amount in controversy. Examples of these would be expenses for rather mechanical acts such as culling documents, indexing discovery, entering documents into a computerized litigation-support system, summarizing depositions, and preparing witnesses. The cost of certain functions that may be expanded in the expectation of strengthening one's case—such as investigation, discovery, motion practice, and trial preparation—would probably increase with larger stakes but finally level off once the basic tasks have been accomplished. There are finite limits on discovery, and today under the "proportionality" provision of Rule 26(b)(2), the court can restrict duplicative or unduly expensive discovery. Although there is little empirical data to demonstrate exactly how aggregation affects litigation costs, descriptive studies suggest that, although both sides may spend more lavishly in a multi-million dollar aggregated case, it does not take very many individual trials to exceed the cost of a single aggregate trial.

* * *

The critics further note that when the decision to aggregate is made, it may be difficult to predict whether there will be economies from aggregation. That is true, but experience provides a variety of bench-

---

22. Epstein, Commentary, The Consolidation of Complex Litigation: A Critical Evaluation of the ALI Proposal, 10 J.L. & Com. 1, 15–16 (1990).

marks for making such predictions. Judges presently must apply efficiency considerations in ruling on mandatory and permissive joinder, in determining whether to transfer to a more convenient forum or to consolidate cases, and in determining whether a class action is superior to other available methods for the fair and efficient adjudication of the controversy. * * * Similarly, the Panel on Multidistrict Litigation has vast experience in applying a number of considerations relating to economy and efficiency to assess whether to transfer and consolidate for pretrial purposes under the Multidistrict Litigation Act of 1968.

* * *

Another aspect of the critics' doubts about economies from aggregation seems more persuasive: could methods less drastic than full aggregation and joint trial achieve many of the cost-saving benefits? Alternatives include voluntary coordination of discovery and pretrial processing, consolidation for pretrial purposes only, and use of collateral estoppel. The question then becomes whether the disadvantages of full aggregation outweigh any incremental economies beyond those that would accrue from less restrictive means.

* * *

B. *Consistency of Result*

It is a fundamental principle of justice that like cases should be accorded like treatment in the interest of achieving consistent results. Aggregate treatment does not guarantee consistent results, but a single proceeding can avoid the widely different outcomes that often result from separate cases brought by similarly situated persons. Aggregate treatment can also avoid the inconsistent outcomes that may result from processing and trying similar cases at different times before different juries. In addition, some parties able to take their cases to trial (or to obtain a trial date that forces the defendant to seriously consider settlement) may reach funds of the defendant that will not be available to later claimants. Thus, when cases are tried individually, the vagaries of timing may make an enormous difference in the relative recovery possibilities of individual plaintiffs.

Experience has shown that in the life cycle of particular litigations, the time when an individual's case is resolved may present markedly different advantages and disadvantages in terms of defendants' willingness to settle, the availability of critical information, and the general judicial climate affecting judges' rulings and jury verdicts. Aggregation avoids such temporal inconsistencies by insuring that all cases will be resolved together at a particular point in time. Inconsistency of individual verdicts may also undercut settlement, as Judge Weinstein has pointed out, because "both claimants and defendants may be more (or less) willing to take their chances in future suits, and the likelihood of fair settlement may be reduced."[55]

---

55. Weinstein, Procedural and Substantive Problems in Complex Litigation Arising   From Disasters, 5 Touro L.Rev. 1, 7 (1988).

Critics of aggregation rightly note that the consistency of treatment accomplished in aggregated cases may fail to give proper regard to individual differences. Critics also question the necessity for, indeed the desirability of, uniform outcome in related cases. Professor Epstein gives the example of two persons receiving identical injuries in identical automobile accidents. The first is anxious about discovery, while the second is better able to withstand its rigors. We might expect different outcomes in their suits because the first plaintiff may not be willing to pursue a course best calculated for an optimal result. A plaintiff who desires a quicker settlement may, through his choice of strategy, receive a lesser compensation than a plaintiff willing to assume the risk and costs of waiting. Furthermore, Epstein says, different lawyers may choose different strategies, which may yield inconsistent results.

It is undoubtedly true that plaintiffs' predilections and their attorneys' strategies can affect litigation outcomes. The concern over inconsistent outcomes, however, does not arise from deliberate choices about those predilections and strategies. We can understand and justify one plaintiff receiving a higher verdict for taking the risk of going to trial. The concern is that it is not such deliberate choices, but much more random procedural and jurisdictional factors (such as where and when a case is tried or the makeup of the particular judge or jury), that account for different outcomes in individually-litigated related cases. When one plaintiff loses a jury verdict after others have won, when one plaintiff receives a nominal recovery after others with similar injuries have received large awards, or when one plaintiff's case is severely undermined because the judge makes pretrial rulings or grants a summary judgment that other judges in other similar cases did not, the inconsistent result springs directly from the fact that there was no single judge, factfinder, and process. Case aggregation can at least insure that the parties are on equal procedural footing in a single case that will provide a definitive outcome for all.

Professor Roger Trangsrud makes the point that "[w]e should not pretend that there is only one proper result in a hotly disputed tort case."[58] Thus, he notes that we do not insist that all injured passengers in a multicar accident bring their claims in one proceeding. It is true that mandatory joinder under Rule 19 has not been interpreted as establishing efficiency standards that would prevent individual plaintiffs in a mass disaster from proceeding in separate suits. [See *infra* pp. 53–54.] But those standards need not govern the use of other devices like class action and consolidation that are more clearly directed at accomplishing efficiency through aggregation. At present, jurisdiction, service, and venue barriers prevent not only the efficient joinder of parties, but also the effective use of the aggregative devices. * * * Removing the barriers, of course, poses its own set of concerns regarding litigant

58. Trangsrud, [Mass Trials in Mass Tort Cases: A Dissent, 1989 U.Ill.L.Rev. 69], at 77.

autonomy, federalism, jurisdictional authority, and appropriate choice of law rules.

* * *

II. Policies Disfavoring Aggregation

A. *Litigant Autonomy*

A principal policy reason often cited for opposing aggregation of claims is individual litigant autonomy. This value encompasses both the right of the plaintiff to select the time and forum for asserting his claim and the right of all parties to control the strategies for individually developing their cases. * * *

The term "litigant autonomy" properly refers to both party and attorney as the "litigant" entity. In fact, the term "attorney autonomy" sometimes better describes the true interest at stake. Parties give up a great deal of their own autonomy when they select an attorney. Often the convenience of the attorney, rather than the party, dictates decisions about party structure and the forum for filing. Indeed, when parties in individual suits resist consolidation or class-action status, their counsel's fear of a loss of control or loss of fees is often a significant factor. This is not to say that the interests of the party and the attorney may not coincide in opposing aggregate treatment, but that attorneys often have distinctive interests in maintaining the individualized structure of a suit.

Aggregation, of course, disrupts both litigant and attorney autonomy much more than do individual cases and can interfere with the proper relationship between attorney and client. Aggregation can upset fee arrangements, undermine attorneys' expectations under contingent-fee contracts, and even create conflicts of interest by forcing attorneys into an unseemly struggle for case control and by reducing their commitment to the client. In a class action, the individual attorney's stake in individualized treatment may conflict with the class-action attorney's stake in aggregate treatment.

These are legitimate concerns, but they are not unique to full case aggregation. Court-management procedures applying to individual as well as aggregated cases can result in an order for coordinated discovery with other related cases that results in lead and liaison counsel or attorney steering committees performing the most time-consuming and compensated functions of the litigation. It is increasingly likely that, for example, an individual plaintiff's attorney will not be able to take her own depositions of the defendant's employees or to conduct her own document discovery. Lead or liaison counsel may assume broad powers over both the formulation and execution of pretrial strategy. Because well over ninety percent of cases are settled, the less restrictive alternative of aggregation only for purposes of pretrial will often determine the outcome of the case.

Nevertheless, courts have given insufficient attention to tailoring the use of class action and consolidation in ways that would permit greater involvement of individual attorneys in the functions they can perform most efficiently. * * * Greater judicial respect for existing attorney-client relationships in original suits is clearly desirable if greater aggregation is to occur.

On the other hand, an individual attorney who objects to losing as large a fee as could have been obtained in an individual case seems to have little equitable claim. A cause of action that is related to other claims arising from similar defendant conduct is by its nature different from the traditional two-party suit, on which rests many of the assumptions about attorney-client relationships and fees. In an age when multiple lawyers often work on aggregated cases and fashion satisfactory fee arrangements, there seems little reason to reject aggregation simply because different circumstances will require different fee structures.

B. Fairness

In evaluating case aggregation, perhaps the most compelling concern is whether the lack of individuation so affects the quality of decision-making that it denies fairness and due process. Clearly due process is denied if the aggregated case is unmanageable, so that the parties are unable to adequately present the facts and law to the jury or the jury is unable to understand the case or to make reasonably discriminating judgments. * * *

1. *Effect on Strategic Advantages.*—Due process concerns are often expressed in terms of strategic adverse effects on the parties. Aggregation could deprive plaintiffs of forum-selection advantages, such as selecting a forum to maximize convenience, minimize cost, utilize the most favorable law, or draw on hometown sympathy. Aggregation could also deny plaintiffs the advantages of individualized control, such as being able to settle individually or not being subjected to an averaging effect in the settlement or award of damages. Defendants also face particular disadvantages. They may experience a sort of averaging effect, arising from either the court's inability to distinguish between defendants with strong and weak defenses or the taint of association with more culpable defendants. Professor Epstein also raises the objection that defendants forced into aggregate proceedings lose the "legitimate interest in having the array of cases brought against them heard by more than one judge," and in "escap[ing] the luck of the draw that could spell ruin."

It is difficult to cast the loss of these strategic advantages in terms of denial of fundamental fairness and due process. Plaintiffs' interests in forum selection, or defendants' insistence on dealing individually with plaintiffs in a divide-and-conquer strategy, may be important to them, but are not fundamental to procedural justice. It is also hard to categorize the possibility of some averaging effect as of fundamental due process proportions. Joining additional parties to even a simple two-party suit may affect the liability determination or dollar amounts that would have resulted had the claims been tried separately. * * * Pursuant to the proper management of litigation, courts can impose on parties a wide range of restrictions and requirements that in some way undercut strategic advantages that parties would otherwise have enjoyed. If such requirements are reasonably related to valid objectives, they are permissible.

2. *Effect on Ability to Raise Individual Issues.*—A more troubling due process issue arises if parties lose certain individual claims or defenses because issue control is ceded to the group attorneys or because of the manner in which the aggregate case is structured. Consolidation and class-action practice have generally allowed a high degree of discretion in the shaping of issues, and some of the benefits of aggregation would be lost if that discretion were too strictly limited. On the other hand, consistent with due process, such discretion should not deprive a party of the chance to have his day in court on individual claims and defenses. There should, therefore, be opportunities for individual parties who so desire to urge their individual claims to group counsel, and, if unsuccessful, to opt out or to sever their individual claims to permit individual assertion of rights. The state of the law regarding the nature and extent of such rights is currently in flux, as the courts wrestle with the difficult issue of whether to forbid opting out from aggregated proceedings where individual suits would considerably undercut the effectiveness and fairness of the aggregation.

C. EVALUATING INNOVATION IN LITIGATION

It should be apparent that complex litigation has served as a sparkplug for innovation across a gamut of procedural issues. The remainder of this book examines many of these issues and invites readers to evaluate them. At first blush, many of these innovations appear to be unexceptional methods of improving the courts' ability to resolve disputes efficiently. As the preceding section shows, however, one must be cautious about such assumptions. Before we turn to detailed consideration of the innovations, it is therefore important to reflect further on competing concerns.

1. JUDICIAL INVOLVEMENT AND MANAGEMENT

The prevailing ethos under the Federal Rules was that the judge's main function was to preside over a trial at which the merits of the case would be resolved on the basis of evidence presented by the parties. Consistent with that attitude, the rules inclined against pleadings decisions and provided broad discovery to permit parties to unearth all pertinent material. Initially, summary judgment was narrowly circumscribed by many courts. Ordinarily the judge might become aware of a case only when the parties notified the court that it was ready for trial. Although the rules contained provisions for pretrial conferences to involve the judge at that point, such events were not frequent.

In a number of areas the "liberal" attitude of this era has eroded. Thus, federal courts have in some instances curtailed the relaxed attitude toward pleading they once displayed. See generally Marcus, The Revival of Fact Pleading Under the Federal Rules of Civil Procedure, 86 Colum.L.Rev. 433 (1986); Marcus, The Puzzling Persistence of Pleading Practice, 76 Texas L.Rev. 1749 (1998). The Supreme Court has emphasized that summary judgment "is properly regarded not as a disfavored procedural shortcut, but rather as an integral part of the Federal Rules as a whole." Celotex Corp. v. Catrett, 477 U.S. 317, 327, 106 S.Ct. 2548, 2554, 91 L.Ed.2d 265 (1986). Thus the assumption that cases could only be adjudicated after trial has been relaxed in many instances. The justification for expanded use of summary judgment has been questioned: "Unfortunately, today's rhetoric about that 'litigation explosion,' a 'liability crisis,' sham or frivolous litigation, and undue burdens on the business community may be encouraging district courts and courts of appeals to rely on the [*Celotex* precedents] to justify resorting to pretrial disposition too readily because they believe that there is a need to alleviate overcrowded dockets or because they disfavor certain substantive claims." Miller, The Pretrial Rush to Judgment: Are the "Litigation Explosion," "Liability Crisis," and Efficiency Cliches Eroding Our Day in Court and Jury Trial Commitments?, 78 N.Y.U. L. Rev. 982, 1133 (2003).

Regarding the generally passive role judges traditionally exhibited in civil litigation, complex litigation provided the stimulus to move in new directions. Whatever the overall tranquility of federal civil litigation in 1938, by the late 1940s there was a widely-felt concern among federal judges about whether "protracted" litigation, particularly antitrust litigation, should be handled differently. A 1951 study by the Judicial Conference of the United States suggested that the solution was greater involvement by judges. "Prettyman Report," 13 F.R.D. 62 (1951). In 1960, a "Handbook of Recommended Procedures for the Trial of Protracted Cases" was issued, providing detailed guidelines for disposition of "big cases" from start to finish. 25 F.R.D. 351 (1960). In the late 1950s, the prosecution of the manufacturers of electronic equipment for price fixing led to attempts to coordinate multiple cases relating to the same matter filed in different courts (there were 2,000 antitrust suits filed in 35 U.S. district courts, containing 25,623 separate claims for damages). A committee of judges appointed by Chief Justice Warren devised a plan for coordinated discovery that became the model for the Multidistrict Litigation Act of 1968. See *infra* p. 142. This act created the Judicial Panel on Multidistrict Litigation (MDL) with the power to assign similar cases pending in federal court for pretrial preparation. The Panel, in turn, published the Manual for Complex Litigation in 1969; now in its fourth edition (2004), it sets out detailed pretrial procedures for complex cases, together with model orders, and relies heavily on active involvement of judges.

Many judges did not restrict their innovations to complex cases. By the late 1970s they began to immerse themselves in the pretrial preparation of a broad range of civil cases. Some began to question the premises of the adversary system on which the passive role of the judge was premised. In a well-known speech, Judge Marvin Frankel proposed modifying the adversary ideal to "consider whether the paramount commitment of counsel concerning matters of fact should be to the discovery of truth rather than to the advancement of the client's interest." He also ventured to "raise the question whether the virginally ignorant judge is always to be preferred to one with an investigative file." See Frankel, The Search for Truth: An Umpireal View, 123 U.Pa.L.Rev. 1031 (1975).

Without explicitly inquiring into the speculations suggested by Judge Frankel, judges who actively managed their cases began to expect counsel to cooperate with them in the development of litigation, and to regard "excessive" adversarial behavior as counterproductive and something to be restrained. As we shall see in Chapter VI, this movement has become widespread and the debate about the proper judicial role continues.

The growth of mass related cases has posed special challenges to innovative judges. Mass related cases usually involve similar discovery and trial preparation, many identical issues, and much the same evidence. If they must be litigated separately there is an enormous duplication of effort and time in preparing and relitigating the same issues again and again. If, however, they could be combined and disposed of together, there might be economies of scale, avoidance of duplication, and consistency of result. But there are barriers to such aggregate disposition. The principal procedural devices for aggregation—joinder, consolidation, and class actions—have limitations that may prevent their use in a number of situations. Furthermore, when lawsuits are pending in state as well as federal courts, jurisdictional barriers can prevent their being brought together in a single forum. Mechanisms in aid of aggregation in federal court—such as transfer, removal, injunctions and stay orders—are also subject to various limitations.

Federal judges faced with huge dockets of mass related cases have found the barriers to case aggregation increasingly onerous. They have turned to innovative techniques for aggregative disposition which have, in turn, drawn criticism based on both constitutional due process and policy grounds. Their frustrations have also lead to proposals for legislative and rule changes which would expand federal jurisdiction to permit combined adjudication of related tort cases. These are also controversial.

2.   DISPUTE RESOLUTION AS GOAL OF CIVIL LITIGATION

The initial reaction of most American law students is probably that the proper goal of courts in civil litigation should be to resolve disputes. To accord that goal preeminence can raise serious concerns, a point that becomes clearest in connection with judicial efforts to encourage settlement. We encounter settlement promotion as a feature of judicial management in Chapter VI, while here raising the initial question whether this should be treated as the paramount goal. Consider the views of Professor Fiss in Against Settlement, 93 Yale L.J. 1073, 1085 (1984):

> The dispute-resolution story makes settlement appear as a perfect substitute for judgment * * * by reducing the social function of the lawsuit to one of resolving private disputes: In that story, settlement appears to achieve exactly the same purpose as judgment—peace between the parties—but at considerably less expense to society. The two quarreling neighbors turn to the court in order to resolve their dispute, and society makes courts available because it wants to aid in the achievement of their private ends or to secure the peace.

> In my view, however, the purpose of adjudication should be understood in broader terms. Adjudication uses public resources, and employs not strangers chosen by the parties but public officials chosen by a process in which the public participates. These officials, like members of the legislative and executive branches, possess a power that has been defined and conferred by public law, not by private agreement. Their job is not to maximize the ends of private parties, nor simply to secure the peace, but to explicate and give force to the values embodied in authoritative texts such as the Constitution and statutes: to interpret those values and to bring reality into accord with them.

Although these remarks are directed toward settlement, the same concerns affect one's attitude toward other issues. Consider, for example, the implications for these issues on whether a court should be free with intervention, a topic addressed in Chapter II. Similarly, consider how these views should affect a court's willingness to grant a protective order that limits disclosure of material in which there may be a public interest, a topic addressed in Chapter V.

3. COMBINED OR INDIVIDUAL TREATMENT

As section B above demonstrates, evaluating current practices and proposed enhancement of the capacity to combine cases raises several of the concerns we have discussed. Purely in efficiency terms, there may be instances in which the addition of more parties or claims or evidence does not enhance the efficiency of the system beyond individualized treatment. To what extent should courts disregard individual differences in order to facilitate combined treatment? Should they try to isolate limited issues in cases that appear to be common to many claims in order to make it possible to resolve those issues in a combined proceeding? Does the value of apparent consistency that might follow from combined adjudication warrant disregarding differences among claimants, or diminishing the claimants' ability to control "their" cases?

Joinder and intervention decisions might further interests in participation in litigation. Similarly, transfer of cases for combined treatment might dilute individual involvement and control, as might the use of the class action device. It is important to keep in mind the costs of complexity, as with the issue of whether the right to jury trials may be suspended in complex cases:

> When a case's complexity results wholly or in part from the joinder of parties and claims permitted or required by procedural rules, there is something odd about reasoning that uses the costs of complexity as the excuse for denying trial by jury. We are confronted by the spectacle of the government denying an explicit constitutional right in order to remedy a supposed constitutional problem for which the government is itself at least partially responsible. This is the case when complexity results from enforced joinder, including by operation of preclusion rules, or from joinder initiated by a party who seeks to avoid a jury trial. Even when the party seeking a jury trial is responsible, one might suppose that before denying the constitutional right the court would explore the option of breaking the lawsuit into smaller, less complex packages, and thus unravelling complexity the government has helped to create.

Burbank, The Costs of Complexity, 85 Mich.L.Rev. 1463, 1480–81 (1987).

Lest it be thought that aggregation invariably deprives individuals of all control over their litigation destinies, consider the following description of how neighbors formed an organization to make claims based on exposure to noxious substances deposited in a waste dump near their homes:

> Despite their lack of common ailments or history, they still had to devise a way to speak with one voice. So they wrote a full constitution, complete with checks and balances. The charter is divided into six articles—only one fewer than the U.S. Constitution. Article II delimits the powers of the Steering Committee and enumerates the duties of the Business, Property, Health and Guardian ad Litem subcommittees. There are definitions of a quorum, methods for the conduct of business, and bylaws regarding the election of officers. Article VI details the proceedings for impeachment.

Hitt, Toxic Dreams: A California Town Finds Meaning in An Acid Pit, Harper's Mag., July 1995, at 57, 61.

4. BROAD v. SPECIFIC RULES

Many of the rules governing important matters such as joinder and class actions are phrased in general language that requires ad hoc application. As a consequence, they grant the judge great latitude in tailoring the treatment of cases under the broad mandate of the rules. It is likely that you will sometimes find yourself in a fog trying to articulate grounds for the different treatment accorded different cases. As you struggle with such difficulties, reflect on the origins and orientation of the rules as explained in Subrin, How Equity Conquered Common Law: The Federal Rules of Civil Procedure in Historical Perspective, 135 U.Pa.L.Rev. 909, 922, 982–83 (1987):

The underlying philosophy of, and procedural choices embodied in, the Federal Rules were almost universally drawn from equity rather than common law. The expansive and flexible aspects of equity were all implicit in the Federal Rules. Before the Rules, equity procedure and jurisprudence historically had applied to only a small percentage of the totality of litigation. Thus the drafters [of the Federal Rules] made an enormous change: in effect the tail of historic adjudication was now wagging the dog.

* * *

As a doctrinal model for the resolution of civil disputes, equity permitted the participation of virtually unlimited numbers of people in trials and the consideration of a similar array of theories and facts. The idea was to escape the confinement of the common law. Because equity wanted the whole picture, without boundaries, in its search for a more perfect answer, it was, in essence, undisciplined. Both recent trends to amend the Federal Rules as well as the developments in alternative dispute resolution have emerged, at least in considerable part, in response to the chaos.

The proponents of the [Rules] Enabling Act and the Federal Rules repeatedly cited the case of Jarndyce v. Jarndyce in Dickens' Bleak House as representative of the type of technicality that they were trying to avoid by the movement for uniform, simple rules. They apparently forgot that a major point of the novel was the perpetual fog surrounding Chancery. * * * It was the search for human perfection, trying to cover everybody and everything, combined with lawyer abuse, that caused the delay, expense, and endless fog in *Jarndyce* and that helps account for the same conditions under the Federal Rules. Equity has no boundaries, and, when standing alone without law, presents a largely lawless system.

As you examine the procedural problems presented in this book, consider whether the elasticity of the rules governing them has added to the complexity and uncertainty of litigation. Do not forget, however, that the urge behind the Federal Rules was to escape a highly formal and rigid past that seemed to work injustice in many cases. Could more structure be given to litigation today without risking similar problems? For further consideration of the inclination toward discretion in modern procedure, see Marcus, Slouching Toward Discretion, 78 Notre Dame L.Rev. 1561 (2003).

5.   IMPACT OF PROCEDURE ON SUBSTANCE

Conceived as the "handmaid to justice," procedure is intended only to effectuate, but not to change, substantive rights. But procedural issues may have a major impact on the viability of a litigation. Consider, for example, the class action seeking redress for a large plaintiff class for relatively small injuries. In such instances the sine qua non for litigation may be access to the class action. Similarly in other contexts, the resolution of procedural disputes may dramatically alter the relative strengths of the parties.

The availability of certain procedures may alter substantive law in more overt ways:

> Arguments regarding the scope of discovery typically have not dealt with the role discovery has played in the evolution of substantive law. It is clear, however, that over the years developments in areas such as products liability, employment discrimination, and consumer protection have been the result at least partly of broadranging discovery provisions. For example, lawyers would not have pushed in the courts and in the legislatures for expanded causes of action hinged on proof that defendants knew or should have known of a product's danger, if such proof were normally unavailable. The ability of plaintiffs' attorneys to obtain a corporate defendant's records, to depose corporate employees, and to send searching interrogatories has had a substantial impact in particular areas of law, and is one important factor in the dramatic increase in cases filed.

Friedenthal, A Divided Supreme Court Adopts Discovery Amendments to the Federal Rules of Civil Procedure, 69 Calif.L.Rev. 806, 818 (1981). But see Marcus, Discovery Containment Redux, 39 Bos.Coll.L.Rev. 747 (1998) (questioning Friedenthal's conclusion).

Courts may also tinker with substantive law to facilitate procedural objectives. For example, courts may be tempted to modify the substantive requirements of a claim to remove troublesome individual issues that could hamper class action treatment or consolidation of cases for common disposition. In such instances, it seems that the substantive law is changed in service to procedure.

6. MODELING PROCEDURES ON COMPLEX CASES

The brief review above of judicial innovation in civil litigation shows that often complex litigation provided the stimulus for innovations that were later adopted for "average" cases as well. Despite uncertainty about the proper definition of complexity in litigation, there is reason to question the extrapolation from those cases to all cases.

There seems little question that there is great diversity in the types of cases currently before the courts. Hence Professor Galanter acknowledges "a growing component of large and complex cases that involve investments of immense amounts of time, exhaustive investigation and research, lavish deployment of expensive experts, and prodigious use of court resources." Galanter, Reading the Landscape of Disputes: What We Know and Don't Know (And Think We Know) About Our Allegedly Contentious and Litigious Society, 31 U.C.L.A.L.Rev. 4, 46 (1983). Nevertheless, he rejects extrapolation from these cases.

> The scholarly foundation of the "litigation explosion" view is the product of a narrow elite of judges (mostly federal), professors and deans at eminent law schools, and practitioners who practice in

large firms and deal with big clients about big cases. Because they
are attuned to the "top" of the system—to appellate courts, to
federal courts, to that small segment of law practice that deals in
large cases, and thus to the concerns of large clients—such elites
tend to have a limited and spotty grasp of what the bulk of the legal
system is really like. For example, they tend to identify as general
problems things such as discovery abuse that apply only in a tiny
minority of cases.

Id. at 61–62; see also Fiss, Against Settlement, 93 Yale L.J. 1073, 1087
(1984) ("All cases are not equal. The Los Angeles desegregation case, to
take one example, is not equal to the allegedly more typical suit involving a property dispute or an automobile accident.").

But our procedural rules outwardly treat all these cases in the same
way. Should we modify that uniform treatment to take account of the
individual characteristics of cases? Consider the following views:

Cadillac-style procedures are not needed to process bicycle-size
lawsuits, yet that is what the rules often appear to require. With few
exceptions (such as the 1983 amendment to Rule 16 permitting
district courts to exempt from elaborate pre-trial procedure categories of actions they deem "inappropriate"), the rules are monolithic
and indiscriminately applicable to all kinds of suits. When that
involves exposing small and medium-size cases to the expansive
discovery weapons the rules provide, the possibilities for abuse are
obvious. * * * The point is simply that for many or possibly most
cases wide-open discovery under the rules is too heavy and powerful
an instrument.

Rosenberg, The Federal Civil Rules After Half a Century, 36 Me.L.Rev.
243, 247 (1984).

Have the courts too frequently assumed that complex litigation
provides the proper model for all litigation? "We should stop designing
processes for the most complex case conceivable and then making these
procedures available for every case." Sipes, Where Do We Go From
Here?, 23 Judges J. 44, 46 (1984). How does one determine which cases
should get high-cost treatment? What should be taken away in other
cases? Would it be best to direct judges to make these determinations on
a case-by-case basis? Could workable distinctions be designed on a
system-wide basis? If so, what would be proper procedures for non-
complex cases?

7. FEDERALISM CONCERNS

When complex litigation procedures involve greater case aggregation, federalism concerns often arise. Mass related cases can often be
filed in a number of different state and federal courts. Federalism
barriers, expressed in federal statutes that limit both federal court
jurisdiction and anti-suit injunctions against pending state court cases,
often prevent aggregation in a single federal district court. Similarly,
where cases are aggregated from a number of states the need to apply

the law of several states may greatly complicate the proceedings or prevent combined adjudication. Courts and legislatures may therefore try to find ways around existing choice of law rules to overcome these difficulties.

For a number of reasons, one may tend to view these restraints on federal court aggregation of cases as undesirable obstacles to valuable innovation. Balanced against such attitudes must be an appreciation that federalism concerns run deep and protect important values. As students should learn from study of the *Erie* problem in first year civil procedure, federal courts must heed these values. See Marcus, They Can't Do That, Can They? Tort Reform Via Rule 23, 80 Cornell L. Rev. 858 (1995) (discussing *Erie* tensions raised by proposed settlements of federal product liability class actions). Moreover, it should not be assumed that the ideal locus for combined adjudication is always a federal court; state courts may, in particular situations, be better suited for comprehensive resolution of major litigation.

Federalism issues often come to the fore concerning class actions. Overlapping class actions in state and federal courts—that is, class actions filed in a number of courts against the same, or some of the same defendants, concerning the same matter, on behalf of classes with some of the same members—have long posed federalism issues concerning stays and injunctions and the preclusive effect to be given to the first case that goes to judgment. In addition, plaintiffs' attorneys in recent years have tended to file class actions in state courts, reflecting a perception that state courts, and in particular certain state courts, are more likely to certify a class action than federal courts. The business community gave strong support to legislation allowing the removal of many large class actions to federal court, known as the Class Action Fairness Act of 2004, that was passed by the House of Representatives and pending in the Senate when this book went to press in Spring 2004. They argued that federal courts could use the MDL device to consolidate overlapping or parallel class actions and that defendants should not be subjected to suits in target state venues that would determine their responsibilities nationwide. Consumer and plaintiffs groups argued that state courts had a legitimate interest in hearing class actions based on their law and that easy removal would overburden federal courts and deprive state courts of an important part of their jurisdiction.

Chapter II

JOINDER AND STRUCTURE OF SUIT IN A UNITARY FEDERAL FORUM

A. PERMISSIVE PARTY JOINDER

MOSLEY v. GENERAL MOTORS CORP.

United States Court of Appeals, Eighth Circuit, 1974.
497 F.2d 1330.

Before Ross and Stephenson, Circuit Judges, and Van Pelt, Senior District Judge.

Ross, Circuit Judge.

Nathaniel Mosley and nine other persons joined in bringing this action individually and as class representatives alleging that their rights guaranteed under 42 U.S.C. § 2000e et seq. and 42 U.S.C. § 1981 were denied by General Motors and Local 25, United Automobile, Aerospace and Agriculture Implement Workers of America [Union] by reason of their color and race. Each of the ten named plaintiffs had, prior to the filing of the complaint, filed a charge with the Equal Employment Opportunity Commission [EEOC] asserting the facts underlying these claims. Pursuant thereto, the EEOC made a reasonable cause finding that General Motors, Fisher Body Division and Chevrolet Division, and the Union had engaged in unlawful employment practices in violation of Title VII of the Civil Rights Act of 1964. Accordingly, the charging parties were notified by EEOC of their right to institute a civil action in the appropriate federal district court, pursuant to § 706(e) of Title VII, 42 U.S.C. § 2000e–5(e).

In each of the first eight counts of the twelve-count complaint, eight of the ten plaintiffs alleged that General Motors, Chevrolet Division, had engaged in unlawful employment practices by: "discriminating against Negroes as regards promotions, terms and conditions of employment"; "retaliating against Negro employees who protested actions made unlawful by Title VII of the Act and by discharging some because they protested said unlawful acts"; "failing to hire Negro employees as a class on the basis of race"; "failing to hire females as a class on the basis of sex"; "discharging Negro employees on the basis of race"; and "discriminating against Negroes and females in the granting of relief time." Each additionally charged that the defendant Union had engaged in unlawful employment practices "with respect to the granting of relief time to Negro and female employees" and "by failing to pursue 6a grievances." The remaining two plaintiffs made similar allegations against General Motors, Fisher Body Division. All of the individual plaintiffs requested injunctive relief, back pay, attorneys fees and costs. Counts XI and XII of the complaint were class action counts against the two individual divisions of General Motors. They also sought declaratory and injunctive relief, back pay, attorneys fees and costs.

General Motors moved to strike portions of each count of the twelve-count complaint, to dismiss Counts XI and XII, to make portions of Counts I through XII more definite, to determine the propriety of Counts XI and XII as class actions, to limit the scope of the class purportedly represented, and to determine under which section of Rule 23 Counts XI and XII were maintainable as class actions. The district court ordered that "insofar as the first ten counts are concerned, those ten counts shall be severed into ten separate causes of action," and each plaintiff was directed to bring a separate action based upon his complaint, duly and separately filed. The court also ordered that the class action would not be dismissed, but rather would be left open "to each of the plaintiffs herein, individually or collectively . . . to allege a separate cause of action on behalf of any class of persons which such plaintiff or plaintiffs may separately or individually represent."

In reaching this conclusion on joinder, the district court followed the reasoning of Smith v. North American Rockwell Corp., 50 F.R.D. 515 (N.D.Okla.1970), which, in a somewhat analogous situation, found there was no right to relief arising out of the same transaction, occurrence or series of transactions or occurrences, and that there was no question of law or fact common to all plaintiffs sufficient to sustain joinder under Federal Rule of Civil Procedure 20(a). Similarly, the district court here felt that the plaintiffs' joint actions against General Motors and the Union presented a variety of issues having little relationship to one another; that they had only one common problem, i.e. the defendant; and that as pleaded the joint actions were completely unmanageable. Upon entering the order, and upon application of the plaintiffs, the district court found that its decision involved a controlling question of law as to which there is a substantial ground for difference of opinion and that any of the parties might make application for appeal under 28 U.S.C. § 1292(b). We granted the application to permit this interlocutory appeal and for the following reasons we affirm in part and reverse in part.

Rule 20(a) of the Federal Rules of Civil Procedure provides:

> All persons may join in one action as plaintiffs if they assert any right to relief jointly, severally, or in the alternative in respect of or arising out of the same transaction, occurrence, or series of transac-

tions or occurrences and if any question of law or fact common to all these persons will arise in the action. . . .

Additionally, Rule 20(b) and Rule 42(b) vest in the district court the discretion to order separate trials or make such other orders as will prevent delay or prejudice. In this manner, the scope of the civil action is made a matter for the discretion of the district court, and a determination on the question of joinder of parties will be reversed on appeal only upon a showing of abuse of that discretion. To determine whether the district court's order was proper herein, we must look to the policy and law that have developed around the operation of Rule 20.

The purpose of the rule is to promote trial convenience and expedite the final determination of disputes, thereby preventing multiple lawsuits. Single trials generally tend to lessen the delay, expense and inconvenience to all concerned. Reflecting this policy, the Supreme Court has said:

> Under the Rules, the impulse is toward entertaining the broadest possible scope of action consistent with fairness to the parties; joinder of claims, parties and remedies is strongly encouraged.

United Mine Workers of America v. Gibbs, 383 U.S. 715, 724, 86 S.Ct. 1130, 1138, 16 L.Ed.2d 218 (1966).

Permissive joinder is not, however, applicable in all cases. The rule imposes two specific requisites to the joinder of parties: (1) a right to relief must be asserted by, or against, each plaintiff or defendant relating to or arising out of the same *transaction or occurrence, or series of transactions or occurrences;* and (2) some *question of law or fact common* to all the parties must arise in the action.

In ascertaining whether a particular factual situation constitutes a single transaction or occurrence for purposes of Rule 20, a case by case approach is generally pursued. No hard and fast rules have been established under the rule. However, construction of the terms "transaction or occurrence" as used in the context of Rule 13(a) counterclaims offers some guide to the application of this test. For the purposes of the latter rule,

> "Transaction" is a word of flexible meaning. It may comprehend a series of many occurrences, depending not so much upon the immediateness of their connection as upon their logical relationship.

Moore v. New York Cotton Exchange, 270 U.S. 593, 610, 46 S.Ct. 367, 371, 70 L.Ed. 750 (1926). Accordingly, all "logically related" events entitling a person to institute a legal action against another generally are regarded as comprising a transaction or occurrence. The analogous interpretation of the terms as used in Rule 20 would permit all reasonably related claims for relief by or against different parties to be tried in a single proceeding. Absolute identity of all events is unnecessary.

This construction accords with the result reached in United States v. Mississippi, 380 U.S. 128, 85 S.Ct. 808, 13 L.Ed.2d 717 (1965), a suit brought by the United States against the State of Mississippi, the election commissioners, and six voting registrars of the State, charging them with engaging in acts and practices hampering and destroying the right of black citizens of Mississippi to vote. The district court concluded that the complaint improperly attempted to hold the six county registrars jointly liable for what amounted to nothing more than individual torts committed by them separately against separate applicants. In reversing, the Supreme Court said:

> But the complaint charged that the registrars had acted and were continuing to act as part of a state-wide system designed to enforce the registration laws in a way that would inevitably deprive colored people of the right to vote solely because of their color. On such an allegation the joinder of all the registrars as defendants in a single suit is authorized by Rule 20(a) of the Federal Rules of Civil Procedure.... These registrars were alleged to be carrying on activities which were part of a series of transactions or occurrences the validity of which depended to a large extent upon "question[s] of law or fact common to all of them."

Here too, then, the plaintiffs have asserted a right to relief arising out of the same transactions or occurrences. Each of the ten plaintiffs alleged that he had been injured by the same general policy of discrimination on the part of General Motors and the Union. Since a "state-wide system designed to enforce the registration laws in a way that would inevitably deprive colored people of the right to vote" was determined to arise out of the same series of transactions or occurrences, we conclude that a company-wide policy purportedly designed to discriminate against blacks in employment similarly arises out of the same series of transactions or occurrences. Thus the plaintiffs meet the first requisite for joinder under Rule 20(a).

The second requisite necessary to sustain a permissive joinder under the rule is that a question of law or fact common to all the parties will arise in the action. The rule does not require that all questions of law and fact raised by the dispute be common. Yet, neither does it establish any qualitative or quantitative test of commonality. For this reason, cases construing the parallel requirement under Federal Rule of Civil Procedure 23(a) provide a helpful framework for construction of the commonality required by Rule 20. In general, those cases that have focused on Rule 23(a)(2) have given it a permissive application so that common questions have been found to exist in a wide range of contexts. Specifically, with respect to employment discrimination cases under Title VII, courts have found that the discriminatory character of a defendant's conduct is basic to the class, and the fact that the individual class members may have suffered different effects from the alleged discrimination is immaterial for the purposes of the prerequisite. In this vein, one court has said:

> [A]lthough the actual effects of a discriminatory policy may thus vary throughout the class, the existence of the discriminatory policy threatens the entire class. And whether the Damoclean threat of a

racially discriminatory policy hangs over the racial class is a question of fact common to all the members of the class.

Hall v. Werthan Bag Corp., 251 F.Supp. 184, 186 (M.D.Tenn.1966).

The right to relief here depends on the ability to demonstrate that each of the plaintiffs was wronged by racially discriminatory policies on the part of the defendants General Motors and the Union. The discriminatory character of the defendants' conduct is thus basic to each plaintiff's recovery. The fact that each plaintiff may have suffered different effects from the alleged discrimination is immaterial for the purposes of determining the common question of law or fact. Thus, we conclude that the second requisite for joinder under Rule 20(a) is also met by the complaint.

For the reasons set forth above, we conclude that the district court abused its discretion in severing the joined actions. The difficulties in ultimately adjudicating damages to the various plaintiffs are not so overwhelming as to require such severance. If appropriate, separate trials may be granted as to any particular issue after the determination of common questions.

BRUNET, A STUDY IN THE ALLOCATION OF SCARCE RESOURCES: THE EFFICIENCY OF FEDERAL INTERVENTION CRITERIA

12 Georgia L.Rev. 701, 710–720 (1978).

* * *

Procedural rules have two basic goals: accurate and economical results. A pragmatic trade-off between the perfect output—a one hundred percent accurate result—and cost constraints is involved. The compromise between these two efficiency considerations is inherent in the blanket assertion of Rule 1 of the Federal Rules of Civil Procedure that the Rules "shall be construed to secure the just, speedy, and inexpensive determination of every action." * * * A "speedy" and "inexpensive" determination is clearly efficiency-based; a "just" determination, although less obviously related to efficiency, will be accurate and will thus allocate resources beneficially by avoiding the uncertainty and duplication of effort often associated with inaccuracy. Efficient rules of procedure will reduce taxpayer expenditures on the court system, thereby advancing an optimal allocation of resources.

The efficiency of the Federal Rules should supplement the adversary model in the quest for efficient dispute resolution. Like the adversary model, many of the Federal Rules facilitate litigant production of the data that courts and juries need to decide cases effectively. Joinder of parties and claims offers the court informational input which theoretically produces a more efficient output or judgment. For example, consolidation of cases under Rule 42(a), joinder of multiple plaintiffs under Rule 20(a), or intervention under Rule 24 should provide the court with more information about each individual claim, revealing strengths and fleshing out weaknesses. The court may analyze differently the information possessed before joinder after it assimilates additional data. Without the information which joinder facilitates judge and jury output quality would suffer. The following graph illustrates this point.

FIGURE A

*Relationship Between Amount of Information
and Quality of Litigation Output*

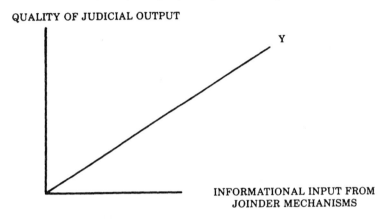

Assuming that the judge or jury can efficiently assimilate the additional information which the federal joinder mechanisms offer, the line *Y*, which is equally distant from the input and the output axes, indicates that the more information the decisionmaker possesses, the more improved (accurate) the result or qualitative output in the individual case. This argument relies on the economies of size or scale present in the production of any product.

The critical assumptions in the previous paragraph may not, of course, be accurate. As informational input deriving from joinder increases, the case may become so complex that additional information would not continue to improve output and may even reduce it. When the marginal utility of additional input is optimal,[69] efficiency would dictate that a judge stop the informational input. For example, when ruling on a motion to consolidate under Rule 42(a) the court has discretion, which can enable it to consider the efficiency effect of the proposed motion. The court "may," in its discretion, order consolidation if the cases present a common question of law or fact and otherwise warrant consolidation. Similarly, the court can use Rule 20(b), which grants a judge the power to "order separate trials or make other orders to prevent delay or injustice," to sever joined claims which merit separate consideration.

---

69. Optimality is the point at which the marginal cost of new input into litigation   equals its marginal utility.

Under some circumstances * * * the court may also deny counterproductive intervention motions.

The following graph illustrates the eventual decrease in productivity which informational input from joinder mechanisms causes.

FIGURE B

*Informational Output From Joinder Mechanisms Beyond
the Optimal Scale Economies in the Court*

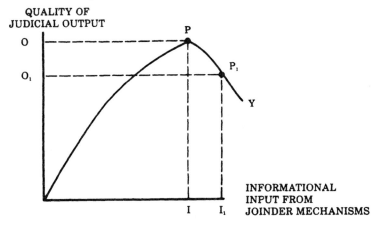

In this graph, the line Y indicates the gains in the quality of judicial output achieved as information input through joinder mechanisms increases. The fall of line Y[73] after point P indicates the decrease in the quality of litigation despite the increased information input. At point P, I units of input produced an output of O. At point P^1, input has increased to I^1, but output has fallen to O^1, a loss in judicial quality of $O—O^1$. The graph corrects the unrealistic assumption of Figure A that decisionmakers can continually make effective use of all added information. Additional input beyond point P may make the earlier input unintelligible or confusing, thereby reducing output accuracy. Thus, at point P a court should deny joinder motions in order to achieve optimal efficiency.

One problem with Figure B is its assumption that line Y will continue to fall after point P. At some point, productive information could follow and cause the slope of Y to rise after falling. Discovery of the "missing link" of a factual morass could increase output to a level higher than point P.[74] Every pretrial motion involving the possibility of addi-

73. If increased information simply stopped improving output after a certain point but never harmed the assimilation of information already received, line Y would not fall but would simply remain horizontal. The decisionmakers thus affected would not be confused by the new input but would be merely indifferent because of their ina-bility to perceive the significance of the information. Although this may be true for some decisionmakers, many will suffer confusion from receiving additional information. It is their confusion that justifies the falling slope of Y.

74. A graph of this point is as follows:

tional information requires the court to assess this risk. If a later rise actually occurred it would be inefficient to limit input at P by denying joinder motions. Fortunately, the exclusion of missing-link input after P, although possible in isolated cases, is unlikely. The adversary system normally would compel counsel to present their best information early in the litigation. In addition, the formalities of joinder, which generally require permission and a statement of reasons supporting the motion, provide a means to present the prospective input to the court and allow it to assimilate the "missing link" input.

Procedural rules must reflect these considerations. The achievement of maximum efficiency in litigation depends on the court's freedom to rule on joinder motions consistent with the variations in optimal input which will necessarily exist in a system of numerous decisionmakers. Each decisionmaker has a different optimal point of informational input and reaches point P of Figure B after differing input quantities. Flexibility in the standards for joinder and broad discretion would appear to be appropriate.

Figure B demonstrates one further characteristic of the litigation process. The relationship between the quality of judicial output and informational input of joinder devices produces an efficiency dynamic that is not limited to the individual case. The judge has many other cases pending when he rules on the joinder motion, and the effect of the additional information on the other pending litigation involves other costs and benefits. Queuing costs may increase as the court assimilates the input. Joinder may also increase the chance of an erroneous judgment which may have a negative impact on other pending and prospective cases since a judgment affects society and guides subsequent cases as stare decisis. The analysis of this section applies to these costs as well. The judge must consider queuing costs and the accuracy of the judgment as factors in the determination of whether he has reached his point P of optimal efficiency. By ruling on joinder motions in terms of efficiency, the judge will enhance output and improve stare decisis.

FIGURE 1

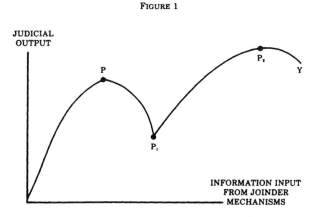

Notes and Questions

1. *Mosley* has been described as "possibly the leading case on joinder of title VII plaintiffs." Miller v. Hygrade Food Products Corp., 202 F.R.D. 142, 144 n. 3 (E.D.Pa.2001). It provides an example of joinder in a single suit of both multiple claims (arising under Title VII of the 1964 Civil Rights Act and § 1981) and multiple parties (ten people who had filed charges of discrimination with the Equal Employment Opportunity Commission). Joinder of multiple claims is permitted by Rule 18(a). Although Title VII and § 1981 have different elements in their statutory causes of action, a central issue in both is that the plaintiff was subjected to race discrimination. Are there occasions when joinder of claims against a single party should not be permitted because the claims are too dissimilar? See Committee Note to Amended Rule 18(a) (1966): "It is emphasized that amended Rule 18(a) deals only with pleading. As already indicated, a claim properly joined as a matter of pleading need not be proceeded with together with the other claims if fairness or convenience justifies separate treatment."

2. It appears, in *Mosley,* that the claim of each of the ten plaintiffs is based on different events by which that plaintiff was allegedly discriminated against as to promotion, conditions of employment, failure to hire, etc. It also seems likely that different G.M. employees were responsible for the alleged acts of discrimination against each plaintiff. How then, can the right to relief which each plaintiff asserts be considered to arise out of "the same transaction, occurrence, or series of transactions or occurrences"? In Duke v. Uniroyal Inc., 928 F.2d 1413 (4th Cir.1991), plaintiffs alleged age discrimination in connection with the company's reduction in force program. The appellate court affirmed the trial court's refusal to sever their cases for trial:

> Both Duke and Fox were terminated on August 15, 1985, as part of the same reduction in force which was implemented by Uniroyal under a uniform policy adopted for selecting employees for discharge. The reduction was implemented by direction of Uniroyal's national sales manager in consultation with its manager of employee relations. Moreover, the decisions with respect to both Duke and Fox were the product of coordinated efforts in the selection of persons for discharge and in making transfers necessitated by restructuring of regions and departments. Plaintiffs' claims arise out of the same transaction, a single reduction in force, raising common questions of law and fact.

> While there was a broad variation of circumstances relating to the merits of the individual performances of each of the plaintiffs, this evidence could be easily distinguished by the jury.

Id. at 1420–21. In Puricelli v. CNA Ins. Co., 185 F.R.D. 139 (N.D.N.Y.1999), the court was willing to overlook "differences in the factual underpinnings" of the claims of two employees who alleged age discrimination, finding a common course of conduct reflecting a "new and aggressive management style" that made excessive demands on older employees. Is it relevant to a finding of the "same transaction" that evidence likely to be offered to prove the claim of discrimination would be applicable to all the joined parties? See Alexander v. Fulton County, 207 F.3d 1303 (11th Cir.2000) (upholding joinder of 18 white employees of the sheriff's department alleging race discrimination by the new sheriff, noting that "each of the Plaintiffs' claims and the evidence of discrimination undoubtedly [is] relevant to every other plaintiff's core allegations of systemic discrimination'').

3. Differences in time, location, and persons involved can prevent joinder of discrimination claims. See Grayson v. K–Mart Corp., 849 F.Supp. 785 (N.D.Ga.1994), in which eleven plaintiffs who had been fired as managers of K–Mart stores in different parts of the country sued claiming that the firings resulted from age discrimination. Defendant moved to sever. Citing *Mosley*, the court said that it was a ''somewhat close question'' whether joinder was proper under Rule 20, but found joinder improper since the employment decisions were made by different managers. ''The decision to demote each plaintiff originated with his district manager and was derived within the context of the business circumstances of each plaintiff's store. Three different regional managers participated in the eleven demotion decisions at issue in these cases.'' Id. at 789. In Randleel v. Pizza Hut of America, Inc., 182 F.R.D. 542 (N.D.Ill.1998), African–American customers claimed they were discriminated against in service at Pizza Hut restaurants in two different cities. The circumstances were somewhat different: denial of service, in one case, for not having an advance reservation, and, in another, after the dining room closed. The court denied joinder on the basis that ''[t]hese are factually discrete and unrelated incidents which occurred two months apart at restaurants in different states, and which involved different management teams and workers.''

4. Although a common course of conduct may be grounds for upholding joinder in discrimination cases, somewhat different circumstances may be required for joinder in product liability cases. Consider the ''common issue'' aspects of Dunavant v. Ford Motor Co., Civ.Ac. No. H–80–1159 (U.S.Dist.Ct., S.D.Tex.,1980): Forty-seven plaintiffs with personal injury and property damage claims, arising out of thirty separate accidents involving the alleged malfunction of the gear shift and transmission on their Ford automobiles, sued Ford in a federal district court in Houston, Texas. The accidents occurred in fourteen different states, over a period of four years. There was no relationship between any of the plaintiffs or any of the accidents other than the common claim that a similar product defect was to blame.

One might ask why a case would be structured in this way. Why didn't each of the plaintiffs file in his or her own state? The answer is often that in such areas as product liability, where considerable expertise, specialized experience, and capital is required of a plaintiff's attorney, cases may be referred by local attorneys to specialists who seek to reduce overall costs (and perhaps to improve their bargaining leverage) by joining a number of cases alleging similar product defects. But this also means that cases involving dissimilar factual situations, and perhaps dissimilar law, may be joined in one suit.

Ford stated in support of its motion for severance: ''These vehicles were manufactured over a thirteen-year period and were equipped with a variety of combinations of various transmission types and transmission control systems. * * * Because the accident date and date of manufacture differ for each vehicle, the evidence which is admissible concerning the failure to warn and adequacy of warning issues and concerning post-accident or post-manufacture design modifications and changes to the language of the owner's manuals will differ from case to case. In addition several states have enacted product liability statutes which affect the materiality of evidence concerning remedial measures, state-of-the-art, presumptions which favor a party, and defensive issues relating to the plaintiff's contributory negligence, comparative fault and use or misuse of the product." What arguments can be made in favor of joinder in this case?

5. Both parties in *Mosley* seem highly concerned with joinder. Defendant cared enough to make a motion to sever, and plaintiffs were sufficiently concerned about the resulting ruling to take an interlocutory appeal. Why would either party attach such importance to the question of joinder in this case? What benefits might defendants receive from preventing joinder? When could joinder actually benefit defendants?

6. Should Rule 20(a) be broadly interpreted as a device for serving the interests of judicial efficiency? The "same transaction or occurrence" test is used in several federal rules, and its exact meaning varies with the context. For example, when used in Rule 13(a) to require the filing of a counterclaim which "arises out of the transaction or occurrence that is the subject matter of the opposing party's claim," it has been interpreted as reflecting a policy of judicial economy; the test is satisfied if the "same evidence" will support the claim and counterclaim. Williams v. Robinson, 1 F.R.D. 211 (D.D.C. 1940). When used in Rule 15(c) to allow an amended pleading to relate back to the date of the original filing if it arose out of the "conduct, transaction, or occurrence set forth" in the original pleading, the test is said to reflect a liberal amendment policy so long as there was adequate notice at time of filing to satisfy the objectives of the statute of limitations. Tiller v. Atlantic Coast Line R. Co., 323 U.S. 574, 581, 65 S.Ct. 421, 424, 89 L.Ed. 465 (1945). Would it be reasonable to read the test in Rule 20(a) as aimed at allowing claims to be tried together when they make a just and efficient trial package? Or is that the purpose of the "common question of law or fact" requirement and thus "same transaction or occurrence" must mean something more?

7. Does the joinder analysis offered by Professor Brunet afford a sensible method for assessing Rule 20 decisions? Is a judge capable of making realistic determinations about such matters as the relative values of different informational inputs or the optimal level of information in any particular situation? How would the judge get this information? Should parties be addressing such information in their briefs on whether joinder is proper? As Professor Brunet notes, this same sort of problem recurs in connection with other joinder issues such as intervention (considered later in this chapter) and class action treatment (Chapter IV), consolidation of separate cases (Chapter III) and the handling of a combined trial (Chapter VII).

STANFORD v. TENNESSEE VALLEY AUTHORITY

United States District Court, Middle District of Tennessee, 1955.
18 F.R.D. 152.

WILLIAM E. MILLER, DISTRICT JUDGE.

The action is before the Court upon the separate motions of defendants, Monsanto Chemical Company and Armour & Company, to dismiss and for alternative relief. The grounds of the motion will be separately discussed.

By an agreed order heretofore entered, the action was dismissed as to the Tennessee Valley Authority, with the result that the complaint, as it is presently framed, seeks to recover damages from the defendants, Monsanto Chemical Company and Armour & Company, jointly and severally, allegedly caused by fluorine gas fumes emitted from the plants of the said defendants located within the vicinity of the plaintiffs' property.

Both defendants move the Court to dismiss the action upon the ground that there is a misjoinder of defendants. It is insisted first, that the defendants, as shown by the averments of the complaint, are not joint tort feasors, and secondly, that the conditions required by Rule 20 of the Federal Rules of Civil Procedure for a permissive joinder of defendants, are not present.

In the alternative, both defendants, in the event the motions to dismiss are overruled, request the Court to order a severance of the claims, requiring that the plaintiffs' claim against each defendant be tried separately.

It appears to be altogether clear from the Tennessee decisions that the defendants, upon the facts set forth in the complaint, are not joint tort feasors and that under the Tennessee practice they may not be joined for the purposes of trial.

But the right to join the defendants for trial, being procedural rather than substantive in character, is governed by the Federal Rules of Civil Procedure, 28 U.S.C.A., and not by the practice obtaining in the state courts.

Rule 20 of the Federal Rules of Civil Procedure permits all persons to be joined in one action as defendants "if there is asserted against them jointly, severally, or in the alternative, any right to relief in respect of or arising out of the same transaction, occurrence, or series of transactions or occurrences and if any question of law or fact common to all of them will arise in the action."

An analysis of the complaint discloses that the defendants' plants are separately owned and operated and that they are located at different distances from the plaintiffs' property. Their activities are separate and distinct from each other although they are engaged in the same general type of business. There is nothing on the face of the complaint from which it could be concluded that the plaintiffs' claims against the two defendants arise out of the same transaction or occurrence, or out of the same series of transactions or occurrences. The transactions are separate as to each defendant. It follows, therefore, that there is a misjoinder of defendants.

Such misjoinder under Rule 21 is not ground for dismissal of the action, but at most would require that the claims be severed and proceeded with separately. On the other hand, Rule 42 authorizes the Court to order a joint hearing or trial of any or all matters in issue in the actions, or to consolidate the actions, if they involve "a common question of law or fact".

In the instant case, it would appear from the averments of the complaint that common questions of law and fact are sufficiently involved to meet the requirements of Rule 42. In the first place, there is a question as to whether the plaintiffs have a cause of action for a permanent nuisance or one of a temporary or recurring nature, a mixed question of law and fact common to both defendants. Also, on a strictly factual basis, the actions against both defendants involve the question whether the fluorine gas fumes are capable of producing and in fact did produce the damage or damages described in the complaint. Still another question of fact, at least in large part common to both defendants, is whether there are devices or processes available which could be used in an operation of this kind to eliminate or curtail the damages allegedly caused by the fumes. Stated in broader terms, the issue is whether the condition is one which can be eliminated by human labor and skill or by the expenditure of money. It is conceivable that other issues, common to both parties, may arise after the answers are filed, or after a further development of the case. It results that the necessary conditions are present to authorize the Court to order a joint trial under Rule 42, and the only remaining question is whether the Court should exercise its discretion to that effect.

The apparent contention of the defendants is that they would be prejudiced by a joint trial because of the difficulty in determining the responsibility of each defendant on account of its alleged contribution to the plaintiffs' damage.

Concededly, in cases of this nature, there is the inherent difficulty of segregating and determining the nature and extent of the contribution made by each party to the common nuisance. This difficulty, however, would not be altogether removed if the claims were tried separately. If the claim against one defendant should be separately tried, the jury would still be confronted with the necessity of determining whether the plaintiffs' damage was caused by the defendant before the Court, or whether it was caused by the other defendant not before the Court. There would also exist the necessity of determining the extent that the activities of the defendant on trial contributed to the plaintiffs' damage as contrasted with the activities of the defendant not on trial.

On the other hand, a joint trial has many advantages, including a saving of trial time, as well as a saving of expense not only to the Government but to the parties. Doubtless in a large measure, the trial of both claims will involve the use of the same witnesses and the same evidence. Upon the whole case, the Court feels that the ends of justice will be met by a joint trial of the claims.

The order should accordingly provide that the claims are severed for all purposes and to be proceeded with separately except that they will be tried together before the same jury.

This will entail the filing of separate complaints against the defendants, and thereafter the filing or entry of separate pleadings, motions, verdicts, judgments, etc. Such an order, as contrasted with a consolidation, will preserve to each defendant the procedural advantages of a separate trial, including the right to peremptory challenges of jurors.

Notes and Questions

1. Is the fact that the defendants' plants were separately owned and operated determinative as to the propriety of joinder in *Stanford*? Should it be relevant whether the plaintiff alleged that the fumes from each plant independently caused him injury or, instead, that they combined to do so? Should it be relevant whether the plaintiff alleged that he could not determine which plant was responsible nor assess the percentage of harm arising from each?

In Poster v. Central Gulf Steamship Corp., 25 F.R.D. 18 (E.D.Pa.1960), plaintiff, a seaman, sued two steamship companies in the same suit for negligence in maintaining sanitary conditions on board their ships. He alleged that, when he was on the ship of the first company in the Suez Canal, he contracted amebiasis from local workers who were allowed on board to assist cooks and use facilities. Some months later, while working on a steamer of the second company, he was again allegedly exposed to unhealthful conditions, resulting in an aggravation of the disease he had contracted on the first ship. The two occurrences were obviously different, and there was no relationship between the two steamship companies. The court nevertheless upheld joinder on the ground that the first steamship company could be held liable for the aggravation as a damage flowing from the original exposure, and therefore that the claim arose out of both exposures.

2. In *Stanford*, the court concludes that although joinder was improper, the cases would be consolidated for a joint trial under Rule 42(a). Note that Rule 42(a) requires only "a common question of law or fact" and not that the actions arise out of "the same transaction or occurrence." What is the sense of maintaining a strict interpretation of the "same transaction or occurrence" requirement as to joinder, if the same result can be achieved by simply using a joint trial under a different rule? Is essentially the same result achieved by a joint trial? How significant are the differences between joinder and a joint trial mentioned in the last paragraph of the opinion? What other differences are there between a joint trial under a consolidation order and a trial where there was joinder from the start? Note that there are a number of other procedural devices, apart from joinder, which attempt to accomplish the efficient disposition of related cases (see Chapter III on duplicative litigation and Chapter IV on class actions).

3. Proof of causation is often a problem in cases of exposure to potentially dangerous products, such as asbestos, tobacco, or pharmaceutical drugs. Since many people are often exposed, joinder or some form of aggregation can offer attractions in terms of judicial economy, efficiency, and uniformity, but the precise language of Rule 20 may dictate otherwise. In Insolia v. Phillip Morris, 186 F.R.D. 547 (E.D.Wis.1999), three individuals suffering from cancer sued five tobacco companies and two industry trade

associations alleging a conspiracy to suppress adverse health reports and hide the dangers of smoking. The court first denied plaintiffs' motion for class action status and then severed the cases for improper joinder, stating:

> Rule 20 demands more than the bare allegation that all plaintiffs are victims of a fraudulent scheme perpetrated by one or more defendants; there must be some indication that each plaintiff has been induced to act by the same misrepresentation. * * *

Misrepresentation and conspiracy are not the only issues difficult to fit into the transaction requirement of Rule 20. Although there are few cases that address the problems associated with joining multiple plaintiffs in a single products liability action, for obvious reasons, these issues are of crucial importance to plaintiffs. As illustrated by In the Matter of Asbestos II Consolidated Pretrial, No. 86–C–1739, 1989 WL 56181 (N.D.Ill. May 10, 1989), medical and legal causation present formidable obstacles under Rule 20. *Asbestos II* involved a group of over 100 former pipefitters who brought a products liability action against several companies responsible for manufacturing asbestos. The district court concluded that these claims did not arise reasonably and logically out of the same series of transactions. Although all of the plaintiffs had contracted pleural asbestosis, the duration and magnitude of this disease varied from plaintiff to plaintiff. Even though all of the plaintiffs had belonged to the same union and had been exposed to asbestos products while working at common sites, exposure did not happen "at the same time [or] at the same place." Given that each claim turned on unique facts, the specter of jury confusion outweighed any benefit that might accrue to the parties and the court system by avoiding multiple lawsuits.

> * * * I conclude that plaintiffs' claims do not arise from the same transaction or series of transactions, as they must in order to satisfy Rule 20. On the abstract level, dissimilarities in the claims brought by plaintiffs suggest that these claims are not related logically to one another. Plaintiffs began smoking at different ages; they brought different brands throughout their years as smokers; and they quit for different reasons and under different circumstances. * * * [P]laintiff Vincent Insolia began smoking almost two decades before the industry hatched its scheme and has not smoked for more than a quarter of a century. By contrast, plaintiffs Billy Mays and Maureen Lovejoy took up the habit in the early '50s and continued to smoke well into the '90s. Even if the conspiracy charged held together, serious questions exist regarding medical causation.

Is there no way to avoid trying separately every case of exposure to a product like asbestos or tobacco? We will return to this question in Chapter IV on class actions.

4. Assume that a railroad, having determined that fifty different persons have separately engaged in acts of vandalism against its property, sues all fifty in the same suit. Is joinder permissible? In Tele–Media Co. v. Antidormi, 179 F.R.D. 75 (D.Conn.1998), 104 people were sued in the same suit for illegally receiving plaintiff company's pay-for-view programs. Plaintiff alleged that the claims arose out of the same transaction because the violations came to light as a result of an electronic countermeasure it had

instituted to detect and disable altered converters. Is joinder proper? In Bridgeport Music, Inc. v. 11C Music, 202 F.R.D. 229 (M.D.Tenn.2001), plaintiff companies that publish, record, and distribute music sued 770 publishing companies, copyright administrators, record labels, and entertainment companies for copyright infringement by "sampling" their music without paying royalties. Defendants challenged joinder, arguing that each infringing song represents a separate transaction requiring a unique set of proof. Plaintiffs argued that the claims were intricately interrelated, that the defendants inflicted the same harm against them, and that a small number of the defendants repeatedly infringed their copyrights and were involved in most of the infringing songs. How should the court rule?

5.   The Rule 20 "same transactions" requirement also allows the claims to arise out of the same "series of transactions or occurrences." Consider Insull v. New York World–Telegram Corp., 172 F.Supp. 615 (N.D.Ill.1959), a suit for libel against nine newspapers of the Scripps–Howard chain which published a 1957 article referring to "racketeering practices" which had sent such "big business tycoons" as Samuel Insull to jail in the 1930's. Also joined as a defendant was Arthur Schlesinger, whose best-selling (and Pulitzer prize-winning) book The Crisis of the Old Order, published some nine months before the article, discussed Mr. Insull's role in bribery, corruption, and embezzlement in the 1930's. The trial court severed the Schlesinger claim from the others under Rule 21, finding they did not arise out of the same transaction or occurrence because there was "no allegation that the alleged libels were published other than independently."

HALL v. E.I. DU PONT DE NEMOURS & CO., INC.

CHANCE v. E.I. DU PONT DE NEMOURS & CO., INC.

United States District Court, Eastern District of New York, 1972.
345 F.Supp. 353.

WEINSTEIN, DISTRICT JUDGE.

These two cases arise out of eighteen separate accidents scattered across the nation in which children were injured by blasting caps. Damages are sought from manufacturers and their trade association, the Institute of Makers of Explosives (I.M.E.). The basic allegation is that the practice of the explosives industry during the 1950's—continuing until 1965—of not placing any warning upon individual blasting caps and of failing to take other safety measures created an unreasonable risk of harm resulting in plaintiffs' injuries.

* * *

I.   THE CHANCE CASE

Thirteen children were allegedly injured by blasting caps in twelve unrelated accidents between 1955 and 1959. The injuries occurred in the states of Alabama, California, Maryland, Montana, Nevada, North Carolina, Tennessee, Texas, Washington and West Virginia. Plaintiffs are citizens of the states in which their injuries occurred. They are now claiming damages against six manufacturers of blasting caps and the

I.M.E. on the grounds of negligence, common law conspiracy, assault, and strict liability in tort. In addition, two parents sue for medical expenses. Federal jurisdiction is based on diversity of citizenship. 28 U.S.C. § 1332.

[None of the *Chance* plaintiffs could identify the manufacturer of the cap that caused his injury, but each alleged that the cap was manufactured jointly and severally by the 6 corporate defendants and I.M.E. The complaint alleged an industry practice of not placing a warning on the caps resulting from a conscious agreement between defendants who also lobbied against labelling legislation.

Defendants moved to dismiss for failure to state a claim, or for severance due to improper joinder. The court reserved ruling on "what choice-of-law principles are to be applied in a case such as this one where planning, design, manufacture, and sale of a product occurred in different states, and injury in yet others." It assumed a national body of state tort law as "a growing consensus on the substantive law in this country permits such a gross first approach to the preliminary motions before us."]

The central question raised by defendants' motion is whether the defendants can be held responsible as a group under any theory of joint liability for injuries arising out of their individual manufacture of blasting caps. Joint tort liability is not limited to a narrow set of relationships and circumstances. It has been imposed in a wide range of situations, requiring varying standards of care, in which defendants cooperate in various degrees, enter into business and property relationships, and undertake to supply goods for public consumption. Developments in negligence and strict tort liability have imposed extensive duties on manufacturers to guard against a broad spectrum of risks with regard to the general population. The reasoning underlying current policy justifies the extension of established doctrines of joint tort liability to the area of industry-wide cooperation in product manufacture and design.

[The court denied the motion to dismiss for failure to state a claim. Surveying modern tort law, Judge Weinstein identified several possibly applicable grounds for joint liability.

First, *concert of action* in creating a dangerous circumstance could support joint liability for resulting harms based either on an explicit agreement or an inference of tacit cooperation based on defendants' parallel behavior. Alternatively, adherence to an industry-wide standard or custom might support such a finding.

Second, *enterprise liability* might apply, given allegations that the entire blasting cap industry could be the logical locus for taking precautions. The judge cautioned, however, that this theory had "special applicability to industries composed of a small number of units."

Third, plaintiffs might avoid the burden of proving that a specific manufacturer produced the harmful cap by *alternative liability* as set forth in § 433B of the Restatement of Torts (Second):

(2) Where the tortious conduct of two or more actors has combined to bring about harm to the plaintiff, and one or more of the actors seeks to limit his liability on the ground that the harm is capable of apportionment among them, the burden of proof as to the apportionment is upon each such actor.

(3) Where the conduct of two or more actors is tortious, and it is proved that harm has been caused to the plaintiff by only one of them, but there is uncertainty as to which one has caused it, the burden is upon each such actor to prove that he has not caused the harm.

In particular, as in the famous case of Summers v. Tice, 33 Cal.2d 80, 199 P.2d 1 (1948) (two hunters negligently shot in the direction of plaintiff, who was hit by one bullet), plaintiffs might be able to show that all defendants owed a duty of care to them. In addition, each plaintiff would have to prove causation by showing by a preponderance of the evidence that the cap that caused the injury was produced by one of the named defendants rather than someone else.]

To justify permissive joinder of parties plaintiffs must show both a "common question of law or fact" and a right to relief "arising out of the same transaction or occurrence or series of transactions or occurrences." Fed.R.Civ.P. 20(a). Defendants move for severance of plaintiffs on the ground that the complaint fails to satisfy either requirement, and for dismissal or transfer of the claims thus severed. 28 U.S.C. § 1404(a). They assert that the substantive law of the ten states will govern liability, and hence the claims present no common question of law.

The question of which state's law will govern which aspects of this case cannot be settled by assertion. In diversity cases, a federal court is bound to apply the choice-of-law principles of the state in which it sits. Klaxon v. Stentor Electric Mfg. Co., 313 U.S. 487, 61 S.Ct. 1020, 85 L.Ed. 1477 (1941). Under New York law, the choice of applicable law in personal injury cases is not determined by the traditional "place of injury" test, but by "the flexible principle that the law to be applied to resolve a particular issue is 'the law of the jurisdiction which, because of its relationship or contact with the occurrence or the parties, has the greatest concern' with the matter in issue and 'the strongest interest' in its resolution."

The locus of defendants' joint activity was allegedly at least in part in New York, the location of the I.M.E. Whether proof of this connection would be sufficient to support the application of New York law to some or all of the claims is a complex question involving consideration of New York choice-of-law principles and federal constitutional law. The parties are directed to supply briefs on this issue and on the general question of the law applicable to the different aspects of this case. Prior to a full consideration of the choice-of-law question, this court cannot rule on whether the plaintiffs' claims contain a common question of law. It should be noted, however, that Rule 20(a) requires only "*any* common question of law or fact." Thus the presence of questions of law not common to all the plaintiffs will not, in itself, defeat joinder.

Plaintiffs' claims do contain, moreover, common questions of fact—for example, whether the defendants exercised joint control over the labeling of blasting caps and operated, for purposes of tort liability, as a joint enterprise with respect to such labeling. The presence of these questions satisfies the requirement of Rule 20(a) that "any question of law *or* fact common to all these persons" arise in the action.

Defendants also contend that because the accidents occurred at different times and places, plaintiffs' rights to relief do not arise out of the same transaction or occurrence, or series of transactions or occurrences. There is no rigid rule as to what constitutes "the same transaction or occurrence" for purposes of joinder under Rule 20(a). "[T]he approach must be the general one of whether there are enough ultimate factual concurrences that it would be fair to the parties to require them to defend jointly" against the several claims. Application of this flexible standard presents a certain challenge in this case. It would be neither fair nor convenient to any of the parties nor to the court to determine in this court all the relevant issues of fact involved in each accident. At the same time it would be unfair and burdensome to require each plaintiff to prove the alleged joint activities in ten separate and (to that extent) repetitive actions.

The solution does not lie in wholesale severance, and the cases cited by defendants do not support that result. * * * Rather, fairness to the parties may be maximized by permitting plaintiffs to litigate the issues of joint activity in this court, and then transferring the questions which turn on the particular facts of each accident to the federal districts in which the accidents occurred. *See* 28 U.S.C. § 1404(a), Rules 20(b) and 42(a) and (b), Federal Rules of Civil Procedure. Whether this procedure would entail full separate trials of different issues, or special findings of fact in this court, or other possible procedures, will be decided after consideration of the choice-of-law problem and in consultation with the parties.

II.   THE HALL CASE

[In this case, three families, one each from New York, Ohio and North Dakota, sued two manufacturers of blasting caps, Du Pont and Hercules. Two families claimed that the offending cap in their cases were from Hercules, and the third asserted that it was from Du Pont. They nevertheless sought to join together in a single suit against the two manufacturers.

The court held that plaintiffs did not properly present a joint liability claim. Although noting that "[a] plaintiff is not required to implead all joint tortfeasors as indispensable parties" and that "the courts will normally honor plaintiff's choice of theory," Judge Weinstein concluded that "there are limits on the plaintiff's choice. One consideration is that some remedies and theories pose substantially more difficult problems of administration than others." Finding that "the redundant naming of an additional manufacturer results from the happenstance of joinder of claims by unrelated plaintiffs," the judge dismissed each family's claims against the manufacturer not accused of producing the cap that injured that child.]

With each plaintiff now having claims only against the manufacturer of the injury-causing cap, defendants' motion for severance under Rule 20(a) of the Federal Rules of Civil Procedure must be granted. While evidence of joint action or responsibility may well be relevant in the claims against each manufacturer, proof of such responsibility will not be necessary for recovery on each plaintiff's claims. Recovery in each case will turn on the legal-factual questions of negligence and strict liability, and on evidence about the circumstances of the separate accidents. The claims by the three groups of plaintiffs present sufficiently diverse questions of law and fact to require severance. [Pursuant to 28 U.S.C.A. § 1404(a), the court transferred the North Dakota and Ohio families' suits to their home jurisdictions, where the incidents in suit occurred.]

Notes and Questions

1.   Judge Weinstein partially reaches a different conclusion about joinder from the judge in *Stanford*. Is that due to differing interpretations of Rule 20 or differing substantive law theories that apply to the cases? Note, for example, § 433B(2) of the Restatement of Torts (Second), quoted in *Chance*. If that doctrine had been accepted in Tennessee when *Stanford* was decided, could it have made a difference on the joinder question presented in that case?

2.   Compare Judge Weinstein's treatment of the joinder questions in *Chance* and *Hall*. In *Hall*, he refused to allow a joint liability theory and did not even allow the two families suing Hercules to join together. Yet in *Chance* he not only upheld the joint liability theory but also allowed all 13 families, from ten states, to join. Is this a consistent application of Rule 20? Although upholding the joinder in *Chance,* Judge Weinstein did indicate that only "the issues of joint activity" would be tried together and then "the questions which turn on the particular facts of each accident" would be transferred "to the federal districts in which the accidents occurred." How would this be accomplished since individual suits were not filed in the districts where the accidents occurred? And what is to be gained if each case has to be tried individually? Judge Weinstein leaves open the question whether this "would entail full separate trials of different issues, or special findings of fact in this court." How would the latter procedure work?

3.   *Choice of law*: Differences in applicable law have presented obstacles to combined treatment of cases through consolidation and also to certifying class actions. Although the law of products liability may have become more uniform under the influence of the Restatement of Torts (Second), there is still considerable diversity in state product liability laws, going to such matters as, for example, standards of liability, burden of proof, availability and scope of defenses, evidentiary requirements, instructions to the jury, and damages. Judge Weinstein's treatment of the problem in the above decision reflects an aggressive view of similarities.

Judge Weinstein deferred a final ruling on whether the Rule 20(a) requirement of a "common question of law" was met until briefs were received on the conflict of laws issue. After considering the issue, he determined that, under the *Erie* doctrine, New York choice-of-law would apply. New York has abandoned the traditional rule requiring that the law of the place of injury be applied; it applies a more flexible rule focusing on the selection of the law most intimately concerned with the outcome of each particular issue. Judge Weinstein determined that in each of these cases New York would apply the substantive law of the state where the accident occurred. For a more detailed discussion of the application of choice of law rules in the class action context to determine whether the forum state can apply its own law, rather than the laws of the states where injury occurred, contracts were breached, etc., see *infra* pp. 412–39.

Should the application of the law of different states automatically prevent joinder? The answer depends, in part, on how different the various state laws are. Minor differences might be dealt with in a joint trial by such techniques as admission of evidence for limited purposes, instructions to the jury clarifying the differences between the various claims, and use of special issues. But as major differences in the laws increase, and more state laws are involved, the possibility of a fair and efficient joint trial wanes. See 371 F.Supp. 439 (S.D.N.Y.1974) for Judge Weinstein's determination and reasoning.

These choice of law problems might be removed if state law were displaced by creation of a federal common law standard, but the federal courts have felt that they lacked authority to do so. See Vairo, Multi–Tort Cases: Cause for More Darkness on the Subject, or a New Role for Federal Common Law?, 54 Fordham L. Rev. 167 (1985) (arguing that "the best of Swift v. Tyson be resurrected" and that federal courts prescribe common law rules): compare Jackson v. Johns–Manville, 750 F.2d 1314 (5th Cir.1985) (refusing to adopt federal common law for asbestos cases).

Another solution would be federal legislation. Proposals for federal legislation on products liability have been made but not adopted. It has also been suggested that in transferred cases federal courts be authorized to select a single rule of law to facilitate combined treatment of the cases. See American Law Institute, Complex Litigation: Statutory Recommendations and Analysis § 6.01 (1994); Rowe & Sibley, Beyond Diversity, Federal Multiparty, Multiforum Jurisdiction, 135 U. Pa. L. Rev. 7 (1986).

4. *The causation problem*: The above cases illustrate recurrent problems in modern tort cases concerning proof of causation. In *Chance*, the plaintiffs cannot identify the specific maker of an allegedly injurious product. Besides the theories outlined by Judge Weinstein, in Sindell v. Abbott Laboratories, 26 Cal.3d 588, 163 Cal.Rptr. 132, 607 P.2d 924 (1980), cert. denied 449 U.S. 912, 101 S.Ct. 285, 66 L.Ed.2d 140 (1982), the court adopted a *market share liability* theory as a variant of the alternative liability theory of Summers v. Tice. The case involved DES, a drug marketed by some 200 companies from the 1940's through the 1960's and often used by patients who did not know the identity of the manufacturer of their product. Absent proof of the identity of the manufacturer, plaintiff could sue defendants who had together manufactured a "substantial share" of the total DES, and the

burden of proof would then shift to the defendants to exonerate themselves. If they failed, it later held, they would shoulder liability to the extent of their percentage share of the market. Brown v. Superior Court, 44 Cal.3d 1049, 245 Cal.Rptr. 412, 751 P.2d 470 (1988); compare Rutherford v. Owens–Illinois, Inc., 16 Cal.4th 953, 67 Cal.Rptr.2d 16, 941 P.2d 1203 (1997) (refusing to apply *Sindell* in asbestos cases).

Consider the implications of use of this theory for joinder under Rule 20. It could provide a basis for satisfying the Rule 20(a) "same transaction or occurrence" requirement in order to join a number of defendants whose activities (such as manufacturing) have been independent of those of other defendants. It also allows a suit to be filed without joining all the possible defendants who might be responsible for the plaintiff's injuries. Note also that the requirement that manufacturers who together hold a "substantial share" of the market be joined operates as something like a substantive compulsory joinder provision.

5.   The *Sindell* majority also did not provide a definition of the relevant market from which the various defendants' market shares would be determined. Is the market national, regional, state, or local? This factor would significantly affect which defendants must be joined in order to represent a "substantial share."

6.   Is the traditional individualized tort process unsuited for resolving mass exposure cases? See Rosenberg, The Causal Connection in Mass Exposure Cases: A "Public Law" Vision of the Tort System, 97 Harv.L.Rev. 851 (1984), proposing a "public law" adjudication model. This model applies a "proportionality rule" whereby liability would be imposed "in proportion to the probability of causation assigned to the excess disease risk in the exposed population" despite the absence of individualized proof of the causal connection. A "market share" standard might often satisfy this rule, although "when market share and risk contribution diverge, ... apportionment should accord with the firm's contribution to risk." Thus a manufacturer's share could be reduced if it took greater care to avoid the risk than did other manufacturers. Is this a workable approach? Should it make class actions mandatory as a prerequisite for use of this liability theory?

B.   COMPULSORY PARTY JOINDER

ELDREDGE v. CARPENTERS 46 NORTHERN CALIFORNIA COUNTIES JATC

United States Court of Appeals, Ninth Circuit, 1981.
662 F.2d 534, *cert. denied,* 459 U.S. 917, 103 S.Ct. 231, 74 L.Ed.2d 183 (1982).

Before FLETCHER and NELSON, CIRCUIT JUDGES, and KEEP, DISTRICT JUDGE.*

FLETCHER, CIRCUIT JUDGE.

Plaintiffs Eldredge and Mazur brought suit under Title VII, 42 U.S.C. § 2000e–2, against the Carpenters 46 Northern California Coun-

* This was the first all woman three judge panel in the history of the U.S. Courts of Appeals. *Eldredge* was the first case the panel heard.—Eds.

ties Joint Apprenticeship and Training Committee (JATC), alleging sex discrimination in the operation of JATC's apprenticeship program. Plaintiffs brought the suit as a class action, but the district court has not yet considered the question of class certification.

Defendant JATC is a joint labor-management committee established under an agreement that provides for a trust fund contributed to by the parties to the master collective bargaining agreements in the Northern California construction industry. JATC is composed of equal numbers of labor and management representatives, and acts as a board of trustees for the administration of the Carpenters Apprenticeship and Training Trust Fund for Northern California. It is responsible for establishing, supporting, and maintaining programs to educate and train journeymen and apprentices in all classifications covered by any collective bargaining agreement that requires employer contributions to the trust fund.

Plaintiffs allege that the process by which JATC selects applicants to its apprenticeship training program discriminates against women. Although JATC has employed other selection procedures in the past, it presently relies on what is known as the "unrestricted hunting license" system. Under this system, an individual must first convince an employer to hire him or her as a beginning apprentice. JATC then places the individual's name on its applicant register. The applicant enters into an apprenticeship agreement with JATC and is dispatched through the union hiring hall. An individual needs no prior training to become an apprentice; all that is required is that he or she be 17 years of age and have a high school diploma or its equivalent.

The master collective bargaining agreements under which JATC operates require employers to hire one apprentice for every five journeymen employed. The apprenticeship is a four-year program. Employers are under no obligation to hire beginning as opposed to experienced apprentices. In May of 1976, only thirteen of JATC's 3220 registered apprentices were women.

The essence of plaintiffs' complaint is that, by relying on the unrestricted hunting license system to recruit apprentices, JATC has adopted an entrance requirement for its program which is known to have a discriminatory effect on women. Plaintiffs argue that JATC knows that individual employers do not hire women under the unrestricted hunting license system, and that JATC's use of this system is therefore illegal under Title VII. The district court assumed for the purposes of its rule 19 analysis that plaintiffs had stated a claim on which relief could be granted.

The district court held that the 4500 employers and 60 union locals covered by the master labor agreement, or adequate representatives of their interests, were indispensable to the litigation under the standards imposed by rule 19(b). It ordered them joined within 60 days. Plaintiffs were granted extensions of time in which to explore the possibilities for joinder, but joinder of all 4500 employers proved impossible. The plaintiffs then sought to join the Northern California Homebuilders' Conference (NCHBC) to represent the absent employers' interests.[3] The court held this inadequate and dismissed the case. We conclude that the employers are not necessary parties under rule 19(a) and thus cannot be indispensable parties under rule 19(b). We reverse.

Rule 19 requires two separate inquiries. First, are there persons who should be joined, either because their own interests or the interests of the parties might be harmed by their absence? Such persons, referred to as "necessary parties," must be joined if feasible. Fed.R.Civ.P. 19(a). Second, if parties determined to be necessary under rule 19(a) cannot be joined, should the action in "equity and good conscience" be dismissed? Only if the court determines that the action should be dismissed is the absent party labeled "indispensable." Fed.R.Civ.P. 19(b).

The nature of the rule 19 inquiry is described at some length in *Provident Tradesmens Bank & Trust Co. v. Patterson,* 390 U.S. 102, 88 S.Ct. 733, 19 L.Ed.2d 936 (1968). The inquiry should focus on the practical effects of joinder and nonjoinder. Rule 19 was revised in 1966 to emphasize its practical focus and to avoid the inflexible approach taken by many courts under the prior version of the rule.

Rule 19(a) describes two categories of persons who should be joined if feasible. If the absent employers fall into either of these two categories, they are "necessary parties."

The first category comprises those persons in whose absence "complete relief cannot be accorded among those already parties." Fed.R.Civ.P. 19(a)(1). This portion of the rule is concerned only with "relief as between the persons already parties, not as between a party and the absent person whose joinder is sought." The district court concluded that the absent employers could frustrate any relief granted against JATC, and that complete relief would therefore not be possible unless the employers were made parties. The court reasoned that the employers could defeat any order against JATC by refusing to hire any apprentices, by hiring only unregistered, nonunion apprentices, or by rejecting all female apprentices dispatched to them. We believe that the district court misapprehended the legal inquiry required by rule 19(a)(1).

If JATC's activities violate Title VII, a question not yet decided, then the court has both the power and the duty to enjoin those activities. The possibility that such an injunction may induce employers to avoid JATC's services, or ultimately to disband the training and referral system altogether, should not defeat the present action against JATC. JATC may not avoid its own liability for practices illegal under Title VII by relying on the employers' possible future conduct that might frustrate the remedial purposes of any court-ordered changes in the apprenticeship program. See, e.g., United States v. Sheet Metal Workers, Local 36, 416 F.2d 123, 132 & n. 16 (8th Cir.1969) (enjoining union from continu-

---

3. The NCHBC is a large employers' organization which negotiated the master labor agreement under which JATC oper- ates. Not all of the employers who subscribe to the master agreement belong to the NCHBC.

ing discriminatory referral practices, even though those practices were required by collective bargaining agreement with absent employers).

The district court appears to assume that the employers would discriminate against women because of their sex, and that they would refuse to hire women training in the apprentice program. There is no evidence to this effect in the record. On the contrary, the employers have previously participated, apparently successfully, in a state-mandated affirmative action program designed to increase the number of minority apprentices.

While it might be desirable to join all 4500 employers in order to eradicate sex discrimination in the industry, we conclude that relief on plaintiffs' claims against JATC as an entity could be afforded by an injunction against JATC alone. Both sides agree that JATC has the power under the trust fund agreement to structure its apprenticeship program in any way it sees fit. It is quite possible that a court-ordered restructuring of the program could effectively increase the participation of women in the apprenticeship program.

The second inquiry required by rule 19(a) concerns prejudice, either to the absent persons or to those already parties. Rule 19(a)(2)(i) provides that a person should be joined if he claims an interest relating to the subject of the action, and the disposition of the action may "as a practical matter impair or impede his ability to protect that interest."

The district court held that the employers should be joined since they have a right to select their own employees, a substantial interest that they have a right to protect. We disagree. The trust fund agreement grants full authority to JATC to structure the apprenticeship program and to select the apprentices. We conclude that the employers have by contract ceded to JATC whatever legally protectible interest they may have had in selecting apprentices to be trained. On the other hand, without the joinder of the employers, any court order that may be entered to enjoin JATC to institute programs cannot go beyond the authority granted JATC under the trust fund agreement. The absent employers are thus assured that an injunction against JATC will not trench on any rights reserved to the employers under the agreement. We must conclude that the employers' ability to protect whatever interest in employee selection they retain will not be "impaired or impeded" if they are not made parties. They are therefore not necessary parties under rule 19(a)(2)(i).

The district court was understandably concerned that the absent employers might have interests that would be unrepresented in the present suit. Although we have concluded that their interests are not the sort that would make the employers necessary under rule 19, on remand it is possible that some employers, or the NCHBC, may move to intervene. The district court may then consider whether to permit intervention under Fed.R.Civ.P. 24.

Notes and Questions

1. Rule 19(a) proposes essentially three criteria for concluding that nonparties should be added to the suit. What facts might support application of each of these criteria in *Eldredge*? Do they really raise different concerns, or are they merely different guises for the same concern about unfair prejudice to the rights of nonparties? For an argument that the rule should be focused only on this concern, see Freer, Rethinking Compulsory Joinder: A Proposal to Restructure Federal Rule 19, 60 N.Y.U.L.Rev. 1061 (1985).

2. The lower court relied heavily on the fact that the individual employers could frustrate the relief ordered against the JATC by refusing to hire women who were referred to them. It thus concluded that "the relief obtained in this lawsuit would serve only to swell the ranks of unemployed apprentices. This surely cannot be the 'complete relief' contemplated by Rule 19(a)." 440 F.Supp. at 520. Is this a proper consideration under Rule 19(a)? Who should be entitled to determine whether the relief available where certain persons are not made parties is satisfactory—the plaintiff or the judge?

Ten years after this decision, things had not changed much for the better. Although federal and state officials had set goals of 20% women in the construction trades in 1978, in 1991 it was reported that women constituted only 2% of the work force, and that the figure had remained virtually unchanged since 1983. Apprenticeship programs, in particular, were criticized as inadequate. See Bishop, Scant Success for California Efforts to Put Women in Construction Trades, N.Y. Times, Feb. 14, 1991 at A16 col. 1. Thereafter, women slipped below even the 2% figure. See Hard Times for Women in Construction, N.Y. Times, Sept. 27, 1992, at B2.

3. Consider Justice Rehnquist's opinion, dissenting from the Supreme Court's denial of certiorari in *Eldredge,* 459 U.S. at 921–22, 103 S.Ct. at 233–34:

> Although the Court of Appeals thought there was "no evidence" that "employers would refuse to hire women admitted to the apprentice program pursuant to any judgment that may be entered against JATC," the substance of respondents' complaint is that *employers* discriminate against women. The District Court correctly perceived the dilemma it and respondents faced. If it ordered relief against the JATC alone, it could not affect the alleged discriminatory practices. Rule 19(a)(1). If it ordered relief against the employers, it would almost certainly affect their right to select apprentices without affording them an opportunity to rebut the charge that they discriminate. Rule 19(a)(2)(i).
>
> The Court of Appeals sought to avoid the force of this argument by claiming that because the agreement that created JATC grants it "full authority to structure the apprenticeship program and to select the apprentices ... the employers have by contract ceded to JATC whatever legally protectible interest they may have had in selecting apprentices to be trained." This is simply not correct. The agreement gives JATC authority only to select persons to refer to employers; an applicant does not become an apprentice and begin the training program until and unless an employer hires him. And, as noted above, employers have bargained to retain their right to reject any applicant for any reason. Yet

the Court of Appeals rather cavalierly found, in a proceeding to which the employers were not parties, that the employers have ceded these rights.

The impropriety of the Court of Appeals' ruling is demonstrated by General Building Contractors Association, Inc. v. Pennsylvania, 458 U.S. 375, 102 S.Ct. 3141, 73 L.Ed.2d 835 (1982), in which we considered a similar apprenticeship system. We held that a district court cannot issue an injunction against employers in an employment discrimination case under 42 U.S.C.A. § 1981 when the employers are not guilty of intentional discrimination. In that case there apparently was no hunting license system, and the discrimination was caused by the JATC and the union, but the bar to an injunction was the same as the bar that will face the District Court on remand in this case: it is improper for a court to act against a person who has not been found to have violated the law.

The Court of Appeals, as if recognizing the unsatisfactory posture of the litigation for providing meaningful adjudication and relief, commented that "on remand it is possible that some employers ... may move to intervene." But to secure full participation only by torturing the meaning of Rule 19 to avoid dismissal, in the hopes that the absent parties will then take it upon themselves to protect their interests, is not an appealing basis for the result reached by the Court of Appeals. It is respondents who have sought to affect the hiring practices of some 4500 employers; it is respondents, and not the absent employers, who should shoulder the responsibility of joining the necessarily affected employers or suffering dismissal of their lawsuit.

* * * Since courts will not, I am confident, begin issuing injunctions against non-parties, the approach of the Court of Appeals will tend to reduce the district courts to issuers of " 'paper' decrees which neither adjudicate nor, in the end, protect rights."

4. Is the central problem in *Eldredge* substantive or procedural? On remand in *Eldredge,* the trial court certified a plaintiff class of women applicants. Then, on cross motions for summary judgment, it entered judgment for defendant on the ground that plaintiffs were trying to hold it liable for discriminatory acts of third parties.

In Eldredge v. Carpenters 46 Northern California Counties JATC, 833 F.2d 1334 (9th Cir.1987), cert. denied 487 U.S. 1210, 108 S.Ct. 2857, 101 L.Ed.2d 894 (1988), the appellate court reversed and directed entry of summary judgment for plaintiffs. It reasoned that, as a matter of substantive anti-discrimination law, a showing that a practice excluded a protected class in disproportionate numbers shifted the burden to the defendant to justify the practice. "The JATC does not contend that some factor other than the 'hunting license' system accounts for women's lower admission rate into its program. It cannot avoid liability for the effects of its own admission procedures by pointing to the discriminatory practices of those to whom it has delegated the power to select apprentices." Id. at 1337.

The district court had reasoned that the JATC stood in the same position as an employment agency, but the appellate court rejected that argument (id. at 1337):

The JATC, however, does not stand in the same position as an employment agency. It is not simply an intermediary between applicant and employer. Rather, it is the JATC that possesses the full authority to select the carpentry apprentices for Northern California. The district court failed to recognize that the employers were merely delegates of the JATC's power to determine which applicants will be admitted into the program. Because the JATC may, under the trust agreement, select apprentices in any way it deems appropriate, it violates Title VII if it used procedures that unjustifiably discriminate against a class of people protected under Title VII.

On further remand, the district court accepted the JATC's proposal to retain the first-job requirement and the hunting license for men and allow women admission to the program's educational aspects without satisfying the first-job requirement. The Court of Appeals reversed again, noting that the JATC had "waged a relentless battle to preserve the status quo" of the hunting license. Eldredge v. Carpenters 46 Northern California Counties JATC, 94 F.3d 1366, 1371 (9th Cir.1996). The appellate court ordered the district judge to adopt a remedy eliminating the hunting license system and requiring that all job applicants be hired from a numerical referral list maintained by the JATC. In addition, it directed that the remedy include a 20% affirmative action program and that the court appoint a monitor of the JATC's compliance. It also directed the district court to consider the plaintiffs' request that all apprentices be instructed regarding workplace harassment. Id. at 1372.

5.   In EEOC v. Pipefitters' Local 120, 235 F.3d 244 (6th Cir.2000), a consent decree was entered in a suit against a union involving alleged racial discrimination in work assignments. When contempt sanctions were sought years later against the union, the court ordered the contractors who hired union members to be joined as defendants pursuant to Rule 19(a). Some contractors objected that this deprived them of their rights, but the court disagreed:

> The district court joined these defendant contractors to ensure complete relief on a prospective basis regarding the record-keeping and reporting requirements of the consent decree. * * * Their joinder did not subject them to liability for past conduct. They are not being deprived of legal rights by a retroactive application of the terms of the consent decree. The impact of joining [the contractors] is *de minimis* and prospective. The district court joined these defendants to enforce the decree against the Union, not for the binding effect it would have on [them]. * * *

> Numerous contractors that utilized the Union's hiring hall were not parties to the original consent decree. Thus, the Union's compliance with the decree, especially in light of the individual claims [of black pipefitters] and lax reporting and record-keeping, was impossible to gauge when non-party contractors hired union workers. This consideration and the need to modify the decree as a result of the Union's alleged contempt justify the district court's concern that "complete relief" could not be attained without joining [the contractors].

6. Contrast Shimkus v. Gersten Companies, 816 F.2d 1318 (9th Cir. 1987). Plaintiffs there demonstrated that defendant, which operated apartment houses, had discriminated against African Americans. The district court ordered that blacks receive preference in allocation of apartments in the future. The court of appeals held that this order was an abuse of discretion because the trial court did not order joinder of non-black minorities against whom the property management firm also discriminated (id. at 1332):

> Under Rule 19(a)(2)(i), these non-black minorities clearly have an interest related to the subject of this action: remedying housing discrimination in Gersten apartments. The disposition of this action without their joinder clearly impairs and impedes their ability to protect that interest. The *Shimkus* decree not only imposes an unfair burden on those minority persons but would require them to bring another federal action seeking [a] consent decree to avoid those burdens. * * * It would be ironic if a decree to remedy discrimination effectively pitted one minority group against another.

Similar issues may arise in employment discrimination litigation. For example, would a change in apprenticeship patterns have a practical impact on the interests of prospective male apprentices? See Martin v. Wilks, *infra* p. 86, suggesting that white males are necessary parties in employment discrimination litigation that results in an affirmative action decree which reduces their chances for promotion. How can a court fashion a remedy without raising at least some risk that it will pit one minority group against another? Are necessary party rules the way to address this problem? See Comment, Compulsory Joinder of Classes, 58 U.Chi.L.Rev. 1453 (1991) (arguing that classes be considered necessary parties).

7. A nonparty is necessary if it has an interest relating to the subject of the action and disposition of the action in its absence may "as a practical matter impair or impede the person's ability to protect that interest." The term "as a practical matter" is used to indicate that even if a person would not be bound by a judgment in the case under claim preclusion (res judicata), it may still be a necessary party if its ability to protect its interest is impaired. See discussion in Chapter VIII regarding the requirement that, to be bound by a judgment, one must be a party or in privity with a party. In some instances an equitable decree can have a practical impact on a nonparty because it changes the status quo. For example, in Ford Motor Co. v. Bisanz Brothers, Inc., 249 F.2d 22 (8th Cir.1957), Ford, a nonparty, was found to be affected as a practical matter by a suit brought by adjoining property owners to enjoin the defendant railroad from using a spur line to the Ford plant since judgment for the plaintiffs could have resulted in Ford's loss of the railroad's services.

Would the fact that the case may result in a precedent that could adversely affect the missing party be enough to make it necessary? See Pulitzer–Polster v. Pulitzer, 784 F.2d 1305 (5th Cir.1986) (finding that co-beneficiaries of a trust who had filed suit in a state court were necessary parties in a similar federal-court suit filed by a different trust beneficiary because, even though they would not be legally bound by the federal-court judgment, the same witnesses would testify on issues of credibility and the federal-court judgment might produce a "negative precedent" in the sense that the state court would respect the credibility findings in the federal suit).

8. The "as a practical matter" standard is also applied to intervention of right under Rule 24(b) ("the applicant is so situated that the disposition of the action may as a practical matter impair or impede the applicant's ability to protect that interest"). Determining the practical effect of a potential judgment is a problem that can arise in environmental cases. In Conner v. Burford, 836 F.2d 1521 (9th Cir.1988), a public interest organization sued the U.S. Forest Service and Fish and Wildlife Service alleging that defendants had issued oil and gas leases on national forest lands without an impact statement as required by the Endangered Species Act and National Environmental Policy Act. Some of the 700 lessees attempted to intervene and filed motions to vacate the lower court's judgment on the ground that they were indispensable parties. The court of appeals found them not to be indispensable because the lower court only enjoined government actions in approving surface-disturbing activity. It reasoned that the lessees were free to assert whatever claims they might have against the government, and if the government complied with the acts, their leases could take effect. Isn't this a classic example of a situation where the missing parties' interests are, as a practical matter, impeded or impaired?

One explanation for indifference to such problems is that the courts take a less-demanding attitude toward compliance with Rule 19 requirements in cases involving "public" rights seemingly on the theory that a "public interest litigant" must have a forum in which to contest governmental activity and vindicate public rights even though some nonparties might be affected as a result. For an argument that there should be no absolute exception to Rule 19 for cases involving "public" rights, and that some mechanism such as participation by representatives of nonparties should be used, see Tobias, Rule 19 and the Public Rights Exception to Party Joinder, 65 N.C.L.Rev. 745 (1987).

9. Rule 20 is designed in part to foster efficiency in litigation by permitting joinder of all interested parties in a single case. Should Rule 19(a) similarly be read broadly to promote combined resolution of related claims? Professor Freer has argued that the rule should be revised to pressure plaintiffs to join all parties in one proceeding: "A plaintiff is entitled to due process, but has no right to sole possession of center stage; we need to tell the prima donna of the legal world that she must work with some co-stars. This can be done by expanding the federal court's power to order joinder for the express purpose of avoiding duplicative litigation." Freer, Avoiding Duplicative Litigation: Rethinking Plaintiff Autonomy and the Court's Role in Defining the Litigative Unit, 50 U.Pitt.L.Rev. 809, 813 (1989).

Whyham v. Piper Aircraft Corp., 96 F.R.D. 557 (M.D.Pa.1982), provides an example of such an approach. Plaintiffs there were injured in a crash in Scotland of a plane manufactured and designed by defendant. Although there appeared to be possible claims against the owner of the plane and the company that serviced it, these were Scottish companies and plaintiffs chose to sue Piper alone in the United States. The district court concluded that all three criteria under Rule 19 applied. First, "[t]he goal of Rule 19(a)(1) is to protect the interests of the parties by affording complete adjudication of the dispute," and this was not possible without the presence of the other possibly liable parties. Second, the interests of the two Scottish companies would be affected because they "are more than key witnesses; rather they are active participants" since Piper argued that they were negligent and partly liable for damages. Third, Piper faced the risk of inconsistent resolution of its claim for indemnification by the Scottish companies if required to pursue that claim in a separate action in Scotland. Citing the desire "[t]o resolve a lawsuit in a single proceeding," the district court dismissed.

Was this a correct reading of Rule 19? In Temple v. Synthes Corp., Ltd., 498 U.S. 5, 111 S.Ct. 315, 112 L.Ed.2d 263 (1990) (per curiam), plaintiff filed a federal court products liability action against the manufacturer of a medical device that had been inserted into his spine. Because he was simultaneously pursuing state-court claims for malpractice against the doctor and hospital involved in the insertion of the device, defendant moved to dismiss for failure to join them in the federal court action, and the district court dismissed in the interest of judicial economy because the doctor and hospital could not be joined without destroying diversity of citizenship.

The Supreme Court reversed because "it is not necessary for all joint tortfeasors to be named as defendants in a single lawsuit." Although its earlier decision in Provident Tradesmens Bank & Trust Co. v. Patterson, 390 U.S. 102, 88 S.Ct. 733, 19 L.Ed.2d 936 (1968), did mention that one focus of Rule 19 was "the interest of the courts and the public in complete, consistent, and efficient settlement of controversies," the Court explained that this consideration only came into play under Rule 19(b), dealing with the court's decision whether to dismiss when necessary parties could not be joined, and that the consideration had no bearing on whether nonparties were necessary within the meaning of Rule 19(a). Is this a sensible result in light of the fact that plaintiff had initiated parallel state-court proceedings against the hospital and doctor? Keep these issues in mind when we turn to duplicative litigation in Chapter III.

THE RULE 19(b) DETERMINATION

Rule 19(a) provides an analysis for determining whether an absentee is a "person to be joined if feasible." Courts and lawyers sometimes still use the old term "necessary party" (from the pre–1966 rule) to describe such a person. If the absentee satisfies the Rule 19(a) criteria, it "shall be joined as a party." However, joinder is not always possible. The usual reasons in a federal court are that the absentee comes from the same state as an opposing party and its joinder would destroy diversity jurisdiction, the absentee has insufficient contacts with the forum to permit personal jurisdiction, or venue would be improper. If the absentee cannot be joined, then Rule 19(b) requires an analysis of four factors to determine whether "equity and good conscience" permit the action to proceed without the absent party. If the court, upon applying the Rule 19(b) criteria, finds that "the action should proceed among the parties before it, or should be dismissed," the absentee will be regarded as "indispensable."

Although the overall "equity and good conscience" orientation of Rule 19(b) is more flexible than Rule 19(a), the rule also provides four factors for making this determination, in part calling for scrutiny of matters very similar to those raised in Rule 19(a). The court is to assess the extent of the threatened prejudice should the case proceed and, rather than indulging theoretical possibilities, to determine whether actual prejudicial consequences are likely to befall either present or absent parties. In considering the adequacy of the judgment that would result, the Supreme Court has said that the court should refer to "the public stake in settling disputes by whole, whenever possible." Provident Tradesmens Bank & Trust Co. v. Patterson, 390 U.S. 102, 88 S.Ct. 733, 19 L.Ed.2d, 936 (1968). Finally, the court is not to dismiss without reflecting on whether plaintiff would have an adequate remedy in the event of dismissal.

The first factor—"the extent to which the judgment rendered in the person's absence might be prejudicial to the person or those already parties"—overlaps with the analysis already made in Rule 19(a). However, while Rule 19(a) analysis asked whether the prejudice could arise from the person's absence, the Rule 19(b) analysis focuses on the extent of the prejudice that will occur now that joinder is not possible. Insufficient prejudice may be found if the absentee's interests are in fact represented by a party. Heckman v. United States, 224 U.S. 413, 444–445, 32 S.Ct. 424, 56 L.Ed. 820 (1912). Where the interests of the absentee and a party are mutually exclusive (for example, rival claimants to a trust), prejudice is likely unless it can be shown to be mitigated under the circumstances. The absentee's ability to intervene may be considered in assessing the extent of prejudice to it. Burger King v. American Nat'l Bank & Trust Co., 119 F.R.D. 672, 678 (N.D.Ill.1988).

The second factor—"the extent to which, by protective provisions in the judgment, by the shaping of relief, or other measures, the prejudice can be lessened or avoided"—requires a creative look at whether the judgment can be tailored to limit the prejudicial effect on a party. In Provident Tradesmens Bank & Trust Co. v. Patterson, 390 U.S. 102, 88 S.Ct. 733, 19 L.Ed.2d 936 L.Ed.2d 936 (1968), the Supreme Court, in reversing a finding of indispensability, noted that payment to parties might have been withheld pending other suits and that the plaintiffs might have been willing to limit the amount of their claims. Prejudice might be reduced by "granting damages but not injunctive relief, delaying relief until litigation elsewhere runs its course, writing a narrowly drawn opinion that makes clear what issues are not being decided, inviting absent parties to intervene, and joining parties likely to protect the interest of the absent party." James, Hazard, & Leubsdorf, Civil Procedure 619 (5th ed. 2001).

The third factor—"whether a judgment rendered in the person's absence will be adequate"—requires an inquiry into whether a truncated suit without the absentee can be adequate for the existing parties. This factor overlaps with the "complete relief" criterion in Rule 19(a). The existing parties are likely to claim that a judgment is adequate since they structured the suit in that way (possibly because joinder of the absentee would have been fatal to the suit jurisdictionally). But it is for the court to decide whether piecemeal justice is adequate enough to warrant the expenditure of both party and judicial resources.

The last factor—"whether the plaintiff will have an adequate remedy if the action is dismissed"—requires an examination of whether there are other courts in which the suit can be brought with all the parties joined. In cases in which plaintiffs can proceed against all interested parties in state court, there are strong arguments for dismissing after review of the Rule 19(b) factors even though plaintiff would prefer to be in federal court. See, e.g., Pulitzer–Polster v. Pulitzer, 784 F.2d 1305 (5th Cir.1986) (dismissing federal court suit where plaintiff already had suit against same defendant pending in state court even though plaintiff objected to delays in state-court suit). Because the availability of an adequate remedy in another court can often obviate the prejudice (although the plaintiff may thereby be denied its preferred choice of forum), this factor is sometimes said to be the most influential of the four if there is no alternative forum.

The Rule 19(b) factors require a case-by-case determination of indispensability. Under the pre–1966 rule analysis, courts sometimes said that certain categories of absentees were not indispensable. The labels should not be determinative under the current Rule 19(b) analysis, but some courts still proclaim that, for example, joint tort-feasors, co-obligors, or potential indemnitors are not indispensable. Consider other categories of absent parties: seller of a product in a suit against the manufacturer, Spiller v. Tennessee Trailers, Inc., 97 F.R.D. 347 (N.D.Ga. 1982); limited partners, Schmidt v. E.N. Maisel & Associates, 105 F.R.D. 157 (N.D.Ill.1985); nonparty to a commercial contract, Northrop Corp. v. McDonnell Douglas Corp., 705 F.2d 1030 (9th Cir.1983).

Consider, however, how the Rule 19(b) analysis should have been done in *Eldredge* had it been concluded that the employers or unions were parties to be joined under Rule 19(a). To begin with, since there would be no jurisdictional obstacle to joining them could the court still decline to insist on their joinder? Compare Rule 23 (authorizing a class action when the members of the class are "so numerous that joinder of all members is impracticable"). The district court in *Eldredge* analyzed the problem as follows:

> Although there is no procedural bar to joinder of the absent parties, the affected employers number 4500, and more than 60 local unions appear to be involved. Plaintiffs have represented that joinder is feasible without explaining how they intend to proceed in light of these numbers. The only alternatives appear to be certification of defendant classes or joinder of contractor associations in lieu of individual employer members, and District Councils, the Carpenters 46 Northern Counties Conference Board, or the International itself in lieu of union locals. That either of these alternatives can provide a feasible and adequate solution to the problems [that justify treating the nonparties as necessary under Rule 19(a)] is open to serious question. The former would raise a host of questions under Rule 23,

while the latter would raise further questions under Rule 19 as to whether individual employers and union locals remain indispensable parties despite the joinder of their representatives. * * *

If joinder cannot be accomplished, the [factors that make the nonparties necessary under Rule 19(a)] will require that the action be dismissed pursuant to Rule 19(b). Any relief directed to the JATC alone would create a substantial possibility of prejudice to both employers and unions, as well as to the JATC itself. No form of decree or protective provisions sufficient to avoid or reduce this prejudice has been suggested, and the Court is aware of none. Most significantly, there is no evidence that a judgment rendered in the absence of these parties would have any significant effect on the evil complained of in this action. Plaintiffs' alternative remedy is, unfortunately, burdensome and expensive: to pursue in individual lawsuits those employers alleged to have discriminated. However, the Court cannot on this ground alone countenance any further expenditure of judicial resources in an action so unlikely to lead to effective relief.

440 F.Supp. at 526–27. Justice Rehnquist expressed agreement with the district court's Rule 19(b) analysis. See 459 U.S. at 922.

SUPPLEMENTAL JURISDICTION FOR JOINDER OF ADDITIONAL PARTIES

Once a person has been determined to be a necessary party under Rule 19(a), the rule provides that the court will order that he or she be made a party, and "if the person should join as a plaintiff but refuses to do so, the person may be made a defendant, or, in a proper case, an involuntary plaintiff." There are, however, three expressed limitations on such joinder. The nonparty cannot be made a party unless (1) subject to service of process, (2) the joinder will not deprive the court of subject matter jurisdiction, and (3) the nonparty does not properly object that its joinder would render venue improper.

The first exception will not be extensively examined in this book. Amenability to service of process—which is the means of insuring that a party can be reached under a long arm statute or other basis for "personal jurisdiction" and has sufficient "minimum contacts" with the forum—is beyond the scope of this book. The other two exceptions—relating to subject matter jurisdiction and venue—can present formidable obstacles to joinder, obstacles which may be overcome, however, through the application of supplemental jurisdiction.

As a refresher, it is useful to recall that federal court subject matter jurisdiction is limited to those jurisdictional categories set out in Article III of the Constitution and in specific authorizing statutes. In cases where jurisdiction is based on diversity of citizenship, the joinder of an additional party will sometimes destroy diversity. Under the diversity statute, 28 U.S.C.A. § 1332, each plaintiff must satisfy the $75,000 amount in controversy requirement, and thus an additional party with a claim not exceeding $75,000 cannot normally be joined. The Supreme Court has also interpreted the statute, since Strawbridge v. Curtiss, 7 U.S. (3 Cranch) 267, 2 L.Ed. 435 (1806), as requiring complete diversity, and thus an additional party will destroy diversity if it is a citizen of the same state as one of the opposing parties. In cases based on federal question jurisdiction, the claims stated in a well-pleaded complaint must arise under the Constitution, laws, or treaties of the United States. Thus, here too, there is no automatic federal court jurisdiction over state-law claims between existing parties or over state-law claims against an additional party sought to be joined.

In these kinds of cases, the question arises whether some form of jurisdiction can be devised to allow new parties to be joined or issues to be raised as to which there would not be federal court jurisdiction. If the jurisdictional requirements were strictly applied, litigation in federal courts would be inflexible and unfair in not allowing related parties and issues to be brought into a law suit. Over a number of decades, the Supreme Court carved out two forms of expanded jurisdiction.

Ancillary jurisdiction permitted the joinder of claims and parties over which a federal court does not have subject matter jurisdiction as an incident to disposition of the entire case before the court. It was particularly useful when procedural devices in the federal rules would otherwise be frustrated, for example, as to compulsory counterclaims (Rule 13(a)) (the landmark case is Moore v. New York Cotton Exchange, 270 U.S. 593, 46 S.Ct. 367, 70 L.Ed. 750 (1926) which allowed defendant to file a state law counterclaim to a federal antitrust claim); cross-claims (Rule 13(g)); impleader of third-party defendants (Rule 14); interpleader (Rule 22); and intervention as of right (Rule 24(a)). But the Supreme Court refused to extend ancillary jurisdiction when it would undercut the intent of the particular jurisdictional statute involved, as with the requirement of complete diversity. See Owen Equipment & Erection Co. v. Kroger, 437 U.S. 365, 98 S.Ct. 2396, 57 L.Ed.2d 274 (1978) (plaintiff would not be allowed to assert a claim against a nondiverse third party defendant properly joined pursuant to Rule 14 because doing so would undercut the complete diversity requirement).

Pendent jurisdiction, like ancillary jurisdiction, developed out of considerations of "judicial economy, convenience and fairness to the litigants." In United Mine Workers v. Gibbs, 383 U.S. 715, 86 S.Ct. 1130, 16 L.Ed.2d 218 (1966), for example, it was invoked to allow a federal court to entertain a state-law claim of conspiracy to interfere with contract rights which was closely related (i.e., derived from "a common nucleus of operative fact") to a federal claim based on violation of the Taft–Hartley Act. Some courts extended the doctrine from "claims" to "parties," as when a federal claim against an existing party is closely enough related to a state claim against another party over whom there would be no independent basis of federal jurisdiction. See C. Wright & M. Kane, Law of Federal Courts 120 (6th ed. 2002). However, the Supreme Court struck down such applications where it found them contrary to the inherent limits of the Article III power and of the congressional intent reflected in the particular federal jurisdictional statute. See Aldinger v. Howard, 427 U.S. 1, 96 S.Ct. 2413, 49 L.Ed.2d 276 (1976) (plaintiff who had claim under 42 U.S.C.A. § 1983 against various county employees could not add claim against county based on state law because it was thought that county was immune to suit under § 1983).

In 1989, the Supreme Court raised doubts about any judicial efforts to justify addition of parties on either ancillary or pendent jurisdiction grounds in Finley v. United States, 490 U.S. 545, 109 S.Ct. 2003, 104 L.Ed.2d 593 (1989). The Court announced a "clear interpretative rule" that "a grant of jurisdiction over claims involving particular parties does not itself confer jurisdiction over additional claims by or against different parties." In closing, the Court noted that Congress could change the statutory scope of jurisdiction.

§ 1367 Supplemental jurisdiction: Congress responded a year and a half later. The Judicial Improvements Act of 1990, 28 U.S.C.A. § 1367, provides a new statutory basis for "supplemental jurisdiction," and this statute is the touchstone for addition of parties not only pursuant to Rule 19, but also Rule 24 (intervention) and Rule 23 (class actions).

Subsection (a) authorizes the district courts to exercise jurisdiction over a supplemental claim whenever it forms "part of the same constitutional case or controversy under Article III" as the claim or claims that provide the basis for the district court's original jurisdiction. It explicitly authorizes exercise of jurisdiction over claims that involve the joinder or intervention of additional parties, thus approving the old "pendent party" jurisdiction. The same case or controversy has been viewed as including all claims arising out of a single transaction or occurrence or related series of transactions or occurrences. 13B C. Wright, A. Miller & E. Cooper, Federal Practice & Procedure § 3567, at 117 (2d ed. 1984).

Subsection (b) prohibits supplemental jurisdiction when it would encourage plaintiffs to evade the complete diversity requirement of § 1332. It thus denies supplemental jurisdiction over "claims by *plaintiffs* against persons made parties under Rule 14, 19, 20, or 24," or over "claims by persons proposed to be joined as *plaintiffs* under Rule 19," or "seeking to intervene as *plaintiffs* under Rule 24" "when exercising supplemental jurisdiction over such claims would be inconsistent with the jurisdictional requirements of § 1332." Notice that subsection (b) denies supplemental jurisdiction over "claims by plaintiffs," or by necessary party plaintiffs joined under Rule 19, or by intervening plaintiffs under Rule 24, but not over claims of additional nondiverse plaintiffs that are joined pursuant to Rule 20. Plaintiff-intervenors would be excluded to the same extent as those sought to be joined as plaintiffs under Rule 19, a change from the prior law regarding intervenors of right. Subsection (b) does not mention Rule 23, which deals with class actions; the importance of this feature of the Act is considered in Chapter IV.

Owen Equipment & Erection Co. v. Kroger, 437 U.S. 365, 98 S.Ct. 2396, 57 L.Ed.2d 274 (1978), is a paradigm for a case in which supplemental jurisdiction would be "inconsistent with the jurisdictional requirements of § 1332" (i.e., a claim by a plaintiff against a nondiverse third-party defendant made a party under Rule 14, which would undermine the complete diversity requirement). See also TIG Ins. Co. v. Reliable Research Co., 334 F.3d 630 (7th Cir.2003) (in suit by insurer, there was no supplemental jurisdiction over intervention on the plaintiff side by a title insurance company that had the same citizenship as defendant); Tell v. Trustees of Dartmouth College, 145 F.3d 417 (1st Cir.1998) (suggesting that alumni association which had the same citizenship as defendant was a necessary and indispensable party on the plaintiff side but that supplemental jurisdiction could not be asserted over it without undermining complete diversity).

Because subsection (b) only applies when federal-court jurisdiction is based solely on grounds of diversity, there are no similar obstacles to using supplemental jurisdiction for the addition of parties in cases relying on federal question jurisdiction, such as *Eldredge, supra* p. 45.

JOINDER PROBLEMS INVOLVING STATE GOVERNMENTAL ENTITIES

Special difficulties may develop if a party that should be joined under Rule 19 is a governmental entity, for such entities usually enjoy some form of sovereign immunity that may preclude proceeding with claims against them. If the entity is made a party, and no exception to sovereign immunity is available, it will be entitled to be dismissed. If it is not made a party and the court finds that the suit should not proceed in its absence, the entire suit will have to be dismissed. See, e.g., Citizen Potawatomi Nation v. Norton, 248 F.3d 993 (10th Cir.2001) (finding, under Rule 19, that nonparty Indian tribes could claim an interest in the funding formulae used by the Department of the Interior that the plaintiff tribe was challenging and that the nonparties' interest could be infringed, but that because they could not be joined due to sovereign immunity the suit had to be dismissed). Thus, when governmental or quasi-sovereign interests are involved, great care must be taken in structuring the suit so as to avoid the barrier of sovereign immunity.

The justification for sovereign immunity has been questioned, particularly as remedial law in the twentieth century came to place primary importance on compensation to the injured and on risk-spreading to those best able to deter harmful conduct and to cope with losses. As a result, there has been some erosion of sovereign immunity, both that of states (as a result of state supreme court decisions and legislative enactments) and of the federal government (under Supreme Court decisions and congressional statutes). Respect for sovereign immunity waxed and waned in the twentieth century, but the 1980s and 1990s witnessed some strengthening of the doctrine under both federal common law and constitutional provisions.

Perhaps the most significant recent development in sovereign-immunity law that affects the ability to join necessary parties in federal courts is in the Eleventh Amendment area. That amendment overruled the result in Chisholm v. Georgia, 2 U.S. (2 Dall.) 419, 1 L.Ed. 440 (1793), which upheld federal court jurisdiction over a suit brought by a citizen of South Carolina against the State of Georgia. The amendment by its terms only forbids the extension of the judicial power of the United States to suits "commenced or prosecuted against one of the United States by Citizens of another State, or by Citizens or Subjects of any Foreign State." However, Hans v. Louisiana, 134 U.S. 1, 10 S.Ct. 504, 33 L.Ed. 842 (1890), held that it applies to a suit by a citizen against his own state. The prohibition of suits against a state cannot be avoided by suing a state official if relief is sought against the state. The Eleventh Amendment applies to a suit against a state official when "the state is the real, substantial party in interest," Ford Motor Co. v. Department of Treasury, 323 U.S. 459, 464, 65 S.Ct. 347, 89 L.Ed. 389 (1945), and "[t]he general rule is that relief sought nominally against an officer is in fact against the sovereign if the decree would operate against the latter." Hawaii v. Gordon, 373 U.S. 57, 58, 83 S.Ct. 1052, 10 L.Ed.2d 191 (1963).

Congress can override states' sovereign immunity by statute in the exercise of its enforcement powers under § 5 of the 14th Amendment, Fitzpatrick v. Bitzer, 427 U.S. 445, 96 S.Ct. 2666, 49 L.Ed.2d 614 (1976), but its intent must be clear and be pursuant to constitutional authority. Compare Seminole Tribe v. Florida, 517 U.S. 44, 116 S.Ct. 1114, 134 L.Ed.2d 252 (1996) (despite congressional intent to abrogate the states' Eleventh Amendment immunity, Congress lacked authority under the Indian commerce clause of the Constitution to do so) with Nevada Dep't of Human Resources v. Hibbs, 538 U.S. 721, 123 S.Ct. 1972, 155 L.Ed.2d 953 (2003) (state employees could recover money damages against a state in federal court for failure to comply with the Family & Medical Leave Act, which made the intention to abrogate unmistakably clear and was a valid exercise of Congress's power under § 5 of the Fourteenth Amendment).

The impact of the Eleventh Amendment was marginalized by the "stripping doctrine" of Ex parte Young, 209 U.S. 123, 28 S.Ct. 441, 52 L.Ed. 714 (1908), which held that the Eleventh Amendment did not prohibit a suit to enjoin a state attorney general from enforcing a state statute alleged to violate the Constitution. The theory was that an unconstitutional statute is void and therefore does not "impart to the [the officer] any immunity from responsibility to the supreme authority of the United States." Since the state could not authorize such unconstitutional action, the officer was "stripped" of his official or representative character and [was] subjected to the consequences of his official conduct. This doctrine thus prevented the application of the Eleventh Amendment to federal court suits for an injunction against state officials alleging violations of constitutional rights.

Cases beginning in the 1970s limited the breadth of Ex parte Young. Edelman v. Jordan, 415 U.S. 651, 94 S.Ct. 1347, 39 L.Ed.2d 662 (1974), held that injunctive relief that awards retroactive monetary relief, as opposed to an injunction as to future conduct, is prohibited under the Eleventh Amendment. Pennhurst State School & Hospital v. Halderman, 465 U.S. 89, 104 S.Ct. 900, 79 L.Ed.2d 67 (1984), held that an injunctive suit against a state official based on state law is contrary to the Eleventh Amendment, even if the official's conduct was ultra vires, and that pendent jurisdiction will not be accorded to the state-law claim even if appended to a federal claim which arose out of the same core events. It reaffirmed, however, the applicability of Ex parte Young to avoid the Eleventh Amendment bar to federal court jurisdiction for suits against state officials who are sued in their official capacity for prospective relief solely to vindicate federal rights. Seminole Tribe v. Florida, *supra*, held that the "stripping doctrine" of Ex Parte Young could not be used to avoid Eleventh Amendment immunity where the federal statute on which the suit was based. (The Indian Gaming Regulatory Act) showed an intent to limit the duty imposed by the act on the states to a "modest set of sanctions" and not to the broad equitable relief sought.

Subdivisions of the state, such as counties and cities, are not entitled to 11th Amendment immunity if they are local in character and their funds are not derived primarily from the state treasury. Mt. Healthy City School District Board of Education v. Doyle, 429 U.S. 274, 280, 97 S.Ct. 568, 572, 50 L.Ed.2d 471 (1977). Lake Country Estates, Inc. v. Tahoe Regional Planning Agency, 440 U.S. 391, 99 S.Ct. 1171, 59 L.Ed.2d 401 (1979), declined to clothe an entity created by an interstate compact with 11th Amendment immunity, but did grant the members of its governing body traditional legislative immunity.

C. INTERVENTION

Intervention provides a means for an outsider who has an interest in a lawsuit to voluntarily join the suit as a party. Joinder of necessary parties under Rule 19, as has been discussed, provides one means of bringing in parties who have sufficient interest in the suit. A class action under Rule 23, as will be discussed in Chapter IV, provides another means of ensuring representation of persons who are not named parties and yet who have interests in the suit. Rule 24 intervention provides a third means of making someone with an interest a party, and it is the principal means for an excluded person to force his or her way into the suit. In recent years, intervention has especially become a means by which organizations or groups with particular interests in a piece of litigation seek to participate directly as parties.

BRUNET, A STUDY IN THE ALLOCATION OF SCARCE RESOURCES: THE EFFICIENCY OF FEDERAL INTERVENTION CRITERIA

12 Georgia L.Rev. 701, 719–20 (1978).

The chief policy advantage of intervention is that it merges into one central dispute additional issues related to the original case and avoids multiple trials on identical or related issues.

The brevity of the articulation of this powerful economy is not commensurate with its significance. Elimination of multiple litigation through intervention represents far more than mere avoidance of a duplicative case. To be sure, intervention avoids the wasted effort of the court in deciding duplicitous motions and presiding at trials. From this efficiency follow three benefits associated with intervention. First, eliminating an additional case carries the independent benefit of reducing queuing time and court clog. Since a lengthy queue of cases is in part the cause of the weighty opportunity cost of litigation, the saving merits emphasis.

Second, intervention can also prevent inconsistencies in fact finding and law determination that might occur if the decisionmaker separately considered the issues combined for consideration through intervention. Inconsistent findings of fact are inefficient for numerous familiar reasons. They fail to perform the conflict-avoidance or law-making functions of dispute resolution that represent the very rationale for a civil litigation system and produce the harmful negative externalities associated with undecided conflict. Lack of confidence in the judicial system damages society and represents another negative externality. Inconsistent determinations of matters of fact and law tend to degrade the public's confidence in the judiciary and government, confidence which is essential to popular acceptance of court decisions and the behavioral concepts (*e.g.,* deterrence of harmful conduct and adherence to law) central to the judiciary's effectiveness in making a rule system effective. Inconsistency harms members of society because if society ignores the deterrence goal of the decision, it frustrates the allocative purpose of the norm.

Third, intervention's integration of similar issues into one action can also avoid complicated issues of collateral estoppel. Although collateral estoppel is designed to achieve efficiency by avoiding duplicative trials on identical issues, the complexity of its preclusion norms warrants minimizing the need to consider whether collateral estoppel applies. The court's determination of intricate questions of issue preclusion increases the likelihood of appeals, thereby adding to the social cost to the litigants and taxpayers of dispute resolution.

These three benefits of intervention can be characterized as system efficiencies because they tend generally to aid the operation of the court system but do not improve the efficiency of individual cases. Intervention can affect the efficiency or decisionmaking accuracy of a single case in a variety of ways, not all of them beneficial. The informational input of intervenors can help the court's fact finding and law determination and thus enrich the quality of litigation. The addition of intervenors can also improve the quality of adversary dispute resolution because the new party possesses a special stake in the outcome. On the other hand, intervention, like other joinder devices, can greatly complicate litigation by introducing new issues. Intervention may also delay the case longer than the time required to resolve the intervenor's independent litigation. Added complexity can adversely affect the quality of the litigation, and added delay may mean a net increase in queuing costs.

PLANNED PARENTHOOD v. CITIZENS FOR COMMUNITY ACTION

United States Court of Appeals, Eighth Circuit, 1977.
558 F.2d 861.

Before GIBSON, CHIEF JUDGE, and WEBSTER and HENLEY, CIRCUIT JUDGES.

GIBSON, CHIEF JUDGE.

The plaintiff, Planned Parenthood of Minnesota, Inc. (Planned Parenthood), has operated a comprehensive family planning clinic in St. Paul, Minnesota, since 1932. In January 1976, it decided to offer first trimester abortion services to its patients in conjunction with its other activities. To accommodate its expanded activities Planned Parenthood in March of 1976 finalized its plan to purchase a building at 1965 Ford Parkway in St. Paul to house its administrative offices, training facilities, research center and a medical clinic for furnishing family planning services including first trimester abortions. The prospective establishment of the abortion clinic met a hostile reception from a number of the residents of the area involved. In response to public protests, the St. Paul City Council temporarily frustrated the construction and operation of the abortion clinic by enacting an ordinance which imposed a six-month moratorium on the construction of "separate abortion facilities and other like facilities within the City of St. Paul" pending a study to determine whether special zoning restrictions should be imposed on such facilities. Planned Parenthood filed the present action challenging the constitutionality of the ordinance and seeking injunctive and monetary relief. The District Court, perceiving serious questions as to the constitutionality of the City Council's action, issued a preliminary injunction against the enforcement of the ordinance.

* * *

An application for intervention was filed by the Citizens for Community Action, a neighborhood association comprised of St. Paul citizens, taxpayers and homeowners. The professed purpose of the association is to preserve property values and insure that abortion facilities do not affect the health, welfare and safety of citizens. The application for intervention was joined by two couples, Donald and Mary Ann Lennon and Norman and Kathleen Vernig, who owned property in the vicinity of the proposed Ford Parkway abortion facility. The Lennons and Vernigs wish to intervene to assure that their property values are not adversely affected by the creation of an abortion clinic in their neighborhood. The District Court refused to allow the applicants to intervene as of right under Fed.R.Civ.P. 24(a)(2) or to intervene permissibly under Fed. R.Civ.P. 24(b).

Upon filing a timely application for intervention as of right under Rule 24(a)(2), the applicant is entitled to intervene if he satisfies the following tripartite test:

> 1) That he has [a] recognized interest in the subject matter of the primary litigation, 2) That his interest might be impaired by the disposition of the suit, and 3) That his interest is not adequately protected by the existing parties.

Edmondson v. Nebraska, 383 F.2d 123, 126 (8th Cir.1967).

In regard to the first requirement, the interest identified must be more than peripheral or insubstantial; the applicant must assert a "significantly protectable interest." *Donaldson v. United States,* 400 U.S. 517, 531, 91 S.Ct. 534, 27 L.Ed.2d 580 (1971). Here, the St. Paul City Council has enacted an ordinance imposing a moratorium on the construction of abortion clinics pending a study to determine whether all abortion clinics should be subjected to special zoning requirements. The applicants for intervention are vigorously defending this ordinance, arguing that such a measure is necessary to preserve their property values.[9] "Interests in property are the most elementary type of right that Rule 24(a) is designed to protect." *Diaz v. Southern Drilling Corp.,* 427 F.2d 1118, 1124 (5th Cir.1970). This litigation, which will establish the validity or invalidity of the ordinance, necessarily bears directly on the property interests the applicants seek to preserve. We conclude that the applicants have a significantly protectable interest in the subject matter of this litigation.

As required by Rule 24(a)(2), the applicants' ability to protect their interest may be impaired or impeded by the disposition of this case. If defendants remain enjoined from enforcing the ordinance, Planned Parenthood can lawfully establish an abortion facility at the Ford Parkway site. A judicial declaration that municipalities can not impose moratoriums on the construction of abortion clinics or, in a broader context, can not subject first trimester abortion clinics to special zoning requirements would have an inhibitive effect on the assertion of applicants' claims. In order to prevent what they view as an incipient erosion of their property values, the applicants must participate in this litigation, and be given the opportunity to present their views to the court in their endeavor to uphold the ordinance as a legitimate and constitutional exercise of municipal power.

---

9. The applicants' contention that the creation of an abortion clinic will lower their property values is not unsubstantiated. The record contains the testimony of a real estate expert who stated that an abortion clinic would lower residential and commercial property values in the immediate area.

Finally, in order to intervene under Rule 24(a)(2), the applicants must carry the "minimal" burden of showing that their interests are not adequately protected by the existing parties. *Trbovich v. United Mine Workers*, 404 U.S. 528, 538 n. 10, 92 S.Ct. 630, 30 L.Ed.2d 686 (1972). The District Court concluded that the applicants are adequately represented by defendants, with whom they seek to align themselves. We disagree.

Concededly, both the applicants and defendants are interested in upholding the constitutionality of the ordinance. However, their respective interests, while not adverse, are disparate. Defendants are accused of invidiously discriminating against Planned Parenthood in particular and abortion clinics in general. Allegations of bad faith have been directed against the defendants. Many of the defendants are seeking to avoid personal liability for allegedly infringing upon Planned Parenthood's constitutional rights. At trial, defendants will argue that the adoption of the ordinance was neither arbitrary nor discriminatory. They will seek to prove that the ordinance is consistent with the City's developing comprehensive zoning plan and existing principles of land use regulation.

The applicants, however, are concerned only with their own property values; they are exposed to no risk of personal liability and are defending no charges of discrimination or bad faith. As stated in *Joseph Skillken and Co. v. City of Toledo*, 528 F.2d 867, 876 (6th Cir.1975), *vacated on other grounds*, 429 U.S. 1068, 97 S.Ct. 800, 50 L.Ed.2d 786 (1977):

> The municipal defendants had enough to do to defend themselves against the charges leveled against them by the plaintiffs. They do not have the same interest in protecting the values of the homeowners' properties as do the homeowners themselves.

In the present case, the City Council is divided on the issue of whether the moratorium ordinance is proper or advisable. The ordinance was passed by a 5 to 2 vote; thus, a switch of two votes could completely change the attitude of the City Council and the municipality in regard to the issues presented in this litigation. The protection of the interests of the individual property owners rests primarily in the hands of a few individual council members, most of whom are threatened with personal liability for their discrete actions in voting favorably on the challenged ordinance. The record shows that the defendants have presented little evidence to show how the operation of an abortion clinic would affect applicants' important property interests.

We, therefore, conclude that the applicants to intervene have presented sufficient evidence to show that defendants are not adequate representatives of the applicants' interests.

Based on the foregoing discussion, the District Court erred in refusing to allow the applicants to intervene under Rule 24(a)(2).

Notes and Questions

1. Is the interest found by the court to justify intervention the protection of the intervenors' property values? What proof should an intervenor be required to present to show a threat to property values? Was the testimony of one real estate expert all that the court should have required? Is the intervenors' concern here really property values or rather the affront to their religious or social beliefs? Should that be enough to justify intervention?

2. Recall that Rule 19(a)(2) also calls for considering the interests of nonparties in determining whether they are necessary and therefore that the court should order their joinder. Should the "interest" provision be interpreted the same under these two rules? Note the different consequences that flow from a finding of interest under the two rules, and consider the views of the court in Smuck v. Hobson, 408 F.2d 175, 178 (D.C.Cir.1969), shortly after the rules were amended in 1966:

> The phrasing of rule 24(a)(2) as amended parallels that of Rule 19(a)(2) concerning joinder. But the fact that the two rules are entwined does not imply that an "interest" for the purpose of one is precisely the same as for the other. The occasions upon which a petitioner should be allowed to intervene under Rule 24 are not necessarily limited to those situations when the trial court should compel him to become a party under Rule 19. And while the division of Rule 24(a) and (b) into "Intervention of Right" and "Permissive Intervention" might superficially suggest that only the latter involves an exercise of discretion by the court, the contrary is clearly the case.

3. In *Planned Parenthood*, the court cites *Donaldson* for the requirement that an intervenor must assert a "significantly protectable interest." Does this mean that it must be a "legal interest" as in a property right? The Supreme Court's previous decision, Cascade Natural Gas Corp. v. El Paso Natural Gas Co., 386 U.S. 129, 87 S.Ct. 932, 17 L.Ed.2d 814 (1967), indicated otherwise. In *Cascade,* the United States sued to prevent El Paso Natural Gas Co. from acquiring the Pacific Northwest Pipeline Corp., alleging violation of the antitrust laws by diminishing competition in the sale of natural gas in California. Several intervenors sought to intervene at the remedy stage after the court had ordered immediate divestiture. They were California, the state affected; Southern California Edison, "a large industrial user of natural gas"; and Cascade, which had used Pacific Northwest as its sole supplier of natural gas. The Court found all three entitled to intervention of right on the ground that they had a sufficient economic interest, though not a legal interest, because they might be adversely affected by the merger. 7C C. Wright, A. Miller & M. Kane, Federal Practice and Procedure: Civil 2nd § 1908 (1986), comments that "[w]ith an occasional rare exception, both the commentators and the lower courts have refused to regard *Cascade* as a significant precedent."

Donaldson seemed to suggest a narrower concept of interest. There the government issued summonses to Donaldson's former employer (Acme) to obtain its records of his compensation. He sought to intervene to prevent disclosure. The Court found that the material sought consisted only of Acme's business records in which Donaldson had "no proprietary interest of any kind." He obviously had an interest in trying to keep the records from falling into the hands of the IRS, but the Court found this not a "significantly protectable interest" sufficient for Rule 24(a). It further observed that "the taxpayer, to the extent that he has such a protectable interest, as, for example, by way of privilege, or to the extent he may claim abuse of process, may always assert that interest or that claim in due course at its proper place in any subsequent trial."

A year later, Trbovich v. United Mine Workers, 404 U.S. 528, 92 S.Ct. 630, 30 L.Ed.2d 686 (1972), further complicated the picture. There a union member sought to intervene in a suit by the Secretary of Labor to set aside an election of union officers on the ground it violated the federal labor statutes. Although the act only authorized the Secretary to file suit, and prohibited members from doing so, the Court ordered intervention. Not mentioning *Donaldson*, it stated: "The Secretary does not contend that petitioner's interest in this litigation is insufficient; he argues, rather, that any interest petitioner has is adequately represented by the Secretary." Would the member's interest qualify as "significantly protectable" under *Donaldson*?

Do the above decisions sufficiently clarify the application of the interest requirement of Rule 24? A leading treatise opines that "[t]here is not any clear definition, either from the Supreme Court or from the lower courts, of the nature of the [Rule 24 interest] that is required for intervention of right. Indeed, it may be, as some courts have suggested, that this is a question not worth answering." 7C Wright, Miller & Kane, § 1908 at 263.

On this question, consider the intervention decision in Grutter v. Bollinger, 188 F.3d 394 (6th Cir.1999), the case in which the Supreme Court ultimately held in 2003 that some race-consciousness in university admissions would be permissible as a way to ensure a diverse learning environment. Plaintiffs, white applicants who had been denied admission, claimed that consideration of race violated their rights. The university defended its admissions policies, but there were requests for intervention by seventeen African–American and Hispanic individuals who claimed that they intended to apply for admission to the university in the future, and by a group that had long supported diversity in education. After the district court denied intervention, the court of appeals reversed, taking an expansive view of the interest needed to justify intervention of right. It found this requirement satisfied by the interest of those who wanted to attend the university. Regarding potentially adverse effects on this interest due to the judgment in the case, the court thought there was "little doubt" that access to the university would be impaired for them if consideration of race and ethnicity were forbidden.

Would any particular potential students have a "significantly protectable interest"? Eventually the Supreme Court upheld the University's program, emphasizing its interest in a diverse educational setting for its students. If the university could achieve its diversity objective by adopting admission policies that would favor other minority applicants but not the ones who sought to intervene, would they nevertheless have an interest sufficient to justify intervention of right? In Texas, the state reacted to a court-imposed ban on considering race by guaranteeing admission to the state university to the top graduates of each high school, thereby ensuring that the racial mix of overall admissions would remain roughly the same. If Michigan could do something similar (perhaps by guaranteeing admission to top graduates of inner-city Detroit schools), should the interests of these particular potential applicants in having the existing admissions policies retained be considered legally protectable?

4. One reason why a clearer definition of interest under the rule might be worthwhile is to determine how it relates to concepts of standing. Standing is one feature of justiciability, a congeries of doctrines designed to satisfy the requirement of Article III that federal courts only exercise jurisdiction over "cases and controversies." In the 1960's, the Supreme Court reformulated the standing test to focus on whether plaintiffs have suffered an injury in fact and whether the legal doctrine they invoke was designed to protect the interest they claim was invaded, but the exact application of this standing doctrine has proven difficult. See generally Chayes, Public Law Litigation and the Burger Court, 96 Harv. L. Rev. 4, 14– 19 (1982). Did the intervenors in *Planned Parenthood* have a right to insist that the City Council take action to prevent the opening of the clinic? If not, did they have a legally-protectable interest? Did they have a legal interest in standing terms?

The question whether intervenors should be required to demonstrate standing has proved difficult for the courts to resolve. See Tobias, Standing to Intervene, 1991 Wis.L.Rev. 415. Consider the following analysis from Chiles v. Thornburgh, 865 F.2d 1197, 1212–13 (11th Cir.1989):

> The reason for this confusion stems from the fact that standing concerns the subject matter jurisdiction of the court. The standing doctrine ensures that a justiciable case and controversy exists between the parties. Intervention under Rule 24 presumes that there is a justiciable case into which an individual wants to intervene. The focus therefore of a Rule 24 inquiry is whether the intervenor has a legally protectable interest in the litigation. It is in this context that the standing cases are relevant, for an intervenor's interest must be a particularized interest rather than a general grievance. We therefore hold that a party seeking to intervene need not demonstrate that he has standing in addition to meeting the requirements of Rule 24 so long as there exists a justiciable case and controversy between the parties already in the lawsuit. The standing cases, however, are relevant to help define the type of interest that the intervenor must assert.

See also Ruiz v. Estelle, 161 F.3d 814 (5th Cir.1998) (the standing doctrine serves to guarantee the existence of a "case or controversy," and once that is established with the principal parties, the presence of additional parties as intervenors does not destroy jurisdiction); Comment, An Attempt to Intervene in the Confusion: Standing Requirements for Rule 24 Intervenors, 69 U.Chi.L.Rev. 681 (2002) (arguing that intervention should be allowed without standing in part because "intervenors frequently lack any political clout and have no other way to protect their rights").

Keissler v. U.S. Forest Service, 157 F.3d 964 (3d Cir.1998), adopted a "flexible" standard for standing. Plaintiffs sued to halt logging in a national forest. Companies wanting to do logging and local governments claiming an entitlement to part of the money paid by the logging companies moved to intervene on the defendant's side. The court said that "rigid rules in such cases contravene a major premise of intervention—the protection of third parties affected by pending litigation" and that intervention should be permitted to enable "private attorneys general" and "public interest" groups to call governmental agencies to task. Judge Becker, concurring, thought this standard was too relaxed, asking rhetorically if the suppliers of the logging company or owners of a local diner, who also faced economic consequences, would not also be entitled to intervene.

Contrast Mausolf v. Babbitt, 85 F.3d 1295 (8th Cir.1996), in which the court held that a conservation group lacked standing and therefore could not intervene in litigation brought by snowmobilers to enjoin limitations on that activity:

> Congress could no more use Rule 24 to abrogate the Article III standing requirements than it could expand the Supreme Court's original jurisdiction by statute.
>
> The Association's position is that once an Article III case or controversy is underway, anybody who satisfies Rule 24's requirements may then join in. As long as the original parties are involved, the Association insists, the lawsuit remains within the scope of the federal "judicial power." We disagree. In our view, an Article III case or controversy, once joined by intervenors who lack standing, is—put bluntly—no longer an Article III case or controversy. An Article III case or controversy is one where all parties have standing, and a would-be intervenor, because he seeks to participate as a party, must have standing as well.

Id. at 1300. If this is correct, should it apply to permissive intervenors as well?

5. Contrast *Planned Parenthood* with Keith v. Daley, 764 F.2d 1265 (7th Cir.1985), in which the court upheld the denial of an application for intervention by the Illinois Pro–Life Coalition (IPC) in an action brought by several doctors to enjoin the enforcement of the Illinois Abortion Law. The court found that IPC had no interest that would justify intervention due to its opposition to abortion (id. at 1270):

> In an America whose freedom is secured by its ever vigilant guard on the openness of its "marketplace of ideas," IPC is encouraged to thrive, and to speak, lobby, promote, and persuade, so that its principles may become, if it is the will of the majority, the law of the land. Such a priceless right to free expression, however, does not also suggest that IPC has a right to intervene in every lawsuit involving abortion rights, or to forever defend statutes it helped to enact. Rule 24(a) precludes a conception of lawsuits, even "public law" suits, as necessary forums for such public policy debates.

6. In *Planned Parenthood*, the court accepted the intervenors' invocation of property values. Should possible financial losses suffice as a "significantly protectable interest?" In New Orleans Public Service, Inc. v. United Gas Pipe Line Co., 732 F.2d 452 (5th Cir.1984), the mayor of New Orleans, acting on behalf of the gas rate payers of the city, sought to intervene in a suit by the gas company against a pipe line company for refunds of alleged

overcharges under a contract between the plaintiff utility and the defendant pipe line company. Since the rate payers were not parties to this contract, the court found that they had no legal rights to enforce. Although they would be affected by the outcome of the case because the utility's costs would affect the rates charged, the court held that this economic interest in the suit was not sufficient to support intervention of right. The court noted that this was not a "public law case," as to which standing is accorded to those within the "zone of interests" intended to be protected by a statute or regulation. The appellate court also upheld the lower court's refusal to allow permissive intervention, over a spirited dissent arguing that the people affected by a significant suit involving their access to energy they must use should have a role in the case. Contrast this attitude toward the interests of nonparties with the approach in United States v. Reserve Mining Co., *infra* p. 73.

7. What happens in *Planned Parenthood* if two votes on the City Council shift and the Council rescinds the ordinance? May the intervenors continue their action? In holding that standing is required to intervene, the Seventh Circuit has emphasized that "a party cannot be forced to settle a case. An intervenor acquires the rights of a party" and, as a consequence, "intervention can impose substantial costs on the parties and the judiciary, not only by making the litigation more cumbersome but also (and more important) by blocking settlement." Solid Waste Agency v. U.S. Army Corps of Engineers, 101 F.3d 503, 507–08 (7th Cir.1996).

The Supreme Court addressed similar issues in Diamond v. Charles, 476 U.S. 54, 106 S.Ct. 1697, 90 L.Ed.2d 48 (1986), holding that an intervenor could not pursue an appeal after the principal defendant decided not to appeal further without demonstrating standing. The suit began as an action by plaintiff doctors against state officials to enjoin application of the 1975 Illinois Abortion Law as unconstitutional. Diamond, also a doctor but a foe of abortion, intervened as a defendant. After the lower courts held many parts of the statute unconstitutional, the state decided not to appeal to the Supreme Court but Diamond sought to pursue the case further himself. The Court ruled that Diamond lacked standing to litigate the legality of the abortion law because (1) one private citizen lacks a judicially cognizable interest in prosecution of another, and (2) Diamond's argument that if the law were enforced he would gain patients relied on "unadorned speculation." The court then held that the fact Diamond had already been allowed to intervene added nothing to his standing: "[A]n intervenor's right to continue a suit in the absence of the party on whose side intervention was permitted is contingent upon a showing by the intervenor that he fulfills the requirements of Art. III." Id. at 68, 106 S.Ct. at 1706. Citing *Planned Parenthood,* the Court also noted that the courts of appeals have disagreed on whether an intervenor must have standing to sue in order to intervene, but it did not resolve the issue. See id. at 69 & n. 21, 106 S.Ct. at 1707 & n. 21.

8. *Intervention for limited purpose*: The foregoing justiciability constraints on intervention may be viewed differently when a party seeks to intervene for a limited purpose and not to litigate the validity of the claim asserted by plaintiff. For example, in Sackman v. Liggett Group, 167 F.R.D. 6 (E.D.N.Y.1996), nonparty tobacco companies were allowed to intervene as of right in a smoker's personal injury action against a cigarette manufactur-

er for the limited purpose of contesting a magistrate judge's order permitting plaintiff to discover certain documents that allegedly disclosed conduct by the intervenors.

9. The requirement that an intervenor not be adequately represented by existing parties "is satisfied if the applicant shows that representation of his interest 'may be' inadequate; and the burden of making that showing should be treated as minimal." Trbovich v. United Mine Workers, 404 U.S. 528, 538 n. 10, 92 S.Ct. 630, 636 n. 10, 30 L.Ed.2d 686 (1972). However, "[w]hen the party seeking intervention has the same ultimate objective as a party to the suit, a presumption arises that its interests are adequately represented, against which the petitioner must demonstrate adversity of interest, collusion, or nonfeasance." International Tank Terminals, Limited v. M/V Acadia Forest, 579 F.2d 964, 967 (5th Cir.1978). That presumption may be hard to overcome.

In Bush v. Viterna, 740 F.2d 350 (5th Cir.1984), the Texas Association of Counties sought to intervene in a class action brought on behalf of the inmates of all 254 Texas counties against the Texas Commission on Jail Standards, alleging that the Commission had failed to perform its duties to ensure that the counties maintained constitutional jails. The court found the counties had no adverse interests from the defendant Commission. The association claimed that the result of the suit might be that the Commission would take action against certain counties and that the counties might challenge the jail standards arising out of this suit. The court found this insufficient to show adversity of interest "in this proceeding," noting that the association's proposed answer in intervention took virtually identical positions to those of the Commission. The court also upheld the denial of permissive intervention, finding that the grant of *amicus* status to the association was more appropriate than full-party status. Observing that the true concern of the association seemed to be that the commission might settle the case adversely to the counties' interests, the court stated that "the mere possibility that a party *may* at some future time enter into a settlement cannot alone show inadequate representation." See also United States v. Carpenter, 298 F.3d 1122 (9th Cir.2002) (denying intervention to environmental groups that objected to a proposed confidential settlement in a suit by the government, since the settlement did not necessarily indicate inadequate representation and the ability of the government to settle cases would be "impaired if every party that the government represents could intervene" because settlement negotiations were confidential).

10. Before the adoption of the supplemental jurisdiction statute, 28 U.S.C.A. § 1367 (see *supra* pp. 57–60, cases had held that independent jurisdictional grounds were not required for intervention of right, which was allowed under pendent or ancillary jurisdiction. See 7C C. Wright, A. Miller, & M. Kane, Federal Practice and Procedure, § 1917, at 472–81 (2d ed. 1986). When an absent party was found to be necessary, but impossible to join because diversity jurisdiction would be destroyed, and the court found that in equity and good conscience the action could proceed in its absence (see Rule 19(b)), cases held that it could intervene of right. See Wright, Miller, & Kane, *supra*, at 479–80 n. 54. This created the anomaly that a party could not be joined under Rule 19, but could intervene under Rule 24(a). Section 1367(b) eliminated this anomaly, excluding Rule 24(a) plaintiff-intervenors

to the same extent as those sought to be joined as plaintiffs under Rule 19. The House Report to § 1367 notes that "[i]f this exclusion threatened unavoidable prejudice to the interests of the prospective intervenor if the action proceeded in its absence, the district court should be more inclined not merely to deny the intervention but to dismiss the whole action for refiling in state court under criteria of Rule 19(b)." House Judiciary Committee, H.R.Rep. No. 734, 101st Cong., 2d Sess.

UNITED STATES v. RESERVE MINING CO.

United States District Court, District of Minnesota, 1972.
56 F.R.D. 408.

[Statement of facts from a later decision in the case, 498 F.2d 1073 (8th Cir.1974):

Reserve Mining Company is a jointly owned subsidiary of Armco Steel Corporation and Republic Steel Corporation which mines low-grade iron ore, called "taconite." The process involves crushing the taconite into fine granules, separating out the metallic iron with huge magnets, and flushing the residue into Lake Superior. Approximately 67,000 tons of this waste product, known as "tailings," are daily discharged into the lake.

The use of Lake Superior for this purpose was originally authorized by the State of Minnesota in 1947, and Reserve commenced operations in 1955. In granting this permit to Reserve, the State of Minnesota accepted Reserve's theory that the weight and velocity of the discharge would insure that the tailings would be deposited at a depth of approximately 900 feet in the "great trough" area of the lake, located offshore from Reserve's facility. The permit provides that:

> [T]ailings shall not be discharged ... so as to result in any material adverse effects on fish life or public water supplies or in any other material unlawful pollution of the waters of the lake....

This enforcement litigation was commenced after state and federal pollution control efforts dating from mid–1969 produced an unsuccessful series of administrative conferences and state court proceedings. On February 2, 1972, the United States Government filed a complaint alleging that Reserve's discharge of tailings into Lake Superior violated Section 13 of the 1899 Refuse Act (33 U.S.C. § 407), Section 10 of the Federal Water Pollution Control Act (33 U.S.C. § 1160), and the federal common law of public nuisance.]

Miles W. Lord, District Judge.

The Court has before it some 15 motions for intervention in this lawsuit. There are 4 applications for intervention as plaintiffs by (1) the State of Wisconsin; (2) the State of Michigan; (3) the Minnesota Environmental Law Institute, Inc., Northern Environmental Council, and Save Lake Superior Association; and (4) the Michigan Student Environmental Confederation, Inc. There are 11 applications for intervention as defendants by (1) Lake County; (2) St. Louis County; (3) the Village of

Babbitt; (4) the Village of Silver Bay; (5) the Village of Beaver Bay; (6) the Town of Beaver Bay; (7) the Lax Lake Property Owners Association; (8) the Northeastern Minnesota Development Association; (9) the Range Municipalities & Civic Association; (10) the Duluth Area Chamber of Commerce; and (11) the Silver Bay Chamber of Commerce.

The State of Wisconsin is seeking to intervene under Rule 24(b)(2), which sets out the requirements of permissive intervention. The State of Michigan is seeking to intervene both as a matter of right under Rule 24(a)(2) and permissively under Rule 24(b)(2). The environmental groups seek to intervene only as a matter of right under Rule 24(a)(2). The applicants seeking to intervene as defendants are moving for intervention under both Rule 24(a)(2) and (b)(2).

* * *

I. APPLICATIONS FOR INTERVENTION AS DEFENDANTS

Because of the similarities in the proposed answers filed by these applicants, their motions for intervention will be considered together.

A. *The Applicants Must Claim an Interest Relating to the Property or Transaction Which Is the Subject Matter of the Action*

The answers filed by the applicants indicate that they have various economic interests which are inextricably intertwined with the fate of Reserve Mining Company. To illustrate, according to the answers filed by the applicants, there are approximately 11,000 people in northeastern Minnesota who are employed either directly by Reserve Mining Company or indirectly by various area businesses and industries supporting Reserve Mining Company. Many of these people live in the villages of Silver Bay, Babbitt, Beaver Bay, and the town of Beaver Bay, and thus in St. Louis and Lake Counties. The individuals employed by Reserve Mining Company and supporting businesses and the families of those individuals are dependent upon these businesses for their livelihood. The local agencies of government are dependent upon both the individuals and Reserve Mining Company and supporting businesses for tax revenues necessary to maintain the efficient operation of local government. The other businesses are also dependent for their continued operation, in part, upon the continued operation of Reserve Mining Company. The disposition of this litigation could, therefore, have a substantial impact on local agencies of government in the area, individuals in the area, and industry and business in the area.

The question, as it appears to this Court, is whether the economic interest asserted by the applicants in their answers is a sufficient interest within the meaning of Rule 24(a)(2). This in turn depends on the construction to be given to Rule 24(a)(2). As stated by the United States Court of Appeals for the District of Columbia:

> We know of no concise yet comprehensive definition of what constitutes a litigable 'interest' for purposes of standing and intervention under Rule 24(a). One court has recently reverted to the

narrow formulation that 'interest' means a 'specific legal or equitable interest in the chose'. Toles v. United States, 371 F.2d 784 (10th Cir.1967). We think a more instructive approach is to let our construction be guided by the policies behind the 'interest' requirement. We know from the recent amendments to the civil rules that in the intervention area the 'interest' test is primarily a practical guide to disposing of lawsuits by involving as many apparently concerned persons as is compatible with efficiency and due process . . .

Nuesse v. Camp, 128 U.S.App.D.C. 172, 385 F.2d 694, 700 (1967).

Viewing the rule in this manner serves as an indication that the "interest" requirement of Rule 24(a)(2) should be viewed as a prerequisite to intervention, rather than a determinative criterion.

Beyond this, the "interest" requirement must be viewed in light of the type of case with which the Court is concerned, since Rule 24(a)(2), while designed to fit ordinary civil litigation, may "require other than literal application in atypical cases." Nuesse v. Camp, 128 U.S.App.D.C. 172, 385 F.2d 694, 700 (1967).

In an action brought under the Federal Water Pollution Control Act, 33 U.S.C. § 1160(g)(1), to secure abatement of alleged pollution, the function of the Court is set forth in, in pertinent part, 33 U.S.C. § 1160(c)(5):

> In any suit brought under the provisions of this subsection the court shall receive in evidence a transcript of the proceedings of the conference and hearing provided for in this subsection, together with the recommendations of the conference and Hearing Board and the recommendations and standards promulgated by the Secretary, and such additional evidence, including that relating to the alleged violation of the standards, as it deems necessary to a complete review of the standards and to a determination of all other issues relating to the alleged violation. The court, giving due consideration to the practicability and to the physical and economic feasibility of complying with such standards, shall have jurisdiction to enter such judgment and orders enforcing such judgment as the public interest and the equities of the case may require.

* * *

A court sitting in an abatement suit brought under subsections (g) and (c) of § 1160 must thus consider a multiplicity of factors in reaching any decision as to whether applicable water quality standards have been violated. The role of a court in such a situation, because of the nature of the proceedings and considerations which must be reviewed and undertaken pursuant to the statute, transcends ordinary civil litigation and makes a reviewing court more of an administrative tribunal than a court in an ordinary adversary civil case.

In such a case, where several factors must be weighed and considered before any final judgment is entered, and where there are several interests at stake, the court is of the opinion that the "interest" requirement in the context of this environmental case, should be viewed as an inclusionary rather than exclusionary device. In addition, because economic factors must be considered and because the Court would have discretion at trial to admit such evidence, this Court is of the opinion that the applicants' interests, within the purview of the Federal Water Pollution Control Act and Rule 24(a)(2), should be cognizable interests.

B. *Disposition of the Action May, as a Practical Matter, Impair or Impede the Ability of the Intervenors to Protect Their Interests*

Following the 1966 amendment to Rule 24(a)(2), it was no longer a requirement that an intervenor be bound by the judgment in a res judicata sense, as a prerequisite to intervention. Subsequent to the amendment the inquiry of the courts appears to have been directed toward the question of whether those interests and the ability of the applicants to protect those interests, will as a practical matter be impaired or impeded.

While any judgment entered against Reserve Mining Company would not be of res judicata effect as to the applicants, they would, as a practical matter, be foreclosed from asserting their claims or defenses if not allowed to do so in this action. Even assuming that another forum would be available in which these intervenors could protect their interests, that factor would not be dispositive. It would, perhaps, be possible for certain of the intervenors to bring subsequent lawsuits, but such hypothecation in no way guarantees an alternative forum for the intervenors. It seems clear to this Court, then, that as a practical matter the ability of the intervenors to protect their substantial economic interests would be seriously impaired or impeded if they were not allowed to intervene in this lawsuit.

C. *Inadequacy of Representation*

Because the first two requisites for intervention as of right have been met, intervention of right will be established unless it is shown that the interests of the applicants are being represented adequately by existing parties.

* * *

In addition, it need not be shown positively that representation will be inadequate. It is sufficient if it is shown that it may be inadequate. As stated by the court in Ford Motor Co. v. Bisanz Bros. Inc., 249 F.2d 22 (8th Cir.1957):

> While there is justification for a belief that the Railroad will, at a trial of this case on the merits, adequately present to the trial court all of the evidence and all of the applicable law necessary to enable the court to consider and decide the issues raised by the pleadings, including the proposed answer of the Ford Motor Company, it cannot be said with certainty that this will be so, and the

Company insists that it will not be so and that it has a special interest that the Railroad does not represent.

The Court is of the opinion that there are substantial similarities between the Bisanz case and the instant case. While Reserve Mining Company would undoubtedly put into evidence at trial the economic conditions of the northeastern Minnesota region, the Court feels that there is a substantial difference between arguments put forth by a corporation which may be only tangentially interested in those economic results, and arguments put forth by those who will be directly affected by whatever happens to Reserve Mining as a result of this litigation.

Reserve Mining has in this case as its primary concern, presumably, its ability to maintain its current operations with a certain profit margin.

* * *

The injury to which Reserve would be subjected if required to take corrective action would be, in relation to Reserve, direct. The injury to the applicants would be, however, of an indirect nature, stemming from the effect, if any, on the internal operations of Reserve. The nature of the injury which the applicants would stand to suffer, as opposed to the injury to Reserve, is thus of a different nature, even though it is similar or would arise from the same litigation. Application of this test leads this Court to the conclusion that it is possible that there would be a possibility of inadequate representation. This is all that is necessary to satisfy the "adequacy of representation" requirement of Rule 24(a)(2).

In relationship to the towns, villages, and counties which seek to intervene, there may be a conceptual problem arising out of the legitimacy of their representation of those people within their boundaries. These political entities represent all individuals within their boundaries to whom the entities are responsible for the furnishing of various governmental services. The conceptual problem arises when the interest is viewed which the United States is seeking to represent and advance. According to the complaint of the United States, Reserve Mining Company has violated the Federal Water Pollution Control Act, 33 U.S.C. § 1160. The alleged violation consists of an allegation, in part, that certain state water quality standards adopted by the State of Minnesota, with federal approval, were violated. Allowing the local agencies of government to intervene as defendants may, as a result, be a contradiction in terms. If the power of municipal corporations is viewed in terms of their legislative power, for example, it can be seen that they are without power to adopt legislation or pass ordinances in violation of a stated state policy or statute to the contrary. If the water quality standards which the Government is attempting to enforce in this action is viewed as a state policy, allowing the municipal corporations to intervene here as defendants would be to allow them to controvert that stated policy.

The Court is of the opinion that in this situation this does not present a substantial problem. In the first place, the State of Minnesota is not a party to this lawsuit. It would thus seem justifiable for the local agencies of government which are directly interested here to intervene as representatives of the individuals within their boundaries. Second, it cannot be presumed that these agencies of government have interests adverse to those of the state. While they are intervening as defendants in this case, they are attempting primarily to protect their economic interests in this lawsuit. If the State were a party it would be presumed that they would do the same. As mentioned previously, while this case may appear to be a strictly adversary proceeding, the fact that there is a statutory mandate requiring the Court to take into consideration various factors, including the economic feasibility of any judgment, makes it imperative for the Court to obtain the fullest possible factual understanding of the conditions in northeastern Minnesota before rendering any judgment. In a sense, then, the parties are advisers of the Court, as in an administrative proceeding, as well as litigants. The Court will thus not be bound by the traditional concepts of adversariness in viewing the right to local governmental agencies to intervene in this lawsuit.

The Court is of the opinion that the requirements of Rule 24(a)(2) have been met, so that the applicants' motions to intervene as defendants are granted.

II. Applications for Intervention as Plaintiffs

A. The States

1. The State of Wisconsin

The State of Wisconsin seeks permissive intervention in this action, pursuant to Rule 24(b)(2). The basis of Wisconsin's proposed complaint is that the suit is brought "in its capacity as *parens patriae* to prevent harm to its quasi-sovereign interests, as trustee over the waters of Lake Superior within her boundaries . . ." * * *

It is clear that the claim of the State of Wisconsin does have a question of fact in common with the main action, since the actions complained of by the United States are the same actions which the State of Wisconsin claims [have] resulted in a public nuisance. Additionally, there is a question of law in common, in that the United States has amended its complaint to include an additional count alleging nuisance violations. It is equally clear that there are independent jurisdictional grounds to support the claim of the State of Wisconsin. Illinois v. City of Milwaukee, 406 U.S. 91, 92 S.Ct. 1385, 31 L.Ed.2d 712 (1972).

Because of the substantial interest of the State of Wisconsin in the subject matter of this lawsuit this Court is in favor of exercising its discretion to permit intervention by the State of Wisconsin.

2. The State of Michigan

The State of Michigan seeks to intervene, both permissively under Rule 24(b)(2) and as of right, under Rule 24(a)(2). The proposed complaint of the State of Michigan alleges violations by Reserve of Minnesota WPC Regulation 15(a)(4), (c)(2); the Federal Water Pollution Control Act, 33 U.S.C. § 1160(c)(5); and the Water Refuse Act of 1899, 33 U.S.C. § 407.

From the proposed complaint filed by the State of Michigan it is quite clear to this Court that Michigan does have a substantial interest relating to the subject of this action. In its capacity as *parens patriae* the State of Michigan is charged with representation of its citizens' interests in Lake Superior, whether the interests be recreational, aesthetic, or property interests. Second, Michigan's ability to protect those interests may be impeded or impaired if she is not allowed to intervene in this lawsuit. While Michigan presumably would have an alternative forum in which to prosecute its cause of action, the possibility of a binding judgment by this Court as well as the possibility of inconsistent or excessive litigation should, as a practical matter, be considered in determining whether intervention should be allowed. Because there would be the possibility of such inconsistent litigation, even presuming the availability of an alternative forum for Michigan, the second criterion for intervention has been met. Intervention as of right will thus be granted unless it can be shown that the representation of Michigan's interests by existing parties is adequate. In this situation the Court is of the opinion that such representation *may* be inadequate, which is all that is required under Rule 24(a)(2). Michigan is representing certain interests of her citizens, which are being substantially affected by Reserve Mining's discharge into Lake Superior. While the United States in prosecuting the action may introduce into evidence the harmful effects of Reserve's discharge on the State of Michigan, this representation could, perhaps, be better undertaken by the direct representative of the people of Michigan. In such a case, where the State of Michigan seeks to intervene in her capacity as *parens patriae,* in a lawsuit where state interests are made an integral part of federal policy, and subject to enforcement by federal action, it is appropriate that the State be allowed to represent the interests which it obviously has in the lawsuit. It is thus the Court's opinion that the interests which the State of Michigan has in the subject matter of this lawsuit may not be adequately represented by existing parties. The State of Michigan is therefore entitled to intervention as of right under Rule 24(a)(2).

This Court is also of the opinion that the State of Michigan would be entitled to permissive intervention under Rule 24(b)(2). * * *

B. The Environmental Groups

1. Minnesota Environmental Law Institute, Inc., Northern Environmental Council, and Save Lake Superior Association

* * *

It appears from the moving papers of these environmental groups that they seek to represent an exceedingly broad interest, while asserting a specific method which they believe will protect that interest. The

Court's attention must be directed, therefore, to the interest asserted by the environmental groups, rather than the method asserted in protection of that interest. The interest is not an interest in on-land disposal of taconite tailings, but rather an interest of specific property owners and an interest of the members of these organizations in Lake Superior as a source of drinking water, recreation, and conservation. This is, within the context of this lawsuit, a substantial interest. Viewing this interest in light of the litigation with which the Court is faced, which is, as stated, very much akin to an administrative proceeding, leads the Court to the conclusion that a representation of those interests would be helpful to any decision reached by this Court.

The Court is thus of the opinion that, considering the type of interest asserted by the environmental groups, and the type of proceedings before the Court, the interests asserted by the environmental groups are sufficient to justify intervention as of right under Rule 24(a)(2), provided the other requirements of the rule are met.

* * * Any judgment entered by this Court, whether maintaining the status quo or forcing Reserve Mining Company to take corrective action, would be of binding force, and would leave the applicants without apparent judicial recourse to assert their claimed interests. As stated in regard to the applications for intervention as defendants, however, the availability of an alternative forum is not necessarily controlling. It should be sufficient to say that the ability of these applicants to represent their interests in the face of a final judgment by the Court or a settlement of this case, would be substantially impaired or impeded.

Since the first two requirements of Rule 24(a)(2) have been satisfied, intervention of right will be established unless it is shown that the interests of the environmental groups will be adequately represented by existing parties to the lawsuit. It is true that the environmental groups represent only a portion of Minnesota citizens interested in this lawsuit, but it is also true that the State of Minnesota is not a party to this lawsuit. This raises the possibility that the interests of the citizens of Minnesota who are represented by the environmental groups would be inadequately represented by the United States. While there may be a similarity of interests asserted between the environmental groups and the United States, the similarity does not necessarily mean that there will be adequate representation of those interests by the United States. Assuming that the end result which the United States is seeking is an abatement of pollution of Lake Superior by Reserve Mining Company, the Court must assume that there is more than one method of achieving that abatement. If the environmental groups maintain an interest in a specific form of abatement, which they feel will better protect their asserted interests, the Court should be willing to hear such evidence, if the best possible judgment is to be rendered. It must be remembered that this litigation is narrowly confined to one particular discharge, by one particular company, and that additional evidence as to alternative methods of abatement, in the event pollution should be proved, will be in the light of the alleged injury of minimal cost and inconvenience to the parties to the lawsuit, but will necessarily lead to a more informed decision by this Court on the merits of the controversy.

In addition, there may be a difference in approach between the environmental groups and the United States. The United States is charged with representing a broad public interest, and, as the Government of the people, must represent varying interests, industry as well as individuals. The Court should at least hear and make of record the views of those groups seeking to represent a more narrow interest.

The environmentalists have already been critical of the Government's failure to pray for the specific relief consisting of on-land disposal of taconite tailings. Were the Court to foreclose this line of inquiry it would leave a substantial portion of the populace and specifically the parties who are most interested, without a forum in which to assert their views. The breadth of 33 U.S.C. § 1160 should, in this Court's opinion, encompass this situation. Because of this factor, this Court is of the opinion that * * * the interests [that] the environmental applicants seek to represent might be inadequately represented by existing parties to this lawsuit. * * *

While the Court here decides that the applicants herein allowed to intervene will come "up to bat" nevertheless the number of "strikes" they will be allowed by way of introducing evidence are matters that can best be answered at a later time. Much will depend upon the actual state of the record during the trial. It is then that the Court can finally determine whether or not it would benefit by further elucidation of a particular point of view of any of the intervenors. The Court will expect and require that its orders curtailing presentations will avoid repetition.

This procedure also points out the genuine possibility that the various parties will work in unison to avoid duplication of discovery efforts and act toward an orderly and expeditious presentation of those evidentiary matters which they have in common.

2. Michigan Student Environmental Confederation, Inc.

* * *

The interests which this group seeks to represent are the same interests advanced by the other three environmental groups. [The court found that the same conclusion that these groups might not be adequately represented by the United States applied to the State of Michigan, which "may give inadequate representation to the narrow interests" asserted by the groups. It viewed intervention as supplementing, rather than usurping, the state's duties in its capacity as parens patriae.]

The motion of the Michigan Student Environmental Confederation, Inc. to intervene is therefore established as a matter of right.

Summary

In summary, the motions of all applicants for intervention in this lawsuit are granted.

In addition, to avoid unnecessary complications in the conduct of this lawsuit, the Court makes the following orders:

(1) The defendants and plaintiffs will each name a spokesman who will act as their representative during all pre-trial proceedings in this Court.

(2) For discovery purposes, each side will work in [unison] to prevent duplication of effort and unnecessary complication.

(3) The right of the parties to bring motions is not susceptible of restriction by the Court, but in all motions which the parties agree should be brought there will be a uniform presentation of such motions.

(4) The number of witnesses and types of witnesses to be called should be agreed upon, insofar as possible, by the parties, prior to trial, subject to further order of this Court.

(5) The type of evidence to be presented should, insofar as possible, be agreed upon by the parties on each side to prevent repetition.

(6) The order of production of witnesses and evidence should also be subject to agreement by the parties on each side.

(7) The United States Government and attorneys for Reserve shall act as liaison counsel and shall insofar as possible outline the basic strategy and presentation of arguments and evidence pending further refinement of procedures herein outlined.

Notes and Questions

1. It should be emphasized at the outset that Judge Lord's aggressive use of intervention in this case strains the outer limits of existing doctrine. His attitude seems to flow from his view that the case "transcends ordinary civil litigation and makes a reviewing court more of an administrative tribunal than a court in an ordinary adversary civil case," and that it is "imperative for the Court to obtain the fullest possible factual understanding of the conditions in northeastern Minnesota before rendering any judgment."

How much legal significance should the effect of the decree on the economic climate of an area usually have on the court fashioning the decree? Consider the reactions of another court to a request to modify a consent decree that required steel companies to reduce pollution by their plants:

> While we cannot help but be moved by the plight of the residents of the Mon Valley, where unemployment is high, all of the considerations put forth by the steel companies in favor of amending the consent decree are the very considerations declared by this Court in *Wheeling–Pitt I* [an earlier decision in the same case] to be insufficient to justify further delay in compliance with the Clean Air Act. As noted above, both [the steel companies'] justifications are economic in nature. And [two state legislators'] entreaties assert no more than that the state's and the Mon Valley's economic interests should prevail over the goals of the Clean Air Act. Yet, in *Wheeling–Pitt I,* we stated that the district court erred,

because it "improperly considered Wheeling's economic straits" and that "removal of pollutants from the air" was a "more compelling public interest" than "a state's economic interest."

United States v. Wheeling–Pittsburgh Steel Corp., 866 F.2d 57, 61–62 (3d Cir.1988).

2. With respect to plaintiff intervenors, does it matter whether they could have sued in their own right? Under the Federal Water Pollution Control Act involved here, they would probably not have been able to sue. What role may they play if the government reaches an agreement with Reserve to settle for entry of a consent decree? Is it consistent to allow them to intervene on the ground that they feel the government's prayer for relief is inadequate but deny them an opportunity to contest the sufficiency of a consent decree? Who else should be heard with respect to any proposed consent decree?

Intervention in governmental environmental enforcement suits has presented a number of problem cases in past years. For example, in United States v. Texas Eastern Transmission Corp., 923 F.2d 410 (5th Cir.1991), the Commonwealth of Pennsylvania tried to intervene in a federal enforcement action to press for compliance with its environmental laws. The court held that the state could not intervene of right because it did not risk sufficient impairment of its interest in enforcing its laws.

Prospective defendants can also seek a role. A recurrent problem is whether "potentially responsible parties" (PRPs) who might be held liable for cleanup expenses under the Comprehensive Environmental Response, Compensation and Liability Act (CERCLA) can intervene to contest the terms of a consent decree the governmental authorities have reached with other PRPs on the ground that the accord cuts off their rights to contribution from the settling parties. In United States v. Union Elec. Co., 64 F.3d 1152 (8th Cir.1995), the court held that PRPs could intervene, rejecting the argument that the intervenors' interests were too speculative or contingent:

The interest does not arise only after the daisy-chain of events identified here by the EPA and settling PRPs and in other decisions by other courts as including litigation against the prospective intervenors, a finding of liability against them, and assessment of excessive liability. Rather, under the terms of [CERCLA] itself, the interest arises at any time during or following litigation pursuant to [the Act] between persons who are or are potentially liable. Thus, no finding of liability is required, nor assessment of excessive liability, before the contribution interest arises. Only the recovery on a contribution claim must await the outcome of this or further litigation, not the right to bring such a claim.

Id. at 1167; compare United States v. Alcan Aluminum, Inc., 25 F.3d 1174 (3d Cir.1994) (dictum that nonsettling PRP's interest in contribution too contingent); United States v. ABC Industries, 153 F.R.D. 603 (W.D.Mich. 1993) (no protectable interest in future contribution claims). Consider the monkey wrench such intervenors could throw into the government's resolution with those it chose to sue. In State of Arizona v. Motorola, Inc., 139 F.R.D. 141 (D.Ariz.1991), the court denied intervention requests by PRPs seeking to challenge a consent decree in a CERCLA action on the ground that CERCLA favors settlement, and "[t]his risk of disproportionate liability encourages parties to resolve their liability early, lest they be found responsible for amounts not paid by settling defendants." Id. at 145. Does this view unduly strengthen the government's hand?

3. A significant use of intervention may arise when members of a class which has been certified under Rule 23(b)(3) assert their right to request exclusion from ("opt out of") the class action. In order to ensure protection of their rights, they may want to intervene directly in the class action suit or to file a separate action (which could, in turn, be consolidated with the class action suit). These matters are discussed in Chapter IV.

4. One factor bearing on the efficiency of intervention is whether the judge, with his or her supporting staff, is capable of synthesizing, digesting, and using the additional input from intervenors. Consider the comments of Brunet, A Study in the Allocation of Scarce Resources: The Efficiency of Federal Intervention Criteria, 12 Georgia L.Rev. 701, 741–42 (1978):

> [I]t would not be optimal for every judge to allow the intervention Judge Lord permitted in *United States v. Reserve Mining Co.,* an action by the government to abate the discharge of taconite into Lake Superior. The court granted intervention to four plaintiffs (Wisconsin, Michigan, and two environmental groups) and eleven defendants (four towns, two counties, two regional development associations, two chambers of commerce, and a property owners' association). [Asking how a particular judge might, or might not, benefit from additional input resulting from intervention] yields valuable information about an efficient intervention policy:
>
> (1) The intervention norm should require an intervention petition to explain the nature and amount of input that the intervenor would inject if the court allowed intervention. Without this data the court cannot evaluate the productivity potential of the information;
>
> (2) Court systems should assign those judges having the greatest scale economies to the cases which involve the largest infusion of information from intervention;
>
> (3) The intervention rules should have sufficient flexibility to permit individual judges to deny intervention if it would provide input which would be counterproductive.

5. Intervention requires "a timely application." Rule 24(a)(2). Stallworth v. Monsanto Co., 558 F.2d 257 (5th Cir.1977), set out four factors for judging timeliness: a) time the intervenor knew or should have known of its interest in the case, b) prejudice to existing parties resulting from the delay in seeking intervention, c) prejudice to the intervenor if intervention is denied, and d) unusual circumstances militating for or against a finding of timeliness.

Regarding when an intervenor should have known of her interest, United Airlines, Inc. v. McDonald, 432 U.S. 385, 97 S.Ct. 2464, 53 L.Ed.2d 423 (1977), found intervention timely when the intervenor, alleging sex discrimination, learned the plaintiffs would not appeal denial of class certification, as that was "as soon as it became clear" that her interests were no longer protected by the class representatives.

Concerning prejudice to existing parties, Garrity v. Gallen, 697 F.2d 452 (1st Cir.1983), found intervention of school districts and an association into a suit challenging conditions at a state mental institution untimely because it would delay relief to the plaintiff class and compel defendant to expend more public resources to defend its stand against the new intervenors. But *Stallworth* emphasized that delay and additional cost must arise from the delay in seeking intervention and not merely from the accommodation of additional intervening parties.

Regarding prejudice to the intervenor, Lelsz v. Kavanagh, 710 F.2d 1040 (5th Cir.1983), found untimely an attempt by a parent association for the retarded to intervene six years after suit was filed by a class of mentally retarded residents against state institutions so it could argue for a different remedy, concluding, *inter alia,* that given the late date, inadequacy of representation was not clear.

6. Note the limitations Judge Lord placed on the intervenors in *Reserve Mining*. How can such limitations be placed on persons who are entitled to intervene "of right"? Consider Stringfellow v. Concerned Neighbors in Action, 480 U.S. 370, 107 S.Ct. 1177, 94 L.Ed.2d 389 (1987). Respondent neighborhood association sought to intervene in an action brought by the United States and the State of California concerning the Stringfellow Acid Pits, an abandoned hazardous waste disposal site in California. The trial court denied intervention of right but allowed permissive intervention that was limited in the following ways: (1) Intervenors could not assert a claim for relief that was not already raised because that would "expand an already complex litigation, and could jeopardize the possibility of settlement"; (2) Intervenors could not seek a share of the government's recovery of clean-up costs; (3) Intervenors could not file motions or discovery without first conferring with all the litigants and obtaining permission from at least one of the other parties. In the process of holding that the order was not appealable, the Court rejected arguments that the district court's limitations were so onerous that they amounted to complete denial of intervention. Concurring, Justice Brennan observed that "restrictions on participation may also be placed on an intervenor of right and on an original party."

Compare Columbus–America Discovery Group v. Atlantic Mut. Ins. Co., 974 F.2d 450 (4th Cir.1992), an action between the discoverer of a shipwreck and the insurers who had paid claims for the lost cargo. Three days before trial was to begin, other potential salvors who claimed plaintiff had improperly used their study of the ocean floor to find the wreck sought to intervene seeking a share of plaintiff's recovery. Although the intervenors had delayed in seeking intervention, the judge allowed them to intervene but denied them any discovery, insisting that the trial go forward as scheduled. After plaintiff defeated their claims, a divided court of appeals held that it was improper to impose conditions on intervenors of right and questioned the Advisory Committee Note to Rule 24 that authorized conditions on intervenors of right. Id. at 469–70. A dissenting judge emphasized that the intervenors had no excuse for waiting so long to join the case, and that the district judge had allowed them some discovery while the trial was underway. See also 7C Federal Practice & Procedure § 1922 (questioning propriety of limitations on intervenors of right).

D. CONSEQUENCES OF FAILURE TO JOIN

MARTIN v. WILKS

Supreme Court of the United States, 1989.
490 U.S. 755, 109 S.Ct. 2180, 104 L.Ed.2d 835.

CHIEF JUSTICE REHNQUIST delivered the opinion of the Court.

A group of white firefighters sued the City of Birmingham, Alabama (City) and the Jefferson County Personnel Board (Board) alleging that they were being denied promotions in favor of less qualified black firefighters. They claimed that the City and the Board were making promotion decisions on the basis of race in reliance on certain consent decrees, and that these decisions constituted impermissible racial discrimination in violation of the Constitution and federal statute. The District Court held that the white firefighters were precluded from challenging employment decisions taken pursuant to the decrees, even though these firefighters had not been parties to the proceedings in which the decrees were entered. We think this holding contravenes the general rule that a person cannot be deprived of his legal rights in a proceeding to which he is not a party.

The litigation in which the consent decrees were entered began in 1974, when the Ensley Branch of the NAACP and seven black individuals filed separate class-action complaints against the City and the Board. They alleged that both had engaged in racially discriminatory hiring and promotion practices in various public service jobs in violation of Title VII of the Civil Rights Act of 1964, 42 U.S.C. § 2000e *et seq.,* and other federal law. After a bench trial on some issues, but before judgment, the parties entered into two consent decrees, one between the black individuals and the City and the other between them and the Board. These proposed decrees set forth an extensive remedial scheme, including long-term and interim annual goals for the hiring of blacks as firefighters. The decrees also provided for goals for promotion of blacks within the department.

The District Court entered an order provisionally approving the decrees and directing publication of notice of the upcoming fairness hearings. Notice of the hearings, with a reference to the general nature of the decrees, was published in two local newspapers. At that hearing, the Birmingham Firefighters Association (BFA) appeared and filed objections as *amicus curiae.* After the hearing, but before final approval of the decrees, the BFA and two of its members also moved to intervene on the ground that the decrees would adversely affect their rights. The District Court denied the motions as untimely and approved the decrees. Seven white firefighters, all members of the BFA, then filed a complaint against the City and the Board seeking injunctive relief against enforcement of the decrees. The seven argued that the decrees would operate to illegally discriminate against them; the District Court denied relief.

Both the denial of intervention and the denial of injunctive relief were affirmed on appeal. The District Court had not abused its discretion in refusing to let the BFA intervene, thought the Eleventh Circuit, in part because the firefighters could "institut[e] an independent Title VII suit, asserting specific violations of their rights." And, for the same reason, petitioners had not adequately shown the potential for irreparable harm from the operation of the decrees necessary to obtain injunctive relief.

A new group of white firefighters, the *Wilks* respondents, then brought suit against the City and the Board in district court. They too alleged that, because of their race, they were being denied promotions in favor of less qualified blacks in violation of federal law. The Board and the City admitted to making race conscious employment decisions, but argued the decisions were unassailable because they were made pursuant to the consent decrees. A group of black individuals, the *Martin* petitioners, were allowed to intervene in their individual capacities to defend the decrees.

The defendants moved to dismiss the reverse discrimination cases as impermissible collateral attacks on the consent decrees. The District Court denied the motions, ruling that the decrees would provide a defense to claims of discrimination for employment decisions "mandated" by the decrees, leaving the principal issue for trial whether the challenged promotions were indeed required by the decrees. After trial the District Court granted the motion to dismiss. The court concluded that "if in fact the City was required to [make promotions of blacks] by the consent decree, then they would not be guilty of [illegal] racial discrimination" and that the defendants had "establish[ed] that the promotions of the black individuals ... were in fact required by the terms of the consent decree."

On appeal, the Eleventh Circuit reversed. It held that "[b]ecause ... [the *Wilks* respondents] were neither parties nor privies to the consent decrees, ... their independent claims of unlawful discrimination are not precluded." *In re Birmingham Reverse Discrimination Employment Litigation,* 833 F.2d 1492, 1498 (1987). The court explicitly rejected the doctrine of "impermissible collateral attack" espoused by other courts of appeals to immunize parties to a consent decree from charges of discrimination by nonparties for actions taken pursuant to the decree. Although it recognized a "strong public policy in favor of voluntary affirmative action plans," the panel acknowledged that this interest "must yield to the policy against requiring third parties to submit to bargains in which their interests were either ignored or sacrificed." The court remanded the case for trial of the discrimination claims, suggesting that the operative law for judging the consent decrees was that governing voluntary affirmative-action plans.

We granted certiorari, and now affirm the Eleventh Circuit's judgment. All agree that "[i]t is a principle of general application in anglo-American jurisprudence that one is not bound by a judgment *in person-*

am in a litigation in which he is not designated as a party or to which he has not been made a party by service of process." *Hansberry v. Lee,* 311 U.S. 32, 40 (1940). This rule is part of our "deep-rooted historic tradition that everyone should have his own day in court." 18 C. Wright, A. Miller & E. Cooper, Federal Practice and Procedure § 4449, p. 417 (1981). A judgment or decree among parties to a lawsuit resolves issues as among them, but it does not conclude the rights of strangers to those proceedings.[2]

Petitioners argue that, because respondents failed to timely intervene in the initial proceedings, their current challenge to actions taken under the consent decree constitutes an impermissible "collateral attack." They argue that respondents were aware that the underlying suit might affect them and if they chose to pass up an opportunity to intervene, they should not be permitted to later litigate the issues in a new action. The position has sufficient appeal to have commanded the approval of the great majority of the federal courts of appeals, but we agree with the contrary view expressed by the Court of Appeals for the Eleventh Circuit in this case.

We begin with the words of Justice Brandeis in *Chase National Bank v. Norwalk,* 291 U.S. 431 (1934):

> "The law does not impose upon any person absolutely entitled to a hearing the burden of voluntary intervention in a suit to which he is a stranger.... Unless duly summoned to appear in a legal proceeding, a person not a privy may rest assured that a judgment recovered therein will not affect his legal rights."

While these words were written before the adoption of the Federal Rules of Civil Procedure, we think the Rules incorporate the same principle; a party seeking a judgment binding on another cannot obligate that person to intervene; he must be joined. Against the background of permissive intervention set forth in *Chase National Bank,* the drafters cast Rule 24, governing intervention, in permissive terms. See Fed.Rule Civ.Proc. 24(a) (intervention as of right) ("[u]pon timely application anyone shall be permitted to intervene"); Fed.Rule Civ.Proc. 24(b) (permissive intervention) ("[u]pon timely application anyone may be permitted to intervene"). They determined that the concern for finality and completeness of judgments would be "better [served] by mandatory joinder procedures." Accordingly, Rule 19(a) provides for mandatory joinder in cir-

---

2. We have recognized an exception to the general rule when, in certain limited circumstances, a person, although not a party, has his interests adequately represented by someone with the same interests who is a party. See *Hansberry v. Lee,* 311 U.S. 32, 41–42 (1940) ("class" or "representative" suits); Fed.Rule Civ.Proc. 23 (same); *Montana v. United States,* 440 U.S. 147, 154–155 (1979) (control of litigation on behalf of one of the parties in the litigation). Additionally, where a special remedial scheme exists expressly foreclosing successive litigation by nonlitigants, as for example in bankruptcy or probate, legal proceedings may terminate preexisting rights if the scheme is otherwise consistent with due process. See *NLRB v. Bildisco & Bildisco,* 465 U.S. 513, 529–530, n. 10 (1984) ("proof of claim must be presented to the Bankruptcy Court ... or be lost"); Tulsa Professional Collection Services, Inc. v. Pope, 485 U.S. 478 (1988) (nonclaim statute terminating unsubmitted claims against the estate). Neither of these exceptions applies, however, in this case.

cumstances where a judgment rendered in the absence of a person may "leave ... persons already parties subject to a substantial risk of incurring ... inconsistent obligations...." Rule 19(b) sets forth the factors to be considered by a court in deciding whether to allow an action to proceed in the absence of an interested party.

Joinder as a party, rather than knowledge of a lawsuit and an opportunity to intervene, is the method by which potential parties are subjected to the jurisdiction of the court and bound by a judgment or decree.[6] The parties to a lawsuit presumably know better than anyone else the nature and scope of relief sought in the action, and at whose expense such relief might be granted. It makes sense, therefore, to place on them a burden of bringing in additional parties where such a step is indicated, rather than placing on potential additional parties a duty to intervene when they acquire knowledge of the lawsuit. The linchpin of the "impermissible collateral attack" doctrine—the attribution of preclusive effect to a failure to intervene—is therefore quite inconsistent with Rule 19 and Rule 24.

Petitioners argue that our decisions in *Penn–Central Merger & N & W Inclusion Cases,* 389 U.S. 486 (1968) and *Provident Tradesmens Bank & Trust Co. v. Patterson,* 390 U.S. 102 (1968) suggest an opposite result. The *Penn–Central* litigation took place in a special statutory framework enacted by Congress to allow reorganization of a huge railway system. Primary jurisdiction was in the Interstate Commerce Commission, with very restricted review in a statutory three-judge district court. Review proceedings were channeled to the District Court for the Southern District of New York, and proceedings in other district courts were stayed. The District Court upheld the decision of the Interstate Commerce Commission in both the merger and the inclusion proceedings, and the parties to that proceeding appealed to this Court. Certain Pennsylvania litigants had sued in the District Court for the Middle District of Pennsylvania to set aside the Commission's order, and this action was stayed pending the decision in the District Court for the Southern District of New York. We held that the borough of Moosic, one of the Pennsylvania litigants, could not challenge the Commission's approval of the merger and inclusion in the Pennsylvania District Court, pointing out the unusual nationwide character of the action and saying "[i]n these circumstances, it would be senseless to permit parties seeking to challenge the merger and the inclusion orders to bring numerous suits in many different district courts."

---

6. The dissent argues on the one hand that respondents have not been "bound" by the decree but rather, that they are only suffering practical adverse effects from the consent decree. On the other hand, the dissent characterizes respondents' suit not as an assertion of their own independent rights, but as a collateral attack on the consent decree which, it is said, can only proceed on very limited grounds. Respondents in their suit have alleged that they are being racially discriminated against by their employer in violation of Title VII: either the fact that the disputed employment decisions are being made pursuant to a consent decree is a defense to respondents' Title VII claims or it is not. If it is a defense to challenges to employment practices which would otherwise violate Title VII, it is very difficult to see why respondents are not being "bound" by the decree.

We do not think that this holding in *Penn–Central,* based as it was upon the extraordinary nature of the proceedings challenging the merger of giant railroads and not even mentioning Rule 19 or Rule 24, affords a guide to the interpretation of the rules relating to joinder and intervention in ordinary civil actions in a district court.

Petitioners also rely on our decision in *Provident Bank, supra,* as authority for the view which they espouse. In that case we discussed Rule 19 shortly after parts of it had been substantially revised, but we expressly left open the question of whether preclusive effect might be attributed to a failure to intervene.

Petitioners contend that a different result should be reached because the need to join affected parties will be burdensome and ultimately discouraging to civil rights litigation. Potential adverse claimants may be numerous and difficult to identify; if they are not joined, the possibility for inconsistent judgments exists. Judicial resources will be needlessly consumed in relitigation of the same question.

Even if we were wholly persuaded by these arguments as a matter of policy, acceptance of them would require a rewriting rather than an interpretation of the relevant Rules. But we are not persuaded that their acceptance would lead to a more satisfactory method of handling cases like this one. It must be remembered that the alternatives are a duty to intervene based on knowledge, on the one hand, and some form of joinder, as the Rules presently provide, on the other. No one can seriously contend that an employer might successfully defend against a Title VII claim by one group of employees on the ground that its actions were required by an earlier decree entered in a suit brought against it by another, if the later group did not have adequate notice or knowledge of the earlier suit.

The difficulties petitioners foresee in identifying those who could be adversely affected by a decree granting broad remedial relief are undoubtedly present, but they arise from the nature of the relief sought and not because of any choice between mandatory intervention and joinder. Rule 19's provisions for joining interested parties are designed to accommodate the sort of complexities that may arise from a decree affecting numerous people in various ways. We doubt that a mandatory intervention rule would be any less awkward. As mentioned, plaintiffs who seek the aid of the courts to alter existing employment policies, or the employer who might be subject to conflicting decrees, are best able to bear the burden of designating those who would be adversely affected if plaintiffs prevail; these parties will generally have a better understanding of the scope of likely relief than employees who are not named but might be affected. Petitioners' alternative does not eliminate the need for, or difficulty of, identifying persons who, because of their interests, should be included in a lawsuit. It merely shifts that responsibility to less able shoulders.

Nor do we think that the system of joinder called for by the Rules is likely to produce more relitigation of issues than the converse rule. The breadth of a lawsuit and concomitant relief may be at least partially shaped in advance through Rule 19 to avoid needless clashes with future litigation. And even under a regime of mandatory intervention, parties who did not have adequate knowledge of the suit would relitigate issues. Additional questions about the adequacy and timeliness of knowledge would inevitably crop up. We think that the system of joinder presently contemplated by the Rules best serves the many interests involved in the run of litigated cases, including cases like the present one.

Petitioners also urge that the congressional policy favoring voluntary settlement of employment discrimination claims, referred to in cases such as *Carson v. American Brands, Inc.,* 450 U.S. 79 (1981), also supports the "impermissible collateral attack" doctrine. But once again it is essential to note just what is meant by "voluntary settlement." A voluntary settlement in the form of a consent decree between one group of employees and their employer cannot possibly "settle," voluntarily or otherwise, the conflicting claims of another group of employees who do not join in the agreement. This is true even if the second group of employees is a party to the litigation:

> "[P]arties who choose to resolve litigation through settlement may not dispose of the claims of a third party ... without that party's agreement. A court's approval of a consent decree between some of the parties therefore cannot dispose of the valid claims of nonconsenting intervenors." *Firefighters v. Cleveland,* 478 U.S. 501, 529, 106 S.Ct. 3063, 92 L.Ed.2d 405 (1986).

Insofar as the argument is bottomed on the idea that it may be easier to settle claims among a disparate group of affected persons if they are all before the Court, joinder bids fair to accomplish that result as well as a regime of mandatory intervention.

For the foregoing reasons we affirm the decision of the Court of Appeals for the Eleventh Circuit. That court remanded the case for trial of the reverse discrimination claims. *Birmingham Reverse Discrimination,* 833 F.2d, at 1500–1502. Petitioners point to language in the District Court's findings of fact and conclusions of law which suggests that respondents will not prevail on the merits. We agree with the view of the Court of Appeals, however, that the proceedings in the District Court may have been affected by the mistaken view that respondents' claims on the merits were barred to the extent they were inconsistent with the consent decree.

Affirmed.

JUSTICE STEVENS, with whom JUSTICE BRENNAN, JUSTICE MARSHALL, and JUSTICE BLACKMUN join, dissenting.

As a matter of law there is a vast difference between persons who are actual parties to litigation and persons who merely have the kind of interest that may as a practical matter be impaired by the outcome of a case. Persons in the first category have a right to participate in a trial and to appeal from an adverse judgment; depending on whether they win or lose, their legal rights may be enhanced or impaired. Persons in the latter category have a right to intervene in the action in a timely fashion, or they may be joined as parties against their will. But if they remain on the sidelines, they may be harmed as a practical matter even though their legal rights are unaffected. One of the disadvantages of sideline-sitting is that the bystander has no right to appeal from a judgment no matter how harmful it may be.

In this case the Court quite rightly concludes that the white fire-fighters who brought the second series of Title VII cases could not be deprived of their legal rights in the first series of cases because they had neither intervened nor been joined as parties. See *Parklane Hosiery Co. v. Shore,* 439 U.S. 322, 327, n. 7 (1979). The consent decrees obviously could not deprive them of any contractual rights, such as seniority or accrued vacation pay, or of any other legal rights, such as the right to have their employer comply with federal statutes like Title VII.[4] There is no reason, however, why the consent decrees might not produce changes in conditions at the white firefighters' place of employment that, as a practical matter, may have a serious effect on their opportunities for employment or promotion even though they are not bound by the decrees in any legal sense. The fact that one of the effects of a decree is to curtail the job opportunities of nonparties does not mean that the nonparties have been deprived of legal rights or that they have standing to appeal from that decree without becoming parties.

Persons who have no right to appeal from a final judgment—either because the time to appeal has elapsed or because they never became parties to the case—may nevertheless collaterally attack a judgment on certain narrow grounds. If the court had no jurisdiction over the subject matter, or if the judgment is the product of corruption, duress, fraud, collusion, or mistake, under limited circumstances it may be set aside in an appropriate collateral proceeding. See Restatement (Second) of Judgments §§ 69–72 (1982); *Griffith v. Bank of New York,* 147 F.2d 899, 901 (CA2) (Clark, J.), cert. denied, 325 U.S. 874 (1945). This rule not only applies to parties to the original action, but also allows interested third

---

4. As Chief Justice Rehnquist has observed:

"Suppose, for example, that the Government sues a private corporation for alleged violations of the antitrust laws and then enters a consent decree. Surely, the existence of that decree does not preclude a future suit by another corporation alleging that the defendant company's conduct, even if authorized by the decree, constitutes an antitrust violation. The nonparty has an independent right to bring his own private antitrust action for treble damages or for injunctive relief. See 2 P. Areeda & D. Turner, Antitrust Law ¶ 330, p. 143 (1978). Similarly, if an action alleging unconstitutional prison conditions results in a consent decree, a prisoner subsequently harmed by prison conditions is not precluded from bringing suit on the mere plea that the conditions are in accordance with the consent decree. Such compliance might be relevant to a defense of good-faith immunity, but it would not suffice to block the suit altogether." *Ashley v. City of Jackson,* 464 U.S. 900, 902 (1983) (opinion dissenting from denial of certiorari).

In suggesting that compliance with a consent decree might be relevant to a defense of good-faith immunity, this passage recognizes that neither due process nor the Rules of Civil Procedure foreclose judicial recognition of a judgment that may have a practical effect on the interests of a nonparty.

parties collaterally to attack judgments. In both civil and criminal cases, however, the grounds that may be invoked to support a collateral attack are much more limited than those that may be asserted as error on direct appeal. Thus, a person who can foresee that a lawsuit is likely to have a practical impact on his interests may pay a heavy price if he elects to sit on the sidelines instead of intervening and taking the risk that his legal rights will be impaired.

In this case there is no dispute about the fact that the respondents are not parties to the consent decrees. It follows as a matter of course that they are not bound by those decrees. Those judgments could not, and did not, deprive them of any legal rights. The judgments did, however, have a practical impact on respondents' opportunities for advancement in their profession. For that reason, respondents had standing to challenge the validity of the decrees, but the grounds that they may advance in support of a collateral challenge are much more limited than would be allowed if they were parties prosecuting a direct appeal.[8]

The District Court's rulings in this case have been described incorrectly by both the Court of Appeals and this Court. The Court of Appeals repeatedly stated that the District Court had "in effect" held that the white firefighters were "bound" by a decree to which they were not parties. And this Court's opinion seems to assume that the District Court had interpreted its consent decrees in the earlier litigation as holding "that the white firefighters were precluded from challenging employment decisions taken pursuant to the decrees." It is important, therefore, to make clear exactly what the District Court did hold and why its judgment should be affirmed.

I

[Justice Stevens described the prior proceedings, including two trials in 1976 and 1979 and the fairness hearing on the consent decrees to which notice was given "to all interested persons" and at which "a group of white firefighters—represented in part by the Birmingham Firefighters Association (BFA)—opposed any race-conscious relief." He

---

8. The Eleventh Circuit, in a decision involving a previous attempt by white firefighters to set aside the consent decrees at issue in this litigation, itself observed: "There are ... limitations on the extent to which a nonparty can undermine a prior judgment. A nonparty may not reopen the case and relitigate the merits anew; neither may he destroy the validity of the judgment between the parties." *United States v. Jefferson County,* 720 F.2d 1511, 1518 (1983). Professors James and Hazard describe the rule as follows:

"Ordinarily, a nonparty has no legal interest in a judgment in an action between others. Such a judgment does not determine the nonparty's rights and obli-

gations under the rules of res judicata and he may so assert if the judgment is relied upon against him. But in some situations one's interests, particularly in one's own personal legal status or claims to property, may be placed in practical jeopardy by a judgment between others. In such circumstances one may seek the aid of a court of equity, but *the grounds upon which one may rely are severely limited.* The general rule is that one must show either that the judgment was void for lack of jurisdiction of the subject matter or that it was the product of fraud directed at the petitioner." James & Hazard, Civil Procedure § 12.15, p. 681 (emphasis supplied).

cited findings in the lower court that "the record provided 'more than ample reason' to conclude that the City would eventually be held liable for discrimination against blacks (who constituted only 49 out of 480 police officers, 3 of 131 sergeants, and none of the 40 lieutenants, captains and battalion chiefs). When, several months after the decrees were entered, a group of white firefighters sued, the lower court, after an evidentiary hearing, found "without merit" their claims that promotions of blacks were contrary to the decrees and that the decrees were illegal and void. While an appeal was pending, the Wilks plaintiffs filed another suit alleging violations of Title VII. After a five-day trial, the lower court ruled orally that "a valid consent decree appropriately limited can be the basis for a defense against a charge of discrimination, even in the situation in which it is clear that the defendant in the litigation did act in a racially conscious manner." The district judge also found that the city had not promoted black officers who were unqualified or were demonstrably less qualified than whites who were not promoted, and concluded that the city had carried its burden of showing that "the promotions of the black individuals in this case were in fact required by the terms of the consent decrees."]

The written conclusions of law that he adopted are less clear than his oral opinion. He began by unequivocally stating: "The City Decree is lawful." He explained that "under all the relevant case law of the Eleventh Circuit and the Supreme Court, it is a proper remedial device, designed to overcome the effects of prior, illegal discrimination by the City of Birmingham." In that same conclusion, however, he did state that "plaintiffs cannot collaterally attack the Decree's validity." Yet, when read in context—and particularly in light of the court's finding that the decree was lawful under Eleventh Circuit and Supreme Court precedent—it is readily apparent that, at the extreme, this was intended as an alternative holding. More likely, it was an overstatement of the rule that collateral review is narrower in scope than appellate review. In any event, and regardless of one's reading of this lone sentence, it is absolutely clear that the court did not hold that respondents were bound by the decree. Nowhere in the District Court's lengthy findings of fact and conclusions of law is there a single word suggesting that respondents were bound by the consent decree or that the court intended to treat them as though they had been actual parties to that litigation and not merely as persons whose interests, as a practical matter, had been affected. Indeed, respondents, the Court of Appeals, and the majority opinion all fail to draw attention to any point in this case's long history at which the judge may have given the impression that any nonparty was legally bound by the consent decree.[20]

20. In Provident Tradesmens Bank & Trust Co. v. Patterson, 390 U.S., at 114, we expressly did not decide whether a litigant might "be bound by [a] previous decision because, although technically a nonparty, he had purposely bypassed an adequate opportunity to intervene." Today, the Court answers this question, at least in the limited context of the instant dispute, holding that "[j]oinder as a party [under Fed.Rule Civ.Proc. 19], rather than knowledge of a lawsuit and an opportunity to intervene [under Fed.Rule Civ.Proc. 24], is the method by which potential parties are subjected

II

Regardless of whether the white firefighters were parties to the decrees granting relief to their black co-workers, it would be quite wrong to assume that they could never collaterally attack such a decree. If a litigant has standing, he or she can always collaterally attack a judgment for certain narrowly defined defects. On the other hand, a district court is not required to retry a case—or to sit in review of another court's judgment—every time an interested nonparty asserts that *some* error that might have been raised on direct appeal was committed. Such a broad allowance of collateral review would destroy the integrity of litigated judgments, would lead to an abundance of vexatious litigation, and would subvert the interest in comity between courts. Here, respondents have offered no circumstance that might justify reopening the District Court's settled judgment.

The implementation of a consent decree affecting the interests of a multitude of nonparties, and the reliance on that decree as a defense to a charge of discrimination in hiring and promotion decisions, raise a legitimate concern of collusion. No such allegation, however, has been raised. Moreover, there is compelling evidence that the decree was not collusive. In its decision approving the consent decree over the objection of the BFA and individual white firefighters, the District Court observed that there had been "no contention or suggestion" that the decrees were fraudulent or collusive. The record of the fairness hearing was made part of the record of this litigation and this finding was not contradicted. More significantly, the consent decrees were not negotiated until after the 1976 trial and the court's finding that the City had discriminated against black candidates for jobs as police officers and firefighters, and until after the 1979 trial, at which substantial evidence was presented suggesting that the City also discriminated against black candidates for promotion in the fire department. Like the record of the 1981 fairness hearing, the records of both of these prior proceedings were made part of the record in this case. Given this history, the lack of any indication of collusion, and the District Court's finding that "there is more than ample reason for ... the City of Birmingham to be concerned that [it] would be in time held liable for discrimination against blacks at higher level positions in the police and fire departments," it is evident that the decree was a product of genuine arm's-length negotiations.

Nor can it be maintained that the consent judgment is subject to reopening and further litigation because the relief it afforded was so out of line with settled legal doctrine that it "was transparently invalid or had only a frivolous pretense to validity." *Walker v. Birmingham,* 388 U.S. 307, 315 (1967) (suggesting that a contemnor might be allowed to challenge contempt citation on ground that underlying court order was "transparently invalid"). To the contrary, the type of race-conscious

to the jurisdiction of the court and bound by a judgment or decree." Because I conclude that the District Court did not hold that respondents were bound by the consent decrees, I do not reach this issue.

relief ordered in the consent decree is entirely consistent with this Court's approach to affirmative action. Given a sufficient predicate of racial discrimination, neither the Equal Protection Clause of the Fourteenth Amendment nor Title VII of the Civil Rights Act of 1964 erects a bar to affirmative action plans that benefit nonvictims and have some adverse effect on non-wrongdoers. * * *

Hence, there is no basis for collaterally attacking the judgment as collusive, fraudulent, or transparently invalid. Moreover, respondents do not claim—nor has there been any showing of—mistake, duress, or lack of jurisdiction. Instead, respondents are left to argue that somewhat different relief would have been more appropriate than the relief that was actually granted. Although this sort of issue may provide the basis for a direct appeal, it cannot, and should not, serve to open the door to relitigation of a settled judgment.

III

The facts that respondents are not bound by the decree and that they have no basis for a collateral attack, moreover, do not compel the conclusion that the District Court should have treated the decree as nonexistent for purposes of respondents' discrimination suit. That the decree may not directly interfere with any of the respondents' legal rights does not mean that it may not affect the factual setting in a way that negates respondents' claim. The fact that a criminal suspect is not a party to the issuance of a search warrant does not imply that the presence of a facially valid warrant may not be taken as evidence that the police acted in good faith. Similarly, the fact that an employer is acting under court compulsion may be evidence that the employer is acting in good faith and without discriminatory intent. Indeed, the threat of a contempt citation provides as good a reason to act as most, if not all, other business justifications.

After reviewing the evidence, the District Court found that the City had in fact acted under compulsion of the consent decree. Based on this finding, the court concluded that the City carried its burden of coming forward with a legitimate business reason for its promotion policy, and, accordingly, held that the promotion decisions were "not taken with the requisite discriminatory intent" necessary to make out a claim of disparate treatment under Title VII or the Equal Protection Clause. For this reason, and not because it thought that respondents were legally bound by the consent decree, the court entered an order in favor of the City and defendant-intervenors.

Of course, in some contexts a plaintiff might be able to demonstrate that reference to a consent decree is pretextual. For example, a plaintiff might be able to show that the consent decree was collusive and that the defendants simply obtained the court's rubber stamp on a private agreement that was in no way related to the eradication of pervasive racial discrimination. The plaintiff, alternatively, might be able to show that the defendants were not bound to obey the consent decree because the court that entered it was without jurisdiction. See *United States v. Mine Workers,* 330 U.S. 258, 291–294 (1947). Similarly, although more tenuous, a plaintiff might argue that the parties to the consent judgment were not bound because the order was "transparently invalid" and thus unenforceable. If the defendants were as a result not bound to implement the affirmative-action program, then the plaintiff might be able to show that the racial preference was not a product of the court order.

In a case such as this, however, in which there has been no showing that the decree was collusive, fraudulent, transparently invalid, or entered without jurisdiction, it would be "unconscionable" to conclude that obedience to an order remedying a Title VII violation could subject a defendant to additional liability. Rather, all of the reasons that support the Court's view that a police officer should not generally be held liable when he carries out the commands in a facially valid warrant apply with added force to city officials, or indeed to private employers, who obey the commands contained in a decree entered by a federal court. In fact, Equal Employment Opportunity Commission regulations concur in this assessment. They assert, "[t]he Commission interprets Title VII to mean that actions taken pursuant to the direction of a Court Order cannot give rise to liability under Title VII." 29 CFR § 1608.8 (1989).[30] Assuming that the District Court's findings of fact were not clearly erroneous—which of course is a matter that is not before us—it seems perfectly clear that its judgment should have been affirmed. Any other conclusion would subject large employers who seek to comply with the law by remedying past discrimination to a never-ending stream of litigation and potential liability. It is unfathomable that either Title VII or the Equal Protection Clause demands such a counter-productive result.

IV

The predecessor to this litigation was brought to change a pattern of hiring and promotion practices that had discriminated against black citizens in Birmingham for decades. The white respondents in this case are not responsible for that history of discrimination, but they are nevertheless beneficiaries of the discriminatory practices that the litigation was designed to correct. Any remedy that seeks to create employment conditions that would have obtained if there had been no violations of law will necessarily have an adverse impact on whites, who must now share their job and promotion opportunities with blacks.[31] Just as white employees in the past were innocent beneficiaries of illegal discriminatory practices, so is it inevitable that some of the same white employees

---

30. Section 1608.8 does not differentiate between orders "entered by consent or after contested litigation." 29 CFR § 1608.8 (1989). Indeed, the reasoning in the Court's opinion today would seem equally applicable to litigated orders and consent decrees.

31. It is inevitable that nonminority employees or applicants will be less well off under an affirmative action plan than without it, no matter what form it takes. For example, even when an employer simply agrees to recruit minority job applicants more actively, white applicants suffer the "nebulous" harm of facing increased competition and the diminished likelihood of eventually being hired.

will be innocent victims who must share some of the burdens resulting from the redress of the past wrongs.

There is nothing unusual about the fact that litigation between adverse parties may, as a practical matter, seriously impair the interests of third persons who elect to sit on the sidelines. Indeed, in complex litigation this Court has squarely held that a sideline-sitter may be bound as firmly as an actual party if he had adequate notice and a fair opportunity to intervene and if the judicial interest in finality is sufficiently strong. See *Penn–Central Merger and N & W Inclusion Cases,* 389 U.S. 486, 505–506 (1968).

There is no need, however, to go that far in order to agree with the District Court's eminently sensible view that compliance with the terms of a valid decree remedying violations of Title VII cannot itself violate that statute or the Equal Protection Clause.[32] The City of Birmingham, in entering into and complying with this decree, has made a substantial step toward the eradication of the long history of pervasive racial discrimination that has plagued its fire department. The District Court, after conducting a trial and carefully considering respondents' arguments, concluded that this effort is lawful and should go forward. Because respondents have thus already had their day in court and have failed to carry their burden, I would vacate the judgment of the Court of Appeals and remand for further proceedings consistent with this opinion.

Notes and Questions

1. *Epilogue on Martin v. Wilks*: Litigation concerning Birmingham's affirmative action plans continued after the above decision by the Supreme Court. On remand in Martin v. Wilks, the district judge rejected plaintiffs' challenges, but the appellate court ruled for the white males on key points in their challenges to actions taken pursuant to the consent decree. In re Birmingham Reverse Discrimination Employment Litig., 20 F.3d 1525 (11th Cir.1994). In particular, the appellate court criticized the provision setting the objective that 50% of promotions be to blacks, even though there were very few black firefighters, as an "arbitrary fixed quota. * * * Because non-black firefighters bear the entire burden of the race-based fire lieutenant promotion remedy in the decree, and because of the immediate and future ramifications of that burden, it is imperative that the remedy be related in some reasonable manner to the representation of blacks among firefighters." Id. at 1542–43.

---

32. In professing difficulty in understanding why respondents are not "bound" by a decree that provides a defense to employment practices that would otherwise violate Title VII, see [majority opinion] n. 6, the Court uses the word "bound" in a sense that is different from that used earlier in its opinion. A judgment against an employer requiring it to institute a seniority system may provide the employer with a defense to employment practices that would otherwise violate Title VII. In the sense in which the word "bound" is used in the cases cited by the Court [earlier in its opinion], only the parties to the litigation would be "bound" by the judgment. But employees who first worked for the company 180 days after the litigation ended would be "bound" by the judgment in the sense that the Court uses when it responds to my argument. The cases on which the Court relies are entirely consistent with my position. Its facile use of the word "bound" should not be allowed to conceal the obvious flaws in its analysis.

Meanwhile, litigation in the original suit also continued when the district judge allowed plaintiffs in Martin v. Wilks to intervene for the limited purpose of arguing for modification of the decree. After the district court made some modifications, but rejected the more aggressive arguments for dismantling the decree, a different panel of the court of appeals found several aspects of the decree's preferential treatment of blacks and women in city employment unconstitutional. Ensley Branch, N.A.A.C.P. v. Seibels, 20 F.3d 1489 (11th Cir.1994). The court of appeals found changed circumstances due to a "falling constitutional ceiling" on such provisions since 1981, when the decree was originally entered. Id. at 1504. It concluded that no showing of a compelling governmental interest justifying affirmative action had been made with regard to any city jobs except those in the fire and police departments. This opinion was later withdrawn, and a decision requiring reconsideration of race-based remedies outside the police and fire departments substituted. Ensley Branch, N.A.A.C.P. v. Seibels, 31 F.3d 1548 (11th Cir.1994).

2.   Martin v. Wilks was one of a number of controversial employment discrimination decisions during the Court's 1988 Term that caused a significant public controversy. Reflect on the impact of the decision on issues you have considered elsewhere in this chapter. For example, does the decision indicate that in Eldredge v. Carpenters 46 Northern California Counties JATC (*supra* p. 45) the male apprentices should have been treated as necessary parties?

3.   In 1991 Congress passed, and the President signed, the Civil Rights Act of 1991. Among the provisions of that Act was an amendment to Title VII, now codified at 42 U.S.C.A. § 2000e–2(n)(1), to provide that "an employment practice that implements and is within the scope of a litigated or consent judgment or order that resolves a claim of employment discrimination under the Constitution or Federal civil rights laws may not be challenged * * * in a claim under the Constitution or Federal civil rights laws":

(i) by a person who, prior to the entry of the judgment or order * * * had—

(I) actual notice of the proposed judgment or order sufficient to apprise such person that such judgment or order might adversely affect the interests and legal rights of such person and that an opportunity was available to present objections to such judgment or order by a future date certain; and

(II) a reasonable opportunity to present objections to such judgment or order; or

(ii) by a person whose interests were adequately represented by another person who had previously challenged the judgment or order on the same legal grounds and with a similar factual situation, unless there has been an intervening change in law or fact.

What impact would this provision have had on the issues raised in Martin v. Wilks and on the application of Rules 19 and 24 in employment discrimination suits brought in the future? Does the statute create the equivalent of "mandatory intervention"? For discussion of the statute, see Catania &

Sullivan, Judging Judgments: The 1991 Civil Rights Act and the Lingering Ghost of Martin v. Wilks, 57 Brooklyn L. Rev. 995 (1992). Note that the act only applies to consent decrees arising in an employment discrimination case. See Wilson v. Minor, 220 F.3d 1297 (11th Cir.2000) (voters who had not sought intervention could file an independent action challenging an injunction issued to remedy a Voting Rights Act violation).

4.   The 1991 Act does not alter the standards for intervention under Rule 24. Edwards v. City of Houston, 78 F.3d 983 (5th Cir.1996), involved a situation similar to that in Martin v. Wilks: African–American and Hispanic–American police officers sued the city, challenging promotional examinations as having a disproportional effect on their racial groups. Groups representing white, female, and Asian–American police officers moved to intervene to contest a proposed consent decree. The court denied intervention as untimely, but permitted the groups to participate in the fairness hearing on the proposed decree. The Fifth Circuit reversed, finding the motion to intervene timely. It pointed out that the 1991 Act had no application as it only dealt with the situation where a nonparty files a subsequent suit collaterally attacking a decree. Here the nonparties simply appealed the denial of intervention. Six dissenting judges would have found the motion to intervene untimely as it came long after all officers had been notified of the suit and three months after the intervenors had received a copy of the proposed settlement. Is the standard for "actual notice" in the Act the same as the standard for timeliness under Rule 24?

5.   In Martin v. Wilks the Court rejects the idea that parties can be required to intervene in order to protect their rights. Does the dissent disagree? Could a party who intervenes be worse off as a result? Consider whether the Martin v. Wilks respondents would have been allowed to make the claims they made in the second suit had they been allowed to intervene in the first action. The United States, which was a party plaintiff in the first suit, joined the plaintiff white firefighters in the second suit. It was held to be collaterally estopped from attacking the consent decree. In re Birmingham Reverse Discrimination Employment Litigation, 833 F.2d 1492, 1501 (11th Cir.1987).

In Independent Federation of Flight Attendants v. Zipes, 491 U.S. 754, 109 S.Ct. 2732, 105 L.Ed.2d 639 (1989), the Court removed one impediment to intervention in Title VII cases by holding that intervenors who unsuccessfully oppose affirmative action decrees sought by Title VII plaintiffs may not be held liable to plaintiffs for the fees they incur resisting intervenors' arguments. The majority emphasized that "[a]n intervenor of the sort before us here is particularly welcome, since we have stressed the necessity of protecting, in Title VII litigation, 'the legitimate expectations of . . . employees innocent of any wrongdoing.'" The Court went on to reason that imposing fee liability on intervenors would "foster piecemeal litigation of complex civil rights controversies—a result that is strongly disfavored." Although unwilling to require intervention, the Court does appear to favor it.

6.   Would a rule forbidding collateral attack on employment discrimination decrees be constitutional? One commentator has concluded that "an unstated premise of the majority's holding is that the due process rights of

the white firefighters necessarily would be violated by giving binding effect to a judgment in a proceeding in which they had not been joined formally as parties either under Rule 19 or 24." Strickler, Martin v. Wilks, 64 Tulane L.Rev. 1557 (1990); see also Issacharoff, When Substance Mandates Procedure—Martin v. Wilks and the Rights of Vested Incumbents in Consent Decrees, 77 Cornell L. Rev. 189 (1992) (emphasizing protected property interests of incumbent public employees). Professor Kramer has argued, however, that with meaningful notice and the sort of opportunity to intervene that Rule 24 affords, such a requirement could be constitutional. See Kramer, Consent Decrees and the Rights of Third Parties, 87 Mich.L.Rev. 321, 338–52 (1988). Would it have been constitutional to foreclose challenge in Martin v. Wilks?

7. When white firefighters did seek to intervene in the first action in Martin v. Wilks their application was rejected by the district court as untimely. Was this proper? "In a title VII suit * * * the remedy can take many forms: damages for back pay, retroactive seniority rights, and even special consideration for future promotions. Because the precise mix of these measures remains unclear until the parties settle or the judge issues a final order, outsiders cannot assess the threat a suit poses to their interests until late in the proceedings." Note, The Supreme Court—Leading Cases, 103 Harv.L.Rev. 310, 314–15 (1989). Are employment discrimination suits really different from other kinds of suits? Compare United States v. Reserve Mining Co., *supra* p. 73. How could the intervenors on the defense side in that case know whether the court's decree really threatened their interests without knowing the terms of the decree?

In Martin v. Wilks, there may have been substantial grounds for uncertainty about the contours of any eventual decree. After prevailing in part on liability, plaintiffs in the original case had a substantial claim for back pay, estimated by some as high as $5 million, but they were more interested in affirmative action in the future than money for the past. The city administration had by then changed, and the consent decree was negotiated by the city's first black mayor. The decree required the city to pay only $300,000, and the mayor stated that it was "the best business deal we had ever struck." See Taylor, Second Class Citizens, American Lawyer, Sept. 1989, at 42. For an argument that consent decrees present inherent risks that the parties to the negotiation will make a deal to maximize their interests at the expense of third parties who are not participating, see Laycock, Consent Decrees Without Consent: The Rights of Nonconsenting Third Parties, 1987 U.Chi.Legal F. 103.

8. Note that the African American plaintiffs from the first action were allowed to intervene in the second action. Were they intervenors of right? What interest did they have in the suit alleging violation of the rights of white firefighters?

9. The dissent emphasizes the difference between impairing the legal rights of third parties and the way in which the outcome of the first litigation might "as a practical matter, seriously impair the interests of third parties who elect to sit on the sidelines." Does the majority disagree with this reasoning? How does the dissent's view compare to the treatment of Rule 19 and Rule 24 proposed by the majority? Recall that both those rules

speak in terms of practical effects on the interests of nonparties, not legal rights of nonparties.

10.   An undercurrent in this case involves difficult problems presented in remedying employment discrimination. This difficulty has affected the handling of a number of procedural issues. In general, there have been debates (not always firmly resolved by the Supreme Court) about the extent to which race conscious remedies (i.e., affirmative action) can be used in cases where there has been no proof of past violations, and the extent to which the remedy must benefit only individuals who have been directly harmed by such discrimination. Much of the dissent is accordingly directed toward establishing that the decree entered in the earlier case was permissible under those cases. To what extent should that issue matter to the questions presented in Martin v. Wilks?

11.   How important is the fact that the first litigation was resolved by a consent decree? There is real concern that in such a situation the parties to the litigation may sacrifice the interests of others who are not involved as the easiest way to compromise their own differences. See Laycock, Consent Decrees Without Consent: The Rights of Nonconsenting Third Parties, 1987 U.Chi.L.Forum 103; Mengler, Consent Decree Paradigms: Models Without Meaning, 29 B.C.L.Rev. 291 (1988). Do these concerns explain the majority's decision?

The dissent points out that in this case the district court had already found that the city had discriminated illegally in making hiring decisions, and had held a trial on whether it had discriminated in promotion as well, indicating that it felt there was a likelihood plaintiffs would prevail on that as well. If there had been no settlement, would an identical decree entered after a finding of discrimination in promotions have altered the majority's reasoning in Martin v. Wilks? To put this question in context, note that "litigated" decrees often involve substantial negotiation between the parties prompted by the court. The reason for this situation is that the court needs detailed input and proposals from the parties to fashion a remedy where the relief that is appropriate does not flow inexorably from the finding of a violation but depends instead on myriad details about the operation of a fairly complicated institution. Does this situation provide support for the "Let everyone join in" attitude toward intervention displayed by Judge Lord in United States v. Reserve Mining Co., *supra* p. 73.

12.   If plaintiffs in the first action had made the white firefighters parties, as the Court says Rule 19 mandated, should they have been added as defendants? What claim could plaintiffs have asserted against them? Cf. Davenport v. International Bhd. of Teamsters, 166 F.3d 356, 366 (D.C.Cir. 1999) ("[W]hile Rule 19 provides for joinder of necessary parties, it does not create a cause of action against them. It is not enough that plaintiffs 'need' an injunction against [their employer] in order to obtain full relief. They must also have a right to such an injunction, and Rule 19 cannot provide such a right").

Chapter III

DISPOSITION OF DUPLICATIVE
OR RELATED LITIGATION

Litigation may be called complex because of the joinder of multiple parties, the difficulty of the issues involved, or the volume of discovery and evidence necessitating substantial court administration. Sometimes, however, cases take on complexities by virtue of their relationship to other cases. Although filed separately, cases can be so clearly related that they should be looked at as part of the same piece of litigation. If such cases are tried separately without considering their relationship to other pending litigation, the objective of just and efficient resolution of disputes may be frustrated. Allowing separate cases between the same parties on the same or similar issues to proceed independently is not only wasteful, but encourages parties to forum shop and to try to obtain an advantage by multiple litigation of the same matters. Even when separate cases have only some of the same parties or issues, separate litigation can be wasteful and can result in inconsistent or conflicting determinations, leading to uncertainty as to what has been decided and as to the impact of judgments in other suits. Thus, the Manual for Complex Litigation (4th) § 20 (2004) observes that "[c]ontrol over the proliferation of cases and coordination of multiple claims is crucial to effective management of complex litigation."

Duplicative litigation is the simultaneous prosecution of two or more suits in which some of the parties or issues are so closely related that the judgment in one will necessarily have a res judicata effect on the other. See Note, Federal Court Stays and Dismissals in Deference to Parallel State Court Proceedings, 44 U.Chi.L.Rev. 641 (1977). Sometimes the terms "parallel proceedings" and "exercise of concurrent jurisdiction" are also used to describe this situation. Three basic types of duplicative litigation have been identified—(1) multiple suits on the same claim by the same plaintiff against the same defendant ("repetitive" suits), (2) a separate suit filed by a defendant to the first action against the plaintiff to the first action, seeking a declaratory judgment that it is not liable under the conditions of the first action or asserting an affirmative claim that arises out of the same transaction or occurrence as the subject matter of the first action ("reactive" suits), and (3) separate actions by class members on the same cause of action raised in the class action, seeking to represent the same or a similar class (this last category will be discussed in the next chapter on class actions). See Vestal, Reactive Litigation, 47 Iowa L.Rev. 11 (1961); Vestal, Repetitive Litigation, 45 Iowa L.Rev. 525 (1960). Under the third category, there may also be "overlapping class actions," that is, class actions filed in a number of courts, either federal or state, against the same (or some of the same) defendants, concerning the same matter, on behalf of classes with some of the same class members. Problems arising in this situation are addressed in Chapter IV.

Apart from strictly duplicative litigation, there are also many situations in which separate suits involve similar parties or issues, but res judicata will not apply. Examples are separate suits by different plaintiffs against the same defendant arising out of the same or a similar cause of action; separate suits involving some of the same and some different parties, having some of the same or similar causes of action; and separate suits by different parties litigating claims to the same rights, property, or *res*. These cases—which we will refer to as *related litigation*—raise somewhat different considerations than duplicative litigation, although some of the same concerns as to efficiency and economy, consistency in outcome, effective judicial administration, and (where applicable) avoidance of friction between state and federal courts arise in both.

When duplicative or related litigation takes place entirely within the federal court system, the principal concerns are efficiency, economy, and justice. However, when there are dual state and federal proceedings, issues of federalism also arise. We will first consider the simpler all-federal context in which the techniques of judicial management have increasingly been brought to bear in the interests of efficiency and economy, and then turn to the more difficult state-federal context. Finally, because it has increasing importance, we conclude with an examination of the power of a bankruptcy court to gather litigation before it.

A. MULTIPLE PROCEEDINGS IN FEDERAL COURT

1. STAY ORDERS OR INJUNCTIONS AGAINST PROSECUTION OF SUITS IN OTHER FEDERAL COURTS

WILLIAM GLUCKIN & CO. v. INTERNATIONAL PLAYTEX CORP.

United States Court of Appeals, Second Circuit, 1969.
407 F.2d 177.

Before MOORE, SMITH and HAYS, CIRCUIT JUDGES.

MOORE, CIRCUIT JUDGE.

International Playtex Corporation (Playtex) appeals from an order entered in the District Court for the Southern District of New York granting a preliminary injunction which restrains Playtex from further prosecuting a patent infringement suit pending in the United States District Court for the Northern District of Georgia until final disposition of the instant case. The underlying suit here in the Southern District of New York was brought by William Gluckin & Co. (Gluckin) against Playtex for a declaration of patent invalidity and/or non-infringement.

Involved here are two patent infringement suits and the question is which takes priority over the other. The first-commenced action was instituted by the patent holder against the customer of an allegedly infringing manufacturer in the Northern District of Georgia. The second action is a declaratory judgment suit against the patent holder in the Southern District of New York.

On April 25, 1968, Playtex brought a patent infringement action against F.W. Woolworth & Co. (Woolworth), alleging in its complaint that Woolworth was selling a brassiere which infringed a patent which it owned. The action was instituted in the Northern District of Georgia ostensibly because Woolworth was selling the allegedly infringing brassiere at its store in Gainesville, Georgia. Playtex, a Delaware corporation, has three of its five manufacturing plants located in Georgia. Its principal place of business is in New York. Woolworth is a New York corporation, with its principal place of business there, and operates retail stores throughout the nation.

The manufacturer of the challenged brassiere sold by Woolworth is Gluckin, a New York corporation with its principal place of business in New York City. It is not licensed to do business in Georgia and, apparently, not subject to suit there. On May 28, 1968, after Playtex had filed its Georgia action, Gluckin brought a declaratory judgment action for patent invalidity and non-infringement against Playtex in the Southern District of New York.

On July 2, 1968, a preliminary injunction was issued by Judge Motley restraining Playtex from further prosecuting the Georgia suit. Judge Motley held that since the first filed suit was against a customer rather than against Gluckin itself and since New York was the most convenient forum for resolving the questions of patent validity and infringement, special circumstances existed which justified giving priority to the second-filed suit.

The general rule in this Circuit is that, as a principle of sound judicial administration, the first suit should have priority, "absent the showing of balance of convenience in favor of the second action." Mattel, Inc. v. Louis Marx & Co., 353 F.2d 421, 423 (2d Cir.1965), petition for cert. dismissed, 384 U.S. 948, 86 S.Ct. 1475, 16 L.Ed.2d 546 (1966), or unless there are special circumstances which justify giving priority to the second. In deciding between competing jurisdictions, it has often been stated that the balancing of convenience should be left to the sound discretion of the district courts. Kerotest Mfg. Co. v. C–O–Two Fire Equipment Co., 342 U.S. 180, 183, 72 S.Ct. 219, 96 L.Ed. 200 (1952).

In *Mattel,* supra, two situations were posed which are said to constitute special circumstances justifying a departure from the "first-filed" rule of priority. The first example is the so-called "customer action" where the first-filed suit is against a customer of the alleged infringer while the second suit involves the infringer himself.

The second example is where forum shopping alone motivated the choice of the situs for the first suit. This, however, is not applicable to the present case because Judge Motley made no specific finding of forum shopping, nor is one inferable and because the reasons Playtex asserts justifying the choice of a Georgia forum are not wholly frivolous.

Judge Motley, relying on the "customer suit" exception to the first-filed rule mentioned in the *Mattel* case, granted the preliminary injunction. Playtex insists, however, that there is no reason why the first suit should be enjoined simply because the defendant happens to be a customer rather than a manufacturer. Section 271 of Title 35 declares manufacturing, using or selling infringing products actionable. Each act is identified as an act of infringement and each is proscribed. 35 U.S.C. § 281. Since Woolworth allegedly has itself "sold thousands of dollars of the infringing merchandise" and is "an infringer of the patent in suit every bit as much as the manufacturer of the infringing article," Playtex argues that it has the statutory right as a patentee to sue an infringing seller.

Playtex asserts, therefore, that before the first-filed suit can be enjoined, there must be a finding of harassment, probable harassment or forum shopping. Moreover, to rely on a "natural theatre" test as the District Court did, is said to be making an application of *forum non conveniens* which is not sanctioned by the statute.

In response Gluckin argues that the manufacturer of allegedly infringing goods is the real party in interest in the event his customer is charged with infringement of patents and this principle lies at the basis of judicial restraint on customer actions. Under the direction of the Supreme Court in *Kerotest,* where it was stated:

> Wise judicial administration, giving regard to conservation of judicial resources and comprehensive disposition of litigation, does not counsel rigid mechanical solution of such problems. The factors relevant to wise administration here are equitable in nature. Necessarily, an ample degree of discretion, appropriate for disciplined and experienced judges, must be left to the lower courts,

lower courts have properly exercised a broad degree of discretion in implementing this basic doctrine.

An inflexible approach to suits of this type is certainly to be avoided. Although the so-called "customer suit" exception to the first-filed rule appears to be in conflict with a flexible approach, as Playtex contends, we nonetheless feel that the issuance of the preliminary injunction in this case was not an abuse of discretion.

This Court, in *Mattel,* stated:

We believe it to be a sound rule that the issues should be tried in the district where suit is first brought unless there are other factors of substance which support the exercise of the court's discretion that *the balance of convenience* is in favor of proceeding first in another district.

Judge Motley found that there were factors of substance indicating that the balance of convenience supported priority for the second-filed suit. The Court noted that (1) since Woolworth is simply a customer of Gluckin and upon whom Woolworth must rely exclusively, the primary party is really Gluckin; (2) the Woolworth employee who has the most knowledge concerning the allegedly infringing item is the Woolworth buyer in New York City; (3) no one connected with Woolworth in Gainesville where the first suit was filed, has any knowledge concerning the patent in suit; (4) the allegedly infringing manufacturer Gluckin is a New York corporation with its main offices in New York City; (5) Gluckin is not licensed to do business in Georgia; (6) the package in which the article is sold by Woolworth is designed, made and supplied by Gluckin, as are all the promotional materials; (7) arrangements for the purchase of the article were negotiated in New York City; (8) Gluckin's manufacturing plants are located in Pennsylvania and its design facility in New York City; (9) it sells and distributes its products to customers nationwide; (10) Playtex, though a Delaware corporation, has its main office and principal place of business in New York City and its design centers in New Jersey; (11) its marketing and purchasing activities are located in New York; (12) the alleged inventor of the Playtex brassiere at issue resides in New Jersey; (13) Playtex's records relating to the invention are in New York City and Georgia; and (14) witnesses who have knowledge of the patent reside in and about New York City.

The reasons for which Playtex chose Gainesville, Georgia, as the place of suit are assertedly (1) because of the location of three of its five plants in that State, (2) because the alleged infringement took place there, and (3) because of the possibility of an earlier trial date in the Northern District of Georgia. It also claims that some of its employees in its Georgia plants will be important witnesses in the action there and that their unique knowledge of the manufacturing process is important to that infringement suit. Playtex contends further that it brought suit in Georgia because of the economic interest in defendant and its employees in Georgia in preserving the substantial volume of business of defendant's patented product.

Judge Motley found Playtex's reasons for bringing suit against Woolworth in Georgia "not very persuasive."

The "whole of the war and all the parties to it" are in the Southern District of New York. Woolworth, the defendant in the Georgia action, has consented to be made a party here and is amenable to process here as well. All the litigants involved have offices and principal places of business in New York City. Most of the witnesses whose testimony is relevant reside in the New York City area. Woolworth must look to Gluckin to supply evidence in its defense in the Georgia action. All counsel are from New York and the convenience of the major witnesses would unquestionably be better served by a New York venue.

Balancing the convenience of the parties and witnesses and with due regard to the weight given to the initial forum, a judgment that the Georgia suit should be restrained in order that the New York suit may proceed does not appear to be at all unreasonable.

Notes and Questions

1.   Could Woolworth have made a Rule 19 objection in Georgia because Gluckin was not a party to that case? Consider the following reasoning from another context:

> At the root of the preference for a manufacturer's declaratory judgment action is the recognition that, in reality, the manufacturer is the true defendant in the customer suit. * * * [I]t is a simple fact of life that a manufacturer must protect its customers, either as a matter of contract, or good business, or in order to avoid the damaging impact of an adverse ruling against its products.

Codex Corp. v. Milgo Electronic Corp., 553 F.2d 735, 737–38 (1st Cir.1977).

2.   Why should the first suit generally have priority? Usually such duplicative litigation is reactive—the defendant in the first suit is filing suit in another court after being sued. In such cases, isn't it reasonable to preserve the first plaintiff's victory in the race to the courthouse in the absence of countervailing considerations like those in *Gluckin*?

3.   A preliminary injunction requiring or forbidding conduct is a forceful remedy that may effectively moot the rest of the lawsuit. Rule 65(a) thus provides that the court may consolidate the application for a preliminary injunction with the hearing on the merits. Whether or not the court does that, the party seeking the injunction normally must show that it is likely to prevail on the merits and that it will suffer irreparable injury unless granted the injunction. See generally Leubsdorf, The Standard for Preliminary Injunctions, 91 Harv.L.Rev. 525 (1978). Rather than focus on such issues, in *Gluckin* the court invokes concepts of "wise judicial administration." With respect to injunctions against the pursuit of collateral litigation, do these concerns supplant the traditional standards for a preliminary injunction?

4.   Rather than seek an injunction, a party involved in duplicative litigation can seek relief from the court in which it does not want to litigate. Specifically, it can ask that court to stay proceedings or to transfer the case to the court in which the other suit is pending under 28 U.S.C. § 1404(a). On the transfer motion, it is likely to make arguments about forum shopping and convenience to the witnesses similar to those considered in *Gluckin*. Would transfer (discussed in greater detail *infra* at p. 128) be preferable to a stay because it would allow both cases to go forward under coordinated judicial handling? If one court refuses to transfer, should that decision affect

the other court's ruling on a motion to enjoin prosecution of the untransferred case?

In ACF Industries, Inc. v. Guinn, 384 F.2d 15 (5th Cir.1967), also a duplicative patent infringement case, one trial judge entered a stay, but, when the case was reassigned, the new judge vacated the stay and denied a transfer motion. The Court of Appeals granted a writ of mandamus, holding that the second judge had abused his discretion. It found the denial of the transfer motion unimportant since "[a] stay order has virtually the same effect, and is granted for practically the same reasons that motivate a court in granting a transfer motion."

SEMMES MOTORS, INC. v. FORD MOTOR CO.

United States Court of Appeals, Second Circuit, 1970.
429 F.2d 1197.

Before WATERMAN, FRIENDLY and FEINBERG, CIRCUIT JUDGES.

FRIENDLY, CIRCUIT JUDGE.

This heated controversy, which at this early stage has already produced four and a half printed pages of docket entries in the District Court for the Southern District of New York, not to speak of those in a related action in the District Court for New Jersey, is between defendant Ford Motor Company and plaintiff Semmes Motors, Inc., Ford's dealer in the plush suburb of Scarsdale, N.Y., since 1949. Federal jurisdiction is predicated both on diverse citizenship and on the Federal Dealer Act, 15 U.S.C. §§ 1221–1225. Part of the acrimony is doubtless due to the fact that William A. Semmes, president of Semmes Motors, has taken an active part in the formation of Ford Dealers Alliance, Inc., a New Jersey corporation joining as a plaintiff, whose "main purpose," as stated in the complaint, "is the protection of dealers from abuse of the franchise system run by" Ford. Semmes considers Ford's termination of his dealership to be a retaliation for these activities and an endeavor to supplant him with a dealership in which Ford would have a financial stake; Ford rejoins that activities on behalf of dealers, however proper, cannot protect against the consequences of what it characterizes as fraud. We affirm the temporary injunction issued by Judge Ryan as being within the discretion afforded him, but order that further proceedings be stayed pending termination of the New Jersey litigation.

* * *

Although there had been a considerable history of dissatisfaction by Ford with Semmes' warranty refund claims, the kick-off for the present fight was an apparently routine letter, dated July 25, 1969, from S.J. Obringer, Ford's New York District Sales Manager, to Semmes. This announced that in accordance with Company policy, Ford auditors would call on him, would "examine warranty claims and their related dealership records, inspect repaired units and may possibly contact customers for whom you have performed warranty work." It continued that the auditors would bring to Semmes' attention "any opportunities they find for improving warranty administration at your dealership," that the audit findings would be discussed with him, and that claims determined to have been improper might be charged back.

The audit was conducted from August 4 through 28; its results were embodied in a report submitted to Semmes on September 18. Not stating the number of claims examined or the period covered, the report found that 253 claims submitted by Semmes for refund, with a price tag of $10,440, were defective. The most serious were 86 claims, aggregating $4,691, where the auditors found that work for which reimbursement had been obtained had not been performed at all. Fifty of these were determined by visual inspection of vehicles that had come in during the audit, presumably for some other cause; the inspectors reported that 87% "of the inspectable units checked had work not performed." The other 36 claims were ascertained in the course of questioning "during telephone contacts made in the form of an owner satisfaction survey." Despite these seemingly serious findings, the auditors' recommendations were rather bland: Semmes should consider appointing a shop foreman, and there should be better control of the return of defective parts, of the recording of mechanics' time, and of the status of repairs in the shop.

The auditors' insistence on contacting customers led the Alliance and Semmes to file, on August 22, 1969, a complaint in a New Jersey state court, later removed by Ford to the District Court for New Jersey, seeking an injunction against such contacts. However, no application for interlocutory relief was then made.[5] The New Jersey action came to the attention of Robert W. Scott, an Associate Counsel in Ford's main office in Dearborn, Michigan. Learning of the results of the audit, Scott decided that Ford would have to consider making a counterclaim for false and fraudulent refund claims and also terminating Semmes' dealership.

On the afternoon of October 7, Ford's New York counsel informed Scott that plaintiffs' New York attorneys had advised them of an intention to file in the Southern District of New York an action on behalf of Semmes and the Alliance substantially identical to the New Jersey action and to seek a temporary restraining order similar to that which had been there refused, see fn. 5. Ford countered by moving on October 8 in the New Jersey action to dismiss Alliance's claim and filing an answer and counterclaim with respect to Semmes. On the same day Judge Ryan, in the Southern District of New York, declined to issue a temporary restraining order against customer contacts pending a hearing on a temporary injunction on October 14.

Meanwhile Scott had been discussing termination of Semmes' dealership with Ford officials in Dearborn, in part, according to him, because of a view that failure to take this step would cast doubt on the sincerity of Ford's counterclaim for fraud. On October 8, a termination notice was signed by the Secretary of Ford and sent to the New York District Sales

---

5. On September 24 Judge Coolahan, in the District Court for New Jersey, declined to issue a temporary restraining order with respect to Ford's investigation.

Office. The next morning Scott cleared this with L.A. Iacocca, Ford's Executive Vice President, and service was made that afternoon. As a result, plaintiffs sought and obtained leave to amend their complaint and their request for a temporary injunction in the Southern District to include the termination of Semmes' dealership.

* * *

On November 5, Judge Ryan issued an opinion in which he denied the motion for a stay of the New York action, limited Ford's contacts with Semmes' customers although not to the extent sought by Semmes, and temporarily enjoined termination of the dealership. An injunction order was entered on December 15. * * *

We must deal at the outset with Ford's contention that the court erred in refusing to stay the New York action until the earlier New Jersey suit had been determined. Since the action was equitable in nature, the denial of the stay would not itself be appealable under 28 U.S.C. § 1292(a)(1) as the denial of an injunction.

When the New York complaint was filed, it was in effect a duplicate of that in New Jersey, although the scope of the New Jersey action had been enlarged by Ford's counterclaim to recover warranty refunds allegedly obtained by Semmes through fraud. Later the New York action was broadened to include Semmes' claim to enjoin termination of the dealership. However, F.R.Civ.P. 13(a) required Semmes to file as a counterclaim in the New Jersey action any claim it had against Ford "at the time of serving the pleading," if the claim arose "out of the transaction or occurrence that is the subject matter of the opposing party's claim." Here "the pleading" was the reply, which was required, F.R.Civ.P. 7(a), to be filed within 20 days after October 8, the very day when Semmes' claim of unlawful termination came into being. This clearly "arose out of the same transaction or occurrence" as Ford's counterclaim.

* * * The New Jersey court therefore should be deemed seized of this claim as well. Semmes' attempted distinction of our holding to substantially that effect in *National Equipment [Rental, Ltd. v. Fowler]*, 287 F.2d at 46 n. 2 [(2d Cir.1961)], on the basis that we were there dealing with a defendant's rather than a plaintiff's failure to file a compulsory counterclaim, is unpersuasive for the reasons stated.

Given this situation, there is no doubt that the New Jersey court could properly have enjoined prosecution of the New York action if Ford had sought this, and might even have been bound to do so. Instead Ford addressed its argument to the New York court. But we can see no reason why the end result should be different when the party seeking to preserve the primacy of the first court moves the second court to stay its hand rather than asking the first court to enjoin prosecution of the second case. Whatever the procedure, the first suit should have priority, "absent the showing of balance of convenience in favor of the second action." See Mattel, Inc. v. Louis Marx & Co., 353 F.2d 421, 424 (2d Cir.1965), where we not only reversed an injunction against prosecution of the first action in New Jersey but ordered a stay of the later action in New York.

We recognize that the instant case differs from the more usual situation where, at least in substance, the plaintiff in the first court is the defendant in the second and *vice versa.* In such instances the plaintiff in the first court is vigorously pressing his desire to proceed in an appropriate forum of his choice and objecting to the defendant's thwarting this by a later suit elsewhere. Here the same party is plaintiff in both actions, prefers to press the second, and has stipulated to discontinue the first if defendant will consent.[7] While Ford's fears of parallel litigation in two courts could be stilled if it were willing to consent to plaintiffs' discontinuing the New Jersey Action, and Ford has no vested right to be proceeded against in the New Jersey rather than the New York federal court, these factors alone are insufficient grounds for departing from the general rule that in the absence of sound reasons the second action should give way to the first.

To begin with, any exception for cases where the same party is plaintiff in both actions would entail the danger that plaintiffs may engage in forum shopping or, more accurately, judge shopping. When they see a storm brewing in the first court, they may try to weigh anchor and set sail for the hopefully more favorable waters of another district. The sequence of events here affords some indication that Semmes might have been attempting to do just that, see fn. 5. The defendant is then put to the Hobson's choice of either going along with this ploy by agreeing to dismissal of the first action if the plaintiff is willing or having to defend two lawsuits at the same time. If he makes the latter election, as is his right, not only the parties but the courts pay a heavy price. "Courts already heavily burdened with litigation with which they must of necessity deal should ... not be called upon to duplicate each other's work in cases involving the same issues and the same parties." Hence, even when the same party is plaintiff in both actions, the instances where the second court should go forward despite the protests of a party to the first action where full justice can be done, should be rare indeed.

We find no considerations sufficient to justify an exception to the general rule in this case. It is true that if we were free to look at the situation in a vacuum, New York is a more logical forum than New Jersey. The cause of action "arose" here, Semmes relies in part on a New York statute, and witnesses from Scarsdale and from Ford's New York office would find it more convenient to come to Foley Square than to Newark. However, these factors must be weighed in the setting created by Semmes' having initiated litigation in New Jersey and the likelihood that failure to stay the New York action will result in

7. Because of Ford's counterclaim the New Jersey court could not dismiss the entire action on plaintiffs' motion even if it were more disposed to do so than it seems to be. F.R.Civ.P. 41(a)(2). Although the pur-pose of this provision was doubtless to prevent a plaintiff's escaping from a counterclaim and that possibility is here precluded by the New York action, the language of the Rule is unqualified.

litigation in two courts[8]—a danger the judge recognized when he made his "denial of the stay subject to further developments in the two actions and further order of the Court." We thus see little force in his observation that the New Jersey action had been pending only a short time; the potential of future waste and conflict exists nonetheless unless Ford consents to dismissal. With respect to the elements favoring New York, the inconvenience to witnesses is exceedingly slight, as Judge Coolahan pointed out in denying a motion by the plaintiffs to transfer the New Jersey action to New York, and the Scarsdale and New York City witnesses are subject to subpoena for a trial in Newark, F.R.Civ.P. 45(e). Insofar as Semmes relies on the Federal Dealer Act, 15 U.S.C. § 1222, a New Jersey federal court is as well equipped to decide the issues as one in New York. So far as the New York statute is concerned, it can scarcely be doubted that a dealer's purposeful submission of false warranty refund claims would constitute "cause" for termination to the extent that this is consistent with the governing contract. Interpretation of that may pose some problems, as we shall see, but the Ford Sales Agreement provides that it is "to be construed in accordance with the laws of Michigan"—a provision to which we assume both New York and New Jersey would give effect. A New Jersey district judge can determine that as well—or badly—as one in New York. None of the factors relied on for giving priority to the second suit comes near the examples given in *Mattel, supra,* 353 F.2d at 424 n. 4. Although a district judge has considerable latitude in these matters, Kerotest Mfg. Co. v. C–O–Two Fire Equip. Co., 342 U.S. 180, 183–184, 72 S.Ct. 219, 96 L.Ed. 200 (1952), we hold that the court below went beyond the allowable bounds of discretion when it refused to grant Ford's motion for a stay and that a stay should be entered, provided that within fifteen days of the issuance of the mandate, Ford stipulates that Semmes, within twenty days thereafter, may file a reply and counterclaim (or, if Semmes prefers, an amended complaint) in the New Jersey action in respect to the termination of the dealership.

Whether the temporary injunction entered by the district court should be set aside is quite another matter. The issues presented by Semmes' motion for a temporary injunction were difficult and complex, and a great deal of time and energy has been spent by Judge Ryan in deciding them and by us in reviewing his action. We see no reason for further expenditure of judicial time on this interlocutory issue when the important thing is to get on with the final hearing. The proper solution is rather to let the temporary injunction stand until the New Jersey action is decided on the merits. In so holding we assume that the New Jersey court will require Semmes to proceed speedily to trial; if that should not occur, the stay should not prevent Ford from asking that the temporary injunction be dissolved.[10]

---

8. Semmes has not sought an injunction against prosecution of the New Jersey action, and, for reasons outlined in the opinion, it would be an abuse of discretion to grant one.

10. We assume also that Semmes will file its counterclaim if Ford stipulates it

This disposition will relieve Ford of its present dilemma of having either to yield to Semmes' forum shopping or to litigate in two courts simultaneously, and the courts from the consequent unnecessary burdens. While it nevertheless allows Semmes to profit in some degree from its initiation of duplicative litigation and what we regard as an error of the court below, this consideration is outweighed by the other factors mentioned. In reaching this result we have been cognizant that in Kerotest Mfg. Co. v. C–O–Two Fire Equip. Co., *supra,* 342 U.S. at 183, 72 S.Ct. at 221, the call for "wise judicial administration, giving regard to conservation of judicial resources and comprehensive disposition of litigation" and the caution against "rigid mechanical solution of such problems" were directed to the courts of appeals as much as to the district courts.

Notes and Questions

1. Was Ford's likelihood of success on the merits in *Semmes* pertinent to the decision whether to grant a stay in the New York suit? Note that the New York court had granted Semmes a preliminary injunction against termination. What showing did he have to make for that relief? Why should that remain in effect? Wasn't the New York court's decision to entertain the injunction motion also an interference with the New Jersey court's authority?

2. The Court of Appeals notes that New York is the "more logical" forum. Should that have any effect on which action may proceed? Could the New Jersey court have refused to enjoin prosecution of the New York suit? Was Semmes forum shopping when he sued there?

3. One suspects that Semmes may have decided to switch courts because he hoped for a friendlier reception in New York. As the court observes, such attempts to pick a favorable judge are disfavored, and the judge-shopping aspects of Semmes' conduct may have influenced the Second Circuit's willingness to rely on the "first filed" standard (note that it says that the New Jersey court should be deemed "seized" of the claim). However, determining who is acting abusively in the context of forum or judge shopping is sometimes complicated. For example, in Northwest Airlines, Inc. v. American Airlines, Inc., 989 F.2d 1002 (8th Cir.1993), the court upheld an injunction issued by a district judge in Minnesota prohibiting defendant American from pursuing litigation it had filed in district court in Texas even though the Texas court had denied plaintiff Northwest's motions to stay or transfer and instead set the Texas case for an early trial. Northwest filed the Minnesota action in response to a letter from American asserting that its hiring of American employees constituted tortious interference, seeking a declaratory judgment that it had acted lawfully. Northwest knew American was contemplating legal action, and sought only declaratory relief in Minnesota, but the appellate court nevertheless held that, despite these "red flags that there may be compelling circumstances," the district judge could adhere to the "first-filed rule" that "the court in which jurisdiction first attached proceed to adjudicate the controversy and should restrain the parties from

may do so, since otherwise a judgment in Ford's favor on the fraud counterclaim would be res judicata on the issue of termination.

proceeding in a later-filed action." Compare National Equipment Rental, Limited v. Fowler, 287 F.2d 43 (2d Cir.1961), in which Chief Judge Lumbard dissented from application of the first filed rule, urging that res judicata should apply where a party invoking the rule has unsuccessfully sought a stay from one court before requesting an injunction from the other.

4.   It is often difficult to determine exactly what has motivated a party to file a duplicative suit and, in the absence of a bad faith motive, one federal court may be hesitant to enjoin suit in another. For example, in Span–Eng Assoc. v. Weidner, 771 F.2d 464 (10th Cir.1985), plaintiffs in a securities fraud case in the federal court in Utah filed a similar suit in the federal court in Arizona after the Utah judge had denied their motion to amend the Utah complaint to add additional defendants. Feeling that the plaintiffs were circumventing his order, the Utah judge enjoined prosecution of the Arizona suit. The Tenth Circuit reversed, stressing that "the right to proceed in court should not be denied except under the most extreme circumstances." Id. at 468. It found that the Utah suit had not progressed to such a point as to warrant an injunction in the interests of judicial economy. It also rejected the Utah court's conclusion that the plaintiffs were forum shopping, observing that they had to file suit to toll the running of limitations with respect to the additional defendants.

2.   PRETRIAL CONSOLIDATION

Rule 42(a) allows a federal district court, "when actions involving a common question of law or fact are pending before the court," to "order a joint hearing or trial of any or all the matters in issue in the actions" or to "order all the actions consolidated." Consolidation was "[o]ne of the earliest examples of case management based on inherent authority," and was viewed as "an inseparable aspect of the powers possessed by common-law and equity courts." Meador, Inherent Judicial Authority in the Conduct of Civil Litigation, 73 Texas L. Rev. 1805, 1807 (1995). "[C]onsolidation is permitted as a matter of convenience and economy in administration, but does not merge the suits into a single cause, or change the rights of the parties, or make those who are parties in one suit parties in another." Johnson v. Manhattan Railway Co., 289 U.S. 479, 496–497, 53 S.Ct. 721, 727, 77 L.Ed. 1331, 1334 (1933).

Consolidation can only take place when the actions are pending in the same division of the same federal district court. However, 28 U.S.C.A. § 1404(b) provides: "Upon motion, consent or stipulation of all parties, any action, suit or proceeding of a civil nature or any motion or hearing thereof, may be transferred, in the discretion of the court, from the division in which pending to any other division in the same district." Local court rules should be looked to for guidance. The Manual for Complex Litigation (4th) § 20.11 (2004) says:

> All related civil cases pending in the same court should initially be assigned to a single judge to determine whether consolidation, or at least coordination of pretrial, is feasible and will reduce conflicts and duplication.

KATZ v. REALTY EQUITIES CORP. OF NEW YORK

United States Court of Appeals, Second Circuit, 1975.
521 F.2d 1354.

Before WATERMAN, FRIENDLY and GURFEIN, CIRCUIT JUDGES.

WATERMAN, CIRCUIT JUDGE.

This appeal concerns an order of a district judge requiring the filing and service of a single consolidated complaint for pretrial purposes upon defendants in a number of related securities cases. We affirm the order which, under the circumstances present, was a proper exercise of the trial judge's authority in the management of the preliminary stages of complex multiparty litigation.

On March 8, 1974 the Securities and Exchange Commission commenced an enforcement action in the United States District Court for the Southern District of New York against Republic National Life Insurance Company ("Republic"), seven of its officers and directors, its auditor Peat Marwick Mitchell & Co., Realty Equities Corporation of New York ("Realty"), two of its officials, its auditor Westheimer, Fine, Berger & Co., and two other individuals. The SEC complaint alleges that the defendants participated in a scheme to defraud the investing public by concealing the actual facts of Realty's financial condition. Republic, which had large investments in Realty, advanced large sums of money, the SEC complaint alleges, through a series of intricate transactions, to Realty or related companies, so that Realty could repay existing indebtedness to Republic.

Patterned on the SEC complaint, twelve private actions were filed in the Southern District of New York based on the Realty–Republic transactions. In addition, four actions were filed in the Northern District of Texas and one action in the Middle District of Tennessee; these five actions were transferred to the Southern District of New York for pretrial purposes by the Judicial Panel on Multidistrict Litigation by order of August 22, 1974, and on August 26, 1974 the district court ordered them consolidated with the pending actions in the Southern District of New York which had been ordered consolidated two months previously.

On June 12, 1974 the district court sua sponte held a hearing to determine whether the actions then pending before it should be consolidated. On June 24, 1974 the district court filed an order of consolidation which provided in part:

Ordered:

(1) The above designated actions (sometimes herein "constituent actions") are hereby consolidated for all pretrial purposes to be had during the pendency of these actions in this District in accordance with the following terms which the Court in the exercise of discretion makes applicable to foster the efficient and proper con-

duct of the claims asserted in the individual complaints in the said actions.

(2) A single consolidated complaint, supplemented and amended, shall be prepared and served herein by liaison counsel which shall set forth the claims for relief asserted in the constituent actions, collated into separately stated counts by class and derivative categories as to each kind of securities holders and at the head of each count shall specifically designate by name or other convenient reference the defendants against whom such count is asserted.

* * *

(11) At the conclusion of the pretrial proceedings, the Court will give consideration to a consolidated trial of the issues herein.

The order of the district court provided for the appointment of lead and liaison counsel for all plaintiffs. The order also stated that the answer of each defendant to the consolidated complaint "shall be deemed" to have asserted cross-claims in the nature of contribution and indemnification against all other defendants.

At the June 12 hearing, the appellants Klein, Hinds & Finke ("KHF") and Alexander Grant & Company ("Grant"), favored the use of consolidated discovery proceedings, but they objected to proceeding under a single consolidated complaint. After the consolidation order was entered the appellants filed a timely notice of appeal which was limited to the portion of the order providing for the consolidation for all pretrial purposes and for the filing of a single consolidated complaint. The sole objection pressed on appeal is to the use of a consolidated complaint.

KHF and Grant had been named as defendants in two of the private complaints, the Herman complaint, a class action brought on behalf of the holders of common stock of Republic, and the Katz complaint, a class action brought on behalf of the holders of common stock in Realty. They had not been named as defendants in the SEC action. In nearly identical language the complaints allege that the appellants violated § 10(b) of the Securities Exchange Act of 1934, 15 U.S.C. § 78j(b), and Rule 10b–5 promulgated thereunder:

Grant and KHF were the independent auditors for Realty during certain relevant portions of the periods above described. Each discovered and knew of certain and many ways of the material problems between Realty and Republic, all as hereinabove described. Grant and KHF informed Realty of the fact that the financial statements of Realty and of FNR [First National Realty & Construction Corp., a Realty affiliate] would not be unqualified and both firms were replaced as auditors for Realty. Yet both firms failed of their obligations to the public and to the SEC and Amex to fully disclose such facts and to alert the responsible authorities thereto. Instead each firm withheld the facts thereof in order to benefit themselves by not involving themselves therein, directly or indirectly, and to prevent damage to themselves and to other defendants, despite the further damage resulting to plaintiff and the class.

Thus the claims against Grant and KHF are limited. There is no allegation that they participated in the complicated real estate and financial transactions between Republic and Realty which are at the core of the SEC complaint and the private complaints based upon the SEC allegations.

The amended consolidated complaint was served on all defendants including KHF and Grant on October 15, 1974. Under it twenty-one plaintiffs sue thirty-nine defendants. Five different classes of plaintiffs allege a total of thirty counts against defendants. The classes consist of: persons who purchased securities in Realty; persons who purchased securities in Republic; holders of shares of Pacific National Life Assurance Company; owners of certain debentures of Realty; and holders of common stock in Mercantile Security Life Insurance Company. Two counts involve derivative claims on behalf of Realty and Republic, and one count is brought individually. Grant and KHF are named in three counts of the consolidated complaint. Each of these counts contains the § 10(b) and Rule 10b–5 allegations of the Katz and Herman complaints and the several plaintiffs are the purchasers of Realty securities, the purchasers of Republic securities, and stockholders of Realty suing derivatively. The remaining bulk of the consolidated complaint concerns the manipulative transactions between Realty and Republic, transactions which allegedly began in September 1970, after Grant and KHF were unable to present unqualified financial statements and after Grant and KHF had been replaced as auditors for Realty.

* * *

Here, under the broad heading that the district court lacked the authority to order a consolidated complaint, the appellants advance various objections to the use of a consolidated complaint: that the order accomplishes an impermissible merger of claims; that the decision in *Garber v. Randell,* [477 F.2d 711 (2d Cir.1973)], excluding the law firm there, is indistinguishable and controlling; that the order inflicts substantial prejudice on the appellants. We are convinced, however, that the trial judge properly exercised his authority when he fashioned this pretrial order, an order appropriate for this complex litigation, and we affirm the order. We are confident that if the claimed prejudice to the appellants, which is now a premature and speculative apprehension, should occur, the trial judge will act vigorously to remedy the situation.

It is axiomatic that consolidation is a procedural device designed to promote judicial economy and that consolidation cannot effect a physical merger of the actions or the defenses of the separate parties. *Johnson v. Manhattan Ry. Co.,* 289 U.S. 479, 496–497, 53 S.Ct. 721, 77 L.Ed. 1331 (1933). There is here, however, no indication that the court below intended a physical merger of claims or that one was accomplished despite the court's intent. Rather, it is evident that the district court limited the use of the consolidated complaint to the controversies' pretrial stages in order to prevent unnecessary duplication and in order to reduce the potential for confusion. At the preliminary hearing on consolidation the trial judge stated:

> It seems to me that the use of a single consolidated complaint need not necessarily foreclose the use of individual complaints at a trial, and in the same way as consolidated discovery would be useful and efficient, a single consolidated complaint during the discovery and pretrial period would be useful and efficient and could be without prejudice to unfurling the separate flags at trial, if necessary, to protect any legitimate interests that may have to be dealt with separately.

> * * *

> I think I am going to try it. I will order a single consolidated complaint for pretrial purposes without prejudice, as I say, to whether or not there will be a consolidated trial and without prejudice to the use of the individual complaints as they stand now at a consolidated trial, and certainly without prejudice to their use in individual trials if that should eventuate.[4]

Also, it is stated in the consolidation order that any decision on a trial consolidation would await the conclusion of the pretrial proceedings. The instructions contained in paragraph 2 of the district court order for the collation of the separately stated counts and for the specific designations of the defendants is a further indication that the trial court, while retaining the particular attributes of each of the several complaints, was attempting to incorporate all the complaints into a single document for convenient pretrial handling.

The use of the consolidated complaint here has significant attractions in keeping the preliminary stages of these cases within reasonable bounds. There are seventeen actions pending against thirty-nine defendants; many of the defendants are sued in most of the actions, some in but a few. A separate answer from each defendant to each complaint in which that defendant is named would involve literally hundreds of answers. As noted previously, all the complaints in the private actions track the SEC complaint, and the answers to each complaint would be substantially the same. The benefits of collecting, for example, sixteen identical answers in each of sixteen cases from one defendant is not readily discernible. It is true that those defendants named in only a

---

4. At a subsequent hearing on September 12, 1974, the district judge stated:

This is a draft, and it isn't even a penultimate draft. It is to coordinate all the claims, and there can be one filed tomorrow and one after that, the day after tomorrow.

The whole purpose of this complaint is to get organized for the discovery and pre-trial phase. The order that I entered specifically recites that the pleadings in each constituent action stand, and when you go back to trial, the constituent actions will determine what will be tried and how, unless when we get to the trial it is agreed that a consolidation of the constituent complaints can be made.

But for present purposes you have got to start somewhere, and the amended consolidated complaint is intended to wrap up all the claims so that we can get on with the business of discovery.

small number of complaints, for example Grant and KHF, would not be overly burdened, but, nevertheless, the overall economies in reducing the proliferation of duplicative papers warrant the trial judge's efforts in the present circumstances. Moreover, it is apparent that a consolidated complaint also aids the consolidated discovery process which all parties, including the appellants, favor. Directing discovery to one complaint, rather than to seventeen complaints, avoids the possible confusion and the possible problems stemming from the situation where each plaintiff pursues his individual complaint. While it is true that carefully supervised and coordinated discovery proceedings would reduce the potential for chaos, the use of a consolidated complaint promotes the desired objective.

It therefore appears clear that in the circumstances here present which involve complex and multifaceted actions with a number of similar complaints, the adoption of a consolidated complaint is a device well-suited to achieving economies of effort on the part of the parties and of the court. Limited presently to the pretrial stages, the consolidated complaint does not supersede the individual complaints and does not impermissibly merge the rights or defenses of the various parties.

Appellants contend that we are not considering this issue afresh and that the Second Circuit's decision in *Garber v. Randell, supra,* compels the result they urge. We disagree. In *Garber* three class actions were instituted against fifty-eight defendants in which the plaintiffs alleged violations of the federal securities laws. The principal thrust of the complaints alleged the artificial inflation of the shares of National Student Marketing Corp. during a four year period through the publication of false and misleading information. One of the complaints, the last filed, also asserted claims that a law firm, White and Case, as counsel for National Student Marketing Corp., had participated in a merger transaction in which it had failed to disclose to stockholders that an accountant's comfort letter did not conform to the terms of the merger; had issued opinions on the validity of the merger agreement; and had transmitted, on behalf of National Student Marketing Corp., a false Form 8K to the SEC. The complaint also alleged that the law firm had on two other occasions rendered opinions on transactions in which the National Student Marketing Corp. had backdated activities.

The district court, in *Garber v. Randell,* after a hearing, issued an order of consolidation [for pretrial purposes, requiring plaintiffs to file a consolidated complaint]. * * * The law firm appealed from this order, as well as from another order denying its motion for severance. The Second Circuit held that joinder of the limited claims against White and Case with the other unrelated claims in a consolidated complaint "would be fundamentally unfair and would violate the principles underlying our decision in *MacAlister v. Guterma,* [263 F.2d 65 (2d Cir.1958)], and the unbroken line of authority going back to *Johnson v. Manhattan Railway Co., supra.*"

The court, however, noted in a footnote that in other circumstances the use of a consolidated complaint might be appropriate, thus recognizing the authority of the district court to so order. * * * The principal reason was the limited and unrelated nature of the alleged misconduct by White and Case which occurred largely on one day and totally within a two-and-a-half month period. In addition, other significant factors were present. Only one of fifteen named plaintiffs brought suit against White and Case, and several of the other plaintiffs had expressly disassociated themselves from these assertions. One Natale, the sole plaintiff alleging the White and Case wrongdoing, had not purchased National Student Marketing Corp. shares on the open market, and it appeared questionable whether he was a proper class representative. White and Case argued that this fact was highly prejudicial because it made it much more difficult, if not impossible, for it to isolate and attack the infirmities of the action by Natale, for not only had he not purchased shares but he also was the only plaintiff seeking to assert claims against White and Case. Also, the only persons who had acquired shares after the date of the alleged concealment by the law firm would be in a position to claim damages, and therefore it would be necessary at some point to separate the claims against White and Case from the claims against the others.

These latter factors, present in *Garber,* are absent here. Thus far there has been no claim that Herman and Katz are improper class representatives. Appellate counsel at oral argument informed the court that the motion for class designation is still pending in the district court. The other plaintiffs have not disassociated themselves from the claims advanced against the appellants; indeed they argue that their acquiescence in proceeding in accord with the order prescribing the consolidated complaint constitutes a de facto amendment of their constituent complaints. The actions of Grant and KHF occurred prior to the transactions which form the bulk of the actions rather than in the midst of the manipulative activity as in *Garber,* and it is plaintiffs' contention that had the auditors been forthright the subsequent alleged wrongs might not have occurred.

These distinctions, however, are not in themselves compelling. Grant and KHF argue forcefully that in the main their fact-situation is analogous to that of White and Case: actors on the periphery of the main activities who must defend against claims having but a remote relation to the principal issues. They also stress that in both cases the order of consolidation limited the consolidation to the pretrial stages of the litigation.

Nevertheless, we choose not to adopt and apply the specific conclusion of *Garber* to the present case. *Garber's* broad holding was that the validity of a consolidated order must be examined with reference to the special underlying facts prompting the order, and with close attention alike to the potential economies of the consolidation on the one hand, and the threatened prejudice to a party or parties, on the other hand. We are not convinced here that the appellants have been presently prejudiced by the consolidated complaint or that the district court will not be alert to the possibility of prejudice to them in the future. Without a firm conviction that prejudice will result, we are most reluctant to interfere, and perhaps disrupt, the efforts of the district court which, without sacrificing the rights of the various parties, seeks to expedite this complex litigation.

The appellants claim that they have been prejudiced in two ways: the expansion of the classes in the consolidated complaint; and the deeming of cross-claims amongst the defendants during the discovery process. As noted *supra,* the Katz and Herman complaints were brought on behalf of purchasers of common stock of Realty and Republic respectively, while the consolidated complaint alleges claims on behalf of "purchasers of securities" in the companies. This expansion of the classes, for which there is no authority in the district court order, would of course increase the potential liability of Grant and KHF in the event that the consolidated complaint was used at trial. This is not the physical merger of claims, which the caselaw forbids, but rather an expansion of classes, which is also troubling. However, the classes have not yet been defined by the district court, and the appropriate place for appellants to object to the proposed definition of the proposed classes is before the district court.

The appellants did not appeal from that portion of the district court order which deemed the answer of each defendant to assert cross-claims for indemnification and contribution against all other defendants.[7] The only issue before us, therefore, is the prejudicial effect to appellants of

---

7. The relevant portion of the district court order reads as follows:

(9) The answer of each defendant to the consolidated complaint (or latest amended complaint) in each of the above-captioned actions shall be deemed to assert cross-claims against all the other defendants therein for such sharing of liability in the nature of contribution and indemnification as exists under the Securities Act of 1933 (15 U.S.C. § 77a *et seq.*) and the Securities Exchange Act of 1934 (15 U.S.C. § 78a *et seq.*) as well as by state statutory and common law, except insofar as any defendant shall in his answer decline to assert such claims against any other defendant; such claims to be deemed asserted in the following form:

"FIRST CROSS–CLAIM AGAINST
ALL OTHER DEFENDANTS

If plaintiffs recover judgment against the cross-claiming defendant, the cross-claiming defendant is, or may be, entitled to contribution under the Securities Act of 1933 (15 U.S.C. § 77(a) [77a] *et seq.*) and the Securities Exchange Act of 1934 (15 U.S.C. § 78(a) [78a] *et seq.*) from some or all of the defendants other than the cross-claiming defendant.

SECOND CROSS–CLAIM AGAINST
ALL OTHER DEFENDANTS

If plaintiffs herein recover judgment against the cross-claiming defendant by reason of any of the acts, transactions or omissions alleged in the amended complaint, such judgment will have been brought about and caused wholly or primarily by the acts, transactions, commissions or omissions of some or all of the defendants and not by, or only secondarily by, any acts, transactions or omissions of the cross-claiming defendant.

By reason of the foregoing, the cross-claiming defendant is, or may be, entitled to indemnification or contribution for all or part of any such judgment recovered by plaintiffs herein,"

and each defendant against whom such cross-claims have been asserted shall be deemed to have interposed answers to said cross-claims controverting the allegations contained therein and denying any liability in the nature of contribution or indemnification.

All cross-claims asserting claims other than for shared liability as hereinbefore described remain unaffected by the foregoing provisions of this order.

this order in connection with the apparently distinct issue of the consolidation of complaints, the issue appealed. It appears from the record that the preservation of cross-claims was designed only to serve as an economical device to facilitate the discovery process and to avoid the proliferation of pleadings. Upon the completion of the discovery and upon a fuller comprehension of the facts, the parties and court can better evaluate the cross-claims worthy of perusal. Appellants do not detail in what manner prejudice will result from this effort to simplify matters, nor do they explain how this is in any way related to the issue they raised before the court, the propriety of the use of a consolidated complaint.

We accordingly find there is no clear showing that the appellants have been prejudiced as a result of the district court's order requiring the filing of a consolidated complaint for pretrial purposes. The appellants' fear, perhaps substantial, that because of their peripheral involvement in the principal transactions involved in the litigation they will suffer prejudice, does not result from the consolidation of the complaints. The Katz and Herman complaints, like the other constituent complaints, parallel the SEC complaint, and are broad in scope; in these complaints the appellants are also peripheral defendants. At the preliminary hearing the district court expressly invited Grant and KHF to move for dismissal of the complaint. In addition, the use of the consolidated complaint for pretrial purposes does not impair appellants' subsequent recourse to the timely motion for severance. At present appellants' fears of prejudice are wholly speculative: if the classes are defined along the present lines, if a motion to dismiss is denied, if a motion for severance is denied, and if the consolidated complaint is used at trial, then appellants' right to their separate defenses may be jeopardized. This possibility is too remote to justify appellate intervention into the pretrial stages of this litigation; and, although we have accepted jurisdiction, we point out that the appeal is taken from an interlocutory order and that an appeal so taken comes close to violating the long-standing and accepted rule statutorily incorporated in 28 U.S.C. § 1291, a rule which has well served the federal courts for years.

Order affirmed.

RHEINGOLD, THE MER/29 STORY—AN INSTANCE OF SUCCESSFUL MASS DISASTER LITIGATION

56 Calif.L.Rev. 116, 125–28, 130–31 (1968).

[In this litigation, 1500 plaintiffs filed individual product liability suits against the manufacturer of the drug MER/29. Because the suits were filed in a number of different state and federal courts, formal consolidation in one federal court action was impossible. The author of this article was counsel for a number of plaintiffs.]

Perhaps the most basic decision for the plaintiffs and the defendant in the MER/29 litigation was whether to consolidate the pending cases, either for all or for a limited number of purposes. The concept of "consolidation" could involve legal joinder of multiple cases for all purposes, including trial, or for some purposes, such as joint discovery, or it could involve extrajudicial cooperation between the plaintiff Group and the defendant by agreement on group procedures. For the defendant there were important considerations on both sides. Consolidation or any form of formal group effort would diminish its law work, reduce the time which its scientific personnel spent in giving discovery, and reduce the chances of inconsistent rulings and trial decisions. On the other hand, consolidation or concerted action by the plaintiffs would also facilitate the plaintiffs' discovery, lend strength through union to the plaintiffs' Group, and probably improve many plaintiffs' cases.

For the plaintiffs, the benefits of concerted action outweighed the dangers in almost every attorney's mind. The individual lawyer was afraid only that he might lose control of his case, which would consequently be less well prepared, or that he would suffer professionally or economically through consolidation. In retrospect, these concerns were not well founded. Far from losing financially, a lawyer in the MER/29 Group enjoyed inexpensive (300 dollars at the most) yet careful preparation of the liability issues which cost the Group as a whole tens of thousands of dollars. No plaintiff's lawyer who resisted joining the Group because he feared loss of identity as an able personal injury lawyer in fact gained anything.

Members were unenthusiastic, however, about consolidating cases for trial purposes, or about any form of Group decision that would directly shape the trial. For every member disappointed because the Group did not take over his case there were dozens who felt themselves perfectly capable of handling their own cases. Thus, concern for one's identity as a trial lawyer and for the potential economic consequences of group trial took real form at the trial stage.

* * *

As a rule, therefore, disposition of the cases was the product of a "free enterprise" system. Without pressure from the Group or from the courts, the lawyer could handle his case as he wished.[43] The members did, however, avidly await from the Group information about other members' cases, including the minutest details available concerning settled cases and the type of trial being put on by both sides. Since Group newsletters could not adequately convey to individual members the Group's collective knowledge about the trial of a MER/29 case, the "MER/29 School," as it was known, came into being. Four two-day sessions were held, operated by the trustee and not the Group, for a total of approximately thirty members. Such was its success, that a member began a trial the day after attending the school—and won.

---

43. The same was true at the pretrials. The Group's role here was confined to providing members with copies of pretrial orders and rulings made in other actions, together with the key documents on liability which could be marked at the conferences. The courts did not work out consolidated pretrials.

The "free enterprise" system returned the balance of power to the defendant at the trial stage. The defendant could and did select the cases it wanted tried. Good cases approaching trial were settled. Finally, when a series of cases came up which favored the defendant because of their facts or for other reasons, the defendant could bring these on to trial. The success of these tactics is evident in verdicts for the defendants in the first three cases tried. Meanwhile, able plaintiff's attorneys with cases buried on long calendars had to wait impatiently for a chance to try a case on their own terms. On the whole, however, members of the Group were not discouraged by the defendant's initial three victories after explanations of the conduct of the trials.

Notes and Questions

1.   "Consolidation holds out a bland, somewhat technocratic, uncontroversial face to the world." Marcus, Confronting the Consolidation Conundrum, 1995 BYU L. Rev. 879, 887. Is that appearance really justified? The standard for consolidation under Rule 42(a) (that the actions involve "a common question of law or fact") is close to the second requirement for permissive joinder under Rule 20(a) ("if any question of law or fact common to all these persons will arise in the action"). It is also close to the requirement for permissive intervention under Rule 24(b) ("when an applicant's claim or defense and the main action have a question of law or fact in common"). Should the "common question" language in these three rules be interpreted in the same way? Is this a less demanding standard than in the "same transaction or occurrence" requirement for party joinder in Rule 20(a)?

2.   The counterweight to the benefits of consolidation is the prejudice that may result from it. Is the more significant prejudice at trial or before trial? What effect will pretrial consolidation have on "bystander" defendants who are named in only one of the consolidated cases and who must decide how to protect their interests during massive discovery of the consolidated actions?

Rule 42(a) leaves a court wide latitude in deciding how much should be consolidated; a consolidation order may apply only to pretrial discovery, or to other aspects of pretrial, or to disposition of particular issues, or may be extended through trial and final judgment. The court has the power to alter its consolidation order or to use Rule 42(b) to order separate trials of any claims or issues "in furtherance of convenience or to avoid prejudice, or when separate trials will be conducive to expedition and economy." Courts sometimes refer to such orders as a severance (Rule 21 provides: "Any claim against a party may be severed and proceeded with separately"), although Rule 42(b) is the appropriate vehicle for ordering separate trials when there has previously been some form of consolidation.

3.   In *Katz,* the court reiterates the familiar adage that consolidation does not "effect a physical merger of the actions." In the same vein, the court assured the parties that the original pleadings would remain in the case after the filing of the consolidated complaint. How reassuring are these statements? Can the individual characteristics of different cases really be preserved? Won't discovery proceed along the lines outlined in the coordinat-

ed complaint, with questions of relevance measured by it? How would such questions of relevance be decided in the absence of a consolidated complaint? The trial court's procedure also deems each defendant to have asserted a cross claim against every other defendant. Would this sort of provision be consistent with Rule 11? If the cases later revert to original pleadings without such cross claims, will these claims then disappear? How much more would be required to violate the rule against "physical merger" of the cases?

4. In contrast to the "free enterprise" model of unofficial coordination described in the Rheingold article, a judge has broad discretionary powers to treat a consolidated case much like a single entity. The judge can appoint (or require the parties on each side to appoint) lead counsel through whom the parties must file motions or otherwise deal with the court. See *infra* p. 664. The parties can be required to file uniform pleadings which could result in the loss of individual claims or defenses.

5. Consolidation can create an action that very much resembles a class action, but with a few differences. Consolidation is restricted to pending cases and cannot encompass "future" parties as can a class action, and parties cannot opt out of a consolidated case (as they can a (b)(3) class action). See Silver, Comparing Class Actions and Consolidations, 10 Rev.Litig. 495, 499–512 (1991); Resnik, From "Cases" to "Litigation," 54 Law & Contemp. Probs 5 (Summer 1991). Consolidation has been invoked in tandem with the class action to accomplish aggregation of asbestos tort cases. See Cimino v. Raymark Indus., Inc., No. B–86–0456–Ca, Mem. and Order 2–3, (1989) ("This court finds that the fairest and most efficient way of processing these cases is to join these 3,031 cases together under Fed. R.Civ.P. 42(a) for a single trial on the issues of state of the art and punitive damages, and to certify a class action under Rule 23(b)(3) for the remaining issues of exposure and actual damages."). Such use raises questions as to whether the two devices should be applied consistently. The American Law Institute's Complex Litigation Project placed principal emphasis on consolidation as a method for aggregating litigations from various locations and handling them together. For an examination of this proposal, contrasting the limitations prescribed by the ALI with those that confine a class action under Rule 23(b)(3), see Marcus, Confronting the Consolidation Conundrum, 1995 BYU L. Rev. 879.

6. *Mass Tort Consolidated Trials*: Using consolidation as a method to combine large numbers of cases for trial has appealed to district courts confronting large numbers of similar tort suits, but appellate courts have sometimes concluded that differences between individual cases may make consolidated trials improper. In Malcolm v. National Gypsum Co., 995 F.2d 346 (2d Cir.1993), the appellate court reversed a verdict entered after a consolidated trial of 600 asbestos personal injury cases. It noted the "herculean task" of coping with mass torts, and acknowledged that "[p]retrial consolidation for the purposes of discovery * * * and, especially, the liberal use of consolidated trials have ameliorated what might otherwise be a sclerotic backlog of cases." Id. at 350. Nevertheless, emphasizing the "cosmic sweep of the factual data the jury had to absorb," it found the combination too sweeping in the case before it. A dissenting judge argued that "[c]onsolidated trials are an indispensable means of resolving the thousands of asbestos claims flooding our state and federal courts, as well as claims from

other types of mass torts." Id. at 354–55 (Walker, J., dissenting). Similarly, in In re Repetitive Stress Injury Litig., 11 F.3d 368 (2d Cir.1993), the court forbade consolidation for trial of 44 personal injury cases involving use of keyboard office equipment because they presented a wide variety of different types of equipment and required consideration of the individual characteristics of the plaintiffs.

The challenges presented by consolidated trials closely correspond to those considered in connection with certification of class actions in such cases in Chapter IV (see *infra* pp. 330-68) and the use of certain innovative trial techniques considered in Chapter VII (see *infra* pp. 762-85). For present purposes, it is important to appreciate that consolidation is increasingly employed in mass tort situations, and is often upheld. For example, in Consorti v. Armstrong World Indus., Inc., 72 F.3d 1003 (2d Cir.1995), vacated on other grounds, 518 U.S. 1031, 116 S.Ct. 2576, 135 L.Ed.2d 1091 (1996), the same court that disapproved consolidated trials in the cases described above affirmed a verdict where four cases involving asbestos exposure were consolidated for trial, saying that the "heyday of individual adjudication of asbestos mass tort lawsuits has long passed," and that "the judiciary, like every other institution, must be open to discarding habits that have outlived their usefulness, and must bend under the pressures of modern life to find greater efficiency in accomplishing its mission." Id. at 1006–07. It also suggested that consolidation could improve the quality of the justice rendered by evening out the awards to different plaintiffs, which often tend to vary significantly when assessed by different juries. Keep these issues in mind as you examine the similar problems in Chapter IV and VII.

7.   The rule of Johnson v. Manhattan Railway Co., *supra* p. 115, was that consolidated cases are not merged into a single case, even though there may be a consolidated complaint applicable to all the cases. In re TMI Litigation, 193 F.3d 613 (3d Cir.1999), consolidated the cases of 2,000 plaintiffs seeking recovery for personal injuries resulting from the release of radioactive discharge from the Three Mile Island nuclear reactor. The court directed a "bellwether" trial of ten "trial plaintiffs." Defendants then moved for summary judgment on the ground that plaintiffs' expert scientific evidence was not admissible. The district court granted summary judgment as to all 2,000 plaintiffs, and not just the ten trial plaintiffs. The appellate court reversed, noting that "consolidation is not intended to affect the substantive rights of the parties to the consolidated cases." The non-trial plaintiffs had not been given an opportunity to object to the motion for summary judgment and therefore should not have been included in the court's judgment. See also Cella v. Togum Constructeur Ensembleier en Industrie Alimentaire, 173 F.3d 909, 912 (3d Cir.1999) ("while a consolidation order may result in a single unit of litigation, such an order does not create a single case for jurisdiction purposes"); compare Schnabel v. Lui, 302 F.3d 1023, 1035 (9th Cir.2002) ("we do not resolve the issue of whether consolidated actions in general retain their separate character under *Johnson* and its progeny, or are merged for purposes of determining personal jurisdiction").

8.   It should be apparent that consolidation can raise a welter of jurisdictional and other issues. For a comprehensive examination of these problems, see Steinman, The Effects of Case Consolidation on the Procedural Rights of Litigants: What They Are, What They Might Be, Part I:

Justiciability and Jurisdiction (Original and Appellate), 42 UCLA L. Rev. 717 (1995); Part II: Non–Jurisdictional Matters, 42 UCLA L. Rev. 967 (1995).

3. TRANSFER TO A MORE CONVENIENT FORUM

In 1948, 28 U.S.C.A. § 1404(a) was passed by Congress in order to modify the strictness of the federal common law doctrine of *forum non conveniens* which, as applied in Gulf Oil Corp. v. Gilbert, 330 U.S. 501, 67 S.Ct. 839, 91 L.Ed. 1055 (1947), allowed a federal court to dismiss a suit, although it had personal and subject-matter jurisdiction and venue was proper, if there were another more convenient forum. Section 1404(a) contains a deceptively simple, one-sentence standard: "For the convenience of the parties and witnesses, in the interest of justice, a district court may transfer any civil action to any other district or division where it might have been brought."

Section 1404(a) can play an important role in helping to accomplish the consolidation of duplicative or related litigation by transferring related cases to the same federal district and allowing consolidation to take place there. But before transfer can be accomplished, it must be established that the transferee district is one "where it might have been brought" and that such transfer is "for the convenience of the parties and witnesses" and "in the interest of justice."

GINSEY INDUSTRIES, INC. v. I.T.K. PLASTICS, INC.

United States District Court, Eastern District of Pennsylvania, 1982.
545 F.Supp. 78.

Louis H. Pollak, District Judge.

Plaintiff, Ginsey Industries, is a Pennsylvania corporation with its principal place of business in Bellmahr, New Jersey, and defendant, I.T.K. Plastics, is a Massachusetts corporation with its principal place of business in Salem, Massachusetts. In the fall of 1981, plaintiff purchased vinyl plastic sheeting manufactured by defendant. After receiving shipment of the plastic, Ginsey determined that the plastic was not, in its view, fit for the purpose for which it was sold. Ginsey then filed this action to recover the payment it made to I.T.K. as well as consequential damages. This matter is now before the court on defendant's motion to dismiss for lack of personal jurisdiction or, in the alternative, for transfer to the District of Massachusetts.

I.T.K. first contends that its limited contact with this forum is insufficient to bring it within the reach of Pennsylvania's long-arm statute, 42 Pa.C.S.A. § 5301 *et seq.*, or to satisfy the due process standards set forth in *International Shoe Co. v. Washington*, 326 U.S. 310, 316, 66 S.Ct. 154, 158, 90 L.Ed. 95 (1945). Alternatively, I.T.K. argues that transfer to the District of Massachusetts is warranted since a civil action involving the same parties and the same plastic products is currently pending there. In response, plaintiff has not come forward with any specific evidence to support this court's exercise of *in personam* jurisdiction over I.T.K. but has instead urged that if transfer is considered appropriate this case should be transferred to the District of New Jersey rather than the District of Massachusetts.

On the basis of the record as it now stands, it seems clear that I.T.K.'s connection with Pennsylvania is so tenuous that this court lacks a proper basis to exercise *in personam* jurisdiction. Perhaps further discovery might reveal some basis for linking I.T.K. to that forum but plaintiff has not sought to pursue this possibility. However, rather than simply dismissing plaintiff's complaint at this point, the better approach, in my view, would be to transfer this matter to a more appropriate forum.[1]

In considering a motion to transfer, a court must first determine that the transferee district is a district where the action "might have been brought." 28 U.S.C. § 1404(a); *Hoffman v. Blaski,* 363 U.S. 335, 80 S.Ct. 1084, 4 L.Ed.2d 1254 (1960). This criterion, however, does not provide any clear guidance in determining which of the two proposed transferee districts—New Jersey or Massachusetts—is more appropriate since both appear to be districts where plaintiff's claim could have been brought. Both courts clearly have jurisdiction over the subject matter of this case under 28 U.S.C. § 1332 by virtue of the diversity of citizenship of the parties, and both courts may properly exercise *in personam* jurisdiction over I.T.K. because of I.T.K.'s contacts with New Jersey and its residence in Massachusetts. Venue would also be proper in both districts under 28 U.S.C. § 1391(a).

I turn therefore to the more difficult question whether the balance of convenience weighs decisively in favor of one of the proposed districts. It is well-settled that "unless the balance is strongly in favor of the defendant, the plaintiff's choice of forum should rarely be disturbed." *Gulf Oil Corp. v. Gilbert,* 330 U.S. 501, 508, 67 S.Ct. 839, 843, 91 L.Ed. 1055 (1947). Therefore, since the District of New Jersey is clearly plaintiff's preferred alternative forum, that preference must be accorded substantial weight.

On the opposing scale, as defendant properly suggests, must be placed the interest in efficient judicial administration which might be advanced by transfer to the District of Massachusetts where an action involving the same parties is pending. By permitting two related cases which are filed initially in different districts to be consolidated, transfer plainly helps avoid needless duplication of effort. For as Justice Black remarked in *Continental Grain Co. v. Barge FBL–585,* 364 U.S. 19, 26, 80 S.Ct. 1470, 1474, 4 L.Ed.2d 1540 (1960): "To permit a situation in which two cases involving precisely the same issues are simultaneously pending in different District Courts leads to the wastefulness of time,

1. In *Goldlawr, Inc. v. Heiman,* 369 U.S. 463, 82 S.Ct. 913, 8 L.Ed.2d 39 (1962), the Court, over Justice Harlan's dissent, construed 28 U.S.C. § 1406(a) to authorize a district court to transfer to a proper district a case filed in a district where venue is improper, notwithstanding that the trans-feror court lacks *in personam* jurisdiction. In *United States v. Berkowitz,* [328 F.2d 358 (3d Cir.1964), *cert. denied,* 379 U.S. 821, 85 S.Ct. 42, 13 L.Ed.2d 32 (1964)], our Court of Appeals extended the *Goldlawr* rationale to § 1404(a).

energy and money that § 1404(a) was designed to prevent." This consideration, of course, loses some of its force where the two pending actions do not stem from precisely the same transaction. A comparison of the complaints filed in Massachusetts and in this action reveals that the actions involve distinct, albeit related, transactions: the Massachusetts allegations speak of an August, 1981 purchase of vinyl plastic valued at $14,000 which Ginsey allegedly failed to pay for; whereas the Pennsylvania claims describe an October or November, 1981 transaction involving a $30,000 payment by Ginsey for vinyl plastic which was rejected as defective. Nevertheless, it would appear that significant economies of time and effort can be achieved if these actions were consolidated in a single district. The essential questions of liability in both actions concern the fitness of I.T.K.'s vinyl products for the commercial purposes Ginsey sought to pursue. The witnesses who will testify about I.T.K.'s product and about Ginsey's reasons for purchasing that product are likely to be the same in both cases. To be sure, consolidation of these actions in the District of Massachusetts imposes a burden on Ginsey. But transfer to that district would, in my judgment, promote efficient judicial administration to such an extent that plaintiff's preference for New Jersey is outweighed. And consolidation ultimately benefits both parties since it is clearly more convenient to conduct related litigation in a single district rather than in two separate forums.

Accordingly, I will order that this matter be transferred to the District of Massachusetts.

Notes and Questions

1. The "where it might have been brought" requirement of § 1404(a) has caused some difficulties. In Hoffman v. Blaski, 363 U.S. 335, 80 S.Ct. 1084, 4 L.Ed.2d 1254 (1960), the Court held that this requirement precluded transfer to a district where defendant would not have been subject to personal jurisdiction even though defendant was willing to waive its objections to jurisdiction. The willingness of the defendant to waive jurisdictional limitations was irrelevant; section 1404(a) was interpreted to require that plaintiff has the right to sue in the transferee district independently of the wishes of defendant. However convenient the transferee forum may be, therefore, it must be a district in which jurisdiction and venue would be proper.

Some lower courts chafed at this restriction on the power to transfer. For example, in A.J. Industries, Inc. v. United States District Court, 503 F.2d 384 (9th Cir.1974), the court upheld a transfer to a district where jurisdiction would not originally have been proper on the ground that the claim made in the transferred suit could have been raised as a counterclaim in a suit filed by the defendant in the transferee district. Thus, at the time the transferred suit was filed the plaintiff in that case could have asserted the same claim in the transferee district. But such situations are rare, and *Hoffman* remains an important limitation on transfer.

2. A § 1404(a) motion may be made at any time, although delay is a factor weighing against granting. Once a motion has been granted, the

transferor court loses jurisdiction, and the suit proceeds in the transferee court as if it had originally been filed there. In Van Dusen v. Barrack, 376 U.S. 612, 84 S.Ct. 805, 11 L.Ed.2d 945 (1964), the Supreme Court held that the transferee court must apply the state law that would have been applied in the transferor court. "Thus if the law is unclear in the state in which the action is commenced, this argues against transfer, since a district judge in that state is presumably better able to fathom its law than is a district judge in the transferee state. Also the fact that the substantive law will not be changed by a transfer may cast doubt on the feasibility of consolidating the transferred case with other cases that were commenced in the court to which transfer is proposed, and may have an effect on the witnesses that will be necessary." C. Wright & M. Kane, Law of Federal Courts 282 (6th ed. 2002). The plaintiff's ability to shop for favorable law received a boost in Ferens v. John Deere Co., 494 U.S. 516, 110 S.Ct. 1274, 108 L.Ed.2d 443 (1990), which held that *Van Dusen* applies to a § 1404(a) transfer even if it is requested by the plaintiff.

3.   Section 1406(a), which is mentioned in footnote 1 in *Ginsey Industries,* is closely related in its purpose to § 1404(a). § 1406(a) provides:

> The district court of a district in which is filed a case laying venue in the wrong division or district shall dismiss, or if it be in the interest of justice, transfer such case to any district or division in which it could have been brought.

Section 1404(a) applies when venue is proper but transfer would serve the convenience of the parties and witnesses, while § 1406(a) allows transfer in the interests of justice when venue was improper in the first place. The holdings of *Goldlawr* and *Berkowitz* [see *Ginsey Industries* footnote 1], that § 1404(a) and § 1406(a) authorize transfer *even in* cases where personal jurisdiction over the defendant is lacking, raise a question as to which section applies when personal jurisdiction is also lacking. Some courts have viewed § 1406(a) as the appropriate mechanism "when there exists an obstacle—either incorrect venue, absence of personal jurisdiction, or both— to a prompt adjudication on the merits in the forum where originally brought." Dubin v. United States, 380 F.2d 813, 816 (5th Cir.1967). Thus, in a case like *Ginsey Industries,* where the original forum lacked personal jurisdiction over the defendant, § 1406(a) would be the proper motion for transfer. Other courts have seen § 1404(a) as allowing transfer when venue is proper but the court lacks personal jurisdiction. Sargent v. Genesco, Inc., 492 F.2d 750, 759 (5th Cir.1974).

4.   Which section is used should make little difference unless it affects the choice of law decision upon transfer. Some courts have been troubled by the possibility that *Van Dusen,* a case of transfer under § 1404(a), would require the transferor law to apply even though personal jurisdiction was lacking in the original forum. That would allow a plaintiff to forum shop for substantive law by filing in any forum, whether or not it could obtain personal jurisdiction over the defendant there, and capture that forum's law. In order to avoid that result, some courts have relied on § 1406(a) to transfer whenever personal jurisdiction or venue is lacking, then applying the transferee's law to prevent unfair forum shopping. See, e.g., Wisland v. Admiral Bev. Corp., 119 F.3d 733, 735–36 (8th Cir.1997); cf. Ellis v. Great

Southwestern Corp., 646 F.2d 1099 (5th Cir.1981) (even if court purports to transfer under § 1404(a), if it lacks personal jurisdiction transferee law applies).

5. We have focused thus far on cases pending within the federal system. In 1991, the National Conference of Commissioners on Uniform State Laws adopted a proposed Uniform Transfer of Litigation Act that would permit courts of participating states to transfer cases among them, but this proposal has not been adopted in any state. For discussion, see Cooper, Interstate Consolidation: A Comparison of the ALI Project with the Uniform Transfer of Litigation Act, 54 La. L. Rev. 897 (1994).

4. DISMISSAL FOR FORUM NON CONVENIENS

Transfer of a case to another federal district court is an efficient mechanism under § 1404(a) or § 1406(a). But what if the only reasonable alternative forum is a foreign court? A federal court, of course, has no power to transfer to another sovereign court, and dismissal may be the only course in such a situation. Common law *forum non conveniens,* where applicable, permits a federal district court to refuse to proceed with a case before it and to dismiss so that an alternative foreign or state jurisdiction can be sought. It also "allows a court to exercise its discretion to avoid the oppression or vexation that might result from automatically honoring plaintiff's forum choice." J. Friedenthal, M. Kane, A. Miller, Civil Procedure 89 (3d ed. 1999).

DE MELO v. LEDERLE LABORATORIES

United States Court of Appeals, Eighth Circuit, 1986.
801 F.2d 1058.

Before JOHN R. GIBSON, CIRCUIT JUDGE, SWYGERT, SENIOR CIRCUIT JUDGE, and FAGG, CIRCUIT JUDGE.

JOHN R. GIBSON, CIRCUIT JUDGE.

Cleonilde Nunes de Melo, a citizen of Brazil, appeals the judgment of the district court dismissing her products liability claims against Lederle Laboratories on grounds of *forum non conveniens.* De Melo argues on appeal that the district court abused its discretion in concluding that Brazil was an adequate alternative forum for this litigation, and that on balance, this litigation would be more convenient for the parties and the available fora if tried in Brazil. We affirm.

Lederle Laboratories, a division of American Cyanamid Corporation, developed, tested, patented, and manufactured the drug Myambutol. American Cyanamid is a Maine corporation with headquarters in New Jersey; Lederle is a New York corporation, and maintains its main laboratories, where Myambutol was developed and manufactured, in New York. Both American Cyanamid and Lederle are licensed to do business in Minnesota. American Cyanamid also licenses the foreign manufacture of Myambutol. Under a licensing agreement, Myambutol is manufactured, marketed and distributed in Brazil by a Brazilian corporation, Cyanamid Quimica de Brasil (CQB), a wholly-owned subsidiary of American Cyanamid.

De Melo, a school teacher in her forties, was treated in Brazil for pulmonary tuberculosis. In 1976, in the course of that treatment, de Melo's Brazilian physicians prescribed Myambutol. After a few months of ingesting the drug, de Melo developed optic atrophy, and became permanently blind. The package insert to Myambutol manufactured by CQB, containing information about the appropriate uses and hazards of the product, is a Portuguese translation of an English version prepared by Lederle for domestic distribution. In 1976, the English-language package insert warned of possible permanent vision loss; the Portuguese version, however, warned only of temporary vision loss. In late 1975, Lederle sent a circular to foreign manufacturers of the drug, including CQB, advising that the package insert be amended to include a statement that repeated ingestion of the drug could cause irreversible reduced visual acuity.

De Melo filed suit in federal district court in Minnesota, seeking recovery under theories of strict liability, negligence, failure to warn, breach of express and implied warranties, and fraudulent concealment. The thrust of de Melo's claims is that Lederle had complete control over the manufacture, packaging, and labeling of Myambutol produced and distributed by CQB; that Lederle knew or should have known that Myambutol causes permanent, not temporary, loss of vision; and that it intentionally or negligently failed to provide the appropriate warnings with Brazilian manufactured Myambutol.

Lederle moved to dismiss the action on the ground of *forum non conveniens,* suggesting that Brazil was the more appropriate forum. The district court, applying the balancing test set forth by the Supreme Court in *Gulf Oil Corp. v. Gilbert,* 330 U.S. 501, 67 S.Ct. 839, 91 L.Ed. 1055 (1947), granted the motion contingent upon Lederle's acceptance of four conditions: first, Lederle consent to suit and accept service of process in Brazil in any civil action brought by de Melo on her claim; second, Lederle agree to make available any documents or witnesses within its control necessary for the fair adjudication of any such claim; third, Lederle consent to pay any judgment rendered against it by a Brazilian court in any such action; and fourth, Lederle agree to waive any statute of limitations defense which did not exist at the time de Melo filed the present action.

The district court first found that Brazil presented an adequate alternative forum to resolve this dispute. * * *

The district court next found that the balance of private interests favored litigation in Brazil. * * *

Finally, the district court found that the public interest factors weighed in favor of Lederle. * * *

A.

Under the doctrine of *forum non conveniens*, federal district courts have inherent power to resist the imposition of jurisdiction even where authorized by statute if "the litigation can more appropriately be conducted in a foreign tribunal." In *Gilbert,* the Supreme Court set out a series of considerations to guide the district court in applying the doctrine: initially, the district court must find that there exists an adequate alternative forum for the litigation; the court must then balance factors relative to the convenience of the litigants, referred to as the private interests, and factors relative to the convenience of the forum, referred to as the public interests, to determine which available forum is most appropriate for trial and resolution. *Piper Aircraft Co. v. Reyno,* 454 U.S. 235, 102 S.Ct. 252, 70 L.Ed.2d 419. The district court's decision to dismiss an action on the grounds of *forum non conveniens* may be reversed only if it is found to be an abuse of discretion. "[W]here the court has considered all relevant public and private interest factors, and where its balancing of these factors is reasonable, its decision deserves substantial deference." *Id.*[2]

B.

The doctrine of *forum non conveniens* "presupposes at least two forums in which the defendant is amenable to process...." *Gilbert,* 330 U.S. at 506–07, 67 S.Ct. at 842. Thus, "[a]t the outset of any *forum non conveniens* inquiry, the court must determine whether there exists an alternative forum." *Piper Aircraft,* 454 U.S. at 254 n. 22, 102 S.Ct. at 265 n. 22. This requirement is satisfied, ordinarily, if the defendant is amenable to process in the alternative jurisdiction, *id.; Gilbert,* 330 U.S. at 506–07, 67 S.Ct. at 842. Here, the district court ensured this by conditioning dismissal on Lederle's concession to jurisdiction and service of process in Brazil. However, "in rare circumstances," the remedy provided in the alternative forum may be "so clearly inadequate or unsatisfactory that it is no remedy at all...." *Piper Aircraft,* 454 U.S. at 254, 102 S.Ct. at 265. In such cases, the alternative forum is not adequate, for "dismissal would not be in the interests of justice." *Id.*

De Melo contends that the unavailability under Brazilian law of punitive damages and recovery for pain and suffering suggests that any recovery she may obtain in Brazil will be grossly inadequate to compensate her for her injuries and deter future misconduct by multinational corporations like the defendant. Moreover, she argues, she is financially unable to prosecute this suit absent some form of contingency arrangement, which, she claims, is rare in Brazil. Thus, the possibility of recovery, however minor, is even more remote.

---

2. We need not decide whether, under *Erie R.R. Co. v. Tompkins,* 304 U.S. 64, 58 S.Ct. 817, 82 L.Ed. 1188 (1938), Minnesota or federal law of *forum non conveniens* applies in this diversity action, *see Piper Air-* *craft,* 454 U.S. at 248, 102 S.Ct. at 262; Minnesota law of *forum non conveniens* is virtually identical to federal law. *See Bergquist v. Medtronic, Inc.,* 379 N.W.2d 508 (Minn.1986).

We do not believe that the district court abused its discretion in finding that Brazil is an adequate alternative forum for this litigation. First, the Supreme Court explicitly held in *Piper Aircraft* that, ordinarily, the fact that the alternative forum's substantive law is decidedly less favorable to the plaintiff should not be given substantial weight in *forum non conveniens* determinations.[3] Where the alternative forum offers a remedy for the plaintiff's claims, and there is no danger that she will be treated unfairly, the foreign forum is adequate. Affidavits from Brazilian attorneys make clear that de Melo's claims state a cause of action under Brazilian law and that she has a direct action against CQB, Lederle's subsidiary. Furthermore, under Brazilian law, de Melo may recover lost wages, indirect losses, and twice the amount of her medical expenses. These damages, whatever they amount to in this case, are not so paltry as to render the available remedy illusory.

The affidavits also establish that contingency fee arrangements are not uncommon, and free legal assistance is available. Although Brazil may be a less favorable forum for de Melo, we cannot conclude that it is inadequate.

C.

The second phase of the *forum non conveniens* inquiry requires the district court to balance the private interest factors, which affect the convenience of the litigants, and the public interest factors, which affect the convenience of the forum. This balance reflects the central purpose of the *forum non conveniens* inquiry: to ensure that the trial is held at a convenient situs.[4]

The factors which bear on the private interest of the litigants include:

> [T]he relative ease of access to sources of proof; availability of compulsory process for attendance of unwilling, and the cost of obtaining attendance of willing, witnesses; possibility of view of premises, if view would be appropriate to the action; and all other practical problems that make trial of a case easy, expeditious and inexpensive. There may also be questions to the enforceability [sic] of a judgment if one is obtained. The court will weigh relative advantages and obstacles to fair trial.

Gilbert, 330 U.S. at 508, 67 S.Ct. at 801.

3. The Court also held that the fact that a defendant may be engaged in reverse forum shopping—filing a motion to dismiss for *forum non conveniens* to obtain a favorable change in law in a foreign forum—should not enter the district court's analysis.

4. There is ordinarily a strong presumption that a plaintiff's choice of forum will not be disturbed, absent a clear indication that it would be unnecessarily burdensome for the defendant or the court. The district court properly acknowledged, however, that the plaintiff's choice is entitled to substantially less deference when the plaintiff is foreign. In such a case, the assumption underlying the presumption, that the plaintiff has chosen the forum for her convenience, is less reasonable. It is thus more likely that the forum was chosen to take advantage of favorable law or harass the defendant, both of which suggest that dismissal for *forum non conveniens* is warranted.

We cannot conclude that the district court erred in finding that the private interest factors weighed in favor of Lederle. De Melo properly points out that ease of access to a substantial body of the relevant evidence favors a domestic forum. Most, if not all, of the evidence relating to the development, testing, and manufacture of Myambutol—and thus the adequacy of warnings accompanying domestically produced Myambutol—presumably is located in New York or New Jersey. Moreover, she points out, litigation in Brazil will require cumbersome translation into Portuguese of all documents located in the United States.

Countervailing considerations, however, indicate that the balance of private interests was properly struck in favor of a Brazilian forum. First, de Melo's argument only accounts for the location of evidence directly relevant to her failure to warn theory, which she obviously views as her most potent claim. Evidence that Lederle is likely to consider relevant to its defense, such as evidence of CQB's manufacture, distribution, advertisement, and labelling of Myambutol, is in Brazil.[5] Additionally, all the evidence relating to de Melo's illness, course of treatment (by approximately ten physicians), ingestion of Myambutol and injuries—evidence necessary regardless of the theory of recovery—is in Brazil. It is clear, therefore, that a substantial amount of testimonial and documentary evidence will be found in Brazil. And, in light of Lederle's evidentiary needs in Brazil, it is apparent that the translation problem will be oppressive regardless of the forum.

It is of considerable importance, moreover, that litigation in the United States would deprive Lederle of compulsory process to much of the evidence located in Brazil, including the circumstances surrounding de Melo's course of treatment before and after ingesting Myambutol. The district court avoided the converse problem—that de Melo would be without compulsory process to secure evidence in this country if the litigation were held in Brazil—by conditioning dismissal on its agreement to make available in the Brazilian courts all relevant witnesses and evidence located in the United States. *Cf. Piper Aircraft*, 454 U.S. at 257 n. 25, 102 S.Ct. at 267 n. 25 (approving use of conditional dismissals to ensure plaintiff access to sources of proof). Although litigation in this country would afford de Melo greater access to sources of proof relevant to *her* theory, it would box out Lederle from access to concededly important evidence upon which its defense may well rest. "Thus, so long as trial were to be conducted in the United States, the inability of both parties to obtain the full panoply of relevant * * * evidence would greatly hinder fair resolution of the dispute." [*Pain v. United Technologies Corp.*, 637 F.2d 775,] 788 [(D.C.Cir.1980)]; *see also Piper Aircraft*,

---

5. De Melo's argument assumes that Lederle Laboratories had total and complete control over the production and distribution of Myambutol and the warnings that accompany the drug. De Melo asserts in her brief that this is an "undisputed fact." She offers portions of the licensing agreement between American Cyanamid and its Brazilian subsidiary, CQB, and statements from depositions of corporate officers of CQB which tend to support this position. However, Lederle "strongly disputes" that it possesses plenary control over CQB's production of Myambutol and product warnings.

454 U.S. at 258, 102 S.Ct. at 267 (witnesses beyond domestic compulsory process a factor in favor of *forum non conveniens* dismissal).

A second private interest strongly favoring dismissal is Lederle's inability to implead potential third-party defendants in domestic litigation. Lederle has indicated that it is likely to implead de Melo's physicians, the pharmacy from which she purchased the drug, and employees of CQB. De Melo correctly notes that Lederle could maintain a suit for indemnity or contribution against potential third-party defendants in Brazil were it found liable in an action here. However, as the Supreme Court noted in *Piper Aircraft* in response to a similar argument, "[i]t would be far more convenient . . . to resolve all claims in one trial. . . . Finding that . . . trial in the plaintiff's chosen forum would be burdensome [to the defendant] . . . is sufficient to support dismissal on grounds of *forum non conveniens*." 454 U.S. at 259, 102 S.Ct. at 268. Therefore, from the standpoint of the convenience of the parties, we believe that the district court reasonably concluded that the litigation was more appropriate in Brazil.

We also believe that the district court's balancing of the public interest factors was reasonable. The public interest factors, which bear on the convenience of the forum, include:

> The administrative difficulties flowing from court congestion; the "local interest in having localized controversies decided at home"; the interest in having the trial of a diversity case in a forum that is at home with the law that must govern the action; the avoidance of unnecessary problems in conflict of laws, or in the application of foreign law; and the unfairness of burdening citizens in an unrelated forum with jury duty.

Piper Aircraft, 454 U.S. at 241 n. 6, 102 S.Ct. at 258 n. 6 (quoting *Gilbert,* 330 U.S. at 509, 67 S.Ct. at 843).

The parties' factual allegations make it clear that neither forum can lay exclusive claim to a "local interest" precisely because this is not an entirely "localized controversy." *See Gilbert,* 330 U.S. at 509, 67 S.Ct. at 843. It is abundantly clear that the forum de Melo has chosen, Minnesota, has no peculiar local interest in this dispute. Further, insofar as there may be a general national interest in resolving this controversy in a domestic forum, we do not believe it is significant in light of Brazil's interests. *Cf. Piper Aircraft,* 454 U.S. at 260, 102 S.Ct. at 268 (plaintiff's argument that "American citizens have an interest in ensuring that American manufacturers are deterred from producing defective products" insufficient because any additional deterrence gained from domestic forum over particular foreign forum "is likely to be insignificant").

The crux of this suit concerns the safety of drugs distributed in Brazil: it involves a Brazilian woman who ingested a drug manufactured, distributed, and labelled in Brazil, pursuant to a course of treatment prescribed by Brazilian physicians, purchased from a pharmacy in Brazil, which resulted in an injury and subsequent treatment in Brazil. It would seem that Brazil has a paramount interest in regulating the quality and distribution of drugs through Brazilian products liability law. *See Dowling [v. Richardson–Merrell, Inc.],* 727 F.2d at 615 [(6th Cir. 1984)] (states where suit brought and where defendant corporation headquartered "have a minimal interest in the safety of products which are manufactured, regulated and sold abroad by foreign entities, even though the development and testing occurred in this country."); *Harrison v. Wyeth Laboratories,* 510 F.Supp. 1, 4 (E.D.Pa.1980), *aff'd mem.,* 676 F.2d 685 (3d Cir.1982) (question as to safety of drugs marketed in foreign country, even if all production and marketing decisions made in defendant's headquarters in United States, properly the concern of the foreign country). Thus, the "local interest in having local controversies decided at home," *Gilbert,* 330 U.S. at 509, 67 S.Ct. at 843, favors litigation in Brazil.

Additionally, the striking fact that this litigation lacks any significant contact with the particular forum chosen by de Melo suggests that it is inappropriate to burden that community with the "enormous commitment of judicial time and resources that would inevitably be required if the case were to be tried there."[6] *Piper Aircraft,* 454 U.S. at 261, 102 S.Ct. at 268. The only states that have any material connection to this litigation are New York and New Jersey. There simply is no justification for adding to the local docket in Minnesota or imposing jury duty on Minnesota residents on a matter which affects the forum and its residents in such a minimal fashion.

Finally, the district court held that, under Minnesota conflict of law rules, Brazilian law would likely govern the litigation. This conclusion, particularly in light of the other public factors favoring a foreign forum, strongly supports dismissal for *forum non conveniens.* There is, as the Court stated in *Gilbert,* a strong interest in resolving a dispute "in a forum that is at home with the law that must govern the action." Our review of these factors leads us to conclude that the district court's balancing of the private and public factors was reasonable.

The judgment of the district court is therefore affirmed.

Swygert, Senior Circuit Judge, dissenting.

I must respectfully dissent from the decision of my brethren to affirm the judgment of the district court dismissing Ms. de Melo's products liability claims against Lederle Laboratories on *forum non conveniens* grounds.

A motion to dismiss on the basis of *forum non conveniens* shall not be granted unless an adequate alternative forum exists. *Gulf Oil Corp. v. Gilbert,* 330 U.S. 501, 67 S.Ct. 839, 91 L.Ed. 1055 (1947). If the remedy provided by a proposed alternative forum is "so clearly inadequate or unsatisfactory that it is no remedy at all" the proposed alternative forum may not be an adequate alternative. *Piper Aircraft Co. v. Reyno,* 454 U.S. 235, 254 and n. 22, 102 S.Ct. 252, 265 and n. 22, 70 L.Ed.2d 419 (1981).

---

6. Minnesota apparently was chosen as a forum because de Melo's attorney, the father of a Peace Corps worker de Melo met in Brazil, lives in Minnesota.

The inquiry into whether an adequate alternative forum exists is a threshold issue that must be crossed before a court may weigh the public and private interests in a suit brought by a foreigner in the courts of the United States.

The evidence before the district court regarding the Brazilian legal system was presented by the parties and was conflicting in many respects: de Melo presented an affidavit from a Brazilian attorney, dos Santos. Lederle submitted a letter from another Brazilian attorney, Ibeas. Dos Santos and Ibeas agree that in Brazil there is no recovery for pain or suffering and that punitive damages are unknown. Ibeas stated that attorneys do take tort cases on a contingent basis. Dos Santos stated that de Melo would be unlikely to find an attorney willing to represent her on that basis. Dos Santos believes the case could take twenty years to be heard. Ibeas believes it will take two to five. Ibeas doubts de Melo could recover even $10,000 despite her permanent blindness. On this sketchy and contradictory evidence concerning applicable Brazilian law, I am unwilling to say that Brazil is an adequate alternative forum.[1]

At the same time, I am troubled by some of the silent assumptions lurking beneath the adequate alternative forum doctrine. The decision to hear a case ought not to depend on a subjective determination of whether another nation's legal system is "adequate." Adequate by what standards? Unfortunately, in litigation crossing national boundaries, comparisons of national legal systems must inevitably be drawn. My chief disagreement with the majority is that I would require more knowledge about a legal system before being willing to sanction the dismissal of a potentially meritorious suit and before entrusting that suit to another country's legal system. Consequently, I would remand for a hearing to determine de Melo's rights and Lederle's responsibilities under Brazilian law.

With respect to the balance of both the private and public interests, the district court adopted an overly-narrow view of those interests. Lederle would be put to relatively little inconvenience in defending de Melo's claim in the United States. Much of the documentary evidence is either in New York or under defendant's control in Brazil. Discovery in Brazil would be no problem to the defendant, and even though it hints there might be third-party defendants in Brazil who could not be impleaded in the present action, there is no disavowal that it would be prevented from seeking contribution or indemnity in Brazil. Indeed, it could be argued that it would be more of a convenience to the defendant to try the case in the United States than in Brazil. Accordingly, we should heed the admonition in *Gulf Oil Corp.*, 330 U.S. at 508, 67 S.Ct. at 843, that "unless the balance is strongly in favor of the defendant, the plaintiff's choice of forum should rarely be disturbed."

1. The district court was also apparently less than completely convinced that Brazilian law, unaided by the four conditions it placed upon the defendant, would provide an adequate alternative forum.

Finally, I cannot help observing that Lederle is a multinational corporation. It has chosen to do business in Brazil. When such companies do business in foreign countries they should not, by that fact, manage to evade the force of American law. De Melo ingested the drug in Brazil. But the decision to warn of only temporary blindness occurred in the United States, and was made by United States citizens in the employ of a United States corporation. These facts suggest that the United States is the most appropriate forum to hear Ms. de Melo's complaint.

Notes and Questions

1. Foreign plaintiffs frequently seem intrigued by American courts:

As a moth is drawn to the light, so is a litigant drawn to the United States. If he can only get his case into their courts, he stands to win a fortune. At no cost to himself, and at no risk of having to pay anything to the other side. The lawyers will conduct the case "on spec" as we say, or on a "contingency fee" as they say. * * * There is also in the United States a right to trial by jury. These are prone to award fabulous damages. They are notoriously sympathetic and know that the lawyers will take their 40 per cent. All this means that the defendant can be readily forced into a settlement. The plaintiff holds all the cards.

Smith Kline & French Laboratories Ltd. v. Bloch, [1983] 1 W.L.R. 730 (C.A.1982).

2. *Forum non conveniens* has increasingly become a potent device with respect to litigation arising out of events occurring in other countries. Consider In re Union Carbide Corp. Gas Plant Disaster, 809 F.2d 195 (2d Cir.1987), *cert. denied,* 484 U.S. 871, 108 S.Ct. 199, 98 L.Ed.2d 150 (1987), dealing with consolidated actions arising out of the gas leak at Union Carbide's plant in Bhopal, India. Many of the injured sued in American courts, and the Government of India also filed an action in this country. All of the cases in federal court were consolidated in the Southern District of New York by the Judicial Panel on Multidistrict Litigation. Carbide moved to dismiss on *forum non conveniens* grounds, and the district judge found that virtually all relevant evidence was in India. He noted further that some records were in Hindi or other Indian languages, and that an Indian court would be better able to handle them. Balanced against these interests in centering the litigation in India, he found no strong American interest in ensuring that American manufacturers are deterred from producing defective products, particularly since there was a strong Indian interest because Carbide's activities in India were licensed by that government and heavily regulated. On appeal, the Second Circuit affirmed, concluding that it might well have been an abuse of discretion to deny dismissal under these circumstances.

The district court conditioned the dismissal, however, on Carbide's consenting to jurisdiction in India, waiving statute of limitations defenses, agreeing to satisfy any judgment by an Indian court that comports with due process and submitting to discovery pursuant to the Federal Rules of Civil Procedure. The Second Circuit nullified two of these conditions. First, it found that the insistence that Carbide consent to enforcement in this country of any judgment that comports with "minimal due process" failed to take account of New York law providing for enforcement of foreign judgments rendered by systems providing "procedures compatible with the requirements of due process." Uncertain whether the district court meant to alter this standard, the appellate court found the condition erroneous. Second, it held that the requirement that Carbide consent to discovery under American rules unfair because it was not a bilateral requirement and "[b]asic justice dictates that both sides be treated equally, with each having equal access to the evidence in the possession or under the control of the other." 809 F.2d at 205.

3.   How much interest is there in this country concerning the distribution in Brazil of a product manufactured by the wholly-owned subsidiary of an American company bearing an allegedly inadequate warning in Portuguese that was never disseminated in this country? Are Judge Swygert's arguments persuasive? Even if there is some American interest, is there any justification for filing this suit in Minnesota?

4.   The court speaks in terms of interest analysis. Similar analysis is often used in making choice of law decisions, and the majority notes that Minnesota choice of law rules might well point toward applying Brazilian law to decide plaintiff's claims. In some instances that might be constitutionally required. See Phillips Petroleum Co. v. Shutts, *infra* p. 412. If Minnesota would apply its own law, should that fact alter the federal court's decision whether to dismiss?

5.   Defendant argues that it wishes to be able to make claims for contribution or indemnity against other potentially responsible parties who are not subject to suit in this country. How much importance will such claims have to a multinational manufacturer?

6.   Notice that the court in *de Melo* conditions dismissal on a number of undertakings by defendant. If a suit were filed in an entirely inappropriate location, why should the judge attach such strings to the *forum non conveniens* dismissal? Doesn't that provide a further incentive for foreign plaintiffs to have a go at the U.S. court system in hopes at least of reaping some advantage in their home-court system? Do the conditions, as Judge Swygert suggests, indicate that the judge mistrusted the Brazilian legal system?

7.   Should de Melo's objections to having to litigate in her home country carry weight? In Piper Aircraft Co. v. Reyno, the Supreme Court cited Phoenix Canada Oil Co. Ltd. v. Texaco, Inc., 78 F.R.D. 445 (D.Del. 1978), in which the alternative forum was Ecuador. The district court refused to dismiss, citing the fact that it was unclear that a tribunal in Ecuador would hear the case, and that there appeared to be no generally codified legal remedy for the unjust enrichment and tort claims asserted. In *Reyno,* by way of contrast, the Court was unconcerned about the fact that Scotland, the alternative forum, did not allow product liability claims.

In Bhatnagar v. Surrendra Overseas, Ltd., 52 F.3d 1220 (3d Cir.1995), the court held that extreme delay in the courts of another country can make suing there so inadequate as to justify denial of a forum non conveniens motion. The district court denied defendant's forum non conveniens motion, finding that India's court system was "in a state of virtual collapse" that could delay resolution of a suit there for 25 years. Although it noted that "delay is an unfortunate but ubiquitous aspect of the legal process," the appellate court held that the district judge had not abused his discretion because the "profound and extreme delay" in India was qualitatively different from that encountered in other countries.

8. In *Ginsey Industries, supra* p. 128, the fact that another case involving similar, but not identical, issues was pending in the forum to which the defendant sought transfer was a factor in granting a § 1404(a) transfer. Is the existence of related suits also significant on a forum non conveniens motion to dismiss? Guidi v. Inter–Continental Hotels Corp., 203 F.3d 180 (2d Cir.2000), was a suit by the widows of two Americans who were killed when a fanatic shot up a hotel in Egypt operated by the defendant (an American company). The suit was dismissed by the district court, which emphasized that suits by two other hotel guests who were killed in the incident were pending in Egypt. The appellate court reversed, finding that pendency of related litigation was relevant to § 1404(a), but not to a forum non conveniens motion. It found that the district judge had not given adequate weight to the plaintiffs' choice of forum, particularly since they were Americans suing an american company at its business headquarters.

In Ravelo Monegro v. Rosa, 211 F.3d 509 (9th Cir.2000), young baseball players from the Dominican Republic sued the San Francisco Giants, claiming that its scout for Latin America had defrauded them when he signed them for the Giants' system. The district court in San Francisco dismissed on forum non conveniens grounds, noting that civil and criminal proceedings had been instituted on the same matter in the Dominican Republic. The appellate court reversed, noting that San Francisco was the defendant's home forum and had a "substantial relation" to the suit because the plaintiffs' goal was to play there. It distinguished the Supreme Court's decision in Piper Aircraft v. Reyno on the ground that there were no additional parties or third-party defendants who could not be joined in the American forum, and found unpersuasive the Giants' assertion that it would be easier to get witnesses to the Dominican Republic than to San Francisco.

5. TRANSFER UNDER MULTIDISTRICT LITIGATION PROCE-DURES

The electrical equipment price-fixing conspiracy that resulted in much-publicized prosecutions of high corporate officials in the early 1960s also brought an unprecedented avalanche of treble-damage antitrust actions in the federal courts. Some 2000 suits were filed in 35 different districts. Because the suits were in different districts, Rule 42(a) consolidation was not possible. Moreover, § 1404(a) *forum non conveniens* procedures were inadequate to ensure that all the cases could be transferred to a single court. The courts were therefore forced to cope with the burden on an *ad hoc* basis, giving impetus to the creation of a Coordinating Committee for Multiple Litigation of the U.S. District Courts, composed of nine federal judges, which supervised nationwide coordinated discovery proceedings for all electrical equipment cases. Out of this experience came the Multidistrict Litigation Act, 28 U.S.C.A. § 1407, enacted in 1968. A number of states also adopted procedures for consolidating cases across the jurisdictional lines of individual courts. See, *e.g.,* California Rules of Court 1500 *et seq.*

HANSEL, EXTREME LITIGATION: AN INTERVIEW WITH JUDGE WM. TERRELL HODGES, CHAIRMAN OF THE JUDICIAL PANEL ON MULTIDISTRICT LITIGATION

2 Me. Bar J. 16–20 (Winter 2004).

Imagine you are minding your own business and litigating a case in federal court. Opening your mail one day, you find an order—from a court you have never heard of—declaring that your case is a "tag along" action and transferring it to another federal court clear across the country for pretrial proceedings. Welcome to the world of multidistrict litigation. Who is this court? How and why can it transfer tens of thousands of perfectly well-situated federal lawsuits to new districts?

Congress created the Judicial Panel on Multidistrict Litigation ("the Panel" or "the JPML") in 1968 pursuant to 28 U.S.C. § 1407. That statute provides, in pertinent part:

> When civil actions involving one or more common questions of fact are pending in different districts, such actions may be transferred to any district for coordinated or consolidated pretrial proceedings. Such transfers shall be made by the judicial panel on multidistrict litigation authorized by this section upon its determination that transfers for such proceedings will be for the convenience of the parties and will promote the just and efficient conduct of such actions. Each action so transferred shall be remanded by the panel at or before the conclusion of such pretrial proceedings to the district from which it was transferred unless it shall have been previously terminated.

The threshold issue for the Panel is *whether* to transfer a case. In deciding that issue, the Panel primarily examines whether the cases are federal civil actions pending in different districts; containing common issues of law and fact; and whether the parties, counsel and judiciary would achieve efficiencies via transfer and centralization. The Panel may also look at the nature of the cases, the number of cases and parties, the Panel's own precedent in similar actions, the chance of inconsistent rulings without centralization and how far along the respective cases are in litigation.

If the Panel is inclined to order transfer, it then considers many factors in deciding *where* to transfer cases. These include the convenience of parties and witnesses, the whereabouts of documents and things, the location of counsel, the site of accidents, the location of related grand juries, the so-called center of gravity of the litigation, the experience of the courts, the speed of courts' dockets, availability of facilities for travel, the location of parties' corporate headquarters, whether cases are pending in possible transferee courts, the level of interest of potential transferee courts and the location of the first-filed case.

Practice before the Panel is governed by the statute and by the Rules of Procedure of the Judicial Panel on Multidistrict Litigation. A "tag along action" is defined as "a civil action pending in a district court involving common questions of fact with actions previously transferred under Section 1407." Tag along actions may be transferred to the same transferee court.

The Panel consists of seven federal circuit and district judges, no two of whom shall be from the same circuit, designated from time to time by the Chief Justice of the United States. The offices and Clerk of the Panel are in Washington, D.C., but the Panel holds periodic hearings around the U.S.

From 1968 to 2002, the Penal centralized 179,071 civil actions for pretrial proceedings. Of that number, 139,975 actions have been terminated and 39,096 remain pending. The Eastern District of Pennsylvania reigns as the most frequent transferee district; the Panel has transferred 104,938 cases there since 1968. Cases before the Panel, colloquially called "MDLs," fall into several categories: air disaster, antitrust, contract, common disaster, employment practices, intellectual property, miscellaneous, products liability, sales practices, and securities.

On July 24, 2003, I interviewed Senior U.S. District Judge Wm. Terrell Hodges of the U.S. District Court for the Middle District of Florida, who serves, by appointment of Chief Justice William Rehnquist, as Chairman of the Panel.

[SELECTED ANSWERS TO INTERVIEW QUESTIONS]

The Panel is given the authority to make orders—centralizing is the word we use rather than consolidation—in a single district called the transferee district for pretrial management but they are not transferred for all purposes for all times. It is only for pretrial management. The statute contemplates, and, in fact, the Supreme Court held in Lexecon Inc. v. Milberg Weiss, Bershad, Hynes & Lerach, 523 U.S. 26, 118 S.Ct. 956, 140 L.Ed.2d 62 (1998), that the statute means what it says when it provides that once the pretrial proceedings have bene completed, then the respective cases have to be remanded or transferred back to the courts from which they came for purposes of trial. I have always assumed the reason for that is to insure that the plaintiff's choice of forum was not completely disrupted and that the right to trial by jury in the district in which the claim arose is preserved that way.

A trial lawyer ought to know that the Panel is there and that it is a mechanism apart from the venue transfer statutes that can result in a case being moved. When a lawyer becomes aware that there are similar cases pending in other districts, he may want to (a) think about whether there may be some advantage to the client in that particular case, reducing the cost of discovery or getting the benefit of the discovery of others and (b) think about possible centralization or take such steps as may be available to avoid centralization if that particular technique is beneficial to his or her client.

We meet the last Thursday of every other month and ten days before each of those sessions, I receive about six linear feet of pleadings with motions and briefs seeking or opposing transfer, etc. We have a staff in Washington of 25 employees with the clerk's office, including four staff attorneys or lawyers working full time under the direction of our executive attorney.

We remand cases frequently and sometimes in the same docket, multiple cases will be remanded to transferor courts for trial, but I'm not aware of any mass confusion resulting from that. In practice, once a case is brought within an MDL docket and centralized somewhere, one judge decides the legal issues that are presented through the dispositive motion process and summary judgment is either granted or denied. At that point, the litigation, like all cases for that matter, tends to settle or is resolved by summary judgment rulings by the transferee judge; so remand for trial is unnecessary. The cases go away through settlement or some other thing.

It is only occasionally that cases are remanded to trial. It would obviously be a lot more efficient if the transferee judge had the authority to try the cases that remain. That would add another settlement tool into the calculus that normally produces settlement anyway. It would probably be more efficient, which is why the Judicial Conference and the Panel supported legislation that would change that part of the statute and alter the result required by *Lexecon*, but I can't say we are not able to function efficiently for the want of it at the moment.

We are just traffic cops deciding whether the case should go, and if so, where. We are not making large technically difficult legal substantive decisions.

Most of the arguments, although it may be the first time around for many of the lawyers in the courtroom, we have heard over and over again. For example, a lawyer will argue that we shouldn't send the case because there is a motion to remand pending in the District Court, the case was improperly removed, and if you will let Judge Jones decide the motion to remand that we are confident is going to be granted, then this case will go away and there is no basis for the panel to act and no reason for it to act until that is done, etc., etc. In the three years I've been on the panel, I've seen the argument certainly a thousand times. Our precedent is clear: that is not a matter that is going to prevent transfer.

By the time a case matures on our docket the judge has ample time, if he or she wishes to, to rule on the remand motion, and if he or she hasn't done so, then the transferee judge can, and in many instances it is probably better if the transferee judge does it, because, again, that would minimize the likelihood of inconsistent rulings on the same issue, at least in that particular docket.

IN RE AVIATION PRODUCTS LIABILITY LITIGATION

Judicial Panel on Multidistrict Litigation, 1972.
347 F.Supp. 1401.

PER CURIAM.

The cases comprising this products liability litigation can be segregated into two broad categories. One category consists of actions by corporate plaintiffs asserting claims for damages allegedly caused by defects in the design, manufacture and installation of a gas turbine helicopter engine produced by the Allison Division of General Motors Corporation. The other category consists of actions asserting claims for personal injuries sustained when a helicopter powered by the same type engine crashed because of an alleged in-flight engine failure.

Plaintiffs in twelve actions pending in seven different districts moved the Panel to transfer these cases (hereinafter referred to as the Schedule A cases) to a single district for coordinated or consolidated pretrial proceedings. The Panel issued an order to show cause why eight apparently related cases (hereinafter referred to as the Schedule B cases) should not also be considered for transfer pursuant to 28 U.S.C. § 1407. On the basis of the papers filed and the hearing held, we find that all of the Schedule A cases and some of the Schedule B cases will clearly benefit from transfer to a single district for coordinated or consolidated pretrial proceedings.

I. SCHEDULE A CASES

A. *Background*

Plaintiffs in the Schedule A cases are represented by the same lead counsel. Each plaintiff is a corporate owner or operator of a commercial helicopter powered by a gas turbine engine designed and manufactured by the Detroit Diesel Allison Division of General Motors Corporation (hereinafter Allison). Each action concerns the design, manufacture and installation of the helicopter engine, known as the Allison 250–C18. Allegations concerning the design and manufacture of the helicopter frame are common to some of the cases, as are charges of improper performance of overhaul, modification and repair service.[1]

The claims for damages in each of the cases are similar: (1) damages to helicopters and to plaintiff's business as a result of crashes or emergency landings caused by premature failures and malfunctions of the helicopter's engine during flight; (2) damages to plaintiff's business

---

1. Textron, Inc. (a division of Bell Helicopter Company) and Fairchild–Hiller Corporation designed and manufactured the helicopters involved in these actions. Aviation Power Supply (Western United States), The Southwest Airmotive Company (Central United States) and Airwork Corporation (Eastern United States) are the authorized distributors of the Allison 250–C18 engine and component parts and are the authorized overhaul and repair facilities for the engines.

as a result of down time required to make engine modifications and repairs specified by the Federal Aviation Agency and Allison.

B. *Arguments of the Parties*

Movants urge that the existence of common questions of fact makes transfer to a single district for coordinated or consolidated pretrial proceedings necessary in order to promote the just and efficient conduct of the litigation and to avoid duplicitous discovery and unnecessary inconvenience to the parties and witnesses. Movants contend that the issue of fact central to each lawsuit is the airworthiness of the Allison 250–C18 engine, including its design, development, manufacture and installation. It is asserted that although the specific defects alleged in each separate case may not be identical they are all interwoven so as to cover the engine's general condition and airworthiness. It is also asserted that discovery common to all cases will concern the extent to which Allison controlled and directed the installation of the engine by the helicopter manufacturers and each incident of engine overhaul modification and repair performed by its authorized distributors.

Allison agrees that consolidation of the Schedule A cases for coordinated pretrial proceedings is necessary, but urges that transfer of the Lametti action [pending in D.Minn.] be denied because discovery is near completion. Allison also points out that transfer of the Freeman action [pending in W.D.Wash.] is unnecessary because that case settled shortly after trial began.

All other defendants[4] oppose transfer of any of the cases in which they are named. Although these defendants generally admit that certain common issues of fact are alleged, they argue that these issues are outnumbered by separate and distinct factual issues peculiar to each case. They assert that since the helicopters were operated in different environments under varying atmospheric conditions, both of which affect the performance of the aircraft and the engine, a substantial amount of local discovery concerning each mishap is necessary and will not be common.

These defendants contend that transfer will restrict their efforts to complete local discovery and will require them to participate in discovery not useful to them. They also contend that an important factor weighing against the desirability of transfer under Section 1407 is the lack of a single district with jurisdiction over all defendants, which precludes any real possibility of a common trial on liability.

C. *The Question of Transfer*

It is clear from the legislative history of Section 1407 that multidistrict products liability litigation was envisioned as susceptible to effective treatment under Section 1407. There is no dispute that two of the three statutory requirements to transfer exist in this litigation: these are civil

---

4. Textron, Inc. (a division of Bell Helicopter Company), Fairchild–Hiller Corpora- tion, Aviation Power Supply and Airwork Corporation.

actions involving one or more common questions of fact which are pending in more than one district. The opposition to transfer, however, strongly urges that the issues of fact are not so common that the convenience of the parties and witnesses and the just and efficient conduct of the litigation will be promoted by transfer under Section 1407. We do not agree.

Each action against Allison will require discovery concerning the design, manufacture and installation of the Allison 250–C18 engine. Even though different component parts are involved in different cases, discovery common to all cases will concern engineers responsible for the overall design and development of the engine. And plaintiffs may also be interested in deposing the company officials who relied on those engineers. Furthermore, if it is true, as plaintiffs assert, that Allison controlled the installation of the engines by the airframe manufacturers and dictated the specifications regarding overhaul, modification and repair to the authorized distributors, discovery on these issues will likely be common.

We are convinced that transfer of the Schedule A cases to a single district for coordinated or consolidated pretrial proceedings is necessary. For the convenience of the parties and witnesses it is highly desirable that witnesses relevant to the common issues be deposed but once. And only through a coordinated pretrial discovery program, tailored to fit the discovery needs of each party and supervised by a single judge, can overlapping and duplicitous discovery be avoided and the just and efficient conduct of the litigation assured.[6]

The Manual for Complex and Multidistrict Litigation specifically resolves defendants' concern that transfer will involve them in unwanted discovery:

> [E]xpenses of counsel in attending depositions on oral interrogatories can be avoided by entry of an order providing an opportunity for a delayed examination by parties who cannot afford to attend all depositions or believe the depositions will not affect their interests. . . .

> Under this order a party with limited means or who in good faith believes the deposition is of no interest to him may without risk, decide not to be represented by counsel at the deposition in question. He may read a copy of the transcript of the initial examination and then decide whether he wishes to request a delayed examination on the ground that his interests were inadequately protected at the initial examination. *Manual* Part I, § 2.31 (1970).

Furthermore, defendants' argument regarding the unavailability of a single district with jurisdiction over all parties is misdirected.[7] Transfer of civil actions pursuant to 28 U.S.C. § 1407 is for pretrial purposes only

---

6. *Cf. In re Plumbing Fixtures Litigation* where the short-line defendants and the full-line defendants were given different discovery schedules.

7. Defendants' argument is better aimed at the appropriateness of a particular transferee forum.

and the fact that all parties are not amenable to suit in a particular district does not prevent transfer to that district for pretrial proceedings where the prerequisites of Section 1407 are otherwise satisfied. Succinctly, venue is not a criterion in deciding the propriety of transfer under Section 1407.

D. Choice of Transferee Forum

The Southern District of Indiana is the most appropriate transferee forum. Allison is the one party involved in all of the transferred cases and the majority of the common discovery will focus on it. Its plant and offices are located in Indianapolis and all its documents and necessary witnesses are there. Also, the transferred cases are fairly well-scattered throughout the country and Indianapolis provides a convenient geographical center for the litigation.

Judge Morell E. Sharp of the Western District of Washington has conducted a complete discovery program in the now-settled *Freeman* action. His familiarity with the issues and discovery involved in this litigation will enable him to expedite the consolidated pretrial proceedings. Pursuant to 28 U.S.C. § 292(c), Judge Sharp has been designated to sit as a district judge in the Southern District of Indiana and this litigation will be assigned to him for pretrial proceedings.

II. Schedule B Cases

A. Cases Transferred

With respect to each action included in the Panel's show cause order, we have examined the complaint, read the briefs filed and heard oral argument. On the basis of our reasoning concerning the Schedule A cases, we conclude that, for the convenience of all parties and witnesses and the just and efficient conduct of the litigation, the following Schedule B cases should be transferred to the Southern District of Indiana for coordinated or consolidated pretrial proceedings.

1. Arizona Helicopters, Inc. v. General Motors Corp. et al., District of Arizona, Civil Action No. Civ.–70–323–PHX

The allegations of plaintiff's complaint closely parallel those made by plaintiffs in the Schedule A cases. Plaintiff, owner of a helicopter powered by an Allison 250–C18 engine, alleges that as a result of engine failures it suffered damage to the aircraft, a loss of revenue due to inability to use the aircraft and additional pecuniary losses. It is alleged that these in-flight failures were a result of defects in the design, material, construction or workmanship (or some combination thereof) regarding the engine and its component parts.

All parties to this action oppose transfer. They claim that discovery is substantially complete, except for a few depositions scheduled to be taken in Indianapolis. Although the case had been scheduled for trial on July 11, 1972, we are advised by counsel that the trial date has been continued for approximately six months. In light of this development and to avoid the possibility of duplicitous discovery and unnecessary inconvenience to the Indianapolis witnesses, we think it best to order this case transferred to the Southern District of Indiana for the completion of pretrial discovery. Certainly if this is the only remaining discovery needed, Judge Sharp can devise a program to accommodate these parties and the action may be considered for remand to the District of Arizona.

2.   Sabine Offshore Services, Inc. v. General Motors Corp., Eastern District of Texas, Civil Action No. 7647

Plaintiff claims that it is entitled to recover damages for two separate helicopter crashes caused by in-flight engine failures. Both the plaintiff and defendant oppose transfer on the ground that this action does not present questions of fact common to the other cases. We do not agree. Plaintiff alleges that the helicopter's engine, an Allison 250–C18, was defective either in "workmanship, design or material at the time the helicopter's engine manufactured by defendant was delivered to plaintiff." Thus, as far as plaintiff's discovery is concerned, there definitely are areas in which questions of fact exist common to the transferred cases. We believe that both parties will benefit from participation in the consolidated pretrial proceedings before Judge Sharp. Once the common discovery is completed, of course, the action may be considered for remand to the Eastern District of Texas.

3.   Ranger et al. v. General Motors Corp. et al., District of Arizona, Civil Action No. Civ.–72–42–PCT

This action, originally filed in state court and subsequently removed to federal court, consists of two claims. The first is a wrongful death claim brought by the personal representative of the estate of a pilot fatally injured in a helicopter crash; the second claim is brought by the corporate owner of two helicopters that were involved in several crashes, one of which resulted in the fatality complained of in the first claim.

A comparison of the second claim with the complaint filed in Elling Halvorsen, Inc., et al. v. Textron, Inc., et al., District of Arizona, Civil Action No. Civ.–71–58–PHX (a Schedule A case), reveals that similar allegations are made in that action involving the same parties and concerning the same helicopters and mishaps. Furthermore, counsel representing the corporate plaintiffs in the second claim also serve as lead counsel for the Schedule A plaintiffs. It is therefore clear that the second claim of the Marvel Ranger action should be consolidated with the other cases for the coordinated pretrial proceedings in the Southern District of Indiana and it is so ordered.

Although plaintiffs in the first claim have no objection to transfer of the second claim for coordinated or consolidated pretrial proceedings, they argue that their claim does not present questions of fact sufficiently common to the other actions to warrant transfer at this time. We agree. Section 1407(a) authorizes the Panel to "separate any claim" from the transferred action and to remand that claim to the transferor district. We therefore remand the first claim of the Marvel Ranger action to the District of Arizona, but without prejudice to later application for transfer should the parties find that discovery will duplicate discovery in the transferee district.

B.   Cases Not Transferred

We have considered each of the remaining Schedule B cases on its own merits and have concluded that none of them present sufficient common questions of fact to warrant transfer to the Southern District of Indiana at this time.

1.   Richard W. Black v. Fairchild Industries, Inc., et al., District of New Jersey, Civil Action No. 63–72 and

John W. Thumann et al. v. Fairchild Industries, Inc., et al., District of Maryland, Civil Action No. 72–433M

Both cases are personal injury actions arising out of the crash of a helicopter en route from Baltimore Friendship Airport to Washington National Airport. Although plaintiffs allege that the crash resulted from a failure of the helicopter's engine, an Allison 250–C18, the complaints do not set forth any specific engine defect and we cannot conclude that discovery will involve issues of fact common to the transferred cases. Transfer is therefore denied without prejudice to later application if it is found during the course of pretrial that discovery will duplicate discovery in the transferee forum.

2.   Mrs. Doyle R. Avant, Jr., et al. v. Fairchild–Hiller Corp. et al., Southern District of Texas, Civil Action No. 70–V–1 and

Barbara G. Hall et al. v. Fairchild–Hiller Corp. et al., Southern District of Texas, Civil Action No. 70–V–2

These cases are wrongful death actions arising from the crash of a helicopter near Goliad, Texas. Transfer is opposed on the ground that discovery is complete and that trial is set for August 14, 1972. It is asserted that any discovery that remains does not involve questions of fact common to the transferred litigation. Transfer of these actions is therefore denied without prejudice to the right of a party to seek reconsideration at a later time.

3.   Petroleum Helicopters, Inc. v. The Southwest Airmotive Co. et al., Western District of Louisiana, Civil Action No. 16224

Plaintiff asserts claims for damages allegedly caused by defendant's negligence in servicing plaintiff's helicopter. Discovery only involves the maintenance and service performed by the defendant and the circumstances surrounding the forced landings. Since it appears that no questions of fact exist common to the transferred cases, transfer is denied, but without prejudice to later application if the parties deem it necessary to expand their discovery to encompass the discovery in the consolidated actions.

Notes and Questions

1.   In the *Aviation Products* litigation, could the various cases have been filed together as one action under Rule 20? Recall Dunavant v. Ford

Motor Co., *supra* p. 33 n. 4. Does the answer to that question bear on the propriety of transfer pursuant to § 1407? How much overlap is necessary? In *Aviation Products,* unrelated crashes or malfunctions are involved and various kinds of injuries are alleged. In some types of cases, the Panel has developed working rules favoring transfer. Consider the following analysis by the Panel with respect to a motion to remand in an action alleging securities fraud:

> We have in the past entertained motions to remand, but our past experience with securities law actions involving both actions against the issuer of securities and against the broker participating in their sale to plaintiff indicates that it is generally preferable to transfer all such actions to a single judge, who can then arrange a schedule for the expeditious completion of pretrial proceedings in the common areas.

In re King Resources Co. Securities Litigation, 342 F.Supp. 1179 (Jud.Pan. Mult.Lit.1972). Is this approach preferable to a detailed analysis of the particular facts of the cases in question? Cf. Comment, The Judicial Panel on Multidistrict Litigation: Time for Rethinking, 140 U. Pa. L. Rev. 711 (1991) (asserting that Panel pays insufficient attention to party interests).

2. It should be apparent that the Panel will transfer cases over the objections of numerous parties. Why would parties oppose transfer? In *Aviation Products,* all defendants except Allison opposed transfer on the ground it would involve them in unwanted discovery. How satisfactory is the Panel's response to that concern? Are "bystander" parties in multidistrict cases entitled to more or less solicitude than in single-district consolidation situations?

Herrmann, To MDL or Not to MDL? A Defense Perspective, 24 Litigation 43 (Summer 1998), examines the practical implications of MDL treatment. For example, a defendant facing an imminent outburst of litigation might inaugurate MDL proceedings simply because these take time and it can use the resulting breather to "organize a defense, negotiate a global settlement, or file a bankruptcy proceeding." Moreover, MDL proceedings in federal court can allow the state court cases (not subject to this delay) to proceed faster. On the other hand, having cases before a number of federal courts permits defense counsel to accelerate cases proceeding before judges the defense likes, or cases involving weak opposing counsel. To shift to the MDL process means that the litigation "takes on a life of its own," and many weaker claims will be filed. Eliminating duplicative discovery is desirable, but "it is difficult to enforce any limitations on discovery in an MDL proceeding based on notions of relevance." On both sides, the ratcheting up of the stakes that MDL produces may lead counsel to adopt extreme positions.

3. Where possibly overlapping class actions have been filed, the Panel has recognized this fact as strongly favoring transfer. In re Piper Aircraft Distribution System Antitrust Litigation, 405 F.Supp. 1402, 1403–04 (Jud. Pan.Mult.Lit.1975); see Note, The Judicial Panel and the Conduct of Multidistrict Litigation, 87 Harv.L.Rev. 1001, 1010 & n. 41 (1974) (asserting that the Panel had as of that date transferred *all* cases involving potentially overlapping classes). In what other situations is such a risk of inconsistency a reason for transferring?

Consider In re Westinghouse Electric Corp. Uranium Contracts Litigation, 405 F.Supp. 316 (Jud.Pan.Mult.Lit.1975). Westinghouse found itself unable to perform its contractual obligation to deliver uranium products to a number of utilities and other customers. Westinghouse notified these customers that it considered itself excused from performance due to commercial impracticability pursuant to § 2–615 of the Uniform Commercial Code, and that it had established an allocation program that would provide each customer with approximately 19% of the amount it should receive under its contract. All the customers sued to enforce their contracts. Although the suits involved different contracts negotiated by different people at different times, the Panel transferred them for combined treatment, noting that transfer would "eliminate the possibility of colliding pretrial rulings by courts of coordinate jurisdiction, and avoid potentially conflicting preliminary injunctive demands on Westinghouse with respect to its delivery of uranium."

4. If the Panel concludes that combined treatment is appropriate, should it, or the transferee judge, be empowered to enjoin prosecution of other suits even if they are in state court? Professor Wright suggests that such cases may fall within the exception to the Anti–Injunction Act (see *infra* pp. 190–99) for injunctions in aid of the federal court's jurisdiction: "This principle would seem to apply to prevent conflicting state actions where many similar suits have been consolidated by the Judicial Panel on Multidistrict Litigation under 28 U.S.C.A. § 1407. The purpose of consolidation is to provide coordinated treatment of these complex cases, and, as in actions in rem and school desegregation cases, it is intolerable to have different orders coming from different courts." C. Wright & M. Kane, The Law of Federal Courts 306 n. 51 (6th ed. 2002).

5. Should the transfer decision be deferred until preliminary motions are decided in the transferor court? In In re King Resources Co. Securities Litigation, 385 F.Supp. 588 (J.P.M.L.1974), one defendant resisted transfer of an action from Ohio to Colorado on the ground that he had pending in the Ohio court a motion to dismiss for lack of personal jurisdiction. The Panel held that the pendency of this motion would not affect the transfer decision because the transferee judge could decide the motion. How likely is the transferee judge to grant the motion? Cf. 28 U.S.C.A. § 1406. See also In re Crown Life Ins. Co. Premium Litig., 178 F.Supp.2d 1365 (J.P.M.L.2001) (transfer not deferred until after decision of plaintiff's motion to remand to state court; transferee judge can rule on that).

6. Despite its broad powers, the Panel ordinarily cannot reach cases in state court. The American Law Institute's Complex Litigation Project (1994) proposed *transfer* from state and federal courts to a transferee court (federal or state) that would then *consolidate* the cases for aggregate disposition. Federal "intrasystem consolidation" would be enhanced by expanding MDL transfer under § 1407 through use of a Complex Litigation Panel and extending authority to the transferee court over trial as well as pretrial. Federal-state "inter-system consolidation" would be accomplished by expanded removal to federal court and consolidation of actions pending in state courts arising out of the same basic transaction that is the basis of a pending federal-court action. See American Law Institute, Complex Litigation: Statutory Recommendations and Analysis § 5.01 (1994). In aid of this mechanism

are provisions for supplemental jurisdiction, § 5.03, anti-suit injunctions, § 5.04, court-ordered notice of intervention and preclusion, § 5.05, and a federal choice of law standard, §§ 6.01–6.07. Despite, or perhaps because of, its broad and comprehensive attempt to deal with duplicative cases in both federal and state courts, the ALI Project's proposals have not been adopted by Congress.

In 2002, Congress did adopt the Multiparty, Multiforum Trial Jurisdiction Act of 2002, 116 Stat. 1826. This Act adds 28 U.S.C. § 1369, which gives district courts original jurisdiction so long as there is minimal diversity in litigation "that arises from a single accident, where at least 75 natural persons have died in the accident at a discrete location." § 1369(a). But if the "substantial majority of all plaintiffs" are citizens of a single state, and the claims will be governed primarily by the law of that state, the federal court should abstain from exercising this jurisdiction. § 1369(b). The district court before which the action is pending is to notify the MDL Panel. § 1369(d). Because accidents causing 75 deaths are relatively rare, this statute is not likely to be invoked often.

WEIGEL, THE JUDICIAL PANEL ON MULTIDISTRICT LITIGATION, TRANSFEROR COURTS AND TRANSFEREE COURTS

78 F.R.D. 575 (1978).

A transfer under Section 1407 becomes effective upon the filing of the Panel's order of transfer with the clerk in the transferee district. Thereafter it is generally accepted that the jurisdiction of the transferor court ceases and the transferee court assumes complete pretrial jurisdiction. The mere pendency of a motion or of an order to show cause before the Panel in no way limits the jurisdiction of the court in which the action is pending. Nor does such pendency before the Panel "affect or suspend orders and pretrial proceedings" in that court. All discovery in progress and all orders of the transferor court remain in effect after transfer unless and until modified by the transferee judge who may modify, expand, or vacate prior orders of the transferor court.

There are no decisions dealing with the question as to whether a transferor judge may [after remand of a case] modify, expand or vacate prior orders of a transferee judge. Modifications or expansions to further the effectiveness of such orders would appear to be proper—perhaps necessary in some instances. However, it would be improper to permit a transferor judge to overturn orders of a transferee judge even though error in the latter might result in reversal of the final judgment of the transferor court. If transferor judges were permitted to upset rulings of transferee judges, the result would be an undermining of the purpose and usefulness of transfer under Section 1407 for coordinated or consolidated pretrial proceedings because those proceedings would then lack the finality (at the trial court level) requisite to the convenience of witnesses and parties and to efficient conduct of actions.

Since the transfer order does deprive the transferor court of jurisdiction, the Panel undertakes to avoid ordering transfer when important motions have been fully submitted and await decision by the prospective transferor court. The Panel often accomplishes that objective informally by a letter from the Chairman of the Panel informing each transferor judge of the prospective transfer. The letter also advises that, if requested, the Panel will defer transfer until the judge decides any matter fully submitted and ripe for decision. Occasionally, the Panel will enter an order deferring decision on the question of transfer until a matter so submitted is decided by the prospective transferor judge. Or the Panel may stay transfer pending such decision.

* * *

The transferee judge assigned to multidistrict litigation possesses all pretrial powers over the transferred actions exercisable by a district court under the Federal Rules of Civil Procedure. In other words, the transferee judge may make any pretrial order that the transferor court might have made in the absence of transfer.

It is the province of the transferee judge to determine the degree and manner in which pretrial proceedings are coordinated or consolidated. The Panel has neither the power nor the inclination to make any determinations regarding the actual conduct of the coordinated or consolidated pretrial proceedings.

The transferee judge has control over all aspects of discovery. The unique discovery interests of any party can be accommodated by him in a schedule providing for discovery on non-common issues to proceed concurrently with those which are common. Or the transferee judge may leave discovery on any unique issue for the supervision of the transferor court upon remand. The transferee judge can make results of completed discovery available to parties in related actions, and to parties in actions that are later filed in the transferee district or in "tag-along" actions, i.e., those transferred by the Panel to be joined with cases previously ordered to be transferred.

* * *

It is generally accepted that a transferee judge has authority to decide all pretrial motions, including motions that may be dispositive, such as motions for judgment approving a settlement, for dismissal, for judgment on the pleadings, for summary judgment, for involuntary dismissal under Rule 41(b), for striking an affirmative defense, for voluntary dismissal under Rule 41(a) and to quash service of process. In several instances, there has been appellate review of the rulings of a transferee court on such motions. In each instance, the authority of the transferee court has either been taken for granted, or expressly affirmed.

Section 1407 provides that each action transferred by the Panel shall be remanded by the Panel, at or before the conclusion of pretrial proceedings, to the district from which the action was transferred unless it shall have been previously terminated. In point of fact, slightly less than five percent of the actions transferred by the Panel have been remanded. Most actions are terminated either in the transferee district (often by settlement) or are transferred by the transferee judge to the transferee district or to another district for trial pursuant to Sections 1404(a) or 1406.

The Panel alone has the power to remand an action or claim. In the exercise of that power, the Panel defers to the views of the transferee judge. Absent a recommendation of remand from the transferee judge, any party advocating remand bears an especially heavy burden.

IN RE FACTOR VIII OR IX CONCENTRATE BLOOD PRODUCTS LITIGATION

United States District Court, Northern District of Illinois, 1996.
169 F.R.D. 632.

GRADY, DISTRICT JUDGE.

The broad question addressed in this opinion is whether a transferee court in multidistrict litigation under 28 U.S.C.A. § 1407 has the authority to limit the number of common-issue expert witnesses at trials which will take place after remand to the transferor districts. If the answer to that question is in the affirmative, then the second question is what the limit should be in this particular litigation.

[Plaintiffs, who suffer from hemophilia, must use "factor concentrates," which contain protein derived from the plasma of blood donors, to deal with their condition. Defendants produce virtually all of the factor concentrates used in the United States. Plaintiffs allege that they have become infected with the Human Immunodeficiency Virus (which causes AIDS) due to use of improperly prepared factor concentrates produced by defendants. Although plaintiffs claim that methods existed to protect against such infection, defendants claim that the risk was unforeseeable during the time plaintiffs became infected and also that no effective means existed to guard against the risk.

The JPML transferred all such cases to Judge Grady, who ultimately had over 190 pending before him. Judge Grady adopted a discovery schedule including a deadline for designation of expert witnesses and providing for depositions of those persons. Defendants designated 137 such expert witnesses, although they conceded that they did not intend to call that many in any particular trial. Unable to depose all 137, and fearing that failure to depose a particular witness before remand of cases that had been transferred might preclude a later deposition, plaintiffs moved for an order requiring defendants to shorten their list of experts. Defendants responded by arguing that Judge Grady lacked authority under § 1407 to make such an order because the statute gives the transferee judge authority over "pretrial" matters only.]

Defendants fundamentally misconceive the nature of multidistrict litigation and "the role of an MDL court." The source of their confusion is their failure to understand, or at least to acknowledge, the relationship between the "pretrial proceedings" referred to in § 1407 and the trial itself. The pretrial and the trial are not, as defendants imply, two unrelated phases of the case. Rather, they are part of a continuum that results in resolution of the case, and the relationship between them is intimate. "Pretrial" proceedings are conducted to prepare for trial. A judge who has no power to impose limits as to what will happen at trial is obviously a judge who has little ability to manage pretrial proceedings in a meaningful way, since there would be no assurance that the judge's efforts are directed toward what is likely to happen at trial. That it is essential for the "pretrial" judge to have the authority to enter orders that will be binding as to the conduct of the trial is recognized by Rule 16(c)(4), (13), (14) and (15), of the Federal Rules of Civil Procedure, which gives the judge conducting pretrial conferences authority to enter a variety of orders that will shape the conduct of the trial, including authority to limit the number of expert witnesses and to establish time limits for presenting evidence at trial. Rule 16 conferences are not necessarily conducted by the same district judge who will ultimately try the case; and some district judges routinely refer Rule 16 conferences to magistrate judges who, in the absence of consent by the parties, could not even be authorized to try the case.

* * * Unless the transferee judge has the authority to enter pretrial orders that will govern the conduct of the trial, there would be little prospect that the "coordinated or consolidated pretrial proceedings" contemplated by [§ 1407] would "promote the just and efficient conduct of such actions." If the transfer is to serve the legislative purpose of § 1407, the transferee judge must have the same authority that any pretrial judge has to enter orders that will ensure the relevance of the pretrial proceedings to the conduct of any trial that occurs after remand to the transferor court. Rule 16 applies to multidistrict proceedings the same as it applies to individual cases, and the transferee court may exercise the authority granted under Rule 16(c)(4) to limit the number of expert witnesses to be called at trial.

* * *

It is true, of course, that no pretrial judge, one managing an individual case as well as one managing consolidated pretrial proceedings in a multidistrict litigation, can anticipate everything that might happen up to the point of trial. Obviously, pretrial orders containing limitations that are overtaken by events are subject to adjustment by the judge who will try the case. For instance, a designated expert witness whose deposition has been taken may die before trial, necessitating the designation of a substitute. But the need for such adjustments is exceptional, not routine. Normally, witness limitations work well. This is especially true in the case of expert witnesses, who often are highly paid and, short of death, likely to be available for trial. Pretrial proceedings have to be conducted on the assumption that the needs of the trial can be fairly anticipated by the pretrial judge. Any other approach would render pretrial proceedings pointless.

This is not to suggest that in the absence of unforeseen developments the transferor judges in this litigation are bound by what this court does. The extent to which any transferor judge might see fit to vary what we do here is a matter of his or her own good judgment. We would expect any error on our part to be corrected before the case went to trial. This is not a matter of trying to tie the hands of the trial judge. It is a matter of defining what this court's authority is to enter orders that will bind the parties at trial to the extent the trial judge sees fit to enforce them. (It is also a matter of determining whether the transferor court can, as a matter of law, safely adhere to the orders of the transferee judge should he or she find it otherwise appropriate to do so.) But it is obvious that the objectives of § 1407 can best be achieved when a departure from the transferee judge's pretrial orders is the exception rather than the rule, and it is this court's impression that such departures are in fact exceptional.[3]

[Drawing in part on his own experience in having presided at one of thirteen factor concentrate cases that went to trial before the MDL consolidation, Judge Grady directed the defendants to designate collectively up to 24 common-issue expert witnesses that they would call to testify in trial of an MDL case.]

Notes and Questions

1. As Judge Weigel's article points out, the transferee judge has authority under § 1407(a) concerning all "pretrial proceedings." There was some sentiment in Congress for permitting the judge to handle only discovery matters, but that seemed unworkable since the scope of discovery could depend on disposition of other motions, such as motions to dismiss or for summary judgment. But it is also clear that the transferee judge cannot hold a trial, and the statute commands that the case be remanded at the conclusion of the "pretrial proceedings."

It may be that Congress assumed there would be a clear line of demarcation between pretrial proceedings and the trial, but that dividing line has become muddy since 1968 due to the development of judicial management of litigation. We will examine this phenomenon in Chapter VI; for the present it is sufficient to appreciate that judges have undertaken to superintend all aspects of pretrial preparation, a shift that is reflected in the extensive expansion of Rule 16. See Rules 16(b) and (c). Should the "pretrial proceedings" provision of § 1407 be interpreted differently against the background of this change in judicial behavior?

2. Should Judge Grady's expert witness order be considered "pretrial" within the meaning of § 1407? Would it matter whether he had reason to think that defendants were trying to take advantage of plaintiffs through the discovery process? In connection with the Bendectin litigation, Professor Green has noted that "Merrell [the defendant] designated every expert witness it might conceivably ask to testify, thereby overwhelming plaintiffs

---

3. The writer happens to be a current member of the Judicial Panel on Multidis-   trict Litigation.

with the number that had to be deposed." M. Green, Bendectin and Birth Defects 131 (1996).

Defendants sought a writ of mandate to overturn Judge Grady's order, but the court of appeals denied the petition. In the Matter of Rhone–Poulenc Rorer Pharmaceuticals, Inc., 138 F.3d 695 (7th Cir.1998). Because this was a petition for a writ of mandate, the court did not have to decide whether the defendants' arguments were correct but only whether the judge's order was usurpative. It offered the following observations:

> A judge presiding over pretrial proceedings has the power to limit the number of witnesses, and Judge Grady's action in limiting the number of the defendants' common-expert witnesses * * * is not so unreasonable in the circumstances that it can be considered usurpative. And, as he pointed out, it is inevitable that pretrial proceedings will affect the conduct of the trial itself, a notable example being a final pretrial order issued under Fed.R.Civ.P.16—an order that a judge presiding over pretrial proceedings by reference from the Multidistrict Litigation Panel has * * * the power to issue. The order challenged here is of that character.

> And the harm to the defendants is not irreparable. They can ask the judges to whom the cases will be retransferred for trial to disregard it, and should the defendants go on to lose that case, they can appeal and challenge the order, just as they can challenge any other interlocutory ruling they think constituted reversible error.

3. In re Asbestos Products Liability Litigation (No. VI), 771 F.Supp. 415 (J.P.M.L.1991), transferred over 26,000 asbestos personal injury cases for combined treatment before a single federal district judge in Philadelphia. The Panel assured the parties (many of whom opposed transfer) that it would not "result in their actions entering some black hole, never to be seen again." Id. at 423 n. 10. More specifically, although it emphasized that "[t]he Panel has neither the power nor the disposition to direct the transferee court in the exercise of its powers and discretion in pretrial rulings," id. at 421, it offered a number of suggestions about how the cases might be streamlined, including (1) a single national class action trial or other types of consolidated trials on product defect, state of the art, or punitive damages; (2) a case deferral program for plaintiffs who are not critically ill (i.e., pleural registries); (3) limited fund class action determinations; and (4) exploration of a global settlement of all cases pending in federal court. It also left open the possibility of developing a "nationwide roster of senior district or other judges available to follow actions remanded back to heavily impacted districts" if that seemed desirable to the transferee judge. Id. at 422. It expressed hope that uniform case management "will, in fact, lead to sizeable reductions in transaction costs (and especially in attorneys' fees)." Id. The Panel concluded that "[w]e emphasize our intention to do everything within our power to provide such assistance in this docket." Id. at 423.

In fact, the asbestos transfer was followed by an attempt to use the class action device to settle all yet-unfiled claims against certain asbestos defendants, but the Supreme Court ruled in 1997 that this effort was unsatisfactory under Rule 23. See Amchem Products, Inc. v. Windsor, *infra* p. 372. As the Court noted in that case, "[i]t is basic to comprehension of this proceeding to notice that no transferred case is included in the settlement at issue, and no case covered by the settlement existed as a civil action at the time of the MDL Panel transfer." See *infra* p. 374 footnote 3.

The judge who chaired the Panel before Judge Hodges was appointed chair praised the transferee judge in the asbestos litigation because "he has been able to keep to a minimum the corporations involved from going into bankruptcy, while at the same time assuring the plaintiffs with the most serious cases a fair and speedy resolution of their case. * * * Judge Weiner has miraculously disposed of approximately 63,500 separate cases, which translates into over 5,000,000 separate claims." Interview, Panel's Long–Time Chair Steps Down, The Third Branch, Dec. 2000, at 10. Not everyone was overjoyed, however. For example, in In re Patenaude, 210 F.3d 135 (3d Cir.2000), the court of appeals with authority to review the transferee judge's handling of these transferred asbestos cases refused to grant a writ of mandate sought by three groups of plaintiffs who sought remand of their asbestos cases to their transferor courts on the ground that they had been mired in the MDL proceeding for seven years while the principal activity there was discussion of settlement. The court held that the transferee court has discretion on when to remand, and that settlement was a proper aspect of pretrial. See also In re Collins, 233 F.3d 809 (3d Cir.2000) (plaintiffs whose claims for compensatory damages but not for punitive damages were returned for trial objected that the transferee judge had undertaken "the substantive task of preserving the assets available to satisfy asbestos claims by refusing to remand the punitive damages issue").

4. At least the statute indicates that the cases will be remanded for trial, but as Judge Weigel points out they rarely get remanded at all. What is the explanation for this? One answer is that most cases settle, including transferred ones, and settlement promotion is among the activities judges have embraced in their management of litigation. Another is that judges can dispose of the merits with pretrial rulings on summary judgment or dismissing claims.

Yet another explanation has depended on a broad reading of the authority of the transferee judge to grant pretrial motions. Within a decade of adoption of § 1407, transferee judges found that § 1404(a) could often be a method for transferring cases for trial. Of course, that was possible only if the judge sat in a district in which the cases could originally have been brought, but if so it became an accepted practice for transferee judges to use § 1404(a). The practice was even embodied in a rule adopted by the Panel.

Despite the broad acceptance of self-transfer pursuant to § 1404(a), the Supreme Court held that it was improper in Lexecon Inc. v. Milberg Weiss Bershad Hynes & Lerach, 523 U.S. 26, 118 S.Ct. 956, 140 L.Ed.2d 62 (1998), because the statute says that at the completion of pretrial proceedings the action "shall be remanded * * * unless it shall have been previously terminated." The transferee judge in that case had resolved all but one of the claims by summary judgment. Over plaintiff's objections, he transferred the case to himself for trial of that claim pursuant to § 1404(a). Defendant prevailed at trial. Even though plaintiff made no claim of error in the conduct of the trial, the Supreme Court reversed because the statute "obligates the Panel to remand any pending case to its originating court when, at the latest, those pretrial proceedings have run their course." It rejected defendant's argument that the granting of the § 1404(a) motion constituted a "termination" that obviated remand, and concluded that defendant "may or may not be correct that permitting transferee courts to make self-assignments would be more desirable than preserving a plaintiff's choice of venue (to the degree that § 1407(a) does so), but the proper venue for resolving that issue remains the floor of Congress."

Might there still be ways for transferee judges to retain control of cases by doing something comparable to a § 1404(a) transfer? The Manual for Complex Litigation (4th) § 20.132 (2004), suggests the following ideas:

> Prior to recommending remand, the transferee court could conduct a bellwether trial of a centralized action or actions originally filed in the transferee district, the results of which (1) may, upon consent of the parties to constituent actions not filed in the transferee district, be binding on those parties and actions, or (2) may otherwise promote settlement in the remaining actions.

> The plaintiffs to an action transferred for pretrial from another district may seek or be encouraged (1) to dismiss their action and refile the action in the transferee district, provided venue lies there, and the defendant(s) agree, if the ruling can only be accomplished in conjunction with a tolling of the statute of limitations or a waiver of venue objections, or (2) to file an amended complaint asserting venue in the transferee district, or (3) to otherwise consent to remain in the transferee district for trial.

> After an action has been remanded to the originating transferor court at the end of section 1407 pretrial proceedings, the transferor court could transfer the action, pursuant to 28 U.S.C. § 1404(a) or 1406, back to the transferee court for trial by the transferee judge.

> The transferee judge could seek an intercircuit or intracircuit assignment pursuant to 28 U.S.C. § 292 or 294 and follow a remanded action, presiding over the trial of the action in that originating district.

As mentioned by Judge Hodges, *supra* p. 145, the Judicial Conference of the United States endorsed legislation to overturn *Lexecon* and allow transferee courts to try transferred actions. Bills have been introduced in Congress. See, e.g., Multidistrict Litigation Restoration Act of 2004, H.R. 1768 (108th Cong.), passed by the House of Representatives in March, 2004, and pending before the Senate as this book went to press, Legislation has not been passed, however.

5.   Despite *Lexecon*, a stipulation between the parties to proceed to trial in the transferee district may continue to be binding. In In re Carbon Dioxide Indus. Antitrust Litigation, 229 F.3d 1321 (11th Cir.2000), after the parties stipulated to trial in the transferee court, many of the claims settled, and the plaintiffs moved to return the cases to the transferor districts. The court refused, and the case was tried. The appellate court ultimately held that the case was distinguishable from *Lexecon* and that § 1404(a) transfer was proper because there was no problem of subject matter jurisdiction and venue can be waived by the parties.

6.   Note that Judge Weigel's article also suggests that, if the case is remanded, the transferor judge can't change orders entered by the transferee judge. Ordinarily, one judge is not bound by the prior rulings of another

judge who previously presided over a case. For example, Amarel v. Connell, 102 F.3d 1494 (9th Cir.1996), a case not involving a transfer to another district, presented a problem like the one confronting a transferor judge after Judge Grady's order. The case was shifted from one district judge to another in the same district. The first judge had sanctioned defendants by prohibiting them from offering any expert testimony at trial because they failed to answer plaintiff's expert witness interrogatories. At trial before the second judge, however, defendants called an expert as a rebuttal witness and the witness was allowed to testify. As the appellate court saw the problem:

> We are confronted here with the delicate problem of two district court judges exercising their "broad discretion" over evidentiary rulings in different phases of the same case and reaching contradictory results. [The first judge] exercised his discretion in sanctioning defendants' discovery violations by prohibiting defendants from introducing expert testimony. The propriety of that decision is uncontested here. [The second judge] exercised her discretion to allow rebuttal testimony by the excluded defense expert.

Id. at 1515. Given the latitude afforded the trial judge to modify pretrial orders, the court of appeals found no error.

In In re New England Mutual Life Ins. Co., 183 F.R.D. 33 (D.Mass. 1998), the transferee court certified a class action that included the MDL cases transferred to it, stating that it did not expect to transfer the MDL cases to itself, but that the class certification was "designed to advance pretrial preparations so that the transferor court will not have to repeat, case by case, all the preparation that will have been completed before the MDL cases are remanded."

7. Under the doctrine "law of the case," a judge customarily will not overturn the orders of a prior judge on the same case unless there are changed circumstances. How should this doctrine apply in multidistrict litigation? Note that Judge Weigel points out that on occasion the Panel will delay transfer to permit the transferor judge to make rulings, and the orders thus entered by the transferor remain in effect unless changed by the transferee. How should the transferee approach orders already entered by the transferor?

In In re Upjohn Co. Antibiotic Cleocin Products Liability Litigation, 664 F.2d 114 (6th Cir.1981), protective orders had been entered in several of the cases before they were transferred, but the transferee judge vacated or modified them and provided instead that plaintiffs could share discovery results with litigants not parties to the multidistrict proceeding. As the appellate court explained, Upjohn claimed that this was improper:

> There is, at first blush at least, some arguable merit in the claim that it is really none of the transferee court's business that the transferor court has earlier prohibited access to the discovery information by parties outside the multidistrict litigation. After all, the Panel's interest in consolidating discovery is to assist the parties to the cases so transferred. * * * [T]he transferor court must ultimately be responsible for the final resolution of the dispute upon remand, and might seem to be better positioned to foresee and thus to avoid the possible abuse of the discovery by its dissemination to outsiders. It can also be said that there

is something unseemly in allowing plaintiffs to relitigate an issue which has already been fairly and fully heard in another court.

Nevertheless, it noted that "[t]he presence of protective orders in some of the cases, while not in others, would inevitably create conflicts which the transferee court would have to resolve." Accordingly, it held that "the transferee judge must necessarily have the final word."

How does law of the case work in such circumstances? As one judge presiding over consolidated antitrust actions put it, "[t]his principle is particularly applicable to multidistrict litigation, in which the presence of a large number of diverse parties might otherwise result in constant relitigation of the same legal issue." Philadelphia Housing Authority v. American Radiator and Standard Sanitary Corp., 323 F.Supp. 381 (E.D.Pa.1970). But doesn't this mean that the "law of the case" should be the rule adopted by the transferee judge for all the transferred cases? For a careful and thorough examination of the law of the case problems that arise in multidistrict litigation, see Steinman, Law of the Case: A Judicial Puzzle in Consolidated and Transferred Cases and in Multidistrict Litigation, 135 U.Pa.L.Rev. 595 (1987).

8.   Even where other judges clearly may regulate matters, they may defer to the transferee judge. In In the Matter of Orthopedic Bone Screw Products Liability Litigation, 79 F.3d 46 (7th Cir.1996), nonparty depositions were scheduled in Wisconsin in connection with MDL proceedings before a district judge in Philadelphia. When the nonparty deponents sought a protective order, three Wisconsin judges "transferred" the motions to the judge in Philadelphia. The appellate court was uncertain whether there was any power so to "transfer," but found the result consistent with the purposes of § 1407 because the Philadelphia judge "is much better situated than is any of the three district judges in Wisconsin to know whether the depositions plaintiffs seek to take, and the questions they propose to ask, are appropriate, cost-justified steps toward resolution of the litigation." Id. at 48.

9.   *Circuit conflicts and multidistrict transfers*: Matters become more complicated yet where the transferred case moves from one circuit to another because the circuits sometimes disagree on issues of federal law. Usually such conflicts relate to merits issues, not procedural questions like class certification or issuance of a protective order. As noted above, § 1407 does not limit transferee judges to deciding discovery issues, and the reality has been that "transferee courts have usually attempted to decide all substantive issues in the litigation." Note, The Experience of Transferee Courts Under the Multidistrict Litigation Act, 39 U.Chi.L.Rev. 588, 607–08 (1972). Should they apply the interpretation of the transferee or transferor circuit in deciding such issues?

In In re Plumbing Fixtures Litigation, 342 F.Supp. 756 (J.P.M.L.1972), the State of North Carolina, having sued in federal court in North Carolina, objected to transfer to Philadelphia because it claimed the court there had decided indirect purchasers could not sue for price fixing under the federal antitrust laws, while the federal circuit court that included North Carolina would allow such a suit. The MDL Panel said that the fears were groundless because, pursuant to Van Dusen v. Barrack, *supra* p. 130 n. 2, a transferee court would apply the transferor circuit's interpretation of federal law.

Should a transferee court be required to decide a federal issue in a way it feels is wrong simply because the transferor court allegedly would have decided it that way? See In re General Motors Class E Stock Buyout Sec. Litig., 696 F.Supp. 1546, 1547 n. 1 (J.P.M.L.1988) (*Plumbing Fixtures* conclusion questionable). For an argument that the transferee court should apply its own interpretation, see Marcus, Conflicts Among Circuits and Transfers Within the Federal Judicial System, 93 Yale L.J. 677 (1984).

In In re Korean Air Lines Disaster of Sept. 1, 1983, 829 F.2d 1171 (D.C.Cir.1987), aff'd on other grounds sub nom. Chan v. Korean Air Lines, Ltd., 490 U.S. 122, 109 S.Ct. 1676, 104 L.Ed.2d 113 (1989), the court held that where federal claims are transferred under § 1407, Van Dusen v. Barrack does not apply and the law of the transferee should determine the result. Noting that the *Erie* considerations that provided some of the impetus behind *Van Dusen* do not apply to transferred federal claims, the court found substantial reasons for limiting *Van Dusen* to state law claims.

A number of circuit courts have followed the In re Korean Air Lines Disaster rationale, holding that where federal law is at issue, transferee courts are obligated to follow their own interpretation (including that of their circuit) of the relevant law. See Murphy v. F.D.I.C., 208 F.3d 959 (11th Cir.2000); Campos v. Ticketmaster Corp., 140 F.3d 1166 (8th Cir.1998); Newton v. Thomason, 22 F.3d 1455 (9th Cir.1994); Menowitz v. Brown, 991 F.2d 36 (2d Cir.1993). But see Eckstein v. Balcor Film Investors, 8 F.3d 1121, 1128 (7th Cir.1993) (stating that the general rule is that "[a] single federal law implies a national interpretation" and "the norm is that each court of appeals considers the question independently and reaches its own decision, without regard to the geographic location of the events giving rise to the litigation," but "when the law of the United States is geographically non-uniform [in this case, differing circuit positions on applicable statutes of limitations], a transferee court should use the rule of the transferor forum in order to implement the central conclusion of *Van Dusen*"). See also In re United Mine Workers of America Employee Ben. Plans Litigation, 854 F.Supp. 914 (D.D.C.1994) (the same standards should apply, whether transfer was pursuant to § 1404 or § 1407).

B. DUAL STATE–FEDERAL PROCEEDINGS

Since state and federal courts are separate judicial systems emanating from separate sovereigns, techniques like consolidation and transfer (which are available only if the duplicative cases are all filed in the same court system) cannot be resorted to for duplicative or related cases in dual state-federal proceedings. Thus the options for combining or harmonizing separate state and federal suits are more limited. The principal possibilities are that one or the other court will *decline jurisdiction* or *stay the proceedings before it* so that the other court can proceed, or will *enjoin the parties from proceeding in the other court,* thus allowing it to proceed unimpeded with the case before it.

Both state and federal courts have the power to decline jurisdiction or to *stay* cases before them. We will look principally at the federal court practice. Some similar considerations relating to efficiency and convenience—such as which suit was filed first, which forum is more convenient for parties and witnesses, and the likelihood of avoidance of piecemeal litigation—affect the willingness of either state or federal courts to stay their proceedings so as to allow a suit to proceed in the other forum. But considerations of federalism are critical to whether a federal court must decline jurisdiction, as will be seen in the cases dealing with the "abstention doctrine." These federalism concerns may require federal courts to abstain from exercising jurisdiction or to stay their proceedings even if there is no pending action in the state court.

As for the converse situation—when a state or federal court wishes to *enjoin* proceedings in the other court—only the federal injunctive practice is relevant. Under the Constitution, states cannot limit the jurisdiction of the federal courts. Thus they cannot enjoin proceedings in a federal court (except, under limited precedents, to protect their jurisdiction over property in their custody or control). C. Wright & M. Kane, Law of Federal Courts 298 (6th ed. 2002). Federal courts, on the other hand, can enjoin state court proceedings, although there are significant limitations, as will be seen from our consideration of the Anti–Injunction Act.

1. FEDERAL COURT'S DECLINE OF JURISDICTION OR GRANT OF STAY ORDER

a. *Traditional Abstention (Pullman and Burford)*

BT INVESTMENT MANAGERS, INC. v. LEWIS

United States Court of Appeals, Fifth Circuit, 1977.
559 F.2d 950.

Before AINSWORTH and MORGAN, CIRCUIT JUDGES, and LYNNE, SENIOR DISTRICT JUDGE.

LYNNE, SENIOR DISTRICT JUDGE.

Appellants sought declaratory and injunctive relief from a Florida statute that prohibited them from operating an "investment advisory" service in that state. The three-judge district court invoked the doctrine of abstention and dismissed the action without prejudice so that plaintiffs might have certain state law issues resolved by the courts of the State of Florida. We reverse.

In 1972 appellant Bankers Trust New York Corporation (BTNYC), a "bank holding company" under the Bank Holding Act, 12 U.S.C. § 1841 *et seq.,* sought to establish its wholly-owned subsidiary, appellant B.T. Investment Managers, Inc. (BTIM), in the activity of "investment advisory" in the State of Florida. Generally, this activity would include providing portfolio investment advice, general economic information and advice, general economic statistical forecasting, and industry studies to persons desiring such services. While BTNYC had pending before the Federal Reserve Board an application for authority to establish BTIM as such an investment advisory service in Palm Beach, Florida, the Florida legislature amended a certain statute so as to prohibit non-Florida bank holding companies from providing investment advisory services to any person in Florida. Bound by a provision of the Bank Holding Act that requires the Federal Reserve Board to deny such an application when the planned activity is prohibited under the law of the "target" state, the Board was obliged to deny BTNYC's application in view of the intervening Florida amendment.

Following the Federal Reserve Board's denial of their application, appellants brought suit in the Northern District of Florida under 28 U.S.C. § 2201, seeking injunctive relief from the operation of the Florida statutes in question and a declaration that the statutes violate the due process and equal protection clauses of the fourteenth amendment as well as the supremacy and commerce clauses of the United States Constitution. A three-judge district court was convened pursuant to 28 U.S.C. § 2281. Pretermitting consideration of the merits of appellants' complaint, that court invoked the doctrine of abstention and accordingly dismissed the action without prejudice.

The sole issue on appeal is whether the district court properly abstained in this case. Although the abstention doctrine is more properly referred to as a *collection* of doctrines, the particular doctrine first articulated in *Railroad Commission of Texas v. Pullman,* 312 U.S. 496, 61 S.Ct. 643, 85 L.Ed. 971 (1941), teaches that in certain federal constitutional challenges to state statutes a federal district court should exercise its discretion to stay its action pending interpretation of the challenged statute by the courts of the enacting state and thereby avoid an unnecessary federal constitutional decision. The doctrine is conceived to enhance comity within our federal system of government: by leaving to a state the interpretation of unsettled questions of that state's laws when such interpretation may dispose of a case short of federal constitutional scrutiny, unnecessary friction between state and national governments may be avoided.

However, *Pullman*-type abstention is a narrow, judicially created exception to the general grant of federal jurisdiction found in article III of the Constitution. Not only is there a presumption in favor of retention of federal jurisdiction once obtained, it is also well established that the doctrine "contemplates that deference to state court adjudication only be made where the issue of state law is uncertain." While it is true, as appellee points out, that the statutes here in question have yet to be construed by the courts of Florida, mere absence of judicial interpretation does not necessarily render their meaning unsettled or uncertain. Indeed, by their very terms the challenged statutes could scarcely be clearer in effect, if not in purpose—that is, to rid Florida banking and trust interests of non-Florida competition in the area of investment counselling. As the Federal Reserve Board observed in denying appellants' application, there is simply no plausible construction of the challenged statutes under which appellants might be permitted to conduct their proposed business in Florida.

Thus, without more, abstention in the present case would appear improper. Appellee, however, contends that since the Florida Constitution contains a provision equivalent to the due process clause of the fourteenth amendment to the United States Constitution, the district court properly abstained in view of the possibility that *state* constitutional scrutiny by the courts of Florida might obviate the necessity of a federal constitutional decision. While appellee's position is not without support in this particularly problematic subcategory of *Pullman*-type abstention cases, we find the instant case controlled by the Supreme Court's holding in *Wisconsin v. Constantineau,* 400 U.S. 433, 91 S.Ct. 507, 27 L.Ed.2d 515 (1971), that where a state statute can be challenged under essentially identical state and federal constitutional provisions, abstention is improper.

The three-judge court alternatively based its abstention on the proposition found in *Burford v. Sun Oil Co.,* 319 U.S. 315, 63 S.Ct. 1098, 87 L.Ed. 1424 (1943), and a line of cases thereunder, that a federal court should refrain from exercising its jurisdiction in order to avoid needless conflict with the administration by a state of its own affairs. Although *Burford*-type abstention shares with *Pullman*-type abstention the goal of "comity" in the broadest sense, the two doctrines differ substantially in both purpose and effect. While the purpose of *Pullman*-type abstention is to avoid unnecessary federal constitutional challenge to state law, a court invoking *Burford*-type abstention essentially defers to a state's overriding interest in the matters *sub judice* and, concomitantly, to the superior competence of the state's courts to adjudicate such matters. Thus, usually at issue in *Burford*-type cases are state regulatory matters such as regulation of natural resources, education, or eminent domain, where a paramount state interest is apparent, where the history of state judicial experience in the area indicates special reliability, or, even absent an established regulatory scheme, where the intrusion of federal adjudication might handicap state government. Unlike *Pullman*-type abstention, *Burford*-type abstention requires neither the presence of a state issue nor unclarity in pertinent state law. Rather, a court abstaining under *Burford* relegates a federal issue to state court adjudication because the federal issue touches some overriding state interest such as those just described. Moreover, rather than merely stay its proceedings pending state court adjudication, as in a *Pullman*-type case, a federal court abstaining under *Burford* normally dismisses the case.

Without considering whether a case may be suitable for abstention under both the *Pullman* and *Burford* doctrines, we find *Burford*-type abstention improper in the present case. Although the challenged statutes are part of a large and perhaps complex regulatory scheme—*i.e.,* the Florida Banking Code—it must be remembered that appellants focus their attack upon a single statute whose possible invalidation could scarcely be expected to disrupt Florida's entire system of banking regulation. In this context we discern no overriding state interest, special state competence, or threat to Florida's administration of its own affairs that would warrant denying appellants access to their chosen federal forum and relegating their various federal claims to the courts of Florida.

Having found neither basis of abstention relied upon by the three-judge district court to be proper, we reverse and remand for that court's consideration of the merits of appellants' complaint.

Notes and Questions

1. In Burford v. Sun Oil Co., 319 U.S. 315, 63 S.Ct. 1098, 87 L.Ed. 1424 (1943), the plaintiff oil companies challenged an order of the state Railroad Commission which permitted Burford to drill four oil wells on a small plot of land because they feared that the Commission would then restrict their opportunity to drill on adjacent properties. Jurisdiction was based on diversity and on a federal question claim that the order denied plaintiffs due process. The court found that the state had established its own elaborate review system for permits and controls governing the complex area of oil and gas regulation, including a provision for judicial review of the Commission's orders that made Texas courts "working partners with the Railroad Commission in the business of a regulatory system for the oil industry." It held that the federal suit would have an impermissibly disruptive effect on state policy for management of the oil fields. Thus, unlike *Pullman,* it is not that the case might have been disposed of by deciding an unsettled state law question and therefore could best have been resolved by the state courts, but that the state had chosen to adopt a comprehensive scheme for regulation of the matter, and federal court intervention might have interfered with that scheme. *Burford* abstention continues to be important. See, e.g., Sierra Club v. City of San Antonio, 112 F.3d 789 (5th Cir.1997) (applying *Burford* to Endangered Species Act suit brought to enjoin overuse of aquifer).

In Quackenbush v. Allstate Insurance Co., 517 U.S. 706, 116 S.Ct. 1712, 135 L.Ed.2d 1 (1996), the Court held that *Burford* abstention is only permitted if the case involves a request for some form of discretionary relief. Plaintiff, the state insurance commissioner and trustee of assets of a defunct insurance company, had sued Allstate in state court for damages, alleging breach of reinsurance agreements. Although there were ongoing liquidation proceedings in state court, Allstate removed to federal court. The district court remanded on *Burford* grounds, but the Court found that the power to dismiss "derives from the discretion historically enjoyed by courts of equity" and that it could not be applied in a suit for money. See Note, Burford Abstention in Actions for Money, 99 Colum.L.Rev. 1871 (1999).

Was it critical in *Burford* that the state regulatory scheme included judicial review in the state courts, or would abstention also have been required for an entirely administrative scheme? Compare nn. 2 and 4, *infra* pp. 181–82.

2. Invocation of *Pullman* abstention should ordinarily result in a stay of proceedings in the federal court with retention of jurisdiction until state remedies have been exhausted, rather than in dismissal. Harris County Commissioners Court v. Moore, 420 U.S. 77, 95 S.Ct. 870, 43 L.Ed.2d 32 (1975). (*Burford* abstention, on the other hand, results in a dismissal.) The plaintiff may "reserve" the federal issues in the state court proceeding,

stating that he seeks state court jurisdiction only as to the state law issues, thus insuring that he continues to have a federal forum for the federal law issues. England v. Louisiana State Board of Medical Examiners, 375 U.S. 411, 84 S.Ct. 461, 11 L.Ed.2d 440 (1964).

An *England* reservation allows a litigant to return to the federal court for a *de novo* determination of its reserved federal claims once the state proceedings are over. It ordinarily avoids the preclusive effect of an adverse state determination, even one that directly rejects its stayed federal claims. An *England* reservation must be timely and may be express or implied. An express reservation may be made by informing the state court that "he is exposing his federal claims there only for the purpose of complying" with the abstention order and that he intends to return to the federal court for disposition of his federal claims. 375 U.S. at 421. For an implied reservation the litigant must take some action which indicates that he has not "freely and without reservation submit[ted] his federal claims for decision by the state courts." *Id.* at 419. Where a federal court declined to rule whether plaintiffs were entitled to return to it after abstention, and they refused to raise their federal claims in the state court proceedings, plaintiffs were found not to have waived or had full and fair opportunity to litigate their federal claims and therefore to be entitled to an *England* reservation. Ivy Club v. Edwards, 943 F.2d 270 (3d Cir.1991).

3. Even if a plaintiff is successful in invoking the *England* reservation to avoid litigating its federal claims in a state court action which it is required to pursue due to federal abstention, it may be difficult to avoid severe effects from the state judgment. Consider Wicker v. Board of Education of Knott County, 826 F.2d 442 (6th Cir.1987), where a federal court abstained in a suit by a school superintendent who alleged that his firing was in violation of his federal constitutional rights. He filed an *England* reservation, and his state court suit, confined to state law issues, went to judgment.

The Sixth Circuit found that the reservation preserved his right to return to federal court and that he was not barred by claim preclusion. However, it accorded issue-preclusive effect to the state court findings of law and fact. It reasoned that the state court necessarily found that he was guilty of inadequate handling of financial affairs, which was a legally sufficient reason for discharge under state law. He was thus prevented from arguing in federal court that he was discharged without legal cause. The appellate court went on, however, to conclude that the state court had not decided whether inadequate handling of finances was the sole cause of his discharge, and thus he was free to raise in the federal court the claim that he was placed in a worse position because of political hostility to his federally-protected rights.

4. The policies underlying *Pullman* and *Burford* abstention are sometimes stated in terms of "our federalism," the need for federal courts, in the exercise of comity, to abstain where there are available state remedies and federal intervention could create friction in the delicate area of federal-state relations. However, there is also an efficiency and expertise rationale unrelated to considerations of federalism. There is a similarity, for example, to the policies underlying the administrative law doctrine of "primary jurisdic-

tion" by which a court refuses to exercise jurisdiction in deference to the special competence of an administrative body whose remedies are still available. See, *e.g.,* United States v. Western Pacific Railroad Co., 352 U.S. 59, 77 S.Ct. 161, 1 L.Ed.2d 126 (1956).

5. In *BT Investment Managers,* the court refers to the "superior competence" of state courts to adjudicate matters that are suitable for *Burford* abstention. Is it assumed that state courts are more competent to adjudicate issues of state law and federal courts to adjudicate issues of federal law? Under conflicts of law rules, state and federal courts are often required to apply the law of other states. Frequently federal courts have jurisdiction to decide state law causes of action, and state courts can decide federal causes of action. What importance should be given to the superior competence of a court in applying its own law when a stay order or injunction is sought regarding litigation in another court?

6. In some cases, federal courts may abstain even when the state law in question in the case is clear, if it is contradicted by other provisions of state law. For example, in Georgevich v. Strauss, 772 F.2d 1078 (3d Cir.1985) (en banc), plaintiffs challenged state parole procedures on equal protection grounds because, due to a complicated series of enactments of state law, there seemed to be no parole procedures for prisoners serving sentences of less than two years who had been transferred from county jails to state correctional facilities. Technically such prisoners remained under the parole jurisdiction of their sentencing judges, but state law did not specify any procedures for handling their paroles. Even though the parole statute seemed unambiguous on its face, the court found *Pullman* applicable. Counsel for the defendant class of state judges apparently conceded at oral argument that some procedures would have to be developed to cope with the problem. Moreover, the court found other provisions of state law that contradicted the unambiguous language to which plaintiffs objected. "The need for state court interpretation results not only from unclear language on the face of a single statute, but also from the juxtaposition of clear, but contradictory state provisions." *Id.* at 1091.

7. What if time is of the essence? In Anderson v. Mills, 664 F.2d 600 (6th Cir.1981), two independent presidential candidates sued in federal court to declare unconstitutional certain provisions of the Kentucky election statute that prevented them from being on the ballot. While noting that the suit was "a prototype of the cause of action to which the abstention doctrine is applicable" because it involved construction of unclear state statutes, the appellate court found that the district court had properly heard the case. The election was only 90 days away, and "the political candidates, as well as the state, required a speedy resolution of the matter." Must it be shown that an action in the state court could not have been decided in time? How would a federal judge obtain sufficient information to determine that?

8. Should a federal court assess the adequacy of the state court remedy for determining the state issues before abstaining? See Chancery Clerk of Chickasaw County, Mississippi v. Wallace, 646 F.2d 151 (5th Cir.1981), declining to abstain in a class action challenging the constitutionality of Mississippi's procedures for involuntary commitment of adults to state mental institutions. The court stated: "[W]e understand that, given the

reluctance of Mississippi courts to countenance class actions at all, the mounting of a similar challenge offering the promise of comparable relief from a state court may be unworkable. Therefore, we doubt the feasibility of resolving the issues presented by this lawsuit in a Mississippi court." If the absence of comparable class action procedures would render a state court remedy inadequate, what other procedural differences from the federal court might also render the state court remedy inadequate?

b. Equitable Abstention under Younger v. Harris

PENNZOIL CO. v. TEXACO, INC.

Supreme Court of the United States, 1987.
481 U.S. 1, 107 S.Ct. 1519, 95 L.Ed.2d 1.

JUSTICE POWELL delivered the opinion of the Court.

The principal issue in this case is whether a federal district court lawfully may enjoin a plaintiff who has prevailed in a trial in state court from executing the judgment in its favor pending appeal of that judgment to a state appellate court.

I

Getty Oil Co. and appellant Pennzoil Co. negotiated an agreement under which Pennzoil was to purchase about three-sevenths of Getty's outstanding shares for $110 a share. Appellee Texaco, Inc. eventually purchased the shares for $128 a share. On February 8, 1984, Pennzoil filed a complaint against Texaco in the Harris County District Court, a state court located in Houston, Texas, the site of Pennzoil's corporate headquarters. The complaint alleged that Texaco tortiously had induced Getty to breach a contract to sell its shares to Pennzoil; Pennzoil sought actual damages of $7.53 billion and punitive damages in the same amount. On November 19, 1985, a jury returned a verdict in favor of Pennzoil, finding actual damages of $7.53 billion and punitive damages of $3 billion. The parties anticipated that the judgment, including prejudgment interest, would exceed $11 billion.

Although the parties disagree about the details, it was clear that the expected judgment would give Pennzoil significant rights under Texas law. By recording an abstract of a judgment in the real property records of any of the 254 counties in Texas, a judgment creditor can secure a lien on all of a judgment debtor's real property located in that county. See Tex.Prop.Code Ann. §§ 52.001–.006 (1984). If a judgment creditor wishes to have the judgment enforced by state officials so that it can take possession of any of the debtor's assets, it may secure a writ of execution from the clerk of the court that issued the judgment. See Tex.Rule Civ.Proc. 627.[1] Rule 627 provides that such a writ usually can be obtained "after the expiration of thirty days from the time a final

---

1. A writ of execution is "[a]ddressed to any sheriff or constable in the State of Texas [and] enables the official to levy on a debtor's nonexempt real and personal prop-   erty, within the official's county." 5 W. Dorsaneo, Texas Litigation Guide § 132.02[1], p. 132–7 (1986).

judgment is signed." But the judgment debtor "may suspend the execution of the judgment by filing a good and sufficient bond to be approved by the clerk." Rule 364(a). See Rule 368.[3] For a money judgment, "the amount of the bond . . . shall be at least the amount of the judgment, interest, and costs." Rule 364(b).[4]

Even before the trial court entered judgment, the jury's verdict cast a serious cloud on Texaco's financial situation. The amount of the bond required by Rule 364(b) would have been more than $13 billion. It is clear that Texaco would not have been able to post such a bond. Accordingly, "the business and financial community concluded that Pennzoil would be able, under the lien and bond provisions of Texas law, to commence enforcement of any judgment entered on the verdict before Texaco's appeals had been resolved." (District Court's Supplemental Finding of Fact 40, Jan. 10, 1986). The effects on Texaco were substantial: the price of its stock dropped markedly; it had difficulty obtaining credit; the rating of its bonds was lowered; and its trade creditors refused to sell it crude oil on customary terms. (District Court's Supplemental Findings of Fact 49–70).

Texaco did not argue to the trial court that the judgment, or execution of the judgment, conflicted with federal law. Rather, on December 10, 1985—before the Texas court entered judgment[5]—Texaco filed this action in the United States District Court for the Southern District of New York in White Plains, New York, the site of Texaco's corporate headquarters. Texaco alleged that the Texas proceedings violated rights secured to Texaco by the Constitution and various federal statutes.[6] It asked the District Court to enjoin Pennzoil from taking any

3. Filing a supersedeas bond would not prevent Pennzoil from securing judgment liens against Texaco's real property. See Tex.Prop.Code Ann. § 52.002 (1984) (directing clerk to issue an abstract of the judgment "[o]n application of a person in whose favor a judgment is rendered"; no exception for superseded judgments). The bond's only effect would be to prevent Pennzoil from executing the judgment and obtaining Texaco's property.

4. A judgment debtor also may suspend execution by filing "cash or other negotiable obligation of the government of the United States of America or any agency thereof, or with leave of court, . . . a negotiable obligation of any bank . . . in the amount fixed for the surety bond." Rule 14c.

5. Later the same day, the Texas court entered a judgment against Texaco for $11,120,976,110.83, including prejudgment interest of approximately $600 million. During the pendency of the federal action—that now concerns only the validity of the Texas judgment enforcement procedures—the state-court action on the merits has pro-

ceeded. Texaco filed a motion for new trial, that was deemed denied by operation of law under Rule 329b(c). See n. 2, *supra*. Subsequently, Texaco appealed the judgment to the Texas Court of Appeals, challenging the judgment on a variety of state and federal grounds. The Texas Court of Appeals rendered a decision on that appeal on February 12, 1987. That decision affirmed the trial court's judgment in most respects, but remitted $2 billion of the punitive damages award, reducing the principal of the judgment to $8.53 billion.

So far as we know, Texaco has never presented to the Texas courts the challenges it makes in this case against the bond and lien provisions under federal law. Three days after it filed its federal lawsuit, Texaco did ask the Texas trial court informally for a hearing concerning possible modification of the judgment under Texas law. That request eventually was denied, because it failed to comply with Texas procedural rules.

6. Texaco claimed that the judgment itself conflicted with the Full Faith and Credit Clause, the Commerce Clause, the

action to enforce the judgment. Pennzoil's response, and basic position, was that the District Court could not hear the case. First, it argued that the Anti–Injunction Act, 28 U.S.C. § 2283, barred issuance of an injunction. It further contended that the court should abstain under the doctrine of *Younger v. Harris,* 401 U.S. 37, 91 S.Ct. 746, 27 L.Ed.2d 669 (1971). * * *

The District Court rejected all of these arguments. * * *

The District Court justified its decision to grant injunctive relief by evaluating the prospects of Texaco's succeeding in its appeal in the Texas state courts. It considered the merits of the various challenges Texaco had made before the Texas Court of Appeals and concluded that these challenges "present generally fair grounds for litigation." It then evaluated the constitutionality of the Texas lien and bond requirements by applying the test articulated in *Mathews v. Eldridge,* 424 U.S. 319, 96 S.Ct. 893, 47 L.Ed.2d 18 (1976). It concluded that application of the lien and bond provisions effectively would deny Texaco a right to appeal. It thought that the private interests and the State's interests favored protecting Texaco's right to appeal. Relying on its view of the merits of the state court appeal, the court found the risk of erroneous deprivation "quite severe." Finally, it viewed the administrative burden on the State as "slight." In light of these factors, the District Court concluded that Texaco's constitutional claims had "a very clear probability of success." Accordingly, the court issued a preliminary injunction.[7]

On appeal, the Court of Appeals for the Second Circuit affirmed. 784 F.2d 1133 (1986). * * *

[T]he court considered whether Texaco had stated a claim under § 1983. The question was whether Texaco's complaint sought to redress action taken "under color of" state law, 42 U.S.C. § 1983. The court noted that "Pennzoil would have to act jointly with state agents by calling on state officials to attach and seize Texaco's assets." Relying on its reading of *Lugar v. Edmondson Oil Co.,* 457 U.S. 922, 102 S.Ct. 2744, 73 L.Ed.2d 482 (1982), the court concluded that the enjoined action would have been taken under color of state law, and thus that Texaco had stated a claim under § 1983. Because § 1983 is an exception to the

Williams Act, and the Securities Exchange Act of 1934. Texaco also argued that application of the Texas bond and lien provisions would violate the Due Process and Equal Protection Clauses of the Fourteenth Amendment to the Federal Constitution.

7. The operative portion of the injunction provided:

"[I]t is hereby ... ORDERED that defendant, Pennzoil Company, its employees, agents, attorneys and servants, and all persons in active concert or participation with them who receive actual notice of this Order by personal service or otherwise, are jointly and severally enjoined and restrained, pending the trial and ulti-

mate disposition of this action, or the further order of this Court, from taking any action of any kind whatsoever to enforce or attempt to enforce the Judgment entered in an action in the District Court for the 151st Judicial District of Texas entitled *Pennzoil Company v. Texaco Inc.,* including, without limitation, attempting to obtain or file any judgment lien or abstract of judgment related to said Judgment (pursuant to Tex.Prop. Code Ann. §§ 52.001, *et seq.,* or otherwise), or initiating or commencing steps to execute on said Judgment...."

The order also required Texaco to post a bond of $1 billion to secure the grant of the preliminary injunction.

Anti–Injunction Act, see *Mitchum v. Foster, supra,* the Court also found that the Anti–Injunction Act did not prevent the District Court from granting the relief sought by Texaco.

Finally, the court held that abstention was unnecessary. First, it addressed *Pullman* abstention, see *Railroad Comm'n v. Pullman Co.,* 312 U.S. 496, 61 S.Ct. 643, 85 L.Ed. 971 (1941). It rejected that ground of abstention, holding that "the mere possibility that the Texas courts would find Rule 364 [concerning the supersedeas bond requirements] unconstitutional as applied does not call for *Pullman* abstention." Next, it rejected *Younger* abstention. It thought that "[t]he state interests at stake in this proceeding differ in both kind and degree from those present in the six cases in which the Supreme Court held that *Younger* applied." Moreover, it thought that Texas had failed to "provide adequate procedures for adjudication of Texaco's federal claims." Turning to the merits, it agreed with the District Court that Texaco had established a likelihood of success on its constitutional claims and that the balance of hardships favored Texaco. Accordingly, it affirmed the grant of injunctive relief.[8]

II

The courts below should have abstained under the principles of federalism enunciated in *Younger v. Harris,* 401 U.S. 37, 91 S.Ct. 746, 27 L.Ed.2d 669 (1971). Both the District Court and the Court of Appeals failed to recognize the significant interests harmed by their unprecedented intrusion into the Texas judicial system. Similarly, neither of those courts applied the appropriate standard in determining whether adequate relief was available in the Texas courts.

A

The first ground for the *Younger* decision was "the basic doctrine of equity jurisprudence that courts of equity should not act, and particularly should not act to restrain a criminal prosecution, when the moving party has an adequate remedy at law." The Court also offered a second explanation for its decision:

> "This underlying reason ... is reinforced by an even more vital consideration, the notion of 'comity,' that is, a proper respect for state functions, a recognition of the fact that the entire country is made up of a Union of separate state governments, and a continuance of the belief that the National Government will fare best if the States and their institutions are left free to perform their separate functions in their separate ways.... The concept does not mean blind deference to 'States' Rights' any more than it means centralization of control over every important issue in our National Government and its courts. The Framers rejected both these courses. What

---

8. Although the District Court had entered only a preliminary injunction, the Court of Appeals concluded that the record was sufficiently undisputed to justify entering a permanent injunction. Thus, it did not remand the case to the District Court for further proceedings on the merits. 784 F.2d 1133, 1156 (1986).

the concept does represent is a system in which there is sensitivity to the legitimate interests of both State and National Governments, and in which the National Government, anxious though it may be to vindicate and protect federal rights and federal interests, always endeavors to do so in ways that will not unduly interfere with the legitimate activities of the States.''

This concern mandates application of *Younger* abstention not only when the pending state proceedings are criminal, but also when certain civil proceedings are pending, if the State's interests in the proceeding are so important that exercise of the federal judicial power would disregard the comity between the States and the National Government.

Another important reason for abstention is to avoid unwarranted determination of federal constitutional questions. When federal courts interpret state statutes in a way that raises federal constitutional questions, "a constitutional determination is predicated on a reading of the statute that is not binding on state courts and may be discredited at any time—thus essentially rendering the federal-court decision advisory and the litigation underlying it meaningless." *Moore v. Sims,* 442 U.S. 415, 428, 99 S.Ct. 2371, 2379, 60 L.Ed.2d 994 (1979).[9] This concern has special significance in this case. Because Texaco chose not to present to the Texas courts the constitutional claims asserted in this case, it is impossible to be certain that the governing Texas statutes and procedural rules actually raise these claims. Moreover, the Texas Constitution contains an "open courts" provision, Art. I, § 13,[10] that appears to address Texaco's claims more specifically than the Due Process Clause of the Fourteenth Amendment. Thus, when this case was filed in Federal Court, it was entirely possible that the Texas courts would have resolved this case on state statutory or constitutional grounds, without reaching the federal constitutional questions Texaco raises in this case. As we have noted, *Younger* abstention in situations like this "offers the opportunity for narrowing constructions that might obviate the constitutional problem and intelligently mediate federal constitutional concerns and state interests." *Moore v. Sims, supra,* 442 U.S., at 429–430, 99 S.Ct., at 2380–2381.

9. In some cases, the probability that any federal adjudication would be effectively advisory is so great that this concern alone is sufficient to justify abstention, even if there are no pending state proceedings in which the question could be raised. See *Railroad Comm'n of Texas v. Pullman Co.,* 312 U.S. 496, 61 S.Ct. 643, 85 L.Ed. 971 (1941). Because appellant has not argued in this Court that *Pullman* abstention is proper, we decline to address Justice Blackmun's conclusion that *Pullman* abstention is the appropriate disposition of this case. [This portion of Justice Blackmun's opinion is not included in this book.] We merely note that considerations similar to those that mandate *Pullman* abstention are rele-

vant to a court's decision whether to abstain under *Younger.* Cf. *Moore v. Sims,* 442 U.S. 415, 428, 99 S.Ct. 2371, 2379, 60 L.Ed.2d 994 (1979). The various types of abstention are not rigid pigeonholes into which federal courts must try to fit cases. Rather, they reflect a complex of considerations designed to soften the tensions inherent in a system that contemplates parallel judicial processes.

10. Article I, § 13 provides: "All courts shall be open, and every person for an injury done him, in his lands, goods, person or reputation, shall have remedy by due course of law.''

Texaco's principal argument against *Younger* abstention is that exercise of the District Court's power did not implicate a "vital" or "important" state interest. This argument reflects a misreading of our precedents. This Court repeatedly has recognized that the States have important interests in administering certain aspects of their judicial systems. In *Juidice v. Vail,* 430 U.S. 327, 97 S.Ct. 1211, 51 L.Ed.2d 376 (1977), we held that a federal court should have abstained from adjudicating a challenge to a State's contempt process. The Court's reasoning in that case informs our decision today:

> "A State's interest in the contempt process, through which it vindicates the regular operation of its judicial system, so long as that system itself affords the opportunity to pursue federal claims within it, is surely an important interest. Perhaps it is not quite as important as is the State's interest in the enforcement of its criminal laws, *Younger, supra,* or even its interest in the maintenance of a quasi-criminal proceeding such as was involved in *Huffman,* [v. Pursue, Ltd., 420 U.S. 592, 95 S.Ct. 1200, 43 L.Ed.2d 482 (1975)]. But we think it is of sufficiently great import to require application of the principles of those cases."

Our comments on why the contempt power was sufficiently important to justify abstention also are illuminating: "Contempt in these cases, serves, of course, to vindicate and preserve the private interests of competing litigants, ... but its purpose is by no means spent upon purely private concerns. It stands in aid of the authority of the judicial system, so that its orders and judgments are not rendered nugatory."

The reasoning of *Juidice* controls here. That case rests on the importance to the States of enforcing the orders and judgments of their courts. There is little difference between the State's interest in forcing persons to transfer property in response to a court's judgment and in forcing persons to respond to the court's process on pain of contempt. Both *Juidice* and this case involve challenges to the processes by which the State compels compliance with the judgments of its courts.[12] Not only would federal injunctions in such cases interfere with the execution of state judgments, but they would do so on grounds that challenge the very process by which those judgments were obtained. So long as those challenges relate to pending state proceedings, proper respect for the ability of state courts to resolve federal questions presented in state court litigation mandates that the federal court stay its hand.[13]

---

12. Thus, contrary to Justice Stevens' suggestion, the State of Texas has an interest in this proceeding "that goes beyond its interest as adjudicator of wholly private disputes." Our opinion does not hold that *Younger* abstention is always appropriate whenever a civil proceeding is pending in a state court. Rather, as in *Juidice,* we rely on the State's interest in protecting "the authority of the judicial system, so that its orders and judgments are not rendered nu-

gatory," 430 U.S., at 336, n. 12, 97 S.Ct., at 1217, n. 12.

13. Texaco also suggests that abstention is unwarranted because of the absence of a state judicial proceeding with respect to which the Federal District Court should have abstained. Texaco argues that "the Texas judiciary plays no role" in execution of judgments. We reject this assertion. There is at least one pending judicial proceeding in the state courts; the lawsuit out

B

Texaco also argues that *Younger* abstention was inappropriate because no Texas court could have heard Texaco's constitutional claims within the limited time available to Texaco. But the burden on this point rests on the federal plaintiff to show "that state procedural law barred presentation of [its] claims." *Moore v. Sims,* 442 U.S., at 432, 99 S.Ct., at 2381. See *Younger v. Harris,* 401 U.S., at 45, 91 S.Ct., at 751 (" 'The accused should first set up and rely upon his defense in the state courts, even though this involves a challenge of the validity of some statute, unless it plainly appears that this course would not afford adequate protection' ").

Moreover, denigrations of the procedural protections afforded by Texas law hardly come from Texaco with good grace, as it apparently made no effort under Texas law to secure the relief sought in this case. Article VI of the United States Constitution declares that "the Judges in every State shall be bound" by the Federal Constitution, laws, and treaties. We cannot assume that state judges will interpret ambiguities in state procedural law to bar presentation of federal claims. Accordingly, when a litigant has not attempted to present his federal claims in related state court proceedings, a federal court should assume that state procedures will afford an adequate remedy, in the absence of unambiguous authority to the contrary.

The "open courts" provision of the Texas Constitution, Article I, § 13, has considerable relevance here. This provision has appeared in each of Texas' six constitutions, dating back to the Constitution of the Republic of Texas in 1836. According to the Texas Supreme Court, the provision "guarantees all litigants . . . the right to their day in court." "The common thread of [the Texas Supreme Court's] decisions construing the open courts provision is that the legislature has no power to make a remedy by due course of law contingent on an impossible condition." *Nelson v. Krusen,* 678 S.W.2d 918, 921 (Tex.1984). In light of this demonstrable and long-standing commitment of the Texas Supreme Court to provide access to the state courts, we are reluctant to conclude that Texas courts would have construed state procedural rules to deny Texaco an effective opportunity to raise its constitutional claims.

Against this background, Texaco's submission that the Texas courts were incapable of hearing its constitutional claims is plainly insufficient. Both of the courts below found that the Texas trial court had the power to consider constitutional challenges to the enforcement provisions. The Texas Attorney General filed a brief in the proceedings below, arguing that such relief was available in the Texas courts. Texaco has cited no statute or case clearly indicating that Texas courts lack such power. Accordingly, Texaco has failed to meet its burden on this point.[16]

of which Texaco's constitutional claims arose is now pending before a Texas Court of Appeals in Houston, Texas. As we explain *infra,* we are not convinced that Texa-co could not have secured judicial relief in those proceedings.

16. We recognize that the trial court no longer has jurisdiction over the case. See

In sum, the lower courts should have deferred on principles of comity to the pending state proceedings. They erred in accepting Texaco's assertions as to the inadequacies of Texas procedure to provide effective relief. It is true that this case presents an unusual fact situation, never before addressed by the Texas courts, and that Texaco urgently desired prompt relief. But we cannot say that those courts, when this suit was filed, would have been any less inclined than a federal court to address and decide the federal constitutional claims. Because Texaco apparently did not give the Texas courts an opportunity to adjudicate its constitutional claims, and because Texaco cannot demonstrate that the Texas courts were not then open to adjudicate its claims, there is no basis for concluding that the Texas law and procedures were so deficient that *Younger* abstention is inappropriate. Accordingly, we conclude that the District Court should have abstained.

III

In this opinion, we have addressed the situation that existed on the morning of December 10, 1985, when this case was filed in the United States District Court for the Southern District of New York. We recognize that much has transpired in the Texas courts since then. Later that day, the Texas trial court entered judgment. On February 12 of this year, the Texas Court of Appeals substantially affirmed the judgment. We are not unmindful of the unique importance to Texaco of having its challenges to that judgment authoritatively considered and resolved. We of course express no opinion on the merits of those challenges. Similarly, we express no opinion on the claims Texaco has raised in this case against the Texas bond and lien provisions, nor on the possibility that Texaco now could raise these claims in the Texas courts, see n. 16, *supra*. Today we decide only that it was inappropriate for the District Court to entertain these claims. If, and when, the Texas courts render a final decision on any federal issue presented by this litigation, review may be sought in this Court in the customary manner.

JUSTICE BRENNAN, with whom JUSTICE MARSHALL joins, concurring in the judgment.

* * *

The District Court was not required to abstain under the principles enunciated in *Younger v. Harris,* 401 U.S. 37, 91 S.Ct. 760, 27 L.Ed.2d 669 (1971). I adhere to my view that *Younger* is, in general, inapplicable to civil proceedings, especially when a plaintiff brings a § 1983 action alleging violation of federal constitutional rights.

Tex.Rule Civ.Proc. 329b(e); n. 5, *supra.* Thus, relief is no longer available to Texaco from the trial court. But Texaco cannot escape *Younger* abstention by failing to assert its state remedies in a timely manner. In any event, the Texas Supreme Court and the Texas Court of Appeals arguably have the authority to suspend the supersedeas requirement to protect their appellate jurisdiction. See *Pace v. McEwen,* 604 S.W.2d 231, 233 (Tex.Civ.App.—San Antonio 1980, no writ) (suggesting that a Texas Court of Appeals has such authority).

The State's interest in this case is negligible. The State of Texas—not a party in this appeal—expressly represented to the Court of Appeals that it "has no interest in the underlying action," except in its fair adjudication. The Court identifies the State's interest as enforcing "the authority of the judicial system, so that its orders and judgments are not rendered nugatory." Yet, the District Court found that "Pennzoil publicly admitted that Texaco's assets are sufficient to satisfy the Judgment even without liens or a bond." "Thus Pennzoil's interest in protecting the full amount of its judgment during the appellate process is reasonably secured by the substantial excess of Texaco's net worth over the amount of Pennzoil's judgment." 784 F.2d, at 1155.

Indeed, the interest in enforcing the bond and lien requirement is privately held by Pennzoil, not by the State of Texas. The Court of Appeals correctly stated that this "is a suit between two private parties stemming from the defendant's alleged tortious interference with the plaintiff's contract with a third private party." 784 F.2d, at 1150. Pennzoil was free to waive the bond and lien requirements under Texas law, without asking the State of Texas for permission. "Since Texas law directs state officials to do Pennzoil's bidding in executing the judgment, it is the decision of Pennzoil, not that of the state judiciary, to utilize state agents to undertake the collection process, and the state officials can act only upon Pennzoil's unilateral determination." 784 F.2d, at 1147. The State's decision to grant private parties unilateral power to invoke, or not invoke, the State's bond and lien provisions demonstrates that the State has no independent interest in the enforcement of those provisions.

Texaco filed this § 1983 suit claiming only violations of *federal* statutory and constitutional law. In enacting § 1983, Congress "created a specific and unique remedy, enforceable in a federal court of equity, that could be frustrated if the federal court were not empowered to enjoin a state court proceeding." *Mitchum v. Foster, supra,* 407 U.S., at 237, 92 S.Ct., at 2159. Today the Court holds that this § 1983 suit should be filed instead in Texas courts, offering to Texaco the unsolicited advice to bring its claims under the "open courts" provision of the Texas Constitution. This "blind deference to 'States' Rights' 'hardly shows' sensitivity to the legitimate interests of *both* State *and National* Governments." *Ante,* at 1525 (quoting *Younger v. Harris, supra,* 401 U.S., at 44, 91 S.Ct., at 750) (emphasis added).

* * *

Justice Blackmun, concurring in the judgment.

I, too, conclude, as do Justice Brennan and Justice Stevens, that a creditor's invocation of a State's post-judgment collection procedures constitutes action under color of state law within the reach of 42 U.S.C. § 1983. I also agree with them that the District Court was correct in not abstaining under the principles enunciated in *Younger v. Harris,* 401 U.S. 37, 91 S.Ct. 760, 27 L.Ed.2d 669 (1971). In my view, to rule otherwise would expand the *Younger* doctrine to an unprecedented extent and would effectively allow the invocation of *Younger* abstention whenever any state proceeding is ongoing, no matter how attenuated the State's interests are in that proceeding and no matter what abuses the federal plaintiff might be sustaining. * * *

JUSTICE STEVENS, with whom JUSTICE MARSHALL joins, concurring in the judgment.

In my opinion Texaco's claim that the Texas judgment lien and supersedeas bond provisions violate the Fourteenth Amendment is plainly without merit. The injunction against enforcement of those provisions must therefore be dissolved. I rest my analysis on this ground because I cannot agree with the grounds upon which the Court disposes of the case. In my view the District Court and the Court of Appeals were correct to hold that a creditor's invocation of a State's post-judgment collection procedures constitutes action "under color of" state law within the meaning of 42 U.S.C. § 1983, and that there is no basis for abstention in this case.[2]

* * *

Notes and Questions

1. There has been speculation as to whether *Pennzoil* was a narrow or a broad extension of *Younger*. A narrow reading would view it simply as an application of *Juidice* which required abstention to avoid interfering with the important state court interest of enforcing its own judgments (in *Juidice*, through state contempt proceedings in aid of a private creditor's enforcement action). There is language in *Pennzoil* to this effect: "Both *Juidice* and this case involve challenges to the processes by which the State compels compliance with the judgments of its courts. Not only would federal injunctions in such cases interfere with the execution of state judgments, but they would do so on grounds that challenge the very process by which those judgments were obtained."

2. As the Court of Appeals explained: "The state interests at stake in this proceeding differ in both kind and in degree" from the cases in which the Court has held *Younger* abstention appropriate. 784 F.2d 1133, 1149 (C.A.2 1986). As Justice Brennan's analysis points out, the issue of whether "proceedings implicate important state interests" is quite distinct from the question of whether there is an ongoing proceeding. Although we have often wrestled with deciding whether a particular exercise of state enforcement power implicates an "important state interest," see *Younger v. Harris,* 401 U.S. 37, 91 S.Ct. 760, 27 L.Ed.2d 669 (1971) (criminal statute); *Huffman v. Pursue, Ltd.,* 420 U.S. 592, 95 S.Ct. 1200, 43 L.Ed.2d 482 (1975) (obscenity regulation); *Juidice v. Vail,* 430 U.S. 327, 97 S.Ct. 1211, 51 L.Ed.2d 376 (1977) (contempt proceedings); *Trainor v. Hernan-* dez, 431 U.S. 434, 97 S.Ct. 1911, 52 L.Ed.2d 486 (1977) (welfare fraud action); *Moore v. Sims,* 442 U.S. 415, 99 S.Ct. 2371, 60 L.Ed.2d 994 (1979) (child abuse regulation); *Middlesex Ethics Comm., supra* (bar disciplinary proceedings); *Ohio Civil Rights Comm. v. Dayton Christian Schools, Inc.,* 477 U.S. 619, 106 S.Ct. 2718, 91 L.Ed.2d 512 (1986) (antidiscrimination laws), we have invariably required that the State have a *substantive* interest in the ongoing proceeding, an interest that goes beyond its interest as adjudicator of wholly private disputes. By abandoning this critical limitation, the Court cuts the *Younger* doctrine adrift from its original doctrinal moorings which dealt with the States' interest in enforcing their criminal laws, and the federal courts' long-standing reluctance to interfere with such proceedings.

The view that *Pennzoil* might be read more broadly focuses on language suggesting that *Younger* abstention applies to all state civil proceedings and not just to enforcement and contempt proceedings: "So long as those challenged statutes related to pending state proceedings, proper respect for the ability of state courts to resolve federal questions presented in state court litigation mandates that the federal court stay its hand." Footnote 9 also seems to suggest deference to state courts when there are "parallel judicial processes." Professor Tribe, one of Pennzoil's attorneys, stated that "[a]s a result of the *Pennzoil* decision, the *Younger* abstention doctrine no longer applies only where there is a pending case.... Instead, it applies to any case where pending state judicial proceedings are structurally capable of resolving the problem." Tribe, Constitutional Law Conference, 56 U.S.L.W. 2333 (1987).

Consider the following analysis by Professor Baker:

[C]loser analysis is that the Supreme Court did not order abstention in a case purely or exclusively between two private parties. In *Pennzoil,* the judgment creditor had in effect risen to the level of a state actor. This holding vindicated a state's interest at least closer to the core of the state court system. * * * Thus understood, the interest in providing for dispute resolution is not alone a sufficiently important state interest to warrant *Younger* abstention. This reading is supported by the repetition in *Pennzoil* of the by now obligatory footnote that the holding does not reach the question whether *Younger* abstention is appropriate whenever a civil proceeding is pending in a state court [footnote 12]. Therefore, the *Pennzoil* holding does not necessarily oblige automatic abstention whenever a state suit is pending. After the state court trial is complete, however, the state court's interest in enforcing the decision is important and justifies federal abstention.

Baker, "Our Federalism" in *Pennzoil Co. v. Texaco, Inc.* or How the *Younger* Doctrine Keeps Getting Older Not Better, 9 Rev.Litig. 303, 342–43 (1990).

2.   The *Younger* doctrine has also been extended to require abstention when there is an on-going state administrative, as opposed to judicial, proceeding. See Middlesex County Ethics Committee v. Garden State Bar Association, 457 U.S. 423, 102 S.Ct. 2515, 73 L.Ed.2d 116 (1982) (federal court must abstain from considering action challenging the constitutionality of state bar disciplinary rules while disciplinary proceedings, involving an administrative board with ultimate review to the state supreme court, are pending). The Court noted that the New Jersey Supreme Court considers its bar disciplinary proceedings to be "judicial in nature." In New Orleans Public Service, Inc. v. Council of City of New Orleans, 491 U.S. 350, 369, 109 S.Ct. 2506, 2519, 105 L.Ed.2d 298 (1989), the Court explained that an administrative agency proceeding will be characterized as judicial or legislative depending on the "nature of the final act" which it is designed to produce. A proceeding is judicial where it "investigates, declares and enforces liabilities as they stand on present and past facts and under laws supposed already to exist." Id. at 2520. See Sun Refining & Marketing Co. v. Brennan, 921 F.2d 635, 637 (6th Cir.1990) (a proceeding before the Ohio Board of Building Appeals, involving investigation of present and past facts

and application of its findings to laws, was an on-going state proceeding "judicial in nature" as to which federal court should abstain).

3. *Younger* only applies to *pending* state proceedings. However, the state proceeding may be initiated after the filing of the federal suit. In Ciotti v. County of Cook, 712 F.2d 312 (7th Cir.1983), plaintiffs' request to the Board of Zoning Appeals for a certificate of nonconforming use for their adult bookstore was denied, and they filed suit in federal court challenging the constitutionality of the ordinance. When plaintiffs continued operations, the county filed a quasi-criminal action in state court for an injunction against further operation and for imposition of a fine. The federal district court dismissed the federal action. The circuit court found that merely filing a federal claim before violating the ordinance did not provide plaintiffs with immunity from state prosecution for post-filing violations and that the district court had properly abstained under *Younger*. "To prevent the state court action, the plaintiffs should have filed their federal action, proved standing, and either attempted to obtain an injunction against state enforcement of the ordinance or ceased operations prior to becoming an illegal use." 712 F.2d at 315.

The risk that the pending state proceedings do not offer the prospect of prompt resolution may not matter, however. Thus, in Marcal Paper Mills, Inc. v. Ewing, 790 F.2d 195 (1st Cir.1986), the Director of the Maine Bureau of Labor Standards sued Marcal in state court to enforce Maine severance pay statutes. Marcal defended on the ground that federal law preempted the state statutes, and filed a declaratory judgment action in federal court raising the same issues, meanwhile asking the state court to stay its proceedings. The state court did issue a stay, but only to permit the state supreme court to address the same issue raised in another state court suit. Notwithstanding the state court stay, the federal court dismissed. On appeal, Marcal argued that even if *Younger* would usually apply, there should be an exception where the federal issue raised is preemption. Accepting this argument *arguendo,* the appellate court nevertheless found special circumstances justifying at least a stay of the federal action due to the pendency of an appeal on the same issues before the state supreme court. Given the complexity of the issues and the risk of a direct conflict between the state and federal courts, it reasoned, a federal stay should issue.

4. Federal courts may, using "sound judicial discretion," abstain until available administrative remedies have been exhausted, but such requests for abstention have often been unsuccessful in civil rights cases. See McCarthy v. Madigan, 503 U.S. 140, 112 S.Ct. 1081, 117 L.Ed.2d 291 (1992) (federal prisoners need not exhaust internal grievance procedure before initiating suit for money damages for violation of constitutional rights); Patsy v. Board of Regents, 457 U.S. 496, 102 S.Ct. 2557, 73 L.Ed.2d 172 (1982) (state university employee need not exhaust internal procedures before filing a § 1983 action in federal court). In Darby v. Cisneros, 509 U.S. 137, 113 S.Ct. 2539, 125 L.Ed.2d 113 (1993), the Court held that a plaintiff suing under the Administrative Procedure Act cannot be required to exhaust administrative remedies where exhaustion is not required by the statute or agency rules.

5. The *Younger* doctrine is not jurisdictional and may, in effect, be waived by the state. See Ohio Bureau of Employment Services v. Hodory, 431 U.S. 471, 480, 97 S.Ct. 1898, 1904, 52 L.Ed.2d 513 (1977). Unlike *Pullman* abstention, *Younger* abstention results in dismissal, and it is doubtful that an *England*-type reservation of federal issues [see discussion of *England, supra* p. 168 n. 2] is available. See Olitt v. Murphy, 453 F.Supp. 354 (S.D.N.Y.1978), aff'd, 591 F.2d 1331 (2d Cir.1978).

6. *The Rooker–Feldman doctrine*: Pennzoil also objected to federal-court jurisdiction on the basis of the *Rooker–Feldman* doctrine. In Rooker v. Fidelity Trust Co., 263 U.S. 413, 44 S.Ct. 149, 68 L.Ed. 362 (1923), a party who had lost in a state-court suit sued in federal court to void the state-court judgment because of constitutional errors. In District of Columbia Court of Appeals v. Feldman, 460 U.S. 462, 103 S.Ct. 1303, 75 L.Ed.2d 206 (1983), a graduate of an unaccredited law school who had sued in the D.C. court for a waiver of its rule that prevented him from sitting for the bar exam sought an injunction in federal court that the local rule not be followed and he be permitted to take the exam. In both cases, the Supreme Court held there was no federal-court subject matter jurisdiction. The essence of the *Rooker–Feldman* doctrine is that an inferior federal court may not act as an appellate tribunal for the purpose of overruling a state-court judgment based on an erroneous resolution of constitutional or federal law and that 28 U.S.C.A. § 1257 (providing for review of judgments by the highest court of a state only by certiorari to the U.S. Supreme Court) is the exclusive procedure for federal-court review in such situations. The test is whether the federal claim is "inextricably intertwined with the state court's denial" so that "the district court is in essence being called upon to review the state-court decision." 460 U.S. at 483.

The Second Circuit found in *Pennzoil* that the federal district court lacked jurisdiction as to that portion of its decision that evaluated the merits of the state-court judgment (on such matters as the propriety of the punitive and compensatory damages award). However, it concluded that Texaco's Due Process and Equal Protection claims, which were not presented to the Texas courts, were within the district court's jurisdiction because they were not "inextricably intertwined" with the state-court action. 784 F.2d at 1141–45. The Supreme Court did not reach this issue since it found that the district court should have abstained under *Younger*.

A claim is inextricably intertwined under *Rooker–Feldman* if it "succeeds only to the extent that the state wrongly decided the issues before it [or] if the relief requested would effectively reverse the state court decision or void its ruling." Charchenko v. City of Stillwater, 47 F.3d 981, 983 (8th Cir.1995). In Fielder v. Credit Acceptance Corp., 188 F.3d 1031 (8th Cir. 1999), plaintiff filed a class action in federal court on behalf of persons who had defaulted on used car loans to enjoin the credit company from enforcing deficiency default judgments entered in state court, alleging illegal fees and interest charges. Jurisdiction was denied under *Rooker–Feldman* because "in granting this relief, the court acted precisely like an appellate court, effectively reversing part of the state court decision."

Noting that "it is commonplace for the lower federal courts to complain that the *Rooker–Feldman* doctrine is difficult to apply," the Ninth Circuit said that the doctrine "applies to defeat federal district court subject matter jurisdiction only when a plaintiff's suit in federal district court is at least in part a forbidden de facto appeal of a state court judgment, and an issue in that federal suit is 'inextricably intertwined' with an issue resolved by the state court judicial decision." Noel v. Hall, 341 F.3d 1148 (9th Cir.2003). In *Noel*, a former partner who had lost in a state-court suit alleging that the other partner had unlawfully wire-tapped him and converted his mobile home, sued in federal court seeking damages for wrongful dissolution of the partnership and conversion of property. Those claims were found not to be barred by *Rooker–Feldman* because plaintiff "neither asserted as a legal wrong an allegedly erroneous decision by the state court in the earlier state court litigation nor sought relief from the state court judgment." Although the claims brought in the state and federal courts were clearly related, the court found that the "inextricably intertwined" analysis of *Rooker–Feldman* did not apply because the federal action was not "a forbidden de facto appeal" from the state-court judgment. There was, however, a remaining question as to whether the federal claims would be barred by claim preclusion. Can *Noel* be reconciled with *Fiedler*?

Rooker–Feldman may also be inapplicable if the state-court order would interfere with the federal court's legitimate exercise of jurisdiction in a related case. See In re Diet Drugs Liability Litigation, 282 F.3d 220 (3d Cir.2002), *infra* p. 391, which rejected a *Rooker–Feldman* challenge to an injunction entered by a federal court that had previously conditionally approved a nationwide settlement class action. The injunction forbade plaintiff's counsel for a proposed statewide class action in a Texas state court from enforcing the state court's order opting the state-court class members out of the federal class action. It found that although the state-court action had the effect of voiding the Texas court's order, that order would interfere with the federal court's jurisdiction over a far-advanced disposition of a national class actions, and "the *Rooker–Feldman* doctrine does not work to defeat a district court's authority over the management of its own case." Notice the similarity between this analysis and that required to determine whether a federal-court injunction satisfied the "in aid of jurisdiction" exception to the Anti–Injunction Act, *infra* p. 190. The court also found the federal court injunction met that exception.

c. *Stay of Federal Suit in Interests of "Wise Judicial Administration"*

LIFE–LINK INTERNATIONAL, INC. v. LALLA

United States Court of Appeals, Tenth Circuit, 1990.
902 F.2d 1493.

Before LOGAN, JONES, and SEYMOUR, CIRCUIT JUDGES.

PER CURIAM.

Plaintiff, Life–Link International, Inc., appeals from an order of the district court dismissing this action with prejudice by virtue of duplicative proceedings pending in state court. We reverse the district court's order.

In February 1988, defendant Ozzie Lalla commenced an action in a Colorado state court against plaintiff for collection of a debt. Plaintiff counterclaimed for trade-mark infringement under 15 U.S.C. § 1114; false designation of origin under 15 U.S.C. § 1125(a); common law unfair competition trademark infringement, and injury to business reputation; deceptive trade practices under Colo.Rev.Stat. § 6–1–105; and breach of contract.

In June 1988, plaintiff commenced this action in federal district court against defendants Ozzie Lalla and Nena Lalla. Nena Lalla is not a party in the state court action. Plaintiff alleged the same claims in this action as it raised in its state court counterclaim. Plaintiff also moved the state court to stay all proceedings, including discovery, pending completion of the federal action. In September 1988, the state court granted that motion. Defendants subsequently moved to dismiss the federal suit on the ground that plaintiff waived its right to invoke the jurisdiction of the federal court by asserting counterclaims in the state court action rather than removing that action to federal court. The district court granted defendants' motion, dismissing with prejudice.

On appeal, plaintiff argues that the district court erred in dismissing its suit and further argues that even if this ruling was correct, dismissal with prejudice was error. Defendant argues only that the district court was correct in dismissing the case, agreeing that dismissal should have been without prejudice. We agree with plaintiff that the district court should not have dismissed this suit.

The district court dismissed this action on the ground asserted by defendants, citing *Paris v. Affleck,* 431 F.Supp. 878 (M.D.Fla.1977). But *Paris* was a removal case regarding whether claims could be concurrently litigated in two federal courts and, thus, is inapplicable to this case of concurrent litigation as between a state and a federal court. *See Colorado River Water Conservation Dist. v. United States,* 424 U.S. 800, 817, 96 S.Ct. 1236, 1246, 47 L.Ed.2d 483 (1976). And the Supreme Court has stated that "[t]his Court never has intimated acceptance of [the] view that the decision of a party to spurn removal and bring a separate suit in federal court invariably warrants the stay or dismissal of the suit under the *Colorado River* doctrine." *Gulfstream Aerospace Corp. v. Mayacamas Corp.,* 485 U.S. 271, 290, 108 S.Ct. 1133, 1144, 99 L.Ed.2d 296 (1988). Therefore, we must hold that the district court erred in dismissing this action solely on the grounds of waiver. So concluding, ordinarily we would remand to the district court with directions to apply the appropriate standard, since "the decision whether to defer to the state courts is necessarily left to the discretion of the district court in the first instance.... [and] such discretion must be exercised under the relevant standard." *Moses H. Cone Memorial Hosp. v. Mercury Constr. Corp.,* 460 U.S. 1, 19, 103 S.Ct. 927, 938, 74 L.Ed.2d 765 (1983). But we believe it would be an abuse of discretion to defer to the state court under the circumstances of this case.

[The court finds that abstention cannot be justified under the *Pullman, Burford,* or *Younger* doctrines.]

Nonetheless, our inquiry cannot stop here:

> "Although this case falls within none of the abstention categories, there are principles unrelated to considerations of proper constitutional adjudication and regard for federal-state relations which govern in situations involving the contemporaneous exercise of concurrent jurisdiction.... These principles rest on considerations of '[w]ise judicial administration, giving regard to conservation of judicial resources and comprehensive disposition of litigation.'"

Colorado River, 424 U.S. at 817, 96 S.Ct. at 1246 (quoting *Kerotest Mfg. Co. v. C–O–Two Fire Equip. Co.,* 342 U.S. 180, 183, 72 S.Ct. 219, 221, 96 L.Ed. 200 (1952)). Even so, we must keep in mind that "the circumstances permitting the dismissal of a federal suit due to the presence of a concurrent state proceeding for reasons of wise judicial administration are considerably more limited than the circumstances appropriate for abstention." We must "ascertain whether there exist 'exceptional' circumstances, the 'clearest of justifications,' that can suffice under *Colorado River* to justify the *surrender* of ... jurisdiction," *Cone,* 460 U.S. at 25–26, 103 S.Ct. at 942 (emphasis in original), "with the balance heavily weighted in favor of the exercise of jurisdiction."

The Supreme Court has announced several factors that guide our analysis: (a) which court first assumed jurisdiction over any property; (b) the inconvenience of the federal forum; (c) the desirability of avoiding piecemeal litigation; and (d) the order in which concurrent jurisdiction was obtained. *Colorado River,* 424 U.S. at 818, 96 S.Ct. at 1246. We must also consider the adequacy of the state court proceedings to protect the parties' rights, whether issues of federal law are presented, and whether the attempt to invoke federal jurisdiction was done in bad faith. [*Cone,* 460 U.S. at 17 n.20, 23–26; 28.]

Neither court has jurisdiction over any property, and defendants concede that both forums are equally convenient. The state court action was commenced first. However, "priority should not be measured exclusively by which complaint was filed first, but rather in terms of how much progress has been made in the two actions." *Cone,* 460 U.S. at 21, 103 S.Ct. at 940. The only additional progress in the state court action appears to be some informal discovery, some formal discovery requests, and a scheduling conference at which the judge stayed the proceedings pending the outcome of this suit. So both actions seem to be at a standstill with no significant progress achieved. The case presents issues of both state and federal law. "Although in some rare circumstances the presence of state-law issues may weigh in favor of ... surrender, the presence of federal-law issues must always be a major consideration weighing against surrender." *Id.* at 26, 103 S.Ct. at 942. Defendants speculate that Nena Lalla was not joined in the state proceedings as justification for plaintiff's forum shopping. But plaintiff argues it might not be able to join Nena Lalla in state court because of improper venue, and therefore, piecemeal litigation and inadequate protection of its rights may result if a federal forum is unavailable. In view of the fact that the state court action has been stayed, there could be no piecemeal litigation or inadequate forum problems if the federal suit is continued.

Federal courts have a "virtually unflagging obligation ... to exercise the jurisdiction given them," *Colorado River,* 424 U.S. at 817, 96 S.Ct. at 1246, therefore, "[o]nly the clearest of justifications will warrant dismissal," *id.* at 819, 96 S.Ct. at 1247. Here, no factor clearly warrants dismissal, and several factors favor retention. Therefore, the district court should accept jurisdiction and hear this case on the merits.

Notes and Questions

1. In *Life–Link,* wasn't plaintiff clearly forum shopping by filing suit on the identical matter in federal court four months after being sued in state court? Didn't plaintiff effectively concede that the state court was an adequate forum by filing its counterclaims? Is it fair to say, as does the court, that there is no problem of piecemeal litigation because the state court has stayed its proceedings? Should the federal judge at least have information as to the state court's reason for staying and the likelihood that it will continue to do so? If the state court case had been further along and the state court had not stayed, would the defendant have overcome the "exceptional circumstances" requirement for a federal court to refuse to exercise its jurisdiction? Or would uncertainty as to joining one defendant in the state court still have justified refusal to abstain? Should the federal judge have been satisfied that the plaintiff just said "it might not be able to join" the other defendant, without further proof?

2. Should a federal court follow the *Colorado River* balancing of factors approach when asked to stay proceedings on a claim as to which there is *exclusive* federal jurisdiction? In Silberkleit v. Kantrowitz, 713 F.2d 433 (9th Cir.1983), the federal suit made claims under § 10(b) of the 1934 Securities Exchange Act and the Employee Retirement and Income Security Act (ERISA), both of which are subject to exclusive federal jurisdiction. The district court stayed its proceedings because there were already four actions in state court between the same parties involving similar issues that might, under principles of collateral estoppel, resolve or limit the issues in the federal case. The Ninth Circuit reversed on the ground that there is no discretion to stay proceedings on a claim as to which there is exclusive federal jurisdiction, citing *Colorado River's* reference to "the virtually unflagging obligation of the federal courts to exercise the jurisdiction given them."

Is such an absolute rule with regard to claims within the exclusive jurisdiction of the federal court consistent with "wise judicial administration"? The Ninth Circuit continues to adhere to the view that a stay cannot be employed in a case within exclusive federal jurisdiction, Intel Corp. v. Advanced Micro Devices, Inc., 12 F.3d 908, 913–14 n. 7 (9th Cir.1993), but this view was rejected by a district court in Allied Machinery Service, Inc. v. Caterpillar Inc., 841 F.Supp. 406 (S.D.Fla.1993). Plaintiff there filed an antitrust suit in a Florida state court based on the Florida antitrust statute.

Three months later it filed suit in the federal district court alleging the same violations, this time based on the federal antitrust statute. The federal court granted defendants' motion to abstain in the interests of wise judicial administration. It especially focused on the *Colorado River* factors that the state court obtained jurisdiction first; that if the federal court did not abstain, there would be duplicate suits over the identical claims; and that plaintiff voluntarily chose state court and only later, after state court proceedings were developing, filed in federal court which appeared to be forum shopping.

The court concluded that "[t]he question of abstention and exclusive federal jurisdiction is unsettled," noting the conflict between the Second Circuit [American Disposal Services, Inc. v. O'Brien, 839 F.2d 84 (2d Cir.1988) (upholding dismissal of a federal § 1983 action under *Colorado River*)] and the Ninth Circuit. It found abstention appropriate because the plaintiff filed first in state court and only filed in federal court after the defendant moved for summary judgment. "Such behavior strains the federal policy against plaintiff removal and forum shopping, and this Court cannot tolerate it. * * * Furthermore, given that the state court has had a three month head start in dealing with the issues presented by these cases, it would be a waste of judicial resources for this Court to revisit issues that may be disposed of by the resolution of the already progressing state proceedings." Id. at 410.

3. If federal courts have expertise for resolving claims within exclusive federal jurisdiction, should state decisions not be accorded collateral estoppel effect with respect to such claims? Cf. Mercoid Corp. v. Mid–Continent Investment Co., 320 U.S. 661, 64 S.Ct. 268, 88 L.Ed. 376 (1944) (limiting res judicata in patent monopolization cases). Otherwise, wouldn't it be more sensible to defer action in federal court until state proceedings are completed if they are likely to be completed before the federal proceedings?

4. In Deakins v. Monaghan, 484 U.S. 193, 108 S.Ct. 523, 98 L.Ed.2d 529 (1988), the Supreme Court clarified the interaction of the *Younger* doctrine and *Colorado River* abstention. Plaintiffs there were subjects of a state grand jury investigation. They claimed that the seizure of their records under a state warrant violated their federal constitutional rights, and sued in federal court for equitable relief and damages. Thereafter, three of them were indicted although the seized records had not been used by the grand jury. The district court dismissed the case in its entirety. On appeal, the Third Circuit held that dismissal of the damages claims was unwarranted, and that they should have been stayed pending completion of the state criminal proceedings, relying on a Third Circuit rule that there only be a stay where the damages claim would not be cognizable in the state court proceedings.

The Supreme Court affirmed. Although it mentioned *Colorado River's* "virtually unflagging obligation" to exercise jurisdiction, the Court endorsed the Third Circuit practice of staying federal actions as prudent because "[i]t allows a parallel state proceeding to go forward without interference from its federal sibling, while enforcing the duty of federal courts to 'assume jurisdiction where jurisdiction properly exists.' " Id. at 202, 108 S.Ct. at 530. Justice White, concurring, argued that the Court should have declared "that *Youn-*

ger requires, not only dismissal of the equitable claim in this case, but also that the damages action not go forward." Id. at 206, 108 S.Ct. at 532.

5. In the lower courts, *Colorado River* has presented problems of application. In Lumen Const., Inc. v. Brant Const. Co., 780 F.2d 691 (7th Cir.1985), plaintiff was first sued in a state interpleader proceeding in which it asserted counterclaims asserting violation of federal civil rights laws. It then filed a federal action asserting "virtually identical" claims and the district court dismissed pending decision of the state court action. Modifying the dismissal into a stay, the appellate court otherwise affirmed. It noted that the state suit was "a good deal more comprehensive than the federal case", id. at 695, and rejected plaintiff's argument that deference was inappropriate because there were additional parties in federal court who were not before the state court. "If the rule were otherwise, the *Colorado River* doctrine could be entirely avoided by the simple expedient of naming additional parties." Id. Accordingly, it was unimportant that the time had passed for adding parties to the state action: "If Lumen can no longer bring in additional parties in the state case, it has only itself to blame." Id. at 696.

In Schomber v. Jewel Cos., 614 F.Supp. 210 (N.D.Ill.1985), the federal court found *Colorado River* to permit a stay of proceedings in a federal class action for injuries resulting from defendant's distribution of milk tainted by salmonella because the Illinois state courts had already embarked on an extensive effort to handle such litigation: "Although the state case has not advanced very far and no class has yet been certified, the state court has undertaken complex administrative procedures to oversee the action. All state court complaints have been consolidated under one number and assigned to one judge, who will oversee all pretrial matters on a consolidated basis." Id. at 217.

Contrast In re Chicago Flood Litigation, 819 F.Supp. 762 (N.D.Ill.1993), in which plaintiffs sued the City of Chicago and others for damages sustained when flooding from the Chicago River disabled many office buildings in downtown Chicago. Almost immediately there were suits filed in Illinois state court. After some rulings in those cases, other plaintiffs filed suits in federal court. The city moved to dismiss or stay the federal suits in deference to the pending state court actions. The court refused to stay. It reasoned that the fact the federal plaintiffs had not sued in state court was not crucial. Instead, the critical consideration would normally be whether issue preclusion might operate to simplify the federal litigation; because the federal cases were "sufficiently parallel," there was a prospect that it would. Nevertheless, relying on "an efficient case management system that speeds resolution of the federal cases and reduces the potential for conflict inherent whenever concurrent litigation occurs," the court decided to proceed. Id. at 765.

6. On occasion one party will file a declaratory judgment action in a federal court to determine the rights and obligations of the parties to a disputed matter, and the other party will then file a suit for full relief based on the same matter in a state court. In Wilton v. Seven Falls Co., 515 U.S. 277, 115 S.Ct. 2137, 132 L.Ed.2d 214 (1995), the Court twice characterized the discretion vested by the Declaratory Judgment Act as "unique" and held that it would "justify a standard vesting district courts with greater discre-

tion in declaratory judgment actions than that presented under the 'exceptional circumstances' test of *Colorado River*.'' Instead, the proper reference in declaratory judgment cases is to Brillhart v. Excess Insurance Co., 316 U.S. 491, 62 S.Ct. 1173, 86 L.Ed. 1620 (1942), which upheld such a stay in a declaratory judgment action. In *Wilton*, the Court explained as follows:

> Although *Brillhart* did not set out an exclusive list of factors governing the district court's exercise of this discretion, it did provide some useful guidance in that regard. The Court indicated, for example, that in deciding whether to enter a stay, a district court should examine "the scope of the pending state court proceeding and the nature of defenses open there." This inquiry, in turn, entails consideration of "whether the claims of all parties in interest can satisfactorily be adjudicated in that proceeding, whether necessary parties have been joined, whether such parties are amenable to process in that proceeding, etc." * * * *Brillhart* indicated that, at least where another suit involving the same parties and presenting opportunity for ventilation of the same state law issues is pending in state court, a district court might be indulging in "[g]ratuitous interference" if it permitted the federal declaratory action to proceed.

2. FEDERAL COURT'S INJUNCTION AGAINST PROSECUTION OF STATE PROCEEDINGS (ANTI–INJUNCTION ACT)

A statute prohibiting federal courts from issuing an injunction "to stay proceedings in any court of a state" was passed by Congress in 1793, 1 Stat. 334, and since that time some form of anti-injunction statute has always existed. The present statute, 28 U.S.C.A. § 2283, was adopted as part of the 1948 Judicial Code, with the intent of specifying clear exceptions in response to a narrow reading of the then-existing statute in Toucey v. New York Life Insurance Co., 314 U.S. 118, 62 S.Ct. 139, 86 L.Ed. 100 (1941). § 2283 reads:

> A court of the United States may not grant an injunction to stay proceedings in a State court except as expressly authorized by Act of Congress, or where necessary in aid of its jurisdiction, or to protect or effectuate its judgments.

The first exception—"as expressly authorized by Act of Congress"—has been interpreted as not requiring specific reference to § 2283 in a statute. Mitchum v. Foster, 407 U.S. 225, 92 S.Ct. 2151, 32 L.Ed.2d 705 (1972), which found an express exception in the § 1983 civil rights statute, described the test as "whether an Act of Congress, clearly creating a federal right or remedy enforceable in a federal court of equity, could be given its intended scope only by the stay of a state court proceeding." Compare Pennzoil Co. v. Texaco, Inc., *supra* p. 171.

The second exception—"where necessary in aid of its jurisdiction"—has traditionally been applied when the "federal court's jurisdiction is *in rem* and the state court action may effectively deprive the federal court of the opportunity to adjudicate as to the res." Standard Microsystems Corp. v. Texas Instruments Inc., 916 F.2d 58, 59 (2d Cir.1990); Mitchum

v. Foster, 407 U.S. 225, 235–37, 92 S.Ct. 2151, 2158–59, 32 L.Ed.2d 705 (1972). *In rem* jurisdiction has been analogized to school desegregation suits to prevent state proceedings that would interfere with the federal court's continuing jurisdiction, see C. Wright & M. Kane, Law of Federal Courts 305–06 (6th ed. 2002), to a class action "so far advanced [toward settlement] that it was the virtual equivalent of a *res*," In re Baldwin–United Corp., 770 F.2d 328, 337 (2d Cir.1985), *infra* p. 199, and to a proceeding regarding a bankruptcy and district court's continuing jurisdiction with respect to a settlement trust's reorganization proceedings, In re Joint Eastern & Southern Dist. Asbestos Litigation, 120 B.R. 648 (Bkrtcy.S.N.Y.1990).

In Carlough v. Amchem Products, Inc., 10 F.3d 189 (3d Cir.1993), the court held that a federal judge considering a settlement of an asbestos class action could enjoin prosecution of a state-court class action which purported to request the judicially-declared opting out of all class members in that state. It reasoned that "the stated purpose of the [state-court] suit is to challenge the propriety of the federal class action, which the district court characterized as a preemptive strike against the viability of the federal suit." See also Winkler v. Eli Lilly & Co., 101 F.3d 1196 (7th Cir.1996) (district court presiding over complex MDL proceeding could issue injunction to protect the integrity of its discovery orders). For further discussion, see In re Diet Drugs, *infra* p. 391.

The third exception—"to protect or effectuate its judgments"—allows an injunction to prevent relitigation of a suit in which a judgment has been entered. Rule 54(a) defines "judgment" as "any order from which an appeal lies."

The effect of § 2283 cannot be avoided by simply enjoining a party from prosecuting his state suit, as opposed to having the federal court stay the state court proceedings. However, § 2283 does not prohibit an injunction against a state officer who is about to institute proceedings to enforce an unconstitutional statute nor against state proceedings in which the state court is not performing a judicial function. C. Wright & M. Kane, *supra,* at 300–01.

STANDARD MICROSYSTEMS CORP.
v. TEXAS INSTRUMENTS, INC.

United States Court of Appeals, Second Circuit, 1990.
916 F.2d 58.

Before OAKES and PRATT, CIRCUIT JUDGES, and LEVAL, DISTRICT JUDGE.

LEVAL, DISTRICT JUDGE:

This appeal seeks to enforce the Anti–Injunction Act, 28 U.S.C. § 2283. In a patent-licensing dispute, the district judge enjoined the defendant-appellant from prosecuting a suit which it had instituted against plaintiff-appellee in the Texas state courts. Because we hold that this order violated the terms of the Act, the injunction is vacated.

The dispute arises out of a patent cross-licensing agreement between Standard Microsystems Corp. ("SMC"), the plaintiff-appellee, and Texas

Instruments, Inc., ("TI"), the defendant-appellant, dated October 1, 1976 (the "Agreement"). The Agreement grants to each party the right to make royalty-free use of semiconductor technology owned by the other. It apparently also contains provisions requiring the parties to keep the agreement confidential, and prohibiting the assignment of rights under the Agreement.

TI has licensed certain Japanese and Korean companies to exploit TI's "Kilby patents," which are part of the cross-licensed technology. SMC now proposes to transfer its rights under the Agreement to make royalty-free use of the same TI technology. It proposes to offer these rights to Japanese and Korean entities. TI apparently advised SMC that it would consider such a sale, and disclosure by SMC in preparation for such a sale, as a violation of the Agreement.

On Friday, January 19, 1990, SMC filed this action against TI in the Eastern District of New York. The complaint alleges violations of federal antitrust and securities statutes and breach of contract, and further seeks declaratory relief that SMC's actions do not breach its Agreement. Simultaneously with the filing of the suit, SMC obtained a temporary restraining order signed by Judge Joseph McLaughlin. The order restrained TI

> from terminating its License Agreement dated October 1, 1976, with plaintiff or revoking any of plaintiff's rights under that Agreement.

Judge McLaughlin's order included an Order to Show Cause setting a hearing before Judge Leonard Wexler, the assigned judge, on SMC's application for a preliminary injunction to be held on Monday, January 22, 1990.

At 8:00 a.m. on Monday morning, January 22, TI filed suit in the Texas state court against SMC. The suit seeks to bar SMC from making disclosures in violation of the Agreement and to bar SMC from interfering with TI's license negotiations in Japan.

On January 22, Judge Wexler continued the TRO and adjourned the preliminary injunction hearing to Friday, January 26.

On January 26, counsel for SMC advised Judge Wexler that SMC "would like [the court] to enjoin TI along the same lines as the temporary restraining order, to begin with. We would also like, Your honor, . . . to enjoin TI from specifically proceeding in the [Texas] State Court action or any other action with respect to the same contract issues. . . ."

Judge Wexler proceeded to make the following order:

> Until there is a determination, Mr. Cooper [TI's counsel], I'm directing [that] you, your firm, your client, [and] anyone connected with you are stayed from doing anything in Texas or in relationship to that action that has previously been filed. Cease and desist immediately.

That is the order from which TI appeals.

TI contends that Judge Wexler's order violates the Anti–Injunction Act, 28 U.S.C. § 2283. The Act provides:

A court of the United States may not grant an injunction to stay proceedings in a State court except as expressly authorized by Act of Congress, or where necessary in aid of its jurisdiction, or to protect or effectuate its judgments.

Its purpose is, *inter alia,* to avoid intergovernmental friction that may result from a federal injunction staying state court proceedings. The Supreme Court has construed the Act to forbid a federal court from enjoining a party from prosecuting a state court action unless one of the three exceptions stated in the statute obtains. The three excepted circumstances are (i) the express provisions of another act of Congress authorizing such an order; (ii) necessity in aid of the federal court's jurisdiction and (iii) the need to protect or effectuate the federal court's judgments. *Atlantic Coast Line R.R. Co. v. Brotherhood of Locomotive Engineers,* 398 U.S. 281, 287–88, 90 S.Ct. 1739, 1743–44, 26 L.Ed.2d 234 (1970).

None of the three statutory exceptions is here pertinent. There is no contrary act of Congress. And the injunction is not necessary either in aid of the federal court's jurisdiction or to protect or effectuate its judgments.

A number of circumstances may justify a finding that the exceptions govern. Where the federal court's jurisdiction is *in rem* and the state court action may effectively deprive the federal court of the opportunity to adjudicate as to the *res,* the exception for necessity "in aid of jurisdiction" may be appropriate. *Compare Kline v. Burke Construction Co.,* 260 U.S. 226, 230, 43 S.Ct. 79, 81, 67 L.Ed. 226 (1922) (declining to uphold federal court injunction against state court proceedings where contract obligations were in dispute, rather than rights relating to a *res*); *Heyman v. Kline,* 456 F.2d 123 (2d Cir.), *cert. denied,* 409 U.S. 847, 93 S.Ct. 53, 34 L.Ed.2d 88 (1972) (Act bars federal court injunction issued in *in personam* proceeding involving employment contract); *Vernitron Corp. v. Benjamin,* 440 F.2d 105 (2d Cir.), *cert. denied,* 402 U.S. 987, 91 S.Ct. 1664, 29 L.Ed.2d 154 (1971) (reversing issuance of injunction justified only by the possibility of collateral estoppel in parallel securities litigations); *with Penn General Casualty Co. v. Pennsylvania ex rel. Schnader,* 294 U.S. 189, 55 S.Ct. 386, 79 L.Ed. 850 (1935) (affirming injunction against state court proceedings to protect court's ability to control and dispose of property in liquidation proceeding). Analogous circumstances may be found where a federal court is on the verge of settling a complex matter, and state court proceedings may undermine its ability to achieve that objective, *see In re Baldwin–United Corp.,* 770 F.2d 328, 337 (2d Cir.1985) (upholding injunction against state court actions to protect ability of federal court to manage and to settle multidistrict class action proceeding which was far advanced and in which court had extensive involvement). Or, where a federal court has made conclusive rulings and their effect may be undermined by threatened relitigation in state courts, the exception may be appropriate. *See, e.g., Necchi Sewing Machine Sales Corp. v. Carl*, 260 F.Supp. 665, 669 (S.D.N.Y.1966) (enjoining state court from hearing claims when federal court had found those claims to be properly heard only before an arbitrator).

The suits at issue here are *in personam* actions, brought on successive business days in two different courts, disputing the interpretation of a contract. The existence of the state court action does not in any way impair the jurisdiction of the federal court or its ability to render justice. It is well-settled that such circumstances as these do not justify invocation of the exceptions of the Anti–Injunction Act. *See Vendo Co. v. Lektro–Vend Corp.*, 433 U.S. 623, 642, 97 S.Ct. 2881, 2893, 53 L.Ed.2d 1009 (1977) (reversing injunction of state court proceedings which, like federal court action, involved dispute arising out of covenant not to compete; "[w]e have never viewed parallel *in personam* actions as interfering with the jurisdiction of either court").

> Each court is free to proceed in its own way and in its own time, without reference to the proceedings in the other court. Whenever a judgment is rendered in one of the courts and pleaded in the other, the effect of that judgment is to be determined by application of the principles of *res adjudicata*. . . .

Vendo Co., 433 U.S. at 642, 97 S.Ct. at 2893; *see also Atlantic Coast Line R.R.*, 398 U.S. at 295, 90 S.Ct. at 1747 ("the state and federal courts had concurrent jurisdiction in this [labor dispute] and neither court was free to prevent either party from simultaneously pursuing claims in both courts").

SMC argues that, nonetheless, Judge Wexler's injunction must be affirmed because it falls within two additional judicially created exceptions to the Act. First, the Act has been held inapplicable to federal injunctions issued prior to the institution of the state court action. *Dombrowski v. Pfister*, 380 U.S. 479, 484 n. 2, 85 S.Ct. 1116, 1119 n. 2, 14 L.Ed.2d 22 (1965); *In re Baldwin–United Corp.*, 770 F.2d 328, 335 (2d Cir.1985). This exception is based both on policy and the explicit terms of the act. Where no state court proceeding exists, there is less danger that a federal court injunction barring the institution of such a proceeding will cause affront to state authority. Furthermore, the Act bars grant of "an injunction to stay *proceedings* in a State court," 28 U.S.C. § 2283 (emph. added), which seems to refer literally to existing proceedings, rather than contemplated proceedings.

SMC contends this case falls within the *Dombrowski* exception because Judge McLaughlin's TRO predated the institution of the Texas action. The contention is frivolous. Although it is true that the TRO predated the Texas action, the TRO did not forbid TI from starting a separate action. The TRO restrained TI only "from terminating [SMC's] License Agreement ... or revoking ... [SMC's] rights under that Agreement." There is no factual basis for SMC's argument that TI's Texas court action was instituted in violation of a federal injunction barring such suit. No order was issued against TI's maintenance of its state court action until January 26, four days after TI started the action.

Second, SMC contends that, notwithstanding the Act, a state court action may be enjoined if a motion to bar the state court action was made before the state court action was started. This argument depends on an exception to the Act created by judicial decision in the Seventh Circuit, *Barancik v. Investors Funding Corp.,* 489 F.2d 933 (7th Cir. 1973), and followed in the First and Eighth Circuits, *see National City Lines, Inc. v. LLC Corp.,* 687 F.2d 1122, 1127–28 (8th Cir.1982) (following *Barancik*); *Hyde Park Partners, L.P. v. Connolly,* 839 F.2d 837 (1st Cir.1988), but rejected in the Sixth, *see Roth v. Bank of the Commonwealth,* 583 F.2d 527 (6th Cir.1978) (criticizing reasoning of *Barancik*), *cert. dismissed,* 442 U.S. 925, 99 S.Ct. 2852, 61 L.Ed.2d 292 (1979). This circuit has never considered the issue.

In *Barancik,* defendants filed an action in state court while plaintiff's preliminary injunction motion was pending in federal court seeking to bar defendants from commencing a separate legal action. The federal district judge enjoined prosecution of the state court action. The Seventh Circuit affirmed, noting that if the federal judge had immediately decided the motion, the injunction would have preceded the filing of the state court action and therefore, under *Dombrowski,* would not have violated the Anti–Injunction Act. The court found anomalous the possibility that the federal court's authority to rule on a pending motion could be terminated by the action of one of the litigants and concluded that the Anti–Injunction Act did not prohibit a stay of state court proceedings if the state court proceeding was commenced *after* filing of a motion seeking to enjoin it.

We have considerable doubt whether the *Barancik* rule should be adopted in this circuit. We do not find its reasoning compelling. The *Barancik* court found it "unseemly" that a court's power to rule could be defeated by the quicker action of a litigant. But it is axiomatic that one is not disabled from acting merely because an adverse litigant has *applied* for an order to bar such action. A party that has not been enjoined is ordinarily free to act, notwithstanding the pendency of applications to enjoin the action. In many circumstances litigants may lawfully moot an application by acting before the court has ruled. To enjoin conduct requires a judge's order, not merely an application for a judge's order. Where speed is needed, the rules of procedure provide for temporary restraining orders, even without notice, to prevent irreparable harm. *See* Fed.R.Civ.Pro.Rule 65. However anomalous it may seem that a party can moot an issue by acting more rapidly than the court, it is far more anomalous and dangerous that a mere application for injunctive relief be deemed equivalent to a court's order issuing an injunction.

The *Barancik* rule, furthermore, creates a still more serious anomaly. Under *Barancik,* merely by filing an application for relief, a party nullifies an Act of Congress. In passing the Anti–Injunction Act, Congress meant to avoid friction in the relationship between federal courts and state courts. The *Barancik* rule places the power in the hands of the plaintiff unilaterally to nullify the effectiveness of an Act of Congress and to create exactly the kind of federal-state conflict that Congress sought to prevent.

We need not decide whether the *Barancik* rule will be followed in this circuit because, in any event, it does not apply to these facts.

At the time of TI's commencement of the Texas action, there was no application before the federal court to bar it from doing so. The Order to Show Cause sought a preliminary injunction barring TI from

> "a. coercing SMC's compliance in TI's interpretation of the License Agreement;
>
> b.   interfering with SMC's dealings . . . ;
>
> c.   attempting to monopolize . . . through the coercive acts alleged herein; and
>
> d.   Terminating the License Agreement and . . . revoking any of SMC's rights thereunder . . . ."

SMC's counsel reaches beyond the limits of ingenuity to contrive an argument that the Order to Show Cause applied for an injunction to bar the filing of a parallel action. The argument is to the effect that the application to enjoin TI's "attempt[s] to monopolize . . . through the coercive acts alleged herein," especially when combined with the concluding prayer for such "other and different relief as [the court] deems proper and just," incorporates by reference the allegation in the complaint of threats of "sham litigation." Taking all this together, SMC contends its application should be construed as having sought an injunction barring institution of the "sham" Texas action. The argument is more convoluted than convincing. In fact, there was no application before the court to bar TI from starting a lawsuit. Thus, even if we were to adopt the reasoning of *Barancik,* it would not apply to this case.

Notes and Questions

1.   Section 2283 eliminates discretion to enjoin state-court proceedings, even if an injunction would prevent duplicative litigation and promote the efficient resolution of disputes. In Atlantic Coast Line Railroad Co. v. Locomotive Engineers, 398 U.S. 281, 90 S.Ct. 1739, 26 L.Ed.2d 234 (1970), the Supreme Court emphasized that "any doubts as to the propriety of a federal injunction against state court proceedings should be resolved in favor of permitting the state courts to proceed in an orderly fashion to finally determine the controversy." In Vendo Co. v. Lektro–Vend Corp., 433 U.S. 623, 97 S.Ct. 2881, 53 L.Ed.2d 1009 (1977), the Court confirmed that "the Act is an absolute prohibition against any injunction of any state-court proceedings, unless the injunction falls within one of the three specifically defined exceptions in the Act. The Act's purpose is to forestall the inevitable friction between the state and federal courts that ensues from the injunction of state judicial proceedings by a federal court."

2. In *Standard Microsystems* the appellate court rejects the argument that the January 19 temporary restraining order should be interpreted to forbid the January 22 filing of the Texas state-court suit. Had plaintiff tried to have defendant held in contempt for filing the Texas suit, this result would seem unavoidable because the order was not clear enough to support a contempt citation. Should the same attitude apply to the Anti–Injunction Act issue? Given Judge Wexler's order on January 26 that the Texas suit not be prosecuted, isn't it reasonable to conclude that Judge McLaughlin would have explicitly forbidden the filing of the suit on January 19 had that been suggested to him? Assuming that the defendant was represented at the January 19 hearing at which the TRO issued, was it under an obligation to disclose its plan to file suit in Texas the following Monday?

3. Note that the court says that the Anti–Injunction Act is designed to avoid "intergovernmental friction." How does it accomplish this objective? So long as the federal court enters an injunction before an action is filed in state court, the Act does not apply even if the party enjoined is a state official acting on behalf of the state. Compare Pennhurst State School and Hospital v. Halderman, 465 U.S. 89, 104 S.Ct. 900, 79 L.Ed.2d 67 (1984) (involving Eleventh Amendment, which precludes federal court judgment against state officials in some circumstances).

4. Even where a federal court cannot enjoin state proceedings, it is possible to ask the state court to stay its action. Would such a stay have been appropriate in *Standard Microsystems* on principles of wise judicial administration?

5. Tender offer situations often involve duplicative litigation, either repetitive or reactive, giving rise to applications to enjoin other actions. In National City Lines, Inc. v. LLC Corp., 687 F.2d 1122 (8th Cir.1982), preliminary injunctions were issued by a federal district court in Missouri to forbid defendants from proceeding in state court to enforce Missouri take-over statutes which were challenged as unconstitutional in the plaintiffs' earlier-filed federal-court action. The court found no cause for *Pullman* or *Younger* abstention, and ruled that "the Anti–Injunction Act is inapplicable when a federal court has first obtained jurisdiction of a matter in controversy by the institution of suit." It further found that "the date on which injunctive relief is *sought* in federal court" governs.

6. The exception to the Anti–Injunction Act for injunctions that will "protect or effectuate" a federal court's judgment has been interpreted narrowly. In Chick Kam Choo v. Exxon Corp., 486 U.S. 140, 108 S.Ct. 1684, 100 L.Ed.2d 127 (1988), the plaintiff seaman sued in federal court to recover for injuries received in Singapore, and the federal court dismissed on forum non conveniens grounds. Plaintiff then sued in state court in Texas, and the defendant reacted by filing an action in federal court to enjoin prosecution of the suit in state court. The Supreme Court invalidated the resulting federal-court injunction against the state court suit. Although it conceded that the earlier federal action had decided that dismissal was proper under federal forum non conveniens law, and that in admiralty actions state courts might be required to apply federal forum non conveniens law, the Court held the injunction was invalid because that question had not been resolved in the earlier federal action. It reasoned that "an essential prerequisite for applying

the relitigation exception is that the claims or issues which the federal injunction insulates from litigation in state proceedings actually have been decided by the federal court." Id. at 147, 108 S.Ct. at 1690. Could defendant have obtained such a ruling in the earlier federal proceeding, which ended *before* the state suit was filed?

It may be that a litigant can re-approach a federal court for a determination of the binding effect of its earlier judgment after a state-court suit has been filed. In Parsons Steel, Inc. v. First Alabama Bank, 474 U.S. 518, 106 S.Ct. 768, 88 L.Ed.2d 877 (1986), the Court held that the Anti–Injunction Act does not permit a party first to argue the binding effect of the federal-court judgment in state court and then, having lost in state court, to try again in federal court. By that time, the Court reasoned, under the Full Faith and Credit clause the state court's resolution of the question was entitled to the same respect in the federal court that it would have received in state court. The Court limited the exception of the Anti–Injunction Act to those situations where the state court had not already ruled on the preclusive effect of a federal-court injunction.

7. Should federal courts take a different attitude toward enjoining prosecution of litigation in other countries? The Anti–Injunction Act certainly poses no obstacle to such injunctions, but principles of comity usually make courts reluctant to issue such injunctions. See Gau Shan Co. v. Bankers Trust Co., 956 F.2d 1349 (6th Cir.1992); China Trade & Dev. Corp. v. M.V. Choong Yong, 837 F.2d 33 (2d Cir.1987); Laker Airways v. Sabena, 731 F.2d 909 (D.C.Cir.1984); compare Kaepa, Inc. v. Achilles Corp., 76 F.3d 624, 627 (5th Cir.1996) ("We decline, however, to require a district court to genuflect before a vague and omnipotent notion of comity every time that it must decide whether to enjoin a foreign action.").

8. Does the Anti–Injunction Act apply to an attempt to enjoin a defendant in federal court who refrains from filing a compulsory counterclaim there and instead sues on that claim in state court? In Bruce v. Martin, 680 F.Supp. 616 (S.D.N.Y.1988), plaintiff investors sued the defendant partnership in federal court alleging both federal claims (based on securities law and RICO) and state causes of action. They sought to rescind their partnership contract and a obtain a declaratory judgment that they were not liable on promissory notes they had executed to defendants. They also moved for a preliminary injunction forbidding defendants from filing suit in state courts to collect on the notes, as they had threatened to do.

The federal court concluded that a claim to collect on the notes would be a compulsory counterclaim in the federal action under Rule 13(a). A federal court may enjoin a party from bringing its compulsory counterclaim in a subsequent federal-court action. See Seattle Totems Hockey Club, Inc. v. National Hockey League, 652 F.2d 852, 854 (9th Cir.1981). But can a federal court enjoin the party from suing on its compulsory counterclaim in *state* court? The Anti–Injunction Act only prohibits injunctions with regard to *pending* state-court suits. However, in determining whether the equitable requirements for an injunction are satisfied (i.e., irreparable injury and likelihood of success on the merits), the court stated that it should look to cases interpreting the Anti–Injunction Act. It noted that precedents allow an injunction to prevent interference by a state-court proceeding where necessary "to protect a judgment that is imminent in proceedings that have already exhausted considerable time and resources in the federal court." The federal court here, however, had not issued any orders or expended much time and resources. Although the Supreme Court in *Vendo* (*supra* note 1) proclaimed that "parallel in personam actions" may not be viewed as interfering with the jurisdiction of state or federal courts, the federal court in *Bruce* found a threat to its jurisdiction by "multiple actions in different states." If the defendants sued in state courts, it said, "prior rulings by state courts that decline to stay such actions may be introduced here to preclude this court from considering a given claim or factual issue," and that this prospect would seriously impair its "flexibility and authority to decide" the case (quoting *Atlantic Coast Line R.R.*, *supra* note 1). It thus found irreparable injury sufficient to justify an injunction under the All Writs Act, 28 U.S.C.A. § 1651.

Would there have been the same result if defendant had already filed suit in state court? See Redish, The Anti–Injunction Act Reconsidered, 44 U.Chi.L.Rev. 717 (1977) (arguing that the standards for the Anti–Injunction Act and All Writs Act should be the same); Gunderson v. ADM Investor Services, Inc., 976 F.Supp. 818 (N.D.Iowa 1997) (Anti–Injunction Act prohibits federal court from enjoining parallel state-court suits filed by defendant one month after the federal-court suit was filed).

9.   The Rule 13(a) compulsory counterclaim rule has been found not to be an express exception to the Anti–Injunction Act. See Seattle Totems Hockey Club, Inc. v. National Hockey League, 652 F.2d 852 (9th Cir.1981); 6 C. Wright, A. Miller & M. Kane, Federal Practice & Procedure § 1418 at 148 (2d ed. 1990). But if the purpose of the rule is "to prevent multiplicity of actions and to achieve resolution in a single lawsuit of all disputes arising out of common matters," Southern Const. Co. v. Pickard, 371 U.S. 57, 83 S.Ct. 108, 9 L.Ed.2d 31 (1962), should that ruling be reconsidered? Cf. Semmes Motors, Inc. v. Ford Motor Co., *supra* p. 111 (federal court "seized" of claim that would be compulsory counterclaim).

3.   ALL WRITS ACT AS AUTHORITY FOR FEDERAL COURT ORDERS RELATING TO STATE–COURT SUITS

IN RE BALDWIN–UNITED CORP.
United States Court of Appeals, Second Circuit, 1985.
770 F.2d 328.

Before PRATT, and MANSFIELD, Circuit Judges, and MACMAHON, District Judge.

MANSFIELD, Circuit Judge:

[More than 100 federal securities suits filed against 26 broker-dealers by 100,000 holders of annuities issued by the bankrupt Baldwin–United Corp. were consoldiated by the MDL panel in the Southern District of New York. For two years, Judge Brieant of that court supervised coordinated settlement talks, resulting in stipulations of settlement signed by 18 of 26 defendants. Judge Brieant provisionally approved a nationwide settlement class on behalf of all holders of Baldwin–United securities. Forty state attorneys general, many of whom had authority under their state law to sue for their citizens in a representational capacity, objected that the settlement did not adequately compensate plaintiffs. Many of the plaintiffs had raised pendent state-law claims, on such grounds as state consumer protection laws, and the proposed settlements would have extinguished all claims arising under federal and state laws.

When some of the attorneys general who were not parties to the MDL class action threatened to sue in state courts on behalf of their citizens on state law claims, Judge Brieant enjoined them and "all other persons having actual knowledge of the Order" from "commencing any action or proceeding of any kind against any defendant * * * on behalf of or derivative of the rights of any plaintiff or purported class member * * * or which action or proceeding may in any way affect the rights of any plaintiff * * * or which action or proceeding seeks money damages arising out of the sale to any plaintiff * * * of the Baldwin annuities."]

Federal courts have authority under the All–Writs Act, 28 U.S.C. § 1651 (1982), to "issue all writs necessary or appropriate in aid of their respective jurisdictions and agreeable to the usages and principles of law." In determining whether the injunction was a permissible exercise of Judge Brieant's authority under the All–Writs Act, we look both to cases interpreting this Act and also to cases interpreting similar language appearing in the Anti–Injunction Act, 28 U.S.C. § 2283 (1982). The latter statute bans injunctions against actions pending in state court, subject to specified exceptions, including an exception for injunctions "necessary in aid of [the federal court's] jurisdiction." While the parties agree that the Anti–Injunction Act is inapplicable here since the injunction below issued before any suits were commenced in state court, see Dombrowski v. Pfister, 380 U.S. 479, 484 n. 2, 85 S.Ct. 1116, 1119 n. 2, 14 L.Ed.2d 22 (1965), cases interpreting this clause of the Anti–Injunction Act have been helpful in understanding the meaning of the All–Writs Act.

We do not find independent authority for the issuance of the injunction in the Fed.R.Civ.P. 23(d) provision empowering the district judge to issue orders appropriate "for the protection of the members of the class or otherwise for the fair conduct of the action"; that rule is a rule of procedure and creates no substantive rights or remedies enforceable in federal court.

When a federal court has jurisdiction over its case in chief, as did the district court here, the All–Writs Act grants it ancillary jurisdiction to issue writs "necessary or appropriate in aid of" that jurisdiction. This provision permits a district court to enjoin actions in state court where necessary to prevent relitigation of an existing federal judgment, notwithstanding the fact that the parties to the original action could invoke res judicata in state courts against any subsequent suit brought on the same matters. Even before a federal judgment is reached, however, the preservation of the federal court's jurisdiction or authority over an ongoing matter may justify an injunction against actions in state court. Such "federal injunctive relief may be necessary to prevent a state court from so interfering with a federal court's consideration or disposition of a case as to seriously impair the federal court's flexibility and authority to decide that case." Atlantic Coast Line R.R. Co. v. Brotherhood of Locomotive Engineers, 398 U.S. 281, 295, 90 S.Ct. 1739, 1747, 26 L.Ed.2d 234 (1970) (dicta) (Anti–Injunction Act); see In re Corrugated Container Antitrust Litigation, 659 F.2d 1332, 1334–35 (5th Cir.1981) (Anti–Injunction Act) (upholding an injunction, issued by a federal judge presiding over multi-district litigation, against actions by the same plaintiffs in state court), cert. denied, 456 U.S. 936, 102 S.Ct. 1993, 72 L.Ed.2d 456 (1982).

On the other hand, the mere existence of a parallel lawsuit in state court that seeks to adjudicate the same *in personam* cause of action does not in itself provide sufficient grounds for an injunction against a state action in favor of a pending federal action. See Vendo Co. v. Lektro–Vend Corp., 433 U.S. 623, 642, 97 S.Ct. 2881, 2893, 53 L.Ed.2d 1009 (1977) ("We have never viewed parallel *in personam* actions as interfering with the jurisdiction of either court."); Kline v. Burke Construction Co., 260 U.S. 226, 230, 43 S.Ct. 79, 81, 67 L.Ed. 226 (1922). This principle does not apply when federal courts have jurisdiction over a res in an in rem action; in such a case, because the "exercise by the state court of jurisdiction over the same *res* necessarily impairs, and may defeat, the jurisdiction of the federal court already attached," the federal court is empowered to enjoin any state court proceeding affecting that res. Kline v. Burke Construction Co., 260 U.S. at 229, 43 S.Ct. at 81.

Here the findings of the district court that the injunction was necessary to preserve its jurisdiction and protect its judgments, if sustainable, would be sufficient to justify the issuance of the injunction under the All–Writs Act. We must therefore examine whether the district court's finding that the maintenance of actions in state court would impair its jurisdiction and authority over the consolidated federal multidistrict actions was clearly erroneous.

At the time when the injunction issued the parties in 18 of the 26 class actions had reached stipulated settlements that had been provisionally approved by the court and were awaiting final court approval, and the parties in the remaining 8 suits were continuing settlement negotiations. Final judgments in the 18 settling actions were entered shortly after the injunction issued. As for the defendants participating in the stipulated settlements, we conclude that the injunction was "necessary or appropriate in aid of" the court's jurisdiction. There is no question that an injunction could have been appropriately ordered after the 18 final federal judgments were entered, since it would properly have forestalled relitigation of those judgments. Because, as a condition of the settlement, the plaintiffs agreed to release all claims arising under federal and state law on account of the purchase of the Baldwin SPDAs [annuities] from the settling defendants, such a post-settlement injunction would have barred the states from bringing state law claims derivative of the plaintiffs' rights. Were this not the case, the finality of virtually any class action involving pendent state claims could be defeated by subsequent suits brought by the states asserting rights derivative of those released by the class members. For instance, as a practical matter no defendant in the consolidated federal actions in the present case could reasonably be expected to consummate a settlement of those claims if their claims could be reasserted under state laws, whether by states on behalf of the plaintiffs or by anyone else, seeking recovery of money to be paid to the plaintiffs. Whether a state represented itself to be acting as a "sovereign" in such a suit or described its prayer as one for "restitution" or a "penalty" would make no difference if the recovery sought by the state was to be paid over to the plaintiffs. The effect would be to threaten to reopen the settlement unless and until it had been reduced to a judgment that would have res judicata consequences.

We recognize that under the line of cases typified by Kline v. Burke Construction Co., until the issuance of a final federal judgment the pendency of duplicative *in personam* actions in state court—even those actions derivative of the rights of parties to the federal action—would not ordinarily justify enjoining the state court actions. Here, however, the potential for an onslaught of state actions posed more than a risk of inconvenience or duplicative litigation; rather, such a development threatened to "seriously impair the federal court's flexibility and authority" to approve settlements in the multi-district litigation. Atlantic Coastline R.R. v. Brotherhood of Locomotive Engineers, 398 U.S. at 295, 90 S.Ct. at 1747. The circumstances faced by Judge Brieant threatened to frustrate proceedings in a federal action of substantial scope, which had already consumed vast amounts of judicial time and was nearing completion. Some 100,000 plaintiffs participated as parties in the action, compared to a mere 50 who chose to opt out. Settlement negotiations in the federal court had been under way for many months, agreements had been reached, and all that remained was approval of the settlement by the district court. Several evidentiary hearings on the settlement had been held, featuring testimony by representatives of the plaintiffs, the defendants, and various state agencies. The district court had before it thousands of pages of materials regarding the rehabilitation proceedings in courts in Arkansas and Indiana. In contrast, although the Baldwin bankruptcy occurred in 1983, the states waited until the eve of settlement approval to take any significant actions against the broker-dealers.

The existence of multiple and harassing actions by the states could only serve to frustrate the district court's efforts to craft a settlement in the multidistrict litigation before it. The success of any federal settlement was dependent on the parties' ability to agree to the release of any and all related civil claims the plaintiffs had against the settling defendants based on the same facts. If states or others could derivatively assert the same claims on behalf of the same class or members of it, there could be no certainty about the finality of any federal settlement. Any substantial risk of this prospect would threaten all of the settlement efforts by the district court and destroy the utility of the multidistrict forum otherwise ideally suited to resolving such broad claims. To the extent that the impending state court suits were vexatious and harassing, our interest in preserving federalism and comity with the state courts is not significantly disturbed by the issuance of injunctive relief. See In re Corrugated Container Antitrust Litigation, supra, 659 F.2d at 1335.

Thus the need to enjoin conflicting state proceedings arises because the jurisdiction of a multidistrict court is "analogous to that of a court in an in rem action or in a school desegregation case, where it is intolerable to have conflicting orders from different courts." 17 C. Wright & A. Miller & E. Cooper, § 4225 at 105 n. 8 (Supp.1985). In effect, unlike the situation in the Kline v. Burke Construction Co. line of cases, the district court had before it a class action proceeding so far advanced that it was the virtual equivalent of a res over which the district judge required full control. Similar authority for the injunction comes from the court's power to protect and effectuate its order provisionally approving the 18 settlements.

Under the circumstances we conclude that the injunction protecting the settling defendants was unquestionably "necessary or appropriate in aid of" the federal court's jurisdiction. Although the question is closer as to the application of the injunction to the 8 defendants who have not yet settled, we cannot find that the injunction was erroneous as to them. Given the extensive involvement of the district court in settlement negotiations to date and in the management of this substantial class action, we perceive a major threat to the federal court's ability to manage and resolve the actions against the remaining defendants should the states be free to harass the defendants through state court actions designed to influence the defendants' choices in the federal litigation. So long as there is a substantially significant prospect that these 8 defendants will settle in the reasonably near future, we conclude that the injunction entered by the district court is not improper. If, however, at some point in the continued progress of the actions against the remaining 8 defendants it should appear that prompt settlement was no longer likely, we anticipate that upon application the injunction against parallel actions by the states might be lifted; in that event the situation would fall within the Burke v. Kline Construction Co. rule that *in personam* proceedings in state court cannot be enjoined merely because they are duplicative of actions being heard in federal court. That situation, however, does not presently exist.

Having found the injunction necessary and appropriate in aid of the district court's jurisdiction we conclude that it is no less valid because it applies to states other than New York. An important feature of the All–Writs Act is its grant of authority to enjoin and bind non-parties to an action when needed to preserve the court's ability to reach or enforce its decision in a case over which it has proper jurisdiction. See, e.g., United States v. New York Telephone Co., 434 U.S. at 174, 98 S.Ct. at 373 ("The power conferred by the Act, extends, under appropriate circumstances, to persons who, though not parties to the original action or engaged in wrongdoing, are in a position to frustrate the implementation of a court order or the proper administration of justice, and encompasses even those who have not taken any affirmative action to hinder justice."); United States v. Hall, 472 F.2d 261, 265 (5th Cir.1972) (upholding a contempt citation based on an injunction enjoining a non-party in a school desegregation case from causing disruption on the school campus because the "integrity of the court's power to render a binding judgment in an action over which it has jurisdiction [was] at stake"). The power to bind non-parties distinguishes injunctions issued under the Act from injunctions issued in situations in which the activities of the third parties do not interfere with the very conduct of the proceeding before the court.

While the issuance of the injunction here did not comply with the requirements that Fed.R.Civ.P. 65 prescribes for the issuance of preliminary injunctions, this is not a fatal defect. Injunctions issued under the authority of the All–Writs Act stem from very different concerns than those motivating preliminary injunctions governed by Fed.R.Civ.P. 65. Preliminary injunctions under Rule 65 are designed to preserve the status quo between the parties before the court pending a decision on the merits of the case at hand. In contrast, injunctions such as that issued here are needed to prevent third parties from thwarting the court's ability to reach and resolve the merits of the federal suit before it. Moreover, there is a difference between the power to enjoin an unrelated non-party pursuant to the All–Writs Act and the narrower authority delineated by Rule 65(d), which confines the application of injunctions to parties, "their officers, agents, servants, employees, and attorneys, and [to] those persons in active concert or participation with them who receive actual notice of the order." We do not believe that Rule 65 was intended to impose such a limit on the court's authority provided by the All–Writs Act to protect its ability to render a binding judgment.

* * *

Here the injunction without any ambiguity bars the states from undertaking actions of a representative character seeking additional restitution for state residents who purchased SPDAs. The decree excepts from that bar suits for "prospective injunctive relief as to any unlawful business practice" by defendants and efforts to "exercise in any way all other state law enforcement and regulatory powers, so long as any such action ... does not seek to in any way affect the rights of any plaintiff or purported class member in any proceeding under MDL 581". The latter provision, standing alone, might appear to be ambiguous. But when it is read in the context of the entire injunction and of the judge's decision upon issuing the injunction, both of which were served on all the states, the import of this language is clear. In approving the injunction the district court states its "absolute" intent that the injunction not "extend to the enforcement of the criminal law against anybody who may be deemed to have violated it, and ... not extend to a request of a state court for prospective injunctive relief as to any business practice on the part of any defendant." On the other hand, the judge made it equally clear that the injunction is directed at actions by the states seeking "restitution, or any judgment directing restitution, or anything at all adjudicating the rights of the class action members vis-a-vis the selling brokers." This focus was based on his expressed conviction that the state actions were improperly being brought for harassing and vexatious purposes and as a means of coercing the defendants to pay more funds into the federal settlement pool. Against this background, there can be no doubt that the plain meaning and intent of this provision is to bar the states from using state actions as leverage to force the defendants to contribute additional sums to the federal settlement pool. Such a restriction is sufficiently specific to put the states on "explicit notice of precisely what conduct is outlawed."

As for notice, the requirements of the All–Writs Act are satisfied if the parties whose conduct is enjoined have actual notice of the injunction and an opportunity to seek relief from it in the district court. These requirements were met here, since each state's attorney general was served with the injunction and since each had the opportunity to present arguments against it to the district court. None sought to introduce evidence. Although it would under many circumstances be desirable for service to be made in advance of any proposed injunction on all non-parties whose conduct would thereby be restricted, we cannot impose such a condition on use of the All–Writs Act. In exercising its powers under that Act, the district court may face circumstances in which such notice is impractical or even impossible. For instance, the type of conduct enjoined here was generally disruptive of the district court proceedings, i.e., actions by states that are derivative of the rights of the plaintiffs in the district court or seeking to change the recoveries to be received by the plaintiffs in settlement of their federal suits. So long as the injunction is limited to those engaged in such conduct with actual notice of the terms of the injunction, as is the injunction here, we cannot say that it must fail for lack of notice, even though it appears that not all of the appellant states were aware in advance that an order of injunction was being entered that would limit their conduct as well as the conduct of the State of New York.

[The court found that the injunction did not offend the sovereign immunity of the states, and thus did not violated the Eleventh Amendment, citing, inter alia, Ex Parte Young, *supra* pp. 61–62.]

Notes and Questions

1. The Anti–Injunction Act did not apply in *Baldwin-United* because the injunction was issued before any state court suit was filed. Why did the court need to find authority for the injunction in the All Writs Act? Did it essentially equate the standards of the Anti–Injunction Act with the scope of the All Writs Act? Would that be proper? See Redish, The Anti–Injunction

Act Reconsidered, 44 U.Chi.L.Rev. 717 (1977) (arguing that the standard should be the same under both statutes).

2. The court relied on the "in aid of its jurisdiction," rather than the "protection of its judgment" exception since the settlements were not final. A post-judgment injunction against state litigation, it said, would clearly be allowed: "[w]ere this not the case, the finality of virtually any class action involving pendent state claims could be defeated by subsequent suits brought by the states asserting rights derivative of those released by the class members." But even though the judgment was not final, "the potential for an onslaught of state actions posed more than a risk of inconvenience or duplicative litigation; rather, such a development threatened to 'seriously impair the federal court's flexibility and authority' to approve settlements in the multi-district litigation." How important to that conclusion was the size, scope, and financial impact of this class action on the federal court's devotion of several years' time to bringing about the settlement?

3. The court in *Baldwin-United* cites In re Corrugated Container Antitrust Litigation, 659 F.2d 1332 (5th Cir.1981), in which some 50 private antitrust actions brought by purchasers and filed in federal courts around the country against 37 corrugated container manufacturers were transferred by the MDL Panel to a Texas federal court which certified the consolidated case as a nationwide class action. Thereafter four corporations that were included in the plaintiff class filed suit in a South Carolina state court, seeking to represent all persons injured by the antitrust conspiracy in violation of South Carolina antitrust laws. The state complaint was almost identical to the consolidated complaint in the Texas federal court, and the plaintiffs' attorneys also represented them in the Texas action.

The Texas federal judge enjoined the four plaintiffs from pursuing their suit in South Carolina or another court, and the Fifth Circuit affirmed, finding the injunction necessary under the "in aid of jurisdiction" exception to the Anti–Injunction Act. The plaintiff class had already entered settlement agreements with most of the defendants, and the South Carolina judge had specifically enjoined the defendants from using any federal court settlement document "in connection with any action pending in any Court" without its prior approval. This, the Fifth Circuit said, was "[s]uch a limitation on the terms of settlement" as "would clearly interfere with the multidistrict court's ability to dispose of the broader action pending before it," invoking the "in aid of jurisdiction" exception to the Anti–Injunction Act. It also invoked the "to protect or effectuate its judgment" exception, finding that the federal court had approved the settlements with most of the defendants at the time it issued the injunction and that final judgments were therefore "predictable if not assured." The "protection of judgment" exception, it said, was intended to apply where the state proceeding would be precluded by res judicata, which it found was the case.

How important to the approval of the injunction was the fact that the South Carolina court had enjoined the defendants from using the federal settlements and thus arguably was directly interfering with the conduct of the federal class action? How important was the fact that the state-court complaint followed the federal complaint almost verbatim, the plaintiff class members' attorneys were identical, and the state suit was also a class action?

Would it have made a difference if these factors were absent? See Sherman, Class Actions and Duplicative Litigation, 62 Ind. L.J. 507, 541–45 (1987).

4. The injunction in *Baldwin-United* was more expansive than the one upheld in *Corrugated Container, supra.* First, the injunction (addressed to "all other persons having actual knowledge of the Order") applied to nonparties as well. Is this appropriate? Second, the court saw no difficulty in extending the injunction to the claims against the eight non-settling defendants "so long as there was a substantially significant prospect" that they would settle. "Given the extensive involvement of the district court in settlement negotiations to date," it said, "and in the management of this substantial class action, we perceive a major threat to the federal court's ability to manage and resolve the actions against the remaining defendants should the states be free to harass the defendants through state court actions designed to influence the defendants' choices in the federal litigation." Is this persuasive?

5. Consider Sherman, Class Actions and Duplicative Litigation, 62 Indiana L.J. 507, 546–47 (1987), concerning *Baldwin–United*:

> The securities laws in some of the states were more favorable to plaintiffs, and thus the class members from those states should have had a stronger bargaining position for a more favorable settlement than other members of the class. * * * The upshot of Judge Brieant's certification of a settlement class, accompanied by an injunction against duplicative litigation, was that the pendent claims of the class members were sacrificed for a gross resolution of the dispute on a nationwide basis. There were other methods by which the pendent claims of class members could have been recognized and preserved. Subclasses could have been created for class members from states or groups of states with distinctive pendent claims, and any settlement would have had to address those claims. The settlement class certified by the court could also have excluded the pendent claims. * * * It is clear, however, that the negotiating defendants and plaintiffs' representatives in *Baldwin-United* did not want to leave open the pendent claims. The defendants demanded the release of all claims the class members had against them, and, as the Second Circuit explained, any substantial risk of duplicative litigation "would threaten all of the settlement efforts by the district court and destroy the utility of the multidistrict forum otherwise ideally suited to resolving such broad claims."

We will encounter these issues again in connection with class actions. See Amchem Products, Inc. v. Windsor, *infra* p. 373.

6. *The All Writs Act as Authority for Removal (Syngenta)*: The Supreme Court stated in United States v. New York Telephone Co., 434 U.S. 159, 172, 98 S.Ct. 364, 54 L.Ed.2d 376 (1977), that the All Writs Act authorizes federal courts "to issue such commands * * * as may be necessary or appropriate to effectuate and prevent the frustration of orders it has previously issued in its exercise of jurisdiction otherwise obtained," and in Pennsylvania Bureau of Correction v. United States Marshals Service, 474 U.S. 34, 41, 106 S.Ct. 355, 88 L.Ed.2d 189 (1985), that the Act "fill[s] the interstices of federal courts' jurisdiction." This led a number of federal courts to rely on the Act to remove state-court cases over which there was no

federal jurisdiction in order to prevent the frustration of orders they had previously issued concerning related issues. See Steinman, The Newest Frontier of Judicial Activism: Removal Under the All Writs Act, 80 Bos. U.L.Rev. 773 (2000).

In Syngenta Crop Protection, Inc. v. Henson, 537 U.S. 28, 123 S.Ct. 366, 154 L.Ed.2d 368 (2002), the Supreme Court rejected this expansive application of the All Writs Act. Plaintiff sued in a Louisiana state court on state tort claims concerning an insecticide (there being no diversity or federal question to provide federal court jurisdiction). A similar action was already underway in a federal court in Alabama, and the Louisiana plaintiff was allowed to intervene in it and participate in a settlement. The plaintiff then returned to the Louisiana court, claiming that the Alabama federal court settlement did not resolve all his claims. When the Louisiana court determined to proceed with his case, the defendants removed to the Louisiana federal court, asserting jurisdiction under the All Writs Act and supplemental jurisdiction under § 1367. The Louisiana federal court then transferred the case to a federal court in Alabama under § 1404(a), and the Alabama federal court dismissed the case as barred by the settlement judgment.

The Supreme Court found the removal improper. "The right of removal is entirely a creature of the statute [28 U.S.C. § 1441(a)]," it said, and under the statute's plain terms there must be original subject-matter jurisdiction in the federal court to which removal is sought. "Because the All Writs Act does not confer jurisdiction on the federal courts, it cannot confer the original jurisdiction required to support removal pursuant to § 1441." It also rejected supplemental jurisdiction as a source since a "court must have jurisdiction over a case or controversy before it may assert jurisdiction over ancillary claims." The fact that the federal court in Alabama had retained jurisdiction over the settlement of the case before it did not establish federal jurisdiction over the Louisiana case.

7. *Overlapping class actions*: Issues that are very similar to those discussed here can arise when there are overlapping class actions, often in both federal and state court. This topic is considered in more detail in Chapter IV, *infra* p. 391, but deserves introduction here. Different lawyers sometimes file similar class actions in different courts, seeking to certify either competing nationwide classes or classes whose membership overlaps with other class actions. There may then be a race to class certification and judgment, typically by settlement, which will preclude competing class actions. Defendants sometimes take advantage of this situation by settling with those plaintiffs' counsel who are least demanding. "[A]n area of concern is the settlement of cases through a 'reverse auction' by which defendants propose a cheap settlement and shop around among plaintiffs' counsel until they find a lawyer willing to settle on their terms." National Association of Consumer Advocates, Standards and Guidelines for Litigating and Settling Consumer Class Actions, 176 F.R.D. 375, 385 (1998).

The MDL device might prevent this phenomenon by transferring competing class actions filed in the federal courts to one court, but no similar device is available to transfer state-court cases across state lines or to a single federal court. However, an MDL judge may, as reflected in *Baldwin United*, enjoin competing class actions in state courts that interfere with an imminent settlement, invoking the All Writs Act and the "in aid of jurisdiction" exception to the Anti–Injunction Act. This can be a potent weapon against attempts to undermine an imminent settlement in the MDL court with a quick "reverse auction" class action in state court.

In re Lease Oil Litigation, 48 F.Supp.2d 699 (S.D.Tex.1998), applied that weapon even when a settlement in a federal MDL court was not imminent. There class actions asserting claims under federal antitrust laws (as to which there is exclusive federal-court jurisdiction) were filed in several federal courts against 24 oil companies. A different group of attorneys then filed a proposed nationwide class action in an Alabama state court based on state antitrust laws and quickly announced a settlement with one of the oil companies (Mobil) as to all claims, state or federal, for a much smaller recovery than had been obtained in settlements with some other oil companies. Meanwhile, a global settlement involving all the companies, which was more favorable to the class, was filed in one of the cases pending in the federal court in Houston. Before that court could consider this settlement, however, all the other federal suits were transferred to the federal district court for the Southern District of Texas by the MDL panel. That court then enjoined all the defendants except Mobil and all named plaintiffs from entering settlement agreements that purported to settle the federal antitrust claims. The fact that the state antitrust claims in the Alabama suit were weaker, the court found, "renders the state court case prone to an inadequate, or possibly even collusive, settlement." Asserting authority under the All Writs Act, the court stated that "to allow these federal claims to be 'hijacked' by a global settlement in state court—where the claims could not even be adjudicated—would effectively destroy those federal rights and the federal procedures designed to safeguard them and to enable their orderly resolution."

The court cited *Baldwin-United* as authority. However, unlike that case, a settlement was not imminent in the federal MDL court (in fact, at the time of the Alabama settlement, the federal cases had not yet been transferred under MDL procedures). Is this a proper application of the All Writs Act? The Fifth Circuit affirmed the issuance of the injunction and also affirmed the district court's refusal to accord full faith and credit to the Alabama judgment. See In re Lease Oil Antitrust Litigation, 200 F.3d 317 (5th Cir.), cert. denied, 530 U.S. 1263, 120 S.Ct. 2722, 147 L.Ed.2d 986 (2000). It found that the Alabama court could not release claims over which it did not have jurisdiction and, that under Alabama preclusion law, the claims within exclusive federal jurisdiction could not have been litigated in the Alabama suit and therefore could not be precluded. Preclusion will be considered in more detail in Chapter VIII. See Matsushita Elec. Indus. Co. v. Epstein, *infra* p. 803. Is the exclusive federal court jurisdiction over the antitrust claims critical to this case? Could the aggressive use of an injunction and refusal to accord full faith and credit be used in a case not involving such claims to prevent "hijacking" of federal claims?

C. BANKRUPTCY PROCEEDINGS

Complex litigation must sometimes be played out in the jurisdictional context of bankruptcy proceedings in a federal court. When a party files a petition in bankruptcy, any claims against it must ordinarily be pursued before the bankruptcy court, and any pending lawsuits against it may be affected by the bankruptcy proceedings.

Congress extended exclusive federal court jurisdiction over bankruptcy proceedings. 28 U.S.C.A. § 1334. Bankruptcy judges, much like magistrate judges, are officers of the district courts. § 151. District judges are instructed to refer bankruptcy cases to bankruptcy judges, who may adjudicate "core proceedings arising under title 11" (which usually means claims by the estate against third parties). § 157. Procedure is governed by the Bankruptcy Rules, adopted in 1983, which generally conform to the Federal Rules of Civil Procedure, the principal differences relating to service of process and setting the dispute for trial.

There are two basic types of bankruptcy proceedings—liquidation and rehabilitation. Chapter 7 of the Act governs liquidation. Debtor rehabilitation is accomplished by Chapters 11 ("reorganization" of debts) or 13 ("adjustment" of debts). Creditors may file involuntary petitions under Chapters 7 or 11, but not 13. A debtor may file a bankruptcy petition under any chapter.

In all liquidation cases a temporary representative of the estate, called an "interim trustee," is appointed by the U.S. Trustee to take charge of the affairs of the debtor's estate (§§ 301 and 701, § 303(g)). The interim trustee becomes the permanent "trustee" unless eligible creditors holding a majority in number and 20% in amount of the unsecured claims elect their own trustee (§ 702). Unsecured creditors may also select a "creditors' committee" of from three to eleven members to aid the trustee (§ 705).

The debtor need not be insolvent in order to invoke the protections of a Chapter 11 reorganization. However, a lack of "good faith," as where the principal purpose for seeking relief is to delay creditors without benefitting them, can constitute "cause" under the Code to justify dismissal of the petition.

The voluntary filing of a bankruptcy petition by a debtor affects all parties who may have a claim against a debtor's assets. A claim is a "right to payment, whether or not such right has been reduced to judgment, liquidated, unliquidated, fixed, contingent, matured, unmatured, disputed, undisputed, equitable, secured, or unsecured." § 101(4)(A). Thus a "claim" that gives rise to a "debt" that is dischargeable in bankruptcy is to be construed broadly to encompass all legal obligations of the debtor, regardless of how remote or contingent they may be.

Proofs of Claims

Under Chapter 11, claimants must file proofs of claim in order to participate in a reorganization and obtain the right to any monetary distribution. Proofs of claim are normally filed individually, but increasingly creditors have sought to file class proofs of claims. Whether this is permitted requires interpreting and reconciling various provisions of the

Bankruptcy Code and Rules with Rule 23, the class action rule. The district and appellate courts have disagreed on this issue.

Automatic Stay and Injunction Against Other Litigation

Bankruptcy jurisdiction is a paradigm for the principle that it is desirable for all claims to be disposed of under a single jurisdiction in order to avoid the pernicious effects of outside litigation. The Bankruptcy Code and Rules provide for an automatic stay against all attempts to collect from the debtor. This includes stays of pending litigation and injunctions against litigation outside the bankruptcy court.

The automatic stay provision of the Code, 11 U.S.C.A. § 362, is designed to prevent a run on the assets of the debtor by enjoining judicial, administrative, or other proceedings from being initiated or continued against it. Upon the filing of a bankruptcy petition, all proceedings against the debtor are automatically stayed. The stay applies to all claims against the debtor, including those that are disputed, contingent, or unliquidated. § 101(4). The automatic stay provides a respite from collection efforts of creditors and the expense of ongoing litigation. It also halts the race of the creditors to obtain judgments and accomplish collection, forcing them to follow the orderly processes of the bankruptcy procedures. This was, indeed, the reason for Texaco's resort to bankruptcy to prevent enforcement of Pennzoil's $11 billion judgment in Pennzoil v. Texaco, Inc., *supra* p. 171. Litigation before a bankruptcy court over the issuance or continuance of the automatic stay and injunctions against other litigation is a frequent occurrence.

Estimation of Claims

A bankruptcy court must make an estimation of the claims against the debtor. The Code provision governing the estimation of claims is evidence of the desire implicit in the Code to have the courts consider all matters concerning the debtor's present and future financial plight. For the purposes of participation in and distribution under the reorganization, § 502 mandates the estimation of any contingent or unliquidated claim, the fixing or liquidation of which hinders the closing of the bankruptcy case. However, when there are potential claims that have not yet been filed, or indeed, have not yet materialized, as with potential tort claims, special problems arise for a bankruptcy court that hopes to make a realistic estimate so that it can fairly allocate assets or future income among claimants.

Right to jury trial

Does a party subject to the jurisdiction of a bankruptcy court have a right to jury trial of its claim? And if so, will it be heard by the district court judge or the bankruptcy judge?

The bankruptcy laws do not address the issue of jury trials. The only relevant statutory provision says that bankruptcy laws "do not affect any right to trial by jury that an individual had under applicable nonbankruptcy law with regard to a personal injury or wrongful death tort claim." 28 U.S.C.A. § 1411. "Since those cases are heard in the district court, the provision suggests that the district court may conduct jury trials in such cases." E. Warren, Business Bankruptcy 155 (Fed. Jud. Ctr. 1993).

There is a long and tortured history of the right to jury trial concerning bankruptcy and related proceedings. In Katchen v. Landy, 382 U.S. 323, 86 S.Ct. 467, 15 L.Ed.2d 391 (1966), the Supreme Court indicated that a bankruptcy court, as part of its equitable power to divide and distribute the estate, could decide without a jury an issue necessary to carry out the division even if a jury trial would have been available had the issue been raised outside the bankruptcy court. It upheld the summary jurisdiction of the bankruptcy court to order a creditor, who had submitted a claim, to surrender voidable preferences.

The 1978 Bankruptcy Reform Act accorded bankruptcy judges a broad grant of power (the "powers of a court of equity, law and admiralty") and specifically gave them the power to hold jury trials. In Northern Pipeline Const. Co. v. Marathon Pipe Line Co., 458 U.S. 50, 102 S.Ct. 2858, 73 L.Ed.2d 598 (1982), the Supreme Court found the broad extension of powers to hold jury trials violated Article III since bankruptcy judges did not enjoy life tenure, fixed and irreducible compensation, and removal only by impeachment as required for an Article III judge.

In response, Congress passed the 1984 Bankruptcy Amendments and Federal Judgeship Act (BAFJA), limiting bankruptcy jurisdiction to matters at the heart of the operation of the bankruptcy system (called "core proceedings" and defined in § 157(b)(2)). Bankruptcy judges are permitted to determine all "core proceedings" arising under Title 11, but the district court may withdraw their jurisdiction over any case or dispute at any time. In non-core proceedings, they are only authorized to submit proposed findings of fact and conclusions of law to the district court, and a majority of courts have ruled that they should not conduct jury trials in non-core proceedings without the consent of the parties. See Macon Prestressed Concrete Co. v. Duke, 46 B.R. 727 (M.D.Ga. 1985); Gibson, Jury Trials in Bankruptcy: Obeying the Commands of Article III and the Seventh Amendment, 72 Minn.L.Rev. 967, 971 n. 5 (1988). The Act provided that it did "not affect any right to trial by jury that an individual has under applicable non-bankruptcy law with regard to a personal injury or wrongful death tort claim." § 1411.

Some courts read *Katchen* as approving the denial of a right to a jury trial in core proceedings. This view, however, was rejected by the Supreme Court in Granfinanciera, S.A. v. Nordberg, 492 U.S. 33, 109 S.Ct. 2782, 106 L.Ed.2d 26 (1989), indicating that the inquiry must focus on the legal and equitable nature of the cause of action and not Congress' "taxonomic changes." The case involved the trustee's attempt to recover an allegedly fraudulent conveyance (which is a core proceeding under § 157(b)(2)(H)) from the bank Granfinanciera (which had not submitted any claim against the bankrupt). The Court stated that whether there was a right to jury trial as to the trustee's preference claim entailed a two-part inquiry: first, a comparison of the statutory action to 18th century actions in England prior to the merger of law and equity, and second, whether the remedy sought is legal or equitable in nature. It found the bank entitled to a jury trial even though the fraudulent conveyance action was a core proceeding, because it was legal in nature. The opinion in *Granfinanciera*, however, reserved the issue of whether Congress had authorized bankruptcy judges to conduct jury trials and whether such authorization would be constitutionally permissible.

THE GATHERING POWER OF BANKRUPTCY COURTS

As we have seen, many factors (including limitations of venue, jurisdiction, and federalism) often militate to prevent aggregating related cases in a single forum. Bankruptcy jurisdiction, on the other hand, is premised on gathering all claims against the debtor in a single bankruptcy court. By virtue of the automatic stay and the obligation to transfer cases to it, a bankruptcy court has a great potential for resolving multiple claims against the debtor, which could not otherwise have been aggregated. As a result, bankruptcy has sometimes been looked to as a model for disposing of mass litigation. Indeed, the Manual for Complex Litigation (4th) (2004) describes bankruptcy as "[t]he most powerful device for aggregating multiple litigation pending in federal and state courts." Id., § 20.

The filing of Chapter 11 petitions by three large corporations embroiled in mass tort litigation arising out of allegedly defective products required bankruptcy courts to address complex issues as to their powers. These bankruptcies resulted in a number of innovative procedures and seminal decisions affecting the disposition of mass tort claims against a defendant in a bankruptcy reorganization.

Johns–Manville Bankruptcy (Asbestos)

In August, 1982, Johns–Manville Corporation, a major producer of asbestos products, filed under Chapter 11. Although a company with assets valued at $2.25 billion and a net worth of $830 million, it was experiencing severe financial difficulties because of an avalanche of personal injury suits, with many more expected, by persons exposed to its product.

The automatic stay operated against all suits against Johns–Manville. However, many of the suits also named other asbestos manufacturers and dealers as co-defendants. These co-defendants petitioned the bankruptcy court to extend the stay to include them. The court refused to do so, ruling that the stay power under § 362 is limited to the debtor, and under § 105 is available only to enjoin third parties from actions that would threaten irreparable injury to the bankruptcy estate. Matter of Johns–Manville Corp., 26 B.R. 405 (Bkrtcy.S.D.N.Y.1983).

The debtor Johns–Manville then moved to enjoin: (1) proceedings against its employees, agents, and others, and discovery proceedings involving them in actions covering the same issues and subject matter as in the stated litigations against it, and (2) direct action suits against insurers and sureties of Manville since the coverage of such policies represented property of the debtors' estate which must be preserved for the creditors. The bankruptcy court issued the stays, enjoining "all actions to obtain possession of or interfere with property from Manville estates." In re Johns–Manville Corp., 26 B.R. 420 (Bkrtcy.S.D.N.Y. 1983).

The Manville bankruptcy court decisions considerably expanded the stay authority. The case also raised difficult questions concerning the "estimation" of claims. Should future claimants—persons who had been exposed to asbestos but had not developed asbestos-related injuries—be included? The bankruptcy judge ordered that all claimants, including future claimants, be included since there was statistical certainty that there would be such claimants against the estate. In re Johns–Manville Corp., 36 B.R. 727, 742 (Bkrtcy.S.D.N.Y.1984). Since the pool of future claimants was likely to be large, the judge also appointed a representative for them, and they were represented on the Official Committee of Asbestos Health Related Litigants. See P. Rheingold, Mass Tort Litigation § 18.24 (1996).

Ultimately, class actions were certified on behalf of the various groups of claimants and, through settlement negotiations, an agreement was reached setting up a trust on behalf of the claimants out of the assets of the corporations. In August, 1986, after four years of negotiations, Johns–Manville proposed a plan of reorganization that was approved and became operative in November, 1988. However, within a short time the cash funds available to the trust had run out, due in part to substantial payments to early claimants and their attorneys. Judge Weinstein, sitting as a judge of the S.D. and E.D. of N.Y., exercised his continuing jurisdiction over the settlement by ordering significant changes in the operation of the trust. In re Joint Eastern & Southern Dist. Asbestos Litigation, 129 B.R. 710 (E. & S.D.N.Y.1991), 120 B.R. 648 (E.D. & S.D.N.Y.1990). His order eliminated the "first in, first out" payment to claimants approach to ensure that claims would be paid in order of their seriousness, and he certified a non-opt-out class for all claimants. (Class action certification on this ground is examined in Chapter IV, *infra* pp. 302-18.) The Second Circuit reversed and remanded. See 982 F.2d 721 (2d Cir.1992). Judge Weinstein then ordered a new plan with six subclasses and a grid and schedule for payments. The first payments were made to claimants who had less than six months to live, and since that time payments to other claimants have continued according to the plan.

A.H. Robins Bankruptcy (Dalkon Shield)

The second seminal bankruptcy case arose in August, 1985, when A.H. Robins Company, Inc., one of the nation's largest pharmaceutical companies, filed for Chapter 11 reorganization. Robins began manufacturing the intrauterine contraceptive device called Dalkon Shield in 1971. It ceased sales three years later after many complaints of injuries from women who used it. By the mid–1970's Dalkon Shield suits were being filed in such numbers that the Judicial Panel on Multi–District Litigation entered a number of orders consolidating suits for pretrial handling.

By the mid–1980's there were over 5,000 Dalkon Shield suits pending, and Robins had already expended more than the half-billion dollar profits it had originally made from the device in defending and settling suits. Faced with an indeterminable number of future suits whose potential claims appeared to exceed its assets, Robins filed a voluntary petition in bankruptcy in 1985. For a lively account of the Dalkon Shield bankruptcy proceedings, see R. Sobol, Bending the Law: The Story of the Dalkon Shield Bankruptcy (1991).

As in the Manville bankruptcy, many suits against the debtor Robins included co-defendants. A number of plaintiffs in those suits, pending in both state and federal courts, moved to sever their claims against Robins and proceed with their claims against the co-defendants. Robins responded by suing a number of those plaintiffs, seeking a declaratory judgment that its product liability insurance policy was an asset of the bankruptcy estate in which all its claimants had an interest (which interest could be adversely affected if suits against its co-defendants were permitted). It also sought an injunction against prosecution of actions against its co-defendants. The district judge concluded, pursuant to 28 U.S.C.A. § 1334(b), that all personal injury and wrongful death claims arising from use of the Dalkon Shield were "related to" the Chapter 11 reorganization, and ordered all such actions removed to bankruptcy jurisdiction.

In July, 1988, 131,000 Dalkon Shield claimants overwhelmingly approved a plan by which Robins provided a consensual fund exceeding $2.6 billion. Robins was given immunity from its Dalkon Shield liability, and all tort claims had to be channeled into the claimants' trust. See In re A.H. Robins Co., Inc., 88 B.R. 742 (E.D.Va.1988), aff'd, 880 F.2d 694 (4th Cir.1989). There was a complicated claims process, including the option of arbitration or jury trial. *Dalkon Shield* provides one relatively successful model for disposition of a mass tort bankruptcy case; first estimate aggregate tort claims; then negotiate a fund to satisfy them; and finally, devise a procedure for fairly apportioning the fund, including various alternative dispute resolution and procedural hurdles for claimants seeking to invoke their ultimate right to a jury trial. See Feinberg, The Dalkon Shield Claimants Trust, 53 Law & Contemp. Probs. 79, 84 (Autumn, 1990).

Dow Corning Bankruptcy (Breast Implants)

The third major bankruptcy that has had to deal with complex procedural issues is that of Dow Corning Corporation. From 1964 to 1994, Dow Corning was a principal manufacturer of silicone-gel breast implants. Various health problems allegedly arose from the implants, including natural reactions to a foreign body, scar tissue causing the implants to become hard and misshapen, and leakage and rupture. In

1977, a jury awarded a recipient $170,000 for complications. V. Mueller & Co. v. Corley, 570 S.W.2d 140 (Tex.Civ.App.1978). In 1984, the first suit to successfully assert that silicone gel caused connective tissue disease resulted in a $2 million jury verdict.

The Multidistrict Panel consolidated the cases pending in federal court and assigned them to the Northern District of Alabama. Negotiations between the defendant manufacturers and a court-appointed plaintiffs steering committee led to a proposed $4.2 billion global settlement class action, pursuant to which Dow Corning would have paid $2.02 billion. Initially, class members were told that, depending upon their injury, they would receive between $200,000 and $2 million. Some 440,000 women filed claims, and the estimated recoveries had to be reduced to $105,000 to $1.4 million. At least 15,000 class members chose to opt out of the proposed settlement, and by May, 1995, the settlement was essentially dead. At the same time, some 90 state trials against Dow Corning were set, each expected to last two to eleven weeks. On May 15, 1995, Dow Corning filed for relief under Chapter 11 in bankruptcy court in the Eastern District of Michigan, where its headquarters were located.

The bankruptcy court appointed counsel for various classes of claimants, and all pending claims against Dow Corning were enjoined and transferred to it. Dow Corning (joined by its shareholders Dow Chemical and Corning, Inc.) then moved to transfer all opt-out breast implant claims pending against the shareholders to the Michigan bankruptcy court. This would include cases in federal courts, the multidistrict forum, and state courts. Then co-defendants in many of these suits (Minnesota Mining, Baxter, Bristol–Myers Squibb, and various physicians) also moved to transfer the opt-out cases in which they were named to the bankruptcy court.

The district judge refused to transfer the cases and enjoin litigation elsewhere with regard to the co-defendants and shareholders, however, finding that they were non-''core'' defendants and that the federal court lacked subject matter jurisdiction under § 1334(b) because those claims were not ''related to'' Dow Corning's bankruptcy proceedings. The Sixth Circuit reversed. It defined ''related to'' as ''whether the outcome of that proceeding could conceivably have any effect on the [bankruptcy] estate.'' The shareholder corporations had asserted cross-claims against Dow Corning, and the co-defendants had claims for contribution and indemnity against Dow Corning. The appellate court found that these contingent claims against the debtor made it possible that the bankruptcy estate would be impaired if the suits went forward outside of bankruptcy. It also upheld transfer of cases against the shareholders based on the fact that they were co-insured, together with Dow Corning, under various insurance policies. That insurance coverage, amounting to over $1 billion, was one of the largest assets in the bankruptcy estate. The court found that this asset might be diminished by allowing separate suits against the shareholders ''to the extent that settlements, judgments and defense costs incurred by the shareholders will exhaust policy limits otherwise available to Dow Corning.''

The bankruptcy judge thereafter was confronted with how to deal with the claims—whether to "estimate" the claims or to allow individual (or multiple) trials to assess Dow Corning's liability, followed by liquidation to pay such claims. The debtor proposed that the court "estimate" the claims and establish a Claims Resolution Facility to make payments to claimants from a trust to be funded by it. The plaintiffs insisted that they had an absolute right to have their claims liquidated by jury trial and proposed a summary jury trial process for 24 plaintiffs, which verdicts would be used by the court to assist in estimating the claims. (The use of statistics and extrapolation in mass tort cases is examined in Chapter VII, *infra* pp. 777–85, and summary jury trials are discussed in Chapter IX, *infra* pp. 939–43.) The bankruptcy court rejected both proposals, finding that "estimation" would cause needless delay and expense and that it should proceed to liquidation of the claims, but not in the manner proposed by the plaintiffs. In re Dow Corning Corp., 211 B.R. 545 (Bkrtcy.E.D.Mich.1997).

The bankruptcy court found a need for aggregation of the cases, namely consolidation under Rule 42, and suggested a phased trial that could first determine general causation and later determine specific causation and damages. It also commented favorably on the use of sampling for such an aggregated trial. It noted that if it concluded that "a consensual plan is unlikely to emerge, and that litigation over the allowance of tort claims is inevitable, we will ask the district court to commence the process of liquidating these claims in the manner we suggest."

After court-ordered mediation and lengthy negotiations, a joint reorganization plan was agreed to by Dow Corning and The Tort Claimants' Committee, providing for a fund of $2.35 billion for personal injury claims with the claimants having a choice to litigate or settle. It created three classes of claimants with less attractive treatment of foreign claimants, did not provide for punitive damages, and released all claims against non-debtor defendants such as Dow Corning's shareholder companies, insurers, physicians, and health care providers. After many challenges, the key features of the plan were upheld. In re Dow Corning Corp., 255 B.R. 445 (E.D.Mich.2000), aff'd in part, 280 F.3d 648 (6th Cir.2002).

As we turn back to litigation outside bankruptcy in the next chapters, consider whether features and settlement provisions used in these bankruptcy mass tort proceedings could influence normal litigation procedures.

Chapter IV

CLASS ACTIONS

The class action is a powerful procedural device, offering enormous savings in time and judicial resources over individual trial of each class member's case while opening up opportunities for both new forms of litigation and potential abuse by litigants. "The class action was an invention of equity * * * mothered by the practical necessity of providing a procedural device so that mere numbers would not disable large groups of individuals, united in interest, from enforcing their equitable rights nor grant them immunity from their equitable wrongs." Montgomery Ward & Co. v. Langer, 168 F.2d 182, 187 (8th Cir.1948). However, the notion of what constituted "unity of interest" among parties entitling them to use the device was more narrowly limited under traditional equity practice than under our present rules.

When the Federal Rules were adopted in 1938, the equitable class action device was extended to all actions under the new merger of law and equity. Class actions were divided into three classifications—*true, hybrid,* and *spurious*—based on the type of "jural relation" between the class members.

A "true" class action involved a right which was "joint, or common, or secondary in the sense that the owner of a primary right refuses to enforce that right and a member of the class thereby becomes entitled to enforce it." Rule 23(a)(1) (1938). Several old precedents nicely exemplified the "true" class action. In Smith v. Swormstedt, 57 U.S. (16 How.) 288, 14 L.Ed. 942 (1853), six ministers, representing 1500 traveling preachers of the southern branch of the Methodist Episcopal Church, sued in federal court against three ministers as representatives of 3800 traveling preachers of the northern branch, seeking a division of church property (the split had resulted from the slavery issue). The court allowed the bill in equity and, despite a Federal Equity Rule to the contrary, indicated that the judgment would bind all class members. Supreme Tribe of Ben–Hur v. Cauble, 255 U.S. 356, 41 S.Ct. 338, 65 L.Ed. 673 (1921), reaffirmed that the decree in a class action involving joint or common rights binds all class members. There a group of certificate holders of a fraternal organization sued on behalf of all the 70,000 certificate holders, seeking to overturn a reorganization plan which had reclassified their certificates. Again, the court's finding that the entire class was bound by the judgment seems fair, given the identity of interest of the class members and the desirability of having the common issue settled once and for all.

Similarly, in a "hybrid" class action—where the right involved was several rather than joint, but the object of the action was the adjudication of claims which affected specific property involved in the action—courts also held that the decree was binding on all class members. The prototype of the hybrid class action was the equity receivership (which has now been largely superseded by reorganization under the Bankruptcy Act).

The "spurious" class action—where the right involved was several but there was a common question of law or fact affecting the several rights and a common relief was sought—was the poor stepchild, treated with suspicion and, unlike the other two types, not accorded a binding effect on all class members. Professor J.W. Moore, one of the principal drafters of the 1938 rule on class actions, viewed the spurious class action as useful, despite its lack of classwide binding effect, as a means of securing joinder in federal courts without incurring the jurisdictional obstacles involved with Rule 20(a) joinder. 2 Moore, Federal Practice ¶ 23.10, p. 3444 (2d ed. 1963). Professor Fleming James observed: "If the spurious class suit judgment were given broader binding effect, however, the device would obviously be a far more efficient one in minimizing litigation. It would, for example, be capable of compelling the settlement in a single lawsuit of all the claims arising out of widespread injury caused by a single untoward event (such as a train wreck, or an explosion, or a miscarriage of atomic energy); and it would be a more effective device in dealing with race relations problems." F. James, Civil Procedure 500 (1965). As will be seen, changes in the federal rules in 1966 recognized this broader potential of the class action, but its applicability to such matters as mass disasters and torts is still in dispute.

A contemporary lawyer can find considerable relief in the fact that the 1966 amendments did away with the three "jural relationship" classifications of class actions. Professor Chafee had criticized the classifications, saying he had as much trouble telling a "common" from a "several" right as in deciding whether some ties were green or blue, and adding that "the situation is so tangled and bewildering that I sometimes wonder whether the world would be any the worse off if the class-suit device had been left buried in the learned obscurity of Calvert on Parties to Suits in Equity." Z. Chafee, Some Problems of Equity 257 (1950).

The 1966 amendments replaced the three classifications with functional tests aimed at ensuring that the underlying policies are satisfied. Four rather general prerequisites for class certification are set out—now often referred to as "numerosity," "commonality," "typicality" and "representativeness" (Rule 23(a)). There are still three kinds of class actions (engagingly referred to as Rule 23(b)(1), 23(b)(2), and 23(b)(3) classes), but they are not tightly defined and mutually exclusive categories as were the pre–1966 classifications. As to a Rule 23(b)(3) class, which bears a superficial resemblance to the old spurious class action, there are special requirements, such as that common questions predominate, that the class action be found superior to other available methods, and that there not be undue management difficulties. Unlike the old spurious class action, the 23(b)(3) class action is binding on all members of the class (as are also the 23(b)(1) and 23(b)(2) class actions).

As Professor Benjamin Kaplan (then Reporter of the Civil Rules Advisory Committee) described the 1966 changes, "[t]he entire reconstruction of the Rule bespoke an intention to promote more vigorously than before the dual missions of the class-action device: (1) to reduce units of litigation by bringing under one umbrella what might otherwise be many separate but duplicating actions; (2) even at the expense of increasing litigation, to provide means of vindicating the rights of groups of people who individually would be without effective strength to bring their opponents into court at all." Kaplan, A Prefatory Note, 10 Boston College Ind. & Com.L.Rev. 497 (1969).

The amendments resulted in a huge increase in the use of class actions. On the one hand, this brought new opportunity for legal redress. Professor Kaplan commented after the first three years: "There are some who are repelled by these massive, complex, unconventional lawsuits because they call for so much judicial initiative and management. We hear talk that it all belongs not to the courts but to administrative agencies. But by hypothesis we are dealing with cases that are not handled by existing agencies, and I do not myself see any subversion of judicial process here but rather a fine opportunity for its accommodation to new challenges of the times. The class action takes its place in a larger search for pliant and sensitive procedures. I confess that I am exhilarated, not depressed, by experimentation which spies out carefully the furthest possibilities of the new Rule." Kaplan, *supra,* 10 Boston College Ind. & Com.L.Rev. at 500. The development of "public law litigation" with its attendant impact upon the morphology of law suits, described by Professor Abram Chayes [see *supra* p. 3] is one of the consequences of the expanded class action.

On the other hand, the expanded class action also led to abuses and court overloading. Professor Arthur Miller noted: "Cases often were certified as class actions on the basis of rather conclusory assertions of compliance with rule 23(a) and (b). Settlements were sometimes approved without an in-depth analysis of the underlying merits of the claim, the economics of the litigation, or the feasibility of distributing the funds to class members. In addition, fee petitions were not scrutinized as carefully as experience now suggests they should have been. Enthusiasm for the class action fed upon itself, and the procedure fell victim to overuse by its champions and misuse by some who sought to exploit it for reasons external to the merits of the case. Mistakes, in most cases honest mistakes of faith, were made. By the end of this first phase, class action practice had been given a very black eye." Miller, Of Frankenstein Monsters and Shining Knights: Myth, Reality, and the "Class Action Problem," 92 Harv.L.Rev. 664, 678 (1979).

The reaction, in the late 1960s and early 1970s, took many forms— proposals for new amendments to the rules, trial court hostility to class actions and to award of attorneys' fees in class actions, and Supreme Court decisions restricting the availability of class actions on jurisdictional and due process grounds. See Snyder v. Harris, 394 U.S. 332, 89 S.Ct. 1053, 22 L.Ed.2d 319 (1969) (class members may not aggregate their claims to satisfy the amount in controversy requirement in federal courts); Zahn v. International Paper Co., 414 U.S. 291, 94 S.Ct. 505, 38 L.Ed.2d 511 (1973) (the claim of each class member must meet the amount in controversy requirement); Eisen v. Carlisle & Jacquelin, 417 U.S. 156, 94 S.Ct. 2140, 40 L.Ed.2d 732 (1974) (individual notice must be given to all class members in a Rule 23(b)(3) class).

Professor Miller saw a third phase, beginning in the mid–1970s, in which the most serious abuses began to die out and courts, in turn, demonstrated less hostility to the class action. "It is a period characterized by increasing sophistication, restraint, and stabilization in class action practice." 92 Harv.L.Rev. at 680. By the 1980s, however, the pace of filings of class actions slowed. See, e.g., Martin, The Rise and Fall of the Class–Action Lawsuit, N.Y.Times, Jan. 8, 1988, at 10 col. 3 (reporting substantial decline in number of cases filed as class actions). In employment discrimination suits, for example, a study showed that by the 1980s class actions had dropped significantly in importance as methods for obtaining legal relief. See Donohue & Siegelman, The Changing Nature of Employment Discrimination Litigation, 43 Stan. L.Rev. 983, 1019–21 (1991).

But at the same time, many of the most important and intractable issues brought before courts in civil cases began to be presented in the class action format. In some areas, such as securities fraud, and consumer rights, class actions continued to be important. More significantly, in mass tort litigation class actions emerged in the 1990s as instruments of major importance in those cases. In testimony before Congress in 1997, the chair of the Civil Rules Advisory Committee said that use of the class action is "transforming the litigation landscape," and that "[c]lass actions are being certified at unprecedented rates, and they are involving a substantial [number], if not a majority of American citizens." Senate Subcommittee Holds Hearing on Class Action Litigation Reform, 66 U.S.L.W. 2294 (Nov. 16, 1997). "[T]he class action device has changed from the more or less rare case fought out by titans of the bar in top financial centers of the nation to the veritable bread and butter of firms of all shapes and sizes across the country." Reid & Coutroulis, Checkmate in Class Actions: Defensive Strategy in the Initial Moves, 28 Litigation 21, 21 (Winter 2002); see also Tempel–Raston, Class–Action Lawsuits Gain Strength on the Web, N.Y. Times, July 28, 2002, at § 3,

p. 10 (asserting that "by some accounts at least 10,000 class-action suits are filed each year"). An experienced judge reported: "In my 27 years on the bench, I have never seen an area in as much ferment as this class action area is." Roundtable Discussion, The Future of Class Action Mass Torts, 66 Fordham L. Rev. 1657, 1667 (1998) (quoting Judge Edward Becker of the Third Circuit). Elsewhere in the world, class actions were beginning to achieve prominence. See Gidi, Class Actions in Brazil—A Model for Civil Law Countries, 51 Amer.J.Comp.L. 311 (2003); Sherman, Group Litigation Under Foreign Legal Systems: Variations and Alternatives to American Class Actions, 52 DePaul L. Rev. 401 (2002); Johnson, Class–Action Suits Let the Aggrieved in China Appeal for Rule of Law, Wall. St.J., March 25, 1999, at A1 ("In what not so long ago was supposed to be a classless society, class-action lawsuits have proliferated in the past few years, as China's frustrated masses have discovered mass litigation.").

The tumult in this country produced calls for change. In 1995, Congress altered some aspects of class actions in securities fraud litigation in the Private Securities Fraud Litigation Act. In 1996, the Advisory Committee on Civil Rules circulated the first formal proposed amendments for Rule 23 since 1966. See Proposed Amendments to the Federal Rules, 167 F.R.D. 523, 559–60 (1996), but controversy about changing the standards for class certification prompted the Committee to shelve the proposals except for addition of a new Rule 23(f) authorizing interlocutory review of class certification decisions. In 2003, extensive amendments to Rules 23(c) and (e) were adopted, and new Rules 23(g) and (h) were added to deal with appointment of class counsel and awards of attorney fees. In addition, Congress seriously considered legislation called the Class Action Fairness Act to move more state-court class actions to federal court. In 2003 the House adopted legislation and the Senate nearly did. See H.R. 1115 and S. 274 (108th Cong.).

The class action therefore deserves study not only as a theoretical construct but also as a procedure of enduring importance. As Professor Chayes has observed, "I think it unlikely that the class action will ever be taught to behave in accordance with the precepts of the traditional model of litigation." Chayes, The Role of the Judge in Public Law Litigation, 89 Harv.L.Rev. 1281, 1291 (1976).

A. ETHICAL CONSIDERATIONS IN CLASS ACTION PRACTICE

J.D. Mark F. Bernstein for *The Recorder*

Copyright © 2003 Mark F. Bernstein. Reprinted by permission.

The class action poses some unique ethical considerations for lawyers and courts. Ethical issues arise from the fact that the named plaintiff is obligated to represent the best interests of the class and yet, at the same time, has personal interests to pursue, interests which at times may not exactly coincide with those of the class. The attorney, as the person who usually structures and guides the suit (indeed, who sometimes has conceived of the suit and found the named plaintiff to bring it) has obligations to both the named plaintiff and the class. The attorney's ethical obligations are further complicated by the fact that she may herself have a very substantial interest in the class action by virtue of a contingent fee contract or the right to recover attorneys' fees if the suit is successful.

KLINE v. COLDWELL, BANKER & CO.

United States Court of Appeals, Ninth Circuit, 1974.
508 F.2d 226, cert. denied 421 U.S. 963, 95 S.Ct. 1950, 44 L.Ed.2d 449 (1975).

Before DUNIWAY and TRASK, CIRCUIT JUDGES, and POWELL, DISTRICT JUDGE.

[A husband and wife sued on behalf of a class of approximately 400,000 purchasers of residential real property in Los Angeles County alleging a conspiracy by realtors to fix an artificially high commission rate for such transactions. The named defendants included the Los Angeles Realty Board and 32 named realtors, who were sued on behalf of a class of approximately 2,000 realtors in the county. The court of appeals reversed orders by the district court certifying both a plaintiffs' and a defendants' class on the ground that plaintiff's reliance on the distribution of a commission schedule by the Los Angeles Realty Board to its members was insufficient to establish a price-fixing conspiracy by generalized means of proof and that the problems of proving conspiracy and injury by individualized proof prevented the case from satisfying the requirements of Rule 23(b)(3) that common questions of fact predominate and that the action be manageable.]

DUNIWAY, CIRCUIT JUDGE (concurring).

I concur in the judgment, but for somewhat different reasons.

* * *

I cannot believe that Rule 23, as amended, was intended or should be construed to authorize the kind of judicial juggernaut that plaintiffs and their counsel seek to create here. The plaintiffs Kline have been designated as the representatives of an estimated 400,000 sellers of real property in Los Angeles County, sellers of residential dwellings containing up to twelve units. The Klines sold one residence, in 1970, for $42,500. They paid a commission to one broker, Lelah Pierson, of 6%, or $2,550. She is a named defendant. Their theory of damages is that, but for the charged conspiracy, the commission would have been less, but they do not tell us how much less. If we assume that the broker would have done her work for nothing, an obviously improper assumption, their maximum damages would be $2,550, which, trebled, would be $7,650. Realistically, this is a grossly exaggerated figure. Yet the plaintiffs seek to parlay their claim into a lawsuit on behalf of 400,000 sellers, not one of whom, so far as we are advised, except the Sherman plaintiffs, has indicated the slightest interest in suing anyone. The Shermans, too, made but one sale. They paid a 6% commission of $2,700, which was divided between two brokers, neither of whom is named as a defendant. The plaintiffs, by this device, seek to recover from Ms. Pierson, among 2,000 others, $750,000,000 in damages, plus attorneys' fees and costs.

The named defendants are 32 real estate brokers and five associations of real estate brokers. They have been designated as representatives of a class of 2,000 brokers. Only one of the "representative" defendants, Ms. Pierson, ever dealt with the "representative" plaintiffs Kline.

At oral argument, plaintiffs explained how easy it will be for them to identify the members of the respective classes. First, they propose, under the aegis of the court, to compel the defendant associations to furnish them with lists showing the name and address of every broker who was a member of any of them at any time during the four year period preceding the filing of this action. These brokers, estimated at 2,000, will be the class of represented defendants. Next, plaintiffs propose, under the aegis of the court, to compel each of these 2,000 brokers to search his files and supply the name and address of every person who, during the same period, paid the broker a commission on a sale of residential property containing twelve units or less. These persons, estimated at 400,000, will be the class of represented plaintiffs. Plaintiffs do not tell us at whose expense all this is to be done.

Next, notice will be sent to each of the 400,000 represented plaintiffs. I would expect that the Rule 23 notice to each "represented" plaintiff, as prepared by plaintiffs' counsel, would give him a brief description of the nature of the case, and then would tell him (Rule 23(c)(2)(A)) that he can "opt out," but would also tell him that, if he does not opt out, he will incur no financial obligation, while, if the suit is won, he will share in the loot. I wonder if this is proper. Why shouldn't a "represented" plaintiff be told that if he elects to participate in the alleged bonanza, he may, by so electing, subject himself to liability for his share of the costs of suit if the bonanza is not forthcoming? Why should the court offer him a free ride in a case in which the defendants' costs, if they win, may be very large, and will probably not be collectible from the named plaintiffs? Why shouldn't what I have said also apply to plaintiffs' attorneys' fees, unless there is an ironclad agreement by the attorneys that they will collect no fees from anyone if the suit is lost? Rule 23(c)(2)(B) states that the notice shall advise each member of the class that "the judgment, whether favorable or not, will include all members who do not request exclusion." In most cases, one of the incidents of an adverse judgment is liability for costs. No doubt it will be said that the potential liability for costs might cause many represented plaintiffs to opt out. If so, what is so wrong about that? It may also be said that the potential liability is meaningless. How would defendants collect? However, there may be a possible alternative. The real bonanza in a case like this, if it is won, will go to counsel. Perhaps the class action order could be conditioned upon an agreement by counsel that they will pay all costs of all defendants if the suit is lost!

* * *

I venture to suggest that none of the class action features of this case was dreamed up by the named plaintiffs, but that all of them are the brain children of their attorneys. In California, barratry is a crime (Cal.Pen.C. § 158). The Rules of Professional Conduct of the State Bar, authorized by Cal.Bus. and Prof.Code § 6076, provide (Rule 2 § a): "a member of the State Bar shall not solicit professional employment by advertisement or otherwise." Does solicitation cease to be solicitation when done under the aegis of a judge? If so, what has become of the centuries old policy of the law against stirring up litigation? Did the Supreme Court, when it adopted Rule 23, as amended, intend to abrogate that policy for a case like this? I am loath to believe that it did. I also have grave doubt whether such a change in the law, if intended, can properly be called a matter of procedure. In other words, I doubt that the Supreme Court has power, by a procedural rule, to abrogate the policy to which I have referred, assuming that that is what the Court intended.

Perhaps more important is the practical effect of such a suit as this. The burden that it can impose on the court—discovery, pre-trial, notice to the classes, etc., and on a jury, if one is ever empanelled, is staggering. It is inconceivable to me that such a case can ever be tried, unless the court is willing to deprive each defendant of his undoubted right to have his claimed liability proved, not by presumptions or assumptions, but by facts, with the burden of proof upon the plaintiff or plaintiffs, and to offer evidence in his defense. The same applies, if he is found liable, to proof of the damage of each "plaintiff." I doubt that plaintiffs' counsel expect the immense and unmanageable case that they seek to create to be tried. What they seek to create will become (whether they intend this result or not) an overwhelmingly costly and potent engine for the compulsion of settlements, whether just or unjust. Most, though by no means all, real estate brokers are small business men. They cannot afford even to participate in such an action as this, much less to defend it effectively. I suspect, for example, that this is true of Ms. Pierson. It is almost inevitable, if the judge's order is permitted to stand, and even if all potential defendants opt out, that many of the named defendants will settle for whatever amount they can bargain for, and without regard as to whether they are really liable or not, with a good chunk of the money going to plaintiffs' lawyers.

I do not say that the Rule 23(b)(3) class action is always unethical and improperly coercive. Doubtless there are circumstances in which it is the only viable means of obtaining relief for classes of truly and actively aggrieved plaintiffs. But courts should not be in the business of encouraging the creation of lawsuits like this one.

Notes and Questions

1. Judge Duniway's concerns seem to go beyond the majority's findings that this was not a proper class action to question the essential wisdom and fairness of the class action device. The debate is ongoing. See RAND, Class Action Dilemmas: Pursuing Public Goals for Private Gain, *supra* p. 7. When the judge objects that "plaintiffs seek to parlay their claim into a lawsuit on behalf of 400,000 sellers," is he challenging the right of any representative class plaintiff to sue on behalf of all? What is the nature of his objection? Is it that the class action gives the representative plaintiff too much leverage and bargaining power against the defendants? But the other side of the coin is that, standing alone, a house seller with a claim of being overcharged a thousand dollars or less not only lacks bargaining power, but cannot afford to litigate the claim which is much smaller than anticipated legal costs. For example, a 1995 study of class actions in four districts by the Federal Judicial Center that showed that the median recovery in class actions in those districts was from $315 to $528 per class member in the examined districts, with the recovery at the 75th percentile ranging from $645 to $3341 per class member. See Willging, Hooper & Niemic, An Empirical Analysis of Rule 23 To Address the Rulemaking Challenges, 71 N.Y.U. L. Rev. 74, 84–85 (1996).

Is Judge Duniway's objection that only two of the 400,000 class members had indicated an interest in suing anyone? But is that surprising at this stage in the litigation when no notice has yet been given the class members? Even if many of the class members are not personally motivated to sue for the relatively small amount they might be entitled to recover, is this a reason not to allow a class action? If so, doesn't the litigation system, with its enormous legal costs, thereby ensure potential defendants that they can get away with violating the rights of others so long as the damages for each is relatively small?

2. How did the Klines happen to file this suit? Is it relevant whether they sought out the lawyer to sue or the lawyer sought them out? Judge Duniway invokes barratry laws, which are premised on the traditional view that the attorney should play a passive role in the initiation of litigation,

only responding to requests from clients. This model has had to undergo revision in light of modern practice involving solicitation by public interest lawyers and also the expanded right of attorneys to advertise. See In re Primus, 436 U.S. 412, 98 S.Ct. 1893, 56 L.Ed.2d 417 (1978) (solicitation of prospective litigants by nonprofit organizations that engage in litigation as a form of political expression and political association constitutes conduct protected by the First Amendment which the government may only regulate with narrow specificity); Bates v. State Bar of Arizona, 433 U.S. 350, 97 S.Ct. 2691, 53 L.Ed.2d 810 (1977) (lawyer advertising is a form of commercial speech protected by the First Amendment which may not be subjected to blanket suppression). In the class action context, is there anything wrong with an effort by a public interest lawyer to find a client to bring a class action challenging illegal governmental activity? Should the rule be different where the lawyer is not so public spirited but interested in profit?

The diminished importance of these traditional concerns of professional responsibility does not mean that ethical issues have vanished as concerns in complex litigation. In mass tort litigation, there are particularly pressing issues regarding the obligations class counsel owe to their clients and the propriety of aggregation. These issues were partly addressed in Chapter I. For a more extensive discussion, see Weinstein, Ethical Dilemmas in Mass Tort Litigation, 88 Nw. L. Rev. 469 (1994). Judge Weinstein opines as follows (id. at 482):

> My own experiences on the bench have led me to conclude that we need to go beyond the rules of the past and provide more realistic guidance to today's lawyers and judges. The ethics issues inherent in litigation of mass torts warrant consideration of whether lawyers can, or judges should, continue to try to adapt their behavior to conform strictly to traditional ethical rules. Do we need a modified set of ethical guidelines to assist us in dealing with these massive cases, just as we have special class action rules of civil procedure? For the attorney, the viability of such ethical imperatives as the duty to communicate with each client effectively, to maintain confidences, and to avoid conflicts of interest in client representation are called into question.

3. As Judge Duniway suggests, the lawyer may be the prime beneficiary of class litigation in a number of areas, notably antitrust and securities suits. In theory the client is to bear the cost of litigation even when the lawyer agrees to a contingent fee arrangement, but the reality is usually different in class actions as in individual cases where a plaintiff is not successful. See Vanderbilt v. Geo–Energy Limited, 725 F.2d 204, 210 (3d Cir.1983) ("It is not uncommon in class actions to have persons other than the named plaintiff pay the costs of the litigation."); In re WorldCom, Inc. Securities Litigation, 219 F.R.D. 267 (S.D.N.Y.2003) (class representatives were adequate although they had not agreed to repay the expenses of litigation). For an argument favoring flexible treatment of such arrangements, see Miller, Payment of Expenses in Securities Class Actions: Ethical Dilemmas, Class Counsel, and Congressional Intent, 22 Rev.Lit. 557 (2003).

4. If there are no ethical restraints on lawyers' solicitation of class representatives and subsequent agreement to maintain the action at their own expense, should there be any limitation on their communication with

class members? Can the Klines' lawyer approach all 400,000 of her new "clients" and ask them to sign retainer agreements? Courts have struggled with these problems [see *infra* p. 470].

5. Judge Duniway is not alone in recognizing the potential for abuse when lawyers become the principal beneficiary of class actions. And yet compensation to plaintiffs is only one of the objectives of a class action, and, in particular cases, deterrence of similar conduct by the defendant or persons similarly situated may replace compensation as the primary purpose. Consider Dam, Class Actions: Efficiency, Compensation, Deterrence, and Conflict of Interest, 4 J.Legal Studies 47, 60–61 (1975):

> [I]n most class actions the attorney has a larger stake in the law suit than any member of the class. The attorney is an entrepreneur. But for his initiative the action would never have been brought. That fact alone will trouble only the more traditional judge; today it is widely appreciated that private enforcement requires for its efficacy a highly motivated plaintiffs' bar. But where the lawyer's stake is large and the stake of each class member is small, it is unlikely that any members of the class will actually receive compensation. * * *

> The absence of actual compensation, however, is not dispositive. Here the concept of deterrence has its true role. Deterrence substitutes as a justification for compensation where compensation is not feasible. The principle of deterrence requires that the wrongdoer pay, but says nothing about who shall receive the payment. Hence the argument for nevertheless favoring the class action even though compensation can never be paid is that if class treatment is not accorded, the deterrent effect of the substantive rule will be forfeited.

> Deterrence, however, is not synonymous with overall efficiency. First, the administrative efficiency of the court system is an element of overall efficiency. Hence, in obtaining an overall efficient solution, any administrative efficiency issues stemming from the impact of class actions on the court system must be weighed against overall efficiency gains from more comprehensive enforcement.

> Second, a penalty system that induced enforcers to invest resources up to the value of an optimal penalty would lead to inefficient overenforcement. This is the economic justification for limiting the role of private attorney general to those members of the citizenry who have actually been injured. To the extent the class action frees the lawyer from weighing the interests of injured class members, the result may be inefficient overenforcement. It seems unlikely, however, that such a consequence would arise often. Although the class action brought by the lawyer-entrepreneur would not be cost-justified if brought on behalf of an individual plaintiff, it is likely to be cost-justified taking into account all of the claims involved. Otherwise, there would be no judgment from which the lawyer could derive his fees.

Consumer class actions are often criticized on the ground that they benefit only the lawyers, but courts emphasize deterrence. In Linder v. Thrifty Oil Co., 97 Cal.Rptr.2d 179 (2000), a case involving alleged overcharges for gasoline, the California Supreme Court concluded that such actions produce "several salutary by-products, including a therapeutic effect upon those sellers who indulge in fraudulent practices, aid to legitimate business enterprises by curtailing illegitimate competition, and avoidance to the judicial process of the burden of multiple litigation involving identical claims."

6. The lawyer's entrepreneurial interest can also lead to conflicts of interest with her "clients" when the issue of settlement arises. Even under the normal contingency fee arrangement there is a potential for conflict. In small-claim class actions like Kline v. Coldwell, Banker, it is likely to be magnified because of the different stakes of the lawyer and the class members. For the class members the suit may resemble a giant lottery that could yield a modest payoff. For the attorney, it is serious business. Having located a class representative, fronted the costs of litigation, and invested years of time, the lawyer is likely to be reluctant to risk all on a trial. Indeed, given the current measure of attorneys' fees awards [discussed *infra* p. 685], which emphasizes hours spent on the case, the lawyer has little to gain and much to lose by going to trial. As a practical matter the lawyer will control the settlement negotiations, and the court is required to scrutinize any proposed settlement and approve it only after a hearing. [See discussion *infra* pp. 509-39].

These conflicts have led some to endorse reconsideration of the effective incentives that affect the behavior of the lawyer for the class. Professor Coffee, for example, has explored the divergence between incentives and goals in a series of articles. See Coffee, The Regulation of Entrepreneurial Litigation: Balancing Fairness and Efficiency in the Large Class Action, 54 U.Chi.L.Rev. 877 (1987); Coffee, The Implications of Economic Theory for Private Enforcement of Law Through Class and Derivative Actions, 86 Colum.L.Rev. 669 (1986); Coffee, The Unfaithful Champion: The Plaintiff as Monitor in Shareholder Litigation, 48 Law & Contemp. Problems 5 (Summer 1985). Using economic analysis, he finds that large class actions such as Kline v. Coldwell, Banker present a number of problems. First, there are "agency cost" problems of relying on a plaintiff with small stakes to monitor the behavior of a lawyer who is in a position to shirk on preparation or sacrifice the interests of the class to the lawyer's own interest in a large and secure fee. Second are the asymmetric stakes that result because the lawyer is the main actor on the plaintiff's side, but he or she may not benefit in a commensurate way from increasing the value of the class recovery. Third is a cost differential that results because plaintiffs' counsel can increase defense costs, and thereby persuade defendants to make substantial "nuisance" settlements (payable principally to the lawyer) to put an end to the litigation. Prof. Coffee blames the hourly billing method of calculating compensation for the lawyer for many of the problems he identifies.

Related but somewhat different concerns can arise when class members, or at least some of them, have substantial claims that might get short shrift in a deal engineered by the lawyers. These concerns are most pronounced in mass tort class actions, particularly those that are confected purely for purposes of settlement. We address some of these concerns *infra* pp. 372-91.

7. Courts have begun to pay attention to incentives for class representatives by granting them bonuses above their share of the recovery for taking the trouble to serve as class representative. Larkin, Incentive Awards

to Class Representatives in Class Action Settlements, 3 BNA Class Action Rep. 195 (March 22, 2002), reports that such awards are "routinely made"; compare Willging, Hooper & Niemic, An Empirical Analysis of Rule 23 to Address the Rulemaking Challenges, 71 N.Y.U. L. Rev. 74, 101 (1996) (reporting that 26% to 40% of settlements in studied districts involved designated awards to class representatives). In Cook v. Niedert, 142 F.3d 1004 (7th Cir.1998), the court reasoned that "[b]ecause a named plaintiff is an essential ingredient of any class action, an incentive award is appropriate if it is necessary to induce an individual to participate in the suit." Id. at 1016. Relevant factors include the actions the plaintiff took to protect the interests of the class, the benefits to the class from those actions, and the time and effort the representative expended in pursuing the litigation. Such awards are not limited to commercial litigation. See Reifenberg, Texaco Settlement in Racial–Bias Case Endorsed by Judge, Wall. St.J., March 26, 1997 (reporting that six African–American lead plaintiffs would receive $800,000 in incentive awards through the settlement); compare Hadix v. Johnson, 322 F.3d 895 (6th Cir.2003) (declining incentive award for class representative in prison conditions suit despite claims that he made sacrifices to pursue the case). On the other hand, in Sonmore v. CheckRite Recovery Serv., Inc., 206 F.R.D. 257 (D.Minn.2001), the court held the class representatives inadequate because they would recover no more than unnamed members of the class. Are incentive awards sometimes essential to make a class action work?

In the Private Securities Litigation Reform Act, Congress provided that, in actions brought under the 1933 Securities Act or the 1934 Securities Exchange Act (including Rule 10b–5 actions), the award to the class representative shall be the same, on a per-share basis, as the award to other members of the class, although the court could also permit payment to the class representative for "reasonable costs and expenses (including lost wages) directly relating to the representation of the class." 15 U.S.C.A. §§ 77z–1(a)(4); 78u–4(a)(4).

8. Lawyers' conduct in asbestos litigation, which has spanned some twenty years and involved millions of claimants, has raised a number of ethical issues as to such matters as solicitation, manipulating expert testimony, coaching claimants' testimony, settlement practices, conflicts of interest, and reasonableness of fees. See Crampton, Lawyer Ethics and the Lunar Landscape of Asbestos Litigation, 31 Pepp. L. Rev. 175 (2003); Brickman, On the Theory Class's Theories of Asbestos Litigation: The Disconnect Between Scholarship and Reality?, 31 Pepp. L. Rev. 33 (2003); Silver, Merging Roles: Mass Tort Lawyers as Agents and Trustees, 31 Pepp. L. Rev. 301 (2003).

B. PREREQUISITES TO A CLASS ACTION

Rule 23(a) sets out four prerequisites for a class action—generally termed numerosity, commonality, typicality, and representativeness. All three functional categories of class actions described in Rule 23(b) must satisfy these prerequisites.

1. ADEQUATE DEFINITION OF THE CLASS

Even before one reaches the four prerequisites for a class action, there must be an adequately defined class. The first dozen words of Rule 23(a) suggest this requirement: "One or more members of a class may sue or be sued * * *." Considerable attention has to be given to the definition of the class that is proposed to the court. It must be clear enough that the court and the parties understand who it includes, though the exact persons and even the exact number of persons it contains is not necessarily required. The exactitude with which the class must be defined depends in part on the relief which is sought. Questions of overinclusiveness and underinclusiveness are frequently raised in objection to proposed classes. It is also sometimes said (although we reserve judgment as to the validity of this statement) that the class definition should be sufficiently clear and precise to show who is affected by res judicata as to the judgment in a class action.

SIMER v. RIOS

United States Court of Appeals, Seventh Circuit, 1981.
661 F.2d 655, cert. denied 456 U.S. 917, 102 S.Ct. 1773, 72 L.Ed.2d 177 (1982).

Before SWYGERT, SENIOR CIRCUIT JUDGE, and PELL and WOOD, CIRCUIT JUDGES.

HARLINGTON WOOD, JR., CIRCUIT JUDGE.

This case raises many issues concerning the legality and eventual vacating of a settlement agreement entered into by the plaintiffs and the Community Services Administration (CSA).

Suit was initiated on September 24, 1979 by eight individuals and Gray Panthers of Chicago, an unincorporated non-profit organization, as a class action. The complaint alleged several claims against CSA for its administration of the Crisis Intervention Program (CIP).

CIP was a program funded under the Emergency Energy Conservation Services Program (EECSP), 42 U.S.C. § 2809(a)(5), and was designed "to enable low income individuals and families, including the elderly ... to participate in the energy conservation programs designed to lessen the impact of the high cost of energy ... and to reduce ... energy consumption."

One aspect of this program provided cash assistance for fuel and utility bills to qualified individuals. The pertinent regulations adopted by CSA conditioned the grant of assistance payments upon the production of a shut-off notice from a utility company. Plaintiffs' complaint alleged that this regulation violated EECSP which provided that "[e]ligibility for any of the programs authorized under this section shall not be based solely on delinquency in payment of fuel bills." 42 U.S.C. § 2809(a)(5).

* * *

Initially we note that our review of the district court's denial of class certification is limited. We can reverse this determination only if the district court's decision denying certification was an abuse of discretion.[23]

The parties, as did the district court, focus on the concept of "manageability" of a class action and whether the issue of each individual plaintiff's state of mind makes the class action unmanageable.[24] We agree that the issue of "state of mind" does make this case difficult to manage as a class action. However, we also conclude that the class action fails for other reasons.

It is axiomatic that for a class action to be certified a "class" must exist. *DeBremaecker v. Short*, 433 F.2d 733, 734 (5th Cir.1970). In the present case serious problems existed in defining and identifying the members of the class. As noted above, the complaint defined the class as those individuals eligible for CIP assistance but who were denied assistance or who were discouraged from applying because of the existence of the invalid regulation promulgated by CSA.

Cases have recognized the difficulty of identifying class members whose membership in the class depends on each individual's state of mind. *DeBremaecker*, 433 F.2d at 734; *Chaffee v. Johnson*, 229 F.Supp. 445, 448 (S.D.Miss.1964), *aff'd on other grounds*, 352 F.2d 514 (5th Cir.1965), *cert. denied*, 384 U.S. 956, 86 S.Ct. 1582, 16 L.Ed.2d 553 (1966); *Capaci v. Katz & Besthoff, Inc.*, 72 F.R.D. 71, 78 (E.D.La.1976). In *DeBremaecker* a class action was filed on behalf of all state residents

23. An initial matter for consideration is whether the dismissal of the claims of the individual class plaintiffs renders the case moot. Recently, the Supreme Court held that "an action brought on behalf of a class does not become moot upon expiration of the named plaintiff's substantive claim, even though class certification has been denied." *United States Parole Comm'n v. Geraghty*, 445 U.S. 388, 404, 100 S.Ct. 1202, 1212, 63 L.Ed.2d 479 (1980) [*infra* p. 484]. Thus, we have jurisdiction to review the district court's denial of class certification.

24. Although the district court did not attempt to categorize which category of Rule 23(b) this class action fell under, its reference to the concept of manageability implies a determination that this was a 23(b)(3) class action. Fed.R.Civ.P. 23(b)(3)(D) (court must consider "difficulties likely to be encountered in the management of a class action.") At one point plaintiffs contend that this is a 23(b)(2) class because their complaint was framed as requesting declaratory, mandamus, and injunctive relief; and that manageability is not a proper consideration in a (b)(2) class determination. For the following reasons we reject plaintiffs' contentions.

First, it is not at all clear that the problems in managing a class action are not relevant in certifying (b)(1) and (b)(2) class actions. Some of the problems which arise in all of the subdivisions of Rule 23(b) are common to all forms of class action—identifying a class, cost of notice of settlement, and administrative burdens on the court in managing the litigation. This is especially true because the purpose of Rule 23 is to allow an efficient mechanism for disposing of multiple claims. *Developments in the Law of Class Actions, supra,* [89 Harv.L.Rev.] at 1322.

Second, the record before us indicates that this case, if certifiable, would have to be certified under Rule 23(b)(3). While plaintiffs attempt to characterize their complaint as one for declaratory and injunctive relief, it is clear that the final form of the relief obtained would be monetary in nature. Class certification under (b)(2) is not appropriate where the relief requested (or in this case obtained) is monetary in nature. Furthermore, although plaintiffs' complaint did request injunctive and declaratory relief, as we note below, the declaration as to the invalidity of the regulation and a judgment awarding relief to members of the class are two completely separate legal issues. The latter depends on proof of whether the existence of the invalid regulation discouraged class members from applying for the assistance. Plaintiffs actually requested that the class members be compensated in some form for these lost benefits—specifically, through the consent decree or funding of programs.

active in the peace movement who had been harassed or intimidated as well as those who feared harassment or intimidation in the exercise of their constitutional rights. The court held that this did not satisfy the requirement of an adequately defined and clearly ascertainable class. First, the court noted the ambiguity inherent in the term "peace movement." Even aside from this ambiguity, however, the court went on to discuss another problem in identifying the class—the theory of the complaint was that state law chilled residents in the exercise of their first amendment rights. It could not be concluded that all state residents were "chilled" in such a manner and therefore there was no way to identify those individuals affected by defendant's policies. *See also Chaffee*, 229 F.Supp. at 448 (class described as all persons working to end race discrimination and encouraging blacks to exercise rights held too vague because depends on each individual's state of mind); *cf. Simon v. Merrill Lynch, Pierce, Fenner and Smith, Inc.*, 482 F.2d 880, 882 (5th Cir.1973) (differences in misrepresentation alleged as well as degrees of reliance thereon made class suit inappropriate).

Problems similar to those in *DeBremaecker* exist in the present case. The first problem is to identify those individuals who qualify for CIP assistance. This by no means is an easy or inexpensive task. *Cf. Ihrke v. Northern States Power Company*, 459 F.2d 566, 572 (8th Cir.), *vacated as moot*, 409 U.S. 815, 93 S.Ct. 66, 34 L.Ed.2d 72 (1972) (deny class certification because of vagueness of class which included all persons who because of poverty are unable to pay for utility service). After completing this task, the court and parties would have to proceed with the Sisyphean task of identifying those individuals who not only qualified for CIP assistance, but also knew of the existence of the regulation and were discouraged from applying for assistance because of the shutoff notice requirement. Such an attempt to identify those individuals who were "chilled" would be a burden on the court and require a large expenditure of valuable court time.[25]

25. In *Developments, supra,* [89 Harv. L.Rev.] at 1478 n. 128 it is observed that the "state of mind" rubric has been applied too loosely to reject class action suits where the class members could be identified by some action or objective manifestation. The article then goes on to critique the holdings in *DeBremaecker* and *Chaffee* because the class in each case actually was defined in terms of actions and not the beliefs of the plaintiffs.

While such a distinction between actions and beliefs may be difficult to articulate in great detail, we believe that even if this distinction has any validity in general, it does not require a different result in the present case. Arguably, the putative class members' state of mind could be described as conduct—failure to apply—rather than their state of mind—discouraged from applying, and therefore the criticism of the article would apply to this case. The change of characterization of the issue in the case from one of state of mind to conduct should not serve as a talisman to decide the difficult issue of whether an identifiable class exists. At best, the general statement that state of mind issues are present serves as a shorthand method of alerting the court and the parties that there might be difficulty in identifying the class members. Also, the classification of an issue as "belief" or "conduct" does not resolve the issue, since many matters of "conduct" by putative class members may nonetheless make the class difficult to identify.

We believe that whether characterized as "state of mind" or "conduct" the putative members of this class would be difficult to identify. In reaching this conclusion we emphasize the cost and time of the court and parties which would have to be expended

Identification of the class serves at least two obvious purposes in the context of certification. First, it alerts the court and parties to the burdens that such a process might entail. In this way the court can decide whether the class device simply would be an inefficient way of trying the lawsuit—for the parties as well as for its own congested docket. Second, identifying the class insures that those actually harmed by defendants' wrongful conduct will be the recipients of the relief eventually provided.

The district court was well aware of problems in identifying the class. At the hearing on January 4, 1980 the district court stated:

> How are we going to find out which persons were chilled from applying because of knowledge of this shutoff notice requirement? How are we going to gather the facts on which persons, other than your named plaintiffs, were turned down on that account in the region? We could spend the 15 million dollars gathering the facts in this case. I say that facetiously, but by the time we gather them, it will be another year down the road and then we would be in the '81 program before we decided who was actually entitled to any money. Is it worth it?

* * *

These statements make it evident that the district court, as well as the parties, were aware of the problems attendant to identifying the members of the class. The district court believed that it would require a great deal of its own time as well as a large amount of money to accomplish this task. In light of these circumstances this certainly was a proper factor for the district court to consider in denying class certification.

[The court also found that the requirement in Rule 23(b)(3) that questions common to the class "predominate" over questions affecting only individual members was not satisfied. Whether the regulation was inconsistent with the statute is a common class issue. However, proof of each member's state of mind would be necessary to show he was discouraged from applying for assistance by the regulation. Each member's damage would also have to be separately proven. The court found that procedural devices, such as subclasses and fluid recovery, would not remedy this problem of lack of predominance of common issues.]

SWYGERT, CIRCUIT JUDGE, dissenting.

* * *

before the class could even possibly be identified. Finally, the presence of state of mind issues should not be an automatic reason for denying class certification, and the above article emphasizes this point. However, in exercising its discretion, the district court may focus on this factor, among others, in considering the viability of a class suit. In the circumstances of this case we observe that not only were there problems in identifying the class, but also with the other requirements of Rule 23.

I believe that the putative class defined in the complaint, met all of the prerequisites for certification imposed by Rule 23(a) and (b)(2).[12] As defendants conceded both in the trial court and in their brief on this appeal, the requirements of Fed.R.Civ.P. 23(a) are met. * * * In addition, defendants stated that "the putative class [meets] the requirements of Rule 23(b)(2), because CSA applied its regulations to the putative class generally. If these regulations were invalid, CSA would have an obligation to the entire putative class to remedy its error."[13]

Policy considerations weigh heavily in favor of certification in the case at bar. If classwide relief is denied, it is highly unlikely that the persons injured by CSA's illegal regulation will receive any relief. Because each putative class member would be entitled to a maximum of only $250.00, individual suits by those persons would be impractical. Further, if the judgment vacating the consent decree is affirmed, the unspent funds from the 1979 CIP will be returned to the Treasury, thus exhausting the funds which would have been available to provide the relief necessitated by the invalid regulation.

The majority notes that there is an argument that the inclusion in the class of persons "discouraged [by the invalid regulation] from applying for assistance" renders the class too ill-defined for certification because identification of class members depends on each individual's state of mind, and cites a line of cases holding that a class including "chilled" applicants cannot be certified. There is, however, a second line of authority that supports the proposition that a class may include "chilled" plaintiffs. *Yaffe v. Powers,* 454 F.2d 1362, 1365–66 (1st Cir. 1972) (class maintainable under Rule 23(b)(2)); *Carpenter v. Davis,* 424 F.2d 257, 260 (5th Cir.1970).

The majority lists several problems that it believes would be encountered by the district court in attempting to identify class members in the instant case. First, the majority notes that identifying those who qualify for CIP aid "by no means is an easy or inexpensive task." That is hardly

12. A class action under 23(b)(2) seeking injunctive or declaratory relief may also include an incidental claim for monetary damages. *Society for Individual Rights, Inc. v. Hampton,* 528 F.2d 905, 906 (9th Cir. 1975).

I disagree with the majority's holding, n. 24 *supra,* that this class suit must be considered a 23(b)(3) rather than a 23(b)(2) action because the relief obtained was monetary in nature. "[A] class action for injunctive relief and damages properly brought under Rule 23(a) and (b)(2) should not be dismissed merely because a subsequent change in policy by the defendant has eliminated the necessity for future injunctive relief, leaving only the question of past damages for determination by the Court." *Arkansas Education Ass'n v. Board of Education,* 446 F.2d 763, 768 (8th Cir.1971).

In the instant case, plaintiffs requested in the complaint a declaration that the regulation at issue was invalid, an injunction prohibiting CSA from returning the unused funds to the Treasury, and an injunction requiring CSA to extend the deadline to apply for 1979 funds. As defendants conceded in the district court and on this appeal, the relief requested by the putative class made it properly a 23(b)(2) action. A different conclusion is not required by the fact that CSA agreed not to return the funds to the Treasury pending the outcome or by the fact that the settlement called for monetary relief.

13. Because I would hold that the instant case is maintainable as a 23(b)(2) class action, there is no need to reach the questions of predominance of common issues of law and fact or manageability as discussed by the majority.

an insurmountable obstacle, because CSA in administering the program had to identify applicants who qualified for aid.

The majority characterizes as "Sisyphean" the job of identifying those qualified persons who were discouraged from applying for assistance. Although I agree with the majority that such a procedure would be a burden on the court, I believe that in certain cases considerations of justice require courts to undertake those tasks; I would find this to be such a case. Further, the problem could be alleviated by giving notice by publication, and by approving the settlement decree which provides for a "fluid" recovery.*

The majority points out that Judge Grady was aware of the problem of identifying class members in the case at bar. Nevertheless, in *Grieg v. Olivarez,* No. 78 C 1646 (Sept. 1, 1978), which concerned the Emergency Energy Assistance Program, the predecessor to the CIP, Judge Grady certified a class very similar to the one described in the complaint in this case:

> (a) The sub-class for all low income persons otherwise eligible for participation in the EEAP who were denied EEAP assistance without written notice or opportunity for written appeal, or were denied the opportunity to submit written applications.

> (b) The sub-class of all low income persons aged 60 and over living alone in households of no more than two persons whose household income is between 125 per cent and 150 per cent of CSA Poverty Guidelines and who were otherwise eligible for EEAP assistance but were denied such assistance due to income or *who were discouraged from applying.*

The problem of identifying "chilled" applicants was the same in both cases, yet the district court granted certification in *Grieg* but denied it here.

Not only would I hold that the denial of certification was an abuse of discretion on the merits, I also believe that the procedure followed by the district court in determining the certification question was inadequate. No hearing was ever held on the issue of certification, and only defendant briefed the question in the district court. "Maintainability [of a class action] may be determined by the court on the pleadings, if sufficient facts are set forth, but ordinarily the determination should be predicated on more information than the pleadings will provide." *Weathers v. Peters Realty Corp.,* 499 F.2d 1197, 1200 (6th Cir.1974). Although an evidentiary hearing on class certification is not required, it is certainly favored and would have been valuable in this case, given the close questions of manageability and identification at issue.

---

* The discussion of the propriety of a "fluid recovery" remedy by the majority and dissent is printed *infra* p. 406.—Eds.

Notes and Questions

1. Judge Wood's majority opinion speaks of "the Sisyphean task of identifying those individuals who not only qualified for CIP assistance, but also knew of the existence of the regulation and were discouraged from applying for assistance because of the shut-off notice requirement." What if notices were posted in places where low income families are likely to see them (for example, low income housing units, post offices, welfare department offices, employment offices, and churches) notifying them of the class action and requesting that they contact the court or class attorney? Would it be sufficient that this might reach a number of persons who qualified for CIP but not all of them? What additional method could be used to show that those persons who responded to such notice also knew of the regulation and were discouraged from applying by the shut-off notice requirement? Could this be done by affidavit? By having such persons examined by a special master? Would it be appropriate to shift the burden to the government to disprove knowledge and chilling effect if an individual so indicated in a sworn affidavit?

As Judge Swygert points out in dissent, other cases have looked more favorably on class definitions that depended on state of mind for inclusion in the class. For example, in Yaffe v. Powers, 454 F.2d 1362 (1st Cir.1972), plaintiffs challenged allegedly harassing police practices during peace demonstrations on behalf of a class of persons "who wish to * * * engage, in the City of Fall River, in peaceful political discussion * * * without surveillance." The district court refused to certify a class or to allow discovery regarding police action involving anyone but the named plaintiffs. The First Circuit reversed, stressing the fact that plaintiffs sued only for injunctive relief and reasoning that "[a]lthough notice to and therefore precise definition of the members of the suggested class are important to certification of a subdivision (b)(3) class, notice to the members of a (b)(2) class is not required, and the actual membership of the class need not therefore be precisely determined. In fact, the conduct complained of is the benchmark for determining whether a subdivision (b)(2) class exists." The appellate court contemplated that further discovery about the police practices would demonstrate whether a definable class existed. Is there less concern with class definition in an injunctive, as opposed to a damage, class action? See In re Monumental Life Ins. Co., *infra* p. 318.

2. In Adashunas v. Negley, 626 F.2d 600 (7th Cir.1980), the parents of two learning disabled children sued on behalf of a class of "all children within the state of Indiana entitled to a public education who have learning disabilities who are not properly identified and/or who are not receiving such special education as to guarantee them [a] minimally adequate education." The suit, filed against state and county educational agency members and a class of local school board members and superintendents, sought to require them to adopt procedures that would identify learning disabled children and accord them special education as allegedly required by the federal Education for All Handicapped Children Act. The court found the class definition inadequate:

> The plaintiff class consists of children entitled to a public education who have learning disabilities and "who are not properly identified

and/or who are not receiving" special education. In the comprehensive discovery undertaken and numerous affidavits filed, it does not appear that there are numerous identifiable children not receiving special education in Indiana, but only suspected-to-exist children with learning disabilities "who are not ... identified." How does one identify class members consisting of persons not identified? This might be conceivably possible if identification were a simple process. However, the record abundantly demonstrates that identifying learning disabled children is a gargantuan task.

The major reason that identification of the learning disabled child is very difficult is that such a child usually possesses a normal or above-average intellectual ability. The two originally named minor plaintiffs were so described in their own pleading. Joseph Adashunas was alleged to be within the bright-normal range of intelligence and has a mental age beyond his chronological age. Plaintiff acknowledged that "it took defendants almost three years to recognize his disability," and defendants included and were assisted by experts in the field of learning disabilities. Shannon Durbin, the other original named plaintiff minor, was alleged to have an above-average Intelligence Quotient and mental age. Despite the extreme pressure of this lawsuit upon the defendants to identify her as learning disabled, it was finally concluded after diligent testing, conferences and observation she was *not* learning disabled and she was dismissed as a plaintiff. If, out of two minors believed by their parents to be learning disabled to the extent that they would file a ponderous lawsuit, three years of testing resulted in one being so found and the other not, how can others be readily identified without parental pressure and without the constraints of a lawsuit?

In Indiana, for the school year 1977–78, there are 6,754 children participating in approved special education programs. However, these children are identified and receiving special education and are therefore outside the class. In other words, those more obviously identifiable have been or are being identified. Those who have not been identified either may not exist or are exceedingly difficult to identify if they do exist.

The plaintiffs' own expert witnesses conceded in affidavits that a "battery" of tests are needed to identify a learning disabled child; that the symptoms are widely diverse; that the only way possibly to identify such a child is to monitor a "clustering" of different test results in order to discover those which may reflect weakness in any given area of potential learning disability. This is a long, arduous process.

Do you agree that a class cannot be defined in terms of "only suspected-to-exist children with learning disabilities 'who are not identified' "? Is the court's discussion of the difficulties of identifying class members in effect a resolution of the merits of plaintiffs' claim? Are all class actions in which the members cannot be identified by name subject to this objection? Compare a class action on behalf of the "homeless." See Joyce v. City and County of San Francisco, 1994 WL 443464 (N.D.Cal.1994), a suit on behalf of the "homeless" in San Francisco challenging a new police measure known as the Matrix Program. The court certified a class consisting of "those persons present in the City and County of San Francisco who (1) are without shelter,

(2) lack the financial resources or mental capacity necessary to provide for their own shelter, and (3) have been cited or arrested for a violation of any of the portions of the Matrix Program now challenged." Is this class definition better than the proposed definition in Adashunas v. Negley?

3. Is it impermissible to certify a class that includes persons who cannot be identified at present? Consider Robertson v. National Basketball Association, 389 F.Supp. 867 (S.D.N.Y.1975), an antitrust action brought by a number of professional basketball players challenging the merger of the N.B.A. and the American Basketball Association. Plaintiffs sought treble damages and injunctive and declaratory relief on behalf of a class of "all presently active players, those who were active at the time the action was originally commenced, and future players in the NBA." Citing an affidavit which stated that "[o]f the literally hundreds of thousands of varsity high school players in the United States and of the thousands of varsity college players, each year fewer than fifty are good enough to join the NBA," defendants objected to inclusion of future players. The court rejected the argument:

> The NBA's claim that the proposed class lacks definition is premised on an erroneous assumption. Defendants misread a portion of the plaintiffs' moving affidavit in asserting that the inclusion of future active players up to the date of judgment raises the specter of a class hundreds of thousands strong. In the affidavit, Laurence Fleisher merely said that out of hundreds of thousands of high school and college ballplayers, fewer than fifty generally are good enough to join the ranks of the NBA each year. The "monster" class cases cited by the NBA are therefore not in point.

> The class is neither amorphous, nor imprecise; at the present time there are three hundred and sixty-five class members. The fact that fifty to a hundred more members may be joining the class does not make it unmanageable. Moreover, it has been held that the "[f]ailure to state the exact number or to identify individually every member of the class does not militate against the maintenance of a class action." This court can determine at any time whether a particular individual is a member of the class, *see* Eisman v. Pan American World Airlines, 336 F.Supp. 543, 547 (E.D.Pa.1971), for it will always be composed of "a well-defined, discrete and limited number of NBA basketball players all of whom are well known and will be readily identifiable by exact name at all stages of this action." This factor makes this case distinguishable from *Eisman, supra* (all past and future purchasers of tickets from Pan American) and from Coniglio v. Highwood Services, Inc., 60 F.R.D. 359, 363 (W.D.N.Y.1972) (all past, present and future ticketholders of the Buffalo Bills).

> Courts have approved classes which included future members. *See, e.g.,* Air Line Stewards & Stewardesses Association Local 550 v. American Airlines, Inc., 490 F.2d 636, 638 (7th Cir.1973), cert. denied, 416 U.S. 993, 94 S.Ct. 2406, 40 L.Ed.2d 773 (1974) ("class consisted of all present and former American stewardesses . . . who had been, desired to be, or would in the future desire to be, pregnant"); Arey v. Providence Hospital, 55 F.R.D. 62, 64 (D.D.C.1972) ("class action brought on behalf

of all black and female employees who have sought, might have sought, seek or might seek, employment and promotion by the defendant"). In view of the size of the class and that plaintiffs have agreed to give notice of the proceedings to all present and future members, the notice requirement does not raise a serious issue.

4. Whether a class definition is adequate may be affected by the class remedy sought. In Tucker v. United States Dept. of Commerce, 135 F.R.D. 175 (N.D.Ill.1991), a class of all Illinois residents alleged that the Census Bureau's procedures undercounted minority and disadvantaged groups. The court denied certification for lack of commonality based on an analysis of whether, under the class definition, the plaintiffs had standing to sue and were entitled to the relief requested. The plaintiffs' claim that all Illinois residents might be harmed from inaccurate counting might be true as far as the federal government was concerned because the count of Illinois residents would affect the allocation of federal funds. However, plaintiffs alleged undercounting only in certain blocks, and their proposed "correction" of the census data could actually benefit other Illinois residents from blocks that were not undercounted "since they will then receive a bigger slice of the state benefit pie." Thus the class of all Illinois residents contained persons who lacked standing and were not entitled to the relief requested. The court also refused to certify an alternative class defined as "residents of the census blocks in which the chronically undercounted reside" on the ground that plaintiffs had not identified such blocks nor had they "provided the court with a principled way of deciding which blocks should be included in the category."

Could the solution be to define the class as limited to those whose rights have been violated? If that class definition were permitted, what would be the binding effect if the defendant won? Consider the objections of the court to such a class definition in Daffron v. Rousseau Assoc., Inc., 1976–2 Tr. Cas. ¶ 61,219 (N.D.Ind.1976): "The new class definition, if allowed, would result in a 'fail-safe' class, a class which would be bound only by a judgment favorable to plaintiffs but not an adverse judgment."

5. The problem of adequate class definition is closely related to the Rule 23(a)(2) requirement of "commonality" and to the further requirement of "representativeness." Problems arising out of the fact that there may be some differences between class members are sometimes analyzed by courts as one of definition and sometimes as one of "commonality" or "representativeness." These problems can sometimes be solved by narrowing the definition of the class to encompass a group with closer interests and which is more easily identifiable, by allowing class members to "opt out" of the class if they believe their interests are too diverse from those of the class, or by use of subclasses. These techniques are discussed in later sections.

6. Sometimes, however, the problems may prove intractable. Consider, for example whether class members' attitudes should be important in a (b)(2) class action. What if some members of the class do not agree with the position proposed to be taken on their behalf? In Pratt v. Chicago Housing Authority, 155 F.R.D. 177 (N.D.Ill.1994), a class action was brought on behalf of residents of the Chicago Housing Authority challenging the constitutionality of the CHA's practices regarding warrantless searches of apart-

ments as violations of the Fourth Amendment. The CHA developed this policy as a response to incidents of violence or gunfire, but owing to logistical problems the "raid" would never occur sooner than two days after the event upon which it was based. The court initially certified a plaintiff class but decertified it after Local Advisory Council presidents for 18 of the 19 CHA developments moved to intervene on the defense side and presented a petition signed by over 5,000 CHA residents applauding the CHA's efforts to respond to violence in the projects. Although the class plaintiffs argued that this opposition within the class was irrelevant, the court was persuaded that the "prominent and vigorous dissent within the class" justified decertification.

Compare Norwalk CORE v. Norwalk Redevelopment Agency, 395 F.2d 920 (2d Cir.1968), a class action was filed on behalf of low-income African Americans and Puerto Ricans who lived in an urban renewal area to ensure their adequate relocation. The court stated that "the fact that some members of the class were personally satisfied with the defendants' relocation efforts is irrelevant." Is that because the class could be limited to those not satisfied with the relocation efforts? See also Bell, Serving Two Masters: Integration Ideals and Client Interests in School Desegregation Litigation, 85 Yale L.J. 470 (1976) (describing tension between goal of integration and parental desires to place more emphasis on educational quality); Rubenstein, Divided We Litigate: Addressing Disputes Among Group Members and Lawyers in Civil Rights Campaigns, 106 Yale L.J. 1623 (1997) (discussing the tension between individualism and group interests).

A number of commentators have urged that the trial court has a duty to deal creatively with potential conflict between members in class actions, especially in "structural reform" suits. See, e.g., Garth, Conflict and Dissent in Class Actions: A Suggested Perspective, 77 Nw.L.Rev. 492, 527 (1982): "Courts should prefer certification, but not automatically grant it, when an accountable legal rights entity represents the class, the class is too diffuse to enforce its rights by any other means, or the court can manage dissent through such mechanisms as subclassing, redefining the class, permitting intervention, and structuring the remedy." See also Fiss, Foreword—The Forms of Justice, 93 Harv.L.Rev. 1, 2 (1979). Keep these issues in mind when you address representativeness, *infra* p. 285.

2. NUMEROSITY

BOARD OF EDUCATION OF TOWNSHIP HIGH SCHOOL v. CLIMATEMP, INC.

United States District Court, Northern District of Illinois, 1981.
1980–81 Trade Cases ¶ 63,863.

LEIGHTON, DISTRICT JUDGE.

[The Attorney General of the State of Illinois and the State's Attorney of Cook County filed suit on behalf of the State, the Chicago Board of Education, and Cook County against 50 enterprises and individuals, alleging bid-rigging and allocation of jobs by sheet metal construction companies in the Chicago area in violation of the federal antitrust laws. The plaintiffs sought to represent a class of governmental entities in the Chicago metropolitan area who had been injured by defendants' conduct.]

Rule 23(a) of the Federal Rules of Civil Procedure specifies that numerosity, typicality, adequacy of representation, and commonality be present as prerequisites to maintenance of a class action. The party seeking to represent an alleged class carries the burden of demonstrating that these elements have been satisfied. In the *State of Illinois* case, plaintiffs have failed to show that the first element, that of numerosity, is satisfied. At best, figures compiled as described above indicate that 135 public sub-entities may have been victims of the alleged antitrust actions. The Attorney General was able to unearth only 56 governmental purchasers of sheet metal services and supplies. While it is reasonable to assume that continued discovery may disclose additional purchasers, this court finds that the number of entities potentially victimized is not so numerous that intervention or joinder of plaintiffs is impractical.

The question of what constitutes impracticability depends on the facts of a given case, and no arbitrary rules concerning satisfaction of numerosity have been imposed by the courts. While joinder has been held to be impracticable with as few as 40 members of a class in *Swanson v. American Consumer Indus., Inc.,* 415 F.2d 1326, 1333 n. 9 (7th Cir.1969), class actions have not been maintainable with as many as 350 potential members. *State of Utah v. American Pipe & Constr. Co.,* 49 F.R.D. 17 (C.D.Cal.1969). There, the state of Utah filed an antitrust action against certain concrete and steel pipe manufacturing companies and sought to represent a class described as those "public bodies and agencies of state and local government in the State of Utah who are end users of pipe acquired from the defendants, co-conspirators and others." Although plaintiffs alleged that its class was so numerous that joinder of all 800 listed potential members was impracticable, the court refused to accept that all public bodies had claims against the defendants. From prior experience, the court concluded that the number of public entities injured by the alleged antitrust conspiracy was more reasonably estimated to be 350, and that joinder of them was not impracticable. The court found that a class action would not achieve economies of time, effort, and expenses or promote any more uniformity of decision than would joinder; to the contrary, joinder and intervention would permit actual determination of actual plaintiffs and damages suffered in a simpler fashion than a class action would permit. *State of Utah v. American Pipe and Constr. Co.,* 49 F.R.D. at 21. See *Minersville Coal Co. v. Anthracite Export Assoc.,* 55 F.R.D. 426 (M.D.Pa.1971), where the court found, in an antitrust case alleging violations of the Sherman and Clayton Acts, that a class numbering 330 plaintiffs was not so numerous that joinder of all members was impracticable.

There is no "magic number" which automatically determines whether or not the numerosity requirement is met. Other factors are to be considered as well. For example, the geographical location of the potential plaintiffs is a major factor to be considered in determining whether joinder is impractical. In the case at bar, potential plaintiffs have been limited by the allegations contained in the complaint to those located in the Chicago metropolitan area, a limitation which lends itself readily to the procedure of joinder or intervention. For the foregoing reasons, this court concludes that the *State of Illinois* case is not maintainable as a class action, and that allegations to the contrary must be stricken.

Notes and Questions

1. Rule 23(a) requires that "the class is so numerous that joinder of all members is impracticable." Why does the fact that the class members in *Climatemp* were all located in the Chicago metropolitan area prevent plaintiffs from satisfying that requirement? Is it that the court felt that the class members would have no difficulty in being joined (or intervening) since they were located locally and would probably have a local attorney or be able to cooperate easily with the main plaintiffs' attorneys? Should that be enough to establish that joinder is impracticable? Should the cost, inconvenience, and unwieldiness of joining 135 (or even 56) class members in *Climatemp* have been a factor?

2. Some courts have found numerosity satisfied "if joinder would result in a burden to the case, be it the cost to the plaintiff of serving each defendant, or the taxation of court resources due to numerous motions filed by several hundred defendants." Alexander Grant & Co. v. McAlister, 116 F.R.D. 583, 586 (S.D.Ohio 1987); Northwestern National Bank of Minneapolis v. Fox & Co., 102 F.R.D. 507, 510 (S.D.N.Y.1984). Having a large number of individual plaintiffs, each of whom must be served with all pleadings, motions, and documents and has the full rights of appearance of a party, can be very unwieldy. The management techniques used in consolidation of cases (such as requiring the parties to act through a single attorney) might be used, but this then comes very much to resemble a class action. When a *defendant* class action is sought, the cost and difficulty of obtaining personal service on each defendant class member may itself demonstrate that joinder is impracticable. In re Alexander Grant & Company Litigation, 110 F.R.D. 528, 532 (S.D.Fla.1986).

3. Some courts have also found impracticability of joinder if the class is so large that individual influence over pleading, discovery, and litigation strategy is effectively eliminated. See Alexander Grant & Co. v. McAlister, 116 F.R.D. 583, 587 (S.D.Ohio 1987) ("[t]here certainly can be no individual influence over litigation involving over 300 counter-defendants spread throughout the nation"); In re Gap Stores Securities Litigation, 79 F.R.D. 283 (N.D.Cal.1978) (joining "ninety-one new parties would be to require that the litigation be conducted through committees, that is, to make joinder a fiction for class adjudication").

4. One of the justifications for a class action is that the individual members may lack incentive to vindicate their rights by separate actions. This can occur because the class members are reluctant to undertake litigation or have such a small monetary interest in the suit as to make it economically unfeasible to sue. Unless a class action is allowed, the defendant will be effectively immunized from suit. Is such a situation grounds for

finding numerosity satisfied by a smaller number of class members? Arkansas Education Association v. Board of Education, 446 F.2d 763, 765 (8th Cir.1971) held it was, finding a race-discrimination suit on behalf of a class of 17 black teachers was sufficiently numerous because of their "natural fear or reluctance" to bring separate actions. See also Mullen v. Treasure Chest Casino, LLC, 186 F.3d 620 (5th Cir.1999) ("potential class members still employed by [defendant] might be unwilling to sue individually or join a suit for fear of retaliation at their jobs"); compare Christiana Mortgage Corp. v. Delaware Mortgage Bankers Association, 136 F.R.D. 372 (D.Del.1991) (joinder not impracticable in class action on behalf of 28 mortgage brokers who had no reluctance to sue, and all the class members were located within a small geographic area). Even in cases that might involve such arguments, at some point classes can be too small. See Harik v. California Teachers Ass'n, 326 F.3d 1042 (9th Cir.2003) (classes of seven, nine, and ten were too small in a suit by teachers against employers and teachers' unions).

5.   What degree of certainty is required to establish numerosity? In Doe v. Charleston Area Medical Center, Inc., 529 F.2d 638 (4th Cir.1975), a suit for declaratory and injunctive relief against enforcement of the anti-abortion policy of a governmental medical center, the circuit court found numerosity satisfied on the basis of an "informal" survey showing that 70 women per month from the area were forced to go outside the state to terminate pregnancies. Should the plaintiff have been required to show that the survey met minimal social science standards for accuracy in its methodology? The *Charleston Area* decision observed that even speculative and conclusory representations as to the size of the class may suffice where only declaratory and injunctive relief is sought. Compare Phillips v. Joint Legislative Committee, Etc., 637 F.2d 1014 (5th Cir.1981) (in a suit against state agencies for discrimination in hiring, evidence that there were 33 unsuccessful black applicants did not satisfy numerosity, especially where the class also included "future and deterred applicants, necessarily unidentifiable"); Male v. Crossroads Associates, 320 F.Supp. 141 (S.D.N.Y.1970) (finding numerosity not satisfied in a suit to enjoin apartment owner from refusing to rent to welfare recipients where no facts were averred or established to show how many welfare recipients were denied housing at the apartment house or deterred from applying there by its policy).

In Vergara v. Hampton, 581 F.2d 1281 (7th Cir.1978), three resident aliens sued U.S. Civil Service officials seeking to have the court declare unconstitutional a policy that barred aliens from taking the federal civil service exam. They sued on behalf of a class of "all other nationals and citizens of foreign states living in Illinois who had been admitted into Illinois for permanent residence and who desire to apply and be eligible for appointment in the U.S. Civil Service." The Seventh Circuit found it "unnecessary in circumstances such as these to establish that every member of the class 'desired' to obtain Civil Service employment" and concluded that numerosity was met by figures showing the number of resident aliens in Illinois and the number of Civil Service positions in the state.

6.   Should less "speculative" proof as to numbers be required if damages, as opposed to injunctive and declaratory relief, are sought? Some courts have found a lack of numerosity when there is no showing of "interest" in

filing suit by a sufficient number of class members who have a sizable economic stake. In Block v. First Blood Associates, 743 F.Supp. 194 (S.D.N.Y.1990), 763 F.Supp. 746 (S.D.N.Y.1991), aff'd, 988 F.2d 344 (2d Cir.1993), a class action was sought on behalf of purchasers of units in a limited partnership that owned the film "Rambo—First Blood," alleging misrepresentations that they would be paid 98% of the net profits and that substantial tax deductions would also be available if the film failed. The court denied class certification with leave to renew within 90 days if plaintiffs "can establish that a meaningful number of limited partners have expressed an identity of interest" in the case. It noted that only 24 of the 57 investors (with investments ranging from $50,000 to $400,000) had expressed interest in the suit and that "the putative class members * * * are easily identifiable and have the financial resources and stake in the partnership which would make joinder practicable." Does the fact that most class members did not express an interest in joining the suit suggest that joinder is practicable or that it is not?

7. In some cases, there is a link between numerosity and the merits. Thus, in Makuc v. American Honda Motor Co., 835 F.2d 389 (1st Cir.1987), plaintiff sued for injuries sustained in a motorcycle crash, claiming that the crash resulted from a defective design. He sought to represent a class consisting of other owners of the motorcycle, and submitted an affidavit from an expert who said that the defect existed in one out of every 50 Honda motorcycle axles to establish that the class was sufficiently numerous. The court held that this was insufficient (id. at 394):

> If taken as true, the expert's claim that one of every fifty axles is defective only shows that other people might have suffered the injury in the same manner as the plaintiff. After two years of discovery, though, the plaintiff was unable to provide any evidence that even one other person was injured due to a defective axle. Nor did plaintiff provide any evidence that even one other Honda axle failed. In view of this lack of similar occurrences, the court could have properly concluded that, standing alone, the plaintiff's contention as to the size of the class was purely speculative.

3. COMMONALITY

The prerequisite in Rule 23(a)(2) that all class actions satisfy "commonality" (that is, that there are questions of law or fact common to the class) is closely related to the requirement in Rule 23(b)(3) class actions that common questions of law or fact must "predominate over any questions affecting only individual class members." The issue of "commonality" is often discussed in Rule 23(b)(3) cases in conjunction with the issue of "predominance" of common questions, and a number of the cases in this section fall under that category. A later section on Rule 23(b)(3) class actions will focus on predominance of common questions in mass tort and similar suits for damages. See *infra* p. 330.

BLACKIE v. BARRACK

United States Court of Appeals, Ninth Circuit, 1975.
524 F.2d 891, cert. denied, 429 U.S. 816, 97 S.Ct. 57, 50 L.Ed.2d 75 (1976).

Before TUTTLE, KOELSCH and BROWNING, CIRCUIT JUDGES.

KOELSCH, CIRCUIT JUDGE.

These are appeals from an order conditionally certifying a class in consolidated actions for violation of Section 10(b) of the Securities and Exchange Act of 1934, 15 U.S.C. § 78j(b), and Rule 10b–5 promulgated thereunder, 17 C.F.R. § 240.10(b)–5.

The litigation is a product of the financial troubles of Ampex Corporation. The annual report issued May 2, 1970, for fiscal 1970, reported a profit of $12 million. By January 1972, the company was predicting an estimated $40 million loss for fiscal 1972 (ending April 30, 1972). Two months later the company disclosed the loss would be much larger, in the $80 to $90 million range; finally, in the annual report for fiscal 1972, filed August 3, 1972, the company reported a loss of $90 million, and the company's independent auditors withdrew certification of the 1971 financial statements, and declined to certify those for 1972, because of doubts that the loss reported for 1972 was in fact suffered in that year.

Several suits were filed following the 1972 disclosures of Ampex's losses. They were consolidated for pre-trial purposes. The named plaintiffs in the various complaints involved in these appeals purchased Ampex securities during the 27 month period between the release of the 1970 and 1972 annual reports, and seek to represent all purchasers of Ampex securities during the period. The corporation, its principal officers during the period, and the company's independent auditor are named as defendants. The gravamen of all the claims is the misrepresentation by reason of annual and interim reports, press releases and SEC filings of the financial condition of Ampex from the date of the 1970 report until the true condition was disclosed by the announcement of losses in August of 1972.

The plaintiffs moved for class certification shortly after filing their complaints in 1972; after extensive briefing and argument the district judge entered an order on April 11, 1974, conditionally certifying as a class all those who purchased Ampex securities during the 27 month period.

* * *

Defendants question this suit's compliance with each of the various requirements of Rule 23(a) and (b)(3) except numerosity (understandably, as it appears that the class period of 27 months will encompass the purchasers involved in about 120,000 transactions involving some 21,000,000 shares). However, all of defendants' contentions can be resolved by addressing 3 underlying questions: 1) whether a common question of law or fact unites the class; 2) whether direct individual proof of subjective reliance by each class member is necessary to establish 10b–5 liability in this situation; and 3) whether proof of liability or damages will create conflicts among class members and with named plaintiffs sufficient to make representation inadequate? We turn to the first issue.

1. COMMON QUESTIONS OF LAW OR FACT

The class certified runs from the date Ampex issued its 1970 annual report until the company released its 1972 report 27 months later. Plaintiffs' complaint alleges that the price of the company's stock was artificially inflated because:

> "the annual reports of Ampex for fiscal years 1970 and 1971, various interim reports, press releases and other documents (a) overstated earnings, (b) overstated the value of inventories and other assets, (c) buried expense items and other costs incurred for research and development in inventory, (d) misrepresented the companies' current ratio, (e) failed to establish adequate reserves for receivables, (f) failed to write off certain assets, (g) failed to account for the proposed discontinuation of certain product lines, (h) misrepresented Ampex's prospects for future earnings."

The plaintiffs estimate that there are some 45 documents issued during the period containing the financial reporting complained of, including two annual reports, six quarterly reports, and various press releases and SEC filings.

Because the alleged misrepresentations are contained in a number of different documents, each pertaining to a different period of Ampex's operation, the defendants argue that purchasers throughout the class period do not present common issues of law or fact. They reason that proof of 10b–5 liability will require inspection of the underlying set of facts to determine the falsity of the impression given by any particular accounting item presented; that the underlying facts fluctuate as the business operates (*i.e.,* inventory is bought and sold, accounts are paid off and created); thus, proof of the actionability of a current accounting representation or omission will apply only to those who purchased while a financial report was current; from which they conclude no common question is presented and a class is improper.

We disagree. The overwhelming weight of authority holds that repeated misrepresentations of the sort alleged here satisfy the "common question" requirement. Confronted with a class of purchasers allegedly defrauded over a period of time by similar misrepresentations, courts have taken the common sense approach that the class is united by a common interest in determining whether a defendant's course of conduct is in its broad outlines actionable, which is not defeated by slight differences in class members' positions, and that the issue may profitably be tried in one suit.

* * *

While the nature of the interrelationship and the degree of similarity which must obtain between different representations in order to come within the outer boundaries of the "common course of conduct" test is somewhat unclear,[19] the test is more than satisfied when a series of financial reports uniformly misrepresent a particular item in the financial statement. In that situation, the misrepresentations are "interrelated, interdependent, and cumulative;" "[l]ike standing dominoes . . . one misrepresentation . . . cause[s] subsequent statements to fall into inaccuracy and distortion when considered by themselves or compared with previous misstatements."

Precisely such a situation is alleged here in at least three respects— the failure to create adequate reserves for uncollectible accounts receivable and for contractually guaranteed royalty payments, and the overstatement of inventory. The 1972 Annual Report shows writedowns of $31.9 million as provision for royalty guarantees, $11.8 million for uncollectible accounts receivable, and $15 million for inventory. Plaintiffs allege that the writedowns had roots tracing back to the beginning

19. Because plaintiffs have alleged specific strands of misrepresentation running throughout financial statements of the class period, they are well within whatever the outer boundaries might be, and we need not resolve the issue. We note, however, that a number of courts have apparently held that allegations simply that earnings and stock price have been inflated over a period of time by a defendant's misrepresentations is sufficient to satisfy the common question requirement (although the cases are somewhat unclear because they fail to specify the precise misrepresentations which allegedly inflated earnings). Appellants point out that allegation of inflation of earnings or price is conclusory, and may derive from altogether unrelated misrepresentations. In their view the common question requirement is met only if all purchasers are injured by the same misrepresentation, or, in a "course of conduct" case, by identical repeated misrepresentations, and if defendant's liability can be established by proof both of the same set of facts and same legal principle. We think that is far too restrictive a view of the common question requirement in the securities fraud context. Rule 10b–5 liability is not restricted solely to isolated misrepresentations or omissions; it may also be predicated on a "practice, or course of business which operates . . . as a fraud . . ." Under that section class members may well be united in establishing liability for fraudulently creating an illusion of prosperity and false expectations.

Moreover, even when misrepresentations are unrelated, class members may share a common question of law or fact. Of course, if an early misrepresentation is undissipat- ed, a later purchaser will present a common question even if another misrepresentation has intervened. But even if the effect of the earlier misrepresentation is dissipated, proof of the earlier misrepresentation may be relevant to the latter purchaser's case. Proof of the earlier fraud and its effects might be relevant circumstantially to establish duty standards, culpability, or damages regarding the later fraud; it would establish background information about the defendant common to both suits. Thus, even when unrelated misrepresentations are alleged as part of a common scheme, class members may share common factual questions, and trial in the same forum avoids duplicative proof. That is a major purpose of a class action; the "common question" requirement should be interpreted to obtain that objective. Naturally, when the component misrepresentations of a "course of conduct" fraud are unrelated, a great many more non-common questions exist. In that situation no representative's claim may be typical of the rest of the class, Rule 23(a)(3), although that depends on how broadly that requirement is construed. We think it is for the predominance and other requirements of Rule 23(b)(3), rather than the common question requirement, to function to keep the balance between the economies attained and lost by allowing a class action. The common question requirement should not be restrictively interpreted to attain that objective, particularly as to do so would eliminate the class action deterrent for those who engage in complicated and imaginative rather than straightforward schemes to inflate stock prices.

of the class period, an allegation somewhat borne out by the auditors' withdrawal of certification of the 1971 report because of uncertainty that the huge losses reported in 1972 were the product of 1972 business operations, and not attributable to earlier years. Plaintiffs contend that the company's financial reports throughout the period uniformly and fraudulently failed to establish reserves in amounts adequate to satisfy accepted accounting principles, injuring all purchasers of the consequently inflated stock.

In this aspect, plaintiffs allege a source of inflation common to every purchaser. The creation of a reserve is of course simply an adjustment made to the balance sheet and income statement to provide a more realistic view of the business and its operations. Failure in any particular period to recognize that a portion of the accounts receivable generated in that period are uncollectible, and to create or adjust a reserve, will have the effect of inflating the balance sheet assets and surplus, and overstating the income for the period; likewise failure to recognize accrued liabilities for royalty payments will inflate surplus by understating liabilities, and will overstate income. Naturally, any inflation in the stock price due to inadequate reserves will persist until the reserves become adequate or until the losses are in fact written off.

Defendants nevertheless contend that a class is improper because each purchaser must depend on proof of a different set of accounting facts to establish the inadequacy of the reserves at the time he bought. Defendants misconceive the requirement for a class action; all that is required is a common issue of law *or* fact. Even were we to assume that the reserves were at some points during the period adequate, the class members still would be united by a common interest in the application to their unique situation of the accounting and legal principles requiring adequate reserves—*i.e.*, by a common question of law. Here, however, in light of the progressive deterioration of Ampex's financial position and the magnitude of the losses at the end of the period, even the fact that reserves were in reality inadequate throughout much if not all of the period may not be in serious dispute; rather, the question will be whether the inadequacy was in some sense culpable because the contingencies which proved them inadequate were foreseen or foreseeable.

The alleged inventory overvaluation likewise presents common issues. Defendants again contend it does not because the valuation of any particular period's closing inventory involves a process of physical estimation based on that inventory's characteristics, and that overstatement of one period's closing inventory, while overstating that period's income, will have an opposite effect on the next period's income by overstating opening inventory, deflating rather than inflating stock price. While true in the abstract, appellants' position disregards the real substance of the plaintiffs' complaint which is again highlighted by the 1972 Report. In explaining the $15 million writedown, the company stated: "Inventories of stereo tapes more than six months old and more than one year old were written down 50% and 100% respectively . . . No significant writedowns of this nature were made in the prior year."

Plaintiffs thus are complaining of the balance sheet effect of inventory overvaluation. They are alleging that by failing throughout the class period to recognize and account for inventory obsolescence each time the inventory was valued, the company consistently inflated the value at which it carried inventory on the balance sheet. In effect, plaintiffs are complaining of a consistent disregard of the accounting principle that inventory be valued at "lower of cost or market." Again, common questions of law and facts are presented.

* * *

2. PREDOMINANCE AND RELIANCE

Defendants contend that any common questions which may exist do not predominate over individual questions of reliance and damages.

The amount of damages is invariably an individual question and does not defeat class action treatment. Moreover, in this situation we are confident that should the class prevail the amount of price inflation during the period can be charted and the process of computing individual damages will be virtually a mechanical task.

Individual questions of reliance are likewise not an impediment—subjective reliance is not a distinct element of proof of 10b–5 claims of the type involved in this case.

The class members' substantive claims either are, or can be, cast in omission or non-disclosure terms—the company's financial reporting failed to disclose the need for reserves, conditions reflecting on the value of the inventory, or other facts necessary to make the reported figures not misleading. The Court has recognized that under such circumstances

> "involving primarily a failure to disclose, positive proof of reliance is not a prerequisite to recovery. All that is necessary is that the facts withheld be material in the sense that a reasonable investor might have considered them important in the making of this decision. This obligation to disclose and this withholding of a material fact establish the requisite element of causation in fact."

Affiliated Ute Citizens of Utah v. United States, 406 U.S. 128, 153–154, 92 S.Ct. 1456, 1472, 31 L.Ed.2d 741 (1972).

Moreover, proof of subjective reliance on particular misrepresentations is unnecessary to establish a 10b–5 claim for a deception inflating the price of stock traded in the open market. Proof of reliance is adduced to demonstrate the causal connection between the defendant's wrongdoing and the plaintiff's loss. We think causation is adequately established in the impersonal stock exchange context by proof of purchase and of the materiality of misrepresentations, without direct proof of reliance. Materiality circumstantially establishes the reliance of some market traders and hence the inflation in the stock price—when the purchase is made the causational chain between defendant's conduct and plaintiff's loss is sufficiently established to make out a prima facie case.

* * *

We merely recognize that individual "transactional causation" can in these circumstances be inferred from the materiality of the misrepresentation, and shift to defendant the burden of disproving a prima facie case of causation. Defendants may do so in at least 2 ways: 1) by disproving materiality or by proving that, despite materiality, an insufficient number of traders relied to inflate the price; and 2) by proving that an individual plaintiff purchased despite knowledge of the falsity of a representation, or that he would have had he known of it.

* * *

Here, we eliminate the requirement that plaintiffs prove reliance directly in this context because the requirement imposes an unreasonable and irrelevant evidentiary burden. A purchaser on the stock exchanges may be either unaware of a specific false representation, or may not directly rely on it; he may purchase because of a favorable price trend, price earnings ratio, or some other factor. Nevertheless, he relies generally on the supposition that the market price is validly set and that no unsuspected manipulation has artificially inflated the price, and thus indirectly on the truth of the representations underlying the stock price—whether he is aware of it or not, the price he pays reflects material misrepresentations. Requiring direct proof from each purchaser that he relied on a particular representation when purchasing would defeat recovery by those whose reliance was indirect, despite the fact that the causational chain is broken only if the purchaser would have purchased the stock even had he known of the misrepresentation. We decline to leave such open market purchasers unprotected. The statute and rule are designed to foster an expectation that securities markets are free from fraud—an expectation on which purchasers should be able to rely.

Thus, in this context we think proof of reliance means at most a requirement that plaintiff prove directly that he would have acted differently had he known the true facts. That is a requirement of proof of a speculative negative (I would not have bought had I known) precisely parallel to that held unnecessary in *Affiliated Ute* and *Mills* [*v. Electric Auto–Lite Co.*, 396 U.S. 375, 90 S.Ct. 616, 24 L.Ed.2d 593 (1970)] (I would not have sold had I known). We reject it here for the same reasons. Direct proof would inevitably be somewhat pro forma, and impose a difficult evidentiary burden, because addressed to a speculative possibility in an area where motivations are complex and difficult to determine. That difficulty threatens to defeat valid claims—implicit in *Affiliated Ute* is a rejection of the burden because it leads to underinclusive recoveries and thereby threatens the enforcement of the securities laws. Here, the requirement is redundant—the same causal nexus can be adequately established indirectly, by proof of materiality coupled with the common sense that a stock purchaser does not ordinarily seek to purchase a loss in the form of artificially inflated stock. Under those circumstances we think it appropriate to eliminate the burden.

Defendants contend that elimination of individual proof of subjective reliance alters and abridges their substantive rights in violation of the Rules Enabling Act, 28 U.S.C. § 2072. The obvious answer is that the standards of proof of causation we have set out apply to all fraud on the market cases, individual as well as class actions. No interpretation of Rule 23 is involved, and the Rules Enabling Act limitation is not implicated.[24]

3. CONFLICTS

Defendants' final major argument is that conflicts among class members preclude class certification. They contend that the interests of class members in proving damages from price inflation (and hence the existence and materiality of misrepresentations subsumed in proving inflation) irreconcilably conflict, because some class members will desire to maximize the inflation existing on a given date while others will desire to minimize it. For example, they posit that a purchaser early in the class period who later sells will desire to maximize the deflation due to an intervening corrective disclosure in order to maximize his out of pocket damages, but in so doing will conflict with his purchaser, who is interested in maximizing the inflation in the price he pays. We agree that class members might at some point during this litigation have differing interests. We altogether disagree, for a spate of reasons, that such potential conflicts afford a valid reason at this time for refusing to certify the class.

Defendants' position depends entirely on adoption of the out of pocket loss measure of damages, rather than a rescissory measure. Under the out of pocket standard each purchaser recovers the difference between the inflated price paid and the value received, plus interest on the difference. If the stock is resold at an inflated price the purchaser-seller's damages, limited by § 28(a) of the Act, 15 U.S.C. § 78bb(a), to "actual damages," must be diminished by the inflation he recovers from his purchaser. Thus, he is interested in proving that some intervening event, such as a corrective release, had diminished the inflation persisting in the stock price when he sold.

While out of pocket loss is the ordinary standard in a 10b–5 suit, it is within the discretion of the district judge in appropriate circumstances to apply a rescissory measure, or to allow consequential damages. It is for the district judge, after becoming aware of the nature of the case, to determine the appropriate measure of damages in the first instance; the possible creation of potential conflicts by that decision does not render

---

24. Indeed, we could, in the exercise of our Article III jurisdiction, transform the 10b–5 suit from its present private compensatory mold by predicating liability to purchasers solely on the materiality of a misrepresentation (*i.e.,* economic damage) regardless of transactional causation, without implicating the Enabling Act limitation.

the class inappropriate now. The Rule provides the mechanism of subsequent creation of subclasses, Rule 23(c)(4), to deal with latent conflicts which may surface as the suit progresses. As a result, courts have generally declined to consider conflicts, particularly as they regard damages, sufficient to defeat class action status at the outset unless the conflict is apparent, imminent, and on an issue at the very heart of the suit.

Here, the conflict, if any, is peripheral, and substantially outweighed by the class members' common interests. Even assuming *arguendo* that the out of pocket standard applies, the class is proper. Every class member shares an overriding common interest in establishing the existence and materiality of misrepresentations. The major portion of the inflation alleged is attributed to causes which allegedly persisted throughout the class period. It will be in the interest of each class member to maximize the inflation from those causes at every point in the class period, both to demonstrate the *sine qua non*—liability—and to maximize his own potential damages—the more the stock is inflated, the more every class member stands to recover. Moreover, because the major portion of the inflation is attributed to causes persisting throughout the period, interim corrective disclosures (of which there appear to have been only two or three) do not necessarily bring predisclosure purchasers into conflict with post-disclosure purchasers. Because both share an interest in maximizing overall inflation, the latter purchaser will no doubt strive to show a substantial market effect from disclosure of the lesser (or partial) causes of inflation to maximize the inflation attributable to more serious causes persisting when he bought—a showing which will increase the recovery of the earlier purchaser. In that light, any conflicting interests in tracing fluctuations in inflation during the class period are secondary, and do not bar class litigation to advance predominantly common interests. Courts faced with the same situation have repeatedly, either explicitly or implicitly, rejected defendants' position, for the potential conflict is present in most prolonged classes involving a series of misrepresentations.

In support of that conclusion, we note that Rule 23 makes no mention of conflicts. The Rule's requirements are that the representative's claims be "typical" and that the class be "fairly and adequately" represented—claims need not be coextensive. Those requirements are in part constitutionally dictated, as due process requires, in order to give collateral res judicata effect to a judgment against class members, that their interests have been adequately represented in the class action. *Hansberry v. Lee,* 311 U.S. 32, 61 S.Ct. 115, 85 L.Ed. 22 (1940) [*infra* p. 285].

Hansberry does not, however, as defendants seem to assume, dictate that any divergence of interest among class members violates due process (thereby necessarily requiring an identity of interests to satisfy Rule 23's adequacy of representation and typicality requirements). Neither the Rule's requirements nor those of due process are so inflexible. The due process touchstone of adequacy and fairness of representation must be judged in light of the seriousness and extent of conflicts involved compared to the importance of issues uniting the class; the alternatives to class representation available; the procedures available to limit and prevent unfairness; and any other facts bearing on the fairness with which the absent class member is represented.

Hansberry is not controlling here—in *Hansberry* there was nothing to satisfy due process. Not only were the members of the purported class of property owners diametrically opposed on the central issue—the validity of racial covenants restricting their property—but the state class action procedure provided absent class members no notice. Here, on the other hand, under the notice and opt-out procedure of Rule 23(b)(3) and 23(c)(2), an absent class member may evaluate his position in the class and decide for himself whether to avail himself of the representation offered. The potential conflicts are at most peripheral. And the district judge will retain constant supervision, through his powers under Rule 23(d) and (e), and through his ability to decertify or create sub-classes, to assure fairness of representation. Finally, and unlike numerous cases in which even one representative has been held adequate to represent a prolonged class, the class members here will be represented by numerous named representatives, with substantial personal stakes, who purchased throughout the class period, and who thus will probably represent whatever conflicting interests there are in the development of plaintiffs' trial strategies. In light of those various factors, we agree with the district judge that the class representatives are typical and will adequately and fairly represent the class.

Notes and Questions

1. Some courts have been quite partial to class actions in securities cases: "Class actions are a particularly appropriate and desirable means to resolve claims based on the securities laws, 'since the effectiveness of the securities laws may depend in large measure on the application of the class action device. * * * [T]he interests of justice require that in a doubtful case . . . any error, if there is to be one, be committed in favor of allowing a class action.'" Eisenberg v. Gagnon, 766 F.2d 770, 785 (3d Cir.1985), quoting Kahan v. Rosenstiel, 424 F.2d 161, 169 (3d Cir.1970), cert. denied, 398 U.S. 950, 90 S.Ct. 1870, 26 L.Ed.2d 290 (1970).

Congress was less enthusiastic about securities fraud class actions, however, and in 1995 passed the Private Securities Litigation Reform Act, which imposes new requirements on securities fraud plaintiffs. Some of these requirements, like upgraded pleading, apply whether or not a suit was brought as a class actions. See Marcus, The Puzzling Persistence of Pleading Practice, 72 Texas L. Rev. 1749 (1998). Other provisions target class actions, particularly provisions regarding control of the case by the lawyer who first files suit. See *infra* pp. 292-93. For general background, see Perino, Did the Private Securities Litigation Reform Act Work?, 2003 U.Ill.L.Rev. 913; Cox, Making Securities Fraud Class Actions Virtuous, 39 Az. L. Rev. 497 (1997).

2. In Basic Inc. v. Levinson, 485 U.S. 224, 108 S.Ct. 978, 99 L.Ed.2d 194 (1988), a 4–2 decision, the Court endorsed class-wide handling of the

reliance issue in many cases by adopting the "fraud on the market" theory. In this securities fraud action, plaintiffs complained of defendants' failure to disclose pending merger negotiations. Citing Blackie v. Barrack in a footnote, the plurality stated that "nearly every court that has considered the proposition has concluded that where materially misleading statements have been disseminated into an impersonal, well-developed market for securities, the reliance of individual plaintiffs on the integrity of the market may be presumed." Id. at 247, 108 S.Ct. at 991. The Court added, however, that "[a]ny showing that severs the link between the alleged misrepresentation and either the price received (or paid) by the plaintiff, or his decision to trade at a fair market price, will be sufficient to rebut the presumption of reliance." Id. at 248, 108 S.Ct. at 992. In dissent, Justice White argued that "in practice the Court must realize * * * that such rebuttal is virtually impossible in all but the most extraordinary case. See Blackie v. Barrack." Id. at 256 n. 7, 108 S.Ct. at 996 n. 7. See also Knapp v. Ernst & Whinney, 90 F.3d 1431 (9th Cir.1996) (suggesting that market inflation shows that sophisticated investors did rely); compare Binder v. Gillespie, 184 F.3d 1059 (9th Cir.1999) (fraud on the market theory not allowed regarding stock sold over the counter); Mirkin v. Wasserman, 5 Cal.4th 1082, 23 Cal.Rptr.2d 101, 858 P.2d 568 (1993) (rejecting fraud on the market theory for common law fraud claims arising from alleged manipulation of stock prices).

3. The court in *Blackie* focuses on misrepresentations as to an adequate reserve and inventory made in reports, press releases, and S.E.C. filings. Would it matter if different figures were given to different class members about the size of the reserve or the inventory? If some purchasers were told that these figures were uncertain or based on an optimistic projection, would they be disqualified as class members? What about purchasers who received inside information that the figures were not correct?

In Crasto v. Kaskel's Estate, 63 F.R.D. 18 (S.D.N.Y.1974), a securities class action was brought on behalf of all the tenants of a cooperative apartment. Plaintiffs alleged they purchased shares in it on the basis of misrepresentations, but the court, in refusing to certify the class, stressed that a variety of different oral and written statements were involved:

Unlike the common securities fraud case, in which a series of documents repeat identical or similar misrepresentations, here, each group of purchasers was relying on a materially different set of documents. When we include the alleged press releases, selling materials and written announcements, which may or may not have reached all the members of the class, the picture becomes even more jumbled and varied. Thus, it seems clear that the alleged misrepresentations are not common to the class even as to the written materials issued by defendants.

The variations in the written material might be remedied by the creation of subclasses, pursuant to Rule 23(c)(4), each subclass containing persons who purchased during similar time periods and who relied on similar representations. Subclasses cannot solve the problem of material variation in these cases, however, because plaintiffs' actions rest in part, at least, on oral misrepresentations.

* * *

Oral representations, by their very nature, differ from person to person, especially where, as here, they are made by and to different people. Thus, at trial, in order to prove that the representations were made, plaintiffs would be required to call each class member who was allegedly deceived by oral representations. We conclude, therefore, that the question of misrepresentation here is an individual, not a common question.

The question of reliance, or causation, also raises serious problems. Although the issues of reliance and damages can await a prior and separate trial of the common issues in a class action, the very nature of the transactions involved here complicates the problem.

4. In Ballan v. Upjohn Co., 159 F.R.D. 473 (W.D.Mich.1994), the court found class certification improper in a securities fraud suit due to conflicts among class members based on when they bought. The court distinguished *Blackie* on the ground that the curative disclosures were relatively ineffective there, while here the curative announcements were effective in causing a much larger decline in the price of the stock. Compare McDonnell Douglas Corporation Securities Litigation, 98 F.R.D. 613 (E.D.Mo.1982), holding that differences in time of purchase did not create irreconcilable conflicts between class members because "[p]laintiffs have a common interest in determining whether a defendant's conduct is actionable in general. *See Blackie v. Barrack.* This is especially true when plaintiffs allege a common course of conduct by defendants. Plaintiffs will attempt to show that each defendant failed to disclose material information about MDC's financial status. In other words, it is a common interest of plaintiffs as a class to show defendants' knowledge of material undisclosed facts before the beginning of the class period, or early in it."

5. Subclassing can sometimes be a solution to commonality and conflict problems caused by potential differences between class members. By subclassing, additional class representatives can be added to the suit to represent a subclass with a more discrete commonality of interests. "By dividing a class, a judge may be able to redefine the responsibilities of class attorneys and named plaintiffs in terms of the interests of distinct and relatively unified portions of a class. The necessity for the ranking of class interests by the parties may therefore diminish, and the likelihood that diverse absentee interests will be presented to the court increase. * * * Subclassing is possible only if different class members coalesce into discrete, identifiable groups. Not all differences among class members, however, will divide along such clear lines. State of mind differences provide an obvious example. Class members may disagree, for example, over the relief that should be sought, or even over whether suit should be brought at all. But while this disagreement may be quite real, it may not be possible for a court to associate it with any particular subset of the class membership." Developments in the Law—Class Actions, 89 Harv.L.Rev. 1318, 1479–82 (1976).

Subclassing does not obviate a careful Rule 23 analysis. To the contrary, "the litigation as to each subclass is treated as a separate law suit. * * * Under the provisions of Rule 23(c)(4)(B), a class may be divided into subclasses and each subclass treated as a class with the provisions of the rule to be construed and applied accordingly to each class." Betts v. Reliable

Collection Agency, Limited, 659 F.2d 1000 (9th Cir.1981). Thus there must be a proper class representative for each subclass, and all other requirements of Rule 23 must be satisfied.

6. Class certification may not be appropriate due to individualized defenses under the doctrine enunciated in Gary Plastic Packaging Corp. v. Merrill Lynch, Pierce, Fenner & Smith, 903 F.2d 176, 179–80 (2d Cir.1990), cert. denied, 498 U.S. 1025, 111 S.Ct. 675, 112 L.Ed.2d 667 (1991) (certification denied because of "danger that absent class members will suffer if their representative is preoccupied with defenses unique to it"). See Hanon v. Dataproducts Corp., 976 F.2d 497, 506–07 (9th Cir.1992) (named plaintiff who had previously bought shares of stock and then filed derivative suits may be subject to defenses not available against other class members); Kovaleff v. Piano, 142 F.R.D. 406, 408 (S.D.N.Y.1992) (no typicality due to the fact that the increase in his holdings in the stock by the named plaintiff after some disclosure of the alleged fraud raised defenses that could adversely impact the interests of the class); Hoexter v. Simmons, 140 F.R.D. 416, 422–23 (D.Ariz.1991) (no typicality where unique defenses could be raised against named plaintiffs); Rolex Employees Retirement Trust v. Mentor Graphics Corp., 136 F.R.D. 658, 664 (D.Or.1991) ("The certification of a class is questionable where it is predictable that a major focus of the litigation will be on an arguable defense unique to the named plaintiff or to a subclass.")

SMILOW v. SOUTHWESTERN BELL MOBILE SYSTEMS, INC.

United States Court of Appeals, First Circuit, 2003.
323 F.3d 32.

Before LYNCH, LIPES, and Howard, Circuit Judges.

LYNCH, Circuit Judge.

This is an appeal from a decision decertifying a class action brought by and on behalf of wireless phone customers of Cellular One, the doing-business name of Southwestern Bell Mobile Systems, Inc. The putative class members are Massachusetts and New Hampshire residents who were charged for incoming calls despite having signed a standard form contract, used mainly between August 1994 and February 1996, purportedly guaranteeing free incoming call service.

Class representative Jill Ann Smilow brought suit in 1997 for breach of contract and violations of Massachusetts General Laws chapter 93A, §§ 2(a), 9, 11 (West 1997), and the Telecommunications Act (TCA) of 1996, 47 U.S.C. § 201(b) (2000). The district court first certified and then decertified the contract, ch. 93A, and TCA classes. * * * We reverse.

Smilow and proposed class representative Margaret L. Bibeau each signed a standard form contract for cellular telephone services with Cellular One in 1995. The form contract says, "Chargeable time for calls originated by a Mobile Subscriber Unit starts when the Mobile Subscriber Unit signals call initiation to C1's facilities and ends when the Mobile

Subscriber Unit signals call disconnect to C1's facilities and the call disconnect signal has been confirmed." The parties contest the meaning of "originated." Smilow alleges that this language precludes Cellular One from charging for incoming calls. It is undisputed that a large group of Cellular One customers signed the same contract and were subject to charges for incoming calls. The contract contains an integration clause providing that changes must be in writing and signed by both parties.

Smilow and Bibeau purport to represent a class of Massachusetts and New Hampshire residents who subscribed for Cellular One services under this contract. The potential class members all signed the standard form contract, which was in broad use from August 1994 to February 1996. They did have a variety of rate plans and usage patterns. Some Cellular One customers paid a flat fee for a fixed number of minutes each month and an additional per-minute charge if they exceeded this fixed amount of air time (for example, $40/month for the first 300 minutes/month and 10 cents/minute thereafter). Many Cellular One customers paid different rates for day and night-time calls.

Cellular One charged Smilow, Bibeau and the potential class members for incoming as well as outgoing calls. Smilow received just one incoming call; Bibeau received many incoming calls. Cellular One invoices clearly indicate that customers are charged for incoming calls. The user guide mailed to new Cellular One customers also states that the company charges for both incoming and outgoing calls. Bibeau paid her invoices knowing she was being charged for incoming calls.

On February 11, 1997, Smilow, as a purported class representative, filed suit in federal district court against Cellular One for breach of contract and violations of ch. 93A and the TCA. The district court had jurisdiction over the federal claims under 28 U.S.C. § 1331 (2000) and over the state law claims under 28 U.S.C. § 1367. The district court originally certified the ch. 93A, breach of contract, and TCA classes on October 9, 1998.

[Thereafter, plaintiffs moved to substitute Bibeau as a new class representative, but defendant opposed this motion on the ground that common issues of fact did not predominate, and therefore neither Bibeau nor any other individual could properly represent the class. The court denied the motion to substitute Bibeau as class represented and decertified the class. Regarding the breach of contract claim, it reasoned that proof that Cellular One customers in Massachusetts and New Hampshire (evidently estimated by plaintiffs to number 275,000) paid for incoming calls did not show any specific amount of damages because phone services were probably provided for those charges. It also concluded that plaintiffs had not shown that causation or the amount of damages could be proven from defendant's records:

> To be a "common issue" in the relevant sense, the issue must be one that does not require separate dispute resolution processes for different individuals who are said to have claims in "common."

In a later opinion, the district court rejected class certification on the ch. 93A claim for two reasons. First, the court held that the class members would fall into two groups: those who waived actual damages in favor of statutory damages of $25 and those who claimed actual damages, which it took to mean that the fact that actual damages could be easily calculated by computer was irrelevant. Second, the court held that individual issues predominated on causation, relying on its earlier rationale that, whatever the common contractual language, "services were received in return for the billed payments." It reasoned that supposed individual differences in the damages calculations showed that causation had no common issues.

Plaintiffs appealed the decertification, and the Court of Appeals agreed to hear the appeal under Rule 23(f) (discussed *infra* p. 370).]

THE PREDOMINANCE REQUIREMENT

The district court's decertification of the classes for the contract, ch. 93A, and TCA claims, as well as its denial of the motion to substitute a new class representative, all rested on fundamental errors of law and fact. Once these errors are corrected, it becomes clear that common issues as to both liability and damages predominate on the elements of the breach of contract and ch. 93A claims. We first consider the contract claim.

BREACH OF CONTRACT CLAIM

The first error was initially contained in the following statement from the district court's March 22, 2001 opinion decertifying the class:

Proof of charges and payments is not evidence of harm or an amount of harm on the basis of which damages could be awarded in the face of (i) a strong likelihood that services were received in return for billed payments and (ii) lack of admissible evidence to rebut that strong likelihood. * * *

From this statement we understand the district court to have believed that the defendant would be entitled to payment for incoming calls on a theory of quantum meruit even if plaintiffs were to prevail on their breach of contract claim. Under the doctrine of quantum meruit, one who renders goods or services in the absence of an enforceable contract may be entitled to payment for those services to the extent the recipient benefitted from them. "If the plaintiff is entitled to recover on a contract, he cannot recover in quantum meruit." Marshall v. Stratus Pharms., Inc., 51 Mass.App.Ct. 667, 749 N.E.2d 698, 703 n. 6 (2001). Though we do not decide the question here, it would similarly seem that where a defendant is clearly not due payment under the terms of an enforceable contract, such defendant cannot claim a right to payment under quantum meruit. "Where ... there is an enforceable express or implied in fact contract that regulates the relations of the parties or that part of their relations about which issues have arisen, there is no room for quasi contract." A.L. Corbin, Corbin on Contracts § 1.20 (J.M. Perillo ed., rev'd ed.1993).

The district court's reliance on the doctrine of quantum meruit led it to overlook questions of law and fact common to all class members. As plaintiffs' brief says, "The plaintiffs' claims are based entirely on a standard form contract which the defendant used with every member of the class." The common factual basis is found in the terms of the contract, which are identical for all class members. The common question of law is whether those terms precluded defendant from charging for incoming calls.

Cellular One's waiver defense is also common to the class. "[A]ffirmative defenses should be considered in making class certification decisions." Again, both the factual basis for and the legal defense of waiver present common issues for all class members.[7] All class members received a user guide and monthly invoices showing that defendant charged the class members for the incoming calls.

Even in the unlikely event that individual waiver determinations prove necessary, the proposed class may still satisfy the predominance requirement. Courts traditionally have been reluctant to deny class action status under Rule 23(b)(3) simply because affirmative defenses may be available against individual members.

Instead, where common issues otherwise predominated, courts have usually certified Rule 23(b)(3) classes even though individual issues were present in one or more affirmative defenses. See, e.g., In re Visa Check/MasterMoney Antitrust Litig., 280 F.3d 124, 138–40 (2d Cir.2001). After all, Rule 23(b)(3) requires merely that common issues predominate, not that all issues be common to the class. If, moreover, evidence later shows that an affirmative defense is likely to bar claims against at least some class members, then a court has available adequate procedural mechanisms. In re Visa Check/MasterMoney Antitrust Litig., 280 F.3d at 141 (describing procedural options and collecting authorities). For example, it can place class members with potentially barred claims in a separate subclass, or exclude them from the class altogether.

Cellular One argues that even if there are common questions of law and fact, the district court did not abuse its discretion by decertifying the class because individual issues predominate on damages. This is largely an issue of whether plaintiffs could use a computer program to extract from Cellular One's computer records information about individual damages. The district court viewed this question as mostly beside the point and its decertification orders rested mainly on other grounds.

The individuation of damages in consumer class actions is rarely determinative under Rule 23(b)(3). Where, as here, common questions predominate regarding liability, then courts generally find the predomi-

---

7. At oral argument defendant first advanced and then wisely withdrew the argument that oral representations made by sales representatives to potential customers would vary the contract terms by customer and so defeat commonality. The contract contains an integration clause.

nance requirement to be satisfied even if individual damages issues remain. In re Visa Check/MasterMoney Antitrust Litig., 280 F.3d at 139; see Blackie v. Barrack, 524 F.2d 891, 905 (9th Cir.1975) [*supra* p. 246] ("The amount of damages is invariably an individual question and does not defeat class action treatment.").[8]

There is even less reason to decertify a class where the possible existence of individual damages issues is a matter of conjecture. Common issues predominate where individual factual determinations can be accomplished using computer records, clerical assistance, and objective criteria—thus rendering unnecessary an evidentiary hearing on each claim.

Still, the parties here dispute whether it will be possible to establish breach, causation, and damages using a mechanical process. Cellular One argues that Smilow has not shown that she could use defendant's computer records either to distinguish the subset of incoming call recipients who exceeded their monthly allotment of "free" minutes or to calculate how much extra each class member was charged as a result of receiving incoming calls.

The plaintiffs' expert, Erik Buchakian, says he could fashion a computer program that would extract from Cellular One's records (1) a list of customers who received incoming calls during the class period; (2) a list of customers who paid extra during the class period because they were billed for incoming calls; and (3) actual damages for each class member during the class period. Buchakian had access to more than adequate materials—including a sample computer tape and the deposition of defendant's expert—and has more than adequate expertise—degrees in business and computer science and thirteen years of relevant work experience. The affidavits of defendant's expert, Susan Quintiliani, are consistent with Buchakian's conclusions.

If later evidence disproves Buchakian's proposition, the district court can at that stage modify or decertify the class, or use a variety of management devices. Indeed, even if individualized determinations were necessary to calculate damages, Rule (23)(c)(4)(A) would still allow the court to maintain the class action with respect to other issues. See, e.g., In re Visa Check/MasterMoney Antitrust Litig., 280 F.3d at 141; Jenkins v. Raymark Indus., Inc., 782 F.2d 468, 470–71 (5th Cir.1986) [*infra* p. 331].

Consideration of the policy goals underlying Rule 23(b)(3) also supports class certification. The class certification prerequisites should be construed in light of the underlying objectives of class actions. Rule 23(b)(3) is intended to be a less stringent requirement than Rule 23(b)(1) or (b)(2). See Amchem Prods., Inc. [v. Windsor], 521 U.S. at 615, 117 S.Ct. 2231 [*infra* p. 373] ("Framed for situations in which class-action treatment is not as clearly called for as it is in Rule 23(b)(1) and (b)(2) situations, Rule 23(b)(3) permits certification where class suit may

---

8. Courts have denied class certification where these individual damages issues are especially complex or burdensome. That does not appear to be the case here.

nevertheless be convenient and desirable.'') The core purpose of Rule 23(b)(3) is to vindicate the claims of consumers and other groups of people whose individual claims would be too small to warrant litigation.[9]

In this case, the claims of most if not all class members are too small to vindicate individually. Smilow, for example, received just a single incoming call and so can obtain only minimal contract damages.

Overall, we find that common issues of law and fact predominate here. The case turns on interpretation of the form contract, executed by all class members and defendant. See W.D. Henderson, Reconciling the Juridical Links Doctrine with the Federal Rules of Civil Procedure and Article III, 67 U. Chi. L.Rev. 1347, 1373–74 (2000) (the fact that prospective class members signed nearly identical consumer contracts might, in itself, satisfy the predominance requirement).

THE CH. 93A CLASS

The decertification of the ch. 93A class is similarly flawed: it also rests on the premise that individual inquiries would be required because "services were received" for the charges on incoming calls.

As plaintiffs' brief says, "the Ch. 93A claim is not an oral misrepresentation claim, but [is] based on the same standard form contract which was signed by all class members." See generally Anthony's Pier Four, Inc. v. HBC Assoc., 411 Mass. 451, 583 N.E.2d 806, 821 (1991) ("[C]onduct in disregard of known contractual arrangements and intended to secure benefits for the breaching party constitutes an unfair act or practice for ch. 93A purposes."). Cellular One points to law to the effect that a mere breach of contract is not a ch. 93A violation. That defense, though, argues for, not against, the commonality of liability issues. Plaintiffs disclaim any intent to rely on oral misrepresentations, and must adhere to that position or risk losing class status.[10]

Our prior discussion is adequate to dispose of any argument that decertification would be required because of a need for individual damages determinations. Since Smilow can compute actual damages using a computer program, we need not address plaintiffs' argument that common issues would predominate only on a claim for statutory damages, and not on a claim for individual damages.[11] As to statutory damages, the

9. Classes such as this one that are made up of consumers are especially likely to satisfy the predominance requirement. See Amchem Prods., Inc., 521 U.S. at 625, 117 S.Ct. 2231 (observing that the predominance requirement is especially likely to be satisfied in consumer fraud and antitrust actions).

10. We doubt that defendants will rely on oral representations. If its sales representatives, familiar with the terms of the contract, represented that there would be a charge for incoming calls without notifying the consumers that the contract language could be read differently, that could be viewed as evidence in plaintiffs' favor of an unfair or deceptive act. If the sales representatives represented that there would be no charge for incoming calls and the customer was charged, then that is also evidence in plaintiffs' favor.

11. Section 9 allows plaintiffs to recover the greater of actual damages or twenty-five dollars; Section 11 allows plaintiffs to recover actual damages. Both sections allow plaintiffs to recover double or treble damages if the violations were willful or knowing or if the refusal to grant relief upon demand was made in bad faith. Mass. Gen. Laws ch. 93A, §§ 9(3), 11.

Supreme Judicial Court has held that plaintiffs who cannot show actual damages under ch. 93A may nonetheless obtain statutory damages if liability is established. This too supports class certification.

We are left with the district court's concern that any ch. 93A class would be composed of two groups: a statutory damages group and an actual damages group. But plaintiffs' position is that should any conflict develop between the two groups, the action would seek only statutory damages, class members would be given notice to that effect, and those who wish to pursue individual claims for actual damages could opt-out. We agree this is an option and, in this context, the hypothetical conflict provides no basis for decertification.

[The court concluded that plaintiffs had waived their federal TCA claim by failing to pursue it on appeal.]

Notes and Questions

1. The court invokes the policies underlying Rule 23 as reasons for favoring certification in consumer class actions. Are there counter-arguments? Some express concern that class actions may be vehicles for enrichment of lawyers more than devices for furthering the interests of class members. In addition, the possibility of aggregation of claims in class actions may result in overenforcement. Recall the concerns noted by Professor Dam (*supra* p. 228 n. 5). In *Smilow*, assuming the plaintiffs are right that there are 275,000 customers who signed the same contract, that would result in an overall recovery of $6,875,000 if plaintiffs' view of the contract is correct. How should that recovery be delivered to class members? How much should plaintiffs' attorneys be paid for bringing this action? Was Rule 23 designed to foster such litigation? If class actions are not available to provide a remedy for behavior such as plaintiffs allege, is there an alternative method of enforcement?

2. Among consumer class actions, *Smilow* may have unusually clear and simple factual circumstances that facilitate class certification. No doubt many would react with anger to learning that a company like defendant was charging for something it said would be provided for no charge. The class relies on an identical contract and seeks recovery for the residents of two states under a state law that provides a specific recovery without proof of actual damages. The court rejects arguments that quantum meruit or other questions bearing on individual circumstances of class members should bear on defendant's liability. Consider whether certification would be as easy to justify if there were a need to determine actual damages for class members, or a defense based on the value of the service provided, or a need to prove reliance by class members. Compare Perrone v. General Motors Acceptance Corp., 232 F.3d 433 (5th Cir.2000) (upholding denial of certification in a suit under the Truth in Lending Act and the Consumer Lending Act claiming that defendant failed to disclose a $400 fee in its form agreements for car financing, because plaintiffs sought to prove actual damages and that required proof of individual reliance).

Other cases are not so simple. Compare Andrews v. American Tel. & Tel. Co., 95 F.3d 1014 (11th Cir.1996), in which the court of appeals reversed class certification in two suits against A.T. & T. and Sprint on behalf of people who called 900 numbers, for which the caller had to pay a hefty additional charge. In one case, plaintiffs claimed that the callers were tricked into making phone calls by solicitations for credit cards that contained misrepresentations. In the other case, plaintiff sued on behalf of customers who called 900 numbers that allowed them to place a bet or wager for some jackpot or prize. Plaintiff claimed that offering these gambling activities by phone was illegal in every state. In both cases, plaintiffs sued on behalf of millions of customers who had made 900 calls. After a six-day hearing, the district judge certified classes in both cases.

The appellate court held that common issues did not predominate in either case. In the credit card solicitation case, the solicitations differed widely in terms of advertising and solicitation used, so that each such program would have to be assessed individually to determine whether fraudulent tactics were used. Even if that were shown, plaintiffs would still have to show actual reliance and resulting injury to recover. These difficulties would be compounded by the need to refer to the laws of 50 states regarding credit cards and consumer protection. Although the district court asserted that it could cope with these difficulties, "litigating the plaintiffs' claims as class actions no matter what the cost in terms of judicial economy, efficiency, and fairness runs counter to the policies underlying Rule 23(b)(3)." Moreover, on at least some of the claims there was a possibility of treble damages or an attorney fee award, so that individual claims may be feasible.

In the gambling case, the court reasoned that

> [A]spects of each 900–number program will have to be individually examined to determine whether a particular program actually involves gambling or runs afoul of state gaming laws. For example, some programs were designed to involve skill or knowledge on the part of callers, while others appear to have depended only upon chance. Many 900–number programs also provided various means of free entry into contests or made more complete disclosures than others. In short, the 900–number programs * * * cannot be lumped together and condemned or absolved en masse.

Id. at 1024. One judge dissented from reversal of class certification in this case on the ground the court should defer to the district court's judgment because there were similarities in the programs (id. at 1027):

> Generally, the schemes offer a chance to win a prize—$20,000, $15,000, a Chevrolet Blazer—in exchange for dialing, and being billed for, the 900 number. Though the prizes and the charges vary (the schemes charge varying amounts by the minute; others charge a flat fee for the call), the schemes generally involve one or more prizes distributed by chance to persons who have paid for a chance to win such a prize.

3. Antitrust price-fixing suits can involve similar complications, even though one would initially think that they should not, because the variety of products involved is often large. For example, in State of Alabama v. Blue Bird Body Co., 573 F.2d 309 (5th Cir.1978), plaintiffs sued six manufacturers

of school bus bodies alleging a conspiracy to fix the price of school buses. Although the district court certified a national class action, the court of appeals reversed. It emphasized that school buses are designed to meet the specifications of individual school districts, and that there are substantial differences in the ways in which public entities purchase school buses. "Because of the unique nature of the product and the different modes of purchase, the defendants assert that an individual examination involving each class member is required before a decision as to impact [of the alleged conspiracy] can be made." Compare In re Screws Antitrust Litigation, 91 F.R.D. 52 (D.Mass.1981) (rejecting argument by defendants that commonality could not be satisfied due to the diversity and complex pricing of their products precluded generalized proof of impact because "[s]crews are not inherently diverse, and distinctions offered are likely to be 'surface distinctions' which should not deter class certification").

4. Often plaintiffs seeking class certification rely, as did plaintiffs in *Smilow*, on experts' assertions that mathematical or mechanical methods exist to demonstrate on a classwide basis that injury has occurred, and in what amount. In *Smilow* the court asserts that plaintiff's expert showed how to extract information that would simplify the task of identifying the customers who had paid extra for incoming calls and the amount they had paid extra. And it was able to add that the affidavits from defendant's experts were consistent.

How should the court approach a case in which there is a disagreement between the experts? In In re Visa Check/Mastermoney Antitrust Litigation, 280 F.3d 124 (2d Cir.2001), plaintiffs sued on behalf of a class of four million merchants. They claimed that the requirement by Visa and Mastercard that merchants wanting to use their credit card services also accept their debit card services constituted an illegal tie-in under antitrust law because the charges for debit card services were the same as for credit card services even though the risks borne by the credit card companies were much lower. Plaintiffs asserted that, in the absence of this requirement, they would have refused to honor the debit card usage unless the charge were lowered, and that defendants would have lowered the charge. Their injury was that they paid higher charges for debit card transactions than they would have in the absence of the requirement. Plaintiffs' expert proposed comparing the charges for merchants to use on-line debit cards, treating any amount above that as an overcharge.

Defendants' expert argued that this analysis was wrong, in part because charges for credit cards would rise as the "package" of credit and debit cards would cease to exist and credit cards would generate a higher charge. He offered examples from the experience with other fees that cut against the analysis on which plaintiffs relied. The district court nonetheless certified the class. On appeal, defendants argued that it should have accepted the testimony of their expert. The majority of the court of appeals disagreed (id. at 135):

> Although a trial court must conduct a "rigorous analysis" to ensure that the prerequisites of Rule 23 have been satisfied before certifying a class, "a motion for class certification in not an occasion for examination of the merits of the case." A district court must ensure that the basis of

the expert opinion is not so flawed that it would be inadmissible as a matter of law. However, a district court may not weigh conflicting expert evidence or engage in "statistical dueling" of experts. The question for the district court at the class certification stage is whether plaintiffs' expert evidence is sufficient to demonstrate common questions of fact warranting certification of the proposed class, not whether the evidence will ultimately be persuasive.

Does this mean that, so long as the testimony of plaintiff's expert is admissible, the court may give no weight to the presentation of defendant's expert? When can the district judge determine whether plaintiff's evidence is persuasive, and can she then change the class certification decision?

Defendants in *Visa/Mastermoney Antitrust Litigation* argued that common issues could not predominate in any event because class members could avoid excess costs by "steering" customers to cheaper ways of paying, such as on-line debit cards. The majority recognized that defenses must be considered in assessing predominance, but the district court found that the formula used by plaintiff's expert might obviate that effort and "was not fatally flawed." Id. at 138. Moreover, there was a common issue in regard to this point about whether defendants' "honor all cards" rule forbade steering. A dissenting judge argued that "[t]he crucial, unresolved difficulty in this litigation concerns individualized proof of damages;" "even if each merchant's claim took no more than a half a day to sort out, the damages phase of trial would last as long as the whole course of Western Civilization from Ur." Id. at 149.

5. In *Smilow* the court suggests that difficult predominance issues could be avoided by using Rule 23(c)(4)(A), which permits a court to certify as to some issues and not others. Wouldn't excising the individual issues and then concluding that the class could be certified as to the remaining ones eviscerate the predominance requirement? But a case can be made that this partial certification was not designed as a method to circumvent the predominance requirement, and that it instead should be available only to permit bifurcation of the case after predominance is satisfied. See Hines, Challenging the Issue Class Action End–Run, 52 Emory L.J. 758 (2003). After carefully examining the drafting of this part of Rule 23, Professor Hines concludes that "[i]n light of the complete absence of evidence that the [Advisory] Committee [on Civil Rules] ever conceived of (c)(4)(A) as anything other than a 'usable detail,' it would be highly ill-advised to allow that provision to be 'transmogrified' into one that authorizes certification of issue class actions as an 'alternative' to dismissing (b)(3) class actions for failure to satisfy the predominance test." Id. at 759.

Is this view too cautious? Other courts have felt that district courts should "take full advantage" of Rule 23(c)(4) to "reduce the range of disputed issues in complex litigation" and to achieve judicial efficiencies. Central Wesleyan College v. W.R. Grace & Co., 6 F.3d 177, 185 (4th Cir.1993); see also Hilao v. Estate of Marcos, 103 F.3d 767, 782–87 (9th Cir.1996).

6. Note the choice between statutory and actual damages measures in *Smilow*. Should the court be concerned about whether an actual damage measure would benefit some class members rather than the statutory

damage award? Must it be certain that plaintiffs have a reliable way of determining on a customer-by-customer basis which measure is best? Or is the difference insignificant in light of the high cost of litigating such claims?

7. Why did plaintiffs want to substitute Bibeau for Smilow as class representative? Would Smilow have been a proper class representative even though she received only one incoming call? Keep this question in mind when we get to representativeness, *infra* p. 285.

8. Note that the state-law claims in *Smilow* were in federal court only on grounds of supplemental jurisdiction, and that plaintiffs abandoned their sole federal claim on appeal. Should the federal court retain jurisdiction over the state-law claims? See 28 U.S.C. § 1367(c)(3). Some argue that federal-court jurisdiction should be available for class actions involving multi-state classes, regardless of complete diversity. For proposed legislation along these lines, see Class Action Fairness Act of 2004, H.R. 1115 and S. 274 (108th Cong.), described *infra* pp. 401-02.

9. As you reflect on the court's grappling with predominance, consider Judge Easterbrook's observation: "Class certifications also have induced some judges to remake some substantive doctrine to render the litigation manageable." Blair v. Equifax Check Services, Inc., 181 F.3d 832, 834 (7th Cir.1999).

4. TYPICALITY

GENERAL TELEPHONE COMPANY OF THE SOUTHWEST v. FALCON

Supreme Court of the United States, 1982.
457 U.S. 147, 102 S.Ct. 2364, 72 L.Ed.2d 740.

JUSTICE STEVENS delivered the opinion of the Court.

The question presented is whether respondent Falcon, who complained that petitioner did not promote him because he is a Mexican–American, was properly permitted to maintain a class action on behalf of Mexican–American applicants for employment whom petitioner did not hire.

I

In 1969 petitioner initiated a special recruitment and training program for minorities. Through that program, respondent Falcon was hired in July 1969 as a groundman, and within a year he was twice promoted, first to lineman and then to lineman-in-charge. He subsequently refused a promotion to installer-repairman. In October 1972 he applied for the job of field inspector; his application was denied even though the promotion was granted several white employees with less seniority.

Falcon thereupon filed a charge with the Equal Employment Opportunity Commission stating his belief that he had been passed over for promotion because of his national origin and that petitioner's promotion policy operated against Mexican–Americans as a class. In due course he received a right to sue letter from the Commission and, in April 1975, he commenced this action under Title VII of the Civil Rights Act of 1964, 74 Stat. 253, as amended, 42 U.S.C. § 2000e *et seq.,* in the United States District Court for the Northern District of Texas. His complaint alleged that petitioner maintained "a policy, practice, custom, or usage of: (a) discriminating against [Mexican–Americans] because of national origin and with respect to compensation, terms, conditions, and privileges of employment, and (b) . . . subjecting [Mexican–Americans] to continuous employment discrimination." Respondent claimed that as a result of this policy whites with less qualification and experience and lower evaluation scores than respondent had been promoted more rapidly. The complaint contained no factual allegations concerning petitioner's hiring practices.

Respondent brought the action "on his own behalf and on behalf of other persons similarly situated, pursuant to Rule 23(b)(2) of the Federal Rules of Civil Procedure." The class identified in the complaint was "composed of Mexican–American persons who are employed, or who might be employed, by GENERAL TELEPHONE COMPANY at its place of business located in Irving, Texas, who have been and who continue to be or might be adversely affected by the practices complained of herein."

After responding to petitioner's written interrogatories,[4] respondent filed a memorandum in favor of certification of "the class of all hourly Mexican–American employees who have been employed, are employed, or may in the future be employed and all those Mexican–Americans who have applied or would have applied for employment had the Defendant not practiced racial discrimination in its employment practices." His position was supported by the ruling of the United States Court of Appeals for the Fifth Circuit in *Johnson v. Georgia Highway Express, Inc.,* 417 F.2d 1122 (1969), that any victim of racial discrimination in employment may maintain an "across the board" attack on all unequal employment practices alleged to have been committed by the employer pursuant to a policy of racial discrimination. Without conducting an evidentiary hearing, the District Court certified a class including Mexican–American employees and Mexican–American applicants for employment who had not been hired.

Following trial of the liability issues, the District Court entered separate findings of fact and conclusions of law with respect first to respondent and then to the class. The District Court found that petitioner had not discriminated against respondent in hiring, but that it did discriminate against him in its promotion practices. The court reached converse conclusions about the class, finding no discrimination in pro-

---

4. Petitioner's Interrogatory No. 8 stated: "Identify the common questions of law and fac[t] which affect the rights of the members of the proposed class."

Respondent answered that interrogatory as follows: "The facts which affect the rights of the members of the class are the facts of their employment, the ways in which evaluations are made, the subjective rather than objective manner in which recommendations for raises and transfers and promotions are handled, and all of the facts surrounding the employment of Mexican–American persons by General Telephone Company. The questions of law specified in Interrogatory No. 8 call for a conclusion on the part of the Plaintiff."

motion practices, but concluding that petitioner had discriminated against Mexican–Americans at its Irving facility in its hiring practices.

After various post-trial proceedings, the District Court ordered petitioner to furnish respondent with a list of all Mexican–Americans who had applied for employment at the Irving facility during the period between January 1, 1973, and October 18, 1976. Respondent was then ordered to give notice to those persons advising them that they might be entitled to some form of recovery. Evidence was taken concerning the applicants who responded to the notice and backpay was ultimately awarded to 13 persons, in addition to respondent Falcon. The total recovery by respondent and the entire class amounted to $67,925.49, plus costs and interest.

Both parties appealed. The Court of Appeals rejected respondent's contention that the class should have encompassed all of petitioner's operations in Texas, New Mexico, Oklahoma, and Arkansas. On the other hand, the court also rejected petitioner's argument that the class had been defined too broadly. For, under the Fifth Circuit's across-the-board rule, it is permissible for "an employee complaining of one employment practice to represent another complaining of another practice, if the plaintiff and the members of the class suffer from essentially the same injury. In this case, all of the claims are based on discrimination because of national origin." The court relied on *Payne v. Travenol Laboratories, Inc.,* 565 F.2d 895 (1978), cert. denied, 439 U.S. 835, 99 S.Ct. 118, 58 L.Ed.2d 131, in which the Fifth Circuit stated:

> "Plaintiffs' action is an 'across the board' attack on unequal employment practices alleged to have been committed by Travenol pursuant to a policy of racial discrimination. As parties who have allegedly been aggrieved by some of these discriminatory practices, plaintiffs have demonstrated a sufficient nexus to enable them to represent other class members suffering from different practices motivated by the same policies."

On the merits, the Court of Appeals upheld respondent's claim of disparate treatment in promotion, but held that the District Court's findings relating to disparate impact in hiring were insufficient to support recovery on behalf of the class.[11] After this Court decided *Texas Department of Community Affairs v. Burdine,* 450 U.S. 248, 101 S.Ct. 1089, 67 L.Ed.2d 207, we vacated the judgment of the Court of Appeals and directed further consideration in the light of that opinion. The Fifth Circuit thereupon vacated the portion of its opinion addressing respondent's promotion claim but reinstated the portions of its opinion approving the District Court's class certification. With the merits of both

---

11. The District Court's finding was based on statistical evidence comparing the number of Mexican–Americans in the company's employ, and the number hired in 1972 and 1973, with the percentage of Mexican–Americans in the Dallas–Fort Worth labor force. Since recovery had been allowed for the years 1973 through 1976 based on statistical evidence pertaining to only a portion of that period, and since petitioner's evidence concerning the entire period suggested that there was no disparate impact, the Court of Appeals ordered further proceedings on the class hiring claims.

respondent's promotion claim and the class hiring claims remaining open for reconsideration in the District Court on remand, we granted certiorari to decide whether the class action was properly maintained on behalf of both employees who were denied promotion and applicants who were denied employment.

II

The class action device was designed as "an exception to the usual rule that litigation is conducted by and on behalf of the individual named parties only." Class relief is "peculiarly appropriate" when the "issues involved are common to the class as a whole" and when they "turn on questions of law applicable in the same manner to each member of the class." For in such cases, "the class-action device saves the resources of both the courts and the parties by permitting an issue potentially affecting every [class member] to be litigated in an economical fashion under Rule 23."

Title VII of the Civil Rights Act of 1964, as amended, authorizes the Equal Employment Opportunity Commission to sue in its own name to secure relief for individuals aggrieved by discriminatory practices forbidden by the Act. See 42 U.S.C. § 2000e–5(f)(1). In exercising this enforcement power, the Commission may seek relief for groups of employees or applicants for employment without complying with the strictures of Rule 23. Title VII, however, contains no special authorization for class suits maintained by private parties. An individual litigant seeking to maintain a class action under Title VII must meet "the prerequisites of numerosity, commonality, typicality, and adequacy of representation" specified in Rule 23(a). These requirements effectively "limit the class claims to those fairly encompassed by the named plaintiff's claims."

We have repeatedly held that "a class representative must be part of the class and 'possess the same interest and suffer the same injury' as the class members." *East Texas Motor Freight System Inc. v. Rodriguez,* 431 U.S. 395, 403, 97 S.Ct. 1891, 1896, 52 L.Ed.2d 453 (quoting *Schlesinger v. Reservists Committee to Stop the War,* 418 U.S. 208, 216, 94 S.Ct. 2925, 2929–2930, 41 L.Ed.2d 706.) In *East Texas Motor Freight,* a Title VII action brought by three Mexican–American city drivers, the Fifth Circuit certified a class consisting of the trucking company's black and Mexican–American city drivers allegedly denied on racial or ethnic grounds transfers to more desirable line-driver jobs. We held that the Court of Appeals had "plainly erred in declaring a class action." Because at the time the class was certified it was clear that the named plaintiffs were not qualified for line-driver positions, "they could have suffered no injury as a result of the allegedly discriminatory practices, and they were, therefore, simply not eligible to represent a class of persons who did allegedly suffer injury."

Our holding in *East Texas Motor Freight* was limited; we noted that "a different case would be presented if the District Court had certified a class and only later had it appeared that the named plaintiffs were not class members or were otherwise inappropriate class representatives." We also recognized the theory behind the Fifth Circuit's across-the-board rule, noting our awareness "that suits alleging racial or ethnic discrimination are often by their very nature class suits, involving classwide wrongs," and that "[c]ommon questions of law or fact are typically present." In the same breath, however, we reiterated that "careful attention to the requirements of Fed.Rule Civ.Proc. 23 remains nonetheless indispensable" and that the "mere fact that a complaint alleges racial or ethnic discrimination does not in itself ensure that the party who has brought the lawsuit will be an adequate representative of those who may have been the real victims of that discrimination."

We cannot disagree with the proposition underlying the across-the-board rule—that racial discrimination is by definition class discrimination. But the allegation that such discrimination has occurred neither determines whether a class action may be maintained in accordance with Rule 23 nor defines the class that may be certified. Conceptually, there is a wide gap between (a) an individual's claim that he has been denied a promotion on discriminatory grounds, and his otherwise unsupported allegation that the company has a policy of discrimination, and (b) the existence of a class of persons who have suffered the same injury as that individual, such that the individual's claim and the class claims will share common questions of law or fact and that the individual's claim will be typical of the class claims.[13] For respondent to bridge that gap, he must prove much more than the validity of his own claim. Even though evidence that he was passed over for promotion when several less deserving whites were advanced may support the conclusion that respondent was denied the promotion because of his national origin, such evidence would not necessarily justify the additional inferences (1) that this discriminatory treatment is typical of petitioner's promotion practices, (2) that petitioner's promotion practices are motivated by a policy of ethnic discrimination that pervades petitioner's Irving division, or (3) that this policy of ethnic discrimination is reflected in petitioner's other employment practices, such as hiring, in the same way it is manifested in the promotion practices. These additional inferences demonstrate the tenuous character of any presumption that the class claims are "fairly encompassed" within respondent's claim.

13. The commonality and typicality requirements of Rule 23(a) tend to merge. Both serve as guideposts for determining whether under the particular circumstances maintenance of a class action is economical and whether the named plaintiff's claim and the class claims are so interrelated that the interests of the class members will be fairly and adequately protected in their absence. Those requirements therefore also tend to merge with the adequacy-of-representation requirement, although the latter requirement also raises concerns about the competency of class counsel and conflicts of interest. In this case, we need not address petitioner's argument that there is a conflict of interest between respondent and the class of rejected applicants because an enlargement of the pool of Mexican–American employees will decrease respondent's chances for promotion. See *General Telephone Co. v. EEOC*, 446 U.S. 318, 331, 100 S.Ct. 1698, 1706–1707, 64 L.Ed.2d 319 ("In employment discrimination litigation, conflicts might arise, for example, between employees and applicants who were denied employment and who will, if granted relief, compete with employees for fringe benefits or seniority. Under Rule 23, the same plaintiff could not represent these classes.")

Respondent's complaint provided an insufficient basis for concluding that the adjudication of his claim of discrimination in promotion would require the decision of any common question concerning the failure of petitioner to hire more Mexican–Americans. Without any specific presentation identifying the questions of law or fact that were common to the claims of respondent and of the members of the class he sought to represent, it was error for the District Court to presume that respondent's claim was typical of other claims against petitioner by Mexican–American employees and applicants. If one allegation of specific discriminatory treatment were sufficient to support an across-the-board attack, every Title VII case would be a potential company-wide class action. We find nothing in the statute to indicate that Congress intended to authorize such a wholesale expansion of class-action litigation.[15]

The trial of this class action followed a predictable course. Instead of raising common questions of law or fact, respondent's evidentiary approaches to the individual and class claims were entirely different. He attempted to sustain his individual claim by proving intentional discrimination. He tried to prove the class claims through statistical evidence of disparate impact. Ironically, the District Court rejected the class claim of promotion discrimination, which conceptually might have borne a closer typicality and commonality relationship with respondent's individual claim, but sustained the class claim of hiring discrimination. As the District Court's bifurcated findings on liability demonstrate, the individual and class claims might as well have been tried separately. It is clear that the maintenance of respondent's action as a class action did not advance "the efficiency and economy of litigation which is a principal purpose of the procedure." *American Pipe & Construction Co. v. Utah,* 414 U.S. 538, 553, 94 S.Ct. 756, 766, 38 L.Ed.2d 713.

We do not, of course, judge the propriety of a class certification by hindsight. The District Court's error in this case, and the error inherent in the across-the-board rule, is the failure to evaluate carefully the legitimacy of the named plaintiff's plea that he is a proper class representative under Rule 23(a). As we noted in *Coopers & Lybrand v. Livesay,* 437 U.S. 463, 98 S.Ct. 2454, 57 L.Ed.2d 351, "the class determination generally involves considerations that are 'enmeshed in the factual and legal issues comprising the plaintiff's cause of action.'" Sometimes the issues are plain enough from the pleadings to determine

---

15. If petitioner used a biased testing procedure to evaluate both applicants for employment and incumbent employees, a class action on behalf of every applicant or employee who might have been prejudiced by the test clearly would satisfy the commonality and typicality requirements of Rule 23(a). Significant proof that an employer operated under a general policy of discrimination conceivably could justify a class of both applicants and employees if the discrimination manifested itself in hiring and promotion practices in the same general fashion, such as through entirely subjective decisionmaking processes. In this regard it is noteworthy that Title VII prohibits discriminatory employment *practices,* not an abstract policy of discrimination. The mere fact that an aggrieved private plaintiff is a member of an identifiable class of persons of the same race or national origin is insufficient to establish his standing to litigate on their behalf all possible claims of discrimination against a common employer.

whether the interests of the absent parties are fairly encompassed within the named plaintiff's claim, and sometimes it may be necessary for the court to probe behind the pleadings before coming to rest on the certification question. Even after a certification order is entered, the judge remains free to modify it in the light of subsequent developments in the litigation. For such an order, particularly during the period before any notice is sent to members of the class, "is inherently tentative." This flexibility enhances the usefulness of the class-action device; actual, not presumed, conformance with Rule 23(a) remains, however, indispensable.

III

The need to carefully apply the requirements of Rule 23(a) to Title VII class actions was noticed by a member of the Fifth Circuit panel that announced the across-the-board rule. In a specially concurring opinion in *Johnson v. Georgia Highway Express, Inc.*, Judge Godbold emphasized the need for "more precise pleadings," for "without reasonable specificity the court cannot define the class, cannot determine whether the representation is adequate, and the employer does not know how to defend." He termed as "most significant" the potential unfairness to the class members bound by the judgment if the framing of the class is overbroad. And he pointed out the error of the "tacit assumption" underlying the across-the-board rule that "all will be well for surely the plaintiff will win and manna will fall on all members of the class." With the same concerns in mind, we reiterate today that a Title VII class action, like any other class action, may only be certified if the trial court is satisfied, after a rigorous analysis, that the prerequisites of Rule 23(a) have been satisfied.

The judgment of the Court of Appeals affirming the certification order is reversed, and the case is remanded for further proceedings consistent with this opinion.

CHIEF JUSTICE BURGER, concurring in part and dissenting in part.

I agree with the Court's decision insofar as it states the general principles which apply in determining whether a class should be certified in this case under Rule 23. However, in my view it is not necessary to remand for further proceedings since it is entirely clear on this record that no class should have been certified in this case. I would simply reverse the Court of Appeals with instructions to dismiss the class claim.

As the Court notes, the purpose of Rule 23 is to promote judicial economy by allowing for litigation of common questions of law and fact at one time. We have stressed that strict attention to the requirements of Rule 23 is indispensable in employment discrimination cases. This means that class claims are limited to those "fairly encompassed by the named plaintiff's claims."

Respondent claims that he was not promoted to a job as field inspector because he is a Mexican–American. To be successful in his claim, which he advances under the "disparate treatment" theory, he must convince a court that those who were promoted were promoted not because they were better qualified than he was, but, instead, that he was not promoted for discriminatory reasons. The success of this claim depends on evaluation of the comparative qualifications of the applicants for promotion to field inspector and on analysis of the credibility of the reasons for the promotion decisions provided by those who made the decisions. Respondent's class claim on behalf of unsuccessful applicants for jobs with petitioner, in contrast, is advanced under the "adverse impact" theory. Its success depends on an analysis of statistics concerning petitioner's hiring patterns.

The record in this case clearly shows that there are no common questions of law or fact between respondent's claim and the class claim; the only commonality is that respondent is a Mexican–American and he seeks to represent a class of Mexican–Americans. We have repeatedly held that the bare fact that a plaintiff alleges racial or ethnic discrimination is not enough to justify class certification.

Moreover, while a judge's decision to certify a class is not normally to be evaluated by hindsight, since the judge cannot know what the evidence will show, there is no reason for us at this stage of these lengthy judicial proceedings not to proceed in light of the evidence actually presented. The Court properly concludes that the Court of Appeals and the District Court failed to consider the requirements of Rule 23. In determining whether to reverse and remand or to simply reverse, we can and should look at the evidence. The record shows that there is no support for the class claim. Respondent's own statistics show that 7.7% of those hired by petitioner between 1972 and 1976 were Mexican–American while the relevant labor force was 5.2% Mexican–American. Petitioner's unchallenged evidence shows that it hired Mexican–Americans in numbers greater than their percentage of the labor force even though Mexican–Americans applied for jobs with petitioner in numbers smaller than their percentage of the labor force. This negates any claim of Falcon as a class representative.

Notes and Questions

1. After remand in *Falcon,* judgment was entered for defendant on the ground that it had rebutted plaintiff's prima facie case of discrimination. See Falcon v. General Telephone Co., 815 F.2d 317 (5th Cir.1987).

2. Perhaps you wondered why the *Falcon* case is put under this section on "typicality." It might as well have been put under the prior section on "commonality." As the court observes in footnote 13, "the commonality and typicality requirements of Rule 23(a) tend to merge," and, indeed, they are also closely related to the "representativeness" requirement. *Falcon* has been taken up here in hopes that the interrelated and overlapping nature of these requirements can be appreciated. Footnote 13 says they "both serve as guideposts for determining whether under the particular circumstances maintenance of a class action is economical and whether the named plaintiff's claim and the class claims are so interrelated that the interests of the class members will be fairly and adequately protected in their absence."

In some instances, however, courts find significant differences between commonality and typicality. In Newton v. Merrill Lynch, Pierce, Fenner & Smith, Inc., 259 F.3d 154 (3d Cir.2001), the court rejected a securities fraud class action for lack of commonality, but found that typicality was not a problem: "[T]ypicality does not require similarity of individual questions concerning reliance or damages on the part of class representatives. In fact, whether the class representatives' claims prove the claims of the entire class highlights important issues of individual reliance and damages that are more properly considered relevant under the predominance and superiority analysis." Id. at 184.

3. With regard to typicality and commonality problems in Title VII employment discrimination class actions, consider Judge Schwarzer's discussion of class certification criteria in Harriss v. Pan American World Airways, Inc., 74 F.R.D. 24 (N.D.Cal.1977):

> In the context of litigation over alleged unlawful employment practices, relevant criteria of commonality include the following:

> (i) What is the nature of the unlawful employment practice charged—is it one that peculiarly affects only one or a few employees or is it genuinely one having a class-wide impact.

> (ii) How uniform or diverse are the relevant employment practices of the employer, considering matters such as: size of the work force; number of plants and installations involved; extent of diversity of employment conditions, occupations and work activities; degree of geographic dispersion of the employees and of intra-company employee transfers and interchanges; degree of decentralization of administration and supervision as opposed to the degree of local autonomy.

> (iii) How uniform or diverse is the membership of the class, in terms of the likelihood that the members' treatment will involve common questions.

> (iv) What is the nature of the employer's management organization as it relates to the degree of centralization and uniformity of relevant employment and personnel policies and practices.

> (v) What is the length of the time span covered by the allegations, as it relates to the degree of probability that similar conditions prevailed throughout the period.

4. What is it about Falcon's claim (that his application for promotion to a field inspector was denied because of his race) that makes this class action noneconomical and Falcon an inappropriate representative? Is it that the class members have a much larger range of discriminatory claims relating to both hiring and employment practices? What does the Court mean when it says proof of his denial of a promotion would not support inferences as to a broader policy affecting other members of the class and that such "inferences demonstrate the tenuous character of any presumption that the class claims are 'fairly encompassed' within respondent's claim"? Is this because of the way in which Falcon put on his evidence and because of the findings of the trial court? Could this have been avoided by a different evidentiary approach by Falcon?

Or is the problem here essentially one of pleading? Could this result have been avoided by different allegations in the complaint? Consider Falcon's response to defendant's interrogatories, quoted in the Court's footnote 4. *Falcon* may signal a more cautious approach to class actions, particularly in employment discrimination cases where the form of discrimination can vary so markedly among class members. Can the problem be met in future cases by a more careful selection of the representative plaintiff or plaintiffs to insure that a broader range of class complaints and situations are encompassed? See Rutherglen, Title VII Class Actions, 47 U.Chi.L.Rev. 688, 707–08 (1980) (urging care in certifying class actions for discrimination).

5. After *Falcon,* some courts strictly refused to allow an employee asserting one type of employment discrimination from representing a class asserting other types. See Roby v. St. Louis Southwestern Ry. Co., 775 F.2d 959, 962 (8th Cir.1985) (plaintiff could not represent class suffering from a different type of discriminatory discharge); Walker v. Jim Dandy Co., 747 F.2d 1360, 1364–65 (11th Cir.1984) (applicants for supervisor position could not represent class of applicants for lower level positions); Holsey v. Armour & Co., 743 F.2d 199, 216 (4th Cir.1984) (plaintiffs asserting promotion discrimination could not represent class of outside applicants, unless same people made both decisions).

However, other courts focused on the language in *Falcon* saying it is error to *presume,* "[w]ithout any specific presentation identifying the questions of law or fact that were common to the claims of [the plaintiff] and of the members of the class he sought to represent." They were willing to find typicality on the basis of specific evidence showing that the plaintiff was discriminated against because of the same characteristics as the class possessed. As one court put it, typicality "does not require that the factual background of each named plaintiff's claim be identical to that of all the class members; rather, it requires that the disputed issue of law or fact 'occupy essentially the same degree of centrality to the named plaintiff's claim as to that of other members of the proposed class.' " Caridad v. Metro–North Commuter R.R., 191 F.3d 283, 293 (2d Cir.1999).

See, for example, Rossini v. Ogilvy & Mather, Inc., 798 F.2d 590 (2d Cir.1986), holding that a female professional employee denied an intracompany transfer could represent a class of women seeking training and promotion by seeking to show that women were discriminated against "in the same general fashion" through use of a subjective evaluation system without formal job descriptions, experience or education requirements, or posting of job openings. In Hartman v. Duffey, 19 F.3d 1459 (D.C.Cir.1994), plaintiffs who had applied for civil service jobs with the U.S. Information Agency sought to represent a class consisting of women who applied for civil service or foreign service positions with the agency even though there was a different examination for foreign service positions. Plaintiffs said that they did not challenge the foreign service examination, but alleged intentional discrimination against women with regard to both categories. Although it found the record insufficient to support such certification, the court added that it was "unwilling to hold as a matter of law, that a named plaintiff who unsuccessfully applied for one job can never represent an employee who unsuccessfully applied for another job simply because the application process for the second job included a separate and different element." Id. at 1472.

6. Compare Jenson v. Eveleth Taconite Co., 139 F.R.D. 657 (D.Minn. 1991), in which plaintiffs were women employed in a mining operation. They claimed their employer and union had discriminated against women in terms of hiring and conditions of employment. They also asserted that the employer had allowed, and perhaps fostered, a hostile work environment. Plaintiffs' attorney took the case thinking it was "a natural class action because the environment of the mine was so clearly hostile to all the women who worked there." C. Bingham & L. Gansler, Class Action 181 (2002). Despite defendants' argument that sexual harassment claims could not be made on a class-wide basis, the court certified a class, finding that plaintiffs had "bridged the gap" between their individual claims and putative class claims (139 F.R.D. at 662):

> Plaintiffs do not purport to raise individual claims of sexual harassment. Rather, plaintiffs advance the view that incidents of sexual harassment constitute but one facet of their discrimination claims. They argue that the systemic offenses were so pervasive as to create an "oppressive work environment." Moreover, plaintiffs do not seek damages based on individual incidents of harassment, but instead seek class-wide injunctive, declaratory, and financial relief.

Compare Elkins v. American Showa, Inc., 219 F.R.D. 414 (S.D. Ohio 2002) (variations in the frequency and severity of harassment of female employees precluded a finding of commonality).

In Harris v. Forklift Systems, Inc., 510 U.S. 17, 114 S.Ct. 367, 126 L.Ed.2d 295 (1993), the Court held that a "reasonable person" standard should be used to determine whether sexual harassment has occurred, rather than making liability turn on whether a specific plaintiff suffered serious psychological injury as a result. Should this standard facilitate or impede class action treatment of such claims?

7. Note the Court's disposition in *Falcon*. On remand, how could the court proceed to adjudicate the claims brought on behalf of job applicants? One possibility would be to create a sub-class, but that would require a typical and adequate representative of the job applicant class. In Johnson v. American Credit Co., 581 F.2d 526 (5th Cir.1978), plaintiff's car was attached on the basis of an affidavit claiming that she was about to remove it from the state, a ground for attachment under the Georgia statute. She filed a class action seeking a declaration that the Georgia attachment scheme violated due process. Because her claim was limited to only one of six grounds for attachment under the statute, the court ruled that she could not represent those affected by the other five provisions. It was cautious, however, about how a court should react to this situation (id. at 533 n. 13):

> When faced with a situation when no named plaintiff can represent a subclass, a trial court should consider whether it is in the interests of justice and judicial economy to postpone dismissal as to the subclass for a specified period in which members of the subclass could become plaintiffs by amendment of the Complaint or by intervention and thereby save the subclass action.

See also Birmingham Steel Corp. v. Tennessee Valley Auth., 353 F.3d 1331 (11th Cir. 2003) (requiring the court to allow class counsel a reasonable time to locate a substitute class representative if the first one is found inadequate).

8. Should similar reasoning apply to discrimination actions outside the employment field? In Jackson v. Motel 6 Multipurpose, Inc., 130 F.3d 999 (11th Cir.1997), plaintiffs claimed that they were denied accommodations in Motel 6 motels, or provided substandard accommodations, due to defendant's policy and practice of racial discrimination at its 750 motels across the country. They sought both money damages and injunctive relief. Concluding that this was a (b)(3) action, the court relied on *Falcon* for the proposition that the alleged common question whether Motel 6 has a practice or policy of discrimination would not outweigh the individual questions:

> The *Jackson* plaintiffs' claims will require distinctly case-specific inquiries into the facts surrounding each alleged incident of discrimination. The issues that must be addressed include not only whether a particular plaintiff was denied a room or was rented a substandard room, but also whether there were any rooms vacant when that plaintiff inquired; whether the plaintiff had reservations; whether unclean rooms were rented to the plaintiff for reasons having nothing to do with the plaintiff's race; whether the plaintiff, at the time that he requested a room, exhibited any non-racial characteristics legitimately counseling renting him a room; and so on. * * * Indeed, we expect that most, if not all, of the plaintiffs' claims will stand or fall, not on the answer to the question whether Motel 6 has a practice or policy of racial discrimination, but on the resolution of these highly case-specific factual issues.

Id. at 1006. Would no amount of anecdotal evidence warrant a conclusion that non-white customers were victims of discrimination? Would limiting the suit to a request for an injunction make a difference? See also Rutstein v. Avis Rent–A–Car Systems, Inc., 211 F.3d 1228 (11th Cir.2000), in which the court found that common questions were not satisfied in a suit alleging that Avis discriminated against customers thought to be Jewish in handling corporate accounts: "[T]he legitimate reasons why Avis might have judged an individual plaintiff to be 'unqualified' for a corporate account are far more various and individualized than in the employment context."

LA MAR v. H & B NOVELTY & LOAN CO.

United States Court of Appeals, Ninth Circuit, 1973.
489 F.2d 461.

Before ELY and SNEED, CIRCUIT JUDGES, and SWEIGERT, DISTRICT JUDGE.

SNEED, CIRCUIT JUDGE.

The common issue of these cases is whether a plaintiff having a cause of action against a single defendant can institute a class action against the single defendant *and* an unrelated group of defendants who have engaged in conduct closely similar to that of the single defendant on behalf of all those injured by all the defendants sought to be included in the defendant class. We hold that he cannot. Under proper circumstances, the plaintiff may represent all those suffering an injury similar to his own inflicted by the defendant responsible for the plaintiff's injury, but in our view he cannot represent those having causes of action against other defendants against whom the plaintiff has no cause of action and from whose hands he suffered no injury.

In a condensed form the facts of these cases are as follows. In *La Mar* the plaintiffs initiated an action against all the pawn brokers licensed to conduct business under the laws of Oregon on behalf of all customers of such pawn brokers to recover either $100 or double the finance charges for alleged violations by the defendant pawn brokers of the Truth-in-Lending Act, 15 U.S.C. §§ 1601–1677. In his complaint La Mar estimated that there were 33,000 such customers and that the recovery should approximate three million dollars. In fact La Mar did business with only one such pawn broker, the H & B Novelty and Loan Company.

* * *

In *Kinsling,* the plaintiff purchased a round trip ticket between Kansas City, Missouri and Augusta, Georgia from Trans World Airlines and Piedmont Aviation Corp. Because there was no published joint fare for the route, a fare construction was required under the applicable tariff rules. The plaintiff alleged that he was overcharged in the amount of $10 in violation of certain provisions of the Federal Aviation Act. This suit was brought against Trans World Airlines and Piedmont Aviation Corp. and the six appellee air carriers on behalf of Kinsling and all others who had suffered a similar overcharge in dealings with these carriers. The aggregate amount of such overcharges in the four years prior to filing the suit was alleged to be approximately eighty million dollars.

[In *Kinsling,* the Court of Appeals affirmed the dismissal of the claims against airlines the named plaintiff had not dealt with. In *La Mar,* it reversed the certification of the class and directed that the claims against pawn brokers other than the H & B Novelty Co. be dismissed.]

In the briefs in *Kinsling* and during oral argument of both cases much attention was devoted to problems of standing. This Court, after reflection, does not believe it is necessary to pass on this issue because in our view, under a proper application of Rule 23 of the Federal Rules of Civil Procedure, the plaintiffs here are not entitled to bring a class action against defendants with whom they had no dealing. That is, for the purposes of these appeals, we are prepared to assume the presence of standing.

* * *

The third prerequisite [of Rule 23(a)] is that the claims of the representative parties be typical of the class. Obviously this requirement is not met when the "representative" plaintiff never had a claim of *any* type against *any* defendant. There is nothing in the rule to suggest that the zeal or talent of the "representative" plaintiff's attorney can supply this omission. We believe that this prerequisite is also lacking when the plaintiff's cause of action, although similar to that of other members of the class, is against a defendant with respect to whom the class members have no cause of action. Those who purchased tickets from the six appellee airlines, from whom the representative plaintiff purchased no tickets, have no cause of action by reason of such purchases against the airlines from whom the representative plaintiff purchased. In brief, typicality is lacking when the representative plaintiff's cause of action is against a defendant unrelated to the defendants against whom the cause of action of the members of the class lies.

The fourth prerequisite is that "the representative parties will fairly and adequately protect the interests of the class." This is particularly troublesome in class actions, such as these, in which the injury to any possible representative party is quite small. Either no one of the injured class is a suitable representative or anyone is. From this it may be said to follow that each possible representative party could "fairly and adequately protect the interests of the class."

The difficulty with this position is that compliance with the prerequisite must necessarily be determined more by examination of the fitness of the counsel of the candidate for representative party status than by the attributes of the candidate. Once the ability of counsel becomes the measure by which compliance with the fourth prerequisite is determined, there remains only a formal and technical reason for insisting that there be a representative party at all.

Assuming, therefore, that in this type of class action the role of the representative party is largely formal, it is reasonable in our view to design its formal characteristics in a manner that is consistent with what we perceive to be the tone of the Advisory Committee's Note [accompanying the 1966 amendment to Rule 23, which the court found to have a tone "of prudence and caution" and not to authorize "massive class actions conducted by attorneys engaged by near-nominal plaintiffs"]. In keeping with that tone and to reduce the incidence of proceedings in which the trial judge and the representative plaintiff's counsel become a part-time regulatory agency, we assert that a plaintiff who has no cause of action against the defendant can not "fairly and adequately protect the interests" of those who do have such causes of action. This is true even though the plaintiff may have suffered an identical injury at the hands of a party other than the defendant and even though his attorney is excellent in every material respect. Obviously this position does not embrace situations in which all injuries are the result of a conspiracy or concerted schemes between the defendants at whose hands the class suffered injury. Nor is it intended to apply in instances in which all defendants are juridically related in a manner that suggests a single resolution of the dispute would be expeditious.

[The court found that the class action could not be maintained under Rule 23(b)(2) because money damages were sought. It also found Rule 23(b)(1)(A) unavailable as the danger faced by a defendant of inconsistent or varying adjudications establishing incompatible standards of conduct rarely arises in actions for money damages: "Certainly the defendants in these proceedings can continue the conduct of which the plaintiffs complain even if the plaintiffs are successful, as the plaintiff in *La Mar* has been, in their individual actions. Their success by its terms does not fix the rights and duties owed by the defendants to others as, for example, would declaration of the invalidity of [a] bond issue."

Likewise, the court found Rule 23(b)(1)(B) inapplicable: "In the cases before us the success or failure of the plaintiffs in their individual actions will not inescapably alter the rights of others similarly situated. Their claims are left untouched by separate actions. Neither the *stare decisis* consequences of an individual action nor the possibility of false reliance upon the improper initiation of a class action can supply either the practical disposition of the rights of the class, or the substantial impairment of those rights, at least one of which is required by Rule 23(b)(1)(B)." [See *infra* p. 302 concerning 23(b)(1) classes.]

If the class actions sought to be initiated in *La Mar* and *Kinsling* are to be authorized it must be done by reliance on Rule 23(b)(3). We do not believe such authorization is required. It is our view that the class actions in question here are inferior to other "available methods for the fair and efficient adjudication of the controversy." While it is not necessary for this decision to pass on the effort of the plaintiffs to initiate a class action against the defendant with whom they dealt on behalf of all others who dealt similarly with that defendant, it must be noted that such suits are more manageable and that nothing said here precludes such actions. Thus, even though La Mar and Kinsling may not represent the classes for whom they here seek to initiate a class action, it may well be that a representative plaintiff injured by each defendant may emerge to undertake the burden which we are preventing La Mar and Kinsling from assuming.

* * *

The trend of the cases supports the results which the holdings above represent. * * *

Clearly the most nearly apposite case of which we are aware is Weiner v. Bank of King of Prussia, 358 F.Supp. 684 (E.D.Pa.1973), in which the plaintiff who borrowed from one national bank within the court's jurisdiction sought to bring suit against all the national banks within the court's jurisdiction on behalf of all the "customers and/or borrowers of national banks in this District". It was held that Rule 23 does not affect the plaintiff's lack of standing to sue those banks with whom he had no dealings.

The cases that are cited to support the result rejected in *Weiner, supra,* predominantly are actions to validate civil rights. While Rule 23 has no "civil rights version", it is not surprising that its interpretation is more generous in this type of case than in others. Even so the cases do not support the plaintiffs here. In Washington v. Lee, 263 F.Supp. 327

(M.D.Ala.1966), the plaintiffs were, or had been, incarcerated in various detention facilities of the State of Alabama, its counties, cities, and towns. Their suit was against the Commissioner of Corrections, members of the Board of Corrections, the Sheriff of Jefferson County and all other sheriffs of Alabama, the Warden of the Birmingham jail and all other wardens and jailers of city and town jails in Alabama. Its purpose was to obtain a declaration of the rights of Negro citizens not to be segregated while incarcerated. Obviously there were many facilities in which the plaintiffs had not been detained even though their wardens or jailers were named defendants. Nonetheless, the fact that the plaintiffs had been confined in several of the facilities was deemed sufficient to provide standing and to satisfy the requirements of Rule 23. Aside from the somewhat broad and accommodating concept of standing in civil rights cases, it is also true that all the defendants were officials of a single state and its subordinate units of government. Their legal relationship distinguishes them from the defendants the plaintiffs La Mar and Kinsling seek to envelop in their class action. Moreover, it was just these juridical links that were used in Broughton v. Brewer, 298 F.Supp. 260 (S.D.Ala. S.D.1969), to fix the identity of those defendants properly included in the plaintiff's class action to declare Alabama's vagrancy laws unconstitutional brought on behalf of "all persons whose poverty or lack of apparent means of livelihood renders them susceptible to arrest under" such laws.

The existence of similar links distinguishes Samuel et al. v. University of Pittsburgh et al., 56 F.R.D. 435 (W.D.Pa.1972). Despite the fact that the representative plaintiffs attended only the University of Pittsburgh, a class action against those state universities which adhered to the rule about which the representative plaintiffs were complaining was sustained. A common rule applied by instrumentalities of a single state presents a situation quite unlike that here before us. It is true that Judge Teitelbaum, who delivered the opinion in *Samuel,* permitted it to lead him into what we believe to be error in Haas v. Pittsburgh National Bank et al., 60 F.R.D. 604 (W.D.Pa.1973), in which he decided the issue before us contrary to what we here hold. In *Haas* Judge Teitelbaum appeared to believe that a common commercial practice was enough to serve as the legal link present in *Washington, Broughton,* and *Samuel.* With this we do not agree.

Notes and Questions

1. In *La Mar* the court expresses disagreement with Haas v. Pittsburgh National Bank, 60 F.R.D. 604 (W.D.Pa.1973), in which plaintiff claimed that the interest charges for credit card accounts were usurious. On behalf of a class of holders of BankAmericard and Master Charge card holders, plaintiff sued three banks although she had had no dealings with one of them, Western Pennsylvania National Bank (WPNB). WPNB moved to dismiss on the ground that plaintiff lacked standing to sue it because she had not dealt with it. The court found that the motion to dismiss "presents a question which lies at the very heart of class actions under the Federal Rules of Civil Procedure ... one which requires the balancing of two important, and here

countervailing, considerations: standing to sue and representative status under Rule 23." It suggested that "it may be implicit in Rule 23 that once the class has been determined, whatever defects may exist as to the standing of the original named plaintiff can be cured by the eventual opting out (or more properly under Rule 23(c)(2) failure to opt out) of class members who possess exactly those elements necessary to standing that the named plaintiff lacked." Does Rule 23 provide a means for granting standing to a plaintiff suing as a class representative if she would not have standing to sue individually? Can the Federal Rules of Civil Procedure expand standing? Keep this issue in mind when we reach mootness, *infra* p. 481.

In *Haas* the court did not rely solely on the standing of unnamed class members. It emphasized WPNB's participation in the credit card scheme as a basis for allowing the action to proceed against it: "[T]he Master Charge card account issued by WPNB supplies the missing link. Here, one plaintiff has brought a class action against three banks, each of whom issues and administers one of two types of credit card account. The essence of plaintiff's complaint goes to the credit cards, rather than the banks themselves. Yet plaintiff is unable to bring BankAmericard and Master Charge, as such, into Court as defendants if BankAmericard and Master Charge are mere labels for service umbrellas which have no existence other than as embodied and administered by member banks." Since WPNB administered Master Charge accounts, the court held that plaintiff could be granted "class representative status" as to it. Could similar reasoning be applied in *La Mar*? Does emphasis on the "missing link" eliminate the objection that Rule 23 may not confer standing on a person who otherwise lacks it?

2. Consider the following criticism of *La Mar*:

A strict application of the requirement that the plaintiff representative possess a claim against each member of the defendant class would effectively prevent actions by a plaintiff class against a defendant class, and a serious question can be raised whether this is an unduly rigid reading of the adequacy of representation requirement. * * * [T]he primary focus of that requirement is whether the representative will vigorously prosecute the action. There is no reason to believe that in a situation such as *La Mar* this will not be the case. It is true, as Judge Sneed noted, that extra administrative burdens may fall on the court in these types of actions. However, that fact is more appropriately considered when determining whether the class action is superior to other methods of handling the dispute.

7A C. Wright, A. Miller & M. Kane, Federal Practice & Procedure § 1770 at 405 (2d ed. 1986).

3. Note that the *La Mar* court specifically limited its rationale to exclude situations in which a conspiracy or concerted scheme is alleged, or a case "in which all defendants are juridically related in a manner that suggests a single resolution of the dispute would be expeditious." An example of the latter standard would seem to be Washington v. Lee, 263 F.Supp. 327 (M.D.Ala.1966), cited by the *La Mar* court, in which plaintiffs incarcerated in several jails were permitted to sue a class consisting of all the sheriffs in the state because they were all officials of a single legal entity. Does the fact that there were common questions of fact in *La Mar* satisfy

that standard? Would the standard be satisfied if all Oregon pawn brokers had adopted identical pawn tickets using a form developed by their trade association?

4. Plaintiffs often include conspiracy allegations in their complaints. Do such allegations solve standing and typicality problems? Consider the Ninth Circuit's reasoning in reversing the certification of a statewide class action under Rule 23(b)(3) in In re Northern District of California "Dalkon Shield" IUD Products Liability Litigation, 693 F.2d 847 (9th Cir.1982):

> From the large California class the court may be able to find plaintiffs whose claims are fairly representative of the varying injuries. In proving liability under a negligence theory, however, the plaintiffs have to prove not only their injuries, but that Robins and each defendant owed them a duty of care and also what those different standards of care were, if they were breached, and—most important—if the breaches proximately caused the plaintiffs' varying injuries. To prove liability under a breach of warranty theory, representative plaintiffs must exist for each type of warranty, assurance, or medical advice each plaintiff received. The difficulty of meeting the typicality requirement seems obvious.

> While we recognize the many differences between this case and *La Mar,* the case is instructive. The district court believed that an exception could be found within the *La Mar* doctrine for this particular case because "plaintiffs have alleged a concerted scheme or conspiracy between defendants in the marketing, design, testing, and production of Dalkon Shields." But this generalization, while partly true, loses sight of the fact that some of the plaintiffs have not alleged that all of their defendants had so conspired. For example, some plaintiffs sued their own doctors and the local suppliers of those doctors, without planning to prove that those defendants were part of a conspiracy.

> The district court's holding was inconsistent with *La Mar.* The financial importance of common questions of law and fact cannot be used to create a class of plaintiffs who have claims against some common defendants and some separate and uncommon defendants. The complexity of issues peculiar to individual claims militates against grouping all plaintiffs into a class for only part of their recovery.

> We do not decide or suggest that the typicality requirement of Rule 23(a)(3) may never be met when multiple plaintiffs sue different defendants. But the requirement is not met in this case.

5. In Angel Music, Inc. v. ABC Sports, Inc., 112 F.R.D. 70 (S.D.N.Y. 1986), plaintiff, the holder of the copyright of music ABC used as background music in its broadcast of the 1984 Olympics, sued on behalf of a class of music publishers against a defendant class of television stations and production affiliates. Plaintiff alleged that the defendant class members had a common practice of using copyrighted music in synchronization with visual images without paying for a license to do so, but the court held that plaintiff lacked standing to sue anyone but ABC. It rejected plaintiff's argument that the allegedly common violation of the Copyright Act established a juridical link escaping the *La Mar* rule: "The juridical link exception has been confined to instances when a class of plaintiffs, usually attempting to

vindicate their civil rights, brings an action against a class of state officials charged with uniformly enforcing an allegedly unconstitutional statute of administrative policy." Id. at 75.

5. REPRESENTATIVENESS

HANSBERRY v. LEE

Supreme Court of the United States, 1940.
311 U.S. 32, 61 S.Ct. 115, 85 L.Ed. 22.

JUSTICE STONE delivered the opinion of the Court.

The question is whether the Supreme Court of Illinois, by its adjudication that petitioners in this case are bound by a judgment rendered in an earlier litigation to which they were not parties, has deprived them of the due process of law guaranteed by the Fourteenth Amendment.

[The Hansberrys, who were African American, bought and moved into a home in Chicago in an area covered by a racially restrictive covenant. In reaction, owners of neighboring homes sued in an Illinois state court to void the sale to the Hansberrys. The Hansberrys defended on the ground that the covenant never became effective because it wasn't signed by 95% of the homeowners in the area (encompassing about 500 homes), as required by its terms. The trial court found that only 54% of the landowners had signed the agreement.

The trial court nevertheless voided the sale to the Hansberrys and ordered them to move out because it found that they were bound by a decision that the covenant was valid in Burke v. Kleiman, an earlier suit to enforce the covenant in an Illinois state court. That suit was filed at the instance of the Woodlawn Property Owners Association, a neighborhood association, against Kleiman, a white property owner who rented to a black, and Hall, his black tenant. It was brought "on behalf of" all landowners in the area and alleged that the covenant had been signed by the required 95% of the owners. Defendants in the Burke case stipulated that the requisite number of signatures had been obtained and defended on the ground that the covenant should no longer be enforceable due to changed conditions. The court in Burke rejected that defense and held the agreement enforceable.

In Hansberry, the trial court found that it could not reopen the issue because Burke had been a class action that was binding on the Hansberry's grantor, and it had decided that there were enough signatures. The Illinois Supreme Court, noting that "[i]t cannot be seriously contended that [the Burke case] was not properly a representative suit," affirmed. It concluded that the stipulation in Burke that 95% had signed the covenant, while factually inaccurate, had not been collusive or fraudulent.]

State courts are free to attach such descriptive labels to litigations before them as they may choose and to attribute to them such consequences as they think appropriate under state constitutions and laws, subject only to the requirements of the Constitution of the United States. But when the judgment of a state court, ascribing to the judgment of another court the binding force and effect of *res judicata,* is challenged for want of due process it becomes the duty of this Court to examine the course of procedure in both litigations to ascertain whether the litigant whose rights have thus been adjudicated has been afforded such notice and opportunity to be heard as are requisite to the due process which the Constitution prescribes.

It is a principle of general application in Anglo–American jurisprudence that one is not bound by a judgment *in personam* in a litigation in which he is not designated as a party or to which he has not been made a party by service of process. *Pennoyer v. Neff,* 95 U.S. 714, 24 L.Ed. 565. A judgment rendered in such circumstances is not entitled to the full faith and credit which the Constitution and statute of the United States prescribes, and judicial action enforcing it against the person or property of the absent party is not that due process which the Fifth and Fourteenth Amendments require.

To these general rules there is a recognized exception that, to an extent not precisely defined by judicial opinion, the judgment in a "class" or "representative" suit, to which some members of the class are parties, may bind members of the class or those represented who were not made parties to it.

* * *

It is familiar doctrine of the federal courts that members of a class not present as parties to the litigation may be bound by the judgment where they are in fact adequately represented by parties who are present, or where they actually participate in the conduct of the litigation in which members of the class are present as parties, or where the interest of the members of the class, some of whom are present as parties, is joint, or where for any other reason the relationship between the parties present and those who are absent is such as legally to entitle the former to stand in judgment for the latter.

In all such cases, so far as it can be said that the members of the class who are present are, by generally recognized rules of law, entitled to stand in judgment for those who are not, we may assume for present purposes that such procedure affords a protection to the parties who are represented, though absent, which would satisfy the requirements of due process and full faith and credit. * * * We decide only that the procedure and the course of litigation sustained here by the plea of *res judicata* do not satisfy these requirements.

The restrictive agreement did not purport to create a joint obligation or liability. If valid and effective its promises were the several obligations of the signers and those claiming under them. The promises ran severally to every other signer. It is plain that in such circumstances all those alleged to be bound by the agreement would not constitute a single class in any litigation brought to enforce it. Those who sought to secure its benefits by enforcing it could not be said to be in the same class with or represent those whose interest was in resisting performance, for the agreement by its terms imposes obligations and confers rights on the owner of each plot of land who signs it. If those who thus seek to secure the benefits of the agreement were rightly regarded by the state Supreme Court as constituting a class, it is evident that those signers or their successors who are interested in challenging the validity of the agreement and resisting its performance are not of the same class in the sense that their interests are identical so that any group who had elected to enforce rights conferred by the agreement could be said to be acting in the interest of any others who were free to deny its obligation.

Because of the dual and potentially conflicting interests of those who are putative parties to the agreement in compelling or resisting its performance, it is impossible to say, solely because they are parties to it, that any two of them are of the same class. Nor without more, and with the due regard for the protection of the rights of absent parties which due process exacts, can some be permitted to stand in judgment for all.

It is one thing to say that some members of a class may represent other members in a litigation where the sole and common interest of the class in the litigation, is either to assert a common right or to challenge an asserted obligation. It is quite another to hold that all those who are free alternatively either to assert rights or to challenge them are of a single class, so that any group, merely because it is of the class so constituted, may be deemed adequately to represent any others of the class in litigating their interests in either alternative. Such a selection of representatives for purposes of litigation, whose substantial interests are not necessarily or even probably the same as those whom they are deemed to represent, does not afford that protection to absent parties which due process requires.

Notes and Questions

1. Can the court resolve differences in strategy or preferences between persons who appear similarly situated? In Green v. Santa Fe Industries, 82 F.R.D. 688 (S.D.N.Y.1979), plaintiff, a former shareholder of a corporation that had been merged into defendant, asserted that the merger was intended to freeze out minority shareholders. Plaintiff sought "restoration of the minority to their status as full shareholders" of the merged corporation. Defendants opposed plaintiff's motion to certify a class of all minority shareholders on the ground that many of those persons had initiated appraisal proceedings in state court. Finding that "[r]escission of the merger would be inconsistent with the relief sought in the appraisal proceeding," the court refused to certify a class. Was this a decision that there was actually no class or that plaintiff was not adequately representing it because he disagreed with some members of the class in his selection of remedies? Recall also the discussion of conflicting objectives affecting class definition in public law litigation, *supra* p. 240-41 n. 6. Can the courts ever resolve such strategic disagreements?

2.   In *Hansberry* the Court points out that the restrictive agreement did not purport to create joint rights but only separate obligations. If joint rights had been involved would the issues have been different? Does it matter whether certification is sought pursuant to Rule 23(b)(2), relating to equitable relief against defendant, or 23(b)(3), which relates to damages? For example, in Green v. Santa Fe Industries, *supra* note 1, was it relevant that plaintiff sought equitable relief against defendant that would affect all minority shareholders? In such situations is it necessary that the suit proceed as a class action? Does class status bear only on the propriety of equitable relief, which is said to be inherently discretionary?

3.   Could the earlier suit in *Hansberry* to enforce the covenant have been redesigned as a bilateral class action to avoid the due process problem? Consider Professor Yeazell's views on *Hansberry*:

> If, as the Court suggested, the validity of a class depends on the subjective desire of the individuals constituting it to assert their rights, classes could consist only of individuals who had, individually, indicated that they wished to assert the rights in question. Because all persons are always free either to assert their claims or not, classes could consist only of volunteers.

> * * *

> Where such representative litigants encompass *both* possible sides of a dispute, one's concern about unrepresented interests may diminish somewhat: one side of the litigation is defending a decision taken by representatives of all the members, and the other side is attacking that decision on behalf of dissatisfied members. Such an alignment may not exhaust every possible position, but it gives some assurances, particularly if the conceived unrepresented interests seem implausible.

> The difficulty with *Hansberry* is that neither of these two conditions obtained. The defendants in [the earlier suit] had not been such representative litigants. In addition, at the time the case was decided it may have been difficult even to define the interests that should have been represented. The residential contiguity meant that the plaintiff and defendant classes had multiple relationships with each other. It was thus far harder to say what the class interest was. The problem posed had two levels. The first was the question of whether interests not usually thought to be economic were at odds with economic ones; did a noneconomic interest in an integrated (or a segregated) neighborhood outweigh the interest in property values? To the extent that the class action is based on easy, objective identification of class interests, a situation like that in *Hansberry,* which involved both material and nonmaterial roles and values, will be almost impossible to handle. One cannot identify a single class interest among the tensions created by multiple relationships, some of which are affective rather than financial. The problem is too *many* interests.

> Moreover, the problem of too many plausible interests repeated itself on the purely material level. Even if one assumes that the class characteristics of the group involved only financial advantage, the picture remains unclear. For one could not with any certainty say whether

it would be to the advantage of the class to increase the available market for its property by opening it to the excluded group, or whether the postulated decline in desirability would offset the greater demand resulting from the larger number of potential buyers.

S. Yeazell, From Medieval Group Litigation to the Modern Class Action 234–35 (1987).

4. Should Hansberry be allowed to argue that he is not bound by the result of the earlier suit due to the mistake made there in stipulating that the required percentage of homeowners had signed the covenant? Can the courts allow such 20/20 hindsight to erode the binding effect of class actions?

5. Is a due process analysis of adequacy of representation mandatory at the class certification stage? Would such an analysis have been helpful in the first suit in *Hansberry?* Is it constitutionally sufficient to examine the adequacy of representation when the res judicata issue is raised? Who benefits from scrutiny at the certification stage, the class members or the defendant? See Woolley, The Availability of Collateral Attack for Inadequate Representation in Class Suits, 79 Texas L. Rev. 383 (2000) (criticizing a trend to foreclose collateral attacks when the earlier court found the class representative adequate). Matsushita Elec. Indus. Co. v. Epstein, *infra* p. 803. Rule 23(a)(4) requires consideration of adequacy of representation at the class certification stage. As you examine the application of its requirements, consider the extent to which they resolve the problems presented in *Hansberry.*

Professor Nagareda finds the analysis of *Hansberry* unsatisfactory, emphasizing that Hansberry was not the only defendant. Instead, James Burke, the white husband of the plaintiff in the earlier case, was also a party. For him, the Court's emphasis on interest alignment is insufficient to explain the result. But the absence of serious consideration of these issues as part of the first suit would, in Professor Nagareda's view, be a ground for declining to bind him: "*Only* the lack of sufficient structural safeguards for adequate representation, not some defect in interest alignment within the class, can explain the lack of preclusive effect accorded the *Burke* class judgment as to James Burke." Nagareda, Administering Adequacy in Class Representation, 82 Tex.L.Rev. 287, 314 (2003).

6. *Hansberry* contines to permit class members to challenge the binding effect of class judgments on them based on inadequacy of representation by class representations and class attorneys. This issue is considered in the context of preclusion and collateral attack in Stephenson v. Dow Chemical Co., *infra* p. 819.

7. For background on the social and political context of *Hansberry,* see Kamp, The History Behind Hansberry v. Lee, 20 U.C.Davis L.Rev. 481 (1987). Professor Kamp reports that, after the Supreme Court held racially restrictive covenants valid in 1926, the Chicago Real Estate Board embarked on a program to impose them on white neighborhoods. This proved to be a massive task, however, owing to the need to get a lot of forms signed by owners (hence the problem with getting 95% of the owners to sign in *Hansberry* itself). Nevertheless, the campaign continued and succeeded in confining African Americans to certain limited areas of the city. The influx of African Americans into Chicago during the Depression put great stress on

these arrangements, as there were estimated to be more than 50,000 more African–American residents of Chicago than units to house them in the areas where they were allowed to live. At the same time, due to the Depression the white population in adjacent areas was declining, and vacant homes in the restricted areas could not be sold or leased to whites at any price while they commanded high prices from blacks, who had nowhere else to go. Professor Kamp explains that one of the reasons the Hansberrys were able to buy their house is that they were the only people who wanted to buy it. For further information, see Tidmarsh, The Story of Hansberry: The Foundation for Modern Class Actions, in Civil Procedure Stories (K. Clermont, ed. 2004), at 217.

PEIL v. NATIONAL SEMICONDUCTOR CORP.

United States District Court, Eastern District of Pennsylvania, 1980.
86 F.R.D. 357.

HANNUM, DISTRICT JUDGE.

Before the Court is the motion of the plaintiff pursuant to F.R.Civ.P. 23(c)(1) for an order determining that the Complaint involved in this litigation and commenced on behalf of similarly situated persons should proceed as a class action. The class that the plaintiff proposes to represent would be defined as consisting of all persons or entities who purchased the common stock of the defendant National Semiconductor Corporation [hereinafter "NSC"] during the period between approximately July 1, 1976 to March 1, 1977 and who sustained damages thereby, whether by selling such securities at reduced prices, continuing to hold them at reduced market values, or otherwise.

The essence of the plaintiff's Complaint alleges that the defendants Charles E. Sporck [hereinafter "Sporck"] and Peter J. Sprague [hereinafter "Sprague"], President and Chairman of the Board of NSC, respectively, engaged in a conspiratorial course of conduct to artificially inflate the value of NSC stock in order to permit Sporck and Sprague to dispose of their privately owned shares at the inflated value. The plaintiff contends that the defendants Sporck and Sprague actively misrepresented and failed to disclose facts that hindered potential and actual investors from gaining an accurate portrayal of the financial condition of NSC and that as a result many investors sustained losses when the market finally reflected the actual value of the stock. The plaintiff seeks to represent the class in rectifying this alleged securities violation because on October 1, 1976, he purchased 500 shares of NSC common stock at $35.75 per share and subsequently sold these same shares on February 3, 1977, at the price of $19.50 per share, a loss of $16.25 per share.

The Complaint instituting this litigation was filed on December 13, 1977, several months after the plaintiff had sold his shares of NSC common stock.

* * *

Adequate Representation. The fourth enumerated requirement of F.R.Civ.P. 23(a) provides that the "representative parties will fairly and adequately protect the interests of the class." In an effort to define this somewhat vague standard for representation, the Third Circuit has adopted the following rule to which a plaintiff must demonstrate his compliance:

> (1) they have no interests which are antagonistic to other members of the class, and (2) their attorney is capable of prosecuting the instant claim with some degree of expertise.

Wetzel v. Liberty Mutual Insurance Co., 508 F.2d 239, 247 (3d Cir.1975).

The defendants apparently recognize the applicability of the rule articulated in *Wetzel* but offer a third requirement for adoption; that the plaintiff have first-hand knowledge of the facts giving rise to the cause of action. Essentially, the defendants contend that the plaintiff's counsel, Richard D. Greenfield, Esquire, is the real party in interest but for his lack of standing because he has unearthed the facts and unraveled the complexities attendant to their application to the securities laws. Reliance for this advancement is upon the decision rendered in *In re Goldchip Funding Co.,* 61 F.R.D. 592, 594–95 (M.D.Pa.1974):

> In my view, facts regarding the personal qualities of the representatives themselves are relevant, indeed necessary, in determining whether "the representative parties will fairly and adequately protect the interests of the class." ... A proper representative can offer more to the prosecution of a class action than mere fulfillment of the procedural requirements of Rule 23. He can, for example, offer his personal knowledge of the factual circumstances, and aid in rendering decisions on practical and nonlegal problems which arise during the course of litigation. An attorney who prosecutes a class action with unfettered discretion becomes, in fact, a representative of the class. This is an unacceptable situation because of the possible conflicts of interest involved.

The *Wetzel* rule, as it presently obtains, implicitly recognizes that a class representative need not be the best of all possible representatives but rather one that will pursue a resolution of the controversy with the requisite vigor and in the interest of the class. What is "requisite" is determined by considering the nature of the litigation and the factual and legal basis underlying it; necessarily a case-by-case analysis. To require a person unschooled in the realm of our complex and abstract securities laws to have first-hand knowledge of facts cloaked in an alleged conspiratorial silence and which present themselves as a wrongdoing that may be actionable would render the class action device an impotent tool. In order to responsibly allege and later adequately prove the accusations contained in the plaintiff's Complaint, the plaintiff's counsel must have engaged in and will engage in extensive investigation and discovery conducted with a working knowledge of the securities laws.

The Court is cognizant of the fact that by it not requiring the class representative to have the degree of first-hand knowledge of the factual basis of this litigation suggested by the defendants, counsel may proceed without various restraints. The Court in *In re Goldchip Funding Co., supra,* expressed a similar concern in its ruling to the effect that such unbridled discretion of counsel may render him a class representative rather than its counsel, thereby creating a conflict of interest. The Court is unmoved by this assertion. Aside from the normal degree of flexibility enjoyed by counsel when presenting a client's case, the Court may intervene, if appropriate, pursuant to its inherent power to protect the class members. Moreover, much influence and control is exercised by the Court by the fact that it controls the fee award to the plaintiff's counsel should the plaintiff prevail. In essence, the Court recognizes the existence of its inherent powers to control the actions of the plaintiff's counsel in the event that a conflict of interest appears. Otherwise, counsel for both parties may exercise the discretion they deserve and enjoy when presenting their respective clients' positions.

Ruling in accordance with the numerous cases that expressly reject the *In re Goldchip Funding Co., supra,* precedent and declining to adopt the defendant's proposed third requirements to the *Wetzel* rule, the Court turns to the two existing requirements: (1) the representative has no antagonistic interests and (2) his counsel has the requisite expertise to prosecute the action. It is not disputed that the plaintiff carries no interest that could conceivably be considered antagonistic to the common interests of the class he seeks to represent. Accordingly, the Court deems this requirement satisfied. In addition, the second requirement is not contested and is therefore deemed satisfied. The plaintiff's counsel's ability to prosecute similar actions with a sufficient degree of expertise has been noted on at least one prior occasion. The Court is of the opinion, and so rules, that the plaintiff is an adequate class representative pursuant to the requirements of F.R.Civ.P. 23(a)(4).

Notes and Questions

1.   The court in *Peil* notes that under Rule 23(a)(4) the class representative "need not be the best of all possible representatives." Given the constitutional concerns identified in *Hansberry*, should the courts insist on selecting the best person? Is judicial control of the lawyer's fee a sufficient surrogate for oversight by a knowledgeable class representative? Despite this concern, *Peil* states the normal view under Rule 23(a)(4). For general examinations of adequacy of representation, see Degnan, Adequacy of Representation in Class Actions, 60 Calif.L.Rev. 705 (1972); Note, The Importance of Being Adequate: Due Process Requirements Under Rule 23, 123 U.Pa. L.Rev. 1217 (1975).

2.   *The PSLRA*: In Weiss & Beckerman, Let the Money Do the Monitoring: How Institutional Investors Can Reduce Agency Costs in Securities Class Actions, 104 Yale L.J. 2053 (1995), the authors argued that the existing practices—particularly rewarding the lawyer who files suit first with an appointment as lead counsel—tended to promote participation of "figure-

head plaintiffs" and deter involvement of institutional investors who might be more effective in monitoring counsel.

Congress found this argument persuasive, and the Private Securities Litigation Reform Act accordingly directs the initial plaintiff in securities fraud actions to provide detailed notice about the claims to other investors, inviting them to express an interest in serving as "lead plaintiff." Thereafter, the court is to appoint as lead plaintiff the person "most capable of adequately representing the interests of class members." 15 U.S.C.A. § 78u–4(a)(3)(B)(i). In evaluating contenders for this position, the court should presume that "the person or group of persons ... that has the largest financial interest in the relief sought by the class" is best qualified, although this presumption can be rebutted. Id., § 78u–4(a)(3)(B)(iii). The lead plaintiff then chooses the class counsel, who can be somebody other than the lawyer who filed the suit.

As might be expected from aggressive legislation on a topic with such high stakes, there has been considerable litigation about the application of the PSLRA. Although extensive coverage of those decisions is beyond the scope of this book, it is useful to canvass some of the issues that have arisen as a contrast to the Rule 23(a)(4) analysis.

A key focus has been on the presumption as to who is best qualified to represent the class. Lawyers involved in securities fraud litigation sometimes arranged to confect a collection of shareholders—sometimes hundreds or thousands—who together can be a "group" with the largest losses. Many have objected that this sort of recruiting by lawyers dilutes the objective of client control over the litigation. For discussion, see Fisch, Aggregation, Auctions, and Other Developments in the Selection of Lead Counsel Under the PSLRA, 64 Law & Contemp. Probs. 53, 65–78) (Spring/Summer 2001) (discerning three types of judicial reactions to this sort of maneuver, and urging that courts should interpret "group" narrowly to avoid undermining the objective of the Act to reduce control by counsel).

Another question has been whether the Act enhances or reduces district court authority over selection of class representatives and appointment of lead counsel. It does direct that such appointments be done under the standards of Rule 23. At least one court opined that the PSLRA "raises the standard adequacy threshold" for class representatives, Berger v. Compaq Computer Corp., 257 F.3d 475, 483 (5th Cir.2001), although the same court later softened its view. But another concluded that the presumption that the one with the largest losses should be preferred did not permit the district judge to favor somebody else on the ground that the judge thought the other potential representative would do a better job. In re Cavanaugh, 306 F.3d 726, 732 (9th Cir.2002):

> So long as the plaintiff with the largest losses satisfies the typicality and adequacy requirements, he is entitled to lead plaintiff status, even if the district court is convinced that some other plaintiff would do a better job.

This can mean that the court must make close calls about who has the largest losses. See In re Advanced Tissue Sciences Securities Litigation, 184 F.R.D. 346 (S.D.Cal.1998) (holding that the nod should go to a group with losses of $3,281,173 rather than another group with losses of $3,096,682).

3. *Expanding the "empowered plaintiff" model*: The PSLRA might be viewed as attempting to empower the class representative to act vigorously and effectively on behalf of the class, in particular by selecting and controlling class counsel. Should Rule 23(a)(4) be changed to require selection of the "best" representative? How would courts identify that person? In securities fraud cases, the amount of a person's financial stake may be a very good guideline. Would it be similarly useful in antitrust cases? Cf. In re Fine Paper Antitrust Litigation, *infra* p. 669, in which a state attorney general objected that at a meeting of plaintiffs' counsel "the mom and pop greeting store with four attorneys got four votes, whereas at that meeting the State of Colorado would get only one vote." Should the State's much larger purchases of the product in question make it a better representative? Who would be the best class representative in a suit seeking to desegregate a school system?

Although recognizing that the empowered lead plaintiff model is not suitable for all class actions, Professor Fisch has urged that it can work outside the securities fraud area when three criteria have been satisfied: (1) the class includes members with a sufficient financial stake to make the effort to do a careful job selecting and monitoring class counsel; (2) the lead plaintiffs must be representative of the interests of class members; and (3) the size of class members' interest must correlate with sophistication in selecting and monitoring class counsel (as with institutional investors in securities fraud suits). Fisch, Lawyers on the Auction Block: Evaluating the Selection of Class Counsel by Auction, 102 Colum.L.Rev. 649, 722 (2002). She suggests that these conditions may exist in shareholder derivative actions, but not in consumer class actions. Similarly, it would be problematic to take this approach in mass tort cases (id. at 726–27):

> Although mass tort cases generally include class members with substantial stakes, the interests of class members may diverge substantially. In particular, the interests of those class members with the largest stakes, often the most seriously injured, are likely to conflict with other class members, such as those with more modest injuries or exposure only plaintiffs. As a result, although the seriously injured plaintiffs may have sufficient motivation to participate actively, they may not be capable of representing the plaintiff class fairly. Additionally, because the process that generates differing class stakes is likely to be fortuitous or random, there is little reason to believe that those with larger interests in the case are likely to be particularly well qualified to serve as lead plaintiff.

4. Representative plaintiffs are sometimes challenged under Rule 23(a)(4) on the basis of their lack of understanding of the case, usually after the opposing attorney grills them on deposition. For example, in In re Crazy Eddie Securities Litigation, 135 F.R.D. 39 (E.D.N.Y.1991), defendant objected to the representativeness of a plaintiff, John Pastamatakis, who had trouble with the English language and showed confusion at deposition about both the facts of the case and his duties to the class members. Having read his deposition, the court found that he was a satisfactory class representative because he was "aware of the basic facts underlying the lawsuit" and not being likely to "abdicate his obligations to fellow class members." Id. at 41. See also In re Monosodium Glutamate Antitrust Litigation, 205 F.R.D. 229 (D. Minn.2001) (the fact that the named plaintiffs could not answer basic

questions about the progress of the litigation or about the allegations did not preclude a finding that they satisfied the adequacy requirement because they possessed enough knowledge to assist their attorney in prosecuting the action). But see Greenspan v. Brassler, 78 F.R.D. 130 (S.D.N.Y.1978) ("the class is entitled to more than blind reliance upon even competent counsel by uninterested and inexperienced representatives," and the representative must do more than play a "superfluous role in the litigation").

5. The attitude of the court in *Peil* is common where the issue is lack of interest on the part of the representative. Consider Kirkpatrick v. J.C. Bradford & Co., 827 F.2d 718, 727 (11th Cir.1987): "[A]dequate class representation generally does not require that the named plaintiffs demonstrate to any particular degree that individually they will pursue with vigor the legal claims of the class. Although the interests of the plaintiff class certainly would be better served if the named plaintiffs fully participate in the litigation, the economics of the class action suit often are such that counsel have a greater financial incentive for obtaining a successful resolution of a class suit than do the individual class members. It is not surprising, then, that the subjective desire to vigorously prosecute a class action * * * quite often is supplied more by counsel than by the class members themselves."

6. For an argument that concern about the individual characteristics of named plaintiffs is simply out of place in class actions, see Burns, Decorative Figureheads: Eliminating Class Representatives in Class Actions, 42 Hastings L.J. 165 (1990). Prof. Burns lists a number of problems that would be solved by dispensing with the class representative altogether. Professors Macey and Miller reach similar conclusions:

> In large-scale, small-claim litigation, the courts should forthrightly acknowledge that the named plaintiff is a figurehead and should accordingly prohibit any inquiry by the defendant into the named plaintiff's intellect, educational achievements, or understanding of the case. Allowing such inquiry merely serves to harass and invade the named plaintiff's privacy and to reduce artificially the supply of representative plaintiffs, further concentrating and limiting the availability of legal services by plaintiffs' attorneys. Indeed, because the named plaintiff is a figurehead, the adequacy of representation would not be harmed if plaintiffs' attorneys could file "Jane Doe" or "Richard Roe" complaints on behalf of a fictitious absent class member without supplying an actual carcass for grilling over the hot coals of a deposition.

Macey & Miller, The Plaintiffs' Attorney's Role in Class Action and Derivative Litigation: Economic Analysis and Recommendations for Reform, 58 U.Chi.L.Rev. at 93–94 (1991).

On the other hand, when applying Rule 23(a)(4) courts do care presently about who the named representative is. Thus, in Kaplan v. Pomerantz, 132 F.R.D. 504 (N.D.Ill.1990), the court refused to certify a class because the representative's deposition testimony was false. "A plaintiff's honesty and integrity are important considerations in allowing him to represent a class." Id. at 510; accord, Deutschman v. Beneficial Corp., 132 F.R.D. 359 (D.Del. 1990); see also Valley Drug Co. v. Geneva Pharmaceuticals, Inc., 350 F.3d 1181 (11th Cir.2003) (holding that class members in price-fixing action who may have been benefitted by certain practices of defendants could not represent those harmed by these practices). At the same time, they do not give in to arguments that might cripple class actions. Thus in Mississippi Protection & Advocacy System, Inc. v. Cotten, 929 F.2d 1054 (5th Cir.1991), the court rejected challenges to a class of retarded persons, noting that defendant's challenges to the representatives' adequacy led to the conclusion that "as a result of the developmental disability which requires their treatment, no patient of the Center is likely to be capable of representing himself in this or any court."

In securities fraud class actions, courts have looked with particular skepticism on "professional plaintiffs." For example, the court in Welling v. Alexy, 155 F.R.D. 654 (N.D.Cal.1994), found a plaintiff who had filed 13 prior securities class actions inadequate to be class representative because he had demonstrated "striking unfamiliarity" with the case, and had "ceded control to his lawyers." See also In re Gibson Greetings Securities Litigation, 159 F.R.D. 499, 501 (S.D.Ohio 1994) (plaintiff who had filed 182 class actions was a "professional class action plaintiff" who would not adequately represent the class). The Private Securities Litigation Reform Act implements this concern in securities fraud class actions by directing that ordinarily no person should be allowed to be class representative in more than five such class actions at once. 15 U.S.C.A. §§ 77z–1(a)(3)(B)(vi); 78u–4(a)(3)(B)(vi).

7. If the representative is found wanting on personal grounds, what should be done? In general, the court will allow the case to continue as an individual action on behalf of the named plaintiff. Under some circumstances, however, it may seek or invite the involvement of another person to act as class representative. See Johnson v. American Credit Co., 581 F.2d 526 (5th Cir.1978). For further discussion, see *supra* p. 277 n. 7. When would such an invitation be appropriate?

8. Putting aside personal failings of the representative, there may be actual conflicts in interest between the representative and some or all of the members of the class. These issues often present challenges for the courts. For example, in Fraser v. Major League Soccer, L.L.C., 180 F.R.D. 178 (D.Mass.1998), plaintiff professional soccer players alleged that defendant's Standard Player Agreement contained provisions forbidden under the antitrust laws. They sought certification of a class consisting all players in the league. Defendants resisted, asserting conflicts with other class members, but the court was not persuaded (id. at 181):

> The defendants argue that there is deep division within the class as to whether plaintiffs should litigate this action or instead seek to negotiate with the defendants. Thus, they say, either class certification should be denied or a subclass of those who favor collective bargaining over litigation should be formed. Certainly, the court has the authority to create such a subclass, or to deny certification completely, when deep divisions exist in the proposed class. However, there is a distinction between a case in which the division between the class plaintiffs and unnamed class members is central to the claims asserted by the class and a case in which the division is a result of disagreements over strategy. An example of the first category is a class complaint where the class includes men who may be beneficiaries of the purported discrimination against women. See, e.g., Payne v. Travenol Labs., Inc, 673 F.2d

798, 812 (5th Cir.1982) [*infra* p. 497] (stating that "[o]rdinarily, if a court discerns a conflict [among named plaintiffs and absent members] the proper solution is to create subclasses of persons whose interests are in accord").

On the other hand, where the asserted division between the named plaintiffs and unnamed class members is simply over a question of strategy rather than a conflict inherent in the structure of the class, denial of class certification has depended upon a strong showing that the disagreement was genuine and fundamental, and that a majority of the class members did not favor litigation. See, e.g., Bailey v. Ryan Stevedoring Co., 528 F.2d 551, 553 (5th Cir.1976) (declining to certify class where named plaintiffs' goal to merge racially segregated unions was opposed by 204 of approximately 230 black union members who filed petition with court).

Here, the defendants' evidence as to disagreement within the class does not demonstrate that a majority of class members oppose this suit. In fact, evidence of *any* opposition at all to this action is tenuous.

See also Robertson v. National Basketball Association, 389 F.Supp. 867 (S.D.N.Y.1975) ("Class action determination will not be denied, nor will the formulation of subclasses be required in the absence of a showing that the alleged potential conflicts are real probabilities and not mere imaginative speculation.").

9.   In addition, the class representative cannot be too closely identified with the lawyer. See London v. Wal–Mart Stores, Inc., 340 F.3d 1246 (11th Cir.2003), a Truth In Lending Act action in which the class representative was a lifelong friend and former stock broker of class counsel. The court held that the longstanding relationship, coupled with the possibility that counsel might again retain the proposed class representative as his stock broker, created an undue potential conflict of interest in this case to favor the lawyer's interests over those of the class. See also Cotchett v. Avis Rent A Car System, 56 F.R.D. 549 (S.D.N.Y.1972) (class representative could not be law partner of class counsel because law partner would benefit financially from enhanced attorney fees, which would come from any recovery by the class). Compare Malchman v. Davis, 706 F.2d 426, 432 (2d Cir.1983) (class representative is sister of chauffeur of class counsel); Lewis v. Goldsmith, 95 F.R.D. 15 (D.N.J.1982) (class counsel is uncle of class representative). Is it likely that the chauffeur's sister is going to be able, as class representative, to provide a meaningful check on the actions of the class attorney who is her brother's employer?

10.   Defendants also like to focus on the ability of the class representative to finance the litigation. In general, the courts have limited the inquiry into such matters. See Note, Discovery of Plaintiff's Financial Situation in Federal Class Actions: Heading 'Em Off at the Passbook, 30 Hast.L.J. 449 (1978). In Rand v. Monsanto Co., 926 F.2d 596 (7th Cir.1991), in which the named plaintiff testified in his deposition that, given his maximum potential recovery of $1,135, he would not agree to be liable for costs up to $25,000. The district court denied class certification on this ground, but the court of appeals reversed in an opinion by Judge Easterbrook: "A conscientious plaintiff is likely to be willing to make some financial commitment to the

case. But no person need be willing to stake his entire fortune for the benefit of strangers. Class lawsuits can be frightfully expensive * * *. No (sane) person would pay the entire costs of a securities class action in exchange for a maximum benefit of $1,135. None would put up $25,000 or even $2,500 against a hope of recovering $1,135." Id. at 599.

11. *Appointment of class counsel*: The traditional adequacy inquiry under Rule 23(a)(4) has also focused on the adequacy of class counsel. Effective 2003, Rule 23(g) explicitly governs the selection of class counsel. As explained, in the Committee Note accompanying the amendment, "Rule 23(a)(4) will continue to call for scrutiny of the proposed class representative, while this subdivision will guide the court in assessing proposed class counsel as part of the certification decision." This topic will be covered in Chapter VI. See *infra* p. 664.

C. TYPES OF CLASS ACTIONS MAINTAINABLE

Class actions that satisfy Rule 23(a) must also meet the requirements of one of the four kinds of class actions described in Rule 23(b)(1)(A), 23(a)(1)(B), 23(b)(2), and 23(b)(3). Even if Rule 23(a) is fully satisfied, a court should certify only if a case satisfies Rule 23(b). See Lowery v. Circuit City Stores, Inc., 158 F.3d 742, 757–58 (4th Cir.1998) (rejecting plaintiffs' argument that the district court was required to certify a class after finding Rule 23(a) satisfied), vacated and remanded for redetermination on issue unrelated to class certification, 527 U.S. 1031, 119 S.Ct. 2388, 144 L.Ed.2d 790 (1999).

This section considers those types of class actions, as well as defendant classes. It also addresses the timing of certification decisions and of appellate review of class certification decisions.

1. RULE 23(b)(1)(A)—"INCOMPATIBLE STANDARDS" CLASS ACTIONS

Rule 23(b)(1)(A) allows a class to be certified when "the prosecution of separate actions by or against individual members of the class would create a risk of inconsistent or varying adjudications with respect to individual members of the class which would establish incompatible standards of conduct for the party opposing the class." This test looks to the impact on the party opposing the class and whether separate actions would subject it to incompatible standards. Notice the similarity to the test in Rule 19(a)(2)(ii) for a necessary party. Owing to concerns like those under Rule 19, such class actions are "mandatory" in the sense that individual class members are ordinarily not allowed to opt out and file separate suits.

Paradigm cases under Rule 23(b)(1)(A) are suits by taxpayers to invalidate municipal action or suits by shareholders to compel the declaration of a dividend. A typical case is Van Gemert v. Boeing Co., 259 F.Supp. 125 (S.D.N.Y.1966), where a class action of debenture holders against the corporation was certified because it sought to determine their right of conversion into common stock. If the corporation had been faced with individual suits by each debenture holder, the outcomes could have been different and it would have been subjected to incompatible standards as to its future conduct.

Defendant classes may also be suitable for Rule 23(b)(1)(A) treatment. For example, in First Federal of Michigan v. Barrow, 878 F.2d 912 (6th Cir.1989), the court upheld certification of two mandatory classes of recipients of preferential payments in connection with a bankruptcy proceeding. The court reasoned (id. at 919):

> The absence of class certification in the instant case would have precipitated a multiplicity of separate actions against the individual members of the certified classes which would have created the risk of inconsistent or varying adjudications with respect to individual class members which, in turn, would have established incompatible standards of conduct for the trustee in pursuing the classes by placing him into a possible conflict of position in seeking satisfaction of individual claims.

Where money damages are central to a case, courts have often refused to certify an "incompatible standards" class. Recall that in *La Mar, supra* p. 278, the Ninth Circuit stated that a (b)(1)(A) class "infrequently, if ever" would arise in a damage action because the defendants could continue their conduct even if the plaintiff were successful and their success would not fix the rights and duties owed by the defendants to others. A good example of this position is found in Alexander Grant & Co. v. McAlister, 116 F.R.D. 583 (S.D.Ohio 1987), which refused to certify an "incompatible standards" class on behalf of some 300 partners of the plaintiff company for purposes of defendant Harris' counterclaim:

> Harris argues that certification under Rule 23(b)(1)(A) is appropriate because if each partner was sued separately, some could be found liable while others could not and this inconsistency is what Rule 23(b)(1)(A) seeks to avoid. [The named class representative] responds that this is all conjecture, as there is no guarantee that there will be inconsistent results, and if different results are reached it may not be due to inconsistency, but rather due to the fact that the Grant partners are situated differently as to tenure as partners and involvement with [the partnership].

> To satisfy the requirements of Rule 23(b)(1)(A), there must be more than the mere possibility that inconsistent judgments and resolutions of identical questions of law would result if numerous actions are held instead of one class action. What is required is well-described in Employers Insurance of Wausau v. FDIC, 112 F.R.D. 52, 54 (E.D.Tenn.1986):

> > The advisory committee notes make it clear that the situation in which a party is faced with inconsistent results requiring it to pay some class members but not others is covered by Rule 23(b)(3) not Rule 23(b)(1). See Advisory Committee Note of

1966 to Rule 23(b)(3). The risk of "incompatible standards of conduct" which Rule 23(b)(1)(A) was designed to protect against involves situations where the non-class party does not know, because of inconsistent adjudications, whether or not it is legally permissible for it to pursue a certain course of conduct. Thus, Rule 23(b)(1)(A) is designed to protect against the nonclass party's being placed in a stalemated or conflicted position and is applicable only to actions in which there is not only a risk of inconsistent adjudications but also where the nonclass party could be sued for *different and incompatible affirmative relief.*

A reading of Harris' arguments made in support of Rule 23(b)(1)(A) certification leads to the conclusion that certification under this provision is not appropriate. Harris is claiming that if there were separate suits, she might win on some and lose on others, even though the legal and factual issues involved are identical. At no point does she argue that anything more might result, and in light of the above law, without more there can be no certification under this provision. This is not like the situation of the validity of a single bond issue, allegedly invalid because of improper authority to issue the bonds, the typical Rule 23(b)(1)(A) type class.

In contrast to *Alexander Grant,* some earlier court cases were willing to invoke Rule 23(b)(1)(A) even when damages were involved. A district court in Robertson v. National Basketball Association, 389 F.Supp. 867 (S.D.N.Y.1975), certified an "incompatible standards" class action on behalf of past, present, and future players in the NBA league for injunctive relief and treble damages in view of the possible conflicting standards that the league would be subjected to if there were individual suits. In Hernandez v. Motor Vessel Skyward, 61 F.R.D. 558 (S.D.Fla. 1973), a (b)(1)(A) class action was certified for damages against a cruise line on behalf of the passengers and crew of a cruise ship who were taken seriously ill due to contaminated food and water. The court reasoned as follows:

> The Court also finds that the prosecution of separate actions by individual members of the class would create a risk of inconsistent or varying adjudications with respect to individual members of the class which would establish incompatible standards of conduct for the parties opposing the class. It is conceivable that the defendants would be taken to task by one passenger after another until a judgment against the defendants was obtained. At that point, future plaintiffs could call the doctrine of collateral estoppel into play to bind the defendants on the issue of negligence in the preparation of food and water.

> But prior to any determination adverse to the defendants, a strong possibility exists that a tremendous amount of needless judicial time and energy may be expended on this litigation. It appears to the Court that the interests of all concerned would be

advanced by a single determination of the negligence issue under the provisions of F.R.Civ.P. 23(c)(4)(A).

Is this reasoning really consistent with the purposes of certification under Rule 23(b)(1)(A)? Compare some Texas caselaw, which explicitly allows a mandatory class action to avoid duplicative litigation. See Morgan v. Deere Credit, Inc., 889 S.W.2d 360 (Tex.App.1994) (allowing "incompatible standards" class action to avoid the possibility of multiple damage suits and noting that "Texas courts have rejected federal law requiring opt-out classes in suits like this one where certification under that rule would compel patently inefficient results").

In In re Federal Skywalk Cases, 93 F.R.D. 415 (W.D.Mo.1982), rev'd, 680 F.2d 1175 (8th Cir.), cert. denied, 459 U.S. 988, 103 S.Ct. 342, 74 L.Ed.2d 383 (1982), the district court certified a (b)(1)(A) class action for compensatory and punitive damages on behalf of all victims injured by the Skywalk collapse. Judge Wright concluded:

> Rule 23(b)(1)(A) certification is necessary as a ready and fair means of achieving unitary adjudication. One or more of the defendants risk being faced with incompatible standards of conduct if varying or inconsistent adjudications with respect to individual members of the class were obtained on the issues of liability for compensatory or punitive damages.

This class certification was reversed by the Eighth Circuit, which found that certification of a mandatory class action had the effect of an injunction in prohibiting class members from prosecuting or settling their pending state court suits in violation of the Anti–Injunction Act. Arguably there is a stronger case for certifying a (b)(1)(A) class where punitive damages are sought because they are addressed to deterring (and therefore affecting) future behavior.

Similar arguments could be made in suits seeking court orders establishing a medical monitoring program. In In re Telectronics Pacing Systems, Inc., 172 F.R.D. 271 (S.D. Ohio 1997), a suit involving alleged defects in wires attached to pacemakers, the district court concluded that "[t]he medical monitoring claim here is an ideal candidate" for Rule 23(b)(1)(A) treatment because separate adjudications would impair defendant's ability to pursue a single uniform medical monitoring program. Id. at 284–85. Compare a California class action in which plaintiffs sought a court order creating a fund to pay for such monitoring activities, but the district court refused to certify one. On appeal, the court emphasized that the suit was basically for money—funding of monitoring—and added that even if differing courts devised separate medical monitoring programs that would lead only to "administrative difficulty" for defendant that would not warrant mandatory class action treatment. Zinser v. Accufix Research Institute, Inc., 253 F.3d 1180, 1194–95 (9th Cir.2001). A dissenting judge denounced the majority's conclusion about the risk of conflicting orders as "altogether speculative and without support." Id. at 1199. Shouldn't it be significant that in this case it was *plaintiff* who was invoking a ground for class certification that is essentially designed to protect *defendant*, who opposed certification?

The admonition in the Advisory Committee Notes still stands as a considerable barrier to the willingness of many courts to accept a broader interpretation of Rule 23(b)(1)(A). From an economy and efficiency point of view, the broader interpretation seems desirable. But if differing jury damage-verdicts in individual cases could establish incompatible standards, wouldn't all cases where a defendant might be sued by multiple plaintiffs fit the (b)(1)(A) definition? Is there a principled way to narrow that broad an approach?

2.   RULE 23(b)(1)(B)—"LIMITED FUND" CLASS ACTIONS

ORTIZ v. FIBREBOARD CORP.

Supreme Court of the United States, 1999.
527 U.S. 815, 119 S.Ct. 2295, 144 L.Ed.2d 715.

JUSTICE SOUTER delivered the opinion of the Court.

This case turns on the conditions for certifying a mandatory settlement class on a limited fund theory under Federal Rule of Civil Procedure 23(b)(1)(B). We hold that applicants for contested certification on this rationale must show that the fund is limited by more than the agreement of the parties, and has been allocated to claimants belonging within the class by a process addressing any conflicting interests of class members.

I

Like Amchem Products, Inc. v. Windsor, 521 U.S. 591, 117 S.Ct. 2231, 138 L.Ed.2d 689 (1997) [*infra* p. 373], this case is a class action prompted by the elephantine mass of asbestos cases, [which] defies customary judicial administration and calls for national legislation. In 1967, one of the first actions for personal asbestos injury was filed in the United States District Court for the Eastern District of Texas against a group of asbestos manufacturers. In the 1970's and 1980's, plaintiffs' lawyers throughout the country, particularly in East Texas, honed the litigation of asbestos claims to the point of almost mechanical regularity, improving the forensic identification of diseases caused by asbestos, refining theories of liability, and often settling large inventories of cases.

Respondent Fibreboard Corporation was a defendant in the 1967 action. * * * As the tide of asbestos litigation rose, Fibreboard found itself litigating on two fronts. On one, plaintiffs were filing a stream of personal injury claims against it, swelling throughout the 1980's and 1990's to thousands of new claims for compensatory damages each year. On the second front, Fibreboard was battling for funds to pay its tort claimants. From May, 1957, through March, 1959, respondent Continental Casualty Company had provided Fibreboard with a comprehensive general liability policy with limits of $1 million per occurrence, $500,000 per claim, and no aggregate limit. Fibreboard also claimed that respondent Pacific Indemnity Company had insured it from 1956 to 1957 under a similar policy. Beginning in 1979, Fibreboard was locked in coverage litigation with Continental and Pacific in a California state trial court, which in 1990 held Continental and Pacific responsible for indemnification as to any claim by a claimant exposed to Fibreboard asbestos products prior to their policies' respective expiration dates. The decree also required the insurers to pay the full cost of defense for each claim covered. The insurance companies appealed.

With asbestos case filings continuing unabated, and its secure insurance assets almost depleted, Fibreboard in 1988 began a practice of "structured settlement," paying plaintiffs 40 percent of the settlement figure up front with the balance contingent upon a successful resolution of the coverage dispute. By 1991, however, the pace of filings forced Fibreboard to start settling cases entirely with the assignments of its rights against Continental, with no initial payment. To reflect the risk that Continental might prevail in the coverage dispute, these assignment agreements generally carried a figure about twice the nominal amount of earlier settlements. Continental challenged Fibreboard's right to make unilateral assignments, but in 1992 a California state court ruled for Fibreboard in that dispute.

Meanwhile, in the aftermath of a 1990 Federal Judicial Center conference on the asbestos litigation crisis, Fibreboard approached a group of leading asbestos plaintiffs' lawyers, offering to discuss a "global settlement" of its asbestos personal-injury liability. Early negotiations bore relatively little fruit, save for the December 1992 settlement by assignment of a significant inventory of pending claims. This settlement brought Fibreboard's deferred settlement obligations to more than $1.2 billion, all contingent upon victory over Continental on the scope of coverage and the validity of the settlement assignments.

In February 1993, after Continental had lost on both issues at the trial level, and thus faced the possibility of practically unbounded liability, it too joined the global settlement negotiations. Because Continental conditioned its part in any settlement on a guarantee of "total peace," ensuring no unknown future liabilities, talks focused on the feasibility of a mandatory class action, one binding all potential plaintiffs and giving none of them any choice to opt out of the certified class.

[As the date for the oral argument of the insurance companies' appeal approached in the California state courts, the parties reached a "Global Settlement Agreement" under which the insurance companies would contribute a total of $1.535 billion to a trust fund to satisfy future asbestos personal injury claims against Fibreboard. Separate "inventory" settlements were reached for those with pending claims against Fibreboard, and the insurers agreed that, if the Global Settlement Agreement were not approved, they would pay Fibreboard $2 billion to defend against such asbestos claims. Fibreboard itself was to contribute only $10 million (out of a net worth estimated at $235 million) to the trust fund for future claims, and 95% of this amount was to come from other insurance proceeds. In addition, the parties negotiated an agreement called the Trilateral Settlement Agreement, which sought to bind all entities that might seek indemnity from Fibreboard for asbestos personal injury claims against them because they distributed Fibreboard products.

The vehicle for accomplishing "total peace" was the filing of a new class action seeking certification for settlement purposes of a mandatory Rule 23(b)(1)(B) class consisting of all who had or might have asbestos personal injury claims against Fibreboard, but who did not have pending lawsuits against the company. Under the agreement, all class members would have to assert claims against the new trust instead of against Fibreboard. These claims would be handled in a streamlined manner compared to ordinary litigation, but claimants could go to court only after exhausting certain ADR procedures, and even then they would face a limit of $500,000 per claim and not be allowed to seek punitive damages or prejudgment interest. The district court provisionally certified the class, and held an eight-day fairness hearing at which objectors intervened and protested features of the settlement. After the fairness hearing, the district court certified the class and approved the settlement. It found that the insurance asset created by the Global Settlement Agreement, or the value of Fibreboard's other assets plus its insurance coverage, constituted a "limited fund" appropriate for Rule 23(b)(1)(B) treatment. The objectors appealed.

The Court of Appeals affirmed by a divided vote, citing expert testimony that Fibreboard faced enormous potential liability in asbestos personal injury litigation, and that it incurred enormous defense costs in that litigation, costs that usually exceeded the amounts paid out to claimants. It concluded that, even combining Fibreboard's net worth with the $2 billion provided under the agreement with the insurers, the company would be unable to pay valid claims within five to nine years. There was also strong testimony that the California courts would probably have reversed the favorable ruling against Continental, leaving no funds from the insurers to pay claimants. The Supreme Court granted certiorari.]

III

A

Although representative suits have been recognized in various forms since the earliest days of English law, class actions as we recognize them today developed as an exception to the formal rigidity of the necessary parties rule in equity, as well as from the bill of peace, an equitable device for combining multiple suits. The necessary parties rule in equity mandated that "all persons materially interested, either as plaintiffs or defendants in the subject matter of the bill ought to be made parties to the suit, however numerous they may be." West v. Randall, 29 F. Cas. 718, 721 (No. 17,424) (C.C.D.R.I.1820) (Story, J.). But because that rule would at times unfairly deny recovery to the party before the court, equity developed exceptions, among them one to cover situations "where the parties are very numerous, and the court perceives, that it will be almost impossible to bring them all before the court; or where the question is of general interest, and a few may sue for the benefit of the whole; or where the parties form a part of a voluntary association for public or private purposes, and may be fairly supposed to represent the rights and interests of the whole. . . ." Id., at 722. From these roots, modern class action practice emerged in the 1966 revision of Rule 23. In drafting Rule 23(b), the Advisory Committee sought to catalogue in "functional" terms "those recurrent life patterns which call for mass litigation through representative parties." Kaplan, A Prefatory Note, 10 B.C. Ind. & Com. L.Rev. 497 (1969).

Rule 23(b)(1)(B) speaks from "a vantage point within the class, [from which the Advisory Committee] spied out situations where lawsuits conducted with individual members of the class would have the practical if not technical effect of concluding the interests of the other members as well, or of impairing the ability of the others to protect their own interests." * * *

Among the traditional varieties of representative suit encompassed by Rule 23(b)(1)(B) were those involving "the presence of property which call[ed] for distribution or management." One recurring type of such suits was the limited fund class action, aggregating "claims . . . made by numerous persons against a fund insufficient to satisfy all claims." * * * As the Advisory Committee recognized, * * * equity required absent parties to be represented, joinder being impractical, where individual claims to be satisfied from the one asset would, as a practical matter, prejudice the rights of absent claimants against a fund inadequate to pay them all.

Equity, of course, recognized the same necessity to bind absent claimants to a limited fund when no formal imposition of a constructive trust was entailed. [The Court described a number of cases from the period 1829–1940.]

B

The cases forming this pedigree of the limited fund class action as understood by the drafters of Rule 23 have a number of common characteristics, despite the variety of circumstances from which they arose. The points of resemblance are not necessarily the points of contention resolved in the particular cases, but they show what the Advisory Committee must have assumed would be at least a sufficient set of conditions to justify binding absent members of a class under Rule 23(b)(1)(B), from which no one has the right to secede.

The first and most distinctive characteristic is that the totals of the aggregated liquidated claims and the fund available for satisfying them, set definitely at their maximums, demonstrate the inadequacy of the fund to pay all the claims. The concept driving this type of suit was insufficiency, which alone justified the limit on an early feast to avoid a later famine. The equity of the limitation is its necessity.

Second, the whole of the inadequate fund was to be devoted to the overwhelming claims. It went without saying that the defendant or estate or constructive trustee with the inadequate assets had no opportunity to benefit himself or claimants of lower priority by holding back on the amount distributed to the class. The limited fund cases thus ensured that the class as a whole was given the best deal; they did not give a defendant a better deal than seriatim litigation would have produced.

Third, the claimants identified by a common theory of recovery were treated equitably among themselves. The cases assume that the class will comprise everyone who might state a claim on a single or repeated set of facts, invoking a common theory of recovery, to be satisfied from the limited fund as the source of payment. * * * Once all similar claims were brought directly or by representation before the court, these antecedents of the mandatory class action presented straightforward models of equitable treatment, with the simple equity of a pro rata distribution providing the required fairness.

* * *

C

The Advisory Committee, and presumably the Congress in approving subdivision (b)(1)(B), must have assumed that an action with these characteristics would satisfy the limited fund rationale cognizable under that subdivision. The question remains how far the same characteristics are necessary for limited fund treatment. While we cannot settle all the details of a subdivision (b)(1)(B) limited fund here (and so cannot decide the ultimate question whether settlements of multitudes of related tort actions are amenable to mandatory class treatment), there are good reasons to treat these characteristics as presumptively necessary, and not merely sufficient, to satisfy the limited fund rationale for a mandatory action. At the least, the burden of justification rests on the proponent of any departure from the traditional norm.

It is true, of course, that the text of Rule 23(b)(1)(B) is on its face open to a more lenient limited fund concept, just as it covers more historical antecedents than the limited fund. But the greater the leniency in departing from the historical limited fund model, the greater the likelihood of abuse in ways that will be apparent when we apply the limited fund criteria to the case before us. The prudent course, therefore, is to presume that when subdivision (b)(1)(B) was devised to cover limited fund actions, the object was to stay close to the historical model. * * *

To begin with, the Advisory Committee looked cautiously at the potential for creativity under Rule 23(b)(1)(B), at least in comparison with Rule 23(b)(3). Although the committee crafted all three subdivisions of the Rule in general, practical terms, without the formalism that had bedeviled the original Rule 23, the Committee was consciously retrospective with intent to codify pre-Rule categories under Rule 23(b)(1), not forward-looking as it was in anticipating innovations under Rule 23(b)(3). Thus, the Committee intended subdivision (b)(1) to capture the "standard" class actions recognized in pre-Rules practice.

Consistent with its backward look under subdivision (b)(1), as commentators have pointed out, it is clear that the Advisory Committee did not contemplate that the mandatory class action codified in subdivision (b)(1)(B) would be used to aggregate unliquidated tort claims on a limited fund rationale. * * * While the Advisory Committee focused much attention on the amenability of Rule 23(b)(3) to ["mass accident"] cases, the Committee's debates are silent about resolving tort claims under a mandatory limited fund rationale under Rule 23(b)(1)(B). It is simply implausible that the Advisory Committee, so concerned about the potential difficulties posed by dealing with mass tort cases under Rule 23(b)(3), with its provisions for notice and the right to opt out, see Rule 23(c)(2), would have uncritically assumed that mandatory versions of such class actions, lacking such protections, could be certified under Rule 23(b)(1)(B). * * *

The Rules Enabling Act underscores the need for caution. As we said in *Amchem*, no reading of the Rule can ignore the Act's mandate that "rules of procedure 'shall not abridge, enlarge or modify any substantive right.' " Petitioners argue that the Act has been violated here, asserting that the Global Settlement Agreement's priorities of claims and compromise of full recovery abrogated the state law that must govern this diversity action under 28 U.S.C. § 1652. Although we need not grapple with the difficult choice-of-law and substantive state-law questions raised by petitioners' assertion, we do need to recognize the tension between the limited fund class action's pro rata distribution in equity and the rights of individual tort victims at law. Even if we assume that some such tension is acceptable under the Rules Enabling Act, it is best kept within tolerable limits by keeping limited fund practice under Rule 23(b)(1)(B) close to the practice preceding its adoption.

Finally, if we needed further counsel against adventurous application of Rule 23(b)(1)(B), the Rules Enabling Act and the general doctrine of constitutional avoidance would jointly sound a warning of the serious constitutional concerns that come with any attempt to aggregate individual tort claims on a limited fund rationale. First, the certification of a mandatory class followed by settlement of its action for money damages obviously implicates the Seventh Amendment jury trial rights of absent class members. We noted in Ross v. Bernhard, 396 U.S. 531, 90 S.Ct. 733, 24 L.Ed.2d 729 (1970), that since the merger of law and equity in 1938, it has become settled among the lower courts that "class action plaintiffs may obtain a jury trial on any legal issues they present." By its nature, however, a mandatory settlement-only class action with legal issues and future claimants compromises their Seventh Amendment rights without their consent.

Second, and no less important, mandatory class actions aggregating damage claims implicate the due process "principle of general application in Anglo–American jurisprudence that one is not bound by a judgment in personam in a litigation in which he is not designated as a party or to which he has not been made a party by service of process," Hansberry v. Lee, 311 U.S. 32, 40, 61 S.Ct. 115, 85 L.Ed. 22 (1940) [*supra* p. 285], it being "our 'deep-rooted historic tradition that everyone should have his own day in court,'" Martin v. Wilks, 490 U.S. 755, 762, 109 S.Ct. 2180, 104 L.Ed.2d 835 (1989) [*supra* p. 86]. * * *

The inherent tension between representative suits and the day-in-court ideal is only magnified if applied to damage claims gathered in a mandatory class. Unlike Rule 23(b)(3) class members, objectors to the collectivism of a mandatory subdivision (b)(1)(B) action have no inherent right to abstain. The legal rights of absent class members (which in a class like this one would include claimants who by definition may be unidentifiable when the class is certified) are resolved regardless either of their consent, or, in a class with objectors, their express wish to the contrary.[23] And in settlement-only class actions the procedural protections built into the Rule to protect the rights of absent class members during litigation are never invoked in an adversarial setting.

* * *

IV

The record on which the District Court rested its certification of the class for the purpose of the global settlement did not support the essential premises of mandatory limited fund actions. It failed to demonstrate that the fund was limited except by the agreement of the parties, and it showed exclusions from the class and allocations of assets at odds with the concept of limited fund treatment and the structural protections of Rule 23(a) explained in *Amchem*.

A

The defect of certification going to the most characteristic feature of a limited fund action was the uncritical adoption by both the District Court and the Court of Appeals of figures agreed upon by the parties in defining the limits of the fund and demonstrating its inadequacy.[26] When

23. It is no answer in this case that the settlement agreement provided for a limited, back-end "opt out" in the form of a right on the part of class members eventually to take their case to court if dissatisfied with the amount provided by the trust. The "opt out" in this case requires claimants to exhaust a variety of alternative dispute mechanisms, to bring suit against the trust, and not against Fibreboard, and it limits damages to $500,000, to be paid out in installments over 5 to 10 years, despite multimillion-dollar jury verdicts sometimes reached in asbestos suits. Indeed, on ap-

proximately a dozen occasions, Fibreboard has settled for more than $500,000.

26. The federal courts have differed somewhat in articulating the standard to evaluate whether, in fact, a fund is limited, in cases involving mass torts. Compare, e.g., In re Northern Dist. of California, Dalkon Shield IUD Products Liability Litigation, 693 F.2d 847, 852 (C.A.9 1982), cert. denied sub nom. A.H. Robins Co., Inc. v. Abed et al., 459 U.S. 1171, 103 S.Ct. 817, 74 L.Ed.2d 1015 (1983) (class proponents must demonstrate that allowing the adjudication

a district court, as here, certifies for class action settlement only, the moment of certification requires "heightene[d] attention," *Amchem*, 521 U.S., at 620, 117 S.Ct. 2231, to the justifications for binding the class members. This is so because certification of a mandatory settlement class, however provisional technically, effectively concludes the proceeding save for the final fairness hearing. * * * Thus, in an action such as this the settling parties must present not only their agreement, but evidence on which the district court may ascertain the limit and the insufficiency of the fund, with support in findings of fact following a proceeding in which the evidence is subject to challenge.

We have already alluded to the difficulties facing limited fund treatment of huge numbers of actions for unliquidated damages arising from mass torts, the first such hurdle being a computation of the total claims. It is simply not a matter of adding up the liquidated amounts, as in the models of limited fund actions. Although we might assume arguendo that prior judicial experience with asbestos claims would allow a court to make a sufficiently reliable determination of the probable total, the District Court here apparently thought otherwise, concluding that "there is no way to predict Fibreboard's future asbestos liability with any certainty." Nothing turns on this conclusion, however, since there was no adequate demonstration of the second element required for limited fund treatment, the upper limit of the fund itself, without which no showing of insufficiency is possible.

The "fund" in this case comprised both the general assets of Fibreboard and the insurance assets provided by the two policies. As to Fibreboard's assets exclusive of the contested insurance, the District Court and the Fifth Circuit concluded that Fibreboard had a then-current sale value of $235 million that could be devoted to the limited fund. While that estimate may have been conservative,[28] at least the District Court heard evidence and made an independent finding at some point in the proceedings. The same, however, cannot be said for the value of the disputed insurance.

The insurance assets would obviously be "limited" in the traditional sense if the total of demonstrable claims would render the insurers

---

of individual claims will inescapably compromise the claims of absent class members), with, e.g., In re "Agent Orange" Product Liability Litigation, 100 F.R.D. 718, 726 (E.D.N.Y.1983), aff'd. 818 F.2d 145 (C.A.2 1987), cert. denied sub nom. Fraticelli v. Dow Chemical Co., 484 U.S. 1004, 108 S.Ct. 695, 98 L.Ed.2d 648 (1988) (requiring only a "substantial probability— that is less than a preponderance but more than a mere possibility—that if damages are awarded, the claims of earlier litigants would exhaust the defendants' assets"). Cf. In re Bendectin Products Liability Litigation, 749 F.2d 300, 306 (C.A.6 1984). Because under either formulation, the class certification in this case cannot stand, it

would be premature to decide the appropriate standard at this time.

28. The District Court based the $235 million figure on evidence provided by an investment banker regarding what a "financially prudent buyer" would pay to acquire Fibreboard free of its personal injury asbestos liabilities, less transaction costs. In 1997, however, Fibreboard was acquired for about $515 million, plus $85 million of assumed debt. See Coffee, Class Wars: The Dilemma of the Mass Tort Class Action, 95 Colum. L.Rev. 1343, 1402 (1995) (noting the surge in Fibreboard's stock price following the settlement below).

insolvent, or if the policies provided aggregate limits falling short of that total; calculation might be difficult, but the way to demonstrate the limit would be clear. Neither possibility is presented in this case, however. Instead, any limit of the insurance asset here had to be a product of potentially unlimited policy coverage discounted by the risk that Fibreboard would ultimately lose the coverage dispute litigation. This sense of limit as a value discounted by risk is of course a step removed from the historical model, but even on the assumption that it would suffice for limited fund treatment, there was no adequate finding of fact to support its application here. Instead of undertaking an independent evaluation of potential insurance funds, the District Court (and, later, the Court of Appeals), simply accepted the $2 billion Trilateral Settlement Agreement figure as representing the maximum amount the insurance companies could be required to pay tort victims, concluding that "[w]here insurance coverage is disputed, it is appropriate to value the insurance asset at a settlement value."

Settlement value is not always acceptable, however. One may take a settlement amount as good evidence of the maximum available if one can assume that parties of equal knowledge and negotiating skill agreed upon the figure through arms-length bargaining, unhindered by any considerations tugging against the interests of the parties ostensibly represented in the negotiation. But no such assumption may be indulged in this case, or probably in any class action settlement with the potential for gigantic fees. [The Court noted that, under a side deal, the attorneys for the class stood to benefit from the "inventory" settlements of their pending cases if the mandatory class action deal could be reached.]

We do not, of course, know exactly what an independent valuation of the limit of the insurance assets would have shown. * * * But objecting and unidentified class members alike are entitled to have the issue settled by specific evidentiary findings independent of the agreement of defendants and conflicted class counsel.

B

The explanation of need for independent determination of the fund has necessarily anticipated our application of the requirement of equity among members of the class. There are two issues, the inclusiveness of the class and the fairness of distributions to those within it. On each, this certification for settlement fell short.

The definition of the class excludes myriad claimants with causes of action, or foreseeable causes of action, arising from exposure to Fibreboard asbestos. While the class includes those with present claims never filed, present claims withdrawn without prejudice, and future claimants, it fails to include those who had previously settled with Fibreboard while retaining the right to sue again "upon development of an asbestos related malignancy," plaintiffs with claims pending against Fibreboard at the time of the initial announcement of the Global Settlement Agreement, and the plaintiffs in the "inventory" claims settled as a supposedly necessary step in reaching the global settlement. The number of those outside the class who settled with a reservation of rights may be uncertain, but there is no such uncertainty about the significance of the settlement's exclusion of the 45,000 inventory plaintiffs and the plaintiffs in the unsettled present cases, estimated * * * at more than 53,000 as of August 27, 1993. It is a fair question how far a natural class may be depleted by prior dispositions of claims and still qualify as a mandatory limited fund class, but there can be no question that such a mandatory settlement class will not qualify when in the very negotiations aimed at a class settlement, class counsel agree to exclude what could turn out to be as much as a third of the claimants that negotiators thought might eventually be involved, a substantial number of whom class counsel represent.

[The Court noted also that "inventory" plaintiffs appeared to have obtained better terms than members of the class.]

On the second element of equity within the class, the fairness of the distribution of the fund among class members, the settlement certification is likewise deficient. Fair treatment in the older cases was characteristically assured by straightforward pro rata distribution of the limited fund. While equity in such a simple sense is unattainable in a settlement covering present claims not specifically proven and claims not even due to arise, if at all, until some future time, at the least such a settlement must seek equity by providing for procedures to resolve the difficult issues of treating such differently situated claimants with fairness as among themselves.

[The Court explained that "homogeneous subclasses" would have to be developed to satisfy its earlier decision in *Amchem*. As structured, the unitary plaintiff class mixed claims of too many whose interests were seriously different. In particular, those exposed before 1959, when the insurance policies in question expired, were certainly in a different position from those exposed only afterwards, but all were included in the same class. Although the Court noted that "at some point there must be an end to reclassification with separate counsel" to deal with such conflicts, no effort was made to provide the sort of "structural protections" demanded by *Amchem*. As in that case, even if all would gain some benefits from creation of a "grand-scale compensation system," that would require a legislative solution, not one designed pursuant to Rule 23(b)(1)(B).]

C

A third contested feature of this settlement certification that departs markedly from the limited fund antecedents is the ultimate provision for a fund smaller than the assets understood by the Court of Appeals to be available for payment of the mandatory class members' claims; most notably, Fibreboard was allowed to retain virtually its entire net worth. Given our treatment of the two preceding deficiencies of the certification, there is of course no need to decide whether this feature of the agreement would alone be fatal to the Global Settlement Agreement. To ignore it entirely, however, would be so misleading that we have decided simply to identify the issue it raises, without purporting to resolve it at this time.

Fibreboard listed its supposed entire net worth as a component of the total (and allegedly inadequate) assets available for claimants, but subsequently retained all but $500,000 of that equity for itself.[34] On the face of it, the arrangement seems irreconcilable with the justification of necessity in denying any opportunity for withdrawal of class members whose jury trial rights will be compromised, whose damages will be capped, and whose payments will be delayed. With Fibreboard retaining nearly all its net worth, it hardly appears that such a regime is the best that can be provided for class members. * * *

The District Court in this case seems to have had a further point in mind, however. One great advantage of class action treatment of mass tort cases is the opportunity to save the enormous transaction costs of piecemeal litigation, an advantage to which the settlement's proponents have referred in this case. Although the District Court made no specific finding about the transaction cost saving likely from this class settlement, estimating the amount in the "hundreds of millions," it did conclude that the amount would exceed Fibreboard's net worth as the Court valued it. If a settlement thus saves transaction costs that would never have gone into a class member's pocket in the absence of settlement, may a credit for some of the savings be recognized in a mandatory class action as an incentive to settlement? It is at least a legitimate question, which we leave for another day.

* * *

The judgment of the Court of Appeals, accordingly, is reversed, and the case is remanded for further proceedings consistent with this opinion.

[Concurring opinion of Chief Justice Rehnquist, joined by Justices Scalia and Kennedy, omitted.]

Justice BREYER, with whom Justice STEVENS joins, dissenting.

[Justice Breyer emphasized factors that the majority recognized but felt insufficient to justify a mandatory class action in the case. First, the "elephantine mass" of asbestos litigation created a problem that conven-

---

34. We need not decide here how close to insolvency a limited fund defendant must be brought as a condition of class certification. While there is no inherent conflict between a limited fund class action under Rule 23(b)(1)(B) and the Bankruptcy Code, it is worth noting that if limited fund certification is allowed in a situation where a company provides only a de minimis contribution to the ultimate settlement fund, the incentives such a resolution would provide to companies facing tort liability to engi-

neer settlements similar to the one negotiated in this case would, in all likelihood, significantly undermine the protections for creditors built into the Bankruptcy Code. We note further that Congress in the Bankruptcy Reform Act of 1994, Pub.L. 103–394 § 111(a), amended the Bankruptcy Code to enable a debtor in a Chapter 11 reorganization in certain circumstances to establish a trust toward which the debtor may channel future asbestos-related liability, see 11 U.S.C. § 524(g), (h).

tional judicial administration could not solve. Second, insisting on a legislative solution seemed an odd reaction to a problem that was the result of relatively conventional litigation, albeit too much of it. Third, the district courts (and particularly the district judge in this case) had much more experience dealing with this problem than the appellate courts. In this instance, that district judge held eight days of hearings and entered 446 findings of fact supporting his class certification and approval of the class settlement. Fourth, owing to delay and unusually high transaction costs, the alternative to a class action is not individual litigation, so that our "deep-rooted historic tradition" that each litigant should have a day in court simply was not applicable.

Against this background, Justice Breyer thought the case could be certified under Rule 23(b)(1)(B) under the majority's standard.]

The case falls within the Rule's language as long as there was a significant "risk" that the total assets available to satisfy the claims of the class members would fall well below the likely total value of those claims, for in such circumstances the money would go to those claimants who brought their actions first, thereby "substantially impair[ing]" the "ability" of later claimants "to protect their interests." And the District Court found there was indeed such a "risk."

[Turning to the three factors cited by the majority, Justice Breyer found them satisfied. Regarding the majority's focus on whether the total of the claims exceeded available funds, Justice Breyer saw no reason to question the district court's valuation of the insurance assets based on the risk that a decision by the California courts might drain them of value. Under those circumstances, giving considerable weight to the settlement arrived at by the parties was reasonable, particularly given that Fibreboard was the one that had negotiated the settlement with the insurers.

On equitable treatment of class members among themselves, Justice Breyer saw no problem with the conflict resulting when lawyers who represented other claimants in negotiated "inventory" settlements also represented the class. Not only would emphasizing this factor foreclose reliance on any experienced asbestos lawyers, it also disregarded the district judge's finding that the "inventory" settlements were used to set the schedule for payments to the class.

Finally, regarding the majority's insistence that the whole of the fund be committed to paying the claims, Justice Breyer pointed out that the Court also would countenance retention of some funds if the class was given the best possible deal.]

Rule 23 itself does not require modern courts to trace every contour of ancient case law with literal exactness. * * * The majority itself recognizes the possibility of providing incentives to enter into settlements that reduce costs by granting a "credit" for cost savings by relaxing the whole-of-the-assets requirement, at least where most of the savings would go to the claimants.

There is no doubt in this case that the settlement made far more money available to satisfy asbestos claims than was likely to occur in its absence. And the District Court found that administering the fund would involve transaction costs of only 15%. A comparison of that 15% figure with the 61% transaction costs figure applicable to asbestos cases in general suggests hundreds of millions of dollars in savings—an amount greater than Fibreboard's net worth. And, of course, not only is it better for the injured plaintiffs, it is far better for Fibreboard, its employees, its creditors, and the communities where it is located for Fibreboard to remain a working enterprise, rather than slowly forcing it into bankruptcy while most of its money is spent on asbestos lawyers and expert witnesses. I would consequently find substantial compliance with the majority's third condition.

Because I believe that all three of the majority's conditions are satisfied, and because I see no fatal conceptual difficulty, I would uphold the determination, made by the District Court and affirmed by the Court of Appeals, that the insurance policies (along with Fibreboard's net value) amount to a classic limited fund, within the scope of Rule 23(b)(1)(B).

Notes and Questions

1. The idea behind certification under Rule 23(b)(1)(B) is to provide a parallel to Rule 19; when proceeding in the absence of nonparties would prejudice them as a practical matter, but they are too numerous to be joined, the class action provision provides a method of representing their interests and binding them. For an historical analysis of the binding effect of early analogues to modern class actions, see Hazard, Gedid & Sowle, An Historical Analysis of the Binding Effect of Class Suits, 146 U.Pa.L.Rev. 1849 (1998).

2. Justice Breyer says that the majority's test for use of Rule 23(b)(1)(B) was satisfied on the record of *Ortiz*. Could any other mass tort case justify certification under this decision?

3. After *Ortiz* was decided, the court in In re Telectronics Pacing Systems, Inc., 221 F.3d 870 (6th Cir.2000), invalidated a limited fund settlement class action in a mass tort litigation. Plaintiffs there were recipients of pacemakers, some of which had defects. About 25,000 people had received these pacemakers in the U.S. The devices were manufactured and distributed by a U.S. company that was the subsidiary of two Australian companies. Plaintiffs sued all three, and the district court early denied the Australian defendants' motions to dismiss for lack of personal jurisdiction.

Thereafter, class counsel and defendants confected a settlement with medical monitoring provisions and a right of those class members who evinced a problem with their pacemakers to obtain a damages payment. The fund to pay for these programs was based on the value of the U.S. subsidiary's assets, and the Australian companies would contribute $10 million but be absolved from further liability. The Court of Appeals found that the settlement did not satisfy the requirements of *Ortiz*. The release of the parent companies was like the release of the insurance companies in *Ortiz*. The district court suggested that it had misgivings about whether personal jurisdiction really existed for the claims against the Australian defendants, but that by itself would not necessarily mean there was a limited fund if plaintiffs could pursue a remedy against them in Australia. The district court also suggested that even if those claims were asserted in this country they probably would not be successful. But the ability to prevail on the merits is different from the ability of a defendant to pay a judgment. And one must be restrained in finding an inability to pay on the ground that the potential liability is large (id. at 880):

> Presumably *all* companies have limited funds at some point—there is always the possibility that a large mass tort action or other litigation will put a company into bankruptcy. Should that eventuality threaten, we have a comprehensive bankruptcy scheme in this country for just such an occurrence. Simply demonstrating that there is a possibility, even a likelihood, that bankruptcy might at some point occur cannot be the basis for finding that there is a "limited fund" in an ongoing corporate concern. The district court cannot discharge the debt in advance of the occurrence, thereby usurping the bankruptcy scheme through settlement, even if it believes such an avenue to be in the best interests of most of the plaintiffs.

See also Doe v. Karadzic, 192 F.R.D. 133 (S.D.N.Y.2000) (holding that even though the current net worth of defendant, the President of a self-proclaimed Bosnian–Serb country, would not cover likely judgments in a human rights class action, there was no showing of a substantial probability that defendant would be unable over the 20–year life of the judgment to pay any awards).

4. In mass tort cases, the determination under Rule 23(b)(1)(B) involves comparing the amount of the claims made and the amount available to pay those claims. How easily can this determination be made? Regarding liabilities, toting up the sum of the prayers for relief seems unwarranted. For one thing, there is no reason to assume that, if one plaintiff is successful in suing the defendant, all other plaintiffs will necessarily be successful. Differences in factual circumstances and applicable principles of state law regarding liability make that unlikely. Therefore, the cumulation of the claims made in all suits is unwarranted. Moreover, even if one could assume all plaintiffs would be successful, assessing the true value of the suits by the prayer, particularly as to punitive damages, is even more dubious. Plaintiff lawyers are notoriously generous in their prayers for relief, and these should not be taken as reliable indicators of probable recovery. Although detailed data on actual results of tried cases (and perhaps settled cases as well) might provide some meaningful indication of likely future recoveries, one would still need to take account as well of the severity of individual injuries. Thus, the actual computation of prospective liability is extremely difficult.

Turning to the assets side of the ledger, the question is much more complicated than obtaining a simple net worth figure from the defendant's books. For example, in a suit against A.H. Robins Co. for injuries resulting from use of the Dalkon Shield, a contraceptive device made by Robins, the district judge concluded that there was a limited fund on the ground that the defendant's assets totalled $280 million, but some six years later bankruptcy proceedings led to the sale of the company and the creation of a fund of

$2.475 billion for claimants. See footnote 28 in *Ortiz*. As *Ortiz* points out, determining the extent of insurance coverage (which should also be considered) is often a difficult proposition.

Another complicating factor in many cases, such as *Ortiz*, is that there are multiple defendants. This circumstance affects both the assets and liabilities. On the assets side, the availability of other defendants may mean that potential plaintiffs face no risks that they will be uncompensated even if this defendant can pay. On the liabilities side, assuming joint liability it may be that only a limited amount of judgments against a given defendant will have to be paid by it, or that it can obtain contribution from other defendants. For discussion of these complications, see Marcus, They Can't Do That, Can They? Tort Reform Via Rule 23, 80 Cornell L. Rev. 858, 878–79 (1995). Does *Ortiz* offer insight about how to handle such problems? See footnote 26.

5. Sometimes there is a legal limit on the amount recoverable, and that may be considered in determining the assets available. For example, a statute limits total damages for certain accidents involving nuclear energy to $560 million. See 42 U.S.C.A. § 2210. That is a large amount, but it could certainly happen that an American "Chernobyl" would produce claims exceeding it. Indeed, that prospect must lie behind the enactment of the statute.

Contractual limitations may also place a cap on the amount recoverable. Cf. State Farm Fire & Cas. Co. v. Tashire, 386 U.S. 523, 87 S.Ct. 1199, 18 L.Ed.2d 270 (1967) (automobile liability insurance policy limiting coverage to $20,000 per occurrence justified interpleader of all claimants when insured's car was involved in accident with Greyhound bus). Compare the insurance coverage dispute in *Ortiz*. The Court suggests that the discounted value of insurance coverage might serve as a measure of the funds available, but doubts that the negotiated figure suffices for that purpose because of concerns about a conflict of interest among those negotiating for the plaintiffs. Could this sort of discounting ever provide an effective guide in valuing "insurance assets?"

6. Another recurrent stimulus for Rule 23(b)(1)(B) arguments in mass tort litigation is the prospect of punitive damages. In 1967, Judge Friendly posited that state law must place some limit on repetitive punitive damage verdicts for the same behavior, but assuming there are such limits they probably will vary from state to state, making consideration of this factor difficult in multistate class actions. Nonetheless, some courts continue to invoke this ground for limited fund class certification. See In re Exxon Valdez, 270 F.3d 1215, 1225 (9th Cir.2001) ("The district court also certified a mandatory punitive damages class, so the award would not be duplicated in other litigation and would include all punitive damages the jury thought appropriate."); In re Simon II Litigation, 211 F.R.D. 86 (E.D.N.Y. 2002) (certifying a nationwide Rule 23(b)(1)(B) punitive damages class in tobacco litigation under the "limited punishment" theory of punitive damages). Should this activity have continued after *Ortiz*?

Another argument to be considered is the possibility that due process places a limit on the aggregate punitive damages awardable against a defendant in mass tort situations. If that were true, it might indicate a nationally uniform maximum. In State Farm Mut. Auto Ins. Co. v. Campbell, 538 U.S. 408, 123 S.Ct. 1513, 155 L.Ed.2d 585 (2003), the Court spoke vigorously of due process limits on punitive damage awards in individual cases; this decision may fortify arguments for limited fund class actions where punitive damages are sought.

For a discussion of the ongoing issues, see Steinman, Managing Punitive Damages: A Role for Mandatory "Limited Generosity" Classes and Anti–Suit Injunctions?, 36 WIll. & Mary L. Rev. 1043 (2001); Nagareda, Punitive Damages Class Actions and the Baseline of Tort, 36 Will. & Mary L. Rev. 943 (2001); Hines, Obstacles to Determining Punitive Damages in Class Actions, 36 Will. & Mary L. Rev. 889 (2001).

7. As the Court suggests (see footnote 34), the bankruptcy system already exists to deal with problems of this sort. In Chapter III we examined the gathering power of bankruptcy. Does it provide advantages over Rule 23(b)(1)(B) in situations that might fit the "limited fund" scenario? A National Commission thought so. See National Bankruptcy Review Commission: The Next Twenty Years 318–19 (1997) (citing the assurance of equality in distribution for similar creditors and preserving the going value of the concern). Judge Edith Jones, a member of the Commission who dissented from its report, objected to the lack of due process afforded in authorizing bankruptcy courts to resolve such future claims. Jones, Rough Justice in Mass Future Claims: Should Bankruptcy Courts Direct Tort Reform?, 76 Texas L. Rev. 1695 (1998).

Professor Gibson, an expert in both civil procedure and bankruptcy, made a detailed comparison of pre-*Ortiz* limited fund mass tort class actions and bankruptcy reorganizations involving mass tort claimants for the Federal Judicial Center. See Gibson, Case Studies of Mass Tort Limited Fund Settlements and Bankruptcy Reorganizations (2000). She concluded that bankruptcy was better (id. at 5–6):

> The confirmation requirement of voting by individual creditors (including tort claimants), the substantive bankruptcy protections for individuals and classes that vote against the plan, and the practice of appointing a future claims representative provide greater protection and opportunity for input for absent tort claimants than is available to them when a district court approves a limited fund class action settlement. Moreover, tort claimants are treated more equitably in a bankruptcy reorganization with respect to the defendant's other creditors, because all are forced to share the defendant's shortfall; in a limited fund class actions settlement, only the tort claimants are forced to compromise their claims.

> Judges presiding over bankruptcy reorganizations also have the advantage of having specific statutory standards for the confirmation of the reorganization plan. The standards for determining whether a limited fund class should be certified and whether a settlement should be approved, by contrast, remain ill defined. * * *

> Where limited fund class action settlements come out ahead, in my view, is with regard to the efficiency of the resolution process and the likelihood that a defendant will invoke that resolution method. A limited fund class settlement can usually be achieved and approved by the court

in much less time than it takes to achieve confirmation of a mass tort defendant's bankruptcy reorganization plan. * * * However, the Supreme Court's recent *Ortiz* decision, by raising doubts about the validity of limited fund class action settlements of mass tort claims, may make a defendant more reluctant in the future to attempt such a settlement to resolve its mass tort liability.

8. The Court invokes the Seventh Amendment as a reason for its disapproval of the settlement in *Ortiz*. Why should the right to jury trial play a role? "It is difficult to understand how the Seventh Amendment bears on settlement, or why it should only affect settlement of mandatory class actions. Is there no similar limitation on the settlement of suits under Federal Rule of Civil Procedure 23(b)(2) for injunctive relief? Is there a reason why the settlement of the scope of defendant's violation of plaintiffs' rights or the proper remedy is different when plaintiff has a right to jury trial? Unless one takes the view that, if the Seventh Amendment does not apply, there is no constitutional right to a 'trial' at all, it is hard to understand why cases subject to the Seventh Amendment are different from those that re not (as would be rare in many 23(b)(2) class actions)." Marcus, Benign Neglect Reconsidered, 148 U.Pa.L.Rev. 2009, 2031–32 n. 113 (2000).

9. There have been repeated calls from judges for legislation to deal with asbestos personal injury claims. Are these efforts to shift the problem to a different branch of government justified? Congress has recently given serious consideration to adopting an administrative scheme to replace litigation for asbestos personal injury claimants. See, e.g., Fairness in Asbestos Injury Resolution Act of 2003, S. 1125 (108th Cong.) (replacing the right of workers exposed to asbestos to sue with no-fault administrative remedies, with dollar amounts based on categories relating to the type of disease, from a trust fund in excess of $100 billion to be contributed by defendant companies and insurers and to be administered by an administrative agency); Asbestos Compensation Fairness Act of 2003, H.R. 1586 (108th Cong.).

3. RULE 23(b)(2) CLASSES

Rule 23(b)(2) allows for a class action when "the party opposing the class has acted or refused to act on grounds generally applicable to the class, thereby making appropriate final injunctive relief or corresponding declaratory relief with respect to the class as a whole." Compared to the complex provisions of Rule 23(b)(1), this language is relatively simple. Indeed, in a broad range of suits seeking injunctive relief (of which the school desegregation and institutional restructuring suits are paradigms), there has been little difficulty in certifying a class. There are, however, questions as to the breadth of this type of class when monetary relief is also sought.

IN RE MONUMENTAL LIFE INS. CO.

United States Court of Appeals, Fifth Circuit, 2004
—— F.3d ——, 2004 WL 718806.

Before SMITH, DENNIS and CLEMENT, Circuit Judges.

JERRY E. SMITH, Circuit Judge.

* * *

In what may be the ultimate negative value class action lawsuit,[1] plaintiffs challenge defendants' alleged practice of paying lower benefits and charging higher premiums to blacks in the sale of low-value life insurance. The district court denied plaintiffs' motion to certify a class pursuant to Fed.R.Civ.P. 23(b)(2), finding, *inter alia*, that the majority of class members would not benefit from injunctive relief. Based primarily on Allison v. Citgo Petroleum Co., 151 F.3d 402 (5th Cir.1998), we reverse and remand.

I.

This is a consolidation of civil rights actions against three life insurance companies: Monumental Life Insurance Company ("Monumental"), American National Insurance Company ("ANICO"), and Western and Southern Insurance Company ("Western and Southern"). Plaintiff policyowners, all of whom are black, allege that, for decades, defendants discriminated against them in the sale and administration of low-value life insurance policies, known as industrial life policies, that have face amounts of $2000 or less and require small weekly or monthly premiums. Defendants comprise over 280 companies that issued industrial life policies over a fifty-to sixty-five-year period.[3]

Plaintiffs allege two overtly discriminatory practices. First, they accuse defendants of placing blacks in industrial policies offering the same benefits as do policies sold to whites, but at a higher premium (dual rates). Second, defendants allegedly placed blacks in specially-designed substandard industrial policies providing fewer or lower benefits than do comparable plans sold to whites (dual plans). These practices are memorialized in the insurer's rate books and records, which explicitly distinguish dual rate and dual plan policies by race. Although, before filing their motion for class certification, plaintiffs challenged the insurers' alleged practice of charging blacks substandard premiums because of non-racial underwriting factors, such as mental condition, occupation, socioeconomic status, educational level, living conditions, and personal habits, plaintiffs no longer complain of such pretextual underwriting procedures.

Defendants state that they issued "hundreds, perhaps thousands, of different industrial life insurance products" encompassing a countless variety of underwriting standards. It is undisputed that all companies that sold dual rate or dual plan policies have not done so since the early 1970's. Also, as early as 1988, some insurers voluntarily adjusted premiums and/or death benefits to equalize the amount of coverage per premium dollar. Still, plaintiffs estimate that over 4.5 million of the 5.6

---

1. A "negative value" suit is one in which class members' claims "would be uneconomical to litigate individually." Phillips Petroleum v. Shutts, 472 U.S. 797, 809, 105 S.Ct. 2965, 86 L.Ed.2d 628 (1985) [*infra* p. 412].

3. Over the years, defendants have acquired other insurance companies and thereby assumed blocks of in-force insurance policies issued by them. Monumental currently administers policies issued by 200 different companies, while Western and Southern administers policies issued by approximately 80 companies. ANICO has assumed an indeterminate number of in-force policies.

million industrial policies issued by defendants remain in-force; many other policies have been terminated, surrendered, or paid-up without remediation. Defendants' expert estimates that the ratio of terminated policies to outstanding policies is approximately five to one, meaning that slightly more than one million policies remain in-force.

Plaintiffs sued for violations of 42 U.S.C. §§ 1981 and 1982, seeking (1) an injunction prohibiting the collection of discriminatory premiums, (2) reformation of policies to equalize benefits, and (3) restitution of past premium overcharges or benefit underpayments. Pursuant to 28 U.S.C. § 1407, the Judicial Panel for Multidistrict Litigation ("MDL") consolidated the actions against Monumental and transferred them to the Eastern District of Louisiana for pretrial proceedings. Later, the MDL Panel took the same action with the cases against ANICO and Western and Southern.

Plaintiffs moved for certification of a class pursuant to rule 23(b)(2), requesting that class members be provided notice and opt-out rights. The district court denied certification, finding that plaintiffs' claims for monetary relief predominate over their claims for injunctive relief, making rule 23(b)(2) certification inappropriate. The court also found that, given the large number of companies and policies involved, individualized hearings were necessary to determine damages and whether claims were barred by the statute of limitations.

* * *

III.

* * * [A] rule 23(b)(2) class may be certified if "the party opposing the class has acted or refused to act on grounds generally applicable to the class, thereby making appropriate final injunctive relief or corresponding declaratory relief with respect to the class as a whole." Fed. R.Civ.P. 23(b)(2). Plaintiffs premise rule 23(b)(2) certification on their request for an injunction prohibiting the further collection of discriminatory premiums.

A.

The [district] court observed that "many" proposed class members—those whose policies have lapsed, those whose policies have already been voluntarily adjusted by defendants, and those whose death benefits already have been paid—would not benefit from injunctive relief. The court concluded that "this is a case in which individuality overrides any bland group-think, and money becomes the prime goal . . . not injunctive relief." Rule 23(b)(2) certification is improper, the court held, where the class's request for injunctive relief merely serves as a bootstrap for a claim of monetary damages.

In *Allison*, we carefully explained the statement in the advisory committee notes that rule 23(b)(2) certification "does not extend to cases in which the appropriate final relief relates exclusively or *predominantly* to money damages." Fed.R.Civ.P. 23 advisory committee notes (emphasis added). *Allison* did not hold, as the district court believed, that monetary relief predominates where it is the "prime goal" or a mere bootstrap to injunctive relief. Instead, "determining whether one form of relief actually predominates in some quantifiable sense is a wasteful and impossible task that should be avoided." In other words, certification does not hinge on the subjective intentions of the class representatives and their counsel in bringing suit.[10]

Instead, *Allison* looked to the nature of the rule 23(b)(2) device in defining when monetary relief predominates. That rule's focus on injunctive and declaratory relief presumes a class best described as a "homogeneous and cohesive group with few conflicting interests among its members." Class certification centers on the defendants' alleged unlawful conduct, not on individual injury. Once monetary damages enter the picture, however, class cohesiveness is generally lost, because "[m]onetary remedies are more often related directly to the disparate merits of individual claims." Where the need to address the merits of individual claims requires separate hearings, the efficiency gained by class litigation is lost.

In *Allison*, therefore, we held that monetary relief, to be viable in a rule 23(b)(2) class, must "flow directly from liability to the class as a whole on the claims forming the basis of the injunctive or declaratory relief." Monetary relief must be incidental, meaning that it is "capable of computation by means of objective standards and not dependent in any significant way on the intangible, subjective differences of each class member's circumstances." Additional hearings to resolve "the disparate merits of each individual's case" should be unnecessary.

[Recognizing that "certification under rule 23(b)(2) is appropriate only if members of the proposed class would benefit from the injunctive relief they request," the court distinguished its earlier decision in Bolin v. Sears Roebuck & Co., 231 F.3d 970 (5th Cir.2000). Plaintiffs in *Bolin* alleged that Sears had improperly coerced payments, but only a "negligible proportion" of the class members faced further harm from Sears, and only they could seek injunctive relief. In *Monumental*, by way of contrast, expert estimates were that between one million (defendant's estimate) and 4.5 to 5.6 million (plaintiffs' estimate) remained in force. "[T]he proportion is sufficient," the court concluded, "that the class as a whole is deemed properly to be seeking injunctive relief."]

B.

* * *

As "fundamental requisites of the constitutional guarantees of procedural due process," notice and opt-out are mandatory for damage classes certified under rule 23(b)(3). Though rule 23 does not explicitly

---

10. But see Molski v. Gleich, 318 F.3d 937, 950 (9th Cir.2003) (expressly rejecting *Allison* and instead "focus[ing] on the language of Rule 23(b)(2) and the intent of the plaintiffs in bringing the suit"); Robinson v. Metro–North Commuter R.R., 267 F.3d 147, 163–64 (2d Cir.2001) (stating that rule 23(b)(2) certification is appropriate only where "reasonable plaintiffs would bring the suit to obtain the injunctive or declaratory relief sought" and "the injunctive or declaratory relief sought would be both reasonably necessary and appropriate were the plaintiffs to succeed on the merits").

extend these safeguards to rule 23(b)(2) classes, due process requires the provision of notice where a rule 23(b)(2) class seeks monetary damages.

On the other hand, there is no absolute right of opt-out in a rule 23(b)(2) class, "even where monetary relief is sought and made available." Under our precedent, should the class be certified on remand, class members must be provided adequate notice, and the district court should consider the possibility of opt-out rights.

Allison's statement that monetary relief may predominate where notice and opt-out are necessary reflects only the inescapable fact that such safeguards are most appropriate where individual issues diminish class cohesiveness. Then, conflicts among class members and issues of adequate representation are most likely to surface. Rule 23(b)(3) is the default vehicle for certification, but only because notice and opt-out rights are mandatory components. A district court is empowered by rule 23(d)(2) to provide notice and opt-out for any class action, so rule 23(b)(2) certification should not be denied on the mistaken assumption that a rule 23(b)(3) class is the only means by which to protect class members.

All of this further demonstrates the futility of the district court's and dissent's inquiry as to whether the "prime goal" of the class is injunctive or monetary relief. The rule 23(b)(2) predominance requirement, by focusing on uniform relief flowing from defendants' liability, "serves essentially the same functions as the procedural safeguards and efficiency and manageability standards mandated in (b)(3) class actions." Therefore, to deny certification on the basis that the damage claims would be better brought as a rule 23(b)(3) class serves no function other than to elevate form over substance.[18] Indeed, interests of judicial economy are best served by resolving plaintiffs' claims for injunctive and monetary relief together.

IV.

Applying *Allison*'s predominance test, the district court determined that the requested monetary relief does not flow from liability to the class as a whole. The court stated that "many and a variety of hearings would be required to determine personalized harm to each individual plaintiff because of the mass of policies involved, differing underwriting practices among some 280 companies, differing built-in benefits, account dividends, and age at policy issuance."

A.

Plaintiffs contend they seek equitable restitution in the form of a constructive trust for class members who no longer have in-force policies. By characterizing this relief as equitable, plaintiffs hope to demon-

---

18. Our view that the rule 23(b)(2) and (b)(3) devices may work in tandem is strengthened by the roots of subdivision (b)(2), which was added "to Rule 23 in 1966 primarily to facilitate the bringing of class actions in the civil rights area." 7A Charles A. Wright et al., Federal Practice and Procedure § 1775, at 470 (2d ed.1986). Before its adoption, the rules made no explicit reference to class actions involving injunctive or declaratory relief, and "there was some uncertainty whether a class action seeking one of those remedies was an appropriate device for vindicating civil rights." Id. at 470–71. Rule 23(b)(2) was adopted to facilitate the use of injunctive relief, not to compartmentalize claims for damages under rule 23(b)(3).

strate that that relief is inherently compatible with rule 23(b)(2) certification, thereby avoiding *Allison*'s monetary predominance inquiry. * * *

Equitable monetary relief is compatible with a rule 23(b)(2) class. Importantly, this pronouncement has been limited to the context of title VII backpay, a remedy designated by statute as "equitable." 42 U.S.C. § 2000e–5(g)(1). Backpay is therefore unique in that it is "an integral component of Title VII's 'make whole' remedial scheme." Not coincidentally, as compared to compensatory damages, "calculation of back pay generally involves less complicated factual determinations and fewer individual issues." In *Allison*, we recognized that, for this reason, backpay generally does not predominate over injunctive or declaratory relief.

It would be mistaken to presume that because backpay—a remedy readily calculable on a classwide basis—is compatible with a rule 23(b)(2) class, any other remedy designated as equitable may automatically piggyback a claim for injunctive relief. To be sure, equitable monetary remedies are less likely to predominate over a class's claim for injunctive relief, but this has more to do with the uniform character of the relief rather than with its label. Therefore, rather than decide whether plaintiffs' claim for restitution is legal or equitable in nature, we apply *Allison* and examine whether the claim predominates over the request for injunctive relief.

B.

This is not a case in which class members are entitled to a one-size-fits-all refund; assuming liability is established, individual damages will depend on the idiosyncracies of the particular dual rate or dual plan policy. For example, the age at which a class member purchased a dual rate policy will have an impact on how long the insured paid premiums and consequently on the amount of damages. Some policies contain built-in benefits covering occurrences outside of death, such as loss of limb; others pay periodic dividends. As we have observed, some defendants, beginning in 1988, voluntarily adjusted premiums and benefits for some policies sold on a race-distinct basis.

Plaintiffs propose using standardized formulas or restitution grids to calculate individual class members' damages. Defendants counter that "thousands" of grids must be constructed to account for the myriad of policy variations. That may be so, but the monetary predominance test does not contain a sweat-of-the-brow exception. Rather, we are guided by its command that damage calculation "should neither introduce new and substantial legal or factual issues, nor entail complex individualized determinations."

In the list of [insurance] policy variables cited by defendants and the district court, none requires the gathering of subjective evidence.[20] This

---

20. Had plaintiffs not limited their proposed class to dual rate and dual plan poli-   cies, individual hearings would be necessary to determine whether pretextual underwrit-

is not, for example, like *Allison*, a title VII case in which class members' claims for compensatory and punitive damages necessarily "implicate[ ] the subjective differences of each plaintiff's circumstances." Rather, assuming that unlawful discrimination is found, class members automatically will be entitled to the difference between what a black and a white paid for the same policy. Not coincidentally, such damages flow from liability in much the same manner that an award of backpay results from a finding of employment discrimination.

We are well aware that, as *Allison* qualifies, the calculation of monetary damages should not "entail complex individualized determinations." Although it is arguable that the construction of thousands of restitution grids, though based on objective data, involves the sort of complex data manipulations forbidden by *Allison*, we read *Allison* to the contrary. The policy variables are identifiable on a classwide basis and, when sorted, are capable of determining damages for individual policyowners; none of these variables is unique to particular plaintiffs. The prevalence of variables common to the class makes damage computation "virtually a mechanical task."[22]

Finally, defendants' records contain the information necessary to determine disparities between, on the one hand, dual rate and dual plan policies, and on the other hand, plans sold to whites. Damage calculations do not require the manipulation of data kept outside defendants' normal course of business. Defendants' complaints to the contrary are belied by the fact that, since 1988, many policies have been adjusted to account for racial disparity.

* * *

The order denying class certification is REVERSED, and this matter is REMANDED for further proceedings consistent with this opinion. We express no view on the district court's ultimate decision whether to certify in light of today's opinion, nor do we opine on the ultimate merits of the substantive claims.

CLEMENT, Circuit Judge, dissenting.

* * * Rule 23(b)(2) only permits monetary relief in the form of "uniform group remedies." Uniform group remedies are consistent with

---

ing practices were used to force the respective class members into substandard plans. In that instance, we agree with the district court that the large number of defendants and underwriting practices would be relevant to finding the predominance of monetary damages.

22. One is left wondering in what circumstances (if any) the dissent would permit monetary damages in a rule 23(b)(2) class. Remarkably, the dissent makes no attempt to explain its view that insurance policy factors such as premium rate, issue age, and benefits paid are based on "intangible, subjective differences." Instead, *Alli-*

son's statement that damages be "capable of computation by means of objective standards" is ideal for refund-type cases such as this, in which damages are calculable using factors developed and maintained in the course of defendants' business. The dissent evidently would limit damages in rule 23(b)(2) classes to instances in which there is no variance among the "specific characteristics of each policy and policyholder," a standard that necessarily would require that each class members' damages be identical. It is safe to say that the dissent's novel approach is unsupported by caselaw.

Rule 23(b)(2) for two reasons: (1) they are "capable of computation by means of objective standards," thus avoiding the need for "complex individualized determinations" and procedural safeguards like notice and opt-out rights; and (2) the group nature of the remedy ensures that the class remains "homogeneous and cohesive."[3] *Allison*, 151 F.3d at 413, 415 (noting that "as claims for individually based money damages begin to predominate, the presumption of cohesiveness decreases"). Therefore, Rule 23(b)(2) class certification is inappropriate where the monetary relief requires "a specific or time-consuming inquiry into the varying circumstances and merits of each class member's individual case."

Under the test articulated in *Allison*, it is clear that Rule 23(b)(2) class certification is inappropriate in this case. First, the majority opinion suggests that notice and opt-out rights are necessary: "Under our precedent, should the class be certified on remand, class members must be provided adequate notice, and the district court should consider the possibility of opt-out rights."

Second, a uniform group remedy is not possible in this case because Plaintiffs seek individualized remedies based on the specific characteristics of each policy and policyholder. Plaintiffs concede that the "amount of the awards vary" based on "factors including the premium rates charged to African–Americans and Caucasians, the issue ages for each policy, and the benefits provided." Monetary relief in a Rule 23(b)(2) class action should not be "dependent in any significant way on the intangible, subjective differences of each class member's circumstances." Therefore, Rule 23(b)(2) class certification is inappropriate here.

Review of the record provides further evidence that Rule 23(b)(2) class certification is inappropriate. Plaintiffs seek: (1) an injunction prohibiting the collection of discriminatory premiums; (2) reformation of existing policies to equalize benefits; and (3) restitution of past premium overcharges or benefit overpayments. The parties appear to agree that: (1) the basis of Plaintiffs' suit is the issuance of hundreds of different industrial life insurance policies by several hundred Defendants over a period of 50 to 65 years; (2) Defendants ceased issuing such policies in the mid–1970s (or, at the latest, the early 1980s); (3) many, if not most, of the industrial life insurance policies are no longer in effect; and (4) a large number of the remaining policies have been modified to some extent by Plaintiffs or Defendants. In this light, the first and second remedies sought by Plaintiffs would seem to be of little consequence to many, if not most, Plaintiffs because the injunction and reformation would only affect those Plaintiffs who still hold industrial life insurance policies that have remained largely unaltered for over 20 years (and up to 75 years). For Plaintiffs who do not fit into this category, the only

3. Footnote 22 of the majority opinion misrepresents the meaning of the term "uniform group remedies". In a Rule 23(b)(2) class action, each class member does not need to receive the exact same amount of monetary relief. However, the monetary relief awarded must be based on the "group nature of the harm alleged" rather than the individual harm suffered by each class member.

relief would be monetary in nature: the restitution of past premium overcharges or benefit overpayments.

In sum, the factual basis of Plaintiffs' suit indicates that injunctive or declaratory relief does not predominate and that the monetary relief is not incidental. As this Court stated in McManus [v. Fleetwood Ent., Inc., 320 F.3d 545 (5th Cir.)], permitting this case to be certified under Rule 23(b)(2)

> would undo the careful interplay between Rules 23(b)(2) and (b)(3) [because] the class members would potentially receive a poor substitute for individualized money damages, without the corresponding notice and opt-out benefits of Rule 23(b)(3)[,] and defendants would potentially be forced to pay what is effectively money damages, without the benefit of requiring plaintiffs to meet the rigorous Rule 23(b)(3) requirements.

This Court should not allow plaintiffs "to shoehorn damages actions into the Rule 23(b)(2) framework" and thus blur the distinctions between the different types of class actions. Therefore, I respectfully dissent.

Notes and Questions

1. For many years, employment discrimination class actions routinely combined requests for injunctive or declaratory relief with requests for back pay and front pay, and the inclusion of those monetary aspects in the suit ordinarily posed no obstacle to certification under Rule 23(b)(2), in part because these remedies were considered equitable.

In Allison v. Citgo Petroleum Corp., 151 F.3d 402 (5th Cir.1998), the court raised questions about the continued viability of this practice, particularly in light of the Civil Rights Act of 1991, which sought to bolster remedies for employment discrimination plaintiffs by permitting them to sue as well for damages for emotional distress and for punitive damages. (Another provision of that Act, dealing with challenges to consent judgments in employment discrimination suits, is described *supra* p. 99 n. 3.) Although some individualized information might be needed for back pay and front pay awards, the amendment magnified that need, and these damages were clearly remedies at law. *Allison* noted that although predominance of common questions was not required in (b)(2) cases, the requirement of cohesiveness of the interests of the class members is anticipated by the limitation to declaratory relief. "Monetary relief predominates in (b)(2) class actions," the court said, "unless it is incidental to requested injunctive or declaratory relief," that is, "damages that flow directly from liability to the class as a whole on the claims forming the basis of the injunctive or declaratory relief." Ideally, incidental damages should be only those to which class members automatically would be entitled once liability to the class (or subclass) as a whole is established. Should *Allison* be read as only allowing damages in (b)(2) class actions in rare situations, such as when there is a statutory penalty to which each class member would be entitled, without the necessity for individualized hearings? See also Jefferson v. Ingersoll International, Inc., 195 F.3d 894 (7th Cir.1999) (agreeing that, although (b)(2) had become the "normal basis" for certification in Title VII pattern-or-practice cases, the 1991 Act made certification more difficult).

As the court notes in *Monumental*, (b)(2) was adopted to facilitate civil rights suits, so it is ironic that legislation designed to aid employment discrimination plaintiffs has complicated use of this kind of class action. One judge on the Fifth Circuit has said that *Allison* may be viewed as "a Title VII exception to Rule 23." Smith v. Texaco, Inc., 263 F.3d 394 (2001) (Reavley, J., dissenting). For discussion, see Note, Evading Friendly Fire: Achieving Class Certification After the Civil Rights Act of 1991, 100 Colum.L.Rev. 1847 (2000); Jordan, Allison v. Citgo Petroleum: The Death Knell for the Title VII Class Action?, 51 Ala.L.Rev. 847 (2000).

2. As *Monumental* makes clear, the attitude that *Allison* introduced is not limited to employment discrimination suits. It also is not limited to civil rights actions. See Bolin v. Sears, Roebuck & Co., 231 F.3d 970 (5th Cir.2000) (class action for improper debt-collection activities not properly certified under (b)(2)). Why would lawyers try to package suits that seem more suited to (b)(3) treatment as (b)(2) actions?

One answer is that "plaintiffs may attempt to shoehorn damages actions into the Rule 23(b)(2) framework, depriving class members of notice and opt-out protections. The incentives to do so are large. Plaintiffs' counsel effectively gathers clients—often thousands of clients—by a certification under (b)(2). Defendants attempting to purchase res judicata may prefer certification under (b)(2) over (b)(3)." *Bolin, supra*, 231 F.3d at 976; see also Jefferson v. Ingersoll Int'l, Inc., 195 F.3d 894 (7th Cir.1999) ("Rule 23(b)(2) gives the class representatives and their lawyers a much freer hand than does Rule 23(b)(3).").

Another answer is that using (b)(2) may lower some hurdles to certification. For example: "Rule 23(b)(2)'s requirement that a defendant have acted consistently towards the class is plainly more permissive than 23(b)(3)'s requirement that questions common to the class *predominate* over individual issues." McManus v. Fleetwood Ent., Inc., 320 F.3d 545, 552 (5th Cir.2003).

3. One might also ask why a plaintiff would seek (b)(2) class certification unless the goal were to provide monetary relief. An injunction against the defendant's continuing the offending behavior would seem sufficient without the complications of a class action. For example, in Doe 1–13 v. Bush, 261 F.3d 1037 (11th Cir.2001), 13 named plaintiffs alleged that the state had systematically violated the rights of developmentally disabled people and sought an injunction against the illegal practices. Finding the state's actions illegal, the district court entered an injunction. Several years later, the state was cited for contempt in failing to provide services to some eligible individuals, and it then argued that the injunction only applied to the 13 plaintiffs who brought the suit because the judge never certified a class. The appellate court rejected this argument on the ground that there was an "implied class" even though it was not certified. Indeed, defendants had opposed class certification on the ground that injunctive relief would inure to the benefits of the putative class members even if there was no formal certification, and had also sought an emergency stay of the injunction when it was entered on the ground that otherwise they would have to retool the statewide system.

One answer to the question why plaintiffs seeking only injunctive relief would seek certification is to assure enforceability of the injunction if it is obtained. For others, consider Daniels v. City of New York, 198 F.R.D. 409 (S.D.N.Y. 2001), a suit challenging police stop and frisk activities as resulting from racial profiling. Defendants offered to stipulate that they would apply any injunctive relief obtained by plaintiffs to any others "similarly situated." The court found that class certification was nonetheless warranted because (1) discovery might be more limited in the absence of class certification, (2) plaintiffs' counsel would not be protected by the attorney-client privilege in communications with unnamed members of the class absent certification, and (3) plaintiffs sought relatively complex relief, which might seem less appropriate in the absence of a class action.

It may also be that class certification is essential to obtaining classwide relief. In Everhart v. Bowen, 853 F.2d 1532 (10th Cir.1988), rev'd on other grounds sub nom. Sullivan v. Everhart, 494 U.S. 83, 110 S.Ct. 960, 108 L.Ed.2d 72 (1990), the court held that the district judge had erred in entering a statewide injunction against certain welfare administrative practices even though it found that the practices were illegal:

> The statewide injunction entered by the district court was tantamount to a grant of classwide relief. * * * At this juncture, there has been no determination on the issue of class certification: indeed, the district court expressly declined to do so. Absent a class certification, the district court should not have treated the suit as a class action by granting statewide injunctive relief, and accordingly should have tailored its injunction "to affect only those persons over [whom] it has power."

See also 18 U.S.C.A. § 2636 (directing that relief in prison conditions cases "shall extend no further than necessary to correct the violation of the federal right to a particular plaintiff").

4. In Robinson v. Metro–North Commuter R.R., 267 F.3d 147 (2d Cir.2001), present or former African–American employees of defendant sued claiming that defendant discriminated against black employees, relying on statistical and anecdotal evidence. They sued on behalf of a class of African–American employees of defendant during an eleven-year period, and sought injunctive relief, back pay, and front pay, as well as compensatory damages for those class members who were the victims of individual acts of intentional discrimination. The district court applied *Allison* and refused to certify under (b)(2). The appellate court reversed, viewing that question as "whether this bright-line bar to (b)(2) class treatment of *all* claims for compensatory damages and other non-incidental damages (e.g., punitive damages) is appropriate." It found a bright-line test inappropriate (id. at 164):

> The district court may allow (b)(2) certification if it finds in its "informed sound discretion" that (1) "the positive weight or value [to the plaintiffs] of the injunctive or declaratory relief sought is predominant even though compensatory or punitive damages are also claimed," and (2) class treatment would be efficient and manageable, thereby achieving an appreciable measure of judicial economy.

> Although the assessment of whether injunctive or declaratory relief predominates will require an ad hoc balancing that will vary from case to case, before allowing (b)(2) certification a district court should, at a

minimum, satisfy itself of the following: (1) even in the absence of possible monetary recovery, reasonable plaintiffs would bring the suit to obtain the injunctive or declaratory relief sought; and (2) the injunctive or declaratory relief sought would be both reasonably necessary and appropriate were the plaintiffs to succeed on the merits. Insignificant or sham requests for injunctive relief should not provide cover for (b)(2) certification of claims that are brought essentially for monetary recovery.

See also Berger v. Xerox Retirement Income Guarantee Plan, 338 F.3d 755 (7th Cir.2003) (suit for declaratory relief regarding determination of lump sum distributions could be certified under Rule 23(b)(2)); Molski v. Gleich, 318 F.3d 937 (9th Cir.2003) (injunctive relief was the predominant form of relief sought in suit seeking improvement of access for mobility-impaired people to gas stations and mini-markets even though claims for statutory damages were also involved).

5.   In Coleman v. General Motors Acceptance Corp., 296 F.3d 443 (6th Cir.2002), plaintiffs sued on behalf of a class of borrowers from defendant, claiming race discrimination and seeking both injunctive relief and compensatory damages. In addressing (b)(2) certification, the court invoked the Advisory Committee Note on (b)(3) regarding predominance of common questions—"[i]t is only where this predominance exists that economies can be achieved by means of the class-action device"—and suggested that the same sort of inquiry should be used under (b)(2). In particular, "one critical factor is whether the compensatory relief requested requires individualized damages determination or is susceptible to calculation on a classwide basis." Id. at 448.

6.   In *Monumental*, defendants also argued that, because so much time had passed since some class members purchased their policies, the statute of limitations had run on those claims, and thus the presence of these individual issues would preclude class certification. The court agreed that individual issues raised by affirmative defenses could defeat class certification, but rejected defendants' argument on the ground that a rebuttable presumption that class members lacked knowledge of defendants' discriminatory practices was warranted at the class certification stage. Should individualized affirmative defenses matter in a (b)(2) action? Do they bear on whether the opposing party has acted on grounds "generally applicable to the class, thereby making appropriate final injunctive relief * * * with respect to the class as a whole"?

7.   The court in *Monumental* notes that the case is a negative value class action. Should that matter in determining whether to allow (b)(2) certification? If class certification were not allowed in that case, would there ever be effective relief for those victims of discrimination?

8.   *Medical monitoring class actions*: Many states recognize some form of tort claim for medical monitoring. States' laws concerning the elements of a cause of action for fear of cancer or other serious disease resulting from exposure to products or environmental conditions fall roughly into two categories. Some states require proof of a reasonable probability that plaintiff will contract cancer. See, e.g., Boyd v. Orkin Exterminating Co., 191 Ga.App. 38, 381 S.E.2d 295 (1989) (children with elevated levels of pesticide

in their blood could not recover for "increased risk of cancer" because they had to prove "to a reasonable medical certainty" that such consequences would occur). Others require an accompanying physical injury of a sufficiently serious nature related to the exposure. See, e.g., Burns v. Jaquays Mining Corp. 156 Ariz. 375, 752 P.2d 28 (App.1987) (rejecting claims of residents of land adjacent to an asbestos-producing mill for risk of cancer and emotional distress based on transitory, non-recurring physical conditions, such as headaches, indigestion, weeping, muscle spasms, depression, and insomnia, on the ground that these did not constitute "substantial bodily harm"). Although people who have been exposed may not have a present cause of action or claim for damages, they are at risk of manifesting disease at some time in the future, and class actions have increasingly been filed seeking "medical monitoring," that is, periodic examinations at defendant's expense to determine their condition. State substantive law varies as to recognition of a claim for medical monitoring. Among states that do recognize such a claim, some view it as a separate cause of action, while others characterize it as a remedy that is supplemental to another cause of action.

How should these claims be treated for purposes of Rule 23(b)(2)? Often such a suit results in a judgment requiring defendant to create a fund to compensate plaintiff for the ongoing cost of monitoring. On the other hand, it may be regarded as providing forward-looking relief (as opposed to compensation) so that it should be considered equitable. Given these uncertainties, the courts have been cautious about certifying (b)(2) mandatory classes for medical monitoring. For discussion, see Note, The Class Certification of Medical Monitoring Claims, 102 Colum. L. Rev. 1659 (2002).

9.   Once the injunctive elements of the case are resolved, should the case continue to be handled under (b)(2)? In Scott v. City of Anniston, 682 F.2d 1353 (11th Cir.1982), a (b)(2) class action under Title VII to enjoin use of written promotional examinations and for back pay, the court held that the case could continue as a (b)(2) action even though the defendant had stopped using the challenged examination. Compare Ardrey v. Federal Kemper Ins. Co., 142 F.R.D. 105 (E.D.Pa.1992) (certification of a (b)(2) class was improper because, although initial injunctive relief was sought, once the court refused to grant that injunctive relief the case became "a matter predominantly concerning monetary damages").

10.   What should the court do if the monetary relief cannot be included with a (b)(2) certification? In many instances, courts will certify only with regard to the injunctive claims, leaving class members free to pursue claims for damages separately. See Rice v. City of Philadelphia, 66 F.R.D. 17 (E.D.Pa.1974). That might lead to preclusion problems, as individual plaintiffs might be challenged for splitting a cause of action if they tried to sue separately for injunctive and damages relief, but courts do not apply preclusion with regard to the claims of unnamed class members. See Cooper v. Federal Reserve Bank of Richmond, *infra* p. 831.

4.   RULE 23(b)(3) CLASSES

We particularly deal in this section with the problems attending the use of the Rule 23(b)(3) class action for mass torts and mass related cases. In 1966, the Advisory Committee Notes accompanying the amendment to Rule 23 observed that "[a] 'mass accident' resulting in injuries to numerous persons is ordinarily not appropriate for a class action because of the likelihood that significant questions, not only of damages but also of liability and defenses of liability, would be present, affecting the individuals in different ways. In these circumstances an action conducted nominally as a class action would degenerate in practice into multiple lawsuits separately tried."

Consistent with the Advisory Committee's admonition, courts were initially cautious about certifying such cases as (b)(3) class actions. For example, in Mertens v. Abbott Laboratories, 99 F.R.D. 38 (D.N.H.1983), twelve New Hampshire residents who had been exposed to the drug DES in utero and claimed to have suffered serious personal injuries as a result sought to sue on behalf of others so exposed in their state. Plaintiffs argued that "the prohibitive cost of individual lawsuits would make the assertion of a claim an economic impossibility for most plaintiffs." But although the court found sufficient common issues to satisfy Rule 23(a)(2), it held that the predominance requirement of Rule 23(b)(3) was not satisfied. Explaining that its task in applying the predominance requirement was to "predict the evidence likely to be introduced at trial," the court saw considerable disparities. Plaintiffs urged that the question whether DES was toxic constituted an issue of "global liability" that should be regarded as predominant, but the court felt that the "details" that would remain unresolved "clearly outweigh the single determination that DES causes injury." The court concluded additionally that a class action would not be superior to adjudication in a more traditional fashion:

> If thousands of claims are brought, they will be dealt with in the same fashion as any other litigation. Indeed, judicial resources applied to each claim on an individual basis would doubtless be more effective than a general pronouncement applied to all cases without any real effect. * * * Other than the possibility of seeking to commit the law of New Hampshire in a particular direction, it is unlikely that anything of real value could be determined that would aid in the resolution of the claims of any individual plaintiff. In addition, it is doubtful if any decision at this level could be as effective as an appellate determination of some of the sweeping and intriguing questions raised in this litigation. Though old fashioned, *stare decisis* is not yet out of fashion.

But as caseloads mounted and certain types of litigation became more familiar to the courts, receptivity to (b)(3) certification grew.

JENKINS v. RAYMARK INDUSTRIES, INC.

United States Court of Appeals, Fifth Circuit, 1986.
782 F.2d 468.

Before GEE, ALVIN B. RUBIN and REAVLEY, CIRCUIT JUDGES.

REAVLEY, CIRCUIT JUDGE.

In this interlocutory appeal, the thirteen defendants challenge the decision of District Judge Robert M. Parker to certify a class of plaintiffs with asbestos-related claims. We affirm.

* * *

About 5,000 asbestos-related cases are pending in this circuit. Much, though by no means all, of the litigation has centered in the Eastern District of Texas. Nearly nine hundred asbestos-related personal injury cases, involving over one thousand plaintiffs, were pending there in December of 1984. Despite innovative streamlined pretrial procedures and large-scale consolidated trials of multiple plaintiffs, the dockets of that district's courts remained alarmingly backlogged. Plaintiffs had waited years for trial, some since 1979—and new cases were (and still are) being filed every day. It is predicted that, because asbestos-related diseases will continue to manifest themselves for the next 15 years, filings will continue at a steady rate until the year 2000.

In early 1985, ten of these plaintiffs responded by moving to certify a class of all plaintiffs with asbestos-related personal injury actions pending in the Eastern District on December 31, 1984. These plaintiffs hoped to determine in the class action one overarching issue—the viability of the "state of the art" defense. Because the trial of that issue consistently consumed substantial resources in every asbestos trial, and the evidence in each case was either identical or virtually so, they argued, a class determination would accelerate their cases.

Following copious briefing and several hearings, the district court granted the motion. In his order of October 16, 1985, Judge Parker carefully considered the request under Rule 23(a), (b)(1) and (b)(3) of the Federal Rules of Civil Procedure. Finding a "limited fund" theory too speculative, he refused to certify the class under Rule 23(b)(1); by contrast, he found all of the elements for a 23(b)(3) action present. Drawing on his past experience, the judge concluded that evidence concerning the "state of the art" defense would vary little as to individual plaintiffs while consuming a major part of the time required for their trials. Considerable savings, both for the litigants and for the court, could thus be gained by resolving this and other defense and defense-related questions, including product identification, product defectiveness, gross negligence and punitive damages, in one class trial.[3] The court further found that the named representatives had "typical" claims, and that they and their attorneys would adequately represent the other class

---

3. The court pointed to the following general issues:

(a) which products, if any, were asbestos-containing insulation products capable of producing dust that contained asbestos fibers sufficient to cause harm in its application, use, or removal;

(b) which of the Defendants' products, if any, were defective as marketed and unreasonably dangerous;

(c) what date each Defendant knew or should have known that insulators and their household members were at risk of contracting an asbestos-related injury or disease from the application, use, or removal of asbestos-containing insulation products; and

(d) what amount of punitive damages, if any, should be awarded to the class as punishment for the Defendants' conduct.

members. Accordingly, it certified the class as to the common questions, ordering them resolved for the class by a class action jury. The class jury would also decide all the individual issues in the class representatives' underlying suits; individual issues of the unnamed members would be resolved later in "mini-trials" of seven to ten plaintiffs. Although the class action jury would evaluate the culpability of defendants' conduct for a possible punitive damage award, any such damages would be awarded only after class members had won or settled their individual cases. The court subsequently appointed a special master to survey the class and prepare a report, detailing the class members and their claims, to apprise the jury of the gravity and extent of the absent members' claims and the typicality of the representatives' claims.

Defendants moved for reconsideration or, in the alternative, certification of the decision for interlocutory appeal. The court granted defendants' alternate motion.

On appeal, defendants challenge the court's decision on three grounds: (1) the class fails to meet the requirements of Rule 23; (2) Texas law proscribes a bifurcated determination of punitive damages and actual damages; and (3) the contemplated class format is unconstitutional.

* * *

RULE 23

Defendants argue that this class meets none of the Rule 23 requirements, except "numerosity." There is no merit to this argument.

The threshold of "commonality" is not high. Aimed in part at "determining whether there is a need for combined treatment and a benefit to be derived therefrom," *In re Agent Orange Product Liability Litigation,* 506 F.Supp. 762, 787 (E.D.N.Y.1980), the rule requires only that resolution of the common questions affect all or a substantial number of the class members. Defendants do not claim that they intend to raise a "state of the art" defense in only a few cases; the related issues are common to all class members.

The "typicality" requirement focuses less on the relative strengths of the named and unnamed plaintiffs' cases than on the similarity of the legal and remedial theories behind their claims. Defendants do not contend that the named plaintiffs' claims rest on theories different from those of the other class members.

The "adequacy" requirement looks at both the class representatives and their counsel. Defendants have not shown that the representatives are "inadequate" due to an insufficient stake in the outcome or interests antagonistic to the unnamed members.[5] Neither do they give us reason to question the district court's finding that class counsel is "adequate" in light of counsel's past experience in asbestos cases, including trials involving multiple plaintiffs.

---

5. Moreover, dissatisfied members have the opportunity to "opt out" of the class.

We similarly find no abuse in the court's determination that the certified questions "predominate" under Rule 23(b)(3). In order to "predominate," common issues must constitute a significant part of the individual cases. It is difficult to imagine that class jury findings on the class questions will not significantly advance the resolution of the underlying hundreds of cases.[6]

Defendants also argue that a class action is not "superior"; they say that better mechanisms, such as the Wellington Facility[7] and "reverse bifurcation,"[8] exist for resolving these claims. Again, however, they have failed to show that the district court abused its discretion by reaching the contrary conclusion. We cannot find that the Wellington Facility, whose merits we do not question, is so superior that it must be used to the exclusion of other forums. Similarly, even if we were prepared to weigh the merits of other procedural mechanisms, we see no basis to conclude that this class action plan is an abuse of discretion.

Courts have usually avoided class actions in the mass accident or tort setting. Because of differences between individual plaintiffs on issues of liability and defenses of liability, as well as damages, it has been feared that separate trials would overshadow the common disposition for the class. The courts are now being forced to rethink the alternatives and priorities by the current volume of litigation and more frequent mass disasters. If Congress leaves us to our own devices, we may be forced to abandon repetitive hearings and arguments for each claimant's attorney to the extent enjoyed by the profession in the past. Be that as time will tell, the decision at hand is driven in one direction by all the circumstances. Judge Parker's plan is clearly superior to the alternative of repeating, hundreds of times over, the litigation of the state of the art issues with, as that experienced judge says, "days of the same witnesses, exhibits and issues from trial to trial."

This assumes plaintiffs win on the critical issues of the class trial. To the extent defendants win, the elimination of issues and docket will mean a far greater saving of judicial resources. Furthermore, attorneys' fees for all parties will be greatly reduced under this plan, not only

---

6. Defendants argue that not all of the defendants in the underlying actions have been named in the class suit; in addition, some 70–80 potential class members have sued none of the class defendants. These arguments go nowhere, however. At worst, these latter "plaintiffs" will simply be unaffected by the class action findings. Conversely, if these "plaintiffs" do not opt out, the district court may decide to redefine the class to include only plaintiffs with claims against the named defendants. As for the plaintiffs who have sued both named and unnamed defendants, even if all class issues must be retried in the mini-trials as to all the unnamed defendants, the evidence will necessarily be significantly less than if no class findings had been made.

7. The Wellington Facility, funded by major asbestos producers, is a newly-operational center designed to resolve asbestos-related claims. The center is named for Dean Wellington of the Yale University Law School, who assisted in its organization.

8. "Reverse bifurcation" originated in the Third Circuit as a means of processing that circuit's backlog of asbestos-related cases. As its name suggests, it is a modified bifurcated trial format whereby plaintiffs in a first trial prove only that exposure to some asbestos product has caused their damages. Thereafter, either the cases are settled or remaining issues are resolved in second or third trials.

because of the elimination of so much trial time but also because the fees collected from all members of the plaintiff class will be controlled by the judge. From our view it seems that the defendants enjoy all of the advantages, and the plaintiffs incur the disadvantages, of the class action—with one exception: the cases are to be brought to trial. That counsel for plaintiffs would urge the class action under these circumstances is significant support for the district judge's decision.

Necessity moves us to change and invent. Both the *Agent Orange* and the *Asbestos School* courts found that specific issues could be decided in a class "mass tort" action—even on a nationwide basis. We approve of the district court's decision in finding that this "mass tort" class could be certified.

OTHER CONTENTIONS

Defendants' remaining arguments challenge the bifurcated trials under Texas law and the United States Constitution. Defendants contend that, under Texas law, punitive damages cannot be determined separately from actual damages because the culpability of their conduct must be evaluated relative to each plaintiff. We disagree.

The purpose of punitive damages is not to compensate the victim but to create a deterrence to the defendant. The focus is on the defendant's conduct, rather than on the plaintiff's. While no plaintiff may receive an award of punitive damages without proving that he suffered actual damages, the allocation need not be made concurrently with an evaluation of the defendant's conduct. The relative timing of these assessments is not critical.

The critical issue in Texas punitive damages law is excessiveness or "reasonable proportionality." Whether a given award is excessive is a question of fact. *See Tatum v. Preston Carter Co.,* 702 S.W.2d 186, 188 (1986). "The reasonable proportion rule does not, standing alone, serve to fix a particular ratio," *Tatum,* 702 S.W.2d at 188; that ratio will vary according to the facts of the case, *id.* at 188. In determining whether an award is excessive the court must consider: (1) the nature of the wrong; (2) the character of the conduct involved; (3) the degree of culpability of the wrongdoer; (4) the situation and sensibilities of the parties concerned; and (5) the extent to which such conduct offends a public sense of justice and propriety.

The format in this case allows for the district court's review of the reasonableness of each plaintiff's punitive damage award and for our review of the standards which the court has applied. Texas law does not require more.

Defendants' constitutional challenges to bifurcation are equally unavailing. Like their other claims, these arguments only recast in constitutional terms their concern that, because the representatives' cases are "better" than the unnamed plaintiffs', the jury's view of the class claims will be skewed.

Although it fails to raise an issue of constitutional magnitude, this concern is nevertheless legitimate. Care must, of course, be taken to ensure fairness. Whatever the jury is told about the claims of the unnamed plaintiffs, it must be made aware that none of those claims have been proved; even after the class trial, they will still be mere allegations. The jury must not assume that all class members have equivalent claims: whatever injuries the unnamed plaintiffs have suffered may differ from the class representatives' as well as from one another's. Should the jury be allowed to award in the aggregate any punitive damages it finds appropriate, it must be instructed to factor in the possibility that none of the unnamed plaintiffs may have suffered *any* damages. Alternatively, the jury could be allowed to award an amount of money that each class member should receive for each dollar of actual damages awarded. Either way, the jury should understand that it must differentiate between proven and still-unproved claims, and that all class members, who recover actual damages from a defendant held liable for punitive damages, will share in the punitive award.

Furthermore, fairness as well as necessity dictates that both the parties and the court ensure that *all* of the necessary findings can be and are made in the class action trial. Sufficient evidence must be adduced for every one of each defendant's products to which a class member claims exposure so that the class jury can make the requisite findings as to *each* product and *each* defendant for such questions as periods of manufacture; areas and dates of distribution; "state of the art" knowledge for each relevant kind of product, use and user; when, if ever, conduct was grossly negligent; and dates and types of warnings if marketing defect is alleged.

The task will not be easy. Nevertheless, particularly in light of the magnitude of the problem and the need for innovative approaches, we find no abuse of discretion in this court's decision to try these cases by means of a Rule 23(b)(3) class suit.

Notes and Questions

1. *Jenkins* may be seen as a symptom of a shift in judicial attitude towards certifying class actions for mass torts occurring over a period of time under different circumstances. Certainly there has been a change in the attitudes of some influential observers from 1966, when Rule 23 was amended. Consider the views of Professor Charles Alan Wright:

> I was an ex officio member of the Advisory Committee on Civil Rules when Rule 23 was amended, which came out with an Advisory Committee Note [*supra* p. 331] saying that mass torts are inappropriate for class certification. I thought then that was true. I am profoundly convinced now that that is untrue. Unless we can use the class action and devices built on the class action, our judicial system is not going to be able to cope with the challenge of the mass repetitive wrong.

Transcript of Oral Argument, July 30, 1984, at 106, in In re Asbestos School Litigation, 594 F.Supp. 178 (E.D.Pa.1984), quoted in H. Newberg, Newberg on Class Actions § 17.06 at 373 (2d ed. 1985).

Similarly, Judge Jack Weinstein noted regarding the Advisory Committee note: "As authority for this warning against attempts to use class actions in torts, the note cites an article [I] wrote as a law professor. As a judge [I have] been forced to ignore this indiscretion when faced with the practicalities of mass tort litigation. In the earlier 1960's we did not fully understand the implications of mass tort demands on our legal system." Weinstein & Hershenov, The Effects of Equity on Mass Torts, 1991 U.Ill.L.Rev. 269, 288.

2. Was it necessary for Judge Parker to limit the class to actions pending in his district? Could he have certified a state-or nation-wide class? Cf. Phillips Petroleum Co. v. Shutts, *infra* p. 412. Need he have limited the action to pending suits? Cf. Amchem Products, Inc. v. Windsor, *infra* p. 373.

3. *Phased trials*. Judge Parker proposed to deal with individual circumstances in relation to remedies for class members. We will address trial of complex cases in Chapter VII, and bifurcation in particular at pp. 762-77. Nonetheless, some introduction now would be helpful:

> Even if proof of damages may require individualized evidence, a class action is not necessarily foreclosed. Some courts have certified classes to determine liability in a common trial and have severed out damages to be determined later through such methods as individual or small-group trials or some form of administrative determination. Courts differ, however, on their willingness to find that such methods comport with standards of efficiency and fairness.
>
> Some courts have also approved dividing up liability issues to be tried in separate phases. For example, in 1986, a federal court in Jenkins v. Raymark Indus., Inc., approved the certification of a class action for persons exposed to asbestos. The trial court ordered a class-wide trial of common issues relating to the defendant manufacturer's conduct, but left for later "phased trials" such individualized issues as the exposure of each class member, affirmative defenses like statute of limitations, and damages. This has been referred to as bifurcation, trifurcation, or polyfurcation. In cases where causation through exposure to defendant's product is a central disputed issue (such as asbestos cases), courts have even approved "reverse bifurcation" by which the issue of generic causation is determined in the first phase, and liability is addressed in the second phase. This ordering is based on the belief that once there has been a determination that the defendant's product could cause the injury (for example, exposure to asbestos could be the cause of asbestosis or smoking could be the cause of lung cancer), the parties are more likely to settle without the need for a full trial.

Sherman, American Class Actions: Significant Features and Developing Alternatives in Foreign Legal Systems, 215 F.R.D. 130, 141–42 (2003).

4. *Trial plan*: Recall that *Falcon, supra* p. 267, focused in part on the manner of proof at trial in determining whether a class action was appropriate. "An increasing number of courts require a party requesting class certification to present a 'trial plan' that describes the issues likely to be presented at trial and tests whether they are susceptible of class-wide proof." Fed. R. Civ. P. 23(c)(1) Committee Note to 2003 amendment. Consider the amount of effort that preparing such a plan may be for counsel who don't know whether there will be a class action. Should they be required

to designate expert witnesses at this point? Should they be allowed to modify the trial plan later if class certification is granted? We will consider the court's management of the trial in Chapter VII.

5. If the goal is to resolve certain issues in a final fashion, is the class action preferable to use of collateral estoppel? There is some problem defining the issues decided in an individual action. Thus, in Hardy v. Johns–Manville, *infra* p. 864, the Fifth Circuit reversed an order by Judge Parker collaterally estopping defendants from relitigating various issues in asbestos cases based on an earlier victory by an individual plaintiff. It found that differences in circumstances between the current cases and the earlier cases made it impossible to say with certainty that the same issues were involved. Would a class action approach solve this problem? If so, would it do so at the expense of attention to individual circumstances?

6. Defendants in *Jenkins* argued that the court should not have certified a class because it would be preferable to use the Wellington Facility. This facility was widely viewed as a failure, Mitchell & Barrett, Novel Effort to Settle Asbestos Claims Fails as Lawsuits Multiply, Wall St.J., June 7, 1988, at 1, col. 6, but it was succeeded by another similar entity known as the Center for Claims Resolution. See Fitzpatrick, The Center for Claims Resolution, 53 Law & Contemp. Probs. 13 (Autumn 1990). For consideration of this ADR technique, see *infra* p. 932. The CCR was an active participant in Amchem Products, Inc. v. Windsor, *infra* p. 373.

7. In Sterling v. Velsicol Chemical Corp., 855 F.2d 1188 (6th Cir.1988), the court also exhibited flexibility about class certification. Plaintiffs in this action sued the operator of a landfill for leakage of toxic substances. Eventually 97 named plaintiffs, who claimed that they had suffered various types of personal injuries, joined the suit. On its own motion, the district court certified a class under Rule 23(b)(3) and directed plaintiffs to select five representative plaintiffs for initial trial to establish liability and damages for their individual cases and for liability to the entire class and punitive damages, if any. After a bench trial, the court found defendant liable to plaintiffs on theories of strict liability, common law negligence, trespass and nuisance.

On appeal, the court upheld the Rule 23(b)(3) certification (id. at 1196–97):

> The procedural device of a Rule 23(b)(3) class action was designed not solely as a means for assuring legal assistance in the vindication of small claims but, rather, to achieve the economies of time, effort, and expense. However, the problem of individualization of issues often is cited as a justification for denying class action treatment in mass tort accidents. While some courts have adopted this justification in refusing to certify such accidents as class actions, numerous other courts have recognized the increasingly insistent need for a more efficient method of disposing of a large number of lawsuits arising out of a single disaster or a single course of conduct. In mass tort accidents, the factual and legal issues of a defendant's liability do not differ dramatically from one plaintiff to the next. No matter how individualized the issue of damages may be, these issues may be reserved for individual treatment with the question of liability tried as a class action. Consequently, the mere fact

that questions peculiar to each individual member of the class remain after the common question of the defendant's liability have been resolved does not dictate the conclusion that a class action is impermissible.

See also In re A.H. Robins Co., 880 F.2d 709, 740 (4th Cir. 1989) (asserting that "the 'trend' is once again to give Rule 23 a liberal rather than a restrictive construction.").

8.   In In re "Agent Orange" Product Liability Litigation, 100 F.R.D. 718 (E.D.N.Y.1983), aff'd, 818 F.2d 145 (2d Cir.1987), Judge Weinstein certified a (b)(3) class action for those claiming injury due to exposure to the defoliant Agent Orange in Viet Nam. The plaintiffs included Viet Nam veterans, their spouses, their parents and their children. They asserted that a variety of illnesses to veterans and their children had resulted from their exposure to the chemical. In an earlier opinion, the court explored some of the difficulties presented by class certification:

> Clearly this is not the "simple" type of "disaster" litigation such as an airplane crash involving a single incident, having a causation picture that is readily grasped through conventional litigation techniques, and presenting comparatively small variations among the claimants as to the effects upon them of the crash. With the Agent Orange litigation, injuries are claimed to have resulted from exposure to a chemical that was disseminated in the air over southeast Asia during a period of several years. Each veteran was exposed differently, although undoubtedly patterns of exposure will emerge. The claimed injuries vary significantly. Moreover, there is a major dispute over whether Agent Orange can cause the injuries in question, and there are separate disputes over whether the exposures claimed in each case did cause the injuries claimed. The picture is further complicated by the use in Vietnam of other chemicals and drugs that also are claimed to be capable of causing many of the injuries attributed to Agent Orange.

In re Agent Orange Product Liability Litigation, 506 F.Supp. 762, 783 (E.D.N.Y.1980). The case was further complicated by plaintiffs' desire to sue the U.S. government as well, and defendants' claim that as military contractors they were immune from liability.

Judge Weinstein reasoned that these problems did not prevent class certification (100 F.R.D. at 723):

> Unlike litigations such as those involving DES, Dalkon Shield and asbestos, the trial is likely to emphasize crucial common defenses applicable to the plaintiffs' class as a whole. They will include such matters as that the substances manufactured could not have caused the injuries claimed; that if any injuries were caused by defendants' product it was because of the particular use and misuse made by the government and that the government, not the manufacturers, were wholly responsible because the former knew of all possible dangers and assumed full responsibility.

* * *

Unlike the asbestos, DES, Dalkon Shield, and Federal Skywalk cases, defendants contest liability not just as to individual members of the class, but as to any members of the class. Thus, unlike other mass product liability cases, a determination of general causation will serve both the interests of judicial economy and assist in the speedy and less expensive resolution of individual class member's claims.

Eventually Judge Weinstein achieved a settlement of the class action for $180 million on the eve of trial, an effort that required a good deal of cajolery and pressure from the court. For a comprehensive examination of the litigation, see P. Schuck, Agent Orange on Trial: Mass Toxic Disasters in the Courts (1986). For an examination of some troubling aspects of the use of the class action and active judicial involvement in the case, see Marcus, Apocalypse Now? (book review), 85 Mich.L.Rev. 1267 (1987).

CASTANO v. THE AMERICAN TOBACCO CO.
United States Court of Appeals, Fifth Circuit, 1996.
84 F.3d 734.

Before SMITH, DUHÉ, and DeMOSS, Circuit Judges.

JERRY E. SMITH, Circuit Judge:

In what may be the largest class action ever attempted in federal court, the district court in this case embarked "on a road certainly less traveled, if ever taken at all," Castano v. American Tobacco Co., 160 F.R.D. 544, 560 (E.D.La.1995) (citing Edward C. Latham, The Poetry of Robert Frost, "The Road Not Taken" 105 (1969)), and entered a class certification order. The court defined the class as:

(a) All nicotine-dependent persons in the United States ... who have purchased and smoked cigarettes manufactured by the defendants;

(b) the estates, representatives, and administrators of these nicotine-dependent cigarette smokers; and

(c) the spouses, children, relatives and "significant others" of these nicotine-dependent cigarette smokers as their heirs or survivors.

The plaintiffs limit the claims to years since 1943.[9]

This matter comes before us on interlocutory appeal, under 28 U.S.C. § 1292(b), of the class certification order. Concluding that the district court abused its discretion in certifying the class, we reverse.

I.

A. THE CLASS COMPLAINT

The plaintiffs filed this class complaint against the defendant tobacco companies and the Tobacco Institute, Inc., seeking compensation

---

9. The court defined "nicotine-dependent" as:

(a) All cigarette smokers who have been diagnosed by a medical practitioner as nicotine-dependent; and/or

(b) All regular cigarette smokers who were or have been advised by a medical practitioner that smoking has had or will

have adverse health consequences who thereafter do not or have not quit smoking.

Id. at 561. The definition is based upon the criteria for "dependence" set forth in American Psychiatric Association, Diagnostic and Statistical Manual of Mental Disorders (4th ed.).

solely for the injury of nicotine addiction. The gravamen of their complaint is the novel and wholly untested theory that the defendants fraudulently failed to inform consumers that nicotine is addictive and manipulated the level of nicotine in cigarettes to sustain their addictive nature. The class complaint alleges nine causes of action: fraud and deceit, negligent misrepresentation, intentional infliction of emotional distress, negligence and negligent infliction of emotional distress, violation of state consumer protection statutes, breach of express warranty, breach of implied warranty, strict product liability, and redhibition pursuant to the Louisiana Civil Code.

The plaintiffs seek compensatory and punitive damages and attorneys' fees. In addition, the plaintiffs seek equitable relief for fraud and deceit, negligent misrepresentation, violation of consumer protection statutes, and breach of express and implied warranty. The equitable remedies include a declaration that defendants are financially responsible for notifying all class members of nicotine's addictive nature, a declaration that the defendants manipulated nicotine levels with the intent to sustain the addiction of plaintiffs and the class members, an order that the defendants disgorge any profits made from the sale of cigarettes, restitution for sums paid for cigarettes, and the establishment of a medical monitoring fund.

The plaintiffs initially defined the class as "all nicotine dependent persons in the United States," including current, former and deceased smokers since 1943. Plaintiffs conceded that addiction would have to be proven by each class member; the defendants argued that proving class membership will require individual mini-trials to determine whether addiction actually exists.

In response to the district court's inquiry, the plaintiffs proposed a four-phase trial plan. In phase 1, a jury would determine common issues of "core liability." Phase 1 issues would include (1) issues of law and fact relating to defendants' course of conduct, fraud, and negligence liability (including duty, standard of care, misrepresentation and concealment, knowledge, intent); (2) issues of law and fact relating to defendants' alleged conspiracy and concert of action; (3) issues of fact relating to the addictive nature/dependency creating characteristics and properties of nicotine; (4) issues of fact relating to nicotine cigarettes as defective products; (5) issues of fact relating to whether defendants' wrongful conduct was intentional, reckless or negligent; (6) identifying which defendants specifically targeted their advertising and promotional efforts to particular groups (e.g. youths, minorities, etc.); (7) availability of a presumption of reliance; (8) whether defendants' misrepresentations/suppression of fact and/or of addictive properties of nicotine preclude availability of a "personal choice" defense; (9) defendants' liability for actual damages, and the categories of such damages; (10) defendants' liability for emotional distress damages; and (11) defendants' liability for punitive damages.

Phase 1 would be followed by notice of the trial verdict and claim forms to class members. In phase 2, the jury would determine compensatory damages in sample plaintiff cases. The jury then would establish a ratio of punitive damages to compensatory damages, which ratio thereafter would apply to each class member.

Phase 3 would entail a complicated procedure to determine compensatory damages for individual class members. The trial plan envisions determination of absent class members' compensatory economic and emotional distress damages on the basis of claim forms, "subject to verification techniques and assertion of defendants' affirmative defenses under grouping, sampling, or representative procedures to be determined by the Court."

The trial plan left open how jury trials on class members' personal injury/wrongful death claims would be handled, but the trial plan discussed the possibility of bifurcation. In phase 4, the court would apply the punitive damage ratio based on individual damage awards and would conduct a review of the reasonableness of the award.

B. THE CLASS CERTIFICATION ORDER

Following extensive briefing, the district court granted, in part, plaintiffs' motion for class certification, concluding that the prerequisites of Fed.R.Civ.P. 23(a) had been met. The court rejected certification, under Fed.R.Civ.P. 23(b)(2), of the plaintiffs' claim for equitable relief, including the claim for medical monitoring. Appellees have not crossappealed that portion of the order.

The court did grant the plaintiffs' motion to certify the class under Fed.R.Civ.P. 23(b)(3), organizing the class action issues into four categories: (1) core liability; (2) injury-in-fact, proximate cause, reliance and affirmative defenses; (3) compensatory damages; and (4) punitive damages. It then analyzed each category to determine whether it met the predominance and superiority requirements of rule 23(b)(3). Using its power to sever issues for certification under Fed.R.Civ.P. 23(c)(4), the court certified the class on core liability and punitive damages, and certified the class conditionally pursuant to Fed.R.Civ.P. 23(c)(1).

1. Core Liability Issues

The court defined core liability issues as "common factual issues [of] whether defendants knew cigarette smoking was addictive, failed to inform cigarette smokers of such, and took actions to addict cigarette smokers. Common legal issues include fraud, negligence, breach of warranty (express or implied), strict liability, and violation of consumer protection statutes."

The court found that the predominance requirement of rule 23(b)(3) was satisfied for the core liability issues. Without any specific analysis regarding the multitude of issues that make up "core liability," the court found that under Jenkins v. Raymark Indus., 782 F.2d 468 (5th Cir. 1986), common issues predominate because resolution of core liability issues would significantly advance the individual cases. The court did not discuss why "core liability" issues would be a significant, rather than just common, part of each individual trial, nor why the individual issues in the remaining categories did not predominate over the common "core liability" issues.

The only specific analysis on predominance analysis was on the plaintiffs' fraud claim. The court determined that it would be premature to hold that individual reliance issues predominate over common issues. Relying on Eisen v. Carlisle & Jacquelin, 417 U.S. 156, 94 S.Ct. 2140, 40 L.Ed.2d 732 (1974), the court stated that it could not inquire into the merits of the plaintiffs' claim to determine whether reliance would be an issue in individual trials. Moreover, the court recognized the possibility that under state law, reliance can be inferred when a fraud claim is based on an omission. Accordingly, the court was convinced that it could certify the class and defer the consideration of how reliance would affect predominance.

The court also deferred substantial consideration of how variations in state law would affect predominance. Relying on two district court opinions, the court concluded that issues of fraud, breach of warranty, negligence, intentional tort, and strict liability do not vary so much from state to state as to cause individual issues to predominate. The court noted that any determination of how state law variations affect predominance was premature, as the court had yet to make a choice of law determination. As for the consumer protection claims, the court also deferred analysis of state law variations, because "there has been no showing that the consumer protection statutes differ so much as to make individual issues predominate."

The court also concluded that a class action is superior to other methods for adjudication of the core liability issues. Relying heavily on *Jenkins*, the court noted that having this common issue litigated in a class action was superior to repeated trials of the same evidence. Recognizing serious problems with manageability, it determined that such problems were outweighed by "the specter of thousands, if not millions, of similar trials of liability proceeding in thousands of courtrooms around the nation."

2. *Injury-in-fact, Proximate Cause, Reliance, Affirmative Defenses, and Compensatory Damages*

Using the same methodology as it did for the core liability issues, the district court refused to certify the issues of injury-in-fact, proximate cause, reliance, affirmative defenses, and compensatory damages, concluding that the "issues are so overwhelmingly replete with individual circumstances that they quickly outweigh predominance and superiority." Specifically, the court found that whether a person suffered emotional injury from addiction, whether his addiction was caused by the defendants' actions, whether he relied on the defendants' misrepresentations, and whether affirmative defenses unique to each class member precluded recovery were all individual issues. As to compensatory damages and the claim for medical monitoring, the court concluded that such claims were so intertwined with proximate cause and affirmative defenses that class certification would not materially advance the individual cases.

3. Punitive Damages

In certifying punitive damages for class treatment, the court adopted the plaintiffs' trial plan for punitive damages: The class jury would develop a ratio of punitive damages to actual damages, and the court would apply that ratio in individual cases. As it did with the core liability issues, the court determined that variations in state law, including differing burdens of proof, did not preclude certification. Rather than conduct an independent review of predominance or superiority, the court relied on *Jenkins* * * * for support of its certification order.

II.

A district court must conduct a rigorous analysis of the rule 23 prerequisites before certifying a class. General Tel. Co. v. Falcon, 457 U.S. 147, 161, 102 S.Ct. 2364, 2372, 72 L.Ed.2d 740 (1982). The decision to certify is within the broad discretion of the court, but that discretion must be exercised within the framework of rule 23. The party seeking certification bears the burden of proof.

The district court erred in its analysis in two distinct ways. First, it failed to consider how variations in state law affect predominance and superiority. Second, its predominance inquiry did not include consideration of how a trial on the merits would be conducted.

Each of these defects mandates reversal. Moreover, at this time, while the tort is immature, the class complaint must be dismissed, as class certification cannot be found to be a superior method of adjudication.[13]

A. Variations in State Law

Although rule 23(c)(1) requires that a class should be certified "as soon as practicable" and allows a court to certify a conditional class, it does not follow that the rule's requirements are lessened when the class is conditional. * * *

In a multi-state class action, variations in state law may swamp any common issues and defeat predominance. Accordingly, a district court must consider how variations in state law affect predominance and superiority. * * * A district court's duty to determine whether the

13. The defendants raise a number of additional challenges to the district court's order, including claims that individual issues predominate, that the use of a punitive damage ratio violates due process, that a multi-state class action inevitably will violate Erie R.R. v. Tompkins, 304 U.S. 64, 58 S.Ct. 817, 82 L.Ed. 1188 (1938), and that bifurcation of core liability issues in a class action violates article III of the Constitution. Given our conclusion that this matter cannot proceed as a class action in any event, we find it unnecessary to address those issues.

plaintiff has borne its burden on class certification requires that a court consider variations in state law when a class action involves multiple jurisdictions. "In order to make the findings required to certify a class action under Rule 23(b)(3) . . . one must initially identify the substantive law issues which will control the outcome of the litigation." Alabama v. Blue Bird Body Co., 573 F.2d 309, 316 (5th Cir.1978).

A requirement that a court know which law will apply before making a predominance determination is especially important when there may be differences in state law. Given the plaintiffs' burden, a court cannot rely on assurances of counsel that any problems with predominance or superiority can be overcome.

The able opinion in [In re] *School Asbestos* [Litigation, 789 F.2d 996 (3d Cir. 1986),] demonstrates what is required from a district court when variations in state law exist. There, the court affirmed class certification, despite variations in state law, because:

> To meet the problem of diversity in applicable state law, class plaintiffs have undertaken an extensive analysis of the variances in products liability among the jurisdictions. That review separates the law into four categories. Even assuming additional permutations and combinations, plaintiffs have made a creditable showing, which apparently satisfied the district court, that class certification does not present insuperable obstacles. Although we have some doubt on this score, the effort may nonetheless prove successful.

789 F.2d at 1010.

A thorough review of the record demonstrates that, in this case, the district court did not properly consider how variations in state law affect predominance. The court acknowledged as much in its order granting class certification, for, in declining to make a choice of law determination, it noted that "[t]he parties have only briefly addressed the conflict of laws issue in this matter." Similarly, the court stated that "there has been no showing that the consumer protection statutes differ so much as to make individual issues predominate."

The district court's review of state law variances can hardly be considered extensive; it conducted a cursory review of state law variations and gave short shrift to the defendants' arguments concerning variations. In response to the defendants' extensive analysis of how state law varied on fraud, products liability, affirmative defenses, negligent infliction of emotional distress, consumer protection statutes, and punitive damages,[15] the court examined a sample phase 1 jury interrogatory

---

15. We find it difficult to fathom how common issues could predominate in this case when variations in state law are thoroughly considered. * * *

The *Castano* class suffers from many of the difficulties that the *Georgine* court [Georgine v. Amchem Prods., 83 F.3d at 626 (3d Cir.1996)] found dispositive. The

class members were exposed to nicotine through different products, for different amounts of time, and over different time periods. Each class member's knowledge about the effects of smoking differs, and each plaintiff began smoking for different reasons. Each of these factual differences impacts the application of legal rules such

and verdict form, a survey of medical monitoring decisions, a survey of consumer fraud class actions, and a survey of punitive damages law in the defendants' home states. The court also relied on two district court opinions granting certification in multi-state class actions.

The district court's consideration of state law variations was inadequate. The surveys provided by the plaintiffs failed to discuss, in any meaningful way, how the court could deal with variations in state law. The consumer fraud survey simply quoted a few state courts that had certified state class actions. The survey of punitive damages was limited to the defendants' home states. Moreover, the two district court opinions on which the court relied did not support the proposition that variations in state law could be ignored. Nothing in the record demonstrates that the court critically analyzed how variations in state law would affect predominance.

The court also failed to perform its duty to determine whether the class action would be manageable in light of state law variations. The court's only discussion of manageability is a citation to *Jenkins* and the claim that "[w]hile manageability of the liability issues in this case may well prove to be difficult, the Court finds that any such difficulties pale in comparison to the specter of thousands, if not millions, of similar trials of liability proceeding in thousands of courtrooms around the nation."

The problem with this approach is that it substitutes case-specific analysis with a generalized reference to *Jenkins*. The *Jenkins* court, however, was not faced with managing a novel claim involving eight causes of action, multiple jurisdictions, millions of plaintiffs, eight defendants, and over fifty years of alleged wrongful conduct. Instead, *Jenkins* involved only 893 personal injury asbestos cases, the law of only one state, and the prospect of trial occurring in only one district. Accordingly, for purposes of the instant case, *Jenkins* is largely inapposite.

In summary, whether the specter of millions of cases outweighs any manageability problems in this class is uncertain when the scope of any manageability problems is unknown. Absent considered judgment on the

as causation, reliance, comparative fault, and other affirmative defenses.

Variations in state law magnify the differences. In a fraud claim, some states require justifiable reliance on a misrepresentation, while others require reasonable reliance. States impose varying standards to determine when there is a duty to disclose facts.

Products liability law also differs among states. Some states do not recognize strict liability. Some have adopted Restatement (Second) of Torts § 402A. Among the states that have adopted the Restatement, there are variations.

Differences in affirmative defenses also exist. Assumption of risk is a complete de-

fense to a products claim in some states. In others, it is a part of comparative fault analysis. Some states utilize "pure" comparative fault, others follow a "greater fault bar," and still others use an "equal fault bar."

Negligent infliction of emotional distress also involves wide variations. Some states do not recognize the cause of action at all. Some require a physical impact.

Despite these overwhelming individual issues, common issues might predominate. We are, however, left to speculate. The point of detailing the alleged differences is to demonstrate the inquiry the district court failed to make.

manageability of the class, a comparison to millions of individual trials is meaningless.

B. Predominance

The district court's second error was that it failed to consider how the plaintiffs' addiction claims would be tried, individually or on a class basis. The district court, based on Eisen v. Carlisle & Jacquelin, 417 U.S. 156, 177–78, 94 S.Ct. 2140, 2152–53, 40 L.Ed.2d 732 (1974), and Miller v. Mackey Int'l, 452 F.2d 424 (5th Cir.1971), believed that it could not go past the pleadings for the certification decision. The result was an incomplete and inadequate predominance inquiry.

The crux of the court's error was that it misinterpreted *Eisen* and *Miller*. Neither case suggests that a court is limited to the pleadings when deciding on certification. Both, instead, stand for the unremarkable proposition that the strength of a plaintiff's claim should not affect the certification decision. In *Eisen*, the Court held that it was improper to make a preliminary inquiry into the merits of a case, determine that the plaintiff was likely to succeed, and consequently shift the cost of providing notice to the defendant. In *Miller*, this court held that a district court could not deny certification based on its belief that the plaintiff could not prevail on the merits.

A district court certainly may look past the pleadings to determine whether the requirements of rule 23 have been met. Going beyond the pleadings is necessary, as a court must understand the claims, defenses, relevant facts, and applicable substantive law in order to make a meaningful determination of the certification issues.

* * * Absent knowledge of how addiction-as-injury cases would actually be tried, however, it was impossible for the court to know whether the common issues would be a "significant" portion of the individual trials. The court just assumed that because the common issues would play a part in every trial, they must be significant.[18] The court's synthesis of *Jenkins* and *Eisen* would write the predominance requirement out of the rule, and any common issue would predominate if it were common to all the individual trials.[19]

---

18. The district court's approach to predominance stands in stark contrast to the methodology the district court used in *Jenkins*. There, the district judge had a vast amount of experience with asbestos cases. He certified the state of the art defense because it was the most significant contested issue in each case. To the contrary, however, the district court in the instant case did not, and could not, have determined that the common issues would be a significant part of each case. Unlike the judge in *Jenkins*, the district judge [in this case] had no experience with this type of case and did not even inquire into how a case would be tried to determine whether the defendants'

conduct would be a significant portion of each case.

19. An incorrect predominance finding also implicates the court's superiority analysis: The greater the number of individual issues, the less likely superiority can be established. [The court quoted the Advisory Committee Note from 1966 disapproving use of class actions in mass accidents, quoted *supra* p. 331.]

The plaintiffs assert that Professor Charles Alan Wright, a member of the Advisory Committee has now repudiated this passage in the notes. See H. Newberg, 3 Newberg on Class Actions § 17.06 (3d ed. 1992) [quoted *supra* p. 321 n. 1]. Professor

The court's treatment of the fraud claim also demonstrates the error inherent in its approach.[20] According to both the advisory committee's notes to Rule 23(b)(3) and this court's decision in Simon v. Merrill Lynch, Pierce, Fenner & Smith, Inc., 482 F.2d 880 (5th Cir.1973), a fraud class action cannot be certified when individual reliance will be an issue. The district court avoided the reach of this court's decision in *Simon* by an erroneous reading of *Eisen*; the court refused to consider whether reliance would be an issue in individual trials.

The problem with the district court's approach is that after the class trial, it might have decided that reliance must be proven in individual trials. The court then would have been faced with the difficult choice of decertifying the class after phase 1 and wasting judicial resources, or continuing with a class action that would have failed the predominance requirement of rule 23(b)(3).[21]

III.

In addition to the reasons given above, regarding the district court's procedural errors, this class must be decertified because it independently fails the superiority requirement of rule 23(b)(3). In the context of mass tort class actions, certification dramatically affects the stakes for defendants. Class certification magnifies and strengthens the number of unmeritorious claims. Aggregation of claims also makes it more likely that a defendant will be found liable and results in significantly higher damage awards.

In addition to skewing trial outcomes, class certification creates insurmountable pressure on defendants to settle, whereas individual trials would not. The risk of facing an all-or-nothing verdict presents too high a risk, even when the probability of an adverse judgment is low. [In re] Rhone–Poulenc [Rorer, Inc.], 51 F.3d [1293,] 1298 [(7th Cir.1995)]. These settlements have been referred to as judicial blackmail.

Wright's recent statements, made as an advocate in *School Asbestos*, must be viewed with some caution. As Professor Wright has stated:

I certainly did not intend by that statement to say that a class should be certified in all mass tort cases. I merely wanted to take the sting out of the statement in the Advisory Committee Note, and even that said only that a class action is "ordinarily not appropriate" in mass-tort cases. The class action is a complex device that must be used with discernment. I think for example that Judge Jones in Louisiana would be creating a Frankenstein's monster if he should allow certification of what purports to be a class action on behalf of everyone who has ever been addicted to nicotine.

Letter of Dec. 22, 1994, to N. Reid Neureiter, Williams & Connolly, Washington, D.C.

20. The court specifically discussed reliance in the context of a fraud claim. Reliance is also an element of breach of warranty claims in some states, and an element of consumer protection statutes in others.

21. Severing the defendants' conduct from reliance under rule 23(c)(4) does not save the class action. A district court cannot manufacture predominance through the nimble use of subdivision (c)(4). The proper interpretation of the interaction between subdivisions (b)(3) and (c)(4) is that a cause of action, as a whole, must satisfy the predominance requirement of (b)(3) and that (c)(4) is a housekeeping rule that allows courts to sever the common issues for a class trial.

It is no surprise then, that historically, certification of mass tort litigation classes has been disfavored.[23] The traditional concern over the rights of defendants in mass tort class actions is magnified in the instant case. Our specific concern is that a mass tort cannot be properly certified without a prior track record of trials from which the district court can draw the information necessary to make the predominance and superiority analysis required by rule 23. This is because certification of an immature tort results in a higher than normal risk that the class action may not be superior to individual adjudication.

We first address the district court's superiority analysis. The court acknowledged the extensive manageability problems with this class. Such problems include difficult choice of law determinations, subclassing of eight claims with variations in state law, *Erie* guesses, notice to millions of class members, further subclassing to take account of transient plaintiffs, and the difficult procedure for determining who is nicotine-dependent. Cases with far fewer manageability problems have given courts pause.

The district court's rationale for certification in spite of such problems—i.e., that a class trial would preserve judicial resources in the millions of inevitable individual trials—is based on pure speculation. Not every mass tort is asbestos, and not every mass tort will result in the same judicial crises.[24] The judicial crisis to which the district court referred is only theoretical.

What the district court failed to consider, and what no court can determine at this time, is the very real possibility that the judicial crisis may fail to materialize.[25] The plaintiffs' claims are based on a new theory

---

23. At the time rule 23 was drafted, mass tort litigation as we now know it did not exist. The term had been applied to single-event accidents. Even in those cases, the advisory committee cautioned against certification. See *supra* note 19. As modern mass tort litigation has evolved, courts have been willing to certify simple single disaster mass torts, see Sterling v. Velsicol Chem. Corp., 855 F.2d 1188, 1197 (6th Cir.1988), but have been hesitant to certify more complex mass torts.

24. There is reason to believe that even a mass tort like asbestos could be managed, without class certification, in a way that avoids judicial meltdown. In a case such as this one, where causation is a key element, disaggregation of claims allows courts to dismiss weak and frivolous claims on summary judgment. Where novel theories of recovery are advanced (such as addiction as injury), courts can aggressively weed out untenable theories. Courts can use case management techniques to avoid discovery abuses. The parties can also turn to mediation and arbitration to settle individual or aggregated cases.

25. The plaintiffs, in seemingly inconsistent positions, argue that the lack of a judicial crisis justifies certification; they assert that the reason why individual plaintiffs have not filed claims is that the tobacco industry makes individual trials far too expensive and plaintiffs are rarely successful. The fact that a party continuously loses at trial does not justify class certification, however. The plaintiffs' argument, if accepted, would justify class treatment whenever a defendant has better attorneys and resources at its disposal.

The plaintiffs' claim also overstates the defendants' ability to outspend plaintiffs. Assuming arguendo that the defendants pool resources and outspend plaintiffs in individual trials, there is no reason why plaintiffs still cannot prevail. The class is represented by a consortium of well-financed plaintiffs' lawyers who, over time, can develop the expertise and specialized knowledge sufficient to beat the tobacco companies at their own game. Courts can also overcome the defendant's alleged advantages through coordination or consolidation of cases for discovery and other pretrial matters.

of liability and the existence of new evidence. Until plaintiffs decide to file individual claims, a court cannot, from the existence of injury, presume that all or even any plaintiffs will pursue legal remedies. Nor can a court make a superiority determination based on such speculation.

Severe manageability problems and the lack of a judicial crisis are not the only reasons why superiority is lacking. The most compelling rationale for finding superiority in a class action—the existence of a negative value suit—is missing in this case.

As he stated in the record, plaintiffs' counsel in this case has promised to inundate the courts with individual claims if class certification is denied. Independently of the reliability of this self-serving promise, there is reason to believe that individual suits are feasible. First, individual damage claims are high, and punitive damages are available in most states. The expense of litigation does not necessarily turn this case into a negative value suit, in part because the prevailing party may recover attorneys' fees under many consumer protection statutes.

In a case such as this one, where each plaintiff may receive a large award, and fee shifting often is available, we find Chief Judge Posner's analysis of superiority to be persuasive:

> For this consensus or maturing of judgment the district judge proposes to substitute a single trial before a single jury.... One jury ... will hold the fate of an industry in the palm of its hand.... That kind of thing can happen in our system of civil justice.... But it need not be tolerated when the alternative exists of submitting an issue to multiple juries constituting in the aggregate a much larger and more diverse sample of decision-makers. That would not be a feasible option if the stakes to each class member were too slight to repay the cost of suit.... But this is not the case.... Each plaintiff if successful is apt to receive a judgment in the millions. With the aggregate stakes in the tens or hundreds of millions of dollars, or even in the billions, it is not a waste of judicial resources to conduct more than one trial, before more than six jurors, to determine whether a major segment of the international pharmaceutical industry is to follow the asbestos manufacturers into Chapter 11.

Rhone–Poulenc, 51 F.3d at 1300. So too here, we cannot say that it would be a waste to allow individual trials to proceed, before a district court engages in the complicated predominance and superiority analysis necessary to certify a class. * * *

The remaining rationale for superiority—judicial efficiency—is also lacking. In the context of an immature tort, any savings in judicial resources is speculative, and any imagined savings would be overwhelmed by the procedural problems that certification of a sui generis cause of action brings with it.

Even assuming arguendo that the tort system will see many more addiction-as-injury claims, a conclusion that certification will save judicial resources is premature at this stage of the litigation. Take for example the district court's plan to divide core liability from other issues such as comparative negligence and reliance. The assumption is that after a class verdict, the common issues will not be a part of follow-up trials. The court has no basis for that assumption.

It may be that comparative negligence will be raised in the individual trials, and the evidence presented at the class trial will have to be repeated. The same may be true for reliance. The net result may be a waste, not a savings, in judicial resources. Only after the courts have more experience with this type of case can a court certify issues in a way that preserves judicial resources.

Even assuming that certification at this time would result in judicial efficiencies in individual trials, certification of an immature tort brings with it unique problems that may consume more judicial resources than certification will save. These problems are not speculative; the district court faced, and ignored, many of the problems that immature torts can cause.

* * *

The district court's predominance inquiry, or lack of it, squarely presents the problems associated with certification of immature torts. Determining whether the common issues are a "significant" part of each individual case has an abstract quality to it when no court in this country has ever tried an injury-as-addiction claim. As the plaintiffs admitted to the district court, "we don't have the learning [curve] that is necessary to say to Your Honor 'this is precisely how this case can be tried and that will not run afoul of the teachings of the 5th Circuit.' "

Yet, an accurate finding on predominance is necessary before the court can certify a class. It may turn out that the defendant's conduct, while common, is a minor part of each trial. Premature certification deprives the defendant of the opportunity to present that argument to any court and risks decertification after considerable resources have been expended.

The court's analysis of reliance also demonstrates the potential judicial inefficiencies in immature tort class actions. Individual trials will determine whether individual reliance will be an issue. Rather than guess that reliance may be inferred, a district court should base its determination that individual reliance does not predominate on the wisdom of such individual trials. The risk that a district court will make the wrong guess, that the parties will engage in years of litigation, and that the class ultimately will be decertified (because reliance predominates over common issues) prevents this class action from being a superior method of adjudication.

* * *

Another factor weighing heavily in favor of individual trials is the risk that in order to make this class action manageable, the court will be forced to bifurcate issues in violation of the Seventh Amendment. This class action is permeated with individual issues, such as proximate causation, comparative negligence, reliance, and compensatory damages. In order to manage so many individual issues, the district court proposed to empanel a class jury to adjudicate common issues. A second jury, or a number of "second" juries, will pass on the individual issues, either on a case-by-case basis or through group trials of individual plaintiffs.

The Seventh Amendment entitles parties to have fact issues decided by one jury, and prohibits a second jury from reexamining those facts and issues. Thus, Constitution allows bifurcation of issues that are so separable that the second jury will not be called upon to reconsider findings of fact by the first:

> [T]his Court has cautioned that separation of issues is not the usual course that should be followed, and that the issue to be tried must be so distinct and separable from the others that a trial of it alone may be had without injustice. This limitation on the use of bifurcation is a recognition of the fact that inherent in the Seventh Amendment guarantee of a trial by jury is the general right of a litigant to have only one jury pass on a common issue of fact. The Supreme Court recognized this principle in Gasoline Products [Co., Inc. v. Champlin Refining Co., 283 U.S. 494, 51 S.Ct. 513, 75 L.Ed. 1188 (1931)].... The Court explained ... that a partial new trial may not be "properly resorted to unless it clearly appears that the issue to be retried is so distinct and separable from the others that a trial of it alone may be had without injustice." Such a rule is dictated for the very practical reason that if separate juries are allowed to pass on issues involving overlapping legal and factual questions the verdicts rendered by each jury could be inconsistent.

Alabama v. Blue Bird Body Co., 573 F.2d 309, 318 (5th Cir.1978).

* * *

Severing a defendant's conduct from comparative negligence results in the type of risk that our court forbade in *Blue Bird*. Comparative negligence, by definition, requires a comparison between the defendant's and the plaintiff's conduct. At a bare minimum, a second jury will rehear evidence of the defendant's conduct. There is a risk that in apportioning fault, the second jury could reevaluate the defendant's fault, determine that the defendant was not at fault, and apportion 100% of the fault to the plaintiff. In such a situation, the second jury would be impermissibly reconsidering the findings of a first jury. The risk of such reevaluation is so great that class treatment can hardly be said to be superior to individual adjudication.

The plaintiffs' final retort is that individual trials are inadequate because time is running out for many of the plaintiffs. They point out that prior litigation against the tobacco companies has taken up to ten years to wind through the legal system. While a compelling rhetorical argument, it is ultimately inconsistent with the plaintiffs' own arguments and ignores the realities of the legal system. First, the plaintiffs' reliance on prior personal injury cases is unpersuasive, as they admit that they have new evidence and are pursuing a claim entirely different from that of past plaintiffs.

Second, the plaintiffs' claim that time is running out ignores the reality of the class action device. In a complicated case involving multiple jurisdictions, the conflict of law question itself could take decades to work its way through the courts. Once that issue has been resolved, discovery, subclassing, and ultimately the class trial would take place. Next would come the appellate process. After the class trial, the individual trials and appeals on comparative negligence and damages would have to take place. The net result could be that the class action device would lengthen, not shorten, the time it takes for the plaintiffs to reach final judgment.

IV.

The district court abused its discretion by ignoring variations in state law and how a trial on the alleged causes of action would be tried. Those errors cannot be corrected on remand because of the novelty of the plaintiffs' claims. Accordingly, class treatment is not superior to individual adjudication.

We have once before stated that "traditional ways of proceeding reflect far more than habit. They reflect the very culture of the jury trial...." In re Fibreboard Corp., 893 F.2d 706, 711 (5th Cir.1990). The collective wisdom of individual juries is necessary before this court commits the fate of an entire industry or, indeed, the fate of a class of millions, to a single jury. For the forgoing reasons, we REVERSE and REMAND with instructions that the district court dismiss the class complaint.

Notes and Questions

1. *Castano* can be viewed as part of a movement in reaction against what some considered excessive use of class actions for mass torts. Shortly before the Fifth Circuit's *Castano* decision, cases in the Sixth and Seventh Circuits also imposed stricter standards on mass tort class actions.

In In re American Medical Systems, Inc., 75 F.3d 1069 (6th Cir.1996), the court issued a writ of mandamus overturning certification of a nationwide class of recipients of defendant's allegedly defective penile implants. It found that individualized issues would predominate since class members had used at least ten different models of the prosthesis and their legal claims would "differ depending upon the model and the year it was issued." The court justified mandamus on the ground that "extraordinary facts" had been presented and because, despite a trend against certifying classes in drug or medical product cases, this judge had done so repeatedly. It emphasized the Supreme Court's admonition in General Telephone v. Falcon (*supra* p. 267) that "it may be necessary for the court to probe behind the pleadings before coming to rest on the certification question." In the face of that admonition, the record before the Sixth Circuit showed "not even the hint of any serious consideration by the judge of commonality" and "no serious consideration" to the typicality requirement in circumstances where "it should have been obvious to the district judge that it needed to 'probe behind the pleadings' " on this subject. The judge also failed even to consider how variations in the law of different jurisdictions would affect handling the claims in one class action.

Mass tort class actions were dealt another blow in In re Rhone–Poulenc Rorer Inc., 51 F.3d 1293 (7th Cir.), cert. denied, 516 U.S. 867, 116 S.Ct. 184, 133 L.Ed.2d 122 (1995), in which the court of appeals granted a writ of mandate overturning Judge Grady's plan for a class action trial of a suit against manufacturers of blood solids. Plaintiffs were hemophiliacs who had become infected with HIV due to tainted blood solids. (Another aspect of this litigation appears as In re Factor VIII or IX Concentrate Blood Products Litig., *supra* p. 156.) Seeking to represent a nationwide class, plaintiffs argued that, even though the risks of AIDS were not known at the time of their exposure, defendants should have used precautions to guard against other infections that would coincidentally have protected them against AIDS. Judge Grady certified an issues-only class limited to negligence under (c)(4) and leading to a special verdict, after which it appeared that further proceedings might be in the home jurisdiction of class members.

Characterizing the case as "truly extraordinary," a majority of a panel of the Seventh Circuit granted a writ of mandate. Judge Posner, writing for the court, saw the class certification as creating irresistible settlement pressure because it would magnify exposure from some $125 million to $25 billion. Moreover, Judge Grady proposed to meld the law of 50 jurisdictions into an "Esperanto instruction" that would not necessarily be the law of any state. Perhaps most significantly, defendants had already gone to trial 14 times on plaintiff's theory in individual cases, and had won 13 of those cases. Based on this statistic, Judge Posner found a "demonstrated great likelihood" that plaintiffs would lose at trial, coupled with an irresistible urge due to class certification for defendants to settle. This, he concluded, "far exceeds the permissible bounds of discretion in the management of federal litigation." Indeed, given the attempt to fashion a combined common law of the states, Judge Posner found that the plan verged on violating *Erie*. One judge dissented.

No absolute bar to mass tort class actions has surfaced, however. In Valentino v. Carter–Wallace, Inc., 97 F.3d 1227 (9th Cir.1996), the court rejected the argument that its earlier decision in In re Northern District of California Dalkon Shield IUD Products Liability Litig. 693 F.2d 847 (9th Cir.1982), supported a rule that certification is never appropriate for a multi-state personal injury class action. The district court had conditionally certified a nationwide product liability class action on behalf of users of an epilepsy drug, claiming the manufacturer had not warned of serious side effects. Because the case involved only one manufacturer, only one product, and a single marketing program over a relatively short period of time, the case was likely to be more manageable than other product liability class actions. Accordingly, certification might become appropriate after further proceedings in the district court, but the court did vacate the brief certification order entered by the district judge.

State-court decisions are sometimes receptive to mass tort class actions, particularly under distinctive laws of the state. For example, in In re West Virginia Rezulin Litigation, 214 W.Va. 52, 585 S.E.2d 52 (2003), the court reversed the trial court's refusal to certify a class in pharmaceutical product litigation. Plaintiffs sought to represent a class of approximately 5,000 West Virginians who took the anti-diabetes drug Rezulin in a suit alleging that it caused liver damage in some users and that defendant manufacturer had concealed this risk. Eschewing absolute reliance on federal class-action cases, which it characterized as a "Pavlovian response to federal decisional law," id. at 61, the state court held that plaintiffs were entitled to class certification under W.Va.R.Civ.P. 23 on a claim for a medical monitoring fund under state consumer protection law. Common issues existed regarding the dangers posed by Rezulin, and proof of a specific loss was not required to support a claim under state consumer law. All that had to be shown was that class members had "a significantly increased risk of contracting a particular disease relative to what would be the case in the absence of exposure." Id. at 73. Moreover, the court found that plaintiffs sought relief that would justify certification under Rule 23(b)(2) as well as Rule 23(b)(3).

2. The *Castano* opinion noted that "in a multi-state class action, variations in state law may swamp any common issues and defeat predominance" and found that the lower court's consideration of state law variations was inadequate. This has been read as "imposing stringent tests on potential class plaintiffs that district courts must apply: The plaintiff has the burden of satisfying the court that class treatment is appropriate, the trial court must conduct a rigorous de novo review of state law, and conditional certification cannot justify a court's overlooking problems with predominance or superiority. *Castano* reflects a new scrutiny that is apprehensive of claims about the social utility of class actions in the mass tort setting." In re: Masonite Corp. Hardboard Siding Products Liability Lit., 170 F.R.D. 417, 423 (E.D.La.1997). In that case, the judge refused to certify a nationwide class of persons and entities whose buildings had Masonite siding, finding the state laws as to such issues as negligence, comparative fault, strict liability, and state of the art defense varied substantially: "this court cannot imagine managing a trial under the law of the jurisdictions on the defectiveness of Masonite siding." Id. at 425.

Since *Castano*, motions to certify nationwide class actions have often been accompanied by a much more careful analysis of state laws. Typically plaintiffs argue either that under choice of law doctrines, the law of one state will apply or that the laws of all the states fall into a small number of categories, allowing a jury to apply the different standards by answering different interrogatories. This harks back to In re School Asbestos Lit., 789 F.2d 996, 1010 (3d Cir.), cert. denied, 479 U.S. 852, 107 S.Ct. 182, 93 L.Ed.2d 117 (1986), which approved a multistate class action for economic harms to property where the state laws would fit into four basic categories. In re Prudential Ins. Co. of America Sales Practices, 962 F.Supp. 450 (D.N.J.1997), approved a settlement class action on behalf of a nationwide class of purchasers of insurance policies based on alleged misrepresentations relating to premiums (the "vanishing premium") and improper inducement to replace policies. The court cited "a series of charts setting forth comprehensive analyses of the various states' laws potentially applicable to their common law claims for fraud, breach of contract, implied obligations of good faith and fair dealing, negligence, and negligent misrepresentation." Id. at 525. It found that the laws fell into "a limited number of predictable patterns" and "a manageable number of jury instructions could be fashioned to comport with the elements of the common law claims in the many jurisdictions." Id. For further discussion, see In re Bridgestone/Firestone, Inc., *infra* p. 429.

3. The *Castano* opinion criticizes the lower court for believing that "it could not go past the pleadings for the certification decision." It says "a court must understand the claims, defenses, relevant facts, and applicable substantive law in order to make a meaningful determination of the certification issues." Does this mean the lower court should have asked how the plaintiffs planned to prove their addiction-as-injury claims and, if persuaded that this would be done with individualized, as opposed to classwide, evidence, should not have certified the class? That courts should not consider the merits on class certification has always been a tenet of faith in class-action procedure, Eisen v. Carlisle & Jacquelin, 417 U.S. 156, 177–78, 94 S.Ct. 2140, 40 L.Ed.2d 732 (1974), but are we moving towards greater scrutiny of the merits? See Bone & Evans, Class Certification and the Substantive Merits, 51 Duke L.J. 1251 (2002) (arguing the *Eisen* rule should be abandoned). If the defendants have a strong defense, or plaintiffs have a weak element in their cause of action, could a court determine that class treatment is not "superior" because of the likelihood that after invoking the expensive and cumbersome class action procedure, the case would still be lost? For further discussion of these issues, see Timing of Class Certification Decisions, *infra* p. 368.

4. The lower court recognized that the issue of reliance might have to be determined later in individual trials. The appellate opinion says that "severing the defendants' conduct from reliance under rule 23(c)(4) does not save the class action." See n. 21. Why not? Isn't that what *Jenkins* approved—that certain common issues would be tried in a class trial while other individualized issues might have to be tried later individually or in mini-trials? *Castano* says "a cause of action, as a whole, must satisfy the predominance requirement." Is that contrary to the notion of "phased trials" approved in *Jenkins, supra* p. 331? Why shouldn't a judge be able to conclude that a class trial of certain common issues will materially advance the termination of the litigation even though some individualized issues of importance are relegated to later phases, possibly requiring individual trials? Is the real problem in *Castano* that there were so many individualized issues that were of such import, and that were so intertwined with the common issues, that little would be gained by trying common issues in a class trial?

In Smith v. Texaco, Inc., 263 F.3d 394 (5th Cir.2001), the Fifth Circuit reiterated its view that "the cause of action, as a whole, must satisfy rule 23(b)(3)'s predominance requirement. Once that requirement is met, rule 23(c)(4) is available to sever the common issues for a class trial. To read the rule not as a housekeeping rule, but instead as allowing the court to pare issues repeatedly until predomination is achieved, would obliterate rule 23(b)(3)'s predominance requirement, resulting in automatic certification in every case in which any common issue exists, a result the drafters of the rule could not have intended." Id. at 409. See Hines, Challenging the Issue Class Action End Run, 52 Emory L.J. 709 (2003) (arguing that Rule 23(c)(4) was not intended to weaken the requirement that predominance be established for the whole case).

5.   How important to the holding in *Castano* is the concern that "class certification creates insurmountable pressure on defendants to settle?" Judge Posner placed great weight on that point in *Rhone-Poulenc, supra* note 1. Class treatment certainly increases the stakes for defendants (Judge Posner's "bet the company" concern), but it has also been seen as an opportunity by defendants to resolve all claims at one time (defendants have particularly embraced settlement classes that allow them to resolve even "future" claims) and to reduce the transaction costs of multiple litigation. Would this superiority analysis prevent certification even if common issues predominated? If so, doesn't it simply conflict with the whole idea of class actions? One federal district judge took issue with the importance given this concern by Judge Posner's "economic theories and distrust of juries." In re Telectronics Pacing Systems, Inc., 172 F.R.D. 271 (S.D.Ohio 1997).

Other courts have been less receptive to the argument that class certification creates improper settlement pressure. As the Second Circuit put it in an antitrust case in which newspaper reports suggested that class-action damages might amount to $39 billion, "[t]he effect of certification on parties' leverage in settlement negotiations is a fact of life for class action litigants. While the sheer size of the class in this case may enhance this effect, this alone cannot defeat an otherwise proper certification." In re Visa Check/Mastermoney Antitrust Litigation, 280 F.3d 124 (2d Cir.2001).

6.   Does the charge of "judicial blackmail" referred to in *Castano* take on added weight because of the lack of prior litigation on the novel issue of liability for nicotine addiction? The opinion notes that with such "immature torts" there is no learning curve. This would increase the likelihood of error (which could be of monumental proportions given class treatment). Consistent with *Castano*'s demand for a "track record of trials from which [to] draw the information necessary to make the predominance and superiority requirements," one court ordered a limited number of individual trials "to familiarize itself and the parties with the contours of this litigation." In re Norplant Contraceptive Prods. Liability Lit., MDL No. 1039, Order of May 17, 1996 (E.D. Tex.).

In 1996, the Advisory Committee on the Civil Rules circulated a tentative draft of possible amendments to Rule 23(b)(3) that would have directed a court to make findings including attention to the "maturity of any related litigation." See Proposed Amendments to the Federal Rules, 167 F.R.D. 523, 559 (1996). The draft Committee Note explained that the possible addition of a maturity factor "reflects the need to support class adjudication by experience gained in completed litigation of several individual claims. If the results of individual litigation begin to converge, class adjudication may seem appropriate. Class adjudication may be inappropriate, however, if individual litigation continues to yield inconsistent results, or if individual litigation demonstrates that knowledge has not yet advanced far enough to support confident decision on a class basis." Id. at 562–63. Should this maturity consideration matter in a securities fraud class action? Eventually, amendments to add a "maturity" factor were shelved.

7. The appellate court in *Castano* faults the lower court for failing to consider "the very real possibility that the judicial crisis may fail to materialize." Must there be a flood of individual case filings before class treatment is justified? That is what happened in asbestos litigation, but why shouldn't a class action be available to resolve a problem that has not yet generated individual cases? The opinion recognizes that "negative-value" cases (cases in which each class member's injury is of such a small dollar value as to make individual litigation economically unfeasible) may be accorded class treatment without a judicial crisis of case filings. Even then, should a court consider that the class members stand to benefit so little that the transaction costs of a class action are not justified? Does deterrence of a defendant's wrongful conduct that affects many people by only a small dollar amount justify all "negative-value" class actions? Is it justified in *Castano* where the class attorneys would likely have settled the class members' claims of nicotine addiction for a relatively small sum for each one (but given a class of perhaps 50 million smokers would have generated huge attorneys' fees for the class attorneys)?

8. In *Castano*, the court also objects that a bifurcated trial might create a risk of violating the Seventh Amendment's prohibition of reexamination of a prior jury verdict. This concern, which is not limited to class actions, is considered further in Chapter VII. See *infra* pp. 767-68.

9. If *Castano* is right, when would it be proper for a court to certify a class action involving a class drawn from more than one state asserting claims based on state law?

10. *Postscript on tobacco class actions*: Following the failure of the nationwide class in *Castano*, plaintiffs' attorneys began filing class actions state-by-state in state court. A statewide class was certified in Florida and a class trial held, but a jury verdict of $12.7 billion in compensatory and $145 billion in punitive damages on behalf of a class of 700,000 smokers was reversed on appeal, and the class was decertified as not having satisfied the class action requirements. Liggett Group, Inc. v. Engle, 853 So.2d 434 (Fla.Ct.App.2003). A statewide class was certified for medical monitoring in Louisiana and a class trial held which resulted in findings by the jury that required the tobacco companies to undertake smoking "cessation" programs. Scott v. American Tobacco Co., 725 So.2d 10 (La.App.1998). A class action was certified on behalf of people who purchased defendants' "light" cigarettes, and the Illinois Circuit Court found the implicit health representations embodied in the term to be a misrepresentation pursuant to a disinformation campaign and awarded $7.1 billion in actual and $3 billion in punitive damages. Miles v. Phillip Morris, Inc. (Cir.Ct., 3d Jud. Cir., Madison County, Ill., March 21, 2003). The Minnesota District Court, Hennepin County, denied class certification for a "light" cigarette suit against Phillip Morris. See Minnesota Court Denies Class Certification in Light Cigarette Suit Against Phillip Morris, 5 Class Action Litigation Report 39 (Jan. 23, 2004). The Ontario, Canada, Superior Court of Justice refused class certification for a suit on behalf of smokers against three tobacco companies, which would have been the largest suit in Canadian history. See Yahoo News, Feb. 11, 2004. For a more general review of the impact of tobacco litigation on procedure, see Marcus, Reassessing the Magnetic Pull of Mega-cases on Procedure, 51 De Paul L.Rev. 457 (2001).

5. DEFENDANT CLASS ACTIONS

Although they are not a different category under Rule 23, defendant class actions present issues somewhat different from plaintiff class actions, and we therefore address them in a different section. It bears noting at the outset that, compared to plaintiff class actions, defendant class actions are rare. For example, in a study of class actions in four judicial districts, the Federal Judicial Center found that there were 192 certified plaintiff class actions and one certified defendant class actions in that district. See Willging, Hooper & Niemic, An Empirical Analysis of Rule 23 to Address the Rulemaking Challenges, 71 N.Y.U.L. Rev. 74, 120 (1996).

THILLENS, INC. v. COMMUNITY CURRENCY EXCHANGE ASSOCIATION OF ILLINOIS

United States District Court, Northern District of Illinois, 1983.
97 F.R.D. 668.

WILLIAM T. HART, DISTRICT JUDGE.

Plaintiff Thillens, Inc. ("Thillens") filed this action in 1981 against the Community Currency Exchange Association of Illinois ("Association"), former and current members of the Association ("individual defendants") and the community currency exchanges owned by those members ("exchange defendants"). Also named are three former Illinois officials ("public defendants"). Thillens alleges that over the past twenty-three years the Association and the individual defendants conspired with the public defendants to restrain Thillens' trade as an ambulatory currency exchange, in violation of federal and state antitrust laws, 42 U.S.C. § 1983, and 18 U.S.C. § 1961 ("RICO"). Also included are various pendent claims. Thillens seeks compensatory and punitive damages, injunctive relief and attorneys' fees.

Thillens is an Illinois corporation, licensed as an "ambulatory currency exchange" providing "mobile check cashing services" within the greater Chicago metropolitan area. Thillens claims to be the only ambulatory currency exchange operating in the Chicago area and perhaps in all of Illinois. Thillens has never belonged to the Association. The Association is an Illinois not-for-profit corporation serving as the trade association for approximately 300 persons who own or control at least 500 "community currency exchanges" in Illinois. Most Chicago area community currency exchanges allegedly belong to the Association. All currency exchanges are required to be licensed by the Illinois Department of Financial Institutions ("DFI").

The gist of Thillens' complaint is that the alleged conspiracy caused the DFI since 1958 to (1) deny Thillens 400 license applications to operate ambulatory currency exchanges in the relevant markets; (2) deprive Thillens of fair hearings to protest the denial of the licenses sought by Thillens; and (3) promulgate unreasonable rules and regulations substantially to Thillens' detriment.

Several motions are before the Court. This Opinion and Order considers only Thillens' motion for certification of a defendant class. The proposed class includes 17 named individual defendants, approximately 350 unnamed individual past and current members of the Association and the more than 500 community currency exchanges owned by those members and represented by the Association. Neither the Association nor the public defendants is named as a class member. Thillens, however, nominates the Association as class representative.

Thillens argues that the class proposed is highly cohesive. In its view, the Association is the logical choice for class representative, precisely because it is the self-selected industry representative of the individual and exchange defendants. Thillens also claims that the Association is financially able to perform representational duties. Finally, Thillens notes that at least 95 individual defendants are represented by the law firm which represents the Association and 16 named defendants.

Thillens also supports its motion for certification of a defendant class by arguing that no unfairness would result: Supposedly each proposed defendant member paid dues to the Association during the relevant period. All of the defendants in the proposed class are alleged to have knowingly participated or acquiesced in the conspiracy and political bribery fund. In light of what Thillens characterizes as virtually identical behaviors, giving rise to identical defenses, Thillens claims that certification will result in substantial savings of judicial and personal resources, without significant sacrifice by class members.

The Association and various individual defendants oppose the motion for certification of a defendant class. They argue that defendant classes are uncommon, especially in antitrust actions. Their primary objection is that certification would be inconsistent with each defendant's due process rights. The defendants also claim that the Association would be an inadequate representative of the [class's] interests because it formerly pled guilty to mail fraud and acknowledged the existence of a political bribery fund, acts which Thillens seeks to prove in this action. According to the Association, it would be collaterally estopped from denying those acts, to the detriment of the class members.

For the reasons stated below, Thillens' motion for certification of a defendant class is granted. The class is certified under Fed.R.Civ.P. 23(b)(3). Each member of the class must be notified personally of its status as a class member consistent with the requirements of Fed. R.Civ.P. 23(c)(2). In the event that liability is determined in Thillens' favor, each member of the class who has not opted out may attempt to prove its nonparticipation in any conspiracy or nonperformance of any unlawful act. Furthermore, each member of the class may be represented by the counsel of its choice.

A. A DEFENDANT CLASS MAY BE CERTIFIED IF DUE PROCESS IS SATISFIED

* * *

[T]he binding nature of the class action poses a dilemma. Fundamental fairness to absentee members must be balanced against judicial savings. Where representative adjudication occurs pursuant to a defendant class, due process concerns not inherent in plaintiff class actions arise. The crux of the distinction is: the unnamed plaintiff stands to gain while the unnamed defendant stands to lose.

It is the hallmark of our system of justice that personal rights cannot be compromised without due process. *See, e.g., International Shoe Co. v. Washington,* 326 U.S. 310, 66 S.Ct. 154, 90 L.Ed. 95 (1945) (foreign defendant must have certain minimum contacts with forum state); *Mullane v. Central Hanover Bank & Trust Co.,* 339 U.S. 306, 70 S.Ct. 652, 94 L.Ed. 865 (1950) (no binding adjudication without reasonable attempts to notify defendant). If, however, a binding judgment depended on the assertion of *in personam* jurisdiction over each member of a class, the action's economies would be dissipated. The Supreme Court has resolved the apparent tension by holding that due process is satisfied and absent members of a class are bound so long as the interests of the absentees are adequately represented. *Hansberry v. Lee,* 311 U.S. 32, 42, 61 S.Ct. 115, 118, 85 L.Ed. 22 (1940) (plaintiff class); *Sam Fox Publishing Co. v. United States,* 366 U.S. 683, 691, 81 S.Ct. 1309, 1313, 6 L.Ed.2d 604 (1961) (defendant class).

Arguably, therefore, a finding that a defendant class is adequately represented should resolve the due process dilemma which attaches to certification of a defendant class. Nonetheless the concern lingers. Defendant classes seldom are certified.

* * * Attempts to certify defendant classes in antitrust actions generally are unsuccessful. *See, e.g., Kline v. Coldwell, Banker & Co.,* 508 F.2d 226 (9th Cir.), *cert. denied,* 421 U.S. 963, 95 S.Ct. 1950, 44 L.Ed.2d 449 (1975) [*supra* p. 223].

The case of *In re Gap Stores Securities Litigation* [79 F.R.D. 283 (N.D.Cal.1978)] illustrates a court's efforts to satisfy the due process interests of a defendant class. *In re Gap* involved 13 cases consolidated in a multidistrict securities litigation arising from alleged misrepresentations in the first public offering of common stock of the Gap Stores, Inc. Plaintiffs, a previously certified class of owners of common stock in Gap Stores, sought to certify a class of 91 defendant underwriters.

The court concluded that "[a]lthough defendant class actions seem to demand greater attention to the due process rights of absent class members, they are not otherwise greatly dissimilar from plaintiff class actions." Building on due process protections for defendants in individual actions, the court held that due process for a defendant class first requires notice to each class member. "[N]otice to the representative cannot be deemed the functional equivalent of notice to the class because the defendant class representative's interests are not necessarily coextensive with the class." Second, the *In re Gap* court held that it would certify a class of defendants only in circumstances fundamentally fair to absentee members, *i.e.,* where subject matter jurisdiction and venue are proper and representation is adequate.

The *In re Gap* opinion also provides a thoughtful framework for understanding why certification of defendant classes often is denied. There is great judicial reluctance to certify a defendant class *when the action is brought by a plaintiff class.* The primary concern with bilateral actions, antitrust or other types, is a fear that each plaintiff member has not been injured by each defendant member. *See, e.g., Adashunas v. Negley,* 626 F.2d 600 (7th Cir.1980) (proposed plaintiff class of all learning disabled children in Indiana improperly identified or not receiving special instruction from proposed defendant class of superintendents and school board members of each Indiana public school failing to identify or educate plaintiff class members); *In re Hotel Telephone Charges,* 500 F.2d 86 (9th Cir.1974) (proposed plaintiff class of 40 million hotel guests alleging nationwide conspiracy among proposed defendant class of 47 hotel chains and 600 individual hotels to increase room rents through disguised telephone charges); *LaMar v. H & B Novelty & Loan Co.,* 489 F.2d 461 (9th Cir.1973) [*supra* p. 278](proposed plaintiff class of 33,000 customers of proposed defendant class of all licensed pawnbrokers in Oregon); *Kline v. Coldwell, Banker, supra,* (proposed plaintiff class of 400,000 plaintiffs who sold their realty to proposed defendant class of 2,000 real estate brokers in Los Angeles area).

Several rules, useful in unilateral as well as bilateral defendant class actions, emerge from *In re Gap* and similar cases: (1) A defendant class will not be certified unless each named plaintiff has a colorable claim against each defendant class member; (2) A defendant class will not be certified under Fed.R.Civ.P. 23(b)(3) without a clear showing that common questions do *in fact* predominate over individual issues; (3) The requirement that each named plaintiff must have a claim against each defendant may be waived where the defendant members are related by a conspiracy or "juridical link."

A "juridical link" is some legal relationship which relates all defendants in a way such that single resolution of the dispute is preferred to a multiplicity of similar actions. *See, e.g., LaMar v. H & B Novelty & Loan Co., supra,* at 470. Absent such juridical link, a defendant class fails the Article III test requiring a case or controversy to support the assertion of jurisdiction.

The *In re Gap* analysis, pertaining to the uncertifiability of bilateral class actions, and the three rules for certification of defendant class actions are significant here. Many of the cases cited by the Association to bolster its opposition to certification of a defendant class are *bilateral* class actions. In those cases, the putative defendant classes often were amorphous: each named plaintiff could not possibly have been harmed by each proposed defendant class member. In contrast, this action is not a bilateral class action. Rather, a single plaintiff, Thillens, alleges that it has been injured by each member of the proposed defendant class.

Instead of being an amorphous entity, the proposed defendant class of currency exchanges and their individual owners is highly cohesive and self-organized. It is juridically linked at least by allegations that each defendant class member voluntarily joined a conspiracy to harm Thillens. Additionally, this Court has subject matter jurisdiction over the claims made.

There are no theoretical roadblocks to certification of this defendant class antitrust action so long as due process safeguards are imposed. However, the proposed class still must be tested by the provisions of Fed.R.Civ.P. 23(a) and (b).

B.   THE DEFENDANT CLASS PROPOSED MEETS THE
        REQUIREMENTS OF FED.R.CIV.P. 23(a)

* * *

Commonality of Legal and Factual Questions

There are both legal and factual questions common to the proposed class of defendants. Fed.R.Civ.P. 23(a)(2). It is sufficient for class certification that the common question be either of fact *or* law. Not all factual or legal questions raised in the lawsuit need be common so long as a single issue is common to all class members. *See, e.g., Blackie v. Barrack,* 524 F.2d 891 (9th Cir.1975), *cert. denied,* 429 U.S. 816, 97 S.Ct. 57, 50 L.Ed.2d 75 (1976) [*supra* p. 246]. Nor should variance in members' positions to the common issue be dispositive of the decision to certify a class action.

Although this is a multi-claim action, Thillens' major claim alleges an antitrust conspiracy. The overriding common issue of law is to determine the existence of a conspiracy.

Thillens also raises as questions common to the antitrust claim (1) whether the Association and members of the defendant class established a secret fund in order to bribe public officials; (2) whether the Association and members conspired to restrain trade in the greater Chicago metropolitan area currency exchange market; (3) whether the Association and members monopolized the greater Chicago metropolitan area currency exchange market; (4) whether the Association and defendants conspired to fix prices in the currency exchange industry; and (5) whether the Association and defendants conspired to improperly divide the relevant geographic currency exchange market. Any one of these legal questions will satisfy the commonality requirement of Fed.R.Civ.P. 23(a)(2).

It is irrelevant for commonality purposes that some members will be able to avoid liability by later showing that they did not take part in any conspiracy proven. * * * [T]he members of the defendant class proposed by Thillens will be presumed to have joined the antitrust conspiracy if such conspiracy is proven. *See, e.g., Phelps Dodge Refining Corp. v. FTC,* 139 F.2d 393 (2d Cir.1943) (mere membership in an association is insufficient to create liability in the members for the acts of the association but a member who knows of his association's wrongs or should have known, becomes a principal by ratification unless he disassociates himself from the association). *But see Kline v. Coldwell, Banker,* (rejecting concept of membership ratification for purpose of finding group liability).

Typicality of Defenses

* * * [T]he paramount representative defense of the Association likely will be to deny the existence of a conspiracy to injure Thillens in violation of antitrust laws. Furthermore, if any joint activity is shown, the Association also will be expected to argue that such activity was not illegal. The nature of these defenses not only is typical but identical to the common defenses of the class members—the nonexistence of the conspiracy and the lawfulness of their joint behaviors.

* * *

The Association Is an Adequate Representative

Because of the serious due process problems which attend the certification of a defendant class, the 23(a)(4) mandate for an adequate representative must be strictly observed. The test of adequacy of representation proposed by Fed.R.Civ.P. 23(a)(4) is two-pronged: (1) the representative must be able to conduct the litigation and (2) the representative's interests must not be antagonistic to those of the class members. Although the representative need not be a member of the class, *see, e.g., [United States v.] Truckee–Carson Irrigation District,* 71 F.R.D. 10 (D.Nev.1975), there is the further requirement that the class representative must have injured the plaintiff in the same way as other defendants have injured him.

The Association allegedly has injured Thillens in precisely the same way as did every individual defendant, exchange defendant and public defendant. All defendants allegedly conspired to ruin Thillens' ambulatory currency exchange business, maintained a secret bribery fund for that purpose and engaged in antitrust and common law violations to Thillens' detriment.

Nonetheless, the Association is an unwilling class representative. That fact alone should not deter a court from naming it as representative, however. In *In re Gap,* the court observed that "[i]ronically the best defendant class representative may well be the one who most vigorously and persuasively opposes certification since he is the one most likely to guarantee an adversary presentation of the issues." If the sheer volume of the briefs which have been filed by the Association (and Thillens) in this case are any indication, adversary presentation of all issues by the Association is guaranteed.

The real concern with a reluctant representative should be for his ability to carry the expense and other practical burdens of a class defense. *See, e.g., Mudd v. Busse,* [68 F.R.D. 522 (N.D.Ind.1975)]. In *Mudd,* the court refused to certify a defendant class of judicial officers in Indiana who allegedly would not release pretrial detainees for failure to make bail. The representative proposed was Judge Busse. The court found that the cost of discovery would be impossible for Judge Busse to bear in so complex a class action.

Here, no serious suggestion can be raised that the Association either is financially unable or without requisite skills to act as the class representative. In fact, the Association does not argue the point. Presumably, the Association is fiscally sound. It owns a bank and at least one currency exchange. No individual defendant could better afford the role of class representative. Furthermore, the Association, through its attorneys, has considerable litigation experience. It has sued to protect the rights of the Association in matters of common interest to its members. The lawyers currently representing the Association, represented the Association and certain individual defendants in the criminal action which prompted Thillens to bring this suit.

Moreover, the Association's directors coincidentally are defendant class members. They have a clear channel of communication from the defendant class to the proposed representative. No doubt the director/defendants will consult on trial strategy and concerns of class members with the Association. Furthermore, the defendant class members fund the Association and, therefore, to some extent control it.

Finally, the Association is the self-selected representative of the member defendants. Each named and unnamed class member allegedly has voluntarily joined the Association seeking to have its business interests represented by the Association. The defendant members pay dues for the very purpose of having the Association represent their interests.

This Association, therefore, is similar to an association named as representative of a defendant class in *United States v. Truckee–Carson Irrigation District.* The *Truckee–Carson* court found that the association, although not a class member, existed for the expressed purpose of representing its members and protecting or asserting their common interests. It was the perfect class representative. Similarly, this Court concludes that the Association is an able, if not the only possible, class representative in this case. Prong one of 23(a)(4) is satisfied.

The second prong of 23(a)(4) also is met. The Association's interests are not antagonistic to the interests of the members of the class. Certification of a class on the grounds of antagonism should be denied only if that antagonism goes to the subject matter of the litigation.

The main subject matter in this case is antitrust. All parties, the representative, defendant class members and public defendants are expected to try to avoid liability by disclaiming an antitrust conspiracy. Arguably, the Association will not passively raise that defense. In defending itself vigorously, the Association necessarily will raise all defenses of the class members except for individual members' claims of nonparticipation in the conspiracy. In fact, this Association has an added incentive to vigorously defend the interests of the members. The Association's bylaws provide that it will indemnify, on request, Association members who are found liable for actions arising out of membership in the Association. Clearly, the interests of the Association are not antagonistic to the interests of the class members.

[The court rejected the Association's claim that it could not adequately represent the members of the class since it had pled guilty to several counts of mail fraud and had admitted the existence of a political bribery fund. Although the Association might be collaterally estopped from denying the existence of the fund, the court found that the admission would not result in an automatic finding of conspiracy in violation of the anti-trust laws nor indicate that Thillens was the target of the conspiracy. Finding the requirements of Rule 23(b)(3) satisfied, the court certified the class.]

Notes and Questions

1. In Rule 23(b)(3) defendant class actions like *Thillens,* why don't all the class members opt out as soon as they receive notice that the class has been certified? Is there anything the court or the plaintiff can do to deter such opting out? Is there anything they would lose by opting out in *Thillens*?

2. In *Thillens,* the class representative was a trade association that was obliged to indemnify individual defendants against certain types of liability. Consider Note, Defendant Class Actions, 91 Harv.L.Rev. 630, 642 (1978): "The structure of certain types of defendant class actions virtually guarantees adequate representation. Suits against the members of a labor union or other unincorporated association, naming the officers as representatives of the class, provide one example. The membership will have already chosen the officers to represent them on a wide variety of matters. Moreover, questions of individual conduct will rarely be in issue, since it is the conduct of the organization that has given rise to the litigation." Is this reasoning applicable to *Thillens*? Would it frequently be applicable to class representatives?

Having a trade association as class representative does not necessarily solve all problems, however. For example, in Monument Builders of Pennsylvania, Inc. v. American Cemetery Association, 206 F.R.D. 113 (E.D.Pa.2002), suit was brought against an association of cemeteries and a defendant class was certified. Thereafter the parties reached a settlement that prescribed limitations on the cemeteries' operations. More than twelve years later, one cemetery was sold to an operator who did not adhere to the limitations, resulting in a contempt proceeding. Because this cemetery operator had no notice of the restrictions (indeed, it had not even been created until years after the suit was settled), the court held that due process forbade holding it in contempt.

3. In Marcera v. Chinlund, 595 F.2d 1231 (2d Cir.1979), vacated on other grounds, 442 U.S. 915, 99 S.Ct. 2833, 61 L.Ed.2d 281 (1979), two New York inmates filed a class action on behalf of pretrial detainees against a defendant class of 42 sheriffs in the state who denied pretrial detainees contact visits. They named the sheriff of the county in which they were detained as the defendant class representative. The Second Circuit reversed the lower court's refusal to certify a defendant class. It found that the named sheriff's claims that contact visits posed a security threat were typical of the

defenses of the other sheriff class members, and rejected his argument that he was unwilling to serve as class representative:

> In contrast with representatives of plaintiff classes, named defendants almost never choose their role as class champion—it is a potentially onerous one thrust upon them by their opponents. It is not surprising, therefore, that Lombard opposes certification on the ground that, as an unwilling representative, he is unlikely to protect the interests of absentees. But courts must not readily accede to the wishes of named defendants in this area, for to permit them to abdicate so easily would utterly vitiate the effectiveness of the defendant class action as an instrument for correcting widespread illegality. Rule 23(a)(4) does not require a willing representative but merely an adequate one. It will often be true that, merely by protecting his own interests, a named defendant will be protecting the class. Where, as here, the legal issues as to liability are entirely common to members of the defendant class, there is little reason to fear unfairness to absentees.

4. *Marcera* was a civil rights case. Are certain kinds of cases more suitable for defendant class treatment? Consider Williams, Some Defendants Have Class: Reflections on the GAP Securities Litigation, 89 F.R.D. 287, 289–90 (1980): "Defendant classes have been employed with good results in several areas of the law. Patent infringement cases may be the most common use of the device because the crucial question of patent validity can be resolved by bringing the class of alleged infringers together. Another common use of defendant classes is challenges to the validity of state laws where the class comprises all state officials who enforce the law. * * * In certain areas, defendant classes provide a fine method of organizing the litigation."

5. The Second Circuit concluded in *Marcera* that a defendant class is permitted under Rule 23(b)(2) despite the rule's authorization only of class actions where "the party *opposing* the class has acted or refused to act on grounds generally applicable to the class." But the virtually unanimous view of other courts, and of the commentators, has been that the rule's language does not permit defendant classes under (b)(2). See Tilley v. TJX Companies, Inc., 345 F.3d 34, 39–40 (1st Cir.2003). One other court has noted, however, that the reference in (b)(2) to declaratory relief against the class could permit a debtor to sue a class of alleged creditors seeking a declaration of nonliability because the "real" plaintiffs were the creditors, and the "real" defendant was the debtor. Henson v. East Lincoln Township, 814 F.2d 410, 414 (7th Cir.1987).

6. Defendant classes can be certified under Rule 23(b)(1), and sometimes are. For example, in Wyandotte Nation v. City of Kansas City, 214 F.R.D. 656 (D.Kan.2003), an Indian tribe sued to recover what it claimed was its land and sought certification of a defendant class of over 1,300 individuals and entities listed as current record owners of the land. One of the defendants was a county government, and it joined in the motion to certify. Citing three earlier cases involving Indian tribes' efforts to obtain recovery of land in which defendant classes had been certified, the court decided that Rule 23(b)(1)(B) authorized certification. It also concluded that a mandatory class would be desirable because "preserving the right of class

members to opt out * * * would inhibit efforts to achieve a resolution of the liability issues." Id. at 664.

In In re Integra Realty Resources, Inc., 354 F.3d 1246 (10th Cir.2004), a trustee in bankruptcy sought relief for allegedly fraudulent transfer and unlawful distribution of a dividend by the bankrupt corporation to its 6,000 shareholders. The bankruptcy court certified a class of defendant shareholder recipients of the dividend under Rule 23(b)(1)(B), and the court of appeals affirmed. It reasoned that, given the centrality of the issue whether the distribution was unlawful, the resolution of the first of the trustee's suits would be dispositive of the rest. The findings in the first case "would almost inevitably prove dispositive" in later cases. Id. at 1264. In part, it relied on the fact that all proceedings would be in the same bankruptcy court, which "further increases the likelihood that the first case would prove dispositive." Id. Compare Tilley v. TJX Companies, Inc., 345 F.3d 34, 42 (1st Cir.2003) (noting that "the vast majority of courts" have ruled that "certification of a class under Rule 23(b)(1)(B) cannot rest solely on an anticipated stare decisis effects").

TIMING OF CLASS CERTIFICATION DECISIONS

Until 2003, Rule 23(c)(1) directed the court to determine whether a case was a proper class action "as soon as practicable" after the case was commenced, and also said that a certification order could be "conditional." In 2003, the rule was changed to say that the certification decision should be made "at an early practicable time." The prior rule's invitation to conditional certification was removed, and Rule 23(c)(1)(C) instead recognizes that the certification order may be altered or amended before final judgment in the action.

The background for these provisions is the notion, central to the 1966 amendments, that the certification question should usually be resolved before the court decided the merits of the suit. In part, that was due to the introduction in 1966 of the (b)(3) class action, with the right to opt out. One goal was to avoid what was called "one-way intervention," which could occur if class members already knew whether the suit was successful before they made their opt-out decisions. Thus, the 1966 version of Rule 23(c) said that modifications in the certification order could only be made before "decision on the merits."

The timing question thus presented issues of two sorts: (1) how much time to allow before ruling on whether the case was a proper class action, and (2) the sequence of decisionmaking (whatever the lapse of time before the certification decision was made). Related to both issues was the question of the amount of preparatory activity, including discovery, that should be done before the court could act. Recall that *Falcon*, *supra* p. 267, emphasizes the need for the court to make an informed decision on whether to certify the class.

In Eisen v. Carlisle & Jacquelin, 417 U.S. 156, 94 S.Ct. 2140, 40 L.Ed.2d 732 (1974), the Court rejected examination of the plaintiffs' likelihood of success as a ground for class certification: "[S]uch a procedure contravenes the Rule by allowing a representative plaintiff to

secure the benefits of a class action without first satisfying the requirements for it. He is thereby allowed to obtain a determination on the
merits of the claims advanced on behalf of the class without any
assurance that a class action may be maintained." Moreover, "a preliminary determination of the merits may result in substantial prejudice to a
defendant, since of necessity it is not accompanied by the traditional
rules and procedures applicable to civil trials."

In the wake of this decision, it sometimes seemed that courts and
parties were locked into a sequence of decisionmaking that forbade
consideration of whether plaintiffs had stated a claim or whether defendants were entitled to summary judgment against plaintiff's claim before
the class certification decision had been made.

To avoid these difficulties, courts might hurry a "conditional"
certification on a thin record in order to open the way for addressing
other issues. The Committee Note to the 2003 amendment makes it clear
that this tactic is not proper: "A court that is not satisfied that the
requirements of Rule 23 have been met should refuse certification until
they have been met."

Over time, the courts evolved solutions to these problems that are
embodied in the 2003 amendments. First, it came to be recognized that a
defendant could challenge the legal sufficiency of the plaintiff's claims,
or seek summary judgment, before certification. True, defendant would
then be giving up the possibility of a judgment against the whole class
instead of defeating only the named plaintiff, but defendants could make
that choice. See, e.g., Curtin v. United Airlines, Inc., 275 F.3d 88
(D.C.Cir.2001) (where district court readily and quickly perceived fatal
flaws in plaintiff's claims, it was proper to reverse the usual order and
grant defendant's motion for summary judgment rather than undertake
determination whether to certify class); Manual for Complex Litigation
(4th) § 21.133 (2004).

Second, the courts developed a nuanced view about what activity
was needed to determine whether class certification should be granted.
At first, they resisted all "merits" discovery, but it was often difficult to
determine where class certification issues left off and merits issues
began. Eventually, courts became more comfortable with the notion that
some consideration of merits questions was necessary for class certification:

> Before deciding whether to allow a case to proceed as a class action,
> therefore, a judge should make whatever factual and legal inquiries
> are necessary under Rule 23. This would be plain enough if, for
> example, the plaintiff alleged that the class had 10,000 members,
> making it too numerous to allow joinder, see Rule 23(a)(1), while the
> defendant insisted that the class contained only 10 members. A
> judge would not and could not accept the plaintiff's assertion as
> conclusive; instead the judge would receive evidence (if only by
> affidavit) and resolve the dispute before deciding whether to certify
> the class. What is true of disputes under Rule 23(a)(1) is equally

true of disputes under Rule 23(b)(3). A court may certify a class under Rule 23(b)(3) only if it finds that all the prerequisites (such as numerosity) have been demonstrated, and in addition the court finds that the questions of law or fact common to the members of the class predominate over any questions affecting only individual members, and that a class action is superior to other available methods for the fair and efficient adjudication of the controversy. * * * Questions such as these require the exercise of judgment and the application of sound discretion; they differ in kind from legal rulings under Rule 12(b)(6). And if some of the considerations under Rule 23(b)(3), such as "the difficulties likely to be encountered in the management of a class action," overlap the merits—as they do in this case, where it is not possible to evaluate impending difficulties without making a choice of law * * *—then the judge must make a preliminary inquiry into the merits.

Szabo v. Bridgeport Machines, Inc., 249 F.3d 672 (7th Cir.2001); see Manual for Complex Litigation (4th) § 21.14 (2004) (on precertification discovery).

This does not mean that the certification decision can be deferred for an unlimited period. Thus, in In re Phillip Morris, Inc., 214 F.3d 132 (2d Cir.2000), the appellate court directed Judge Weinstein to decide whether to certify a class before trial in a tobacco liability case. Although certification could perhaps be deferred until after trial in some cases, "Rule 23(c) imposes on the district court an immediate obligation to decide the issue of class certification and thereby abate the multi-billion dollar specter of a risk-free intervention decision by many decisions of putative plaintiffs." Compare Pyke v. Cuomo, 209 F.R.D. 33 (S.D.N.Y. 2002) (class certification motion ten years after action commenced not too late).

Because (b)(1) and (b)(2) classes don't involve advance notice and a right to opt out, it has been held that there is more flexibility about the timing of class certification in such cases. See Jimenez v. Weinberger, 523 F.2d 689, 698 (7th Cir.1975), cert. denied, 427 U.S. 912, 96 S.Ct. 3200, 49 L.Ed.2d 1204 (1976) (in such cases it may be permissible to enter a single order determining the merits and the identity of class members). Similarly, merits-affecting sanctions can be entered before class certification is decided. See In re Consolidated Pretrial Proceedings in Air West Securities Litigation, 73 F.R.D. 12, 16 (N.D.Cal.1976) (entry of defendant's default when he refused to appear as ordered for his deposition did not violate *Eisen* because defendant forced the court to take the action that had the effect of determining the merits).

TIMING OF APPEALS FROM CLASS CERTIFICATION DECISIONS

Another critical timing issue for class certification is the timing of appellate review. Until recently, obtaining prompt review of class certification was extremely difficult because certification decisions are by definition interlocutory. The Supreme Court rejected arguments for immediate appeal if the refusal to certify would be the death knell of the case because plaintiffs couldn't continue individually, and the "collateral order" ground for immediate review usually would be unavailable because the certification decision was not completely separate from the merits. Coopers & Lybrand v. Livesay, 437 U.S. 463, 98 S.Ct. 2454, 57 L.Ed.2d 351 (1978). On occasion, district courts would designate certification orders for immediate appeal under 28 U.S.C.A. § 1292(b). In some cases, appellate courts would grant a writ of mandate to address the correctness of class certification. See, e.g., In re Rhone–Poulenc Rorer, Inc., 51 F.3d 1293 (7th Cir.1995) (emphasizing the "intense pressure to settle" produced in that case by class certification).

In 1998, Rule 23(f) was adopted to provide an avenue for appellate review of certification decisions. It grants a court of appeals discretion to permit an immediate appeal for a district court decision granting or denying certification, and provides that an appeal does not automatically stay proceedings before the district court. Although it was expected that courts of appeals would not often grant such review, this amendment provided an avenue for development of a fuller body of appellate caselaw on certification standards.

In Blair v. Equifax Check Serv., Inc., 181 F.3d 832 (7th Cir.1999), the court explored the criteria that bear on whether to accept an appeal under new Rule 23(f), albeit eschewing a bright line approach. It suggested that where class certification is denied the "death knell" idea might suffice, cautioned that courts be "wary lest the mind hear a bell that is not tolling" in cases that will be pursued despite the denial of class certification. The obverse is in cases in which certification is granted if "the stakes are large and the risk of a settlement or other disposition that does not reflect the merits of the claim is substantial." In those situations, however, the appellant must demonstrate that the certification is questionable. Finally, allowing an appeal may facilitate in the development of the law, thereby making rule amendments unnecessary. If an appeal is allowed, "a stay would depend on a demonstration that the probability of error in the class certification decision is high enough that the costs of pressing ahead in the district court exceed the costs of waiting."

Other courts have followed suit. See, e.g., Prado–Steiman v. Bush, 221 F.3d 1266 (11th Cir.2000) (decisions whether to accept interlocutory appeals should look to (1) whether the ruling made by the district court is likely to be the "death knell" of the case, (2) whether there is a substantial weakness in the class certification decision, (3) whether the issue presented is important, (4) the pretrial posture of the case, and (5) whether there is an ongoing train of events, such as settlement discussions, that might obviate review). In Tilley v. TJX Companies, Inc., 345 F.3d 34 (1st Cir.2003), the court applied the same basic analysis to appeal of certification of a defendant class.

For general discussion, see Solimine & Hines, Deciding to Decide: Class Action Certification and Interlocutory Review by the United States Courts of Appeals Under Rule 23(f), 41 Will. & Mary L. Rev. 1531 (2000).

D. SETTLEMENT CLASS ACTIONS

The question of certifying a class action may be viewed somewhat differently if the case is certified only for purposes of possible settlement, or tentatively certified while settlement is explored. In those circumstances, the court might be spared the need to make difficult class certification determinations while the settlement negotiations are underway; at the same time, the court has some supervisory role in connection with those negotiations if it designates the lawyer who may negotiate on behalf of the class. Moreover, the class certification decision itself may be significantly eased because some of the manageability complications that would be presented by attempting to manage a trial might be less pressing, and the difficulties presented by conflicting legal regimes might be avoided. Finally, class members deciding whether to opt out should have a clearer idea of the value of staying in the class since the settlement deal will then be a known quantity. These concerns led courts presented with Rule 23(b)(3) cases to uphold tentative certification for purposes of settlement negotiation even though certification might not be proper if a trial were necessary. See Mars Steel Corp. v. Continental Illinois Nat'l Bank, 834 F.2d 677 (7th Cir.1987); Weinberger v. Kendrick, 698 F.2d 61 (2d Cir.1982), cert. denied, 464 U.S. 818, 104 S.Ct. 77, 78 L.Ed.2d 89 (1983).

There are, however, serious potential drawbacks to this practice. Defendants may be able to "shop" for a favorably-inclined plaintiffs' lawyer. See Ace Heating & Plumbing Co. v. Crane Co., 453 F.2d 30, 33 (3d Cir.1971) ("a person who unofficially represents the class during settlement negotiations may be under strong pressure to conform to the defendant's wishes [because] a negotiating defendant may not like his 'attitude' and may try to reach settlement with another member of the class"). In addition, the failure of the court to make an expeditious determination on class certification may have a negative effect on the court's ability to scrutinize the settlement. See Mars Steel Corp. v. Continental Illinois Nat. Bank, 834 F.2d 677, 681 (7th Cir.1987):

> The danger of a premature, even a collusive, settlement is increased when as in this case the status of the action as a class action is not determined until a settlement has been negotiated with all the momentum that a settlement agreement generates * * *. And when notice of the class action is, again as in this case, sent simultaneously with the notice of the settlement itself, the class members are presented with what looks like a fait accompli.

Nevertheless, the common attitude was that "as the law now stands, tentative or temporary settlement classes are favored when there is little or no likelihood of abuse, and the settlement is fair and reasonable and under the scrutiny of the trial judge." In re Beef Industry Antitrust Litigation, 607 F.2d 167, 174 (5th Cir.1979), cert. denied, 452 U.S. 905, 101 S.Ct. 3029, 69 L.Ed.2d 405 (1981).

AMCHEM PRODUCTS, INC. v. WINDSOR

Supreme Court of the United States, 1997.
521 U.S. 591, 117 S.Ct. 2231, 138 L.Ed.2d 689.

JUSTICE GINSBURG delivered the opinion of the Court.

This case concerns the legitimacy under Rule 23 of the Federal Rules of Civil Procedure of a class-action certification sought to achieve global settlement of current and future asbestos-related claims. The class proposed for certification potentially encompasses hundreds of thousands, perhaps millions, of individuals tied together by this commonality: each was, or some day may be, adversely affected by past exposure to asbestos products manufactured by one or more of 20 companies. Those companies, defendants in the lower courts, are petitioners here.

The United States District Court for the Eastern District of Pennsylvania certified the class for settlement only, finding that the proposed settlement was fair and that representation and notice had been adequate. That court enjoined class members from separately pursuing asbestos-related personal-injury suits in any court, federal or state, pending the issuance of a final order. The Court of Appeals for the Third Circuit vacated the District Court's orders, holding that the class certification failed to satisfy Rule 23's requirements in several critical respects. We affirm the Court of Appeals' judgment.

I

A

The settlement-class certification we confront evolved in response to an asbestos-litigation crisis. * * *

[In 1991,] the MDL Panel transferred all asbestos cases then filed, but not yet on trial in federal courts to a single district, the United States District Court for the Eastern District of Pennsylvania; pursuant to the transfer order, the collected cases were consolidated for pretrial proceedings before Judge Weiner. See In re Asbestos Products Liability Litigation (No. VI), 771 F. Supp. 415, 422–424 (JPML 1991) [*supra* p. 159, n. 3]. The order aggregated pending cases only; no authority resides in the MDL Panel to license for consolidated proceedings claims not yet filed.

B

After the consolidation, attorneys for plaintiffs and defendants formed separate steering committees and began settlement negotiations. Ronald L. Motley and Gene Locks—later appointed, along with Motley's law partner Joseph F. Rice, to represent the plaintiff class in this action—co-chaired the Plaintiffs' Steering Committee. Counsel for the Center for Claims Resolution (CCR), the consortium of 20 former asbestos manufacturers now before us as petitioners, participated in the Defendants' Steering Committee. Although the MDL order collected, transferred, and consolidated only cases already commenced in federal courts, settlement negotiations included efforts to find a "means of resolving . . . future cases."

* * *

[Initially, negotiations with Plaintiffs' Steering Committee were unsuccessful. Thereafter,] CCR counsel approached the lawyers who had headed the Plaintiffs' Steering Committee in the unsuccessful negotiations, and a new round of negotiations began; that round yielded the mass settlement agreement now in controversy. At the time, the former heads of the Plaintiffs' Steering Committee represented thousands of plaintiffs with then-pending asbestos-related claims—claimants the parties to this suit call "inventory" plaintiffs. CCR indicated in these discussions that it would resist settlement of inventory cases absent "some kind of protection for the future."

Settlement talks thus concentrated on devising an administrative scheme for disposition of asbestos claims not yet in litigation. In these negotiations, counsel for masses of inventory plaintiffs endeavored to represent the interests of the anticipated future claimants, although those lawyers then had no attorney-client relationship with such claimants.

Once negotiations seemed likely to produce an agreement purporting to bind potential plaintiffs, CCR agreed to settle, through separate agreements, the claims of plaintiffs who had already filed asbestos-related lawsuits. In one such agreement, CCR defendants promised to pay more than $200 million to gain release of the claims of numerous inventory plaintiffs. After settling the inventory claims, CCR, together with the plaintiffs' lawyers CCR had approached, launched this case, exclusively involving persons outside the MDL Panel's province—plaintiffs without already pending lawsuits.[3]

C

The class action thus instituted was not intended to be litigated. Rather, within the space of a single day, January 15, 1993, the settling parties—CCR defendants and the representatives of the plaintiff class described below—presented to the District Court a complaint, an answer, a proposed settlement agreement, and a joint motion for conditional class certification.

The complaint identified nine lead plaintiffs, designating them and members of their families as representatives of a class comprising all persons who had not filed an asbestos-related lawsuit against a CCR defendant as of the date the class action commenced, but who (1) had been exposed—occupationally or through the occupational exposure of a spouse or household member—to asbestos or products containing asbestos attributable to a CCR defendant, or (2) whose spouse or family

---

3. It is basic to comprehension of this proceeding to notice that no transferred case is included in the settlement at issue, and no case covered by the settlement existed as a civil action at the time of the MDL Panel transfer.

member had been so exposed. Untold numbers of individuals may fall within this description. All named plaintiffs alleged that they or a member of their family had been exposed to asbestos-containing products of CCR defendants. More than half of the named plaintiffs alleged that they or their family members had already suffered various physical injuries as a result of the exposure. The others alleged that they had not yet manifested any asbestos-related condition. The complaint delineated no subclasses; all named plaintiffs were designated as representatives of the class as a whole.

The complaint invoked the District Court's diversity jurisdiction and asserted various state-law claims for relief, including (1) negligent failure to warn, (2) strict liability, (3) breach of express and implied warranty, (4) negligent infliction of emotional distress, (5) enhanced risk of disease, (6) medical monitoring, and (7) civil conspiracy. Each plaintiff requested unspecified damages in excess of $100,000. CCR defendants' answer denied the principal allegations of the complaint and asserted 11 affirmative defenses.

A stipulation of settlement accompanied the pleadings; it proposed to settle, and to preclude nearly all class members from litigating against CCR companies, all claims not filed before January 15, 1993, involving compensation for present and future asbestos-related personal injury or death. An exhaustive document exceeding 100 pages, the stipulation presents in detail an administrative mechanism and a schedule of payments to compensate class members who meet defined asbestos-exposure and medical requirements. The stipulation describes four categories of compensable disease: mesothelioma; lung cancer; certain "other cancers" (colon-rectal, laryngeal, esophageal, and stomach cancer); and "non-malignant conditions" (asbestosis and bilateral pleural thickening). Persons with "exceptional" medical claims—claims that do not fall within the four described diagnostic categories—may in some instances qualify for compensation, but the settlement caps the number of "exceptional" claims CCR must cover.

For each qualifying disease category, the stipulation specifies the range of damages CCR will pay to qualifying claimants. Payments under the settlement are not adjustable for inflation. Mesothelioma claimants—the most highly compensated category—are scheduled to receive between $20,000 and $200,000. The stipulation provides that CCR is to propose the level of compensation within the prescribed ranges; it also establishes procedures to resolve disputes over medical diagnoses and levels of compensation.

Compensation above the fixed ranges may be obtained for "extraordinary" claims. But the settlement places both numerical caps and dollar limits on such claims.[6] The settlement also imposes "case flow maxi-

---

6. Only three percent of the qualified mesothelioma, lung cancer, and "other cancer" claims, and only one percent of the total number of qualified "non-malignant condition" claims can be designated "extraordinary." Average expenditures are specified for claims found "extraordinary"; mesothelioma victims with compensable extraordinary claims, for example, receive, on average, $300,000.

mums," which cap the number of claims payable for each disease in a given year.

Class members are to receive no compensation for certain kinds of claims, even if otherwise applicable state law recognizes such claims. Claims that garner no compensation under the settlement include claims by family members of asbestos-exposed individuals for loss of consortium, and claims by so-called "exposure-only" plaintiffs for increased risk of cancer, fear of future asbestos-related injury, and medical monitoring. "Pleural" claims, which might be asserted by persons with asbestos-related plaques on their lungs but no accompanying physical impairment, are also excluded. Although not entitled to present compensation, exposure-only claimants and pleural claimants may qualify for benefits when and if they develop a compensable disease and meet the relevant exposure and medical criteria. Defendants forgo defenses to liability, including statute of limitations pleas.

Class members, in the main, are bound by the settlement in perpetuity, while CCR defendants may choose to withdraw from the settlement after ten years. A small number of class members—only a few per year—may reject the settlement and pursue their claims in court. Those permitted to exercise this option, however, may not assert any punitive damages claim or any claim for increased risk of cancer. Aspects of the administration of the settlement are to be monitored by the AFL–CIO and class counsel. Class counsel are to receive attorneys' fees in an amount to be approved by the District Court.

D

On January 29, 1993, as requested by the settling parties, the District Court conditionally certified, under Federal Rule of Civil Procedure 23(b)(3), an encompassing opt-out class. The certified class included persons occupationally exposed to defendants' asbestos products, and members of their families, who had not filed suit as of January 15. Judge Weiner appointed Locks, Motley, and Rice as class counsel, noting that "[t]he Court may in the future appoint additional counsel if it is deemed necessary and advisable." At no stage of the proceedings, however, were additional counsel in fact appointed. Nor was the class ever divided into subclasses. In a separate order, Judge Weiner assigned to Judge Reed, also of the Eastern District of Pennsylvania, "the task of conducting fairness proceedings and of determining whether the proposed settlement is fair to the class." Various class members raised objections to the settlement stipulation, and Judge Weiner granted the objectors full rights to participate in the subsequent proceedings.

In preliminary rulings, Judge Reed held that the District Court had subject-matter jurisdiction, and he approved the settling parties' elaborate plan for giving notice to the class. The court-approved notice informed recipients that they could exclude themselves from the class, if they so chose, within a three-month opt-out period.

Objectors raised numerous challenges to the settlement. They urged that the settlement unfairly disadvantaged those without currently compensable conditions in that it failed to adjust for inflation or to account for changes, over time, in medical understanding. They maintained that compensation levels were intolerably low in comparison to awards available in tort litigation or payments received by the inventory plaintiffs. And they objected to the absence of any compensation for certain claims, for example, medical monitoring, compensable under the tort law of several States. Rejecting these and all other objections, Judge Reed concluded that the settlement terms were fair and had been negotiated without collusion. He also found that adequate notice had been given to class members, and that final class certification under Rule 23(b)(3) was appropriate.

As to the specific prerequisites to certification, the District Court observed that the class satisfied Rule 23(a)(1)'s numerosity requirement, a matter no one debates. The Rule 23(a)(2) and (b)(3) requirements of commonality and preponderance were also satisfied, the District Court held, in that "[t]he members of the class have all been exposed to asbestos products supplied by the defendants and all share an interest in receiving prompt and fair compensation for their claims, while minimizing the risks and transaction costs inherent in the asbestos litigation process as it occurs presently in the tort system. Whether the proposed settlement satisfies this interest and is otherwise a fair, reasonable and adequate compromise of the claims of the class is a predominant issue for purposes of Rule 23(b)(3)." The District Court held next that the claims of the class representatives were "typical" of the class as a whole, a requirement of Rule 23(a)(3), and that, as Rule 23(b)(3) demands, the class settlement was "superior" to other methods of adjudication.

Strenuous objections had been asserted regarding the adequacy of representation, a Rule 23(a)(4) requirement. * * *

[T]he District Court rejected these objections. Subclasses were unnecessary, the District Court held, bearing in mind the added cost and confusion they would entail and the ability of class members to exclude themselves from the class during the three-month opt-out period. Reasoning that the representative plaintiffs "have a strong interest that recovery for all of the medical categories be maximized because they may have claims in any, or several categories," the District Court found "no antagonism of interest between class members with various medical conditions, or between persons with and without currently manifest asbestos impairment." Declaring class certification appropriate and the settlement fair, the District Court preliminarily enjoined all class members from commencing any asbestos-related suit against the CCR defendants in any state or federal court.

The objectors appealed. The United States Court of Appeals for the Third Circuit vacated the certification, holding that the requirements of Rule 23 had not been satisfied.

E

The Court of Appeals, in a long, heavily detailed opinion by Judge Becker, first noted several challenges by objectors to justiciability, subject-matter jurisdiction, and adequacy of notice. These challenges, the court said, raised "serious concerns." However, the court observed, "the jurisdictional issues in this case would not exist but for the [class action] certification." Turning to the class-certification issues and finding them dispositive, the Third Circuit declined to decide other questions.

On class-action prerequisites, the Court of Appeals referred to an earlier Third Circuit decision, In re General Motors Corp. Pick–Up Truck Fuel Tank Products Liability Litigation, 55 F. 3d 768 (CA3), cert. denied, 516 U.S. 824 (1995) (hereinafter *GM Trucks*), which held that although a class action may be certified for settlement purposes only, Rule 23(a)'s requirements must be satisfied as if the case were going to be litigated. The same rule should apply, the Third Circuit said, to class certification under Rule 23(b)(3). While stating that the requirements of Rule 23(a) and (b)(3) must be met "without taking into account the settlement," the Court of Appeals in fact closely considered the terms of the settlement as it examined aspects of the case under Rule 23 criteria.

* * *

In contrast to mass torts involving a single accident, class members in this case were exposed to different asbestos-containing products, in different ways, over different periods, and for different amounts of time; some suffered no physical injury, others suffered disabling or deadly diseases. "These factual differences," the Third Circuit explained, "translate[d] into significant legal differences." State law governed and varied widely on such critical issues as "viability of [exposure-only] claims [and] availability of causes of action for medical monitoring, increased risk of cancer, and fear of future injury."[14] "[T]he number of uncommon issues in this humongous class action," the Third Circuit concluded, barred a determination, under existing tort law, that common questions predominated.

The Court of Appeals next found that "serious intra-class conflicts preclude[d] th[e] class from meeting the adequacy of representation requirement" of Rule 23(a)(4). Adverting to, but not resolving charges of attorney conflict of interests, the Third Circuit addressed the question whether the named plaintiffs could adequately advance the interests of all class members. The Court of Appeals acknowledged that the District Court was certainly correct to this extent: " '[T]he members of the class are united in seeking the maximum possible recovery for their asbestos-related claims.' " "But the settlement does more than simply provide a general recovery fund," the Court of Appeals immediately added;

---

14. Recoveries under the laws of different States spanned a wide range. Objectors assert, for example, that 15% of current mesothelioma claims arise in California, where the statewide average recovery is $419,674—or more than 209% above the $200,000 maximum specified in the settlement for mesothelioma claims not typed "extraordinary."

"[r]ather, it makes important judgments on how recovery is to be allocated among different kinds of plaintiffs, decisions that necessarily favor some claimants over others."

In the Third Circuit's view, the "most salient" divergence of interests separated plaintiffs already afflicted with an asbestos-related disease from plaintiffs without manifest injury (exposure-only plaintiffs). The latter would rationally want protection against inflation for distant recoveries. They would also seek sturdy back-end opt-out rights and "causation provisions that can keep pace with changing science and medicine, rather than freezing in place the science of 1993." Already injured parties, in contrast, would care little about such provisions and would rationally trade them for higher current payouts. These and other adverse interests, the Court of Appeals carefully explained, strongly suggested that an undivided set of representatives could not adequately protect the discrete interests of both currently afflicted and exposure-only claimants.

The Third Circuit next rejected the District Court's determination that the named plaintiffs were "typical" of the class, noting that this Rule 23(a)(3) inquiry overlaps the adequacy of representation question: "both look to the potential for conflicts in the class." Evident conflict problems, the court said, led it to hold that "no set of representatives can be 'typical' of this class."

The Court of Appeals similarly rejected the District Court's assessment of the superiority of the class action. * * * "A series of statewide or more narrowly defined adjudications, either through consolidation under Rule 42(a) or as class actions under Rule 23, would seem preferable," the Court of Appeals said.

* * *

We granted certiorari, and now affirm.

II

Objectors assert in this Court, as they did in the District Court and Court of Appeals, an array of jurisdictional barriers. Most fundamentally, they maintain that the settlement proceeding instituted by class counsel and CCR is not a justiciable case or controversy within the confines of Article III of the Federal Constitution. In the main, they say, the proceeding is a nonadversarial endeavor to impose on countless individuals without currently ripe claims an administrative compensation regime binding on those individuals if and when they manifest injuries.

Furthermore, objectors urge that exposure-only claimants lack standing to sue: Either they have not yet sustained any cognizable injury or, to the extent the complaint states claims and demands relief for emotional distress, enhanced risk of disease, and medical monitoring, the settlement provides no redress. Objectors also argue that exposure-only claimants did not meet the then-current amount-in-controversy requirement (in excess of $50,000) specified for federal-court jurisdiction based upon diversity of citizenship. See 28 U.S.C. § 1332(a).

As earlier recounted, the Third Circuit declined to reach these issues because they "would not exist but for the [class action] certification." We agree that "[t]he class certification issues are dispositive;" because their resolution here is logically antecedent to the existence of any Article III issues, it is appropriate to reach them first. We therefore follow the path taken by the Court of Appeals, mindful that Rule 23's requirements must be interpreted in keeping with Article III constraints, and with the Rules Enabling Act, which instructs that rules of procedure "shall not abridge, enlarge or modify any substantive right," 28 U.S.C. § 2072(b). See also Fed. Rule Civ. Proc. 82 ("rules shall not be construed to extend ... the [subject matter] jurisdiction of the United States district courts").

III

To place this controversy in context, we briefly describe the characteristics of class actions for which the Federal Rules provide. [Justice Ginsburg described the evolution of Rule 23, noting that Rule 23(b)(3) was "the most adventuresome" innovation in the 1996 amendments. She quoted the Advisory Committee Note that (b)(3) applied in situations in which "class-action treatment is not as clearly called for" as under (b)(1) and (b)(2). She also noted that the rulemakers intended for courts to look carefully at the individual interests involved before certifying classes under (b)(3), quoting the Third Circuit's observation that "[e]ach plaintiff [in any action involving claims for personal injury and death] has a significant interest in individually controlling the prosecution of [his case]," and that each "ha[s] a substantial stake in making individual decisions whether to settle."]

In the decades since the 1966 revision of Rule 23, class action practice has become ever more "adventuresome" as a means of coping with claims too numerous to secure their "just, speedy, and inexpensive determination" one by one. See Fed. Rule Civ. Proc. 1. The development reflects concerns about the efficient use of court resources and the conservation of funds to compensate claimants who do not line up early in a litigation queue.

Among current applications of Rule 23(b)(3), the "settlement only" class has become a stock device. Although all Federal Circuits recognize the utility of Rule 23(b)(3) settlement classes, courts have divided on the extent to which a proffered settlement affects court surveillance under Rule 23's certification criteria.

In *GM Trucks* and in the instant case, the Third Circuit held that a class cannot be certified for settlement when certification for trial would be unwarranted. Other courts have held that settlement obviates or reduces the need to measure a proposed class against the enumerated Rule 23 requirements.

* * *

IV

We granted review to decide the role settlement may play, under existing Rule 23, in determining the propriety of class certification. The Third Circuit's opinion stated that each of the requirements of Rule 23(a) and (b)(3) "must be satisfied without taking into account the settlement." That statement, petitioners urge, is incorrect.

We agree with petitioners to this limited extent: settlement is relevant to a class certification. The Third Circuit's opinion bears modification in that respect. But, as we earlier observed, the Court of Appeals in fact did not ignore the settlement; instead, that court homed in on settlement terms in explaining why it found the absentees' interests inadequately represented. The Third Circuit's close inspection of the settlement in that regard was altogether proper.

Confronted with a request for settlement-only class certification, a district court need not inquire whether the case, if tried, would present intractable management problems, see Fed. Rule Civ. Proc. 23(b)(3)(D), for the proposal is that there be no trial. But other specifications of the rule—those designed to protect absentees by blocking unwarranted or overbroad class definitions—demand undiluted, even heightened, attention in the settlement context. Such attention is of vital importance, for a court asked to certify a settlement class will lack the opportunity, present when a case is litigated, to adjust the class, informed by the proceedings as they unfold. See Fed. Rule Civ. Proc. 23(c), (d).

And, of overriding importance, courts must be mindful that the rule as now composed sets the requirements they are bound to enforce. Federal Rules take effect after an extensive deliberative process involving many reviewers: a Rules Advisory Committee, public commenters, the Judicial Conference, this Court, the Congress. See 28 U.S.C. §§ 2073, 2074. The text of a rule thus proposed and reviewed limits judicial inventiveness. Courts are not free to amend a rule outside the process Congress ordered, a process properly tuned to the instruction that rules of procedure "shall not abridge . . . any substantive right." § 2072(b).

Rule 23(e), on settlement of class actions, * * * was designed to function as an additional requirement, not a superseding direction, for the "class action" to which Rule 23(e) refers is one qualified for certification under Rule 23(a) and (b). Cf. Eisen [v. Carlisle & Jacquelin], 417 U.S., at 176–177 [*infra* p. 440](adequate representation does not eliminate additional requirement to provide notice). Subdivisions (a) and (b) focus court attention on whether a proposed class has sufficient unity so that absent members can fairly be bound by decisions of class representatives. That dominant concern persists when settlement, rather than trial, is proposed.

The safeguards provided by the Rule 23(a) and (b) class-qualifying criteria, we emphasize, are not impractical impediments—checks shorn of utility—in the settlement class context. First, the standards set for the protection of absent class members serve to inhibit appraisals of the chancellor's foot kind—class certifications dependent upon the court's gestalt judgment or overarching impression of the settlement's fairness.

Second, if a fairness inquiry under Rule 23(e) controlled certification, eclipsing Rule 23(a) and (b), and permitting class designation despite the impossibility of litigation, both class counsel and court would be disarmed. Class counsel confined to settlement negotiations could not use the threat of litigation to press for a better offer, and the court would face a bargain proffered for its approval without benefit of adversarial investigation, see, e.g., Kamilewicz v. Bank of Boston Corp., 100 F. 3d 1348, 1352 (C.A.7 1996) (Easterbrook, J., dissenting from denial of rehearing en banc) (parties "may even put one over on the court, in a staged performance"), cert. denied, 520 U.S. 1204 (1997).

Federal courts, in any case, lack authority to substitute for Rule 23's certification criteria a standard never adopted—that if a settlement is "fair," then certification is proper. Applying to this case criteria the rulemakers set, we conclude that the Third Circuit's appraisal is essentially correct. Although that court should have acknowledged that settlement is a factor in the calculus, a remand is not warranted on that account. The Court of Appeals' opinion amply demonstrates why—with or without a settlement on the table—the sprawling class the District Court certified does not satisfy Rule 23's requirements.

A

We address first the requirement of Rule 23(b)(3) that "[common] questions of law or fact ... predominate over any questions affecting only individual members." The District Court concluded that predominance was satisfied based on two factors: class members' shared experience of asbestos exposure and their common "interest in receiving prompt and fair compensation for their claims, while minimizing the risks and transaction costs inherent in the asbestos litigation process as it occurs presently in the tort system." The settling parties also contend that the settlement's fairness is a common question, predominating over disparate legal issues that might be pivotal in litigation but become irrelevant under the settlement.

The predominance requirement stated in Rule 23(b)(3), we hold, is not met by the factors on which the District Court relied. The benefits asbestos-exposed persons might gain from the establishment of a grand-scale compensation scheme is a matter fit for legislative consideration, but it is not pertinent to the predominance inquiry. That inquiry trains on the legal or factual questions that qualify each class member's case as a genuine controversy, questions that preexist any settlement.[18]

---

18. In this respect, the predominance requirement of Rule 23(b)(3) is similar to the requirement of Rule 23(a)(3) that "claims or defenses" of the named representatives must be "typical of the claims or defenses of the class." The words "claims or defenses" in this context—just as in the context of Rule 24(b)(2) governing permis- sive intervention—"manifestly refer to the kinds of claims or defenses that can be raised in courts of law as part of an actual or impending law suit." Diamond v. Charles, 476 U.S. 54, 76–77 (1986) (O'Connor, J., concurring in part and concurring in judgment).

The Rule 23(b)(3) predominance inquiry tests whether proposed classes are sufficiently cohesive to warrant adjudication by representation. The inquiry appropriate under Rule 23(e), on the other hand, protects unnamed class members "from unjust or unfair settlements affecting their rights when the representatives become fainthearted before the action is adjudicated or are able to secure satisfaction of their individual claims by a compromise." But it is not the mission of Rule 23(e) to assure the class cohesion that legitimizes representative action in the first place. If a common interest in a fair compromise could satisfy the predominance requirement of Rule 23(b)(3), that vital prescription would be stripped of any meaning in the settlement context.

The District Court also relied upon this commonality: "The members of the class have all been exposed to asbestos products supplied by the defendants...." Even if Rule 23(a)'s commonality requirement may be satisfied by that shared experience, the predominance criterion is far more demanding. Given the greater number of questions peculiar to the several categories of class members, and to individuals within each category, and the significance of those uncommon questions, any overarching dispute about the health consequences of asbestos exposure cannot satisfy the Rule 23(b)(3) predominance standard.

The Third Circuit highlighted the disparate questions undermining class cohesion in this case:

"Class members were exposed to different asbestos-containing products, for different amounts of time, in different ways, and over different periods. Some class members suffer no physical injury or have only asymptomatic pleural changes, while others suffer from lung cancer, disabling asbestosis, or from mesothelioma.... Each has a different history of cigarette smoking, a factor that complicates the causation inquiry.

"The [exposure-only] plaintiffs especially share little in common, either with each other or with the presently injured class members. It is unclear whether they will contract asbestos-related disease and, if so, what disease each will suffer. They will also incur different medical expenses because their monitoring and treatment will depend on singular circumstances and individual medical histories."

Differences in state law, the Court of Appeals observed, compound these disparities.

No settlement class called to our attention is as sprawling as this one. Predominance is a test readily met in certain cases alleging consumer or securities fraud or violations of the antitrust laws. Even mass tort cases arising from a common cause or disaster may, depending upon the circumstances, satisfy the predominance requirement. The Advisory Committee for the 1966 revision of Rule 23, it is true, noted that "mass accident" cases are likely to present "significant questions, not only of damages but of liability and defenses of liability, ... affecting the individuals in different ways." And the Committee advised that such cases are "ordinarily not appropriate" for class treatment. But the text of the rule does not categorically exclude mass tort cases from class certification, and district courts, since the late 1970s, have been certifying such cases in increasing number. The Committee's warning, however, continues to call for caution when individual stakes are high and disparities among class members great. As the Third Circuit's opinion makes plain, the certification in this case does not follow the counsel of caution. That certification cannot be upheld, for it rests on a conception of Rule 23(b)(3)'s predominance requirement irreconcilable with the rule's design.

B

Nor can the class approved by the District Court satisfy Rule 23(a)(4)'s requirement that the named parties "will fairly and adequately protect the interests of the class." The adequacy inquiry under Rule 23(a)(4) serves to uncover conflicts of interest between named parties and the class they seek to represent. "[A] class representative must be part of the class and 'possess the same interest and suffer the same injury' as the class members." East Tex. Motor Freight System, Inc. v. Rodriguez, 431 U.S. 395, 403 (1977).[20]

As the Third Circuit pointed out, named parties with diverse medical conditions sought to act on behalf of a single giant class rather than on behalf of discrete subclasses. In significant respects, the interests of those within the single class are not aligned. Most saliently, for the currently injured, the critical goal is generous immediate payments. That goal tugs against the interest of exposure-only plaintiffs in ensuring an ample, inflation-protected fund for the future. Cf. General Telephone Co. of Northwest v. EEOC, 446 U.S. 318, 331 (1980) ("In employment discrimination litigation, conflicts might arise, for example, between employees and applicants who were denied employment and who will, if granted relief, compete with employees for fringe benefits or seniority. Under Rule 23, the same plaintiff could not represent these classes.")

The disparity between the currently injured and exposure-only categories of plaintiffs, and the diversity within each category are not made insignificant by the District Court's finding that petitioners' assets suffice to pay claims under the settlement. Although this is not a "limited fund" case certified under Rule 23(b)(1)(B), the terms of the

---

20. The adequacy-of-representation requirement "tend[s] to merge" with the commonality and typicality criteria of Rule 23(a), which "serve as guideposts for determining whether ... maintenance of a class action is economical and whether the named plaintiff's claim and the class claims are so interrelated that the interests of the class members will be fairly and adequately protected in their absence." General Tele- phone Co. of Southwest v. Falcon, 457 U.S. 147, 157, n. 13 (1982). The adequacy heading also factors in competency and conflicts of class counsel. Like the Third Circuit, we decline to address adequacy-of-counsel issues discretely in light of our conclusions that common questions of law or fact do not predominate and that the named plaintiffs cannot adequately represent the interests of this enormous class.

settlement reflect essential allocation decisions designed to confine compensation and to limit defendants' liability. For example, as earlier described, the settlement includes no adjustment for inflation; only a few claimants per year can opt out at the back end; and loss-of-consortium claims are extinguished with no compensation.

The settling parties, in sum, achieved a global compromise with no structural assurance of fair and adequate representation for the diverse groups and individuals affected. Although the named parties alleged a range of complaints, each served generally as representative for the whole, not for a separate constituency. In another asbestos class action, the Second Circuit spoke precisely to this point:

> "[W]here differences among members of a class are such that subclasses must be established, we know of no authority that permits a court to approve a settlement without creating subclasses on the basis of consents by members of a unitary class, some of whom happen to be members of the distinct subgroups. The class representatives may well have thought that the Settlement serves the aggregate interests of the entire class. But the adversity among subgroups requires that the members of each subgroup cannot be bound to a settlement except by consents given by those who understand that their role is to represent solely the members of their respective subgroups."

In re Joint Eastern and Southern Dist. Asbestos Litigation, 982 F. 2d 721, 742–743 (C.A.2 1992), modified on reh'g sub nom. In re Findley, 993 F. 2d 7 (C.A.2 1993). The Third Circuit found no assurance here—either in the terms of the settlement or in the structure of the negotiations—that the named plaintiffs operated under a proper understanding of their representational responsibilities. That assessment, we conclude, is on the mark.

C

Impediments to the provision of adequate notice, the Third Circuit emphasized, rendered highly problematic any endeavor to tie to a settlement class persons with no perceptible asbestos-related disease at the time of the settlement. Many persons in the exposure-only category, the Court of Appeals stressed, may not even know of their exposure, or realize the extent of the harm they may incur. Even if they fully appreciate the significance of class notice, those without current afflictions may not have the information or foresight needed to decide, intelligently, whether to stay in or opt out.

Family members of asbestos-exposed individuals may themselves fall prey to disease or may ultimately have ripe claims for loss of consortium. Yet large numbers of people in this category—future spouses and children of asbestos victims—could not be alerted to their class membership. And current spouses and children of the occupationally exposed may know nothing of that exposure.

Because we have concluded that the class in this case cannot satisfy the requirements of common issue predominance and adequacy of representation, we need not rule, definitively, on the notice given here. In accord with the Third Circuit, however, we recognize the gravity of the question whether class action notice sufficient under the Constitution and Rule 23 could ever be given to legions so unselfconscious and amorphous.

V

The argument is sensibly made that a nationwide administrative claims processing regime would provide the most secure, fair, and efficient means of compensating victims of asbestos exposure. Congress, however, has not adopted such a solution. And Rule 23, which must be interpreted with fidelity to the Rules Enabling Act and applied with the interests of absent class members in close view, cannot carry the large load CCR, class counsel, and the District Court heaped upon it. As this case exemplifies, the rulemakers' prescriptions for class actions may be endangered by "those who embrace [Rule 23] too enthusiastically just as [they are by] those who approach [the rule] with distaste."

* * *

For the reasons stated, the judgment of the Court of Appeals for the Third Circuit is affirmed.

JUSTICE O'CONNOR took no part in the consideration or decision of this case.

JUSTICE BREYER, with whom JUSTICE STEVENS joins, concurring in part and dissenting in part.

Although I agree with the Court's basic holding that "settlement is relevant to a class certification," I find several problems in its approach that lead me to a different conclusion. First, I believe that the need for settlement in this mass tort case, with hundreds of thousands of lawsuits, is greater than the Court's opinion suggests. Second, I would give more weight than would the majority to settlement-related issues for purposes of determining whether common issues predominate. Third, I am uncertain about the Court's determination of adequacy of representation, and do not believe it appropriate for this Court to second-guess the District Court on the matter without first having the Court of Appeals consider it. Fourth, I am uncertain about the tenor of an opinion that seems to suggest the settlement is unfair.

* * *

I believe the majority understates the importance of settlement in this case. [Justice Breyer reviewed the evolution of asbestos litigation, emphasizing its high transaction costs and uneven compensation. He also emphasized the vigor and contentiousness of the negotiations that produced the agreement presented to the district court, and the district court's conclusion that the agreement improved class members' chances of compensation.]

[T]he majority, in reviewing the District Court's determination that common "issues of fact and law predominate," says that the predominance "inquiry trains on the legal or factual questions that qualify each class member's case as a genuine controversy, questions that preexist any settlement." I find it difficult to interpret this sentence in a way that could lead me to the majority's conclusion. If the majority means that these pre-settlement questions are what matters, then how does it reconcile its statement with its basic conclusion that "settlement is relevant" to class certification, or with the numerous lower court authority that says that settlement is not only relevant, but important?

Nor do I understand how one could decide whether common questions "predominate" in the abstract—without looking at what is likely to be at issue in the proceedings that will ensue, namely, the settlement.

* * *

[C]ertain details of the settlement that are not discussed in the majority opinion suggest that the settlement may be of greater benefit to future plaintiffs than the majority suggests. The District Court concluded that future plaintiffs receive a "significant value" from the settlement due to variety of its items that benefit future plaintiffs, such as: (1) tolling the statute of limitations so that class members "will no longer be forced to file premature lawsuits or risk their claims being time-barred"; (2) waiver of defenses to liability; (3) payment of claims, if and when members become sick, pursuant to the settlement's compensation standards, which avoids "the uncertainties, long delays and high transaction costs [including attorney's fees] of the tort system"; (4) "some assurance that there will be funds available if and when they get sick," based on the finding that each defendant "has shown an ability to fund the payment of all qualifying claims" under the settlement; and (5) the right to additional compensation if cancer develops (many settlements for plaintiffs with noncancerous conditions bar such additional claims). For these reasons, and others, the District Court found that the distinction between present and future plaintiffs was "illusory."

Notes and Questions

1. Does the agreement reached through negotiation in *Amchem* seem unfair? If it appears to be a reasonable deal for class members in general, do you think that the promising features of the agreement should have mattered more to the Court, as Justice Breyer argues? One way of viewing *Amchem* is that it represented a contest between the advocates of substantive justice for claimants and those who insisted on fealty to procedural principles. See Issacharoff, "Shocked": Mass Torts and Aggregate Asbestos Litigation after Amchem and Ortiz, 80 Tex. L.Rev. 1926 (2002) (asserting that the proceduralists won hands down in the Court's decision). Some might argue that this is an example of the old maxim "The perfect is the enemy of the good."

Asbestos litigation did not vanish as a result of this decision. To the contrary, after *Amchem* and *Ortiz, supra* p. 302, the level of asbestos personal injury filings rose dramatically. The CCR disbanded, having paid out some $5 billion to approximately 350,000 claimants, and at least five members of the CCR filed petitions in bankruptcy. For details, see Hensler, As Time Goes By: Asbestos Litigation After Amchem and Ortiz, 80 Texas L.Rev. 1899 (2002). As Professor Hensler details, it is far from clear that asbestos claimants are better off than they would have been under the *Amchem* settlement. Most asbestos claims were resolved by inventory settlements, and individual claimants had virtually no role in setting the terms of those settlements. In general, the settlements employed some sort of grid based on the amounts paid to prior claimants, like the one in the settlement in *Amchem*. Claimants in bankruptcy proceedings, meanwhile, appeared not to fare very well. But it is, of course, impossible to say whether the bankruptcy filings would have occurred anyway had the Supreme Court reached a different result. For further examination of the implications of aggregate treatment outside the class action setting, see Erichson, Beyond the Class Action: Lawyer Loyalty and Client Autonomy in Non–Class Collective Representation, 2003 U.Chi. Legal F. 519.

2. One thing is clear from the Court's opinion—the Third Circuit rule that the terms of a settlement are irrelevant to class certification is wrong, or "bears modification," in the Court's gentle phrase. But how clear is the Court on the manner in which settlement should bear on class certification in a case such as *Amchem*? On one hand, Justice Ginsburg says that "the district court need not inquire whether the case, if tried, would present intractable management problems." On the other hand, she emphasizes that a Rule 23(e) fairness inquiry is not a "superseding factor" that obviates application of the Rule 23(a) and (b) requirements. Indeed, in some instances the fact of settlement should incline the court to be more skeptical about certification. What exactly is the predominance provision of (b)(3) supposed to mean in the settlement context? Compare Justice Breyer's criticism of the Court's explanation of how predominance of common questions bears on settlement-class certification.

3. In 1996 the Advisory Committee circulated a draft of a proposed amendment to Rule 23 adding a new subdivision (b)(4) authorizing certification when "the parties to a settlement request certification under subdivision (b)(3) for purposes of settlement, even though the requirements of subdivision (b)(3) might not be met for purposes of trial." See Proposed Amendments to the Federal Rules, 167 F.R.D. 523, 559 (1996). This change would have formally recognized in Rule 23 that certification for settlement is different from certification for trial. After the Court's decision in *Amchem*, the Advisory Committee decided to defer further action on a rule amendment. Could changing Rule 23 profitably clarify the requirements of *Amchem*?

4. What effect should *Amchem* have had on certification for settlement in cases not involving asbestos claims? Shortly after the case was decided, one district judge concluded that "*Amchem* decimated the notion of some circuits that Rule 23 requisites were relaxed in the settlement context." Walker v. Liggett Group, 175 F.R.D. 226 (S.D.W.Va.1997). But an experienced class action lawyer saw things differently: "We should expect that the

long-term impact of *Amchem* will be essentially favorable to those class actions that pit individuals of average means against modern corporations involving claims too small to litigate feasibly on a case-by-case basis." Cabraser, Life After Amchem: The Class Struggle Continues, 31 Loyola L.A. L. Rev. 373, 378 (1998).

A possible example is a case handled by Ms. Cabraser, the lawyer just quoted—Hanlon v. Chrysler Corp., 150 F.3d 1011 (9th Cir.1998), a nationwide class action alleging that defendant's minivans had defective rear latches. After litigation skirmishing in several courts that led to settlement discussions, an agreement was reached by which various cases were consolidated in one nationwide class action on behalf of some 3.3 million minivan owners. Three days after this suit was filed, the parties submitted a class-action settlement agreement that excluded any personal injury or death claims from its coverage. The settlement obligated defendant to replace latches on minivans and engage in outreach to alert owners of their right to a replacement. It also obligated defendant to make the minivans safe. The district court approved the settlement.

Objecting class members appealed. The court of appeals affirmed (id. at 1021):

> Unlike the class in *Amchem*, this class of minivan owners does not present an allocation dilemma. Potential plaintiffs are not divided into conflicting discrete categories, such as those with present health problems and those who may develop symptoms in the future. Rather, each potential plaintiff has the same problem: an allegedly defective rear latchgate which requires repair or commensurate compensation. The differences in severity of personal injury present in *Amchem* are avoided here by excluding personal injury and wrongful death claims. Similarly, there is no structural conflict of interest based on variations in state law, for the named representatives include individuals from each state, and the differences in state remedies are not sufficiently substantial so as to warrant the creation of subclasses. Representatives of other potential subclasses are included among the named representatives, including owners of every minivan model. However, even if the named representatives did not include a broad cross-section of claimants, the prospects for irreparable conflict of interest are minimal in this case because of the relatively small differences in damages and potential remedies.

5.   Recall the problem of maturity discussed in *Castano*, *supra* p. 340. There is no mass tort litigation more familiar to American courts than asbestos litigation. If even in that litigation the uncertainties of future developments limit class certification, when would any personal injury litigation be sufficiently "mature" to permit settlement class certification?

6.   Note the question whether lawyers like Motley and Lock, who had many current claimants, would properly represent the interests of future claimants. If the court could look only to lawyers who have no current clients, how would it find one with sufficient experience to negotiate a suitable settlement?

7.   The dilemma of how to deal with "future" members of classes who have been exposed to a toxic product but have not yet manifested disease

remains. State substantive law often requires proof of some present physical injury in order to have standing to sue. In the asbestos context, hundreds of thousands of people have been exposed, but have not manifested disease or injury. Many others have only "scarring" or "pleural thickening" that causes no immediate health hazard. Attempts to deal with this problem have included "medical monitoring" classes and "pleural registries" created by local rule in a number of courts to permit a filing that will toll the statute of limitations. Consider Priest, The Cumulative Sources of the Asbestos Litigation Phenomenon, 31 Pepp. L. Rev. 261, 264 (2004):

> [T]ypically, judicial decisions in asbestos cases proceed with rhetoric that allows recovery in the case before the court, yet still claims to retain some limiting principle with respect to future claims. The recent United States Supreme Court opinion in Norfolk & Western Railway Co. v. Ayers, [538 U.S. 135, 123 S.Ct. 1210 (2003)], is illustrative. In that case, the Supreme Court allowed for first-time claims from exposure to asbestos, though the Court insisted that the claim could only proceed if the worker could show some physical manifestation of exposure. Thus the Court vastly expanded grounds for recovery based upon asbestos exposure (the only claimed injury was mental anguish) while purporting to retain some limit on the expansion. Cumulatively, however, this rhetoric of limitation has proved meaningless. In subsequent cases, the limitations of one case have been realized for another, and the availability of recovery has continued to expand.

8.   One idea mentioned by Justice Ginsburg is providing class members with "sturdy back-end opt-out rights." Would provision of such rights be a way of dealing with the problem of future claimants? See Nagareda, Autonomy, Peace, and Put Options in the Mass Tort Class Action, 115 Harv.L.Rev. 747 (2002). Prof. Nagareda suggests that a class action settlement that exchanges the right to sue for punitive damages in return for the choice between a pre-set payment and the right to sue the manufacturer for damages if class members get sick is like a put option. He argues that this would preserve the claimants' autonomy and protect defendant against a serious problem in "over-mature" mass tort litigation, which is that plaintiff counsel will press forward with claims for those who are not impaired as well as for the injured.

9.   Recall that *Ortiz*, *supra* p. 302, involved a settlement class under Rule 23(b)(1). Could party agreement ever ease certification of a class action under that provision? Should mandatory class action treatment ever be allowed on relaxed terms because the class representatives (or their lawyers) are willing?

10.   What is the significance of *Amchem* for (b)(3) certification for litigation purposes? The Court seems to back away from the 1966 Advisory Committee Note about the impropriety of class actions in mass tort situations. Should this decision be read to endorse class action treatment in cases such as Jenkins v. Raymark Industries, Inc., *supra* p. 331? Does it also support the decision in Castano v. American Tobacco Co., *supra* p. 340?

One possible impact would be on the court's attitude toward settlement. In In re Integra Realty Resources, Inc., 354 F. 3d 1246 (10th Cir.2004), objectors to a class-action settlement urged that there had to be heightened scrutiny of the settlement under *Amchem*. The court rejected the argument (id. at 1262):

> We reject appellant's argument that the heightened scrutiny dictated by Amchem Prods., Inc. v. Windsor for settlement-only certifications applies to this case since here, unlike in *Amchem*, the class was certified before settlement negotiations began and the designated class counsel acted as the negotiator for the class.

11. For more discussion of present treatment of settlement class actions, see Manual for Complex Litigation (4th) § 21.132 (2004).

E.   OVERLAPPING CLASS ACTIONS

IN RE DIET DRUGS

United States Court of Appeals, Third Circuit, 2002.
282 F.3d 220.

Before: SCIRICA, GREENBERG, COWEN, Circuit Judges.

SCIRICA, Circuit Judge.

In this matter involving competing mass tort class actions in federal and state courts, we address an interlocutory appeal in a complex multidistrict federal class action comprising six million members from an order enjoining a mass opt out of a state class. We will affirm.

I.

The underlying case involves two drugs, both appetite suppressants, fenfluramine—marketed as "Pondimin"—and dexfenfluramine—marketed as "Redux." Both drugs were in great demand. Between 1995 and 1997, four million people took Pondimin and two million people took Redux. In 1997, data came to light suggesting a link between the drugs' use and valvular heart disease. In July 1997, the United States Food and Drug Administration issued a public health advisory alert. On September 15, 1997, American Home Products removed both drugs from the market. Subsequent clinical studies support the view the drugs may cause valvular heart damage.

Following the FDA's issuance of the public health warning, several lawsuits were filed. The number of lawsuits increased exponentially after American Home Products withdrew the diet drugs from the market. Approximately eighteen thousand individual lawsuits and over one hundred putative class actions were filed in federal and state courts around the country. American Home Products removed many of the state cases to federal courts, increasing the number of federal cases. In December 1997, the Judicial Panel for Multidistrict Litigation transferred all the federal actions to Judge Louis Bechtle in the United States District Court for the Eastern District of Pennsylvania, creating Multidistrict Litigation 1203 ("MDL 1203").

In April 1999, American Home Products began "global" settlement talks with plaintiffs in the federal action together with several plaintiffs in similar state class actions. The parties reached a tentative settlement agreement for a nationwide class in November 1999. Known as the "*Brown* class," the proposed class included all persons in the United States, as well as their representatives and dependents, who had ingested either or both of the diet drugs. The global settlement contemplated different kinds of relief, including medical care, medical screening, payments for injury, and refunds of the drugs' purchase price.

The purchase-price-relief provisions were separated into two sections, one for those who had taken the drugs for sixty days or less, the other for those who had taken the drugs for more than sixty days. Short term users were to be paid $30 per month's use of Pondimin, and $60 per month's use of Redux. Long term users would receive the same amounts per month, subject to a $500 cap and the availability of sufficient money in an overall settlement fund. Unlike short term users, long term users were entitled to other benefits, such as medical screening.

The District Court entered an order on November 23, 1999, conditionally certifying a nationwide settlement class and, concurrently, preliminarily approving the settlement. To opt out, a class member was to "sign and submit written notice to the Claims Administrator[s] with a copy to American Home Products, clearly manifesting the Class Member's intent to opt out of the Settlement." The opt-out period extended until March 23, 2000. The court scheduled a fairness hearing for May 1, 2000 on class certification and final settlement approval. On August 28, 2000, the District Court entered a final order certifying the class and approving the settlement.

In July 1997—after the FDA warning, but before American Home Products withdrew the drugs from the market—appellants filed a putative class action in [Hidalgo County,] Texas state court, Gonzalez et al. v. Medeva Pharmaceuticals, Inc., et al. The *Gonzalez* case was one of the first cases filed and preceded the creation of MDL 1203 by several months. The proposed *Gonzalez* class, including all Texas purchasers of the two diet drugs, was a subset of what would become the *Brown* class. The Gonzalez action was limited insofar as it sought actual purchase-price recovery only, together with treble damages under the Texas Deceptive Trade Practices Act–Consumer Protection Act ("DTPA"), Tex. Bus. & Comm.Code, § 17.41 et seq.

[Although the *Gonzalez* complaint did not assert a federal claim, American Home Products removed in early 1998 on ground of diversity, contending that the nondiverse defendant had been fraudulently joined, and the case was transferred under MDL 1203 to Philadelphia. Plaintiffs moved to remand, assuring the federal judge that the nondiverse defendant was a proper defendant, and also claiming that the amount in controversy requirement was not satisfied because they did not seek an award of statutory attorney fees. Eventually, during the MDL 1203 opt-out period in early 2000, the federal judge in Philadelphia granted the motion to remand, finding the nondiverse defendant to be a proper defendant.

A month after remand, the *Gonzalez* plaintiffs filed an amended complaint dropping all claims against the nondiverse defendant and adding a claim for attorney fees. A week after that, the Hidalgo County court certified a class of all who purchased the drugs in Texas. On the same day it certified the class, the Texas court set a hearing for the following morning on plaintiffs' motion to opt all members of the *Gonzalez* class out of *Brown*. At that time, there were eight days remaining before the end of the opt-out period in *Brown*.

Slightly before noon on the following day, American Home Products obtained a TRO from the federal court in Philadelphia to prevent the application to the Texas court. But on the same morning the Texas court granted the order requested by the *Gonzalez* plaintiffs. The Texas court later issued an order "clarifying" that it had acted before the federal court had entered its order.

Shortly after that, American Home Products again removed *Gonzalez* on grounds of diversity. Along with class counsel in *Brown*, it also moved the federal court in Philadelphia for a permanent injunction, and the federal court entered PTO 1227.]

PTO 1227, entitled "Permanent Injunction and Declaration Regarding Purported Class–Wide Opt–Outs," contains two main parts. The first is an injunction directed primarily at counsel for the *Gonzalez* class:

> Counsel for the named plaintiffs in Gonzalez v. Medeva Pharmaceuticals, Inc., et al., originally filed in Hidalgo County, Texas ... and removed to the United States District Court for the Southern District of Texas on March 28, 2000, and all those acting in concert with them, are hereby permanently enjoined from taking any action to effect, secure, or issue notice of any purported class opt out, on behalf of the unnamed absent members of any class which may have been certified in *Gonzalez*, from the class action settlement which this Court has conditionally certified and preliminary [sic] approved. . . .

The second part is declaratory in nature. It states, "Insofar as the Hidalgo County order purports to affect or determine the opt out status of any member of the MDL 1203 class it is null and void and of no effect." The District Court also stated, "The Hidalgo County's order is also null and void and of no effect insofar as it purports to authorize or effect a partial opt-out on behalf of any member of the MDL 1203 class." This was because the Texas order "interfere[d] with [the District] Court's authority to determine the means and methods by which members of such class may elect to opt out of the MDL–1203 class."

[The *Gonzalez* plaintiffs thereafter moved to remand, but the federal judge in Texas referred the issue to the judge in Philadelphia. After the case was transferred to Philadelphia by the MDL Panel, plaintiffs made no further attempt to obtain a remand. But they did appeal PTO 1227.

Thereafter, the district court approved the settlement in *Brown* and, in conjunction with that, issued a blanket injunction against commencement or prosecution of parallel actions in other courts by class members.]

This case illustrates the remarkable extent to which lawsuits can be turned into procedural entanglements. One view of this may be that the actions taken here represent nothing more than astute lawyering. Another is that the legal jockeying employed by both sides exhibits a proclivity to attempt to manipulate the rules for immediate tactical advantage—a use at odds with the purposes of these rules, and one dissonant with the equitable nature of class action proceedings.

Rather than enter this tenebrous world of procedural machinations, we think it preferable to address the *Gonzalez* plaintiffs' main arguments. As we discuss, the District Court's order was an appropriate exercise of its authority regardless of the status of the Texas opt-out order.

IV.

a. Anti-Injunction Act/All Writs Act.

The District Court issued PTO 1227 under the All Writs Act, which provides "all courts established by Act of Congress may issue all writs necessary or appropriate in aid of their respective jurisdictions and agreeable to the usages and principles of law." 28 U.S.C. § 1651. The power granted by the All Writs Act is limited by the Anti–Injunction Act, 28 U.S.C. § 2283, which prohibits, with certain specified exceptions, injunctions by federal courts that have the effect of staying a state court proceeding. Appellants contend the District Court's order was prohibited by the Anti–Injunction Act. American Home Products and the *Brown* plaintiffs claim the injunction falls under one of the Act's exceptions. We hold the District Court's order was not barred by the Anti Injunction Act and was a valid exercise of its power under the All Writs Act.

[Because PTO 1227 had the effect of staying the Texas court's proceedings, it is subject to the Anti–Injunction Act, and the only possibly applicable exception to that Act is the "in aid of jurisdiction" exception. The court recognized that ordinarily in personam actions in state and federal court may proceed concurrently, with the effect of any judgment ultimately rendered determined by preclusion rules. But a federal injunction may issue "to prevent a state court from so interfering with a federal court's consideration or disposition of a case as to seriously impair the federal court's flexibility and authority to decide that case."]

Several factors are relevant to determine whether sufficient interference is threatened to justify an injunction otherwise prohibited by the Anti–Injunction Act. First, we look to the nature of the federal action to determine what kinds of state court interference would sufficiently impair the federal proceeding. Second, we assess the state court's actions, in order to determine whether they present a sufficient threat to the federal action. And finally, we consider principles of federalism and comity, for a primary aim of the Anti–Injunction Act is "to prevent needless friction between the state and federal courts."

We turn first to the nature of the federal action. While, as noted, the "necessary in aid of jurisdiction" exception does not ordinarily permit injunctions merely to prevent duplicative actions in personam, federal courts are permitted to stay later-initiated state court proceedings over the same res in actions in rem, because "the exercise by the state court of jurisdiction over the same res necessarily impairs, and may defeat, the jurisdiction of the federal court already attached." Federal courts may also issue such injunctions to protect exclusive federal jurisdiction of a case that has been removed from state court.

We have recognized another category of federal cases for which state court actions present a special threat to the jurisdiction of the federal court. Under an appropriate set of facts, a federal court entertaining complex litigation, especially when it involves a substantial class of persons from multiple states, or represents a consolidation of cases from multiple districts, may appropriately enjoin state court proceedings in order to protect its jurisdiction. Carlough v. Amchem Prods., Inc., 10 F.3d 189, 202–04 (3d Cir.1993). *Carlough* involved a nationwide class of plaintiffs and several defendants—primarily manufacturers of asbestos-related products—and third-party defendants—primarily insurance providers. We found the complexity of the case to be a substantial factor in justifying the injunction imposed.

Implicit in *Carlough* is the recognition that maintaining "the federal court's flexibility and authority to decide" such complex nationwide cases makes special demands on the court that may justify an injunction otherwise prohibited by the Anti–Injunction Act. Several other courts have concurred.[12] See, e.g., Hanlon v. Chrysler Corp., 150 F.3d 1011 (9th Cir.1998); Winkler [v. Eli Lilly & Co.], 101 F.3d at 1203 [(7th Cir.1996)] ("[T]he Anti–Injunction Act does not bar courts with jurisdiction over complex multidistrict litigation from issuing injunctions to protect the integrity of their rulings."); In re Corrugated Container Antitrust Litig., 659 F.2d 1332, 1334–35 (5th Cir.Unit A 1981) (approving injunction in a "complicated antitrust action [that] has required a great deal of the

---

12. In several cases, courts have analogized complex litigation cases to actions in rem. As one court reasoned, "the district court had before it a class action proceeding so far advanced that it was the virtual equivalent of a res over which the district judge required full control." [In re] Baldwin–United, 770 F.2d at 337 [(2d Cir. 1985)]; see also Battle [v. Liberty Nat'l Life Ins. Co.] 877 F.2d at 882 [(11th Cir.1987)] ("[I]t makes sense to consider this case, involving years of litigation and mountains of paperwork, as similar to a res to be administered."). The in rem analogy may help to bring into focus what makes these cases stand apart. In cases in rem, "the jurisdiction over the same res necessarily impairs, and may defeat, the jurisdiction of the federal court already attached." Similarly, where complex cases are sufficiently developed, mere exercise of parallel jurisdiction by the state court may present enough of a threat to the jurisdiction of the federal court to justify issuance of an injunction. See *Baldwin-United*, 770 F.2d at 337 (noting such cases, like cases in rem, are ones in which "it is intolerable to have conflicting orders from different courts").

district court's time and has necessitated that it maintain a flexible approach in resolving the various claims of the many parties.").

This is not to say that class actions are, by virtue of that categorization alone, exempt from the general rule that in personam cases must be permitted to proceed in parallel. Federal courts ordinarily refrain from enjoining a state action even where the state court is asked to approve a settlement substantially similar to one the federal court has already rejected. That a state court may resolve an issue first (which may operate as res judicata), is not by itself a sufficient threat to the federal court's jurisdiction that justifies an injunction, unless the proceedings in state courts threaten to "frustrate proceedings and disrupt the orderly resolution of the federal litigation." Still, while the potentially preclusive effects of the state action may not themselves justify an injunction, they might do so indirectly. If, for example, the possibility of an earlier state court judgment is disruptive to settlement negotiations in federal court, the existence of the state court action might sufficiently interfere with the federal court's flexibility to justify an injunction.

The threat to the federal court's jurisdiction posed by parallel state actions is particularly significant where there are conditional class certifications and impending settlements in federal actions. Many—though not all—of the cases permitting injunctions in complex litigation cases involve injunctions issued as the parties approached settlement. Complex cases in the later stages—where, for instance, settlement negotiations are underway—embody an enormous amount of time and expenditure of resources. It is in the nature of complex litigation that the parties often seek complicated, comprehensive settlements to resolve as many claims as possible in one proceeding. These cases are especially vulnerable to parallel state actions that may "frustrate the district court's efforts to craft a settlement in the multi-district litigation before it," thereby destroying the ability to achieve the benefits of consolidation. In complex cases where certification or settlement has received conditional approval, or perhaps even where settlement is pending, the challenges facing the overseeing court are such that it is likely that almost any parallel litigation in other fora presents a genuine threat to the jurisdiction of the federal court.

This case amply highlights these concerns. MDL 1203 represented the consolidation of over two thousand cases that had been filed in or removed to federal court. The *Brown* class finally certified comprised six million members. The District Court entered well over one thousand orders in the case. This massive consolidation enabled the possibility of a global resolution that promised to minimize the various difficulties associated with duplicative and competing lawsuits. The central events in this dispute occurred after two years of exhaustive work by the parties and the District Court, and after a conditional class certification and preliminary settlement had been negotiated and approved by the District Court. There can be no doubt that keeping this enormously complicated settlement process on track required careful management by the District Court. Any state court action that might interfere with the District

Court's oversight of the settlement at that time, given the careful balancing it embodied, was a serious threat to the District Court's ability to manage the final stages of this complex litigation.[13] Duplicative and competing actions were substantially more likely to "frustrate proceedings and disrupt the orderly resolution" of this dispute at the time PTO 1227 was issued than they would be in ordinary actions in personam. This is especially true where, as here, the litigants in state court have the ability to tailor their state actions to the terms of the pending federal settlement.

Determining the applicability of the *Carlough* rule also requires assessment of the character of the state court action, for we must assess the level of interference with the federal action actually threatened by the state court proceeding. In *Carlough*, our approval of the injunction was supported by the direct threat to the federal action the state court action represented. After the district court had provisionally certified the *Carlough* class, and after a preliminary settlement had been negotiated and presented to the court, a parallel action was filed in West Virginia. As here, the plaintiffs in that case—Gore v. Amchem Products, Inc.— sought an order of the state court opting out the members of the West Virginia class from the federal class. They also sought a declaration that *Carlough* would not be binding on the members of the West Virginia class.

We viewed the filing of the West Virginia action as an intentional "preemptive strike" against the federal action. The purpose of the West Virginia filing was "to challenge the propriety of the federal class action." Id. We found "it difficult to imagine a more detrimental effect upon the district court's ability to effectuate the settlement of this complex and far-reaching matter then would occur if the West Virginia state court was permitted to make a determination regarding the validity of the federal settlement."

* * *

The interference that would have been caused by the Hidalgo County court's order implicates the same concerns that animated our decision in *Carlough*. The Texas court's order directly affected the identity of the parties to MDL 1203 and did so contrary to a previous District Court order. It sought to "declare what the federal court should and should not do with respect to the federal settlement." Furthermore, as in *Carlough*, the Texas order would have created confusion among those who were members of both the federal and the state classes. It would be difficult to discern which, if any, action one was a party to,

---

13. Among other vulnerabilities, it is worth highlighting one example. The settlement agreement in this case expressly permitted American Home Products to terminate the settlement agreement, at its discretion, based on the number of opt outs. That provision was, of course, created with the complicated opt-out provisions crafted specifically for MDL 1203 in mind. External actions that would disturb that balance, by altering the number of opt outs through a different mechanism, clearly would substantially interfere with MDL 1203.

especially since the Texas order was entered during, and shortly before the end of, the MDL 1203 opt-out period.

[The court rejected the argument that the order entered by the Texas suit presented a situation different from *Carlough* because *Gonzalez* had been filed before *Brown* was filed. The key act in *Gonzalez* was not the filing of the suit but the motion for a class-wide opt-out order, and that occurred after *Brown* was at an advanced stage.]

Because an injunction must be necessary in aid of jurisdiction to fall under this application to the Anti–Injunction Act, it is important to carefully tailor such injunctions to meet the needs of the case. Notably, the relief we approved in *Carlough* was substantially broader than the relief granted by the District Court here. The federal order in *Carlough* enjoined the West Virginia plaintiffs, as well as their attorneys and representatives, from pursuing the *Gore* action or initiating similar litigation in any other forum. The injunction in *Carlough* effectively stayed the entire parallel state action, not only the attempted opt out, or other portions directed squarely at the federal action. Here, by contrast, the District Court's order enjoined only the pursuit of the attempted mass opt out-the part of *Gonzalez* that unquestionably interfered with the management of MDL 1203. It did not prevent the *Gonzalez* plaintiffs from individually opting out. Furthermore, the injunction was not directed at a proceeding in which plaintiffs had merely requested relief that threatened to interfere with the federal action, it was directed at a proceeding in which the state court had actually granted such a request, making the interference substantially more manifest. Under these circumstances, we find the District Court's injunction to be well within its "sound discretion."

The propriety of an injunction directed at the Texas order is also consistent with considerations of federalism and comity. The Texas plaintiffs who wished to opt out of the *Brown* class were given an adequate opportunity to individually opt out of the federal action, a factor we found significant in *Carlough*. As such, Texas residents retained the option to commence lawsuits in the forum of their choice. Furthermore, the injunction only prevented application of a particular order that was directed squarely at the federal action. It did not so much interfere with the state court proceeding as prevent state court interference with the federal proceeding. Failing to act on the Hidalgo County order threatened to "create the very 'needless friction between state and federal courts' which the Anti Injunction Act was designed to prevent." "While the Anti–Injunction Act is designed to avoid disharmony between federal and state systems, the exception in § 2283 reflects congressional recognition that injunctions may sometimes be necessary in order to avoid that disharmony."

* * *

Our holding that PTO 1227 was necessary in aid of the District Court's jurisdiction for purposes of the Anti-Injunction Act necessarily implies it was authorized under the All Writs Act as well. For the All

Writs Act grants federal courts the authority to issue all writs "necessary or appropriate in aid" of a court's jurisdiction. 28 U.S.C. § 1651(a). * * *

b. Full Faith and Credit Act.

[The *Gonzalez* plaintiffs argued that the federal court was obligated to give full faith and credit to the Texas court's order. The court rejected this argument on the ground that Texas law does not extend preclusive effect to orders that are "collateral or incidental to the main suit," such as the order in question.]

c. The Rooker–Feldman Doctrine.

Appellants claim PTO 1227 exceeded the District Court's authority under the related *Rooker-Feldman* doctrine, which prohibits review of state court decisions by federal courts other than the United States Supreme Court. D.C. Court of Appeals v. Feldman, 460 U.S. 462, 103 S.Ct. 1303, 75 L.Ed.2d 206 (1983); Rooker v. Fidelity Trust Co., 263 U.S. 413, 44 S.Ct. 149, 68 L.Ed. 362 (1923). [See *supra* p. 183 n. 6] According to the *Gonzalez* plaintiffs, the District Court did so in declaring the Texas order "null and void and without effect."

Under the *Rooker-Feldman* doctrine, inferior federal courts lack subject matter jurisdiction to review, directly or indirectly, state court adjudications. Review of such adjudications must be pursued in the state appellate system, and, if necessary, by way of review of the state's highest court in the United States Supreme Court.

In most cases, where consideration of an issue is precluded under the *Rooker-Feldman* doctrine, the issue will also be res judicata, and therefore precluded from consideration under the Full Faith and Credit Clause. * * *

We need not decide here the extent to which the doctrine is to apply to other kinds of interlocutory orders—and, in particular, procedural ones—because we believe, in any event, the District Court's order did not constitute "review" for purposes of the *Rooker-Feldman* doctrine.

American Home Products argues—correctly in our view—that the District Court did not review the Texas opt-out order, it simply applied its indisputable authority to determine the opt-out rules for the plaintiff class before it, and to determine who had properly opted out under those rules. Making determinations concerning the identity of the parties to a case before it is at the core of the District Court's authority. The Texas opt-out order purported to make a determination with respect to the parties to the federal action. It was, in other words, effectively an attempt to make an interlocutory procedural ruling in a case pending before another court.

* * *

The *Rooker-Feldman* doctrine does not work to defeat a district court's authority over the management of its own case. Because PTO

1227 did not reach beyond that authority, it did not run afoul of the *Rooker-Feldman* doctrine.

Appellants' approach would permit a state court to issue orders directed squarely at the inner workings of federal cases, subject only to reversal by superior state courts and the United States Supreme Court. This approach would undermine the federalism values the doctrine seeks to protect. We have recognized the doctrine seeks to preserve finality and respect for state courts. But permitting a state court to interfere with a federal court's management of its cases would serve neither purpose and would facilitate the kind of interference between state and federal courts the doctrine is meant to avoid. Accordingly, we hold that where, as here, a federal court's proper exercise of its jurisdiction to manage its cases has the secondary effect of voiding a state court determination, it is not a review of that order for purposes of the *Rooker-Feldman* doctrine.

Notes and Questions

1. Concern about overlapping class actions began to increase in the mid–1990s, but the difficulties it can cause are not new. Recall In re Baldwin–United Corp., *supra* p. 199. To take a prominent example, in In re Federal Skywalk Cases, 97 F.R.D. 370 (W.D.Mo.1983), there were simultaneous plaintiff class actions in state and federal court asserting claims resulting from the collapse of a skywalk in the lobby of the Kansas City Hyatt Regency Hotel. Shortly before Christmas, 1982, as the country was in a recession, defendants and the state-court plaintiffs presented a proposed settlement to the state court judge under which any person present in the hotel at the time of the collapse could receive an immediate payment of $1,000 in return for a full release without having to make any proof of injury. The state court tentatively approved the settlement and the sending of notice to class members. Immediately after the state court hearing, the plaintiffs called a press conference to publicize the settlement. On the following day, two named plaintiffs from the state-court suit appeared with their lawyers on a nationally televised morning news show to discuss the proposed settlement. With economic times tough, and Christmas approaching, $1,000 in cash may have looked good to many class members.

Neither the federal judge nor class counsel in the federal-court class action had been told about the proposed settlement of the state-court suit. But the federal court was immediately inundated with inquiries about it, and the number of opt-outs from the federal action increased substantially. The federal judge held defendants in contempt for their role in the state-court settlement proceedings, in part for failing to apprise the state-court judge of all pertinent developments in the federal case. The federal judge reasoned:

> If this Court permits the defendants to make an end-run around its supervisory authority, the principle that will be established for future class actions is unconscionable. Defendants would, from this day forward, be free to select the counsel of their choice in attempting to defeat a class action. If one group of counsel did not agree with them, they would be at liberty to persuade another group of counsel to file a class action in another forum where jurisdiction is possible.

Accordingly, the federal judge invalidated all opt-outs from the federal case received after announcement of the state-court settlement and provided that any class members who had received $1,000 from defendants could keep the money as an "advance" on any future recovery in the federal case.

2. The current concern about overlapping class actions is not about evasion of federal court by defendants but rather, as in *Diet Drugs*, about plaintiff counsel who file additional class actions. If these filings are in federal court, the risk of conflicting orders is minimized by the power of the MDL Panel to transfer all the actions to a single judge. See Note, the Judicial Panel and the Conduct of Multidistrict Litigation, 87 Harv.L.Rev. 1001, 1010 & n. 41 (1974) (asserting that the Panel had, by that date, transferred all cases involving potentially overlapping class actions to a single judge).

The problem, then, arises when a class action in a state court overlaps with one in a federal court, as was true in *Diet Drugs*. In such situations, one concern is that plaintiff counsel may be "shopping" the case seeking a judge willing to certify a large class, perhaps a nationwide class. It was sometimes said that such counsel would seek out certain state courts known for "drive-by certifications." Because their independence of action would be compromised if the case were in federal court, such counsel might attempt to design their state-court cases to make them immune from removal. Do you see reasons to suspect something of the sort was afoot in *Diet Drugs*? Why did plaintiffs there initially sue the nondiverse defendant and forgo attorneys' fees?

3. *The Class Action Fairness Act*: The Class Action Fairness Act of 2004 was designed in part to nullify such efforts by making state-court class actions removable based on minimal diversity. The Act, which had been introduced in somewhat similar form in each session of Congress from 1998 to 2004, passed the House in 2003, and awaited an expected vote in the Senate when this book went to press. Strongly supported by business interests (and opposed by consumer, civil rights, environmental, and plaintiff attorneys' organizations), the bill contains procedural changes that are likely to continue to hang over class action practice whether or not it becomes law. The Act adopts a "minimal diversity" standard for federal court jurisdiction, allowing federal courts to hear class actions so long as any member of the plaintiff class is a citizen of a state different from that of any defendant.

Under current jurisdictional rules, many state-law class actions, including those involving parties from different states, are not eligible for federal-court jurisdiction because of the complete diversity requirement the courts found in 28 U.S.C. § 1332. Although only the citizenship of the named plaintiff(s) is to be considered for purposes of determining if diversity exists, class counsel who want to avoid removal to federal court can often structure a suit so that at least some of the defendants are citizens of the same state as some class representatives. In addition, the jurisdictional minimum requirement has been interpreted to forbid aggregation of smaller claims of class members to satisfy the $75,000 requirement. For further discussion of these issues, see Subject Matter Jurisdiction Limitations on State–Law Class Actions, *infra* p. 427.

The Class Action Fairness Act proposes to overcome those jurisdictional limitations so long as minimal diversity exists and the aggregate claims reach a certain amount. The proponents of the Act's expansion of federal-court jurisdiction argued that it was urgently needed because, under the existing regime, counsel can avoid federal court by filing in certain "magnet" state courts that have reputations for being pro-plaintiff and applying loose standards for class certification. This has meant, they argued, that class actions against national corporations in magnet venues would determine the proper standards that would govern the corporations's activities nationwide. Further, they expressed the concern that the existing system allowed over-lapping, conflicting, and duplicative class actions to be filed in multiple jurisdictions and that only the federal courts had available the MDL procedure for transferring and consolidating cases across state lines.

Opponents of the Act, on the other hand, maintained that a broad minimal diversity standard would sweep into federal court many cases in which there was no federal interest outweighing the interest of the forum state where the cause of action arose under its law. They viewed the Act as violating the principles of federalism by denying state courts the right to apply their own class-action rules in cases involving their own citizens and their own laws. They argued that state courts are capable of properly conducting class actions and that, in fact, the abuses of some magnet-venue state courts are currently being addressed by the legislatures and higher courts of those states.

The Act did include restrictions on minimal diversity jurisdiction for class actions, requiring that there be $5 million in controversy and 100 class members. In addition, it proposed to except class actions based on state law in which the primary defendant and two-thirds of the members of the plaintiff class are residents of the forum state. Opponents argued that these provisions were inadequate to keep many class actions in which there is no significant federal interest from being subject to removal to federal court.

4. Is it always true that state courts will be less careful or protective than federal courts? Reynolds v. Beneficial National Bank, 288 F.3d 277 (7th Cir.2002), involved a settlement of a federal class action that was enforced by a federal injunction against prosecution of a class action in a Texas state court. But in this instance the Texas case was set for trial and seemed to offer class members a much better recovery than the federal-court settlement. Indeed, there were intimations that the federal-court class settlement was arranged to reduce the settlement value of the Texas case. "Remarkably in view of the progress and promise of the Texas suit relative to the half-hearted efforts of the settlement class counsel, the district judge enjoined the Texas suit." Id. at 283. The district judge also enjoined the lawyers for the Texas class from notifying the members of that class about the status of the Texas action to assist them in deciding whether to opt out of the settlement being considered in federal court. Finding that the district judge had improperly approved the dubious settlement, the Seventh Circuit reversed and ordered that the injunction against the Texas case be vacated.

5. One alternative to dueling orders is cooperation. For discussion of examples of cooperation between federal judges and state-court judges, see Schwarzer, Weiss & Hirsch, Judicial Federalism in Action: Coordination of

Litigation in State and Federal Courts, 78 Va.L.Rev. 1689 (1992); Manual for Complex Litigation (4th) §§ 20.3–20.31. Might this approach have been helpful in *Diet Drugs*?

6. Despite all these concerns, the court in *Diet Drugs* emphasizes some remarkable features of that litigation to justify the order there. There were over 2,000 cases consolidated before a single federal court that had before it a class of over six million and had already entered 1,000 orders in that case. How often would such circumstances be presented? One example was Carlough v. Amchem Prods., Inc., 10 F.3d 189 (3d Cir.1993), involving an injunction entered by the federal district court in *Amchem, supra* p. 372, to prevent a dissident plaintiff lawyer from obtaining a state-court order that would result in the secession of all the West Virginians in that nationwide class action.

More generally, injunctive power has been upheld in the context of imminent settlement of actions consolidated by the MDL Panel. In re Baldwin–United Corp., *supra* p. 199; see also In re Joint E. & S. Dists. Asbestos Litig., 120 B.R. 648 (Bkrtcy., E. & S.D.N.Y.1990), rev'd on other grounds, In re Johns–Manville Corp., 27 F.3d 48 (2d Cir.1994).

But most cases do not present such circumstances. Consider In re General Motors Corp. Pick–Up Truck Fuel Tank Prod. Liabil. Lit., 134 F.3d 133 (3d Cir.1998). The district court, presiding over an MDL coordination in Philadelphia, approved a nationwide class action settlement of this action charging that G.M. pickup trucks were unsafe because of the placement of the fuel tank. The Third Circuit reversed, however, on the ground (later rejected by the Supreme Court in *Amchem, supra* p. 372 that settlement classes could only be certified in circumstances in which a litigation class would be allowed. After the Third Circuit remanded for further proceedings, some plaintiffs' lawyers "repaired to the 18th Judicial District for the Parish of Iberville, Louisiana, where a similar suit had been pending, restructured their deal, and submitted it to the Louisiana court, which ultimately approved it" as a nationwide class action.

Dissident class members asked the federal judge in Philadelphia to enjoin the proceedings in state court in Louisiana, but the judge refused. The Third Circuit affirmed, distinguishing its earlier decision in *Carlough, supra*:

> Here, none of the *Carlough* circumstances exist. There is no class-wide settlement pending before the district court (indeed, the conditional class certification by the district court no longer subsists), and no stipulation of settlement or prospect of settlement in that court is imminent. Furthermore, it simply cannot be said that the Louisiana court is attempting to dictate to the district court the scope and terms of a settlement, since none is pending before the district court. Finally, there can be no confusion by class members [due to receipt of competing notices from the state and federal courts], for only one set of notices has been sent out (from the Louisiana court).

Id. at 145. The plaintiffs in the MDL proceeding could opt out of the Louisiana class action. Accordingly, the injunction would not be in aid of jurisdiction. The court did note, however, that unless the Louisiana settlement approval was overturned, except for those who opted out of that case, "no court will have any plaintiffs left with which to proceed."

Would an injunction be warranted under *Diet Drugs* to constrain a parallel state-court class action if one had been filed, for example, in Smilow v. Southwestern Bell Mobile Systems, *supra* p. 257, or in In re Monumental Life. Ins. Co., *supra* p. 318? For further discussion of these problems, see Sherman, Complimentary Devices to Prevent Duplicative Litigation, 1995 B.Y.U. L.Rev. 943.

7. In *Diet Drugs*, the federal court had certified a nationwide class action, while the Texas state court had certified an in-state class action. Under *Castano*, *supra* p. 340, which certification is easier to justify? Should federal courts defer to state-court statewide class actions? Note that the proposed Class Action Fairness Act of 2004 seems to recognize the legitimacy of state courts entertaining statewide class actions from its removal provisions. The Act (see *supra* note 3) attempted to limit the broad sweep of minimal diversity federal-court jurisdiction to larger class actions (those with more than $5 million in controversy and 100 class members) and to exclude even those class actions if state interests were paramount (e.g., those based on the forum's law and in which the primary defendant and two-thirds of the plaintiff class members were residents of the forum state). But that would mean, for example, that a class action in a Texas state court brought under Texas consumer protection, tort, or environmental laws against a national corporation that was incorporated in Delaware and whose principal place of business was in New York that injured Texas residents by its activities in Texas could be removed to federal court.

8. When there are parallel class actions, the entry of final judgment in one may lead to preclusion in the other. Ordinarily, a state-court class action judgment is res judicata against the claims of class members in a federal-court class action, even if the federal action includes claims within exclusive federal jurisdiction. See Matsushita Electric Indus. Co. v. Epstein, *infra* p. 803. But that is only true if state preclusion law would foreclose the federal claims. See In re Lease Oil Antitrust Litigation, 200 F.3d 317 (5th Cir.2000) (refusing to order dismissal of federal-court class action claims based on settlement of Alabama state-court class action on grounds that Alabama preclusion law does not call for preclusion regarding claims outside the jurisdiction of the Alabama courts).

If the federal case reaches final judgment, another exception of the Anti–Injunction Act, comes into play, because the federal court may then act "to protect or effectuate its judgments." In In re Prudential Ins. Co. Sales Practices Litigation, 314 F.3d 99 (3d Cir.2002), class members obtained the relief that was available under the ADR procedure specified in the settlement but then filed individual actions in state court seeking more, claiming that the ADR procedures were inadequate. Although plaintiffs contended that they were objecting to events that occurred after judgment was entered, the appellate court upheld an injunction based on the "relitigation exception" to the Act because "plaintiffs' claims here constitute a direct challenge to the system of remedies specified in the class action settlement."

9. Could the relitigation exception to the Anti–Injunction Act be applied to federal-court orders entered before final judgment? That might be a way to restrict "shopping" for lax class certification attitudes of state courts. In In re Bridgestone/Firestone, Inc., Tires Products Liability Lit., 333 F.3d

763 (7th Cir.2003), the court directed an injunction against all members of a putative class forbidding them from seeking nationwide class certification in another court after the federal court decided that nationwide class certification would be improper given the differences among the laws of many states. See In re Bridgestone/Firestone, Inc., Tires Products Liability Litig., *infra* p. 429. But at least five proposed nationwide class actions were filed in various state courts by lawyers who had been involved in the federal case. One state court judge certified a nationwide class on the day the complaint was filed, without awaiting a response from the defendants and without explaining the certification.

Defendants responded by asking the district judge to enjoin all other class actions, nationwide or otherwise, and the district judge refused. Defendants appealed, and the court of appeals held that an injunction was appropriate to forbid further pursuit of nationwide class certification despite the strictures of the Anti–Injunction Act, but that plaintiffs could pursue statewide class actions. Because its earlier decision had held nationwide class certification improper, the court relied on issue preclusion on the ground its earlier decision was sufficiently final even though the litigation in which it was rendered continued. The decision focused directly on "shopping" class certification (id. at 766–67):

> Relitigation can turn even an unlikely outcome into reality. Suppose that every state in the nation would as a matter of first principles deem inappropriate a nationwide class covering these claims and products. What this might mean in practice is something like "9 of 10 judges in every state would rule against certifying a nationwide class." * * * Although the 10% that see things otherwise are a distinct minority, one is bound to turn up if plaintiffs file enough suits—and, if one nationwide class *is* certified, then all the no-certification decisions fade into insignificance. A single positive trumps all the negatives. * * * Section 2283 permits a federal court to issue an injunction to stop such a process in its tracks and hold *both* sides to a fully litigated outcome, rather than perpetuating an asymmetric system in which class counsel can win but never lose.

Is this a proper reading of the relitigation clause? Does it bind class members to an implicit ruling that class counsel were adequate in the prior proceedings in the federal case? Should it matter if counsel who brought the state-court cases had different arguments, or if the state-court standards for class certification were different?

F. CLASS ACTION REMEDIES

Devising a proper remedy for a class often requires considerable ingenuity. Recall In re Monumental Life Ins. Co., *supra* p. 318. As we have seen, courts may certify classes despite the existence of non-common issues among various members and despite the fact that the ultimate remedy may not be clearly ascertainable at the time of certification. A recurring concern is whether individual differences between various class members must always be taken into account or whether a broad classwide remedy, ideally based on an easily ascertainable formula, can be devised.

SIMER v. RIOS

United States Court of Appeals, Seventh Circuit, 1981.
661 F.2d 655.

Before SWYGERT, SENIOR CIRCUIT JUDGE, and PELL and WOOD, CIRCUIT JUDGES.

HARLINGTON WOOD, JR., CIRCUIT JUDGE.

[The portion of this opinion dealing with problems of certification of a class of persons eligible for assistance under the Crisis Intervention Program who were either refused or discouraged from applying because of invalid regulations is contained *supra* at p. 231.]

Another possible procedural alternative, and one which actually is reflected in the settlement decree, is the use of a fluid recovery. The fluid recovery is used where the individuals injured are not likely to come forward and prove their claims or cannot be given notice of the case. In a fluid recovery the money is either distributed through a market system in the way of reduced charges or is used to fund a project which will likely benefit the members of the class.

Plaintiffs similarly contend that in the instant case the fluid recovery remedy will provide redress for the general class of individuals harmed by defendants' conduct. In raising this contention plaintiffs rely on *Bebchick v. Public Utilities Commission,* 318 F.2d 187 (D.C.Cir.) *(en banc), cert. denied,* 373 U.S. 913, 83 S.Ct. 1304, 10 L.Ed.2d 414 (1963).

Bebchick concerned a challenge to a rate increase by the Washington, D.C. transit system. The court of appeals invalidated the rate increase and in a supplemental opinion addressed the issue of how to structure a judgment to carry out the opinion of the court—since the illegal rate had been in effect for a time prior to invalidation. The court acknowledged that it was not possible to order refunds to individuals who had paid the increased fare. Nevertheless, the court ordered that the Transit should utilize the money for the benefit of the users of the system.

The analogy of *Bebchick* to the present case is not unfounded. Yet, we believe that an analysis of the fluid recovery mechanism must take a more critical tack. Plaintiffs apparently contend that the harmed individuals cannot be identified and therefore a fluid recovery should be utilized. Strictly speaking, plaintiffs' contention proves too much. It sets forth no criteria for determining when class certification is unnecessary and when the requirements of class certification may be restructured. Indeed, to accept plaintiffs' position would be to ignore the requirements of Rule 23, such as whether an identifiable class exists and whether notice to the class can be executed.[40] Therefore, we reject any approach

---

40. There can be little doubt that the use of a fluid recovery mechanism allows a court to avoid some of the manageability problems in a Rule 23(b)(3) class action. See *Windham* [*v. American Brands, Inc.*], 565 F.2d at 72 (cannot use fluid recovery to

which would automatically utilize a fluid recovery mechanism as a procedural alternative to class action disposition.

At the other extreme is the position that a fluid recovery mechanism is unconstitutional. The argument raised is that it violates defendant's right to trial by jury. In *Windham v. American Brands, Inc.,* 565 F.2d 59, 72 (4th Cir.1977), the Fourth Circuit Court of Appeals apparently rejected the use of a fluid recovery. The court stated:

> Nor ... can the difficulties inherent in proving individual damages be avoided by use of a form of "fluid recovery." Such a method of computing damages in a class action has been branded as "illegal, inadmissible as a solution of the manageability problems of class actions and wholly improper."

We need not adopt either of the two extreme positions—that is, whether a fluid recovery always can be used to surmount problems in the going forward of a class action or whether a fluid recovery is per se unconstitutional.[42] Rather, we believe that a careful case-by-case analysis of use of the fluid recovery mechanism is the better approach. In this approach we focus on the various substantive policies that use of a fluid recovery would serve in the particular case. The general inquiry is whether the use of such a mechanism is consistent with the policy or policies reflected by the statute violated. This matter can be more particularized into an assessment of to what extent the statute embodies policies of deterrence, disgorgement, and compensation.

First, we focus on whether a fluid recovery is needed to deter the defendant from illegal conduct. We think not. CSA has been charged with administering a large and complex program and it is inevitable that problems arise. While in no way do we applaud or encourage the passage of invalid regulations, there is no indication that CSA's actions have been in bad faith or with the specific intent of disobeying its statutory obligation. This is not a case where the defendant has intentionally violated a statute which was intended to regulate socially opprobrious conduct—such as that reflected in the antitrust or securities laws. Thus, the deterrence factor weighs against the use of a fluid recovery.

The second factor, that of disgorging illegally obtained profits, also counsels against use of a fluid recovery. Those cases where a corporate defendant engages in unlawful conduct and illegally profits is most appropriate for a fluid recovery. In this manner, the *Bebchick* decision also involved the disgorging of profits illegally obtained. The transit system of Washington relied on private investment and profits were

---

avoid manageability problems inherent in proving individualized damages).

42. Another objection raised to the use of a fluid recovery is that it alters the substantive rights of the defendant and therefore exceeds the scope of the Rules Enabling Act. In *Al Barnett & Son, Inc. v. Outboard Marine Corp.,* 64 F.R.D. 43 (D.Del.1974), the court refused to certify a class because common issues did not predominate, the issues of injury and damage being individual to each class member. The court rejected use of a fluid recovery holding that it would alter the substantive law of antitrust by essentially eliminating plaintiffs' proof of injury and damage. Such a result, the court stated, would exceed the scope of the Rules Enabling Act.

returned to investors. The court of appeals properly ordered that the Transit not retain the illegally obtained profits. In the present case neither CSA, nor any shareholders, benefited financially from its allegedly illegal conduct. Rather, if anything, CSA would have been able to disburse more funds had the regulation not been in effect. The money CSA refused to spend merely reverted to the Treasury. In sum, this is not a case where the defendant would retain illegally obtained profits— once the termination date of the program passed CSA no longer had the money to spend and did not benefit from its unlawful conduct.

The final factor, whether the statute has a compensatory purpose, does weigh in favor of fluid recovery. The Act authorizing CSA to administer assistance programs had as its chief aim assisting low income individuals in dealing with the high cost of energy. Indeed, the purpose of the statute is purely compensatory.

However, we believe that even this factor does not clearly require fluid recovery. For fiscal year 1980 Congress funded a much larger energy assistance program and therefore absence of fluid recovery will not deprive plaintiffs of relief. * * *

In light of these three factors we believe that the use of a fluid recovery mechanism is not necessary to further the substantive policies at issue. The policies of deterrence and disgorgement are inapplicable and therefore weigh heavily against fluid recovery. To be sure, the compensatory policy is seriously implicated by the withholding of this relief. Yet, as we note above, the needy individuals continued to receive assistance through appropriations for 1980. Thus, even the compensatory policy does not definitively lead one to conclude that fluid recovery is needed. In sum, the relevant policies weigh against fluid recovery.

Notes and Questions

1. Judge Swygert dissented in Simer v. Rios, arguing as follows: "The statute's purpose, to reduce the impact of high energy costs on low income people including the elderly and near poor, is served by [using fluid recovery]. Further, a fluid recovery is necessary in the instant case, where providing individual recovery would be difficult and procedurally costly but where such a recovery would remedy, at least in part, the wrong suffered by the class members as a result of the invalid regulation." Is it significant to this analysis that defendants apparently derived no profit from their violation of federal guidelines? Is fluid recovery needed to accomplish the goals of the statute?

2. The idea behind fluid recovery is to determine in the aggregate the damages suffered by the class, thus vastly simplifying the task of managing class actions. In Eisen v. Carlisle & Jacquelin, 417 U.S. 156, 172 n. 10, 94 S.Ct. 2140, 2150 n. 10, 40 L.Ed.2d 732 (1974), the Supreme Court carefully reserved passing on the fluid recovery issue. Congress, meanwhile, has seemed sympathetic to the approach in certain situations. Thus, the Hart–Scott–Rodino Antitrust Improvements Act of 1976 provides that state attorneys general can sue for "aggregate damages" sustained by citizens of their states, based on a "reasonable system of estimating aggregate damages."

During the Congressional consideration of this statute, it was even proposed, albeit unsuccessfully, that the statute provide such a damage measure in all antitrust class actions. See Handler, Antitrust—Myth and Reality in an Inflationary Era, 50 N.Y.U.L.Rev. 211, 255 (1975). If the device can be used in a suit by a public official, why not in a suit brought by a private person found by the court to be an adequate representative?

Opposition to fluid recovery has been vigorous. Consider the views of Judge Medina in Eisen v. Carlisle & Jacquelin, 479 F.2d 1005 (2d Cir.1973), vac'd and remanded, 417 U.S. 156, 94 S.Ct. 2140, 40 L.Ed.2d 732 (1974): "Even if amended Rule 23 could be read so as to permit any such fantastic procedure, the courts would have to reject it as an unconstitutional violation of the requirement of due process of law. * * * We hold the 'fluid recovery' concept and practice to be illegal, inadmissible as a solution of the manageability problems of class actions and wholly improper." Are serious due process issues involved? Is it significant that when settlements of class actions are negotiated the parties in essence bargain in fluid recovery terms—discussing figures that would be paid for a classwide settlement?

For a more receptive approach to fluid class recovery, see State of California v. Levi Strauss & Co., 41 Cal.3d 460, 224 Cal.Rptr. 605, 715 P.2d 564 (1986) (court tries to provide "a source of guidance * * * for other courts in confronting the largely uncharted area of fluid recovery in consumer class actions"). In Gordon v. Boden, 224 Ill.App.3d 195, 166 Ill.Dec. 503, 586 N.E.2d 461 (1991), the court held that fluid recovery could be used in Illinois state-court class actions, quoting Simer v. Rios. Plaintiffs sued on behalf of a nationwide class of consumers, claiming that defendants had disseminated adulterated orange juice. The court stressed the "it must be remembered that this is a consumer class action. Our courts have recognized that, '[i]n a large and impersonal society, class actions are often the last barricade of consumer protection.' The consumer class action is an inviting procedural device to address frauds that cause small damages to large groups." 166 Ill.Dec. at 509, 586 N.E.2d at 467.

3. Some sort of fluid recovery approach may be the only realistic way to provide a remedy in a consumer class action. For example, in In re Compact Disc Minimum Advertised Price Antitrust Litigation, 216 F.R.D. 197 (D.Me.2003), over fifty private class actions against distributors and retailers of CDs for antitrust violations through illegal overcharges averaging 23 cents per CD were consolidated by the MDL Panel in the federal district court in Maine. The aggregate amount of the overcharges was estimated at between $103 and $245 million. The judge approved a class settlement valued at $143 million that would pay some $13 to each claimant who had completed a sworn affidavit on line that she had purchased CDs. The defendants would also distribute 5.6 million CDs for public use in libraries and educational institutions on a pro rata basis to every state (to encompass a wide range of musical genres and not simply "discount bin" items). The judge rejected an argument by objecting class members that an all-cash settlement was required, noting that "people do not keep records to remember or prove their purchases" and that "where a case settlement will not reach every injured member of the class and administratively cannot be calibrated reliably to the actual loss suffered by each member—there is positive value to the class members in the so-called 'cy pres program' that

the parties have developed." However, he rejected that part of the settlement that gave coupon discounts to class members who had purchased CDs through clubs, finding no evidence that they were likely to be used or of benefit. (In comparison, a class action settlement in a suit against H & R Block that provided for discounts on services and tax software was rejected as being of little value. See H & R Block Accord Draws Fire, Wall St.J., Dec. 24, 2002.) Finally, the judge found that, given the risks of litigation, the value of the settlement (estimated at $143 million) was appropriate, even though it was only about 58% of the potential recovery estimated by plaintiffs' expert.

4. The fluid recovery approach should be contrasted with a classwide formula method of determining individual damages. In a price-fixing case, for example, once the amount of illegal price inflation is determined, the measurement of individual damages becomes a matter of arithmetic. Defendants retain the right to challenge any class member's assertion that he bought the claimed quantity of the price-fixed product, but once that is established the determination of his recovery becomes automatic. Is this approach significantly different from a fluid recovery approach for due process purposes?

In some instances, the law itself may provide a formula. For example, in Six Mexican Workers v. Arizona Citrus Growers, 904 F.2d 1301 (9th Cir. 1990), plaintiffs sued on behalf of a class of undocumented Mexican workers, claiming that defendants failed to comply with the Farm Labor Contractor Registration Act (FLCRA). Having found violations of a number of provisions of the Act, the district court awarded set amounts per plaintiff for each such violation. The Ninth Circuit affirmed, despite objections that this was an improper use of the fluid recovery concept, rejecting defendant's reliance on cases refusing to use the method in antitrust cases (id. at 1306):

> The plaintiff class sought statutory not actual damages. Statutory damages under FLCRA, unlike damages under the antitrust laws * * * are not dependent on proof of actual injury. Congress intended these damages to promote enforcement of FLCRA and deter future violations. Therefore, the district court was not obligated to require individual proof of injury from each class member. The concerns * * * about the impermissible circumvention of individual proof requirements are not at issue where the underlying statute permits awards without a showing of actual damage. The district court's use of *cy pres* involved only the "distribution of damages" aspect of class action manageability.

5. There may be other circumstances in which a classwide determination could be superior. Consider an employment discrimination case in which the employer had a finite number of jobs that could have been provided to class members who were the victims of discrimination. How should the remedy for the class be fashioned? In Pettway v. American Cast Iron Pipe Co., 681 F.2d 1259 (11th Cir.1982), the court noted that there was "no way of determining which jobs the class members would have bid on and have obtained" absent discrimination, and reasoned that in light of this "quagmire of hypothetical judgments * * * a class-wide approach to the measure of back pay is necessitated." But it proved difficult to fashion such a remedy, and the district court reverted to requiring class members to demonstrate

that they would have obtained a certain job or promotion. The appellate court insisted that "[u]nless the [district] court determines that relief *cannot* be given upon a classwide basis, * * * it should proceed to determine the back pay issue on that basis." If back pay is so determined, which class members should receive what amounts?

6. *The cy pres possibility.* Obviously determination of classwide damages can involve an element of speculation. Moreover, some class members entitled to compensation may fail to contact the court or file for their share. As a result, there may be a surplus left after all class members' claims have been satisfied. The courts have differed on proper disposition of the surplus, although generally approving exercise of *cy pres* authority over the funds. As explained by one court, the concept has been borrowed from a doctrine dealing with redirecting testamentary gifts. In class actions, "the unclaimed funds should be distributed for a purpose as near as possible to the legitimate objectives underlying the lawsuit, the interests of class members, and the interests of those similarly situated." In re Airline Ticket Comm'n Antitrust Litigation, 307 F.3d 679, 682 (8th Cir.2002).

In Powell v. Georgia–Pacific Corp., 119 F.3d 703 (8th Cir.1997), nearly $1 million was left over after settlement of a Title VII action brought by a class of African–American workers. Rather than distribute the remaining funds to class members, the district court ordered the parties to design a scholarship program to be administered by the Georgia–Pacific Corporation. Under the program, scholarships would be awarded to African–American high school students in the three counties in Arkansas and the three parishes in Louisiana where most of the class members lived. A district court does not have total discretion in deciding what to do with such funds. See In re Airline Ticket Comm'n Antitrust Litigation, *supra*, in which the district court directed that the funds be distributed to various local law schools and charities, and then to a public interest law organization. Twice the appellate court held that this was improper, and eventually it ordered that the money be paid instead to travel agencies in Puerto Rico and the U.S. Virgin Islands.

Sometimes the amounts involved can be remarkable. For example, Toshiba Corporation was sued in a class action alleging that there was a defective chip in its computers and reached a settlement valued at about $2 billion. After all distributions and payment of class counsel, some $350 million were left and, under the terms of the settlement, this money was used to create a foundation that used the money to fund various projects to make computers available to students in low income locations across the country. See Hells Angels, American Lawyer, June 2003, at 15.

California Cal. Code Civ. Proc. § 384 contains explicit *cy pres* authority. It is designed "to ensure that the unpaid residuals in class action litigation are distributed, to the extent possible in a manner designed either to further the purposes of the underlying causes of action or to promote justice for all Californians." Accordingly, the court is to determine the total amount that would be paid to all class members and set a date for a report on how much was actually paid to the class members. On receiving that report, "the court shall amend the judgment to direct the defendant to pay the sum of the unpaid residue * * * to nonprofit organizations or foundations to support projects that will benefit the class or similarly situated persons, or that promote the law consistent with the objectives and purposes of the underlying cause of action; to child advocacy groups, or to nonprofit organizations providing civil legal services to the indigent."

7.　In Van Gemert v. Boeing Co., 739 F.2d 730 (2d Cir.1984), the court upheld return of the surplus from a litigated damage judgment to the defendant in a securities action. It reasoned that the plaintiff class members could not share in the surplus because "that would constitute a form of fluid class recovery." It also rejected arguments that returning the money to Boeing would undermine the deterrent value of the award by stressing the lower court's conclusion that "Boeing had acted without malice, without bad faith and relied on the advice of others" before taking the challenged actions. Might this approach give defendants an incentive to try to cripple the claims process, thereby increasing the likelihood that there will be a surplus?

8.　Even where monetary relief is not involved, fashioning relief in a class action may present special problems. For example, in Giles v. Secretary of the Army, 627 F.2d 554 (D.C.Cir.1980), plaintiffs complained that they had improperly been denied honorable discharges from the Army on the basis of urinalysis test results that were illegally obtained, and they sought relief on behalf of a class comprised of all who had suffered downgraded discharges due to such test results. The district court found that their rights had been violated and directed that all class members be upgraded to honorable discharges. Noting that there might be *other* grounds for less-than-honorable discharges for some class members, the appellate court found it necessary to "prevent a remedial windfall." It therefore permitted the Army to initiate new proceedings with respect to any class member whose file indicated other grounds for less-than-honorable discharge.

G.　PROBLEMS OF JURISDICTION AND CHOICE OF LAW

PHILLIPS PETROLEUM CO. v. SHUTTS

United States Supreme Court, 1985.
472 U.S. 797, 105 S.Ct. 2965, 86 L.Ed.2d 628.

JUSTICE REHNQUIST delivered the opinion of the Court.

Petitioner is a Delaware corporation which has its principal place of business in Oklahoma. During the 1970's it produced or purchased natural gas from leased land located in 11 different States, and sold most of the gas in interstate commerce. Respondents are some 28,000 of the royalty owners possessing rights to the leases from which petitioner produced the gas; they reside in all 50 States, the District of Columbia, and several foreign countries. Respondents brought a class action against petitioner in the Kansas state court, seeking to recover interest on royalty payments which had been delayed by petitioner. They recovered judgment in the trial court, and the Supreme Court of Kansas affirmed the judgment over petitioner's contentions that the Due Process Clause of the Fourteenth Amendment prevented Kansas from adjudicating the claims of all the respondents, and that the Due Process Clause and the

Full Faith and Credit Clause of Article IV of the Constitution prohibited the application of Kansas law to all of the transactions between petitioner and respondents. We granted certiorari to consider these claims. We reject petitioner's jurisdictional claim, but sustain its claim regarding the choice of law.

Because petitioner sold the gas to its customers in interstate commerce, it was required to secure approval for price increases from what was then the Federal Power Commission, and is now the Federal Energy Regulatory Commission. Under its regulations the Federal Power Commission permitted petitioner to propose and collect tentative higher gas prices, subject to final approval by the Commission. If the Commission eventually denied petitioner's proposed price increase or reduced the proposed increase, petitioner would have to refund to its customers the difference between the approved price and the higher price charged, plus interest at a rate set by statute.

Although petitioner received higher gas prices pending review by the Commission, petitioner suspended any increase in royalties paid to the royalty owners because the higher price could be subject to recoupment by petitioner's customers. Petitioner agreed to pay the higher royalty only if the royalty owners would provide petitioner with a bond or indemnity for the increase, plus interest, in case the price increase was not ultimately approved and a refund was due to the customers. Petitioner set the interest rate on the indemnity agreements at the same interest rate the Commission would have required petitioner to refund to its customers. A small percentage of the royalty owners provided this indemnity and received royalties immediately from the interim price increases; these royalty owners are unimportant to this case.

The remaining royalty owners received no royalty on the unapproved portion of the prices until the Federal Power Commission approval of those prices became final. Royalties on the unapproved portion of the gas price were suspended three times by petitioner, corresponding to its three proposed price increases in the mid–1970's. In three written opinions the Commission approved all of petitioner's tentative price increases, so petitioner paid to its royalty owners the suspended royalties of $3.7 million in 1976, $4.7 million in 1977, and $2.9 million in 1978. Petitioner paid no interest to the royalty owners although it had the use of the suspended royalty money for a number of years.

Respondents Irl Shutts, Robert Anderson, and Betty Anderson filed suit against petitioner in Kansas state court, seeking interest payments on their suspended royalties which petitioner had possessed pending the Commission's approval of the price increases. Shutts is a resident of Kansas, and the Andersons live in Oklahoma. Shutts and the Andersons own gas leases in Oklahoma and Texas. Over petitioner's objection the Kansas trial court granted respondents' motion to certify the suit as a class action under Kansas law. Kan.Stat.Ann. § 60–223 et seq. (1983). The class as certified was comprised of 33,000 royalty owners who had royalties suspended by petitioner. The average claim of each royalty owner for interest on the suspended royalties was $100.

After the class was certified respondents provided each class member with notice through first-class mail. The notice described the action and informed each class member that he could appear in person or by counsel; otherwise each member would be represented by Shutts and the Andersons, the named plaintiffs. The notices also stated that class members would be included in the class and bound by the judgment unless they "opted out" of the lawsuit by executing and returning a "request for exclusion" that was included with the notice. The final class as certified contained 28,100 members; 3,400 had "opted out" of the class by returning the request for exclusion, and notice could not be delivered to another 1,500 members, who were also excluded. Less than 1,000 of the class members resided in Kansas. Only a minuscule amount, approximately one quarter of one percent, of the gas leases involved in the lawsuit were on Kansas land.

After petitioner's mandamus petition to decertify the class was denied, the case was tried to the court. The court found petitioner liable under Kansas law for interest on the suspended royalties to all class members. The trial court relied heavily on an earlier, unrelated class action involving the same nominal plaintiff and the same defendant, *Shutts, Executor v. Phillips Petroleum Co.*, 222 Kan. 527, 567 P.2d 1292 (1977), cert. denied, 434 U.S. 1068, 98 S.Ct. 1246, 55 L.Ed.2d 769 (1978). The Kansas Supreme Court had held in *Shutts, Executor* that a gas company owed interest to royalty owners for royalties suspended pending final Commission approval of a price increase. No federal statutes touched on the liability for suspended royalties, and the court in *Shutts, Executor* held as a matter of Kansas equity law that the applicable interest rates for computation of interest on suspended royalties were the interest rates at which the gas company would have had to reimburse its customers had its interim price increase been rejected by the Commission. The court in *Shutts, Executor* viewed these as the fairest interest rates because they were also the rates that petitioner required the royalty owners to meet in their indemnity agreements in order to avoid suspended royalties.

The trial court in the present case applied the rule from *Shutts, Executor,* and held petitioner liable for prejudgment and postjudgment interest on the suspended royalties, computed at the Commission rates governing petitioner's three price increases. The applicable interest rates were: 7% for royalties retained until October 1974; 9% for royalties retained between October 1974 and September 1979; and thereafter at the average prime rate. The trial court did not determine whether any difference existed between the laws of Kansas and other States, or whether another State's laws should be applied to non-Kansas plaintiffs or to royalties from leases in States other than Kansas.

Petitioner raised two principal claims in its appeal to the Supreme Court of Kansas. It first asserted that the Kansas trial court did not possess personal jurisdiction over absent plaintiff class members as required by *International Shoe Co. v. Washington,* 326 U.S. 310, 66 S.Ct. 154, 90 L.Ed. 95 (1945), and similar cases. Related to this first claim was petitioner's contention that the "opt-out" notice to absent class members, which forced them to return the request for exclusion in order to avoid the suit, was insufficient to bind class members who were not residents of Kansas or who did not possess "minimum contacts" with Kansas. Second, petitioner claimed that Kansas courts could not apply Kansas law to every claim in the dispute. The trial court should have looked to the laws of each State where the leases were located to determine, on the basis of conflict of laws principles, whether interest on the suspended royalties was recoverable, and at what rate.

The Supreme Court of Kansas held that the entire cause of action was maintainable under the Kansas class-action statute, and the court rejected both of petitioner's claims. First, it held that the absent class members were plaintiffs, not defendants, and thus the traditional minimum contacts test of *International Shoe* did not apply. The court held that nonresident class-action plaintiffs were only entitled to adequate notice, an opportunity to be heard, an opportunity to opt out of the case, and adequate representation by the named plaintiffs. If these procedural due process minima were met, according to the court, Kansas could assert jurisdiction over the plaintiff class and bind each class member with a judgment on his claim. The court surveyed the course of the litigation and concluded that all of these minima had been met.

The court also rejected petitioner's contention that Kansas law could not be applied to plaintiffs and royalty arrangements having no connection with Kansas. The court stated that generally the law of the forum controlled all claims unless "compelling reasons" existed to apply a different law. The court found no compelling reasons, and noted that "[t]he plaintiff class members have indicated their desire to have this action determined under the laws of Kansas." The court affirmed as a matter of Kansas equity law the award of interest on the suspended royalties, at the rates imposed by the trial court. The court set the postjudgment interest rate on all claims at the Kansas statutory rate of 15%.

[The Court held that Phillips had standing to raise the question of jurisdiction over unnamed plaintiffs: "Petitioner seeks to vindicate its own interests. As a class-action defendant, petitioner is in a unique predicament. If Kansas does not possess jurisdiction over this plaintiff class, petitioner will be bound to 28,100 judgment holders scattered across the globe, but none of these will be bound by the Kansas decree."]

* * *

II

Reduced to its essentials, petitioner's argument is that unless out-of-state plaintiffs affirmatively consent, the Kansas courts may not exert jurisdiction over their claims. Petitioner claims that failure to execute and return the "request for exclusion" provided with the class notice cannot constitute consent of the out-of-state plaintiffs; thus Kansas courts may exercise jurisdiction over these plaintiffs only if the plaintiffs possess the sufficient "minimum contacts" with Kansas as that term is used in cases involving personal jurisdiction over out-of-state defendants. *E.g., International Shoe Co. v. Washington,* 326 U.S. 310, 66 S.Ct. 154, 90 L.Ed. 95 (1945); *Shaffer v. Heitner,* 433 U.S. 186, 97 S.Ct. 2569, 53 L.Ed.2d 683 (1977); *World–Wide Volkswagen Corp. v. Woodson,* 444 U.S. 286, 100 S.Ct. 559, 62 L.Ed.2d 490 (1980). Since Kansas had no prelitigation contact with many of the plaintiffs and leases involved, petitioner claims that Kansas has exceeded its jurisdictional reach and thereby violated the due process rights of the absent plaintiffs.

In *International Shoe* we were faced with an out-of-state corporation which sought to avoid the exercise of personal jurisdiction over it as a defendant by a Washington state court. We held that the extent of the defendant's due process protection would depend "upon the quality and nature of the activity in relation to the fair and orderly administration of the laws. . . ."

We noted that the Due Process Clause did not permit a State to make a binding judgment against a person with whom the State had no contacts, ties, or relations. If the defendant possessed certain minimum contacts with the State, so that it was "reasonable and just, according to our traditional conception of fair play and substantial justice" for a State to exercise personal jurisdiction, the State could force the defendant to defend himself in the forum, upon pain of default, and could bind him to a judgment.

The purpose of this test, of course, is to protect a defendant from the travail of defending in a distant forum, unless the defendant's contacts with the forum make it just to force him to defend there. As we explained in *Woodson, supra,* the defendant's contacts should be such that "he should reasonably anticipate being haled" into the forum. 444 U.S., at 297, 100 S.Ct., at 567. In *Insurance Corp. of Ireland v. Compagnie des Bauxites de Guinee,* 456 U.S. 694, 702–703, and n. 10, 102 S.Ct. 2099, 2104–2105, and n. 10, 72 L.Ed.2d 492 (1982), we explained that the requirement that a court have personal jurisdiction comes from the Due Process Clause's protection of the defendant's personal liberty interest, and said that the requirement "represents a restriction on judicial power not as a matter of sovereignty, but as a matter of individual liberty."

Although the cases like *Shaffer* and *Woodson* which petitioner relies on for a minimum contacts requirement all dealt with out-of-state defendants or parties in the procedural posture of a defendant, petitioner claims that the same analysis must apply to absent class-action plaintiffs. In this regard petitioner correctly points out that a chose in action is a constitutionally recognized property interest possessed by each of the plaintiffs. *Mullane v. Central Hanover Bank & Trust Co.,* 339 U.S. 306, 70 S.Ct. 652, 94 L.Ed. 865 (1950). An adverse judgment by Kansas courts in this case may extinguish the chose in action forever through res judicata. Such an adverse judgment, petitioner claims, would be every bit as onerous to an absent plaintiff as an adverse judgment on the merits would be to a defendant. Thus, the same due process protections should apply to absent plaintiffs: Kansas should not be able to exert jurisdiction over the plaintiff's claims unless the plaintiffs have sufficient minimum contacts with Kansas.

We think petitioner's premise is in error. The burdens placed by a State upon an absent class-action plaintiff are not of the same order or magnitude as those it places upon an absent defendant. An out-of-state defendant summoned by a plaintiff is faced with the full powers of the forum State to render judgment *against* it. The defendant must generally hire counsel and travel to the forum to defend itself from the plaintiff's claim, or suffer a default judgment. The defendant may be forced to participate in extended and often costly discovery, and will be forced to respond in damages or to comply with some other form of remedy imposed by the court should it lose the suit. The defendant may also face liability for court costs and attorney's fees. These burdens are substantial, and the minimum contacts requirement of the Due Process Clause prevents the forum State from unfairly imposing them upon the defendant.

A class-action plaintiff, however, is in quite a different posture. The Court noted this difference in *Hansberry v. Lee,* 311 U.S. 32, 40–41, 61 S.Ct. 115, 117–118, 85 L.Ed. 22 (1940), which explained that a "class" or "representative" suit was an exception to the rule that one could not be bound by judgment *in personam* unless one was made fully a party in the traditional sense. *Ibid.,* citing *Pennoyer v. Neff,* 95 U.S. (5 Otto) 714, 24 L.Ed. 565 (1878). As the Court pointed out in *Hansberry,* the class action was an invention of equity to enable it to proceed to a decree in suits where the number of those interested in the litigation was too great to permit joinder. The absent parties would be bound by the decree so long as the named parties adequately represented the absent class and the prosecution of the litigation was within the common interest.[1]

Modern plaintiff class actions follow the same goals, permitting litigation of a suit involving common questions when there are too many plaintiffs for proper joinder. Class actions also may permit the plaintiffs to pool claims which would be uneconomical to litigate individually. For example, this lawsuit involves claims averaging about $100 per plaintiff; most of the plaintiffs would have no realistic day in court if a class action were not available.

In sharp contrast to the predicament of a defendant haled into an out-of-state forum, the plaintiffs in this suit were not haled anywhere to

---

1. The holding in *Hansberry,* of course, was that petitioners in that case had not a sufficient common interest with the parties to a prior lawsuit such that a decree against those parties in the prior suit would bind the petitioners. But in the present case there is no question that the named plaintiffs adequately represent the class, and that all members of the class have the same interest in enforcing their claims against the defendant.

defend themselves upon pain of a default judgment. As commentators have noted, from the plaintiffs' point of view a class action resembles a "quasi-administrative proceeding, conducted by the judge."

A plaintiff class in Kansas and numerous other jurisdictions cannot first be certified unless the judge, with the aid of the named plaintiffs and defendant, conducts an inquiry into the common nature of the named plaintiffs' and the absent plaintiffs' claims, the adequacy of representation, the jurisdiction possessed over the class, and any other matters that will bear upon proper representation of the absent plaintiffs' interest. See, *e.g.*, Kan.Stat.Ann. § 60–223 (1983); Fed.Rule Civ. Proc. 23. Unlike a defendant in a civil suit, a class-action plaintiff is not required to fend for himself. See Kan.Stat.Ann. § 60–223(d) (1983). The court and named plaintiffs protect his interests. Indeed, the class-action defendant itself has a great interest in ensuring that the absent plaintiff's claims are properly before the forum. In this case, for example, the defendant sought to avoid class certification by alleging that the absent plaintiffs would not be adequately represented and were not amenable to jurisdiction.

The concern of the typical class-action rules for the absent plaintiffs is manifested in other ways. Most jurisdictions, including Kansas, require that a class action, once certified, may not be dismissed or compromised without the approval of the court. In many jurisdictions such as Kansas the court may amend the pleadings to ensure that all sections of the class are represented adequately. Kan.Stat.Ann. § 60–223(d) (1983); see also, *e.g.*, Fed.Rule Civ.Proc. 23(d).

Besides this continuing solicitude for their rights, absent plaintiff class members are not subject to other burdens imposed upon defendants. They need not hire counsel or appear. They are almost never subject to counterclaims or cross-claims, or liability for fees or costs.[2] Absent plaintiff class members are not subject to coercive or punitive remedies. Nor will an adverse judgment typically bind an absent plaintiff for any damages, although a valid adverse judgment may extinguish any of the plaintiff's claims which were litigated.

Unlike a defendant in a normal civil suit, an absent class-action plaintiff is not required to do anything. He may sit back and allow the litigation to run its course, content in knowing that there are safeguards provided for his protection. In most class actions an absent plaintiff is provided at least with an opportunity to "opt out" of the class, and if he takes advantage of that opportunity he is removed from the litigation entirely. This was true of the Kansas proceedings in this case. The Kansas procedure provided for the mailing of a notice to each class member by first-class mail. The notice, as we have previously

2. Petitioner places emphasis on the fact that absent class members might be subject to discovery, counterclaims, cross-claims, or court costs. Petitioner cites no cases involving any such imposition upon plaintiffs, however. We are convinced that such burdens are rarely imposed upon plaintiff class members, and that the disposition of these issues is best left to a case which presents them in a more concrete way.

indicated, described the action and informed the class member that he could appear in person or by counsel, in default of which he would be represented by the named plaintiffs and their attorneys. The notice further stated that class members would be included in the class and bound by the judgment unless they "opted out" by executing and returning a "request for exclusion" that was included in the notice.

Petitioner contends, however, that the "opt out" procedure provided by Kansas is not good enough, and that an "opt in" procedure is required to satisfy the Due Process Clause of the Fourteenth Amendment. Insofar as plaintiffs who have no minimum contacts with the forum State are concerned, an "opt in" provision would require that each class member affirmatively consent to his inclusion within the class.

Because States place fewer burdens upon absent class plaintiffs than they do upon absent defendants in nonclass suits, the Due Process Clause need not and does not afford the former as much protection from state-court jurisdiction as it does the latter. The Fourteenth Amendment does protect "persons," not "defendants," however, so absent plaintiffs as well as absent defendants are entitled to some protection from the jurisdiction of a forum State which seeks to adjudicate their claims. In this case we hold that a forum State may exercise jurisdiction over the claim of an absent class-action plaintiff, even though that plaintiff may not possess the minimum contacts with the forum which would support personal jurisdiction over a defendant. If the forum State wishes to bind an absent plaintiff concerning a claim for money damages or similar relief at law,[3] it must provide minimal procedural due process protection. The plaintiff must receive notice plus an opportunity to be heard and participate in the litigation, whether in person or through counsel. The notice must be the best practicable, "reasonably calculated, under all the circumstances, to apprise interested parties of the pendency of the action and afford them an opportunity to present their objections." *Mullane,* 339 U.S., at 314–315, 70 S.Ct., at 657; cf. *Eisen v. Carlisle & Jacquelin,* 417 U.S. 156, 174–175, 94 S.Ct. 2140, 2151, 40 L.Ed.2d 732 (1974). The notice should describe the action and the plaintiffs' rights in it. Additionally, we hold that due process requires at a minimum that an absent plaintiff be provided with an opportunity to remove himself from the class by executing and returning an "opt out" or "request for exclusion" form to the court. Finally, the Due Process Clause of course requires that the named plaintiff at all times adequately represent the interests of the absent class members. *Hansberry,* 311 U.S., at 42–43, 45, 61 S.Ct., at 118–119, 120.

We reject petitioner's contention that the Due Process Clause of the Fourteenth Amendment requires that absent plaintiffs affirmatively "opt in" to the class, rather than be deemed members of the class if they

---

3. Our holding today is limited to those class actions which seek to bind known plaintiffs concerning claims wholly or predominately for money judgments. We intimate no view concerning other types of class actions, such as those seeking equitable relief. Nor, of course, does our discussion of personal jurisdiction address class actions where the jurisdiction is asserted against a *defendant* class.

do not "opt out." We think that such a contention is supported by little, if any precedent, and that it ignores the differences between class-action plaintiffs, on the one hand, and defendants in nonclass civil suits on the other. Any plaintiff may consent to jurisdiction. The essential question, then, is how stringent the requirement for a showing of consent will be.

We think that the procedure followed by Kansas, where a fully descriptive notice is sent first-class mail to each class member, with an explanation of the right to "opt out," satisfies due process. Requiring a plaintiff to affirmatively request inclusion would probably impede the prosecution of those class actions involving an aggregation of small individual claims, where a large number of claims are required to make it economical to bring suit. See, *e.g., Eisen, supra,* 417 U.S., at 161, 94 S.Ct., at 2144. The plaintiff's claim may be so small, or the plaintiff so unfamiliar with the law, that he would not file suit individually, nor would he affirmatively request inclusion in the class if such a request were required by the Constitution.[4] If, on the other hand, the plaintiff's claim is sufficiently large or important that he wishes to litigate it on his own, he will likely have retained an attorney or have thought about filing suit, and should be fully capable of exercising his right to "opt out."

In this case over 3,400 members of the potential class did "opt out," which belies the contention that "opt out" procedures result in guaranteed jurisdiction by inertia. Another 1,500 were excluded because the notice and "opt out" form was undeliverable. We think that such results show that the "opt out" procedure provided by Kansas is by no means *pro forma,* and that the Constitution does not require more to protect what must be the somewhat rare species of class member who is unwilling to execute an "opt out" form, but whose claim is nonetheless so important that he cannot be presumed to consent to being a member of the class by his failure to do so. Petitioner's "opt in" requirement would require the invalidation of scores of state statutes and of the class-action provision of the Federal Rules of Civil Procedure, and for the reasons stated we do not think that the Constitution requires the State to sacrifice the obvious advantages in judicial efficiency resulting from the "opt out" approach for the protection of the *rara avis* portrayed by petitioner.

We therefore hold that the protection afforded the plaintiff class members by the Kansas statute satisfies the Due Process Clause. The interests of the absent plaintiffs are sufficiently protected by the forum State when those plaintiffs are provided with a request for exclusion that

---

4. In this regard the Reporter for the 1966 amendments to the Federal Rules of Civil Procedure stated:

"[R]equiring the individuals affirmatively to request inclusion in the lawsuit would result in freezing out the claims of people—especially small claims held by small people—who for one reason or another,

ignorance, timidity, unfamiliarity with business or legal matters, will simply not take the affirmative step."

Kaplan, Continuing Work of the Civil Committee: 1966 Amendments of the Federal Rules of Civil Procedure (I), 81 Harv.L.Rev. 356, 397–398 (1967).

can be returned within a reasonable time to the court. Both the Kansas trial court and the Supreme Court of Kansas held that the class received adequate representation, and no party disputes that conclusion here. We conclude that the Kansas court properly asserted personal jurisdiction over the absent plaintiffs and their claims against petitioner.

III

The Kansas courts applied Kansas contract and Kansas equity law to every claim in this case, notwithstanding that over 99% of the gas leases and some 97% of the plaintiffs in the case had no apparent connection to the State of Kansas except for this lawsuit.[6] Petitioner protested that the Kansas courts should apply the laws of the States where the leases were located, or at least apply Texas and Oklahoma law because so many of the leases came from those States. The Kansas courts disregarded this contention and found petitioner liable for interest on the suspended royalties as a matter of Kansas law, and set the interest rates under Kansas equity principles.

Petitioner contends that total application of Kansas substantive law violated the constitutional limitations on choice of law mandated by the Due Process Clause of the Fourteenth Amendment and the Full Faith and Credit Clause of Article IV, § 1. We must first determine whether Kansas law conflicts in any material way with any other law which could apply. There can be no injury in applying Kansas law if it is not in conflict with that of any other jurisdiction connected to this suit.

Petitioner claims that Kansas law conflicts with that of a number of States connected to this litigation, especially Texas and Oklahoma. These putative conflicts range from the direct to the tangential, and may be addressed by the Supreme Court of Kansas on remand under the

---

6. The Commission approved petitioner's price increases in Opinion Nos. 699, 749, and 770. Petitioner reimbursed royalty owners $3.7, $2.9, and $4.7 million in suspended royalties, respectively. The States where the leases were located and their resident plaintiffs are as follows:

OPINION 699

States	No. leases in state	Royalties to state leases	No. royalty owners in state
Oklahoma	1,266	$ 83,711.35	2,653
Texas	4,414	839,152.73	9,591
Kansas	3	152.88	496
Arkansas	6	3,228.22	173
Louisiana	68	2,187,548.06	1,244
New Mexico	941	433,574.85	621
Illinois	—	—	397
Wyoming	690	148,906.93	413
Mississippi	—	—	67
Utah	—	—	29
West Virginia	—	—	20
No State Code	1	[.05]	1,025
	7,389	$3,696,274.97	

OPINION 749

States	No. leases in state	Royalties to state leases	No. royalty owners in state
Oklahoma	1,948	$243,163.49	3,591
Texas	3,479	2,171,217.36	7,881
Kansas	15	2,619.24	553
Arkansas	32	1,769.33	171
Louisiana	178	352,539.45	740
New Mexico	350	22,670.27	339
Illinois	1	1.30	357
Wyoming	68	67,570.01	37
Mississippi	3	694.93	88
Utah	1	184.60	18
West Virginia	32	10,364.61	246
No State Code	2	1,032.59	1,553
	6,109	$2,873,827.18	

OPINION 770

States	No. leases in state	Royalties to state leases	No. royalty owners in state
Oklahoma	1,430	$471,122.53	2,684
Texas	3,702	2,615,744.46	8,550
Kansas	4	115.10	504
Arkansas	2	552.83	162
Louisiana	26	516,248.13	361
New Mexico	591	194,799.95	469
Illinois	1	.01	353
Wyoming	476	945,441.09	272
Mississippi	—	—	36
Utah	—	—	18
West Virginia	—	—	22
No State Code	—	—	1,046
	6,232	$4,744,024.10	

correct constitutional standard. For example, there is no recorded Oklahoma decision dealing with interest liability for suspended royalties: whether Oklahoma is likely to impose liability would require a survey of Oklahoma oil and gas law. Even if Oklahoma found such liability, petitioner shows that Oklahoma would most likely apply its constitutional and statutory 6% interest rate rather than the much higher Kansas rates applied in this litigation.

Additionally, petitioner points to an Oklahoma statute which excuses liability for interest if a creditor accepts payment of the full principal without a claim for interest, Okla.Stat., Tit. 23, § 8 (1951). Petitioner contends that by ignoring this statute the Kansas courts created liability that does not exist in Oklahoma.

Petitioner also points out several conflicts between Kansas and Texas law. Although Texas recognizes interest liability for suspended royalties, Texas has never awarded any such interest at a rate greater than 6%, which corresponds with the Texas constitutional and statutory rate. Moreover, at least one court interpreting Texas law appears to have held that Texas excuses interest liability once the gas company offers to take an indemnity from the royalty owner and pay him the suspended royalty while the price increase is still tentative. Such a rule is contrary to Kansas law as applied below, but if applied to the Texas plaintiffs or leases in this case, would vastly reduce petitioner's liability.

The conflicts on the applicable interest rates, alone—which we do not think can be labeled "false conflicts" without a more thoroughgoing treatment than was accorded them by the Supreme Court of Kansas— certainly amounted to millions of dollars in liability. We think that the Supreme Court of Kansas erred in deciding on the basis that it did that the application of its laws to all claims would be constitutional.

Four Terms ago we addressed a similar situation in *Allstate Ins. Co. v. Hague*, 449 U.S. 302, 101 S.Ct. 633, 66 L.Ed.2d 521 (1981). In that case we were confronted with two conflicting rules of state insurance law. Minnesota permitted the "stacking" of separate uninsured motorist policies while Wisconsin did not. Although the decedent lived in Wisconsin, took out insurance policies and was killed there, he was employed in Minnesota, and after his death his widow moved to Minnesota for reasons unrelated to the litigation, and was appointed personal representative of his estate. She filed suit in Minnesota courts, which applied the Minnesota stacking rule.

The plurality in *Allstate* noted that a particular set of facts giving rise to litigation could justify, constitutionally, the application of more than one jurisdiction's laws. The plurality recognized, however, that the Due Process Clause and the Full Faith and Credit Clause provided modest restrictions on the application of forum law. These restrictions required "that for a State's substantive law to be selected in a constitutionally permissible manner, that State must have a significant contact or significant aggregation of contacts, creating state interests, such that choice of its law is neither arbitrary nor fundamentally unfair." The dissenting Justices were in substantial agreement with this principle. *Id.* at 332, 101 S.Ct., at 650 (opinion of Powell, J., joined by Burger, C.J., and Rehnquist, J.). The dissent stressed that the Due Process Clause prohibited the application of law which was only casually or slightly related to the litigation, while the Full Faith and Credit Clause required the forum to respect the laws and judgments of other States, subject to the forum's own interests in furthering its public policy.

The plurality in *Allstate* affirmed the application of Minnesota law because of the forum's significant contacts to the litigation which supported the State's interest in applying its law. Kansas' contacts to this litigation, as explained by the Kansas Supreme Court, can be gleaned from the opinion below.

Petitioner owns property and conducts substantial business in the State, so Kansas certainly has an interest in regulating petitioner's conduct in Kansas. Moreover, oil and gas extraction is an important business to Kansas, and although only a few leases in issue are located in Kansas, hundreds of Kansas plaintiffs were affected by petitioner's suspension of royalties; thus the court held that the State has a real interest in protecting "the rights of these royalty owners both as individual residents of [Kansas] and as members of this particular class of plaintiffs." The Kansas Supreme Court pointed out that Kansas courts are quite familiar with this type of lawsuit, and "[t]he plaintiff class members have indicated their desire to have this action determined under the laws of Kansas." Finally, the Kansas court buttressed its use of Kansas law by stating that this lawsuit was analogous to a suit against a "common fund" located in Kansas.

We do not lightly discount this description of Kansas' contacts with this litigation and its interest in applying its law. There is, however, no "common fund" located in Kansas that would require or support the application of only Kansas law to all these claims. As the Kansas court noted, petitioner commingled the suspended royalties with its general corporate accounts. There is no specific identifiable res in Kansas, nor is there any limited amount which may be depleted before every plaintiff is compensated. Only by somehow aggregating all the separate claims in this case could a "common fund" in any sense be created, and the term becomes all but meaningless when used in such an expansive sense.

We also give little credence to the idea that Kansas law should apply to all claims because the plaintiffs, by failing to opt out, evinced their desire to be bound by Kansas law. Even if one could say that the plaintiffs "consented" to the application of Kansas law by not opting out, plaintiff's desire for forum law is rarely, if ever controlling. In most cases the plaintiff shows his obvious wish for forum law by filing there. "If a plaintiff could choose the substantive rules to be applied to an action ... the invitation to forum shopping would be irresistible." *Allstate, supra,* 449 U.S., at 337, 101 S.Ct., at 652 (opinion of POWELL, J.). Even if a plaintiff evidences his desire for forum law by moving to the forum, we have generally accorded such a move little or no significance. In *Allstate* the plaintiff's move to the forum was only relevant because it was unrelated and prior to the litigation. Thus the plaintiffs' desire for Kansas law, manifested by their participation in this Kansas lawsuit, bears little relevance.

The Supreme Court of Kansas in its opinion in this case expressed the view that by reason of the fact that it was adjudicating a nationwide class action, it had much greater latitude in applying its own law to the transactions in question than might otherwise be the case:

> "The general rule is that the law of the forum applies unless it is expressly shown that a different law governs, and in case of doubt, the law of the forum is preferred.... Where a state court determines it has jurisdiction over a nationwide class action and procedural due process guarantees of notice and adequate representation are present, we believe the law of the forum should be applied unless compelling reasons exist for applying a different law.... Compelling reasons do not exist to require this court to look to other state laws to determine the rights of the parties involved in this lawsuit."

We think that this is something of a "bootstrap" argument. The Kansas class-action statute, like those of most other jurisdictions, requires that there be "common issues of law or fact." But while a State may, for the reasons we have previously stated, assume jurisdiction over the claims of plaintiffs whose principal contacts are with other States, it may not use this assumption of jurisdiction as an added weight in the scale when considering the permissible constitutional limits on choice of substantive law. It may not take a transaction with little or no relationship to the forum and apply the law of the forum in order to satisfy the procedural requirement that there be a "common question of law." The issue of personal jurisdiction over plaintiffs in a class action is entirely distinct from the question of the constitutional limitations on choice of law; the latter calculus is not altered by the fact that it may be more difficult or more burdensome to comply with the constitutional limitations because of the large number of transactions which the State proposes to adjudicate and which have little connection with the forum.

Kansas must have a "significant contact or significant aggregation of contacts" to the claims asserted by each member of the plaintiff class, contacts "creating state interests," in order to ensure that the choice of Kansas law is not arbitrary or unfair. *Allstate,* 449 U.S., at 312–313, 101 S.Ct., at 639–640. Given Kansas' lack of "interest" in claims unrelated to that State, and the substantive conflict with jurisdictions such as Texas, we conclude that application of Kansas law to every claim in this case is sufficiently arbitrary and unfair as to exceed constitutional limits.

When considering fairness in this context, an important element is the expectation of the parties. See *Allstate, supra,* 449 U.S., at 333, 101 S.Ct., at 650 (opinion of Powell, J.). There is no indication that when the leases involving land and royalty owners outside of Kansas were executed, the parties had any idea that Kansas law would control. Neither the Due Process Clause nor the Full Faith and Credit Clause requires

Kansas "to substitute for its own [laws], applicable to persons and events within it, the conflicting statute of another state," *Pacific Employers Ins. Co. v. Industrial Accident Comm'n*, 306 U.S. 493, 502, 59 S.Ct. 629, 633, 83 L.Ed. 940 (1939), but Kansas "may not abrogate the rights of parties beyond its borders having no relation to anything done or to be done within them." *Home Ins. Co. v. Dick*, 281 U.S., at 410, 50 S.Ct., at 342.

Here the Supreme Court of Kansas took the view that in a nationwide class action where procedural due process guarantees of notice and adequate representation were met, "the law of the forum should be applied unless compelling reasons exist for applying a different law." Whatever practical reasons may have commended this rule to the Supreme Court of Kansas, for the reasons already stated we do not believe that it is consistent with the decisions of this Court. We make no effort to determine for ourselves which law must apply to the various transactions involved in this lawsuit, and we reaffirm our observation in *Allstate* that in many situations a state court may be free to apply one of several choices of law. But the constitutional limitations laid down in cases such as *Allstate* and *Home Ins. Co. v. Dick, supra,* must be respected even in a nationwide class action.

We therefore affirm the judgment of the Supreme Court of Kansas insofar as it upheld the jurisdiction of the Kansas courts over the plaintiff class members in this case, and reverse its judgment insofar as it held that Kansas law was applicable to all of the transactions which it sought to adjudicate. We remand the case to that court for further proceedings not inconsistent with this opinion.

It is so ordered.

Justice Powell took no part in the decision of this case.

[Opinion of JUSTICE STEVENS, concurring in part and dissenting in part, omitted.]

Notes and Questions

1. Is the Court's personal jurisdiction reasoning persuasive? To the extent that the sole concern is unfairness to absent plaintiffs due to litigation in the forum, plaintiffs' ability to consent to jurisdiction there can provide a solution. But consider a claim by a Texas resident concerning royalties on a Texas well arising out of a royalty agreement entered into in Texas between the claimant and Phillips. Could that claimant overcome Phillips' personal jurisdiction objections to her suit in Kansas? Perhaps the overall level of Phillips' activities in Kansas would be such as to render it answerable to such a suit on some general jurisdiction theory. Otherwise, however, doesn't the class action device alter Phillips' due process rights to object to jurisdiction? Would it make a difference in terms of personal jurisdiction if the suit had been filed in Alaska by the only Alaskan who held a royalty interest in the affected wells? Professor Kennedy argued that "the opinion implies that there was no alternative remedy to the multistate class action in Kansas and ignores and avoids the real issue that Kansas lawyers

were engaged in abusive forum shopping for the Oklahoma plaintiffs. Contrary to the implied premise of the opinion, the plaintiff multistate class would still have an effective alternative remedy if the Court were to require that the action be brought in a state with a dominant nexus to the multistate class." Kennedy, The Supreme Court Meets the Bride of Frankenstein: Phillips Petroleum Co. v. Shutts and the State Multistate Class Action, 34 U.Kan.L.Rev. 255, 285 (1985).

2. The Court is careful to point out that the personal jurisdiction issues might be different for a defendant class. Certainly there is a sense among some courts that defendants have more to lose than plaintiffs have to gain from litigation. See, e.g., Thillens, Inc. v. Community Currency Exchange Assoc. of Illinois, *supra* p. 359 ("The crux of the distinction is: the unnamed plaintiff stands to gain while the unnamed defendant stands to lose."). Is this a persuasive reason for treating plaintiff and defendant classes differently? If unnamed plaintiffs only stand to gain, why were there concerns in Amchem Products, Inc. v. Windsor, *supra* p. 373, about the rights of plaintiff class members?

3. The Court in *Shutts* solves the personal jurisdiction problem by treating the failure to opt out as consent to jurisdiction. Does this mean that the right to opt out is required by due process? If so, what is to become of "mandatory" class actions? Consider the views of Professors Miller (who argued the case for Phillips in the Supreme Court) and Crump in Jurisdiction and Choice of Law in Multistate Class Actions After Phillips Petroleum v. Shutts, 96 Yale L.J. 1, 39; 54 (1986): "Although *Shutts* does not address the issue directly, the concept, expressed in *Shutts,* that the right to opt out is a fundamental due process requirement seems to contradict the mandatory class action that has developed under Federal Rule 23 and its state counterparts. There can be no mandatory class if the members have the constitutional right to opt out. The conclusion seems to follow that *Shutts* prohibits mandatory class actions. * * * The difficulty with this absolute approach, however, is that it prevents rational adjudication of genuine Rule 23(b)(1) class claims which, by definition, require unified disposition. * * * If individual adjudication truly would be impossible, and the case must be adjudicated uniformly, it seems unlikely that *Shutts* is intended to prevent that resolution."

4. In Ortiz v. Fibreboard Corp., *supra* p. 302, the Court noted that "[i]n *Shutts,* as an important caveat to our holding, we made clear that we were only examining the procedural protections attendant on binding out-of-state class members whose claims were 'wholly or predominately for money judgments.'" Recall the analysis required under Rule 23(b)(2) to determine whether a case may be certified on the ground that the class seeks injunctive or declaratory relief. See In re Monumental Life Ins. Co., *supra* p. 318. Would the same standard apply to the due process limitations on personal jurisdiction regarding absent plaintiff class members?

5. In *Shutts*, the Court cites Hansberry v. Lee, *supra* p. 285, for the proposition that "the named plaintiff at all times adequately represent the interests of the absent class members." Keep that admonition in mind as we examine the preclusive effect of class actions in Chapter VIII. See Matsushita Elec. Indus. Co. v. Epstein, *infra* p. 803.

6.   What impact does *Shutts* have on state law claims in class actions in federal court? With regard to personal jurisdiction, it probably places the same limits on such cases as actions in state court. See Miller & Crump, *supra,* 96 Yale L.J. at 29–31.

7.   If the right to opt out is fundamental in cases involving claims primarily for money damages, does that apply in cases where there is no problem with personal jurisdiction over the class members? Consider, for instance, a class consisting solely of residents of the state in which the suit was filed. For other reasons, such as choice of law difficulties, plaintiffs might elect such a class definition. If the action is filed in a state court, and the state's class action provisions do not assure notice and a right to opt out, would due process require a right to opt out?

SUBJECT MATTER JURISDICTION LIMITATIONS ON STATE–LAW CLASS ACTIONS

Shutts was in state court, in part, because it could not be brought in federal court. When class action claims are in federal court on grounds of diversity of citizenship, 28 U.S.C.A. § 1332, subject matter jurisdiction problems may arise.

Complete Diversity: The Supreme Court's requirement of complete diversity, see Strawbridge v. Curtiss, 7 U.S. (3 Cranch) 267, 2 L.Ed. 435 (1806); Owen Equipment & Erection Co. v. Kroger, 437 U.S. 365, 98 S.Ct. 2396, 57 L.Ed.2d 274 (1978), would present substantial difficulties if it had to be satisfied as to all class members.

These difficulties were solved by Supreme Tribe of Ben–Hur v. Cauble, 255 U.S. 356, 41 S.Ct. 338, 65 L.Ed. 673 (1921), which held the diversity statute satisfied in a class action provided only that all the *named* plaintiffs were diverse to all the defendants. Plaintiff, a fraternal benefit association organized under the laws of Indiana, filed a bill in the federal district court to enjoin defendants, who were members of the association, from prosecuting actions against it in state court. The association's theory was that the defendants were bound by the result in an earlier federal court case in which they were members of a class that made the same claims against the association. Since all the defendants were Indiana citizens, the district court held that they were not bound because including them in the earlier class action would have defeated federal jurisdiction.

The Supreme Court reversed, finding: "Diversity of citizenship gave the District Court jurisdiction. Indiana citizens were of the class represented. The intervention of the Indiana citizens in this suit would not have defeated the jurisdiction already acquired. Being thus represented, we think it must necessarily follow that their rights were concluded by the original decree." This suggestion of ancillary jurisdiction, however, would not serve to distinguish *Ben–Hur* from *Strawbridge,* and thus *Ben–Hur* can be viewed as weakening the "complete diversity" rule in class actions. It conveniently serves the exigencies of class actions by providing that only the citizenship of the named plaintiffs will be considered for purposes of satisfying diversity.

In Devlin v. Scardeletti, 536 U.S. 1, 122 S.Ct. 2005, 153 L.Ed.2d 27 (2002), the Court explained that "[t]he rule that nonnamed class members cannot defeat complete diversity is * * * justified by the goals of class action litigation. Ease of administration of class actions would be compromised by having to consider the citizenship of all class members, many of whom may even be unknown, in determining jurisdiction."

Although the rule that only the citizenship of named class representatives need be considered permits plaintiffs to obtain access to federal court even though there is not complete diversity, sometimes plaintiffs may not want to be in federal court. Recall In re Diet Drugs, *supra* p. 391. The Class Action Fairness Act of 2004 was designed to permit removal to federal court if there is minimal diversity in certain circumstances. See *supra* p. 401 n. 3 for discussion of that Act.

Jurisdictional Amount: 28 U.S.C.A. § 1332 also requires that "the matter in controversy exceeds the sum or value of $75,000." This requirement has become a substantial impediment to federal class actions involving state claims that are small or modest.

In Snyder v. Harris, 394 U.S. 332, 89 S.Ct. 1053, 22 L.Ed.2d 319 (1969), none of the named plaintiffs seeking to represent a Rule 23(b)(3) class had an individual claim in excess of the jurisdictional minimum, although the aggregate of the claims on behalf of the class was well over the jurisdictional minimum. Plaintiffs argued that the 1966 amendments to Rule 23 authorized such aggregation for jurisdictional purposes. The Court disagreed, relying by analogy on joinder cases, and holding that aggregation is allowed *only* where "two or more plaintiffs unite to enforce a single title or right in which they have a common and undivided interest." *Snyder* still applies. See, e.g., In re Brand Name Prescription Drugs, 123 F.3d 599, 607 (7th Cir.1997) ("The court cannot just add up the damages sought by each member of the class.")

The Supreme Court took *Snyder* a step farther in Zahn v. International Paper Co., 414 U.S. 291, 94 S.Ct. 505, 38 L.Ed.2d 511 (1973). The named plaintiffs there had claims in excess of the jurisdictional minimum, but other members of the plaintiff class did not. Plaintiffs argued that there was ancillary jurisdiction over the claims of the class members, but the Court held that every member of the class must satisfy the jurisdictional minimum if the claims are not joint. The rule of *Zahn* is clear enough, but its result is difficult to reconcile with *Ben–Hur* unless one emphasizes differences between "joint" rights (which were involved in *Ben–Hur*) and "separate" rights. But in *Ben–Hur* the Court did not limit its holding to joint interests, and such a limitation makes no policy sense. As Professor Currie has written, "it is when interests are several that an out-of-state party is most likely to need the jurisdiction provided by *Ben–Hur* to protect him from bias in the local court; when interests are joint, a biased tribunal may be unable to injure the outsider without harming a local coparty as well." Currie, Pendent Parties, 45 U.Chi. L.Rev. 753, 762–63 (1978); *see also* Goldberg, The Influence of Procedural Rules on Federal Jurisdiction, 28 Stan.L.Rev. 397 (1976). Whatever the difficulties in reconciling *Ben–Hur* and *Zahn,* they co-exist in class action suits so that diversity is governed by the citizenship of the named plaintiffs, but the amount in controversy is not.

The supplemental jurisdiction statute, 28 U.S.C.A. § 1367, appears on its face to overrule *Zahn.* § 1367(a) grants district courts that have original jurisdiction over the claim of one plaintiff supplemental jurisdiction over any other claims that form a part of the same case or controversy, which would include "pendent" claims of other class members. This grant is limited in diversity cases by § 1367(b), but that limitation does not appear to apply in class actions. The legislative history nevertheless says that "[t]his section is not intended to affect the jurisdictional requirements of 28 U.S.C. § 1332 in diversity-only class actions, as those requirements were interpreted prior to *Finley.*" H.R.Rep. No. 734, 101st Cong., 2d Sess., 1990 U.S.Cong. & Admin.News 6860, 6875 (citing *Zahn* and *Ben–Hur*).

In In re Abbott Laboratories, 51 F.3d 524 (5th Cir.1995), aff'd by an equally divided court, 529 U.S. 333, 120 S.Ct. 1578 (2000), the court held that § 1367 does overrule *Zahn* and authorize supplemental jurisdiction over the claims of class members without regard to amount in controversy if some class members have claims that satisfy the amount in controversy requirement. Speaking for the court, Judge Higginbotham acknowledged that the omission of Rule 23 from § 1367(b) may have been a "clerical error," but concluded that "the statute is the sole repository of congressional intent when the statute is clear and does not demand an absurd result." *Id.* at 528–29. The courts have split on this question, with the majority agreeing with *Abbott Laboratories, supra.* Compare Allapattah Serv., Inc. v. Exxon Corp., 333 F.3d 1248 (11th Cir.2003) (§ 1367 creates supplemental jurisdiction over claims of class members that don't individually satisfy the jurisdictional minimum); Kanter v. Warner–Lambert Co., 265 F.3d 853 (9th Cir.2001) (same); Rosmer v. Pfizer, Inc., 263 F.3d 110 (4th Cir.2001) (same), with Meritcare, Inc. v. St. Paul Mercury Ins. Co., 166 F.3d 214 (3d Cir.1999) (§ 1367 did not change the requirement that each class member's claim satisfy the jurisdictional minimum requirement); Leonhardt v. Western Sugar Co., 160 F.3d 631 (10th Cir.1998) (same); see Pfander, Supplemental Jurisdiction and Section 1367: The Case for a Sympathetic Textualism, 148 U.Pa.L.Rev. 109 (1999).

IN RE BRIDGESTONE/FIRESTONE, INC.

United States Court of Appeals, Seventh Circuit, 2002.
288 F.3d 1012, cert. denied, 537 U.S. 1105, 123 S.Ct. 870, 154 L.Ed.2d 774, 2003.

Before EASTERBROOK, MANION and KANNE, Circuit Judges.

EASTERBROOK, Circuit Judge.

Firestone tires on Ford Explorer SUVs experienced an abnormally high failure rate during the late 1990s. In August 2000, while the National Highway Transportation Safety Administration was investigating, Firestone recalled and replaced some of those tires. Ford and Firestone replaced additional tires during 2001. Many suits have been filed as a result of injuries and deaths related to the tire failures. Other suits were filed by persons who own (or owned) Ford Explorers or Firestone tires that have so far performed properly; these persons seek compensation for the *risk* of failure, which may be reflected in diminished resale value of the vehicles and perhaps in mental stress. The Judicial Panel on Multidistrict Litigation transferred suits filed in, or removed to, federal court to the Southern District of Indiana for consolidated pretrial proceedings under 28 U.S.C. § 1407(a). Once these have been completed, the cases must be returned to the originating districts for decision on the merits. In an effort to prevent retransfer, counsel representing many of the plaintiffs filed a new consolidated suit in Indianapolis and asked the judge to certify it as a nationwide class action, which would make all other suits redundant. The district court obliged and certified two nationwide classes: the first includes everyone who owns, owned, leases, or leased a Ford Explorer of model year 1991 through 2001 anytime before the first recall, and the second includes all owners and lessees from 1990 until today of Firestone ATX, ATX II, Firehawk ATX, ATX 23 Degree, Widetrack Radial Baja, or Wilderness tire models, or any other Firestone tire "substantially similar" to them. More than 60 million tires and 3 million vehicles fit these definitions.

No class action is proper unless all litigants are governed by the same legal rules. Otherwise the class cannot satisfy the commonality and superiority requirements of Fed.R.Civ.P. 23(a), (b)(3). Yet state laws about theories such as those presented by our plaintiffs differ, and such differences have led us to hold that other warranty, fraud, or products-liability suits may not proceed as nationwide classes. The district judge, well aware of this principle, recognized that uniform law would be essential to class certification. Because plaintiffs' claims rest on state law, the choice-of-law rules come from the state in which the federal court sits. See Klaxon v. Stentor Electric Manufacturing Co., 313 U.S. 487, 61 S.Ct. 1020, 85 L.Ed. 1477 (1941). The district judge concluded that Indiana law points to the headquarters of the defendants, because that is where the products are designed and the important decisions about disclosures and sales are made. Ford and Firestone engaged in conduct that was uniform across the nation, which the district court took to imply the appropriateness of uniform law. This ruling means that all claims by the Explorer class will be resolved under Michigan law and all claims by the tire class will be resolved under Tennessee law. According to the district court, other obstacles (such as the fact that the six named tire models represent 67 designs for different sizes and performance criteria, and that half of all 1996 and 1997 model Explorers came with Goodyear tires) are worth overcoming in light of the efficiency of class treatment. Nor did the district court deem it important that Firestone's tires were designed in Ohio, and many were manufactured outside Tennessee, as many of Ford's vehicles are manufactured outside Michigan.

[The court explained that it decided to review the decision under Rule 23(f) because the stakes were so large that settlement became "almost inevitable" after class certification.]

Indiana is a *lex loci delicti* state: in all but exceptional cases it applies the law of the place where harm occurred. See Hubbard Manufacturing Co. v. Greeson, 515 N.E.2d 1071 (Ind.1987). Those class members who suffered injury or death as a result of defects were harmed in the states where the tires failed. As a practical matter, these class members can be ignored; they are sure to opt out and litigate independently. These classes therefore effectively include only those consumers whose loss (if any) is financial rather than physical: it is the class of persons whose tires did *not* fail, whose vehicles did *not* roll over. Many class members face no future threat of failure either, because about 30 million tires were recalled and replaced, while other tires have been used up and discarded. Financial loss (if any, a qualification we will not repeat) was suffered in the places where the vehicles and tires were purchased at excessive prices or resold at depressed prices. Those injuries occurred in all 50 states, the District of Columbia, Puerto Rico, and U.S. territories such as Guam. The *lex loci delicti* principle points to the places of these injuries, not the defendants' corporate headquarters, as the source of law.

Plaintiffs concede that until 1987 this would have been Indiana's approach. They contend, however, that *Hubbard* changed everything by holding that when the place of the injury "bears little connection to the legal action" a court may consider other factors, such as the place of the conduct causing the injury and the residence of the parties. It is conceivable, we suppose, that Indiana might think that a financial (or physical) injury to one of its residents, occurring within the state's borders, "bears little connection to the legal action", but the proof of that pudding is in the eating. Has Indiana since 1987 applied the law of a state where a product was designed, or promotional materials drafted, to a suit arising out of an injury in Indiana? As far as we can tell, the answer is no—not even once, and the state has had plenty of opportunities. Yet since 1987 both Indiana and this court have routinely applied Indiana law when injury caused by a defective product occurred in Indiana to Indiana residents. Neither Indiana nor any other state has applied a uniform place-of-the-defendant's-headquarters rule to products-liability cases. It is not hard to devise an argument that such a uniform rule would be good on many dimensions, but that argument has not carried the day with state judges, and it is state law rather than a quest for efficiency in litigation (or in product design decisions) that controls.

"Ah, but this is not a products-liability case!" So plaintiffs respond to the conspicuous lack of support from state decisions. And indeed it is not a products-liability suit, since all who suffered physical injury are bound to opt out. No injury, no tort, is an ingredient of every state's law. Plaintiffs describe the injury as financial rather than physical and seek to move the suit out of the tort domain and into that of contract (the vehicle was not the flawless one described and thus is not merchantable, a warranty theory) and consumer fraud (on the theory that selling products with undisclosed attributes, and thus worth less than represented, is fraudulent). It is not clear that this maneuver actually moves the locus from tort to contract. If tort law fully compensates those who are physically injured, then any recoveries by those whose products function properly mean excess compensation. As a result, most states would not entertain the sort of theory that plaintiffs press. [The court cited cases from a number of states.]

Obviously plaintiffs believe that Michigan and Tennessee are in the favorable minority; we need not decide. If recovery for breach of warranty or consumer fraud is possible, the injury is decidedly where the *consumer* is located, rather than where the seller maintains its headquarters. A contract for the sale of a car in Indiana is governed by Indiana law unless it contains a choice-of-law clause, and plaintiffs do not want to enforce any choice-of-law clause. Plaintiffs have not cited, and we could not find, any Indiana case applying any law other than Indiana's to warranty or fraud claims arising from consumer products designed (or contract terms written) out of state, unless a choice-of-law clause was involved. State consumer-protection laws vary considerably, and courts must respect these differences rather than apply one state's law to sales in other states with different rules. See BMW of North America, Inc. v. Gore, 517 U.S. 559, 568–73, 116 S.Ct. 1589, 134 L.Ed.2d 809 (1996). We do not for a second suppose that Indiana would apply Michigan law to an auto sale if Michigan permitted auto companies to conceal defects from customers; nor do we think it likely that Indiana would apply Korean law (no matter *what* Korean law on the subject may provide) to claims of deceit in the sale of Hyundai automobiles, in Indiana, to residents of Indiana, or French law to the sale of cars equipped with Michelin tires. Indiana has consistently said that sales of products in Indiana must conform to Indiana's consumer-protection laws and its rules of contract law. It follows that Indiana's choice-of-law rule selects the 50 states and multiple territories where the buyers live, and not the place of the sellers' headquarters, for these suits.

Against all of this plaintiffs set a single decision: KPMG Peat Marwick v. Asher, 689 N.E.2d 1283 (Ind.App.1997). This decision holds that the adequacy of services rendered by an accountant in Missouri to a business whose headquarters were in Missouri is governed by Missouri law, even when a suit is filed by unpaid lenders who live in Indiana. This is a straightforward application of *lex loci delicti*. The injury, if any, was suffered by the business, which hired and paid the accountant for professional services rendered directly to the client; those who dealt with the audited firm, such as the plaintiffs in *KPMG Peat Marwick*, suffer a derivative injury. Similarly a malpractice claim against a firm's lawyer is determined by the law of the state where the services are performed, for that state's law supplies the standard of performance and that is where the client normally would suffer injury. Investors may be able to step into a corporation's shoes and assert a derivative claim, and in some states * * * investors may have a direct claim too; but because the firm remains the lawyer's or accountant's client one body of law must apply to this single transaction. Sales of a consumer product in 50 states do not lead to derivative claims, and each sale is a separate transaction in the place of the sale. *KPMG Peat Marwick* accordingly has no bearing on consumers' suits against manufacturers of allegedly defective products.

Because these claims must be adjudicated under the law of so many jurisdictions, a single nationwide class is not manageable. Lest we soon see a Rule 23(f) petition to review the certification of 50 state classes, we add that this litigation is not manageable as a class action even on a statewide basis. About 20% of the Ford Explorers were shipped without Firestone tires. The Firestone tires supplied with the majority of the vehicles were recalled at different times; they may well have differed in their propensity to fail, and this would require sub-subclassing among those owners of Ford Explorers with Firestone tires. Some of the vehicles were resold and others have not been; the resales may have reflected different discounts that could require vehicle-specific litigation. Plaintiffs contend that many of the failures occurred because Ford and Firestone advised the owners to underinflate their tires, leading them to overheat. Other factors also affect heating; the failure rate (and hence the discount) may have been higher in Arizona than in Alaska. Of those vehicles that have not yet been resold, some will be resold in the future (by which time the tire replacements may have alleviated or eliminated any discount) and some never will be resold. Owners who wring the last possible mile out of their vehicles receive everything they paid for and have claims that differ from owners who sold their Explorers to the second-hand market during the height of the publicity in 2000. Some owners drove their SUVs off the road over rugged terrain, while others never used the "sport" or "utility" features; these differences also affect resale prices.

Firestone's tires likewise exhibit variability; that's why fewer than half of those included in the tire class were recalled. The tire class includes many buyers who used Firestone tires on vehicles other than Ford Explorers, and who therefore were not advised to underinflate their tires. (Note that this description does not reflect any view of the merits; we are repeating rather than endorsing plaintiffs' contention that Ford counseled "underinflation.") The six trade names listed in the class certification order comprise 67 master tire specifications: "Firehawk ATX" tires, for example, come in multiple diameters, widths, and tread designs; their safety features and failure modes differ accordingly. Plaintiffs say that all 67 specifications had three particular shortcomings that led to excess failures. But whether a particular feature is required for safe operation depends on *other* attributes of the tires, and as these other attributes varied across the 67 master specifications it would not be possible to make a once-and-for-all decision about whether all 60 million tires were defective, even if the law were uniform. There are other differences too, but the ones we have mentioned preclude any finding "that the questions of law or fact common to the members of the class predominate over any questions affecting only individual members, and that a class action is superior to other available methods for the fair and efficient adjudication of the controversy." Fed.R.Civ.P. 23(b)(3). Regulation by the NHTSA, coupled with tort litigation by persons suffering physical injury, is far superior to a suit by millions of *uninjured* buyers for dealing with consumer products that are said to be failure-prone.

The district judge did not doubt that differences within the class would lead to difficulties in managing the litigation. But the judge thought it better to cope with these differences than to scatter the suits to the winds and require hundreds of judges to resolve thousands of claims under 50 or more bodies of law. Efficiency is a vital goal in any legal system—but the vision of "efficiency" underlying this class certification is the model of the central planner. Plaintiffs share the premise of the ALI's Complex Litigation Project (1993), which devotes more than 700 pages to an analysis of means to consolidate litigation as quickly as possible, by which the authors mean, before multiple trials break out. The authors take as given the benefits of that step. Yet the benefits are elusive. The central planning model—one case, one court, one set of rules, one settlement price for all involved—suppresses information that is vital to accurate resolution. What *is* the law of Michigan, or Arkansas, or Guam, as applied to this problem? Judges and lawyers will have to guess, because the central planning model keeps the litigation far away from state courts. (Ford asked us to certify legal questions to the Supreme Court of Michigan, to ensure that genuine state law was applied if Michigan's law were to govern the whole country; the plaintiffs stoutly resisted that proposal.) And if the law were clear, how would the facts (and thus the damages per plaintiff) be ascertained? One suit is an all-or-none affair, with high risk even if the parties supply all the information at their disposal. Getting things right the first time would be an accident. * * * When courts think of efficiency, they should think of market models rather than central-planning models.

Our decision in [In re] Rhone–Poulenc Rorer, [51 F.3d 1293 (7th Cir.1995)], made this point, and it is worth reiterating: only "a decentralized process of multiple trials, involving different juries, and different standards of liability, in different jurisdictions" (51 F.3d at 1299) will yield the information needed for accurate evaluation of mass tort claims. Once a series of decisions or settlements has produced an accurate evaluation of a subset of the claims (say, 1995 Explorers in Arizona equipped with a particular tire specification) the others in that subset can be settled or resolved at an established price.

No matter what one makes of the decentralized approach as an original matter, it is hard to adopt the central-planner model without violence not only to Rule 23 but also to principles of federalism. Differences across states may be costly for courts and litigants alike, but they are a fundamental aspect of our federal republic and must not be overridden in a quest to clear the queue in court. See BMW v. Gore, 517 U.S. at 568–73, 116 S.Ct. 1589. Tempting as it is to alter doctrine in order to facilitate class treatment, judges must resist so that all parties' legal rights may be respected. Amchem Products, Inc. v. Windsor, 521 U.S. 591, 613, 117 S.Ct. 2231, 138 L.Ed.2d 689 (1997).

Notes and Questions

1. As demonstrated by Castano v. American Tobacco Co., *supra* p. 340, differences in state law may pose a powerful obstacle to class certification. *Shutts* places constitutional limits on efforts by states to solve those problems by applying one set of legal rules to all class members. On remand, the Kansas Supreme Court determined that, on the question whether prejudgment interest was due, the law of Kansas was not different from that of the other five states whose law was briefed by Phillips, and that the prejudgment interest rate applied by all would be the same. Shutts v. Phillips Petroleum Co., 240 Kan. 764, 732 P.2d 1286 (1987), cert. denied, 487 U.S. 1223, 108 S.Ct. 2883, 101 L.Ed.2d 918 (1988). As to post-judgment interest, however, there were disparities in the rates of the different states. On that issue, the court directed that the interest be determined by the law of the state in which the lease was located without explaining how it decided on that standard. See 732 P.2d at 1314. Should the court instead have tried to determine which law, within the range allowed by due process, would best further the interests of plaintiffs or defendants, or give claimants a choice between the law of their state of residence and the law of the state in which the lease was located where those differed?

2. Should courts approach choice of law in class actions in the same way they do in individual suits? *Shutts'* emphasis on the need to examine each claim to assess the constitutional limits on choice of law strengthen the argument that the class action should be viewed that way. But in consolidated cases courts have seemed to strain to find a single set of legal rules applicable. For example, In re Air Crash Disaster Near Chicago, Illinois, on May 25, 1979, 644 F.2d 633 (7th Cir.1981), involved cases gathered pursuant to a multidistrict transfer. Presented with the question whether plaintiffs could seek punitive damages, the court surveyed the choice-of-law doctrines of many states and ended up concluding, rather remarkably, that all of these states would choose to apply Illinois law. Cf. Boardman Petroleum, Inc. v. Federated Mut. Ins. Co., 135 F.3d 750 (11th Cir.1998) (in transferred consolidated cases, court uses "balancing of interests" test because "of necessity only one state's law may be applied").

In *Firestone/Bridgestone*, the court notes and rejects the "central planning" attitude of the ALI Complex Litigation Project. That Project proposed that where otherwise-applicable laws conflict in consolidated proceedings for transactionally related cases under proposed expanded transfer and removal provisions, the transferee judge be directed to choose a single controlling law for all cases, and it proposed choice of law guidelines that could be used for the purpose. See American Law Institute, Complex Litigation: Statutory Recommendations and Analysis §§ 6.01 (mass torts); 6.02–6.03 (mass contracts); 6.04 (statutes of limitation); 6.05 (monetary relief generally); 6.06 (punitive damages) (1994).

Note that, as the court recognizes, the conduct of defendants in *Firestone/Bridgestone* was uniform and directed from a single place. Do those circumstances support efforts to find a single set of rules to measure the legality of that conduct?

3.   As the plaintiffs suggest in *Bridgestone/Firestone*, one seemingly fair choice would be the law of the defendant's home state. In *Shutts*, would there have been any constitutional objection to applying the law of Oklahoma to determine the obligations of Phillips Petroleum? Obviously, the Seventh Circuit holds here that Indiana would not reach that conclusion under its choice of law rules.

Other choice of law regimes might present similar difficulties. Consider Zinser v. Accufix Research Institute, Inc., 253 F.3d 1180 (9th Cir.2001), in which plaintiffs proposed that Colorado law be applied to the claims of all class members in a proposed nationwide products liability class action. Because the case was in a California federal court, the pertinent choice of law rules were the California version of the "governmental interest" analysis, which looks to which state's interests would be "more impaired" were its law not applied. As applied to this proposed nationwide class action, this analysis led to a byzantine choice of law determination (id. at 1188):

> As the district court explained, "the three-part California choice of law inquiry requires comparison of each non-forum state's law and interest with California's law and interest *separately*." As required by California law, Zinser thus must apply California's three-part conflict test to *each* non-forum state with an interest in the application of its law. Also, because Zinser seeks certification of three separate claims—negligence, products liability, and medical monitoring—this conflicts test must be applied to *each* claim upon which certification is sought.

The reality is that choice of law is hard to do. Thus, a district judge trying to navigate this thicket complained that "[t]he law on 'choice of law' in the various states and in the federal courts is a veritable jungle, which, if the law can be found out, leads not to a 'rule of action' but a reign of chaos dominated in each case by the judge's 'informed guess' as to what some other state than the one in which he sits would hold its law to be." In re Paris Air Crash of March 3, 1974, 399 F.Supp. 732, 739 (C.D.Cal.1975). This situation has not improved dramatically since.

4.   At the same time, the Supreme Court has emphasized the limits on states that may be tempted to reach out to apply their own law to distant transactions. In BMW of North America v. Gore, 517 U.S. 559, 116 S.Ct. 1589, 134 L.Ed.2d 809 (1996), cited by the court in *Bridgestone/Firestone*, plaintiff in an individual suit received a large punitive damages award that the state court recognized was premised in large measure on proof that defendant had treated other customers in other states the same way it treated him. But there was no showing that the conduct in question was unlawful in the states where these customers resided, and the Court concluded that "Alabama does not have the power * * * to punish BMW for conduct that was lawful where it occurred and had no impact on Alabama or its residents." Id. at 572–73. In State Farm Mut. Auto. Ins. Co. v. Campbell, 538 U.S. 408, 123 S.Ct. 1513, 155 L.Ed.2d 585 (2003), it reiterated that "[a] state cannot punish a defendant for conduct that may be been lawful where it occurred."

The same constraints would seem to matter in class actions. Urging that choice of law should be understood as an integral part of substantive law, Professor Kramer has argued that impulses toward class-action choice of law practices that facilitate aggregate treatment should be resisted:

> Because choice of law is part of the process of defining the parties' rights, it should not change simply because, as a matter of administrative convenience and efficiency, we have combined many claims in one proceeding; whatever choice-of-law rules we use to define substantive rights should be the same for ordinary and complex cases.

Kramer, Choice of Law in Complex Litigation, 71 N.Y.U.L. Rev. 547, 549 (1996); cf. In re Bendectin Litigation, *infra* p. 773 ("Simply because a litigant shares his complaint with eight hundred other claimants is not a reason to deprive him of the day in court he would have enjoyed had he been the sole plaintiff.") (Jones, J. concurring).

5. In *Bridgestone/Firestone*, the court says that "[n]o class action is proper unless all litigants are governed by the same legal rules." Professor Kramer does not think that the problem is necessarily insurmountable:

> [C]omplex litigation could really become unmanageable if, once the various substantive laws were compiled and organized, the judge still had to perform hundreds or thousands of individualized choice-of-law analyses. But because variation in the legal rules is not great, once the state-by-state survey is completed, judges will find a relatively small number of conflicts and an equally small number of approaches to choice of law. At that point, claims can be grouped and the task of resolving the conflicts completed in a fairly efficient manner. It may not be fun, but it is far from impossible.

Kramer, *supra*, 71 N.Y.U.L. Rev. at 584. At least one court has taken such an approach. In In re School Asbestos Litigation, 789 F.2d 996, 1010 (3d Cir.1986), the appellate court initially approved a (b)(3) action:

> To meet the problem of diversity in applicable state law, class plaintiffs have undertaken an extensive analysis of the variances in products liability among the jurisdictions. That review separates the law into four categories. Even assuming additional permutations and combinations, plaintiffs have made a creditable showing, which apparently satisfied the district court, that class certification does not present insuperable obstacles.

But the court in *Castano* (supra p. 340, 84 F.3d at 751 n. 33), raised questions about the *School Asbestos* experience:

> The plaintiffs rely on *School Asbestos* for the proposition that variations in state law do not preclude predominance. Putting that issue aside, the case is instructive for what happened after the Third Circuit remanded to the district court. Almost nine years after the first complaint was filed, and eight years after the court of appeals had affirmed certification, the conflict of law issues had yet to be resolved. See In re Sch. Asbestos Litig., 977 F.2d 764, 771 (3d Cir.1992) (granting mandamus to disqualify judge but refusing to address whether district court's trial plan properly resolved any problems with variations in state law because new judge may adopt a different trial plan).

In Washington Mutual Bank v. Superior Court, 24 Cal.4th 906, 103 Cal.Rptr.2d 320, 15 P.3d 1071 (2001), the California Supreme Court insisted on a careful analysis of these questions at the outset in state-court class actions:

> [W]e hold that a class action proponent must credibly demonstrate, through a thorough analysis of the applicable state laws, that state law variations will not swamp common issues and defeat predominance. Additionally, the proponent's presentation must be sufficient to permit the trial court, at the time of certification, to make a detailed assessment of how any state law differences could be managed fairly and efficiently at trial, for example, through the creation of a manageable number of subclasses.

6. State courts, applying choice of law standards, have sometimes certified nationwide or multi-state class actions upon finding that the law of a single state applies. For example, Ysbrand v. DaimlerChrysler Corp., 81 P.3d 618 (Okla.2003), was a suit alleging defective installation of air bags in minivans. The court held that, under the "most significant relationship" test, the law of Michigan, defendant's principal place of business, would apply to breach of warranty claims. This conclusion was based on Michigan's interest "in having its regulatory scheme applied to the conduct of a Michigan manufacturer." But the court found that the law of the states in which the class members were domiciled should be applied to fraud claims, making a class action on those claims unmanageable. In Farmer's Ins. Exch. v. Leonard & Sawyer, 125 S.W.3d 55 (Tex.App.2003), a contract-claim class action by agents against their company for failure to pay bonuses as promised, the court applied the law of California to the claims of all class members because the insurance group had its principal place of business in California, and administered the bonus contracts from there. These factors outweighed the interests of the states in which the agents performed their duties.

7. Is state law likely to be more uniform on some subjects than others? Recall that there are Restatements and Uniform Laws that have many adherents. But even on those topics, uniformity may prove elusive. Consider the views of a leading treatise: "The Uniform Commercial Code is not uniform." J. White & R. Summers, Uniform Commercial Code 7 (2d ed.1980).

8. The same difficulties should not arise, it should be kept in mind, if the governing substantive law is federal law, although they can reappear if federal law incorporates standards drawn from the local law of the place of a transaction.

9. Could an argument be made that the *Bridgestone/Firestone* court is simply antagonistic toward class actions? Why should it matter if "[o]ne suit is an all-or-nothing affair"? Isn't that the goal of a class action?

10. In In re Bridgestone/Firestone, Inc., Tires Products Liability Litigation, 333 F.3d 763 (7th Cir.2003), defendants sought an injunction against efforts by putative class members to obtain nationwide class certification in various state courts. The court held that it could enjoin these efforts on the ground its decision in the principal case above foreclosed any such certification because it was sufficiently final to be enforceable by injunction under

the exception of the Anti–Injunction Act for injunctions to "effectuate" the federal court's judgment. See *supra* p. 404–05 n. 9.

But the injunction was issued against the putative members of a class that the court said could not properly be constituted. Under *Shutts*, could there be jurisdiction for such an injunction? In In re Real Estate Title and Settlement Services Antitrust Litigation, 869 F.2d 760 (3d Cir.), cert. denied, 493 U.S. 821, 110 S.Ct. 77, 107 L.Ed.2d 44 (1989), the court certified a class action under Rule 23(b)(1) and (b)(2) on charges that defendants conspired to fix prices for settlement of real estate transactions. The class actions were "hybrid" actions seeking both damages and equitable relief. After a settlement of the class actions, one class member attempted to opt out and filed an individual action for damages in its home jurisdiction. The class action court enjoined prosecution of the damages action, and the court of appeals reversed. Noting that there was no right to opt out, the appellate court reasoned that the situation was different from *Shutts* even though it was dealing with a plaintiff class member:

> The only issue we address is whether an absent class member can be enjoined from relitigation if the member does not have minimum contacts with the forum. On that issue, we hold that, given that the absent member in this case loses more than the plaintiffs lost in *Shutts,* if the member has not been given the opportunity to opt out in a class action involving both important injunctive relief and damage claims, the member must either have minimum contacts with the forum or consent to jurisdiction in order to be enjoined by the district court that entertained the class action. We also hold that a plaintiff does not consent to personal jurisdiction to have an injunction levied against it if it merely appeared in the district court to make a motion to opt out.

Compare Grimes v. Vitalink Communications Corp., 17 F.3d 1553 (3d Cir.1994), in which the court held that by purchasing stock in a Delaware corporation, plaintiff class members established a sufficient connection with the state for it to bind them by res judicata under the class action judgment of a Delaware state court. It distinguished In re *Real Estate Title, supra,* on the ground that case involved an injunction against class members rather than preclusive effect of the state-court judgment.

In *Bridgestone/Firestone*, the court held that it had jurisdiction to enjoin class members even though they were not part of a proper class. In part, this was because the case had involved a claim based on the federal RICO statute, which authorizes nationwide service of process (on defendants). Beyond that, the court reasoned that class members "have the status of parties for many purposes," so that "[j]ust as they receive the fruits of victory, so an adverse decision is conclusive against them." 333 F.3d at 768. All that was needed, the court said, was that the class members have been adequately represented, and that was determined by the class certification granted by the district court initially and not challenged on defendants' appeal from that certification. Therefore, "[o]ur prior judgment is binding *in personam* with respect to the unnamed class members." Id. at 769.

The court was careful, however, to limit the injunction to proposals for certification of a nationwide class. Note the comments the court made in the principal case about the difficulties in the way of a state-wide class certification. In the later decision, the court adverted to those comments, but added that "this assessment did not become part of our judgment," adding that "advice designed to ward off what a federal court deems an unproductive investment of judicial time does not create a 'judgment' that *forbids* any state tribunal to make the effort."

H. PREJUDGMENT NOTICE TO CLASS MEMBERS

EISEN v. CARLISLE & JACQUELIN

Supreme Court of the United States, 1974.
417 U.S. 156, 94 S.Ct. 2140, 40 L.Ed.2d 732.

JUSTICE POWELL delivered the opinion of the Court.

[The district court certified a Rule 23(b)(3) class action on behalf of all persons who traded odd lots of shares (blocks of less than 100 shares or not in multiples of 100 shares) on the New York Stock Exchange between 1962 and 1966. Plaintiff alleged that defendants conspired to fix the commissions charged on such trades in violation of the antitrust and securities laws. The class had an estimated six million members. The district court found that some 2,250,000 of those could be identified with reasonable effort. The cost of mailing notice to these persons would have been $225,000. The class representative's claim was estimated at $70. Rather than impose the postage cost on the class representative, the district court authorized a notice procedure costing approximately $22,000. It involved individual notice to all identifiable class members who had ten or more odd-lot trades during the period and to 5,000 others selected at random. In addition, there would be prominent advertisements in the Wall Street Journal and other newspapers in New York and California. Based on its preliminary assessment of plaintiff's probabilities of success, the district court directed defendants to pay 90% of the cost of this notice procedure.]

Turning to the merits of the case, we find that the District Court's resolution of the notice problems was erroneous in two respects. First, it failed to comply with the notice requirements of Rule 23(c)(2), and second, it imposed part of the cost of notice on respondents.

A

Rule 23(c)(2) provides that, in any class action maintained under subdivision (b)(3), each class member shall be advised that he has the right to exclude himself from the action on request or to enter an appearance through counsel, and further that the judgment, whether favorable or not, will bind all class members not requesting exclusion. To this end, the court is required to direct to class members "the best notice practicable under the circumstances, *including individual notice to all members who can be identified through reasonable effort.*" We think the import of this language is unmistakable. Individual notice must be sent to all class members whose names and addresses may be ascertained through reasonable effort.

The Advisory Committee's Note to Rule 23 reinforces this conclusion. The Advisory Committee described subdivision (c)(2) as "not merely discretionary" and added that the "mandatory notice pursuant to subdivision (c)(2) . . . is designed to fulfill requirements of due process to which the class action procedure is of course subject." The Committee explicated its incorporation of due process standards by citation to *Mullane v. Central Hanover Bank & Trust Co.,* 339 U.S. 306, 70 S.Ct. 652, 94 L.Ed. 865 (1950), and like cases.

In *Mullane* the Court addressed the constitutional sufficiency of publication notice rather than mailed individual notice to known beneficiaries of a common trust fund as part of a judicial settlement of accounts. The Court observed that notice and an opportunity to be heard were fundamental requisites of the constitutional guarantee of procedural due process. It further stated that notice must be "reasonably calculated, under all the circumstances, to apprise interested parties of the pendency of the action and afford them an opportunity to present their objections." The Court continued:

> "But when notice is a person's due, process which is a mere gesture is not due process. The means employed must be such as one desirous of actually informing the absentee might reasonably adopt to accomplish it. The reasonableness and hence the constitutional validity of any chosen method may be defended on the ground that it is in itself reasonably certain to inform those affected."

The Court then held that publication notice could not satisfy due process where the names and addresses of the beneficiaries were known. In such cases, "the reasons disappear for resort to means less likely than the mails to apprise them of [an action's] pendency."

* * *

Viewed in this context, the express language and intent of Rule 23(c)(2) leave no doubt that individual notice must be provided to those class members who are identifiable through reasonable effort. In the present case, the names and addresses of 2,250,000 class members are easily ascertainable, and there is nothing to show that individual notice cannot be mailed to each. For these class members, individual notice is clearly the "best notice practicable" within the meaning of Rule 23(c)(2) and our prior decisions.

Petitioner contends, however, that we should dispense with the requirement of individual notice in this case, and he advances two reasons for our doing so. First, the prohibitively high cost of providing individual notice to 2,250,000 class members would end this suit as a class action and effectively frustrate petitioner's attempt to vindicate the policies underlying the antitrust and securities laws. Second, petitioner contends that individual notice is unnecessary in this case, because no prospective class member has a large enough stake in the matter to justify separate litigation of his individual claim. Hence, class members lack any incentive to opt out of the class action even if notified.

The short answer to these arguments is that individual notice to identifiable class members is not a discretionary consideration to be waived in a particular case. It is, rather, an unambiguous requirement of Rule 23. As the Advisory Committee's Note explained, the Rule was intended to insure that the judgment, whether favorable or not, would bind all class members who did not request exclusion from the suit. Accordingly, each class member who can be identified through reasonable effort must be notified that he may request exclusion from the action and thereby preserve his opportunity to press his claim separately or that he may remain in the class and perhaps participate in the management of the action. There is nothing in Rule 23 to suggest that the notice requirements can be tailored to fit the pocketbooks of particular plaintiffs.[13]

Petitioner further contends that adequate representation, rather than notice, is the touchstone of due process in a class action and therefore satisfies Rule 23. We think this view has little to commend it. To begin with, Rule 23 speaks to notice as well as to adequacy of representation and requires that both be provided. Moreover, petitioner's argument proves too much, for it quickly leads to the conclusion that no notice at all, published or otherwise, would be required in the present case. This cannot be so, for quite apart from what due process may require, the command of Rule 23 is clearly to the contrary. We therefore conclude that Rule 23(c)(2) requires that individual notice be sent to all class members who can be identified with reasonable effort.[14]

B

We also agree with the Court of Appeals that petitioner must bear the cost of notice to the members of his class. The District Court reached the contrary conclusion and imposed 90% of the notice cost on respondents. * * *

The usual rule is that a plaintiff must initially bear the cost of notice to the class. The exceptions cited by the District Court related to situations where a fiduciary duty pre-existed between the plaintiff and defendant, as in a shareholder derivative suit.[15] Where, as here, the relationship between the parties is truly adversary, the plaintiff must

---

13. Petitioner also argues that class members will not opt out because the statute of limitations has long since run out on the claims of all class members other than petitioner. This contention is disposed of by our recent decision in *American Pipe & Construction Co. v. Utah,* 414 U.S. 538, 94 S.Ct. 756, 38 L.Ed.2d 713 (1974), which established that commencement of a class action tolls the applicable statute of limitations as to all members of the class.

14. We are concerned here only with the notice requirements of subdivision

(c)(2), which are applicable to class actions maintained under subdivision (b)(3). By its terms subdivision (c)(2) is inapplicable to class actions for injunctive or declaratory relief maintained under subdivision (b)(2). Petitioner's effort to qualify his suit as a class action under subdivisions (b)(1) and (b)(2) was rejected by the Court of Appeals.

15. See, *E.g., Dolgow v. Anderson,* 43 F.R.D. 472, 498–500 (E.D.N.Y.1968). We, of course, express no opinion on the proper allocation of the cost of notice in such cases.

pay for the cost of notice as part of the ordinary burden of financing his own suit.

Petitioner has consistently maintained, however, that he will not bear the cost of notice under subdivision (c)(2) to members of the class as defined in his original complaint. We therefore remand the cause with instructions to dismiss the class action as so defined.[16]

[Dissenting opinion of Justice Douglas omitted.]

Notes and Questions

1. One may argue that *Eisen* represented either the best or the worst use of the class action device. The case had been labelled a "Frankenstein monster posing as a class action" by Chief Judge Lumbard of the Second Circuit, dissenting from an earlier ruling. Eisen v. Carlisle and Jacquelin, 391 F.2d 555, 572 (2d Cir.1968). On the other hand, it seems unlikely that the claims of these millions of people would be litigated outside the class action context. Noting that the named plaintiff's claim was only $70, Justice Powell acknowledged that "[n]o competent attorney would undertake this complex antitrust action to recover so inconsequential an amount." 417 U.S. at 161, 94 S.Ct. at 2144.

In such cases, does requiring individual notice make sense if it entails such cost? Consider the views of Professors Macey and Miller:

> There is little to recommend the *Eisen* rule from the standpoint of economic analysis. The pecuniary costs of notice in large class actions can run well over half a million dollars. In addition, the costs of identifying absent class members and preparing the notice, as well as the opportunity costs to class members of interpreting the notice, can be substantial. These costs would be justified if they were outweighed by compensating benefits that might exist in such a case with substantial individual claims. In the large-scale, small-claim class action, however, the benefits of notice appear minimal at best. It is doubtful whether notice has any social utility other than that of informing the class members of the claim. Most plaintiffs are unlikely to place any significant value on such information.

Macey & Miller, The Plaintiffs' Attorney's Role in Class Action and Derivative Litigation: Economic Analysis and Recommendations for Reform, 58 U.Chi.L.Rev. 1, 27–28 (1991); see also Rand v. Monsanto Co., 926 F.2d 596, 599 (7th Cir.1991) ("No (sane) person would pay the entire costs of a securities class action in exchange for a maximum benefit of $1,135"). It has even been suggested that in antitrust cases *Eisen* led to the filing of an increased number of class actions because it "lowered the optimal size of the class, encouraging more filings to cover the same number of damaged cartel customers." Marvel, Netter & Robinson, Price Fixing and Civil Damages, 40 Stan.L.Rev. 561, 568 (1988).

16. The record does not reveal whether a smaller class of odd-lot traders could be defined, and if so, whether petitioner would be willing to pay the cost of notice to members of such a class. We intimate no view on whether any such subclass would satisfy the requirements of Rule 23. We do note, however, that our dismissal of the class action as originally defined is without prejudice to any efforts petitioner may make to redefine his class either under Rule 23(c)(4) or Fed. Rule Civ.Proc. 15.

Could technology reduce the costs associated with giving notice? E-mail might provide a much cheaper and easier method of giving of notifying class members. Would there be a greater risk that class members would regard it as unwanted spam than that they would regard regular mail about a class action as junk mail? At least some lawyers are trying to use the Internet to communicate about pending class actions. See Temple–Raston, Class–Action Suits Gain Strength on the Web, N.Y.Times, July 28, 2002, § 3 at 10 (reporting that law firms are posting information about class actions on websites).

2.   What are the advantages to class members of notice? There seem to be basically two:

(a) *Monitoring*: Class members who are aware of the pendency of the class action can monitor it and protect their interests. But how important is it that they all be notified for this purpose? Consider the views of the Supreme Court in a different context in Mullane v. Central Hanover Bank & Trust Co., 339 U.S. 306, 70 S.Ct. 652, 94 L.Ed. 865 (1950):

> The individual interest does not stand alone but is identical with that of a class. The rights of each in the integrity of the fund and the fidelity of the trustee are shared by many other beneficiaries. Therefore notice reasonably certain to reach most of those interested in objecting is likely to safeguard the interests of all, since any objections sustained would inure to the benefit of all.

Was the plan adopted by the district court in *Eisen* deficient in light of these concerns?

(b) *Opt-out*: In (b)(3) class actions class members may opt out, but to do so they may need notice. For this purpose, notice to some class members seems not to be a substitute for notice to all. But if that is true, why is there no concern with the 3.75 million class members not identified in *Eisen* ? If most of those identified opt out of the class action does that provide a reason to reconsider class certification?

3.   Rule 23(c)(2) calls for "the best notice practicable under the circumstances." With a large class, how should notice be given? In Amchem Products, Inc. v. Windsor, *supra* p. 373, the Supreme Court adverted to the problems presented in giving adequate notice to a large class of persons, many of whom did not at the time suffer from any asbestos-related disease, and cited the court of appeals decision in that case which said that "[i]t is unrealistic to expect every individual with incidental exposure to asbestos to realize that he or she could some day contract a deadly disease and make a reasoned decision about whether to stay in this class action." See 83 F.3d at 633. Moreover, there was no listing of class members, so many could not be sent mailed notice. It was true, however, that 35 labor unions had collaborated in an effort to get out the word and there had been a great deal of advertising about the case, and possible class members were invited to call a toll-free number to obtain information packets on the class action settlement. The district court concluded that over 6.8 million people received individually-delivered notice packets. See Georgine v. Amchem Products, Inc., 157 F.R.D. 246, 333 (E.D.Pa.1994).

Could adequate notice ever be given in such a sprawling class action with regard to such inchoate claims? Compare In re Agent Orange Product Liability Litigation, 818 F.2d 145 (2d Cir.1987), cert. denied, 484 U.S. 1004, 108 S.Ct. 695, 98 L.Ed.2d 648 (1988), where the court relied in part on media publicity of the litigation in holding notice efforts adequate. In addition to mailed notice to veterans listed in the Agent Orange Registry, there was notice in newspapers, radio and television. "We also take judicial notice of the widespread publicity this litigation has received. Given the grave doubt as to whether anyone at all was injured by Agent Orange, the fact that some 240,000 claims have been filed suggests that no practical problem exists as to the adequacy of notice." Id. at 169. Does the doubt about actual injury distinguish the asbestos situation from the Agent Orange case?

4. Was *Eisen* based on Rule 23 or the due process clause? If it was based on the Constitution, why did the court reserve the question of notice in actions under Rule 23(b)(1) or (b)(2)? Some courts have held that prejudgment notice is constitutionally required in those cases as well. See Johnson v. General Motors Corp., 598 F.2d 432 (5th Cir.1979). Others have contended that mandatory class actions are different. Consider Larionoff v. United States, 533 F.2d 1167, 1186 (D.C.Cir.1976), *affirmed on other grounds,* 431 U.S. 864, 97 S.Ct. 2150, 53 L.Ed.2d 48 (1977):

> Unlike the situation with respect to members of a Rule 23(b)(3) class, the members of a Rule 23(b)(1) class are likely to be more unified in the sense that there will probably be little interest on the part of individual members in controlling and directing their own separate litigation on the question at issue in the class suit. Indeed, in a Rule 23(b)(1)(B) class action, adjudications with respect to individual members would as a practical matter dispose of the interests of the absent members or substantially impair or impede their ability to protect their interests. At best, then, notice provides absent members with an opportunity to monitor the representation of their rights. In such cases, we think that due process is satisfied if the procedure adopted "fairly insures the protection of the interests of absent parties who are to be bound by it." *Hansberry v. Lee,* 311 U.S. 32, 42, 61 S.Ct. 115, 118, 85 L.Ed. 22, 27 (1940).

Is Hansberry v. Lee, *supra* p. 285, even relevant to the issue of notice? If so, is there any constitutional requirement for notice at all if the representation is adequate? See Weber, Preclusion and Procedural Due Process in Rule 23(b)(2) Class Actions, 21 U.Mich.J.Law Reform, 347 (1988) (arguing that preclusion of unnamed class members without notice violates due process in (b)(2) class actions). Keep these issues in mind in connection with the possible constitutional right to opt out, *infra* p. 457 n. 4.

In 2001, an amendment to Rule 23(c)(2) was proposed that would have provided that "[f]or any class certified under Rule 23(b)(1) or (2), the court must direct notice by means calculated to reach a reasonable number of class members." See Preliminary Draft of Proposed Amendments to the Federal Rules of Bankruptcy, Civil and Criminal Procedure and Rules of Evidence, 201 F.R.D. 560, 606 (2001). The proposal prompted criticism that it could impose prohibitive costs in some suits for injunctions, particularly civil rights class actions, and it was not included in the 2003 amendments.

5. As amended in 2003, Rule 23(c)(2) provides that the class notice in (b)(3) cases "must concisely and clearly state in plain, easily understood language" a number of things that would likely be important to class members. In the past, class action notices have proved difficult for recipients to understand. Consider the observations of Professor Arthur R. Miller, a former Reporter of the Judicial Conference's Advisory Committee on Civil Rules, in Problems of Giving Notice in Class Actions, 58 F.R.D. 313, 321–22 (1972):

> Obviously, the federal courts should not involve themselves in Madison Avenue activities. I am not advocating the use of gayly colored judicial mail embossed: "Important! Open this envelope! You may be entitled to a cash reward!!" The courts cannot act as if they were hawking the *Reader's Digest*. Nevertheless, the notice-giving process under Rule 23 must be reasonably pragmatic. The sad truth is that notices issued by courts or attorneys typically are much too larded with legal jargon to be understood by the average citizen.

> A good illustration of this also is offered by the tetracycline cases. The Attorney General of North Carolina sent notice of the action to citizens of his state who had paid income taxes during a particular period. The theory underlying this procedure was sound enough. Given the wide use of the medication it was important to send notice to a broadly based list of citizens. Some of the responses are worth reading because they are symptomatic of the difficulty with the wording of most notices and reflect the problem of communicating to lay people about legal matters.

> > Dear Mr. Clerk: I have your notice that I owe you $300 for selling drugs. I have never sold any drugs, especially those you have listed; but I have sold a little whiskey once in a while.

> > Dear Sir: I received this paper from you. I guess I really don't understand it, but if I have been given one of those drugs, nobody told me why. If it means what I think it does, I have not been with a man in nine years.

> > Dear Sir: I received your pamphlet on drugs, which I think will be of great value to me in the future. I am unable to attend your class, however.

> > Dear Mr. Attorney General: I am sorry to say this, but you have the wrong John Doe, because in 1954, I wasn't but three years old and didn't even have a name. Mother named me when I got my driver's license. Up to then, they just called me Baby Doe.

6. Consider how a notice that provides meaningful information should be drafted. Should the court leave it to the lawyers to draft the notice? Won't the plaintiff lawyers want to paint the case in a favorable light? Won't the defendant lawyers want to emphasize that class members take a risk unless they opt out? Can the judge insist on a proper assessment of the case's chances of success? Recall that the judge is not to make a class certification decision based on the likelihood of success of the case. See Timing of Class

Certification Decisions, *supra* p. 370. Some reflection may suggest why such notices often tend to be rather bland and technical affairs. The Manual for Complex Litigation (4th) § 21.31 (2004) points out that question-and-answer formats can make information easier for many readers to absorb, and makes other suggestions for enhancing comprehension.

7. Some courts have specified that, in addition to the matters required by Rule 23(c)(2) to be included in the notice of class certification, the notice include a verified proof-of-claim form to be completed and returned. See Minnesota v. United States Steel Corp., 44 F.R.D. 559, 577 (D.Minn.1968). It is argued that the power to require such affirmative action may be implied from Rule 23(d), as necessary for determining who should be in the class for purposes of scheduling phases of the action such as damage issues, and furthers expediency, cost-saving, and fairness to defendant. See 7B C. Wright, A. Miller & M. Kane, Federal Practice & Procedure § 1787, at 215 (2d ed. 1986). On the other hand, this looks suspiciously like an "opt in" requirement that seems contrary to Rule 23(c)(2). Requiring a class member to get together sufficient information to file a claim form seems likely to result in the exclusion of persons who are confused or dilatory about legal matters or simply unwilling to invest time and effort when there is as yet no assurance of recovery. This procedure might be seen as especially inappropriate where there are a large number of class members with small claims, see In re Antibiotic Antitrust Actions, 333 F.Supp. 267 (S.D.N.Y.1971), the class members are unsophisticated, see Enterprise Wall Paper Mfg. Co. v. Bodman, 85 F.R.D. 325 (S.D.N.Y.1980), or class members may need the benefit of discovery or further case developments (such as expert testimony as to the availability of a damage formula) in order to assess their claim. It has been suggested that each case should be considered on its facts: "This has the effect of recognizing the court's discretion to utilize this procedure except when it only will confuse the absentees, some class members can demonstrate that it will prejudice their rights, it will be employed prematurely or administered in an inappropriate fashion, or it will serve only to reduce the efficiencies of the class action." Federal Practice & Procedure, *supra,* at pp. 218–19.

8. In *Eisen,* defendants offered to supply plaintiff with a list of 2,250,-000 class members at their own expense, leaving plaintiff to pay the cost of mailing notice. What happens if defendants are not so helpful?

In Oppenheimer Fund, Inc. v. Sanders, 437 U.S. 340, 98 S.Ct. 2380, 57 L.Ed.2d 253 (1978), the Court held that plaintiff must also pay the cost of identifying class members. Plaintiff sued on behalf of all purchasers of shares in the defendant Fund during 1968–69, asserting violations of the securities laws. Discovery revealed that the class numbered approximately 121,000. To cull out the names and addresses of the members of the class would require computer operations costing over $16,000. Concluding that this cost was "insubstantial," the district court directed defendant to provide the list for free. The Supreme Court reversed. It held that the compilation of the list of class members was not discovery since the information sought did not bear on any substantive issue in dispute. The Court acknowledged that discovery could be used "to illuminate issues upon which a district court must pass in deciding whether a suit should proceed as a class action under Rule 23, such as numerosity, common questions and adequacy of representation," but concluded that the requested list did not serve that function. The Court found authority under Rule 23(d) to order defendant to prepare the list only if the burden of doing so would be substantially less than the burden on plaintiffs to compile the list on their own. Under those circumstances, the defendant would be entitled to reimbursement for the cost unless the expense was "so insubstantial as not to warrant the effort required to calculate it and shift it to the representative plaintiff."

The cost of identifying class members could become enormous. Consider In re Domestic Air Transportation Antitrust Litigation, 141 F.R.D. 534 (N.D.Ga.1992), a suit on behalf of all persons in the United States who purchased an airline ticket from one of the defendant airlines for travel to or from a hub airport of that airline during a three-and-a-half year period. Defendants took the position that plaintiffs had to glean the needed information from microfiche records of tickets, a process estimated to take some 1.2 million hours of work for United Airlines customers alone. The court refused to find that Rule 23(c)(2) required this effort, which it said "would require decades to accomplish." See also Southern Ute Indian Tribe v. Amoco Production Co., 2 F.3d 1023 (10th Cir.1993) (Because defendants had already compiled such a list for business purposes before the litigation began, it was improper to impose any of the "enormous" cost on the plaintiffs, particularly since defendants favored the class treatment and stood to benefit from it.).

9.   If defendant has regular mailings to the class, it can be required to include the notice in those mailings as a cost-saving measure. For example, in Mountain States Tel. & Tel. Co. v. District Court, 778 P.2d 667 (Colo. 1989), cert. denied, 493 U.S. 983, 110 S.Ct. 519, 107 L.Ed.2d 520 (1989), the court ordered defendant to send notice to nearly 1.5 million of its customers. The state supreme court upheld this requirement under Oppenheimer Fund, Inc. v. Sanders, *supra* note 8, on the ground that "the representative plaintiffs in the class action would incur such substantial costs in mailing the notices as to possibly preclude the litigation, and * * * Mountain Bell has the ability to notify the class members, at no significant additional expense to itself, by merely enclosing the class notices in billing envelopes routinely sent to its customers." The court also rejected defendant's argument that this requirement violated its first amendment rights by requiring it to disseminate adverse information.

10.   Keep in mind that where personal jurisdiction issues arise, the due process right to notice and an opportunity to opt out will be governed in part by Phillips Petroleum Co. v. Shutts, *supra* p. 412.

I.   INTERVENTION AND OPT–OUT

WOOLEN v. SURTRAN TAXICABS, INC.

United States Court of Appeals, Fifth Circuit, 1982.
684 F.2d 324.

Before BROWN, GOLDBERG and POLITZ, CIRCUIT JUDGES.

BROWN, CIRCUIT JUDGE.

This case presents us with both unique facts and issues within the context of an antitrust class action challenging the Dallas/Fort Worth airport's restriction of solicitation of taxicab passengers to limited holders of permits. The controversy surrounding the antitrust claim which forms the merits of this case pales in comparison to this donnybrook between two factions of plaintiffs, the Woolen/Campisi (Campisi) group and the Whorton group. The loser in the first round, the Whorton plaintiffs, sought exclusion from the class suit filed by the Campisi plaintiffs, or intervention in that suit, alleging inadequate representation and imposition of a class attorney antagonistic to their interests. The District Court denied intervention, certified the class as a F.R.Civ.P. 23(b)(2) suit, and thus in practical effect denied exclusion.[1] * * *

A TOUCH OF CLASS

The underlying litigation in which the Whorton plaintiffs seek to intervene or from which they seek to be excluded is an antitrust action stemming from the establishment by the cities of Dallas and Fort Worth of the D/FW Surtran System to provide ground transportation for the D/FW airport. Surtran apparently accepted competitive bids for the privilege of picking up passengers at the airport. The winning bid was submitted by Yellow Cab of Dallas, Inc. and Fort Worth Cab and Baggage Company who together formed Surtran Taxicabs, Inc., which contracted with Surtran System to pick up taxicab passengers at the airport for transportation to points in the ten counties surrounding the airport. The contract between Surtran System and Surtran Taxicabs set

---

1. Although the Whorton plaintiffs filed a request for exclusion from the Campisi suit, at least through the time of oral argument in this case, the District Court had not ruled on the motion. The District Judge certified the class action in this case as a (b)(2) action. Although there is some debate whether in certain circumstances notice must be given to the members of the class with the attendant right to opt out in a (b)(2) action, F.R.Civ.P. 23 requires notice and the opportunity to be excluded specifically only in a (b)(3) action. Thus, at least at this point, the practical effect of certification under (b)(2) is to deny the motion for exclusion. However, since the District Court has not ruled on this motion for exclusion, we need not reach the issue of whether the Whorton plaintiffs have a right to opt out of the class action.

This Court has considered the right to opt out of a class under Rule 23(b)(2) and the right to notice generally within the context of settlements or consent decrees in Title VII cases. In *Johnson v. General Motors Corp.*, 598 F.2d 432 (5th Cir.1979), we found that where monetary relief was sought in a Title VII case certified under Rule 23(b)(2), notice was required before an absent class member could be barred from pursuing an individual damage claim. In *Penson v. Terminal Transport Co.*, 634 F.2d

989, 992–95 (5th Cir.1981), after surveying prior Circuit law, we held that a member of a class certified under Rule 23(b)(2) had no absolute right to opt out of the class, although a District Court has the power to require an opt out right under Rule 23(d)(2). Thus, this Court had addressed the opt out requirement in retrospect in the context of the res judicata effect of a prior action and the due process requirements necessary for a prior action to be binding on absent members of a class. The inquiry then generally becomes one of adequacy of representation under the standard of *Hansberry v. Lee*, 311 U.S. 32, 61 S.Ct. 115, 85 L.Ed.22 (1940). For instance, in this case should the Campisi class action continue as a (b)(2) action without the intervention of the Whorton plaintiffs or the consolidation of these two cases, and should the Campisi plaintiffs either lose on the merits or settle with the defendants, the Whorton plaintiffs could argue in this case or in a separate action the flip-side of the opt out argument, that of adequacy of representation. Although there may be no right to opt out in a (b)(2) action, the judgment is always subject to attack on the premise that those absent members were inadequately represented and thus are not bound. For this reason, it is essential that representation of absent class members be adequate from the start.

the rates to be charged, and provided that Surtran System would be paid seventy-five cents per trip plus fifty percent of all profits above a five percent operating profit. Both Dallas and Fort Worth adopted ordinances providing that only holders of permits issued by the airport board may provide ground transportation from the airport. The effect of these ordinances was that only Surtran Taxicabs, as the sole holder of a permit, could pick up taxi passengers at the airport.

On May 22, 1978, plaintiffs John Woolen, Jack Stephens, and John D. Campisi, individually and on behalf of a class of taxi drivers, filed suit against Surtran Taxicabs, the City of Dallas, City of Fort Worth, and three surrounding cities. The Campisi class action suit alleged that the arrangement between the cities and Surtran Taxicabs violated the Sherman Act by both restraining trade and creating a monopoly, in violation of Section 1 and 2 of the Act, 15 U.S.C.A. §§ 1, 2. The initial complaint sought both injunctive relief and treble damages on behalf of taxicab drivers who held permits to operate cabs within the ten-county region surrounding the airport. Two weeks later, on June 6, 1978, the Campisi plaintiffs amended their complaint to add Yellow Cab as a defendant and to add approximately 50 additional named representatives as class members, including the Dallas Taxicab Association. On that same day, the Whorton plaintiffs filed over 200 requests for exclusion from the Campisi suit, alleging that they would not be represented adequately and that the suit would not be prosecuted vigorously since at least two of the three named members of the Woolen class suit were members of the Dallas Taxicab Association, a nonprofit association of taxicab drivers operating in Dallas and formed by Yellow Cab Co., itself a defendant in this lawsuit. Ten days later, the Whorton plaintiffs filed a separate suit naming over 200 individual plaintiffs, but not in the form of a class action, seeking to recover treble damages for the antitrust violations.

On June 29, 1978, the Campisi plaintiffs filed a motion to consolidate their action with the Whorton plaintiffs and to designate the Campisi's attorney, Tom Thomas, as lead counsel. In November 1978, the defendants' subsequent motion to dismiss was denied by the District Court. In December 1978, the Campisi plaintiffs moved for class certification [under Rules 23(b)(2) and (b)(3)] to represent a class of all licensed taxicab drivers in the ten county area, a class estimated to be between 2,000 and 2,500 persons. The class included Woolen and 50 other named plaintiffs as well as the Dallas Taxicab Association. * * *

TRYING TO GET TO THE HEAD OF THE CLASS

In August 1979, four of the Whorton plaintiffs filed a motion to intervene in the Campisi case under Rule 24(a)(2), alleging that they had an interest in the transaction, were so situated that the disposition of the action might impair or impede their ability to protect that interest, and were not adequately represented by existing parties.

In October 1979, the four Whorton plaintiffs seeking to intervene filed "Requested Findings of Fact and Conclusions of Law in Opposition to Class Certification,'' alleging that the Campisi case should not be certified as a class action. The filing of this opposition is one of the more graphic examples of the antagonism and conflict between the Campisi and Whorton groups. The relations between the Campisi and Whorton plaintiffs continued to deteriorate for the next year as the attorneys for both groups were less than cooperative in discovery attempts.

* * * [O]n December 31, 1980, the District Judge filed an order certifying the Campisi suit as a 23(b)(2) class action and finding the Campisi plaintiffs adequate representatives for purposes of the class action. The class was defined as all taxicab operators who held permits to operate taxicabs issued by the municipalities located within the ten county area. Campisi's attorney, Tom Thomas, was appointed lead class action counsel. In addition, the District Judge denied the motion of the four Whorton plaintiffs to intervene. Although the District Judge did not rule on the motion for exclusion from the class suit, filed by the Whorton plaintiffs, the practical effect of certification under (b)(2) was to deny the right to opt out to these class members. See note 1, *supra*. From this December 31, 1980 order the Whorton plaintiffs appeal.

UNITED WE FALL, DIVIDED WE STAND

Why, one might wonder, would two groups of taxicab drivers whom one would expect to be aligned against one common set of defendants, instead attempt to keep the other from active participation in the lawsuit? Each set of plaintiffs has tried to inhibit discovery by the other set. The Campisi group has worked to keep the Whorton group from intervening while the Whorton group has been busy trying to defeat the certification of the Campisi group. What we have in the final analysis is two factions of plaintiffs, each seeking to be represented by the attorney of their choice, and each seeking to get through the courtroom door first. While the underlying claim is the same, the Campisi plaintiffs seek injunctive relief as evident from their initial motion for certification. The Whorton group, on the other hand, is concerned primarily with damages.

TAX(I)ATION WITHOUT REPRESENTATION

In this appeal, the Whorton plaintiffs basically argue that the District Judge's order of December 31, 1980 results in their being locked into a class action in which they are not adequately represented, in which their interests are antagonistic to other members of the class, and in which they have no desire to participate unless they are allowed representation by the attorney of their choice. They assert that the class action device has been abused to preempt their claim through a sham class action filed by the Campisi group and that the District Judge's orders have conclusively determined their rights in such a way that review on appeal from a final judgment will be ineffective. Through certification under Rule 23(b)(2), they fear that their claims for damages may eventually be lost should the Campisi class action fail on the merits or settle. To support these claims, the Whorton plaintiffs allege a pattern of delays, less than diligent prosecution by Campisi and the class attorney, antagonism between the two groups of plaintiffs, and conflicts of interest, both within the class and between Campisi and the defendants. For instance, they allege that the Dallas Taxicab Association, certified to represent the drivers, has members from only one of the ten counties, and was originally formed by Yellow Cab, one of the defendants, for the purpose of helping Yellow Cab drivers. Thus, the Whorton plaintiffs contend that the representation is inadequate. In addition, they allege that three of the four named Campisi plaintiffs are members of the Dallas Taxicab Association. Not only are there connections between the class representatives and defendant Yellow Cab, but, according to the Whorton group, there are connections between Campisi's lawyer and Yellow Cab. The Whorton plaintiffs charge that Campisi's attorney chose certification as a (b)(2) class action and included the denial of the request for intervention, without any specific request by the court, an assertion substantiated in a letter to the District Judge from the attorney for the defendants. Through a series of statements and examples, the Whorton plaintiffs attempt to demonstrate inadequate representation by class members and their counsel and to create the implication that the Campisi representatives are likely to compromise the Whorton claims for damages because of the connections between the Campisi plaintiffs and the defendants. While several examples are given of the inadequacy of representation, both by the named class representatives and their attorney, we find it unnecessary to provide more than the bare outline so far sketched.

In this appeal, the Whorton plaintiffs raise several issues. First they contend that they have an absolute right to intervene under F.R.Civ.P. 24(a)(2) because their interest is not adequately represented. Second, they maintain that the District Judge's order of December 31, 1980 was an abuse of discretion by eliminating the representation of the Whorton plaintiffs, including those 200 who originally requested exclusion from the Campisi suit. This abuse is demonstrated by certifying a class action with no opportunity to opt out or without any subclasses, denying exclusion to the 200 drivers, denying intervention to the representatives of these 200 drivers, staying the individual damage actions of these drivers, and imposing antagonistic class representation and counsel on these drivers through mandatory inclusion in the class action.

* * *

When analyzed properly—unfortunately the District Judge in this case failed to do so adequately—intervention of right under Rule 24(a) and class action certification under Rule 23 are two separate and distinct theories. * * *

[T]he notion of adequacy of representation sufficient to satisfy the prerequisites for a class action under Rule 23(a)(4) [is not] necessarily equivalent to the adequacy of representation contemplated by Rule 24 within the context of intervention of right. In the Advisory Committee's note to the 1966 amendment to Rule 24(a), the Committee indicated that the rule, as amended, no longer contained the prior requirement that as a condition of intervention an applicant be bound. Rather, "[a] class member who claims that his 'representative' does not adequately represent him, and is able to establish that proposition with sufficient probability, should not be put to the risk of having a judgment entered in the action which by its terms extends to him, and be obliged to test the validity of the judgment as applied to his interest by a later collateral attack. Rather he should, as a general rule, be entitled to intervene in the action."

From this statement it is clear that the Committee contemplated that one who was already a class member could intervene in a lawsuit. It is also apparent that the notion of adequacy for purposes of Rule 23(a)(4) is one having more concern with the res judicata effects of a judgment on absent members of a class. Without adequate representation a judgment cannot bind those absent class members. Rule 24(a), as amended, specifically drops the requirement that a party is or may be bound by a judgment, substituting instead a practical test, requiring only that the disposition of the action "*may* as a *practical* matter impair or impede his ability to protect that interest, ..." (emphasis added). As revised, the Rule clearly leaves room for a situation where one's interest may be impaired by inadequate representation without necessarily requiring a res judicata effect. One therefore could intervene, claiming inadequacy of representation without necessarily claiming that he will be precluded by the other action. This would appear to establish a lower threshold or showing of inadequacy for purposes of intervention as opposed to class action certification. The adequacy of representation in Rule 23(a)(4) is that essential to due process under *Hansberry v. Lee* before absent class members can be bound. The problem of intervention within a class action would appear to arise most likely in a class certified under 23(b)(1) or (b)(2), rather than in a class certified under 23(b)(3). A class member who does not consider that he is being represented adequately has the option in a (b)(3) action to opt out under 23(c)(2) or to enter an appearance through counsel of his choosing. Should he choose to opt out of the lawsuit, the plaintiff would not be bound. The concept of intervention within a class certified under 23(b)(2) balances the more likely impairment of the individual's interest since he is unable to opt out of this class. Also by allowing intervention, subsequent collateral attacks on the due process preclusive effect of a judgment are avoided.

* * *

Rule 24(a)(2) establishes three conditions which must be met for intervention of right. The applicant must (1) claim "an interest relating to the property or transaction which is the subject of the action"; (2) be "so situated that the disposition of the action may as a practical matter impair or impede his ability to protect that interest"; *and* (3) his interest is not adequately represented by existing parties. In this case the Whorton plaintiffs have claimed an interest in the transaction which is the subject of the action, that is in the alleged antitrust violations. However, the interest is not identical to that of the Campisi plaintiffs who have clearly indicated that at this point their interest is in injunctive relief, while that of the Whorton plaintiffs is in damages. The Whorton plaintiffs have alleged that the disposition of the Campisi class action *may* as a *practical matter* impair their ability to protect their interest. Should the Campisi plaintiffs fail on the liability issue in the class action, at least as a practical matter, the Whorton plaintiffs' ability to recover may be impaired. It is possible that any judgment on the issue of liability in the Campisi (b)(2) class action may be binding on the Whorton plaintiffs in a separate action unless they can demonstrate in a subsequent or collateral attack that they were inadequately represented and thus denied due process. Finally, the Whorton plaintiffs have alleged that their interest is not adequately represented by the existing parties. They contend that neither the class representatives nor their attorney adequately presents their position and [that they] have failed to protect their interest. On the basis of the pleadings and motions before the District Court, it is clear that the Whorton plaintiffs are "without a friend in this litigation." The Whorton plaintiffs have alleged that the Campisi plaintiffs have attempted to hamper their discovery, have encouraged burdensome damage interrogatories against the Whorton plaintiffs, and have abandoned any interest in the damage claims. From proceedings in this Court, it is clear that the Campisi plaintiffs, through opposing the motion of intervention and subsequent appeal, are not aligned with the Whorton plaintiffs.

The District Court held a hearing on the question of class certification at which the intervenors were allowed to participate. In its order of December 31, 1980, the District Court denied intervention. * * * In the order certifying the Campisi class, the District Judge made findings of fact that the class representatives would fairly and adequately protect the interest of the class. The first of the subfindings is that "there is no significant antagonism or conflict between the class action representatives and the class." This finding is perhaps the only relevant one to the issue of intervention and it is not clear whether at the time the District Court was considering the intervenors as members of the class. If so, this finding is clearly erroneous since the antagonism between the Whorton plaintiffs who, at least as defined by the District Court, are members of the class, and the class action representatives is too blatant to be ignored. For example, the Whorton plaintiffs had earlier attempted to defeat certification. Based on the filings in this case and the hearing, the District Court could not possibly find no antagonism. However, we think that given the lack of findings of fact specifically relating to the issue of intervention, in this case where the credibility of the parties, both the Campisi representatives and the Whorton plaintiffs, is so essential, this action should be remanded to the District Court to consider again the right to intervene under Rule 24(a)(2) so that this Court is provided with an adequate record on the merits of intervention of right, should this Court need to consider again the right to intervene.

KEEPING THE METER RUNNING

From our disposition of this case, we are in no way intimating our opinion on the merits of the claim of intervention of right, other than to indicate that the Whorton plaintiffs have alleged a colorable claim which needs further exploration, perhaps evidentiary detail and findings by the District Court before we could pass on the merits. Nor are we indicating that we consider intervention the best route through this Serbonian Bog. Were this case before us in a different posture we would be free to indicate that consolidation of the Whorton and Campisi cases would offer the most, and perhaps *only,* manageable solution. Under consolidation, the issue of liability could be tried *once* and *only once,* while allowing the parties to be represented by counsel of their choice. With representation satisfactory to each of the two groups, the court could likely avoid a subsequent attack on the adequacy of representation under the guise of res judicata effects should the defendants succeed on the issue of liability or should the Campisi plaintiffs settle with the defendants. Nor need consolidation hinder the Campisi plaintiffs' efforts to proceed. The District Court may stay discovery on the issue of damage until the issue of liability is resolved since the District Court need not, indeed should not, assume that the defendants will be held liable. Discovery exploration of possible potential damages at this early [stage] in the detail sought is obviously inefficient and wasteful of services of counsel. Consolidation also avoids the question of which lawsuit proceeds first. Obviously consolidation will succeed only if the attorneys for both the Whorton and Campisi plaintiffs mend their differences and unite in their efforts to defeat what one assumes is their common enemy, the defendants. Certainly consolidation would benefit the class members, who after all are, or should be, the true focus of these lawsuits.

* * * Obviously the problems in this case would not have arisen had the District Court certified the action as a (b)(3) action, in which case the Whorton plaintiffs would have had the opportunity to opt out. Certification as a (b)(3) action would also have protected their damage claim. Generally antitrust actions are certified under 23(b)(3) since the usual focus is on treble damages and the Advisory Committee note makes clear that certification under (b)(2) is not appropriate where the primary relief sought is not injunctive.

Notes and Questions

1. Is the Court of Appeals' real concern that the *Campisi* case should never have been certified under Rule 23(b)(2)? Under Rule 23(b)(3), class members have a right to "enter an appearance through counsel." What does this mean? The commentators early disagreed on whether automatic intervention was allowed. Compare Cohn, The New Federal Rules of Civil Procedure, 54 Geo.L.J. 1204, 1224 (1966), with Kaplan, Continuing Work of the Civil Committee: The 1966 Amendments of the Federal Rules of Civil Procedure, 81 Harv.L.Rev. 356, 392 n. 137 (1967). The consensus now seems to be that "[i]ntervention in class actions is governed by the same principles as apply in any other proceeding." 7B C. Wright, A. Miller & M. Kane,

Federal Practice & Procedure § 1799 at 442 (2d ed. 1986). How much help would that be in *Woolen*?

In some ways, at least, intervention issues may be unique to class actions. Newberg, for example, suggests that intervention may sometimes result in benefits peculiar to such cases: bolstering adequacy of representation, preventing mootness, facilitating assessment of individual damages claims, and protecting claims from limitations imposed by the court. 3 H. Newberg & A. Conte, Newberg on Class Actions § 16.09 (3d ed. 1992).

2. The court in *Woolen* argues that a lesser showing of inadequacy of representation is needed for intervention of right under Rule 24(a) than to defeat class certification under Rule 23(a)(4). Isn't it backwards to impose a lower standard of inadequacy for intervention? The class member will be bound by res judicata from the judgment in the class action, but the intervenor need not be bound, but only have an interest. Consider Lelsz v. Kavanagh, 710 F.2d 1040, 1044 (5th Cir.1983): "the overlapping character of the inquiries into adequacy of representation suggests that when intervention of right is appropriate, class certification may also be called into question." Would decertification or designation of the intervenor as class representative be the more appropriate remedy? Is the effort by the *Woolen* court to ease intervention a wise middle ground between denying intervention and decertifying the class? Compare Jenkins by Jenkins v. State of Missouri, 78 F.3d 1270 (8th Cir.1996) (upholding refusal to allow intervention in school desegregation class action because it was based on "disagreements over the details of the remedy" and that "a difference of opinion concerning litigation strategy or individual aspects of a remedy does not overcome the presumption of adequate representation"). Contrast Woolley, Rethinking the Adequacy of Adequate Representation, 75 Texas L. Rev. 571, 578 (1997) (finding that *Shutts*, *supra* p. 412, creates a "fundamental right to be heard and participate in the litigation" that applies even if there is adequate representation).

3. Rule 23 provides for opting out only in (b)(3) cases. Should there be such a right in so-called "hybrid" Rule 23(b)(2) class actions in which some form of monetary relief is also sought, such as actions under Title VII for employment discrimination? In such cases, it has been held that the court has discretion under Rule 23(d) to permit opting out. The Eleventh Circuit has held that under some circumstances refusal to allow an opt-out in a "hybrid" class action is an abuse of discretion. Holmes v. Continental Can Co., 706 F.2d 1144 (11th Cir.1983).

In Eubanks v. Billington, 110 F.3d 87 (D.C.Cir.1997), an employment discrimination action, the court agreed that opting out may be authorized in a case certified pursuant to (b)(2), but held that it was not required. After the case was settled, two class members dissatisfied with the amounts they would receive as back pay under the settlement insisted they had a right to opt out and sue for larger amounts, but the district court refused. Recognizing that such opting out might jeopardize settlement of class actions, the appellate court nevertheless found that the question involved evaluation of several factors (id. at 94–95):

> Although, as a general matter, courts should not permit opt-outs when doing so would undermine the policies behind (b)(1) or (b)(2) certifica-

tion, where both injunctive and monetary relief are sought, the need to protect the rights of individual class members may necessitate procedural protections beyond those ordinarily provided under (b)(1) and (b)(2). As the Eleventh Circuit observed in *Holmes*, 706 F.2d at 1156–57, the underlying premise of (b)(2) certification—that the class members suffer from a common injury that can be addressed by classwide relief—begins to break down when the class seeks to recover back pay or other forms of monetary damages to be allocated based on individual injuries. In that situation, an employment discrimination case will implicate the concerns that led to adoption of more stringent procedural protections in (b)(3) actions, and the potential for conflicts of interest may necessitate measures, such as permitting opt-outs, that safeguard the due process rights of the individual class members.

The court concluded, however, that there was no need for such treatment in the case before it because the objectors had been treated in the same manner as all other class members. It distinguished Holmes v. Continental Can Co., *supra*, because in that case a disproportionate share of the money was to go to class representatives. Compare Thomas v. Albright, 139 F.3d 227 (D.C.Cir. 1998) (holding district court abused discretion in allowing opt-outs in (b)(2) action because the class appeared cohesive and dissidents' claims were not atypical).

4. Some argue that Phillips Petroleum Co. v. Shutts, *supra* p. 412, requires a right to opt out as a matter of due process whenever monetary claims are presented on behalf of class members. The Supreme Court has twice granted certiorari to determine the scope of a constitutional right to opt out, but not decided the issue. In Brown v. Ticor Title Insurance Co., 982 F.2d 386 (9th Cir.1992), a class action alleging price fixing in the sale of title insurance sought injunctive relief and damages. Over the objection of some class members, the court certified a (b)(1) & (2) class action, denying the objectors the right to opt out and approving a settlement for injunctive relief but not damages. Thereafter some of the objectors filed a new suit based on the same claim. The Ninth Circuit held that the objector class members had been denied minimal due process by not being allowed to opt out and, therefore, that they were not bound by the settlement or barred by res judicata.

The Supreme Court granted certiorari but later dismissed on the ground certiorari was improvidently granted because the case might require resolution of a constitutional question that could be entirely hypothetical. Ticor Title Insurance Co. v. Brown, 511 U.S. 117, 114 S.Ct. 1359, 128 L.Ed.2d 33 (1994). Justice O'Connor, joined by the Chief Justice and Justice Kennedy, dissented, commenting that "lower courts have consistently held that the presence of monetary damage claims does not preclude class certification under Rules 23(b)(1)(A) and (b)(2)." "Whether or not," she stated, "those decisions are correct (a question we need not, and indeed should not, decide today), they at least indicate that there are a substantial number of class members in exactly the same position as respondents." She expressed particular concern over continuing uncertainty as to the binding effect of judgments in such cases, observing that "individuals, corporations, and governments that have successfully defended against class actions or reached appropriate settlements" are now "subject to relitigation of the same claims with individual class members."

In Adams v. Robertson, 520 U.S. 83, 117 S.Ct. 1028, 137 L.Ed.2d 203 (1997), the Court granted certiorari "to decide whether the Alabama courts' approval of the class action and the settlement agreement in this case, without affording all class members the right to exclude themselves from the class or the agreement, violated the Due Process Clause." The class plaintiffs charged an insurance company with fraudulently persuading customers to exchange existing health insurance policies for new policies that provided less coverage. When a settlement was proposed that precluded further suits by class members, petitioners objected but the Alabama courts approved the settlement. Although petitioners pointed to references to *Ticor, supra,* in their brief in the Alabama Supreme Court, that court did not address the argument. Because the Alabama court could have concluded that the federal contention was not before it, the Supreme Court felt compelled to dismiss certiorari as improperly granted since "[o]ur continuing interest in an issue * * * does not affect the application of our rules [regarding proper presentation in the courts below.]"

5. Putting aside the provisions of Rule 23 and due process requirements, does the difference in treatment between (b)(3) and (b)(2) class actions regarding the right to opt out make sense? Consider the views of Professor Yeazell in S. Yeazell, From Medieval Group Litigation to the Modern Class Action 252–54 (1987):

> [T]he rule requires notice just when discrepancy of interest among the class members is least likely. Most (b)(3) actions will involve an active plaintiff, frequently bolstered by a lawyer, seeking monetary recovery on behalf of some group that the defendant has allegedly damaged. Under such circumstances the absentees might be quite concerned that the active litigant and the lawyer have at least as great a financial stake in the suit as they, that the active litigant will press the suit vigorously, and that the counsel representing them is competent. But the threshold inquiries of 23(a) focus on such questions. What is not likely is that, if such conditions are fulfilled, the absentees would prefer not to sue at all. It is an axiom of modern social and economic life that we all wish to command more of the world's wealth; there is not much sense in asking someone whether one dollar or two would be preferable.

* * *

If the treatment of (b)(3) actions seems to overprotect individual autonomy, the treatment of (b)(2) actions seems equally puzzling for the opposite reason. For suits falling into this category the rule requires no notice, relying entirely on the threshold findings of common interest, typicality, and adequate representation. Yet the rule does so in circumstances where it is much more likely than in the (b)(3) cases that the interests of the group's members will conflict and will be least amenable to abstract assessment. An example will make the point. Like many American cities, Boston in the 1970s found itself in the throes of a lawsuit over school integration. Managed by the NAACP, the plaintiffs' suit alleged numerous discriminatory acts by the Boston School Committee and sought a widespread integration decree that involved busing black children into the schools of South Boston, where they encountered a hostile reception. Derrick Bell has reported that many of Boston's black parents, on whose behalf the case was brought, would have preferred a remedy that did not require their children to attend school in a section of the city with poor schools and a tradition of violence. Indeed, some of them might have preferred entirely to forgo the legal vindication of their rights if such was the only foreseeable remedy. Under such circumstances, Bell argued, some more searching assessment of interest than the one called for by Rule 23(b)(2) is necessary.

6. If opting out is a "right," can the court do anything that tends to deter people from exercising it? A Special Committee on Class Action Improvements of the ABA Section of Litigation, 110 F.R.D. 195 (1986), recommended amending Rule 23(c)(2) to permit a court to impose limitations on opt-outs, including a prohibition against maintaining an independent action on some or all of the matters at issue in the class action. In Premier Elec. Const. Co. v. National Elec. Contractors Ass'n, 814 F.2d 358 (7th Cir.1987), the court adopted a "categorical rule" against allowing opt-outs to use the result in the class action for offensive collateral estoppel purposes; see also Note, Offensive Assertion of Collateral Estoppel by Persons Opting Out of a Class Action, 31 Hast.L.J. 1189 (1980).

Another possibility is, in effect, to recapture the actions via consolidation. See W. Schwarzer, Managing Antitrust and Other Complex Litigation 182 (1982) ("Individual actions ancillary to the class action should be managed so as to minimize duplication of activity. Consolidating them with the main action for pretrial and trial reduces such duplication."). Some have even argued for a good cause requirement for leave to opt out. See Note, Constrained Individualism in Group Litigation: Requiring Class Members to Make a Good Cause Showing Before Opting Out of a Federal Class Action, 100 Yale L.J. 745 (1990).

There are limits to the ability of courts to curtail the activities of opt-outs, however. Rule 23 presently insists that (b)(3) class members have the right to opt out, at least as a matter of form. Other laws may also limit the court's power. In In re Glenn W. Turner Enterprises Litigation, 521 F.2d 775 (3d Cir.1975), the trial court tried to require class members who held state court judgments against a defendant in shaky financial condition to choose between the state and federal cases by enjoining enforcement of the state court judgments by class members who did not opt out. The appellate court did not hold that this order exceeded the court's powers under Rule 23, but did find that it violated the Anti–Injunction Act because it was not "necessary in aid of jurisdiction": "Parties opting out of the class undoubtedly would be free to continue the prosecution of any state actions and execute upon any resulting judgment even if the execution totally depleted the common defendants' coffers. Since Rule 23 by its own terms creates a mechanism leaving parties in a (b)(3) action free to continue with any state proceedings, we cannot hold that a Rule 23(b)(3) class action can 'be given its intended scope only by way of the stay of a state court proceeding.' " Id. at 781.

7. The parties may be able by agreement make opting out less attractive. In In re Vitamins Antitrust Class Actions, 215 F.3d 26 (D.C.Cir.2000),

the settlement agreement included a "most favored nation" clause that required the settling defendants to pay the class plaintiffs more if they agreed to better terms for others (including the opt-outs). The opt-outs sought to intervene to object to the settlement under Rule 23(e) on the ground that this provision unfairly undercut their ability to make a better deal. The court denied intervention because the only question before the court under Rule 23(e) is whether the agreement is fair to the class, not whether it may disadvantage others. The court rejected the argument that this provision burdened the right to opt out, although it recognized that "the defendants may well [have liked] a Ulysses-tied-to-the-mast arrangement that enables them to convincingly stiff opt-outs who demand more."

8. "The right to participate, or to opt out, is an individual one and should not be made by the class representative or the class counsel." Hanlon v. Chrysler Corp., 150 F.3d 1011, 1024 (9th Cir.1998). Accordingly, it has been held that one cannot obtain an order "opting out" the members of a class from a competing class action. See In re Diet Drugs, *supra* p. 391.

9. What are the rights of a class member who does not intervene or opt out? One, which we will examine later, is to object to a proposed settlement submitted for the court's approval under Rule 23(e). For some time there was a question about whether such an objector could appeal approval of the settlement. In Devlin v. Scardelletti, 536 U.S. 1, 122 S.Ct. 2005, 153 L.Ed.2d 27 (2002), the Court held that an objecting class member is sufficiently a "party" for purposes of obtaining review of her objection to appeal the court's approval of the settlement. But this right is limited to the objections made by this class member, and does not include review of objections made by other class members.

J. STATUTES OF LIMITATIONS

In an individual action the filing of the suit usually is the event that tolls the running of the statute of limitations. Class actions complicate the picture, however, because they involve the claims of other people as well. Before 1966, statutes of limitations had posed difficulties in class actions in which class members had to intervene to prosecute their right to relief. In an ordinary action, a plaintiff who sought intervention after the limitations period had run could be barred from suing. If the same rule applied to absent class members, the pendency of the class action might be cold comfort for the class member whose claim expired before intervention, robbing the procedure of its efficiency value.

Another timing problem that troubled the courts was "one way intervention," which was said to occur when an unnamed member of the class sat on the sidelines until the merits of the class action were determined and then intervened if the outcome was favorable. This tactic seemed unfair to defendants, who could still have to confront the claims of such free riders if they successfully defended the class action.

The 1966 amendments included Rule 23(c)(3), which provides that the judgment in the class action is binding on the members of the class whatever the outcome, and whether or not they intervene. That being the case, courts held that for purposes of intervening or otherwise sharing in the class recovery, the filing of the class action tolled the running of the statute of limitations as to all members of the class. See 7B C. Wright, A. Miller & M. Kane, Federal Practice & Procedure § 1800.

There remained, however, the problem presented when class status was denied. Rule 23(c)(1) directed that the court determine whether the case was a proper class action "[a]s soon as practicable after the commencement" of the suit, but in some instances substantial delays might occur before that ruling was made. See Timing of Class Certification Decisions, *supra* p. 370. In those circumstances other claimants might have no choice but to file their own suits or seek to intervene to protect their rights.

In American Pipe & Const. Co. v. Utah, 414 U.S. 538, 94 S.Ct. 756, 38 L.Ed.2d 713 (1974), the Supreme Court addressed this problem and adopted a tolling rule. The underlying suits grew out of prosecutions for illegal price rigging in the sale of concrete and steel pipe; eleven days before the limitations period expired the State of Utah filed a class action for price fixing against a variety of the defendants on behalf of a class of all public bodies and agencies in the state that were end users of the products involved. The case was consolidated with more than 100 others making such claims against defendants. The judge presiding over the consolidated cases found that all the other prerequisites of Rule 23(a) had been satisfied but that, given his experience with such cases, he was confident that the class members were not too numerous to join and therefore class certification should be denied under Rule 23(a)(1).

Eight days after denial of class certification (but seven months after suit was filed), more than 60 Utah towns, municipalities and water districts moved to intervene. The district court held that limitations barred the claims, but the court of appeals held that the pendency of the class action tolled the running of limitations for the intervenors.

The Supreme Court affirmed. It noted the former problem of "one way intervention" and the present rule's requirement that the class action determination come early in the case, which meant that "potential class members retain an option to participate in or withdraw from the class action only until a point in the litigation * * * when the suit is allowed to continue as a class action." It ruled that "the commencement of the original class suit tolls the running of the statute for all purported members of the class who make timely motions to intervene after the court has found the suit inappropriate for class action status." It found this rule essential to the class action procedure:

> To hold to the contrary would frustrate the principal function of a class suit, because then the sole means by which members of the class could assure their participation in the judgment if notice of the class suit did not reach them until after the running of the limitations period would be to file earlier individual motions to join or intervene as parties—precisely the multiplicity of activity which

Rule 23 was designed to avoid in those cases where a class action is found "superior to other available methods for the fair and efficient adjudication of the controversy."

The Court found no significant interests of the defendants that would offset these concerns:

> This rule is in no way inconsistent with the functional operation of the statute of limitations. * * * [S]tatutory limitation periods are "designed to promote justice by preventing surprises through the revival of claims that have been allowed to slumber until evidence has been lost, memories have faded, and witnesses have disappeared. The theory is that even if one has a just claim it is unjust not to put the adversary on notice to defend within the period of limitation and that the right to be free of stale claims in time comes to prevail over the right to prosecute them." The policies of ensuring essential fairness to defendants and of barring a plaintiff who has "slept on his rights" are satisfied when, as here, a named plaintiff who is found to be representative of a class commences a suit and thereby notifies the defendants not only of the substantive claims being brought against them, but also of the number and generic identities of the potential plaintiffs who may participate in the judgment. Within the period set by the statute of limitations, the defendants have the essential information necessary to determine both the subject matter and the size of the prospective litigation.

Finally, the Court saw no need why this rule of tolling should turn on actual reliance by absent class members on the pendency of the action:

> Rule 23 is not designed to afford class action representation only to those who are active participants in or even aware of the proceedings in the suit prior to the order that the suit shall or shall not proceed as a class action. During the pendency of the District Court's determination in this regard * * * potential class members are mere passive beneficiaries of the action brought in their behalf. Not until the existence and limits of the class have been established and notice of membership has been sent does a class member have any duty to take note of the suit or to exercise any responsibility with respect to it in order to profit from the eventual outcome of the case.

Although *American Pipe* settled a great deal, it left important problems unresolved.

CROWN CORK & SEAL CO. v. PARKER

Supreme Court of the United States, 1983.
462 U.S. 345, 103 S.Ct. 2392, 76 L.Ed.2d 628.

JUSTICE BLACKMUN delivered the opinion of the Court.

The question that confronts us in this case is whether the filing of a class action tolls the applicable statute of limitations, and thus permits all members of the putative class to file individual actions in the event that class certification is denied, provided, of course, that those actions are instituted within the time that remains on the limitations period.

[Respondent, an African American male fired by petitioner in July 1977, filed a timely charge of discrimination with the Equal Employment Opportunity Commission. In November, 1977, the EEOC determined there was no reason to believe he had been the victim of discrimination and issued him a Notice of Right to Sue within 90 days. By that time, however, two other black males formerly employed by petitioner had filed a class action alleging discrimination in violation of Title VII. Petitioner was a putative member of the class. In May, 1979, plaintiffs in the class action moved for class certification. In September, 1980, the district court denied that motion, finding that the named plaintiffs' claims were not typical, that the named plaintiffs would not be adequate class representatives, and that the class was not so numerous that joinder was not feasible. Within 90 days after that ruling, but almost two years after issuance of his Notice of Right to Sue, respondent filed an individual Title VII suit against petitioner. The district court dismissed the case as time-barred, and the Court of Appeals reversed, relying on *American Pipe & Construction Co. v. Utah.*]

* * *

Petitioner asserts that the rule of *American Pipe* was limited to intervenors, and does not toll the statute of limitations for class members who file actions of their own. Petitioner relies on the Court's statement in *American Pipe* that "the commencement of the original class suit tolls the running of the statute for all purported members of the class *who make timely motions to intervene* after the court has found the suit inappropriate for class action status." While *American Pipe* concerned only intervenors, we conclude that the holding of that case is not to be read so narrowly. The filing of a class action tolls the statute of limitations "as to all asserted members of the class," not just as to intervenors.

The *American Pipe* Court recognized that unless the statute of limitations was tolled by the filing of the class action, class members would not be able to rely on the existence of the suit to protect their rights. Only by intervening or taking other action prior to the running of the statute of limitations would they be able to ensure that their rights would not be lost in the event that class certification was denied. Much the same inefficiencies would ensue if *American Pipe's* tolling rule were limited to permitting putative class members to intervene after the denial of class certification. There are many reasons why a class member, after the denial of class certification, might prefer to bring an individual suit rather than intervene. The forum in which the class action is pending might be an inconvenient one, for example, or the class member might not wish to share control over the litigation with other plaintiffs once the economies of a class action were no longer available.

Moreover, permission to intervene might be refused for reasons wholly unrelated to the merits of the claim.[4]

A putative class member who fears that class certification may be denied would have every incentive to file a separate action prior to the expiration of his own period of limitations. The result would be a needless multiplicity of actions—precisely the situation that Federal Rule of Civil Procedure 23 and the tolling rule of *American Pipe* were designed to avoid.

Failure to apply *American Pipe* to class members filing separate actions also would be inconsistent with the Court's reliance on *American Pipe* in *Eisen v. Carlisle & Jacquelin,* 417 U.S. 156, 94 S.Ct. 2140, 40 L.Ed.2d 732 (1974). In *Eisen,* the Court held that Rule 23(c)(2) required individual notice to absent class members, so that each class member could decide whether to "opt out" of the class and thereby preserve his right to pursue his own lawsuit. The named plaintiff in *Eisen* argued that such notice would be fruitless because the statute of limitations had long since run on the claims of absent class members. This argument, said the Court, was "disposed of by our recent decision in *American Pipe* ... which established that commencement of a class action tolls the applicable statute of limitations as to all members of the class." *Id.,* at 176, n. 13, 94 S.Ct., at 2152, n. 13.

If *American Pipe's* tolling rule applies only to intervenors, this reference to *American Pipe* is misplaced and makes no sense. *Eisen's* notice requirement was intended to inform the class member that he could "preserve his opportunity to press his claim *separately*" by opting out of the class. But a class member would be unable to "press his claim separately" if the limitation period had expired while the class action was pending. The *Eisen* Court recognized this difficulty, but concluded that the right to opt out and press a separate claim remained meaningful because the filing of the class action tolled the statute of limitations under the rule of *American Pipe.* If *American Pipe* were limited to intervenors, it would not serve the purpose assigned to it by *Eisen;* no class member would opt out simply to intervene. Thus, the *Eisen* Court necessarily read *American Pipe* as we read it today, to apply to class members who choose to file separate suits.

The Court noted in *American Pipe* that a tolling rule for class actions is not inconsistent with the purposes served by statutes of limitations. * * * [A] class complaint "notifies the defendants not only of the substantive claims being brought against them, but also of the

---

4. Putative class members frequently are not entitled to intervene as of right under Fed.Rule Civ.Proc. 24(a), and permissive intervention under Fed.Rule Civ.Proc. 24(b) may be denied in the discretion of the District Court. *American Pipe,* 414 U.S., at 559–560, 94 S.Ct., at 769; *id.,* at 562, 94 S.Ct., at 700 (concurring opinion). In exercising its discretion the District Court considers "whether the intervention will undu-ly delay or prejudice the adjudication of the rights of the original parties," Fed.Rule Civ. Proc. 24(b), and a court could conclude that undue delay or prejudice would result if many class members were brought in as plaintiffs upon the denial of class certification. Thus, permissive intervention well may be an uncertain prospect for members of a proposed class.

number and generic identities of the potential plaintiffs who may participate in the judgment." *American Pipe,* 414 U.S., at 555, 94 S.Ct., at 767.
The defendant will be aware of the need to preserve evidence and
witnesses respecting the claims of all the members of the class. Tolling
the statute of limitations thus creates no potential for unfair surprise,
regardless of the method class members choose to enforce their rights
upon denial of class certification.

JUSTICE POWELL, joined by JUSTICE REHNQUIST and JUSTICE O'CONNOR,
concurring.

* * *

In *American Pipe* we noted that a class suit "notifies the defendants
not only of the substantive claims being brought against them, but also
of the number and generic identities of the potential plaintiffs who
participate in the judgment. Within the period set by the statute of
limitations, the defendants have the essential information necessary to
determine both the subject matter and size of the prospective litigation."
When thus notified, the defendant normally is not prejudiced by tolling
of the statute of limitations. It is important to make certain, however,
that *American Pipe* is not abused by the assertion of claims that differ
from those raised in the original class suit. * * * [W]hen a plaintiff
invokes *American Pipe* in support of a separate lawsuit, the district court
should take care to ensure that the suit raises claims that "concern the
same evidence, memories, and witnesses as the subject matter of the
original class suit," so that "the defendant will not be prejudiced."
Claims as to which the defendant was not fairly placed on notice by the
class suit are not protected under *American Pipe* and are barred by the
statute of limitations.

Notes and Questions

1. In *Crown Cork* the Court asserts that defendants were as well aware
of the claims they would face as in *American Pipe.* But in *Crown Cork*
certification was denied on the ground that the class representative's claims
were not typical. Should that be a basis for distinguishing the two cases?

Mass tort class actions have largely developed since the decision in
Crown Cork. In *Amchem, supra* p. 373, the Court characterized the class as
"sprawling." Should tolling operate in such amorphous suits? Consider the
argument in Lowenthal & Feder, The Impropriety of Class Action Tolling for
Mass Tort Statutes of Limitations, 64 Geo.Wash.L.Rev. 532, 537 (1996):

> [T]he costs of class action tolling are exorbitant, at least when applied to
> modern mass tort litigation. The individual nature of the personal
> injuries that lie at the core of most mass tort actions prevents the class
> action defendant from gathering the evidence necessary to test and
> challenge absent plaintiffs' claims. Indeed, the defendants generally do
> not even know the identity of the absent class members and, therefore,
> are unable to discover evidence about that claimant, or marshall appro-
> priate medical, economic, and other witnesses to comment on that
> claimant's circumstances.

How different are these arguments from the ones defendants have directed at the propriety of certifying class actions in mass tort suits? Should that similarity matter more to the tolling question? The issue in mass tort cases is complicated further by the fact that the underlying limitations period, like the claims being asserted on behalf of class members, is governed by state law. See Vaught v. Showa Denko K.K., 107 F.3d 1137 (5th Cir.1997) (refusing tolling with regard to products liability suit brought by putative class member on ground that state law precluded application of the tolling doctrine).

2. In *American Pipe* Justice Blackmun, the author of *Crown Cork,* concurred with the admonition that the decision "must not be regarded as encouragement to lawyers in a case of this kind to frame their pleadings as a class action, intentionally, to attract and save members of the purported class who have slept on their rights." Does *Crown Cork* provide protection against such behavior? Consider Justice Powell's remarks in his concurring opinion.

Some lower courts find overly general complaints insufficient to justify tolling of limitations. In Camotex v. Hunt, 741 F.Supp. 1086 (S.D.N.Y.1990), the court found the class complaint to be a "generalized laundry list" and that *Crown Cork* did not permit such "pyramiding" of claims. It reasoned that "[i]t would be contrary to the *American Pipe* doctrine to hold that class complaints asserting the generalized grievances of an open-ended group alert the defendant to the identity of those likely to participate in the action against him." Id. at 1091; see also Rochford v. Joyce, 755 F.Supp. 1423, 1428 (N.D.Ill.1990) ("[t]o ensure fairness, the later action must be similar enough to the earlier action so that the defendants are notified of the substantive claims against them, as well as the number and generic identities of the potential plaintiffs").

3. In *American Pipe,* the Court stressed the requirement of Rule 23(c)(1) that class certification be decided promptly. If certification is denied for undue delay should that fact bear on the issue of tolling the statute of limitations?

4. Should notice of denial of class certification be given so that class members can pursue their individual remedies? For an argument that such notice is not required, see Wheeler, Predismissal Notice and Statutes of Limitation in Federal Class Actions After American Pipe and Construction Co. v. Utah, 48 So.Cal.L.Rev. 771 (1975).

A related issue has been confronted in actions under the Fair Labor Standards Act, 29 U.S.C.A. § 216(b), which authorizes an action by an employee on behalf of other employees but requires that the action is binding only if the other employee "gives his consent in writing," in effect requiring an "opt-in." In Hoffmann–La Roche Inc. v. Sperling, 493 U.S. 165, 110 S.Ct. 482, 107 L.Ed.2d 480 (1989), the Court interpreted a related provision in the Age Discrimination in Employment Act, 29 U.S.C.A. § 623, to permit a court to give notice to all potential class members of their right to participate in this fashion in the litigation.

On the other hand, even where a class has been tentatively certified and certification is later withdrawn, the court may not be required to notify class members of this development unless there are indications they have relied in fact on the pendency of the action. See Payne v. Travenol Laboratories, Inc., *infra* p. 497.

5. Can the putative class member file another class action after denial of certification and rely on the *American Pipe* tolling rule? In Korwek v. Hunt, 827 F.2d 874 (2d Cir.1987), the court held that the tolling accomplished by the filing of one class action does not apply to a second. The court discussed *American Pipe* and *Parker,* noting that in those cases the earlier decision not to certify would foreclose *any* future class action (for lack of numerosity or common questions), while in the suit before it the ground for refusal to certify was the existence of intraclass conflicts and manageability problems. Despite these differences, the court held that no second chance should be allowed:

> [T]he tolling rule established by *American Pipe,* and expanded upon by *Crown, Cork,* was not intended to be applied to suspend the running of statutes of limitation for class action suits filed after a definitive determination of class certification; such an application of the rule would be inimical to the purposes behind statutes of limitations and the class action procedure.
>
> * * * Appellants filed a complaint alleging class claims identical theoretically and temporally to those raised in a previously filed class action suit which was denied class certification mainly because of overwhelming manageability difficulties. Appellants ignored the district court's express finding that the original action was unwieldy * * * when filing what was essentially a duplicate of the original complaint. The Supreme Court in *American Pipe* and *Crown, Cork* certainly did not intend to afford plaintiffs the opportunity to argue and reargue the question of class certification by filing new but repetitive complaints.

Id. at 879; accord, Robbin v. Fluor Corp., 835 F.2d 213 (9th Cir.1987); Basch v. Ground Round, Inc., 139 F.3d 6 (1st Cir.1998).

Contrast situations in which there was no adverse certification decision in the first case. In Schur v. Friedman & Shaftan, P.C., 123 F.R.D. 611 (N.D.Cal.1988), the court held that an earlier class action did toll the running of limitations with respect to defendants dismissed from the earlier case and thereby preserved the later-filed class action against a limitations defense:

> We find that *Robbin* and *Korwek* are inapplicable to this case. Though defendant was previously dismissed from the [earlier] action, that dismissal had nothing to do with the propriety of class certification. Instead, we dismissed defendant because there was no transactional nexus between any named plaintiff and defendant. Thus, plaintiff Schur is not attempting to relitigate an unsuccessful class certification motion by filing a new claim against this defendant, since we have not made a class certification determination with respect to Friedman and Shaftan. Therefore, we find that class members are entitled to tolling.

Id. at 613; see also Catholic Social Services, Inc. v. Immigration & Naturalization Serv., 232 F.3d 1139 (9th Cir.2002) (second case not seeking to relitigate an earlier denial of class certification). Does this reasoning make sense? Why should plaintiffs who seek to cure other deficiencies in the first case get the benefit of a "double" toll while those who try to cure the class certification problems do not?

Intervening in the first case offers an alternative. In McKowan Lowe & Co. v. Jasmine, Ltd., 295 F.3d 380 (3d Cir.2002), the original putative class representative was rejected as inadequate, and another class member intervened to cure the problem and seek certification. Because there was no final decision that the earlier case was an improper class action that the intervenor sought to relitigate, the court held that the *American Pipe* toll still applied. Compare Griffin v. Singletary, 17 F.3d 356 (11th Cir.1994) (holding that the rule against a second certification decision bars an intervenor from seeking class certification).

6. If class certification is granted but a class member opts out, "the statute begins running anew from the date when the class member exercises the right to opt out." Tosti v. City of Los Angeles, 754 F.2d 1485, 1488 (9th Cir.1985). But such an opt-out plaintiff gets the benefit of the tolling effect of the class action even after abandoning it. Should this be true?

One might argue that allowing tolling for opt-outs defeats the Court's objective of deterring the filing of individual actions, and that a class member who elects to forego the benefits of the class action should forego them all, including tolling. For arguments that tolling should not operate with respect to the claim of a class member who opts out after certification is granted, see Note, The American Pipe Dream: Class Actions and Statutes of Limitations, 67 Iowa L.Rev. 743, 752–58 (1982); Note, Statutes of Limitations and Opting Out of Class Actions, 81 Mich.L.Rev. 399 (1982).

On the other hand, until certification is decided the class member does not know the terms on which it will be granted, or the qualities of the representatives. Rather than try to intervene, she may find it sensible to commence a separate action. Moreover, in terms of the statute of limitations concerns of the defendant, it hardly matters that it must defend another lawsuit with respect to the claim of the class member who opts out, given the alternative of facing possible liability to that same claimant in the class action.

7. Does the putative class member who does not file her own action or move to intervene after denial of certification lose all rights? In United Airlines, Inc. v. McDonald, 432 U.S. 385, 97 S.Ct. 2464, 53 L.Ed.2d 423 (1977), the trial court granted defendant's motion to strike class action allegations in an employment discrimination suit. The prospective class representatives indicated that they would appeal this ruling after judgment, but after prevailing on the merits they decided not to appeal the class certification ruling. At that point, a class member filed a motion to intervene to appeal the class determination order. The district court denied the motion on the ground it was not timely. The Supreme Court held that the motion to intervene was timely, but only to appeal the question of class certification. Where it is clear early on that the interests of the class members will not be protected by the class representatives, class members' delay may preclude intervention after judgment is entered. *Cf.* In re Fine Paper Antitrust Litigation, 695 F.2d 494, 501 (3d Cir.1982).

In United Airlines v. McDonald, the Court discussed permissive intervention under Rule 24(b). After the named plaintiff decides not to appeal the denial of class certification, should the intervention for purposes of appeal be treated as intervention of right under Rule 24(a)? Particularly where the statute of limitations would otherwise bar the claim, is it not clear that denial of intervention would, as a practical matter, impair the class member's ability to protect her interest within the meaning of Rule 24(a)(2)? See Lane v. Bethlehem Steel Corp., 93 F.R.D. 611 (D.Md.1982).

Because the court can reconsider class certification at any time before final judgment is entered, there is potential uncertainty about whether excluded class members can continue to rely on the tolling effect of the class action pending an appellate ruling on whether they were properly excluded. Generally such litigants cannot reasonably continue to rely on the class action after denial of certification or exclusion of their claims. See Nelson v. County of Allegheny, 60 F.3d 1010 (3d Cir.1995) (tolling ceased upon district court's denial of class certification); Calderon v. Presidio Valley Farmers Ass'n, 863 F.2d 384 (5th Cir.1989), cert. denied, 493 U.S. 821, 110 S.Ct. 79, 107 L.Ed.2d 45 (1989) (tolling ends upon denial of certification even if district court later reconsiders the issue). But in Armstrong v. Martin Marietta Corp., 93 F.3d 1505 (11th Cir.1996), a divided panel concluded that the possibility the district judge may reconsider the certification ruling meant that tolling continued pending appellate review unless the excluded class members filed individual actions, which would moot any appeal from the class action ruling. The majority reasoned that this holding avoided needless suits by excluded class members who intended to appeal the class certification ruling, while a dissenter concluded that there could not be reasonable reliance at this point.

8. *Tolling and defendant class actions*: From the perspective of an unnamed member of a plaintiff class, tolling is attractive. But a member of a defendant class would probably prefer that the limitations period continue to run, at least until it is notified of the pendency of the suit. Should *American Pipe* apply?

In Appleton Elec. Co. v. Graves Truck Line, Inc., 635 F.2d 603 (7th Cir.1980), cert. denied, 451 U.S. 976, 101 S.Ct. 2058, 68 L.Ed.2d 357 (1981), the court was asked to hold that the limitations period was tolled as to all members of a defendant class. Noting that "[u]nlike the Court in *American Pipe*, we are confronted here with a true conflict between the operation of the statute of limitations and Rule 23," it held that tolling should apply even in the absence of notice to defendant class members:

> A contrary rule would sound the death knell for suits brought against a defendant class, nullifying that part of Rule 23 that specifically authorizes such suits. This, in turn, would have a potentially devastating effect on the federal courts. Plaintiffs would, in each case, be required to file protective suits, pending class certification, to stop the running of the statute of limitations. In the present instance, this could have resulted in the filing of a staggering number of complaints.

See also In re Activision Securities Litigation, 1986–87 Fed.Sec.L.Rep. (CCH) ¶ 92,998 (N.D.Cal.1986) ("all class defendants concede they had actual notice both that the suit was filed and that they were included as defendant class members"); compare Meadows v. Pacific Inland Securities Corp., 36 F.Supp.2d 1240 (S.D.Cal.1999) (rejecting tolling in defendant class action);

Chevalier v. Baird Savings Association, 72 F.R.D. 140 (E.D.Pa.1976) (court refused to toll as to a defendant class, noting that "[o]therwise, defendants would be required to defend against actions of which they had no knowledge whatsoever until the statute of limitations had run."). For an argument that a precertification notice should be sent to members of a putative defendant class, see Note, Statutes of Limitation and Defendant Class Actions, 82 Mich.L.Rev. 347 (1983). Unless there is a toll, won't all defendants opt out?

K. COMMUNICATIONS WITH UNNAMED MEMBERS OF CLASS

GULF OIL CO. v. BERNARD

Supreme Court of the United States, 1981.
452 U.S. 89, 101 S.Ct. 2193, 68 L.Ed.2d 693.

JUSTICE POWELL delivered the opinion of the Court.

This is a class action involving allegations of racial discrimination in employment on the part of petitioners, the Gulf Oil Co. (Gulf) and one of the unions at its Port Arthur, Tex., refinery. We granted a writ of certiorari to determine the scope of a district court's authority to limit communications from named plaintiffs and their counsel to prospective class members, during the pendency of a class action. We hold that in the circumstances of this case the District Court exceeded its authority under the Federal Rules of Civil Procedure.

[The Equal Employment Opportunity Commission entered into a conciliation agreement regarding alleged discrimination against black and female employees by Gulf Oil Co. pursuant to which Gulf sent notices to current employees eligible for backpay under the agreement in return for a release for Gulf. Shortly thereafter, respondents filed a class action against Gulf on behalf of all current and former black employees charging racial discrimination.

Nine days after the class action was filed, Gulf moved the court to limit communications between class counsel and the class members. It asserted that one of plaintiffs' lawyers attended a meeting of class members and advised them not to sign releases because they could receive at least double the amounts Gulf was offering through the class action. Class counsel opposed Gulf's motion, admitting that they had attended the meeting with Gulf employees, but denying that they had advised them to reject Gulf's offers or promised that the law suit would produce more. They also argued that they needed to communicate with class members in order to obtain information about the case and advise class members of their rights. They asserted that they had a First Amendment right to contact class members.

The district court adopted an order modeled on the sample pretrial order in the first edition of the Manual for Complex Litigation prohibiting respondents' communications with class members, although it eventually permitted Gulf to continue soliciting releases. The court made no findings of fact. The Fifth Circuit reversed on the ground that the order violated respondents' First Amendment rights, although eight concurring judges insisted that the case should be decided under Rule 23 without reaching the constitutional issues.]

Rule 23(d) of the Federal Rules of Civil Procedure provides: "(d) ORDERS IN CONDUCT OF ACTIONS. In the conduct of actions to which this rule applies, the court may make appropriate orders: . . . (3) imposing conditions on the representative parties or on intervenors . . . [and] (5) dealing with similar procedural matters." As the concurring judges below recognized, prior to reaching any constitutional questions, federal courts must consider nonconstitutional grounds for decision. As a result, in this case we first consider the authority of district courts under the Federal Rules to impose sweeping limitations on communications by named plaintiffs and their counsel to prospective class members.

More specifically, the question for decision is whether the limiting order entered in this case is consistent with the general policies embodied in Rule 23, which governs class actions in federal court. Class actions serve an important function in our system of civil justice. They present, however, opportunities for abuse as well as problems for courts and counsel in the management of cases.[12] Because of the potential for abuse, a district court has both the duty and the broad authority to exercise control over a class action and to enter appropriate orders governing the conduct of counsel and parties. * * *

In the present case, we are faced with the unquestionable assertion by respondents that the order created at least potential difficulties for them as they sought to vindicate the legal rights of a class of employees. The order interfered with their efforts to inform potential class members of the existence of this lawsuit, and may have been particularly injurious—not only to respondents but to the class as a whole—because the employees at that time were being pressed to decide whether to accept a backpay offer from Gulf that required them to sign a full release of all liability for discriminatory acts. In addition, the order made it more difficult for respondents, as the class representatives, to obtain information about the merits of the case from the persons they sought to represent.

Because of these potential problems, an order limiting communications between parties and potential class members should be based on a clear record and specific findings that reflect a weighing of the need for a limitation and the potential interference with the rights of the parties. Only such a determination can ensure that the court is furthering,

---

12. * * * The potential abuses associated with communications to class members are described in *Waldo v. Lakeshore Estates, Inc.,* 433 F.Supp. 782 (E.D.La.1977). That court referred, *inter alia,* to the "heightened susceptibilities of nonparty class members to solicitation amounting to barratry as well as the increased opportunities of the parties or counsel to 'drum up' participation in the proceeding." The court added that "[u]napproved communications to class members that misrepresent the status or effect of the pending action also have an obvious potential for confusion and/or adversely affecting the administration of justice."

rather than hindering, the policies embodied in the Federal Rules of Civil Procedure, especially Rule 23. In addition, such a weighing—identifying the potential abuses being addressed—should result in a carefully drawn order that limits speech as little as possible, consistent with the rights of the parties under the circumstances. As the court stated in *Coles v. Marsh*, 560 F.2d 186, 189 (C.A.3, 1977), cert. denied, 434 U.S. 985, 98 S.Ct. 611, 54 L.Ed.2d 479 (1977):

> "[T]o the extent that the district court is empowered . . . to restrict certain communications in order to prevent frustration of the policies of Rule 23, it may not exercise the power without a specific record showing by the moving party of the particular abuses by which it is threatened. Moreover, the district court must find that the showing provides a satisfactory basis for relief and that the relief sought would be consistent with the policies of Rule 23 giving explicit consideration to the narrowest possible relief which would protect the respective parties."

In the present case, one looks in vain for any indication of a careful weighing of competing factors. Indeed, in this respect, the District Court failed to provide any record useful for appellate review. The court made neither factual finding nor legal arguments supporting the need for this sweeping restraint order. Instead, the court adopted *in toto* the order suggested by the Manual for Complex Litigation.

* * *

We conclude that the imposition of the order was an abuse of discretion. The record reveals no grounds on which the District Court could have determined that it was necessary or appropriate to impose this order. Although we do not decide what standards are mandated by the First Amendment in this kind of case, we do observe that the order involved serious restraints on expression. This fact, at minimum, counsels caution on the part of a district court in drafting such an order, and attention to whether the restraint is justified by a likelihood of serious abuses.

We recognize the possibility of abuses in class-action litigation, and agree with petitioners that such abuses may implicate communications with potential class members. But the mere possibility of abuses does not justify routine adoption of a communications ban that interferes with the formation of a class or the prosecution of a class action in accordance with the rules. There certainly is no justification for adopting verbatim the form of order recommended by the Manual for Complex Litigation, in the absence of a clear record and specific findings of need. Other, less burdensome remedies may be appropriate.[20] Indeed, in many cases there will be no problem requiring remedies at all.

---

20. For example, an order requiring parties to file copies of nonprivileged communications to class members with the court may be appropriate in some circumstances.

In the present case, for the reasons stated above, we hold that the District Court abused its discretion.[21] Accordingly, the judgment below is affirmed.

KLEINER v. FIRST NATIONAL BANK OF ATLANTA

United States Court of Appeals, Eleventh Circuit, 1985.
751 F.2d 1193.

Before HILL, VANCE and ANDERSON, CIRCUIT JUDGES.

VANCE, CIRCUIT JUDGE.

[Plaintiff sued on behalf of a class of borrowers alleging defendant Bank had fraudulently failed to disclose that in fact it loaned money to favored borrowers at rates below its stated "prime" rate. The district court certified a class under Rule 23(b)(3). Before notice was sent to the class, the Bank noticed the depositions of 25 class members. The district court granted a protective order prohibiting the taking of more than five depositions and indicated that there should be no other contact between the Bank and class members about the suit. The Bank's lawyer argued that the Bank had a constitutional right to communicate with class members about the case, and the judge directed briefing on that issue. Before the district court had decided the constitutional question, the Bank's Chairman, after consulting with counsel, organized a campaign in which all loan officers were directed to contact borrowers by telephone and to "do the best selling job they had ever done" to persuade class members to opt out. One loan officer who refused to use pressure tactics was fired. In a few days some 3,000 borrowers were contacted. Of these, 2,800, representing total loans of almost $700 million, opted out.

When the trial court learned of the Bank's campaign, the Bank claimed it was purely informational. The court nevertheless invalidated the opt outs, held the lawyer for the Bank in contempt and disqualified him from further work on the case, imposed over $50,000 in costs on the Bank and imposed a $50,000 fine on counsel for the Bank. Thereafter, the Bank settled with the plaintiff class. The Bank's counsel, however, appealed from the finding of contempt and the fine.

The appellate court affirmed, finding the basic issue to be whether the district court had authority to forbid defense contacts with a plaintiff class for the purpose of eliciting opt outs.]

When confronted with claims pressed by a plaintiff class, it is obviously in defendants' interest to diminish the size of the class and thus the range of potential liability by soliciting exclusion requests. Such conduct reduces the effectiveness of the 23(b)(3) class action for no reason except to undermine the purposes of the Rule.

---

21. In the conduct of a case, a court often finds it necessary to restrict the free expression of participants, including counsel, witnesses, and jurors. Our decision regarding the need for careful analysis of the particular circumstances is limited to the situation before us—involving a broad restraint on communication with class members. We also note that the rules of ethics properly impose restraints on some forms of expression. See, *e.g.*, ABA Code of Professional Responsibility, DR 7–104 (1980).

A unilateral communications scheme, moreover, is rife with potential for coercion. "[I]f the class and the class opponent are involved in an ongoing business relationship, communications from the class opponent to the class may be coercive." This litigation is illustrative. The class consisted of Bank borrowers, many of whom were dependent on the Bank for future financing. Bank customers affected by the litigation included "those who anticipated seeking a note 'rollover,' new loans, extension of lines of credit, or any type of discretionary financial indulgence from their loan officers, and who did not have convenient access to other credit sources." As the district court pointed out, the high number of exclusion requests was witness to the inherent coercion of the Bank's machinations.

In view of the tension between the preference for class adjudication and the individual autonomy afforded by exclusion, it is critical that the class receive accurate and impartial information regarding the status, purposes and effects of the class action. This is especially important since the court must not consider the probable outcome of the case in passing on class certification. The "best practicable notice" envisioned by the Rule is notice that conveys objective, neutral information about the nature of the claim and the consequence of proceeding as a class.

Unsupervised, unilateral communications with the plaintiff class sabotage the goal of informed consent by urging exclusion on the basis of a one-sided presentation of the facts, without opportunity for rebuttal. The damage from misstatements could well be irreparable. Concomitantly, a solicitations scheme relegates the essential supervision of the court to the status of an "afterthought." In this case, the carefully constructed edifice of check and countercheck, notice and reply, was obliterated when the telephones were lifted from their cradles. The Bank's actions obstructed the district court in the discharge of its duty to "protect both the absent class and the integrity of the judicial process by monitoring the actions before it." The Bank's subterfuge and subversion constituted an intolerable affront to the authority of the district court to police class member contacts. Accordingly, we hold that the trial court had ample discretion under Rules 23(b)(3) and 23(d) to prohibit the Bank's overtures.

* * *

In general, an order limiting communications regarding ongoing litigation between a class and class opponents will satisfy first amendment concerns if it is grounded in good cause and issued with a "heightened sensitivity" for first amendment concerns. In ascertaining the existence of good cause, four criteria are determinative: the severity and the likelihood of the perceived harm; the precision with which the order is drawn; the availability of a less onerous alternative; and the duration of the order.

Consistent with the Supreme Court's clear concern with ensuring the effective regulation of advertising and other forms of solicitation, it is unnecessary for a trial court to issue particularized findings of abusive conduct when a given form of speech is inherently conducive to over-reaching and duress. The Supreme Court has acknowledged that unsupervised oral solicitations, by their very nature, are wont to produce distorted statements on the one hand and the coercion of susceptible individuals on the other.

> [I]n-person solicitation may exert pressure and often demands an immediate response, without providing an opportunity for comparison or reflection. The aim and effect of in-person solicitation may be to provide a one-sided presentation and to encourage speedy and perhaps uninformed decisionmaking; there is no opportunity for intervention or counter-education.

Ohralik [*v. Ohio State Bar Ass'n*], 436 U.S. at 457, 98 S.Ct. 1919. Under such circumstances, "the absence of explicit proof or findings of harm or injury is immaterial," and the trial court is empowered to enter prophylactic orders designed to prevent harm before it happens. The Bank's telephone solicitation canvass is a classic example of a major potential abuse which necessitates restraint.[27]

In the realm of litigation, a fair and just result often presupposes restraints on the speech of the parties. *Seattle Times Co. v. Rhinehart,* 467 U.S. 20, 104 S.Ct. 2199, 2207 n. 18, 81 L.Ed.2d 17 (1984) [*infra* p. 574]. Inroads on the principle forbidding the solicitation of exclusion requests in 23(b)(3) class actions could spell the ultimate extinction of that form of relief. Given the inherent coercion conveyed by the Bank's covert campaign, we agree that the district court possessed the authority to regulate such contacts without the predicate record and findings required in *Bernard.*

Notes and Questions

1. Since *Gulf Oil* the position of the Manual has changed, and it now admonishes that judicial intervention into pre-certification contacts is justified only with a clear record of abuse, and then with a carefully drawn order. Manual for Complex Litigation (4th) § 21.12 (2004).

What should suffice to justify such a limitation? In Great Rivers Cooperative v. Farmland Industries, 59 F.3d 764 (8th Cir.1995), plaintiffs accused

---

27. This case illustrates precisely the same dangers discussed in *Ohralik.* The telephone campaign left the court and counsel powerless to corroborate the supposedly innocent content of the conversations. The Bank's claims of innocence are suspect, moreover, because the briefing materials used to answer customer questions insinuated reprisals or distortions of fact, as the court justifiably found. "[B]oth the Bank's top management and its counsel knew that by verbally providing information to customers through Defendant's employees there was a high likelihood that the facts would become even further skewed in transmission. This likelihood was further heightened by the Bank's election to use a non-lawyer, who had little familiarity with the case, but good persuasive skills, to make the primary presentation to those who would be contacting absent class members." Worse yet, the loan officers who made the telephone calls were the ones who controlled the customer's line of credit, and their on-the-spot entreaties pressured the listener to reach an immediate decision to comply before hearing the opposite point of view. The "usual cure for false speech is more speech," but in this case the Bank left "no time for more speech before the party opted out." It comes as no surprise that over seventy-five percent of those contacted decided to opt out.

defendant, an agricultural cooperative, of fraud. After the suit was filed, defendant published a two-page opinion piece about the suit in its newsletter to members. Plaintiffs thereupon sought relief from the district judge, who concluded that the article "appears to contain somewhat misleading representations" and "to constitute an implied solicitation to potential class members to opt out." The court therefore required defendant to publish a rebuttal article from plaintiffs and to refrain from further communications that could be taken as an invitation to opt out. The court of appeals held that this order was improper because the district court made insufficient findings. "That a statement 'appears' 'in certain respects' to be 'somewhat misleading' is not sufficient to require a party to print a rebuttal without serious and careful weighing of that party's First Amendment rights." One judge dissented regarding the prohibition on invitations to opt out due to the "unique circumstances" of class actions, but agreed regarding the order to publish a rebuttal.

2. Note the risks of communication with class members identified by the Court in *Gulf Oil*. Are these serious concerns? In some circumstances there is a constitutional right for attorneys to solicit clients. See Zauderer v. Office of Disciplinary Counsel, 471 U.S. 626, 105 S.Ct. 2265, 85 L.Ed.2d 652 (1985). For an argument that this protection should cover class counsel's efforts to solicit class members, see Camisa, The Constitutional Right To Solicit Potential Class Members in a Class Action, 25 Gonzaga L.Rev. 95 (1989); compare American Computer Trust Leasing v. Jack Farrell Implement Co., 136 F.R.D. 160 (D.Minn.1991) (class counsel forbidden to use list of class members obtained through discovery subject to protective order for purposes of soliciting them).

Arguably class counsel have a duty to communicate with class members. See Note, Conflicts in Class Actions and Protection of Absent Class Members, 91 Yale L.J. 590, 603–14 (1982). In Oppenheimer Fund, Inc. v. Sanders, 437 U.S. 340, 354 n. 20, 98 S.Ct. 2380, 2391 n. 20, 57 L.Ed.2d 253 (1978), the Court acknowledged that there may be instances where the class representative needs to contact class members to obtain information bearing on whether the case should proceed as a class action. May defendant attempt to prevent such communication? See Nagy v. Jostens, Inc., 91 F.R.D. 431 (D.Minn.1981), in which the defendant in an employment discrimination action obtained "confidentiality" agreements with its employees that forbade communication with plaintiff's lawyers. The court held that such agreements could not apply to material pertinent to the lawsuit.

In some instances, however, courts continue to voice concern about communications on behalf of putative class representatives. In Jackson v. Motel 6 Multipurpose, Inc., 130 F.3d 999 (11th Cir.1997), plaintiffs filed two class actions charging defendant (operator of over 750 motels nationwide) with discriminating against patrons on grounds of race and discriminating against employees who refused to implement defendant's policy of discriminating against nonwhite patrons. The district court had a local rule forbidding communication with class members. On plaintiffs' motion, however, the district judge authorized their establishment of an 800 telephone number for potential class members to call about problems at defendant's motels, and also authorized nationwide publication and mass mailings by the class representatives about their allegations, soliciting information regarding plaintiffs' allegations of discrimination. The appellate court concluded that the district judge's later conditional class certification was erroneous (see *supra* p. 278 n. 8), and that the communications order was improper:

> In sum, we hold that the district court abused its discretion in entering an order allowing communication with potential class members when the authorized communications would be nationwide in scope and would cause serious and irreparable injury to the defendant, when a decision on class certification was not imminent, and when the proposed *Jackson* class was clearly not certifiable. Under these circumstances, there was no need for the plaintiffs immediately to begin the highly injurious publication of their claims authorized by the order—publication that could and did continue for months, as the court contemplated the plaintiffs' motions for class certification.

Id. at 1007. Was the district court's local rule valid under *Gulf Oil*? Could the court forbid plaintiffs from publicizing their allegations in the law suit?

3.   Are the concerns about subverting Rule 23 values greater when the communication comes from the class opponent? Consider the situation in *Kleiner*. How can the court meaningfully monitor communications the bank has with class members with whom it has an ongoing business relationship?

For another case like *Kleiner*, consider Air Communication and Satellite, Inc. v. EchoStar Satellite Corp., 38 P.3d 1246 (Colo. S. Ct. 2002), a class action on behalf of 20,000 retailers alleging that defendant had breached its sales agreements. Defendant mailed "information packets" with a new sales agreement to class members. The agreement conditioned the retailers' continued receipt of defendant's merchandise (satellite TV receivers) on waiving any claims they had against the defendant. The trial court ordered a corrective notice and directed that all future communications between defendant and the retailers had to be approved in advance. The state supreme court upheld the requirement that defendant send a corrective notice to undo the effect of the earlier mailing, but found that there was no sufficient basis in the record for the blanket requirement that future communications be reviewed in advance by the court.

The defendant is not the only potential source of efforts to subvert the class action. In Georgine v. Amchem Products, Inc., 160 F.R.D. 478 (E.D.Pa. 1995), the judge invalidated the opt-outs of class members on the ground that many of them had been misled about the terms of the settlement by objecting plaintiff lawyers. Some 235,000 class members had sent in opt-out forms, but more than 95% of these had evidently been on forms provided by the objectors rather than the court. The judge found that over 62,500 misleading letters had been sent out by objectors, and that at least 667,550 people had been misled by these letters or by advertisements the objectors placed in newspapers. He therefore ordered that those who opted out be noticed again and given another opportunity to decide whether to opt out. Thereafter, the Supreme Court upheld objectors' arguments that the class had been certified improperly. See Amchem Products, Inc. v. Windsor, *supra* p. 373.

4.   The rules change once a court has determined that the action can be maintained as a class action. Before certification it may be said that the class members are not "represented by" counsel for purposes of A.B.A. Model

Rule of Professional Conduct 4.2 (formerly Disciplinary Rule 7–104), which forbids communication by an attorney with an opposing party represented by counsel. *Cf.* Cada v. Costa Line, Inc., 93 F.R.D. 95 (N.D.Ill.1981) (upholding settlements with class members in certified class action). Once the class has been certified and class counsel appointed, however, the rules governing communications apply as though each class member is the client of class counsel. Manual for Complex Litigation (4th) § 21.33 (2004). Compare Parks v. Eastwood Ins. Serv., Inc., 235 F.Supp.2d 1082 (C.D.Cal.2002) (in action under Fair Labor Standards Act, which requires employees to "opt in" to become plaintiffs, the court would not limit defendant employer's communications with employees before they opted in, except to forbid any that undermine or contradict the court's own notice to prospective plaintiffs about the right to opt in).

5. In *Kleiner,* the court stresses the oral nature of the communications. Should the court have more control over the manner of communication than over its content?

6. How much control can the court exercise over the content of communications? Consider Williams v. United States District Court, 658 F.2d 430 (6th Cir.1981), cert. denied 454 U.S. 1128, 102 S.Ct. 980, 71 L.Ed.2d 116 (1981), an action alleging racial discrimination by an employer and a union. After certifying the class, the district court directed that class members be sent a notice and questionnaire that included the following questions:

"Do you consent to Mizell Williams and his attorneys representing your interests in this lawsuit?"

"Do you wish to intervene and be represented by an attorney of your own choosing?"

"Have the defendants discriminated against you personally because of your race in the selection of employees for training to become locomotive engineers? If your answer is 'yes,' please explain how they have done so."

"Has the United Transportation Union failed to represent your interests with regard to the subjects of selection of employees for engineering training or the operation of the seniority system? If the answer is 'yes', please explain how the United Transportation Union has failed to represent your interests."

The district court forbade counsel for plaintiff to communicate with the class members about these questions. To what extent can a court intrude into the relationship between the attorney for the class and the class? The appellate court held that the district court local rule on which the district court had relied was invalid under *Gulf Oil.*

7. Sometimes the court has to worry about communications by strangers to the litigation. For example, in In re Synthroid Marketing Litigation, 197 F.R.D. 607 (N.D.Ill.2000), a nonparty organization wrote to class members telling them that unless they "opted out" of its efforts it would proceed to obtain benefits they were to receive due to the settlement of the class action. Worried that class members who got this letter and the court's official notice of the settlement (setting forth the claims procedure) might be

confused, the court decided that a corrective notice had to be sent. See also In re Domestic Air Transportation Antitrust Litigation, 24 Fed. R. Serv. 3d 515 (N.D.Ga.1992) (court enjoins company that was offering to sell class members information that was available free from class counsel from continuing this practice).

8. *Postscript on Kleiner*: After being affirmed, the district judge did not hold defendant's lawyers in contempt, but did impose fines based on professional-conduct rules and the court's own rules. Meanwhile, 15 years after the decision in *Gulf Oil* that district continued to have a local rule automatically restricting communications with class members. See Abdallah v. Coca–Cola Co., 186 F.R.D. 672 (N.D.Ga.1999) (despite arguments by both plaintiffs and defendant that the rule was unconstitutional, the court declined to reach those questions).

DISCOVERY FROM UNNAMED CLASS MEMBERS

In Kleiner v. First National Bank of Atlanta, *supra* p. 473, the opening salvo regarding contacts with class members was precipitated by defendant's notice setting the depositions of 25 of them. The district court granted a protective order prohibiting the taking of more than five such depositions even though there were about 3,000 class members. Ordinarily, a defendant is not limited in taking the deposition of a plaintiff (except by limitations on the number of depositions permitted parties, see Fed.R.Civ.P. 30(a)(2)(A)), but class actions are different. Consider why the court might grant such protection. How much effort would be required to respond to discovery on behalf of 3,000 class members, and how much useful information would be likely to emerge? Given that the existence of common questions is the reason for allowing a class action in the first place, the need for discovery from individual class members often may not loom large. Thus, the Supreme Court was able to say that few burdens would be placed on absent class members in handling the personal jurisdiction issues raised in Phillips Petroleum Co. v. Shutts, *supra* p. 412, and specifically shrug off concerns about their need to respond to discovery.

In general, courts are quite cautious about allowing the class opponent to pursue discovery from unnamed class members. See Manual for Complex Litigation (4th) § 21.41 (2004). As the Eleventh Circuit put it, "a discovery order threatening dismissal for non-compliance amounts to no more than an affirmative 'opt-in' device—that is, it requires passive class members to take some positive action to stay in the suit." Cox v. American Cast Iron Pipe Co., 784 F.2d 1546, 1557 (11th Cir.), cert. denied, 479 U.S. 883, 107 S.Ct. 274, 93 L.Ed.2d 250 (1986); see also On the House Syndication v. Federal Express Corp., 203 F.R.D. 452 (S.D.Cal.2001) (discovery from class members should be allowed only "upon a showing of unique circumstances"); see generally 7B C. Wright, A. Miller & M. Kane, Federal Practice & Procedure § 1796.1. Compare Cal.R.Ct. 1858 (providing that discovery from class members is allowed, if they are served with subpoenas, without a court order).

Class members are not absolutely immune to discovery, however. In Brennan v. Midwestern United Life Ins. Co., 450 F.2d 999 (7th Cir.

1971), cert. denied, 405 U.S. 921, 92 S.Ct. 957, 30 L.Ed.2d 792 (1972), the appellate court affirmed a district court order that class members respond to interrogatories and document requests, and later dismissed with prejudice the claims of those who failed to respond. In dissent, then-judge John Paul Stevens argued that these class members should have been afforded a renewed opportunity to exclude themselves from the class after receipt of the discovery requests.

Notes and Questions

1. The risk of abuse of class discovery by defendants is fairly apparent. Will unbridled access to discovery usually demoralize class members? Consider the views of a lawyer who represented a plaintiff class in an antitrust action where the judge initially granted defendants latitude to conduct what the author describes as a discovery "assault": "The class saw the defense tactics for what they were and became more, not less, cohesive. The defense gave away much of its case in the course of this discovery. The judge eventually got angry and began enforcing his [discovery] rulings very strictly against the defendants. In the end the useful information learned from the class members was minimal." Gruenberger, Discovery From Class Members: A Fertile Field for Abuse, 4 Litigation No. 1 at 35 (Fall 1977).

2. Failure to initiate discovery from class members may have adverse consequences, however. In Dellums v. Powell, 566 F.2d 167, 187 (D.C.Cir. 1977), cert. denied, 438 U.S. 916, 98 S.Ct. 3146, 57 L.Ed.2d 1161 (1978), defendant argued that his Rule 60 motion should have been granted because he had been the victim of "surprise" testimony from unnamed class members at trial. The court of appeals rejected this argument, noting that the testimony came as a surprise because defendant had never attempted discovery as to those class members. If he had attempted and been denied discovery by the trial court, would the witnesses nevertheless have been allowed to testify at trial? See also Dondore v. NGK Metals Corp., 152 F.Supp.2d 662 (E.D.Pa.2001) (defendant not allowed to interview potential witnesses listed by plaintiff because they were class members).

3. Failure to opt out may waive a privilege the class members might otherwise assert against discovery. In Doe v. Meachum, 126 F.R.D. 444 (D.Conn.1989), a class of HIV-infected prison inmates challenged the policies of the state Department of Corrections. Because the inmates' mental condition was an element of their case, the court held that they had waived their privilege to deny access to their mental health records. Cf. Rhone–Poulenc Rorer, Inc. v. Home Indemnity Co., *infra* p. 619.

4. Should the court notify class members of the possibility of intrusive or burdensome discovery before they have to decide whether to opt out? Noting that "[d]iscovery of non-named plaintiffs is both rare and usually inappropriate," the court rejected defendant's request to include such warnings in the initial notice in Roberts v. Heim, 130 F.R.D. 416, 423 (N.D.Cal. 1988).

5. How should the discovery problem be handled with a defendant class? Should a more or less stringent standard be used to determine whether discovery is allowed? Should default be allowed against the absent

class member if he fails to respond to discovery? If default can't be entered, what incentive does the unnamed defendant have to respond?

6. The issue of discovery from an absent class member should be distinguished from the question of discovery from the class representative. There is no question that the class representative may be subjected to discovery, but courts may limit its scope. In particular, many courts are inclined to restrict questions about the class representative's financial resources, which are sought on the ground that he will have to pay the cost of litigation. See, e.g., Kaplan v. Pomerantz, 131 F.R.D. 118 (N.D.Ill.1990); compare Ralston v. Volkswagenwerk, A.G., 61 F.R.D. 427, 433–34 (W.D.Mo. 1973).

L. MOOTNESS

DEPOSIT GUARANTY NATIONAL BANK v. ROPER

Supreme Court of the United States, 1980.
445 U.S. 326, 100 S.Ct. 1166, 63 L.Ed.2d 427.

CHIEF JUSTICE BURGER delivered the opinion of the Court.

[Holders of BankAmericard credit cards issued by petitioner bank sued on behalf of a class of some 90,000 Mississippi credit card holders alleging that the bank charged usurious interest rates. The district court refused to certify the class. The bank then tendered to respondents the maximum they could recover on their individual claims, $889.42 and $423.54 respectively, but respondents rejected the offer because it was conditioned on their waiver of the right to appeal the denial of class certification. On motion by the bank, the district court entered judgment in respondents' favor in the above amounts and dismissed the action. On appeal, the court of appeals held that respondents had a right to challenge the class action ruling under United Airlines, Inc. v. McDonald, 432 U.S. 385, 97 S.Ct. 2464, 53 L.Ed.2d 423 (1977), *supra* p. 468 n. 7.]

* * *

As parties in a federal civil action, respondents exercised their option as putative members of a similarly situated cardholder class to assert their claims under Rule 23. Their right to assert their own claims in the framework of a class action is clear. However, the right of a litigant to employ Rule 23 is a procedural right only, ancillary to the litigation of substantive claims. Should these substantive claims become moot in the Art. III sense, by settlement of all personal claims for example, the court retains no jurisdiction over the controversy of the individual plaintiffs.

The factual context in which this question arises is important. At no time did the named plaintiffs accept the tender in settlement of the case; instead, judgment was entered in their favor by the court without their consent and the case was dismissed over their continued objections. Neither the rejected tender nor the dismissal of the action over plaintiffs' objections mooted the plaintiffs' claim on the merits so long as they retained an economic interest in class certification. Although a case or controversy is mooted in the Art. III sense upon payment and satisfaction of a final, unappealable judgment, a decision that is "final" for purposes of appeal does not absolutely resolve a case or controversy until the time for appeal has run. Nor does a confession of judgment by defendants on less than all the issues moot an entire case; other issues in the case may be appealable. We can assume that a district court's final judgment fully satisfying named plaintiff's private substantive claims would preclude their appeal on that aspect of the final judgment; however, it does not follow that this circumstance would terminate the named plaintiffs' right to take an appeal on the issue of class certification.

* * *

We cannot say definitively what will become of respondents' continuing personal interest in their own substantive controversy with the petitioner when this case returns to the District Court. Petitioner has denied liability to the respondents, but tendered what they appear to regard as a "nuisance settlement." Respondents have never accepted the tender of judgment as satisfaction of their substantive claims. The judgment of the District Court accepting petitioner's tender has now been set aside by the Court of Appeals. We need not speculate on the correctness of the action of the District Court in accepting the tender in the first instance, or on whether petitioner may now withdraw its tender.

* * *

The use of the class-action procedure for litigation of individual claims may offer substantial advantages for named plaintiffs; it may motivate them to bring cases that for economic reasons might not be brought otherwise.[9] Plainly there has been a growth of litigation stimulated by contingent-fee agreements and an enlargement of the role this type of fee arrangement has played in vindicating the rights of individuals who otherwise might not consider it worth the candle to embark on litigation in which the optimum result might be more than consumed by the cost. The prospect of such fee arrangements offers advantages for litigation by named plaintiffs in class actions as well as for their attorneys. For better or worse, the financial incentive that class actions offer to the legal profession is a natural outgrowth of the increasing

9. A significant benefit to claimants who choose to litigate their individual claims in a class-action context is the prospect of reducing their costs of litigation, particularly attorney's fees, by allocating such costs among all members of the class who benefit from any recovery. Typically, the attorney's fees of a named plaintiff proceeding without reliance on Rule 23 could exceed the value of the individual judgment in favor of any one plaintiff. Here the damages claimed by the two named plaintiffs totaled $1,006.00. Such plaintiffs would be unlikely to obtain legal redress at an acceptable cost, unless counsel were motivated by the fee-spreading incentive and proceeded on a contingent-fee basis. This, of course, is a central concept of Rule 23.

reliance on the "private attorney general" for the vindication of legal rights; obviously this development has been facilitated by Rule 23.

The aggregation of individual claims in the context of a classwide suit is an evolutionary response to the existence of injuries unremedied by the regulatory action of government. Where it is not economically feasible to obtain relief within the traditional framework of a multiplicity of small individual suits for damages, aggrieved persons may be without any effective redress unless they may employ the class-action device. That there is a potential for misuse of the class-action mechanism is obvious. Its benefits to class members are often nominal and symbolic, with persons other than class members becoming the chief beneficiaries. But the remedy for abuses does not lie in denying the relief sought here, but with re-examination of Rule 23 as to untoward consequences.

A district court's ruling on the certification issue is often the most significant decision rendered in these class-action proceedings. To deny the right to appeal simply because the defendant has sought to "buy off" the individual private claims of the named plaintiffs would be contrary to sound judicial administration. Requiring multiple plaintiffs to bring separate actions, which effectively could be "picked off" by a defendant's tender of judgment before an affirmative ruling on class certification could be obtained, obviously would frustrate the objectives of class actions; moreover it would invite waste of judicial resources by stimulating successive suits brought by others claiming aggrievement. It would be in the interests of a class-action defendant to forestall any appeal of denial of class certification if that could be accomplished by tendering the individual damages claimed by the named plaintiffs. Permitting appeal of the district court's certification ruling—either at once by interlocutory appeal, or after entry of judgment on the merits—also minimizes problems raised by "forum shopping" by putative class representatives attempting to locate a judge perceived as sympathetic to class actions.

That small individual claims otherwise might be limited to local and state courts rather than a federal forum does not justify ignoring the overall problem of wise use of judicial resources. Such policy considerations are not irrelevant to the determination whether an adverse procedural ruling on certification should be subject to appeal at the behest of named plaintiffs. Courts have a certain latitude in formulating the standards that govern the appealability of procedural rulings even though, as in this case, the holding may determine the absolute finality of a judgment, and thus, indirectly, determine whether the controversy has become moot.

We conclude that on this record the District Court's entry of judgment in favor of named plaintiffs over their objections did not moot their private case or controversy, and that respondents' *individual* interest in the litigation—as distinguished from whatever may be their representative responsibilities to the putative class[12]—is sufficient to permit their appeal of the adverse certification ruling.

[Concurring opinions of JUSTICES REHNQUIST, STEVENS and BLACKMUN, and dissenting opinion of JUSTICE POWELL, joined by JUSTICE STEWART, omitted.]

UNITED STATES PAROLE COMMISSION v. GERAGHTY

Supreme Court of the United States, 1980.
445 U.S. 388, 100 S.Ct. 1202, 63 L.Ed.2d 479.

JUSTICE BLACKMUN delivered the opinion of the Court.

This case raises the question whether a trial court's denial of a motion for certification of a class may be reviewed on appeal after the named plaintiff's personal claim has become "moot." The United States Court of Appeals for the Third Circuit held that a named plaintiff, respondent here, who brought a class action challenging the validity of the United States Parole Commission's Parole Release Guidelines, could continue his appeal of a ruling denying class certification even though he had been released from prison while the appeal was pending. We granted certiorari to consider this issue of substantial significance under Art. III of the Constitution, to class-action litigation, and to resolve the conflict in approach among the Courts of Appeals.

I

[In 1973, the United States Parole Board adopted parole release guidelines. In 1976, Congress enacted the Parole Commission and Reorganization Act (PCRA), which expressly authorized parole release guidelines and indicated the nature of appropriate criteria for making parole decisions. Respondent John M. Geraghty was convicted of conspiracy to commit extortion and sentenced to serve 30 months. He twice applied for parole. On both occasions his application was denied because of his high "salient factor score" under the 1973 guidelines. At that point he had been in custody for nine months. Under the guidelines, he would not be released until he served his full sentence minus good-time credits.]

* * *

He then instituted this civil suit as a class action in the United States District Court for the District of Columbia, challenging the guidelines as inconsistent with the PCRA and the Constitution, and questioning the procedures by which the guidelines were applied to his case.

Respondent sought certification of a class of "all federal prisoners who are or who will become eligible for release on parole." Without

---

12. Difficult questions arise as to what, if any, are the named plaintiffs' responsibilities to the putative class *prior* to certification; this case does not require us to reach these questions.

ruling on Geraghty's motion, the court transferred the case to the Middle District of Pennsylvania, where respondent was incarcerated. Geraghty continued to press his motion for class certification, but the court postponed ruling on the motion until it was prepared to render a decision on cross-motions for summary judgment.

The District Court subsequently denied Geraghty's request for class certification and granted summary judgment for petitioners on all the claims Geraghty asserted. The court regarded respondent's action as a petition for a writ of habeas corpus, to which Federal Rule of Civil Procedure 23 applied only by analogy. It denied class certification as "neither necessary nor appropriate." A class action was "necessary" only to avoid mootness. The court found such a consideration not comprehended by Rule 23. It found class certification inappropriate because Geraghty raised certain individual issues and, inasmuch as some prisoners might be benefited by the guidelines, because his claims were not typical of the entire proposed class. On the merits, the court ruled that the guidelines are consistent with the PCRA and do not offend the *Ex Post Facto* Clause, U.S. Const., Art. I, § 9, cl. 3.

Respondent, individually "and on behalf of a class," appealed to the United States Court of Appeals for the Third Circuit. Thereafter, another prisoner, Becher, who had been denied parole through application of the guidelines and who was represented by Geraghty's counsel, moved to intervene. Becher sought intervention to ensure that the legal issue raised by Geraghty on behalf of the class "will not escape review in the appeal in this case." The District Court, concluding that the filing of Geraghty's notice of appeal had divested it of jurisdiction, denied the petition to intervene. Becher then filed a timely notice of appeal from the denial of intervention. The two appeals were consolidated.

On June 30, 1977, before any brief had been filed in the Court of Appeals, Geraghty was mandatorily released from prison; he had served 22 months of his sentence, and had earned good-time credits for the rest. Petitioners then moved to dismiss the appeals as moot. The appellate court reserved decision of the motion to dismiss until consideration of the merits.

The Court of Appeals, concluding that the litigation was not moot, reversed the judgment of the District Court and remanded the case for further proceedings. If a class had been certified by the District Court, mootness of respondent Geraghty's personal claim would not have rendered the controversy moot. See, *e.g., Sosna v. Iowa,* 419 U.S. 393, 95 S.Ct. 553, 42 L.Ed.2d 532 (1975). The Court of Appeals reasoned that an erroneous *denial* of a class certification should not lead to the opposite result. Rather, certification of a "certifiable" class, that erroneously had been denied, relates back to the original denial and thus preserves jurisdiction.

* * *

II

Article III of the Constitution limits federal "judicial Power," that is, federal-court jurisdiction, to "Cases" and "Controversies." This case-or-controversy limitation serves "two complementary" purposes. It limits the business of federal courts to "questions presented in an adversary context and in a form historically viewed as capable of resolution through the judicial process," and it defines the "role assigned to the judiciary in a tripartite allocation of power to assure that the federal courts will not intrude into areas committed to the other branches of government." Likewise, mootness has two aspects: "when the issues presented are no longer 'live' or the parties lack a legally cognizable interest in the outcome."

It is clear that the controversy over the validity of the Parole Release Guidelines is still a "live" one between petitioners and at least some members of the class respondent seeks to represent. This is demonstrated by the fact that prisoners currently affected by the guidelines have moved to be substituted, or to intervene, as "named" respondents in this Court. We therefore are concerned here with the second aspect of mootness, that is, the parties' interest in the litigation. The Court has referred to this concept as the "personal stake" requirement.

The personal-stake requirement relates to the first purpose of the case-or-controversy doctrine—limiting judicial power to disputes capable of judicial resolution. The Court in *Flast v. Cohen,* 392 U.S., at 100–101, stated:

> "The question whether a particular person is a proper party to maintain the action does not, by its own force, raise separation of powers problems related to improper judicial interference in areas committed to other branches of the Federal Government.... Thus, in terms of Article III limitations on federal court jurisdiction, the question of standing is related only to whether the dispute sought to be adjudicated will be presented in an adversary context and in a form historically viewed as capable of judicial resolution. It is for that reason that the emphasis in standing problems is on whether the party invoking federal court jurisdiction has 'a personal stake in the outcome of the controversy,' and whether the dispute touches upon 'the legal relations of parties having adverse legal interests.' "

The "personal stake" aspect of mootness doctrine also serves primarily the purpose of assuring that federal courts are presented with disputes they are capable of resolving. One commentator has defined mootness as "the doctrine of standing set in a time frame: The requisite personal interest that must exist at the commencement of the litigation (standing) must continue throughout its existence (mootness)."

III

On several occasions the Court has considered the application of the "personal stake" requirement in the class-action context. In *Sosna v. Iowa,* 419 U.S. 393, 95 S.Ct. 553, 42 L.Ed.2d 532 (1975), it held that mootness of the named plaintiff's individual claim *after* a class has been duly certified does not render the action moot. It reasoned that "even though appellees ... might not again enforce the Iowa durational residency requirement against [the class representative], it is clear that they will enforce it against those persons in the class that appellant sought to represent and that the District Court certified." The Court stated specifically that an Art. III case or controversy "may exist ... between a named defendant and a member of the class represented by the named plaintiff, even though the claim of the named plaintiff has become moot."

Although one might argue that *Sosna* contains at least an implication that the critical factor for Art. III purposes is the timing of class certification, other cases, applying a "relation back" approach, clearly demonstrate that timing is not crucial. When the claim on the merits is "capable of repetition, yet evading review," the named plaintiff may litigate the class certification issue despite loss of his personal stake in the outcome of the litigation. The "capable of repetition, yet evading review" doctrine, to be sure, was developed outside the class-action context. But it has been applied where the named plaintiff does have a personal stake at the outset of the lawsuit, and where the claim may arise again with respect to that plaintiff; the litigation then may continue notwithstanding the named plaintiff's current lack of a personal stake. See, *e.g., Roe v. Wade,* 410 U.S. 113, 123–125, 93 S.Ct. 705, 711–712, 35 L.Ed.2d 147 (1973). Since the litigant faces some likelihood of becoming involved in the same controversy in the future, vigorous advocacy can be expected to continue.

When, however, there is no chance that the named plaintiff's expired claim will reoccur, mootness still can be avoided through certification of a class prior to expiration of the named plaintiff's personal claim. Some claims are so inherently transitory that the trial court will not have even enough time to rule on a motion for class certification before the proposed representative's individual interest expires. The Court considered this possibility in *Gerstein v. Pugh,* 420 U.S., at 110, n. 11, 95 S.Ct., at 861 n. 11. *Gerstein* was an action challenging pretrial detention conditions. The Court assumed that the named plaintiffs were no longer in custody awaiting trial at the time the trial court certified a class of pretrial detainees. There was no indication that the particular named plaintiffs might again be subject to pretrial detention. Nonetheless, the case was held not to be moot because:

> "The length of pretrial custody cannot be ascertained at the outset, and it may be ended at any time by release on recognizance, dismissal of the charges, or a guilty plea, as well as by acquittal or conviction after trial. It is by no means certain that any given individual, named as plaintiff, would be in pretrial custody long enough for a district judge to certify the class. Moreover, in this case the constant existence of a class of persons suffering the deprivation is certain. The attorney representing the named respondents is a

public defender, and we can safely assume that he has other clients with a continuing live interest in the case."

In two different contexts the Court has stated that the proposed class representative who proceeds to a judgment on the merits may appeal *denial* of class certification. First, this assumption was "an important ingredient," *Deposit Guaranty Nat. Bank v. Roper, ante,* in the rejection of interlocutory appeals, "as of right," of class certification denials. *Coopers & Lybrand v. Livesay,* 437 U.S. 463, 469, 470 n. 15, 98 S.Ct. 2454, 2459, 57 L.Ed.2d 351 (1978). The Court reasoned that denial of class status will not necessarily be the "death knell" of a small-claimant action, since there still remains "the prospect of prevailing on the merits and reversing an order denying class certification."

Second, in *United Airlines, Inc. v. McDonald,* 432 U.S. 385, 393–395, 97 S.Ct. 2464, 2469–2471, 53 L.Ed.2d 423 (1977), the Court held that a putative class member may intervene, for the purpose of appealing the denial of a class certification motion, after the named plaintiffs' claims have been satisfied and judgment entered in their favor. Underlying that decision was the view that "refusal to certify was subject to appellate review after final judgment at the behest of the named plaintiffs." And today, the Court holds that named plaintiffs whose claims are satisfied through entry of judgment over their objections may appeal the denial of a class certification ruling. *Deposit Guaranty Nat. Bank v. Roper, ante.*

Gerstein, McDonald, and *Roper* are all examples of cases found not to be moot, despite the loss of a "personal stake" in the merits of the litigation by the proposed class representative. The interest of the named plaintiffs in *Gerstein* was precisely the same as that of Geraghty here. Similarly, after judgment had been entered in their favor, the named plaintiffs in *McDonald* had no continuing narrow personal stake in the outcome of the class claims. And in *Roper* the Court points out that an individual controversy is rendered moot, in the strict Art. III sense, by payment and satisfaction of a final judgment.

These cases demonstrate the flexible character of the Art. III mootness doctrine. As has been noted in the past, Art. III justiciability is "not a legal concept with a fixed content or susceptible of scientific verification." "[T]he justiciability doctrine [is] one of uncertain and shifting contours." *Flast v. Cohen,* 392 U.S., at 97, 88 S.Ct., at 1951.

IV

Perhaps somewhat anticipating today's decision in *Roper,* petitioners argue that the situation presented is entirely different when mootness of the individual claim is caused by "expiration" of the claim, rather than by a judgment on the claim. They assert that a proposed class representative who individually prevails on the merits still has a "personal stake" in the outcome of the litigation, while the named plaintiff whose claim is truly moot does not. In the latter situation, where no class has been certified, there is no party before the court with a live claim, and it follows, it is said, that we have no jurisdiction to consider whether a class should have been certified.

We do not find this distinction persuasive. As has been noted earlier, Geraghty's "personal stake" in the outcome of the litigation is, in a practical sense, no different from that of the putative class representatives in *Roper*. Further, the opinion in *Roper* indicates that the approach to take in applying Art. III is issue by issue. "Nor does a confession of judgment by defendants on less than all the issues moot an entire case; other issues in the case may be appealable. We can assume that a district court's final judgment fully satisfying named plaintiffs' private substantive claims would preclude their appeal on that aspect of the final judgment; however, it does not follow that this circumstance would terminate the named plaintiffs' right to take an appeal on the issue of class certification."

Similarly, the fact that a named plaintiff's substantive claims are mooted due to an occurrence other than a judgment on the merits does not mean that all the other issues in the case are mooted. A plaintiff who brings a class action presents two separate issues for judicial resolution. One is the claim on the merits; the other is the claim that he is entitled to represent a class. "The denial of class certification stands as an adjudication of one of the issues litigated," *Roper*. We think that in determining whether the plaintiff may continue to press the class certification claim, after the claim on the merits "expires," we must look to the nature of the "personal stake" in the class certification claim. Determining Art. III's "uncertain and shifting contours," see *Flast v. Cohen*, 392 U.S., at 97, 88 S.Ct., at 1951, with respect to nontraditional forms of litigation, such as the class action, requires reference to the purposes of the case-or-controversy requirement.

Application of the personal-stake requirement to a procedural claim, such as the right to represent a class, is not automatic or readily resolved. A "legally cognizable interest," as the Court described it in *Powell v. McCormack*, 395 U.S., at 496, 89 S.Ct., at 1950, in the traditional sense rarely ever exists with respect to the class certification claim.[8] The justifications that led to the development of the class action include the protection of the defendant from inconsistent obligations, the protection of the interests of absentees, the provision of a convenient and economical means for disposing of similar lawsuits, and the facilitation of the spreading of litigation costs among numerous litigants with similar claims. Although the named representative receives certain benefits from the class nature of the action, some of which are regarded as desirable and others as less so, these benefits generally are byproducts of the class-action device. In order to achieve the primary benefits of class suits, the Federal Rules of Civil Procedure give the proposed class representative the right to have a class certified if the requirements of the Rules are met. This "right" is more analogous to the private attorney general

8. Were the class an indispensable party, the named plaintiff's interests in certifi- cation would approach a "legally cognizable interest."

concept than to the type of interest traditionally thought to satisfy the "personal stake" requirement.

As noted above, the purpose of the "personal stake" requirement is to assure that the case is in a form capable of judicial resolution. The imperatives of a dispute capable of judicial resolution are sharply presented issues in a concrete factual setting and self-interested parties vigorously advocating opposing positions. We conclude that these elements can exist with respect to the class certification issue notwithstanding the fact that the named plaintiff's claim on the merits has expired. The question whether class certification is appropriate remains as a concrete, sharply presented issue. In *Sosna v. Iowa* it was recognized that a named plaintiff whose claim on the merits expires *after* class certification may still adequately represent the class. Implicit in that decision was the determination that vigorous advocacy can be assured through means other than the traditional requirement of a "personal stake in the outcome." Respondent here continues vigorously to advocate his right to have a class certified.

We therefore hold that an action brought on behalf of a class does not become moot upon expiration of the named plaintiff's substantive claim, even though class certification has been denied.[10] The proposed representative retains a "personal stake" in obtaining class certification sufficient to assure that Art. III values are not undermined. If the appeal results in reversal of the class certification denial, and a class subsequently is properly certified, the merits of the class claim then may be adjudicated pursuant to the holding in *Sosna*.

Our holding is limited to the appeal of the denial of the class certification motion. A named plaintiff whose claim expires may not continue to press the appeal on the merits until a class has been properly certified. If, on appeal, it is determined that class certification properly was denied, the claim on the merits must be dismissed as moot.

Our conclusion that the controversy here is not moot does not automatically establish that the named plaintiff is entitled to continue litigating the interests of the class. "[I]t does shift the focus of examination from the elements of justiciability to the ability of the named representative to 'fairly and adequately protect the interests of the class.' Rule 23(a)." *Sosna v. Iowa,* 419 U.S., at 403, 95 S.Ct., at 559. We hold only that a case or controversy still exists. The question of who is to represent the class is a separate issue.

We need not decide here whether Geraghty is a proper representative for the purpose of representing the class on the merits. No class as yet has been certified. Upon remand, the District Court can determine whether Geraghty may continue to press the class claims or whether

---

10. We intimate no view as to whether a named plaintiff who settles the individual claim after denial of class certification may, consistent with Art. III, appeal from the adverse ruling on class certification. See *United Airlines, Inc. v. McDonald,* 432 U.S. 385, 393–394, and n. 14, 97 S.Ct. 2464, 2469–2470, and n. 14, 53 L.Ed.2d 423 (1977).

another representative would be appropriate. We decide only that Geraghty was a proper representative for the purpose of appealing the ruling denying certification of the class that he initially defined. Thus, it was not improper for the Court of Appeals to consider whether the District Court should have granted class certification.

JUSTICE POWELL, with whom the CHIEF JUSTICE, JUSTICE STEWART; and JUSTICE REHNQUIST join, dissenting.

* * *

I

As the Court observes, this case involves the "personal stake" aspect of the mootness doctrine. There is undoubtedly a "live" issue which an appropriate plaintiff could present for judicial resolution. The question is whether respondent, who has no further interest in this action, nevertheless may—through counsel—continue to litigate it.

Recent decisions of this Court have considered the personal stake requirement with some care. When the issue is presented at the outset of litigation as a question of standing to sue, we have held that the personal stake requirement has a double aspect. On the one hand, it derives from Art. III limitations on the power of the federal courts. On the other, it embodies additional, self-imposed restraints on the exercise of judicial power. The prudential aspect of standing aptly is described as a doctrine of uncertain contours. But the constitutional minimum has been given definite content: "In order to satisfy Art. III, the plaintiff must show that he personally has suffered some actual or threatened injury as a result of the putatively illegal conduct of the defendant." Although noneconomic injuries can confer standing, the Court has rejected all attempts to substitute abstract concern with a subject—or with the rights of third parties—for "the concrete injury required by Art. III."

As the Court notes today, the same threshold requirement must be satisfied throughout the action. Prudential considerations not present at the outset may support continuation of an action in which the parties have invested substantial resources and generated a factual record. But an actual case or controversy in the constitutional sense " 'must be extant at all stages of review.' "

* * *

[T]he core requirement of a personal stake in the outcome is not "flexible." Indeed, the rule barring litigation by those who have no interest of their own at stake is applied so rigorously that it has been termed the "one major proposition" in the law of standing to which "the federal courts have consistently adhered ... without exception." We have insisted upon the personal stake requirement in mootness and standing cases because it is embedded in the case-or-controversy limitation imposed by the Constitution, "founded in concern about the proper—and properly limited—role of the courts in a democratic society." In this way we have, until today, "prevent[ed] the judicial process from becoming no more than a vehicle for the vindication of the value interests of concerned bystanders."

II

The foregoing decisions establish principles that the Court has applied consistently. These principles were developed outside the class action context. But Art. III contains no exception for class actions. Thus, we have held that a putative class representative who alleges no individual injury "may [not] seek relief on behalf of himself or any other member of the class." *O'Shea v. Littleton,* 414 U.S. 488, 494, 94 S.Ct. 669, 675, 38 L.Ed.2d 674 (1974). Only after a class has been certified in accordance with Rule 23 can it "acquir[e] a legal status separate from the interest asserted by [the named plaintiff]." *Sosna v. Iowa, supra,* 419 U.S. at 399, 95 S.Ct. at 557. "Given a properly certified class," the live interests of unnamed but identifiable class members may supply the personal stake required by Art. III when the named plaintiff's individual claim becomes moot. *Franks v. Bowman Transportation Co.,* 424 U.S. 747, 755–756, 96 S.Ct. 1251, 1259–1260, 47 L.Ed.2d 444 (1976); *Sosna v. Iowa, supra,* 419 U.S. at 402, 95 S.Ct. at 558.

This case presents a fundamentally different situation. No class has been certified, and the lone plaintiff no longer has any personal stake in the litigation.[6] In the words of his own lawyer, respondent "can obtain absolutely no additional personal relief" in this case. Even the lawyer has evinced no interest in continuing to represent respondent as named plaintiff, as distinguished from other persons presently incarcerated. In these circumstances, Art. III and the precedents of this Court require dismissal. But the Court views the case differently, and constructs new doctrine to breathe life into a lawsuit that has no plaintiff.

The Court announces today for the first time—and without attempting to reconcile the many cases to the contrary—that there are two categories of "the Art. III mootness doctrine": "flexible" and "less flexible." The Court then relies on cases said to demonstrate the application of "flexible" mootness to class action litigation. * * *

In *Sosna,* the Court simply acknowledged that actual class certification gives legal recognition to additional adverse parties.[8] And in *Ger-*

---

6. No one suggests that respondent could be affected personally by any ruling on the class certification question that is remanded today. In fact, the Court apparently concedes that respondent has no personal stake—"in the traditional sense"—in obtaining certification.

Several prisoners now in federal custody have filed a motion to intervene as parties respondent in this Court. Although the Court does not rule on that motion, I note that the motion was received well over a year after respondent was released from prison. In the interim, respondent obtained a ruling from the Court of Appeals and filed

his petition for certiorari in this Court. Such untimely intervention comes too late to save the action under *United Airlines, Inc. v. McDonald,* 432 U.S. 385, 97 S.Ct. 2464, 53 L.Ed.2d 423 (1977).

8. Certification is no mere formality. It represents a judicial finding that injured parties other than the named plaintiff exist. It also provides a definition by which they can be identified. Certification identifies and sharpens the interests of unnamed class members in the outcome; only thereafter will they be bound by the outcome. After certification, class members can be certain that the action will not be settled or

stein, the Court applied a rule long established, outside the class action context, by cases that never have been thought to erode the requirement of a personal stake in the outcome. *Gerstein* held that a class action challenging the constitutionality of pretrial detention procedures could continue after the named plaintiffs' convictions had brought their detentions to an end. The Court did not suggest that a personal stake in the outcome on the merits was unnecessary. The action continued only because of the transitory nature of pretrial detention, which placed the claim within "that narrow class of cases" that are "distinctly 'capable of repetition, yet evading review.' "

McDonald and *Roper* sanction some appeals from the denial of class certification notwithstanding satisfaction of the class representative's claim on the merits. But neither case holds that Art. III may be satisfied in the absence of a personal stake in the outcome. In *McDonald,* a putative class member intervened within the statutory time limit to appeal the certification ruling. Because the Court found that her claim was not time-barred, the intervenor in *McDonald* possessed the stake necessary to pursue the action. Indeed, the Court devoted its entire opinion to showing that the intervenor's claim for relief had not expired.[11] At most, *McDonald* holds only that an action which is kept alive by interested parties within prescribed periods of limitations does not "die" in an Art. III sense.

* * * In *Roper* the Court holds that the named plaintiffs, who have refused to accept proffered individual settlements, retain a personal stake in sharing anticipated litigation costs with the class. Finding that Art. III is satisfied by this alleged economic interest, *Roper* reasons that the rules of federal practice governing appealability permit a party to obtain review of certain procedural rulings that are collateral to a generally favorable judgment. The Court concludes that the denial of class certification falls within this category, as long as the named plaintiffs "assert a continuing stake in the outcome of the appeal."

III

While the Court's new concept of "flexible" mootness is unprecedented, the content given that concept is even more disturbing. The Court splits the class aspects of this action into two separate "claims":

dismissed without appropriate notice. Fed. Rule Civ.Proc. 23(e). Vigorous advocacy is assured by the authoritative imposition on the named plaintiffs of a duty adequately to represent the entire class. If the named plaintiff's own claim becomes moot after certification, the court can re-examine his ability to represent the interests of class members. Should it be found wanting, the court may seek a substitute representative or even decertify the class. Fed.Rules Civ. Proc. 23(c)(1), 23(d). After certification, the case is no different in principle from more traditional representative actions involving,

for example, a single party who cannot participate himself because of his incompetence but is permitted to litigate through an appointed fiduciary.

11. This extensive inquiry would have been unnecessary if, as the Court holds today, the intervenor had a personal stake in the class certification issue itself. Since the present respondent's claim long since has "expired," he stands in the same position as a member of the putative class whose claim has "expired" by reason of the statute of limitations.

(i) that the action may be maintained by respondent on behalf of a class, and (ii) that the class is entitled to relief on the merits. Since no class has been certified, the Court concedes that the claim on the merits is moot. But respondent is said to have a personal stake in his "procedural claim" despite his lack of a stake in the merits.

* * *

The Court reasons that its departure from precedent is compelled by the difficulty of identifying a personal stake in a "procedural claim," particularly in "nontraditional forms of litigation." But the Court has created a false dilemma. As noted in *Roper,* class certification issues are "ancillary to the litigation of substantive claims." Any attempt to identify a personal stake in such ancillary "claims" often must end in frustration, for they are not claims in any ordinary sense of the word. A motion for class certification, like a motion to join additional parties or to try the case before a jury instead of a judge, seeks only to present a substantive claim in a particular context. Such procedural devices generally have no value apart from their capacity to facilitate a favorable resolution of the case on the merits. Accordingly, the moving party is neither expected nor required to assert an interest in them independent of his interest in the merits.

Class actions may advance significantly the administration of justice in appropriate cases. Indeed, the class action is scarcely a new idea. Rule 23 codifies, and was intended to clarify, procedures for dealing with a form of action long known in equity. That federal jurisdiction can attach to the class aspect of litigation involving individual claims has never been questioned. But even when we deal with truly new procedural devices, our freedom to "adapt" Art. III is limited to the recognition of different " 'means for presenting a case or controversy *otherwise cognizable by the federal courts.*' " *Aetna Life Ins. Co. v. Haworth,* 300 U.S., at 240, 57 S.Ct., at 464 (Declaratory Judgment Act). The effect of mootness on the vitality of a device like the class action may be a relevant prudential consideration. But it cannot provide a plaintiff when none is before the Court, for we are powerless to assume jurisdiction in violation of Art. III.

Notes and Questions

1. In County of Riverside v. McLaughlin, 500 U.S. 44, 111 S.Ct. 1661, 114 L.Ed.2d 49 (1991), the Supreme Court reaffirmed the relation-back rule of Gerstein v. Pugh, 420 U.S. 103, 95 S.Ct. 854, 43 L.Ed.2d 54 (1975). Plaintiffs challenged the county's delays in providing probable cause determinations for prisoners arrested without an arrest warrant. The district court certified a class. The county raised mootness because the named plaintiffs had either received probable cause determinations or been released by the time the class was certified. The Supreme Court rejected this argument because, as stated in Geraghty, the relation-back doctrine should apply whenever claims "are so inherently transitory that the trial court will not have even enough time to rule on a motion for class certification before the proposed representative's individual interest expires."

2. In *Geraghty,* what stake, personal or otherwise, did the original plaintiff have in obtaining a determination whether the challenged standards could be applied to other people? See Lee, Deconstitutionalizing Justiciability: The Example of Mootness, 105 Harv.L.Rev. 603, 625 (1992) ("what stake could Geraghty have had in class certification, other than the satisfaction of inflicting a wound on the 'system' that wounded him?"). Where regulations or standards are at issue, should there be a requirement that some affected person stand up for the people affected by the rule? Doesn't this turn into litigation by lawyers challenging governmental behavior that is outside the ambit of traditional private litigation? Of course, if there is no person affected before the court, the challenged rules may benefit all such people and they would all oppose changes allegedly made on their behalf. But what does the court do when some of the affected individuals like the rule and others do not? Does mootness or standing solve that problem, or even address it?

Another way of looking at the problem is to view the "party" whose continuing interest is important as the class itself. As Professor Chayes has put it, if one uses this approach to mootness "[i]t is as if the class were a more familiar juridical person—a corporation, for instance, that changed its president." Chayes, Foreword: Public Law Litigation and the Burger Court, 96 Harv.L.Rev. 4, 42 (1982). Would the initial question of standing then be determined with reference to the class claims rather than the class representative's claims? For an argument that, for standing purposes, an action should be treated as a class action from the date of filing, see Greenstein, Bridging the Mootness Gap in Federal Court Class Actions, 35 Stan.L.Rev. 897 (1983). See also Shapiro, Class Actions: The Class as Party and Client, 73 Notre Dame L. Rev. 913 (1998) (arguing that the class should be considered an entity somewhat separate from the class members).

Should *Geraghty* apply to a proposed subclass? In Twelve John Does v. District of Columbia, 117 F.3d 571 (D.C.Cir.1997), a group of prisoners dissatisfied with the handling of a prison conditions class action sought to intervene to represent the allegedly-large proportion of the prison population that shared their opposition. When their motion to intervene was denied they appealed, but by the time the appeal was heard they had all been transferred to other institutions. The court of appeals nevertheless held that their appeal was not moot:

> The Court reasoned in *Geraghty* that the proposed class representative's interest was akin to that of a private attorney general, a right deliberately created in order to make it possible to realize the benefits of the class action form. *Geraghty*'s logic, in finding that the interest was significant enough to preserve the case from mootness, appears to apply to the interest of a party that has sought to intervene as representative of a subclass. Superficially, it may not seem within the stated purpose of *Geraghty* to allow the representative interest of persons seeking to *splinter* a class to save that splintering effort from mootness. But the use of a subclass makes it possible to preserve the class action form where the named representative cannot be found to adequately represent all the interests in the class, so application of *Geraghty* to subclass claims seems within its spirit.

3. "The Supreme Court has consistently distinguished between individual actions and class actions in applying the doctrine of mootness." Lewis v. Tully, 99 F.R.D. 632, 638 (N.D.Ill.1983). The difference in treatment between class actions and individual actions is illustrated by comparing *Geraghty* to Murphy v. Hunt, 455 U.S. 478, 102 S.Ct. 1181, 71 L.Ed.2d 353 (1982), where the court applied the mootness doctrine to bar an individual suit in analogous circumstances. Hunt was denied bail pending trial in state court because the state constitution forbade bail in cases of forcible sexual assault, the charge against Hunt. He sued in federal court, claiming that the state constitutional provision constituted cruel and unusual punishment. Meanwhile, Hunt was convicted in state court and sentenced to prison. The Supreme Court held that the case was moot: "The question was no longer live because even a favorable decision on it would not have entitled Hunt to bail. For the same reason, Hunt no longer had a legally cognizable interest in the result in this case. He had not prayed for damages nor had he sought to represent a class of pretrial detainees." Isn't it more reasonable to say that the case was moot because Hunt's lawyer decided not to file a class action? Should the lawyer's decision determine the question of mootness?

4. In *Roper,* the Court suggests that the class representatives had a "personal stake" in the class certification in order to spread the cost of litigation among all members of the class. Could the defendant moot that by tendering an additional amount to cover attorneys' fees and costs incurred to date? Does this prospect raise ethical problems for plaintiff's attorney?

5. The Court's personal stake analysis in class actions may undermine much of its Article III jurisprudence. Consider the following views:

> Arguably, the Court's approach does signal a recognition of the class as a personal stakeholder. Moreover, it suggests a willingness to tolerate representation of that class by one who no longer shares its personal stake. If so, this raises far-reaching questions about the idea of the Article III case. One question is why recognition of the class as stakeholder should depend on certification * * *. The more fundamental question is whether this principle can be confined to class representation. If not, it could ultimately lead to the abandonment of traditional adversity doctrine and to acceptance of a theory that so long as there is *some* party adverse to the defendant, the case requirement is met.

Bandes, The Idea of a Case, 42 Stan.L.Rev. 227, 249 (1990).

6. If the availability of class action treatment is a personal right of the class representative, can she barter it away for a price? In at least one reported case, a court upheld a settlement between the named plaintiff and defendant, after denial of certification, that provided plaintiff would not appeal the certification issue. Burkhalter v. Montgomery Ward & Co., 92 F.R.D. 361 (E.D.Ark.1981), aff'd, 676 F.2d 291 (8th Cir.1982). Another court vacated its order striking class action allegations to prevent plaintiffs from using them as "leverage" in settlement talks. Yaffe v. Detroit Steel Corp., 50 F.R.D. 481 (N.D.Ill.1970). Doesn't the approach in *Roper* tacitly approve such conduct?

Perhaps the solution lies in confronting the "difficult questions" regarding the named plaintiff's responsibilities to the putative class members before class certification so that one can evaluate the continuing duty after certification is denied. Surely the duty after denial of certification is less. Arguably the prospect of intervention by class members in order to appeal the class certification issue is sufficient to protect them. Will this safety valve work if the action is dismissed pursuant to the settlement?

7. In *Geraghty,* the Court suggests that the controversy is "live" because other prisoners have sought to intervene. Can the class action continue with the original plaintiff as class representative even though he has executed a release? How would he then be an adequate representative? *Cf.* Love v. Turlington, 733 F.2d 1562 (11th Cir.1984) (court holds challenge to class certification denial not moot although named plaintiff settled her individual claim). Contrast Dugas v. Trans Union Corp., 99 F.3d 724 (5th Cir.1996) (plaintiff who accepts Rule 68 offer of judgment that does not reserve right to appeal denial of class certification may not appeal that decision); Shores v. Sklar, 885 F.2d 760 (11th Cir.1989) (en banc) (class representative who settles individual claim must expressly reserve right to appeal denial of class certification).

Under the Fair Labor Standards Act, 29 U.S.C. § 216(b), an opt-in class is required by statute. In Cameron–Grant v. Maxim Healthcare Servs., Inc., 347 F.3d 1240 (11th Cir.2003), the district court refused to give notice to putative class members of their right to opt in because the plaintiffs who had filed the suit had settled. The appellate court ruled that, having settled, plaintiffs had nothing to appeal. *Geraghty* held that proposed class representatives have some enduring stake in class certification, it reasoned, but that holding did not apply in the opt-in situation, which makes representation dependent on affirmative consent by those to be represented. Because of this "fundamental, irreconcilable difference" between the statute and Rule 23, "[i]n contrast to the Rule 23 plaintiff, a § 216(b) plaintiff has no claim that he is entitled to represent other plaintiffs." Id. at 1249.

8. Note that the decision in *Geraghty* could be different if the challenged regulations themselves had been abandoned because that would undermine the "live controversy" prong of the mootness requirement as to all members of the class. Care must be taken, however, in determining whether there is a likelihood that the defendant will revert to the challenged practice.

M. DECERTIFICATION AND MODIFICATION OF CLASS DEFINITION

PAYNE v. TRAVENOL LABORATORIES, INC.

United States Court of Appeals, Fifth Circuit, 1982.
673 F.2d 798, cert. denied 459 U.S. 1038, 103
S.Ct. 451, 452, 74 L.Ed.2d 605 (1982).

Before CLARK, CHIEF JUDGE, GOLDBERG and WILLIAMS, CIRCUIT JUDGES.

JERRE S. WILLIAMS, CIRCUIT JUDGE.

I. BACKGROUND

Nearly a decade old at the time of this appeal, this case began on March 2, 1972 when Willie Mae Payne, a black female, and several other named plaintiffs obtained right-to-sue letters and filed suit under Title VII, 42 U.S.C. § 2000e *et seq.* and also filed claims under 42 U.S.C. § 1981 against Travenol Laboratories. Payne attacked a battery of Travenol's employment practices at its Cleveland, Mississippi, pharmaceutical plant as being racially discriminatory. The complaint was later amended to include charges of sex discrimination as well.

* * *

In 1975 the case was tried on the issue of liability, Payne representing a class of black females. The district court rendered its decision in 1976, finding that Travenol had discriminated on the basis of race and sex. The court enjoined certain employment practices and directed the parties to submit suggestions on further relief, including constructive seniority and backpay.

* * *

II.   LIMITATIONS ON THE CLASS CERTIFIED BY THE DISTRICT COURT

* * *

We now turn to Payne's challenge to the exclusion of black males from the class. To place this challenge in perspective we review the history of the district court's treatment of the class as it bears on this issue. This case was filed as a class action on March 2, 1972, by three named plaintiffs: two black females, Willie Mae Payne and Alma Jean Williams, and one black male, James Williams. The complaint alleged that Travenol discriminated against all three and the class they represented on the basis of race. On November 16, 1972, the court conditionally certified the plaintiff class to include all black applicants and employees.

On May 1, 1973 the court permitted Willie Mae Payne to amend her complaint. The amended complaint alleged sex discrimination as well as race discrimination. On May 8, 1973, the court granted James Williams' motion to withdraw from the case because of his religious views. More than one year later, on July 31, 1974, two black females, Delilah Cherry and Birdie Lee Griffin, were permitted to intervene in the case alleging race and sex discrimination. These developments prompted the defendants to move the district court to redefine the class, and on December 20, 1974, the district court did so. The new class excluded black males, and other changes were made in the composition of the class.

The district court made no written findings on its reasons for excluding black males, but the transcript of a hearing on the issue reveals that the district court was swayed by two factors. First, the district court noted that no male plaintiff remained in the case after James Williams' withdrawal. The only remaining plaintiffs were black females. Second, the court believed that a conflict existed between the interests of black males and the black female plaintiffs who sought to represent them. The black females charged sex discrimination in the assignment of material handlers. According to the court, this created a conflict because to the extent that females proved sex discrimination, the interests of males would be impaired. The court thus concluded that black females could not adequately represent the interests of black males.

After this ruling, counsel for the plaintiffs requested that black males be sent notice of their provisional exclusion from the class and of the need for one of them to step forward if black males were to remain in the case, but the district court declined. The court directed, however, that members of the new provisional class receive notice of their inclusion in the case and be given an opportunity to opt out. On December 8, 1976, after trial, the court made its class-definition order final.

The appellants contest the redefinition of the class to exclude black males on two grounds. First, Payne denies the existence of a conflict between black females and black males that warrants excluding males from the class. Second, Payne argues that black males had a stake in the litigation because of their provisional inclusion in the class, and the district court had an obligation to protect their interest. The district court, therefore, should have sent notice to black males to permit one to intervene as a plaintiff. Had this been done, the class could have been subdivided to remove the conflict between the interests of black females and black males.

* * *

The conflict found by the district court here is straightforward: the female plaintiffs asserted that Travenol discriminates against females by typically assigning them to the lower-paying job of assembler while typically assigning males to the higher-paying job of material handler. The females, therefore, sought to establish that males were favored at their expense. This claim plainly draws the interests of males into conflict with the interests of females. We are aware of no case holding that a black female plaintiff is an adequate representative of black males in a sex and race discrimination suit when the interests of the two groups conflict. On the contrary, a host of district courts have refused to permit black females to represent black males in class actions alleging both race and sex discrimination when a conflict of interest appears.

* * *

The plaintiffs argue that because both blacks and women were adequately represented at trial, the existence of a possible conflict between the two before trial is not relevant. We reject this argument. It is true that the court's responsibility to assess the adequacy of representation is an ongoing one. The district court may decertify a class after trial if plaintiff's trial performance showed him or her to be an inadequate class representative. But the trial court is not required to hypothesize about the effect of an actual conflict of interests on the adequacy of plaintiffs' representation. It is enough to deny representation that the conflict is actual at the outset of the trial.

The plaintiffs also argue that black males have no "legally cognizable" interest in perpetuating sex discrimination at Travenol's plant, and we agree. But black males do have an interest in representation of their interests with undivided loyalty. The existence *vel non* of sex discrimination is at issue in this case. Black males are entitled to a class representative who is free from a desire to prove a claim that will impair their interests.

Finally, the plaintiffs contend that we must balance the harms to black males flowing from their inclusion in the class against the harms flowing from their exclusion. Payne maintains that the harms of excluding black males overshadow the potential harms of including them. The district court's ruling deprives black males of the benefits accorded to class members, including constructive seniority and back pay. To include them in the class despite the conflict of interest, Payne argues, would have brought them much less harm. This argument diverts attention from the proper inquiry under Rule 23. Rule 23 forces a court to measure the adequacy of representation because of the sensitive considerations involved in binding parties not before the court to a judgment won or lost by class representatives. See *Hansberry v. Lee,* 311 U.S. 32, 61 S.Ct. 115, 85 L.Ed. 22 (1940) [*supra* p. 285]. A court need not look beyond the issues in the suit before it to determine when a conflict of interest precludes adequate representation. We conclude, therefore, that the district court was within its discretion in excluding black males from the class.

Ordinarily, if a court discerns a conflict like the one in this case, the proper solution is to create subclasses of persons whose interests are in accord. Of course, each subclass must be headed by a person who claims the same injury as the subclass, but who lacks the fatal conflict. In this case, after the sole black male plaintiff, James Williams, withdrew from the case, no named plaintiff existed to head a class of black males. Payne therefore argues that having provisionally included black males in the class, the district court owed black males a duty to send them notice of their pending exclusion from the case to allow one of them to step forward to intervene. We do not find this obligation in the law.

Rule 23 requires a district court to give notice to absent class members of developments in the suit in only two situations. The first is when the court certifies a class under Rule 23(b)(3) because of common questions of law or fact that predominate over other aspects of the suit and render a class action the appropriate vehicle to resolve the claims. Fed.R.Civ.P. 23(c)(2); *Eisen v. Carlisle & Jacquelin,* 417 U.S. 156, 94 S.Ct. 2140, 40 L.Ed.2d 732 (1974) [*supra* p. 440]. The second is when a class action is to be dismissed or compromised. Fed.R.Civ.P. 23(e).[14] In all other cases, notice lies within the district court's discretion. Fed. R.Civ.P. 23(d)(2). The district court thus had discretionary power to give black males notice of their impending exit from the case. Such action in

---

14. The plaintiffs have not argued that the redefinition of the class in this case is a dismissal within the meaning of Rule 23(e), and we do not consider it to be one.

general is to be encouraged.[15] We cannot say, however, that the court transgressed its authority in failing to recruit a new black male plaintiff to intervene to permit subdivision of the class. *Cf. United States Parole Commission v. Geraghty,* 445 U.S. 388, 100 S.Ct. 1202, 1214, 63 L.Ed.2d 479 (1980) [*supra* p. 484] (after denying class certification, a district court must give the representative of the plaintiff class an opportunity to propose subclasses, but has no obligation to construct them itself).

Were we to accept Payne's reasoning, a district court that provisionally certified a class but later concluded that the existing class representative was inadequate would have to send notice soliciting a new class representative. Plainly, that is not the rule in this Circuit, nor should it be. The rule that Payne proposes would shift a burden onto the district court that properly remains with the plaintiff.[16] Only if the black males had received notice of their initial inclusion in the class, had relied on the class suit to protect their rights, and would be prejudiced as a practical matter by exclusion from the class might the district court be obligated to take some action to safeguard their interests. Here, there is no showing that black males relied to their detriment on the district court's provisional inclusion of them in the class. In the absence of such a showing, we decline to hold that the district court abused its discretion in failing to give them notice. In sum, the district court on this record was justified in its discretion in believing that recruiting black males after the one black male had dropped out almost two years before would constitute the stimulation of a new law suit by the court rather than a continuation of the old.

GOLDBERG, CIRCUIT JUDGE, dissenting in part:

* * * I believe the district court committed two analytically distinct errors in excluding black males from the plaintiff class. First, the district court should not have excluded black men from a class represented by

---

15. In *Silva v. Vowell,* 621 F.2d 640, 649 (5th Cir.1980), *cert. denied,* 449 U.S. 1125, 101 S.Ct. 941, 67 L.Ed.2d 111 (1981), we stated that if the court had found no named plaintiff qualified to represent a subclass, "the court could have considered 'whether it is in the interest of justice and judicial economy to postpone dismissal as to the subclass for a specified period in which members of the subclass could become plaintiffs by amendment of the Complaint or by intervention and thereby save the subclass action.'" In *Sullivan v. Winn–Dixie Greenville Inc.,* 62 F.R.D. 370, 377 (D.S.C.1974), the court followed this procedure but did not require notice to the subclass members. *But see Alexander v. Avco Corp.,* 380 F.Supp. 1282, 1286 (M.D.Tenn. 1974), (the court gave notice to class members to give them an opportunity to intervene as individuals before dismissing the class action) *modified,* 565 F.2d 1364 (6th Cir.1977), *cert. denied,* 436 U.S. 946, 98 S.Ct. 2849, 56 L.Ed.2d 787 (1978).

16. At oral argument, plaintiff's counsel advised this Court that counsel failed to seek a black male plaintiff to intervene on his own because of doubts that attorneys for the plaintiffs could freely communicate with class members. *Gulf Oil Co. v. Bernard,* 452 U.S. 89, 101 S.Ct. 2193, 68 L.Ed.2d 693 (1981) [*supra* p. 470], made clear that a district court may not curtail communications between the attorney for the plaintiff and class members, at least in the absence of specific findings that such an order is appropriate or necessary to prevent abuses. Although in 1974 the plaintiffs lacked the guidance of *Gulf Oil,* nothing in the record indicates that the plaintiffs asked the district court to allow them to communicate with the class. We cannot impose a duty on the district court to fill the void created by the plaintiffs' failure to press their rights to communicate with persons excluded from the class.

black women on the grounds of a potential conflict of interest which in fact never materialized. Second, even if the district court was correct in its theory that black women could not represent black men, the district court erred in failing to inform the absent class members that their sole representative had withdrawn from the suit and they would be excluded from the action.

Each of these errors, standing alone, mandates that the district court's decision on exclusion of black males be reversed and remanded with instructions to rectify these mistakes.

II.   EXCLUSION OF BLACK MALES FROM THE PLAINTIFF CLASS: ANOTHER VIEW

A.   *The Pretrial Ruling*

* * *

The trial court's decision to exclude black men was based on a mere hypothesis that a conflict *might* develop between male and female class members *if* females were allowed to compete with males for the better paying jobs of material handler. This is not a case where the testimony of the named plaintiffs revealed identifiable antagonism toward other class members. Thus, I believe that this is a case of mere possible and *not* actual conflict.

* * *

In fact, the only potential conflict I can find in this case is that of competition between black males and females seeking material handler jobs. However, the "conflict" among these class members is indistinguishable from the conflicts inherent in any Title VII class action. Whenever a Title VII plaintiff class prevails, the class members are thrown into competition with one another, as well as with non-class members, for a limited number of jobs. However, as the Majority acknowledges, this Court has consistently rejected the contention that job competition among class members creates a conflict sufficient to defeat class certification under F.R.Civ.P.Rule 23. To hold otherwise would effectively destroy the class action as a procedural device for enforcing Title VII rights, for it is impossible to imagine a Title VII class action that does *not* involve a potential conflict among class members at the relief stage of the litigation.

* * *

In fact, it is *only* through the procedural device of a class action that the competing claims of Title VII plaintiffs can be equitably resolved. The very purpose of a class action is to gather before the court all parties entitled to relief. When all are assembled, the court can distribute relief fairly among the class members rather than awarding relief to any one plaintiff at the expense of other similarly injured individuals.

As will be discussed more fully *infra,* the district court in this case specifically found that black males, as well as females, were the victims of unlawful discrimination. However, as a consequence of the Majority's decision, the Magistrate is now actually forbidden to consider the interests of black men in designing those portions of his proposed order which deal with individualized relief. Because all the parties entitled to relief were not gathered together in this one action, the trial court is now unable to equitably distribute the limited available relief in the remedial phase of the litigation.

Finally, the Majority justifies the exclusion of black males from the class as necessary to vindicate the black males' right to be represented with "undivided loyalty" by "a class representative who is free from a desire to prove a claim that will impair their interests."

The Platonic ideal of adequate representation is realized when one attorney zealously represents the individual interests of one client. Every class action is necessarily a departure from this ideal. In a class action, attorneys advocate several interests which are common to all class members. Therefore, no one class member's interests are ever represented with "undivided loyalty": counsel's loyalty is necessarily owed to the goals shared by the class as a whole.

Under this system of advocacy, there is always the danger that a class attorney will not urge all class members' interests with equal vigor. This possibility exists even in the most homogeneous of classes. For instance, as a matter of trial strategy, an attorney may choose to press the claims which are easiest or least expensive to prove, ignoring others. Or, an attorney may advocate the named plaintiff's interests more strongly than the interests of absentees. However, the ever-present possibility of less than vigorous representation of some class members' claims has not necessitated abandonment of the class action as a procedural device for vindicating rights. Instead, the trial judge presiding over a class action is charged with the duty to protect the interests of absentees by monitoring the adequacy with which their interests are represented throughout the litigation. If at trial the class attorney does not fulfill his or her duty to adequately represent all class interests, the trial court may at that time decertify the class.

In this case, plaintiffs' attorneys sought to prove both race and sex discrimination. Of course, there was a possibility that counsel might concentrate on proving sex discrimination, leaving the class members' race discrimination claims to languish unproven. In that event, it would be the trial court's duty to decertify the class, so that black men would not be bound by the judgment. However, until class counsel actually proved, by their trial performance, that they would not represent both race and sex claims with equal vigor, there was no inherent reason to assume inadequate representation of black males' interests.

* * *

There was no disagreement between black men and women as to the outcome of this case: both groups sought to prove that defendant had discriminated against them in violation of Title VII; and that accordingly, they were entitled to appropriate relief. There was no reason, based on the law in this Circuit, why a black female could not represent all black employees in their mutual jihad against Travenol Laboratories.

B. *The Post–Trial Exclusion of Black Males From The Plaintiff Class*

* * *

In considering the class representatives' claims that defendant Travenol discriminated on the basis of both race and sex, the district court necessarily reviewed evidence bearing on the effect of Travenol's policies on blacks. However, the district court did not confine itself to an examination of evidence bearing upon discrimination against black women. Instead, the court specifically found that Travenol's hiring policies, educational requirements, failure to post job vacancies, and system of promotion adversely affected *all* blacks. In some cases, the findings were actually broken down to show the specific effect of discriminatory policies on black men. Thus, although black males were excluded by pretrial order from the class of plaintiffs bringing this action, the district court proceeded to try the case and make findings predicated on the assumption that black men were properly included in the class. In doing so, the district judge quite properly exercised his duty to monitor the class representative and to protect the interests of absentees.

After trial, however, the district judge refused to modify his original definition of the class. Instead of redefining the class to include black males, the district judge, in his Order of December 8, 1976, reiterated the class definition given in his pretrial order, without, however, providing any new explanation for this decision. In view of the district court's finding that black males had indeed been the victims of unlawful racial discrimination, the December 8, 1976 decision was completely unjustified and should be reversed.

The district court's rationale for continuing to exclude black males from the plaintiff class even after trial was that there existed a *potential* conflict of interest between black females and black males. In this case, to paraphrase an old adage, the proof of plaintiff's ability to represent the interests of black males was in the representation thereof. Clearly, any potential conflicts at the relief stage of the litigation did not hinder plaintiffs' counsel from presenting sufficient evidence of discrimination against black men to support the district court's findings that black men as well as women were victims of defendant's discriminatory hiring policies. What more should be required to sustain a finding that the interests of black males had been adequately represented for the purposes of Rule 23?

Based on the district court's own findings following the trial on the merits, its post-trial order excluding black males from the plaintiff class compels reversal.

III. THE TRIAL COURT ERRED IN FAILING TO NOTIFY ABSENT CLASS MEMBERS THAT THEY WOULD BE EXCLUDED FROM THE ACTION

* * *

F.R.Civ.P. 23(e) provides that " ... a class action shall not be dismissed or compromised without the approval of the Court, and notice of the proposed dismissal *shall* be given to all members of the class ..." (emphasis added). One "purpose of [Rule 23(e)] is to protect the nonparty members of the class ... when the representatives become fainthearted before the action is adjudicated." Wright and Miller, *Federal Practice and Procedure* § 1797. I believe that there is no question but that the mandatory notice requirement of Rule 23(e) was triggered in this case and that the trial court erred in failing to provide notice to the soon-to-be-excluded absentee class members.

Once a plaintiff class has been certified, the provisions of Rule 23(e) become applicable. As the Majority correctly notes, the notice requirement set forth in Rule 23(e) is mandatory. However, the Majority has asserted that Mr. Williams' withdrawal as class representative and the resultant exclusion of black males from the plaintiff class did not constitute a "dismissal" within the meaning of Rule 23(e). Thus, the Majority concludes that Mr. Williams' departure and the exclusion of black males did not trigger the mandatory notice requirement.[19] I must take exception to this conclusion. When Mr. Williams withdrew from the action, his departure was arranged through the use of F.R.Civ.P. 21 (motion to drop a party). However, it is clear that " ... the parties [should] not be allowed to circumvent [Rule 23(e)] simply by classifying a dismissal as a motion to drop one or more parties under Rule 21; the court is obliged to determine if the change in parties will affect the rights of the other class members so that notice of the motion should be given." Wright & Miller, 7A *Federal Practice and Procedure* § 1797.

Rule 23(e) is designed to serve at least two important purposes. First, it protects absent class members who may be relying upon the pendency of a class action from being prejudiced if their named representative should choose to drop his (and their) action. Second, the Rule is a prophylactic device, a safeguard designed to discourage collusion. Without Rule 23(e), class action defendants might seek to "buy off" class representatives in an effort to "turn off" a class action.

Without in any way questioning the piety or sincerity of the named plaintiff who chose to withdraw from this case, we must recognize that his fortuitous departure from the lawsuit did result in the exclusion of all black males from the plaintiff class—a valuable boon to defendants. Thus, one can readily see the grave potential for abuse which will follow from the Majority's holding that Rule 23(e) notice is not required in a

---

19. In their footnote 14, the Majority seems to suggest that insofar as the plaintiff-appellants have failed to specifically cite Rule 23(e) in their argument regarding the trial court's refusal to provide notice, the issue need not be seriously considered by this Court. This reasoning defeats the very purpose of Rule 23. Rule 23(e) is designed to protect absent class members from being sold out or abandoned by their own class representatives. It would turn the rule on its head to hold that Rule 23(e) will only be enforced if the class representative invokes it. In a case involving a "sell out" or abandonment of absent class members by the class representative, we could hardly expect the class representative to invoke Rule 23(e). That is why the mandatory notice requirements of Rule 23(e) can and must be raised by the court *sua sponte*.

case such as this. Under the rule set forth by the Majority, future class action defendants may be tempted to quietly secure the withdrawal of the named class representative and thereby "turn off" the class action. If, as the Majority holds, Rule 23(e) can be ignored, there will be nothing to prevent such collusion.

Although the Majority holds that Rule 23(e) is inapplicable in this case, the Majority does indicate that if the absent class members were aware "of their initial inclusion in the plaintiff class, had relied on the class suit to protect their rights, and would be prejudiced as a practical matter by exclusion from the class," notice would indeed be mandatory. However, the Majority concludes that because "there is no showing that black males relied to their detriment" on their provisional inclusion in the class, notice of their exclusion was not required.

As the Majority suggests, there is some authority for the proposition that 23(e) notice need not be provided if the trial court determines that the absent class members have not detrimentally relied upon their inclusion in the class. However, in those cases where district courts have seen fit to dispense with the 23(e) notice requirement, they have done so only after making a specific finding of fact concerning the question of whether absent class members may have detrimentally relied upon their inclusion in the plaintiff class. In each of these cases, the district court recognized its affirmative duty to safeguard the interests of absent class members. If the court determined that absent class members may have detrimentally relied upon inclusion in the plaintiff class, notice was ordered. Only if the court specifically found that absent class members could not have detrimentally relied was the Rule 23(e) notice dispensed with.

* * *

Although the absent class members in this case may never have received formal written notice of their inclusion in the plaintiff class, we cannot just assume that they were unaware of the existence of this action. The record indicates that Travenol Laboratories was the major employer in a small Mississippi town. Thus, many of the absent class members might well have learned of the pendency of this suit by word of mouth.

In this case, Rule 23(e) notice was required because "[c]lass members ... may have relied upon informal publicity about the existence of the class suit and abstained from filing individual or class claims.... If a class member learned that a suit had been filed, but not that it had been terminated, he might lose his claim." Developments in the Law—Class Actions, 89 Harv.L.Rev. 1318, 1541 (1976). * * *

The Majority seems to suggest it was the plaintiff's burden to establish that absent class members had detrimentally relied upon their initial inclusion in the plaintiff class. Of course, this cannot be the rule. Rule 23(e) is designed to protect absent class members from collusion or abandonment *by their own representatives*. Certainly the representative parties cannot be relied upon to establish that 23(e) notice is required. Rather, it is the *trial court's* affirmative duty as monitor and guardian for the interests of absent class members to determine whether Rule 23(e) notice is necessary.

Notes and Questions

1. In Forehand v. Florida State Hospital, 89 F.3d 1562 (11th Cir.1996), the court initially certified a class for an employment discrimination suit, and a 55–day trial was held by a special master, after which the special master concluded that most of the claimants should lose. Over two years after that, and ten years after the case was filed, the district judge decertified the class. Finding that the district judge was correct in concluding that class certification had been wrong in light of *Falcon, supra* p. 267, and that there had been no prejudice to absent class members, the court of appeals affirmed while noting that "a class decertification order entered ten years after commencement of the action is unusual and perhaps disfavored." Id. at 1566.

2. After the complaint in Payne v. Travenol was amended to add claims of sex discrimination, but before Mr. Williams withdrew from the suit, was there a solution to the problem of possible conflicts between the interests of black men and black women? After Mr. Williams' departure, was that avenue no longer available? Consider the following view:

> When faced with a situation when no named plaintiff can represent a subclass, a trial court should consider whether it is in the interests of justice and judicial economy to postpone dismissal as to the subclass for a specified period in which members of the subclass could become plaintiffs by amendment of the complaint and thereby save the subclass action.

Johnson v. American Credit Co., 581 F.2d 526, 533 n. 13 (5th Cir.1978).

In Birmingham Steel Corp. v. Tennessee Valley Authority, 353 F.3d 1331 (11th Cir.2003), the court announced the following directions regarding decertification (id. at 1338):

> A district court that is about to decertify a class on the ground of inadequate representation by the named plaintiff will, except in extraordinary circumstances, not be required to take on itself the responsibility of notifying the class members of imminent decertification in order to allow these members an opportunity to intervene or substitute themselves as the class representative; this is the job of class counsel or the class representative. * * * [But] once a district court has decertified a class, it must ensure that notification of this action be sent to the class members, in order that the latter can be alerted that the statute of limitations has begun to run again on their individual claims.

3. Does the majority's emphasis in *Payne* on showing reliance by black males on the pendency of the action provide a reason in "hybrid" class actions such as this one (including elements of both (b)(2) and (b)(3)) for favoring notice to the class after class determination?

4. Does the posture of the case at the time of the modification of the class description matter? It is generally held that where the modification on

grounds of conflicts is made after trial, it can be justified only on grounds of actual failure, not merely possible failure, to represent the interests of the class. See, e.g., Scott v. City of Anniston, 682 F.2d 1353, 1357 (11th Cir.1982). How should the court remedy the problem at trial? Where the prospective conflict is identified at the time of the initial motion to certify, the court may give much more weight to it. Should there be any limitation on the court's power, at that stage, to revise the class description without notice to the excluded former class members?

5.   Should a different approach be taken to *expansion* of the class after a merits determination? In Kilgo v. Bowman Transportation, Inc., 789 F.2d 859 (11th Cir.1986), the court upheld expansion of the class definition after a finding was made of illegal discrimination against women (id. at 877–78):

> While it is apparent that expansion of a class after trial should be viewed with caution, we find no abuse of discretion in the instant case. The district court's post-trial expansion of the disparate impact class to include company-wide applicants simply conformed to what had been proved at trial. * * * Bowman cannot assert that it was prejudiced because it did not have the opportunity and incentive to introduce evidence on the percentage of female truck drivers in the area covered by the expanded class. It was clear early in this litigation that the class would include persons who applied initially at all other Bowman terminals when the applications were processed through the Atlanta terminal.

Contrast Betts v. Reliable Collection Agency, Ltd., 659 F.2d 1000 (9th Cir.1981), in which the court declared the state statute regarding garnishment unconstitutional in a class action on behalf of recipients of Aid to Families with Dependent Children. After judgment was entered, a Social Security recipient moved for redefinition of the class to include a subclass of recipients of Social Security (who were not included in the original definition of the class). Although the district court did so, the Ninth Circuit reversed: "We have found no authority * * * which permits the district judge to follow a procedure of allowing potential 'subclass representatives' the opportunity to 'create' additional subclasses seeking to benefit by an earlier ruling."

6.   Are there similar concerns about expansion of the class as part of a settlement? Consider Rebney v. Wells Fargo Bank, 220 Cal.App.3d 1117, 269 Cal.Rptr. 844 (1990), a class action brought on behalf of customers charged a certain fee by the bank. As part of the settlement package, the class was expanded to include people who paid a number of other types of fees. Because approval of the settlement cut off the right of customers to challenge these other fees, several of the original class representatives objected even though they had not paid the other fees. The objectors claimed that there was not enough information about the scope of the claims of these people, and accordingly a high risk that the settlement was too cheap. The appellate court concluded that they lacked standing to challenge the expansion, noting that the people who had paid the other fees did not appear and object: "Ralph Abascal's dual role as named plaintiff and objector makes for a particularly strange paradox: he contends he was not an appropriate advocate at the trial level for class members who paid [the other fees], yet he argues in their behalf on appeal. How can he have it both ways?" Id. at 852.

Would it be reasonable to expect these other customers to be as alert to their interests as the class representatives who brought the original suit?

7. Does the continuing power to modify the class raise a risk in cases where the defendant does not initially resist "certification"? Some courts have said that "ordinarily the district court must take some action to find an appropriate class representative if it finds the named plaintiff inadequate." Newby v. Johnston, 681 F.2d 1012, 1014 (5th Cir.1982). Unless there is some such duty, isn't there a problem that a defendant will attempt the reverse of one-way intervention? Consider the views of the Supreme Court of California in Green v. Obledo, 29 Cal.3d 126, 147, 172 Cal.Rptr. 206, 218–19, 624 P.2d 256, 268–69 (1981):

> Without the requirement that class issues be resolved prior to a decision on the merits, a defendant could take advantage of decertification by a strategy similar to that of "one-way intervention." Thus he could appear to acquiesce in the plaintiff's motion to certify the class, holding back his evidence and arguments on the issue. If the judgment on the merits then goes in his favor, it will bind all members of the class who were notified and bar further lawsuits against him on the same cause of action by all such unnamed class members; indeed, the larger the class, the more he will be insulated from such litigation. Yet if instead he loses on the merits, he can undo most of the damage by bringing out his evidence and arguments and mounting a belated attack on the certification order. To be sure, if he fails in his effort to decertify the class he will have given away the chance to enter into a settlement for potentially less than the liability flowing from a judgment on the merits. But that is all he loses. The strategy of acquiescence thus affords the defendant the inexpensive option of seeking to bind as large a plaintiff class as possible while taking no commensurate risk.

8. Note that the class representatives vigorously fought the limitation of the class to females in *Payne*. Were they obligated to do so? Cf. Oppenheimer Fund, Inc. v. Sanders, 437 U.S. 340, 98 S.Ct. 2380, 57 L.Ed.2d 253 (1978), where the class representatives sought to redefine the class when they found out how much it would cost to give notice to the class as originally described in their complaint. Defendant opposed redefinition of the class on the ground it would be arbitrary to exclude 18,000 people for this reason, and the district court denied the request for redefinition. On appeal with regard to other issues, the Supreme Court indicated that the district court had acted properly in this regard.

9. If the plaintiffs in *Payne* had sought only back pay, would it matter whether the black representative was male or female? Should the relief sought influence the selection of the class representative?

N. JUDICIAL CONTROL OF SETTLEMENT

Like most lawsuits, most class actions are settled. But unlike almost all other settlements, class action settlements are subject to substantive review by the court. As amended in 2003, Rule 23(e)(1) says that the claims of a certified class can only be settled after the court finds that it is "fair, reasonable, and adequate" and after notice and an opportunity to object is given to the class. While there is a similar requirement for approval by the court in derivative actions under Rule 23.1, Rule 23(e) involves the court in a highly unusual and unaccustomed supervisory role. Note, however, that judicial promotion of settlements raises some similar issues. See *infra* pp. 639-43.

Settlement before certification can require a Rule 23(e) analysis if it purports to dispose of a class claim. See Amchem Products, Inc. v. Windsor, *supra* p. 373. Before 2003, it was regularly held that Rule 23(e) also required some court scrutiny of a proposed individual settlement with the class representative before certification had been decided. See, e.g., Shelton v. Pargo, Inc., 582 F.2d 1298 (4th Cir.1978) (district court to determine "whether the settling plaintiff has used the class action claim for unfair personal aggrandizement in the settlement, with prejudice to absent putative class members"). The 2003 amendments to Rule 23(e) changed that, however, and the court is now directed to scrutinize only a "settlement, voluntary dismissal, or compromise of the claims, issues, or defenses of a certified class."

Settlement review can be one of the most difficult and demanding tasks a district judge must perform. As indicated in Amchem Products, Inc. v. Windsor, *supra* p. 373, settlement review is not a substitute for careful evaluation of the class-certification criteria of Rules 23(a) and (b), but it is highly important even though those criteria have been satisfied. In recognition of the importance of this task, Rule 23(e) was substantially expanded in 2003 to provide a roadmap for the court in approaching class-action settlements.

As recommended by the Manual for Complex Litigation (4th) § 21.632 (2004), it is a two-tiered process, beginning with a preliminary review of the proposal by the court based on a presentation from the advocates for the settlement. If this preliminary determination about the adequacy of the settlement suggests that giving notice to the class is worthwhile, the court must direct notice to the class under Rule 23(e)(1)(B). It has been said that the court has "virtually complete discretion" in selecting the kind of notice. Franks v. Kroger Co., 649 F.2d 1216, 1222 (6th Cir.1981). The Committee Note to the 2003 amendments to Rule 23(e) points out, however, that individual notice may be appropriate if there is a right to opt out, or if class members must file claims to qualify for the benefits of the settlement. The notice should describe the terms of the settlement adequately to allow class members to decide whether to opt out (if allowed at that point) or to object. In addition, it may include information on the proposed attorney fee award to class counsel. Rule 23(h)(1), also adopted in 2003, requires notice to the class of the motion for attorney fees, so combining the two items in one notice would save effort.

The notice should afford class members a reasonable time to review the proposed settlement and inform them of the deadline for objecting to the settlement. If there are objectors, the court has the benefit of an adversary presentation in connection with its final review of the proposed settlement. As explained by the Manual for Complex Litigation (4th) § 21.62:

> Rule 23(e)(1)(C) establishes that the settlement must be fair, reasonable, and adequate. Fairness calls for a comparative analysis of the treatment of class members vis-a-vis each other and vis-a-vis similar individuals with similar claims who are not in the class. Reasonableness depends on an analysis of the class allegations and claims and the responsiveness of the settlement to those claims. Adequacy of the settlement involves a comparison of the relief granted relative to what class members might have obtained with using the class action process.

Often the hearing addressing these issues is lengthy, and results in detailed findings by the district court. For example, in *Amchem, supra* p. 373, the fairness hearing lasted 18 days, and the court entered 300 findings of fact and 103 conclusions of law based on that hearing.

We turn first to the roles of class counsel, class representatives, and objectors during the settlement review process, and then examine the application of these standards to the substance of the settlement.

PARKER v. ANDERSON

United States Court of Appeals, Fifth Circuit, 1982.
667 F.2d 1204, cert. denied 459 U.S. 828, 103 S.Ct. 63, 74 L.Ed.2d 65 (1982).

Before THORNBERRY, REAVLEY and POLITZ, CIRCUIT JUDGES.

POLITZ, CIRCUIT JUDGE.

We review the district court's approval of a settlement of a class action suit against Bell Helicopter Company and its award of attorneys' fees. The court's approval was granted over the objection of all but one of the eleven named plaintiffs as well as over the objections of a number of class plaintiffs. Improprieties are claimed to have occurred in the settlement negotiations and the agreement is challenged as inadequate in its terms.

[Seven employment discrimination suits were brought by a total of eleven named plaintiffs against Bell Helicopter Co. After the suits were consolidated, the court conditionally certified a class under Rule 23(b)(2) and designated lead counsel. Shortly before trial was to commence, class counsel Howard Specter opened settlement discussions with counsel for defendant.]

* * *

During March 1980, class counsel met with the various named plaintiffs and discussed the tentative settlement proposal. Each of the eleven named plaintiffs authorized their counsel to note their approval of the class settlement, subject to Bell's acceptance of their individual demands which included a demand of $100,000 for one plaintiff, $84,000 for another, and guarantees of promotion to specific jobs for others. Bell countered with an offer of $1,500 each for ten of the named plaintiffs and $2,500 plus a future promotion for the eleventh.

On March 26, 1980, associate class counsel Barber met with all named plaintiffs to discuss the suit and proposed settlement. A discussion of the evidence, particularly the statistics plaintiffs were relying on, was planned. No serious discussion of the lawsuit was possible; plaintiffs were interested primarily in discussing their personal monetary demands. Apparently convinced that Bell's offer to them was too little, nine of the eleven plaintiffs expressed opposition to the settlement.[3]

On March 29, 1980, the attorneys for the parties approved a proposed Stipulation of Compromise and Agreement which embodied 18 of the 19 points contained in the tentative agreement confected on February 19, 1980. The proposal required Bell to deposit $1,250,000 in an interest bearing account to be distributed to the class members when and as directed by the court. Certain affirmative relief measures projected to cost Bell approximately $1,000,000 to implement and maintain, were included. The proposal was made applicable only to the members of the class; Bell agreed to sever the individual claims of the named plaintiffs. Those claims are still pending.

[All but one of the named plaintiffs fired class counsel and, through new counsel, attacked the adequacy of the settlement. The trial court nevertheless gave notice to the class, held a hearing, and approved the settlement over the objections of the ten original plaintiffs plus some objecting unnamed class members. The ten original plaintiffs, now objectors, appealed.]

* * *

Objectors contend that the attorneys did not represent the class fairly and adequately during negotiations. They contend that counsel failed to consult with them, withheld certain information, and misrepresented material matters. The record does not support any of these assertions.

This inquiry must be placed in proper perspective. Objectors' personal claims were not before the district court and are not before us; they were severed and are still pending. Rather, the objectors stand before us as representatives of the absentee class members. The question presented by this appeal is whether class counsel provided fair and adequate legal representation to the class as a whole. Necessarily, much of what counsel does for the class is by and through the class representatives, but that is neither the ultimate nor the key determinant. The compelling obligation of class counsel in class action litigation is to the group which makes up the class. Counsel must be aware of and motivat-

---

3. The trial court capsulated the evidence about the meeting as follows:

Angry and offended at what seemed to them small counteroffers, and fortified with a case of beer, the plaintiffs were ill disposed to listen to any explanation of the deficiencies of the statistical case against Bell. Posturing and wild talk took the place of reasoned analysis. At the close of the meeting, the plaintiffs voted to "reject" the settlement.

ed by that which is in the maximum best interests of the class considered as a unit.

The duty owed to the client sharply distinguishes litigation on behalf of one or more individuals and litigation on behalf of a class. Objectors emphasize the duty of counsel in non-class litigation. The prevailing principles in that situation cannot be imported wholesale into a class action setting. The fairness and adequacy of counsel's perform-ance cannot be gauged in terms of the representation of the named plaintiffs. In addressing this point in our recent decision of *Kincade v. General Tire & Rubber Co.,* 635 F.2d 501, 508 (5th Cir.1981), we stated:

> Appellants' argument that the settlement cannot be applied to them because they did not authorize their attorney ... to settle the case or otherwise consent to the settlement is also easily disposed of. Because the "client" in a class action consists of numerous unnamed class members as well as the representatives, and because "[t]he class itself often speaks in several voices ...," it may be impossible for the class attorney to do more than act in what he believes to be the best interests of the class as a whole...." *Pettway v. American Cast Iron Pipe Co.,* 576 F.2d 1157, 1216 (5th Cir.1978).

The courts have recognized that the duty owed by class counsel is to the entire class and is not dependent on the special desires of the named plaintiffs. It has been held that agreement of the named plaintiffs is not essential to approval of a settlement which the trial court finds to be fair and reasonable. "Because of the unique nature of the attorney-client relationship in a class action, the cases cited by appellants holding that an attorney cannot settle his individual client's case without the authori-zation of the client are simply inapplicable." *Kincade,* 635 F.2d at 508; *Flinn v. FMC Corp.,* 528 F.2d 1169, 1174 n. 19 (4th Cir.1975), cert. denied, 424 U.S. 967, 96 S.Ct. 1462, 47 L.Ed.2d 734 (1976) ("Appellants do not argue, nor may they under the authorities, that the assent of the class plaintiffs is essential to the settlement, provided the trial court finds it fair and reasonable."). The rationale implicit in these decisions is sound: the named plaintiffs should not be permitted to hold the absentee class hostage by refusing to assent to an otherwise fair and adequate settlement in order to secure their individual demands. The trial court was not impressed favorably by the motivation of the objectors, finding as a fact that: "Plaintiff-objectors opposed the settlement in bad faith, primarily to gain leverage in settling their individual claims against Bell at exorbitant figures."

We measure class counsel's performance of the duty to represent the class fairly and adequately as we gauge the fairness and adequacy of the settlement. It will follow generally that an attorney who secures and submits a fair and adequate settlement has represented the client class fairly and adequately. In this instance, we affirm the trial judge's findings as to the settlement and necessarily reject the contention that the attorneys' performance in confecting the settlement was inadequate.

* * *

Objectors complain of the inadequacy of contacts between counsel and the class members, especially as regards discussions of relative strengths and weaknesses of their case. Objectors point to the paucity of contact between counsel and the class representatives, pointing particularly to the five month period immediately preceding the February 29, 1980, tentative accord. The record does not support this assertion.

We note over 30 contacts between a member of Specter's staff and the class representatives during that period. In addition, the record reflects substantial contacts between class counsel and the representatives during March and April of 1980. During that period, the class attorneys advised the representatives of the terms of the proposed settlement, evaluated the evidentiary bases for the case, held meetings to discuss the settlement, and attempted to negotiate a monetary increase for some of the individual representatives.[9] Objectors suggest that these contacts are immaterial, contending that the February 29 letter was, in effect, the final settlement agreement. This objection is not well taken. As appellees point out, the tentative agreement was conditional, incomplete, and subject to approval, including the ultimate approval of the court.

The trial court reached the following conclusions: "Counsel consulted regularly and frequently with the class representatives throughout the case"; during March "all named plaintiffs consulted their attorneys about the class action settlement and authorized them to convey binding offers to Bell and to approve class settlement on their behalf if accepted," and "lead counsel behaved appropriately in negotiating the tentative settlement as spokesman for the class, immediately advising the named plaintiffs and associate counsel of its terms by letter, and ascertaining the named plaintiffs' reaction to the settlement before presenting it to the court." We perceive no error in these findings.

Notes and Questions

1. What are the varying incentives for the players in the settlement approval process? There may be various types of conflicts of interest at work. Class representatives might seek an unfair share of the fruits of settlement. Class counsel might be primarily concerned with making certain that they will collect a fee (which might often not occur if the case is lost) and with making that fee as large as possible. See Coffee, Class Action Accountability:

9. For example, in a letter to plaintiff Mackey, dated March 25, 1980, lead counsel devoted approximately four pages to a detailed evaluation of the strengths and weaknesses of the case. In summarizing his purpose for writing he stated: "I want you to have a clear understanding of the risks which you are running before you decide what course to take and whether to seek to settle or take your chances in court." A similar letter was sent to plaintiff Odom.

In addition, on at least two occasions, it was the named plaintiffs that refused to accept counseling and evaluations offered by class counsel. After the February 29 letter [between counsel regarding tentative settlement] but before the final settlement agreement, associate counsel Barber met with plaintiffs to discuss the case. Instead of rational discussion, he was confronted with hostility and anger. After the March 28 agreement, but before the settlement hearing, lead counsel offered to discuss settlement with plaintiffs individually. The invitation went begging.

Reconciling Exit, Voice, and Loyalty in Representative Litigation, 100 Colum. L. Rev. 370, 391 (2000) (arguing that the reluctance of counsel to risk all on a litigated outcome is more likely to incline lawyers to accept "cheap settlements" than corrupt payoffs in which they get overpaid). Recall also the allegations of conflicts in *Amchem, supra* p. 373, and *Ortiz, supra* p. 302, concerning the "inventory settlements" class counsel had made for their own clients.

2.   Consider the proper role of class representatives and class counsel in the settlement process. Under Rule 23(a)(3) and (a)(4), the class representatives have been found to be both typical and adequate representatives. In theory they are to check the otherwise untrammelled action of class counsel. In the settlement context are their opinions entitled to any greater weight than the opinions of other class members? In *Parker,* does the class representatives' behavior in the settlement process indicate that they were not adequate after all? Is it improper for the class representatives to want something "extra" from the case? In some instances the class representatives may be able to obtain "bonus" compensation for having undertaken the rigors of representing the class, but that amount should somewhat reflect the efforts they have made. The Private Securities Litigation Act, for example, directs that class representatives in securities fraud cases may be paid extra only upon a showing that they have incurred actual costs or losses of income as a result of their service as class representatives. 15 U.S.C.A. §§ 77z–1(a)(4); 78u–4(a)(4). In other cases the limitations are not so severe, but the concerns are similar. Could the arrangements demanded by the class representatives in *Parker* be justified?

3.   Rule 23(g)(1)(B), adopted in 2003, directs that class counsel "must fairly and adequately represent the interests of the class." As the Committee Note accompanying Rule 23(g) explains, this obligation applies even before class certification: "Whether or not formally designated interim counsel, an attorney who acts on behalf of the class before certification must act in the best interests of the class as a whole. For example, an attorney who negotiates a pre-certification settlement must seek a settlement that is fair, reasonable, and adequate for the class."

In *Parker*, the class representatives commanded class counsel to reject the settlement, but counsel went ahead to present it to the court. Aren't clients usually the principals, and lawyers required to follow their dictates, whether or not they agree with them? Does the duty of loyalty that usually applies to lawyers stop applying in the class action context?

The reality is that these tethers are somewhat relaxed in the class-action setting. See ALI, Restatement (Third) of the Law Governing Lawyers § 128 comment d(iii) (2000) (recognizing that a different approach is taken in the class actions); Green, Conflicts of Interest in Litigation: The Judicial Role, 65 Fordham L.Rev. 71, 127 (1996) ("the conflict rules do not appear to be drafted with class action procedures in mind and may be at odds with the policies underlying the class action rules"). For example, in Lazy Oil Co. v. Witco Corp., 166 F.3d 581 (3d Cir.1999), three of four class representatives objected to the proposed settlement and argued that class counsel ("their" lawyer) could not represent the class and oppose their objections. The appellate court adopted a balancing approach to the disqualification issue, comparing the interest of the class in continued representation by experienced counsel against the actual prejudice to the objectors due to being opposed by their former counsel. It explained (id. at 589):

> In many class actions, one or more class representatives will object to a settlement and become adverse parties to the remaining class representatives (and the rest of the class). If, by applying the usual rules on attorney-client relations, class counsel could easily be disqualified in these cases, not only would the objectors enjoy great "leverage," but many fair and reasonable settlements would be undermined by the need to find substitute counsel after months or even years of fruitful settlement negotiations.

In the same vein, it is held that class representatives cannot "fire" class counsel, who is selected by the court. See Maywalt v. Parker & Parsley Petroleum Co., 67 F.3d 1072 (2d Cir.1995) (class counsel can be removed only for failure to perform obligations to the class).

4. It should be clear that the power of the judge in approving a class action settlement contrasts with the power of the judge in other settings. As we will see in Chapter VI, judges nowadays often urge settlement, but they cannot force it on parties. To what extent can they do so in class actions, with the support of class counsel, if they find that the settlement is fair, reasonable, and adequate? Consider whether a judge should be empowered in other litigation to accept and implement a settlement found to be fair, reasonable and adequate. Should the desires of the class members ever be controlling?

At least on occasion, substantial opposition fails to derail proposed settlements. For example, in Lazy Oil Co. v. Witco Corp., 166 F.3d 581 (3d Cir.1999), mentioned in the previous note, not only did three of the four class representatives oppose the settlement, but they were joined in opposition by 384 unnamed members of the class. The district court approved the settlement anyway, and the court of appeals affirmed. How could this be? Consider TBK Partners, Limited v. Western Union Corp., 675 F.2d 456, 462–63 (2d Cir.1982), in which the trial court accepted a settlement in a shareholder class action even though it was opposed by holders of between 54% and 58% of the outstanding shares:

> A settlement can, of course, be fair notwithstanding a large number of objectors. *See, e.g., Cotton v. Hinton,* 559 F.2d 1326, 1331 (5th Cir.1977) (approving settlement over objections of counsel purporting to represent almost 50% of class). But although majority rule should not necessarily be a litmus test for the fairness of a proposed settlement, the opposition to a settlement by a majority of a class is significant. Especially when a dispute centers on the sufficiency of a settlement fund rather than the allocation of a fund, majority opposition to a settlement tends to indicate that the settlement may not be adequate since class members presumably know what is in their own best interests. Nevertheless, majority opposition to a settlement cannot serve as an automatic bar to a settlement that a district judge, after weighing all the strengths and weaknesses of a case and the risks of litigation, determines to be manifestly reasonable. Preventing settlement in such circumstances not only deprives other class members of the benefits of a

manifestly fair settlement and subjects them to the uncertainties of litigation, but, in this case, would most likely have resulted in the eventual disappointment of the objecting class members as well.

5. Should courts view objectors with suspicion or gratitude? Courts might feel grateful because the objectors could be relied upon to identify and illuminate the areas on which the judge should focus in determining whether the settlement is adequate. As noted above, in the first tier of settlement review the court is usually deprived of an adversary presentation. The objectors are fighting an uphill battle by the time they get involved, for the settlement is being urged by class counsel, whom the court has appointed to that position, and objectors are not nearly so familiar with the case as the proponents of settlement. Sometimes they may be able to obtain discovery to overcome some of this disparity of knowledge. So objectors who ferret out deficiencies in the settlement are doing a genuine service, and if their efforts result in a significant improvement in the settlement they may be awarded attorney fees for their efforts. See Shaw v. Toshiba America Information Systems, Inc., 91 F.Supp.2d 942, 974 (E.D.Tex.2000) (objectors awarded $6 million in attorney fees for successfully getting redemption time for coupons doubled).

But there is also ample room for suspicion. Indeed, it is not an over-statement that experienced class action lawyers regard objectors as a group as "bottom feeders" who are actually interested in feathering their own nests rather than furthering the class interests. The reason for this mistrust has long been recognized by courts. As the Second Circuit explained in City of Detroit v. Grinnell Corp., 495 F.2d 448, 464 (2d Cir.1974):

> In general the position taken by the objectors is that by merely objecting, they are entitled to stop the settlement in its tracks, without demonstrating any factual basis for their objections, and to force the parties to expend large amounts of time, money and effort to answer their rhetorical questions, notwithstanding the copious discovery available from years of prior litigation and extensive pre-trial proceedings. To allow the objectors to disrupt the settlement on the basis of nothing more than their unsupported suppositions would completely thwart the settlement process. On their theory no class action would ever be settled, so long as there was at least a single lawyer around who would like to replace counsel for the class and start the case anew. * * * Although the parties reaching the settlement have the obligation to support their conclusion to the satisfaction of the District Court, once they have done so, they are not under any recurring obligation to take up their burden again and again *ad infinitum* unless the objectors have made a clear and specific showing that vital material was ignored by the District Court.

More recently, courts have become more emphatic. In Shaw v. Toshiba America Information Systems, Inc., 91 F.Supp.2d 942 (E.D.Tex.2000), the court denounced "professional objectors who seek out class actions to simply extract a fee by lodging generic, unhelpful protests." Some say that objections to class action settlements have become "a cottage industry" in which free riders exploit their ability to delay implementation of settlements. See Schmitt, Objecting to Class–Action Pacts Can be Lucrative for Attorneys,

Wall.St.J., Jan. 10, 1997, at B1. In Vollmer v. Publishers Clearing House, 248 F.3d 698 (7th Cir.2001), the district court imposed a $50,000 Rule 11 sanction on objectors, which was remanded by the appellate court.

Such concerns have prompted changes in the rules. Thus, Rule 23(e)(4)(B) provides that an objection may be withdrawn only with the court's approval. Should the courts be concerned about efforts by objectors to exploit their ability to tie up the settlement for personal advantage? In Duhaime v. John Hancock Mut. Life Ins. Co., 183 F.3d 1 (1st Cir.1999), objectors appealed after their objections were rejected by the trial court. While their appeal was pending, these objectors reached a side settlement on terms their lawyer characterized as "very, very good." Those acting on behalf of the class then sought discovery of these terms, saying that if the terms were really substantially more favorable they would insist on the same terms for the class as well. The court rejected this request on the ground that it need not ensure that all class members are treated the same.

> We simply have no tradition of court intervention to ensure that similarly victimized plaintiffs who have retained separate counsel and have made different litigation decisions get similar results. * * * A fundamental assumption of our adversary system is that adversaries represented by persons with presumably undivided loyalties will tend to negotiate acceptably fair resolutions of their disputes. * * * [C]ourts oversee class-action settlements only because factors unique to the class-action context—the already noted tendency towards a coincidence of interests between class representatives and the party opposing the class, and the chasm between representatives and faceless, absent class members—call into question whether the representatives' loyalties are in fact undivided.

Shouldn't courts be concerned about the possibility that objectors can exploit their ability to obstruct the settlement? Under Rule 23(e)(4)(B), which did not apply when this case was decided, should the court take action to address a situation like this one? At least, courts are very wary about efforts by objectors to obtain broad discovery in support of broadly-phrased objections.

On the other hand, it is not so clear that "professional objectors" exist in large numbers, and unavoidably true that an adversarial airing of the merits of the settlement can assist the district court in deciding whether to approve it. Brunet, Class Action Objectors: Extortionist Free Riders or Fairness Guarantors, 2003 U.Chi.Legal F. 403, provides a thorough and thoughtful examination of the various issues and methods of providing meaningful input for the judge. Besides private objectors, Professor Brunet considers the role of public officials and bodies as monitors of class counsel's performance, and also the role of public interest organizations such as the Public Citizen Litigation Group and the Trial Lawyers for Public Justice, which have begun challenging a number of settlements. In particular, he suggests that objections to the fee that was paid class counsel rather than the settlement terms for the class may invite abusive efforts to extort a portion of the fee. See id. at 442. The 2003 amendments to Rule 23 may also play a role. Thus, Rule 23(e)(2) requires the parties seeking approval of a settlement to identify any "agreement made in connection the proposed settlement," and Rule 23(e)(4)(B) permits withdrawal of objections only with the court's approval. Together, these provisions may foster transparency about special deals made with those who try to "hold up" the proponents of settlement. But Rule 23(h)(2) explicitly recognizes the right to object to class counsel's motion for attorney fees, which may foster some extortive objections.

6.   In Devlin v. Scardeletti, 536 U.S. 1, 122 S.Ct. 2005, 153 L.Ed.2d 27 (2002), the Court ruled that class members who object may appeal without having been permitted to intervene. Otherwise, the district court could constrain their ability to delay or disrupt proceedings by denying leave to intervene on the ground that their objections were unwarranted. Yet saying that parties may not even obtain review of a decision terminating their rights might be too aggressive. What effect will the decision have on negotiation of settlements? "After the *Devlin* decision, it became clear that objectors are players in class action settlements. Counsel for the class, knowing that one or more objectors are likely to emerge, has the incentive to try to increase a settlement demand to include an incremental part of the settlement for likely objectors. In a sense, the prospect of subsequent objections and the need to pay for them has been bid into the dynamic negotiation process and accounted for by the parties." Brunet, Class Action Objectors: Extortionist Free Riders or Fairness Guarantors, 2003 U.Chi.Legal F. 403, 432.

7.   Was it critical in *Parker* that the ten original plaintiffs were allowed to withdraw their individual claims? Could the court have forced them to accept a settlement that included those claims?

One feature that the court might favor would be to allow class members to opt out a second time if the initial time period to opt out has expired. See Rule 23(e)(3). Would class members have a firmer ground for deciding whether to remain in the class once they know the terms of settlement than the did when the class was initially certified?

8.   Note that confidential communications between class counsel and her clients, the class representatives, may be disclosed on behalf of the other clients, the unnamed members of the class. Should class counsel so advise the class representatives?

IN RE PRUDENTIAL INSURANCE CO. SALES PRACTICES LITIGATION

United States Court of Appeals, Third Circuit, 1998.
148 F.3d 283.

Before SCIRICA, ROTH and RENDELL, Circuit Judges.

SCIRICA, Circuit Judge.

This is an appeal from the approval of the settlement of a nationwide class action lawsuit against Prudential Life Insurance Company alleging deceptive sales practices affecting over 8 million claimants throughout the fifty states and the District of Columbia.

The class is comprised of Prudential policyholders who allegedly were the victims of fraudulent and misleading sales practices employed by Prudential's sales force. The challenged sales practices consisted primarily of churning, vanishing premiums and fraudulent investment plans, and each cause of action is based on fraud or deceptive conduct. There are no allegations of personal injury; there are no futures classes. The settlement creates an alternative dispute resolution mechanism and establishes protocols to determine the kind and amount of relief to be granted. The relief awarded includes full compensatory damages consisting of what plaintiffs thought they were purchasing from the insurance agent. There is no cap on the amount of compensatory damages for those who qualify, and although punitive damages are not included in the settlement, Prudential has agreed to pay a remediation amount in addition to the payments made through dispute resolution process.

* * *

We hold the district court properly evaluated the settlement, finding it fair, reasonable and adequate. Prudential's deceptive practices occurred nationwide. It may be argued that problems national in scope deserve the attention of national courts when there is appropriate federal jurisdiction. Because of the extraordinary number of claims, fairness counsels that plaintiffs similarly injured by the same course of deceptive conduct should receive similar results with respect to liability and damages. The proposed class settlement offers plaintiffs several advantages, including full compensation for their injuries, no obligation to pay attorneys' fees, and a relatively speedy resolution of their claims. The alternative dispute resolution process is sensible and provides adequate safeguards for individual treatment of claims, including appeals. We will affirm the district court's approval of the class certification and the settlement.

[Beginning in 1994, many individual and class action suits were filed against Prudential, the nation's largest life insurer, alleging that it had developed and implemented a fraudulent scheme to sell life insurance policies. These practices included "churning," "vanishing premium," and "investment plan" sales tactics. Eventually, the Judicial Panel on Multidistrict Litigation transferred more than 100 cases from around the country to federal district court in New Jersey, and a consolidated complaint charging federal securities fraud and various kinds of state-law fraud was filed.

Meanwhile, some 30 states formed a Multi–State Life Insurance Task Force to investigate Prudential's sales practices during the period 1985 to 1995. The Task Force interviewed 283 agents and 27 sales management executives, and reviewed voluminous materials provided by Prudential. In 1996, the Task Force issued a report citing widespread evidence of fraudulent sales practices and inadequate supervision by Prudential's management. Although some sales were not tainted by fraud, the Task Force recommended the adoption of a remediation plan that would include outreach to all who purchased Prudential life insurance policies. Policyholders would receive the option of either an ADR process or an alternative no-fault remedy known as Basic Claim relief.

Eventually 43 states and the District of Columbia adopted a consent order embodying the Task Force plan.

In the litigation, Prudential approached lead counsel in the private litigation and initiated settlement discussions, but lead counsel refused to discuss settlement until they had completed significant discovery even though they had interviewed approximately 30 former Prudential agents and customers. On May 10, 1996, the district court ordered Prudential to provide plaintiffs with copies of the materials already provided to the Task Force, and Prudential provided counsel with over 70 boxes of documents by August 8, 1996. By that time, preliminary negotiations on the terms of settlement had been completed. By September 22, the parties had negotiated the details of the settlement agreement, and they worked out the final details of the agreement by late October, at which time it was presented to the district court.

The district court conditionally certified a national settlement class and scheduled a fairness hearing for January, 1997. Notice of the settlement was sent to each of more than 8 million class members by mail by November 4, 1996, and gave them until December 19, 1996, to file objections or opt out of the class.]

The Proposed Settlement

The proposed settlement was largely based on the Task Force Report and its proposed remediation plan. Like the Task Force plan, the settlement proposed a remediation scheme by which class members had the option of either pursuing their claims through an Alternate Dispute Resolution procedure or electing Basic Claim Relief. The proposed settlement class included all persons who owned one or more Prudential insurance policies between January 1, 1982 and December 31, 1995, with certain exceptions. The class included approximately eight million Prudential policyholders who own or owned approximately 10.7 million policies.

a.   The Alternative Dispute Resolution Process

Under the ADR process contained in the proposed settlement, class members who believed they had been misled could submit a claim to Prudential. The claim form provided to all potential class members contained both narrowly drawn questions designed to elicit information relating to specific evidentiary scoring criteria established under the settlement, as well as more open-ended questions allowing claimants to explain the exact nature of their claims. Claimants were also asked to submit any supporting documents in their possession. Prudential established a toll-free hotline to allow claimants to speak to a Claimant Support team, whose members are specially trained to answer policyholder inquiries, assist with filling out claim forms, and advise them with respect to the collection of supporting documents. Once the claim form was submitted, Prudential was obligated to locate all of its records pertaining to the claim and submit them for consideration.

Once a claim has been filed and all the relevant materials gathered, the claim is subject to a four tier review process. At the first level, the claim would be examined by a member of the Claim Evaluation Staff, who will apply a set of specific criteria for each of four general categories of sales complaints: (1) financed insurance (taking a loan against an existing policy in order to pay the premiums on a new policy); (2) abbreviated payment plans (using dividends from a policy to pay the premiums on that policy); (3) life insurance sold as an investment; and (4) other improper sales practices. Based on the application of the established criteria, the reviewers then assign a score from zero to 3 to each claim.[18] The Claim Evaluation Staff is comprised of specially trained Prudential employees who are not associated with Prudential's individual life insurance sales force.

Any claim not receiving a score of "3" will automatically be reviewed by a team of independent claim evaluators who are selected by class counsel and representatives of the state regulators. This team will apply the same criteria as the Claim Evaluation Staff, and make a written recommendation if it believes the claimant's score should be adjusted.

That recommendation is then examined by a member of the Claim Review Staff, which is comprised of Prudential employees who have not worked as or had supervisory authority over Prudential sales agents. The determination of the Claim Review Staff may not be appealed by Prudential. The claimant, however, may appeal the decision to the fourth level of review, the Appeals Committee. The Appeals Committee is selected by class counsel and representatives of the state regulators from a list agreed upon by class counsel, the state regulators, and Prudential. While the Appeals Committee must apply the same criteria, its review of the claim is de novo.

The relief afforded a claimant varies depending on the final score he or she is awarded. Those obtaining a score of zero are afforded no relief. Those with a score of "1" may obtain relief only through Basic Claim

---

18. The scoring system set forth in the Stipulation of Settlement is as follows:

—A score of "3" is assigned in the event that either (i) Company Documentation expressly supports the Misstatement, or (ii) the Agent Statement confirms the Claimant's allegation of the Misstatement and this confirmation is not undermined by Available Evidence.

—A score of "2" is assigned in the event that the alleged Misstatement is not expressly in writing and the Agent Statement denies the allegations, but (i) Available Evidence, on balance, supports the Claimant's allegation of the Misstatement, or (ii) the Agent has a Complaint History.

—A score of "1" is assigned in the event that the alleged Misstatement is not expressly in writing and the Agent Statement denies the allegation, and Available Evidence, on balance, neither supports nor undermines the Claimant's allegation of the Misstatement.

—A score of "0" is assigned in the event that Available Evidence exists which undermines the Claimant's allegation of the Misstatement and suggests that no Misstatement occurred.

—A score of "N/A" is assigned in the event that the Claim Resolution Factor is "not applicable" to the Claim submitted.

Relief. Those with scores of "2" or "3" are entitled to compensatory relief.[20]

b. Basic Claim Relief

Basic Claim Relief allows the class member to obtain one or more forms of relief without having to demonstrate liability on Prudential's part. The available forms of Basic Claim Relief include: (1) low interest loans to help policy holders make premium payments on existing policies; (2) enhanced value policies which allow members to purchase new policies with additional coverage paid for by Prudential; (3) deferred annuities enhanced by contributions from Prudential; and (4) the opportunity to purchase shares in designated mutual funds enhanced by a contribution from Prudential.

[The district court held a one-day fairness hearing at which all parties who requested time to speak, including objectors, were allowed to speak. Among the objectors were Krell, who had filed a class action in Ohio state court seeking relief under Ohio law. Krell took the position that the Ohio customers, particularly those whose claims were based on "replacement" insurance policies, would be better off with claims based on Ohio law. Krell attacked the settlement on a number of grounds. In addition, a number of representatives of state governments were allowed to participate either as intervenors under Rule 24(b) or as amicus curiae. Several of these states initially objected to the settlement but later withdrew their objections when Prudential made concessions that enhanced the terms of the settlement for the class.

About two weeks later, the district court issued an order certifying the class and approving the settlement, with a lengthy (almost 250 pages) opinion explaining the decision. Among other things, the district court found that the settlement provided enhancements for the remediation plan developed by the Task Force in several ways. First, it improved the ADR process by including class counsel and their representatives in the monitoring process and improving the claim scoring criteria and by obtaining a blanket waiver of the statute of limitations and other defenses. Second, it provided minimum financial guarantees that were

---

20. Under the Stipulation of Settlement, the following relief is available based on the category of claim proven:

Financed Insurance—The policyholder may obtain a refund of the loans, dividends, or values improperly used, with interest in some cases. The policyholder also may be entitled to cancel the "new" policy and get back some or all of the premiums paid, with interest in some cases.

Abbreviated Payment—The policyholder may be permitted to cancel the policy and obtain a refund of some or all of the premiums paid, with interest in some cases. Alternatively, the policyholder may be permitted to keep the policy without having to make any additional out-of-pocket payments for some or all of the premiums due.

Investment Product—The policyholder may be allowed to cancel the policy and obtain a refund of some or all of the premiums paid, with interest in some cases. Alternatively, the policyholder may be able to exchange the policy for an annuity.

Other Claims—If a policyholder was misled in some other way, the policyholder may be allowed to cancel the policy and obtain a refund of some or all of the premiums paid, with interest in some cases, or may be able to use the refund to purchase another policy.

not present in the Task Force plan. Prudential guaranteed it would pay at least $260 million for each 110,000 claims remedied, with a minimum overall payment of $410 million. In addition, Prudential was to pay an additional remediation amount of between $50 and $300 million, depending on the number of claims remedied. Third, the settlement agreement provided a very aggressive outreach program including mailed individual notice and newspaper notices in a number of major papers.

Krell appealed approval of the settlement, raising an array of arguments. Before reaching the fairness of the settlement, the court held that it had supplemental jurisdiction over state-law claims because federal securities fraud claims were asserted on behalf of some class members and the state-law claims had a close nexus with those federal claims. It also held that class certification was proper under Rule 23(b)(3) because the predominant questions in the case revolved around Prudential's fraudulent scheme. Krell argued that variations in state law precluded certification, but the appellate court noted that "relatively minor differences in state law could be overcome at trial by grouping similar state laws together and applying them as a unit." It reasoned that "Krell has failed to demonstrate that the differences in applicable state law were sufficient to foreclose a similar approach."]

THE FAIRNESS OF THE PROPOSED SETTLEMENT

Even if it has satisfied the requirements for certification under Rule 23, a class action cannot be settled without the approval of the court and a determination that the proposed settlement is "fair, reasonable and adequate." "Rule 23(e) imposes on the trial judge the duty of protecting absentees, which is executed by the court's assuring the settlement represents adequate compensation for the release of the class claims."

In deciding the fairness of a proposed settlement, we have said that "[t]he evaluating court must, of course, guard against demanding too large a settlement based on its view of the merits of the litigation; after all, settlement is a compromise, a yielding of the highest hopes in exchange for certainty and resolution." At the same time, we have noted that cases such as this, where the parties simultaneously seek certification and settlement approval, require "courts to be even more scrupulous than usual" when they examine the fairness of the proposed settlement. This heightened standard is designed to ensure that class counsel has demonstrated "sustained advocacy" throughout the course of the proceedings and has protected the interests of all class members.

"The decision of whether to approve a proposed settlement of a class action is left to the sound discretion of the district court." Girsh v. Jepson, 521 F.2d 153, 156 (3d Cir.1975). Because of the district court's proximity to the parties and to the nuances of the litigation, we accord great weight to the court's factual findings.

As the district court recognized, our decision in *Girsh* sets out appropriate factors to be considered when determining the fairness of a proposed settlement. Those factors are:

(1) the complexity, expense and likely duration of the litigation ... ; (2) the reaction of the class to the settlement ... ; (3) the stage of the proceedings and the amount of discovery completed ... ; (4) the risks of establishing liability ... ; (5) the risks of establishing damages ... ; (6) the risks of maintaining the class action through trial ... ; (7) the ability of the defendants to withstand a greater judgment; (8) the range of reasonableness of the settlement fund in light of the best possible recovery ... ; (9) the range of reasonableness of the settlement fund to a possible recovery in light of all the attendant risks of litigation. . . .

Girsh, 521 F.2d at 157 (quoting City of Detroit v. Grinnell Corp., 495 F.2d 448, 463 (2d Cir.1974)) (the "*Girsh* factors"). The court examined each of these factors and found "the Proposed Settlement is indeed fair, reasonable, and adequate and should be approved."

* * *

THE *GIRSH* FACTORS

Although Krell has not directly challenged the court's analysis with respect to each of the nine *Girsh* factors, we will examine each of them in turn.

1. *The complexity and duration of the litigation*

Citing the myriad complex legal and factual issues which would arise at trial, the district court found the "anticipated complexity, costs, and time necessary to try this case greatly substantiate the fairness of the settlement." The court found that litigation would require expensive and time-consuming discovery, would necessitate the use of several expert witnesses, and would not be completed for years. Consequently, the court concluded this factor weighed in favor of settlement.

We agree. Examining the sheer magnitude of the proposed settlement class as well as the complexity of the issues raised, we conclude the trial of this class action would be a long, arduous process requiring great expenditures of time and money on behalf of both the parties and the court. The prospect of such a massive undertaking clearly counsels in favor of settlement.

2. *The reaction of the class to the settlement*

This factor attempts to gauge whether members of the class support the settlement. Although the response rate in a 23(b)(3) class action is relevant to the fairness determination, "a combination of observations about the practical realities of class actions has led a number of courts to be considerably more cautious about inferring support from a small number of objectors to a sophisticated settlement."

The district court found that, of the 8 million policyholders to whom Prudential sent the class notice, approximately 19,000 policyholders or 0.2 per cent of the class opted out.[62] The court also noted that approxi-

---

62. The court found that approximately 700 of those who opted out wrote "to indi-   cate they do not feel they were misled in the purchase of their insurance, are satis-

mately 300 policyholders filed objections to the settlement. The court found the small percentage of opt outs and objectors was "truly insignificant," and noted that the "most vociferous objectors to the Proposed Settlement are a handful of litigants represented by counsel in cases that compete with or overlap the claims asserted in the Second Amended Complaint." Consequently, the court concluded the limited number of objections filed also weighed in favor of approving the settlement.

We see no abuse of discretion. While we do not read too much into the low rate of response, we believe the district court properly analyzed this factor.[63]

3. *The stage of the proceedings and amount of discovery completed*

The parties must have an "adequate appreciation of the merits of the case before negotiating." To ensure that a proposed settlement is the product of informed negotiations, there should be an inquiry into the type and amount of discovery the parties have undertaken. Krell contends that class counsel's discovery was insufficient to support the proposed settlement, claiming that Lead Counsel's pre-settlement discovery consisted only of 70 boxes of documents received in August 1996 pursuant to informal letter requests, and a number of meetings with Prudential's chairman, Arthur Ryan. Krell questions how Lead Counsel could have been in "second stage settlement negotiations" before receiving Prudential's production of over 1 million documents, videotapes, audio tapes and computer tapes in mid-August. Finally, Krell contends there was no vigorous, adversarial discovery because "virtually all of Prudential's discovery obligations" were stayed between October 1995 and September 10, 1996, and the parties didn't agree on a free exchange of information until August 20, 1996, only a few weeks before the proposed settlement was announced.

The district court found that "counsel for plaintiffs and Prudential did not commence serious settlement discussions until 18 months of vigorous litigation had transpired," noting the parties had filed and argued a multitude of motions, including consolidation motions, jurisdictional motions, motions to stay competing class actions, case management motions, and Prudential's motion to dismiss under F.R.C.P. 12(b)(6). In addition to its in-court efforts, the district court concluded that class counsel's pursuit of discovery also supported the settlement. The court found class counsel reviewed a multitude of documents provided by Prudential,[64] conducted its own interviews with hundreds of current and former Prudential employees, took twenty depositions, and had access to all of the materials collected by the Task Force. The

---

fied with their policies, and do not want to participate in the action against Prudential."

63. Krell argues that the low response rate was the result of inadequate notice. We disagree. * * * [W]e believe the class notice adequately apprised the class members of

their right to enter an appearance, file objections, or opt out of the proposed class, and provided a detailed explanation of the procedures for doing so.

64. This discovery included over 1 million documents, 160 computer diskettes, 500 audio and video tapes.

district court also found class counsel took sufficient time to review the discovery materials it collected, noting that class counsel refused to discuss settlement on two separate occasions because it believed it needed further discovery. Finally, the court found class counsels' "use of informal discovery was especially appropriate in this case because the Court stayed plaintiffs' right to formal discovery for many months, and because informal discovery could provide the information that plaintiffs needed." Based on the foregoing, the district court concluded "the volume and substance of Class Counsel's knowledge of this case are unquestionably adequate to support this settlement." We see no error here.

4.   *The risks of establishing liability and damages*

The fourth and fifth *Girsh* factors survey the possible risks of litigation in order to balance the likelihood of success and the potential damage award if the case were taken to trial against the benefits of an immediate settlement. Examining plaintiffs' ability to establish liability and damages at trial, the court concluded "the risks of establishing liability weigh in favor of approving the settlement."

We believe the district court properly examined the risks faced by the putative class. The court found plaintiffs would face a difficult burden at trial demonstrating, inter alia, (1) class members were deceived by Prudential's written disclosures and illustrations; (2) their contract claims were not barred by the parol evidence rule because they conflict with the unambiguous language in the insurance contracts; (3) the necessary reliance to support their federal securities claims; and (4) their federal securities claims were not barred by the one year statute of limitations and the three year statute of repose. As further evidence of the barriers facing plaintiffs, the district court took notice of a similar life insurance sales practice case in Alabama state court in which the judge overturned a substantial jury verdict against Prudential. We believe the district court offered substantial reasons for its findings.

Krell argues the district court failed to consider separately the likelihood of success at trial for those class members who alleged "replacement claims," contending those claims require a lesser degree of proof and may be established by an objective review of the documents in Prudential's files. Both Prudential and Lead Counsel contend that "replacement policyholders faced similar burdens to those of other Class Members in establishing liability and damages against Prudential."

The district court did not believe that "replacement claims" are easier to prove and therefore required separate consideration. We agree. Krell offers no authority or analysis to support this blanket assertion. In addition, the findings of the Multi–State Task Force undermine Krell's argument.

The primary focus of the Multi–State Task Force was the practice known as "churning" or "twisting," which it defined as "the sale of any policy based upon incomplete or misleading comparisons." According to the Multi–State Task Force Report, the transactions most frequently the subject of churning or twisting complaints were financed sales and abbreviated payment plans. Replacement transactions are a subcategory of financed sales in which at least 25% of an existing policy's value is used to fund the purchase of a new policy.

The Task Force Report makes clear that "none of these types of sales, financed, replacement or abbreviated pay, is in violation of the replacement regulation if properly done." It also notes that, during the late 1970s and early 1980's, the previous industry-wide disinclination for replacement sales began to give way. In 1978, for example, the National Association of Insurance Commissioners modified its model replacement regulations to reflect the growing acceptance of replacement sales, provided those sales were accompanied by necessary information and disclosure to allow consumers to "make an informed choice."

Turning to its examination of Prudential, the Task Force acknowledged its goal was "to determine whether during the sale of new policies, those involving financing or replacement, consumers were adequately advised of the potential failings of the new policies or the funding basis on which they were sold." The Report notes that although all of the required disclosure forms may have been completed and filed by Prudential, "[o]ne must look beyond the required forms to determine whether or not presentations were accurate and not misleading." In its discussion of the remediation protocol, the Task Force explained "the documentation received from Prudential did not always support the consumer's assertion," and consequently "[w]hat was or was not agreed upon at the time of sale became a question of fact."

Consequently, it appears that misrepresentation, rather than compliance with bookkeeping requirements, was the primary concern of the Task Force examination of Prudential's replacement sales. As the Task Force Report states, it is incorrect "to assume that in any and every case where a replacement was not identified or the regulatory requirements were not met, the policyholder did not understand the transaction or that it was not properly explained." We also find it significant that the state insurance regulators who crafted the initial Task Force Report did not incorporate a lesser burden of proof or otherwise distinguish "replacement claims" from other types of claims.[67] Consequently, we believe the district court properly considered the role of replacement claims when analyzing the fourth and fifth *Girsh* factors.

---

67. We note that even if the different claims alleged by plaintiffs require proof of different elements to establish liability, those differences are adequately addressed during the ADR process. ADR claims will be examined using a set of criteria specific to the type of claim filed. For example, the evidentiary considerations for a churning claim include misstatements by a Prudential agent concerning the applicable interest rate on a policy loan, the policyholder's annual income, and the use of blank, signed disbursement forms. Considerations for a vanishing premium claim include whether the policyholder was advised to disregard notices from Prudential, whether the policyholder made a "significant financial decision" in reliance on the belief that premium payments would cease, and whether the policyholder received altered or unclear sales materials from an agent.

5. *The risks of maintaining the class action through trial*

Under Rule 23, a district court may decertify or modify a class at any time during the litigation if it proves to be unmanageable. In this instance, the district court concluded that although "this case is manageable as a class action and [ ] the class action device is the most appropriate means to adjudicate this controversy, as the case evolves, maintaining the class action may become unworkable" and require decertification. The court also noted Prudential had sought to preserve its objections to class certification, and would likely contest certification if the case proceeded to trial. Consequently, the court concluded that there was a risk the case might eventually be decertified, all of which weighed in favor of settlement.

Although we agree with the district court's analysis and find there was some risk of decertification which supports settlement, we pause to comment on the application of this factor in "settlement-only" class actions following the Supreme Court's decision in *Amchem*. Because the district court always possesses the authority to decertify or modify a class that proves unmanageable, examination of this factor in the standard class action would appear to be perfunctory. There will always be a "risk" or possibility of decertification, and consequently the court can always claim this factor weighs in favor of settlement. The test becomes even more "toothless" after *Amchem*. The Supreme Court in *Amchem* held a district court could take settlement into consideration when deciding whether to certify a class, and that, "[c]onfronted with a request for settlement-only class certification, a district court need not inquire whether the case, if tried, would present intractable management problems . . . for the proposal is that there be no trial." 521 U.S. at 620, 117 S.Ct. at 2248. It would seem, therefore, that after *Amchem* the manageability inquiry in settlement-only class actions may not be significant.

6. *The ability of the defendants to withstand a greater judgment*

The district court found "Prudential's ability to withstand a greater judgment is a matter of concern." Noting that the settlement was valued between $1 billion and $2 billion, the court found a larger judgment could negatively impact Prudential's declining credit rating.[70] The court also expressed concern that, because Prudential is a mutual insurer, non-class member policyholders could conceivably be adversely affected by an excessive settlement in the form of lower dividends.

Krell claims the district court erred by finding that Prudential could not withstand a greater judgment because "neither Lead Counsel nor Prudential submitted any reliable evidence of the true value of the ADR relief." Krell speculates that even the $410 million minimum is inaccurate because it does not account for "profits, if any" generated by Basic Claim Relief.

70. The court found that Prudential's credit rating had already declined during the course of the litigation.

We see no error here. As the district court noted, the value of the proposed settlement is difficult to determine because both the compensatory relief available under the ADR and the additional relief available through Basic Claim Relief are uncapped. The parties' experts offered valuations between $1 and $2 billion, with an absolute minimum of $410 million. While these numbers are imprecise, they are a sufficient basis for the district court to decide whether Prudential could withstand a greater judgment. In addition, Prudential's credit rating during the course of the litigation may be an appropriate indicator, among others, for the court's consideration, and its decline would support the court's analysis.

7. *The range of reasonableness of the settlement fund in light of the best possible recovery and all the attendant risks of litigation*

The last two *Girsh* factors ask whether the settlement is reasonable in light of the best possible recovery and the risks the parties would face if the case went to trial. In order to assess the reasonableness of a proposed settlement seeking monetary relief, "the present value of the damages plaintiffs would likely recover if successful, appropriately discounted for the risk of not prevailing, should be compared with the amount of the proposed settlement." On appeal, Krell argues the district court declined to address this issue, instead finding the analysis unnecessary because all injured policyholders would receive full compensatory relief.

Krell has mischaracterized the district court's opinion. The district court applied the final two *Girsh* factors, although it did not attempt to reduce its analysis to a concrete formula. The district court found that calculating the best possible recovery for the class in the aggregate would be "exceedingly speculative," and in this instance such a calculation was unnecessary because the reasonableness of the settlement could be fairly judged. The court instead examined the nature of the settlement and the range of possible outcomes for those participating in either the ADR process or Basic Claim Relief, and concluded that "an individual's recovery exceeds the value of the best possible recovery discounted by the risks of litigation."

For example, the court found class members who have clear claims against Prudential will receive scores of "3" and will "receive a choice between full rescissionary or compensatory relief plus interest." Thus they will receive full compensation without paying attorneys fees and without undue delay. The court concluded this relief "is not only fair, it is exceptional." Those class members who received a score of "2"— where the evidence on balance supports the claim—would receive 50% of their damages without having to pay litigation costs or fees, an award the court concluded was equivalent to what the claimant would have received at trial. The court also found the settlement was fair for those receiving a score of "1" in the ADR process and for those electing Basic Claim Relief—those who would not have had a claim or not elected to bring one—because the Basic Claim Relief recovery is greater than what they would have gotten at trial.

We believe the district court adequately addressed these factors and agree its examination "accounts appropriately for the nuances of this Proposed Settlement." As the court noted, both the structure of the settlement and the uncapped nature of the relief provided make it difficult to determine accurately the actual value of the settlement. Consequently, the traditional calculus suggested by the Manual for Complex Litigation 2d * * * cannot be applied to this case. But we cannot find the district court abused its discretion when it found that the remedies available under the proposed settlement provided extraordinary relief. When balanced against the best possible recovery and the risks of taking this case to trial, these remedies weighed in favor of the proposed settlement.

It is worth noting that since *Girsh* was decided in 1975, there has been a sea-change in the nature of class actions, especially with respect to mass torts. In this regard, it may be useful to expand the traditional *Girsh* factors to include, when appropriate, these factors among others: the maturity of the underlying substantive issues, as measured by experience in adjudicating individual actions, the development of scientific knowledge, the extent of discovery on the merits, and other factors that bear on the ability to assess the probable outcome of a trial on the merits of liability and individual damages; the existence and probable outcome of claims by other classes and subclasses; the comparison between the results achieved by the settlement for individual class or subclass members and the results achieved—or likely to be achieved—for other claimants; whether class or subclass members are accorded the right to opt out of the settlement; whether any provisions for attorneys' fees are reasonable; and whether the procedure for processing individual claims under the settlement is fair and reasonable.[73] Of these factors, the

73. * * * Other related factors that also may be relevant to this inquiry are discussed by Judge William Schwarzer in his article, Settlement of Mass Tort Class Actions: Order Out of Chaos, 80 Cornell L.Rev. 837, 843–44 (May 1995). The factors suggested by Judge Schwarzer include:

(1) Whether the prerequisites set forth in subdivisions (a) and (b) [of Rule 23] have been met;

(2) Whether the class definition is appropriate and fair, taking into account among other things whether it is consistent with the purpose for which the class is certified, whether it may be overinclusive or underinclusive, and whether division into subclasses may be necessary or advisable;

(3) Whether persons with similar claims will receive similar treatment, taking into account any differences in treatment between present and future claimants;

(4) Whether notice to members of the class is adequate, taking into account the ability of persons to understand the notice and its significance to them;

(5) Whether the representation of members of the class is adequate, taking into account the possibility of conflicts of interest in the representation of persons whose claims differ in material respects from those of other claimants;

(6) Whether opt-out rights are adequate to fairly protect interests of class members;

(7) Whether provisions for attorneys' fees are reasonable, taking into account the value and amount of services rendered and the risks assumed;

(8) Whether the settlement will have significant effects on parties in other actions pending in state or federal courts;

only one relevant here is the fairness and reasonableness of the ADR procedure.

* * *

CONCLUSION

As we have noted, a review of the *Girsh* factors strongly supports the district court's conclusion that the proposed settlement is fair and reasonable. In addition, the parties have fully satisfied the notice requirements of Rule 23, and provided the class with both individual and publication notice regarding the terms of the settlement. There are also other facets of the settlement which counsel in favor of its approval.

First, we are impressed with the nature and extent of the relief provided under the settlement. The ADR process provides an efficient and individually tailored approach to the remediation of claims. Rather than offering 8 million class members a small refund or a coupon towards the purchase of other policies (which we believe would have failed the fairness evaluation), the ADR process responds to the individual claims of the class and provides compensation based on the harm they have suffered. As a result, the potential class recovery is uncapped, a fact which weighs strongly in favor of the settlement.

Second, we are also impressed with the procedural safeguards created by the settlement. The four tier review process, in which the first and third levels of review are conducted by Prudential employees and the second and fourth levels are conducted by independent reviewers selected by class counsel, provide assurance that the ADR process will accurately assess and compensate the claims of injured class members.

Third, we are mindful of the external indicia of fairness which attach to this settlement. In particular, we are cognizant that the original framework of this settlement resulted from the efforts of the Multi–State Task Force. The involvement of the various state insurance regulators, with their vast experience and expertise, provides great support in favor of the fairness of the settlement. In addition, we are impressed by the seal of approval this settlement has received from the insurance regulators of each of the 50 states and the District of Columbia.

Fourth, that Prudential will bear all administrative costs associated with the remediation process and will pay class counsel's fees and costs weighs in favor of the settlement. By agreeing to cover these expenses, Prudential has ensured that the administrative and legal costs of the settlement will not diminish the class recovery.

(9) Whether the settlement will have significant effects on potential claims of class members for injury or loss arising out of the same or related occurrences but excluded from the settlement;

(10) Whether the compensation for loss and damage provided by the settlement is within the range of reason, taking into account the balance of costs to defendant and benefits to class members; and

(11) Whether the claims process under the settlement is likely to be fair and equitable in its operation.

Based on the foregoing, we conclude that the district court's finding that the proposed settlement was fair, reasonable and adequate was well within its sound discretion.

[The court then reviewed the district court's fee award to class counsel. Under the settlement agreement, Prudential agreed to pay class counsel's fees separately from the payments to class members, and not to oppose a request for fees up to $90 million. Class counsel sought to justify this fee by offering the affidavit of a partner from Arthur Andersen & Co. who estimated that the total value of the settlement would be slightly under $2 billion, with somewhat less than $1.2 billion attributable to the ADR program and the remainder to the Basic Claim Relief. The accountant also estimated that some $860 million of the settlement's value was produced by the Task Force plan, and the remainder, over $1.1 billion, from the provisions of the settlement.

Krell claimed that the fee provisions of the agreement showed that class counsel had a conflict of interest, but the court rejected this argument in part on the ground that the fee provisions of the settlement agreement were not negotiated until after the substantive provisions had been settled. Nonetheless, it vacated the fee award because the district court had credited class counsel with the entire value of the settlement, including the portion attributable to the Task Force plan. Even the enhancements in the Task Force plan were partly produced by negotiations by states that initially objected to the settlement negotiated by class counsel. In addition, the appellate court was concerned that the district judge used too large a percentage to calculate the proper fee given the huge dimensions of the fund, noting that the fee award worked out to nearly $1,150 per hour worked by class counsel on the case. Given uncertainty about the method used by the Arthur Andersen expert in calculating the values ascribed to the settlement, it noted that it might be appropriate to permit Krell to do limited discovery on that topic on remand.]

Notes and Questions

1. Reviewing proposed settlements is obviously a difficult process for district judges. A number of courts have developed lists of considerations like the *Girsh* factors used by this courts. See, e.g., City of Detroit v. Grinnell Corp., 495 F.2d 448, 463 (2d Cir.1974) (listing what have become known in the Second Circuit as the "*Grinnell* factors"). The Committee Note to Rule 23(e)(1)(C), adopted in 2003, cites *Prudential* as providing "[a] helpful review of many factors that deserve consideration." How useful are these lists? Note the additional factors mentioned by the court in footnote 73. At some point, could the inquiry become too diffuse?

The Manual for Complex Litigation, meanwhile, has a list of potential abuses of class action settlements that courts should worry about during the Rule 23(e) review. See Manual for Complex Litigation (4th) § 21.61 (2004)(including the risk of a "reverse auction" in which defendant selects the most pliant plaintiff attorney, illusory "benefits" for class members such as coupons for more of defendant's products along with large fees for class counsel, strict eligibility conditions for compensation that make it unlikely many class members will actually receive benefits, special benefits for certain class representatives, releases of claims of class members who receive any benefits, and setting a high attorney fee based on hypothetical values of nonmonetary relief).

2.　Reflect on whether all the considerations mentioned by the court in *Prudential* provide useful ways of evaluating the settlement. For example, should the prospect that the court will ultimately not approve a class action for litigation purposes cut in favor of approval of the settlement? Isn't it at least arguable that the reasons why class action treatment would be refused are also reasons for disapproving the settlement? If that is true, wouldn't it mean that a relaxed attitude toward the certification criteria for purposes of settlement would be undermined by this factor? Yet, as many have observed, in situations in which settlement is the only outcome that can be achieved on a classwide basis, class counsel are really in a disadvantageous bargaining position because they can only settle, and not litigate. See Coffee, Class Wars: The Dilemma of the Mass Tort Class Action, 95 Colum. L. Rev. 1343, 1370–73 (1995) (describing the "reverse auction" that results when contending plaintiff counsel compete with each other to make a deal with defendant). Shouldn't that make the court suspicious about whether class counsel have gotten full value for the class?

As a possible example such a reverse action, consider Reynolds v. Beneficial National Bank, 288 F.3d 277 (7th Cir.2002), in which there were two class actions. One was a state-court class action in Texas, which was set for trial with a certified class against two defendants. The other was a proposed nationwide class action in federal court in Chicago, which had languished for some time when the lawyer for one of the defendants suggested to the lawyers who filed the federal case that his client might be willing to settle within a certain dollar range. Eventually, the lawyers for the Chicago class reached an agreement with both defendants for a figure in the range first suggested by one of them. Even though their efforts were "singularly feeble," class counsel in Chicago were allowed $4.25 million in attorney fees, a figure that was evidently kept secret from the class. (Note that Rule 23(h)(1) now requires that notice of class counsel's attorney fee motion to be given to the class.) The settlement offered class members only a certificate for a discount on further services from defendants, even though the Texas case seemed likely to produce a large money judgment for the class there, and the federal judge in Chicago enjoined further pursuit of the Texas case as a means of enforcing the settlement. Reversing approval of the settlement, Judge Posner admonished that judges must use "the highest degree of vigilance in scrutinizing proposed settlements" to protect the class from "lawyers for the class who may * * * place their pecuniary self-interest ahead of that of the class." Id. at 279.

But note that the judge's concern should ordinarily be limited to the interests of class members. For example, in In re Vitamins Antitrust Class Actions, 215 F.3d 26 (D.C.Cir.2000), the settlement agreement had a "most favored nation" provision that if defendants made a better deal with opt-outs than class members had received, the class would also have to get the benefit. Opt-outs objected to this provision, which would hamper them in their negotiations with defendants, but the court held that they had no standing to object to the settlement.

3. Another factor mentioned in *Prudential* is the ability of Prudential to pay more. In *Ortiz, supra* p. 302, the Court ruled that this sort of concern cannot easily form the basis for class certification under Rule 23(b)(1)(B). Should it count in favor of a settlement class certified under Rule 23(b)(3)?

4. Krell claims that differences in state law prevent class certification and show that some class members have been short-changed in *Prudential*. The court in part emphasizes that the claims made show that this problem is "national in scope." Should that feature of a case make a court less concerned about differences in state law when confronting settlement proposals? The appellate court says that Krell has not made a sufficient showing that state-law differences would defeat class certification. For purposes of certification, shouldn't the burden be the other way around, with the burden on class counsel to show how the case could be tried despite state-law differences?

If the state-law differences are significant, what should be done? The conventional response would be to create subclasses. How should that be handled in connection with a proposed settlement? Consider In re Chicken Antitrust Litigation, 669 F.2d 228 (5th Cir.1982), an antitrust price-fixing action brought for a class that included "indirect purchasers" as well as those who bought directly from defendant. Counsel initially agreed in an allocation formula for settlement proceeds, but then the Supreme Court ruled that indirect purchasers could not sue under the federal antitrust laws (although they had some state-law claims). This led to a hurried renegotiation of the allocation formula to reduce the amount for indirect purchasers, and the court upheld allowing the indirect purchasers to receive something on the ground that they still had state-law claims. Except for relying on arms-length negotiation by the various sub-classes, there seems to be no solution to this sort of allocation problem.

In *Prudential*, isn't there an implicit allocation accomplished by the rating system employed in the ADR process? What is the legal basis for that allocation? Is it an assumed general consistency of state law on the handling of different sorts of claims?

5. The court in *Prudential* asserts that the settlement provides "full compensation" except for waiving punitive damages. To reach that conclusion, what assumptions have to be made about the ADR process? Must one assume that it will always reach the same conclusion as litigation on whether a class member is entitled to relief and as to the amount of relief the class member should receive? Or should the small size of the claims and the unlikelihood that they would be litigated outside the class-action context reduce the importance of those considerations? Compare the treatment of state-law differences in *Amchem, supra* p. 373.

6. Note the difficulty the court had in assigning a monetary value to the deal struck in *Prudential*. That sort of difficulty often arises when class action settlements provide mainly nonmonetary relief, but it is also true of settlements that in form provide monetary relief if class members must make claims to get paid. In *Prudential*, for example, a major difficulty in determining the value of the settlement was that it depended on a prediction

of how many claims would be submitted, and of the categorization of those claims by the ADR process.

Should courts favor or disfavor nonmonetary settlements? Settling by providing coupons that can be used to purchase more of its products or services may be considerably more attractive to defendant than paying out large sums of money. At least some have urged that courts look with great suspicion on coupon settlements, sometimes pointing out that class counsel are not willing to be paid in coupons. For discussion, see Leslie, A Market–Based Approach to Coupon Settlements, 49 UCLA L. Rev. 991 (2002) (arguing that, due to the agency problems that exist if counsel get cash while class members get coupons, counsel should be paid in coupons also). Couldn't a discount on defendant's goods or services be of real value to class members, but not necessarily of value to class counsel? For a general discussion, see Miller & Singer, Nonpecuniary Class Action Settlements, 60 Law & Contemp. Probs. 97 (Fall 1997). In In re Compact Disc Minimum Advertised Price Antitrust Litigation, 216 F.R.D. 197 (D. Me.2003), the court was confronted with arguments from objectors that only an all-cash settlement should be used in a case in which the proposal was to include some $75 million worth of CDs as part of the deal. Noting the small size of claims and the difficulties purchasers would have detailing their purchases of CDs, the court rejected the argument. See id. at 208–09.

Consider Sherman, Consumer Class Actions: Who are the Real Winners?, 56 Maine L. Rev. 225 (2004):

One of the most criticized aspects of consumer class actions has been the use of "coupon settlements." They have been criticized by both plaintiff and defense organizations. See Richard H. Middleton, Jr. (President of Association of Trial Lawyers of America), Save Class Actions: Drop the Coupon Scams, http://www.atla.org/hmepage/classact.ht (Dec. 5, 2001); Hensler, et al., Class Action Dilemmas: Pursuing Public Goals for Private Gain, at 94–98 (Rand Institute for Civil Justice 2000) (discussing objections raised by Public Citizen to various class settlements). There are cases where the recovery for each class member would be small and a discount or coupon for future purchases is worth more to the class member than its costs to the defendant. This can be fair where class members will have to continue buying the defendant's service—as in a suit for overcharges by a utility. However, a class member's relief should not be conditioned on continued purchase of a service or product that is deficient. For example, class members in a suit claiming a product defect in certain Ford pickup trucks were given a nontransferable coupon for $1000 off the purchase of a new Ford pickup, which could, alternatively, be exchanged for a $500 coupon transferable to someone who wanted to buy a GM vehicle. The appellate court refused to approve the settlement, finding it "a sophisticated GM marketing program" that had little benefit for a class member. In re Gen. Motors Corp. Pick-up Truck Fuel Tank Prod. Liab. Litig., 55 F.3d 768, 807 (3d Cir. 1995). See also, disapproving coupon settlements, Gen. Motors Corp. v. Bloyed, 916 S.W.2d 949 (Tex. 1996) (refusing to approve coupon settlement); In re Ford Motor Co. Bronco II Prod. Liab. Litig., 177 F.R.D. 360 (E.D.La. 1997). Since the public outcry over coupon settlements, courts have more carefully scrutinized coupon settlements, appreciating that "coupons that are not redeemed impose no real cost on the defendant, and a settlement composed wholly or largely of such coupons is not worth its face value." Hensler et al., supra, at 488. The amended Federal Rule of Civil Procedure 23(e) that went into effect in December, 2003 imposes specific responsibilities on federal judges to approve settlements "only after a hearing and on finding that [it] is fair, reasonable, and adequate."

7. Even settlements with large monetary payouts may be challenged. For example, in In re Cendant Corp. Litigation, 264 F.3d 201 (3d Cir.2001), the settlement in a securities fraud litigation provided for a total of $3.2 billion in payments by defendants, but it was nonetheless vigorously challenged by objectors.

In In re Corrugated Container Antitrust Litigation, 643 F.2d 195 (5th Cir.1981), an antitrust price-fixing action, 18 of 36 defendants had reached settlements with class counsel totalling some $300 million (a very large settlement at the time). The amounts of the settlements varied according to defendants' market share in the product involved, and in accordance to their seeming culpability. Class members who claimed that class counsel should have gotten more money objected to their economic analysis of the case. The district judge approved the proposed settlement, noting that it was clear that these defendants would not pay more in settlement. The appellate court rejected this approach because "there is no reason to approve an otherwise inadequate settlement solely because it was the best offer defendants were willing to make." Instead, it ruled, the district judge must methodically examine and evaluate the arguments made by objectors. At the same time, it cautioned that "this type of evaluation is not and cannot involve a trial on the merits" and recognized that a settlement necessarily involves some concessions on each side. After remand, the district court approved the same settlement, but with more extensive findings, and the appellate court then upheld the settlement approval, noting that "a just result is often no more than an arbitrary point between competing notions of reasonableness." In re Corrugated Container Antitrust Litigation, 659 F.2d 1332 (5th. Cir.1981), cert. denied, 456 U.S. 936, 102 S.Ct. 1993, 72 L.Ed.2d 456 (1982).

8. When the judge has been actively involved in settlement promotion (see *infra* pp. 639-43), that involvement may further complicate the settlement approval task. For example, the settlement in the Agent Orange litigation resulted in large measure from the active involvement of Judge Weinstein and special settlement masters he appointed. Consider Professor Schuck's comments about the judge's approval of the settlement:

> The settlement, after all, was not an agreement that the lawyers had negotiated and drafted by themselves and brought to the court for its evaluation and approval. It was in fact Weinstein's own creation in every sense of the word. If he had not contrived the settlement, by all accounts it would not have occurred when and in the form it did; indeed, it might not have occurred at all. His hand (and those of his special masters) appeared in every provision, every detail, of the document. * * * He had staked a great deal, including numerous possibilities for appellate court reversal of his many innovative rulings, upon his ability

to craft a settlement that would terminate the case and foreclose an appeal.

Weinstein had also invested an enormous amount of the court's resources in the effort; the special masters' fees alone already totalled hundreds of thousands of dollars and would exceed one million before the case was over. He had devoted a great deal of his own time and energy to the search for settlement and had placed his considerable personal and judicial reputation on the line in extracting concessions and accommodations from both sides in the interests of securing an agreement. * * * He had quite literally dictated the principal terms of the settlement * * * and had cajoled the lawyers into accepting them.

Given these firm commitments to a settlement almost entirely of his own construction, it was inconceivable that Judge Weinstein would fail to find the agreement "fair, reasonable, and adequate." In effect, he was acting as judge in what had come to be his own case insofar as the settlement was concerned. As to that issue, at least, he was plainly interested in the outcome. For this reason alone, he should have left the Rule 23(e) evaluation of the settlement to another, more detached judge.

P. Schuck, Agent Orange on Trial 178–79 (1986). Judge Weinstein himself has offered some cogent thoughts about the problems facing the judge confronted with pre-certification fairness review in Weinstein & Schwartz, Notes From the Cave: Some Problems of Judges in Dealing With Class Action Settlements, 163 F.R.D. 369 (1995). He notes that the pre-fairness hearing creates a risk that the fairness hearing appears to be a sham because the judge seems to have decided already. He also notes that the give-and-take between the judge and the lawyers could confer on the judge something like a line-item veto, but that this is undesirable because it might deter settlements. Id. at 382–83.

9. If one judge disapproves a settlement, what can the proponents of the settlement do? One reaction would be to renegotiate the settlement and present a different one to the judge. Another would be to "shop" the settlement to another judge. Should that be allowed? In In re General Motors Corp. Pick–Up Fuel Tank Prod. Liabil. Lit., 134 F.3d 133 (3d Cir.1998), the federal court had disapproved a settlement, and plaintiff counsel then "repaired to the 18th Judicial District for the Parish of Iberville, Louisiana, where a similar suit had been pending, restructured their deal, and submitted it to the Louisiana court, which ultimately approved it." See *supra* p. 403 n.6. The court held that it could not enjoin these state-court proceedings. There were contentions that the deal proposed to the Louisiana court was significantly different from the one disapproved by the Third Circuit. Should there be a rule that requires the parties to return to the court that originally disapproved the settlement if they want to try again?

10. The proposed Class Action Fairness Act of 2004, *supra* p. 401 n.3, contained a number of limitations on what a settlement agreement could contain, and on the judge's approval authority: The court could only approve a settlement involving noncash benefits after a hearing and written finding that the settlement was "fair, reasonable, and adequate." S. 1751, 108th Cong. § 1712. The court could only approve a settlement under which a class

member would be obligated to pay sums to class counsel that would result in a net monetary loss to the class member upon a written finding that "nonmonetary benefits to the class members substantially outweigh the monetary loss." Id., § 1713. The court could not approve a settlement providing for the payment of:

> (1) greater sums to some class members than to others solely on the basis that the class members to whom the greater sums are to be paid are located in closer geographic proximity to the court. § 1714.

> (2) a greater share of the award to a class representative on the basis of a formula of distribution to all other class members (but not for reasonable time or costs the representative was required to expend in fulfilling obligations as class representative). § 1715.

If these requirements were adopted, and conflicted with case law, or the court's interpretation of Rule 23, which would take precedence?

DISTRIBUTING THE SETTLEMENT FUNDS

Unlike settlements of one-on-one litigation, there is usually considerable work to be done after the settlement is approved and implemented. Consider on the tasks that will be necessary to implement the settlement in *Prudential*, supra p. 519.

In some cases, notably suits for injunctive or declaratory relief under Rule 23(b)(2), there may be no need for individualized distribution of relief under the settlement. But otherwise some technique needs to be developed to invite and evaluate claims to relief. The settlement should provide specifics on how that is to be done, since the court should ensure that the criteria and procedures are fair to class members. Although some proof should accompany claims, it need not be of the quality or quantity that might be required in a contested trial. If defendant is to get back whatever is left over after all claims are paid, the court should be particularly vigilant about high barriers that class members have to surmount to get paid. For general discussion, see Manual for Complex Litigation (4th) § 21.66 (2004).

In general, class members who do not satisfy claims procedures are barred from future litigation even though they do not share in the proceeds of the settlement. Kyriazi v. Western Electric Co., 647 F.2d 388 (3d Cir.1981). But courts often grant dispensation to those who file late. As explained by one court:

> Settlement administration in a complex class action often requires courts to use their equitable powers under Rule 23 to manage the disparate interests competing over a finite pool of assets with which to satisfy the class. As stated in the Manual for Complex Litigation, "[t]he equitable powers of the court may be invoked to deal with other problems that commonly arise during administration of the settlement." These equitable powers are retained by the court until the settlement fund is actually distributed. A primary use of these equitable powers is balancing the goals of expedient settlement

distribution and the consideration due to late-arriving class members.

In re Orthopedic Bone Screw Products Liability Litigation, 246 F.3d 315, 321 (3d Cir.2001). In addition, with regard to court-imposed deadlines Rule 60(b)(2) permits the court to allow belated actions where the delay is due to "excusable neglect." See In re Cendant Corp. Prides Litigation, 311 F.3d 298 (3d Cir.2002) (holding that district court improperly rejected late claims); compare Waters v. International Precious Metals Corp., 237 F.3d 1273 (11th Cir.2001) (elaborate protocol for claims in settlement agreement precluded judge from extending deadlines for submission of claims).

Should class counsel be responsible for ensuring that all their "clients" get their claims in on time? In Zimmer Paper Prods., Inc. v. Berger & Montague, P.C., 758 F.2d 86 (3d Cir.1985), only 12% of the class members submitted claims forms after being sent notice by first class mail, and the settlement proceeds were distributed to these class members (after payment of 20% to class counsel as attorney fees). Several months later, Zimmer contacted class counsel, claiming that it had not received notice and that it was entitled to $250,000 for its claim. When told that the money was gone, Zimmer sued counsel for malpractice, asserting that counsel should have followed up due to the low response rate. The Third Circuit upheld dismissal of the suit, rejecting the contention that the response rate was unusually low and observing that "[i]f class counsel in this case have breached their fiduciary duties, attorneys throughout the country who have complied with court orders * * * may well be subject to malpractice lawsuits by anyone who alleges that he or she did not receive notice of the opportunity to file a claim." A dissenting judge argued that "[t]he fiduciary obligation of class counsel may go beyond the notice requirements of Rule 23(e)."

Even where claims are filed on time, there may be disputes on the application of criteria for eligibility. For example, the settlement for litigation involving fen-phen, the popular diet drug combination (see In re Diet Drugs, *supra* p. 391), required medical certification of claims. The trust administering the settlement fund later sued a doctor, asserting that she had signed off on claims for people who did not qualify. The doctor in question had reviewed more than 10,000 echocardiograms at the behest of 25 plaintiff law firms, to determine whether claimants qualified for payment. Supposedly she found that some 40 to 70 percent of claimants reviewed had serious heart damage, and received several million dollars for her efforts. The judge overseeing the settlement described this doctor's process as "a mass production operation that would have been the envy of Henry Ford." Other doctors supposedly had fee arrangements under which they were paid a premium for cases in which they found heart disease. The judge ordered an audit of all claims submitted to the trust. See Abelson & Glater, Tough Questions are Raised on Fen–Phen Compensation, N.Y.Times, Oct. 7, 2003, at C1.

Chapter V

DISCOVERY

J.D.

MARK F. BERNSTEIN for THE RECORDER

Copyright © 2001 Mark Bernstein. Reprinted by permission.

Nowhere has the metamorphosis of litigation been more apparent to lawyers than in discovery. The Federal Rules of Civil Procedure were intended to work a revolution in the nature of pretrial preparation, and they did. See Subrin: Fishing Expeditions Allowed: The Historical Background of the 1938 Federal Discovery Rules, 39 Bos.Coll.L.Rev. 691 (1998). Indeed, it is routinely been said that discovery is the arena in which lawsuits are won and lost. The trial lawyer of the past has been replaced by the "litigator" of today. Since discovery often commands the bulk of the litigator's efforts, it deserves substantial attention. Students should have a good grasp of the basic concepts from introductory civil procedure; the coverage here builds on that base.

The metamorphosis of discovery owes a great deal to technological development. The photocopier geometrically increased the amount of paper contained in the files of most business and governmental organizations. It also enabled the lawyer to make copies of the opposing party's files. The computer compounded this increase in information subject to discovery. Although computers have made it easier for lawyers to manage the material generated in complex litigation, the emergence of e-mail as a major medium for communication and the proliferation of computer backup systems pose new challenges for discovery.

Discovery can become very expensive, but it is also extremely effective in many cases in rooting out the truth. In complex litigation, however, there is considerable concern that discovery's expense could outweigh its value in revealing the truth. The amount of effort required to glean a kernel of material information from a mountain of discovery is often astonishing. Tactically, the task for the lawyer is to devise a discovery strategy that maximizes the utility of the available tools. Socially, the question repeatedly asked is whether the information obtained by the broad discovery available under the Federal Rules is worth the price. The American answer has largely been that the game is still worth the candle. See Marcus, Retooling American Discovery for the Twenty–First Century: Toward a New World Order?, 7 Tulane J. Int'l & Comp. L. Rev. 153 (1999) (concluding that U.S. discovery remains, and will remain, uniquely broad and intrusive).

A. OVERVIEW OF LARGE CASE DISCOVERY

We live in an information age, so discovery—the litigation method of generating information—is a central concern. But since the photocopier was introduced in the 1950s, the amount of information that could be gathered through discovery has multiplied. The introduction of the computer magnified this development. In 2003, for example, an article in the ABA Journal reported that a litigation-support company found that "a small e-discovery job * * * involves about 500 gigabytes of data. One gigabyte is the equivalent of between 50,000 and 100,000 printed pages, depending on the kind of computer files being searched. Some major cases now involve one terabyte of information, which, if printed to paper, would fill the Sears Tower four times." Krause, What a Concept!, ABA Journal, Aug. 2003, at 60.

Coping with massive quantities of information has been a challenge in complex litigation for decades. Consider the following description of discovery in Class Plaintiffs v. City of Seattle, 955 F.2d 1268 (9th Cir.1992), a suit arising out of default on bonds for construction of nuclear power plants in Washington (id. at 1275):

> Discovery was comprehensive. An estimated 200 million document pages were produced. Depositions of more than 300 persons were taken over a period of three and one-half years. Approximately 285 fact witnesses were deposed over a two year period. In addition, 34 expert witnesses were deposed.

Lawyers addressing such quantities of data had to develop a systematic method of coping with it. Obviously no one person could review or absorb so much information. Instead, large numbers of people had to be marshalled to digest and sort this information. By the 1970s, lawyers had recognized the need to use a computer for this activity as described in Halverson, Coping With the Fruits of Discovery in the Complex Case—The Systems Approach to Litigation Support, 44 Antitrust L.J. 39 (1975):

> In a complex case, there is, in my opinion, no other viable alternative to the computer for the control, indexing, and retrieval

of documentation of all types, and for the analysis of complex sets of data which is necessary to prepare economic and statistical models and charts and to prepare the experts for their testimony at trial.

Planning for such an effort is critical. Moreover, the Federal Rules direct that some of this planning is supposed to be collaborative, to happen early in the litigation, and to involve the judge. Thus, Rule 26(a)(1) calls for initial disclosure of certain information, and Rule 26(f) directs the lawyers to confer to devise a discovery plan for the case that should be submitted to the court before it enters a scheduling order. Meanwhile, Rule 26(d) interdicts formal discovery until the conference about a discovery plan has occurred. Judicial oversight of discovery and other aspects of pretrial litigation is examined in Chapter VI. In complex cases, judges will increasingly insist on such a sequence. Lawyers must therefore think through their discovery strategy early in the litigation.

The transformation worked by the computer in the business world has had similar implications for discovery practice. In part, that is because so much information is only available from computers. "In fact, currently 93 percent of business documents are created electronically; most are never printed." Burke & Kummer, Controlling Discovery Costs, Legal Times, Aug. 18, 2003, at 19. Largely for that reason, we are told that "the document production of 2003 bears little resemblance to that of the 1980s and 1990s. * * * [T]echnology has changed forever the way lawyers produce their client's documents." Horrigan, Producing Those Documents, Nat. L.J., March 17, 2003, at C3. This transition has prompted one leader in the field of electronic discovery to predict: "Within three years, I'm sure almost all evidence collected in discovery will be electronic-based." Byron, Computer Forensics Sleuths Help Find Fraud, Wall. St. J., March 18, 2003, at B1.

Owing to the importance of computer-based information, we turn in the next section to the difficulties—particularly regarding cost—that have attended its centrality in modern discovery. Before doing so, however, we should introduce some practices developed in hard-copy discovery that remain of importance. One reason why they remain important is that hard copy discovery still plays a major role, even if digital material may be more prominent.

Litigation support systems: First, there is the role of the computer in analyzing the fruits of discovery—a computerized litigation support system. As noted above, the speed and accuracy of computer retrieval has long played a central role in managing the voluminous fruits of discovery. "The function of a computer-based litigation support system is conceptually similar to the trial notebooks, tab locators, or card indexes which lawyers have long used to find relevant material." Sherman & Kinnard, The Development, Discovery and Use of Computer Support Systems in Achieving Efficiency in Litigation, 79 Colum. L. Rev. 267, 268 (1979). Technology makes it possible now to input most or all documentary materials into such a system.

Searching such materials using a key word technique is also a familiar method of identifying relevant items. But it is important to appreciate the possible imperfections of that mode of searching. In a well-known experiment using an actual litigation support system containing a full-text database of 40,000 documents with 350,000 pages, it was found that searches turned up only about 20% of the relevant materials. Blair & Maron, An Evaluation of Retrieval Effectiveness for a Full–Text Document–Retrieval System, 28 Commun. of the A.C.M. 289 (1985). These results surprised the lawyers involved in the experiment, who believed that they had found 75% of the relevant documents. Blair and Maron theorized that it was inevitable that, in large-scale databases, searches would have to be limited to avoid overload in ways that would curtail their ability to locate many of the relevant documents. Careful lawyers must therefore consider alternate methods for identifying important materials, such as having a person review those most likely to be important. Moreover, the arresting predictions of those in the business of selling computer-based services about displacing hard copy discovery may well understate the ongoing importance of review of hard copy materials. But improvements in search techniques are likely to make computer searching increasingly reliable in retrieving responsive materials.

The litigation support system is the lawyer's device. Can *it* be the subject of discovery? This question raises problems as to both (a) *ordinary work product* (the conditional protection accorded materials prepared in anticipation of litigation under Rule 26(b)(3), requiring the discovering party to show "substantial need" and inability "without undue hardship to obtain a substantial equivalent") and (b) *opinion work product* (the greater protection accorded by Rule 26(b)(3) to "mental impressions, conclusions, opinions, and legal theories of an attorney or other representative of a party").

The application of work product protection against efforts to use discovery to obtain a copy of a litigation support system turns in part on whether the system's creation depends on the lawyer's case analysis. To the extent that it reveals the lawyer's analysis of the case, it should qualify for opinion work product protection. Thus, fields like those for subject classification of documents, often included in litigation support systems and based on a legal analysis of the case, should be entitled to the protection afforded opinion work product. See Shipes v. BIC Corp., 154 F.R.D. 301 (M.D.Ga.1994) (in-house legal department's computer database created in anticipation of litigation). But if the system is a created in a mechanical way from materials generated through discovery, it may not even be considered ordinary work product. See Hines v. Widnall, 183 F.R.D. 596 (N.D.Fla.1998) (database consisting of defendant's imaging of documents produced in the litigation, without any ingredient of legal opinion reflected, was not protected as work product). "[T]here would seem to be many situations in which a court could predict that limited access to a support system for the purpose of locating documents would not risk substantial disclosure of opinion work

product." Sherman & Kinnard, *supra*, 79 Colum. L. Rev. at 288. For
general discussion, see A. Cohen & D. Lender, Electronic Discovery
§ 8.04 (2003); Poirier, Robb & Mosher, Computer–Based Litigation
Support Systems: The Discoverability Issue, 54 UMKC L. Rev. 440
(1986).

Collaborative handling of discovery in related litigation: Second,
there is what might be called the collaboration issue. This issue can be
important both in litigation involving a large number of parties on a
given side, and in situations in which there are many related suits, often
involving a number of unrelated parties against a common foe. Recall the
consideration of consolidated and transferred cases in Chapter III. In
each instance, the parties must decide how much sharing they should do
in preparation of their cases. With numerous parties on a the same side
of a single suit, there is likely to be an inevitable impulse toward
collaboration due to tactical reasons and pressure from the court. We
will see this topic again in Chapter VI. See *infra* p. 666 n.1. Generally
the related suit situation involves numerous unrelated plaintiffs suing a
common defendant. In that situation, the question whether to collabo-
rate presents choices for the plaintiff lawyers, and for the defendant.

An early example of collaboration was presented by the litigation
concerning the pharmaceutical MER/29, profiled in Rheingold, The
MER/29 Story—An Instance of Successful Mass Disaster Litigation, 56
Cal.L.Rev. 116 (1968) (partly excerpted *supra* p. 123), an article by one
of the plaintiff lawyers. The experience is one that plaintiff lawyers have
emulated repeatedly since, and bears description here:

After MER/29 was withdrawn from the market by its manufacturer,
Richardson–Merrell, 33 lawyers with suits against Merrell met during a
convention of the Association of Trial Lawyers of America (ATLA), an
organization of plaintiff lawyers, to coordinate their efforts. Thereafter,
the lawyers created the "MER/29 Group" to supervise discovery from
Merrell and provide a clearinghouse for resulting materials. The clearinghouse function was performed primarily by issuance of group newsletters to members of the group. Although these were confidential, ultimately some got into the defendant's hands. Indeed, "later issues were
written somewhat for the defendant's consumption." For the defendant,
the advantage was that all group members agreed to make use of the
common discovery, and the defendant therefore had to provide discovery
only once. The plaintiffs then would look to the centralized repository for
documents rather than to the defendant, and in depositions the questioning of defense witnesses was done by a representative of the group.
See Manual for Complex Litigation (4th) § 11.444 (2004) (discussing
document depositories).

As explained by Rehingold, "[s]uch unified action by the plaintiffs
served to counteract the defendant's natural advantages. The defendant
in any mass disaster situation is inherently well organized to deal with
multiple litigation. It can coordinate its activities and to an extent even
control the course of litigation." 56 Cal.L.Rev. at 124. But defendants

may resist this sort of cooperation in some instances. For example, consider the following description of a later litigation also involving Merrell in which an individual suit was followed by consolidated multi-district treatment:

> [I]n the [individual] case Merrell enjoyed and exploited a resource advantage, and it was the aggressor in discovery. This difference in resources is graphically illustrated by the way in which one of [the individual plaintiff's] lawyers dealt with production of the lengthy new drug applications produced by Merrell: he rented a microfilm machine in Florida, loaded it in his car, drove to New York where Merrell's lawyers had their office, and microfilmed the documents himself. There are many microfilm services that do this sort of work, and no defense lawyer would undertake it personally. In short, try as they did, plaintiffs' lawyers in the individual suit "did not have the resources or capacity that Merrell did." The formation of the plaintiffs' litigation committee in connection with the multidistrict litigation "afforded plaintiffs' lawyers a far more level playing field in terms of stakes and available resources," and plaintiffs' discovery in the multidistrict litigation was accordingly much broader than in the individual suit.

Marcus, Reexamining the Bendectin Litigation Story, 83 Iowa L.Rev. 231, 243–44 (1997) (reviewing M. Green, Bendectin and Birth Defects: The Challenge of Mass Toxic Substances Litigation (1996)).

Of course, pooling of efforts does not depend on multidistrict or other coordinated treatment. In the years since the MER/29 litigation, elements of the plaintiffs' bar have become much more sophisticated in their cooperative approach to discovery. Under the auspices of ATLA, members of that organization of plaintiff lawyers have access to the "ATLA Exchange," which provides a centralized data bank of information discovered in litigation involving various products. In addition, the exchange offers advice including case abstracts, expert lists and technical information. See Note, Seattle Times: What Effect on Discovery Sharing?, 1985 Wis.L.Rev. 1055, 1057. Users of this service must pay for it. Does this go too far in redressing the imbalance Rheingold perceives? Keep these issues in mind in connection with the material below on how protective orders may impede collaboration by plaintiff lawyers.

B. E–DISCOVERY

ZUBULAKE v. UBS WARBURG LLC

United States District Court, Southern District of New York, 2003.
217 F.R.D. 309.

SCHEINDLIN, District Judge.

The world was a far different place in 1849, when Henry David Thoreau opined (in an admittedly broader context) that "[t]he process of discovery is very simple."[1] That hopeful maxim has given way to rapid technological advances, requiring new solutions to old problems. The issue presented here is one such problem, recast in light of current technology: To what extent is inaccessible electronic data discoverable, and who should pay for its production?

I. INTRODUCTION

The Supreme Court recently reiterated that our "simplified notice pleading standard relies on liberal discovery rules and summary judgment motions to define disputed facts and issues and to dispose of unmeritorious claims." Thus, it is now beyond dispute that "[b]road discovery is a cornerstone of the litigation process contemplated by the Federal Rules of Civil Procedure." The Rules contemplate a minimal burden to bringing a claim; that claim is then fleshed out through vigorous and expansive discovery.

In one context, however, the reliance on broad discovery has hit a roadblock. As individuals and corporations increasingly do business electronically—using computers to create and store documents, make deals, and exchange e-mails—the universe of discoverable material has expanded exponentially.[6] The more information there is to discover, the more expensive it is to discover all the relevant information until, in the end, "discovery is not just about uncovering the truth, but also about how much of the truth the parties can afford to disinter."

This case provides a textbook example of the difficulty of balancing the competing needs of broad discovery and manageable costs. Laura Zubulake is suing UBS Warburg LLC, UBS Warburg, and UBS AG (collectively, "UBS" or the "Firm") under Federal, State and City law for gender discrimination and illegal retaliation. Zubulake's case is certainly not frivolous[8] and if she prevails, her damages may be substantial.[9] She contends that key evidence is located in various e-mails exchanged among UBS employees that now exist only on backup tapes and perhaps other archived media. According to UBS, restoring those e-mails would cost approximately $175,000.00, exclusive of attorney time in reviewing the e-mails. Zubulake now moves for an order compelling UBS to produce those e-mails at its expense.

1. Henry David Thoreau, A Week on the Concord and Merrimack Rivers (1849).

6. Rowe Entm't, Inc. v. William Morris Agency, Inc., 205 F.R.D. 421, 429 (S.D.N.Y. 2002) (explaining that electronic data is so voluminous because, unlike paper documents, "the costs of storage are virtually nil. Information is retained not because it is expected to be used, but because there is no compelling reason to discard it").

8. Indeed, Zubulake has already produced a sort of "smoking gun": an e-mail suggesting that she be fired "ASAP" after her EEOC charge was filed, in part so that she would not be eligible for year-end bonuses.

9. At the time she was terminated, Zubulake's annual salary was approximately $500,000. Were she to receive full back pay and front pay, Zubulake estimates that she may be entitled to as much as $13,000,000 in damages, not including any punitive damages or attorney's fees.

II. Background

UBS hired Zubulake on August 23, 1999, as a director and senior salesperson on its U.S. Asian Equities Sales Desk (the "Desk"), where she reported to Dominic Vail, the Desk's manager. At the time she was hired, Zubulake was told that she would be considered for Vail's position if and when it became vacant.

In December 2000, Vail indeed left his position to move to the Firm's London office. But Zubulake was not considered for his position, and the Firm instead hired Matthew Chapin as director of the Desk. Zubulake alleges that from the outset Chapin treated her differently than the other members of the Desk, all of whom were male. In particular, Chapin "undermined Ms. Zubulake's ability to perform her job by, inter alia: (a) ridiculing and belittling her in front of co-workers; (b) excluding her from work-related outings with male co-workers and clients; (c) making sexist remarks in her presence; and (d) isolating her from the other senior salespersons on the Desk by seating her apart from them." No such actions were taken against any of Zubulake's male co-workers.

Zubulake ultimately responded by filing a Charge of (gender) Discrimination with the EEOC on August 16, 2001. On October 9, 2001, Zubulake was fired with two weeks' notice. On February 15, 2002, Zubulake filed the instant action, suing for sex discrimination and retaliation under Title VII, the New York State Human Rights Law, and the Administrative Code of the City of New York. UBS timely answered on March 12, 2002, denying the allegations. UBS's argument is, in essence, that Chapin's conduct was not unlawfully discriminatory because he treated everyone equally badly. * * *

Discovery in this action commenced on or about June 3, 2002, when Zubulake served UBS with her first document request. At issue here is request number twenty-eight, for "[a]ll documents concerning any communication by or between UBS employees concerning Plaintiff." The term document in Zubulake's request "includ[es], without limitation, electronic or computerized data compilations." On July 8, 2002, UBS responded by producing approximately 350 pages of documents, including approximately 100 pages of e-mails. UBS also objected to a substantial portion of Zubulake's requests.

[After negotiations, and a conference with a magistrate judge, the parties reached an agreement under which UBS would produce e-mails from the accounts of five named individuals "if retrieval is possible." But UBS actually produced no additional e-mails, contending that searching backup tapes would cost approximately $300,000.]

Zubulake * * * objected to UBS's nonproduction. In fact, Zubulake *knew* that there were additional responsive e-mails that UBS had failed to produce because she herself had produced approximately 450 pages of e-mail correspondence. Clearly, numerous responsive e-mails had been created and deleted[19] at UBS, and Zubulake wanted them.

On December 2, 2002, the parties again appeared before [Magistrate] Judge Gorenstein, who ordered UBS to produce for deposition a person with knowledge of UBS's e-mail retention policies in an effort to determine whether the backup tapes contained the deleted e-mails and the burden of producing them. In response, UBS produced Christopher Behny, Manager of Global Messaging, who was deposed on January 14, 2003. Mr. Behny testified to UBS's e-mail backup protocol, and also to the cost of restoring the relevant data.

In the first instance, the parties agree that e-mail was an important means of communication at UBS during the relevant time period. Each salesperson, including the salespeople on the Desk, received approximately 200 e-mails each day. Given this volume, and because Securities and Exchange Commission regulations require it,[21] UBS implemented extensive e-mail backup and preservation protocols. In particular, e-mails were backed up in two distinct ways: on backup tapes and on optical disks.

UBS employees used a program called HP OpenMail, manufactured by Hewlett–Packard, for all work-related e-mail communications. With limited exceptions, all e-mails sent or received by any UBS employee are stored onto backup tapes. To do so, UBS employs a program called Veritas NetBackup, which creates a "snapshot" of all e-mails that exist on a given server at the time the backup is taken. Except for scheduling the backups and physically inserting the tapes into the machines, the backup process is entirely automated.

UBS used the same backup protocol during the entire relevant time period, from 1999 through 2001. Using NetBackup, UBS backed up its e-mails at three intervals: (1) daily, at the end of each day, (2) weekly, on Friday nights, and (3) monthly, on the last business day of the month. Nightly backup tapes were kept for twenty working days, weekly tapes

---

19. The term "deleted" is sticky in the context of electronic data. " 'Deleting' a file does not actually erase that data from the computer's storage devices. Rather, it simply finds the data's entry in the disk directory and changes it to a 'not used' status— thus permitting the computer to write over the 'deleted' data. Until the computer writes over the 'deleted' data, however, it may be recovered by searching the disk itself rather than the disk's directory. Accordingly, many files are recoverable long after they have been deleted—even if neither the computer user nor the computer itself is aware of their existence. Such data is referred to as 'residual data.' " Shira A. Scheindlin & Jeffrey Rabkin, Electronic Discovery in Federal Civil Litigation: Is Rule 34 Up to the Task?, 41 B.C. L.Rev.

327, 337 (2000). Deleted data may also exist because it was backed up before it was deleted. Thus, it may reside on backup tapes or similar media.

21. SEC Rule 17a–4, promulgated pursuant to Section 17(a) of the Securities Exchange Act of 1934, provides in pertinent part:

Every [ ] broker and dealer shall preserve for a period of not less than 3 years, the first two years in an accessible place ... [o]riginals of all communications received and copies of all communications sent by such member, broker or dealer (including inter-office memoranda and communications) relating to his business as such.

17 C.F.R. § 240.17a–4(b) and (4).

for one year, and monthly tapes for three years. After the relevant time period elapsed, the tapes were recycled.[25]

Once e-mails have been stored onto backup tapes, the restoration process is lengthy. Each backup tape routinely takes approximately five days to restore, although resort to an outside vendor would speed up the process (at greatly enhanced costs, of course). Because each tape represents a snapshot of one server's hard drive in a given month, each server/month must be restored separately onto a hard drive. Then, a program called Double Mail is used to extract a particular individual's e-mail file. That mail file is then exported into a Microsoft Outlook data file, which in turn can be opened in Microsoft Outlook, a common e-mail application. A user could then browse through the mail file and sort the mail by recipient, date or subject, or search for key words in the body of the e-mail.

Fortunately, NetBackup also created indexes of each backup tape. Thus, Behny was able to search through the tapes from the relevant time period and determine that the e-mail files responsive to Zubulake's requests are contained on a total of ninety-four backup tapes.

In addition to the e-mail backup tapes, UBS also stored certain e-mails on optical disks. For certain "registered traders," probably including the members of the Desk, a copy of all e-mails sent to or received from outside sources (i.e., e-mails from a "registered trader" at UBS to someone at another entity, or vice versa) was simultaneously written onto a series of optical disks. Internal e-mails, however, were not stored on this system.

UBS has retained each optical disk used since the system was put into place in mid–1998. Moreover, the optical disks are neither erasable nor rewritable. Thus, UBS has every e-mail sent or received by registered traders (except internal e-mails) during the period of Zubulake's employment, even if the e-mail was deleted instantaneously on that trader's system.

The optical disks are easily searchable using a program called Tumbleweed. Using Tumbleweed, a user can simply log into the system with the proper credentials and create a plain language search. Search criteria can include not just "header" information, such as the date or the name of the sender or recipient, but can also include terms within the text of the e-mail itself. For example, UBS personnel could easily run a search for e-mails containing the words "Laura" or "Zubulake" that were sent or received by [the five UBS employees covered by the agreement to produce].

25. Of course, periodic backups such as UBS's necessarily entails the loss of certain e-mails. Because backups were conducted only intermittently, some e-mails that were deleted from the server were never backed up. For example, if a user both received and deleted an e-mail on the same day, it would not reside on any backup tape. Similarly, an e-mail received and deleted within the span of one month would not exist on the monthly backup, although it might exist on a weekly or daily backup, if those tapes still exist. As explained below, if an e-mail was to or from a "registered trader," however, it may have been stored on UBS's optical storage devices.

III. LEGAL STANDARD

[The court surveyed the general attitude of the Federal Rules toward discovery. Rule 26(b)(1) defines relevance broadly, but Rule 26(b)(2) directs the court to guard against disproportionate discovery costs.]

The application of these various discovery rules is particularly complicated where electronic data is sought because otherwise discoverable evidence is often only available from expensive-to-restore backup media. That being so, courts have devised creative solutions for balancing the broad scope of discovery prescribed in Rule 26(b)(1) with the cost-consciousness of Rule 26(b)(2). By and large, the solution has been to consider cost-shifting: forcing the requesting party, rather than the answering party, to bear the cost of discovery.

By far, the most influential response to the problem of cost-shifting relating to the discovery of electronic data was given by United States Magistrate Judge James C. Francis IV of this district in Rowe Entertainment [Inc. v. William Morris Agency, 205 F.R.D. 421 (S.D.N.Y.2002)]. Judge Francis utilized an eight-factor test to determine whether discovery costs should be shifted. Those eight factors are:

(1) the specificity of the discovery requests; (2) the likelihood of discovering critical information; (3) the availability of such information from other sources; (4) the purposes for which the responding party maintains the requested data; (5) the relative benefits to the parties of obtaining the information; (6) the total cost associated with production; (7) the relative ability of each party to control costs and its incentive to do so; and (8) the resources available to each party.

Both Zubulake and UBS agree that the eight-factor *Rowe* test should be used to determine whether cost-shifting is appropriate.

IV. DISCUSSION

* * *

UBS argues that Zubulake is not entitled to any further discovery because it already produced all responsive documents, to wit, the 100 pages of e-mails. This argument is unpersuasive for two reasons. *First*, because of the way that UBS backs up its e-mail files, it clearly could not have searched all of its e-mails without restoring the ninety-four backup tapes (which UBS admits that it has not done). UBS therefore cannot represent that it has produced all responsive e-mails. *Second*, Zubulake herself has produced over 450 pages of relevant e-mails, including e-mails that would have been responsive to her discovery requests but were never produced by UBS. These two facts strongly suggest that there are e-mails that Zubulake has not received that reside on UBS's backup media.

Because it apparently recognizes that Zubulake is entitled to the requested discovery, UBS expends most of its efforts urging the court to shift the cost of production to "protect [it] ... from undue burden or expense." Faced with similar applications, courts generally engage in some sort of cost-shifting analysis, whether the refined eight-factor *Rowe* test or a cruder application of Rule [26(b)(2)'s] proportionality test, or something in between.

The first question, however, is whether cost-shifting must be considered in every case involving the discovery of electronic data, which—in today's world—includes virtually all cases. In light of the accepted principle, stated above, that electronic evidence is no less discoverable than paper evidence, the answer is, "No." The Supreme Court has instructed that "the presumption is that the responding party must bear the expense of complying with discovery requests...." [Oppenheimer Fund, Inc. v. Sanders, 437 U.S. 340, 358, 98 S.Ct. 2380 (1978)]. Any principled approach to electronic evidence must respect this presumption.

Courts must remember that cost-shifting may effectively end discovery, especially when private parties are engaged in litigation with large corporations. As large companies increasingly move to entirely paper-free environments, the frequent use of cost-shifting will have the effect of crippling discovery in discrimination and retaliation cases. This will both undermine the "strong public policy favor[ing] resolving disputes on their merits," and may ultimately deter the filing of potentially meritorious claims.

Thus, cost-shifting should be considered *only* when electronic discovery imposes an "undue burden or expense" on the responding party. [Fed.R.Civ.P. 26(c)] The burden or expense of discovery is, in turn, "undue" when it "outweighs its likely benefit, taking into account the needs of the case, the amount in controversy, the parties' resources, the importance of the issues at stake in the litigation, and the importance of the proposed discovery in resolving the issues." [Fed.R.Civ.P. 26(b)(2)(iii)]

Many courts have automatically assumed that an undue burden or expense may arise simply because electronic evidence is involved. This makes no sense. Electronic evidence is frequently cheaper and easier to produce than paper evidence because it can be searched automatically, key words can be run for privilege checks, and the production can be made in electronic form obviating the need for mass photocopying.

In fact, whether production of documents is unduly burdensome or expensive turns primarily on whether it is kept in an *accessible or inaccessible* format (a distinction that corresponds closely to the expense of production). In the world of paper documents, for example, a document is accessible if it is readily available in a usable format and reasonably indexed. Examples of inaccessible paper documents could include (a) documents in storage in a difficult to reach place; (b) documents converted to microfiche and not easily readable; or (c) documents kept haphazardly, with no indexing system, in quantities that make page-by-page searches impracticable. But in the world of electronic data, thanks to search engines, any data that is retained in a machine readable format is typically accessible.

Whether electronic data is accessible or inaccessible turns largely on the media on which it is stored. Five categories of data, listed in order from most accessible to least accessible, are described in the literature on electronic data storage: [(1) *active, online data* includes data on a magnetic disk and accessible almost immediately; (2) *near-line data* is stored in a robotic storage library, and can be accessed in a minute or two; (3) *offline storage/archives* are maintained on an optical disk or magnetic tape for archival or disaster recovery purposes so that the likelihood of retrieval is minimal, and access involves manual intervention and is much slower, perhaps taking hours or even days; (4) *backup tapes* contain all data from a system and are created for disaster-recovery purposes, often use some sort of data-compression method, and are much more difficult to restore; (5) *erased, fragmented, or damaged data* include items that can be accessed only after significant forensic efforts].

Of these, the first three categories are typically identified as accessible, and the latter two as inaccessible. The difference between the two classes is easy to appreciate. Information deemed "accessible" is stored in a readily usable format. Although the time it takes to actually access the data ranges from milliseconds to days, the data does not need to be restored or otherwise manipulated to be usable. "Inaccessible" data, on the other hand, is not readily usable. Backup tapes must be restored using a process similar to that previously described, fragmented data must be de-fragmented, and erased data must be reconstructed, all before the data is usable. That makes such data inaccessible.

The case at bar is a perfect illustration of the range of accessibility of electronic data. As explained above, UBS maintains e-mail files in three forms: (1) active user e-mail files; (2) archived e-mails on optical disks; and (3) backup data stored on tapes. The active (HP OpenMail) data is obviously the most accessible: it is online data that resides on an active server, and can be accessed immediately. The optical disk (Tumbleweed) data is only slightly less accessible, and falls into either the second or third category. The e-mails are on optical disks that need to be located and read with the correct hardware, but the system is configured to make searching the optical disks simple and automated once they are located. For these sources of e-mails—active mail files and e-mails stored on optical disks—it would be wholly inappropriate to even consider cost-shifting. UBS maintains the data in an accessible and usable format, and can respond to Zubulake's request cheaply and quickly. Like most typical discovery requests, therefore, the producing party should bear the cost of production.

E-mails stored on backup tapes (via NetBackup), however, are an entirely different matter. Although UBS has already identified the ninety-four potentially responsive backup tapes, those tapes are not currently accessible. In order to search the tapes for responsive e-mails,

UBS would have to engage in the costly and time-consuming process detailed above. It is therefore appropriate to consider cost shifting.

In the year since *Rowe* was decided, its eight factor test has unquestionably become the gold standard for courts resolving electronic discovery disputes. But there is little doubt that the *Rowe* factors will generally favor cost-shifting. Indeed, in the handful of reported opinions that apply *Rowe* or some modification thereof, *all of them* have ordered the cost of discovery to be shifted to the requesting party.

[The court criticized the *Rowe* test on several grounds. The test was incomplete in leaving out consideration of the amount in controversy and the importance of the issues involved in the litigation. It did not take account of the relative ability of the parties to pay for discovery. In addition, its focus on the purpose for which the party resisting discovery maintained the information was misdirected, because the focus should be on accessibility.]

Set forth below is a new seven-factor test based on the modifications to *Rowe* discussed in the preceding sections.

1. The extent to which the request is specifically tailored to discover relevant information;

2. The availability of such information from other sources;

3. The total cost of production, compared to the amount in controversy;

4. The total cost of production, compared to the resources available to each party;

5. The relative ability of each party to control costs and its incentive to do so;

6. The importance of the issues at stake in the litigation; and

7. The relative benefits to the parties of obtaining the information.

Whenever a court applies a multi-factor test, there is a temptation to treat the factors as a check-list, resolving the issue in favor of whichever column has the most checks. But "we do not just add up the factors." When evaluating cost-shifting, the central question must be, does the request impose an "undue burden or expense" on the responding party? Put another way, "how important is the sought-after evidence in comparison to the cost of production?" The seven-factor test articulated above provides some guidance in answering this question, but the test cannot be mechanically applied at the risk of losing sight of its purpose.

Weighting the factors in descending order of importance may solve the problem and avoid a mechanistic application of the test. The first two factors—comprising the marginal utility test—are the most important. These factors include: (1) The extent to which the request is specifically tailored to discover relevant information and (2) the availability of such information from other sources. The substance of the marginal utility test was well described in McPeek v. Ashcroft [202 F.R.D. 31 (D.D.C.2001)]:

The more likely it is that the backup tape contains information that is relevant to a claim or defense, the fairer it is that the [responding party] search at its own expense. The less likely it is, the more unjust it would be to make the [responding party] search at its own expense. The difference is "at the margin."

The second group of factors addresses cost issues: "How expensive will this production be?" and, "Who can handle that expense?" These factors include: (3) the total cost of production compared to the amount in controversy, (4) the total cost of production compared to the resources available to each party and (5) the relative ability of each party to control costs and its incentive to do so. The third "group"—(6) the importance of the litigation itself—stands alone, and as noted earlier will only rarely come into play. But where it does, this factor has the potential to predominate over the others. Collectively, the first three groups correspond to the three explicit considerations of Rule 26(b)(2)(iii). Finally, the last factor—(7) the relative benefits of production as between the requesting and producing parties—is the least important because it is fair to presume that the response to a discovery request generally benefits the requesting party. But in the unusual case where production will also provide a tangible or strategic benefit to the responding party, that fact may weigh against shifting costs.

Courts applying *Rowe* have uniformly favored cost-shifting largely because of assumptions made concerning the likelihood that relevant information will be found. [Thus, *Rowe* relied on assumptions rather than proof.] But such proof will rarely exist in advance of obtaining the requested discovery. The suggestion that a plaintiff must not only demonstrate that probative evidence exists, but also prove that electronic discovery will yield a "gold mine," is contrary to the plain language of Rule 26(b)(1), which permits discovery of "any matter" that is "relevant to [a] claim or defense."

The best solution to this problem is found in *McPeek* [*supra*, 202 F.R.D. at 34–35]:

> Given the complicated questions presented [and] the clash of policies . . . I have decided to take small steps and perform, as it were, a test run. Accordingly, I will order DOJ to perform a backup restoration of the e-mails attributable to Diegelman's computer during the period of July 1, 1998 to July 1, 1999. . . . The DOJ will have to carefully document the time and money spent in doing the search. It will then have to search in the restored e-mails for any document responsive to any of the plaintiff's requests for production of documents. Upon the completion of this search, the DOJ will then file a comprehensive, sworn certification of the time and money spent and the results of the search. Once it does, I will permit the parties an opportunity to argue why the results and the expense do or do not justify any further search.

Requiring the responding party to restore and produce responsive documents from a small sample of backup tapes will inform the cost-shifting analysis laid out above. When based on an actual sample, the marginal utility test will not be an exercise in speculation—there will be tangible evidence of what the backup tapes may have to offer. There will also be tangible evidence of the time and cost required to restore the backup tapes, which in turn will inform the second group of cost-shifting factors. Thus, by requiring a sample restoration of backup tapes, the entire cost-shifting analysis can be grounded in fact rather than guess-work.

IV. CONCLUSION AND ORDER

In summary, deciding disputes regarding the scope and cost of discovery of electronic data requires a three-step analysis:

First, it is necessary to thoroughly understand the responding party's computer system, both with respect to active and stored data. For data that is kept in an accessible format, the usual rules of discovery apply: the responding party should pay the costs of producing responsive data. A court should consider cost-shifting only when electronic data is relatively inaccessible, such as in backup tapes.

Second, because the cost-shifting analysis is so fact-intensive, it is necessary to determine what data may be found on the inaccessible media. Requiring the responding party to restore and produce responsive documents from a small sample of the requested backup tapes is a sensible approach in most cases.

Third, and finally, in conducting the cost-shifting analysis, the [seven] factors [above] should be considered, weighted more-or-less in the [order presented].

Accordingly, UBS is ordered to produce all responsive e-mails that exist on its optical disks or on its active servers (i.e., in HP OpenMail files) at its own expense. UBS is also ordered to produce, at its expense, responsive e-mails from any five backup tapes selected by Zubulake. UBS should then prepare an affidavit detailing the results of its search, as well as the time and money spent. After reviewing the contents of the backup tapes and UBS's certification, the Court will conduct the appropriate cost-shifting analysis.

Notes and Questions

1. *Epilogue*: In Zubulake v. UBS Warburg LLC, 216 F.R.D. 280 (S.D.N.Y.2003), the court reviewed the information resulting from the examination of five backup tapes selected by plaintiff. UBS hired an outside vendor to restore those five tapes, a process that revealed that a total of 8,344 e-mails were on the five tapes. After eliminating duplicates, 6,203 unique e-mails were identified. A search of these using "Laura," "Zubulake," and "L.Z.," culled 1,075 e-mails, of which UBS deemed approximately 600 to be responsive to plaintiff's document request. The outside vendor billed UBS approximately $11,500 for this activity, and UBS paid its outside counsel approximately $7,500 to review these materials before production. Based on this experience, UBS estimated that the cost of restoring the

remaining backup tapes would be approximately $166,000 for restoration, and that attorney review would cost another $107,000. It asked that plaintiff be directed to bear this entire cost.

The court rejected UBS's request for reimbursement for the cost of reviewing and producing the data once the tapes had been restored. "Documents stored on backup tapes can be likened to paper records locked inside a sophisticated safe to which no one has the key or combination. The cost of accessing those documents may be onerous, and in some cases the parties should split the cost of breaking into the safe. But once the safe is opened, the production of the documents found inside is the sole responsibility of the responding party." Id. at 291.

Regarding the restoration cost, the court directed that plaintiff pay 25% using the seven-factor test. Considering her first two factors, the judge noted that plaintiff identified 68 of the roughly 600 e-mails unearthed in the five tapes examined so far as important to her case. The judge concluded that "they tell a compelling story of the dysfunctional atmosphere" at plaintiff's workplace, and that she would presume these 68 to be reasonably representative of what was on the other backup tapes. At the same time, these documents did not show that the animosity between plaintiff and her supervisor was gender-related. The fact that UBS had produced only 100 e-mails before this restoration effort was made showed that a significant number of e-mails were only accessible by this method. In view of these results, the judge found that plaintiff's discovery request was narrowly tailored, and that the marginal utility was quite high.

On the second group of factors—regarding expense—the judge noted that UBS had "exponentially more resources" than Zubulake, despite her high salary, particularly since the plaintiff had been unemployed for nearly two years. Moreover, there was nothing plaintiff could do to focus the discovery more precisely and thereby avoid additional costs.

Finally, looking to the last two factors, the court concluded that this discrimination case was not distinctive, so that the issues at stake did not affect the cost-shifting determination, and that plaintiff surely would gain far more than UBS did from the effort involved in restoring the other tapes. Without using a strictly arithmetic method of determining the outcome, the judge decided that "some cost-shifting is appropriate in this case," and that 25% suitably was not too much for this plaintiff to bear and assured that UBS's expenses would not be unduly burdensome.

2. Discovery of computer-based data has prompted widespread concerns, largely about cost. As the court points out in *Zubulake*, the American assumption is that ordinarily the responding party should bear the costs of responding. Should the volume of data involved in this form of discovery might call for a different attitude? The Supreme Court long ago recognized that "although it may be expensive to retrieve information stored in computers when no program yet exists for the particular job, there is no reason to think that the same information could be extracted any less expensively if the records were kept in less modern forms. Indeed, one might expect the reverse to be true, for otherwise computers would not have gained such widespread use in the storing and handling of information." Oppenheimer Fund, Inc. v. Sanders, 437 U.S. 340, 362, 98 S.Ct. 2380, 2395, 57 L.Ed.2d 253

(1978). Parties are sometimes required only to search computer records because a search of hard copies would be too burdensome. See, e.g., Hayes v. Compass Group USA, Inc., 202 F.R.D. 363 (D.Conn.2001) (defendant required to produce all computerized information on age discrimination cases or grievances, but not to search manually through its hard copy files for similar information).

Is e-discovery qualitatively different from hard copy discovery? See generally, Marcus, Confronting the Future: Coping With Discovery of Electronic Material, 64 Law & Contemp. Probs. 253, 258–71 (Spring/Summer 2001) (exploring the comparison). Long before e-discovery had become a possibility, there was much tumult about the burden of hard copy discovery. Often, it was said, discovery requests were easy to write but hugely expensive to satisfy, and often the effort produced little of real value to the case. For a description of these views, see Marcus, Discovery Containment Redux, 39 Bos.Col.L.Rev. 747, 752–53 (1998).

In McPeek v. Ashcroft, 202 F.R.D. 31 (D.D.C.2001), the court described and rejected an early judicial reaction to the costs of such discovery (id. at 33):

> The one judicial rationale that has emerged is that producing backup tapes is a cost of doing business in the computer age. But that assumes an alternative. It is impossible to walk ten feet into the office of a private business or government agency without seeing a network computer, which is on a server, which, in turn, is being backed up on a tape (or some other media) on a daily, weekly, or monthly basis. What alternative is there? Quill pens?

With time, judges have become more sophisticated about the problems as well as the potentials for extracting information from computers.

Note the judge's cautious attitude toward defendant's arguments for cost-bearing in *Zubulake*. She emphasizes that the earlier *Rowe* approach had usually led to cost-shifting. Why would that approach have led to that result? Was that a bad thing? At least some think that the American attitude should shift toward making parties pay for the response costs their discovery forays impose on others. Cooter & Rubinfeld, Reforming the New Discovery Rules, 84 Geo. L.J. 61 (1995), define as "abusive" any discovery request for which the cost of complying exceeds the expected value of the evidence in improving the other side's case. Would *Zubulake*'s approach be consistent with that argument? Focusing on the specificity of the discovery request and the availability of alternative sources of information (factors 1 and 2) seems consistent. Compare Wright v. AmSouth Bancorporation, 320 F.3d 1198 (11th Cir.2003) (district court properly refused to order production of "all word processing files created, modified and/or accessed by, or on behalf of" five of defendant's employees over a period exceeding two years). But should the greater wealth of the corporate defendant be a ground for imposing the costs of compliance on it despite plaintiff's prosperity? Is the consideration of the relative benefits to the parties (factor 7) of obtaining the information consistent? Consider what emphasizing the cost of compliance might mean for retrieving information from "accessible sources." For an argument that cost-shifting should be favored, see Redish, Electronic Discovery and the Litigation Matrix, 51 Duke L.J. 561 (2001).

Keep in mind that plaintiff in *Zubulake* made important showings in support of her desire for information from backup tapes. She could show that e-mails contained important information, and (from the collection she already had) that defendant's initial production omitted many that were pertinent. Further, the experiment with five tapes showed that there were in fact numerous responsive items on backup tapes. Would most plaintiffs be able to make a similar showing? Would more conventional discovery put them in a position to do so?

3. Should it be presumed that e-mail messages on backup tapes usually contain useful information? E-mail is quite a new phenomenon, but it has achieved great importance. For example, in In re Prudential Ins. Co. of America Sales Practices Lit., 169 F.R.D. 598 (D.N.J.1997), the court faulted defendant's notice to its agents to preserve evidence because only 1100 of the 2700 employees had e-mail and many of those who had it did not use it. Compare the description of UBS's reliance on e-mail in *Zubulake*. See Nimsger, Digging for E-data, Trial, Jan., 2001, at 56 ("In 2001, businesses in North America sent an estimated 2.5 trillion e-mail messages, expected to grow to 3.25 trillion in 2002.").

Are e-mail communications as important as other evidence? Many have noted that "[e]mployees say things in e-mail messages that would never be stated directly to a person or consciously memorialized in writing." Pooley & Shaw, Finding What's Out There: Technical and Legal Aspects of Discovery, 4 Tex. Intell. Prop. L.J. 57, 63 (1994); see also Thunderstruck, The Economist, May 25, 2002, at 14 ("to put in a near-indestructible e-mail the sorts of comments you might give vent to round the water-cooler is to invite trouble"). Are e-mail messages very good evidence or relatively unhelpful? That could bear on the level of effort that would be justified to retrieve these items. One could argue that the comments made in e-mail messages are particularly valuable because they are candid, or particularly misleading because they are offhand remarks. At least some employers have begun trying to get employees to think in these terms. See Varchaver & Bonamici, The Perils of E-mail, Fortune, Feb. 17, 2003 (reporting that Merrill Lynch ordered its employees to attend "a re-education camp of sorts" about e-mail use, and to ask themselves "How would I feel if this message appeared on the front page of a newspaper?"). Obviously the SEC thinks that it is important to review these communications (see the court's footnote 21 in *Zubulake*).

4. The *Zubulake* decision delves deeply into the details of defendant's information management systems. Should this sort of detail ordinarily be important to resolution of disputes about discovery about electronic information? At least one court has adopted a local rule that requires counsel to review their client's information management systems at the outset of litigation in order to understand how information is stored and how it can be retrieved. See D.N.J. L.R. 26.1(d)(1) (adopted 2003). Whether or not this is required by rule, it may be good practice. For example, in GTFM, Inc. v. Wal–Mart Stores, Inc., 2000 WL 335558 (S.D.N.Y.2000), counsel for defendant told the court that certain electronic records concerning its stores' purchases were not available. The lawyer relied on an official of the client who was not involved in information management in making the assurance. A year later during a deposition, an officer of defendant's information

management department revealed that defendant's computers had possessed the ability to track the desired information at the time the representation was made to the court, but that the material no longer existed by the time of the deposition because it had been erased. The court imposed sanctions on defendant. It may often be necessary for parties to explore and explain such details to justify their objections on grounds of burden to discovery of electronic materials, and important to assure that those with reliable information are consulted.

5. E-mail is hardly the only kind of information that parties possess in electronic form. Indeed, *most* business records are kept electronically, and often in a format that cannot be rendered into hard copy. UBS's records of activity in customers' accounts, for example, are central to the business but not in a form that can be "produced" for examination by an opposing party. Instead, the computer system relies on databases that can be instructed to deliver information that, in turn, may be provided to other parties. Should such discovery be handled under Rule 33 (interrogatories) or Rule 34 (document production)? If the former, how should Rule 33(d)'s option to produce business records be applied? Must the producing party provide all necessary software (possibly proprietary) to the other side so that it can derive information from the computerized data?

6. An increasing proportion of Americans have home computers that they use for e-mail communication and other purposes. How should efforts to discover material on such devices be handled? In Playboy Enterprises, Inc. v. Welles, 60 F.Supp.2d 1050 (S.D.Cal.1999), plaintiff charged defendant (a former Playboy Playmate) with violating its copyright in operation of her Internet business, and it served discovery requests for all communications about certain of defendant's business activities. Having learned that defendant usually deleted e-mail communications shortly after receiving them, plaintiff sought discovery of defendant's computer's hard drive. But defendant used her computer for both personal and business purposes, and objected to permitting plaintiff access to information about her personal affairs. The court decided to appoint as a special master a computer expert (at plaintiff's expense) to make a "mirror image" copy of defendant's hard drive and determine whether there were relevant e-mail messages still retrievable from it even though "deleted" (see footnote 19 in *Zubulake*) to determine whether there appeared to be relevant materials, and then to deliver them to defendant's attorney for review for production.

Does this form of discovery raise serious privacy concerns? Many have expressed concern about unlimited employer access to computers used by employees in their offices. Cf. Fraser v. Nationwide Mut. Ins. Co., 352 F.3d 107 (3d Cir.2003) (holding that an employer's sifting through an employee's e-mail did not violate federal privacy protections). Consider that many employees of large organizations "telecommute" by working from home on their home computers. Should litigation involving their employers justify discovery of the sort done in Playboy Enterprises v. Welles? Note that Rule 34 permits discovery only of documents under the custody or control of a party, but that Rule 45 permits service of a subpoena on nonparties to obtain production of relevant documents.

7. *Form of production*: In *Zubulake* defendant produced 100 pages of e-mail messages. In what form should materials stored electronically be produced? If they are stored (and often created) in a format that is electronically searchable, should production in a format that is not be considered adequate?

8. For further information about e-discovery, see Manual for Complex Litigation (4th) § 11.446 (2004); A. Cohen & D. Lender, Electronic Discovery: Law and Practice (2003); M. Overly, Electronic Evidence in California (1999).

C. DOCUMENT PRESERVATION

NATION–WIDE CHECK CORP. v. FOREST HILLS DISTRIBUTORS, INC.

United States Court of Appeals, First Circuit, 1982.
692 F.2d 214.

Before DAVIS, CAMPBELL and BREYER, CIRCUIT JUDGES.

BREYER, CIRCUIT JUDGE.

Appellants Joseph Braunstein, Stephen Gordon, and Victor Dahar (the "assignees") are assignees for the benefit of creditors of Forest Hills Distributors, Inc., and Forest Hills of New Hampshire, Inc. ("Forest Hills"). Appellee Nation–Wide Check Corporation ("Nation–Wide") sells money orders. Forest Hills sold Nation–Wide's money orders on Nation–Wide's behalf. After Forest Hills assigned its assets for the benefit of its creditors, Nation–Wide sued the assignees for the proceeds of the money order sales. The district court found in its favor. The assignees appeal, claiming that the court rested its decision in part upon an impermissible inference based upon the fact that the assignees allowed the destruction of certain Forest Hills documents in their possession. We believe the district court's inference was permissible, and we therefore affirm its decision.

I

In October 1973 Nation–Wide agreed with Forest Hills that Forest Hills would sell Nation–Wide's money orders to the public in return for a commission. The agreement specifically provided that Forest Hills would hold the sale proceeds apart from all its other assets and revenues, depositing those proceeds in a separate account with The First National Bank of Boston. This procedure, however, was not followed. Instead, the proceeds were deposited in various Forest Hills accounts in local banks near Forest Hills' stores, then transferred to various other Forest Hills accounts in Boston banks. From there, Forest Hills periodically remitted amounts due to Nation–Wide. Moreover, the proceeds were commingled with general Forest Hills revenues when they reached the Boston banks.

In late 1974 Forest Hills encountered financial difficulties and stopped sending money order proceeds to Nation–Wide. On December 18, Forest Hills executed an assignment of all its assets for the benefit of its creditors. At the time of the assignment, Forest Hills owed Nation–Wide $71,417.69 for money orders issued between early November (when Forest Hills stopped paying Nation–Wide) and December 18 (when the assignment took place and money order sales were halted).

The assignees quickly liquidated most of Forest Hills' assets. By the end of December 1974 they apparently accumulated a fund of more than $600,000. Nation–Wide with equal promptness told the assignees about its claim against Forest Hills. Nation–Wide said that its claim took precedence over the claims of Forest Hills' general unsecured creditors because of the "separate-fund" provisions in its 1973 money order agreement. Nation–Wide's lawyers spoke to assignee Gordon around December 19 and wrote to Gordon about their claim a few days later. The assignees rejected Nation–Wide's priority claim and Nation–Wide filed suit against the assignees and Forest Hills on April 1, 1975, seeking payment of its $71,000 out of the $600,000 the assignees had accumulated.

On April 11, Gordon, an associate in a Boston law firm, wrote a letter to a senior partner in the same office about Forest Hills' business records. He noted that the records were being stored at some expense and asked if they should be discarded. In accordance with advice he received from the firm's partner, he then abandoned many of the documents—including all 1974 checks—to the landlord of the storage premises. Gordon's act of abandonment lies at the center of the controversy on this appeal.

[In order to recover $71,000, plaintiff needed to trace the funds Forest Hills received from purchasers of its money orders to the funds ultimately received by the assignees. It was aided in this effort by legal presumptions that provided that where a trustee such as Forest Hills commingles a beneficiary's money with its own, it is presumed to withdraw its own first. Hence, if Forest Hills retained sufficient money in accounts to cover the amounts deposited from sales of plaintiff's money orders, or if it transferred that money to other accounts from which the assignees received the money, plaintiff's priority would stand. But plaintiff could not use the documents abandoned by Gordon, and most of the banks involved had scanty or no records or transactions involving Forest Hills' accounts. Although it did trace $1,204.85 from a Seabrook, New Hampshire store into the assignees' hands, plaintiff was unable to produce parallel documentation of the proceeds from the other accounts.]

The district court filled this evidentiary gap by drawing an inference from the destruction of Forest Hills' business records by Gordon. The court found that Gordon had known as early as December 1974, from his communications with Nation–Wide's attorney, that the business records might be needed to trace the money order funds into the hands of the assignees. The court concluded that while Gordon had not acted in actual bad faith, he had "intentionally discarded" the documents "in knowing disregard of the plaintiff's claims," and that it was therefore proper to infer that the documents would have allowed Nation–Wide to trace the balance of the money order proceeds into the hands of the assignees.

The most recent authority in this circuit on the inferences to be drawn from the destruction of documents is *Allen Pen v. Springfield Photo Mount Co.*, 653 F.2d 17 (1st Cir.1981). *Allen Pen* held that without some evidence that documents have been destroyed "in bad faith" or "from the consciousness of a weak case," it is "ordinarily" improper to draw an adverse inference about the contents of the documents. 653 F.2d at 23–24. The district court expressly found that Gordon did not act in bad faith, not because it believed that Gordon's behavior was in any sense proper, but because it felt that Gordon, as an assignee for the benefit of creditors, had no direct stake in the disposition of Forest Hills' assets among the claimants. However, the court did not interpret *Allen Pen* as establishing a *per se* requirement that bad faith be found before an adverse inference is drawn. It concluded that the inference was proper in this case because Gordon's conduct was not merely negligent but "purposeful" and "in knowing disregard" of Nation–Wide's claim. Unless an adverse inference were drawn, the court feared that other assignees might act like Gordon; they would be encouraged to destroy relevant documents and claimants in Nation–Wide's position would be denied their rightful property.

II

The general principles concerning the inferences to be drawn from the loss or destruction of documents are well established. When the contents of a document are relevant to an issue in a case, the trier of fact generally may receive the fact of the document's nonproduction or destruction as evidence that the party which has prevented production did so out of the well-founded fear that the contents would harm him. Wigmore has asserted that nonproduction is not merely "some" evidence, but is sufficient by itself to support an adverse inference even if no other evidence for the inference exists:

> The failure or refusal to produce a relevant document, or the destruction of it, is evidence *from which alone* its contents may be inferred to be unfavorable to the possessor, provided the opponent, when the identity of the document is disputed, first introduces some evidence tending to show that the document actually destroyed or withheld is the one as to whose contents it is desired to draw an inference.

2 *Wigmore on Evidence* § 291, at 228 (Chadbourn rev. 1979) (emphasis added). The inference depends, of course, on a showing that the party had notice that the documents were relevant at the time he failed to produce them or destroyed them.

The adverse inference is based on two rationales, one evidentiary and one not. The evidentiary rationale is nothing more than the common sense observation that a party who has notice that a document is relevant to litigation and who proceeds to destroy the document is more likely to have been threatened by the document than is a party in the same position who does not destroy the document. The fact of destruction satisfies the minimum requirement of relevance: it has some tendency, however small, to make the existence of a fact at issue more probable than it would otherwise be. *See* Fed.R.Evid. 401. Precisely how the document might have aided the party's adversary, and what evidentiary shortfalls its destruction may be taken to redeem, will depend on the particular facts of each case, but the general evidentiary rationale for the inference is clear.

The other rationale for the inference has to do with its prophylactic and punitive effects. Allowing the trier of fact to draw the inference presumably deters parties from destroying relevant evidence before it can be introduced at trial. The inference also serves as a penalty, placing the risk of an erroneous judgment on the party that wrongfully created the risk. In McCormick's words, "the real underpinning of the rule of admissibility [may be] a desire to impose swift punishment, with a certain poetic justice, rather than concern over niceties of proof." *McCormick on Evidence* § 273, at 661 (1972).

That this policy rationale goes beyond a mere determination of relevance has been clear from the beginning. In the famous case of *Armory v. Delamirie,* 1 Stra. 505, 93 Eng.Rep. 664 (K.B.1722), the chimney sweep who sued the jeweler for return of the jewel he had found and left with the jeweler, was allowed to infer from the fact that the jeweler did not return the jewel that it was a stone "of the finest water." Were relevance all that was at issue, the inference would not necessarily be that the jewel was "of the *finest* water"; the fact that the jeweler kept the jewel proved that the jewel had value, but it did not prove the value of the jewel. Nonetheless, the judge instructed the jury to "presume the strongest against him, and make the value of the *best* jewels the measure of their damages"—a clear sign that the inference was designed to serve a prophylactic and punitive purpose and not simply to reflect relevance.

In this case, both the evidentiary and the policy rationales support the inference drawn by the district court. It is important as an initial matter to recall how much Nation–Wide had shown, directly or indirectly, without resort to the inference. It had established the precise dates and amounts of the money orders and the probable initial route of the proceeds into the local accounts. It had shown that at least some of the Massachusetts accounts had sufficient balances at all relevant times to cover the proceeds. Although it was unable to introduce cancelled checks or other records to trace most inter-account transfers, it was able to do so with regard to the Seabrook proceeds, and the court found that the flow of money from the Seabrook store's local account to the central accounts was "typical" of the flows from the other stores. Finally, it showed that some $88,000 came into the assignees' hands from a specific Forest Hills central account, and while it could not prove where the rest of the money collected by the assignees came from, it was not unreasonable to assume that some portion of it came from other Forest Hills accounts. In short, even without the inference from the destruction of the records, the court had significant circumstantial evidence that the proceeds were not dissipated before they could reach the assignees. The issue before the court was not whether the destruction was sufficient, standing alone, to warrant an adverse inference about the documents' contents; it was simply whether the destruction was at all relevant to the tracing issue, and if so, whether it was sufficiently probative in conjunction with the other evidence to support the tracing conclusion.

That the destruction was relevant is clear. As the district court found, Gordon had notice that the documents might be necessary to Nation–Wide's claim at the time he destroyed them. The assignees argue to the contrary on appeal, but there is sufficient evidence in the record to support the court's finding that Gordon was put on notice as early as late December 1974, four months before he destroyed the documents, by his communications with Nation–Wide's attorney. More importantly, the court found that Gordon's conduct transcended mere negligence and amounted to "knowing disregard" of Nation–Wide's claim. The court's reluctance to label Gordon's conduct as "bad faith" is not dispositive: "bad faith" is not a talisman, as *Allen Pen* itself made clear when it stated that the adverse inference "ordinarily" depended on a showing of bad faith. Indeed, the "bad faith" label is more useful to summarize the conclusion that an adverse inference is permissible than it is actually to reach the conclusion. Here, although the court found that Gordon might not have been "completely aware" of the significance of the records, he proceeded to destroy them without further inquiry even though they theoretically could have disproven as well as proven Nation–Wide's tracing claim. This conscious abandonment of potentially useful evidence is, at a minimum, an indication that Gordon believed the records would not *help* his side of the case—by proving, through the checks written, for example, that the accumulated funds could not contain the sale proceeds. In turn, such a belief by an assignee who was presumably familiar with records that included all 1974 checks, who knew of the assignee's denial of Nation–Wide's claim, and who knew of Nation–Wide's suit against him, is some (though perhaps weak) evidence that the records would have helped Nation–Wide.

Once this minimum link of relevance is established, however, we believe that the district court has some discretion in determining how much weight to give the document destruction, and prophylactic and punitive considerations may appropriately be taken into account. The court did consider the innocuous reason that Gordon claimed had led to his discarding the records—avoiding storage costs. The court also took account of the fact that an assignee ordinarily is supposed to be "neutral" as among claimants and thus would not wish to destroy evidence that would support a meritorious claim. It is also true that Gordon did not "destroy" the documents in an orthodox sense; he simply left them for the landlord to destroy.

While these considerations arguably reduce the probative value of Gordon's acts, they do not destroy the relevance of the acts altogether.

Gordon's letter to his partners could be seen as self-serving. His neutrality also can be called into question, both because he had been made an assignee by the general creditors rather than by Nation–Wide, and because he was a defendant in Nation–Wide's suit. Moreover, while the mitigating circumstances surrounding Gordon's conduct might provide a basis for tempering a prophylactic or punitive use of the inference, the court was entitled to consider countervailing factors. Among these were the improper nature of Gordon's conduct, the desirability of deterring other assignees from engaging in similarly reckless behavior, and the extent to which fairness dictates making the assignees, rather than Nation–Wide, bear the financial risks arising from document loss. The court could also take into account the other evidence tending to show that the money flows satisfied the "tracing" requirements and reasonably conclude that the evidentiary gap was not a large one. Taking these matters into account, the district court decided to give the act of document destruction sufficient weight to satisfy, in context, the tracing burden the law imposed upon Nation–Wide. Given that the act of destruction was logically connected to the ultimate fact proved and that the policy considerations militated in favor of according that act significant weight, we believe the district court's decision was reasonable and within its discretion.

Notes and Questions

1. In the late 1980s, commentators wrote: "In the past 15 years, evidence destruction has come out of the closet. News reports of document destruction, if not a daily feature, have lost their novelty. Richard Nixon believed in retrospect that he should have destroyed the Watergate tapes. Oliver North did destroy documents." Solum & Marzen, Destruction of Evidence, 16 Litigation 11, 11 (Fall 1989). Since then, attention to these issues has continued. In 2002, for example, Arthur Andersen was convicted of obstruction of justice for destroying documents pertinent to Enron Corp., and many others have been charged with similar crimes.

2. *Document retention policies*: The focus on the needs of document retention has spawned renewed attention to policies on what should be maintained. Some say that " 'document retention policy' is one of the great Orwellian misnomers of modern litigation practice. It invariably refers to a policy requiring the periodic destruction of documents." Yablon, Stupid Lawyer Tricks: An Essay on Discovery Abuse, 96 Colum. L. Rev. 1618, 1632 n. 47 (1996). Yet having such a policy and following it can protect a party against an adverse consequence when documents have been discarded. See Stevenson v. Union Pacific R.R., 354 F.3d 739, 747 (8th Cir.2004) ("Where a routine document retention policy has been followed in this context, * * * there must be some indication of an intent to destroy the evidence for the purpose of obstructing or suppressing the truth in order to sanction an adverse inference instruction."). Coates v. Johnson & Johnson, 756 F.2d 524, 551 (7th Cir.1985) (because documents were destroyed under routine procedures, there is no ground for inferring that defendant's agents were conscious of a weak case when they destroyed them). No organization can keep all materials forever, and consistency about what should be retained is a sensible measure.

Thoughtful preservation is also a measure that is required by various regulations. Recall the SEC requirement on retention of materials about communications by securities brokers in Zubulake v. UBS Warburg LLC, *supra* p. 549 n. 21. Failure to comply can have quite adverse consequences even without litigation. See McGeehan, Wall St. Banks May be Fined for Discarding E–Mail Traffic, N.Y.Times, Aug. 2, 2002, at C1 (reporting that the SEC proposed fines of $10 million for failure to keep e-mail messages as required). For general discussion of legal requirements that businesses preserve records, see Fedders & Guttelplan, Document Retention and Destruction: Practical, Legal and Ethical Considerations, 56 Notre Dame Law. 5 (1980). Besides complying with such regulatory requirements, a sensible policy would take account of the possible needs for materials as evidence, as for other purposes, in deciding how long to keep such things. But many companies evidently don't have such policies. See Krause, Frequent Filers, ABAJ, Aug. 2003, at 52, 53 (reporting that barely half of firms surveyed by the ABA in 2002 had such a policy). What sort of policy should the assignees in *Nation-Wide Check* have adopted? What policy should Forest Hills have had?

Retention issues take on new dimensions with electronic materials. On the one hand, storage space is not a concern. But at least some materials are altered or overwritten by ordinary operation of computer systems, and that could be characterized as evidence destruction. Data storage enterprises evidently have recognized data-retention issues as a marketing opportunity. See Austen, New Economy, N.Y. Times, April 21, 2003, at C4 (reporting that makers of storage technology are successfully marketing high-margin software for managing data due to "[t]he renewed emphasis on keeping records in a way that will satisfy regulators"). Even well-thought-out methods may not work. See Krause, *supra*, ABAJ, Aug. 2003, at 52–53 (reporting on a case in which outside counsel for a company found that none of its backup tapes worked, and then learned that the company had never tested its backup system).

3. In cases in which parties have embarked on a calculated plan to destroy evidence that would support claims against them, courts have sometimes decided cases against them as a sanction for such conduct. In Carlucci v. Piper Aircraft Corp., 102 F.R.D. 472 (S.D.Fla.1984), aff'd in part, rev'd in part, 775 F.2d 1440 (11th Cir.1985), plaintiffs sued for wrongful death in connection with the crash of a plane manufactured by defendant. The court eventually entered default on the issue of liability, finding that defendant had continuously obstructed discovery. It also found persuasive the testimony of two former employees that Piper had embarked on an extensive document-destruction policy (102 F.R.D. at 481):

> The policy was initiated in the late 1960's or the early 1970's when [the employees] received the instruction from J. Myers, the flight test supervisor and their direct superior, to "purge" the department's files. The stated purpose of the destruction of records was the elimination of documents that might be detrimental to Piper in a law suit. Wrisley and Lister were delegated the discretion to determine which documents were to be destroyed. The initial purging involved hundreds of flight test department documents. They were also directed to retrieve copies of the detrimental documents from other departments. Thereafter, the destruction of all potentially harmful documents was an ongoing process.

Should this have been sufficient, standing alone, to justify a default? Note that at the time these documents were destroyed there was evidently no pending litigation or claims regarding the products in question.

Even after discovery begins, parties sometimes engage in such brazen destruction. For example, in Kucala Ent., Ltd. v. Auto Wax Co., 2003 WL 21230605 (N.D.Ill.2003), defendant sought access to plaintiff's hard drive to locate missing e-mail communications. After persistent inquiry, plaintiff's attorney was able to learn which program defendant's expert planned to use to locate materials on the hard drive the day before the examination was to occur. At 4:00 a.m. on the day of the examination, plaintiff used software called "Evidence Eliminator" to delete and destroy more than 12,000 files from his hard drive. "Evidence Eliminator" is advertised as able to "clean * * * deadly evidence" from a hard drive, and as capable of defeating the software that defendant intended to use for plaintiff's hard drive. The court dismissed plaintiff's complaint as a sanction for destroying the files.

4. The abandonment of records in *Nation–Wide Check* hardly seems comparable. Note the court's treatment of bad faith. Should more be required before adverse consequences result from the disappearance of documents or other evidence? Is it significant that Gordon was a lawyer and therefore that he might realize the importance of the records to plaintiff's claim?

In Residential Funding Corp. v. DeGeorge Financial Corp., 306 F.3d 99 (2d Cir.2002), plaintiff had agreed to produce relevant e-mail messages from backup tapes, and had repeatedly assured defendant and the court that it was having an outside expert retrieve those messages. But on the eve of trial, after stalling with repeated assurances that production would soon be forthcoming, it reported that its expert could not restore the tapes, and even then it was laggard in providing copies of the tapes to defendant so that its expert could try to restore them. Within four days, without working overtime, defendant's expert had located 950,000 e-mail messages on the tapes. But defendant never used any of them in the trial, or showed that they were important, and the court refused to instruct the jury that it could infer that the unproduced e-mail messages would harm plaintiff's case. Plaintiff won a $96 million verdict.

Defendant appealed, and the court of appeals treated plaintiff's failure to produce as tantamount to destruction. It vacated plaintiff's judgment and remanded because the district judge should have approached the question of sanctions differently. It intimated that plaintiff's stalling looked like bad faith, and noted that the district judge said plaintiff was guilty of "purposeful sluggishness," but ruled further that "[t]he sanction of an adverse inference may be appropriate in some cases involving the negligent destruction of evidence because each party should bear the risk of its own negligence." Id. at 108. It directed that a new trial would be appropriate if defendant showed prejudice due to plaintiff's delay in producing the e-mail messages. Even if defendant could not show prejudice, it added, there should be some penalty for plaintiff, and it suggested that plaintiff be denied postjudgment interest on its verdict for the time from the original entry of judgment to the district court's ruling on remand, a considerable sum since the district court's judgment was already a year old when the appellate court ruled.

5. Once litigation is underway, there is a heightened obligation to retain possibly relevant materials. The obligation often begins even before litigation is formally commenced. For example, in Zubulake v. UBS Warburg, 2003 WL 22410619 (S.D.N.Y.2003), the court addressed the question of sanctions against defendant for failure to retain three backup tapes and parts of four others that were to be restored under the cost-sharing arrangement directed by the court (see *supra* p. 556 n. 1). Defendant had directed its employees to retain relevant documents at the time plaintiff filed her EEOC charge of gender discrimination. The court found, however, that the duty to preserve relevant documents attached four months earlier because "it appears that almost everyone associated with Zubulake recognized the possibility that she might sue" by that time. Indeed, some of defendant's employees began titling e-mail messages pertaining to Zubulake "UBS Attorney Client Privilege." On the scope of the preservation duty, the court observed:

> Must a corporation, upon recognizing the threat of litigation, preserve every shred of paper, every e-mail or electronic document, and every backup tape? The answer is clearly, "no." Such a rule would cripple large corporations, like UBS, that are almost always involved in litigation. As a general rule, then, a party need not preserve all backup tapes even when it reasonably anticipates litigation.

But because there was reason to believe that e-mail messages of the relevant persons at UBS were on these particular backup tapes, the court held that these tapes should have been retained.

This sort of obligation is not necessarily limited to defendants, or to corporations, or to materials owned by the party. Consider Silvestri v. General Motors Corp., 271 F.3d 583 (4th Cir.2001). Plaintiff there was injured in an automobile collision, and claimed that his injuries were worsened because the air bag failed to deploy. The car belonged to the husband of plaintiff's landlord. While he was in the hospital recovering from his injuries in the crash, plaintiff's parents hired a lawyer who sent accident reconstruction experts to examine the crash scene and the car, but neither plaintiff nor his lawyer made efforts to have the car retained in its post-crash condition until GM inspected it. Instead, the owner (not the plaintiff) sold the car to a collision repair outfit that repaired it and sold it.

When plaintiff sued GM three years later, it located the car in Quebec, where the new owner lived, but due to the repairs it could not then test the airbag equipment that plaintiff claimed had malfunctioned. Applying "the federal law of spoliation," id. at 590, the court upheld dismissal of plaintiff's suit. Plaintiff clearly had access to the car, because his experts inspected it, but he made no effort to buy it, preserve it against change, or notify GM. Dismissal was appropriate because plaintiff's conduct was "so prejudicial that it substantially denied the defendant the ability to defend the claim." Id. at 593. If the plaintiff were impecunious, what should have been done?

6. If documents disappear due to fault of a party, what remedy should the court use? In *Nation–Wide Check,* the court finds that an adverse inference should be employed even in the absence of a finding of bad faith. How should the court determine what should be inferred? Do we really have

any basis for predicting what was in the materials Gordon abandoned? Does this inference invite the jury to overemphasize the disappearance of evidence? Consider, Oesterle, A Private Litigant's Remedies for an Opponent's Inappropriate Destruction of Relevant Documents, 61 Texas L.Rev. 1185, 1235 (1983) (arguing that such an instruction is probably overvalued by a jury). In Zubulake v. UBS Warburg LLC, 2003 WL 22410619 (S.D.N.Y.2003), the court declined to direct that the jury be given an adverse inference instruction as a sanction for defendant's improper failure to retain backup tapes:

> In practice, an adverse inference instruction often ends the litigation—it is too difficult a hurdle for the spoliator to overcome. The *in terrorem* effect of an adverse inference is obvious. When a jury is instructed that it may "infer that the party who destroyed potentially relevant evidence did so out of a realization that the [evidence was] unfavorable," the party suffering this instruction will be hard-pressed to prevail on the merits. Accordingly, the adverse inference instruction is an extreme sanction and should not be given lightly.

Was the sanction used in *Nation-Wide Check* more moderate?

7. Putting aside the other risks of destruction of evidence, consider the possibility that, despite efforts to destroy inculpatory materials, copies may survive. Shouldn't the fact that the party tried to destroy the documents be admissible? Perhaps this risk explains the rather remarkable lengths to which some will go to make sure destroyed documents remain destroyed. Consider the following observations by a corporate lawyer concerning methods for destruction of hard-copy corporate files:

> Incineration or simple burial, for example, may not fully destroy compacted materials or materials enclosed in fileboxes or other containers, and transportation to a dump may result in loss or theft before or after delivery. Shredding, while time-consuming, can be effective although with a substantial effort, it is reversible.
>
> More complete pulverization is available for paper as well as nonshreddible materials, as are off-site processing concerns that will chemically reduce disposable items to masses of pulp. Particular care must be taken with magnetically recorded information, such as audio and computer tapes and computer disks. Recovery techniques are readily available to reconstruct data thought to have been erased from the tape or disk.

Lenkowsky, Goal is to Safeguard Confidentiality, Nat.L.J., May 14, 1990, at 23.

8. Leading commentators, having outlined these various problems, conclude: "It comes down to this: Only if you have one of those rare documents so damaging that its discovery would equal unconditional surrender should you consider destroying it, and only then after making sure that destruction is lawful. In most cases document destruction—even if it is certainly legal—is ill-advised if litigation is on the horizon." Solum & Marzen, *supra* note 1, 16 Litigation at 13.

9. *Document preservation orders*: Unsatisfied with reliance on such deterrents, courts may enter orders requiring preservation of evidence.

Sometimes courts enter such orders ex parte at the very inception of litigation. For example, in Hester v. Bayer Corp., 206 F.R.D. 683 (M.D.Ala. 2001), plaintiff sued defendant in state court claiming that defendant's drug Baycol caused health problems. The state court entered an ex parte order requiring Bayer to preserve all information about Baycol, and to "suspend all routine destruction of documents, including, but not limited to, recycling backup tapes, automated deletion of e-mail, and reformatting hard drives." On removal to federal court, defendant filed an emergency motion to vacate the order, pointing out compliance costs of approximately $50,000 per month. Citing the obligation to preserve that exists without a specific order, the court found this order "superfluous" and vacated it. It also criticized plaintiff's counsel for providing no evidence at all when they made their ex parte request to the state-court judge.

The Manual for Complex Litigation recognizes that it may be appropriate to enter a preservation order early in the case, but its sample order emphasizes negotiation of terms between the parties. See Manual for Complex Litigation (4th) § 40.25 (2004). The Manual also notes that "[a] blanket preservation order may be prohibitively expensive and unduly burdensome for parties dependent on computer systems for their day-to-day operations. In addition, a preservation order will likely be ineffective if it is formulated without reliable information from the responding party regarding what data-management systems are already in place, the volume of data affected, and the costs and technical feasibility of implementation." Id., § 11.422.

If such an order is entered, however, a party subject to it should make substantial efforts to comply. For example, in In re Prudential Ins. Co. of America Sales Practices Lit., 169 F.R.D. 598 (D.N.J.1997), the judge ordered Prudential to preserve all sales promotion materials for the insurance products that were the subject of the litigation. Unfortunately, Prudential had already undertaken a program of culling outdated materials from its files, and such materials were destroyed in at least four of its branch offices. The court ruled that Prudential had not done enough to notify its employees of their obligations under the order. The company did send out e-mail messages about the need to preserve documents, threatening adverse employment action against employees who failed to preserve materials, but at that time only 1100 of its 2700 agents had e-mail, and many of those 1100 did not know how to use it. "While there is no proof that Prudential * * * engaged in conduct intended to thwart discovery through purposeful destruction of documents, its haphazard and uncoordinated approach to document retention indisputably denies its party opponents potential evidence to establish facts in dispute." The judge therefore imposed sanctions on Prudential.

D.   DISCOVERY CONFIDENTIALITY AND PROTECTIVE ORDERS

"Complex litigation will frequently involve information or documents that a party considers sensitive." Manual for Complex Litigation (4th) § 11.432 (2004). Beginning in the 1970s, one reaction to this problem was that the court would enter a protective order to restrict dissemination of materials obtained through discovery. An example is provided by Zenith Radio Corp. v. Matsushita Elec. Indus. Co., 529 F.Supp. 866 (E.D.Pa.1981), a massive antitrust litigation. As the judge explained, a reading of the complaints, "which spanned the law of antitrust and focused on defendants' price behavior," showed that "large quantities of sensitive commercial data would be sought in discovery." Id. at 892.

One way of handling questions of confidentiality would be for the producing party to object to discovery, leading to a contested protective order motion, either on motion of the producing party or in response to a motion to compel discovery. In such a proceeding, the burden would be on the party seeking the court's protection to establish that the materials were eligible for that protection. To show "good cause" for a protective order under Rule 26(c), the moving party would have to make a specific showing (a) that the materials contained sensitive information that was kept secret, (b) that disclosure would likely cause a specific harm, and (c) that issuance of the order was supported by "good cause."

In *Zenith*, as in many case, the parties took a different course. They stipulated to what is called an "umbrella" protective order, which permitted parties to designate materials they produced as confidential and limited dissemination of materials so designated. The judge observed that he was "unaware of any case in the past half-dozen years of even a modicum of complexity where an umbrella protective order similar * * * has not been agreed to by the parties and approved by the court. Protective orders have been used so frequently that a degree of standardization is appearing." Id. at 889. For an example of such an order, see Manual for Complex Litigation (4th) § 40.27 (2004).

The designation process provided by an umbrella order relies on the first instance on the party's lawyer. "[T]here is a danger here that counsel will err on the side of caution by designating confidential any potentially sensitive document," but "[t]he designation of a document as confidential may be viewed as equivalent to a motion for protective order and subject to the sanctions of Fed.R.Civ.P. 26(g)." Cipollone v. Liggett Group, Inc., 785 F.2d 1108, 1122 n. 17 (3d Cir.1986), cert. denied, 484 U.S. 976, 108 S.Ct. 487, 98 L.Ed.2d 485 (1987). See Procter & Gamble Co. v. Bankers Trust Co., 78 F.3d 219 (6th Cir.1996) (objecting to a stipulated protective order because "the parties were allowed to adjudicate their own case based upon their own self-interest"). The sample order in the Manual for Complex Litigation (4th) (2004) provides as follows (§ 40.27(c)):

> Only documents containing trade secrets, special formulas, company security matters, customer lists, financial data, projected sales data, production data, matters relating to mergers and acquisitions, and data which touch upon the topic of price may be designated confidential. * * * [T]he information subject to a confidentiality designation may include the following: customer names; proprietary licensing, distribution, marketing, design, development, research,

and manufacturing information—not publicly filed with any federal or state regulatory authority—regarding products and medicines, whether currently marketed or under development; clinical studies not publicly filed with any federal or state regulatory authority; information concerning competitors; production information; personnel records and information; financial information not publicly filed with any federal or state regulatory authority.

In *Zenith, supra*, the parties produced some 35 million documents after entering into the protective order. One defendant stamped over 77,000 documents confidential, and plaintiff produced over 100,000 documents on paper preprinted with a confidentiality designation. As trial approached, the judge directed the parties to file pretrial statements in connection with summary judgment motions. Plaintiff's pretrial statement was 17,000 pages long and cross-referenced over 250,000 documents. After a five-week hearing to determine the admissibility of this material, the court granted defendants' motion for summary judgment. The Supreme Court later affirmed this ruling. Matsushita Elec. Indus. Co. v. Zenith Radio Corp., 475 U.S. 574, 106 S.Ct. 1348, 89 L.Ed.2d 538 (1986).

After the district judge granted defendants' motion for summary judgment, plaintiff sought to have the confidentiality provisions lifted, seemingly in part so that it could supply copies of discovery materials to governmental authorities. Plaintiff made an across-the-board challenge to the restrictions on releasing the documents, claiming that defendants had overused the confidentiality stamp, and that continued protection had to be justified document-by-document. Defendants submitted affidavits concerning the ways in which the information could be used to their commercial disadvantage. One method would be to discern defendants' pricing strategies. "Of equal if not greater concern to defendants is the possible consequence of exposure of [details about their arrangements with retailers], in that customer relationships could be impaired if those retailers knew the terms on which a manufacturer sold to the retailer's competitors." In at least some instances, defendants had accorded more favorable treatment to some retailers than others.

Plaintiff urged that defendants had to make a detailed showing to justify continued protection. The judge acknowledged that "[i]n practical terms, it may well be that courts apply a less rigorous standard to consent [protective] orders, although we doubt that any judge would approve a consent order not demonstrably rooted in Rule 26(c), both as a matter of judicial authority and out of concern for potential public access rights." Id. at 889 n. 40. The judge concluded that the defendants' showing was sufficient because it demonstrated with adequate specificity that defendants maintained the confidentiality of the information and risked competitive disadvantage should it be disclosed. A document-by-document showing was not necessary. Moreover, the judge rejected plaintiff's argument for wholesale declassification because it was not raised at the time of production of the documents, concluding that a party could not "sit on its hands while the mountain of discovery materials grows and then attempt to challenge the protection of such material with the same ease with which it could have raised an objection contemporaneously." Id. at 893–94. He added:

> In terms of complex case management, we also believe that wholesale declassification is a poor, inappropriate, and unfair tool, not only with respect to the interests of the litigants, but also with respect to the interests of third parties who are frequently drawn into the vortex. It is common that, in response to a subpoena to attend a deposition and produce related documents, and in reliance upon an umbrella confidential order, third parties divulge sensitive commercial information * * *.

It should be apparent that there are many efficiency considerations that can be furthered by entry of protective orders in complex litigation, but there are countervailing considerations. We turn to those now.

SEATTLE TIMES CO. v. RHINEHART

Supreme Court of the United States, 1984.
467 U.S. 20, 104 S.Ct. 2199, 81 L.Ed.2d 17.

JUSTICE POWELL delivered the opinion of the Court.

This case presents the issue whether parties to civil litigation have a First Amendment right to disseminate, in advance of trial, information gained through the pretrial discovery process.

I

Respondent Rhinehart is the spiritual leader of a religious group, the Aquarian Foundation. The Foundation has fewer than 1,000 members, most of whom live in the State of Washington. Aquarian beliefs include life after death and the ability to communicate with the dead through a medium. Rhinehart is the primary Aquarian medium.

In recent years, the Seattle Times and the Walla Walla Union–Bulletin have published stories about Rhinehart and the Foundation. Altogether 11 articles appeared in the newspapers during the years 1973, 1978 and 1979. The five articles that appeared in 1973 focused on Rhinehart and the manner in which he operated the Foundation. They described seances conducted by Rhinehart in which people paid him to put them in touch with deceased relatives and friends. The articles also stated that Rhinehart had sold magical "stones" that had been "expelled" from his body. One article referred to Rhinehart's conviction, later vacated, for sodomy. The four articles that appeared in 1978 concentrated on an "extravaganza" sponsored by Rhinehart at the Walla Walla State Penitentiary. The articles stated that he had treated 1,100 inmates to a 6–hour-long show, during which he gave away between $35,000 and $50,000 in cash and prizes. One article described a "chorus line of girls [who] shed their gowns and bikinis and sang...." The two articles that appeared in 1979 referred to a purported connection between Rhinehart and Lou Ferrigno, star of the popular television program, "The Incredible Hulk."

[Rhinehart and his Foundation sued the newspapers in Washington state court for defamation and invasion of privacy. Alleging that the articles were false and would discourage contributions to the Foundation, they sought over $14 million in damages. After answering, defendants initiated extensive discovery including requests for lists of donors and members of the Foundation and certain financial information about the Foundation. The trial court ordered production of the information and initially denied plaintiffs' request for a protective order despite a showing that defendants intended to continue publishing articles about the Foundation. Plaintiffs then submitted affidavits detailing attacks and threats against the Foundation and asserting that disclosure of the information would subject members to harassment and adversely affect Foundation membership. The trial court then entered a protective order pursuant to Wash.Super.Ct.R. 26(c) forbidding use of financial or membership information turned over through discovery for any purpose except preparation for trial. The Supreme Court of Washington affirmed, noting that its holding conflicted with *In re Halkin*, 598 F.2d 176 (D.C.Cir.1979).]

* * *

III

Most states, including Washington, have adopted discovery provisions modeled on Rules 26 through 37 of the Federal Rules of Civil Procedure.[14] Rule 26(b)(1) provides that a party "may obtain discovery regarding any matter, not privileged, which is relevant to the subject matter involved in the pending action." It further provides that discovery is not limited to matters that will be admissible at trial so long as the information sought "appears reasonably calculated to lead to the discovery of admissible evidence."

The rules do not differentiate between information that is private or intimate and that to which no privacy interests attach. Under the rules, the only express limitations are that the information sought is not privileged, and is relevant to the subject matter of the pending action. Thus, the rules often allow extensive intrusion into the affairs of both litigants and third parties. If a litigant fails to comply with a request for discovery, the Court may issue an order directing compliance that is enforceable by the Court's contempt powers.

Petitioners argue that the First Amendment imposes strict limits on the availability of any judicial order that has the effect of restricting expression. They contend that civil discovery is not different from other

---

14. The Washington Supreme Court has stated that when the language of a Washington rule and its federal counterpart are the same, courts should look to decisions interpreting the federal rule for guidance. The Washington rule that provides for the scope of civil discovery and the issuance of protective orders is virtually identical to its counterpart in the Federal Rules of Civil Procedure.

sources of information, and therefore the information is "protected speech" for First Amendment purposes. Petitioners assert the right in this case to disseminate any information gained through discovery. They do recognize that in limited circumstances, not thought to be present here, some information may be restrained. They submit, however, that:

> "When a protective order seeks to limit expression, it may do so only if the proponent shows a compelling governmental interest. Mere speculation and conjecture are insufficient. Any restraining order, moreover, must be narrowly drawn and precise. Finally, before issuing such an order a court must determine that there are no alternatives which intrude less directly on expression."

We think the rule urged by petitioners would impose an unwarranted restriction on the duty and discretion of a trial court to oversee the discovery process.

IV

It is, of course, clear that information obtained through civil discovery authorized by modern rules of civil procedure would rarely, if ever, fall within the classes of unprotected speech identified by decisions of this Court. In this case, as petitioners argue, there certainly is a public interest in knowing more about respondents. This interest may well include most—and possibly all—of what has been discovered as a result of the court's order under Rule 26(b)(1). It does not necessarily follow, however, that a litigant has an unrestrained right to disseminate information that has been obtained through pretrial discovery. For even though the broad sweep of the First Amendment seems to prohibit all restraints on free expression, this Court has observed that "freedom of speech . . . does not comprehend the right to speak on any subject at any time." *American Communications Assn. v. Douds,* 339 U.S. 382, 394–395, 70 S.Ct. 674, 681–682, 94 L.Ed. 925 (1950).

The critical question that this case presents is whether a litigant's freedom comprehends the right to disseminate information that he has obtained pursuant to a court order that both granted him access to that information and placed restraints on the way in which the information might be used. In addressing that question it is necessary to consider whether the "practice in question [furthers] an important or substantial governmental interest unrelated to the suppression of expression" and whether "the limitation of First Amendment freedoms [is] no greater than is necessary or essential to the protection of the particular governmental interest involved." *Procunier v. Martinez,* 416 U.S. 396, 413, 94 S.Ct. 1800, 1811, 40 L.Ed.2d 224 (1974).

A

At the outset, it is important to recognize the extent of the impairment of First Amendment rights that a protective order, such as the one at issue here, may cause. As in all civil litigation, petitioners gained the information they wish to disseminate only by virtue of the trial court's discovery processes. As the rules authorizing discovery were adopted by the state legislature, the processes thereunder are a matter of legislative grace. A litigant has no First Amendment right of access to information made available only for purposes of trying his suit. *Zemel v. Rusk,* 381 U.S. 1, 16–17, 85 S.Ct. 1271, 1280–1281, 14 L.Ed.2d 179 (1965) ("The right to speak and publish does not carry with it the unrestrained right to gather information."). Thus, continued court control over the discovered information does not raise the same spectre of government censorship that such control might suggest in other situations.[18]

Moreover, pretrial depositions and interrogatories are not public components of a civil trial.[19] Such proceedings were not open to the public at common law, *Gannett Co. v. DePasquale,* 443 U.S. 368, 389, 99 S.Ct. 2898, 2910, 61 L.Ed.2d 608 (1979), and, in general, they are conducted in private as a matter of modern practice. See *id.,* at 396, 99 S.Ct., at 2913–2914 (Burger, C.J., concurring); Marcus, Myth and Reality in Protective Order Litigation, 69 Cornell L.Rev. 1 (1983). Much of the information that surfaces during pretrial discovery may be unrelated, or only tangentially related, to the underlying cause of action. Therefore, restraints placed on discovered, but not yet admitted, information are not a restriction on a traditionally public source of information.

Finally, it is significant to note that an order prohibiting dissemination of discovered information before trial is not the kind of classic prior restraint that requires exacting First Amendment scrutiny. As in this case, such a protective order prevents a party from disseminating only that information obtained through use of the discovery process. Thus, the party may disseminate the identical information covered by the protective order as long as the information is gained through means independent of the court's processes. In sum, judicial limitations on a party's ability to disseminate information discovered in advance of trial implicate the First Amendment rights of the restricted party to a far lesser extent than would restraints on dissemination of information in a different context. Therefore, our consideration of the provision for pro-

---

18. Although litigants do not "surrender their First Amendment rights at the courthouse door," *In re Halkin,* 598 F.2d, at 186, those rights may be subordinated to other interests that arise in this setting. For instance, on several occasions this Court has approved restriction on the communications of trial participants where necessary to ensure a fair trial for a criminal defendant. See *Nebraska Press v. Stuart,* 427 U.S. 539, 563, 96 S.Ct. 2791, 2804–2805, 49 L.Ed.2d 683 (1976). "In the conduct of a case, a court often finds it necessary to restrict the free expression of participants, including counsel, witnesses, and jurors." *Gulf Oil Co. v. Bernard,* 452 U.S. 89, 104 n. 21, 101 S.Ct. 2193, 2201–2202 n. 21, 68 L.Ed.2d 693 (1981).

19. Discovery rarely takes place in public. Depositions are scheduled at times and places most convenient to those involved. Interrogatories are answered in private. Rules of civil procedure may require parties to file with the clerk of the court interrogatory answers, responses to requests for admissions, and deposition transcripts. See Fed.Rule Civ.Proc. 5(d). Jurisdictions that require filing of discovery materials customarily provide that trial courts may order that the materials not be filed or that they be filed under seal. See *ibid.* Federal district courts may adopt local rules providing that the fruits of discovery are not to be filed except on order of the court. Thus, to the extent that courthouse records could serve as a source of public information, access to that source customarily is subject to the control of the trial court.

tective orders contained in the Washington Civil Rules takes into account the unique position that such orders occupy in relation to the First Amendment.

B

Rule 26(c) furthers a substantial governmental interest unrelated to the suppression of expression. The Washington Civil Rules enable parties to litigation to obtain information "relevant to the subject matter involved" that they believe will be helpful in the preparation and trial of the case. Rule 26, however, must be viewed in its entirety. Liberal discovery is provided for the sole purpose of assisting in the preparation and trial, or the settlement, of litigated disputes. Because of the liberality of pretrial discovery permitted by Rule 26(b)(1), it is necessary for the trial court to have the authority to issue protective orders conferred by Rule 26(c). It is clear from experience that pretrial discovery by depositions and interrogatories has a significant potential for abuse. This abuse is not limited to matters of delay and expense; discovery also may seriously implicate privacy interests of litigants and third parties.[21] The Rules do not distinguish between public and private information. Nor do they apply only to parties to the litigation, as relevant information in the hands of third parties may be subject to discovery.

There is an opportunity, therefore, for litigants to obtain—incidentally or purposefully—information that not only is irrelevant but if publicly released could be damaging to reputation and privacy. The government clearly has a substantial interest in preventing this sort of abuse of its processes. As stated by Judge Friendly in *International Products Corp. v. Koons*, 325 F.2d 403, 407–408 (C.A.2 1963), "[w]hether or not the Rule itself authorizes [a particular protective order] ... we have no question as to the court's jurisdiction to do this under the inherent 'equitable powers of courts of law over their own process, to prevent abuses, oppression, and injustices.'" The prevention of the abuse that can attend the coerced production of information under a state's discovery rule is sufficient justification for the authorization of protective orders.[22]

C

We also find that the provision for protective orders in the Washington rules requires, in itself, no heightened First Amendment scrutiny. To

21. Rule 26(c) includes among its express purposes the protection of a "party or person from annoyance, embarrassment, oppression, or undue burden or expense." Although the Rule contains no specific reference to privacy or to other rights or interests that may be implicated, such matters are implicit in the broad purpose and language of the Rule.

22. The Supreme Court of Washington properly emphasized the importance of ensuring that potential litigants have unimpeded access to the courts: "[A]s the trial court rightly observed, rather than expose themselves to unwanted publicity, individuals may well forego the pursuit of their just claims. The judicial system will thus have made the utilization of its remedies so onerous that the people will be reluctant or unwilling to use it, resulting in frustration of a right as valuable as that of speech itself."

be sure, Rule 26(c) confers broad discretion on the trial court to decide when a protective order is appropriate and what degree of protection is required. The legislature of the State of Washington, following the example of the Congress in its approval of the Federal Rules of Civil Procedure, has determined that such discretion is necessary, and we find no reason to disagree. The trial court is in the best position to weigh fairly the competing needs and interests of parties affected by discovery. The unique character of the discovery process requires that the trial court have substantial latitude to fashion protective orders.

V

The facts in this case illustrate the concerns that justifiably may prompt a court to issue a protective order. As we have noted, the trial court's order allowing discovery was extremely broad. It compelled respondents—among other things—to identify all persons who had made donations over a five-year period to Rhinehart and the Aquarian Foundation, together with the amounts donated. In effect the order would compel disclosure of membership as well as sources of financial support. The Supreme Court of Washington found that dissemination of this information would "result in annoyance, embarrassment and even oppression." It is sufficient for purposes of our decision that the highest court in the state found no abuse of discretion in the trial court's decision to issue a protective order pursuant to a constitutional state law. We therefore hold that where, as in this case, a protective order is entered on a showing of good cause as required by Rule 26(c), is limited to the context of pretrial civil discovery, and does not restrict the dissemination of the information if gained from other sources, it does not offend the First Amendment.

[Concurring opinion of JUSTICE BRENNAN omitted.]

Notes and Questions

1. The issue in this case is whether a court may prevent a party—here a newspaper—from disclosing information that it properly obtained through discovery. Concern about the First Amendment could arise whenever a litigant is prevented from revealing what it has learned through discovery. In In re Halkin, 598 F.2d 176 (D.C.Cir.1979), plaintiffs alleged that a number of governmental agencies, including the Central Intelligence Agency, had conducted illegal surveillance against them because they opposed the war in Viet Nam. Through discovery, plaintiffs obtained copies of documents relating to Operation Chaos, the CIA's program with regard to anti-war activities. After reviewing the documents, plaintiffs notified defendants that they intended to release several of them at a press conference. Defendants then obtained a protective order against such release from the district court on the ground that disclosure would endanger their right to a fair trial.

A divided panel of the court of appeals granted a writ of mandate overturning the protective order. The majority reasoned that "[t]he inherent value of speech in terms of its capacity for informing the public does not turn on how or where the information was acquired. Even where information has been stolen, New York Times Co. v. United States, 403 U.S. 713, 91 S.Ct. 2140, 29 L.Ed.2d 822 (1971), or retained in violation of a security agreement, United States v. Marchetti, 466 F.2d 1309, 1317 (4th Cir.1972), *cert. denied* 409 U.S. 1063, 93 S.Ct. 553, 34 L.Ed.2d 516, individuals who obtain such information have been held to have First Amendment rights in its dissemination. A party's right to disseminate information is far stronger for discovery materials than for information that has been stolen or obtained in breach of contract."

Does the Court in *Seattle Times* adequately respond to these arguments? It does emphasize that a party is not restricted by the protective order in making use of materials not obtained through the discovery process. How much consolation does this offer the newspapers? In other contexts, proving an independent source may prove exceedingly difficult. *Cf.* 5 W. LaFave, Search and Seizure § 11.4 (3d ed. 1996) (discussing proof of independent source in criminal cases where a Fourth Amendment violation is involved). Won't the protective order chill the newspapers' ability to print stories about the Foundation?

2. Professor Post finds that the Court's analysis "place[s] the Court at odds with a long line of precedents holding that the First Amendment deeply disfavors 'official discretionary power to control' speech in the absence of 'narrowly drawn, reasonable and definite standards for the officials to follow.'" Post, The Management of Speech, Discretion and Rights, 1984 Sup.Ct.Rev. 169, 179. Nevertheless, he concludes that the thrust of the case is actually elsewhere (id. at 196):

> [T]he crux of *Rhinehart* is neither the protection of privacy interests nor the diminishment of litigants' First Amendment interests, but rather the Court's perception that discretionary authority to issue restraining orders is essential for the administration of pretrial discovery. In this sense, the government's interests in restraining orders may be analogous to its interests in the management of other government institutions such as schools or prisons. These interests are quite different from those at stake when the government regulates the speech of the general public, as in the many cases where the Court has struck down discretionary authority to suppress speech.

3. After *Seattle Times,* how can umbrella protective orders be justified? Two answers seem possible:

First, if the order is entered by consent it would seem that all parties waived their First Amendment rights to the extent limited by the order.

Second, given the Court's emphasis on management of discovery, it may be that the interest in smooth discovery would suffice as good cause, and thus to satisfy any First Amendment concerns. As one court has noted, such orders "allow the parties to make full disclosure in discovery without fear of public access to sensitive information and without the expense and delay of protracted disputes over every item of sensitive information, thereby promoting the overriding goal of the Federal Rules of Civil Procedure, 'to secure the just, speedy, and inexpensive determination of every action.'" United Nuclear Corp. v. Cranford Ins. Co., 905 F.2d 1424, 1427 (10th Cir.1990), cert. denied, 498 U.S. 1073, 111 S.Ct. 799, 112 L.Ed.2d 860 (1991). How does the court determine whether such interests justify a protective order in a given case?

Is Rule 26(c) intended to serve such interests? One court asserted that "general concerns of trial administration" do not suffice to justify a protective order: "Rule 26(c), however, does not empower individual courts to make such policy decisions. The Rule allows a court to 'protect a party or person'—the focus is on injury to a specific individual, not on general concerns of case administration." Cipollone v. Liggett Group, Inc., 113 F.R.D. 86, 92 (D.N.J.1986), aff'd, 822 F.2d 335 (3d Cir.), cert. denied, 484 U.S. 976, 108 S.Ct. 487, 98 L.Ed.2d 485 (1987). Is this view consistent with the Supreme Court's attitude in *Seattle Times*?

4. Note that under Rule 26(c) one way for a court to avoid the harms that a protective order guards against is to refuse discovery altogether. For example, in Litton Indus., Inc. v. Chesapeake & Ohio Ry. Co., 129 F.R.D. 528 (E.D.Wis.1990), plaintiff claimed that defendants had excluded it from building ships in violation of the antitrust laws. To bolster its case on damages, it sought to force two nonparties to disclose financial data on their operations. Recognizing that the materials were relevant, the court nevertheless refused to order disclosure even subject to a protective order because "[t]here is a constant danger inherent in disclosure of confidential information pursuant to a protective order. Therefore, the party requesting disclosure must make a strong showing of need, especially when confidential information from a nonparty is sought." Id. at 531. Would this be a better reaction than the frequent granting of protective orders?

5. Is there a legitimate basis for objecting to publicizing lawsuits? Consider Koster v. Chase Manhattan Bank, 93 F.R.D. 471 (S.D.N.Y.1982), where plaintiff alleged she was fired for refusing sexual advances. After the suit was filed plaintiff was interviewed on three different television shows, and her attorney was interviewed on the radio. In addition, her story appeared in a number of newspapers under headlines such as the following: "No Sex, No Job, Woman Charges," "Bank Boss Forced Me To Have Sex," "Sexploited and Fired: Exec." and "I've Had It With Men." Defendant moved for a protective order against disclosure of material previously provided through discovery. Citing First Amendment concerns, the court denied the motion but warned that "the penchant of the plaintiff to try her case in the media may become a consideration in determining the scope of discovery to be afforded her." Is plaintiff's penchant relevant to the scope of discovery?

6. *Public trial:* Both constitutional and common law protections guarantee that trials be public. In a series of criminal cases, the Supreme Court has overturned the closure of the trial and certain pretrial events. In Globe Newspaper Co. v. Superior Court, 457 U.S. 596, 102 S.Ct. 2613, 73 L.Ed.2d 248 (1982), the Court explained that this right was based both on the historical openness of courts and on certain functional considerations:

> [T]he right of access to criminal trials plays a particularly significant role in the functioning of the judicial process and the government as a whole. Public scrutiny of a criminal trial enhances the quality and safeguards the integrity of the factfinding process, with benefits to both the defendant and to society as a whole. Moreover, public access to the criminal trial fosters an appearance of fairness, thereby heightening

public respect for the judicial process. And in the broadest terms, public access to criminal trials permits the public to participate in and serve as a check upon the judicial process—an essential component in our structure of self-government.

In *Seattle Times,* the Court announces that pretrial discovery is not a public component of a civil trial. Should this position be reconsidered given the increasingly important role discovery has come to play in civil litigation? Consider the views of the court in Mokhiber v. Davis, 537 A.2d 1100, 1112 (D.C.App.1988):

> [T]he public should enjoy the right to view new kinds of proceedings when they are like traditional ones in this significant respect: that access will serve the same values and policies which underlie the common law's recognition of the public right to view other parts of court procedure and which, indeed, are similar to those values and policies upon which asserted first amendment rights are justified. * * *
>
> The discovery process is clearly an important element of civil litigation. The manner in which it proceeds may prove decisive to the outcome of particular disputes, and the availability of mandatory discovery has greatly affected the way in which our courts do justice. Moreover, discovery procedures have become a continuing focus of controversy and reform within the judiciary and the legal community. This debate has arisen precisely because discovery is so important in trial practice. * * * We disagree with the view that "discovery proceedings are fundamentally different from proceedings to which the courts have recognized a public right of access."

Are these arguments persuasive? Consider the contrasting views of the court in Anderson v. Cryovac, Inc., 805 F.2d 1, 12 (1st Cir.1986):

> Nor does public access to the discovery process play a significant role in the administration of justice. Indeed, if such access were to be mandated, the civil discovery process might actually be made more complicated and burdensome than it already is. * * * The public's interest is in seeing that the process works and the parties are able to explore the issues without excessive waste or delay. But rather than facilitate an efficient and complete exploration of the facts and issues, a public right of access would unduly complicate the process.

For an effort to balance the confidentiality recognized by *Seattle Times* and public access to court proceedings, see Comment, The First Amendment and Pretrial Discovery Hearings: When Should the Public and Press Have Access?, 36 UCLA L.Rev. 609 (1989).

CHICAGO TRIBUNE CO. v. BRIDGE-STONE/FIRESTONE, INC.

United States Court of Appeals, Eleventh Circuit, 2001.
263 F.3d 1304.

Before BLACK, RONEY and COX, Circuit Judges.

PER CURIAM:

This is an appeal of the district court's order unsealing documents previously filed pursuant to a protective order entered by stipulation of the parties. See Fed.R.Civ.P. 26(c)(7). We vacate and remand with instructions for the district court to determine whether "good cause" exists for maintaining the documents under seal.

I. BACKGROUND

Daniel Van Etten, an eighteen-year old football player from West Virginia University, died as a result of injuries sustained in a roll-over automobile accident. In April of 1998, his parents filed suit in the Southern District of Georgia, claiming that Bridgestone/Firestone, Inc.'s negligent design and manufacture of the tires on Daniel's Ford Explorer were the proximate cause of his death. At the beginning of the litigation, in what has become commonplace in the federal courts, the parties stipulated to a protective order allowing each other to designate particular documents as confidential and subject to protection under Federal Rule of Civil Procedure 26(c)(7). See Fed.R.Civ.P. 26(c)(7). This method replaces the need to litigate the claim to protection document by document, and postpones the necessary showing of "good cause" required for entry of a protective order until the confidential designation is challenged. As the district court noted, this allowed Bridgestone/Firestone, Inc. (Firestone) to temporarily enjoy the protection of Rule 26(c), making Firestone's documents presumptively confidential until challenged.[2]

Consistent with local rule, documents produced pursuant to discovery requests were not filed with the court. The protective order required the parties filing confidential material with the court in connection with a pleading or motion to place the documents in a sealed, marked envelope. The documents were to be used only for preparation and conduct of the action, and only counsel, their paralegals and technical consultants, as well as the court and its staff, were privy to the content of any confidential document. Of the nearly three hundred documents filed in the action, fifteen were placed under seal.

Following discovery, Firestone moved for summary judgment. The district court denied the motion, and shortly thereafter the parties settled. In accordance with the terms of the protective order, the confidential documents remained sealed.

In the months following settlement, media scrutiny of tire tread separation accidents intensified, and members of the media, now appellees[3] (collectively, "the Press"), sought leave to intervene for the purpose of unsealing Firestone's documents. Firestone agreed to unseal some of the material, but objected to disclosure of nine documents and ten pages excerpted from legal briefs, claiming that these particular items contain trade secrets. In support of this claim, Firestone appended a privilege log

---

2. See Manual for Complex Litigation (Third) § 21.432 (1995) (noting that "[u]mbrella orders provide that all assertedly confidential material disclosed ... is presumptively protected unless challenged. The orders are made without a particularized showing to support the claim for pro- tection, but such a showing must be made whenever a claim under an order is challenged.").

3. Appellees are: the Chicago Tribune Company; the Washington Post Company; CBS Broadcasting, Inc.; and Los Angeles Times Communications, L.L.C.

and the affidavit of John Goudie, the Senior Product Engineer in Firestone's Product Analysis Department.

The district court granted the Press's motion to intervene as well as its consolidated motion to unseal the remaining documents, determining that the Goudie affidavit was too general and conclusory to carry Firestone's burden of showing "that the closure of the records filed with this Court is necessitated by a compelling interest and that the closure is narrowly tailored to that compelling interest." Accordingly, the district court ordered the documents unsealed, but, granting in part Firestone's motion to stay disclosure pending appeal, delayed the unsealing. We granted Firestone's emergency motion for a stay pending Firestone's appeal.

* * *

IV. DISCUSSION

Firestone's main contention is that the district court applied the wrong standard when it required Firestone to show that sealing the documents is necessitated by a compelling governmental interest and is narrowly tailored to that interest. Firestone argues for application of Rule 26's "good cause" standard, which balances the asserted right of access against the other party's interest in keeping the information confidential.

The Press argues that two sources supply a right of access to Firestone's documents, both requiring application of the standard used by the district court. The Press first relies on the common-law right to inspect and copy judicial records, a right grounded in the democratic process, as "[t]he operations of the courts and the judicial conduct of judges are matters of utmost public concern." Landmark Comm. v. Virginia, 435 U.S. 829, 839, 98 S.Ct. 1535, 1541, 56 L.Ed.2d 1 (1978). The Press argues that in cases concerning health and safety or where there is a particularly strong public interest in court records, the common-law right of access is measured by the compelling interest standard.

Additionally, the Press contends that there is a First Amendment right of access to court records and documents in civil cases. The Press cites Newman v. Graddick, 696 F.2d 796 (11th Cir.1983), for the proposition that the compelling interest standard applies to civil as well as criminal proceedings. Accordingly, the Press argues that whether the right of access is grounded in the common law or the Constitution, the compelling interest standard applies.

Because the parties' arguments concern three different bases for disclosure of the sealed documents, it is necessary for us to limn the bounds of the common-law right of access, the constitutional right of access, and Federal Rule of Civil Procedure 26(c). We consider first the constitutional right of access.

A. Constitutional Right of Access

The media and general public's First Amendment right of access to criminal trial proceedings [is] firmly established * * *. For a court to exclude the press and public from a criminal proceeding, "it must be shown that the denial is necessitated by a compelling governmental interest, and is narrowly tailored to serve that interest."

The constitutional right of access has a more limited application in the civil context than it does in the criminal. Nonetheless, this court has extended the scope of the constitutional right of access to include civil actions pertaining to the release or incarceration of prisoners and their confinement. [Newman v. Graddick, 696 F.2d 796 (11th Cir.1983).] Materials merely gathered as a result of the civil discovery process, however, do not fall within the scope of the constitutional right of access's compelling interest standard.

Public disclosure of discovery material is subject to the discretion of the trial court and the federal rules that circumscribe that discretion. See Seattle Times Co. v. Rhinehart, 467 U.S. 20, 33, 104 S.Ct. 2199, 2208, 81 L.Ed.2d 17. (1984). Where discovery materials are concerned, the constitutional right of access standard is identical to that of Rule 26(c) of the Federal Rules of Civil Procedure. Accordingly, where a third party seeks access to material disclosed during discovery and covered by a protective order, the constitutional right of access, like Rule 26, requires a showing of good cause by the party seeking protection.

The district court required Firestone to meet a compelling interest standard. To the extent this was predicated on a constitutional right of access, it was error. All of the documents were produced during the discovery phase of the litigation, and the protective order did not restrict the dissemination of information gained from other sources. As we later discuss more fully, the adequacy of Firestone's good cause showing remains to be determined upon remand; because the Rule 26 standard is identical, the resolution of that issue will necessarily decide the Press's constitutional right of access claim.

B. Common–Law Right of Access

The common-law right of access to judicial proceedings, an essential component of our system of justice, is instrumental in securing the integrity of the process. See Richmond Newspapers [v. Virginia], 448 U.S. at 564–74, 100 S.Ct. at 2821–26 (providing panegyric on the value of openness). Beyond establishing a general presumption that criminal and civil actions should be conducted publicly, the common-law right of access includes the right to inspect and copy public records and documents. Nixon v. Warner Comm., Inc., 435 U.S. 589, 597, 98 S.Ct. 1306, 1312, 55 L.Ed.2d 570 (1978). The right to inspect and copy is not absolute, however, and a judge's exercise of discretion in deciding whether to release judicial records should be informed by a "sensitive appreciation of the circumstances that led to ... [the] production [of the particular document in question]." Not unlike the Rule 26 standard, the common-law right of access requires a balancing of competing interests.

Although there is some disagreement about where precisely the line should be drawn, when applying the common-law right of access federal courts traditionally distinguish between those items which may properly be considered public or judicial records and those that may not; the media and public presumptively have access to the former, but not to the latter. An illustrative example is the treatment of discovery material, for which there is no common-law right of access, as these materials are neither public documents nor judicial records.

In certain narrow circumstances, the common-law right of access demands heightened scrutiny of a court's decision to conceal records from the public and the media. Where the trial court conceals the record of an entire case, making no distinction between those documents that are sensitive or privileged and those that are not, it must be shown that "the denial [of access] is necessitated by a compelling governmental interest, and is narrowly tailored to that interest." * * *

The common-law right of access standard as it applies to particular documents requires the court to balance the competing interests of the parties. We turn now to an examination of the documents at issue, and the context of the proceeding in which they were submitted to the court.

The Firestone documents were produced during discovery, but all of them were also filed with the court, under seal, in connection with pre-trial motions. Some of the documents were submitted to support motions to compel discovery; others were submitted to support summary judgment motions. Significantly, all the documents were submitted under seal, and all were submitted by the Van Ettens: Firestone did not submit the documents for judicial consideration.

The Press contends, and the district court agreed, that because the documents were filed with the court they are judicial records and therefore subject to the common-law right of access. Such an approach does not distinguish between material filed with discovery motions and material filed in connection with more substantive motions.[10] We think a more refined approach is called for, one that accounts both for the tradition favoring access, as well as the unique function discovery serves in modern proceedings. The better rule is that material filed with discovery motions is not subject to the common-law right of access, whereas discovery material filed in connection with pretrial motions that require judicial resolution of the merits is subject to the common-law right, and we so hold. This means that the Firestone documents filed in connection with motions to compel discovery are not subject to the common-law right of access.

10. We note that absent a contrary court order or local rule, the default rule under the Federal Rules of Civil Procedure is that discovery materials must be filed with the district court. See Fed.R.Civ.P. 5(d). The prospect of all discovery material being presumptively subject to the right of access would likely lead to an increased resistance to discovery requests.

Additionally, where a party has sought the protection of Rule 26, the fact that sealed material is subsequently submitted in connection with a substantive motion does not mean that the confidentiality imposed by Rule 26 is automatically forgone. Before disclosure is appropriate, a court must first conduct the common-law right of access balancing test. Because in this context the common-law right of access, like the constitutional right, requires the court to balance the respective interests of the parties, the Press's common-law right to the Firestone documents filed in connection with the motion for summary judgment may be resolved by the Rule 26 good cause balancing test. We turn next to a discussion of Rule 26.

C. *Federal Rule of Civil Procedure 26(c)*

Rule 26(c) permits a court upon motion of a party to make a protective order requiring "that a trade secret or other confidential research, development, or commercial information not be revealed or be revealed only in a designated way." Fed.R.Civ.P. 26(c)(7). The prerequisite is a showing of "good cause" made by the party seeking protection. Federal courts have superimposed a balancing of interests approach for Rule 26's good cause requirement. This standard requires the district court to balance the party's interest in obtaining access against the other party's interest in keeping the information confidential.

Since the confidential designation was not challenged until the Press intervened, Firestone's Response to Intervenors' Motion to Unseal is the document that must establish good cause for continued protection under Rule 26. Although the district court discusses the adequacy of Firestone's Response in the order unsealing Firestone's documents, we do not find a determination by the district court that the request for a protective order was not supported by good cause. Because this conclusion is necessary to a resolution of the matter, we must remand to the district court for a determination of whether good cause exists for a protective order under Rule 26.

The first question that must be addressed on remand is whether Firestone's presumptively confidential documents do in fact contain trade secrets. Firestone argues that the sealed documents meet all of the commonly accepted criteria that define this category. These criteria require that Firestone must have consistently treated the information as closely guarded secrets, that the information represents substantial value to Firestone, that it would be valuable to Firestone's competitors, and that it derives its value by virtue of the effort of its creation and lack of dissemination.[13] Firestone argues that the Goudie affidavit and privilege log established each of these criteria.

---

13. See Ruckelshaus v. Monsanto Co., 467 U.S. 986, 1001, 104 S.Ct. 2862, 2872, 81 L.Ed.2d 815 (1984) (noting that Restatement of Torts defines a trade secret as "any formula, pattern, device or compilation of information which is used in one's business, and which gives him an opportunity to obtain an advantage over competitors who do not know or use it"); Unif. Trade Secrets Act § 1(4), 14 U.L.A. 438 (1985) (defining "trade secret" as "information, including a formula, pattern, compilation, program, de-

* * * Because trade secret status is the only basis Firestone provides for nondisclosure, should the district court conclude that Firestone's documents do not fall within this category, good cause does not support the protective order, and the documents may be unsealed.

Should the district court determine that these documents do in fact contain trade secrets, the district court must balance Firestone's interest in keeping the information confidential against the Press's contention that disclosure serves the public's legitimate interest in health and safety. In its order the district court stated that "[e]ven assuming that the sealed material could be classified as trade secrets, concerns of public health and safety trump any right to shield such material from public scrutiny." The district court made no factual findings, however, that support the conclusion that the public's health and safety are sufficiently impacted by the information contained in these specific documents to trump Firestone's interest in keeping trade secret information confidential.[15] See generally Ruckelshaus v. Monsanto Co., 467 U.S. 986, 104 S.Ct. 2862, 81 L.Ed.2d 815 (1984) (discussing takings of proprietary trade secret information and attendant Fifth Amendment implications). Because whether good cause exists for a protective order is a factual matter to be decided by the nature and character of the information in question, this determination, supported by findings of fact, must be conducted upon remand.

BLACK, Circuit Judge, specially concurring:

I concur fully in the Court's holding regarding the press's rights under the Constitution, the common law, and Fed.R.Civ.P. 26(c). I write separately to express my concern about third parties—who have no cause of action before the court—using the discovery process as a means to unearth documents to which they otherwise would have no right to inspect and copy.

This Court has previously commented:

vice, method, technique, or process, that: (i) derives independent economic value, actual or potential, from not being generally known to, and not being readily ascertainable by proper means by, other persons who can obtain economic value from its disclosure or use, and (ii) is the subject of efforts that are reasonable under the circumstances to maintain its secrecy").

15. We also note that the district court did not discuss Firestone's reliance on the terms of the stipulated protective order. As we noted in United States v. Anderson, 799 F.2d 1438 (11th Cir.1986), agreements to treat certain materials voluntarily produced during discovery as confidential facilitate the discovery process: "[l]itigants should not be discouraged from putting their discovery agreements in writing, and district judges should not be discouraged from facilitating voluntary discovery." This is particularly the case where the party filing the

presumptively confidential discovery material with the court is not the party claiming confidentiality, but that party's adversary, as is the case here. As the District of Columbia Court of Appeals noted in Mokhiber v. Davis, 537 A.2d 1100 (D.C.App.1988), "[b]y submitting pleadings and motions to the court for decision, one enters the public arena of courtroom proceedings and exposes oneself . . . to the risk . . . of public scrutiny." The assumption is that one voluntarily foregoes confidentiality when one submits material for dispute resolution in a judicial forum. There is no voluntariness, of course, where one's adversary submits the presumptively confidential material. On remand, the district court should consider the fact that Firestone has exhibited behavior consistent with its claim of reliance in connection with the good cause balancing test.

Discovery, whether civil or criminal, is essentially a private process because the litigants and the courts assume that the *sole purpose* of discovery is to assist trial preparation. That is why parties regularly agree, and courts often order, that discovery information will remain private.

If it were otherwise and discovery information and discovery orders were readily available to the public and the press, the consequences to the smooth functioning of the discovery process would be severe. Not only would voluntary discovery be chilled, but whatever discovery and court encouragement that would take place would be oral, which is undesirable to the extent that it creates misunderstanding and surprise for the litigants and the trial judge.

United States v. Anderson, 799 F.2d 1438, 1441 (11th Cir.1986). Simply stated, the purpose of discovery is to resolve legal disputes between parties, not to provide newsworthy material.

To facilitate prompt discovery and the timely resolution of disputes, this Court has upheld the use of umbrella protective orders similar to the one used in this case. In these cases, we did not permit the media to challenge each and every document protected by the umbrella order. Instead, the media was permitted only to challenge the umbrella order as being too broad, based on a variety of factors. We have restricted the scope of the media's challenge because a document-by-document approach would not only burden the trial court, but, more importantly, it would interfere with the free flow of information during discovery.[3] Such interference by parties who have no interest in the underlying litigation could seriously impair an Article III court from carrying out its core function—resolving cases and controversies.

In light of the strong interest in having unimpeded discovery, third parties may be barred from accessing documents even when the documents are not protected by a privilege (like the trade-secret privilege), as long as the umbrella order itself meets the good cause requirement. Here, however, the Court concludes that "trade secret status is the only basis Firestone provides for nondisclosure...." Therefore, absent a showing that the challenged documents are trade secrets, "good cause does not support the [umbrella] order, and the documents may be unsealed." Id. (footnote omitted). In some future case, however, a party may argue that, although the individual documents fail to qualify as privileged material, they nonetheless should be sealed because the umbrella order is necessary to facilitate the free flow of information and thus satisfies the good cause requirement. Since the Court has concluded that Firestone has not adequately preserved this argument, I concur in its holding.

3. In this case, the litigation has ceased, and therefore the press is not disrupting an active discovery proceeding. Nonetheless, the free flow of information will cease if parties resist entering umbrella orders because they fear such orders could be subject to document-by-document, post-judgment attacks.

Notes and Questions

1. Is the information subject to the protective order in this case of greater or lesser public interest than the information involved in *Seattle Times*? Compare Cipollone v. Liggett Group, 785 F.2d 1108 (3d Cir.1986), cert. denied, 484 U.S. 976, 108 S.Ct. 487, 98 L.Ed.2d 485 (1987), in which the appellate court reversed the district court's decision to release all discovery in litigation over tobacco, and directed the district judge to determine whether there was good cause for vacating a protective order. On remand, the judge found that defendants had failed to establish good cause:

> Discovery may well reveal that a product is defective and its continued use dangerous to the consuming public. The public disclosure of that information will certainly embarrass that party and cause it financial loss. It is inconceivable to this court that under such circumstances the public interest is not a vital factor to be considered in determining whether to further conceal that information, and whether a court should be a party to that concealment.

Cipollone v. Liggett Group, Inc., 113 F.R.D. 86 (D.N.J.1986), aff'd, Cipollone v. Liggett Group, Inc., 822 F.2d 335 (3d Cir.1987).

Should litigation be viewed as a method to uncover risks? Can judges determine whether discovered information really indicates that there is a public risk involved in a case? Note the views of Judge Black in *Chicago Tribune* that discovery is essentially a private process. Should it be? For discussion of this point, see Morrison, Protective Orders, Plaintiffs, Defendants and the Public Interest in Disclosure: Where Does the Balance Lie?, 24 U.Rich.L.Rev. 109 (1989) (arguing for judicial involvement in determining whether confidential information implicates public interest); Marcus, The Discovery Confidentiality Controversy, 1991 U.Ill.L.Rev. 457 (criticizing broad public access approach); Miller, Confidentiality, Protective Orders, and Public Access to the Courts, 105 Harv.L.Rev. 427 (1991).

Contrast Newman v. Graddick, 696 F.2d 796 (11th Cir.1983), a class action by inmates in the Alabama prisons challenging overcrowding. After a consent decree was entered but overcrowding worsened, the district court directed prison officials to submit lists of prisoners "least deserving of further incarceration," with an eye to possibly directing the release of specific prisoners to reduce crowding. Two newspapers sought to obtain copies of the lists, and the appellate court reversed the district judge's refusal to permit access. Should this issues involved in *Chicago Tribune* be considered comparable? Note that the litigation involved the operation of a public facility, and the materials were being considered by a judge in connection with a possible order to release specific prisoners before they had completed their sentences. See Marcus, Myth and Reality in Protective Order Litigation, 69 Cornell L. Rev. 1, 50–52 (1983) (discussing the public interest in governmental acts).

2. If it is important that there is a public interest in the discovered information in *Chicago Tribune*, should that lead to disclosure only of the materials filed in court under seal? Note that the Rule 26(c) is in no sense limited to materials filed in court. Should all discovery materials be treated as equally available to the public as those filed in court? Many courts have seemed to think so: "It is well-established that the fruits of pre-trial

discovery are, in the absence of a court order to the contrary, presumptively public. Rule 26(c) authorizes a district court to override this presumption when 'good cause' is shown." San Jose Mercury News, Inc. v. United States District Court, 187 F.3d 1096, 1103 (9th Cir.1999). Is this view consistent with the purpose of discovery? Would Judge Black, who concurred in *Chicago Tribune*, agree with it?

Note that the court in *Chicago Tribune* invokes Fed.R.Civ.P. 5(d), saying that discovery materials should usually be filed. But that was never true of documents obtained by Rule 34 requests, and in 2000 Rule 5(d) was amended to forbid filing of all discovery materials until they are "used in the proceeding." In S.E.C. v. TheStreet.com, 273 F.3d 222 (2d Cir.2001), the court dealt with an argument that the Federal Rules create a "statutory right of access to discovery materials," and noted that "the recent amendment to [Rule 5(d)] provides no presumption of filing of all discovery materials, let alone public access to them. Indeed, the rule now *prohibits* the filing of certain discovery materials unless they are used in the proceeding or the court orders filing." Id. at 233 n. 11. Although the good cause requirement would appear to apply to restrictions on a party's use of materials obtained through discovery, as in *Seattle Times*, it may be that the notion that others have a right to obtain access to these materials will abate.

3. Some states have embraced the public access approach to discovery. The Florida "Sunshine in Litigation Act," Fla.Stats. § 69.081, provides in part as follows:

(2) As used in this section, "public hazard" means an instrumentality, including but not limited to any device, instrument, person, procedure, product, or a condition of a device, instrument, person, procedure or product, that has caused or is likely to cause injury.

(3) Except pursuant to this section [requiring a noticed motion and hearing at which any interested person may be heard], no court shall enter an order or judgment which has the purpose or effect of concealing a public hazard or any information concerning a public hazard, nor shall the court enter an order or judgment which has the purpose or effect of concealing any information which may be useful to members of the public in protecting themselves from injury which may result from the public hazard.

Similarly, Texas Rule of Civil Procedure 76a provides that "court records" are open to the general public, and treats unfiled discovery as a "court record" if it contains "matters that have a probable adverse effect upon the general public health or safety." How could a court make a determination about these issues regarding materials inspected in discovery but never filed in court? Similar proposed legislation has been introduced in Congress. See, e.g., Sunshine in Litigation Act of 2003, S. 817, 108th Cong. See generally Rooks, Let The Sun Shine In, Trial, June 2003, at 26 (arguing that the evidence shows that sunshine does not chill settlements).

4. Should courts take the initiative in dealing with possible public hazards? In Wyeth Laboratories v. U.S. District Court, 851 F.2d 321 (10th Cir.1988), the trial court entered judgment for plaintiff in a suit claiming injuries due to DTP, a vaccine manufactured by defendant. Plaintiff thereupon moved to vacate the stipulated protective order to permit use of

discovered material in other litigation. The trial court granted the motion, but went beyond that and directed that a "Wyeth Laboratory DTP Vaccine Litigation Discovery Library" be established at the courthouse to house information developed in this case and other cases as well. He explained that this facility would assist in the preparation of other cases, and expressed the hope that it would have wider use:

> [B]ecause the trial record of this case will be of interest to researchers, academics, institutions, consumer groups, members of the medical profession or associations, private or governmental, legal associations such as the ATLA and/or Defense Research Institute, and even law students, all in the interest of stimulating scientific and/or public discourse or learning regarding whooping cough vaccinations and their ramifications, they are all welcomed here.

Graham v. Wyeth Laboratories, 118 F.R.D. 511, 514 (D.Kan.1988). Although sympathetic to the district court's motivations, the court of appeals directed that the order creating the library be vacated because the district court had no jurisdiction to create such a facility. See 851 F.2d at 324.

5. If public disclosure should not be presumptively allowed, should sharing for litigation purposes be fostered? In Cipollone v. Liggett Group, Inc., *supra* note 1, plaintiffs argued that "defendants' real purpose [in seeking protective order restrictions] was to make it impossible for plaintiffs in other suits against the cigarette companies to share information gathered from the defendants. The defendants' strategy, said plaintiffs, was to raise the expense of litigation for future plaintiffs, thus making the cost of suits prohibitive." Some view sharing of discovered information among plaintiff lawyers as essential to redress imbalances between the plaintiffs and defense sides:

> In sharp contrast to the resources of the defendant-manufacturer are those of the typical plaintiff's attorney. Plaintiffs' attorneys generally practice in groups of three or less. Furthermore, plaintiffs' attorneys generally are not familiar with the defendant's product nor do they have the unlimited access to experts who are familiar with the product. For this reason, plaintiffs' attorneys have formed cooperative discovery mechanisms similar to those of defendant-manufacturers that facilitate the exchange of information.

Hare, Gilbert & Ellenberger, Confidentiality Orders in Products Liability Cases, 13 Am.J.Trial Advocacy 597, 599 (1989).

Some courts view cooperation among counsel as a proper ground for disclosure. E.g., Deford v. Schmid Products Co., 120 F.R.D. 648, 654 (D.Md. 1987) ("The plaintiffs' primary argument in favor of disclosure is their desire to share information with other litigants and their counsel. This is an appropriate goal under the Federal Rules of Civil Procedure"). Compare Poliquin v. Garden Way, Inc., 154 F.R.D. 29 (D.Me.1994) (counsel for plaintiff in a product liability action violated a protective order by advising co-counsel in a similar case against the same defendant to contact the court reporter to obtain a copy of a deposition). If sharing is a valid goal, should the court allow counsel to advertise the fruits of the discovery campaign and charge those who wish access? See Note, Seattle Times: What Effect on Discovery Sharing, 1985 Wis.L.Rev. 1055, 1058 ("Almost always, litigants must pay for the previously discovered information"); Note, Mass Products Liability Litigation: A Proposal for Dissemination of Discovered Material Covered by a Protective Order, 60 N.Y.U.L.Rev. 1137, 1158 (1985) ("Successful marketing of discovery materials will require advertising."). The sample order in the Manual for Complex Litigation (4th) § 40.27 (2004) includes a provision that would permit confidential discovered information from one action to be used in other related litigation.

6. In *Chicago Tribune*, the court emphasizes that the only ground put forward for protection under Rule 26(c) was that the items in question were trade secrets. How readily can a court determine whether something is a genuine trade secret? Trade secret is "at best a nebulous concept which * * * is somewhat incapable of definition," Kodekey Elecs., Inc. v. Mechanex Corp., 486 F.2d 449, 453–54 n. 3 (10th Cir.1973), and "[t]he subject matter that has been awarded trade secret protection can be extraordinarily broad." Klitzke, Trade Secrets: Important Quasi–Property Right, 41 Bus. Law. 555, 558 (1986). Would the materials in *Seattle Times* be viewed as trade secrets? Compare the information involved in Zenith Radio Corp. v. Matsushita Elec. Indus. Co., *supra* pp. 572-74, which would reveal that defendants had made more favorable deals with some customers than with others. Assuming that is confidential and important information, should courts prevent parties from revealing it?

Note that Rule 26(c)(7) goes beyond trade secrets and includes "other confidential research, development or commercial information." That is not the limit of the court's power to grant protective orders: "Although courts may be more likely to grant protective orders for the information listed in Rule 26(c)(7), courts have consistently granted protective orders that prevent disclosure or many types of information." Phillips ex rel. Estate of Byrd v. General Motors Corp., 307 F.3d 1206, 1212 (9th Cir.2002). In *Phillips*, the appellate court vacated the district judge's decision not to provide protection for a confidential settlement agreement because the district judge seemed unaware that Rule 26 would permit that protection.

7. In her concurring opinion, Judge Black emphasizes facilitating "prompt discovery" and cautions against stimulating producing parties to resist entering umbrella orders rather than insisting on document-by-document review of allegedly sensitive items. If parties are obligated to provide discovery, why should these factors matter? Recall the reaction of the judge in Zenith Radio Corp. v. Matsushita Elec. Indus. Co., *supra* pp. 572-74, to reviewing tens of thousands of documents.

8. Could there be constitutional difficulties were courts to order discovery without providing protective orders? It has been argued that, when a party is required to provide discovery of information that it is in the business of selling, the discovery works an unconstitutional taking without compensation. See Gelfand, "Taking" Informational Property Through Discovery, 66 Wash.U.L.Rev. 703 (1988). Consider, for example, the formula for Coca–Cola. Could a court order that formula produced through discovery without a protective order limiting dissemination? Cf. Coca–Cola Bottling Co. v. Coca–Cola Co., 107 F.R.D. 288 (D.Del.1985) (court ordered discovery of formula subject to strict limitations on disclosure). With regard to other information, however, Professor Gelfand sees a protective order as the solution to the

constitutional problem: "a typical trade secret * * * may likewise be disclosed during litigation under suitable protective orders and not be 'taken' by disclosure." Gelfand, *supra,* at 708.

9. If material covered by a protective order is disclosed, the aggrieved party may even sue. In Westinghouse Elec. Corp. v. Newman & Holtzinger, 39 Cal.App.4th 1194, 46 Cal.Rptr.2d 151 (1995), the court held that no tort or contract claim was stated based on allegations of a conspiracy to reveal materials covered by a protective order. In an earlier suit in federal court, defendants had acted as counsel for a party suing plaintiff and had stipulated to a protective order that limited disclosure of materials deemed confidential. In violation of that order, plaintiff alleged, they revealed these materials to others who promptly sued plaintiff on the basis of the contents and thereby caused plaintiff to incur substantial litigation expenses. Plaintiff sued the lawyers for damages, attempting to state both tort and contract claims. The court rejected the contract claim because violation of a protective order does not give rise to such a claim even if the order was based on prior consent to entry of the order. The court could "conceive of situations in which wrongful disclosure of information covered by a protective order could be both a discovery violation and a tort," such as disclosure of a trade secret or of intimate and embarrassing facts about a party. But this could not be true, it concluded, where the only alleged harm is that other parties filed lawsuits based on the confidential materials. Indeed, plaintiff did not even claim that the suits lacked merit.

E. PRESERVING PRIVILEGE PROTECTION

A large part of the litigator's time and energy is spent asserting and preserving privilege claims. In complex litigation, the difficulties of protecting privilege may increase enormously as larger amounts of information are involved. We proceed from the assumption that the general contours of privilege law come from other courses; our primary focus is the loss of that protection due to waiver in some form. The main privileges that litigators worry about are the attorney-client privilege and the work product doctrine. The former depends on satisfying a somewhat elaborate definition. The Supreme Court has said in a different context that it should be available when "[a]pplication of the attorney-client privilege * * * puts the adversary in no worse position than if the communications had never taken place." Upjohn Co. v. United States, 449 U.S. 383, 101 S.Ct. 677, 66 L.Ed.2d 584 (1981). Arguably that same attitude could inform decisions about whether to rule that a waiver has occurred. The work product doctrine, now partly codified in Rule 26(b)(3), covers a wide variety of litigation preparation activities by lawyers and others.

A few additional observations about privileges are in order to introduce the topic. First, Rule 26(b)(5) requires that claims of privilege be made with sufficient specificity to enable other parties to assess the applicability of the privilege. Failure to do so may vitiate privilege protection. Second, under Fed. R. Evid. 501, privilege issues are governed by state law as to substantive issues governed by state law, but otherwise federal common law of waiver applies. Third, owing to the large number of "clients" in class actions, the privilege protection may be very broad but also, in some ways, less confining. Thus, in Parker v. Anderson, *supra* p. 511, class counsel could submit privileged materials to the court reviewing the proposed settlement to counter assertions by former class representatives about whether the settlement should be approved.

Throughout discovery and trial preparation, litigators need to be conscious of preserving privilege protection. We focus on four recurrent scenarios that pose risks of waiver of privilege protection: (1) Disclosure of privileged material to an adversary; (2) disclosure of privileged material to a non-adversary; (3) use of privileged material in witness preparation; and (4) putting privileged material into issue. For an argument that in each of these situations a fairness standard should be used to determine whether there has been a waiver, see Marcus, The Perils of Privilege: Waiver and the Litigator, 84 Mich.L.Rev. 1605, 1627–48 (1986).

By way of background, it is important to appreciate two propositions about classical waiver doctrine. First, waiver is not limited to the privileged item that has been disclosed. Instead, it usually is said to extend to all privileged matters dealing with the same *subject matter*. Second, waiver extends to *the entire world*. Thus, disclosure to one person may operate as a waiver of the right to assert the waived privilege against any adversary. With these features of waiver doctrine in mind, examine the circumstances in which waiver may occur.

TRANSAMERICA COMPUTER CO. v. INTERNATIONAL BUSINESS MACHINES CORP.

United States Court of Appeals, Ninth Circuit, 1978.
573 F.2d 646.

Before WATERMAN, CARTER and KENNEDY, CIRCUIT JUDGES.

WATERMAN, CIRCUIT JUDGE.

On this interlocutory appeal brought pursuant to 28 U.S.C. § 1292(b) we are required to address the narrow issue of whether defendant-appellee International Business Machines Corporation ("IBM"), by virtue of its inadvertent production of certain documents in accelerated discovery proceedings in a prior unrelated antitrust lawsuit in which it was a defendant, has waived its right to claim here that those documents are privileged and therefore not discoverable by plaintiff-appellant Transamerica Computer Company, Inc. ("TCC"). The district court below held that under the circumstances in that prior antitrust case there had been no waiver by IBM. We affirm.

On October 5, 1973 TCC commenced the present private antitrust action against IBM by filing a complaint in the United States District Court for the Northern District of California. Pursuant to an order of the Judicial Panel on Multidistrict Litigation, TCC's antitrust suit was consolidated with six other similar suits which had been instituted against IBM. As part of its pretrial discovery, TCC requested that IBM produce numerous documents, and these documents included a group which the parties have designated, and which have come to be known as, the "JJ documents." Although IBM produced those portions of these documents which it believed were not privileged, IBM refused to comply with TCC's request that the documents be produced in their entirety, principally justifying its refusal on the grounds that the documents being withheld were protected by either the attorney-client privilege or the attorney's work product doctrine.[1] Following this refusal, TCC sought, pursuant to Rule 37(a) of the Federal Rules of Civil Procedure, an order from the district court compelling the production of the portions of the JJ documents which had been withheld by IBM. In support of its request that IBM be compelled to produce the withheld documents, TCC took the position that, even assuming arguendo that the documents had, in fact, been privileged when originally prepared, IBM had waived its right to rely upon the privilege as it had produced these very documents to Control Data Corporation in the antitrust action previously brought by that corporation against IBM (*Control Data Corporation v. International Business Machines Corporation*, Doc. No. 3–68 Civ. 312 (D.Minn.)) (The "CDC case"). The district court below, McNichols, J., denied TCC's motion, "find[ing] that the JJ documents were produced in connection with accelerated discovery proceedings [in the CDC case] wherein the Presiding Judge sought and intended to protect the parties against assertions of waiver." * * *

It is critical to our disposition of this appeal that we describe the unique circumstances under which IBM produced the so-called JJ documents in the CDC litigation. On October 19, 1970 United States District Judge Philip Neville of the U.S. District Court for the District of Minnesota, who was overseeing the pretrial proceedings in that case, issued a pretrial order which dramatically accelerated the document inspection program which had been in progress there. The effect of the order was to require IBM to produce within a three-month period for inspection and for adversary copying approximately 17 million pages of documents. To say the least, the logistical problems confronting IBM were monumental and were exacerbated by a number of factors. For example, the documents which CDC sought to have IBM produce for inspection had not been produced during any previous litigation and they were not grouped or batched together so as to be readily accessible.

---

1. IBM claims that the documents at issue are protected by either the attorney-client privilege or by the attorney's work product doctrine. While there is an important distinction between the rules governing when each type of protection has been waived, this distinction is unimportant here where the third person to whom the disclosure was made, a disclosure supposedly resulting in a waiver, was IBM's adversary in litigation. Thus, if IBM's inadvertent production of documents in the prior antitrust lawsuit constituted a waiver of the attorney-client privilege, under the circumstances it also resulted in a waiver of the protection of the work product doctrine. In this opinion, therefore, we shall loosely refer to both as either the "privilege" or "the attorney-client privilege."

Most of the documents were particularly difficult to screen for privilege, for they were letters and memoranda contained in myriad headquarters-type files randomly strewn throughout various IBM branch offices and divisional headquarters.

To achieve compliance with the court's onerous production order, while at the same time seeking to preserve all its rights of privilege, IBM mounted a herculean effort to review and produce the material which had been requested. Inasmuch as much of the material was only partially privileged it was necessary that each and every one of the 17 million pages be carefully examined. In view of this fact, and because time was short and the amount of material to be produced so incredibly voluminous, IBM was compelled to seek assistance from outside attorneys unfamiliar with IBM's business or with the specifics of this particular lawsuit and to employ outside clerical help who lacked the motivation or the competence that full-time IBM employees would normally be expected to possess. Despite expedited training given to these outside personnel, the extensive use of workers who had been previously unfamiliar with the case obviously increased the risk that privileged material would be accidentally produced, and the probability that this might occur necessitated an additional IBM review of the material being examined by the outside help. This supplemental review was needed not only to prevent inadvertent production of privileged material but also to insure that documents which the outside reviewers had preliminarily classified as privileged documents were, in fact, properly withholdable by IBM. Furthermore, the existence of a substantial amount of material only partially privileged meant not only that every one of the 17 million pages had to be assiduously inspected, but also that, once partially privileged material was discovered, a cumbersome masking process had to be employed so that the unprivileged, properly discoverable portions of each document could be produced in compliance with the district court's production order. These logistical difficulties confronting IBM in the CDC case were further exacerbated by the fact that at the very time IBM was being compelled to produce the documents to CDC, it was also being compelled to produce the same documents to the United States Department of Justice in the gargantuan civil suit instituted by the United States against IBM in the United States District Court for the Southern District of New York.

In order to comply with the order compelling production, while at the same time doing all it possibly could do to preserve its right to withhold privileged documents, IBM attempted, in the minimal amount of time available to it, to develop effective screening procedures. In an affidavit submitted in support of IBM's motion in the CDC case for an order determining that under the unique circumstances there, any inadvertent production by IBM of certain allegedly privileged documents did not constitute a waiver of the privilege, Frederick A.O. Schwarz, Jr., a member of one of the law firms representing IBM, succinctly described "the various steps [taken by IBM], from initial review through [ultimate] production":

(a) The responsive files of 103 executives, 60 departments and other miscellaneous files had to be found in the files of 30 Branch Offices, 1 District Office, 5 Regional Headquarters, 1 Plant, Corporate Headquarters, Data Processing Group Headquarters, Data Processing Division Headquarters, Systems Development Division Headquarters, and World Trade Headquarters;

(b) Over 17 million pages had each to be separately turned by the reviewers, page by page;

(c) Once a page is turned over, it must be examined to determine if it may be privileged or partially privileged;

(d) Once a document is found which may be privileged, it must be (i) removed from its original file folder, (ii) placed in a specially colored green folder, and (iii) that folder must be turned up on end within the original folder to enable a clerk to see it in the box or file receptacle;

(e) Once that is done, a clerk must then (i) find and remove the green folder from the box of producible documents, and (ii) make certain that the green folder has the box number, folder name, etc., information to associate it with its source;

(f) The material in a green folder must then be re-reviewed by a more experienced lawyer (i) to determine if it is in fact privileged or partially privileged, and (ii) if partially privileged to indicate which material is partially privileged and which must then be blocked out (masked) by placing a strip of paper over the partially privileged material and then preparing a Xerox copy for reinsertion in the file and production to the plaintiffs;

(g)(i) The material found not to be privileged at all must then be placed back in the original file folder; (ii) the partially privileged material is then placed in another (blue colored) folder within the green folder with instructions for masking, and (iii) the wholly privileged material is passed on to another group required to fill out logs pursuant to the Court's Order;

(h)(i) The nonprivileged material is then removed and returned to the box of producible material, and (ii) the partially privileged material must be removed, masked and then returned for production.

Not surprisingly, after this process had been in effect for a short time, IBM realized that, despite its intensive screening efforts, a small number of privileged documents were evading detection by its reviewers and were slipping through the filtering net. In an attempt to prevent any further instances of such accidental production, an attorney characterized as the "interceptor" was placed by IBM in the room where CDC was inspecting the documents. His function, as his imposing appellation suggests, was to review all documents selected by CDC for copying and then to withhold from those so selected any privileged documents which the IBM reviewers had overlooked. CDC objected to the presence of this so-called "interceptor" and sought from the district court an order requiring his removal. Pursuant to CDC's request, a hearing was held on November 2, 1970 at which time Judge Neville ruled that the interceptor should be removed. More important, however, was the judge's contemporaneous ruling that henceforth the inadvertent production of allegedly privileged material by either party would not constitute a waiver of that party's right to claim the attorney-client privilege, provided only that the party disclaiming waiver had continued to employ procedures reasonably designed to screen out privileged material. Prior to November 2, CDC had procured 24 documents which IBM claimed were either completely or partially privileged and Judge Neville expressly reserved ruling on the question of whether IBM had waived any privilege it might have for these 24 documents.

Incredibly, IBM met the court's three-month production demand, and, in so complying, notwithstanding the previously described extensive screening procedures which resulted in the withholding of about 491,000 pages of documents, a relatively small number, 1138 (approximately 5800 pages) of supposedly privileged documents were inadvertently produced to CDC. These are the so-called "JJ documents."

The final significant event in the CDC case was an order issued by Judge Neville on April 18, 1972. The judge, noting that his ruling of November 2, 1970 had left open the question of the privileged status of any documents turned over to the opposing party prior to that date, now addressed that question, and, as well, the broader question of whether claims of privilege had been preserved for any documents produced at any time during the three-month period of accelerated discovery. Observing that "[c]ertain confusion and errors were bound to result in such a strenuous program," the judge ruled that all claims of privilege were preserved for documents produced prior to November 2, 1970 as well as for those produced after that date, and this preservation of privilege would be lost only if the parties had failed to employ reasonable screening techniques.

Turning now to the legal theory upon which this important case must be decided, we note first of all that the parties initially address the issue of whether a party having no subjective intention of waiving the attorney-client privilege may nonetheless waive that privilege if he produces privileged documents which he would not have produced had he realized their privileged status. In support of its position that under such circumstances there would be no waiver, IBM directs our attention to cases which IBM claims stand for the proposition that mere "inadvertent" production of privileged documents does not constitute a waiver of the privilege. TCC, on the other hand, adverting to cases such as *Underwater Storage, Inc. v. United States Rubber Co.,* 314 F.Supp. 546, 549 (D.D.C.1970), argues that, although under *Johnson v. Zerbst,* 304 U.S. 458, 58 S.Ct. 1019, 82 L.Ed. 1461 (1938), a party certainly cannot effectively waive a *constitutional* right without knowledge on his part that he possesses such a right, the attorney-client privilege, being "a mere evidentiary privilege," is so easily waived that it may be waived by a party who, though not desiring to waive the privilege, nonetheless voluntarily produces or allows examination of privileged documents because at the moment he produces them he is unaware that they are, in fact, privileged documents.

We do not decide, however, whether this sort of "inadvertent" disclosure constitutes a waiver of the attorney-client privilege, for we believe that this case is properly decided upon the basis of a legal principle upon which the parties are in complete accord. Specifically, IBM asserts, and TCC concedes, that a party does not waive the attorney-client privilege for documents which he is *compelled* to produce. Of course, despite this accord, the parties are in sharp disagreement over the result which should obtain when this legal principle is applied to the circumstances surrounding IBM's inadvertent production of privileged documents in the CDC case. IBM urges that under the rather extraordinary circumstances of the accelerated discovery proceedings in that case IBM's inadvertent production there of a limited number of privileged documents was, in effect, "compelled," and therefore no waiver of the privilege could be predicated upon such involuntary production. We agree.

* * *

Despite this general acceptance of the principle that waiver cannot result from compelled production, we have not found any case, other than the CDC case, which has considered the precise issue of whether de facto compulsion can result from the imposition of an extremely rigorous schedule for discovery. TCC, while conceding that "Judge Neville ordered IBM to produce a large number of documents to CDC in a relatively short time" and that "the volume of document production in the CDC case was unusually high," nonetheless strenuously maintains that, inasmuch as "he did not order IBM to produce documents which it considered privileged," Judge Neville did not "compel" IBM to produce the JJ documents. TCC further warns that the federal courts will be engulfed in a flood of collateral litigation should we hold that the inadvertent production of a privileged document in the context of accelerated discovery proceedings does not constitute a waiver of the privilege. To be sure, such a possibility exists. We think it fairly remote, however, for we are convinced that the accelerated discovery proceedings in the CDC litigation represent what is probably a truly exceptional and a unique situation. Having reviewed those proceedings, we experience no difficulty in holding, as we do here, that there the document inspection program imposed such incredible burdens on IBM that it would be disingenuous for us to say that IBM was not, in a very practical way, "compelled" to produce privileged documents which it certainly would have withheld and would not have produced had the discovery program proceeded under a less demanding schedule. This is not to say that Judge Neville did not have the authority under Fed.R.Civ.P. 26(c) to require that discovery proceed at such a strenuous pace. There are, however, limits upon the power of the district court to accelerate pretrial discovery, and it may well be that a demanding discovery schedule of the sort imposed by Judge Neville would be an unreasonable exercise of the district court's discretion unless it was, as it was there, coupled with an express preservation of claims of privilege.

We have already described at length the extraordinary logistical difficulties with which IBM was confronted in its efforts to comply, as it eventually did, with the demanding timetable Judge Neville had established for the document inspection program. We believe that there is merit in IBM's argument that that timetable deprived IBM of the opportunity to claim the privilege inasmuch as it was statistically inevitable that, despite the extraordinary precautions undertaken by IBM, some privileged documents would escape detection by the IBM reviewers.

* * *

Although our conclusion that IBM did not waive its claim to its privilege because IBM did not have an adequate enough opportunity to claim it is based on our independent analysis of the circumstances surrounding IBM's inadvertent production of the JJ documents in the CDC case, we also find Judge Neville's rulings of November 2, 1970 and April 18, 1972 to be of especial importance. As the judicial officer directly in charge of supervising the discovery proceedings in that litigation, he was in an ideal position to determine whether the timetable he himself had imposed was so stringent that, as a practical matter, it effectively denied IBM the opportunity to claim the attorney-client privilege for documents it was producing for inspection by CDC. TCC acknowledges that waiver cannot be directly compelled, and Judge Neville's rulings recognize and we so hold, that neither can it be indirectly compelled.

Moreover, any documents produced after November 2, 1970, were produced under Judge Neville's ruling explicitly protecting and preserving all claims of privilege, provided only that the parties wishing to preserve privilege had engaged in suitable screening techniques. Obviously, IBM did not waive its right to claim the privilege as to any documents produced after that date. We point out that under Fed. R.Civ.P. 26(c)(2) the district judge presiding over discovery proceedings can dictate "the specified terms and conditions" upon which discovery may be had. This rule, which merely clarifies the former rule that allowed the issuance of " 'any other order which justice requires,' " certainly empowers the court, inter alia, to set deadlines for completion of discovery. Particularly in "exceptional" cases, though, this power to establish deadlines is not unlimited, for the parties must be given a fair and adequate opportunity to develop their cases. Of course, rule 26(c)(2) is broad enough to empower the district judge to achieve this objective in a number of ways. One reasonable method of accelerating the discovery proceedings without impinging upon the parties' right to prepare their cases properly was to do precisely what Judge Neville did, that is, to issue an order preserving claims of privilege.

[Concurring opinion of KENNEDY, CIRCUIT JUDGE, omitted.]

WEIL v. INVESTMENT/INDICATORS, RESEARCH & MANAGE-
MENT, INC., 647 F.2d 18 (9th Cir.1981):

TRASK, CIRCUIT JUDGE.

[In connection with review of an order requiring plaintiff to post
security for costs in a securities action, the court held that defendant
waived its privilege as to certain documents produced by its attorney to
plaintiff's attorney during discovery.]

Appellees contend that the Fund cannot be found to have waived its
attorney-client privilege because it did not intend waiver when it made
the disclosure. It argues that waiver must be express to be effective, and
that waiver cannot result from inadvertent disclosure.

We are not persuaded by this argument. All three cases cited by
appellees in support of it were decided under state law, and thus their
holdings are distinguishable from cases such as this one in which federal
law must be applied. In contrast to appellees' position, the federal cases
presuppose that waiver may be effected by implication. *See, e.g.,* Tasby v.
United States, 504 F.2d 332, 336 (8th Cir.1974), *cert. denied,* 419 U.S.
1125, 95 S.Ct. 811, 42 L.Ed.2d 826 (1975); United States v. Woodall, 438
F.2d 1317, 1324 (5th Cir.1970), *cert. denied,* 403 U.S. 933, 91 S.Ct. 2262,
29 L.Ed.2d 712 (1971). Moreover, the subjective intent of the party
asserting the privilege is only one factor to be considered in determining
whether waiver should be implied. Finally, "inadvertence" of disclosure
does not as a matter of law prevent the occurrence of waiver.

As with all evidentiary privileges, the burden of proving that the
attorney-client privilege applies rests not with the party contesting the
privilege, but with the party asserting it. One of the elements that the
asserting party must prove is that it has not waived the privilege. The
Fund has disclosed the content of a privileged communication which is
relevant and material to an issue in the case. Against this, the Fund's
bare assertion that it did not subjectively intend to waive the privilege is
insufficient to make out the necessary element of non-waiver.[13]

Notes and Questions

1. *Weil* represents classical waiver doctrine at work. Was the disclosure
in that case really any more volitional than in *Transamerica?* See also
Suburban Sew 'N Sweep, Inc. v. Swiss–Bernina, Inc., 91 F.R.D. 254 (N.D.Ill.
1981) (privileged materials stolen from defendant's garbage); cf. Sanders v.
Shell Oil Co., 678 F.2d 614 (5th Cir.1982) (former employee purloined
internal memoranda and turned them over to plaintiff in an employment
discrimination action).

---

13. Indeed, when, as here, the privileged communication is voluntarily disclosed without objection by the asserting
party's counsel and in the absence of surprise or deception by opposing counsel, it
may be unnecessary to look beyond the
objective fact of disclosure in ruling on the
question of waiver.

Compare von Bulow by Auersperg v. von Bulow, 114 F.R.D. 71 (S.D.N.Y. 1987), a suit by the children of Martha von Bulow against Claus von Bulow for assault on their mother. Claus von Bulow had been represented in criminal proceedings about the same events by Alan Dershowitz, a Harvard Law School professor who wrote a book about his experiences (later made into a movie) called *Reversal of Fortune*. The book included material that was covered by the attorney-client privilege, and further confidences were breached on a television program called *The Phil Donahue Show* with Claus von Bulow present. Emphasizing von Bulow's support for publication of the book and presence during the filming of the television show, the court held that he had waived the privilege. The Second Circuit upheld the waiver finding, but limited the scope of the waiver the matters actually disclosed rather than applying it also to related matters not disclosed. In re von Bulow, 828 F.2d 94 (2d Cir.1987). It reasoned that "so long as such disclosures are and remain extrajudicial, there is no *legal* prejudice that warrants a broad court-imposed subject matter waiver." Id. at 103. Should mistaken disclosure through discovery be treated differently?

2. "The inadvertent production of a privileged document is a specter that haunts every document intensive case." F.D.I.C. v. Marine Midland Realty Credit Corp., 138 F.R.D. 479, 479–80 (E.D.Va.1991). Should classical waiver doctrine be suspended in instances of inadvertent disclosure through discovery? Some have developed an inadvertent disclosure exception to waiver where a party has made reasonable efforts to cull privileged materials before producing them. E.g., Lois Sportswear, U.S.A., Inc. v. Levi Strauss & Co., 104 F.R.D. 103, 105 (S.D.N.Y.1985) (relying on "the reasonableness of the precautions to prevent inadvertent disclosure"); Note, Inadvertent Disclosure of Documents Subject to the Attorney–Client Privilege, 82 Mich. L.Rev. 598, 616–19 (1983); Meese, Inadvertent Waiver of the Attorney–Client Privilege by Disclosure of Documents: An Economic Analysis, 23 Creighton L.Rev. 513, 523–26 (1990). How close to the "herculean" efforts of IBM must such culling come?

Other courts reject the inadvertent production exception. Consider the views of the court in In re Sealed Case, 877 F.2d 976, 980 (D.C.Cir.1989):

> To hold, as we do, that an inadvertent disclosure will waive the privilege imposes a self-governing restraint on the freedom with which organizations such as corporations, unions, and the like label documents related to communications with counsel as privileged. To readily do so creates a greater risk of "inadvertent" disclosure and thereby the danger that "waiver" will extend to all related matters, perhaps causing grave injury to the organization. But that is as it should be. Otherwise, there is a temptation to seek artificially to expand the content of privileged matter. In other words, if a client wishes to preserve the privilege, it must treat the confidentiality of attorney-client communications like jewels— if not crown jewels.

For an overview, see 8 C. Wright, A. Miller & R. Marcus, Federal Practice & Procedure, § 2016.2 at 241–46 (2d ed. 1994) (describing three views adopted by courts—waiver always found, waiver never found without client approval, and waiver dependent on circumstances).

Should a different attitude be applied to inadvertent production in e-discovery? In Zubulake v. UBS Warburg LLC, 216 F.R.D. 280 (S.D.N.Y. 2003), the court ruled that the cost of reviewing e-mail messages from restored backup tapes for privilege should be borne by the producing party because the distinctive cost with this form of e-discovery was for restoring the backup tapes. In other situations, however, it may seem that electronic discovery is distinctive. For example, in In re Ford Motor Co., 345 F.3d 1315 (11th Cir.2003), the court of appeals granted a writ of mandate to overturn a district court order in a products liability suit that required Ford to permit plaintiff's lawyer to access various databases of Ford that plaintiff claimed contained relevant information. The court of appeals ruled that the order was unjustified in this case because Ford had not been given an opportunity to respond, but it recognized that "some kind of direct access [to party databases] might be permissible in certain cases." Id. at 1317. In such cases, what should be the consequences of plaintiff's accessing privileged material?

3. Note that in *Transamerica* the judge in Minnesota entered an order immunizing inadvertent disclosures from waiver and that the Ninth Circuit stated that it was "obvious" that production after that date did not waive the privilege. At least in complex cases, such an order can facilitate discovery. Consider the experience of Professors Hazard and Rice as special masters in a large antitrust case in which the judge entered such an order: "By eliminating the risk of inadvertent waiver through the production of documents, the order eliminated the necessity of hypercareful scrutiny of each document prior to its disclosure. * * * This permitted relatively free exchange of the exceptionally large mass of demanded and subpoenaed materials." Hazard & Rice, Special Masters as Case Managers, 1982 A.B.F.Res.J. 375, 399–400.

How does this solution prevent a waiver? Consider the following argument:

> But the stipulation or order approach is inconsistent with classical waiver doctrine, which holds that *any* disclosure to an outsider destroys the attorney-client privilege. The fact that the parties have agreed in advance that disclosure should not have that effect, with or without the court's blessing, has no bearing on that conclusion. Even if such an agreement estops the recipient of the material from claiming waiver, it would have no effect on a nonparty's right to claim the disclosure established waiver. Yet the courts choose to disregard this theoretical glitch, presumably because the concrete reality of protracted discovery is more immediate than the abstract operation of classical waiver doctrine.

Marcus, The Perils of Privilege: Waiver and the Litigator, 84 Mich.L.Rev. 1605, 1612 (1986). Thus the Manual for Complex Litigation (4th) § 11.431 n. 129 notes that some courts have refused to enforce such agreements.

Can a court speed discovery up by ordering that production occur without any privilege review, but that production of privileged material works no waiver? In In re Dow Corning Corp. 261 F.3d 280 (2d Cir.2001), the court rejected such an attempt. "[W]e have found no authority * * * that holds that imposition of a protective order like the one issued by the district court permits a court to order disclosure of privileged attorney-client communications. The absence of authority no doubt stems from the common sense observation that such a protective order is an inadequate surrogate for the privilege."

4. If inadvertent production does not result in a waiver, what should be done with the materials revealed? Should courts try to "suppress" the documents by refusing to allow them into evidence? For an argument that such a "now you see it, now you don't" approach would create a risk of undermining the appearance of justice and unduly weaken the normal incentive to screen out privileged material before production, see Marcus, *supra,* 84 Mich.L.Rev. at 1635–36. In some cases, courts may decline to find a waiver even though the documents have received widespread attention. In Smith v. Armour Pharmaceutical Co., 838 F.Supp. 1573 (S.D.Fla.1993), a memorandum by an in-house lawyer had been inadvertently produced in earlier litigation, and accounts of the memorandum had been published in a variety of newspapers "from Alaska to Florida." Many courts had allowed it to be used at trial, finding a waiver, but this court found that Florida law authorizes a waiver only when the client so authorizes and therefore that the disclosure did not constitute a waiver. "The fact that the contents of a privileged document have become widely known is insufficient by itself to eliminate the privilege that covers the document." Id. at 1577.

5. Are there any limits on what counsel may do with privileged materials erroneously delivered to her? In State Compensation Ins. Fund v. WPS, Inc., 70 Cal.App.4th 644, 82 Cal.Rptr.2d 799 (1999), materials stamped privileged were nonetheless produced. After receipt, counsel refused to return the documents and shared them with another lawyer litigating against the same opponent. Based on ABA Formal Opinion 92–368, the court sanctioned the lawyers, saying that in such circumstances the lawyer must refrain from examining the materials any more than necessary to determine that they are privileged and to notify the other side of the mistake. Disqualification is an available punishment for violation of these directives.

6. Even if the actual privileged materials were not produced, an inadequate specification of the grounds for withholding, as required by Rule 26(b)(5), may be argued to constitute a waiver. In complex cases, courts will hopefully approach such arguments with caution. The Advisory Committee Note accompanying the 1993 addition of Rule 26(b)(5) explained that "[d]etails concerning time, persons, general subject matter, etc., may be appropriate if only a few items are withheld, but may be unduly burdensome when voluminous documents are claimed to be privileged or protected, particularly if the items can be described by categories." 146 F.R.D. at 639. For a discussion, see 8 C. Wright, A. Miller & R. Marcus, Federal Practice & Procedure § 2016.1 (2d ed. 1994).

7. *Waiver by agreement.* Sometimes, unlike the situation in *Weil*, the client may consciously waive the privilege. Federal prosecutors, for example, sometimes insist on waiver of privilege by corporations suspected of misconduct to demonstrate cooperation. Reportedly, "[p]rosecutors readily acknowledge that waiver and disclosure are a lot like voting in Chicago elections: Corporations must do it early and often, or be treated as uncooperative." Gibeaut, Junior G–Men, ABA J., June 2003, at 46, 51.

Another ground of waiver that could occur is contract, but it is rare. It may also be narrow. In Tennenbaum v. Deloitte & Touche, 77 F.3d 337 (9th

Cir.1996), defendant had explicitly agreed to waive the privilege in a settlement of another case but refused to answer questions in a deposition that inquired into a privileged area. The court held that the agreement to waive does not, absent disclosure, constitute an enforceable waiver. Based on its earlier decision in *Weil*, the court found that the focus of waiver should be actual disclosure, and that a mere intention to disclose is not sufficient to effect a waiver. Of course, there might be a breach of contract claim for damages, but proving damages on such a claim seems difficult.

8. *Postscript:* In New York, where the United States was proceeding with its own antitrust action against IBM, Judge Edelstein ordered IBM to produce the same materials involved in *Transamerica.* When IBM refused, the judge found it in contempt and imposed a fine of $150,000 per day until the documents were produced. Although a panel of the Second Circuit reversed, that court later held *en banc* that it lacked jurisdiction to review Judge Edelstein's order before final judgment. International Business Machines Corp. v. United States, 493 F.2d 112 (2d Cir.1973), *cert. denied,* 416 U.S. 995, 94 S.Ct. 2409, 40 L.Ed.2d 774 (1974).

UNITED STATES v. AMERICAN TELEPHONE & TELEGRAPH CO.

United States Court of Appeals, District of Columbia Circuit, 1980.
642 F.2d 1285.

Before TAMM, ROBINSON and WILKEY, CIRCUIT JUDGES.

WILKEY, CIRCUIT JUDGE.

[Parallel suits were pending in the Northern District of Illinois and the District of Columbia charging AT & T with monopolizing the market for long-distance telephone communications. In the Illinois action, the plaintiff was MCI Telecommunications Corp. The United States had filed the District of Columbia action. In its suit, MCI had obtained production of some 7 million documents from AT & T subject to a protective order.]

Upon a motion by the United States in the Northern District of Illinois, the judge presiding there over MCI's antitrust suit against AT & T granted a modification of an existing protective order to allow MCI to make available to the United States all discovery materials it had acquired from AT & T in the case, including documents, deposition transcripts, and exhibits referred to in depositions. In addition, this order permitted MCI to furnish to the Department of Justice "any explanatory material or information which would be helpful to an understanding of the items produced." To preserve the confidentiality of any material provided by MCI pursuant to the order, the order prohibited the Government from using such materials for any purpose other than its case against AT & T in the District Court for the District of Columbia. It is this latter, explanatory material, which is in issue in the case at bar.

Following the Seventh Circuit's affirmance of this modification of the protective order, MCI furnished the Government the documents, depositions, and exhibits that MCI had discovered from AT & T. MCI also furnished certain documents pertaining to a "database" consisting of computerized abstracts of documents, deposition transcripts, and exhibits received from AT & T during discovery. MCI's counsel had prepared the database for the Northern District of Illinois litigation. The "database documents" furnished by MCI and at issue in the current appeal describe the structure of the database and explain how information can be entered and retrieved. MCI claims to have maintained strictly the secrecy of the database documents from AT & T—although they relate to the original documents discovered from AT & T and furnished the Government—and to have provided them to the United States under the confidentiality provision of the Northern District of Illinois order.

Since AT & T had already given microfilm copies to the Government for documents selected by MCI in discovery, the major additional effect of the modification of the protective order was to permit MCI to produce their depositions and analyses of data for Government counsel's use. Much of this analysis of data and documents was contained in MCI's computerized litigation support system, to which the now disputed database documents pertain. *Unlike the documents and data themselves, none of the analytical or descriptive material in the database documents is admissible as evidence.* But the database documents enable the United States to gain access to the analysis contained in the computerized support system, and might well enable AT & T to determine which documents a plaintiff's counsel would consider important, why counsel might consider them to be important, and what portions of those documents counsel might think are most important for the issues in this suit.

The controversy leading to the district court's discovery order now challenged by MCI began on 23 February 1979, when AT & T served a document request on the United States seeking discovery of the database documents furnished by MCI. The United States raised MCI's work product privilege as a defense against this request.

* * *

[The court concluded that "[d]iscoverability in this situation should properly turn on whether the transferor MCI waived any work product privilege by giving the documents to the United States."]

MCI claims that the database documents at issue in this case were prepared by or for MCI's attorneys specifically in anticipation of litigation in MCI's antitrust suit against AT & T in the Northern District of Illinois. On such facts the work product privilege would attach to the documents in the Northern District case and they could not be discovered by AT & T in that case without a showing of substantial need. The question for our consideration is whether the work product privilege applies also in the case between AT & T and the United States in the District of Columbia.

A number of district court opinions have considered whether the work product privilege is waived when a party that created documents in anticipation of litigation provides those documents to another party for use in litigation in a related case. Several of the decisions have turned on whether the transferor has "common interests" with the transferee. In applying this standard courts have held the work product privilege not to be waived by disclosures between attorneys for parties "having a mutual interest in litigation," or between parties which were potential co-defendants to an antitrust suit, or between attorneys representing parties "sharing such a common interest in litigation, actual or prospective," or between parties one of whose interests in prospective litigation may turn on the success of the other party in a separate litigation. The earlier opinions in this line of decisions tended to employ a narrow definition of "common interests," restricted to situations in which the relationship of the parties was similar to that between co-parties in a suit.

* * *

We do not consider the strict standard of waiver in the attorney-client privilege context * * * to be appropriate for work product cases. *The attorney-client privilege exists* to protect confidential communications, to assure the client that any statements he makes in seeking legal advice will be kept strictly confidential between him and his attorney; in effect, *to protect the attorney-client relationship.* Any voluntary disclosure by the holder of such a privilege is inconsistent with the confidential relationship and thus waives the privilege.

By contrast, the *work product privilege* does not exist to protect a confidential relationship, but rather *to promote the adversary system by safeguarding the fruits of an attorney's trial preparations from the discovery attempts of the opponent.* The purpose of the work product doctrine is to protect information against opposing parties, rather than against all others outside a particular confidential relationship, in order to encourage effective trial preparation. In the leading case on the work product privilege, the Supreme Court stated: "Proper preparation of a client's case demands that he assemble information, sift what he considers to be the relevant from the irrelevant facts, prepare his legal theories and plan his strategy without undue and needless interference." [Hickman v. Taylor, 329 U.S. 495, 511, 67 S.Ct. 385, 393, 91 L.Ed. 451 (1947)]. A disclosure made in the pursuit of such trial preparation, and not inconsistent with maintaining secrecy against opponents, should be allowed without waiver of the privilege. We conclude, then, that *while the mere showing of a voluntary disclosure to a third person will generally suffice to show waiver of the attorney-client privilege, it should not suffice in itself for waiver of the work product privilege.*

We do not endorse a reading * * * so broad as to allow confidential disclosure to *any* person without waiver of the work product privilege. The existence of common interests between transferor and transferee is relevant to deciding whether the disclosure is consistent with the nature of the work product privilege. But "common interests" should not be construed as narrowly limited to co-parties. So long as transferor and transferee anticipate litigation against a common adversary on the same issue or issues, they have strong common interests in sharing the fruit of the trial preparation efforts. Moreover, with common interests on a particular issue against a common adversary, the transferee is not at all likely to disclose the work product material to the adversary. When the transfer to a party with such common interests is conducted under a guarantee of confidentiality, the case against waiver is even stronger.

In the present case, MCI shares common interests with the United States, in the sense that they are proceeding on overlapping antitrust issues against a common adversary, AT & T. The United States and MCI shared common interests in developing legal theories and analyses of documents on which to proceed on those issues where they both made the same antitrust claims against AT & T. Moreover, the Northern District of Illinois court order authorizing the transfer of the database documents also ordered the Government to maintain their confidentiality. This transfer is consistent with the promotion of trial preparation within the adversary system. Further, because of the Government's interests adverse to AT & T on these issues, the transfer poses very little likelihood of AT & T gaining access to the documents through the United States.

In their second opinion and order the Special Masters observed in dictum that the Government and MCI were aligned in interest in light of the facts that "the same transaction is in litigation, the adversary is the same, and the positions of the parties involved in the exchange were substantially identical as against that adversary." They went on to observe: "The exchange seems to us to partake of a consultation on tactics and strategy, the very things the work product privilege is designed to protect."

We believe our holding on the waiver issue furthers the purpose of the work product privilege by protecting attorneys' preparations for trial and encouraging the fullest preparation without fear of access by adversaries. *The work product privilege rests on the belief that such promotion of adversary preparation ultimately furthers the truth-finding process.* For MCI to contribute the fruit of its analysis to the Government on those issues common to their two cases will further the Government's preparation for trial and eliminate some duplication of effort. The advantages of such sharing led the judge in MCI's Northern District of Illinois case against AT & T to remark, "we believe the court should not only encourage the sharing of discovery in cases with common fact questions but order it on its own motion even where the parties do not suggest it."

We recognize that the truth-finding process might be further enhanced *in the short term* in this particular case if AT & T gained access to the documents in question. In the long run, however, this would discourage trial preparation and vigorous advocacy and would discourage any party from turning over work product to the government.

The Government has the same entitlement as any other party to assistance from those sharing common interests, whatever their motives. This is clearly true in antitrust cases, where Congress has established a policy of private enforcement to supplement governmental action against offenders. This policy should not be thwarted by allowing an alleged antitrust offender to acquire the trial preparations of his private adversaries when they cooperate with Government lawyers in a related suit by the Justice Department. It is important to bear in mind that this case involves the sharing of legal analysis and other forms of materials created by attorneys; it does not involve the sharing of evidence. If a person shares *evidentiary* material with the Government, that material is of course subject to discovery by those against whom the Government uses it. But attorney work product, such as the database documents in question here, is not generally admissible as evidence, and should not be any more easily discoverable from the Government than from any other party.

Notes and Questions

1. The common interest exception to the waiver doctrine discussed in United States v. AT&T is extremely important in multi-party cases. Operating under this doctrine, parties with the same alignment can coordinate strategies and share information useful to the combined effort. Does it make sense to differentiate between the attorney-client and the work product materials in applying this exception to the waiver doctrine? The distinction may be justified because the attorney-client privilege is more likely to prevent access to evidence (as opposed to inadmissible attorney opinion). In addition, once invoked, the attorney-client privilege is absolute, while the work product protection may be overcome by a sufficient showing of necessity. Is the court's argument that one is designed to protect confidential information against the world while the other is intended to guard it only as against adversaries persuasive? See Bartel, Reconceptualizing the Joint Defense Doctrine, 65 Fordham L.Rev. 871 (1996) (arguing that doctrine should not be treated as feature of attorney-client privilege because the strictures of that privilege are too confining); Note, Waiver of Attorney–Client Privilege on Inter–Attorney Exchange of Information, 63 Yale L.J. 1030 (1954) (arguing in favor of insulating exchanges of attorney-client privileged information among co-parties).

2. Why should revelation of privileged material to *A* work a waiver of the privilege to refuse to reveal the material to *B*? Consider the following reasoning from Permian Corp. v. United States, 665 F.2d 1214 (D.C.Cir. 1981): "Because the attorney-client privilege inhibits the truth-finding process, it has been narrowly construed, and courts have been vigilant to prevent litigants from converting the privilege into a tool for selective disclosure. *See* Green v. Crapo, 181 Mass. 55, 62 N.E. 956, 959 (1902) (Holmes, J.) ('the privacy for the sake of which the privilege was created was gone by the appellant's own consent, and the privilege does not remain in such circumstances for the mere sake of giving the client an additional

weapon to use or not at his choice'). The client cannot be permitted to pick and choose among his opponents, waiving the privilege for some and resurrecting the claim of confidentiality to obstruct others, or to invoke the privilege as to communications whose confidentiality he has already compromised for his own benefit."

Is there something inherently unfair about permitting revelation to some but not to others? Recall that the Supreme Court noted that application of the attorney-client privilege "puts the adversary in no worse position than if the communications had never taken place." Upjohn Co. v. United States, 449 U.S. 383, 101 S.Ct. 677, 66 L.Ed.2d 584 (1981). Does that reasoning suggest that the proper question is whether the revelation of information to A put B in a worse position than if the revelation to A had never taken place? If so, shouldn't that support a waiver in United States v. AT & T? If not, isn't B getting a windfall if the privilege is held waived due to revelation to A even though B was in no way harmed by that revelation?

3. Should certain types of revelations be favored? In Diversified Industries, Inc. v. Meredith, 572 F.2d 596 (8th Cir.1977), the court adopted a "limited waiver" doctrine in a case involving voluntary delivery of privileged material to the S.E.C. in order to promote cooperation with that agency. Most courts, however, have rejected this approach. See In re Weiss, 596 F.2d 1185 (4th Cir.1979); Westinghouse Elec. Corp. v. Republic of the Philippines, 951 F.2d 1414, 1425–26 (3d Cir.1991); Note, The Limited Waiver Rule: Creation of an SEC–Corporation Privilege, 36 Stan.L.Rev. 789 (1984). Is it unfair to allow a person to disclose privileged information to a governmental agency but still assert privilege against private opponents? For an argument that a strict waiver approach is unfair to corporations trying to cooperate with governmental agencies, see Note, Permian Corporation v. United States and the Attorney–Client Privilege for Corporations: Unjustified Severity on the Issue of Waiver, 77 Nw.L.Rev. 223 (1982).

4. Note that in United States v. AT&T the government and MCI shared a common litigation interest—in separate lawsuits they were suing a common opponent. Courts are wary about treating common interests not relating to litigation as sufficient to permit sharing. In Cheeves v. Southern Clays, Inc., 128 F.R.D. 128 (M.D.Ga.1989), a company negotiating a sale of assets shared privileged materials with the company that ultimately bought the seller's assets. Noting that under state law the transaction was not a de facto merger, the court held that this sharing operated as a waiver because the two companies did not have a shared legal (v. economic) interest.

Compare Hewlett–Packard Co. v. Bausch & Lomb, Inc., 115 F.R.D. 308 (N.D.Cal.1987), a patent infringement suit in which plaintiff shared an attorney's opinion letter about its patent claims with a prospective purchaser of the division that manufactured the product in question. Although the sale ultimately did not go through, Magistrate Judge Brazil held there was a sufficient common interest to insulate the disclosure (id. at 311):

> Holding that this kind of disclosure constitutes a waiver could make it appreciably more difficult to negotiate sales of businesses and products that arguably involve interests protected by laws relating to intellectual property. Unless it serves some significant interest courts should not create procedural doctrine that restricts communication between buyers

and sellers, erects barriers to business deals, and increases the risk that prospective buyers will not have access to important information that could play key roles in assessing the value of the business or product they are considering buying. Legal doctrine that impedes frank communication between buyers and sellers also sets the stage for more lawsuits, as buyers are more likely to be unpleasantly surprised by what they receive. By refusing to find waiver in these settings, courts create an environment in which businesses can share more freely information that is relevant to their transactions. This policy lubricates business deals and encourages more openness in transactions of this nature.

Is this a proper extension of the common interest idea? See also United States v. Gulf Oil Corp., 760 F.2d 292, 296 (Temp.Emer.Ct.App.1985) (information sharing among potential merger partners who later became adversaries is not a waiver). Compare U.S. Information Systems, Inc. v. International Bhd. of Elec. Workers Local Union No. 3, 2002 W 31296430 (S.D.N.Y., Oct. 11, 2002) (letters sent by an electrical contractor's counsel to an assistant district attorney in an attempt to persuade him to take action against plaintiff were prepared in anticipation of litigation, and thus, initially qualified as protected work product, but the privilege was waived by the disclosure to the assistant district attorney with whom it shared a common interest). What other sorts of business arrangements should qualify?

5. Serious sharing problems can also arise in connection with outside audits. Auditors may demand access to privileged information before issuing an unqualified opinion about a company. Yet there is no privilege for such disclosures, see United States v. Arthur Young & Co., 465 U.S. 805, 104 S.Ct. 1495, 79 L.Ed.2d 826 (1984), and the sharing may work a waiver. Thus, in In re John Doe Corp., 675 F.2d 482 (2d Cir.1982), the company argued that the disclosure was "coerced by the legal duty of due diligence and the millions of dollars riding on the public offering of registered securities." The court, however, found this factor irrelevant because "[f]ederal securities laws put a price of disclosure upon access to interstate capital markets. Once materials are utilized in that disclosure, they become representations to third parties by the corporation." Id. at 489.

BERKEY PHOTO, INC. v. EASTMAN KODAK CO.

United States District Court, Southern District of New York, 1977.
74 F.R.D. 613.

FRANKEL, DISTRICT JUDGE.

Plaintiff, Berkey Photo, Inc., has charged defendant, Eastman Kodak Company, with violations of Sections 1 and 2 of the Sherman Act. By order of October 29, 1976, the court referred all remaining discovery matters in this case and its companion case to Magistrate Sol Schreiber "to determine ... whenever possible, or, if necessary, to hear and report." The result has been, as expected, a course of crisp, efficient management of pretrial proceedings bringing us now close to the eve of trial. The single discovery problem requiring the court's attention since the reference to the Magistrate is the close question now presented. It arises from one aspect of the Magistrate's order that all expert witnesses be deposed, and that, in connection with these depositions, and pursuant to Rule 612 of the Federal Rules of Evidence, all material given to the expert during his preparation be produced to opposing counsel.

The dispute concerns the refusal of Kodak to produce four notebooks ("the Doar notebooks") all or parts of which were shown to Kodak's economic experts as "background" during their preparation for this case.[1] According to the affidavit of defendant's counsel, John Doar, Esq., the notebooks were prepared by him in the course of readying the case for trial; they consist of his synthesis of the facts and factual issues. The material in the notebooks is said to "represent [counsel's] legal analysis, mental impressions and ... legal judgment as to what facts were needed to be understood, mastered, and possibly presented in the trial of the Berkey case."

At his deposition, one of defendant's experts, Prof. Merton J. Peck, testified that he had received the Doar notebooks at some point during the past winter, probably in January. To the question whether he had the notebooks in his possession when he prepared the outline of his "witness book" for production to plaintiff, the witness replied: "I don't recall, because we did not use them. We may have read them before or after, but we didn't use them, and I don't recall." Another of the experts, in an affidavit offered on this motion, states that he read the Color Slide and Movie volume and that this "served to fill in details about the development of various Kodak movie and slide films, and movie camera products. By reading the volume I gained a further appreciation of the technological details about the development of specific Kodak products." Although he did not read the CP & P volume carefully, he "did gain some appreciation of the photofinishing industry" from it.

On the record at the deposition, and later before Magistrate Schreiber, Kodak's counsel claimed a work product privilege with respect to the Doar notebooks and argued that they were not properly within the Magistrate's production order. The Magistrate overruled the objection and ordered the notebooks produced to plaintiff's counsel; defendant now moves for reversal of the Magistrate's ruling.

The Magistrate ordered production of the Doar notebooks pursuant to Rule 612, Fed.R.Evid. That rule provides in pertinent part that

"... [I]f a witness uses a writing to refresh his memory for the purpose of testifying, ...

(2) before testifying, if the court in its discretion determines it is necessary in the interests of justice,

an adverse party is entitled to have the writing produced at the hearing, to inspect it, to cross-examine the witness thereon, and to

1. The notebooks are entitled "Color Prints 1942–1976" (2 vols.), "Amateur Reversal Color Films 1928–1955, Amateur Color Slides 1955–1975, Amateur Color Movies 1955–1975" and "CP & P." Prof. Merton J. Peck received all four volumes; Prof. M.A. Adelman received at least two (he is uncertain whether he saw the "Color Prints" volumes); and Prof. R.C. Levin received all but the "Color Prints" volumes.

introduce in evidence those portions which relate to the testimony of the witness."

Defendant argues that Rule 612 is inapplicable to this case because "the four volumes at issue were not used for assisting [the experts] in preparing [their] substantive testimony regarding the economic matters within [their] expertise." Therefore, the argument proceeds, the witnesses did not use the material to "refresh [their] memor[ies] for the purposes of testifying" within the meaning of Rule 612.

As defendant notes, Rule 612 is not intended "as a pretext for wholesale exploration of an opposing party's files...." It was designed to permit "access ... to those writings which may fairly be said in fact to have an impact upon the testimony of the witness." More broadly stated, "the purpose of the rule is the same as that of the *Jencks* statute, 18 U.S.C. § 3500: to promote the search of credibility and memory."

The question, then, is whether the Doar notebooks can be said to have had sufficient "impact" on the experts' testimony to trigger the application of Rule 612.

At the hearing on this motion, when the court asked why the Doar notebooks were given to the experts, defense counsel stated: "Because I thought it might be useful for them to have a review of the factual organization that I have prepared in connection with the history of the product development of the Eastman Kodak Company.... [I]t is useful to the client to have the expert as fully familiar with the background and operation of the company as he can [be]...." This confirms and reinforces impressions given by the expert who reported that the notebooks "served to fill in details" and to enhance his "appreciation" of the facts concerning which his expertise was to be presented.

It is evident that the Doar notebooks, at least to a strongly arguable degree, may be supposed to have had "an impact upon the testimony of the witness." To state a less reducible minimum, they have the sound and quality of materials appropriate "to promote the search of credibility and memory." Accordingly, unless a privilege bars production, or is deemed so far to outweigh the benefits of production that this should not be held "necessary in the interests of justice," plaintiff's demand should be honored.

We are led to assess, therefore, the countervailing force of the work product privilege invoked by defendant. We come for this subject to the wealth of learning embraced in materials ranging from the landmark decision in *Hickman v. Taylor*, 329 U.S. 495, 67 S.Ct. 385, 91 L.Ed. 451 (1947), to the more recent (1970) codification in F.R.Civ.P. 26(b)(3). In this light the court has inspected the four notebooks in question. It seems clear that they are indeed "work product" in an essential sense of the term. They are counsel's ordering of the "facts," referring to the prospective proofs, organizing, aligning, and marshaling empirical data with the view to combative employment that is the hallmark of the adversary enterprise. The pages collate the expected or imagined or hoped-for proofs of the propositions counsel has learned and written.

There is the evident residue and reflection of "interviews, statements, memoranda, correspondence ... mental impressions, personal beliefs," and other products of the advocate's professional interaction with the materials of his art. *Hickman v. Taylor, supra.*

Characterizing the notebooks as "work product" does not end the problem. The privilege sheltering such materials may be waived. It is not, in any event, absolute.

As to waiver, there is less enlightenment than might be desired from precedent and legislative history. We are cautioned not to confuse the work product privilege with the attorney-client privilege, ruling mechanically that any disclosure to third persons destroys the former. There are intimations that Rule 612 was intended to leave privileges generally untouched, but other evidences weigh against a conclusion that the subject can approach such simplicity. In the setting of modern views favoring broad access to materials useful for effective cross-examination, embodied in rules like 612 and like the Jencks Act, 18 U.S.C. § 3500, it is disquieting to posit that a party's lawyer may "aid" a witness with items of work product and then prevent totally the access that might reveal and counteract the effects of such assistance. There is much to be said for a view that a party or its lawyer, meaning to invoke the privilege, ought to use other and different materials, available later to a cross-examiner, in the preparation of witnesses. When this simple choice emerges the decision to give the work product to the witness could well be deemed a waiver of the privilege.

Similar thoughts apply in considering how absolute or qualified the privilege should be deemed to be. The answer will vary, of course, with the nature of the materials sought from the lawyer's files. Starting with *Hickman v. Taylor,* and extending to now, the authoritative pronouncements come close to, or arrive at, an "absolute immunity" from discovery of the attorney's "mental impressions, conclusions, opinions, or legal theories.... " F.R.Civ.P. 26(b)(3).[8] Again, however, the sweeping language of the cited authorities has never been challenged by an instance where such immunized materials have been deliberately employed to prepare—and thus, very possibly, to influence and shape—testimony, with the anticipation that these efforts should remain forever unknowable and undiscoverable. It ought not to be comfortably supposed that a claim that extreme must necessarily be sustained.

There would appear, in short, to be room for allowing discovery, either on a theory of waiver or of qualified privilege, where an attempt is made to exceed decent limits of preparation on the one hand and concealment on the other. But the circumstances presented here do not on balance warrant such a ruling. There is no indication at all of a

---

8. In view of the decision against required disclosure, it is not necessary to decide whether the attorney's "mental impressions" could be excised feasibly and less sensitive materials given to plaintiffs. Suffice it to say the task would be difficult, if possible at all. Obviously, given the enormous and amorphous world of available "facts," counsel's selection and ordering come close to the vital area of maximum protection under *Hickman.*

calculated plan to exploit the work product in a significant way for preparing the experts while planning to erect the shield of privilege against discovery. The materials actually made available for cross-examination are evidently voluminous and appear, so far as any evidence discloses, to cover all the concrete and specifically identifiable points on which the experts were instructed or advised for their testimony. No less importantly, given the current development of the law in this quarter, it seems fair to say that counsel were not vividly aware of the potential for a stark choice between withholding the notebooks from the experts or turning them over to opposing counsel.

All things considered, then, altering an earlier inclination and overruling the Magistrate without any sure conviction that this is an ineluctably right course, the court will order that plaintiff's demand for the notebooks should be denied.

* * *

[T]his court notes now, with hindsight, that there is not a compelling rationale for the view that counsel may (1) deliver work product to an expert or other witness to be "useful to the client," but then (2) withhold the material from an adversary who seeks to exploit the fact of this assistance in cross-examining the witness. From now on, as the problem and the pertinent legal materials become more familiar, there should be a sharp discounting of the concerns on which defendant is prevailing today. To put the point succinctly, there will be hereafter powerful reason to hold that materials considered work product should be withheld from prospective witnesses if they are to be withheld from opposing parties.

In this instance, however, for the reasons outlined above, defendant need not make the disclosure plaintiff seeks.

Notes and Questions

1. It is unclear whether Rule 612 was intended to affect either pretrial proceedings or privileged materials. Thus, one might argue that it applied only to materials used to refresh a witness for testimony at trial (not a deposition) and not to materials protected by a privilege. In fact, neither limiting avenue has been taken, as suggested by *Berkey Photo.* For a criticism of the breadth of the language in *Berkey Photo,* see Note, Interactions Between Memory Refreshment Doctrine and Work Product Protection Under the Federal Rules, 88 Yale L.J. 390 (1978).

2. To a large extent the expansive approach to Rule 612 resulted from concern about abuse of privilege protection. Thus, Judge Frankel noted that there was no showing of "a calculated plan to exploit the work product," and another court spoke of "the unfair disadvantage which could be placed upon the cross-examiner by the simple expedient of using only privileged writings to refresh recollection." Bailey v. Meister Brau, Inc., 57 F.R.D. 11, 13 (N.D.Ill.1972). How likely is such abuse? Could it be effective in a large documents case in which reams of material, usually including correspon-

dence and internal memoranda, have been turned over to the cross examiner?

3. The concern underlying Rule 612 is the fabrication of testimony. To what extent is such fabrication assisted by preserving the privileged character of materials used to refresh the witness' testimony? The most famous instance of allegedly fabricated testimony in American annals was the testimony by one of the prosecution's witnesses at the criminal trial following the death of over 100 women in the Triangle Shirtwaist Co. in 1911 in New York. Max Steuer, attorney for the defendants, impeached the witness, who had survived the fire, by having her repeat her story to show that she used the same words each time. Whether or not the prosecutor originated this story, there is no indication that any documents were used in preparing the witness; fabrication hardly depends upon them. See A. Steuer, Max Steuer, Trial Lawyer 89–109 (1950). Yet Rule 612 gives the cross-examiner no right to a transcript of the oral preparation of opposing witnesses.

Should the court impose limitations on *ex parte* oral communications with witnesses? In International Business Machines Corp. v. Edelstein, 526 F.2d 37 (2d Cir.1975), the trial judge ordered that any witness interview conducted by one party outside the presence of opposing counsel be transcribed by a court reporter. The court of appeals granted a writ of mandamus to overturn the order. It noted that "[t]his is part of an attorney's so-called work product. It is the common experience of counsel at the trial bar that a potential witness, upon reflection, will often change, modify or expand upon his original statement and that a second or third interview will be productive of greater accuracy." In addition, it reasoned that the order was "contrary to time-honored and decision-honored principles, namely, that counsel for all parties have a right to interview an adverse party's witnesses (the witness willing) in private, without the presence or consent of opposing counsel and without a transcript being made." Is the risk of fabrication eliminated if the witness is not aligned with the lawyer?

4. Balanced against the risk of fabrication is the reality that lawyers must prepare witnesses for their testimony; failure to do so might be a dereliction of professional duty. This "can involve a rehearsal process that exceeds the length of the actual deposition." Coffee, The Unfaithful Champion: The Plaintiff as Monitor in Shareholder Litigation, 48 Law & Contemp. Probs. 5, 17 (Summer 1985). The fact of witness preparation—called "woodshedding the witness"—does not give rise to an inference of falsification of testimony. Indeed, the preparation process may qualify as work product. See Ford v. Philips Electronics Instruments Co., 82 F.R.D. 359, 361 (E.D.Pa.1979) (court refuses to require revelation of exact questions asked by counsel while preparing nonparty witness).

From the perspective of the lawyer, this process is ordinarily best handled face to face. Particularly when the lawyer and the witness are located at a distance from one another, however, this may be difficult and expensive to arrange, and the lawyer may find it necessary to put in writing many of the thoughts that could, under other circumstances, be communicated orally. To the extent those writings are subject to disclosure under Rule 612, would the rule tend to make litigation even more labor-intensive by rewarding the party who is willing to pay a lawyer across the country to meet personally with the witness rather than relying on a memorandum? If the concern is falsification of testimony, is face-to-face or written preparation more likely to present problems? Compare Ohralik v. Ohio State Bar Ass'n, 436 U.S. 447, 98 S.Ct. 1912, 56 L.Ed.2d 444 (1978) (discipline of lawyer permitted for face-to-face solicitation due to inherently coercive nature of interaction) with In re Primus, 436 U.S. 412, 98 S.Ct. 1893, 56 L.Ed.2d 417 (1978) (discipline forbidden where solicitation was through public presentation with written follow-up).

5. Interpreted broadly, Rule 612 could interdict any written communications between attorney and client. There is no guarantee that the passage of time between the communication and the examination precludes a finding that the writing was used to refresh the witness' recollection. Indeed, that may have been the purpose of the lawyer as part of her own internal investigation at the beginning of the case. Is there an easy limiting principle that would assure the lawyer and the client of protection against a later argument for disclosure based on Rule 612?

6. Different problems are presented when the witnesses are, as in *Berkey Photo,* retained experts. Well-prepared lawyers often work up background analyses like the Doar notebooks that provide a starting point for the assistance they seek from experts. Should the price for showing such documents to experts be waiver of privilege if the experts testify at trial? How otherwise can the lawyer effectively identify for the expert the areas in which the lawyer needs the expert's advice?

Under Rule 26(a)(2), added in 1993, parties are to provide extensive reports from their expert witnesses that should contain "the data or other information considered by the witness in forming the opinions." The Advisory Committee Note accompanying this provision seems stronger than Judge Frankel's admonition in *Berkey Photo*: "Given this obligation of disclosure, litigants should no longer be able to argue that materials furnished to their experts to be used in forming their opinions—whether or not ultimately relied upon by the expert—are privileged or otherwise protected from disclosure when such persons are testifying or being deposed." 146 F.R.D. at 634. Prior to the adoption of Rule 26(a)(2), there was authority insulating against disclosure where privileged materials were provided to an expert witness. See Bogosian v. Gulf Oil Corp., 738 F.2d 587 (3d Cir.1984); compare Intermedics, Inc. v. Ventritex, Inc., 139 F.R.D. 384 (N.D.Cal.1991) (allowing discovery). Under the new rule, the courts disagree on whether disclosure applies to all work product. See 8 C. Wright, A. Miller & R. Marcus § 2016.2 n. 41 (2004 Pkt.Pt.).

7. If all the documents reviewed by the witness in preparation for his or her deposition have already been produced through discovery, should the interrogating party be entitled to a list of the documents selected by counsel for review by the witness? See Sporck v. Peil, 759 F.2d 312 (3d Cir.), cert. denied, 474 U.S. 903, 106 S.Ct. 232, 88 L.Ed.2d 230 (1985) ("Proper application of Rule 612 should never implicate an attorney's selection, in preparation for a witness' deposition, of a group of documents that he believes critical to a case").

8. *Practice tip*: "[W]hile many good lawyers forget to do so, it is always worth asking the witness if she brought any documents to the deposition.

This question often is so productive that seasoned practitioners routinely ask it. You are taking a big chance if you do not do so. It is simply astounding how many witnesses, sophisticated and unsophisticated, show up for depositions with a sheaf of documents in their briefcases. Often, their own attorneys have not even seen the documents. You have to remember to get them to open the briefcase. My practice is to bury this question in a series of routine background questions. I try to ask it when the witness has become comfortable with me and the opposing attorney does not appear to be paying too much attention. Almost every time, witnesses, especially non-parties, respond that, yes, they did bring documents. Some have even handed them to me before an opposing attorney could object. At least half the time, the question unearths a useful document that was not previously produced in discovery, such as a calendar, notebook or personal file." Mills, Taking Chances at Depositions, Litigation, Fall 2001, at 30, 33.

RHONE–POULENC RORER, INC.
v. HOME INDEMNITY CO.

United States Court of Appeals, Third Circuit, 1994.
32 F.3d 851.

Before MANSMANN, LEWIS, CIRCUIT JUDGES. and McKELVIE, DISTRICT JUDGE.

McKELVIE, DISTRICT JUDGE.

In this insurance coverage case, the district court has ordered the insureds, their attorneys and their accountants to produce documents that would normally be protected from disclosure by the attorney client privilege * * * or as attorney work product. The documents to be produced were created before the insureds purchased coverage, and contain evaluations of the insureds' potential liability to consumers of their products.

The district court found the information in the documents relevant to matters in issue in the action in that it may tend to show whether or not the insureds expected or intended the claims for which they seek coverage. The court held the insureds had waived any right to maintain confidentiality of these documents by filing this action for coverage and by putting in issue the matter of their knowledge of facts relating to the claims.

[In 1985, Rhone–Poulenc began negotiating the purchase of a company named Armour that marketed a blood clotting product sold primarily for use by hemophiliacs. It formally acquired Armour in January, 1986, and three months later Armour was named as a defendant in the first of a series of lawsuits brought by plaintiffs who claimed they had become infected with HIV due to use of Armour's blood clotting product. Over 200 such cases have been filed against Armour. (See In re Factor VIII or IX Concentrate Blood Products Litigation, *supra* p. 156.)

Rhone–Poulenc and Armour brought this suit against Home Indemnity Co., seeking a declaration that the general liability policy Home issued Rhone–Poulenc effective December 31, 1985, provided coverage with regard to these suits. They also sued Pacific Employers Insurance Co. (PEIC) on similar grounds with regard to a blanket excess policy PEIC issued in July, 1986. Defendants denied coverage and also asserted as an affirmative defense that claims for HIV infection were not "occurrences" within the meaning of the policies because covered "occurrences" were limited to events not "expected" by the insured, while these suits were foreseen. They also asserted that Rhone–Poulenc had wrongfully obtained the coverage by intentionally failing to disclose its knowledge of the potential for such claims.

A relatively-tangled series of discovery disputes followed concerning the information Rhone–Poulenc and Armour possessed when the insurance coverage was issued. Rhone–Poulenc's CEO testified in deposition about the investigation undertaken with regard to Armour before Rhone–Poulenc bought it. He said that the company obtained advice from outside legal counsel on potential liabilities in connection with the contemplated acquisition. Thereafter, defendants pressed for production of all documents possessed by Rhone–Poulenc relating to assessments of potential AIDS-related claims in 1985 or early 1986, and also served subpoenas for a wide range of similar materials on several law firms that had advised Rhone–Poulenc about the contemplated acquisition of Armour.

The district court ordered that plaintiffs produce the requested documents and that the law firms comply with the subpoenas. It explained:

> At issue is Plaintiffs' knowledge of the liabilities associated with the acquisition of Armour. The issues put into question by this lawsuit focus around Plaintiffs' knowledge of the underlying claims and when they became aware of such claims. This court finds that the documents The Home and PEIC seek will aid in disclosing what and when Plaintiffs knew of the underlying claims. Thus, the information contained in the requested documents is directly relevant. Therefore, in this instance this court finds it necessary to invade the attorney-client privilege.

As the court of appeals explained, the district court held: (1) in filing the action for a declaration of insurance coverage, Rhone–Poulenc and Armour had put in issue the knowledge they had as to potential AIDS-related claims at the time they purchased the coverage; (2) by putting their knowledge of those matters in issue, they had waived the privilege to prevent the disclosure of attorney client and accountant client communications relevant to those matters; and (3) by putting their knowledge of these matters in issue, they had also waived the protection from disclosure of the work product of their attorneys. Finding that the district court had committed clear error, the court of appeals issued a writ of mandate.]

There is authority for the proposition that a party can waive the attorney client privilege by asserting claims or defenses that put his or her attorney's advice in issue in the litigation. For example, a client may waive the privilege as to certain communications with a lawyer by filing a malpractice action against the lawyer. A defendant may also waive the privilege by asserting reliance on the advice of counsel as an affirmative defense. Chevron Corp. v. Pennzoil Co., 974 F.2d 1156 (9th Cir.1992) (party's claim that its tax position was reasonable because it was based on advice of counsel puts advice in issue and waives privilege); see also Hunt v. Blackburn, 128 U.S. at 470, 9 S.Ct. at 127, (client waives privilege when she alleges as a defense that she was misled by counsel). In an action for patent infringement, where a party is accused of acting willfully, and where that party asserts as an essential element of its defense that it relied upon the advice of counsel, the party waives the privilege regarding communications pertaining to that advice. Mellon v. Beecham Group PLC, 17 U.S.P.Q.2d 1149, 1151, 1991 WL 16494 (D.N.J. 1990); see also, e.g., W.L. Gore & Associates, Inc. v. Tetratec Corp., 15 U.S.P.Q.2d 1048, 1051, 1989 WL 144178 (E.D.Pa.1989) (client waived privilege by asserting reliance upon advice of counsel as an essential element of his defense).

In these cases, the client has made the decision and taken the affirmative step in the litigation to place the advice of the attorney in issue. Courts have found that by placing the advice in issue, the client has opened to examination facts relating to that advice. Advice is not in issue merely because it is relevant, and does not necessarily become in issue merely because the attorney's advice might affect the client's state of mind in a relevant manner. The advice of counsel is placed in issue where the client asserts a claim or defense, and attempts to prove that claim or defense by disclosing or describing an attorney client communication.

Thus, in a patent suit, where an infringer is alleged to have acted willfully, the advice of the infringer's lawyer may be relevant to the question of whether the infringer acted with a willful state of mind. However, the advice of the infringer's counsel is not placed in issue, and the privilege is not waived, unless the infringer seeks to limit its liability by describing that advice and by asserting that he relied on that advice. When the advice of counsel is asserted as a defense by the infringer, the patent owner may explore facts that would make it more probable than not that the infringer did not rely in good faith on that advice, including for example, what the advice was, when it was given, whether the alleged infringer's conduct suggests he had relied on the advice and whether he had knowledge of facts that would have led him to believe it would not be reasonable to rely on that advice.

Finding a waiver of the attorney client privilege when the client puts the attorney's advice in issue is consistent with the essential elements of the privilege. That is, in leaving to the client the decision whether or not to waive the privilege by putting the attorney's advice in issue, we provide certainty that the client's confidential communications will not be disclosed unless the client takes an affirmative step to waive the privilege, and we provide predictability for the client concerning the circumstances by which the client will waive that privilege. This certainty and predictability as to the circumstances of a waiver encourage clients to consult with counsel free from the apprehension that the communications will be disclosed without their consent.

Some decisions have extended the finding of a waiver of the privilege to cases in which the client's state of mind may be in issue in the litigation. These courts have allowed the opposing party discovery of confidential attorney client communications in order to test the client's contentions. See, e.g., Hearn v. Rhay, 68 F.R.D. 574 (E.D.Wash.1975). These decisions are of dubious validity. While the opinions dress up their analysis with a checklist of factors, they appear to rest on a conclusion that the information sought is relevant and should in fairness be disclosed. Relevance is not the standard for determining whether or not evidence should be protected from disclosure as privileged, and that remains the case even if one might conclude the facts to be disclosed are vital, highly probative, directly relevant or even go to the heart of an issue.

As the attorney client privilege is intended to assure a client that he or she can consult with counsel in confidence, finding that confidentiality may be waived depending on the relevance of the communication completely undermines the interest to be served. Clients will face the greatest risk of disclosure for what may be the most important matters. Furthermore, because the definition of what may be relevant and discoverable from those consultations may depend on the facts and circumstances of as yet unfiled litigation, the client will have no sense of whether the communication may be relevant to some future issue, and will have no sense of certainty or assurance that the communication will remain confidential.

A party does not lose the privilege to protect attorney client communications from disclosure in discovery when his or her state of mind is put in issue in the action. While the attorney's advice may be relevant to the matters in issue, the privilege applies as the interests it is intended to protect are still served by confidentiality.

It appears that one matter in issue in this case is whether or not the insureds knew, before they obtained coverage, that Armour's pharmaceutical products were causing the transmission of HIV. Rhone–Poulenc has not waived the attorney client privilege by filing this lawsuit or by placing its state of mind in issue. As Rhone–Poulenc and Armour have not interjected the advice of counsel as an essential element of a claim in this case, the district court erred in * * * finding they must disclose documents relating to the AIDS-related evaluation that would otherwise be protected from disclosure by the attorney client privilege.

In summary, we emphasize that our holding is not meant to preclude disclosure of the knowledge the insureds possessed at the time they obtained coverage. Facts are discoverable, the legal conclusions regarding those facts are not. A litigant cannot shield from discovery the knowledge it possessed by claiming it has been communicated to a lawyer; nor can a litigant refuse to disclose facts simply because that information came from a lawyer. Rather than separately review each subpoena served on the law firms, it should suffice to say that each subpoena seeks the production of both privileged and discoverable documents. Because some documents may contain both discoverable and privileged information it would be appropriate, if not too burdensome, to redact them accordingly. On remand the insurers may redraft the subpoenas in a manner consistent with this opinion.

[The appellate court also concluded that the district judge erred in finding that a waiver of the attorney client privilege on this ground would justify production of work product materials. For one thing, work product that was not shown to the client could have no effect on the client's state of mind. Moreover, work product belongs to the lawyer, not the client, and care should be taken in assessing the reach of any waiver. Because the subpoenas to the law firms, as written, were generally directed toward documents for which a waiver by the client would not be effective, the court held that they should be quashed.]

Notes and Questions

1. The starting point for this kind of waiver is that the client's state of mind with regard to certain legal issues is relevant to the outcome of the case, and the client seeks to present privileged material to prove its state of mind. Under these circumstances, one confronts a risk of a different kind of selective disclosure. As Judge Learned Hand put it regarding the Fifth Amendment, United States v. St. Pierre, 132 F.2d 837 (2d Cir.1942): "It must be conceded that the privilege is to suppress the truth, but that does not mean that there is a privilege to garble it; although its exercise deprives the parties of evidence, it should not furnish one side with what may be false evidence and deprive the other of any means of detecting the imposition."

Thus, where one uses privileged matter affirmatively as evidence one may not select only the favorable material and deny access to the rest. This insight explains the subject matter scope of waiver. For example, in a patent infringement case the court applied the subject matter scope to opinions of counsel about the validity of a patent: "If the rule were limited to only a particular counsel, a party might get several viewpoints and assert reliance on only one, thus barring an inquiry as to the actuality and reasonableness of that reliance." Technitrol, Inc. v. Digital Equip. Corp., 181 U.S.P.Q. (BNA) 731, 732 (N.D.Ill.1974).

Where such a waiver occurs, therefore, the opponent needs access to all materials bearing on the subject matter at hand. Recognizing the need to prepare to meet such material, some courts therefore have required parties to decide in advance of trial whether they will use privileged material as affirmative evidence at trial so that there will be time to review related privileged materials before trial and prepare to rebut the showing. See Handgards, Inc. v. Johnson & Johnson, 413 F.Supp. 926, 932–33 (N.D.Cal. 1976); International Tel. & Tel. Corp. v. United Tel. Co., 60 F.R.D. 177, 186 (M.D.Fla.1973).

2. The doctrine does not stop with cases in which the party uses privileged material as evidence, however. As the court notes, where an

element of a claim or defense involves the party's state of mind regarding legal matters, the assertion of that claim or defense waives the privilege regarding legal advice the client received at the pertinent time about that subject. Why does this rule not apply in *Rhone-Poulenc*? Note the connection between the burden of pleading and this waiver doctrine. Is the allocation of burden of pleading a sensible way of apportioning this waiver consequence? Consider whether the insurers in *Rhone-Poulenc* could be required to reveal privileged materials regarding their understanding of the risks of HIV contamination litigation involving Armour at the time the insurance was issued.

3. Should this waiver doctrine be limited to cases in which the advice of counsel is an element of the claim or defense of the party alleged to have waived the privilege? Compare *Rhone-Poulenc* with Pitney–Bowes, Inc. v. Mestre, 86 F.R.D. 444 (S.D.Fla.1980), in which Pitney–Bowes sued for reformation of a contract, claiming that the actual agreement had expired although the written agreement appeared to remain in force. The court held that Pitney–Bowes had waived the attorney-client privilege:

> Here, P–B has injected a narrow issue into the dispute, namely, *the intent of the parties.* * * * [P–B] asserted that it had intended to enter into modifications of pure patent licensing agreements. It then sought to withhold communications between its attorneys and executives that might reveal the true intent behind the agreements. P–B has placed in issue the very soul of this litigation—the intent of the parties with regard to construction of certain terms of the Agreements.

To what extent is this conclusion justified by P–B's intention to relinquish the privilege? Is that the price for suing to reform a contract? Has Rhone–Poulenc similarly injected the question of its intent into this case?

See also United States v. Exxon Corp., 94 F.R.D. 246 (D.D.C.1981), in which the government sued to recover $183 million from Exxon alleged overcharges in violation of Department of Energy (DOE) regulations. Exxon asserted an affirmative defense claiming that it had relied in good faith on the regulations. Reasoning that "a party waives the protection of the attorney-client privilege when he voluntarily injects into the suit the question of his state of mind," the court held that disclosure was required as to all advice Exxon had received from its attorneys about the regulations. It explained:

> Exxon's affirmative defenses necessarily revolve around whether Exxon did, in fact, primarily or solely rely upon a particular DOE regulation or communication when the company made its pricing decisions. Thus, the only way to assess the validity of Exxon's affirmative defenses, voluntarily injected into this dispute, is to investigate attorney-client communications where Exxon's interpretation of various DOE policies and directives was established and where Exxon expresses its intentions regarding compliance with those policies and directives. There is no other reasonable way for plaintiff to explore Exxon's corporate state of mind, a consideration now central to this suit.

Other courts have taken an aggressive attitude toward this justification for access to privileged material. For example, in Hearn v. Rhay, 68 F.R.D. 574 (E.D.Wash.1975), the court held that, by invoking the defense of qualified immunity in a suit under 42 U.S.C.A. § 1983, the defendant had impliedly waived any privilege it had with regard to information "germane" to that defense. It reasoned that plaintiff needed access to privileged information to "defend against defendant's affirmative defense," a need it found to be "inextricably merged with the elements of plaintiff's case and defendant's affirmative defense." In Russell v. Curtin Matheson Scientific, Inc., 493 F.Supp. 456 (S.D.Tex.1980), plaintiffs claimed that their ADEA suit was not time-barred because the running of the limitations period should be equitably tolled because defendant misled them about how and when to file their suit. The court held that by raising the tolling issue in response to defendant's limitations defense plaintiffs had waived the privilege with regard to any communications they had with their attorney concerning how to file their suit.

4. Some courts have expressed concern about the potential breadth of this ground for waiver. For example, in United States v. White, 887 F.2d 267 (D.C.Cir.1989), White was prosecuted for having created an illegal relationship with a government officer. The district court held that, by denying his criminal intent, White waived the privilege with respect to his conversations with his lawyer about whether the arrangement would be legal. The appellate court disagreed (id. at 270):

> A rule thus forfeiting the privilege upon denial of mens rea would deter individuals from consulting with their lawyers to ascertain the legality of contemplated actions; it would therefore undermine the animating purpose of the privilege.

> The district court apparently equated White's denial of criminal intent with a reliance-upon-advice-of-counsel defense, which would have waived the privilege. Reliance on advice of counsel is an affirmative defense, an assertion more positive and specific than a general denial of criminal intent. To be acquitted for lack of criminal intent, White did not need to introduce any evidence of communications to and from [his lawyer], and he did not do so. Indeed, White carefully refrained from relying on any statements of counsel and expressly disavowed any intent to rely on an advice-of-counsel defense.

* * *

> In fact, to be acquitted for lack of criminal intent, White need not have presented any evidence. Intent is an element of the offense the government must prove. It was White's constitutional right to put the government to its proof on all the elements of the offense.

5. In *Rhone-Poulenc*, the court also says that facts are discoverable and that a litigant cannot refuse to disclose facts simply because they came from its lawyer. If the communications between the lawyer and client are not discoverable, how can one know whether the litigant has fully disclosed the facts it knew?

6. Note that, unlike other waivers, this sort can be withdrawn; if waiver applies to a party but the party values its privilege sufficiently it may withdraw its claim or defense and avoid disclosure.

Chapter VI

JUDICIAL CONTROL OF PRETRIAL LITIGATION

We have already seen in Chapter I that public law litigation focused attention on the judge as the central actor in civil litigation. Since the 1970s, active judicial control of all litigation has become much more prevalent in the American federal courts. See Marcus, Reining in the American Litigator: The New Role of American Judges, 27 Hast. Int'l & Compar.L.Rev. 3 (2003). This chapter examines a *potpourri* of issues raised by this active judicial involvement in litigation before trial. In the next chapter we will consider innovative ways of handling the trial itself.

The issues in this chapter share a single theme—the extent to which the judge should play a more active role than simply serving as the impartial and remote decider of the merits. The chapter begins with an overview of increased judicial management of litigation and promotion of settlement, and the debate that these activities have spawned. It then examines the use of sanctions to deal with what the judge perceives as inappropriate behavior. More specific issues follow: delegation to special masters, appointment of counsel for parties in class actions and consolidated litigation; awards of attorneys' fees, and disqualification of the judge.

A. THE CASE MANAGEMENT MOVEMENT

Until the 1970s, lawyers and parties largely controlled the pretrial development of lawsuits, and judges took little interest in them until the parties demanded attention by filing motions or seeking a trial date. That has changed.

In the federal courts, the change began in metropolitan courts in the 1960s, partly due to the adoption of the "single assignment system" under which a case would be assigned to a single judge at filing, and that judge would ordinarily preside over the case until final judgment was entered. This arrangement fostered a sense in which the judge had greater responsibility for the case than had been true with the "master calendar" system prevailing before, under which specific tasks regarding given cases—deciding a motion, etc.—were assigned to available judges even though they might not before have presided in the case, and might not see it again.

At much the same time, the rate of civil filings in federal court appeared to increase significantly. Whether that increase is real, or significant, is a matter of some controversy. Coupled with the single assignment system, the sense of increased work prompted innovation by judges. As one judge who was a strong proponent of active judicial management wrote in 1981:

> Federal district court filings have more than doubled during the last twelve years, and an increasing number of these cases are complex and protracted. In the last decade, the number of trials lasting over thirty days has increased by 344 percent. But in spite of burgeoning caseloads—perhaps because of them—federal courts have become more efficient. In the last twelve years, the median time from filing to disposition has dropped by twenty percent, and in the last year alone the case output per district judge has increased by six percent.

Peckham, The Federal Judge as Case Manager: The New Role in Guiding a Case From Filing to Disposition, 69 Calif. L. Rev. 770, 770 (1981).

Further changes resulted from judges' increasingly active supervision of cases before them. Although not specifically mandated by the original Federal Rules of Civil Procedure, this activity could be pursued through pretrial conferences under Rule 16 and was designed to accomplish the objectives of Rule 1, that suits be resolved in a just, speedy, and inexpensive manner.

A judge using this approach would summon counsel for a conference early in the litigation, and use the occasion to establish a plan for the development of the case, and in particular the discovery that needed to be done. As the same time, the judge could "be alert to the particularly combative attorney who, if the case is not actively managed during pretrial, might succeed in turning a trial that should be a molehill into a mountain. * * * The meeting itself warns the attorneys that they have a vigilant judge, and it may therefore prod attorneys who might otherwise be less than diligent into transferring the case to their 'active' files. The conference can also give the judge a 'feel' for the case and the attorneys; he may pick up early signals that an attorney tends to be careless or to procrastinate, perhaps warranting a fairly rigid timetable and a warning that it will be strictly enforced. * * * He may glean that one or both attorneys are confused about important legal or other issues in the action, so that the later, formal pretrial conference and order should be comprehensive." Peckham, *supra*, 69 Cal.L.Rev. at 781–82.

The case management movement was a "bottom up" development that began with innovation on the local level in metropolitan courts. But national rule changes have made some such effort mandatory in most federal litigation. Rule 26(d) provides that the parties should not commence formal discovery until they confer pursuant to Rule 26(f) to develop a discovery plan. That discovery plan must then be submitted to the court for consideration in connection with a scheduling order under Rule 16(b), which should be entered only after the judge interacts with the lawyers, and must set deadlines for adding parties, filing motions, and completing discovery. The Rule 16(b) order may also deal with a variety of other things. Congress itself embraced some notions of case management in the Civil Justice Reform Act of 1990, 104 Stat. 5089, which expired in 1997. According to the legislative history, the CJRA sought to implement the "benefits of enhanced case management" because "greater and earlier judicial control over civil cases yields faster rates of disposition." S.Rep. 101–416 (101st Cong., 1st Sess.) at 16. So the message that began as a bottom up movement is also being touted from on high.

Although case management has been widely embraced in federal courts, it has also been questioned. We turn to some of these questions now.

RESNIK, MANAGERIAL JUDGES
96 Harv.L.Rev. 374, 380, 424–31 (1982).

In the rush to conquer the mountain of work, no one—neither judges, court administrators, nor legal commentators—has assessed whether relying on trial judges for informal dispute resolution and for case management, either before or after trial, is good, bad, or neutral. Little empirical evidence supports the claim that judicial management "works" either to settle cases or to provide cheaper, quicker, or fairer dispositions. Proponents of judicial management have also failed to consider the systemic effects of the shift in judicial role. Management is a new form of "judicial activism," a behavior that usually attracts substantial criticism. Moreover, judicial management may be teaching judges to value their statistics, such as the number of case dispositions, more than they value the quality of their dispositions. Finally, because managerial judging is less visible and usually unreviewable, it gives trial courts more authority and at the same time provides litigants with fewer procedural safeguards to protect them from abuse of that authority. In short, managerial judging may be redefining sub silentio our standards of what constitutes rational, fair, and impartial adjudication.

* * *

[Professor Resnik finds insufficient empirical information to support the conclusion that judicial management shortened the time to dispose of cases, increased the number of cases that were resolved, or reduced costs.]

In the rush to conquer case loads, few proponents of managerial judging have examined its side effects. Judicial management has its own techniques, goals, and values, which appear to elevate speed over deliberation, impartiality, and fairness. * * *

Vast New Powers.—Judges are very powerful: they decide contested issues, and they alone can compel obedience by the threat of contempt. As a result, those subject to judges' authority may challenge it only at great risk. Under the individual calendar system, a single judge retains control over all phases of a case. Thus, litigants who incur a judge's displeasure may suffer judicial hostility or even vengeance with little hope of relief.

[Professor Resnik finds that judicial management expands the opportunities for judges to use their power, but that it tends to undermine traditional constraints on the use of that power without providing norms or standards to guide judges in the use of this power.]

Given the lack of established standards, judges are forced to draw on their own experience. Judges certainly are familiar with the problems of the courts; they were among the first to identify the need for reform. But awareness of the problems does not necessarily qualify judges to design the solutions, especially on an individual, ad hoc basis. As familiar adages discouraging self-medication by doctors and self-representation by lawyers suggest, self-interest often makes professionals less objective, dispassionate, and adept at their work. Moreover, judges may well overestimate the extent of their wisdom. Many have been trial lawyers; they have some appreciation for which litigant tactics are well founded and which are dilatory. But because few have practiced in all of the diverse areas of federal court jurisdiction, they may reach ill-founded conclusions in cases about which they really know very little.

The Threat to Impartiality.—Privacy and informality have some genuine advantages; attorneys and judges can discuss discovery schedules and explore settlement proposals without the constraints of the formal courtroom environment. But substantial dangers also inhere in such activities. The extensive information that judges receive during pretrial conferences has not been filtered by the rules of evidence. Some of this information is received ex parte, a process that deprives the opposing party of the opportunity to contest the validity of information received. Moreover, judges are in close contact with attorneys during the course of management. Such interactions may become occasions for the development of intense feelings—admiration, friendship, or antipathy. Therefore, management becomes a fertile field for the growth of personal bias.

Further, judges with supervisory obligations may gain stakes in the cases they manage. Their prestige may ride on "efficient" management, as calculated by the speed and number of dispositions. Competition and peer pressure may tempt judges to rush litigants because of reasons unrelated to the merits of disputes. * * *

In the past, such exposure to parties and issues and such a comparable interest in the proceedings might have resulted in recusal or disqualification. Despite a flexible approach to the procedural safeguards required to ensure due process, the Supreme Court has consistently required an "impartial" judge—an individual with no prior involvement or interest in the dispute. Interest is broadly defined; indirect as well as direct benefits suffice to require disqualification. * * * Nevertheless, neither the Supreme Court, the lower federal courts, nor Congress has considered the effect of judicial management on impartiality.

I recognize that case management is not the only anomaly in the rules governing judicial disqualification and recusal. Many current practices assume that trial judges can compartmentalize their minds, disregard inappropriate evidence, and reconsider past decisions in light of new information. * * * Yet reconsideration by the same judge who first heard a case is far less worrisome than factfinding by the judge who *managed* the case. As "repeat adjudicators," judges are generally confined to the record. They rely upon traditional adversarial exchanges, publicly explain their decisions, and know that their work may be reviewed on appeal. In contrast, as pretrial case managers, judges operate in the freewheeling arena of informal dispute resolution. Having supervised case preparation and pressed for settlement, judges can hardly be considered untainted if they are ultimately asked to find the facts and adjudicate the merits of a dispute.

Unreviewable power, casual contact, and interest in outcome (or in aggregate outcomes) have not traditionally been associated with the "due process" decisionmaking model. These features do not evoke images of reasoned adjudication, images that form the very basis of both our faith in the judicial process and our enormous grant of power to federal judges. The literature of managerial judging refers only occasionally to the values of due process: the accuracy of decisionmaking, the adequacy of reasoning, and the quality of adjudication. Instead, commentators and the training sessions for district judges emphasize speed, control, and quantity. District court chief judges boast of vast statistics on the number of cases terminated, the number and type of discrete events (such as trial days and oral arguments) supervised, and the number of motions decided. The accumulation of such data may cause— or reflect—a subtle shift in the values that shape the judiciary's comprehension of its own mission. Case processing is no longer viewed as a means to an end; instead, it appears to have become the desired goal. Quantity has become all important; quality is occasionally mentioned and then ignored. Indeed, some commentators regard deliberation as an obstacle to efficiency.

Proponents of management may be forgetting the quintessential judicial obligations of conducting a reasoned inquiry, articulating the reasons for decision, and subjecting those reasons to appellate review— characteristics that have long defined judging and distinguished it from other tasks.

PECKHAM, A JUDICIAL RESPONSE TO THE COST OF LITIGATION: CASE MANAGEMENT, TWO–STAGE DISCOVERY PLANNING AND ALTERNATIVE DISPUTE RESOLUTION

37 Rutgers L.Rev. 253, 260–67 (1985).

The most outspoken critic of case management, Professor Judith Resnik, has charged that the "new" emphasis on judicial case supervision is a departure from the traditional role of judges and is inconsistent with our notions of due process and the proper functioning of the adversarial system. Furthermore, she has asserted that, contrary to the claims of its proponents, case management may not be cost-effective.

At the outset it should be noted that the recent emphasis on early judicial involvement in the litigation process may not be either as new or as much a departure from tradition as Professor Resnik's article intimates. A judge's duty has never been purely adjudication. Judges have long engaged in some form of case and calendar management as well as court administration, mediation, regulation of the bar, and other professional activities. Nevertheless, Professor Resnik has performed an important service by forcing us to focus on the potential benefits and dangers of case management.

* * *

A.   IMPARTIALITY

* * *

An impartial adjudicator must indeed refrain from prejudging the merits of an action. All would agree that at trial a judge must analyze the parties' legal arguments, consider only that evidence which is properly before the court, and reach a reasoned decision based upon coherent legal principles. Although a judge must exhibit the qualities of dispassion and disengagement, he or she need not be ignorant in order to be impartial, nor remote in order to be dispassionate.

Traditionally, throughout the course of a lawsuit, a judge is exposed to the theories and contentions of the parties in order to render rulings. In determining motions to sever or bifurcate, a judge is required to anticipate, and sometimes to restrict, the parties' litigative strategies. Similarly, in evaluating a discovery motion, a judge legitimately may inquire whether a particular avenue of investigation is reasonable in relation to the theory of the case. Indeed, the 1983 amendments to rule 26 of the Federal Rules of Civil Procedure explicitly inject the concept of proportionality into the judicial calculus. A court performs the same balancing calculus when it rules on an evidentiary objection. In making such evidentiary rulings, a judge must be exposed to what Professor Resnik terms "extraneous and impermissible information," by way of offers of proof. Yet, in the latter situation, we do not consider the judicial

632 JUDICIAL CONTROL OF LITIGATION Ch. VI

mind to be contaminated. When all status conferences and discovery disputes are conducted on the record with all parties represented, the numerous pretrial rulings which issue from those hearings are similar in character to the traditional rulings which cause us no concern.

Admittedly, in limiting the scope of discovery, setting schedules, and narrowing issues, the court restricts somewhat the attorneys' freedom to pursue their actions in an unfettered fashion and eliminates entirely some theories or lines of inquiry. Motions to dismiss some claims or for partial summary judgment similarly may result in the drastic alteration of the contours of a lawsuit, yet we do not question the legitimacy of judges' deciding such motions.

Impartiality is a capacity of mind—a learned ability to recognize and compartmentalize the relevant from the irrelevant and to detach one's emotional from one's rational faculties. Only because we trust judges to be able to satisfy those obligations do we permit them to exercise such power and oversight. On the basis of this trust, we permit the same judge who presides over a pretrial suppression hearing, where defendants may solemnly proclaim their ownership of the seized evidence in order to establish their standing, to sit in the subsequent trial and issue further rulings. Moreover, the type of information a judge receives when resolving discovery disputes or making scheduling decisions is not of a prejudicial nature.

Unreported or ex parte communications do indeed provide a temptation for abuse and, more importantly, may create the appearance or suspicion of coerciveness. To alleviate this potential abuse, however, all status and pretrial conferences should be on the record with all counsel present. The informal setting may still be preserved by the use of the telephone or holding the conference in chambers. * * *

Professor Resnik has also opined that the emphasis on litigation management may cause judges to become overly concerned with the quantity, as opposed to the quality, of dispositions in their courtrooms. Since the federal court system began keeping statistical records in 1940, there have been no allegations that its judges have been improperly influenced by knowledge or their statistical performances. * * * Surely, if federal judges are not swayed by the possible impact of their rulings upon their political or social prestige, they will not become preoccupied with the numerical state of their calendars. Thus, the trend toward case supervision is not likely to cause judges to take an improper interest in the quantitative character of their calendars.

B. ACCOUNTABILITY

* * *

Professor Resnik correctly states that, under our present system, pretrial judicial decisions concerning scheduling or discovery are not likely to be reviewed by mandamus. This, however, is not anomalous. Many, if not most, interlocutory rulings which may significantly affect the future progress of the case (for example, amendment of the pleadings or joinder) are also reviewable only in unusual instances. Furthermore, even if review should be granted, an appellate court will generally defer to the broad discretion of the trial court on issues of trial procedure and management.

Professor Resnik's concern with the unreviewability of such rulings is related to her fear that they may result in a settlement that is unfair to one of the parties. As previously noted, however, this possibility is presented by numerous common interlocutory rulings. Furthermore, a settlement which results from one party's collapse in the face of the other party's unsupervised dilatory tactics is a far more probable example of an unfair and unreviewable termination of the action. Pretrial judicial intervention serves to promote equitable and informed settlements by insuring diligent and economical trial preparation.

* * *

C.   PRESERVATION OF THE ADVERSARY SYSTEM

Professor Resnik raises a serious issue when she questions whether judicial supervision will ultimately weaken the adversarial system. * * * Professor Resnik places the onus of responsibility for the orderly and prompt disposition of litigation with the bar, whereas I place that responsibility equally, if not primarily, on the shoulders of the judge. She wishes to preserve the laissez-faire character of the adversarial system. I contend, however, that our adversarial system has run amok and that the movement toward judicial oversight represents an effort to preserve the best qualities of the system. * * *

Furthermore, there is nothing sacrosanct about the adversarial system. It is a mere instrument by which to achieve the just resolution of disputes. If it can no longer fulfill that function effectively, it must be modified. From many quarters one hears the cry that the adversarial system is seriously flawed and cannot be retained in its present form. Under the laissez-faire model, the costs and delays of litigation have multiplied apace.

* * *

Earlier in this century, we recognized that the laissez-faire [type] of capitalism, in its pure form, was no longer appropriate for our complex modern society, that individual liberty would not be adequately protected by a government which served only as a passive night watchman, and that limited regulation would in fact enhance true freedom and preserve the best aspects of our system. Similarly, the cause of justice can no longer be served by a laissez-faire judicial model. Our controlled inaction is an affirmative choice, an abdication of our responsibility to use our power to assist in restoring the health of the system. We are not lowered by our participating in the movement but rather by our failing to do so. Professor Resnik wishes to bring back the judicial blindfold, but we cannot remain blind to the fact that the court's traditional remoteness contributes to the devastating abuses which threaten to subvert our system of due process.

D. COST EFFECTIVENESS

Professor Resnik's charge that early judicial intervention is unnecessarily costly is similarly unfounded. Status conferences serve a valuable function by clearly defining and limiting the scope of the lawsuit and reducing the costs of delay and unnecessary discovery. Early attorney preparedness facilitates early settlement before substantial costs are incurred.

Professor Resnik further overestimates the time a judge spends on these matters. I estimate that a judge could easily conduct all status conferences for a full caseload in one day per month and certainly in no more than two. This is very little time to expend in facilitating the prompt and fair disposition of cases. * * * [P]roperly conducted, these conferences will indirectly promote settlements. Case management simply brings cases to settlement or to trial sooner than if their progress were left entirely to the impetus of the parties.

Notes and Questions

1. Is something more significant than attorney latitude lost if the judge supplants the lawyers as the one primarily responsible for conduct of the litigation? To the extent that lawyers are responsive to their clients, this could shift control of litigation away from clients. Research in social psychology has suggested that allowing litigants to control the development and presentation of proof in their cases is an important factor governing their satisfaction with the litigation process. Thus, a 1975 study concluded that "[f]or participants, the evidence that an adversary procedure significantly enhances the acceptability of the outcome suggests that civil and criminal processes should be designed to facilitate personal participation by the parties." Walker, Lind & Thibaut, The Relation Between Procedural and Distributive Justice, 65 Va.L.Rev. 1401, 1417 (1979); see also E. Lind & T. Tyler, The Social Psychology of Procedural Justice 30–40 (1988).

But this vision of client control may be overstated in many cases. Empirical research has also indicated that "lawyer-client relations are more often perfunctory and superficial than intimate; the locus of control is shifted toward lawyers rather than clients; lawyers educate their clients to a view of the legal process that serves the lawyer's interests as much, if not more than the clients' interests; [and] litigants are frequently only names to both lawyers and court personnel." Hensler, Resolving Mass Toxic Torts: Myths and Realities, 1989 U.Ill.L.Rev. 89, 92. Are Professor Resnik's criticisms similarly premised on a mythical vision of the role and actions of judges?

2. Judge Peckham criticizes Professor Resnik's "laissez-faire" attitude toward the adversary system, concluding that this method of resolving disputes is a "mere instrument by which to achieve the just resolution of disputes." This attitude places little weight on the value to the participants of controlling the proceedings. Does it adequately recognize the problems

that may be associated with active judicial involvement in the refinement of the issues? Professor Fuller has warned against having the judge attempt to develop the case for either side rather than leaving that to the adversaries:

> [F]ailure generally attends the attempt to dispense with the distinct roles traditionally implied in adjudication. What generally occurs in practice is that at some early point a familiar pattern will seem to emerge from the evidence; an accustomed label is wanting for the case and, without awaiting further proofs, this label is promptly assigned to it. It is a mistake to suppose that this premature cataloguing must necessarily result from impatience, prejudice or mental sloth. Often it proceeds from a very understandable desire to bring the hearing into some order and coherence, for without some tentative theory of the case there is no standard of relevance by which testimony may be measured. But what starts as a preliminary diagnosis designed to direct the inquiry tends, quickly and imperceptibly, to become a fixed conclusion, as all that confirms the diagnosis makes a strong imprint on the mind, while all that runs counter to it is received with diverted attention.

> An adversary presentation seems the only effective means for combatting this natural human tendency to judge too swiftly in terms of the familiar that which is not yet fully known. The arguments of counsel hold the case, as it were, in suspension between two opposing interpretations of it. While the proper classification of the case is thus kept unresolved, there is time to explore all of its peculiarities and nuances.

Fuller, The Forms and Limits of Adjudication, 92 Harv.L.Rev. 353, 383 (1978).

3.   Professor Resnik questioned whether case management "works," in terms of expedited, fair, and less expensive outcomes. The question whether empirical data showed that it worked remained uncertain. See Marcus, Deja Vu All Over Again? An American Reaction to the Woolf Report, in Reform of Civil Procedure, at 219, 232–35 (A. Zuckerman ed. 1995). The Civil Justice Reform Act provided one method of assessing the effects of case management because it directed that a study be done of ten "pilot" districts designed in the legislation.

Under contract with the federal government to conduct the study, the RAND Corporation gathered data on some 12,000 cases pending in the ten "pilot" districts designated in the statute to implement specific case management techniques, and in ten "comparison districts" selected as comparable to the pilot districts. Based on its analysis of this data, RAND concluded that case management had an effect, albeit not necessarily the one that was envisioned by its proponents. Thus, early case management did result in a significant reduction of the time to disposition of cases, but it also added significantly to the litigation cost. This increase in cost was not mere acceleration of expenses that would occur anyway, but an overall increase in the amount spent on the case. The only "win-win" measure that RAND identified was imposition of a short time limitation for completion of discovery; it found that use of this technique significantly accelerated the disposition of litigation without affecting overall cost. See J. Kakalik et al., An Analysis of Judicial Case Management Under the Civil Justice Reform Act (1997). Compare T. Willging, J. Shapard, D. Stienstra & D. Miletich, Discovery and Disclosure Practice, Problems, and Proposals for Change 52–55 (1997) (finding no substantial relationship between discovery cutoffs and cost or duration of litigation).

4. According to Judge Peckham, "[d]elineation of the issues * * * helps to illuminate possible grounds for motions to dismiss and for summary judgment." Peckham, *supra*, 69 Cal.L.Rev. at 780. At least in this regard, case management is said to work:

> Regardless of whether case management accomplishes its stated goals, its aggressive use clearly facilitates pretrial disposition. Rule 16 conferences, for example, often clarify what factual or legal issues may be in dispute, thus permitting focused discovery and identification of claims and defenses suitable for summary resolution. In addition, a judge who actively participates throughout the pretrial phase and is familiar with the dispute's facts and theories may be more inclined to believe that having the same evidence presented at trial is unnecessary and to resolve the case on summary judgment.

Miller, The Pretrial Rush to Judgment: Are the "Litigation Explosion," "Liability Crisis," and Efficiency Cliches Eroding Our Day in Court and Jury Trial Commitments?, 78 N.Y.U.L. Rev. 982, 1006 (2003).

Professor Miller deplores case management's tendency to prompt summary judgment dispositions. Professor Molot, by contrast, sees increased reliance on summary judgment as preferable to other features of case management, particularly settlement promotion (discussed below). In his view, "the controversy that surrounds judicial use of the summary judgment mechanism is more tepid than that surrounding the settlement conference." Molot, An Old Judicial Role for a New Litigation Era, 113 Yale L.J. 27, 45 (2003). Concerned with the lack of legal standards for much judicial management, he borrows from the 19th century's development of reviewable standards for judges to control trials and suggests that "[i]f we were to follow the pattern established in nineteenth-century trial practice * * * we would promote formal tools like summary judgment, formalize those management tools that are susceptible to formalization, like those governing discovery, and either reject or substantially revise management tools that are not susceptible to formalization, like the settlement conference." Id. at 88. Is Professor Molot simply acquiescing in the undesirable trend that Professor Miller laments?

Consider Acuna v. Brown & Root Inc., 200 F.3d 335 (5th Cir.2000), which involved claims for injuries due to exposure to uranium on behalf of about 1,600 plaintiffs. After the cases were removed from state court, the district court entered "Lone Pine" orders (based on Lore v. Lone Pine Corp., No. L–33606–85, N.J. Super. Ct., 1986) requiring that before discovery began plaintiffs establish certain elements of their claims (about causation and their medical conditions) through expert affidavits. When plaintiffs filed form affidavits from a single expert, the court found these insufficient, and when supplemental affidavits did not supply the desired information, the court dismissed most of the claims. The appellate court affirmed, emphasizing that 1,600 plaintiffs were suing over 100 defendants for a range of injuries occurring over a 40–year period. Because the pleadings did not give notice of which plaintiffs claimed to suffer which diseases, or which facilities were involved in the alleged problems of which plaintiff, the district court had authority to "take steps to manage the complex and potentially very burdensome discovery." The court also noted that the information sought was the sort that Fed. R. Civ. P. 11(b)(3) calls for plaintiffs to possess before filing suit.

5. Assuming that fostering disposition of cases via summary judgment or motions to dismiss is a desirable goal, there still might be reason for concern about doing so through the pretrial conference medium. Those motions are ordinarily granted only after notice and an opportunity to fashion a response. Should case management foster a more flexible power to decide the merits of a case? In United Food & Commercial Workers Union Local v. Armour & Co., 106 F.R.D. 345 (N.D.Cal.1985), Judge Peckham granted defendant only partial sanctions due to plaintiff's groundless suit because defendant's lawyers had not informally called his attention to the factual baselessness of the suit soon enough, and had therefore unnecessarily incurred additional costs thereafter.

> Once Armour had pointed out, in the presence of the court, that it had agreed to arbitrate, it seems likely that Unions' counsel would have had to acknowledge his failure to investigate and would have dropped the suit. And if Unions' counsel refused to drop the suit, the court could have asserted its powers of oversight of litigation to dismiss the suit.

Generally courts have been uneasy about granting oral motions for summary judgment. See, e.g., Hanson v. Polk County Land, Inc., 608 F.2d 129 (5th Cir.1979). Should "powers of oversight of litigation" be used in place of formal motions to dismiss or for summary judgment?

Proceeding informally can have pitfalls. Consider the following observations by Magistrate Judge Brazil:

> Prompt rulings can save parties considerable expense and expedite the pretrial process. But the depth of consideration, by both counsel and the neutral, is necessarily limited. I have been forced to acknowledge that fact by parties urging reconsideration of my tentative discovery rulings. In some instances my initial instinct was misplaced, the situation was more complex than I appreciated, and after more careful consideration I have reversed my original decision. These sobering experiences have not led me to conclude that most discovery disputes require formal briefing and argument. But I have become more sensitive to the dangers inherent in speedy and wholly oral proceedings.

Brazil, Special Masters in Complex Cases: Extending the Judiciary or Reshaping Adjudication?, 53 U.Chi.L.Rev. 394, 420 (1986).

6. Some trappings of the adversary system have been found to give way before judicial management. For example, in In re San Juan Dupont Plaza Hotel Fire Litigation, 859 F.2d 1007 (1st Cir.1988), the trial court required the lawyers to provide a list of the exhibits to be used in a deposition in advance of the deposition. The appellate court rejected arguments that this order improperly invaded work product, the doctrine designed to insulate the adversary fact-gathering process (id. at 1015):

> The evolution of the work product doctrine—which sprouted and grew in the fruited plains of pretrial discovery—explains what we see as

a lacuna: the need/hardship balance, such as is precisely enunciated in Rule 26(b)(3), has traditionally been a barometer only of the relative interests of the opposing litigants. This makes abundant good sense for the resolution of discovery rhubarbs, but leaves the circle unclosed in the Rule 16 milieu. Insofar as we can tell, concerns for maximizing the efficient use of judicial and litigant resources (such as are served by broadening judicial management powers) have never heretofore been a relevant consideration in formulating the work product doctrine. Given the rigors of modern-day litigation, and the increased emphasis on case management, the omission looms as intolerable.

When case management, rather than conventional discovery, becomes the hammer which bangs against the work product anvil, logic demands that the district judge must be given greater latitude than provided by the routine striking of the need-hardship balance. Because of "the taxing demands of modern day case management," the requirements of the litigation and the court must, we think, be weighed in determining whether a management technique impermissibly impinges upon the protected zone of work product privacy. In this context the vista is not exclusively head-to-head, A against B, plaintiff versus defendant; the relationship is triangular, with the court itself as a third, important player. There is no reason, then, why the crying need for efficient use of scarce judicial resources cannot—and should not—be factored into the equation. We hold that it must.

Should such efficiency interests generally overcome the precepts of the adversary system?

7.   Do the sorts of regulation explicitly required by Rule 16(b)—schedules for motions and completing discovery—raise similar concerns? Consider Marcus, Slouching Toward Discretion, 78 Notre Dame L. Rev. 1561, 1589–90 (2003):

Without case management, the growing centrality of the pretrial phase meant that the lawyers would be free of substantial constraint from anyone in their use of very substantial powers—most notably in discovery—that modern American procedure conferred on them. * * * Viewed in this light, case management might be seen not just as an increase in judicial discretion, but also as a consequence of the increased lawyer discretion provided under the new rules. Of necessity case management escaped frequent oversight by appellate courts, but a laissez-faire attitude toward lawyer latitude hardly seems preferable.

8.   How should the court develop a schedule for cases before it? Judge Peckham estimated that little effort would be required, but couldn't the preparation of individualized schedules become a burden? Would standard schedules be appropriate? Consider Subrin, Federal Rules, Local Rules, and State Rules: Uniformity, Divergence, and Emerging Procedural Patterns, 137 U.Pa.L.Rev. 1999, 2049 (1989): "Case-by-case management developed because the transaction costs of procedural rules with broad attorney latitude were too high. As a result of federal local rules and state experimentation, the judiciary has already demonstrated that it thinks the transaction costs of ad hoc case-by-case management are also too high. Judges are

already turning to formal limitations and definitions in order to reduce transaction costs."

Should such standardized limitations be avoided in complex litigation? Consider Freehill v. Lewis, 355 F.2d 46, 48 (4th Cir.1966): "A set rule limiting the time within which pretrial discovery may be had may be appropriate for routine cases, indeed, for most cases. The exceptional case requires different treatment, however, and the spirit of the rules does not require that completeness in the exposure of the issues in the pretrial discovery proceedings be sacrificed to speed in reaching the ultimate trial on the merits."

Keep in mind that cutoff dates can loom very large in ordinary litigation. For example, in Otero v. Buslee, 695 F.2d 1244 (10th Cir.1982), defendant delayed discovery past the cutoff date while awaiting the court's ruling on cross motions for summary judgment. As the cutoff date approached, defendant moved for an extension, but the court did not rule on either motion until after the cutoff date, and then denied both motions. The appellate court upheld the denial of leave to conduct discovery after the cutoff date. Should defendant have been required to embark on (possibly expensive) discovery while potentially dispositive motions were pending?

9. *The California Experience*: Dealing with somewhat similar concerns about delay and cost of litigation, California took a different course in the 1980s with its Trial Court Delay Reduction Act, which was added to its Government Code, not its Code of Civil Procedure. See Marcus, Malaise of the Litigation Superpower, in Civil Justice in Crisis (A. Zuckerman, ed., 1999), at 71, 103–04. This legislation commanded prompter handling of litigation and led to computer-generated deadlines that prompted strong objections from lawyers. See id. at 106–07. In light of these concerns, the Legislature modified the Act in 1990 to introduce more flexibility. Despite that injection of flexibility, concerns about rigidity remained and the implementing rules were amended again effective January 1, 2004, to ensure that continuances would be flexibly granted and that multiple factors were considered in setting trial dates. See, e.g., Cal. Rule of Court 375(d) (requiring courts ruling on a motion for a continuance to consider all facts and circumstances relevant to the determination and listing eleven factors to be considered).

10. *Case Management in England*: Based on a comprehensive study of English civil litigation in the mid–1990s, England adopted new Civil Procedure Rules in 1998 that "transformed English civil procedure" and represent "a radical departure from past practice." A. Zuckerman, Civil Procedure 1 (2003). One "cornerstone" of this new regime is case management. N. Andrews, English Civil Procedure 337 (2003). For discussion of the features of English case management, see Zuckerman, *supra*, chp. 10 and 11, and Andrews, *supra*, chp. 2 and 13.

JUDICIAL SETTLEMENT PROMOTION

Case management has certainly come to include judicial promotion of settlement in many cases. See Rule 16(c)(9) (authorizing the court to take action with regard to "settlement and the use of special procedures to assist in resolving the dispute"). Some find this activity deeply troubling:

> The most controversial of all judicial management tools—the judicial settlement conference—is the one that strays the furthest from the judiciary's traditional adjudicative role. When a judge calls parties into his or her chambers to urge a settlement, his or her actions bear almost no resemblance to the traditional judicial role. Parties do not file motions to trigger, or prevent, judicial intervention. There are no legal standards to govern judicial conduct in settlement negotiations. And there generally is no appellate review either of the judge's tactics or the judge's views regarding the merits of the case.

Molot, An Old Judicial Role for a New Litigation Era, 113 Yale L.J. 27, 43–44 (2003).

Skepticism about adjudicated results seems to play a role in some judicial promotion of settlement. Thus, an experienced judge encouraging newly-appointed judges to promote settlement opined that "[o]ptimal justice is usually found somewhere between the polar positions of the litigants. Trial is likely to produce a polar solution, and often the jury or the judge has no choice except all or nothing. Settlement is usually the avenue that allows a more just result than trial." Tone, The Role of the Judge in the Settlement Process, in Seminars for Newly Appointed United States District Judges 57 (1975). But the change in judicial behavior may not be producing results that are as large as some suggest. "There have always been a lot of settlements in American civil courts. It remains unclear whether the percentage of cases terminated by settlement has increased in recent years. And, if there has been an increase, it is unclear whether it is caused by the increased intervention of judges." Galanter, The Emergence of the Judge as a Mediator in Civil Cases, 69 Judicature 257, 257 (1986).

Moreover, settlement conferences may be an integral part of overall case management: "[S]ettlement conferences allow courts to *manage* their dockets efficiently. At these conferences, courts receive important information from the parties concerning the status of cases. Relying on this information, courts then plan ahead, scheduling trials, hearings, and other necessary matters. * * * [S]ettlement conferences, like all pretrial conferences, benefit courts by providing them an opportunity to gather information they need to manage the judicial process efficiently." In re Novak, 932 F.2d 1397, 1404 (11th Cir.1991).

It is difficult to determine whether the judge's involvement really furthers the settlement process. A study of settlement trends in asbestos litigation concluded that while active judicial promotion of settlement did work, "the traditional scheduling of a firm trial date, coupled with benign neglect until the day of trial, also works." T. Willging, Trends in Asbestos Litigation 70–76 (1987). Willging concludes: "Efforts to produce earlier settlements appear justifiable only on grounds of improving the quality of settlements; efficiency grounds will support little more than a system of imposing fines for delayed settlements or a brief judge-hosted conference." Id. at 73.

Lawyers feel that the effort is worthwhile. A major national survey found that "in overwhelming numbers, litigators say judges should get *actively* involved in settlement negotiations in most cases in federal court. Lawyers clearly believe that federal judges can make important contributions to the settlement dynamic and can significantly improve the prospects that the parties will reach an agreement." Brazil, What Lawyers Want From Judges in the Settlement Arena, 106 F.R.D. 85, 85 (1985). The study also found that "[t]he factor cited far and away the most often is willingness to express an opinion, to comment specifically on the strengths or weaknesses of evidence or arguments, or to offer a valuation of the case." Id. at 86.

Thus, although some view settlement as "a capitulation to the conditions of mass society," Fiss, Against Settlement, 93 Yale L.J. 1073, 1075 (1984), this activity will continue to be an important feature of case management.

Notes and Questions

1. Should the judge be able to *order* the parties to discuss settlement? Consider In re Air Crash Disaster at Stapleton International Airport, 720 F.Supp. 1433 (D.Colo.1988), involving 36 suits arising out of an airplane crash that were consolidated by the MDL Panel. After settlement conference with the judge led to settlements in 16 of the cases, the judge ordered the parties in the other 20 cases to meet and discuss settlement at the offices of plaintiffs' counsel. Challenged by defendants, the judge held he had authority to make such an order because "[i]n a consolidated multidistrict case, the goal of efficiency takes on special importance and broadens the range of alternatives available." Id. at 1436. Court orders that the parties go through other forms of "dispute resolution" are discussed in Chapter IX, *infra* p. 938.

2. Can the judge sanction parties for not settling? In Newton v. A.C. & S., Inc., 918 F.2d 1121 (3d Cir.1990), the trial court entered an order setting a time limit for settlement of asbestos personal injury cases set for trial and providing a $1,000 fine in the event the cases were settled after such a date. Although it found that the fixed fine was arbitrary, the appellate court concluded that there was authority under Rule 16 for such a program (id. at 1126):

> Rule 16 does not specifically grant authority to the district court to impose sanctions for settling after a certain date. However, imposing sanctions for unjustified failure to comply with the court's schedule for settlement is entirely consistent with the spirit of Rule 16. The purpose of Rule 16 is to maximize the efficiency of the court system by insisting that attorneys and clients cooperate with the court and abandon practices which unreasonably interfere with the expeditious management of cases. * * *

> The intent and spirit of Rule 16 is to allow courts to actively manage the timetable of case preparation so as to expedite the speedy disposition of cases. Thus, the imposition of sanctions for failure to

comply with a settlement schedule is entirely consistent with the purpose of Rule 16.

3. Should the judge try to mold the substance of the settlement or merely try to facilitate a deal without reference to the terms? One's attitude may depend upon the perspective from which one views the problem. Consider the results of the survey of lawyers mentioned above:

> The question that produces the most extreme differences of opinion cuts right to the core of beliefs about the adversary system. It is: "Should a judge who believes that a party is about to accept a settlement that clearly is unreasonable take some step to encourage that party to reconsider its position?" Among all lawyers only 29% say yes; 54% say no and 16% are not sure. * * * Dramatic differences emerge, however, when we compare the views of attorneys grouped by their practice situations. Lawyers who practice in big firms or who primarily represent defendants are much more likely to object to a judge taking some action in this situation than are lawyers who practice in small firms or who spend most of their time representing plaintiffs. For example, almost 70% of the defense counsel we polled object to judicial intervention on behalf of a party who is about to accept an offer the court feels is clearly unreasonable; by contrast, only 36% of plaintiffs' lawyers share this view. Similarly, while only 18% of the lawyers in our sample who work in the legal aid/public interest field believe a judge should take no action in this situation, that figure jumps to almost 70% among the attorneys we polled who are direct employees of private companies.

Brazil, What Lawyers Want From Judges in the Settlement Arena, 106 F.R.D. 85, 89 (1985). Given this disparity of views on a fundamental issue, why is it that the same lawyers were so near unanimity about the desirability of active judicial involvement in the settlement process?

4. If the judge who presides over settlement discussions will also try the case, does she have too much power to sway the lawyers? Consider Schuck, The Role of Judges in Settling Complex Cases: The Agent Orange Example, 53 U.Chi.L.Rev. 337, 358 (1986):

> The essential, unvarnished fact is this: The lawyers know—and the judge knows that the lawyers know—that the judge is in a position to make many decisions of vital concern to them and their clients in the future, both in this case and in subsequent cases in which they will appear before that judge. Many of these decisions entail the exercise of some judicial discretion. Some, like the pace and nature of discovery, the time of trial, and the admissibility of expert testimony, are almost wholly discretionary. Especially in a complex case, even those decisions that are in principle not discretionary are often not appealable as a legal or practical matter. Some of the most important decisions from the lawyers's selfish point of view—class certification, appointment of lead counsel, and the award of attorneys' fees and costs—may turn upon the judge's perception of a particular lawyer's ability and performance. Rightly or wrongly, lawyers believe that these decisions are more likely to be favorable, at least at the margin, if the judge regards the lawyers as reasonable and cooperative. It would be astonishing, under these

circumstances, if lawyers did not seek to present themselves as conciliatory actors who are anxious to please the court.

5. In addition to participating in settlement discussions, the judge may become an enforcer of a settlement agreement if disputes arise about it. In Lynch, Inc. v. SamataMason Inc., 279 F.3d 487 (7th Cir.2002), a magistrate judge concluded at the end of an off-the-record settlement conference that the parties had reached a settlement. When they later could not agree on one provision for the written settlement agreement, the magistrate judge directed both to submit proposed provisions to him, so he could determine whether the issue had been settled and, if so, which version correctly reflected the settlement that had been reached. Thereafter, he determined that the defendant's version was the correct one and directed the parties to execute an agreement including that provision. When plaintiff refused, the magistrate judge dismissed with prejudice. The court of appeals affirmed, finding that under Illinois law (which applied because the case was in federal court in Illinois) an oral settlement agreement could be binding unless barred by the statute of frauds, which plaintiff did not contend applied. It emphasized that putting the settlement terms into the record and getting the parties to agree on the record is not only the standard practice but the better practice. But both parties assumed the risk of a disagreement by not requesting that be done. See also Doi v. Halekulani Corp., 276 F.3d 1131 (9th Cir.2002) (plaintiff sanctioned for trying to renegotiate settlement agreement after saying she agreed to the settlement when pressed by the judge in open court).

6. *Settling multiparty cases*: In cases involving many defendants, settlement may become more intricate when settlements are reached with some but not other defendants. Sometimes plaintiffs engage in log-rolling to ratchet up settlement amounts and to provide a "litigation war chest" as the litigation evolves. See, e.g., In re Corrugated Container Antitrust Litigation, 643 F.2d 195 (5th Cir.1981) (plaintiffs gradually increased the settlement price for defendants as settlements were reached). Settlement agreements can include provisions going beyond price, such as agreements to provide discovery. They may even reduce the amount due from defendants who settle early if later settlements are cheaper. For example, in Cintech Industrial Coatings, Inc. v. Bennett Indus., Inc., 85 F.3d 1198 (6th Cir.1996), a settling defendant obtained a "most favored nation" clause that entitled it to better terms if plaintiffs later settled on such terms with another defendant. Then plaintiffs dismissed as to another defendant because they lacked evidence against it, and the settling defendant asked for all of its money back. The court held the clause inapplicable to this situation, which was not a "settlement" covered by the agreement. Finally, the possibility that the nonsettling defendants will seek contribution from those ready to settle may prevent settlement. See Franklin v. Kaypro Corp., 884 F.2d 1222 (9th Cir.1989) (observing that a defendant that refuses to settle can force all to trial because of the risk of liability for contribution should the remaining defendant lose at trial). In some instances, however, the court can cut off that ability. See, e.g., Cal.Code Civ.Proc. § 877.6 (authorizing the court to cut off contribution claims on finding that the settlement has been made in good faith); Note, Multiple Defendant Settlement in 10b–5: Good Faith Contribution Bar, 40 Hast.L.J. 1253 (1989).

B. SANCTIONS

Judges may use sanctions to enforce their case management orders. But sanctions—whether imposed on attorneys or parties—generate enormous hostility and have a way of becoming the subject of significant "satellite litigation." Sanctions that affect the outcome of the case also raise troubling questions about entering judgments on the merits to enforce case management orders. Such results are particularly troubling where the main wrongdoer appears to be the attorney, and the sanction in effect punishes the client for the sins of the lawyer. In complex litigation, sanctions can be seen as a symptom of a failure of judicial management. Consider the admonition in § 10.151 of the Manual for Complex Litigation (4th) (2004):

> [A] resort to sanctions may reflect a breakdown of case management. Close judicial oversight and a clear, specific, and reasonable management program, developed with the participation of counsel, will reduce the potential for sanctionable conduct because the parties will know what the judge expects of them.

CHAPMAN v. PACIFIC TELEPHONE & TELEGRAPH CO.

United States Court of Appeals, Ninth Circuit, 1979.
613 F.2d 193.

Before WRIGHT and ANDERSON, CIRCUIT JUDGES, and SOLOMON, SENIOR DISTRICT JUDGE.

EUGENE A. WRIGHT, CIRCUIT JUDGE.

Deborah Halvonik was one of the attorneys for multiple plaintiffs in a Title VII action. During pretrial proceedings, she refused to comply with the order of the district court, asserting that the order was confusing and invalid for unconstitutionality. The court found that the order was clear and definite.

The issue here is whether the district court may hold an attorney in criminal contempt for willfully refusing to comply with a clear and definite order, even though the attorney asserts that the order is unconstitutional and that she was confused. We hold that the court had that right and affirm the order holding the attorney in criminal contempt.

At a pretrial conference on January 6, 1978, the district court orally ordered Mrs. Halvonik, lead counsel, to submit a written narrative statement of the direct testimony of each witness whom plaintiffs intended to call at the trial. The court observed that such statements would be helpful to the court in understanding the issues and would compel the parties to prepare adequately for trial. Appellant was given ten days to comply.

She made no attempt to prepare the statements. Instead, on January 16, she petitioned this court for a writ to prohibit the district court from enforcing the order. We denied the petition as premature.

On January 26, she attended another pretrial conference. The court inquired what progress had been made in preparing the witness statements. Mrs. Halvonik informed the court that nothing had been done. The court held her in contempt but withheld fixing punishment until after the conclusion of the Title VII trial.

When the court informed Mrs. Halvonik she was in contempt, she asked for and was granted a recess to consult with co-counsel. After the recess, Mrs. Halvonik said she did not intend to comply with the order because she was confused. The court found her confusion "self-induced and self-perpetuated."

On that day, the court reduced its order to writing. Mrs. Halvonik still did not make even a good faith attempt to prepare witness statements.

On January 30, the trial date, plaintiffs were unable to proceed because Mrs. Halvonik was not present and co-counsel were not prepared to examine their witnesses. The case was continued to February 6, when it was tried essentially without the aid of Mrs. Halvonik's witness statements. Despite this inauspicious beginning, two of the plaintiffs prevailed.

On June 9, 1978, the district court asked for post-trial briefs addressing the issues of awarding attorney's fees and certifying contempt. Mrs. Halvonik did not submit the requested materials.

On September 1, the court issued its final judgment, including an award of $3,624 for attorney's fees to Mrs. Halvonik. On that day, the court certified Mrs. Halvonik's criminal contempt for refusing to comply with the January 6 oral order. She was fined $500.

Elements of Contempt

Mrs. Halvonik's non-compliance was found contumacious under 18 U.S.C. § 401(3) which provides:

> A court of the United States shall have power to punish by fine or imprisonment, at its discretion, such contempt of its authority, and none other, as—

* * *

> (3) Disobedience or resistance to its lawful writ, process, order, rule, decree, or command.

Criminal contempt is established when:

> (1) there is a clear and definite order, and the contemnor knows of the order; and

> (2) the contemnor willfully disobeys the order.

Clear and Definite Order

Mrs. Halvonik argues that the order was not clear and definite. She portrays the court's infinite patience, its repeated explanations of the order and its attempts to mollify Mrs. Halvonik as vacillation. We are at a loss to see what more the court could have done to clarify and define its order.

WILLFUL DISOBEDIENCE

Mrs. Halvonik also argues that willfulness cannot be established because she was confused. The district court characterized her confusion as "self-induced and self-perpetuated," a finding amply supported by the record.

No recitation of particulars can adequately communicate the agonizing frustration the district court endured here. We recite in the margin only one example of Mrs. Halvonik's conduct but it alone would be sufficient to sustain the court's finding of willfulness.[1]

1. THE COURT: All right. Now, I come to the statements of the witnesses—of the lay witnesses for the plaintiffs, and I'd like to hear the status of that matter from counsel.

MRS. HALVONIK: As this Court knows, we filed a writ regarding the issue presented by this Court's order of January 6th, and it's our position that the plaintiffs are entitled to a public trial, that they are prevented from having their public trial, because the testimony in chief of their case must be in writing.

Secondly, that the plaintiffs are entitled to, by Rule 43, present in all trials on the merits, oral testimony in open court, and that this Court's rule or order of January 6th violates that rule. So, we do not have prepared testimony of the witnesses.

THE COURT: Did you get an order relieving you of the necessity of complying with this Court's order?

MRS. HALVONIK: We have been contacted twice recently by the Ninth Circuit.

THE COURT: Well, the question is, did you get an order?

MRS. HALVONIK: Their problem has been that there's been a delay in preparing the transcript. I was contacted just a few moments before this hearing took place, and they've just received the transcript, but they do not know whether a decision can come—

THE COURT: Is the answer no?

MRS. HALVONIK: The answer is no.

THE COURT: Well, you're in contempt of the Court's order, Mrs. Halvonik, and the Court will consider appropriate sanctions at the conclusion of the trial after a decision has been rendered.

* * *

The question is, do you intend to comply with the Court's order insofar as it requires you to submit a written, narrative statement of the direct testimony of each witness you intend to present prior to trial? Do you intend to comply with that part of the order?

MRS. HALVONIK: To the extent that that's direct—written statement is a substitute for direct testimony, we intend to seek review of that order.

THE COURT: So, you don't—the answer is you don't intend to comply with the order of the Court.

MRS. HALVONIK: That's why I asked the Court if I could ask a question. I might ask this Court for—in view of the seriousness of holding me in contempt at this moment, if I could have a five-minute recess to consult with counsel?

THE COURT: Well, you've violated the order, and you're now taking the position that you continue to refuse to comply with the order, what choice do I have? Am I supposed to now say, well, if counsel feels that the order of the District Court is wrong, well, that's their right, and I guess there's nothing I can do about enforcing that order. If I took that position, soon we'd be living in a lawless society. Your clients wouldn't be any better off than anyone else. I'm duty bound to enforce the orders of the Court, and I intend to do so. I see no necessity at this point of having a recess. We can take one at the end of the hour.

MRS. HALVONIK: Then, there is one further matter that I want to be sure is brought to this Court's attention. That is, that we were not certain on January 6th that this Court ordered the testimony to be in affidavit form. Nowhere in the transcript does the word affidavit appear. We contacted your Clerk, Mr. Driscoll, and he informed us Tuesday or Wednesday of last week that it was to be in affidavit form. To the extent this Court feels that our presentation to the Ninth Circuit is not in keeping with what actually transpired, I would appreciate elucidation on that point.

THE COURT: Well, Mrs. Halvonik, I won't ask you whether you can read. I will ask you whether you've taken the trouble since you made these representations about what this Court did to the Ninth Circuit, whether you've taken the trouble to read the Reporter's transcript of what the Court did? The transcript of January 6th?

MRS. HALVONIK: I received the transcript a few hours ago and I looked at it, yes.

THE COURT: I think that answers the question. I went over it in great detail, but just to summarize it, again, and I'll refer you to, for example, Page 10, Pages 39 to 42, and Page 45. In summary, what is explained—I don't know why I should go through this again, but I will—also on Pages 50 to 51.

What the transcript says over and over again is that I expected to have both sides prepare in advance of trial a statement, and I said the word statement over again, in narrative form of the testimony of each witness, which they intend to offer. Not an affidavit, but a statement. Then, if the other side—opposing party wishes to cross-examine the witness on the statement he has to be at the trial. If not, he may be at the trial anyway, and the procedure for handling the statements will be that the witness takes the stand, and he says, first, he takes the oath, and then having been sworn, he says, this is my testimony and I adopt it, and then, as I indicated to counsel quite clearly on a number of occasions, if counsel wishes to ask some further questions in order to bring out particular matters that counsel thinks are important, they will have the right to do so, but I want the statements to be complete and contain all of the testimony that is proposed to be offered, but I will permit counsel to cover some of the grounds again in question and answer form if there are particular areas where there may be questions of credibility or other particular problems. At no time did the Court order or suggest—just a minute. At no time did the Court ever order, direct or suggest that plaintiffs may not present their case orally by direct examination in open court. Never did the Court suggest, direct or ask that plaintiffs must present their entire case by written affidavit two weeks in advance of trial. Those statements are totally false and are a total misconception of what the transcript said, and I think that in view of the fact I went over it three

or four, five times during the course of the conference on January 6th, counsel should have understood that that was so.

So, I've explained it adequately, now. I don't think I need to explain it another time, and that is the way I intended to proceed, and that's still the way I intend to proceed, and what steps I will take ultimately based on counsel's deliberate refusal to comply with this order, I will consider after the case has been decided.

Now, if you wish to advise me of what your position is or if you wish at this time to consult with co-counsel, I'll give you leave to do so.

MRS. HALVONIK: I appreciate that.

THE COURT: Do you have any questions, Mrs. Halvonik, that you would require clarification from the Court?

MRS. HALVONIK: Only the remaining question of whether we were misinformed as to whether this should have been in affidavit form, and I call to the Court's—

THE COURT: That's a false issue, Mrs. Halvonik. It hasn't anything to do with whether you should submit the statement or not. You didn't submit it in any form, affidavit or otherwise. I don't see what that has to do with it.

Neither side has been shy in getting in touch with the Court and asking for clarification from the Court. We've been doing that quite regularly for quite a while. If you felt uncertain on that point, the way to do that is to get in touch with the Court and ask for clarification.

I'll give you five minutes to consult with counsel. Perhaps you'd let me know what your positions are.

(Court in recess.)

(Continued proceedings.)

THE COURT: All right, Mrs. Halvonik. Now, you've had a recess, ten minutes, and I will renew the question.

Do you intend to comply with the Court's order and submit, as I've stated before, narrative statements of the witnesses in advance of the trial? Yes or no?

MRS. HALVONIK: The answer is no, because—

THE COURT: All right.

MRS. HALVONIK: Your Honor, I wish to state this for the record—

THE COURT: You can state the reasons if you wish. . . .

MRS. HALVONIK: Your Honor, for the record, the reason I have said, no, is that we still do not understand what the Court is ordering by way of testimony. Either the

ETHICAL DUTY OF COUNSEL

Attorneys, as officers of the court, have a duty to cooperate with the court to preserve and promote the efficient operation of our system of justice.

The Code of Professional Responsibility, Disciplinary Rule 7–106(A) provides:

> A lawyer shall not disregard or advise his client to disregard a standing rule of a tribunal or a ruling of a tribunal made in the course of a proceeding, but he may take appropriate steps in good faith to test the validity of such rule or ruling.

The Code further exhorts the lawyer that:

> Rules of evidence and procedure are designed to lead to just decisions and are part of the framework of the law. Thus while a lawyer may take steps in good faith and within the framework of the law to test the validity of rules, he is not justified in consciously violating such rules and he should be diligent in his efforts to guard against his unintentional violation of them.

Ethical Code 7–25. Mrs. Halvonik's conduct in this case far surpassed the bounds of a good faith testing of the district court's order.

We cannot believe Mrs. Halvonik was ignorant of her ethical duties. Her counsel seeks to excuse her conduct, arguing that she is "young and inexperienced." She is 37 years old. At oral argument, her counsel estimated she had practiced law for six years. She is sufficiently mature and experienced to understand her obligation to comply with a court order. If she is not, she lacks the basic competence to practice law.

VALIDITY OF THE ORDER

Mrs. Halvonik argues she was privileged to disobey the court's order because it was invalid. An attorney who believes a court order is erroneous is not relieved of the duty to obey it. The proper course of action, unless and until the order is invalidated by an appellate court, is to comply and cite the order as reversible error should an adverse judgment result. *Maness v. Meyers,* 419 U.S. 449, 95 S.Ct. 584, 42 L.Ed.2d 574 (1975).

Mrs. Halvonik attempts to avoid the *Maness* rule by insisting that the court's order was unconstitutional.[2] We disagree. We believe the

testimony is written testimony or it is not written testimony, and for the elucidation the Court has attempted to give us, we still do not understand what the Court wants.

2. Appellant contends *Maness* creates an exception to the general rule: an unconstitutional order need not be obeyed. In *Maness,* the contemnor was an attorney who advised his client to assert Fifth Amendment rights against self-incrimina-

tion by retaining material the trial court ordered him to produce. We note that the "exception" to the general rule derives not from the unconstitutionality of the order but from the exercise of a specific constitutional right not to cooperate with the judicial process. We need not rest our opinion on this reading of *Maness,* however, because we find the district court's order in this case constitutional.

district court acted properly, in a laudable effort to save trial time and to assure adequate representation by counsel.

The procedure employed by the court in this case was not "trial by affidavit" as appellant insists. Indeed, it was commendable. Direct oral testimony was to be permitted to supplement the written narrative statement "where there may be questions of credibility or other particular problems." Oral cross-examination and oral redirect were also contemplated.

Submission of direct testimony in written form is expressly provided for by the court rules of other districts and has been employed productively by other trial courts. We should think that Mrs. Halvonik would have welcomed, rather than resisted the court's plan to clarify and simplify the issues at trial.

ADEQUACY OF CONTEMPT PROCEDURE

The district court purported to hold Mrs. Halvonik summarily in contempt under Rule 42(a) [of the Federal Rules of Criminal Procedure]. She argues that summary disposition was inappropriate. We need not decide this issue because the procedure employed complied with the notice and hearing requirements of Rule 42(b).

This court, in *In Re Allis,* 531 F.2d 1391 (9th Cir.1976), cert. den., 429 U.S. 900, 97 S.Ct. 267, 50 L.Ed.2d 185 (1976), held that Rule 42(b) is satisfied if a "reasonable time for the preparation of the defense" is provided. Allis, an attorney, made a tardy appearance before the court. The court told him there was imminent likelihood he would be held in contempt. After a ten-minute recess, during which Allis conferred with counsel, the court asked whether he could excuse his conduct. Allis offered no excuse and was held in contempt. This court affirmed the contempt citation though the trial court purported to act summarily under Rule 42(a).

The present case is similar to *Allis* except that Mrs. Halvonik was never at a loss for excuses. This is not a compelling distinction. We find *Allis* controlling.

Notes and Questions

1. *Chapman* illustrates one way in which case management can carry over into the handling of the trial itself, a topic we will examine in detail in Chapter VII. See *infra* p. 755. For the present, it is important that you appreciate that attorney Halvonik may have had serious tactical reasons for resisting the judge's program of using written substitutes for direct testimony. Given those reasons, is there any way in which she could have avoided the confrontation with the judge that occurred?

2. Under 18 U.S.C.A. § 401, a court may punish as a crime "such contempt of its authority, and none other, as (1) Misbehavior of any person in its presence or so near thereto as to obstruct the administration of justice; * * * (3) Disobedience or resistance to its lawful writ, process, order, rule,

decree or command." Consider how many orders a court might make in the process of case management that would come within the statute.

Punishment under 18 U.S.C.A. § 401 falls within the category of criminal contempt, in which a sanction is imposed on the contemnor for violation of the court's order. It is considered a separate proceeding, and the conviction is immediately appealable although the underlying litigation continues. Other possibilities also exist. Thus, the court can proceed with civil contempt, in which the remedy is compensation to the victim of the misconduct for the actions involved. Alternatively, the court may use coercive civil contempt designed to prod the contemnor into compliance with the court's order. For example, in International Business Mach. Corp. v. United States, 493 F.2d 112 (2d Cir.1973), cert. denied, 416 U.S. 995, 94 S.Ct. 2409, 40 L.Ed.2d 774 (1974), a judge in New York imposed a fine of $150,000 per day on IBM for each day it disobeyed his order to produce the documents that the Ninth Circuit held to be privileged in Transamerica Computer Co. v. IBM, *supra* p. 595. Because such orders do not employ criminal contempt, they are not appealable until final judgment is entered in the case. Often the dividing line between criminal and civil contempt is difficult to identify.

3. *Chapman* involves criminal contempt. In such cases, one may not disobey the order and later challenge its validity because "an order may be 'lawful,' and sufficient to uphold a contempt finding, even though the order is void for lack of jurisdiction or because it is unconstitutional. This is on the basis that the courts must have jurisdiction to determine their jurisdiction, and that their interim orders must be obeyed." 3A C. Wright, N. King & S. Klein, Federal Practice & Procedure § 702 at 434 (3d ed. 2004). This is known as the "collateral bar" doctrine. See Walker v. City of Birmingham, 388 U.S. 307, 87 S.Ct. 1824, 18 L.Ed.2d 1210 (1967) (civil rights marchers properly held in contempt for disobeying order banning march on basis of unconstitutional ordinance). Thus, even if an order is beyond the broad authority of the court to manage cases counsel may not disregard it with impunity. How often would there even be an argument that the order is beyond the court's pretrial management authority? See Rule 16(c).

4. Courts engaged in active case management have used contempt as a tool to aid in settlement promotion. For example, in In re Novak, 932 F.2d 1397 (11th Cir.1991), a district court in Georgia ordered Novak, a claim analyst who worked at the home office of defendant's insurer in Illinois, to appear at a settlement conference in Savannah after learning that plaintiff would not accept the highest settlement offer made by defendant and that Novak was the individual with authority to approve higher offers. Although Novak authorized a 50% increase in the settlement offer, he did not appear at the settlement conference because he believed that the order was void because the court did not have personal jurisdiction over him. After issuing an order to show cause concerning contempt, the district court fined Novak $500.

The appellate court held that the district court's order was beyond its authority, but affirmed Novak's conviction for criminal contempt. It rejected Novak's personal jurisdiction objection because it found that if the order was properly based on the inherent power of the court "personal jurisdiction, or lack thereof, over Novak is irrelevant. A federal court certainly has the power to issue any order necessary to preserve its ability to manage and adjudicate a case or controversy properly before it." Id. at 1403. Recognizing an inherent power to order a represented party to attend a settlement conference, the appellate court concluded that this power did not extend to employees of nonparty insurers and that the district court's order to Novak was therefore beyond its authority. Nevertheless, under the collateral bar doctrine Novak was foreclosed from relying on the order's invalidity because he had simply disregarded the order rather than challenging it.

5. Fed.R.Crim.P. 42(a) permits criminal contempt to be punished summarily "if the judge certifies that the judge saw or heard the conduct constituting the contempt and that it was committed in the actual presence of the court." This limitation can be traced to early legislation that was intended to provide strict limitations on the power of summary contempt. See generally In re McConnell, 370 U.S. 230, 82 S.Ct. 1288, 8 L.Ed.2d 434 (1962). Could *Chapman* have been treated in a summary fashion? How often will violations of case management orders be within the summary contempt power?

If the event is not within the summary power, the risk of satellite litigation increases but, as *Chapman* illustrates, substantial hearings are not essential. Although the person charged must be given notice of the charges and an opportunity to be heard, a full scale trial is not required. Unless the contempt is treated as a petty offense, however, a jury trial is required. Bloom v. Illinois, 391 U.S. 194, 88 S.Ct. 1477, 20 L.Ed.2d 522 (1968). There is some uncertainty about what constitutes a petty offense. For jail sentences, six months is the dividing line, but for fines, as in *Chapman,* it is not so clear. 18 U.S.C.A. § 1(3) defines a petty offense as one involving a fine of less than $500. Nevertheless, in Muniz v. Hoffman, 422 U.S. 454, 95 S.Ct. 2178, 45 L.Ed.2d 319 (1975), the Court held that no jury trial was required where a union local was fined $10,000, noting that the local collected dues from 13,000 members and therefore the fine was not a "serious risk" to it. Compare United States v. Twentieth Century Fox Film Corp., 882 F.2d 656 (2d Cir.1989), cert. denied, 493 U.S. 1021, 110 S.Ct. 722, 107 L.Ed.2d 741 (1990) (jury trial required for criminal contempt whenever the fine imposed on an organization exceeds $100,000). How should fines against lawyers be treated?

6. Recall Professor Resnik's concerns about the risk to impartiality that could result from the court's more intense involvement in litigation due to active case management. Does the colloquy between Judge Schwarzer and attorney Halvonik suggest some reason for concern along these lines? Fed.R.Crim.P. 42(b) provides that "[i]f the contempt charged involves disrespect to or criticism of a judge, that judge is disqualified from presiding at the trial or hearing [regarding contempt] except with the defendant's consent." The Supreme Court has indicated that where the judge has become "embroiled in a running controversy" with counsel, a different judge should handle the contempt proceeding. Taylor v. Hayes, 418 U.S. 488, 501, 94 S.Ct. 2697, 2704, 41 L.Ed.2d 897 (1974). In *Chapman,* is it reassuring to note that when the case was tried "essentially without the aid of Mrs. Halvonik's witness statements," the district judge found in favor of two of the plaintiffs?

7. *Merits sanctions*: Rather than punishing for contempt, a court may react to disobedience of its management orders by deciding the case against the disobedient party. In Link v. Wabash R.R.Co., 370 U.S. 626, 82 S.Ct. 1386, 8 L.Ed.2d 734 (1962), the district court dismissed a suit when plaintiff's lawyer failed to appear for a pretrial conference even though the lawyer called in advance and advised the court that he would be unable to appear because he was preparing papers for filing in state court. Relying on Rule 41(b), and noting that the case was "the oldest case on the court docket," the district judge dismissed for failure to prosecute. Plaintiff appealed, noting that one reason why the case was the oldest case on the docket was that the district judge had erroneously dismissed for failure to state a claim, and further progress in the case was delayed while plaintiff successfully appealed that dismissal.

The Supreme Court upheld the dismissal on the ground that the district judge did not abuse his discretion. It observed that "[w]e need not decide whether unexplained absence from a pretrial conference *alone* would justify a dismissal with prejudice if the record showed no other evidence of dilatoriness" because it understood the district judge to have relied on "all the circumstances" in the case. It also rejected plaintiff's argument that he should not be deprived of his claim due to his lawyer's mistake in failing to appear for the conference because "each party is deemed bound by the acts of his lawyer":

> There is certainly no merit to the contention that dismissal of petitioner's claim because of his counsel's unexcused conduct imposes an unjust penalty on the client. Petitioner voluntarily chose the attorney as his representative in the action, and he cannot now avoid the consequences of the acts or omissions of this freely selected agent.

In a later case involving dismissal as a sanction for failure to meet a discovery deadline, the Court added that "the most severe in the spectrum of sanctions provided by statute or rule must be available to the district court, not merely to penalize those whose conduct may be deemed to warrant such a sanction, but to deter those who might be tempted to such conduct in the absence of such a deterrent." National Hockey League v. Metropolitan Hockey Club, Inc., 427 U.S. 639, 96 S.Ct. 2778, 49 L.Ed.2d 747 (1976).

Should these sorts of sanctions be favored to enforce case management orders? Consider Rogers v. Kroger Co., 669 F.2d 317 (5th Cir.1982), an employment discrimination action in which plaintiff's counsel was unready to proceed to trial at the appointed time and the court dismissed the case under Rule 41(b). The court of appeals reversed, noting that it would affirm Rule 41(b) dismissals with prejudice only in cases that involved "egregious and sometimes outrageous delays." In *Rogers*, the court explained, there was no "clear record of delay by Rogers," nothing indicating that less severe sanctions were considered, and no evidence that Rogers himself was personally responsible for the delay. Thus, in general the lower courts have not ordinarily pursued the most aggressive use of sanctions that the Supreme Court decisions might seem to authorize.

Indeed, sometimes there may be obstacles to using severe sanctions even when a party's behavior is outrageous. In Phoceene Sous–Marine v. U.S. Phosmarine, Inc., 682 F.2d 802 (9th Cir.1982), defendant obtained a continuance of his trial by submitting a forged "doctor's note" stating that he was too ill for the rigors of a trial, and later tried to cover up his deception by suborning perjury. The district court entered defendant's default as a sanction when it found out about the deception, but the court of appeals reversed because the sanction would violate due process. Although defendant's behavior could readily be treated as contempt of court, "a court could not, consistent with the requirements of due process, strike a defendant's answer and enter default as punishment for contempt." This limitation is necessary unless the disobedience implies a view as to the merits of the case, because contempt is not a ground for depriving a party of the opportunity to present or defend based on factors unrelated to the merits. Although plaintiff contended that defendant's lying to delay the start of trial supported an inference that he expected to lose, the court found that "[m]ere dilatory tactics provide too insubstantial a foundation to support such a presumption."

8. *Inherent authority:* In very limited situations, courts also have inherent authority to impose sanctions on litigants or lawyers for bad faith conduct that threatens to undermine the court's jurisdiction. In Chambers v. NASCO, Inc., 501 U.S. 32, 111 S.Ct. 2123, 115 L.Ed.2d 27 (1991), defendant and its lawyer tried to frustrate specific performance through a phony transfer of the assets in question and other bad faith actions. Although neither the federal rules nor any statute authorized sanctions, the Supreme Court upheld a sanction of nearly $1 million (the entire amount of plaintiff's litigation costs including attorneys' fees) based on the inherent power of the court. It noted, however, that this inherent power must be used with restraint.

C. RELIANCE ON JUDICIAL SURROGATES

For decades, federal courts have relied on special masters in complex cases, but the rules had no explicit provisions for much of this activity. Rule 53, governing special masters, was extensively amended in 2003. The Committee Note accompanying that amendment explains: "The appointment of masters to participate in pretrial proceedings has developed extensively over the last two decades as some district courts have felt the need for additional help in managing complex litigation." As the court explained in Cardoza v. Pacific States Steel Corp., 320 F.3d 989, 995 (9th Cir.2003), "in this era of complex litigation, special masters may, subject to judicial review, be called upon to perform a broad range of judicial functions—supervising discovery, issuing stipulations of fact, and in exceptional circumstances, hearing and making recommendations with regard to motions to dismiss and for summary judgment." A master may also play a crucial role in implementing the court's decree in a complex case, particularly in the sort of "public law" litigation described by Professor Chayes (*supra* p. 3). Indeed, Professor Silberman has observed that "there has developed an almost Pavlovian response to the complicated case—delegation to a special master." Silberman, Judicial Adjuncts Revisited: The Proliferation of Ad Hoc Procedure, 137 U.Pa. L.Rev. 2131, 2158 (1989).

COBELL v. NORTON

United States Court of Appeals, District of Columbia Circuit, 2003.
334 F.3d 1128.

Before GINSBURG, Chief Judge, and HENDERSON and RANDOLPH, Circuit Judges.

GINSBURG, Chief Judge.

[Beneficiaries of Individual Indian Money (IIM) trust accounts filed a class action against the Secretary of the Interior and other federal officials, charging them with breaching their fiduciary duties in managing these accounts. The accounts were originally set up pursuant to legislation in 1887 that allotted lands previously set aside for Indian tribes to individual Indians. An individual account was to be set up for each Indian with an interest in the allotted lands, and the accounts (and 11 million acres of land) would be managed for their benefit by the Government. The Indian Trust Fund Management Reform Act of 1994 modified the Government's fiduciary duties in handling these accounts and created the new position of Special Trustee in the Department of the Interior to supervise reform of the trust account system. In 1996, plaintiffs filed this suit claiming that the Government had breached its responsibilities.

In 1999, the district court found that the Government did not even know the precise number of IIM trust accounts, or know the proper balances in these accounts. It therefore held that the Secretary of the Interior and other defendants had breached their fiduciary duties and issued a declaratory judgment remanding the case to the Interior and Treasury Departments, directing them to bring themselves into compliance with the law and to take specific steps the court deemed necessary to provide an accounting of the IIM trust and provide for suitable recognition and protection of the rights of the 300,000 individual beneficiaries of the trust. The decree directed the Government to file quarterly reports with the court on its progress in accomplishing these tasks, and the court retained jurisdiction over the enforcement of the decree.

In April, 2001, the district court appointed Joseph S. Kieffer III to be the "Court Monitor" with the consent of the parties. The order of appointment authorized Kieffer to "monitor and review all of the Interior defendants' trust reform activities and file written reports of his findings with the Court. These reports shall include a summary of the defendants' trust reform progress and any other matter Mr. Kieffer deems pertinent to trust reform." Mr. Kieffer was also "permitted to make and receive ex parte communications with all entities necessary or proper to effectuate his duties." The Department was told to "assist Mr. Kieffer in the execution of his duties and responsibilities," and to "provide Mr. Kieffer with access to any Interior offices or employees to gather information necessary or proper to fulfill his duties." Cobell v. Norton, 226 F.Supp.2d 163, 165 (D.D.C.2002) (the Monitor Order). The order said Kieffer would serve for one year.

In April, 2002, the district court proposed to extend Kieffer's term for at least another year. The Department of the Interior objected to the extension unless several conditions were met, but the court reappointed Kieffer without satisfying all those conditions. Four days later, Kieffer attended a meeting with the Deputy Secretary of the Interior during which Kieffer discussed with Interior officials his concerns about the way they were doing their jobs. Plaintiffs were not notified of this meeting. After Kieffer reported to the court about the meeting, the district judge characterized his actions as "an effort to set the stage to convince the parties attending the meeting to find some way to work together." Thereafter, the Government moved to revoke Kieffer's appointment on the ground that he was purporting to assert powers reserved to the Executive Branch. Meanwhile, Kieffer's report on the Department's activities prompted the district court to order the Secretary to show cause why she should not be held in contempt for failure to comply with the 1999 declaratory judgment.

The district court then entered an order holding the Secretary in contempt, saying that she had been guilty of "litigation misconduct" due to "intransigence" about the court's orders for rectifying the breach of fiduciary duty. The contempt order added that if the Secretary or others at the Department felt that "as a result of the Court's ruling they are unable or unwilling to perform their duties," they should "leave the Department forthwith." The court also denied the Government's motion to revoke the appointment of Kieffer, found that his participation in the meeting with the Deputy Secretary was not inappropriate or beyond his authority, and appointed Kieffer to the position of Special Master–Monitor, with added duties as special master for the management of discovery.

The Secretary appealed. The appellate court held that the orders were not appealable, but that the case presented an appropriate occasion for use of mandamus.]

We turn now to the merits of the Department's claim the district court erred by retaining Kieffer in this case. Specifically, the Department argues both that the court had no authority to reappoint Kieffer as Court Monitor over its objection, and that Kieffer was disqualified from serving as Special Master–Monitor due to his personal knowledge of the case and the resulting appearance of partiality.

1. COURT MONITOR

Kieffer was appointed Court Monitor on April 16, 2001, with the consent of the parties, for a term of one year. In April 2002 the Government objected to Kieffer's reappointment unless certain conditions were placed upon the scope of his powers. On April 15, 2002, the district court reappointed him without regard to one of those conditions. The Department claims this was a clear error. We agree.

The district court claimed authority to appoint the Monitor in the first instance based upon the "consent of the [parties], and . . . the

Court's inherent powers." The Government claims it did not consent to Kieffer's reappointment, however, and neither the district court nor the plaintiffs point to any case or other authority suggesting a district court has inherent power to appoint a court monitor. Indeed, in their brief the plaintiffs, tellingly, do not address the Department's argument that the district court could not appoint a court monitor over its objection. At oral argument the plaintiffs instead rested upon the assertion that the DOI's consent to Kieffer's original appointment as Court Monitor was temporally unlimited and irrevocable.

The plaintiffs' position is untenable on the facts of this case. First, the district court did not propose or purport to appoint Kieffer permanently, so the DOI had no occasion to consent to his having an unlimited tenure. As we noted earlier, the order appointing him stated that Kieffer would "serve for at least 1 year from this date. Upon order of the Court, after comment or objection thereto by the parties, his term of service may be extended for additional terms." The plaintiffs' suggestion that this order, which explicitly grants the parties the right to object to Kieffer's reappointment, actually served as consent to his unlimited tenure, is absurd. We conclude the Department effectively withheld its consent to the court's reappointment of Kieffer as Monitor, which brings us to the question whether the district court has inherent power to appoint a monitor without the consent of the party to be monitored.

A judicial claim to an "inherent power" is not to be indulged lightly, lest it excuse overreaching "[t]he judicial Power" actually granted to federal courts by Article III of the Constitution of the United States, and the customs and usages that inform the meaning of that phrase. Such a claim, therefore, must either be documented by historical practice, see, e.g., Link v. Wabash R.R. Co., 370 U.S. 626, 629–30, 631, 82 S.Ct. 1386, 1388–89, 1389, 8 L.Ed.2d 734 (1962) (noting court's inherent power to dismiss suit for failure to prosecute dates to Blackstone's Commentaries and "has long gone unquestioned"), or supported by an irrefutable showing that the exercise of an undoubted authority would otherwise be set to naught. See, e.g., Chambers v. NASCO, 501 U.S. 32, 43, 111 S.Ct. 2123, 2132, 115 L.Ed.2d 27 (1991) ("It has long been understood that certain implied powers must necessarily result to our Courts of justice from the nature of their institution, powers which cannot be dispensed with in a Court, because they are necessary to the exercise of all others"); cf. All Writs Act, 28 U.S.C. § 1651(a) (granting federal courts power to "issue all writs necessary or appropriate in aid of their respective jurisdictions and agreeable to the usages and principles of law"). Often the two go hand in hand. In this case, however, we find nothing but the district court's assertion it has inherent power to appoint a monitor, which can hardly be self-supporting. Therefore, we hold the district court does not have inherent power to appoint a monitor—at least not a monitor with the extensive duties the court assigned to Kieffer—over a party's substantial objection, here the Government's objection that the appointment violated the separation of powers. As the foregoing sentence conveys, our holding is a narrow one, tethered to the peculiar facts recounted below.

In this case the Court Monitor was charged to "monitor and review all of the Interior defendants' trust reform activities" and to report to the district court on "any ... matter [he] deem[ed] pertinent to trust reform." The court authorized the Monitor to engage in ex parte communications, and required the DOI to "facilitate and assist" the Monitor, to "provide [him] with access to any ... offices or employees to gather information," and to pay his hourly fees and expenses. In short, the Monitor acted as an internal investigator, not unlike a departmental Inspector General except that he reported not to the Secretary but to the district court.

Although the Department initially consented to this arrangement, after a year's experience it conditioned its renewed consent upon a narrower and more specific definition of the Monitor's role: The DOI sought to limit the scope of the Monitor's investigation to "steps taken by the Department to rectify the breaches of trust declared by the Court or steps taken that would necessarily delay rather than accelerate the ultimate provision of an adequate accounting." It later augmented its objection to the Monitor's role, arguing that the Monitor's broad-ranging investigation interfered with the Department's deliberative process privilege * * * and that the Monitor otherwise intruded unduly into the function of the Executive Branch. We need not decide, however, whether the Department's objection was meritorious; it is enough for present purposes that the objection was colorable.

Regardless whether the district court has any inherent authority to appoint an agent to monitor the conduct of a party in litigation before it, it was surely impermissible to invest the Court Monitor with wide-ranging extrajudicial duties over the Government's objection. The Monitor's portfolio was truly extraordinary; instead of resolving disputes brought to him by the parties, he became something like a party himself. The Monitor was charged with an investigative, quasi-inquisitorial, quasi-prosecutorial role that is unknown to our adversarial legal system. When the parties consent to such an arrangement, we have no occasion to inject ourselves into their affairs. When a party has for a nonfrivolous reason denied its consent, however, the district court must confine itself (and its agents) to its accustomed judicial role.

Although the plaintiffs did not bring it to our attention, we are aware of the practice of a federal district court appointing a special master pursuant to Rule 53 to supervise implementation of a court order, especially a remedial order requiring major structural reform of a state institution. See, e.g., Ruiz v. Estelle, 679 F.2d 1115, 1161–62 (5th Cir.1982) (prison reform); Halderman v. Pennhurst State Sch. & Hosp., 612 F.2d 84, 111 (3d Cir.1979) (en banc) (reform of institution for the mentally retarded), rev'd on other grounds, 451 U.S. 1, 101 S.Ct. 1531, 67 L.Ed.2d 694 (1981); Ross Sandler & David Schoenbrod, Democracy by Decree 55–57 (2003). Putting aside the question whether those cases shed any light whatsoever upon the propriety of a federal court authorizing its agent to interfere with the affairs of another branch of the federal government, we think the present case goes far beyond the practice that has grown up under Rule 53.

Ruiz illustrates the limits of the mandate a district court may permissibly give its agent. There the district court, having found the defendant state department of corrections subjected inmates to cruel and unusual conditions, entered an injunction and appointed a special master, assisted by several "monitors," "to monitor implementation of the relief ordered." The special master was given "unlimited access to [the defendants'] premises and records as well as the power to conduct confidential interviews with . . . staff members and inmates." On appeal, the State argued the appointment was improper because there was no "exceptional condition" warranting it, as required by Rule 53. In rejecting that argument, the court of appeals approved the special master's mandate, namely, "to report on [the department's] compliance with the district court's decree and to help implement the decree," thereby "assum[ing] one of the plaintiffs' traditional roles."

The role of the special master in *Ruiz* was not nearly as broad as the role of the Monitor in this case. There the master was specifically instructed "not to intervene in the administrative management of [the department] and . . . not to direct the defendants or any of their subordinates to take or to refrain from taking any specific action to achieve compliance." Most important, the court of appeals clarified that the special master and the monitors were "not to consider matters that go beyond superintending compliance with the district court's decree," thereby assuring the special master would not be an "advocate" for the plaintiffs or a "roving federal district court."

The last requirement highlights the problems with the role of the Monitor in this case, and with his appointment. The Monitor was not limited to "superintending compliance with the district court's decree," but was instead ordered to "monitor and review all of the . . . defendants' trust reform activities," including "the defendants' trust reform progress and any other matter Mr. Kieffer deems pertinent to trust reform." Nor could the Monitor have been limited to enforcing a decree, for there was no decree to enforce, let alone the sort of specific and detailed decree issued in *Ruiz* and typical of such cases. *See* Sandler & Schoenbrod, above, at 9 (referring to "court decrees that are as thick as phone books"). The case had been remanded to the Department "for further proceedings not inconsistent with" the opinion of the district court in order "[t]o allow defendants the opportunity to promptly come into compliance." Cf., e.g., *Halderman*, 612 F.2d at 111 (allowing special master to administer implementation of injunction and noting that "[m]asters are peculiarly appropriate in the implementation of complex equitable decrees which require ongoing judicial supervision"). In this case, the district court's appointment of the Monitor entailed a license to intrude into the internal affairs of the Department, which simply is not permissible under our adversarial system of justice and our constitutional system of separated powers. Accordingly, the district court should not have reappointed the Court Monitor on April 15, 2002 over the Department's objection.

2. SPECIAL MASTER–MONITOR

In its June 14 motion to revoke Kieffer's appointment and clarify the role of the Court Monitor, the Department among other things complained that Kieffer's actions at the April 19, 2002 ex parte meeting had created an appearance of partiality. The district court not only rejected the Department's arguments, it supplemented Kieffer's role by appointing him Special Master–Monitor. Again the Department claims this was clear error. Again we agree.

The relevant standard is to be found at 28 U.S.C. § 455(a): A judicial officer must be disqualified from "any proceeding in which his impartiality might reasonably be questioned," that is, questioned by one fully apprised of the surrounding circumstances. It is clear, notwithstanding the plaintiffs' objections, that in this Circuit the ethical restrictions of § 455 apply to a special master. So much for the law; for the facts we rely solely upon the district court's own recitation, which establishes that Kieffer's prior role and personal involvement in this case as Court Monitor would cause a reasonable person to doubt his ability to remain impartial while serving as Special Master.

For instance, Kieffer was "permitted to make and receive ex parte communications with all entities," Monitor Order, 226 F.Supp.2d at 165, and in fact engaged in numerous ex parte communications with officials of Interior. Moreover, in the course of his investigation Kieffer acquired information upon the basis of which he "apprised the Deputy Secretary that there was a dispute developing between the Secretary and the Special Trustee [appointed pursuant to the Indian Trust Management Act of 1994] ... regarding the appropriate role of the Special Trustee." The Court Monitor was also present at the "heated" ex parte meeting on April 19, 2002, about which he reported to the Court that "defendants were unwilling to fully accept the Congressionally-mandated role of the Special Trustee." At that meeting, Kieffer "expressed his concerns to the Deputy Secretary about the actions of the Secretary and the Deputy Secretary regarding the Special Trustee." In particular, he "apprise[d] the Deputy Secretary in the presence of the Special Trustee of the obvious risks faced by the defendants in this litigation and the additional concerns he had regarding" some of the Secretary's views, in "an effort to set the stage to convince the parties attending the meeting to find some way to work together rather than continue the internecine warfare patently obvious in their own dueling memoranda."

The district court's account of these events demonstrates that Kieffer had a settled opinion about what the Department should and should not do on remand to comply with the order of the district court, which opinion he developed in his extrajudicial role as Court Monitor with access to the internal deliberations of the Department regarding the lawsuit. The district court's account also demonstrates that Kieffer's opinion was based in part upon ex parte communications received in his extra-judicial capacity as Monitor. These facts so clearly cast a shadow over Kieffer's impartiality that the district court abused its discretion in appointing Kieffer to be Special Master (in addition to Monitor).

The plaintiffs argue the April 19 meeting was not "extrajudicial" because it took place with the knowledge and approval of the district court and of the parties. That does not change the key fact: The district court appointed Kieffer to a judicial role in a case in which he had significant prior knowledge obtained in his role as a Court Monitor, on the basis of which he had formed and expressed opinions of continuing relevance to the litigation. A newly appointed judge may not hear a case in which he previously played any role. See 28 U.S.C. § 455(b)(3) (a judge shall recuse himself "[w]here he has served in governmental employment and in such capacity participated as counsel, adviser or material witness concerning the proceeding or expressed an opinion concerning the merits of the particular case in controversy"); ABA Model Code of Judicial Conduct Canon 3(E)(1)(b) (a judge is disqualified when "the judge served as a lawyer in the matter in controversy, or a lawyer with whom the judge previously practiced law served during such association as a lawyer concerning the matter, or the judge has been a material witness concerning it"). Similarly here, Kieffer's experience as Court Monitor disqualified him from later assuming a judicial role in this case. Accordingly, the order appointing Kieffer to be a Special Master–Monitor must be vacated.*

[The court then held that the Secretary could not be held in contempt, largely because she could not be held in contempt for actions of her predecessor.]

Notes and Questions

1. There is no provision in the Federal Rules of Civil Procedure for appointment of a "court monitor." Rule 53(a)(1)(C) now provides that a court may appoint a master to "address pretrial and post-trial matters that cannot be addressed effectively and timely by an available district judge or magistrate judge of the district." Should there be some additional authority to appoint a "monitor" to do the tasks that the district court assigned Kieffer? Note the appellate court's concern that the monitor might become a

* In light of this disposition we need not and do not pass upon the DOI's objections to the propriety of Kieffer's actions at the April 19 meeting or at any other time prior to his appointment as Special Master–Monitor. The events of April 19 do, however, suggest the Department's concerns about the scope of the Court Monitor's role were well-founded. The district court's findings indicate that the Court Monitor's duties were so wide-ranging as to have a potentially significant effect upon the DOI's deliberative process. See Monitor Order, 226 F.Supp.2d at 172 (Court Monitor's presentation was "an effort to set the stage to convince the parties attending the meeting to find some way to work together"); id. (Court Monitor "sought to ... enable [DOI officials] to better carry out [their] trust reform fiduciary obligations"); id. at 172 n. 6 (Court Monitor, with authorization of district court, "attempt[ed] to facilitate a resolution of the continuing dispute between the Secretary, the Deputy Secretary, and the Special Trustee").

"roving federal district court," and consider its discussion of inherent authority.

Could the court have appointed Kieffer a master under Rule 53 to accomplish the assigned tasks? Note that the oversight involved identification and accounting for the accounts of 300,000 beneficiaries. Note also the duties assigned to the master in Ruiz v. Estelle, 679 F.2d 1115 (5th Cir.1982), cited by the court in *Cobell*. Would it be reasonable to assign a district judge or magistrate judge to undertake these tasks?

2. *Decree implementation*: Decree implementation has long been a task assigned to masters in complex litigation. In a famous example, Judge Weinstein appointed a law professor to implement a school desegregation decree. See Berger, Away From the Courthouse and Into the Field, The Odyssey of a Special Master, 78 Colum.L.Rev. 707 (1978). See also Williams v. Lane, 851 F.2d 867 (7th Cir.1988), cert. denied, 488 U.S. 1047, 109 S.Ct. 879, 102 L.Ed.2d 1001 (1989) (appointment of special master is proper where record is replete with evidence of administrative recalcitrance by defendant and court discerned need for supervision of defendant's future compliance). As Professor Silberman notes, "[t]here is substantial evidence to indicate that violations of constitutional rights, when asserted against institutional defendants, can be remedied only when effective follow-up takes place, usually by the special master. * * * Moreover, masters often have particular expertise which enables them to bring a realistic and practical approach to their shaping, monitoring, and/or compliance functions." Silberman, *supra*, 137 U.Pa.L.Rev. at 2162–63.

But there are potential drawbacks. Consider the following cautions based on a case in which the court appointed a law professor to develop solutions to pollution problems (Brazil, Special Masters in Complex Cases: Extending the Judiciary or Reshaping Adjudication?, 53 U.Chi.L.Rev. 394, 419 (1986)):

> [W]hen a special master is employed to investigate a complex situation and propose solutions, or to lend the court expertise in some sophisticated technological or other esoteric subject, serious dangers may face our dispute resolution system. Because parties often lack an opportunity to challenge the master's findings, and generalist judges may be tempted to rely too heavily on the master's expertise, the resulting decision may be less well reasoned and less acceptable to affected parties than if a court-appointed expert had been utilized instead. The rules applying to experts incorporate mechanisms to test publicly the appointee's work and to guard against the problems that can arise when the court's agent is not limited, in forming his opinions, to information on the record. This issue is especially sensitive in public law cases, where a master can affect important policies or social institutions.

In connection with decree implementation, some find that Rule 70 and the court's inherent authority permit reference to a special master without sole reliance on Rule 53. See Levine, The Authority for the Appointment of Remedial Special Masters in Federal Institutional Reform Litigation: The History Reconsidered, 17 U.C. Davis L.Rev. 753 (1984); Note, Rule 53, Inherent Powers, and Institutional Reform: The Lack of Limits on Special Masters, 66 N.Y.U.L.Rev. 800 (1991). In 1994, Congress prescribed criteria and limitations for use of special masters in prison conditions cases. See 18 U.S.C.A. § 3626(f).

In *Cobell*, the court contrasts the district court's directions to the monitor with the specifics provided in the decree in Ruiz v. Estelle, 679 F.2d 1115 (5th Cir.1982), which specifically instructed the master not to interfere in the administrative management of the corrections department. Often such decrees include great detail about operation of the facility, which presents the court with a problem in drafting such detailed directives. As *Cobell* makes clear, this potential intrusion into the operation of public institutions may produce tension between the judiciary and executive department officials. For federal courts, it may also raise federalism concerns when state institutions are the objects of such orders. Should these issues affect the decision whether to appoint a master to enforce a decree, and the specificity of the court's directives about the tasks and authority of the master? The Committee Note accompanying the 2003 amendment to Rule 53(b) observes that "[c]are must be taken to make the order as precise as possible" and adds: "Clear identification of any investigating or enforcement duties is particularly important. Clear delineation of topics for any reports or recommendations is also an important part of this process."

3. *Discovery and pretrial management*: Another task assigned to Kieffer when he was formally appointed a master was supervision of discovery. In cases involving time-intensive supervision of discovery, courts often appoint masters to resolve disputes about privilege and related matters. For a description of extensive supervision by masters of massive document discovery, see Hazard & Rice, Judicial Management of the Pretrial Process in Massive Litigation: Special Masters as Case Managers, 1982 A.B.F.Res.J. 375. The Manual for Complex Litigation (4th) § 11.424 (2004) observes that "[s]pecial masters can successfully oversee discovery, particularly where there are numerous issues—such as claims of privilege—to resolve or where the parties are extraordinarily contentious," but cautions about the cost of the practice and says that appointments should ordinarily not be made over the parties' objections.

E-discovery has presented a special need for designation of a master when access to a party's hard disk is involved. Permitting the opposing party such access could lead to a privilege waiver, a problem courts have solved by appointing a master or other court emissary to gather material from the hard disk, and then allowing the party's lawyer to review the material before it is turned over to the opposing party, and to raise any privilege objections at that time. See, e.g., Playboy Ent., Inc. v. Welles, 60 F.Supp.2d 1050 (S.D.Cal.1999) (appointing computer specialist as an "Officer of the Court" so that disclosure to the specialist would not result in a waiver of privilege).

Beyond supervision of discovery, judges in some cases have appointed masters to organize the pretrial phases of litigation. For example, District Judge Lambros in Cleveland appointed two law professors as masters to design a special procedure for handling personal injury asbestos litigation pending before him. See Brazil, Special Masters in Complex Cases: Extending the Judiciary or Reshaping Adjudication?, 53 U.Chi.L.Rev. 394, 399–402 (1986). The Committee Note to the 2003 amendment to Rule 53 cautions that "[d]irect judicial performance of judicial functions may be particularly important in cases that involve important public issues or many parties. At the extreme, a broad delegation of pretrial responsibility as well as a delegation of trial responsibilities can run afoul of Article III."

4. *Settlement promotion*: One of the things Kieffer was to attempt was to persuade the parties to "work together." In large cases judges have appointed masters to facilitate settlement. For example, in the Agent Orange litigation Judge Jack Weinstein appointed experienced lawyers to engage in "shuttle diplomacy" between the attorneys for the plaintiffs and the defendants. See P. Schuck, Agent Orange on Trial 144–67 (1986).

5. *Trial*: Rule 53 has long authorized judges to assign cases to a master for trial, but only if some "exceptional condition" made that necessary. In La Buy v. Howes Leather Co., 352 U.S. 249, 77 S.Ct. 309, 313, 1 L.Ed.2d 290 (1957), the Court granted mandamus to overturn a district judge's assignment of complex antitrust case to a master for trial. The district court had justified the assignment on the ground that the case was a complex antitrust matter. The Supreme Court responded: "But most litigation in the antitrust field is complex. It does not follow that antitrust litigants are not entitled to a trial before a court. On the contrary, we believe that there is an impelling reason for trial before a regular, experienced trial judge rather than before a temporary substitute appointed on an ad hoc basis and ordinarily not experienced in judicial work." The 2003 amendment was not meant to permit more frequent appointment of masters for trial.

6. *Disqualification*: In *Cobell*, the court applies the judicial disqualification standard, 28 U.S.C. § 455, to the master. Rule 53(a)(2) now makes it clear that this standard must be satisfied in all appointments of a master. In that connection, note that Rule 53(c) authorizes a master to impose sanctions provided by Rule 37 or 45, and to recommend a contempt sanction.

7. In *Cobell*, one problem was that the Kieffer had ex parte communications with the parties. Rule 53(b)(2) prescribes that the court's order of appointment should specify the exact duties that the master has, the circumstances, if any, in which the master may communicate ex parte with the court or a party, and provide other details on the master's service.

8. For an examination of recent experience with masters, see T. Willging, L. Hooper, M. Leary, D. Miletich, T. Reagan & J. Shapard, Special Masters' Incidence and Activity (Fed.Jud.Ctr.2000). This study found that special masters were appointed in about two cases per 1,000, and that trial activities were the focus of about half the appointments, with the other half roughly equally divided between pretrial and post-trial activities. About one quarter of the people appointed were not lawyers. The compensation received by special masters was considerable. The median amount was $63,000, but a quarter of the appointments involved total payments of $315,000 or more. Ex parte communications between the master and the parties or the court were common. Most respondents thought that the benefits of appointing the masters used in their cases outweighed any drawbacks.

9. *Magistrate judges*: Besides masters under Rule 53, district judges may assign matters to magistrate judges, who are appointed for eight-year terms by district courts. Under 28 U.S.C. § 636(b), all pretrial matters may be assigned to magistrate judges for either decision (if they are "nondisposi-

tive" matters) or a report and recommendation (if they are "dispositive" matters). See Rule 72. The distinction between "dispositive" and "nondispositive" matters often depends on the importance of the order to the case. See Ocelot Oil Corp. v. Sparrow Industries, Inc., 847 F.2d 1458 (10th Cir.1988) (striking of pleadings with prejudice as a discovery sanction was "dispositive"). The difference does not affect the authority of the magistrate judge, but only the standard of review the district judge is to use if a party objects to what the magistrate judge did. For "nondispositive" matters, the district judge should not disturb the ruling unless it is clearly erroneous or contrary to law; with "dispositive" matters, the district court should review the matter de novo. 28 U.S.C. § 636(c) permits cases to be assigned to magistrate judges for all purposes if the parties consent. See Fed. R. Civ. P. 73.

D. JUDICIAL SELECTION OF COUNSEL

In complex litigation, judges may, in effect, be called upon to hire lawyers through designation of lead counsel or class counsel. As we shall see, courts have long understood that they had authority and a responsibility to designate lawyers to act in litigation in a variety of circumstances, but the situations in which such appointments must be made have increased in frequency and importance. Effective in 2003, Rule 23(g) directs the court to appoint class counsel when certifying a class action. Discharging such appointment responsibilities involves assessments that differ some from traditional judicial duties. The Manual for Complex Litigation (4th) § 10.224 (2004) observes:

> Few decisions by the court in complex litigation are as difficult and sensitive as the appointment of designated counsel. There is often intense competition for appointment by the court as designated counsel, an appointment that may implicitly promise large fees and a prominent role in the litigation. Side agreements among lawyers may also have a significant effect on positions taken in the proceedings. At the same time, because appointment of designated counsel will alter the usual dynamics of client representation in important ways, attorneys will have legitimate concerns that their clients' interests be adequately represented.

McALLISTER v. GUTERMA
United States Court of Appeals, Second Circuit, 1958.
263 F.2d 65.

Before SWAN and MOORE, Circuit Judges, and KAUFMAN, District Judge.

KAUFMAN, District Judge.

[In ruling on the consolidation of a number of stockholders' derivative actions, the appellate court described the power of a trial court to appoint lead counsel.]

The court below questioned its power to consolidate actions for purposes other than for trial. We think such power exists. The purpose of consolidation is to permit trial convenience and economy in administration. Toward this end Rule 42(a), in addition to providing for joint trials in actions involving common questions of law and fact, specifically confers the authority to "make such orders concerning proceedings therein as may tend to avoid unnecessary costs or delay." Certainly, overlapping duplication in motion practices and pre-trial procedures occasioned by competing counsel representing different plaintiffs in separate stockholder derivative actions constitute the waste and efficiency sought to be avoided by the lucid direction contained in the rule. Special treatment is often called for in stockholders' derivative actions where the stockholder sues, not in his own right, but in that of the corporation and on behalf of his fellow stockholders. Often many such suits by other stockholders are brought, attacking the same transactions. The cost of defending these multiple actions may well do serious harm to the very corporation in whose interest they are supposedly brought. An order consolidating such actions during the pre-trial stages, together with the appointment of a general counsel, may in many instances prove the only effective means of channeling the efforts of counsel along constructive lines and its implementation must be considered within the clear contemplation of the rule. It certainly does not clash with the oft repeated policy underlying consolidation under Rule 42, to wit, "[C]onsolidation is permitted as a matter of convenience and economy in administration, but does not merge the suits into a single cause, or change the rights of the parties, or make those who are parties in one suit parties in another." Johnson v. Manhattan Ry. Co., 1933, 289 U.S. 479, 496–497, 53 S.Ct. 721, 727, 77 L.Ed. 1331.

By such a procedure, one general counsel is not substituted for the counsel of each party plaintiff's choice. The function of general counsel is merely to supervise and coordinate the conduct of plaintiffs' cases. The separate actions are not merged under the direction of one court appointed master of litigation—each counsel is still free to present his own case, to examine witnesses and to open and close before the jury, if there be one. But even if the rule were more restricted in its scope we would be most reluctant to deny such inherent power to the district courts. The power to order consolidation prior to trial falls within the broad inherent authority of every court "to control the disposition of the causes on its docket with economy of time and effort for itself, for counsel and for litigants." Cardozo, J. in Landis v. North American Co., 1936, 299 U.S. 248, 254, 57 S.Ct. 163, 166, 81 L.Ed. 153.

We see no reason nor has any been suggested by counsel why the considerations permitting consolidation for trial are not equally apposite in connection with consolidation in the period before trial. Indeed, an orderly and expeditious disposition at trial is dependent in large part on the manner in which the pre-trial proceedings are conducted. If one of the purposes of consolidation for trial be to expedite the proceedings and avoid needless time and expense to the litigants and to the court, such objectives are as desirable and as attainable in the period utilized in preparing for the trial.

Consolidation for all purposes and the appointment of general counsel is not new. It has long been recognized by the courts in New York as an expeditious means for handling litigation.[2] Nor is its employment unknown to the federal courts.

* * *

The benefits achieved by consolidation and the appointment of general counsel, i.e. elimination of duplication and repetition and in effect the creation of a coordinator of diffuse plaintiffs through whom motions and discovery proceedings will be channeled, will most certainly redound to the benefit of all parties to the litigation. The advantages of this procedure should not be denied litigants in the federal courts because of misapplied notions concerning interference with a party's right to his own counsel.

Notes and Questions

1. Can the economies sought by the court be achieved without inappropriately inhibiting the freedom of the lawyers? Some sacrifice of individual freedom of action is essential to achieve overall fairness. Even in the absence of action by the court, the parties may voluntarily decide to act in a coordinated fashion. One antitrust practitioner summarized the situation in antitrust class actions as follows:

> Even where the court does not formally appoint liaison counsel or lead counsel, everything in an antitrust class action is handled by committee, anyway. Those of you who have participated in meetings of counsel in such cases know that your experience in the courtroom does you precious little good; what you would need, ideally, is experience in a state legislature. In fact, it is often the best trial lawyers who have the hardest time adapting to what have become the accepted procedures for handling antitrust class actions. A good trial lawyer's tenacious pursuit of his own theory of the case and his unwillingness to compromise his own client's interests in the slightest respect for the good of the majority are almost immediately taken as signs of pigheadedness on the part of his fellow counsel. The result is that he is quickly ostracized from the decision-making inner circle of lawyers on his side of the case, thereby further diminishing his ability to influence the course of the proceedings.

Cellini, An Overview of Antitrust Class Actions, 49 Antitrust L.J. 1501, 1505 (1980). What effect should this process have on the court's imprimatur in designating lead counsel?

2. Once lead counsel is appointed, should the court make an effort to monitor the lawyer's performance? The Manual for Complex Litigation (4th)

---

2. As noted by the court in Manning v. Mercantile Trust Co., 1899, 26 Misc. 440, 57 N.Y.S. 467, 468:

"[T]here can be but one master of a litigation on the side of the plaintiffs. It is also plain that it would be as easy to drive a span of horses pulling in diverging directions, as to conduct a litigation by separate, independent action of various plaintiffs, acting without concert, and with possible discord."

(2004) suggests (in § 40.22) the following sample order prescribing those responsibilities:

> Plaintiffs' Lead Counsel shall be generally responsible for coordinating the activities of plaintiffs during pretrial proceedings and shall
>
> (a) determine (after such consultation with other members of Plaintiffs' Steering Committee and other co-counsel as may be appropriate) and present (in briefs, oral argument or such other fashion as may be appropriate, personally or by a designee) to the court and opposing parties the position of the plaintiffs on all matters arising during the pretrial proceedings;
>
> (b) coordinate the initiation and conduct of discovery on behalf of plaintiffs consistent with the requirements of Fed.R.Civ.P. 26(b)(1), 26(b)(2), and 26(g), including the preparation of joint interrogatories and requests for production of documents and the examination of witnesses in depositions;
>
> (c) conduct settlement negotiations on behalf of plaintiffs, but not enter binding agreements except to the extent expressly authorized;
>
> (d) delegate specific tasks to other counsel or committees of counsel, as authorized by the court, in a manner to assure that pretrial preparation for the plaintiffs is conducted effectively, efficiently, and economically;
>
> (e) enter into stipulations with opposing counsel, necessary for conduct of the litigation;
>
> (f) prepare and distribute periodic status reports to the parties;
>
> (g) maintain adequate time and disbursement records covering services as lead counsel;
>
> (h) monitor the activities of cocounsel to assure that schedules are met and unnecessary expenditures of time and expenses are avoided; and
>
> (i) perform such other duties as may be incidental to proper coordination of plaintiffs' pretrial activities or authorized by further order of the court.

Counsel for plaintiffs who disagree with lead counsel (or those acting on behalf of lead counsel) or who have individual or divergent positions may present written and oral arguments, conduct examinations of deponents, or otherwise act separately on behalf of their clients as appropriate, provided that in doing so they do not repeat arguments, questions, or actions of lead counsel.

How effectively will the above order limit the actions of lead counsel and preserve the autonomy of individual plaintiffs to pursue their own cases as they desire? If such discord appears, what effect will that have on plaintiffs' chances of success? How is one to decide whether a single position need be taken by all plaintiffs?

3. Should the court formally limit the actions of non-lead counsel? Unless they are forbidden from taking actions without the consent of lead

counsel, these attorneys might disrupt the orderly pretrial preparation by pursuing their own strategies. Accordingly, courts have upheld orders that forbid non-lead counsel from initiating discovery or filing motions without securing permission from lead counsel. See, e.g., Vincent v. Hughes Air West, Inc., 557 F.2d 759 (9th Cir.1977). Under these circumstances, can it really be said that the parties who hired the other lawyers got the representation of their choice? Can the non-lead counsel who disagreed with lead counsel really get effective relief from the court?

4.   In class actions, the authority granted lead counsel can include the power to accept settlement terms that will be presented to the court for approval pursuant to Rule 23(e) (discussed *supra* pp. 511-18). In In re Ivan F. Boesky Securities Litigation, 948 F.2d 1358 (2d Cir.1991), class members who objected to a settlement challenged the authority of lead counsel to settle their claims. The appellate court rejected the challenge: "So long as the district court ensures that the interests of all members of the class are adequately taken into account during negotiations, the authority of Lead/Liaison Counsel to negotiate and propose a settlement is largely what the district court says it is. * * * We are most disinclined to cabin the authority of lead counsel by requiring the explicit agreement of every lawyer for a named plaintiff or subclass to the proposed settlement. To empower each representative of a named plaintiff or subclass to veto the very proposal of a settlement to the district court would generally not serve the purposes of Rule 23." Id. at 1364–66.

5.   In Link v. Wabash Railroad, 370 U.S. 626, 82 S.Ct. 1386, 8 L.Ed.2d 734 (1962), the Supreme Court said that because plaintiff "voluntarily chose this attorney as his representative" he could not disavow the actions of his "freely selected agent." How realistic is that attitude where the real authority rests with lead counsel? Should the court remove lead counsel if she is found to have taken actions that warrant sanctions?

6.   *Interim class counsel*: As we saw in Chapter IV, considerable litigation may be necessary before the court decides whether to certify a class. During this period, Rule 23(g)(2)(A) authorizes the judge to designate interim counsel to act on behalf of the class. Whether or not formally so designated, an attorney who acts on behalf of the class before certification is obliged to act in the best interests of the class, as provided in Rule 23(g)(1)(B).

7.   *The judge's task in selecting the lawyer or lawyers*: We turn now to the problem of choosing the lawyers for the task, not merely riding herd on them. The Manual for Complex Litigation (4th) § 10.224 (2004) admonishes that "the judge is advised to take an active part in the decision on the appointment of counsel. Deferring to proposals by counsel without independent examination, even those that seem to have the concurrence of a majority of those affected, invites problems down the road if designated counsel turn out to be unwilling or unable to discharge their responsibilities satisfactorily or if they incur excessive costs." We begin with a famous example of some of the "problems down the road" that the court should seek to ward off by taking an "active part in the selection."

IN RE FINE PAPER ANTITRUST LITIGATION

United States District Court, Eastern District of Pennsylvania, 1983.
98 F.R.D. 48,* reversed and remanded, 751 F.2d 562 (3d Cir.1984).

McGLYNN, DISTRICT JUDGE.

[In mid–1977, 15 complaints were filed in eight different districts alleging a price-fixing conspiracy by the manufacturers of fine paper. In 1978, the Judicial Panel of Multidistrict Litigation transferred all 15 cases to the Eastern District of Pennsylvania. Thereafter 23 more lawsuits were filed and transferred as tag-along actions. Almost all of the 38 actions were either class actions or suits by state attorneys general as *parens patriae*.

In mid–1978, negotiations commenced between attorneys for plaintiffs and certain defendants. Between July, 1978, and January, 1979, six of the fifteen defendants settled for an aggregate amount of $30 million. In early 1979, the court certified two plaintiff classes, and left certain states to pursue their claims on their own. As the September, 1980, trial date approached, settlement negotiations resumed and all of the private cases were settled before trial for an additional $20 million, bringing the total settlement fund to $50 million. The remaining claims asserted by state attorneys general went to trial. At the close of plaintiffs' case, defendants rested without offering any evidence, and the jury returned a verdict for the defendants. In discussing the attorneys' fee petitions of the various class counsel, the court provided a rare glimpse into the dynamics of self-government by class counsel.]

The lawyers representing the private plaintiffs' class created an organizational structure consisting of tiers of committees and subcommittees with numerous "Chairmen" and scores of "Co–Chairmen" for virtually every task in the case. This arrangement succeeded in utilizing the services of over three dozen law firms and state attorneys general and resulted in enormous charges against the fund by lawyers and numerous paralegals. This top-heavy structure was a model of inefficiency and worked to the detriment of thousands of unnamed class members on whose behalf counsel purported to act. For a three-year period, approximately 97,000 hours were billed to the class—70,000 in lawyer hours and over 16,000 in paralegal hours. Most of this time, approximately 85,000 hours, was spent in the two-year period after the initial $30 million in settlements had been obtained. * * *

(A) FORMATION OF THE ORGANIZATIONAL STRUCTURE

On July 18, 1977 Specks & Goldberg, Ltd. filed a complaint in the Northern District of Illinois on behalf of Herst Litho, Inc., a New York based company. Specks' co-counsel on this initial complaint was the New York firm of Robinson, Silverman, Pearce, Aronsohn & Berman. On October 11, 1977, Specks and Goldberg, Ltd. filed a second *Fine Paper*

---

* The opinion, which is 189 pages long, has been heavily edited.—Eds.

case in the District of Connecticut, this time on behalf of Phillip and Ruth Meroney of New Orleans. Specks' co-counsel on this complaint was Fine, Waltzer & Bagneris, a New Orleans law firm. Each of these actions was brought on behalf of a national class of direct purchasers of fine paper similar to the class eventually certified by the court.

After filing these two complaints, Specks circulated copies of them to several lawyers with whom he had worked in prior class actions, including Jack Chestnut's firm in Minneapolis, Leonard Barrack of Philadelphia, Lawrence Walner of Chicago, Gene Mesh of Cincinnati, David Berger of Philadelphia and Harold E. Kohn of Philadelphia. These lawyers in turn filed actions in various United States District Courts. For example, Leonard Barrack filed a complaint for his Philadelphia-based client in the District of Connecticut. David Berger filed a complaint for his client in the Eastern District of Pennsylvania, although Specks had asked Berger to file his complaint in the District of Connecticut. Harold Kohn filed his complaint on behalf of his firm's client in the Southern District of New York in November of 1977. Kohn testified that although his client was a member of the national class sought by Specks in his initial complaint, he decided to file his complaint because Specks "begged" him to "over a period of several months." Lawrence Walner filed a complaint on behalf of Campbell Office Supply Company of Chicago in the Northern District of Illinois. Four other law firms were co-counsel with Walner on this complaint. Harold Kohn claims that one of these firms, Saveri & Saveri, was added by Walner to his complaint "as a favor" to Specks.

At the time the Judicial Panel on Multidistrict Litigation entered its transfer order in March of 1978, there were fifteen actions filed in eight different federal districts. "All the actions were filed as purported class actions. While there ... [were] some variations in the descriptions of the classes sought, most ... [were] national classes of all, or some group of fine paper purchasers." Opinion of Panel, 446 F.Supp. at 759. Within a year of the Panel's transfer order, twenty-three additional cases had been filed by various lawyers, despite the fact that their clients' interests were already protected by the previously-filed class actions. Indeed, many of these complaints were filed as late as 1979, after the first $30 million of settlements had been obtained and the class already had been certified. As noted by the class objectors, the only logical reason for these new filings was to permit counsel to participate in the case and thereby to obtain attorneys' fees.

(B) PREORGANIZATION MEETINGS AMONG COUNSEL

As the complaints were being filed, Granvil I. Specks and others began planning for the distribution of patronage, that is, deciding to which firms the work assignments would be allocated. The planning appears to have begun in January 1978 in anticipation of the February 3, 1978 "organizational meeting" in Chicago (discussed below) at which the structure of the case was formally proposed, voted upon and determined by various plaintiffs' counsel. * * *

In addition to these conferences in Chicago, on January 29, 1978, there was a meeting of plaintiffs' counsel in Atlanta, Georgia where many of the same lawyers were attending a hearing in the *Armored Car Antitrust Litigation*. This meeting was referred to by Aaron M. Fine of Philadelphia, an experienced antitrust lawyer, who wrote to Specks on March 8, 1978 to complain about not being invited to participate in the Atlanta session. Certain documents, including Mr. Fine's letter, are quoted at length because they provide some insight into the workings of the class action bar and help to demonstrate that the polestar of plaintiffs' organizational structure in this case was patronage, not efficiency:

> I called you on Thursday, February 2, 1978, after receiving your notice that there was to be an organizational meeting of all plaintiffs' counsel to be held on the following day in Chicago, because I had heard disquieting reports from a number of sources. As I told you, I had heard that there had been a meeting of selected plaintiffs' counsel in Atlanta at which an Executive Committee had been agreed upon, and that Harold [Kohn] had made disparaging remarks about our firm and stated that we could not serve on any such committee.

> When I called you on February 2, you told me that there had indeed been a meeting in Atlanta; and that we could not be on the Executive Committee, because Harold had said so. You stated, however, that we would certainly not be barred from serving on other committees and, indeed, you said that you had the highest regard for the legal abilities of our firm. When I asked you who was going to be on the Executive Committee, you identified lawyers in five Philadelphia firms, including Dave Berger. While I have great respect and admiration for Dave's legal abilities, I questioned you about his inclusion on the Executive Committee when we were to be excluded, in view of the fact that he had not yet to our knowledge filed a fine paper case and that we had not only filed a case, but taken an active part in obtaining the impoundment of the Grand Jury documents and in the transfer hearing before the Multidistrict Panel. You replied that Dave would certainly have to have a case on file to be on the committee and that he was selected to be on the committee because of his "position in the industry." I asked whether you meant his position in the fine paper industry, and you replied that you meant his position in the plaintiffs' antitrust industry, which may, in fact, be an apt description of what is going on. I later learned that Dave did file a case on February 2, 1978, but instead of putting Dave on the Executive Committee, you put Laddie Montague of his firm on it. Again, I have great respect for Laddie and his abilities, but question why he should be on to the exclusion of somebody from our firm.

* * *

We have not received your status report of March 3, 1978, addressed to all plaintiffs' counsel, except counsel for the states of Arizona and Colorado. The status report disclosed that the members of the Plaintiffs' Executive Committee had approved the establishment of standing committees. A list of the members of those committees was annexed to the report. We are not represented on any of the committees. A number of plaintiffs' counsel, on the other hand, have multiple assignments, including yourself and Messrs. Kohn, Montague, Walner, Barrack, Rubin and others.

I would appreciate it if you would let me know on what basis the committee assignments were made and on what basis our firm was excluded from any assignment. I hope that it was not done in response to Harold Kohn's expressed feelings about us. Particularly now that the litigation has been transferred to Philadelphia as a result of the applications made by Sy Kurland and us, I suggest that you may want to reconsider our exclusion from the Executive and other meaningful committees.

(C) The February 3, 1978 Organizational Meeting

The formal organizational meeting was held in Chicago on February 3, 1978. The minutes of this meeting show that 21 private law firms representing 13 clients (5 law firms represented Campbell Office Supply) and 11 state attorneys general were in attendance. The minutes state that "it was the consensus, voting on both a case basis and a counsel basis, that for the purpose of this meeting each Attorney General and each private law firm should have one vote on any matter...."

Following the above procedure, the meeting elected a four-man lead counsel team: Granvil Specks, Harold Kohn, Joseph Cotchett and John Noel. Later Seymour Kurland was added to this group. The meeting then elected a dozen-member Executive Committee (later expanded to 14), with two Co–Chairmen, Specks and Kohn, which had the power to appoint standing committees. The minutes of the meeting concluded with a "Statement of Guiding Principles":

The Chairman [Granvil I. Specks] stated that the members of the Executive Committee were of the opinion that the Fine Paper Antitrust Litigation should be governed by two guiding principles:

(1) There will be a fair and equitable allocation of work so that all plaintiffs' counsel can actively participate in the litigation.

(2) That plaintiffs' counsel will be reasonably compensated for services actually and productively rendered. As a corollary of this principle, the litigation should be run as efficiently as possible and duplicative work should be avoided.

Within a matter of a few weeks a host of committees and subcommittees had been formed by the Executive Committee. A plaintiffs' Discovery Committee was formed with one chairman and three vice-chairmen. Fifteen individual defendants' Discovery Subcommittees were formed with two chairmen for each subcommittee. Other committees included a Plaintiff's Rule 37 Subcommittee, a Consolidated Amended Complaint Subcommittee, an Industrial Analysis Committee, and a Finance Committee, most with a chairman and a vice-chairman.

At this court's first pretrial conference on April 19, 1978, certain states' attorneys general objected to the makeup of the Executive Committee established at the February 3rd organizational meeting. In particular, Michael Spiegel, Deputy Attorney General of California, complained at length about the organization of the case and about the voting procedures used by the private law firms:

> "I think what we are coming down to in this case is what really is at stake here. In this litigation you have got a group of States who have filed cases. These States are claiming damages for purchases that they have made. They have got clients, that is, the attorneys general representing them have clients with purchases, they have something at stake in this litigation.

> * * *

> "On the other side we have a group of private attorneys here without substantial clients.[5] If you go down that list and look at the clients they represent you have three or four of the most prominent antitrust attorneys in this country representing a mom and pop greeting card store, a fishmonger from Fort Bragg, California who buys wrapping paper to wrap fish, and these people, just because they have had the ingenuity to allege a national class action representing the Fortune 500 corporations who also buy fine paper, it doesn't seem to me that that ought to give them a position to walk into a courtroom and say we're going to run this thing.

> "What have they got at stake here? Their clients have nothing at stake. The defendants could buy all their clients for less than probably a month's attorneys' fees.

> "What is really at stake here is attorneys' fees. These lawyers have filed these cases. They hope to proceed in this case so that at the end they can have an award of attorneys' fees. That is their interest. From my point of view that is a conflict of interest.

> * * *

> "The interesting thing that occurred at the meeting in ... Chicago is that they decided to vote based on one attorney, one vote.

> "I could have brought a 400–man staff out there and packed that meeting if I wanted to. They didn't vote in terms of one client, one vote, you see, so that the mom and pop greeting card store with four attorneys got four votes, whereas at that meeting the State of Colorado would only get one vote.

5. Indeed, eight clients who are represented by 11 law firms have not filed claims for any portion of the settlement fund mainly because their claims are too insignificant.

"Now that is the way this thing was set up and, of course, this was set up before the cases were even transferred. So that whatever was done had no authority in terms of any court order, by any request of any court to have this committee set up.

"My experience in the past has simply been that this is the way that this is done, if somebody wants to make a run for it and grab the power and run the case you do it before anybody else has got together, before the panel has made any transfer, before anybody knows what happens.

"Then you walk into court and say now we have this executive committee and I am in charge of it and here are my four co-lead plaintiffs and we are going to run this thing and everybody else should sit down and be quiet."

* * *

In retrospect, I can recognize the force of Mr. Spiegel's argument but at the time the court was persuaded by the array of distinguished counsel for the private plaintiffs and had no reason to anticipate that the case would not be prosecuted in the best interests of the class.

(D) THE ADDITION OF NEW LAW FIRMS AND THE EXCLUSION OF OTHERS

The number of law firms appearing as counsel for the class continued to grow even after the organizational structure was in place. For example, eight of the petitioning firms did not become involved in the case until well after the first $30 million in settlements were in the bank and the class had been certified. Kohn repeatedly objected to the entry of additional firms, but Specks and other members of the Executive Committee nonetheless assigned work to the newcomers. Incredibly, while new counsel were being invited to participate, other counsel, including some who had been involved from the outset, were frozen out of the case.

* * *

[As time went by, disputes grew between Harold Kohn and Granvil Specks about pretrial preparation.]

An acknowledged leader of the class action bar with vast experience in the antitrust field, Kohn asserted that the 97,000 hours claimed by the plaintiffs' lawyers were excessive, and that the same work could have been accomplished with an expenditure of 5,000 to 15,000 hours by one competent firm. Kohn alleged that much of the time claimed was unnecessary and duplicated the work of others, pointing particularly to time charged for travel and attendance at hearings at which attorneys did nothing but sit and listen to other counsel make presentations. He also complained about the many hours charged by lawyers who on their own undertook to "review" the work of others.

* * *

Even more serious, Kohn claimed that five firms, Specks & Goldberg, Ltd., Saveri & Saveri, Sloan & Connelly, Lawrence Walner & Associates, Ltd. and Freeman, Atkins & Coleman, Ltd., gained control of the litigation through a voting block formed by lawyers who were importuned to file additional redundant class actions or who were simply added as co-counsel to complaints already filed. This coterie elected lead counsel and the Executive Committee who were responsible for handing out committee and other work assignments to themselves and to attorneys who voted for them. Such assignments were highly desirable because they enabled firms to increase their lodestar billing, frequently just for mere meetings and review tasks, and to claim multipliers for their leadership roles.

* * *

In the final months before the scheduled trial, a schism developed between Kohn and Specks over control of the case. It was nothing more than an out-and-out power struggle that began with name calling[89] and ended with the establishment of separate camps (rival trial headquarters) in Philadelphia in anticipation of the trial.

Notes and Questions

1. No doubt the district judge in *Fine Paper* wished that he had taken an active role at the outset in selecting class counsel. How should he have done so? What should the judge have done differently? The lawyers who were appointed were well-known and had established track records in handling cases of this sort successfully. Was there any reason for the judge to mistrust them? Compare In re Wirebound Boxes Antitrust Litigation, 128 F.R.D. 256, 258 (D.Minn.1989) (citing *Fine Paper* in deciding not to appoint Granvil Specks lead counsel). So far as the class members are concerned, is it clear that Specks did a poor job in *Fine Paper*? Evidently no one objected to the settlement amounts obtained for class members. Is the appointment of multiple firms to represent a plaintiff class something to be avoided? The Committee Note accompanying Rule 23(g) explains:

> The rule states that the court should appoint "class counsel." In many instances, the applicant will be an individual attorney. In other cases, however, an entire firm, or perhaps numerous attorneys who are not otherwise affiliated but are collaborating on the action will apply. No rule of thumb exists to determine when such arrangements are appropriate; the court should be alert to the need for adequate staffing of the

---

89. In an August 21, 1980 letter, Specks took Kohn to task for "your repeated efforts to cripple the preparation of Plaintiffs' Trial Memorandum by the drafting committee and your continuing failure and refusal to abide by the decisions of Plaintiffs' Executive Committee and to cooperate with other counsel in preparing the case for trial." On August 23, Kohn responded, "I don't propose to waste further time reviewing or responding to the manic minutiae of your letter of August 21st. In view of the tone of the letter and your prior communications, I think the matter must be referred forthwith to the Court for resolution. If you and your two conferees [Sloan and Saveri] want to repeat your folly before Judge Singleton, so be it." Specks replied that, "it is clear from the record who is 'manic' ... [E]very effort has been made by the other members of the trial team to conciliate your hostile, uncooperative and counter-productive actions, but apparently to no avail."

case, but also to the risk of overstaffing or an ungainly counsel structure.

Will Rule 23(g) help courts avoid problems like those that eventually plagued the judge in *Fine Paper?*

2. The ultimate focus of the court's opinion, and of much of the effort of counsel, was the attorneys' fee award. In *Fine Paper,* the district court cut the fee requests substantially. On appeal, the Third Circuit reversed and remanded as to certain matters regarding fees. It noted in conclusion, however, that "[w]e have found more in the trial court's opinion of which we wholeheartedly approve than we have found necessary to reverse." In re Fine Paper Antitrust Litigation, 751 F.2d 562 (3d Cir.1984). We will consider the court's role in setting attorney fee awards *infra* at p. 680.

Should prospective fees be considered at the outset? Rule 23(g)(1)(C)(iii) authorizes the court to direct proposed class counsel to "propose terms for attorney fees and nontaxable costs," and Rule 23(g)(2)(C) says the court may include provisions about an attorney fee award in the order appointing class counsel. How often will this be possible?

3. Was the sort of bartering for votes that *Fine Paper* illustrates inevitable? Professor Coffee attributed the situation to the court's abdication of the responsibility for selection and control of lead counsel:

> Until recently, the Manual for Complex Litigation instructed the trial court to let the plaintiffs' attorneys elect their own lead counsel. The result was the legal equivalent of an unsupervised political convention without procedural rules or even a credentials committee. Rival slates would form. Competing groups would invite other attorneys into the action in order to secure their vote for lead counsel. Eventually, a political compromise would emerge. The price of such a compromise was often both overstaffing and an acceptance of the free-riding or marginally competent attorney whose vote gave him leverage his ability did not.

Coffee, The Regulation of Entrepreneurial Litigation: Balancing Fairness and Efficiency in the Large Class Action, 54 U.Chi.L.Rev. 877, 907–08 (1987). Professors Macey and Miller treat these arrangements as barriers to entry into the market for lead counsel positions, and suggest that "a reduction of barriers to entry might well increase the level of quality competition among plaintiffs' attorneys, presumably to the benefit of both clients and the litigation system." Macey & Miller, The Plaintiffs' Attorney's Role in Class Action and Derivative Litigation: Economic Analysis and Recommendations for Reform, 58 U.Chi.L.Rev. 1, 68 (1991).

4. Lest it appear that judges are always unhappy with the performance of lead counsel, consider In re MGM Grand Hotel Fire Litigation, 660 F.Supp. 522 (D.Nev.1987), in which the court praised the performance of the Plaintiffs' Legal Committee: "To the court's knowledge, the results of the PLC's efforts have never been equalled in any other mass disaster litigation. Indeed, of the dozens of mass disaster cases that were pending or begun during the pendency of this case, none of them have concluded except this one, and from the court's viewpoint, that says it all." Id. at 529.

5. Rule 23(g)(1)(C) directs the court to consider a variety of factors in deciding on class counsel. It must consider the work counsel has done in the

case, counsel's experience in handling class actions, other complex litigation and claims of the type asserted in the case, counsel's knowledge of the applicable law, and the resources counsel will commit to representing the class. It may consider "any other matter pertinent to counsel's ability to fairly and adequately represent the interests of the class." On any of these topics, the court may direct counsel to provide information to the court. See also Manual for Complex Litigation (4th) § 10.224 (2004) (listing criteria to be used for selection of appointed counsel, including the qualifications of the designated lawyer, the lawyer's resources, the attorneys' "ability to command the respect of their colleagues and work cooperatively with opposing counsel and the court" and other factors). In *Fine Paper*, would such an approach have produced a different result in appointment of class counsel?

Rule 23(g)(2)(B) provides that, if there are multiple adequate applicants for the class counsel position, the court should appoint "the applicant best able to represent the interests of the class." Sometimes, lawyers have been found to be inadequate. For example, in Kingsepp v. Wesleyan Univ., 142 F.R.D. 597 (S.D.N.Y.1992), the court rejected an applicant for the class counsel position who had been sanctioned by other judges for misconduct and whose filings in the current case confirmed the low opinion of his competence. Except in such cases, how can judges make confident choices between contending lawyers?

6. *Auctioning the position*: In In re Oracle Securities Litigation, 131 F.R.D. 688 (N.D.Cal.1990), a securities fraud class action, the judge was frustrated that proposed class counsel who vied for the position of class counsel "displayed a rather cavalier indifference to at least the spirit of the antitrust laws" when he directed them to bid for the position by making proposals emphasizing the fees that they would charge. Rather than do so, they formed an alliance and made a combined bid. Eventually, the judge obtained bids for several firms and, concluding that "[a]ll of the bidders are prominent, well established firms specializing in the type of litigation at bar," concluded that he could not choose among them on the basis of the likely quality of their work on the case. See In re Oracle Securities Litigation, 132 F.R.D. 538 (N.D.Cal.1990). A few other judges experimented with variations of this technique. See generally Hooper & Leary, Auctioning the Role of Class Counsel, 209 F.R.D. 519 (2001).

Should competition of this sort be promoted as a better way of selecting class counsel? How can the judge compare varying bids? Is there a sensible way to factor in the quality, tenacity, commitment, etc. of the lawyers or law firms involved? The auction approach excited considerable interest, and the Third Circuit appointed a task force to investigate its possibilities, but the task force reached rather negative conclusions. See Third Circuit Task Force Report on the Selection of Class Counsel, 74 Temple L. Rev. 689 (2001). The Task Force thought that the auction method would work only when the defendant's liability appears clear (perhaps due to a government investigation or admission by the defendant), the damages appear both large and collectible, and the lead plaintiff is not a sophisticated litigant that has already retained counsel of its choice through a reasonable arm's-length process that would be upset by appointment of a different lawyer. In most class actions, however, these circumstances do not obtain and the traditional methods of selecting class counsel should be used, albeit with caution about overstaffing by lawyer groups. Regarding adopting attorney fee provisions at the point of appointment of class counsel, the Task Force concluded that Rule 23 ultimately requires that the court examine the fairness of the fees at the conclusion of the case, and that advance directives may prove to be premature.

7. *The Private Securities Litigation Reform Act (PSLRA) Approach*: The PSLRA refashions the securities fraud class action to place primary responsibility on the lead plaintiff, who to be the class member "most capable of adequately representing the class members." 15 U.S.C. § 78u–4(a)(3)(B)(i). The Act adds that the applicant for the position with the greatest financial stake in the outcome of the case is presumed to be the most capable unless that presumption is rebutted. Id., § 78u–4(a)(3)(B)(iii). One reaction entrepreneurial lawyers have had to this provision has been to try to put together a group of claimants who together would serve as lead plaintiff in order to come up with the largest aggregate prospective recovery. See Fisch, Aggregation, Auctions, and Other Developments in the Selection of Lead Counsel Under the PSLRA, 64 Law & Contemp. Probs. 53 (Spring/Summer 2001) (evaluating this practice).

What role does the court have under the PSLRA? The judge is to determine whether the proposed lead plaintiff satisfies the requirements of Rule 23, such as adequacy of representation. See *supra* p. 285 for discussion of adequacy of representation. In In re Cavanaugh, 306 F.3d 726 (9th Cir.2002), the district judge (the same one who first tried the auction method mentioned in note 6 above) concluded that the group with the largest stake in the recovery would not be an adequate representative because this group had hired a prominent law firm on terms that the judge thought were too generous to the firm, and therefore disadvantageous for the class. The judge accordingly appointed another lead plaintiff, who had a different arrangement with a smaller firm.

The Ninth Circuit held that this appointment went beyond the judge's authority under the PSLRA. "So long as the plaintiff with the largest losses satisfies the typicality and adequacy requirements, he is entitled to lead plaintiff status, even if the district court is convinced the some other plaintiff would do a better job." Id. at 732. Choice of counsel is not a ground for preferring one lead plaintiff over another, for that is customarily left to the client. "Selecting a lawyer in whom a litigant has confidence is an important client prerogative and we will not lightly infer the Congress meant to take away this prerogative from securities plaintiffs." Id. at 734. Ultimately, the court will have to pass on the reasonableness of the fee award, but that will not occur until the end of the case, and only if the case is won. Moreover, "[a] plaintiff facing large losses and a tough case may rationally conclude that he will be better off by hiring the more expensive, and more formidable, advocate, who may intimidate defendants into a prompt settlement on favorable terms." Id. at 735. If judges making class counsel appointments under Rule 23(g)(2)(B) must choose the "best" applicant, how often will they be able to make the same sort of determination, as the Ninth Circuit says that the lead plaintiff may?

8. *Expanding the "empowered plaintiff" model*: If the selection of the best lawyer is really better made by the client than by the court, can the PSLRA experience be the basis for a new approach to appointment of class

counsel more generally? Professor Fisch argues that, under existing practices for appointment of counsel and without the need of statutory assistance, the courts might properly favor that approach over trying to make their own selection. See Fisch, Lawyers on the Auction Block: Evaluating the Selection of Class Counsel by Auction, 102 Colum.L.Rev. 650 (2002). She proposes three criteria for selecting cases in which her approach would be workable (id. at 722):

> First, the class must include members with a sufficient financial stake in the litigation. Only if the empowered lead plaintiff has a sufficient interest in the case will it incur the costs of identifying, negotiating with, and monitoring class counsel. Second, the potential lead plaintiffs must be sufficiently representative of the interests of other class members. * * * Third, the size of a class member's interest should be correlated with its sophistication and ability to handle the selection, negotiation, and monitoring processes.

Would these criteria have been satisfied in *Fine Paper*? Would lawyers who file class actions seek out class representatives who fit Professor Fisch's description?

Professor Fisch recognizes that this approach won't work in many class actions. "In particular, it is unlikely to work well in cases that fall toward either end of the spectrum of class actions—small claimant cases, on the one hand, and mass tort cases on the other." Id. at 725. Regarding mass tort class actions, she adds (id. at 726–27):

> Although mass tort class actions generally include class members with substantial stakes, the interests of class members may diverge substantially. In particular, the interests of those class members with the largest stakes, often the most seriously injured, are likely to conflict with other class members, such as those with more modest injuries or exposure only plaintiffs. As a result, although the severely injured plaintiffs may have sufficient motivation to participate actively, they may not be capable of representing the plaintiff class fairly. Additionally, * * * there is little reason to believe that those with larger interests in the case are likely to be particularly well qualified to serve as lead plaintiff.

9. *Public entities*: In *Fine Paper*, one of the objectors was the California Attorney General. Should courts regard such actors as preferable voices for the interests of the class because they are "above the fray"? Brunet, Class Action Objectors: Extortionist Free Riders or Fairness Guarantors, 2003 U.Chi.Legal F. 403, notes that "[p]articipation in class actions by states is increasingly common." Id. at 449. Although Professor Brunet examines the role of governmental agencies as objectors, might they be preferred as lead plaintiffs or class representatives where willing to serve, and relied upon to select appropriate counsel? Professor Brunet notes that "[g]overnment attorneys have different incentives than class action counsel. * * * Rather than aspire to monetary awards, the typical agency attorney seeks prominence generally, and peer group acceptance, particularly." Id. at 454. Would this orientation be preferable to the profit seeking of private counsel?

10. As you reflect on the difficulties that the court confronts in selecting and dealing with lead counsel, keep in mind that in many instances

the reason why this becomes necessary is that broad joinder rules and related doctrines create more complex litigation. Should these kinds of difficulties temper the impulse toward aggregation of claims? Do the rules regarding aggregation adequately take account of these problems? Cf. Fed. R.Civ.P. 23(b)(3) (directing court to determine whether a class action is "superior to other available methods for the fair and efficient adjudication of the controversy").

11. *Disqualification of counsel*: Besides being responsible for selecting counsel in a number of situations, courts are called upon with some frequency to remove privately-retained counsel. In general, such motions are based on the alleged breach of the challenged attorney's duties to another client through service to the one involved in this case. "Lawyers have discovered that disqualifying opposing counsel is a successful trial strategy, capable of creating delay, harassment, additional expense, and perhaps even resulting in the withdrawal of a dangerously competent counsel." Developments in the Law, Conflicts of Interest in the Legal Profession, 94 Harv.L.Rev. 1224, 1285 (1981).

In complex litigation, disqualification of counsel can be highly disruptive. For example, in Westinghouse Elec. Corp. v. Rio Algom Ltd., 448 F.Supp. 1284 (N.D.Ill.1978), a major law firm had represented Westinghouse throughout the litigation. It emerged, however, that the Washington office of the firm had provided some advice to a trade association that included several defendants as prominent members, and defendants moved to disqualify plaintiff's firm. Emphasizing that the firm had taken hundreds of depositions and participated in a trial that lasted six months, the district judge declined to disqualify the firm in "a case of the present complexity and magnitude" because the objection to its involvement fell in the "twilight zone of ethical transgressions." The appellate court, however, held that the district judge had no choice, and that disqualification was required. See Westinghouse Elec. Corp. v. Kerr–McGee Corp., 580 F.2d 1311 (7th Cir.), cert. denied, 439 U.S. 955, 99 S.Ct. 353, 58 L.Ed.2d 346 (1978). Perhaps to ward off such disruptions, the Manual for Complex Litigation (4th) § 10.23 (2004), advises that "[i]n view of the number and dispersion of parties and interests in complex litigation, the court should remind counsel to be alert to present or potential conflicts of interest."

E. ATTORNEYS' FEES AWARDS

In the 1980s, many noted that attorneys' fee awards became a sort of cottage industry for the legal profession, and this trend has gained momentum since. At first blush, awards of attorneys' fees may not seem to be tools of judicial control of litigation. In operation, however, they can serve that purpose. Recall Peil v. National Semiconductor Corp., *supra* p. 292 ("much influence and control is exercised by the Court by the fact that it controls the fee award to plaintiffs' counsel"). Particularly in complex litigation, the judge's authority to determine how much one set of lawyers will be paid exerts a considerable influence on the way those lawyers approach the litigation.

In class actions, this authority has increasingly been viewed as important to the healthy functioning of this procedural device. "In a

class action, whether the attorneys' fees come from a common fund or
are otherwise paid, the district court must exercise its inherent authority
to assure that the amount and mode of payment of attorneys' fees are
fair and proper." Zucker v. Occidental Petroleum Corp., 192 F.3d 1323,
1328 (9th Cir.1999); see also In re Cendant Corp. PRIDES Litigation,
243 F.3d 722, 730 (3d Cir.2001) (referring to "the special position of the
courts in connection with class action settlements and attorneys' fee
awards"); RAND, Executive Summary, Class Action Dilemmas 33 (1999)
("The single most important action that judges can take to support the
public goals of class action litigation is to reward class action attorneys
only for lawsuits that actually accomplish something of value to class
members and society."). Does the "American rule" against fee awards
serve a valid purpose in limiting judicial intrusion into the performance
of the lawyer?

1. AUTHORITY TO AWARD ATTORNEYS' FEES

The United States adheres generally to the "American Rule" that
each litigant must pay its own lawyer, so that some exception to that
rule must be found to justify fee-shifting. Manual for Complex Litigation
(4th) § 14.11 (2004) outlines many of the grounds for fee awards.
Perhaps the most common is a fee-shifting statute, such as the one
involved in Hensley v. Eckerhart, *infra* p. 686. Each of these statutes
provides in some way that the prevailing party is entitled to an award of
attorney fees. In complex litigation there are often claims that invoke a
fee-shifting statute. Besides those, some other fee-shifting grounds deserve mention:

Common fund: Where the litigation activities of one person created
a fund for a number of other persons or conferred a benefit on them,
American courts early allowed the litigant to recover from the fund thus
created an amount including the attorneys' fees incurred in creating the
fund. The premise was a theory of unjust enrichment—the passive
beneficiaries of litigation should shoulder their fair share of the cost of
creating the fund if they were to receive it. See Trustees v. Greenough,
105 U.S. (15 Otto) 527, 26 L.Ed. 1157 (1881); Central Railroad &
Banking Co. v. Pettus, 113 U.S. 116, 5 S.Ct. 387, 28 L.Ed. 915 (1885).

The common fund notion is most important in complex litigation in
two contexts. First, it fits easily into the derivative action mold in which
a disgruntled shareholder takes up the cudgel for the injured corporation
and obtains a recovery for it. Second, the common fund or benefit
doctrine provides a basis for awarding class counsel their fees out of the
proceeds of a class action before distributing the residue to the class
members. In Boeing Co. v. Van Gemert, 444 U.S. 472, 100 S.Ct. 745, 62
L.Ed.2d 676 (1980), some class members did not claim their shares of the
class-wide damage award. Defendant asserted that the attorneys' fee
award could not be paid in part from these unclaimed shares. Rejecting
this argument, the Court broadly endorsed application of the common
fund doctrine to class actions:

To claim their logically ascertainable shares of the judgment fund, absentee class members need prove only their membership in the injured class. Their right to share the harvest of the lawsuit upon proof of their identity, whether or not they exercise it, is a benefit in the fund created by the efforts of the class representatives and their counsel. Unless absentees contribute to the payment of attorney's fees incurred on their behalves, they will pay nothing for the creation of the fund and their representatives may bear additional costs. The judgment entered by the District Court and affirmed by the Court of Appeals rectifies this inequity by requiring every member of the class to share attorney's fees to the same extent that he can share the recovery. Since the benefits of the class recovery have been "traced with some accuracy" and the costs of recovery have been "shifted with some exactitude to those benefiting," *Alyeska Pipeline Service Co. v. Wilderness Society,* [421 U.S.] at 265, n. 39, we conclude that the attorneys' fee award in this case is a proper application of the common-fund doctrine.

The *Boeing* analysis applies relatively easily to a class action under Rule 23(b)(3) in which the objective is to generate a fund of class damages. Can a similar argument provide a basis for the award of attorneys' fees in (b)(1) or (b)(2) class actions? Would the result depend on whether the defendant were required to pay over some fund of money to the plaintiff class members? If not, could the same common benefit argument be made in cases where the relief granted would operate to the advantage of nonparties? Where would the money come from? In the derivative action context, the doctrine has been held to authorize an award of fees even where no fund is created. Mills v. Electric Auto–Lite Co., 396 U.S. 375, 90 S.Ct. 616, 24 L.Ed.2d 593 (1970).

This principle can also apply to class members who object to proposed settlements during proceedings under Rule 23(e). See *supra* pp. 509-39. If the objections produce improvements in the settlement, the objectors may be eligible for a fee award to compensate them for the efforts expended in improving the settlement. See, e.g. White v. Auerbach, 500 F.2d 822, 828 (2d Cir.1974) (objectors entitled to attorneys' fees for producing improved settlement). It is even possible that successful objectors to the attorney fee motion of class counsel could obtain attorney fee awards for their efforts. See, e.g., Gottlieb v. Barry, 43 F.3d 474 (10th Cir.1994) (fee award to objectors who brought about reduction in fee awarded from settlement fund).

Lead counsel: The common fund doctrine has been used to justify fee shifting in consolidated cases where lead counsel is appointed. As the Manual for Complex Litigation (4th) § 14.215 (2004) explains, "[l]ead and liaison counsel may have been appointed by the court to perform functions necessary for the management of the case but not properly charged to their clients." Accordingly, it advises, the court should make a determination early in the case of how these lawyers are to be compensated for this work, "including setting up a fund to which designated parties should contribute in specified proportions." This approach is more common with respect to fees for plaintiff's attorneys. For example, in Vincent v. Hughes Air West, Inc., 557 F.2d 759 (9th Cir.1977), a number of actions were filed to recover damages for passengers killed in the crash of a commercial airliner. After consolidation, the district court appointed lead counsel, who were authorized to conduct all discovery and file motions, and directed that no other plaintiff's attorneys take such actions without the approval of lead counsel. Thereafter, the court ordered that 5% of any judgment or settlement in favor of any plaintiff be deposited into a fund that could be used to pay lead counsel. To the extent plaintiffs had agreed to pay their own lawyers more than 20% of their recovery as a contingency fee, the deposit into the fund was to come from the lawyers' share; otherwise it was to come from the client's share of the settlement. Over time, some $450,000 accumulated in the fund. After all the cases were settled, the district court awarded the entire fund to lead counsel. The Ninth Circuit affirmed, rejecting the argument that the court had artificially created a fund out of which to pay lead counsel:

> Yet the Special Class Fund is not the only asset in this case which can be used to satisfy the requirements of the common fund doctrine. Taking a broader view, we see that lead counsel helped "create" a fund consisting of the various settlements negotiated in these consolidated actions. The court found as a matter of fact that the efforts of lead counsel were instrumental in persuading Hughes and the United States not to contest liability and accordingly were a significant cause-in-fact of the settlements.

Accord, In re Air Crash Disaster at Florida Everglades, 549 F.2d 1006 (5th Cir.1977); see also In re Linerboard Antitrust Litigation, 292 F.Supp.2d 644 (E.D.Pa.2003) (court could create fund out of the proceeds of tag-along suits brought by opt-outs in order to compensate class counsel). Is it really fair to say that the lead counsel's efforts created a fund for non-lead counsel in those cases where they had to contribute to the fund?

There are limits to the court's power to "tax" other plaintiffs, however. In In re Showa Denko K.K. L–Tryptophan Products Liability Litigation, 953 F.2d 162 (4th Cir.1992), the district court was presiding over some 470 actions transferred by the Judicial Panel on Multidistrict Litigation, and it ordered each plaintiff to contribute $1,000 into a common fund to defray the costs of discovery incurred by plaintiffs' steering committee. It imposed the same order with regard to plaintiffs in other federal cases not transferred by the Panel, and with regard to plaintiffs in some 680 cases pending in state courts. The appellate court held that this effort to require contributions from plaintiffs not before the court was beyond its power and, with regard to cases in state court, raised federalism issues because it had "the very real potential of interfering with discovery proceedings in state court." Id. at 166. It therefore reversed with respect to cases not pending before the district court.

Should similar reasoning justify allocating the costs of lead counsel for the *defense* to other defendants? In In re Two Appeals Arising Out of San Juan Dupont Plaza Hotel Fire Litigation, 994 F.2d 956 (1st Cir. 1993), the district court ordered the creation of a joint document depository and appointment of liaison counsel and imposed assessments on both plaintiff's management committee and on defendants to finance these undertakings. Defendants which were eventually found not liable challenged the district judge's refusal to refund their payments of approximately $585,000, urging that this cost should be reallocated to other parties because the objectors won. The appellate court found that district court judges have power to allocate costs in complex cases, based principally on then-existing authority in Rule 26(f) (since removed) to enter orders for "the allocation of expenses as are necessary for the proper management of discovery." See id. at 965. This power included the ability to reallocate such costs on the basis of "equitable principles" that look to derived benefit as the basis for imposition of costs. Accordingly, "there is no basis for a * * * presumption that the winners' case-management expenses should be borne by the losers." Id. at 966. It left to the district court the proper application of these principles in this case.

In In re Three Additional Appeals Arising Out of the San Juan Dupont Plaza Hotel Fire Litigation, 93 F.3d 1 (1st Cir.1996), the court rejected the arguments of certain insurers added as defendants late in the litigation that they should not have to pay the $41,000 assessed for the Joint Document Depository and related centralized services, noting that these defendants had made use of these services. "[I]t is of no moment that [these defendants] might have preferred to go it alone. The case-management system that the district court so painstakingly devised could not have operated on a voluntary basis." Id. at 5.

Private attorney general: Beginning in the 1960s the notion that litigants acting as "private attorneys general" enforcing various statutes against violators should be allowed to recover their attorneys fees threatened for a time to eclipse the common fund doctrine as the principal judge-made exception to the American rule. For federal claims, that development was scotched by Alyeska Pipeline Service Co. v. Wilderness Society, 421 U.S. 240, 95 S.Ct. 1612, 44 L.Ed.2d 141 (1975), which rejected this new exception. Some states have been more receptive. Most notably, California provides by statute for an award of attorneys' fees in specified circumstances to a plaintiff whose suit enforced "an important right affecting the public interest." Cal. Code Civ. Proc. § 1021.5.

2. DETERMINING THE AMOUNT TO BE AWARDED

"He's illuminating something called 'The Book of Billable Hours.'"

It would be pleasing to be able to report that the computation of fee awards has proved to be straightforward, but it has not. "Of all the tasks facing trial court judges in class action litigation, one of the most difficult is determining the appropriate fee." Eisenberg & Miller, Attorney Fees in Class Action Settlements: An Empirical Study, 1 J. Empir. Legal Stud. 27, 27 (2004). Indeed, there are entire books devoted to the problems of attorneys' fee awards. See, e.g., A. Hirsch & D. Sheehey, Awarding Attorneys' Fees and Managing Fee Litigation (1994); H. Newberg, Attorney Fee Awards (1986). Setting the fee is, however, one means by which the judge can wield power over the lawyers, albeit often retrospectively. In 1993, Rule 54(d)(2) was added to provide procedures for fee award litigation. In 2003, Rule 23(h) was added to deal directly with fee awards in class actions; it recognizes the importance of this regulatory effort by the court to make class actions operate properly.

In large measure, the challenge of fee litigation results from changes within the legal marketplace. In general terms, most lawyers tended not to be terribly "businesslike" about their fee arrangements and billing until the 1960s or 1970s. By the early 1970s, however, those concerned with law office economics had begun to urge lawyers to focus on the amount of time they spent on matters in determining the amount they charged for their services. Some contend that the broadened discovery authorized by the Federal Rules acted as a catalyst for the broad adoption of hourly billing in litigation. See Shepherd & Cloud, Time and

Money: Discovery Leads to Hourly Billing, 1999 U.Ill.L.Rev. 91. In any event, billing on the basis of hourly rates became widespread, along with such law firm management techniques as billable budgets setting the number of hours lawyers should bill in a year.

Beginning in the 1980s, both clients and lawyers have expressed reservations about hourly billing. From the clients' perspective, there were concerns that this billing approach magnified fees by allowing lawyers to run up their hours on a case or overstaff it. See Report of ABA Commission on Professionalism, 112 F.R.D. 243, 283–84 (1986) (describing overbilling by lawyers using hourly billing). From the lawyers' perspective, the hourly method of billing might undercompensate them when they achieved outstanding results with the investment of little time. During the 1980s, at least in the area of mergers and acquisitions, a new concept of "value billing" was introduced to justify increases over the amount determined on an hourly basis if results were good. For a discussion of the problems, see R. Reed, Beyond the Billable Hour (1989).

Against this background, the problem of determining the amount to award where fees are to be shifted has proved, like other problems of fee shifting, to be "surprisingly complex." Rowe, Predicting the Effects of Attorney Fee Shifting, 47 Law & Contemp.Probs. 139, 140 (Winter 1984). In this section, we will look at the conventional approach developed by the lower courts—often called the "lodestar"—and then turn to criticisms that have been levelled against this approach in certain common fund cases.

a. The Emergence of the Lodestar

Until the mid–1980s, the Supreme Court did not venture into the question of setting fee awards, and the task was left to the lower courts. Basically two models emerged. First, in Lindy Brothers Builders, Inc. v. American Radiator & Standard Sanitary Corp., 487 F.2d 161 (3d Cir. 1973), the court emphasized an hourly approach, concluding that the product of hours spent on a case times hourly rate "should be the lodestar of the court's fee determination." This figure could then be increased or decreased on the basis of the quality of the lawyer's work and success, and on the basis of the contingency of the action.

The Fifth Circuit adopted a twelve-factor approach, based on the ABA rules concerning ethical limitations on billing, in Johnson v. Georgia Highway Express, Inc., 488 F.2d 714 (5th Cir.1974): (1) the time and labor required; (2) the novelty and difficulty of the questions; (3) the skill requisite to perform the legal service properly; (4) the preclusion of employment by the attorney due to acceptance of the case; (5) the customary fee; (6) whether the fee is fixed or contingent; (7) time limitations imposed by the client or the circumstances; (8) the amount involved and the results obtained; (9) the experience, reputation, and ability of the attorneys; (10) the "undesirability" of the case; (11) the nature and length of the professional relationship with the client; and (12) awards in similar cases. The Fifth Circuit continues to employ this technique. See Singer v. City of Waco, 324 F.3d 813, 829 (5th Cir.2003).

By the late 1970s problems had begun to emerge with the handling of fee awards under these standards. Results seemed haphazard to some observers, and many noted a "public interest discount" that meant that lawyers who brought securities fraud, antitrust, or other commercial cases would be paid much more handsomely than those who brought civil rights or similar cases. See Berger, Court Awarded Attorneys' Fees: What is Reasonable?, 126 U.Pa.L.Rev. 281, 310 (1977) (1975 study showed that in antitrust cases lawyers received $181 per hour but that in civil rights cases they received only $40 per hour). During the 1980s, the Supreme Court increasingly involved itself in the area.

HENSLEY v. ECKERHART

Supreme Court of the United States, 1983.
461 U.S. 424, 103 S.Ct. 1933, 76 L.Ed.2d 40.

JUSTICE POWELL delivered the opinion of the Court.

Title 42 U.S.C. § 1988 provides that in federal civil rights actions "the court, in its discretion, may allow the prevailing party, other than the United States, a reasonable attorney's fee as part of the costs." The issue in this case is whether a partially prevailing plaintiff may recover an attorney's fee for legal services on unsuccessful claims.

I

A

Respondents brought this lawsuit on behalf of all persons involuntarily confined at the Forensic Unit of the Fulton State Hospital in Fulton, Mo. The Forensic Unit consists of two residential buildings for housing patients who are dangerous to themselves or others. Maximum-security patients are housed in the Marion O. Biggs Building for the Criminally Insane. The rest of the patients reside in the less restrictive Rehabilitation Unit.

In 1972 respondents filed a three-count complaint in the District Court for the Western District of Missouri against petitioners, who are officials at the Forensic Unit and members of the Missouri Mental Health Commission. Count I challenged the constitutionality of treatment and conditions at the Forensic Unit. Count II challenged the placement of patients in the Biggs Building without procedural due process. Count III sought compensation for patients who performed institution-maintaining labor.

Count II was resolved by a consent decree in December 1973. Count III largely was mooted in August 1974 when petitioners began compensating patients for labor pursuant to the Fair Labor Standards Act, 29 U.S.C. § 201 et seq. In April 1975 respondents voluntarily dismissed the lawsuit and filed a new two-count complaint. Count I again related to the constitutionality of treatment and conditions at the Forensic Unit. Count II sought damages, based on the Thirteenth Amendment, for the value of past patient labor. In July 1976 respondents voluntarily dismissed this backpay count. Finally, in August 1977 respondents filed an amended one-count complaint specifying the conditions that allegedly violated their constitutional right to treatment.

In August 1979, following a three-week trial, the District Court held that an involuntarily committed patient has a constitutional right to minimally adequate treatment. 475 F.Supp. 908, 915 (1979). The court then found constitutional violations in five of six general areas: physical environment; individual treatment plans; least restrictive environment; visitation, telephone, and mail privileges; and seclusion and restraint.[1] With respect to staffing, the sixth general area, the District Court found that the Forensic Unit's staffing levels, which had increased during the litigation, were minimally adequate. Petitioners did not appeal the District Court's decision on the merits.

B

In February 1980 respondents filed a request for attorney's fees for the period from January 1975 through the end of the litigation. Their four attorneys claimed 2,985 hours worked and sought payment at rates varying from $40 to $65 per hour. This amounted to approximately $150,000. Respondents also requested that the fee be enhanced by 30 to 50 percent, for a total award of somewhere between $195,000 and $225,000. Petitioners opposed the request on numerous grounds, including inclusion of hours spent in pursuit of unsuccessful claims.

The District Court first determined that respondents were prevailing parties under 42 U.S.C. § 1988 even though they had not succeeded on every claim. It then refused to eliminate from the award hours spent on unsuccessful claims:

> "[Petitioners'] suggested method of calculating fees is based strictly on a mathematical approach comparing the total number of issues in the case with those actually prevailed upon. Under this method no consideration is given for the relative importance of various issues, the interrelation of the issues, the difficulty in identifying issues, or the extent to which a party may prevail on various issues."

Finding that respondents "have obtained relief of significant import," the District Court awarded a fee of $133,332.25. This award differed

---

1. Under "physical environment" the court found that certain physical aspects of the Biggs Building were not minimally adequate.

Under "individual treatment plans" the court found that the existing plans were adequate, but that the long delay in preparation of initial plans after patients were admitted and the lack of regular review of the plans operated to deny patients minimally adequate plans.

Under "least restrictive environment" the court found unconstitutional the delay in transfer of patients from the Biggs Building to the Rehabilitation Unit following a

determination that they no longer needed maximum-security confinement.

Under "visitation, telephone and mail" the court found that the visitation and telephone policies at the Biggs Building were so restrictive that they constituted punishment and therefore violated patients' due process rights.

Under "seclusion and restraint" the court rejected respondents' claim that patients were given excessive medication as a form of behavior control. The court then found that petitioners' practices regarding seclusion and physical restraint were not minimally adequate.

from the fee request in two respects. First, the court reduced the number of hours claimed by one attorney by 30 percent to account for his inexperience and failure to keep contemporaneous records. Second, the court declined to adopt an enhancement factor to increase the award.

The Court of Appeals for the Eighth Circuit affirmed on the basis of the District Court's memorandum opinion and order. 664 F.2d 294 (1981). We granted certiorari, 455 U.S. 988, 102 S.Ct. 1610, 71 L.Ed.2d 847 (1982), and now vacate and remand for further proceedings.

II

In *Alyeska Pipeline Service Co. v. Wilderness Society,* 421 U.S. 240, 95 S.Ct. 1612, 44 L.Ed.2d 141 (1975), this Court reaffirmed the "American Rule" that each party in a lawsuit ordinarily shall bear its own attorney's fees unless there is express statutory authorization to the contrary. In response Congress enacted the Civil Rights Attorney's Fees Awards Act of 1976, 42 U.S.C. § 1988, authorizing the district courts to award a reasonable attorney's fee to prevailing parties in civil rights litigation. The purpose of § 1988 is to ensure "effective access to the judicial process" for persons with civil rights grievances. H.R.Rep. No. 94–1558, p. 1 (1976). Accordingly, a prevailing plaintiff " 'should ordinarily recover an attorney's fee unless special circumstances would render such an award unjust.' " S.Rep. No. 94–1011, p. 4 (1976), U.S.Code Cong. & Admin.News 1976, p. 5912 (quoting *Newman v. Piggie Park Enterprises, Inc.,* 390 U.S. 400, 402, 88 S.Ct. 964, 966, 19 L.Ed.2d 1263 (1968)).

The amount of the fee, of course, must be determined on the facts of each case. On this issue the House Report simply refers to 12 factors set forth in *Johnson v. Georgia Highway Express, Inc.,* 488 F.2d 714 (C.A.5 1974). The Senate Report cites to *Johnson* as well and also refers to three District Court decisions that "correctly applied" the 12 factors. One of the factors in *Johnson,* "the amount involved and the results obtained," indicates that the level of a plaintiff's success is relevant to the amount of fees to be awarded. The importance of this relationship is confirmed in varying degrees by the other cases cited approvingly in the Senate Report.

[The Court concluded that in these cases plaintiffs obtained "essentially complete relief," and that they therefore did not offer a standard for cases in which plaintiff obtains only limited success.]

In this case petitioners contend that "an award of attorney's fees must be proportioned to be consistent with the extent to which a plaintiff has prevailed, and only time reasonably expended in support of successful claims should be compensated." Respondents agree that a plaintiff's success is relevant, but propose a less stringent standard focusing on "whether the time spent prosecuting [an unsuccessful] claim in any way contributed to the ultimate results achieved." Both parties acknowledge the discretion of the district court in this area. We take this opportunity to clarify the proper relationship of the results obtained to an award of attorney's fees.

III

A

A plaintiff must be a "prevailing party" to recover an attorney's fee under § 1988. The standard for making this threshold determination has been framed in various ways. A typical formulation is that "plaintiffs may be considered 'prevailing parties' for attorney's fees purposes if they succeed on any significant issue in litigation which achieves some of the benefit the parties sought in bringing suit." *Nadeau v. Helgemoe,* 581 F.2d 275, 278–279 (C.A.1 1978). This is a generous formulation that brings the plaintiff only across the statutory threshold. It remains for the district court to determine what fee is "reasonable."

The most useful starting point for determining the amount of a reasonable fee is the number of hours reasonably expended on the litigation multiplied by a reasonable hourly rate. This calculation provides an objective basis on which to make an initial estimate of the value of a lawyer's services. The party seeking an award of fees should submit evidence supporting the hours worked and rates claimed. Where the documentation of hours is inadequate, the district court may reduce the award accordingly.

The district court also should exclude from this initial fee calculation hours that were not "reasonably expended." S.Rep. No. 94–1011, p. 6 (1976). Cases may be overstaffed, and the skill and experience of lawyers vary widely. Counsel for the prevailing party should make a good-faith effort to exclude from a fee request hours that are excessive, redundant, or otherwise unnecessary, just as a lawyer in private practice ethically is obligated to exclude such hours from his fee submission. "In the private sector, 'billing judgment' is an important component in fee setting. It is no less important here. Hours that are not properly billed to one's *client* also are not properly billed to one's *adversary* pursuant to statutory authority." *Copeland v. Marshall,* 205 U.S.App.D.C. 390, 401, 641 F.2d 880, 891 (1980) (en banc) (emphasis in original).

B

The product of reasonable hours times a reasonable rate does not end the inquiry. There remain other considerations that may lead the district court to adjust the fee upward or downward, including the important factor of the "results obtained."[9] This factor is particularly crucial where a plaintiff is deemed "prevailing" even though he succeeded on only some of his claims for relief. In this situation two questions must be addressed. First, did the plaintiff fail to prevail on claims that

---

9. The district court also may consider other factors identified in *Johnson v. Georgia Highway Express, Inc.,* 488 F.2d 714, 717–719 (C.A.5 1974), though it should note that many of these factors usually are subsumed within the initial calculation of hours reasonably expended at a reasonable hourly rate.

were unrelated to the claims on which he succeeded? Second, did the plaintiff achieve a level of success that makes the hours reasonably expended a satisfactory basis for making a fee award?

In some cases a plaintiff may present in one lawsuit distinctly different claims for relief that are based on different facts and legal theories. In such a suit, even where the claims are brought against the same defendants—often an institution and its officers, as in this case— counsel's work on one claim will be unrelated to his work on another claim. Accordingly, work on an unsuccessful claim cannot be deemed to have been "expended in pursuit of the ultimate result achieved." The congressional intent to limit awards to prevailing parties requires that these unrelated claims be treated as if they had been raised in separate lawsuits, and therefore no fee may be awarded for services on the unsuccessful claim.

It may well be that cases involving such unrelated claims are unlikely to arise with great frequency. Many civil rights cases will present only a single claim. In other cases the plaintiff's claims for relief will involve a common core of facts or will be based on related legal theories. Much of counsel's time will be devoted generally to the litigation as a whole, making it difficult to divide the hours expended on a claim-by-claim basis. Such a lawsuit cannot be viewed as a series of discrete claims. Instead the district court should focus on the significance of the overall relief obtained by the plaintiff in relation to the hours reasonably expended on the litigation.

Where a plaintiff has obtained excellent results, his attorney should recover a fully compensatory fee. Normally this will encompass all hours reasonably expended on the litigation, and indeed in some cases of exceptional success an enhanced award may be justified. In these circumstances the fee award should not be reduced simply because the plaintiff failed to prevail on every contention raised in the lawsuit. Litigants in good faith may raise alternative legal grounds for a desired outcome, and the court's rejection of or failure to reach certain grounds is not a sufficient reason for reducing a fee. The result is what matters.[11]

If, on the other hand, a plaintiff has achieved only partial or limited success, the product of hours reasonably expended on the litigation as a whole times a reasonable hourly rate may be an excessive amount. This will be true even where the plaintiff's claims were interrelated, nonfrivolous, and raised in good faith. Congress has not authorized an award of fees whenever it was reasonable for a plaintiff to bring a lawsuit or

11. We agree with the District Court's rejection of "a mathematical approach comparing the total number of issues in the case with those actually prevailed upon." Such a ratio provides little aid in determining what is a reasonable fee in light of all the relevant factors. Nor is it necessarily significant that a prevailing plaintiff did not receive all the relief requested. For example, a plaintiff who failed to recover damages but obtained injunctive relief, or vice versa, may recover a fee award based on all hours reasonably expended if the relief obtained justified that expenditure of attorney time.

whenever conscientious counsel tried the case with devotion and skill. Again, the most critical factor is the degree of success obtained.

Application of this principle is particularly important in complex civil rights litigation involving numerous challenges to institutional practices or conditions. This type of litigation is lengthy and demands many hours of lawyers' services. Although the plaintiff often may succeed in identifying some unlawful practices or conditions, the range of possible success is vast. That the plaintiff is a "prevailing party" therefore may say little about whether the expenditure of counsel's time was reasonable in relation to the success achieved. In this case, for example, the District Court's award of fees based on 2,557 hours worked may have been reasonable in light of the substantial relief obtained. But had respondents prevailed on only one of their six general claims, for example the claim that petitioners' visitation, mail, and telephone policies were overly restrictive, see n. 1, *supra,* a fee award based on the claimed hours clearly would have been excessive.

There is no precise rule or formula for making these determinations. The district court may attempt to identify specific hours that should be eliminated, or it may simply reduce the award to account for the limited success. The court necessarily has discretion in making this equitable judgment. This discretion, however, must be exercised in light of the considerations we have identified.

C

A request for attorney's fees should not result in a second major litigation. Ideally, of course, litigants will settle the amount of a fee. Where settlement is not possible, the fee applicant bears the burden of establishing entitlement to an award and documenting the appropriate hours expended and hourly rates. The applicant should exercise "billing judgment" with respect to hours worked, and should maintain billing time records in a manner that will enable a reviewing court to identify distinct claims.[12]

We reemphasize that the district court has discretion in determining the amount of a fee award. This is appropriate in view of the district court's superior understanding of the litigation and the desirability of avoiding frequent appellate review of what essentially are factual matters. It remains important, however, for the district court to provide a concise but clear explanation of its reasons for the fee award. When an adjustment is requested on the basis of either the exceptional or limited nature of the relief obtained by the plaintiff, the district court should

---

12. We recognize that there is no certain method of determining when claims are "related" or "unrelated." Plaintiff's counsel, of course, is not required to record in great detail how each minute of his time was expended. But at least counsel should identify the general subject matter of his time expenditures. See *Nadeau v. Helgemoe,* 581 F.2d 275, 279 (C.A.1 1978) ("As for the future, we would not view with sympathy any claim that a district court abused its discretion in awarding unreasonably low attorney's fees in a suit in which plaintiffs were only partially successful if counsel's records do not provide a proper basis for determining how much time was spent on particular claims").

make clear that it has considered the relationship between the amount of the fee awarded and the results obtained.

In this case the District Court began by finding that "[t]he relief [respondents] obtained at trial was substantial and certainly entitles them to be considered prevailing . . . , without the need of examining those issues disposed of prior to trial in order to determine which went in [respondents'] favor." It then declined to divide the hours worked between winning and losing claims, stating that this fails to consider "the relative importance of various issues, the interrelation of the issues, the difficulty in identifying issues, or the extent to which a party may prevail on various issues." Finally, the court assessed the "amount involved/results obtained" and declared: "Not only should [respondents] be considered prevailing parties, they are parties who have obtained relief of significant import. [Respondents'] relief affects not only them, but also numerous other institutionalized patients similarly situated. The extent of this relief clearly justifies the award of a reasonable attorney's fee." *Id.,* at 231.

These findings represent a commendable effort to explain the fee award. Given the interrelated nature of the facts and legal theories in this case, the District Court did not err in refusing to apportion the fee award mechanically on the basis of respondents' success or failure on particular issues.[13] And given the findings with respect to the level of respondents' success, the District Court's award may be consistent with our holding today.

We are unable to affirm the decisions below, however, because the District Court's opinion did not properly consider the relationship between the extent of success and the amount of the fee award.[14] The court's finding that "the [significant] extent of the relief clearly justifies the award of a reasonable attorney's fee" does not answer the question

13. In addition, the District Court properly considered the reasonableness of the hours expended, and reduced the hours of one attorney by 30 percent to account for his inexperience and failure to keep contemporaneous time records.

14. The District Court expressly relied on *Brown v. Bathke,* 588 F.2d 634 (C.A.8 1978), a case we believe understates the significance of the results obtained. In that case a fired school-teacher had sought reinstatement, lost wages, $25,000 in damages, and expungement of derogatory material from her employment record. She obtained lost wages and the requested expungement, but not reinstatement or damages. The District Court awarded attorney's fees for the hours that it estimated the plaintiff's attorney had spent on the particular legal issue on which relief had been granted. The Eighth Circuit reversed. It stated that the results obtained may be considered, but that this factor should not "be given such weight that it reduces the fee awarded to a prevailing party below the 'reasonable attorney's fee' authorized by the Act." The court determined that the unsuccessful issues that had been raised by the plaintiff were not frivolous, and then remanded the case to the District Court.

Our holding today differs at least in emphasis from that of the Eighth Circuit in *Brown.* We hold that the extent of a plaintiff's success is a crucial factor that the district courts should consider carefully in determining the amount of fees to be awarded. In *Brown* the plaintiff had lost on the major issue of reinstatement. The District Court found that she had "'obtained only a minor part of the relief she sought.'" In remanding the Eighth Circuit implied that the District Court should not withhold fees for work on unsuccessful claims unless those claims were frivolous. Today we hold otherwise. It certainly was well within the *Brown* District Court's discretion to make a limited fee award in light of the "minor" relief obtained.

of what is "reasonable" in light of that level of success.[15] We emphasize that the inquiry does not end with a finding that the plaintiff obtained significant relief. A reduced fee award is appropriate if the relief, however significant, is limited in comparison to the scope of the litigation as a whole.

V

We hold that the extent of a plaintiff's success is a crucial factor in determining the proper amount of an award of attorney's fees under 42 U.S.C. § 1988. Where the plaintiff has failed to prevail on a claim that is distinct in all respects from his successful claims, the hours spent on the unsuccessful claim should be excluded in considering the amount of a reasonable fee. Where a lawsuit consists of related claims, a plaintiff who has won substantial relief should not have his attorney's fee reduced simply because the district court did not adopt each contention raised. But where the plaintiff achieved only limited success, the district court should award only that amount of fees that is reasonable in relation to the results obtained. On remand the District Court should determine the proper amount of the attorney's fee award in light of these standards.

The judgment of the Court of Appeals is vacated, and the case is remanded for further proceedings consistent with this opinion.

It is so ordered.

[Concurring opinion of CHIEF JUSTICE BURGER omitted.]

JUSTICE BRENNAN with whom JUSTICE MARSHALL, JUSTICE BLACKMUN and JUSTICE STEVENS join, concurring in part and dissenting in part.

* * *

I do not join the Court's opinion. In restating general principles of the law of attorney's fees, the Court omits a number of elements crucial to the calculation of attorney's fees under § 1988. A court that did not take account of those additional elements in evaluating a claim for attorney's fees would entirely fail to perform the task Congress has entrusted to it, a task that Congress—I think rightly—has deemed crucial to the vindication of individuals' rights in a society where access to justice so often requires the services of a lawyer.

Furthermore, whether one considers all the relevant factors or merely the relationship of fees to results obtained, the District Court in this case awarded a fee that was well within the court's zone of

---

15. The dissent errs in suggesting that the District Court's opinion would have been acceptable if merely a single word had been changed. We note, for example, that the District Court did not determine whether petitioners' unilateral increase in staff levels was a result of the litigation. Petitioners asserted that 70%–80% of the attorney time in the case was spent on the question of staffing levels at the Forensic Unit. If this is true, and if respondents' lawsuit was not a catalyst for the staffing increases, then respondents' failure to prevail on their challenge to the staffing levels would be material in determining whether an award based on over 2,500 hours expended was justifiable in light of respondents' actual success. The District Court's failure to consider this issue would not have been obviated by a mere conclusory statement that this fee was reasonable in light of the success obtained.

discretion under § 1988, and it explained the amount of the fee meticulously. The Court admits as much. Vacating a fee award such as this and remanding for further explanation can serve only as an invitation to losing defendants to engage in what must be one of the least socially productive types of litigation imaginable: appeals from awards of attorney's fees, after the merits of a case have been concluded, when the appeals are not likely to affect the amount of the final fee. * * *

I

In *Alyeska Pipeline Co. v. Wilderness Society,* 421 U.S. 240, 269, 95 S.Ct. 1612, 1627, 44 L.Ed.2d 141 (1975), this Court held that it was beyond the competence of judges to "pick and choose among plaintiffs and the statutes under which they sue and to award fees in some cases but not in others." Congress, however, has full authority to make such decisions, and it responded to the challenge of *Alyeska* by doing the "picking and choosing" itself. Its legislative solution legitimates the federal common law of attorney's fees that had developed in the years before *Alyeska* by specifying when and to whom fees are to be available. Section 1988 manifests a finely balanced congressional purpose to provide plaintiffs asserting specified federal rights with "fees which are adequate to attract competent counsel, but which do not produce windfalls to attorneys." S.Rep. No. 94–1011, p. 6 (1976). The Court today emphasizes those aspects of judicial discretion necessary to prevent "windfalls," but lower courts must not forget the need to ensure that civil rights plaintiffs with bona fide claims are able to find lawyers to represent them.

* * *

As nearly as possible, market standards should prevail, for that is the best way of ensuring that competent counsel will be available to all persons with bona fide civil rights claims. This means that judges awarding fees must make certain that attorneys are paid the full value that their efforts would receive on the open market in non-civil-rights cases, both by awarding them market-rate fees and by awarding fees only for time *reasonably* expended. If attorneys representing civil rights plaintiffs do not expect to receive full compensation for their efforts when they are successful, or if they feel they can "lard" winning cases with additional work solely to augment their fees, the balance struck by § 1988 goes awry.

The Court accepts these principles today. As in litigation for fee-paying clients, a certain amount of "billing judgment" is appropriate, taking into account the fact that Congress did not intend fees in civil rights cases, unlike most private-law litigation, to depend on obtaining relief with substantial monetary value. Where plaintiffs prevail on some claims and lose on others, the Court is correct in holding that the extent of their success is an important factor for calculating fee awards. Any system for awarding attorney's fees that did not take account of the relationship between results and fees would fail to accomplish Congress' goal of checking insubstantial litigation.

At the same time, however, courts should recognize that reasonable counsel in a civil rights case, as in much litigation, must often advance a number of related legal claims in order to give plaintiffs the best possible chance of obtaining significant relief. As the Court admits, "[s]uch a lawsuit cannot be viewed as a series of discrete claims." And even where two claims apparently share no "common core of facts" or related legal concepts, the actual work performed by lawyers to develop the facts of both claims may be closely intertwined. For instance, in taking a deposition of a state official, plaintiffs' counsel may find it necessary to cover a range of territory that includes both the successful and the unsuccessful claims. It is sometimes virtually impossible to determine how much time was devoted to one category or the other, and the incremental time required to pursue both claims rather than just one is likely to be small.

Furthermore, on many occasions awarding counsel fees that reflect the full market value of their time will require paying more than their customary hourly rates. Most attorneys paid an hourly rate expect to be paid promptly and without regard to success or failure. Customary rates reflect those expectations. Attorneys who take cases on contingency, thus deferring payment of their fees until the case has ended and taking upon themselves the risk that they will receive no payment at all, generally receive far more in winning cases than they would if they charged an hourly rate. The difference, however, reflects the time-value of money and the risk of nonrecovery usually borne by clients in cases where lawyers are paid an hourly rate. Courts applying § 1988 must also take account of the time-value of money and the fact that attorneys can never be 100% certain they will win even the best case.

Therefore, district courts should not end their fee inquiries when they have multiplied a customary hourly rate times the reasonable number of hours expended, and then checked the product against the results obtained. They should also consider both delays in payment and the prelitigation likelihood that the claims which did in fact prevail would prevail.[8] These factors are potentially relevant in every case. Even if the results obtained do not justify awarding fees for all the hours spent on a particular case, no fee is reasonable unless it would be adequate to induce other attorneys to represent similarly situated clients seeking relief comparable to that obtained in the case at hand.

8. Thus, the Court's opinion should not be read to imply that "exceptional success" provides the only basis for awarding a fee higher than the reasonable rate times the reasonable number of hours. To the contrary, the Court expressly approves consideration of the full range of *Johnson v. Georgia Highway Express, Inc.*, 488 F.2d 714 (C.A.5 1974), factors. If the rate used in calculating the fee does not already include some factor for risk or the time-value of money, it ought to be enhanced by some percentage figure. By the same token, attorneys need not obtain "excellent" results to merit a fully compensatory fee; merely prevailing to some significant extent entitles them to full compensation for the work reasonably required to obtain relief.

II

Setting to one side theoretical issues about how district courts should approach attorney's fees questions under § 1988, I fear the Court makes a serious error in vacating the judgment in this case and remanding for further proceedings. There is simply no reason for another round of litigation between these parties, and the lower courts are in no need of guidance from us.

[Justice Brennan argued that the district court adequately explained the reasonableness of the fee award, stressing the judge's conclusion that the case "involves the constitutional and civil rights of the plaintiff class and resulted in a number of changes regarding their conditions and treatment at the state hospital. * * * The extent of this relief clearly justifies the award of a reasonable attorney's fee." Justice Brennan argued that changing the word "a" in the last sentence to "this" would have satisfied the majority of the Court.

Justice Brennan further opined that the language of Brown v. Bathke (see majority footnote 14) suggesting that full fees should be recoverable for all nonfrivolous claims, whether or not successful, had not been followed and provided no justification for reversing this judgment. He decried any "paragraph-by-paragraph" scrutiny of district court explanations for fee awards, noting that such scrutiny would give defendants an incentive to challenge fee awards and protract litigation.]

Few, if any, differences about the basic framework of attorney's fees law under § 1988 divide the Court today. Apart from matters of nuance and tone, largely tangential to the case at hand, I object to only two aspects of today's judgment. First, I see no reason for us to have devoted our scarce time to hearing this case, and I fear that the sudden appearance of a new Supreme Court precedent in this area will unjustifiably provoke new litigation and prolong old litigation over attorney's fees. More fundamentally, the principles that the Court and I share should have led us, once we had granted a writ of certiorari, to affirm the judgment below. To that extent, I dissent.

Notes and Questions

1. Despite Congress's citation to the 12–factor approach of the Fifth Circuit, the Supreme Court has favored the lodestar method of measuring attorneys' fee awards. In 1992, it declared that the lodestar approach had "become the guiding light of our fee-shifting jurisprudence." City of Burlington v. Dague, 505 U.S. 557, 112 S.Ct. 2638, 120 L.Ed.2d 449 (1992).

2. The lodestar may not be so simple to apply in all cases as it might seem because problems can arise with regard to both components of the formula:

(a) *Hours worked:* Note that the Court emphasizes the need for detailed information about the hours worked by the lawyers. Law offices now use computers for this task, and they can generate very detailed reports about the lawyer time on a case. The court is then to scrutinize these reports to determine whether all hours should be compensated.

One ground for refusing to pay for lawyer work is that it was wasteful or inefficient. In re Fine Paper Antitrust Litigation, *supra* p. 669, is a famous example of a case in which a judge determined that waste had occurred. How easily could a court make such determinations in more ordinary cases? Was the percentage discount used by the lower court in *Hensley* a reasonable way of correcting for inefficiency?

One development in the legal marketplace that may offer promise to judges called upon to assess fee requests is "task-based billing," which lumps together all the lawyer time on discrete tasks in the litigation and therefore is more easily understood by the client. See, e.g, Rickerson, Law Firm Profits Increase With Strategic Legal Management, 68 Def.Couns.J. 228, 229 (2001) (describing the development of the uniform task-based management system by a consortium of corporations and law firms); Connell, The Task–Based Billing Express, Calif. Lawyer, Aug. 1995, at 25. Advocates of this method sing its praises in terms that might be attractive to judges called upon to assess legal bills also:

> Task-based billing enables a company to assess whether a particular project was handled efficiently. It shows if too much time was spent on particular projects; if work should have been downstreamed to personnel at a lower billing rate; if work could have been consolidated to fewer personnel at a particular work level; if the bill reflects costs associated with rotating staff through the matter; or if staff members duplicated each others' work.

Rangel & Epstein, Efficiency Analysis Driving the Need for Task–Based Billing, Corp. Legal Times, Feb. 1993, at 33.

The court is also to exclude from consideration hours that were not spent on the successful claims. The Supreme Court has emphasized that plaintiffs are entitled to a fee award if they succeed on "any significant issue in litigation which achieves some of the benefit the parties sought in bringing the suit." Texas State Teachers Ass'n v. Garland Independent School Dist., 489 U.S. 782, 109 S.Ct. 1486, 103 L.Ed.2d 866 (1989). Thus, there may often be occasions in which the court must screen out time spent on unsuccessful issues or claims. How easily can it do that? Won't plaintiffs usually claim that all of the work contributed to the victory?

Note the way in which the problem was presented in *Hensley*. Will the court's involvement in the fashioning of relief in such a case give it a good feel for which hours should be disallowed?

(b) *Billing rate:* Justice Brennan emphasizes the need to use a market measure for fee awards. The basic problem in many fee award cases, however, is that there is no market in the usual sense to assist in setting fees. See, e.g., Vizcaino v. Microsoft Corp., 290 F.3d 1043, 1049 (9th Cir. 2002) ("in employment class actions like this one, no ascertainable 'market' exists. The 'market' is simply counsel's expectation of court-awarded fees."). This problem can become obvious in determining the billing rate for lawyers. In *Hensley,* for instance, the plaintiffs' lawyers worked for a legal services organization that provided representation for people unable to pay. Where did the quoted billing rates come from?

The ordinary reaction of lawyers without usual rates is to rely on an analogy to lawyers who do bill by the hour. In Blum v. Stenson, 465 U.S. 886, 104 S.Ct. 1541, 79 L.Ed.2d 891 (1984), defendant objected that the proper approach for the plaintiff's lawyers, who worked for a nonprofit legal aid organization, should be based on the lawyers' salaries (which were low) since that determined the cost to the organization of providing representation to the plaintiffs. The Court disagreed, holding that hourly rate is "to be calculated according to the prevailing market rates in the relevant community." This may sometimes allow public interest lawyers to collect "silk stocking" rates. See New York State Ass'n for Retarded Children, Inc. v. Carey, 711 F.2d 1136 (2d Cir.1983) (plaintiff's lawyers awarded fees based on a schedule used by Wall Street firm Cravath, Swain & Moore for associate time). In general, the comparisons look to lawyers of roughly the same experience as counsel for plaintiff.

If lawyers in fact have a billing rate, should that be used? Ordinarily it is, but in some instances the courts may deviate from the lawyer's actual billing rate. Consider Judge Easterbrook's views in overturning a decision by a district judge to award rates below those usually charged by the lawyers on the ground that the lawyers' usual rates were too high:

> When the lawyers sell their time in the market, the market provides the starting point: the lawyer's hourly rate. Lawyers do not come from cookie cutters. Some are fast studies and others require extra preparation. * * * A $225 per hour lawyer may end up costing less than a $150 per hour lawyer for the same results or may produce better results for the same total bill. Only an assumption that all lawyers are identical could support the averaging approach.

> * * * [T]he best measure of the cost of an attorney's time is what that attorney could earn from paying clients. For a busy attorney, this is the standard hourly rate. * * *

> A judge who departs from this presumption must have some reason other than the ability to identify a different average rate in the community.

Gusman v. Unisys Corp., 986 F.2d 1146 (7th Cir.1993). Compare Student Public Interest Res. Group v. AT & T Bell Laboratories, 842 F.2d 1436 (3d Cir.1988), in which the court held that a public interest law firm that customarily charged its clients rates dramatically lower than those charged by commercial law firms could use those commercial rates for purposes of a fee award. How can it be that the commercial law firms are in the same market? Is the reason for this decision that there are "public interest" matters, or that there is something wrong with the market in which these lawyers must charge low fees?

3. *Multipliers:* Once the lodestar is determined, the court may alter it using what the lower courts have come to call "multipliers." The lower courts were often rather free with such multipliers. The Supreme Court has cut back on them:

(a) *Quality:* Many lower courts increased the lodestar amount on the ground that the work the lawyers did was of high quality, or that the litigation was particularly challenging. In Blum v. Stenson, 465 U.S. 886, 104

S.Ct. 1541, 79 L.Ed.2d 891 (1984), the district court calculated the lodestar and then applied a 50% multiplier to enhance that figure on the ground that the issues were novel and the litigation was complex. The Supreme Court held that neither the plaintiffs nor the lower court had indicated anything extraordinary about the litigation to justify the bonus. It emphasized that novelty and complexity of litigation are usually reflected in the number of hours expended and that quality is reflected in the hourly rate of compensation, so that neither should justify an increase over the lodestar. See also Van Gerwen v. Guarantee Mut. Life Co., 214 F.3d 1041 (9th Cir.2000) (holding that a downward multiplier should not ordinarily be used because the low quality of the lawyering would be factored into the lower billing rate). The Court has since reemphasized its concern that the award be enhanced on grounds of quality of representation only in exceptional cases. See Pennsylvania v. Delaware Valley Citizens' Council (I), 478 U.S. 546, 106 S.Ct. 3088, 92 L.Ed.2d 439 (1986).

As *Hensley* indicates, the results obtained may also be considered in determining whether to award or enhance the lodestar amount. Justice Powell says that "[w]here a plaintiff has obtained excellent results, his attorney should recover a fully compensatory fee." Does this mean that the lawyer should not be fully compensated unless the results are excellent? How would that affect the ability of civil rights plaintiffs to obtain representation? Justice Powell does acknowledge that there may be cases of "exceptional success" that would justify enhancement above the lodestar.

How does one measure success if the judgment is for money? Note that Justice Brennan observes in *Hensley* that "Congress did not intend fees in civil rights cases * * * to depend on obtaining relief with substantial monetary value." In City of Riverside v. Rivera, 477 U.S. 561, 106 S.Ct. 2686, 91 L.Ed.2d 466 (1986), the Court addressed, but left rather unclear, the handling of attorneys' fee requests that far exceed the amount recovered. In this civil rights case, plaintiffs sued a variety of police officers for illegal arrest and ultimately obtained judgments against some of them totalling $33,000. The district court then awarded $245,000 in attorneys' fees, characterizing the results obtained as "excellent." The district court also suggested that it would have granted an injunction had one been requested, and observed that the police misconduct "had to be stopped and * * * nothing short of having a lawsuit like this would have stopped it."

Defendants appealed. Writing for a plurality of four, Justice Brennan upheld the award, stressing the public benefit advanced by civil rights litigation. Justice Rehnquist, joined by three other justices, dissented. He denounced Justice Brennan for adopting a "revisionist interpretation" of *Hensley* that would turn § 1988 into "a relief Act for lawyers." He urged that "billing judgment" required scaling back the award in view of the small proceeds of the suit. Justice Powell cast a deciding vote for affirmance, concurring in the judgment on the ground that the district court's findings concerning the broader public importance of the suit were not clearly erroneous. He added, however, that the fee seemed unreasonable on its face, and that in his view "[w]here recovery of private damages is the purpose of a civil rights litigation, a district court in fixing fees, is obligated to give primary consideration to the amount of damages awarded as compared to the amount sought." The lower courts have struggled to implement this ruling. See, e.g., Morales v. City of San Rafael, 96 F.3d 359 (9th Cir.1996) (Because $17,500 damages award was more than nominal, it was improper to limit attorneys' fees to $20,000); Washington v. Philadelphia County Court of Common Pleas, 89 F.3d 1031 (3d Cir.1996) (ratio between fees and damages not authorized); compare Cole v. Wodziak, 169 F.3d 486 (7th Cir.1999) (in wrongful eviction case, asking for fees that were higher than the prayer and nearly 20 times the recovery was "off the map").

(b) *Contingency:* For some time, lower courts regularly increased the lodestar to compensate lawyers for the risk that they would not be paid at all, often doubling the lodestar. See Leubsdorf, The Contingency Factor in Attorney Fee Awards, 90 Yale L.J. 473 (1981). In City of Burlington v. Dague, 505 U.S. 557, 112 S.Ct. 2638, 120 L.Ed.2d 449 (1992), the Court held that contingency enhancement is not allowed. Justice Scalia, writing for the Court, contended that there was a risk of encouraging non-meritorious litigation and that allowing enhancement for contingency causes double counting because the difficulty of establishing the merits will be reflected in the hourly rate (better lawyers are needed for tougher cases) and the amount of time spent on the case (lawyers take longer on tougher cases). In the process, the Court disregarded the argument that a lawyer with an ordinary billing rate presented with a choice between a contingent case and one in which payment was certain would always choose the latter if money were the only consideration. In any event, the Court embraced the lodestar as its preferred method, even though it "often (perhaps generally) results in a larger fee award than the contingent-fee model." Id. at 565, 112 S.Ct. at 2643. Compare Coleman v. Kaye, 87 F.3d 1491 (3d Cir.1996) (New Jersey law rejects *Dague*, so the lodestar must be adjusted to reflect risk of nonrecovery because the fee award is based on New Jersey law).

Despite *Dague*, lower courts continue to allow multipliers on occasion. See Wing v. Asarco Inc., 114 F.3d 986 (9th Cir.1997) (multiplier of two due to class counsel's continuing obligations under decree); Guam Soc'y of Obstetricians v. Ada, 100 F.3d 691 (9th Cir.1996) (enhancement for extreme undesirability of case).

4.   Should the fact that the lawyer in question has agreed to handle the case for a share of the recovery have a bearing on the fee determination? The Supreme Court has held that it should not. See Venegas v. Mitchell, 495 U.S. 82, 110 S.Ct. 1679, 109 L.Ed.2d 74 (1990) (attorney may enforce agreement to pay percentage fee of over $400,000 even though district court found that reasonable fee calculated on lodestar method—after doubling for quality of work—was $75,000); Blanchard v. Bergeron, 489 U.S. 87, 109 S.Ct. 939, 103 L.Ed.2d 67 (1989) (contingency fee figure not a cap on amount to be awarded under § 1988); compare Alexander v. Chicago Park Dist., 927 F.2d 1014 (7th Cir.1991) (where settlement agreement in class action provided that counsel would accept figure determined by court, he may not later enforce contractual right to receive more pursuant to a contingent fee contract).

5.   To what extent is the judge responsible for preventing waste efforts before they crop up in attorneys fee awards? In Jaquette v. Black Hawk County, 710 F.2d 455 (8th Cir.1983), the district court substantially reduced the lodestar on the ground that plaintiff's attorneys had spent excessive time on issues of "marginal merit" and had been guilty of "misconduct" in

handling the case. The appellate court affirmed, but admonished that "[i]n almost all cases the key to avoiding excessive costs and delay is early and stringent judicial management of the case. * * * With such management procedure, we are confident that litigation such as this, extending almost three years in the district court, would be avoided." Does that mean that once the court has permitted counsel to make certain maneuvers it must compensate them for these efforts?

Some courts address the question of fees explicitly at the outset of cases in which there might be a fee application later. See generally Manual for Complex Litigation (4th) § 14.211 (2004) (recommending consideration of this practice); In In re Continental Illinois Securities Litigation, 572 F.Supp. 931 (N.D.Ill.1983), the judge specified early in the case that only one lawyer should appear for plaintiffs at hearings, that the billing rates would reflect the nature of the services performed (i.e., associate rates for "associate" work), and that no fees would be awarded for reviewing the work product of another lawyer. In Matter of Continental Illinois Securities Litigation, 962 F.2d 566 (7th Cir.1992), the appellate court found many mistakes in the district court's approach. The judge set a ceiling of $175 per hour, but that was not the correct approach. Defendants had hired "a crowd of pricey lawyers to defend the case," and the district judge nevertheless "thought he knew the value of the class lawyers' legal services better than the market did" and tried "to determine the equivalent of the medieval just price." Id. at 568. See also Uniroyal Goodrich Tire Co. v. Mutual Trading Corp., 63 F.3d 516 (7th Cir.1995), in which the court rejected arguments that it was wasteful for more than one lawyer to appear at a hearing, reasoning that "[i]n a case of this size, it would have been sensible for the attorneys to divide up the responsibilities of the pretrial litigation, thereby necessitating that each attorney be present for court appearances." See also Rule 23(g)(1)(C)(iii), which authorizes the judge to direct potential class counsel to propose terms for an eventual fee award, a proposal that is likely to be given considerable weight when fees are later awarded under Rule 23(h).

6. Note that the Court in *Hensley* says that the fee-setting process should not result in "a second major litigation." How reasonable is this hope? Judge Easterbrook has described it as "an unattainable dream." He explains: "The stakes—in this case the request for fees was double the judgement, and in others the request for fees may be millions of dollars—ensure that the parties will pursue all available opportunities for litigation. The fuzziness of the criteria (what is a 'reasonable' number of hours) ensures that people seeking opportunities to contest the fees will not need to search hard." Kirchoff v. Flynn, 786 F.2d 320, 325 (7th Cir.1986). Are fees more likely to be contested in commercial or civil rights cases?

7. Although it is usually said that the right to demand fees belongs to the plaintiff, it should be apparent that the focus is on the lawyer. Can the defendant use the fees to divide the lawyer and the client? In Evans v. Jeff D., 475 U.S. 717, 106 S.Ct. 1531, 89 L.Ed.2d 747 (1986), the Court held that defendants can condition a favorable settlement on the merits on waiver of the fees. Like *Hensley,* that case involved treatment rights of people housed by the state, in this case children with handicaps. On the eve of trial, defendants offered plaintiffs "virtually all the injunctive relief" they had sought in the suit, providing plaintiffs waived fees. Because this was "the

best result [plaintiffs] could have gotten in this court or in any court,'' the lawyer recommended accepting it, subject to his argument that the fee waiver condition was unenforceable. The Supreme Court held the waiver enforceable. What strategy could lawyers use to guard against this risk? See Venegas v. Mitchell, 495 U.S. 82, 110 S.Ct. 1679, 109 L.Ed.2d 74 (1990) (lawyer's contract with plaintiff forbids plaintiff from waiving attorneys' fee award).

b.   *The Challenge to the Lodestar*

The lodestar has been widely assailed. The Third Circuit, which created the lodestar in Lindy Brothers Builders, Inc. v. American Radiator & Standard Sanitary Corp., 487 F.2d 161 (3d Cir.1973), appointed a task force to study the lodestar a decade later. The task force catalogued a variety of objections to this method of fee calculation: (1) that it overtaxes already busy judges; (2) that it is insufficiently objective and has led to wide variations in awards; (3) that billing rates for the same lawyer vary widely from judge to judge; (4) that judges can manipulate it to arrive at a result that is a favored percentage of the recovery; (5) that it has encouraged lawyers to spend excessive hours on fee-shifting cases; (6) that it creates a disincentive for early settlement of cases; (7) that it unduly curtails the district court's discretion; (8) that it has worked to the disadvantage of the public interest bar, which tended to receive lower awards; and (9) that it is too unpredictable in operation. See Report of the Third Circuit Task Force, Court Awarded Attorney Fees, 108 F.R.D. 237, 246–49 (1985). The lower courts have begun innovating to deal with these sorts of problems.

IN RE ACTIVISION SECURITIES LITIGATION

United States District Court, Northern District of California, 1989.
723 F.Supp. 1373.

PATEL, DISTRICT JUDGE.

This case has followed the all too familiar path of large securities cases. It was filed as a class action by a number of well-recognized lawyers who specialize in plaintiffs' securities litigation. The complaint named the usual cast of defendants—the corporation issuing the shares, in this case when the corporation went public; the officers and directors; the underwriters; the corporation's accountants; and a variety of venture capital defendants who sold their shares at or near the time the corporation went public. Various defendants moved to dismiss and the case moved lugubriously through the pleadings phase. Discovery assumed its usual massive proportions, and finally, as the case wound down toward trial, settlement negotiations became serious and were aggressively pursued. On the eve of trial, after the parties had expended significant attorneys' time and, hence, accumulated the routinely anticipated hours and fees, the case was settled.

Then began the process which all too often consumes a disproportionate share of the court's time, the application for attorneys' fees. It is at this point in these and other common fund cases that the court is abandoned by the adversary system and left to the plaintiff's unilateral application and the judge's own good conscience. Rarely do the settling defendants, who have created the pool of money from which the attorneys' fees are awarded, offer any counterpoint; rarely do members of the class come forward with any response or opposition to the fees sought. There are no *amici curiae* who volunteer their advice.

For its guidance during this solitary inquiry, the court is confronted with a mountain of computerized billing records and, of course, the obligatory [lodestar] factors. * * *

Courts have pursued a number of alternatives at the fee application stage. Some, by themselves or with the assistance of a magistrate, have waded through the computer printouts, which often represent years of work by several firms, their partners, associates, and paralegals. Others have appointed special masters familiar with the field and with attorney billing to perform the details of the task and to make a recommendation. The special master is then paid from the common fund. This court has used both of these alternatives. Undoubtedly, there are more creative ones that other courts have found. What is curious is that whatever method is used and no matter what billing records are submitted to the [lodestar] regimen, the result is an award that almost always hovers around 30% of the fund created by the settlement.

The question this court is compelled to ask is, "Is this process necessary?" Under a cost-benefit analysis, the answer would be a resounding, "No!" Not only do the [lodestar] analyses consume an undue amount of court time with little resulting advantage to anyone, but, in fact, it may be to the detriment of the class members. They are forced to wait until the court has done a thorough, conscientious analysis of the attorneys' fee petition. Or, class members may suffer a further diminution of their fund when a special master is retained and paid from the fund. Most important, however, is the effect the process has on the litigation and the timing of settlement. Where attorneys must depend on a lodestar approach there is little incentive to arrive at an early settlement. The history of these cases demonstrates this as noted below in the discussion of typical percentage awards.

Adoption of a policy of awarding approximately 30% of the fund as attorneys' fees in the ordinary case is well-justified in light of the lengthy line of cases which find such an award appropriate and reasonable before or after superimposing the *Lindy* * * * factors. Several years of this practice and the body of case law across the circuits validate this approach. The Supreme Court has accepted it. In *Blum v. Stenson,* 465 U.S. 886, 900 n. 16, 104 S.Ct. 1541, 1550 n. 16, 79 L.Ed.2d 891 (1984), the Court noted approvingly the use of a percentage of the common fund to set attorneys' fees in common fund cases. In fact, the language of the note appears to assume that the percentage approach is routine. Distinguishing attorneys' fee determinations under fee shifting statutes such as 42 U.S.C. § 1988, the Court observed:

Unlike the calculation of attorney's fees under the "common fund doctrine," where a reasonable fee is based on a percentage of the fund bestowed on the class, a reasonable fee under § 1988 reflects the amount of attorney time reasonably expended on the litigation.

The Third Circuit, home of the *Lindy* formulation, recently criticized its application in common fund cases and recommended a return to a percentage of the fund approach. In the Report of the Third Circuit Task Force, Court Awarded Attorney Fees, 108 F.R.D. 237 (1985), the Task Force concluded that the *Lindy* method was a "cumbersome, enervating, and often surrealistic process of preparing and evaluating fee petitions that now plagues the Bench and Bar...." According to the Task Force, the percentage scheme with appropriate judicial supervision would ordinarily be adequate to protect the integrity of the fee award process. It recommended that early in the litigation the court set or "negotiate" a percentage-based fee and offered a number of suggestions for fashioning a mechanism for fee setting. This court agrees with the Task Force's conclusion that a number of salutary effects can be achieved by this procedure, including removing the inducement to unnecessarily increase hours, prompting early settlement, reducing burdensome paperwork for counsel and the court and providing a degree of predictability to fee awards.

* * *

It has been wisely stated by Professor Coffee that:

If one wishes to economize on the judicial time that is today invested in monitoring class and derivative litigation, the highest priority should be given to those reforms that restrict collusion and are essentially self-policing. The percentage of the recovery award formula is such a "deregulatory" reform because it relies on incentives rather than costly monitoring. Ultimately, this "deregulatory" approach is the only alternative to converting the courts into the equivalent of public utility commissions that oversee the plaintiff's attorney and elaborately fix the attorney's "fair" return.

Coffee, *Understanding the Plaintiffs' Attorney: The Implications of Economic Theory for Private Enforcement of Law Through Class and Derivative Actions,* 86 Colum.L.Rev. 669, 724–25 (1986).

* * *

[T]he court is compelled to conclude that the accepted practice of applying the lodestar * * * regime to common fund cases does not achieve the stated purposes of proportionality, predictability and protection of the class. It encourages abuses such as unjustified work and protracting the litigation. It adds to the work load of already overworked district courts. In short, it does not encourage efficiency, but rather, it adds inefficiency to the process.

Therefore, this court concludes that in class action common fund cases the better practice is to set a percentage fee and that, absent extraordinary circumstances that suggest reasons to lower or increase the percentage, the rate should be set at 30%. This will encourage plaintiffs' attorneys to move for early settlement, provide predictability for the attorneys and the class members, and reduce the time consumed by counsel and court in dealing with voluminous fee petitions.

[Because the Special Master had done a thorough job, the court adopted his lodestar award, which worked out to be 32.8% of the fund.]

MATTER OF SUPERIOR BEVERAGE/GLASS CONTAINER CONSOLIDATED PRETRIAL

United States District Court, Northern District of Illinois, 1990.
133 F.R.D. 119.

WILL, DISTRICT JUDGE.

[In this antitrust price fixing nationwide class action, plaintiffs sought an attorneys' fee award after concluding a settlement with the principal defendant under which this defendant agreed to issue discount purchase certificates to class members with a total value between $49 million and $70 million. The agreement also provided that this defendant would pay the attorneys' fee found proper by the court.

A total of 12 law firms applied for fees for the work of 50 lawyers and 40 paralegals over a four-year period. The court reviewed "every entry on every time sheet for every lawyer and paralegal in every firm." The judge also compared the time logged by plaintiffs' counsel with that billed by defendant's counsel. Based on this review under the lodestar, the court awarded fees totalling between 15.6% and 17.3% of the total amount obtained for the class (depending on the actual redemption of certificates).]

Quite recently, at least three district courts have inveighed against lodestars, one of them abandoning the lodestar approach altogether [citing, *inter alia,* In re Activision Securities Litigation, *supra* p. 703.]. In 1984, the Supreme Court seemed, in a glancing footnote, to assume that a "reasonable fee" in a common fund case "is based on a fair percentage of the fund," *Blum v. Stenson,* 465 U.S. 886, 900 n. 16, 104 S.Ct. 1541, 1550 n. 16, 79 L.Ed.2d 891 (1984), and some lawyers have wondered in print whether "[t]he movement against the lodestar [isn't] turning into a stampede." Solovy and Kaster, *Re–Examining The Lodestar,* National Law Journal, April 9, 1990, p. 13. * * *

We remain convinced, as we were in 1979, that rigid application of any method, whether lodestar or percentage, is a mistake but that some form of time/rate multiplier analysis modified, if necessary, to reflect a reasonable percentage of the recovery, is the best way to calculate reasonable and fair fees. We note that neither class counsel nor the defendants have suggested that fees should be awarded on a straight percentage basis in this case and that all the firms that have petitioned for fees have submitted lodestar figures.

A. THE PROBLEMS WITH PERCENTAGES

The notion of awarding fees out of a common fund on a straight percentage-of-the-pot basis, without regard to billed hours, is overly simplified and shortsighted. In a case where the class is represented by more than one law firm (and that happens almost always) how does the court divide up a percentage award between (or among) the firms? Sometimes, the division is left to the firms themselves. In some cases, the firms stipulate to their "cuts" or "points" at the end of the case, in others, at the beginning. If the firms cannot agree, then the dispute falls back into the court's lap, and we see only one way to resolve such a dispute—by returning to the time sheets and calculating who toiled how many hours doing what. In other words, percentages frequently end up with lodestars when there is more than one firm in the case. In this case, there were twelve firms representing the class. How often firms will be able to negotiate fee arrangements among themselves—and plaintiffs' lawyers do manage such divisions in some cases—is an empirical question. There are, though, still other more serious problems with percentages.

In this case, the settlement provides for up to $70 million but in no event less than $49 million dollars in discount certificates, all redeemable in installments over a period of ten years. What is 30% of *up to* $70 million payable over a period of years? And how are fees, to be awarded in cash, to be compared to a recovery that consists of certificates, warrants or chits? Similar problems, of course, are presented in a personal injury case where part of the settlement provides for an annuity, and economists and accountants in such cases calculate the present value of the annuity and then calculate the contingent fee from the discounted value. Calculating the cash value of certificates is trickier than calculating the present cash value of an annuity but is still possible. Nonetheless, what is the present cash value of a class recovery that provides for certificates, redeemable over time, in an undetermined amount to range from 49 to 70 million?

Percentage contingent fees also present a problem of "sell-out" settlements:

> Suppose a defendant offers $100,000, the contingent fee [or percentage of the common fund promised by the court] is 30 percent regardless of when the litigation ends, and the lawyer is sure he can get a judgment for $120,000 if the case is tried but knows that it will cost him, in time and other expenses, $8,000 to try it. [The class] will be better off if the case is tried, for after paying the lawyer's fee [class members will still collect] $84,000 . . . rather than $70,000 if it is settled. But the lawyer will be worse off, since his additional fee, $6,000 ($36,000 minus $30,000) will be less than the trial costs of $8,000. . . .

Chesny v. Marek, 720 F.2d 474, 477 (7th Cir.1983) [*rev'd on other grounds,* 473 U.S. 1, 105 S.Ct. 3012, 87 L.Ed.2d 1 (1985)].

Finally, a still more fundamental problem, and the major problem, with pure fixed percentage awards arises from the very notion of using fixed percentages at all. *Fixed percentages will drastically overcompensate lawyers in some cases and drastically undercompensate them in others.* Twenty-five or thirty percent might be an appropriate award on a recovery of a million dollars. It is likely, on the other hand, to result in a windfall in a case where the recovery totals many millions of dollars. The same reasoning also works in reverse. Seven percent will usually be a "paltry" award on a recovery of four million, depending on the hours worked and the risk incurred in bringing the case, but may be an appropriate award on a recovery of two hundred million. The point is that "percentage" is a relational concept. Percentage *of what*? Fifty percent is neither a lot nor a little, until one knows what the underlying whole is. Half of one cookie isn't much. Half of a full cookie jar may well be a lot.

There is no necessary logical connection between percentages and reasonable compensation. At best, percentages are simply a rough and ready way of estimating contingency plus effort. It is our opinion that there are better ways of estimating both.

B.   The Objections to Lodestars

Many, though not all, of the objections to lodestars seem to us to be overstated. We will address eight of them.

First, there is no question but that calculating lodestars takes more time than awarding fees by percentages, and this is a drawback. We suspect that many courts frown on lodestars for this reason alone. There are a number of time consuming steps in calculating lodestars—(1) reviewing the time records to weed out hours not spent benefiting the class, (2) going back and tallying the hours left, in many cases separately per firm and per lawyer and paralegal, since different firms or different lawyers within a firm will be compensated with different hourly rates, (3) determining a reasonable hourly rate for each lawyer or paralegal, (4) calculating a lodestar for each firm, (5) determining the proper multiplier, if any, and (6) multiplying the lodestar by the multiplier. In our experience, it is the second step, which consumes by far the most time. But it need not. If courts required firms to submit time records for each lawyer or paralegal on disk in Lotus or some other spreadsheet format specified by the court, there would be no trick to tallying the hours. Running spreadsheet programs is neither burdensome nor time-consuming. More time-consuming than percentages to be sure, but for a more reasonable result.

Second, there is no reason why under a lodestar approach there should necessarily be widespread variation in fees awarded by different judges to the same lawyers in the same community. The rate to be awarded is the rate a lawyer normally charges paying clients, unless that rate is unreasonable—i.e., unless it exceeds the going rate for comparable work. There may be some dispute as to what the going rate is, but note that there will also be disputes, under a percentage approach, over what a reasonable percentage is.

Third, we have not found, either in this case or others we have handled, that lodestars lead most lawyers to pad their time records. And to the extent that there is either padding, in terms of fictitious hours, or "lodestarring," careful judges and their staffs should be able to spot the worst, if not all, abuses.

Along the same lines, we also have not found that lodestars lead most lawyers to inflate their "normal" billing rates. A policy of not awarding rates that are clearly out of line with the going rate certainly acts as a restraint. We have occasionally seen some lawyers raise their billing rates dramatically during the course of a case, perhaps in hopes of "lodestarring" the court. But abuses of that sort are fairly easily identified by asking all lawyers to submit fee schedules showing historical rates and by comparing rate hikes in one firm with rate hikes in another. If most firms have, in any given year, raised their rates by ten or twenty dollars an hour, but one firm has raised rates by fifty-five, the possibility of lodestarring is plain.

Fourth, lodestar fee awards, properly calculated, take into account skill as well as time. It is not true that lodestar fees leave talent unrewarded. The greatest fear in this regard seems to relate to the scenario of the difficult case that is settled very quickly as the result of a brilliant effort by an extraordinarily skilled lawyer for the class. The lodestar in that kind of a case is de minimis. Few hours were expended. But compensation should not be de minimis, and need not be, even if a pure percentage method is not used. It is obvious that one hour well spent may produce more and better results than one hundred plodding hours of mediocrity. And that one hour should be compensated equally, even more generously, than the one hundred hours. Obviously, one hour makes for a smaller lodestar than one hundred. But that is where multipliers step in. *There is no reason that multipliers, in such cases, should be low.* We recognize that historically multipliers have been low in most cases. That is primarily because the quick, magnificent recovery rarely occurs in the real world. We see no reason, however, that they must be or that any court should ever set an upper limit on multipliers applicable to all cases. Many, even most, of the objections to lodestars posed by plaintiffs' lawyers appear to us to stem from fears about low multipliers. But multipliers need not be low. Frequently when they are, it is because a higher multiplier would result in an unreasonable fee.

Fifth, there is no per se reason that lodestars should create disincentives for the early settlement of cases generally. The objections here seem to be of two types. First is a concern about "slam dunk" cases. If fees are awarded by lodestar, so goes the argument, then there is no incentive to settle a slam dunk case early on, though it *should* be settled early on, because settling early results in a low lodestar and a low lodestar means low fees. The answer to this is that in the hands of a capable judge a slam dunk case will not settle late and hours need not be padded to obtain a reasonable fee. If liability is clear, then there should be case dispositive motions, either to dismiss or for summary judgment, and no further discovery should be allowed until the motions have been ruled on. If no dispositive motions are filed, but it is apparent to the judge that the case would have been or was an easy win, long hours will not be remunerated or can be remunerated against a *negative* multiplier.

The second objection is broader and stems from the view that lodestars encourage long hours, not just padded hours, and in all cases not just slam dunks. This is a serious concern but is often grossly exaggerated. Most lawyers prefer to be paid as soon as possible and the nature of deferred fees in itself discourages excessive hours. A lawyer who thinks and acts as a rational maximizer will not log more hours than are necessary in a case where, because it is contingent, there may not be fees at all in the end. In common fund cases fees are always uncertain—absent a favorable judgment or a settlement, there is no compensation. Class litigation is risky, and a lawyer as a rational maximizer will not compound his or her risks by logging long hours that might wind up unrewarded.

Further, in no case, even under a time/rate analysis, should a fee award consume an untoward portion of the class recovery. And in this sense, even judges who use time/rate analyses always blend lodestars and percentages. No judge reasonably awards fees by looking *only* at hours. What is left for the class, after fees have been awarded, is always a paramount consideration. *The size of the settlement necessarily suggests upper (and lower) limits on permissible fees, in a common fund case, no matter how many hours were logged.* That is axiomatic. Hours are not rewarded simply because they were toiled. They are rewarded, consistent with the common fund theory, because they brought benefit to the class. Recognition among lawyers and judges that long hours will not be fully compensated where the result is a fee award that dwarfs what's left for the class should deter many of the abuses of lodestarring.

Sixth, there is no per se reason that lodestars should encourage opportunistic litigation. The manner by which fees are awarded clearly structures incentives. Overly generous fee awards may encourage nuisance suits and "strike" litigation with no merit. Lawyers *should* be made to think twice before filing massive, complicated cases of clearly marginal merit. Lodestars, however, provide stronger incentives for opportunistic litigation than percentages do only if lodestar awards are more generous than percentage awards. And there is no per se reason that they should be. (Many plaintiffs' attorneys, in fact, tend to believe that lodestar awards are frequently lower than percentage awards.)

There undoubtedly are cases brought by opportunistic counsel who, by logging long hours and forcing defense counsel to log similar hours, harass defendants into settling by running up costs and fees and creating bad press. But in these cases, and particularly where only a modest settlement is reached, full compensation for long hours may be inappropriate. As we have said, where the lodestar is large and the recovery is small adjustments may be called for.

Seventh, while defense lawyers frequently express concern that lodestars encourage opportunistic litigation, plaintiffs' lawyers frequently complain that lodestars discourage meritorious litigation. One form of this fear is related, again, to the slam dunk case—massive damages, quick settlement. Many plaintiffs' lawyers seem to feel that it is not worth bringing such cases on behalf of a class for lodestar fees, that their time is better spent bringing contingent fee cases where compensation is much more generous, that the opportunity costs involved in bringing lodestar cases make them a very poor investment where time could be spent on contingent, percentage recoveries instead. This argument, however, reveals less about the inadequacy of lodestars than it does about an information failure in a market where clients are willing to sign high-percentage contingent fee contracts (40% percent in many of the asbestos cases currently pending in this district) to have lawyers bring cases where liability is clear or almost certain and the work is minimal.

The plaintiffs' bar, however, also has a much more serious and legitimate concern about lodestars, namely that they may undercompensate for risk. But a lodestar, enhanced by an appropriate multiplier, should not undercompensate for risk.

Fees that are contingent on success present definite risks. Payment, if any, is deferred, and there is always a risk, often a very substantial risk, that there may be no payment at all. Unless a case settles or ends in a favorable judgment for the class, work goes uncompensated. The "best" case can be lost and the "worst" case can be won, and juries may find liability but no damages. None of these risks should be underestimated.

It is axiomatic that risk demands a premium. And, as a general rule, the greater the uncertainty of payment the greater the premium should be. Risk must be assessed ex ante. Lawyers make decisions about whether to bring lawsuits on the basis of the risks and rewards they perceive at the beginning and must be compensated on the basis of the risks as they appeared at the beginning, not as the court perceives them at the end of the litigation. Obviously, the hard question is what the compensation for risk should be. Many cases do not present a better than 50–50 chance of success at the beginning, before discovery has been conducted and the evidence is in, which suggests that often a multiplier of at least 2 for risk would be appropriate at least for the principal counsel in the case who invest the most in time and money and have the least choice about doing so.

The essential point is that a straight hourly rate is not reasonable compensation in most contingent cases. Class counsel run risks of nonpayment in every class case and those risks must be compensated. How much the compensation should be will depend on how much incentive lawyers need to bring class cases. Much more research is needed on that subject. In any event, fees must bear some relationship to the time spent and amount recovered.

Eighth, and finally, a number of courts and commentators, after reviewing common fund awards, have concluded that the majority of common fund fee awards fall between 20 and 30 percent of the fund, no matter what method is used. See *In re Activision,* 723 F.Supp. at 1377–78; Third Circuit Task Force Report, *supra,* 108 F.R.D. at 247 n. 32; H. Newberg, *Attorney Fee Awards,* § 2.08 at 51–56 (1986). The empirical basis for this conclusion escapes us. Certainly, the size of the award has, and should, vary with the size of the fund. Newberg himself states that "[e]mpirical analysis of fee precedents tends to show that for common fund and derivative shareholder suit recoveries of approximately $40–$75 million, fee awards usually fall in the *13–16 per cent range.*" Newberg, *Attorney Fee Awards,* § 2.09 (Supp.1990 at 12) (emphasis added). And the tables in Newberg reflect that, for whatever reasons, in antitrust suits with recoveries in excess of $25 million, fee awards have been closer to 12% than 20 to 30. In cases with recoveries in the $100 million and over range, fees have been less than 10% and even less than 7%.

C. A HYBRID APPROACH

Fee determinations call for the exercise of informed discretion. There are no easy formulas. This is not an exact science. The best short statement may be that the size of an award should be reasonably arbitrary—meaning that there is no magic in the precise final numbers but that they must be reasonable, which is to say, the result of considered, articulated and fair judgments. The aim is neither to chisel lawyers nor to enrich them at the expense of the class.

Any method used should be flexible. Every case is different, and considerations that are significant in one case may not be in the next. But there are some fairly constant principles, which generally hold true.

Thus, it is our firm belief that no final fee determination can reasonably be made without considering the size of the settlement. Lawyers should be fairly compensated. But settlements must ultimately be negotiated for the benefit of the class, and no fee award should either fleece the class of its recovery or result in a windfall to their lawyers in excess of any efforts those counsel made or risks they ran.

Notes and Questions

1. The Manual for Complex Litigation (4th) § 14.121 (2004) reports that "the vast majority of courts of appeals now permit or direct district courts to use the percentage method in common-fund cases." The Private Securities Litigation Reform Act of 1995 directed that in suits governed by that Act "[t]otal attorneys' fees * * * shall not exceed a reasonable percentage of the amount of any damages and prejudgment interest paid to the class." 15 U.S.C. § 77z–1(a)(6). Given the low recoveries in civil rights and like cases, no such movement has surfaced in cases like Hensley v. Eckerhart, *supra* p. 687.

2.   Judge Patel voices a frequent criticism of the lodestar when she suggests that it prompts lawyers to delay settlement and load hours into a case as a way to bolster later fee applications. To the extent such problems exist, are they less likely to be true in cases like *Hensley,* which do not involve large damage claims? Might there be a temptation for lawyers in such cases to bolster their fee-generating value by putting in more hours in cases that seemed to be sure winners before discussing settlement? See Simon, Fee Sharing Between Lawyers and Public Interest Groups, 98 Yale L.J. 1069, 1074 (1989):

> Virtually every public interest organization requires its staff attorneys to turn over all court-awarded fees. These fees finance many litigation activities that do not generate fees * * *. In addition, fee awards finance such things as educational activities, client screening, capital improvements, policy development, scholarships, recruitment and training programs, supervision of cooperating attorneys, and general overhead expenses.

Could a percentage approach cause problems in public interest cases? Consider the Supreme Court's explanation for refusing to limit recovery in a civil rights case to the percentage of the monetary recovery that the lawyer had agreed to accept from the plaintiff: "If a contingent fee agreement were to govern as a strict limitation on the award of attorney's fees, an undesirable emphasis might be placed on the importance of the recovery of damages in civil rights litigation. The intention of Congress was to encourage successful civil rights litigation, not to create a special incentive to prove damages and shortchange efforts to seek effective injunctive or declaratory relief." Blanchard v. Bergeron, 489 U.S. 87, 95, 109 S.Ct. 939, 945, 103 L.Ed.2d 67 (1989).

3.   Another goal of the fee measurement process is to avoid windfalls for the lawyer. Would there be a risk of such windfalls if a percentage method were adopted in large dollar cases? Consider Dawson, Lawyers and Involuntary Clients in Public Interest Litigation, 88 Harv.L.Rev. 849, 922 (1975):

> It is in the massive class action that sharing-of-benefit formulas for measuring fees appear in the most lurid light. It is to be expected that the classes will grow large as the purposes to be served grow more ambitious, to prevent or redress injuries to broad sectors of the population or to scattered but very numerous individuals. These features of the modernized class action when combined with sharing-of-benefit formulas provide an advantage that is not even to be found in stockholders' suits. It enables lawyers, almost miraculously, to increase the importance and usefulness of their public service and, in the same proportion, to magnify their own income, usually without adding significantly to their own workload. For if such formulas control, multiplying the members in the class and thereby the recovery will automatically multiply fees.

In securities class actions, there may be particular problems in this regard. Professor Alexander found that settlements in securities class actions appear not to reflect the merits of the claims. Based on this conclusion, she cautioned against a percentage approach:

If outcomes do not reflect the merits, changing to a percentage of the recovery formula is exactly the wrong thing to do. At least the lodestar method assures that discovery will be done and the lawyers will be exposed to the facts of the case. To guarantee a fee as a fixed percentage of any recovery, however, regardless of the amount of work done, would add one more incentive to ignore the merits. If the benchmark percentage applies to fees plus expenses, it would work even more strongly against taking account of the merits by giving plaintiffs' attorneys an incentive to minimize expenses, which generally are related to information-gathering (experts, depositions, and so on).

Alexander, Do the Merits Matter? A Study of Settlements in Securities Class Actions, 43 Stan.L.Rev. 497, 579 (1991).

In In re Cendant PRIDES Litigation, 243 F.3d 722 (3d Cir.2001), the class action settlement had a value of over $340 million. Noting that this settlement enabled participating class members to recover fully, the district judge concluded that "counsel should not be penalized by a slavish application of the lodestar," given counsel's "gifted execution of responsibilities." Id. at 734. It awarded a fee of $19 million, some 5.7% of the award. The appellate court noted that, even taking the highest billing rates and accepting all hours worked, this would involve a multiplier of seven beyond the lodestar. Moreover, "this case was neither legally nor factually complex and did not require significant motion practice or discovery by [counsel], and the entire duration of the case from the filing of the Amended Complaint to the submission of a Settlement Agreement to the District Court was only four months." Id. at 742–43. It compared the fee awards in more than a dozen other cases with large recoveries (id. at 737–38), and concluded that the award in the PRIDES case could not be justified on the record made.

4. What is the effect of the lodestar on the interests of the plaintiffs? One effect may be that the residue left after fees are paid (i.e., the amount actually distributed to plaintiff class members) is depleted by the tendency of lawyers to overwork the case. Professor Coffee has vigorously suggested that in cases where the relief is not money, the lodestar may invite collusive settlements in which defendants agree to unimportant cosmetic equitable relief in return for allowing plaintiffs' attorneys to run up time on the case with no opposition from defendants at the fee award stage. See, e.g., Coffee, The Unfaithful Champion: The Plaintiff as Monitor in Shareholder Litigation, 48 Law & Contemp.Probs. 5 (Summer 1985). Could a court avoid this problem by adhering to Hensley's emphasis on the results obtained? How could it value those results in corporate litigation involving such things as proxy solicitations?

5. If a percentage is to be used, what is the right percentage? Judge Patel concludes that 30% is correct, although the Ninth Circuit had observed that "25 percent has been a proper benchmark figure." Paul, Johnson, Alston & Hunt v. Graulty, 886 F.2d 268, 273 (9th Cir.1989). Note the range in the figures Judge Patel encountered in her survey of other cases. Professor Dawson, examining efforts earlier in the 20th century to determine the "nationwide average," criticized them because the cases cited "showed wild variations ranging up and down the scale from two and one-half to forty-nine

percent." Dawson, Lawyers and Involuntary Clients in Public Interest Litigation, 88 Harv.L.Rev. 849, 876 (1975). Given the magnitude of dollar difference that results from a change in the percentage, is there a way to derive a proper percentage?

Some courts have questioned the use of a "benchmark." See Goldberger v. Integrated Resources, Inc., 209 F.3d 43 (2d Cir.2000) (insisting on a multifactor analysis because the court is "disturbed by the essential notion of a benchmark" since "we cannot know precisely what fees common fund plaintiffs in an efficient market for legal services would agree to"). The Seventh Circuit, on the other hand, directs district judges to try to estimate the terms of a contract that private plaintiffs would negotiate with their lawyers at the outset of the case, and concluded that "[t]he second circuit's consider-everything approach, by contrast, lacks a benchmark: a list of factors without a rule of decision is just chopped salad." In re Synthroid Marketing Litigation, 264 F.3d 712 (7th Cir.2001).

In In re Synthroid Marketing Litigation, *supra*, the Seventh Circuit also endorsed making the percentage determination early in the case, and also rejected the district court's announcement that in "megafund" cases (over $75 million) she would not award more than 10% of the fund. "On remand, the district court must estimate the terms of the contract that private plaintiffs would have negotiated with their lawyers, had bargaining occurred at the outset of the case." Id. at 718. How readily can a court do this? Could it ever result in an "escalating" percentage, in which counsel get a larger percentage of amounts recovered over a baseline? Would that be justified on the ground that the first $10 million would be "easy" to get, while the next $10 million would be "hard" to get.

6.   There may also be a debate about what a settlement is worth. How easily can the court determine the value of the case in order to apply the percentage to that amount? If plaintiffs win a money judgment payable at present, this should not be a challenge. But what if plaintiffs receive, through judgment or settlement, something else? Then the judge must determine what that something else is worth before giving the lawyer her share of it. As Judge Will says, "What is 30% of *up to* $70 million payable over a period of years?" Coupons can cause a greater difficulty. See, for example, In re Domestic Air Transportation Antitrust Litigation, 148 F.R.D. 297 (N.D.Ga.1993), in which the settlement called for the airlines to provide discount coupons to class members. Plaintiffs' lawyers contended that the correct measure of the value conferred on the class was the aggregate face value of the coupons, but the judge concluded that the real value was considerably less. See discussion, *supra* p. 535 n.6. Are judges better able to make this sort of determination than whether lawyers have spent too much time on the case?

A Texas statute passed in 2003 provides that "if any portion of the benefits recovered for the class are in the form of coupons or other noncash common benefits, the attorney's fees awarded in the action must be in cash and noncash amounts in the same proportion as the recovery for the class." V.T.C.A., Civ. Prac. & Rem. Code § 26.003(b). It also provides that "the trial court shall use the Lodestar method to calculate the amount of attorney's fees to be awarded class counsel." Id. at § 23.003(a).

7. Unless there is only one set of lawyers on the winning side, some method must also be found for allocating the fees between them. In In re Thirteen Appeals Arising Out of the San Juan Dupont Plaza Hotel Fire Litigation, 56 F.3d 295 (1st Cir.1995), the court addressed the allocation of fees between lead counsel and individual counsel in mass tort litigation. The pot was certainly large—$68 million in fees—and the district judge decided that 70% should go to the court-appointed steering committee members and only 30% to the individually retained representatives of individual plaintiffs (which included members of the court-appointed steering committee). The appellate court vacated this division, finding it unlikely that in any mass tort case the steering committee could be entitled to more than half. The court noted that "the power to appoint lead counsel gives the trial judge an unusual degree of control over the livelihood of the lawyers who practice before the court," and that "in mass tort litigation * * * free rider concerns are minimized." It distinguished other types of class actions, notably securities class actions, because in the mass tort context the victims' losses are almost always keenly felt, and interaction with individual retained counsel therefore should be important. Moreover, the district judge had praised all the lawyers for doing a good job and recognized that the individually retained lawyers had done a substantial amount of work. See id. at 309–12. Compare In re FPI/Agretech Securities Litig., 105 F.3d 469 (9th Cir.1997) (district court's refusal to accept negotiated allocation of fees among plaintiffs' counsel was not erroneous).

8. Yet another way of calculating fees would be to blend the percentage and hourly approaches. For an argument that such an approach would avoid the negative features of the pure hourly and the pure percentage approach, see Clermont & Currivan, Improving on the Contingent Fee, 63 Cornell L.Rev. 529 (1978). Many courts use the lodestar as a cross-check on the percentage method. See Manual for Complex Litigation (4th) § 14.121 (2004).

9. In 2004, Professors Eisenberg and Miller published a study of fee awards in hundreds of class actions settled during the period 1993 to 2002. Somewhat underscoring arguments in favor of the percentage approach, they found "an overwhelming correlation between class recovery and attorney fees." Eisenberg & Miller, Attorney Fees in Class Action Settlements: An Empirical Study, 1 J. Empir. Legal Stud. 27, 72 (2004). The summarize their results as follows (id. at 28):

> The relation between fees and recovery is remarkably linear on a log scale, and is similar between cases in which no fee-shifting statute applies and cases in which the plaintiff had a right to seek reimbursement under a fee-shifting statute. The presence of high risk is associated with a higher fee, as is the presence of the case in federal rather than state court. Contrary to popular belief, we found no robust evidence that either recoveries for plaintiffs or fees of their attorneys as a percentage of the class recovery increased during the time period studied. Nor does the presence or absence of objectors to settlement have a discernable effect on fees.

F. RECUSAL

UNITED STATES v. STATE OF ALABAMA

United States Court of Appeals, Eleventh Circuit, 1987.
828 F.2d 1532, cert. denied, 487 U.S. 1210, 108
S.Ct. 2857, 101 L.Ed.2d 894 (1988).

Before VANCE and KRAVITCH, CIRCUIT JUDGES, and BROWN, SENIOR CIRCUIT JUDGE.

PER CURIAM.

[This action claimed racial discrimination in Alabama's public higher education. The case was assigned to a African–American district judge who had formerly been a civil rights lawyer and a state senator. Defendants moved to disqualify the judge on grounds of both bias and interest.]

LEGAL STANDARD

"The guarantee to the defendant of a totally fair and impartial tribunal, and the protection of the integrity and dignity of the judicial process from any hint or appearance of bias is the palladium of our judicial system." To ensure that the courts remain above reproach, the Congress passed statutory provisions governing the disqualification of federal judges. The relevant statutes are 28 U.S.C. §§ 144 and 455.[21] These two statutes control appellants' claim that the lower court erred

---

21. 28 U.S.C. § 144 provides:

Whenever a party to any proceeding in a district court makes and files a timely and sufficient affidavit that the judge before whom the matter is pending has a personal bias or prejudice either against him or in favor of any adverse party, such judge shall proceed no further therein, but another judge shall be assigned to hear such proceeding.

The affidavit shall state the facts and the reasons for the belief that bias or prejudice exists, and shall be filed not less than ten days before the beginning of the term at which the proceeding is to be heard, or good cause shall be shown for failure to file it within such time. A party may file only one such affidavit in any case. It shall be accompanied by a certificate of counsel of record stating that it is made in good faith.

28 U.S.C. § 455 provides, in pertinent part:

(a) Any justice, judge, or magistrate of the United States shall disqualify himself in any proceeding in which his impartiality might reasonably be questioned.

(b) He shall also disqualify himself in the following circumstances:

(1) Where he has a personal bias or prejudice concerning a party, or personal knowledge of disputed evidentiary facts concerning the proceeding;

(2) Where in private practice he served as lawyer in the matter in controversy, or a lawyer with whom he previously practiced law served during such association as a lawyer concerning the matter, or the judge or such lawyer has been a material witness concerning it;

(3) Where he has served in governmental employment and in such capacity participated as counsel, adviser or material witness concerning the proceeding or expressed an opinion concerning the merits of the particular case in controversy;

(4) He knows that he, individually or as a fiduciary, or his spouse or minor child residing in his household, has a financial interest in the subject matter in controversy or in a party to the proceeding, or any other interest that could be substantially affected by the outcome of the proceeding;

(5) He or his spouse, or a person within the third degree of relationship

in failing to disqualify Judge Clemon from presiding over this case.[22]

Disqualification under § 144 requires that a party file an affidavit demonstrating the judge's personal bias or prejudice against that party or in favor of an adverse party. The statute mandates that the affidavit be filed within a specified time period and that it be accompanied by a certificate of good faith by a counsel of record. If an affidavit is timely and technically correct, the trial judge may not pass upon the truthfulness of the facts stated in the affidavit even when the court knows these allegations to be false. The statute restricts the trial judge to determining whether the facts alleged are legally sufficient to require recusal. The test for legal sufficiency adopted by this Court requires a party to show:

1. The facts are material and stated with particularity;

2. The facts are such that, if true they would convince a reasonable person that a bias exists.

3. The facts show that the bias is personal, as opposed to judicial, in nature.

In 1974, Congress rewrote 28 U.S.C. § 455 to correct perceived problems in the disqualification statutes. Prior to 1974, both the technical and legal sufficiency requirements of § 144 had been construed strictly in favor of judges. Courts also operated under the so-called "duty to sit" doctrine which required a judge to hear a case unless a clear demonstration of extra-judicial bias or prejudice was made. Consequently, disqualification of a judge was difficult under § 144. In passing the amended 28 U.S.C. § 455, Congress broadened the grounds and loosened the procedure for disqualification in the federal courts. Although a party still is permitted to make a motion and submit affidavits to bring about a judge's disqualification, the statute places a judge under a self-enforcing obligation to recuse himself where the proper legal grounds exist. The statute also did away with the "duty to sit" so the benefit of the doubt is now to be resolved in favor of recusal. Section 455(a) requires a judge to disqualify himself when "his impartiality might reasonably be questioned." Thus, under § 455(a) an actual demonstrated prejudice need

to either of them, or the spouse of such a person:

> (i) Is a party to the proceeding, or an officer, director, or trustee of a party;

> (ii) Is acting as a lawyer in the proceeding;

> (iii) Is known by the judge to have an interest that could be substantially affected by the outcome of the proceeding;

> (iv) Is to the judge's knowledge likely to be a material witness in the proceeding.

* * *

(e) No justice, judge, or magistrate shall accept from the parties to the pro-

ceeding a waiver of any ground for disqualification enumerated in subsection (b). Where the ground for disqualification arises only under subsection (a), waiver may be accepted provided it is preceded by a full disclosure on the record of the basis for disqualification.

22. The right to a fair trial before an impartial judge is a basic requirement of due process and thus guaranteed by the United States Constitution. However, because the statutory grounds for disqualification are stricter than the requirements of due process, it is not necessary to address the constitutional dimensions of disqualification.

not exist in order for a judge to recuse himself: "disqualification should follow if the reasonable man, were he to know all the circumstances, would harbor doubts about the judge's impartiality." Congress expressly intended the amended § 455 to promote public confidence in the impartiality of the courts by eliminating even the appearance of impropriety. Although the courts retained the requirement that the alleged bias or prejudice "stem from an extrajudicial source" and now permitted the factual accuracy of affidavits submitted under § 455 to be scrutinized, the general effect of this statute was to liberalize greatly the scope of disqualification in the federal courts.

The amended § 455 also established a number of bright line rules for disqualification. Mandatory disqualification is provided for in certain situations where the potential for conflicts of interest [is] readily apparent. For example, under subsection (b), a judge must disqualify himself when he has a financial interest or when a member of his family "within the third degree of relationship" is a party or lawyer in the case. The statute also states that the parties cannot waive the *per se* rules of disqualification set out in § 455(b).

DISCUSSION

Defendants assert a number of grounds for the disqualification of Judge Clemon. Defendants first allege in their affidavits that Judge Clemon has two minor children and thus is disqualified because these children are members of the plaintiff class. Judge Clemon proudly admits to having two children who were ages 9 and 16 at the time of appellants' motions. The class certified by the trial judge includes all children "who are eligible to attend the public institutions of higher education in the Montgomery, Alabama, area." Consequently, Judge Clemon's children are technically members of this class and possess an interest in the outcome of this litigation. Section 455 provides for disqualification where the judge knows that a "minor child residing in his household, has a financial interest ... or any other interest that could be substantially affected by the outcome of the proceeding" or if "[h]e or his spouse, or a person within the third degree of relationship, is a party to the proceeding." Defendants argue that the trial judge should be disqualified under this provision.

We conclude that the interests of Judge Clemon's children are not "substantial" enough to merit disqualification. Any beneficial effects of this suit upon these children were remote, contingent and speculative. There is no evidence that Judge Clemon's children have any desire or inclination to attend a Montgomery area institution. Any potential interest, moreover, is shared by all young black Alabamians. "[A]n interest which a judge has in common with many others in a public matter is not sufficient to disqualify him." * * *

To disqualify Judge Clemon on the basis of his children's membership in the plaintiff class could come dangerously close to holding that minority judges must disqualify themselves from all major civil rights actions. * * * To disqualify minority judges from major civil rights litigation solely because of their minority status is intolerable. This court cannot and will not countenance such a result. The recusal statutes do not contemplate such a double standard for minority judges. The fact that an individual belongs to a minority does not render one biased or prejudiced, or raise doubts about one's impartiality: "that one is black does not mean, ipso facto, that he is anti-white; no more than being Jewish implies being anti-Catholic, or being Catholic implies being anti-Protestant." * * *

Nor can we countenance defendants' claim that Judge Clemon is prejudiced and no longer impartial by virtue of his background as a civil rights lawyer. Appellants point to Judge Clemon's representation of black plaintiffs in race discrimination actions prior to joining the bench as evidence of personal bias in this action. It is well settled that "the facts pleaded ... will not suffice to show the personal bias required by the statute if they go to the background and associations of the judge rather than to his appraisal of a party personally." All judges come to the bench with a background of experiences, associations and viewpoints. * * *

Similarly, the views expressed by Judge Clemon as a political figure and member of the Alabama State Senate do not mandate disqualification. As judges on this court have recognized, "[i]t appears to be an inescapable part of our system of government that judges are drawn primarily from lawyers who have participated in public and political affairs." Since the funding and control of public institutions in the instant case are important issues in the Alabama political arena, it is not surprising that Judge Clemon took public positions concerning these institutions prior to becoming a judge. The fact that prior to joining the bench a judge has stated strong beliefs does not indicate that he has prejudged the legal question before him. As noted above, judges have frequently heard cases concerning subjects about which they have previously expressed some views.

Judge Clemon's involvement in the issues before this court went beyond the mere making of public statements, however. During his tenure in the state legislature, the trial judge actively participated in the very events and shaped the very facts that are at issue in this suit.

[The court recounted events in the judge's political career that were directly involved in the litigation, noting that as a result he was "forced to make factual findings about events in which he was an active participant." In addition, it found that his involvement as a lawyer in a school desegregation case left him "with knowledge of facts that were in dispute in the instant case" in that it involved proof of alleged discrimination in employment of school officials that was at issue in the current case. It therefore ordered the judge disqualified, noting that "[w]e consider the future of higher education in Alabama too important to be decided under a cloud."]

IN RE INTERNATIONAL BUSINESS MACHINES CORP.

United States Court of Appeals, Second Circuit, 1980.
618 F.2d 923.

Before MULLIGAN, VAN GRAAFEILAND and MESKILL, CIRCUIT JUDGES.

MULLIGAN, CIRCUIT JUDGE.

More than a decade ago, on January 17, 1969, the United States of America, by its attorneys, acting under the direction of the Attorney General, filed a complaint in the United States District Court for the Southern District of New York which alleged that International Business Machines Corporation (IBM), commencing in or about 1961, had monopolized and attempted to monopolize the market for general purpose electronic digital computers in violation of Section 2 of the Sherman Act (15 U.S.C. § 2). In addition to injunctive relief the Government sought such "divorcement, divestiture and reorganization" of IBM as might be appropriate to restore competitive conditions. On January 26, 1972, Hon. David N. Edelstein, Chief Judge of the Southern District, assumed control of the case. After extensive pretrial discovery, the bench trial was commenced on May 19, 1975. Counsel for the Government estimated that its case would take two to three months and IBM's counsel predicted that its defense would take six to eight months.

These estimates in fact proved to be grossly erroneous. The Government's direct case lasted for almost three years, ending on April 26, 1978. IBM's defense began on that date and it continues as of this writing. Eleven years have elapsed since the filing of the initial complaint, pre-trial depositions commenced some eight years ago, and more than four and one-half years of trial time have been consumed. A mammoth record of trial transcript and exhibits has been assembled. To the best of our knowledge no litigation has taken so much time and involved such expense.

* * *

On July 19, 1979 five distinguished members of the Board of Directors of IBM (William T. Coleman, Jr., Carla Anderson Hills, John N. Irwin II, William W. Scranton and Irving S. Shapiro), acting as a special committee of the Board, filed an affidavit stating their belief, as noted above, that Chief Judge Edelstein "has a personal bias and prejudice against IBM and in favor of plaintiff, that his impartiality in this action may reasonably be questioned, that he has a bent of mind that will prevent impartiality of judgment, and that his bias and prejudice could not have come from any source other than an extrajudicial source." The committee requested his recusal and the assignment of another judge to hear the case. The affidavit was filed pursuant to the Fifth Amendment of the United States Constitution, and Sections 144 and 455 of Title 28, United States Code. * * * In substance, IBM's charge of bias and prejudice is based upon the following allegations:

1) The Chief Judge has become an advocate for the plaintiff, disrupting the direct testimony of IBM's witnesses, cross-examining IBM witnesses himself, shielding plaintiff's witnesses from cross-examination, and routinely abusing IBM's witnesses and counsel.

2) His rulings on questions of evidence, procedure and discovery have been inconsistent and the general conduct of the trial has been in favor of the Government and against IBM.

3) He has expressed an antipathy toward IBM counsel which manifests an attitude that they can do no right.

4) He has deliberately attempted to create a record that cannot be subject to full and adequate appellate review by refusing to file papers submitted by IBM, refusing to hand down timely rulings in matters of importance to IBM, and secretly making alterations in and deletions from the trial transcript.

IBM's petition recognizes that the alleged prejudice of the trial judge must be extrajudicial, that it must arise by virtue of some factor which creates partiality arising outside of the events which occur in the trial itself. The Supreme Court has held, "The alleged bias and prejudice to be disqualifying must stem from an extrajudicial source and result in an opinion on the merits on some basis other than what the judge has learned from his participation in the case." *United States v. Grinnell Corp.,* 384 U.S. 563, 583, 86 S.Ct. 1698, 1710, 16 L.Ed.2d 778 (1966). Section 144 *in haec verba* requires that the party's affidavit of prejudice state that the judge before whom the matter is pending have a "personal bias or prejudice either against him or in favor of any adverse party." The mandamus petition is also based on section 455. Section 455(b) lists five instances which mandate the recusal of a judge. The only relevant subdivision is section 455(b)(1), which requires recusal where the judge "has a personal bias or prejudice concerning a party...." This language is taken directly from section 144. We agree with the Fifth Circuit's holding that, "[c]onstruing §§ 144 and 455 *in pari materia* we believe the test is the same under both.... The determination should be made on the basis of conduct extrajudicial in nature as distinguished from conduct within a judicial context."

IBM has not shown and does not purport to establish or identify any personal connection, relationship or extrajudicial incident which accounts for the alleged personal animus of the trial judge. IBM's claim of prejudice is based completely on Chief Judge Edelstein's conduct and rulings in the case at hand. These we have repeatedly held form no basis for a finding of extrajudicial bias. Thus in *King v. United States,* 576 F.2d 432, 437 (2d Cir.1978), we stated:

> "The grounds urged for disqualification are for the most part rulings made by [the trial judge] during the trial or statements made by him in the course of his judicial duties.... Nothing of this kind, what the judge has learned from or done in the proceedings before him, is any basis for disqualification; to be sufficient for disqualifica-

tion the alleged bias or prejudice must be from an extrajudicial source.''

IBM urges that disqualification is also required under section 455(a). Section 455(a) provides for recusal where the judge's "impartiality might reasonably be questioned.'' This section sets up an objective standard for recusal, creating the so-called "appearance of justice" rule. Thus it may well be, for example, that if a judge's first cousin is a party to a case and no disqualification arises under section 455(b)(5) since he is not within the third degree of kinship, reasonable men might well question his impartiality where a close personal relationship exists between the two. However, we cannot agree that adverse rulings by a judge can per se create the appearance of bias under section 455(a). A trial judge must be free to make rulings on the merits without the apprehension that if he makes a disproportionate number in favor of one litigant, he may have created the impression of bias. Judicial independence cannot be subservient to a statistical study of the calls he has made during the contest. As Mr. Justice Frankfurter noted in *Wilkerson v. McCarthy,* 336 U.S. 53, 65, 69 S.Ct. 413, 419, 93 L.Ed. 497 (1949) (Frankfurter, J., concurring), "A timid judge, like a biased judge, is intrinsically a lawless judge." We conclude that under section 455(a) the bias to be established must be extrajudicial and not based upon in-court rulings.

A reading of the cases supporting the general proposition that the bias which requires recusal must be personal and cannot rest upon trial rulings or conduct, reveals two practical considerations which have influenced the courts. The first is quite obvious. As the Supreme Court noted in *Ex parte American Steel Barrel Co.,* 230 U.S. 35, 44, 33 S.Ct. 1007, 1010, 57 L.Ed. 1379 (1913), "[The recusal statute] was never intended to enable a litigant to oust a judge for adverse rulings made, for such rulings are reviewable otherwise . . . .''

IBM claims that 86% of the some 10,000 oral motions made and 74 out of 79 written motions have been decided against the petitioner and in favor of the Government. The United States counters that some 70% of these motions were made by IBM, which allegedly has adopted an increasingly hostile and uncooperative trial strategy, making unnecessary or frivolous objections for the purpose of creating the very statistics upon which it now depends. IBM would have us contrast the favorable rulings made in the Government's favor in its presentation with those which it claims were made inconsistently against IBM in its defense. The Government, asserting that IBM's statistics are flawed, claims that the IBM appendices refer only to a small fraction of the motions made and that no pattern of bias emerges. IBM has made further computations which refute those of the Government and allegedly re-establish that a disproportionate number of rulings have been adverse to its interest.

It seems evident that statistics alone, no matter how computed, cannot establish extrajudicial bias. There is no authority for, and no logic in, assuming that either party to a litigation is entitled to a certain percentage of favorable decisions. The inquiry to be at all meaningful would necessarily require this court to examine each and every ruling to determine whether it was, initially, legally valid. If we determined that some adverse rulings were correctly made, obviously they could not be tainted by bias. Even if they were deemed to be incorrect, it of course does not follow that they were motivated by personal bias. We would next have to ask whether the error could be attributed to the judge's misunderstanding of the facts or the law. The exercise would require this court to become intimately familiar with a 90,000 page trial transcript and to examine thousands of underlying documents and exhibits. That in turn would require us to become familiar with the highly technical and complicated engineering issues involved. There is no precedent for such an undertaking on this scale at this interim stage of the litigation. The exercise is futile in any event, since it is impossible from the record before us to ascribe extrajudicial animus to an evidentiary ruling. There is no ruling or comment by the judge which gives any clue or inkling of extrajudicial bias against IBM. If material legal or factual error has been committed it can be dealt with on plenary appeal.

This brings us to the second policy consideration underlying the rule that the bias necessary for recusal must be extrajudicial and not based upon what the judge has learned in this case. Chief Judge Edelstein is the sole finder of the fact here. His role is not that of a passive observer. His obligation is to determine the facts in a field which is exceedingly complex and technical. * * *

The point of this comment is perhaps best illustrated by IBM's complaint that Chief Judge Edelstein's treatment of its witnesses and its counsel has been marked by asperity, incivility and hostility. We have examined the affidavits of the nine IBM witnesses, all of whom state that his conduct demonstrates an unidentified personal bias. Much of this is not discernible from the record. Many complain of his "stares," "glares" and "scowls." One urges that the Chief Judge "would often glower at me, scowl and then turn and make bold notes on a pad of paper, as if threatening me with the contents."

There is no question but that these witnesses have felt that the judge's conduct was intimidating. However, the burden of IBM is to establish clearly and convincingly that his attitude can only be attributed to his personal prejudice. * * * [T]he trial judge has the obligation to form judgments as to the veracity of the witnesses before him. His asperity and incivility may well be due to his feeling that a witness is not forthright, that he is trying to protect a position, or is otherwise attempting to obfuscate the fact finding process. IBM complains, for example, that Chief Judge Edelstein has asked its witnesses too many questions, has required them to draw meaningless charts and diagrams, to answer questions "yes" or "no" when they are not susceptible to such simplistic solutions. He has, we are assured, interrupted plaintiff's 52 witnesses "only 846 times and has interrupted IBM's first 19 witnesses over 1200 times." Accepting all of these contentions at face value we do not find them to be of the stuff upon which one can sensibly premise extrajudicial bias.

What may be a simple technical issue to the expert witness or even to IBM counsel, who have been given technical training in preparation for this litigation, may well be arcane to the jurist. His questioning, his interruption, his insistence on clarification may well be prompted by his struggle to determine the truth in a field in which he is not sophisticated. His asperity may well be prompted by a feeling that the witnesses for IBM (three are long time employees) are dissembling. We do not know and cannot on this record determine whether his conduct has been guided by what he has learned during the trial, in which case his reaction is licit, or whether it is due to a personal prejudice which is clearly impermissible. The point is that IBM has not met its burden of showing that the Chief Judge is personally biased against the petitioner.

There is of course another factor at play here—the seemingly interminable length of the trial. The IBM witnesses did not begin to testify until almost three years of trial time had elapsed. Even the most stoic might well lose patience in these circumstances. The judge's allegedly hostile attitude to IBM witnesses as compared to Government witnesses may be due to the natural factor of fatigue in a case of this difficulty and duration. At any rate, while the duration of trial is certainly the responsibility of the trial judge, the marathon here is as wearing on the Government as it is upon IBM and cannot constitute evidence of extrajudicial bias against IBM.

Our reading of the record does disclose that on several occasions Chief Judge Edelstein has expressed his dissatisfaction with counsel for IBM. There have been exchanges in the courtroom and in robing room conferences which indicate that he has, whether justifiably or not, reached the conclusion that he has been "baited" by counsel by their persistence in raising points which he believed had already been determined by previous rulings. The issues here are hotly contested, much is at stake and charges and countercharges of intransigence have continued to be made in the papers before us. Although we cannot condone intemperate behavior on the part of a trial judge, we have observed following a trial of only nine days, "Judges, while expected to possess more than the average amount of self-restraint, are still only human. They do not possess limitless ability, once passion is aroused, to resist provocation."

We have examined the record and are persuaded that while occasional flareups toward counsel have undoubtedly occurred, there is no indication that this is other than sporadic. Such isolated instances are undoubtedly endemic to a trial of this dimension, and do not provide any basis for finding personal prejudice against IBM, as distinct from its counsel.

In sum we conclude that the rulings and conduct of the trial judge complained of here are legally insufficient to warrant recusal under Title 28, §§ 144, 455 or under the due process clause of the Fifth Amendment of the United States Constitution.

Notes and Questions

1. "To decide when a judge may not sit is to define what a judge is. To define what a judge is is to decide what a system of adjudication is all about." Leubsdorf, Theories of Judging and Judge Disqualification, 62 N.Y.U.L.Rev. 237, 237 (1987). Professor Leubsdorf strongly criticizes the distinctions that current law on judicial disqualification draws in determining when a judge may or may not sit in a case. Do they make sense to you? Recall the disagreement between Professor Resnik and Judge Peckham about the risks that active case management may pose for impartiality. See *supra* pp. 628-34. Do the current rules for disqualification provide good protection against partiality? Whatever the wisdom of the current rules, disqualification has become sufficiently important that there is now an entire book dedicated to the topic. See R. Flamm, Judicial Disqualification (1997).

2. The basic starting point is due process. In Aetna Life Ins. Co. v. Lavoie, 475 U.S. 813, 106 S.Ct. 1580, 89 L.Ed.2d 823 (1986), the Court held that a judgment of the Alabama Supreme Court was invalid because of the participation of a justice who was a plaintiff in a similar action. The underlying claim asserted that an insurer had wrongfully refused to pay a $3,028 medical bill, and the jury had awarded $3.5 million in punitive damages. The state supreme court affirmed 5–4, with that court's decision written by a justice who was himself a plaintiff in a bad faith nonpayment case against another insurer. The Supreme Court rejected the insurer's argument that this justice's general hostility to insurers deprived it of due process, but held that the pendency of his own suit did so owing to the similarity between the issues in the two cases, and the previously unclear law on those issues. Under the circumstances, it concluded, the justice acted "as a judge in his own case." Id. at 822, 106 S.Ct. at 1586. But it rejected the further argument that other justices were disqualified because they had not withdrawn as members of the class that this justice sought to represent: "With the proliferation of class actions involving broadly defined classes, the application of the constitutional requirement of disqualification must be carefully limited. Otherwise constitutional disqualification arguments could quickly become a standard feature of class action litigation." Id. at 826, 106 S.Ct. at 1588.

3. The disqualification statutes go beyond situations in which due process requires removal of the judge, and the 1975 amendment to § 455 was designed to broaden the scope of disqualification. Although these changes abandoned the "duty to sit" doctrine, courts continue to state that "[t]he judge is, of course, obligated not to recuse himself without reason just as he is obligated to recuse himself when there is reason." Suson v. Zenith Radio Corp., 763 F.2d 304, 308–09 n. 2 (7th Cir.1985). Is there reason to be concerned about judges disqualifying themselves too easily?

4. Judges have been disqualified for a financial interest that is very attenuated. For example, in In re Cement Antitrust Litigation, 673 F.2d 1020 (9th Cir.1981), affirmed for absence of a quorum, 459 U.S. 1190, 103 S.Ct. 1173, 75 L.Ed.2d 425 (1983), 21 separate actions for price fixing in the cement industry were filed in a variety of districts. The Judicial Panel on Multidistrict Litigation transferred them to the District of Arizona for

consolidation, in part because the judge there was familiar with the cases. Thereafter, he certified a nationwide class of over 210,000 purchasers of cement. Two years later, several defendants moved to recuse him on the ground that his wife owned stock in seven of the 210,000 companies in the plaintiff class. At first the judge responded by reference to Mr. Bumble in *Oliver Twist* that "If the law supposes that . . . the law is an ass—an idiot." Ultimately, however, he concluded that 28 U.S.C.A. § 455(b)(4) requires automatic disqualification for *any* financial interest held by any member of a judge's family, and the Ninth Circuit affirmed.

Eventually Congress amended the statute to add 28 U.S.C. § 455(f), which permits the judge to divest herself of the interest in question if the judge learns of the interest after "substantial judicial time has been devoted to the matter." In In re Initial Public Offering Securities Litigation, 294 F.3d 297 (2d Cir.2002), the district judge was presiding over 1,000 class actions asserting securities fraud in connection with IPOs against 263 issuers, 42 underwriters and hundreds of individuals, and some defendants moved to recuse her on the ground that she had bought stock in some IPOs. The judge promptly sold the stock in question, and announced she would opt out of any class if one were certified. Citing the "herculean organizational effort" the district judge had to undertake upon assignment of all these cases, the appellate court denied a petition for a writ of mandate on the ground that divestment was effective under § 455(f). "Organizational work may be the grunt work of the judicial system, but it is as necessary and vital to its success as motion and trial practice."

5. In United States v. State of Alabama, does the court properly evaluate the judge's claimed interest in the outcome? "Every judge has a race and a view of religion, so that, by itself, does not disqualify." Leubsdorf, *supra,* 62 N.Y.U.L.Rev. at 241.

Contrast other grounds for recusal. For example, Judge Clemon, the district judge in United States v. State of Alabama, may also have been the object of a technique designed to remove him from employment discrimination cases. Orey, Uncle and Nephew Find Legal Ethics Strain Family Ties, Wall St.J., Aug. 7, 2002, at A1, reports that some in Birmingham, Ala. (including some judges), believe that defendants hire the firm in which Judge Clemon's nephew is a partner in order to cause Judge Clemon's recusal from cases. Another district judge, in a written opinion, cited 15 cases over a two and a half year period in which Judge Clemon recused himself because his nephew's firm represented the defendant.

6. In re IBM focuses on the problem of possible bias resulting from the judge's involvement in the litigation in her role as judge. As the court states, the normal view was that the only grounds for disqualification must be extrajudicial. Are there persuasive reasons for this rule?

In Liteky v. United States, 510 U.S. 540, 114 S.Ct. 1147, 127 L.Ed.2d 474 (1994), a criminal case, the Court held that the extrajudicial source of the judge's alleged bias is indeed a "factor" in recusal, but that concern with this factor should not be viewed as a "doctrine" that absolutely precludes disqualification on such grounds. It explained that "[a] favorable or unfavorable predisposition can also deserve to be characterized as 'bias' or 'prejudice' because, even though it springs from the facts adduced or the events occurring at trial, it is so extreme as to display clear inability to render fair judgment." The Court suggested, however, that recusal would be justified only in the rarest circumstances. See In re Martinez–Catala, 129 F.3d 213, 219 (1st Cir.1997) ("Judges constantly form personal opinions during proceedings. It may be wiser not to express such views, and almost always prudent to avoid epithets, but disqualification is almost never required where the judge's opinions are based on the proceedings.").

Such circumstances may sometimes occur in complex litigation. For example, consider Gardiner v. A.H. Robins Co., 747 F.2d 1180 (8th Cir.1984). Judge Miles Lord of the District of Minnesota required representatives of the company, which was a defendant in a Dalkon Shield litigation pending before him, to appear in court and receive criticism from the judge about the way the company had reacted to the problem of injuries traced to the IUD. Since the case had settled, there was no occasion to consider recusal, but the Eighth Circuit reprimanded him, rejecting the argument that discipline was not appropriate because the source of the judge's attitude was not extrajudicial: "Those comments in such a context exhibit a pervasive bias and prejudice as to deprive Robins of its due process right to a hearing before an impartial judge." Id. at 1192.

7. Could similar arguments have been made in the IBM case? Consider these later developments: The Department of Justice and IBM reached a settlement pursuant to which the government voluntarily dismissed. Judge Edelstein then *sua sponte* directed briefs on whether the settlement was invalid under the Antitrust Procedures and Penalties Act (the Tunney Act) because of consulting activity that Assistant Attorney General William Baxter had done for IBM before he joined the government. In response, IBM renewed its motion to recuse the judge, and the judge again denied it. The Second Circuit then granted a writ of mandate directing Judge Edelstein to cease his consideration of the Tunney Act issues. In re International Business Machines Corp., 687 F.2d 591 (2d Cir.1982). It did so because "we believe that the district court, even without ruling on the merits of the Tunney Act claim, has evinced a 'usurpation of power' and a 'clear abuse of discretion.'" This conclusion flowed from the appellate court's finding that there was not even "colorable jurisdiction" under the Tunney Act to review a voluntary dismissal. The court noted further that Judge Edelstein was quoted in the Wall Street Journal as criticizing Baxter's handling of the case, that he delayed one hearing 40 minutes to allow the press to arrive, and that he refused to authorize destruction of billions of pages of unused documents despite costs of $100,000 per week for storage. Does this episode suggest that the earlier motion to recuse the judge had more merit than the appellate court acknowledged when the recusal issue was decided?

Nearly a decade later, the wounds had reportedly not healed. Thus, the Wall Street Journal reported in 1989 that when another suit against IBM was assigned to Judge Edelstein, from the perspective of IBM "the prospect of defending another antitrust case before Judge Edelstein was something like the U.S. Army mobilizing and going back into Vietnam." Miller, This Case May Lead Spectators to Shout "Order in the Court," Wall St.J., Feb. 16, 1989, at 1 col. 4. IBM moved to disqualify the judge once again, albeit admitting it had no new grounds not included in its motion in the government's antitrust suit. In part the explanation was that IBM and its lawyers "suspect their new opponent * * * of steering the case before Judge Edelstein specifically because it believes he hates IBM." For the resulting order denying the motion to recuse, see Allen–Myland, Inc. v. IBM, 709 F.Supp. 491 (S.D.N.Y.1989).

The Second Circuit did remove Judge Edelstein in In re International Business Mach. Corp., 45 F.3d 641 (2d Cir.1995), a suit filed in 1952 that antedated the one giving rise to the decision above. This case had been pending before Judge Edelstein for 43 years, although nothing of substance had happened since 1970. In mid–1994, however, IBM moved to terminate the consent decree entered in 1956 and also to recuse Judge Edelstein. The judge denied the recusal motion, but the Second Circuit took what it acknowledged was the extraordinary step of removing him from the case by writ of mandate. Finding the question to be "whether a reasonable observer, fully informed as to the circumstances of the Judge's refusal promptly to terminate his authority over the 1969 Case, after the parties had stipulated for its dismissal, would question the Judge's ability fairly and impartially to decide whether to grant the pending motion to terminate his authority over the 1952 Case," the court concluded that it was "manifestly clear" that an observer would. Id. at 644. It also noted that under the Supreme Court's decision in *Liteky*, (described in note 6 above), judicial rulings could be considered in conjunction with other matters in ruling on a recusal motion.

8. Some activities by the judge in relation to the case can lead to disqualification. A notable example is the government's monopolization case against Microsoft, United States v. Microsoft Corp., 253 F.3d 34 (D.C. Cir.2001), which holds that the district judge's practice of talking to reporters about the case while the trial was proceeding violated a variety of provisions of the Code of Conduct for U.S. Judges and called for recusal under 28 U.S.C. § 455(a). Among other things, the judge's activities raised questions about such delicate possibilities as insider trading by the reporters who knew what nobody else (including the parties) knew about what the judge thought of the case. Indeed, "[j]udges who covet publicity, or convey the appearance that they do, lead any objective observer to wonder whether their judgments are being influenced by the prospect of favorable coverage in the media."

Must judges remain oblivious to what the papers say? In In re Boston's Children First, 244 F.3d 164 (1st Cir.2001), the court disqualified a district judge who reacted to a newspaper story about a case suggesting that she was partial to the one side by writing a letter to the reporter who wrote the article, and then talking to the reporter. The appellate court rejected the judge's view that "it was her 'obligation to make certain that people receive accurate information regarding the proceedings over which [she] preside[s].'" Id. at 166. To the contrary, "in newsworthy cases where tensions may be high, judges should be particularly cautious about commenting on pending litigation." Id. at 170.

9. Objections are sometimes raised to judges' attendance at educational seminars that could be criticized as slanted. In In re Aguinda, 241 F.3d 194 (2d Cir.2001), a case against Texaco, Inc., for alleged pollution, the district judge attended a five-day conference put on by a group that received 3% of its funding from Texaco, and a former chief executive of Texaco spoke at the

conference. Plaintiffs moved to disqualify the judge, and the appellate court held that recusal was not required. "No reasonable person would believe that expense-paid attendance at such events would cause a judge to be partial." Id. at 203. Even if this conference was "unbalanced," the fact the judge attend it does not support an inference of partiality. Judges often receive "unbalanced" books, journals, magazines and other materials, and are expected to be able to winnow from these materials that which is useful. Nonetheless, the court did caution about accepting invitations from organizations that receive a significant amount of their funding from litigants or counsel appearing before the judge, and from participating in events that relate to particularized issues pending before the judge.

10. Given the uncertainties of recusal motions under federal law, should parties be given a peremptory challenge to judges? A number of states provide, in effect, that parties may remove a judge once by filing a pro forma affidavit. See, e.g. West's Ann.Cal.Code Civ.Proc. § 170.6. Proposals have been made in Congress for a similar provision in federal court.

Chapter VII

TRYING COMPLEX CASES

In the mid-twentieth century, a thoughtful observer of the American litigation scene could declare that "[t]he heart of the judicial process is the trial in court. All that precedes the trial is but preparation. All that follows is but the correction of error, if error there be."[1] Into the 1980s, courts still declared that trial was "the centerpiece of the litigation."[2] But these declarations no longer ring true. With the evolution from the trial lawyer to the litigator, and the emergence of the case management movement, there has been a widespread and overt shift of focus of judicial activity to the pretrial stage. Although the court may be involved in a number of aspects of most civil cases, very few of these cases reach trial.

Nevertheless, even complex cases must be tried if they are not settled or otherwise resolved before trial. Indeed, the first study of protracted litigation—the Prettyman Report of 1951—dealt principally with problems arising in the trial of such cases.[3] The case management movement has largely focused on changing the court's pretrial role, but it has gradually led to innovations in the manner of trial as well. This section considers a number of these techniques and innovations.

Before turning to the new, however, it is useful to revisit the features of the traditional trial. Like pretrial development of the case, the conduct of the trial until recently tended largely to be left to the lawyers. Although Rule 16 had prescribed a pretrial conference from the promulgation of the Federal Rules of Civil Procedure in 1938, courts often did not impose precise guidelines for trials. At trial, the lawyers were given substantial freedom and, despite the revelations of discovery, surprise could still be an effective weapon.

The trial itself followed the format that had gradually developed in Anglo–American jurisprudence. After jury selection, if necessary, the lawyers would introduce their case through opening statements (or

1. Simpson, The Problem of Trial, in D.D. Field, Centenary Essays 141, 142 (1949).

2. Walters v. Inexco Oil Co., 440 So.2d 268, 275 (Miss.1983).

3. See Report, Procedure in Anti–Trust and Other Protracted Cases, 13 F.R.D. 62 (1951).

perhaps trial briefs if trial were to the court). Plaintiff would then call witnesses, who would customarily testify on direct and cross examination in open court. Documentary evidence would be introduced through witnesses who could authenticate it. When plaintiff rested, defendant could call witnesses and offer evidence, and plaintiff would then be allowed to rebut. All issues in the case were ordinarily before the court at the same time, and each party had the burden of putting on evidence sufficient to support a finding in its favor on the issues it had the burden of proving. Once the evidence was in, the lawyers would be allowed to argue the case and, in jury trials, the jury would be instructed.

This traditional format can be, and increasingly has been, modified in the trial of complex cases. As you consider the modifications explored in this chapter, reflect on the values that might be furthered by the traditional trial. At least where credibility determinations were important, in-court assessment of the demeanor of witnesses while testifying has been considered critical to accurate decision making. The opportunity to tell their story to the judge and/or jury could also be important to litigants anxious to have their "day in court." As a semi-theatrical event, the trial could also bring out-of-court events to life for the persons who had to decide the outcome. Similarly, by setting out the facts in a single continuous proceeding, the trial could allow the observing public to understand the underlying dispute and its resolution in court. Finally, as concluded by a 1992 ABA–Brookings symposium, "the jury provides an important check on the bureaucratization and professionalization of the legal system. The involvement of jurors prevents adjudication from becoming technical and routinized, perhaps even distant and insensitive, as cases with similar fact patterns recur over and over before the same decisionmaker (the judge)." Brookings Institution, Charting a Future for the Civil Jury System 10 (1992). On the values of the traditional trial system, see generally Morgan, Completing Equity's Conquest? Reflections on the Future of Trial Under the Federal Rules of Civil Procedure, 50 U.Pitt.L.Rev. 725, 754–82 (1989).

Some empirical evidence supports continuing concern with these values, at least as compared to settlement and similar alternatives in tort cases. Consider the following description of social science surveys of litigants:

> Litigants may be the only participants in the litigation process who actually like trials. In a survey of tort litigants * * * trials were seen as providing more careful and more thorough decision making than other resolution mechanisms like arbitration, judicial settlement conferences, and bilateral bargaining. Compared to litigants whose cases were arbitrated or disposed through a judicial settlement conference, litigants whose cases went to trial had as high, if not higher, levels of perceived control, perceived participation, and felt comprehension. Trials were also accorded the highest dignity and fairness ratings. Next to trial, court-administered arbitration, involving in-court hearings, was accorded the highest mark, with

settlement conferences, generally not attended by litigants, trailing behind.

Data from another survey, limited to tort litigants whose cases were arbitrated through the New Jersey court arbitration program, suggest why trials and arbitration may receive higher marks from litigants than nonadjudicatory procedures. * * * [T]he most frequently cited objective of lay litigants in adjudicatory proceedings was to "tell my side of the story," a function not generally provided by bargaining or court-mediated settlement processes.

Hensler, Resolving Mass Toxic Torts: Myths and Realities, 1989 U.Ill. L.Rev. 89, 98–99.

The open-ended format of trial that results from granting principal latitude to the attorneys can, at least in tort trials to a jury, also have value:

The jury constructs its own understanding of a case from the testimony of witnesses. Every observer has a limited point of view. Each side has a bias; the perceptions of each witness have been filtered through a unique web of apperception. * * * The jury cannot, therefore, simply choose sides; its role is to form an understanding of the circumstances from its own shared and intermediate perspective. This intermediate perspective is obtained through a complex process of analyzing and comparing a number of different descriptions.

To create an intermediate perspective, the jury must recognize the partial perspective of each observer. * * * [N]o observer has an ideal position from which to offer a perspective-free account of the underlying controversy. Instead, a final account can be reached only by receiving multiple reports and interpreting those reports within a framework that includes the exact position of each observer.

* * *

The dominant consideration is that all relevant information should be admitted so long as it is possible through the technique of cross examination or otherwise to place the information in its proper perspective. This is because the jury, in coming to a shared interpretation of the relevant evidence, is not simply weighing the credibility of witness accounts; it is instead performing the more complicated task of piecing together a fabric of observations and partial perspectives that begins to tell a coherent story about "what happened."

Wells, Tort Law as Corrective Justice: A Pragmatic Justification for Jury Adjudication, 88 Mich.L.Rev. 2348, 2403–04 (1990).

This catalogue of values may be more a theoretical possibility than a present reality, however. Moreover, these values must be measured in light of the values of Rule 1, which says that courts should strive to ensure that cases are determined in a way that is speedy and inexpensive as well as just. At least in complex cases, courts and commentators have increasingly doubted that trials have functioned effectively. This reaction has prompted the innovations to which we turn. As you consider these innovations, reflect on what might be lost if they were more widely adopted.

A. JUDICIAL MANAGEMENT OF THE TRIAL

In Chapter VI, we saw that American judges have considerably expanded their supervision of pretrial activities in recent decades. See *supra* pp. 626-43. Regarding regulation of the conduct of the trial itself, expanded judicial authority dates from an earlier period:

> Just as judges in the late twentieth century enhanced their control of the pretrial process, so too did nineteenth-century judges enhance their power over trial practice. If American judges at the time of the Founding played a more passive role in litigation than their English counterparts, the American judiciary bolstered its power dramatically over the century that followed. In part because of growing concerns that juries could not be trusted to do justice without guidance from judges, and in part because of changes in the legal profession that yielded an ever greater number of upstart lawyers who "elevated emotional intensity over intellect or traditional doctrinal authority" and actively sought to play upon juror emotion and confusion, judges felt a need to exert a greater influence over the trial process.

Molot, An Old Judicial Role for a New Litigation Era, 113 Yale L.J. 27, 77–78 (2003). Thus, the nineteenth century saw the growth of judicial regulation of admission of evidence, and the increasing recognition that the court could direct a verdict or, in some cases, grant summary judgment without a trial.

Against that background, the judicial management movement extended the judge's control over the trial into the pretrial period. Building on the pretrial conferences to manage pretrial activities, judges have come to rely increasingly on the final pretrial conference under Rule 16(d) as a method of resolving in advance issues that formerly would be addressed at trial. Rule 26(a)(3) requires the parties to disclose some information about their evidence at trial. In class actions, early judicial attention to the manner of trial may be important in making the class-certification decision. "An increasing number of courts require a party requesting class certification to present a 'trial plan' that describes the issues likely to be presented at trial and tests whether they are susceptible to class-wide proof." Committee Note to Rule 23(c)(1) amendment (2003).

Local rules often require pretrial statements for final pretrial conferences to include much more. In the Northern District of California, for example, a local rule requires lead counsel to meet and confer at least 30 days before the final pretrial conference to discuss a variety of matters in anticipation of preparing a *joint* pretrial statement to be submitted before the Rule 16(d) conference. This pretrial statement must cover a wide range of topics: (1) a "plain and concise statement" of all undisputed facts and of all disputed factual issues; (2) a "concise statement of each disputed point of law," along with citation to briefs setting forth each party's contentions on that legal point; (3) lists of all witnesses likely to be called and of all items to be offered as exhibits. N.D.Cal. L.R. 16–15. In addition, local rules require the filing before trial of all requested voir dire questions and proposed forms of verdict in jury trials, and proposed findings of fact and conclusions of law in bench trials. The pretrial statement must also address settlement negotiations and the possibility of bifurcation of the trial.

Satisfying such requirements requires a lot of work, and may call for compromises to satisfy the judge. As recognized by a former Chief Judge of the Northern District of California, this aspect of judicial management of litigation is "the phase that the bar finds most objectionable." Peckham, The Federal Judge as Case Manager: The New Role in Guiding a Case From Filing to Disposition, 69 Cal.L.Rev. 770, 785 (1981). Moreover, it is "indisputably not as productive in proportion to the amount of preparation required as is the status conference." Id. But the stakes are high. (id. at 787):

> I regard the pretrial order as fully binding on the parties. If an attorney can show that he entered into an agreement or waiver by honest mistake, and that there will be no possible prejudice to the other side, I may allow deviations from the pretrial order, but generally I believe that strict enforcement of pretrial orders is essential to maintaining effective pretrial procedures. If pretrial orders are not strictly enforced, their purposes are often frustrated: orders that are not enforced will usually have wasted rather than saved time and expense.

Notes and Questions

1. How much of the lawyers' work that is required by pretrial judicial management should be done anyway? Should judges insist that lawyers who would not otherwise do this "homework" prepare adequately? Should this effort be required even if settlement appears likely?

2. Lawyers criticize extensive pretrial order requirements on the ground they resemble code and common law pleading systems. These systems insisted on highly detailed statements of the grounds for a suit, often resulting in decision on a point of pleading rather than the merits of the case. Is judicial insistence on detailed pretrial preparation by the lawyers comparable? Consider that the final pretrial process occurs only after discovery has been completed, and at a time when lawyers should be making strategic choices about which issues and evidence to emphasize.

In some instances, appellate courts have concluded that the effort involved in preparing pretrial orders has gotten out of hand. For example, in McCargo v. Hedrick, 545 F.2d 393 (4th Cir.1976), the trial court's local rule on joint pretrial statements filled eleven single-spaced pages. After completing the 120–day discovery period allowed in the case, counsel for both sides began a 16–month effort to prepare a pretrial statement that satisfied the rule, only to have each version rejected as inadequate. Eventually the district court dismissed for failure to comply with the local rule and the appellate court reversed, noting that "[t]he facts of this case illustrate the burden put upon litigants and their counsel by a pretrial procedure that appears to have become an end in itself." Id. at 396.

3.   How easily can the court identify issues on which it should press for stipulations or agreements? How hard should it push to obtain such agreements? Consider the attitude of another well-known judge from the Northern District of California: "[L]awyers, if permitted, will try every issue, present every witness and offer every exhibit that might possibly persuade a jury to return a verdict in their favor. Understandably, lawyers do not take chances. That is no reason, however, why judges should not take active part in the pretrial process." Schwarzer, Reforming Jury Trials, 132 F.R.D. 575, 577 (1991).

Contrast the views of Judge Charles Clark, who drafted the original Rule 16 as promulgated in 1938:

> [Rule 16] calls for a *conference* of counsel with the court to *prepare* for, not avert, trial, leading to an order which shall recite the "agreements made by the parties as to any of the matters considered." * * * Nothing in the rule affords a basis for clubbing the parties into admissions they do not willingly make; but it is a way of advancing the trial ultimately to be had by setting forth the points on which the parties are agreed after a conference with a trained judge.

Padovani v. Bruchhausen, 293 F.2d 546, 548 (2d Cir.1961). Is this attitude a relic of a bygone era?

4.   Before courts began to require thorough pretrial orders, some of the matters considered in that process could be raised by motions in limine. These motions seek rulings in advance of trial on the admissibility of specific items of evidence or on legal issues expected to arise during the trial. Traditionally, American judges have hesitated to make such rulings until trial for a variety of reasons including the belief that evidentiary rulings should be made in the context of all the evidence and not in a vacuum, the belief that a trial should be unrehearsed and spontaneous, and the desire not to commit the time necessary to decide the motions in cases that will settle before trial. Have these considerations lost their former force?

5.   Would lawyers prepare differently for trial if judges did not impose demanding final pretrial order requirements on them? At least in complex cases, it may be essential for lawyers to be concrete about what they will use at trial in order to be able to present the case. Consider another experienced judge's description of "dolly cases":

> Such characterization conjures up the all-too-familiar image of lawyers and paralegals lugging dollies loaded with boxes of documents into the courthouse. The image also, unfortunately, includes the frantic search through these boxes to retrieve a document for use on direct or cross-examination. A typical "dolly case" is interspersed with dozens of "I'm sorry, your Honor, we're trying to locate the exhibit," while the jury, witnesses, counsel, and court wait. All too often the lawyer abandons the

search and proceeds without benefit of the document "in the interest of time."

Parker, Streamlining Complex Cases, 10 Rev.Lit. 547, 548–49 (1991). In this vein, note that a study conducted in the 1960's concluded that pretrial conferences did not accelerate the disposition of litigation, but that they did increase the chance that the case would be well-presented and also eliminated inefficiencies at trial. See M. Rosenberg, The Pretrial Conference and Effective Justice (1964).

6. Once the pretrial order is entered, how readily should the court permit deviations or additions at trial? Note that Rule 16(e) permits changes in the final pretrial order "only to prevent manifest injustice." Contrast Rule 15(b), which allows amendment of the pleadings to conform to trial "freely when the presentation of the merits will be subserved thereby." Many courts, like Judge Peckham, firmly resist changes in final pretrial orders. "Unless pretrial orders are honored and enforced, the objectives of the pretrial conference to simplify issues and avoid unnecessary proof by obtaining admissions of fact will be jeopardized if not entirely nullified. * * * Disregard of these principles would bring back the days of trial by ambush and discourage timely preparation by the parties for trial." United States v. First National Bank of Circle, 652 F.2d 882, 886 (9th Cir.1981).

When the pretrial order lists witnesses and evidence, resistance to changing it may cause the court to refuse to accept relevant evidence. Surprise expert witnesses may be particularly unwelcome. On a related issue, the Supreme Court upheld the conviction of a criminal defendant who had been denied the right to present a witness not listed in pretrial discovery. Defendant claimed that the exclusion of this witness violated his rights under the Compulsory Process clause of the Sixth Amendment, but the Court disagreed, stressing the need for notice to permit the opposing party to meet the new evidence: "The adversary process could not function effectively without adherence to rules of procedure that govern the orderly presentation of facts and arguments to provide each party with a fair opportunity to assemble and submit evidence to contradict or explain the opponent's case." Taylor v. Illinois, 484 U.S. 400, 108 S.Ct. 646, 98 L.Ed.2d 798 (1988).

7. With these general considerations about the judge's role in designing the trial in mind, we turn to specific actions the court may take in complex cases.

B. STRIKING JURY DEMANDS

The Seventh Amendment provides that "In Suits at common law * * * the right of trial by jury shall be preserved." As you may have learned in introductory civil procedure, the customary debate about whether there is a right to jury trial has focused on whether an issue should be characterized as "legal" or "equitable" and relied heavily on historical materials. In 1970, however, the Supreme Court suggested an expanded inquiry in its famous footnote 10 in Ross v. Bernhard, 396 U.S. 531, 90 S.Ct. 733, 24 L.Ed.2d 729 (1970), which stated that the right to jury trial "is determined by considering, first, the pre-merger custom with reference to such questions; second, the remedy sought; and third, the practical abilities and limitations of juries." During the 1970s, defendants seized upon the third prong to argue against jury trials in complex cases and persuaded some judges. As the court put it in one such case, "at some point, it must be recognized that the complexity of a case may exceed the ability of a jury to decide the facts in an informed and capable manner." In re Boise Cascade Securities Litigation, 420 F.Supp. 99, 104 (W.D.Wash.1976).

Since *Ross,* there has been disagreement among the lower courts as to whether there is a "complexity exception" to the Seventh Amendment. The Third Circuit, in In re Japanese Electronic Products Antitrust Litigation, 631 F.2d 1069 (3d Cir.1980), an immense antitrust case, held that the Seventh Amendment right to jury trial may be outweighed by the requirements of Fifth Amendment due process if a jury would not be able to render a rational decision with a reasonable understanding of the evidence and legal standards. It reasoned:

> Any assessment of a jury's ability to decide complex cases should include consideration not only of a jury's particular strengths and the possible enhancement of its capabilities but also of the particular constraints that operate on a jury in complex cases. The long time periods required for most complex cases are especially disabling for a jury. A long trial can interrupt the career and personal life of a jury member and thereby strain his commitment to the jury's task. The prospect of a long trial can also weed out many veniremen whose professional backgrounds qualify them for deciding a complex case but also prohibits them from lengthy jury service. Furthermore, a jury is likely to be unfamiliar with both the technical subject matter of a complex case and the process of civil litigation. The probability is not remote that a jury will become overwhelmed and confused by a mass of evidence and issues and will reach erroneous decisions. The reality of these difficulties that juries encounter in complex cases is underscored by the experience of some federal district judges who have found particular suits to have exceeded the practical abilities of a jury.

* * *

> A general presumption that a judge is capable of deciding an extraordinarily complex case, by contrast, is reasonable. A long trial would not greatly disrupt the professional and personal life of a judge and should not be significantly disabling. In fact, the judge's greater ability to allocate time to the task of deciding a complex case can be a major advantage in surmounting the difficulties posed by the suit. Although we cannot presume that a judge will be more intelligent than a jury or more familiar with technical subject matters, a judge will almost surely have substantial familiarity with the process of civil litigation, as a result of experience on the bench or in practice. This experience can enable him to digest a large

amount of evidence and legal argument, segregate distinct issues and the portions of evidence relevant to each issue, assess the opinions of expert witnesses, and apply highly complex legal standards to the facts of the case. The judge's experience also can enable him to make better use of special trial techniques designed to help the factfinder in complex cases, like colloquies with expert witnesses. The requirement that a judge issue findings of fact and conclusions of law offsets the substantial tendency to overlook issues in order that a verdict might be reached in these difficult cases. Fed.R.Civ.P. 52(a). Finally, if after trial and during deliberation a judge finds himself confused on certain matters or unable to decide certain issues, he can reopen the trial for the purpose of obtaining clarification or additional evidence. Fed.R.Civ.P. 59(a).

Given these relative abilities, the Third Circuit resolved the balance between due process and right to jury trial as follows:

The due process objections to jury trial of a complex case implicate values of fundamental importance. If judicial decisions are not based on factual determinations bearing some reliable degree of accuracy, legal remedies will not be applied consistently with the purposes of the laws. There is a danger that jury verdicts will be erratic and completely unpredictable, which would be inconsistent with evenhanded justice. Finally, unless the jury can understand the evidence and the legal rules sufficiently to rest its decision on them, the objective of most rules of evidence and procedure in promoting a fair trial will be lost entirely. We believe that when a jury is unable to perform its decisionmaking task with a reasonable understanding of the evidence and legal rules, it undermines the ability of a district court to render basic justice.

* * *

Therefore, we find the most reasonable accommodation between the requirements of the fifth and seventh amendments to be a denial of jury trial when a jury will not be able to perform its task of rational decisionmaking with a reasonable understanding of the evidence and the relevant legal standards. In lawsuits of this complexity, the interests protected by this procedural rule of due process carry greater weight than the interests served by the constitutional guarantee of jury trial. Consequently, we shall not read the seventh amendment to guarantee the right to jury trial in these suits.

Presented with essentially the same due process arguments in a massive securities case, In re U.S. Financial Securities Litigation, 609 F.2d 411 (9th Cir.1979), cert. denied 446 U.S. 929, 100 S.Ct. 1866, 64 L.Ed.2d 281 (1980), the Ninth Circuit rejected any attempt to limit the right to jury trial:

Many cases appear overwhelmingly complicated in their early stages. Nevertheless, by the time such cases go to trial, what had initially appeared as an impossible array of facts and issues has been synthesized in a coherent theory by the efforts of counsel. Moreover, in answering the Seventh Amendment question, courts should take into consideration the various procedural developments which serve to simplify and facilitate the trial of a "complex" case to a jury.

The assumption that attorneys cannot develop and present complex cases to a jury underestimates the abilities of the bar, especially the experienced and capable counsel associated with the present litigation. Whether a case is tried to a jury or to a judge, the task of the attorney remains the same. The attorney must organize and assemble a complex mass of information into a form which is understandable to the uninitiated. In fact, one judge has suggested attorneys may do a better job of trying complex cases to a jury than to a judge.

Also, the trial judge has the power and the authority to control, manage and direct the course of complex cases. The Federal Judicial Center developed the *Manual for Complex Litigation* for just such cases. The *Manual* is designed to provide for the fair, firm, and efficient judicial control of complex litigation. A district judge is not left in the position of a captain whose ship, lacking a rudder and throttle, proceeds at its own speed in its own direction. Instead, the Manual encourages and provides suggestions as to how the district judge should exercise control over the parties and give the case direction.

Notes and Questions

1. There is little empirical information on the ability of a jury to handle a complex case. For an argument that methods exist to develop such information, see Lempert, Civil Juries and Complex Cases: Let's Not Rush to Judgment, 80 Mich.L.Rev. 68 (1981). Professor Lempert suggested four methods: (1) Review of existing records of complex cases to devise strategies to simplify them; (2) Interviewing judges and jurors who have been involved in such cases; (3) Using "shadow juries" consisting of persons eligible for jury duty but not serving, and interviewing them; (4) Simulation of trials of complex cases combined with tests to measure comprehension.

At least some research of this sort has occurred. See Jury Comprehension in Complex Cases (ABA 1989) (special committee of ABA Section of Litigation studied deliberations of alternate jurors and interviewed jurors in four complex cases). Heuer & Penrod, Trial Complexity, 18 Law & Human Behav. 29 (1994), attempted to identify aspects of complexity in litigation and, on the basis of 160 civil and criminal trials, to assess the effects of complexity on jury action. The results were ambivalent. Although an increased quantity of information or complexity of evidence caused jurors difficulty in reaching decisions, increased complexity of the evidence also made them more confident they were well informed by the trial. See id. at 41–42. Assessing whether that confidence is warranted is, of course, a different question, but the study showed that trial complexity did not correlate to whether the judge and the jury agreed about the outcome. Id. at

48. Should further action on the right to jury trial in complex cases be deferred until more research has been done?

2. In ILC Peripherals Leasing Corp. v. IBM Corp., 458 F.Supp. 423 (N.D.Cal.1978), IBM was sued for $300 million for monopolization of a segment of the computer market. After a five-month trial, the jury reported itself unable to agree on a verdict. The judge questioned the jurors about some of the technical aspects of the case:

The Court:	... Do you know what demand substitutability is, [Juror A]?
Juror [A]:	Well, I would like to kind of look into that.
The Court:	Okay. And how about the barrier to entry, [Juror B]?
Juror [B]:	I would have to read about it.
The Court:	And how about F.T.P., [Juror C]?
Juror [C]:	That's fixed term plan.
The Court:	And you understand the ramifications of that, do you think?
Juror [C]:	Yes, your honor.
The Court:	All right. And how about reverse engineering? [Reverse engineering is a method of copying a competitor's product.]
Juror [C]:	That's when you would take a product and you would alter it in a, or modify it for your own purpose; that is, you would reverse its function and use it in your own method.
The Court:	And [Juror D], what is software?
Juror [D]:	It's software.
The Court:	Well, what is software?
Juror [D]:	That's the paper software.
The Court:	What's the hardware?
Juror [D]:	That's the wires and hardware.
The Court:	And what is—do you know what an interface is? [An interface is the connection between a computer and an auxiliary piece of equipment.]
Juror [D]:	Yes.
The Court:	What's that?
Juror [D]:	The interface is the—I am not good in English, your honor.
The Court:	No, that's all right.
Juror [D]:	But it's the interface, you know.
The Court:	Can you give me an example of that?
Juror [D]:	Well, if you take a blivet, turn it off one thing and drop it down, it's an interface change; right?

Quoted in Note, The Right to a Jury Trial in Complex Civil Litigation, 92 Harv.L.Rev. 898, 908 n. 60 (1979).

After the jury had deadlocked in *ILC Peripherals,* the judge granted IBM's motion for a directed verdict. In addition, he struck the jury demand in the event that the appellate court granted a retrial, explaining his decision as follows (458 F.Supp. at 447):

Throughout the trial, the court felt that the jury was having trouble grasping the concepts that were being discussed by the expert witnesses, most of whom had doctorate degrees in their specialties. This perception was confirmed when the court questioned the jurors during the course of their deliberations and after they were discharged. When asked by the court whether a case of this type should be tried to a jury, the foreman of the jury said, "If you can find a jury that's both a computer technician, a lawyer, an economist, knows all about that stuff, yes, I think you could have a qualified jury, but we don't know anything about that."

Would a 21st century jury have similar problems understanding computer terms and operations?

Concern about juror confusion shifted in the 1980s and 1990s from cases involving technology and voluminous business information to issues of science. Many question the ability of jurors in product liability cases to evaluate novel scientific theories often offered on issues of causation. Some contend that the majority of Americans lack basic understanding of science and the scientific method, and that this ignorance among jurors causes them to accept pseudo science that has no support in valid scientific work. See, e.g., Huber, Junk Science and the Jury, 1990 U.Chi.Legal Forum 273.

3. Short of striking the jury altogether, courts might foster use of more knowledgeable jurors for cases involving especially difficult issues. See Note, A More Rational Approach to Complex Civil Litigation in the Federal Courts: The Special Jury, 1990 U.Chi.Legal Forum 575. How should courts identify cases suited to this special treatment?

4. Does the power of the judge to grant judgment as a matter of law under Rule 50 protect against jury incompetence? Should a court presented with such a motion interrogate the jury as the judge did in *ILC Peripherals* (*supra* note 2)? Federal Rule of Evidence 606 states that, where the validity of the verdict is in question, "a juror may not testify . . . concerning the juror's mental processes in connection" with the verdict. Doesn't this rule preclude the sort of inquiry made by the court in *ILC Peripherals* when a J.N.O.V. motion is made? How then can the judge assess the jury's understanding of the case?

5. How good are judges at deciding complicated or technical cases? They have no greater expertise in a variety of a technical matters than many jurors. Indeed, there are some who assert that in patent cases, for example, district judges often are unable to understand the technical issues involved.

6. Does having the judge try the case raise other problems? If the judge is the fact-finder, isn't it more important to scrutinize her potential bias? Wouldn't there be a greater incentive for judge shopping? After taking an active role in case management, isn't it likely that she will develop some foretaste of the issues that is inconsistent with our notion that a verdict should be based on the evidence presented at trial, and not the prejudices of the fact-finder?

7. In *Japanese Electronics*, defendants relied in part on 17th and 18th century English cases. They argued that in England in 1791, the chancellor controlled the boundary between law and equity and could exercise jurisdiction when the procedures at law, including the abilities of a jury, were inadequate to do justice. The Third Circuit noted that "we are aware of no federal court decision that employs history in this manner" although "many have determined the legal or equitable nature of a suit by comparing it with suits actually tried in courts of common law or equity." It "chose not to pioneer in this use of history," relying instead upon its conclusion that due process could override the right to jury trial. Do 18th century precedents provide useful guidance at the end of the 21st century? Don't many of the

complexities of litigation now result from joinder and other procedural mechanisms that did not exist then? Can other procedural mechanisms be used to ameliorate the difficulties posed by these procedural innovations? Keep this question in mind as you consider the other techniques examined in this chapter.

8. The viability of reliance on the jury competence factor of Ross v. Bernhard's famous footnote 10 is questionable. The Supreme Court itself has observed that "the Court has not used these considerations [of the practical limitations of jurors] as an independent basis for extending the right to a jury trial under the Seventh Amendment." Tull v. United States, 481 U.S. 412, 418 n. 4, 107 S.Ct. 1831, 1835 n. 4, 95 L.Ed.2d 365 (1987); see Leach v. Pan American World Airways, 842 F.2d 285 (11th Cir.1988) (questioning "whether the third tenet of *Ross* retains any vitality in light of the fact that the Supreme Court has several times considered the right to a jury trial without analyzing or even mentioning the third factor"). The lower courts, meanwhile, have not actually used this factor as a ground for denial of a jury trial in complex cases. See, e.g., Rieff v. Evans, 672 N.W.2d 728 (Iowa S.Ct.2003) (declining to find a complex litigation exception to the right to jury trial).

C. IMPROVED TRIAL METHODS

A variety of techniques can be used to improve the trial, in somewhat overlapping ways. Particularly in jury trials, these methods may overcome problems that would otherwise cause concerns about the ability of the jury to understand the issues presented and render a responsible decision. We begin with an experienced judge's exhortation.

SCHWARZER, REFORMING JURY TRIALS
132 F.R.D. 575, 575–76; 588–90 (1991).

Do juries understand cases sufficiently to be able to decide them intelligently? The increasing complexity of modern litigation has raised the concern that often they do not. The jury system developed at a time when the issues that came before jurors were generally within their common experience. For the most part, these issues revolved around credibility and reasonableness of behavior. That, of course, is no longer true. Jurors must now render verdicts on complex and technical issues arising under securities, environmental, patent, product liability, antitrust, and other laws in cases that are often lengthy and involve vast amounts of complicated evidence.

The challenge today is how to make these cases understandable to jurors. Much of their complexity is the product of lawyers' work—excessive discovery and proliferation of evidence and issues—and judges' passivity and permissiveness. And much of the difficulty they present to jurors flows from the way they are tried.

* * *

Although much has been written and said about how to try cases effectively to juries, the fundamental truth is often overlooked: a trial is an exercise in education. The most effective advocacy is not a slashing argument but a clear and well-organized exposition of the facts. Yet lawyers allow their preoccupation with the adversary process to get in the way of their teaching function.

The presentation of evidence should serve to teach the jury, especially in complex cases. A number of techniques have proven effective. * * *

Much evidence becomes more comprehensible when presented with visual aids, such as a chart summarizing data, a chronology, an enlarged picture of an object, a diagram of a building, or a map. Juror surveys have shown that charts and diagrams have a powerful impact. In one survey, 92 percent of jurors said they were a major (50 percent) or at least a minor (42 percent) factor in their decision. Diagrams, models or videotapes make testimony about a physical object more meaningful and less time-consuming. Videotapes are particularly effective because jurors are accustomed to acquiring information from the television screen and thus react favorably to video presentations. Occasionally, lawyers may want, with the court's consent, to use visual aids for demonstration only without offering them as exhibits.

When the subject matter is technical, a tutorial before the trial for both jurors and the judge can be very helpful. * * * Experts acceptable to the parties make the presentation, which is sufficiently basic to be non-controversial.

A mix of methods can be used to help jurors organize and remember the evidence. The court should take advantage of Federal Rule of Evidence 1006, which permits the use of summaries to present the contents of voluminous writings. The underlying evidence on which the summary is based need not be received into evidence, so long as it is made available to the opponent. Jurors should have access to exhibits while witnesses are testifying about them. Overhead projectors or juror notebooks can serve this purpose. Loose-leaf notebooks, provided by the court, may include, in addition to copies of key exhibits, fact stipulations, the preliminary instructions, chronologies or time line charts, lists of witnesses, a glossary of technical terms, and other relevant items. Mounting pictures of each witness, as he or she testifies, on a poster board in the courtroom or jury room, will also help jurors remember testimony.

These are some of the techniques for improving the presentation of evidence in complex cases. While their use is the lawyers' responsibility, the judge should encourage it to enhance jury comprehension and expedite the trial. At the same time, the judge should urge the lawyers to avoid techniques having the opposite effect. Reading depositions is a prime example: Few courtroom activities are less informative and more boring to jurors, who constantly complain about it in post-trial interviews. While occasionally a particular snippet of verbatim testimony can be important, for the most part the information in depositions can be presented in summaries. Often counsel will arrive at summaries by stipulation, especially when encouraged by the court. In a major antitrust case recently tried, the court required each side to submit, in advance of trial, summaries of deposition testimony it proposed to use. The opponent could object and submit counter-summaries. Differences the parties were unable to resolve were then submitted to the judge or magistrate for decision before trial.

Another perennial problem is that the volume of exhibits may overwhelm the jurors during deliberations. Common sense should tell us that jurors will not know what to do with exhibits during deliberations if they comprise thousands of pages. Should each juror read all of them? Should some read all? Should each read only arbitrarily selected excerpts? Lawyers should not offer, and the judge should not receive, more written material than any juror could read and absorb within an hour or two. For what is the point of exhibits jurors will not read? Instead, summaries and excerpts should be used as much as possible, and for those exhibits that must be received in their entirety, jurors should be given finding aids to help them locate what they need during deliberations.

———

Judge Schwarzer's discussion touches on a number of methods for improving jury trials. Before turning to some specifics, note that many of these simplification techniques could profitably be used in court trials as well.

1. JURY "EMPOWERMENT"

Empowerment is a term used in a variety of contexts where there is a desire to give people involved in a process a feeling of involvement and control. The traditional trial format did little to empower the jurors. Designed by lawyers and judges, the format required the jurors to remain passive and observe, without even the outlet of discussing the case among themselves until deliberations began. Many courts have broken with some of these traditions in a number of areas:

Instructions: Whatever their other talents, jurors do not begin a case with an understanding of the law that should be applied. Because some grounding in the applicable legal principles can be helpful to the jurors in focusing on the important parts of the evidence, judges may begin the trial with preinstructions on the area of law that will be involved in the case. In 1995, the Arizona Supreme Court directed that jurors be given oral and written preliminary instructions. See Dann & Logan, Jury Reform: The Arizona Experience, 79 Judicature 280, 281 (1996) ("In complex or technical cases, [preliminary instructions should include] definitions of terms and other information that would help orient the jury to the case."); see also Manual for Complex Litigation (4th) § 12.432 (2004) (providing suggestions about preliminary instructions).

Likewise, judges have long made efforts to simplify instructions, particularly in complicated areas of the law, to assist the jury in understanding the law. "[T]he object of a charge to a jury is not to satisfy an appellate court that you have repeated the right rigmarole of words, but to try to make jurors who are laymen understand what you are talking about." Cape Cod Food Products v. National Cranberry Association, 119 F.Supp. 900, 907 (D.Mass.1954). For similar reasons, "[m]ost judges give jurors copies of the instructions to use during deliberations." Manual for Complex Litigation (4th) § 12.434 (2004).

Note-taking: Most law students take notes in class as an aid to recalling points made. Note-taking may also help to focus attention on key points because it involves selectivity, which in turn may prompt jurors to sift through evidence in choosing the items to record.

Juror notebooks: Jurors can be supplied with notebooks containing key documents and/or pictures of witnesses (if they are numerous). This may focus their attention on the pertinent portions of the documentary evidence while they are being discussed by the witnesses, and assist the jurors in remembering the testimony during their deliberations.

Juror questioning of witnesses: Traditionally, except for occasional questions from the judge, only the lawyers asked questions. Some courts have begun to allow jurors to ask questions, although usually only by writing them out and having the judge screen them. This technique is intended to ensure that the jury clears up basic misunderstandings about the case that might otherwise go unrepaired and, perhaps, to enable the jury to unearth evidence overlooked by the lawyers.

Interim argument: In lengthy trials, some courts will allow the lawyers to make interim arguments during the presentation of evidence to explain how the pieces of evidence fit together or to emphasize their view about the importance or believability of given pieces of evidence.

Juror discussion of evidence: Customarily jurors are told at the outset of the trial that they may not discuss the evidence with anyone until the end of the trial. This admonition has long been thought unrealistic, and particularly so in long, complex cases. In 1995, Arizona authorized such discussions in civil cases, provided that they occur in the jury room when all jurors are present. See Az. R. Civ. P. 39(f). Hannaford, Hans & Munsterman, Permitting Jury Discussions During Trial: Impact of the Arizona Reform, 24 Law & Human Behav. 359 (2000), reports on a study of this innovation, comparing cases in which the jurors were told that this practice was permitted with others that did not. Although jurors liked being able to discuss the case while the trial was ongoing, it was not clear that their understanding was measurably enhanced by this activity. Discussions did lessen the degree of uncertainty jurors felt about the result they favored before deliberations began. See also Vidmar, Juror Discussion During Civil Trials: Studying an Arizona Innovation, 45 Az. L. Rev. 1 (2003); Hannaford, "Speaking Rights": Evaluating Juror Discussions During Civil Trials, 85 Judicature 237 (2002).

Notes and Questions

1. Are these modifications of the traditional trial format more reasonable reactions to problems of jury understanding than striking jury demands on grounds of complexity? Used with care, should they solve the problem of jury understanding?

2. Jury "empowerment" may be an important way of furthering the goals of the Seventh Amendment. Professor Friedland has argued, for example, that the jury is "an essential political institution:"

> A more active jury model maintains this democratic tradition of citizen participation. Furthermore, if an active jury model improves the accuracy of the decisionmaking process and enhances the credibility of the jury, it also strengthens the conceptual legitimacy of the verdict. Similarly, even if the active model improves only the perception of the jury as an able decisionmaker, it still would enhance public confidence in the decisionmaking process.

> In addition to its representative role within a democratic system, the jury serves "as a check upon the judge's power in each case." [Higginbotham, Continuing the Dialogue: Civil Juries and the Allocation of Judicial Power, 56 Texas L.Rev. 47, 58 (1977).] This limitation on the judicial branch enhances the tripartite division of government set forth in the Constitution. The jury, as well as the judges who review lower court decisions on appeal, prevent the trial judge from becoming the equivalent of a benevolent despot. It is precisely the symbolism associated with the jury's role that is so significant to the legitimacy of a trial by jury. In essence, according the jury a greater voice during trial reallocates the division of power, providing a symbolic and perhaps even an actual check on the court. The symbolism of juror participation strengthens the conceptualization of the jury as the representative of the people.

> An expanded jury role reallocates the symbolic division of power in at least one other significant respect. Lawyers usually are afforded primary control over the evidence offered at trial, the strategy by which the case is tried, and the questions asked of the witnesses. * * * A more active jury tends to oppose this considerable power of the trial lawyer.

Friedland, The Competency and Responsibility of Jurors in Deciding Cases, 85 Nw.L.Rev. 190, 207–08 (1990). In the context of increased judicial control of all aspects of litigation, including the trial, are these points valid?

3. Many of these techniques may seem unexceptional, but that does not mean that they are risk free. Regarding juror note-taking, for example, consider the comments of Judge Jack Weinstein, who often is in the forefront of innovation in handling complex litigation: "This solution too has serious problems. Notetakers may miss some of what is going on in the courtroom, and the notes of one juror may tend to have too much weight in deliberations; they may well overemphasize some points." Weinstein, The Power and Duty of Federal Judges to Marshall and Comment on the Evidence in Jury Trials and Some Suggestions on Charging Juries, 118 F.R.D. 161, 168 (1988). But a 1994 study indicated that note-taking did not produce a distorted view of the case, although it also did not show that note

taking aided memory or increased satisfaction. Heuer & Penrod, Juror Notetaking and Question Asking During Trials, 18 Law & Human Behav. 121 (1994). The Manual for Complex Litigation (4th) § 12.421 (2004) notes that "[a]rguments for juror notetaking are particularly compelling in long and complicated trials."

Similarly, many have been troubled by allowing jurors to ask questions. Objections include the risk that jurors will become partisan, that they will react negatively when their questions are not asked due to objections by one of the parties, or that they might disrupt the orderly presentation of the trial. Empirical investigation, however, indicates that the feared problems do not arise in either simple or complex litigation. See Heuer & Penrod, Trial Lawyers in the Box, The Docket 4 (Fall 1988). Capello & Strenio, Jury Questioning: The Verdict Is In, Trial, June 2000, at 44, reports growing acceptance of juror questioning in state courts, with only Mississippi completely forbidding the practice. See also United States v. Richardson, 233 F.3d 1285 (11th Cir.2000); United States v. Hernandez, 176 F.3d 719 (3d Cir.1999); compare United States v. Collins, 226 F.3d 457 (6th Cir.2000) ("the routine practice of juror questioning should be discouraged," and it should be a "rare practice").

Given such concerns, innovative techniques may be limited to complex cases. Thus, judges involved in experimental use of note-taking by jurors in the Second Circuit indicated that "the benefits of note taking increase in proportion to the length and complexity of the trial." Sand & Reiss, A Report on Seven Experiments Conducted by District Court Judges in the Second Circuit, 60 N.Y.U.L.Rev. 423, 450 (1985).

4. An empirical assessment of use of techniques for improving juror performance indicated that they had differing effectiveness. Allowing juror questions and using a detailed verdict form consistently were beneficial from jurors' perspectives, but notetaking, judges' comments on the evidence and pattern instructions were not. As evidence complexity increased, juror confidence went up if juror questioning was allowed, and it went down if questioning was not allowed. Heuer & Penrod, Trial Complexity, 18 Law & Human Behav. 29 (1994).

5. For a general review and assessment of such efforts at improving juror performance, see Hannaford & Munsterman, Beyond Note Taking, Innovations in Jury Reform, Trial, July 1997, at 48.

2. USE OF TECHNOLOGY

In many ways, technology has transformed the pretrial handling of litigation, as it has transformed many other aspects of life and business. Increasingly, some of the possibilities of technology have been employed in trials.

———

BUXTON & GLOVER, MANAGING A BIG CASE DOWN TO SIZE, 15 Litigation 22, 22–23 (Summer 1989):

[The authors served as counsel for plaintiff in ETSI Pipeline Project v. Burlington Northern, Inc., No. B–84–979–CA (E.D.Tex.), which is also the case described in the next excerpt. They describe the innovative trial procedures used by the court.]

The most dramatic of the innovative procedures was the video presentation of deposition testimony at trial. Videotaped depositions themselves are not unusual, but the manner and extent of their use in this case seem unprecedented. The court gave the parties wide latitude in editing and rearranging deposition testimony, allowing interspersal of narrated lawyer summaries with the excerpts of testimony. The result was a presentation that closely resembled a television documentary or news report.

Here is how it went: Because most of the witnesses were beyond the subpoena power of the court, both sides videotaped depositions. Of the 52 trial witnesses for the plaintiffs, 32 testified by videotape deposition. Thus, when the president of one of the defendant railroads testified at trial about a meeting that ultimately led to the formation of the alleged conspiracy, he did so by deposition—but in living color on a eight-foot-square video screen. What the jury saw was the creation of a production studio, and not merely the playback of a tape made in the deposition room. Included with the deposition excerpts on the videotape were narrative summaries of the deposition testimony by one of ETSI's lawyers.

Preparing such video summaries was time-consuming and demanding because of the visual production requirements and the procedures for advising the other side. The first step was to choose testimony that would be played for the jury. Well before trial, each side was required to notify the other of these selections. The excerpts, which might be as short as a single question and answer, or as long as several minutes, were then spliced together in a way that provided the most logical, effective presentation. There was no requirement that the deposition's original chronology be preserved. Interruptions, as well as repetitious or irrelevant material, were eliminated. Careful editing allowed rambling deposition transcripts to be transformed into cohesive trial testimony.

Selected testimonial excerpts were combined with summaries of other relevant testimony by that witness. These summaries served a variety of purposes, from providing background for the excerpts to explaining a complicated technical point. The only real limitation on combining testimonial excerpts and summaries was that the end product had to be fair and accurate—it could not distort the testimony by taking it out of context.

* * *

The use of deposition summaries and tightly edited videotape deposition excerpts was obviously more interesting for all concerned. It also saved a lot of time. In all, videotaped testimony of 33 witnesses was presented in segments lasting from a few minutes to four hours. Had the parties been forced to read depositions into the record, or even just to present all the background testimony in lieu of summaries, juror attention might have waned and evidentiary points might have been lost. The pace of the trial would have slowed to a crawl.

PARKER, STREAMLINING COMPLEX CASES, 10 Review of Litigation 547, 549 (1991):

[Judge Parker, who presided over the trial in the case described in the previous excerpt, explained how technology avoided the problem of the "dolly case," in which counsel cannot find the pertinent documents in the mountain of material developed in discovery. See *supra* p. 736 n. 5.]

Contrast the "dolly case" scene with that of the lawyer who can, using a simple bar-code scanner, instantly show the jury documents stored on a laser disk. Laser disk technology permits the storage of more than 50,000 pages of documents on a single twelve-inch disk. The disk also can store both the audio and video portions of depositions and computer-generated graphics in the form of traditional graphs and charts, as well as animated graphic presentations. Documents may be printed out in the courtroom or shown on monitors. This technology has random-access, freeze-frame, slow-motion, and enlargement capabilities. By using a bar-code notebook and a scanner, the lawyer has at his fingertips reliable, instantaneous document retrieval in a form that is also more effective as a method of communication.

In addition, expert witnesses can use computer-generated graphics as a powerful means of illustrating the subject matter of the testimony for the jury. Plaintiff's counsel in *ETSI Pipeline Project* used such technology to visually construct a spider-web illustration of an alleged antitrust conspiracy, and to cause a pipeline to snake its way from Wyoming to the Gulf Coast before the jury's eyes, thus indelibly imprinting plaintiff's basic theories of recovery on the minds of the jury.

McCRYSTAL & MASCHARI, WILL ELECTRONIC TECHNOLOGY TAKE THE WITNESS STAND?, 11 U.Tol.L.Rev. 239, 250–51 (1980):

[The authors, an Ohio state court judge and his law clerk, describe the use in Ohio state courts of the pre-recorded videotape trial (PRVTT), in which all testimony in simpler cases is recorded on videotape and played to the jury, with the only live presentations to the jury being the opening statements and closing arguments of the lawyers.]

Critics [of legal applications of the electronic media] continue to urge the McLuhanistic proposition that "the medium is the message," expressing fear that the videotape medium changes the message from that conveyed in a live proceeding. Years of experimentation have revealed, however, that jurors watching videotaped materials do not react any differently than those observing a live trial. Jurors render similar judgments without any significant difference in the magnitude of money awards. In addition, jurors' powers of perception and retention are not negatively affected by the videotape medium, rather such qualities become more acute as the trial progresses.

What of the theory that a witness' mannerisms may be as important as what he says—that the absence of non-verbal cues from the videotape trial may affect jurors' ability to judge the credibility of witnesses? Studies reveal that jurors, at best, are poor detectors of witness deception regardless of whether the testimony is live, taped, or read. Experiments have disclosed that in no instance do observers watching live testimony "outjudge" those viewing taped presentations, and surprisingly, the highest percentage of correct judgments as to credibility of witnesses occurs among observers *reading* written transcripts.

Jurors participating in a PRVTT are freed from the effects of many distracting and prejudicial tactics employed in a live trial which, while objectionable, are unavoidable. When videotaping testimony the camera is focused only on the witness box, filtering out extraneous movement and providing jurors with a less complex stimulus field. A juror's attention is not diverted by the bench conferences, the objections by—or comments between—counsel, the attorneys' charisma, the charged atmosphere of the courtroom, or the judge's demeanor, all of which may seriously affect a jury's decision-making process. In a pre-recorded trial the effects of such external factors are minimized.

The responses of jurors who have actually participated in pre-recorded videotape trials are of great significance. In response to the question, "If you were involved [as a litigant] in a civil case similar to the one in which you served, and you were offered the choice of a live or videotape trial, which would you choose?," over sixty percent of former jurors indicated they would select a PRVTT.

Notes and Questions

1. Obviously these writers are strong proponents of use of technological techniques to alter trial methods. But Fed.R.Civ.P. 43(a) still says that "[i]n every trial, the testimony of witnesses shall be taken in open court, unless a federal law, these rules, or other rules adopted by the Supreme Court provide otherwise."

Are such videotaped trials within the powers of federal judges? Consider District Judge Richey's description of his innovations in Richey, Rule 16 Revisited: Reflections For the Benefit of Bench and Bar, 139 F.R.D. 525, 535 (1992):

> In one recent medical malpractice case, I ordered, with the agreement of the parties, that all testimony can be taken on videotape. I then directed the parties, pursuant to a Rule 16 order, to file proposed findings of fact and conclusions of law, and to direct me, in their submissions, to the most crucial portions of the testimony taken. After the videotapes and requisite documents are submitted, I will view the videotapes and then hear oral argument from the parties. In this way, the parties can have a

resolution of their case much sooner than if they were forced to await a date on my overcrowded trial calendar.

Should the court pressure the parties to agree to this method? Considering the values that may be furthered by the traditional manner of trial, are there reasons for tempering enthusiasm for the new techniques?

If the "video trial" permitted jurors to view the videotape from their own home, there might be additional questions about the method. In Stine v. Marathon Oil Co., 976 F.2d 254 (5th Cir.1992), the district court directed that copies of excerpts of depositions be provided to the jurors rather than being read to them. Characterizing this as "evidence to go" or "take-out evidence," the court of appeals found that this practice raised undue problems:

> Such a practice requires the jury to spend time outside the courtroom, over and above a full day in the courtroom. The jury's reading of the deposition excerpts was thus totally outside the supervision of the trial judge. Indeed, the procedure followed incurs a real risk that the jurors merely took the excerpts home and brought them back the next day unread and, thus, reached a verdict without having considered all the evidence.

2. *Testimony via video conference*: Improvements in the operation of video conferencing open the possibility that witness testimony or party participation could be handled from a remote location without physical presence. This would not involve delayed conveyance of testimony to the jury, but would remove the in-court testimony that has been a hallmark of our legal system.

In Edwards v. Keen Mountain Correctional Officer Logan, 38 F.Supp.2d 463 (W.D.Va.1999), the court moved toward embracing the virtual trial as a cost-saving measure. Plaintiff was a prisoner who claimed a guard forced him into a fist fight with another guard while he was incarcerated in Virginia. Plaintiff had since been transferred to New Mexico and it would cost more than $8,000 to transport him back for trial. The court therefore ordered that the trial be conducted with plaintiff participating by video conferencing, whereby plaintiff "will be virtually present at his trial and will have the ability to confront witnesses, and participate fully." Although it recognized that "it is to be expected that the ability to observe demeanor, central to the fact-finding process, may be lessened in a particular case by video conferencing," the court thought the problem not great because the case was "relatively simple and straightforward." For further discussion of such ideas, see Carrington, Virtual Civil Litigation: A Visit to John Bunyan's Celestial City, 98 Colum. L. Rev. 1516, 1524–29 (1998) (discussing "virtual trials").

Nonparty witnesses might also testify by video transmission. In F.T.C. v. Swedish Match North America, Inc., 197 F.R.D. 1 (D.D.C.2000), the court permitted plaintiff to present a witness who resided in Oklahoma by live video feed during a hearing. The judge opined that there is no difference between live testimony and live video transmission. He also suggested that the Committee Notes accompanying Rule 43(a)'s requirement of live testimony "are more hostile than I am to live video transmission." See also Beltran–Tirado v. I.N.S., 213 F.3d 1179 (9th Cir.2000) (permitting use of telephonic testimony from out-of-state witness during an administrative hearing). For further discussion, see Manual for Complex Litigation (4th) § 12.334 (2004).

3. There is substantial psychological research indicating that people do a poor job of detecting deception from observing a person telling a lie, largely because they rely on facial expressions. Unfortunately, most people take behavior that merely indicates the speaker is nervous as indicating lying, while they commonly credit behaviors that are in fact indicia of lying—making eye contact, smiling less, and gesturing more—as signs of honesty. This credulity can be manipulated, and no doubt has been manipulated in court on occasion.

Although this research may provide a reason for changing rules such as the hearsay rule, see Wellborn, Demeanor, 76 Cornell L.Rev. 1075 (1991), it does not necessarily warrant abandonment of the traditional live trial. Instead, most of the research is done in significantly different contexts from a traditional trial. It does not call for collaborative decision-making, as does a jury trial, and does not involve subjects alert to the possibility of deception. In addition, it does not offer subjects the opportunity to compare competing versions of events, or to check the story they are told against physical or other evidence. See generally Marcus, Completing Equity's Conquest? Reflections on the Future of Trial Under the Federal Rules of Civil Procedure, 50 U.Pitt.L.Rev. 725, 761–62 (1989).

4. Judge McCrystal and his law clerk (later a judge of the same court) urged that videotaped trials avoid "the charged atmosphere of the courtroom." Is this a desirable thing? Contrast the following view, which considers a variety of alternative bases for decision including summary judgment:

> Live trials convey texture and intensity in a way that written materials probably cannot. As reading a play is a far different experience from seeing the play performed, so is reading a trial transcript qualitatively different from actually observing the trial. The written version would seem bloodless by contrast to a live version. Even a videotaped presentation of evidence would often lack significant emotive elements that live presentation offers; movies and television are not the same as legitimate theater. Here demeanor evidence—the array of sensory impressions about a person that are available to the decider who observes the live in-court trial—could make a difference in a way that matters, perhaps more than demeanor matters as a method of detecting lying. The experience of observing the trial as a live event would add an important dimension to the decision-making process.

* * *

As Professor Damaska explains, "A genuinely concentrated trial, even if well prepared, requires that decisions be based largely on fresh impressions, including surprise, shock, the spell of superficial rhetoric, and perhaps even theatrics." Should we try to drain off this emotion through alternative trial methods?

Removing the intuitive element of trials seems an undesirable idea. Our law is not a bloodless thing, to be administered mechanically through automatic application of clear rules. It is, instead, full of standards that look to the reasonable person, seemingly requiring a comprehensive understanding of the circumstances giving rise to the out-of-court event that precipitated the litigation. * * *

Actually observing the plaintiff, while testifying and otherwise, provides information that is important to the decision entirely apart from the question who is telling the truth.

Marcus, *supra,* 50 U.Pitt.L.Rev. at 762–63; 766; 768.

In Traylor v. Husqvarna Motor, 988 F.2d 729 (7th Cir.1993), one defendant's expert witness announced at the end of his direct testimony (on a Friday) that he could not appear to be cross-examined on the following Monday. The judge therefore ordered that his cross-examination be video-taped over the weekend and shown to the jury. After reversing on other grounds, Judge Posner criticized this action (id. at 734):

Although we have no objection to videotaped testimony and do not believe that the fact that this witness's direct testimony was live and his cross-examination taped was reversible error, we do think that this sort of "dual media" testimony is generally, and was in this instance, a bad idea. Psychologists and decision theorists point out, what is anyway common sense, that a living person generally conveys a stronger impres-sion than does his resume, or a transcript of his remarks. * * * By presenting its expert witness's direct testimony live but his cross-examination taped, [defendant] Omark was able to give artificially greater salience to the part of this examination that favored Omark than to the part that favored its opponent. There was a thumb on the scale. It should be removed in the retrial.

5. If jury decisions are preferred because of perceived accuracy, would decisions based on a presentation that "closely resembled a television documentary or news report" be similarly credited?

6. Note the effort involved in preparing the video presentations in the *ETSI* antitrust case. Would most litigants be able to mount such an effort? Might poorer litigants prefer to take their chances with live testimony as a way to save money?

7. If allowing the jury to question the witnesses is important, how is that to be accomplished in a videotaped trial? One state-court trial judge who supported juror questioning of witnesses found that it was inappropriate if there is substantial video deposition testimony on one side. Frankel, A Trial Judge's Perspective on Providing Tools for Rational Decisionmaking, 85 Nw.L.Rev. 221, 223 (1990).

8. One of the rationales behind the common law right of the public to attend trials is that the presence of the public encourages truthful testimo-ny. Should the public be entitled, perhaps encouraged, to attend depositions when a videotape of the deposition is expected to be used at trial?

9. Would reliance on technology at trial change the way discovery is done? "Were depositions, for example, to be used to replace live testimony, both plaintiffs and defendants would be forced to elicit the planned testimo-ny of their witnesses during depositions, thus disclosing at that time their entire trial strategy." R.B. Matthews, Inc. v. Transamerica Transportation Services, Inc., 945 F.2d 269, 272–73 (9th Cir.1991). Would this development

be undesirable? How much trial strategy can lawyers hold back if the court requires a thorough final pretrial statement?

10. Innovation using computer imaging to present documentary material to jurors is more easily fit into the traditional trial framework. Like Judge Parker (*supra* p. 750), another judge has described his use of these techniques:

> Before trial, counsel "scan" the documents they intend to present to the jury. With a witness on the stand, the interrogating lawyer directs the courtroom deputy to display a specific document. The document is displayed on all terminals with the exception of those facing the jury. Once the document is identified, the interrogating counsel moves its admission. If the document is admitted, the monitors facing the jury are activated. The witness and the lawyer can discuss the document displayed, with the jury following the interrogation.

Rubin, A Paperless Trial, 19 Litigation 5 (Spring 1993). Judge Rubin found that jurors much prefer this method, having been brought up on television.

3. ALTERNATIVES TO IN–COURT TESTIMONY

There has been a gradual movement in courts towards the selective replacement of live testimony with written or summarized testimony. Submission of a witness' direct testimony in written or summarized form has long been the practice in administrative hearings. The practice is justified as a more efficient way to present evidence, especially when the information is technical. Horne, Presenting Direct Testimony in Writing, 3 Litigation 30 (1977). It has also been observed that "the question and answer method is a strained device for obtaining information in an orderly fashion." McElhaney, An Introduction to Direct Examination, 2 Litigation 37 (1976).

In Kuntz v. Sea Eagle Diving Adventures Corp., 199 F.R.D. 665 (D.Haw.2001), plaintiff challenged the district court's practice of requiring that the direct testimony of witnesses in court trials be provided in declaration form three working days before the commencement of the trial., Witnesses would take the stand only for cross-examination, and the court encouraged the parties to provide cross-examination by declaration as well. Even with hostile witnesses, parties were expected to attempt to obtain declarations. In all instances, however, parties could be excused from this requirement on a showing of good cause. The court justified this practice on grounds of efficiency.

In *Kuntz*, the plaintiff made no showing of good cause to excuse the court's requirement for direct testimony by declaration, but claimed that these requirements were invalid. Despite the provisions of Fed. R. Civ. P. 43(a) (*supra* p. 751, n.1), the court found that the declarations procedure was authorized by Fed. R. Evid. 611(a), which gives the court "reasonable control over the mode and order of interrogating witnesses." It also rejected plaintiff's other objections, stressing that the declaration requirement would be relaxed based on a showing that it was inappropriate. Thus, "in a particular case, a child witness should be allowed to present live direct testimony to avoid the trauma of beginning with cross-examination." Even hostile witnesses sometimes sign declarations prepared by opposing counsel. The court also recognized "that some professionals in this jurisdiction, particularly surgeons, may refuse even to review a draft of a declaration before trial." And damages testimony might present grounds for using a live witness if, for example, a plaintiff argues that her emotional distress is such that the court can only comprehend it through live direct testimony. Might this court's approach be criticized as favoring declarations too strongly?

Other courts have been less aggressive in use of this technique. A judge endorsing the approach wrote as follows:

> It should be immediately cautioned that requiring the preparation of written direct testimony in advance of trial may be neither appropriate nor beneficial for use in the ordinary case. It may, however, be particularly useful in complex litigation where control and management of a case generally require the intervention and participation of the court.

Richey, A Modern Management Technique for Trial Courts to Improve the Quality of Justice: Requiring Direct Testimony to be Submitted in Written Form Prior to Trial, 72 Geo.L.J. 73, 74 (1983).

Notes and Questions

1. As long ago as the mid–1970s, some courts required, even in jury trials, that the parties submit "written narrative statements" before trial for all witnesses, particularly expert witnesses. See Solomon, Techniques for Shortening Trials, 65 F.R.D. 485, 489 (1975). When the witness is sworn, the judge informs the jury that the testimony was reduced to writing and a copy given to opposing counsel and asks the witness whether there is any need to change the written version. If not, the witness reads the written statement to the jury, using visual aids if desired. Judge Solomon reported that under this method direct and cross examination often took less than an hour for witnesses he estimated would have been on the stand four hours under the usual question-and-answer method. "If the contents of a deposition are a necessary element of a party's proof, the preferred mode of presentation is a succinct stipulated statement or summary of the material facts that can be read to the jury." Manual for Complex Litigation (4th) § 12.331 (2004).

In the same vein, Judge Parker, in the *ETSI* antitrust case (see *supra* pp. 748-50), required counsel to summarize the depositions and exchange them with opposing counsel in advance of trial to facilitate counter-summary designations. Parker, Streamlining Complex Cases, 10 Rev. of Litigation 547, 551 (1991). Counsel were then free to "combine a video presentation with summary techniques." This was done by showing a portion of the video deposition and then having counsel summarize the remainder, or by interrupting a summary to permit the jury to see and hear part of the witness' actual testimony. In Oostendorp v. Khanna, 937 F.2d 1177 (7th Cir.1991), the trial court required 5–page written narratives of depositions and refused to admit depositions of two witnesses for plaintiff that were not summarized. The appellate court affirmed.

2. Recall the resistance of plaintiff's counsel to such techniques in Chapman v. Pacific Tel. & Tel., *supra* p. 644. Besides concern about the effort involved in preparing written direct testimony, what objection would a lawyer have to this method of trying a case? Consider the following points:

> The most obvious and serious disadvantage of written direct is the reduced impact the direct case is likely to have on the presiding officer. * * * [O]ften the presiding officer actually sees the witness largely in the context of cross-examination. Thus, except in the happy event that the cross-examination is completely ineffective, the live impression your witness makes is one of making concessions that detract from your case or struggling with mixed effectiveness to avoid making them.

Horne, Presenting Direct Testimony in Writing, 3 Litigation 30, 32 (Winter 1977).

3. Who should draft the written testimony? It would seem that, even with nonparty witnesses, the most likely candidate is the lawyer who calls the witness. Is this a reason to hesitate to use written testimony? With live testimony, the lawyer can (and should) prepare the witness. Yet if the lawyer gives the witness a script, that can be brought out and could discredit the testimony. Cf. Fed.R.Evid. 612. Does allowing the lawyer to draft the testimony essentially permit counsel to use the witness as a ventriloquist's dummy?

4. If the testimony is in writing, should it be read aloud in open court? If not, what effect will this have on the right of public access to the trial? "The fact that the adjudicators are unfamiliar with the case, as well as the fact that the trial is a continuously unfolding event, makes the cognitive needs of both the decision maker and the attending public identical; informing and persuading the former implies informing and persuading the latter as well." M. Damaska, The Faces of Justice and State Authority 62 (1986). Will the public be able to understand the proceedings without oral presentation of the whole story?

5. One of the features of a trial that may have value to the participants is the ability to tell their story in court. There is ample research indicating that people value this opportunity. Is a plaintiff in a personal injury case likely to be satisfied with submission of written direct about her injury?

In this connection, consider First National Bank and Trust Co. v. Hollingsworth, 931 F.2d 1295 (8th Cir.1991), a RICO action in which defendant's deposition testimony was read into the record during plaintiff's case-in-chief, a process that consumed six hours of trial time. When defendant sought to testify regarding the RICO claims during his own defense, the trial court barred him from the stand. The appellate court found no basis in the record for concluding that defendant's testimony would be cumulative and therefore ruled that this was plain error, despite defendant's failure to object, because it was "fundamentally unfair" (id. at 1305):

> Whether or not Hollingsworth's testimony is cumulative to that given in the deposition is immaterial. As a party and a material witness, he should be given every opportunity to allow the jury to observe his demeanor and pass upon his credibility. If Hollingsworth's testimony

has any evidentiary value helpful to the defense, the jury should be given an opportunity to pass on it.

6. Might these innovations offer desirable alternatives to traditional summary judgment procedure in cases that would be tried to the court? Considering the following views:

> A court may determine [in response to a motion for summary judgment in a case that would be tried to the court] that a full trial would add nothing to the paper record and, after proper notice, decide a case on that record, making a decision on a "trial without witnesses" rather than on summary judgment. However one interprets Rule 56, courts have considerable discretion in fashioning a procedure for factual development other than a full trial.

Schwarzer, Hirsch & Barrans, The Analysis and Decision of Summary Judgment Motions, 139 F.R.D. 441, 474 (1992). See Acuff–Rose Music, Inc., 155 F.3d 140 (2d Cir.1998) (upholding use of this approach if the parties forgo their right to a full trial).

4. LIMITING THE AMOUNT OF EVIDENCE AND DURATION OF TRIAL

MCI COMMUNICATIONS CORP. v. AMERICAN TELEPHONE AND TELEGRAPH CO.

United States Court of Appeals, Seventh Circuit, 1983.
708 F.2d 1081, cert. denied, 464 U.S. 891, 104 S.Ct. 234, 78 L.Ed.2d 226 (1983).

Before WOOD and CUDAHY, CIRCUIT JUDGES, and FAIRCHILD, SENIOR CIRCUIT JUDGE.

CUDAHY, CIRCUIT JUDGE.

In this extraordinary antitrust case, defendant American Telephone and Telegraph Company ("AT & T") appeals from a judgment in the amount of $1.8 billion, entered on a jury verdict, in a treble damage suit brought by plaintiffs MCI Communications Corporation and MCI Tele-communications Corporation (collectively "MCI") under section 4 of the Clayton Act, 15 U.S.C. § 15.

[MCI claimed that AT & T had violated the antitrust laws in 22 different ways. After MCI completed its case in chief, the trial court granted AT & T a directed verdict as to seven of these alleged violations. The jury eventually found for MCI on ten of the fifteen remaining charges submitted to it, and awarded damages of $600 million, which were trebled.

AT & T challenged the verdict on a variety of grounds on appeal, and the appellate court found that the jury's verdict lacked evidentiary support in certain respects but that it was proper in other respects. It remanded for a new trial limited to damages. AT & T also challenged the trial court's order that it present its case in 26 trial days.]

We also reject AT & T's argument that the district court did not allow AT & T sufficient time to present its case in an intelligible manner. Originally, AT & T predicted that it would take approximately eighteen months to try the case. Understandably chagrined, the district court directed the parties to submit lists of their witnesses and a summary of the testimony of each, together with a more precise estimate of the time required for trial. MCI's list named seventeen witnesses and predicted that it would require twenty-six days to present its case-in-chief. AT & T's list, by contrast, named 162 witnesses and described a minimum of twenty-one more by category. At that time, AT & T predicted that trial of the entire case would take eight to nine months. The district court reviewed those materials and only then imposed a twenty-six day time limit on the presentation of each side's case-in-chief.[130] The district court did not place a limit on the time allotted for rebuttal or surrebuttal. On appeal, AT & T argues that the limits which were imposed were wholly arbitrary and amounted to a denial of due process. We cannot agree.

* * *

The time limits ordered by Judge Grady had the effect of excluding cumulative testimony, although in setting those limits the district court apparently fixed a period of time for the trial as a whole. This approach is not, *per se,* an abuse of discretion. This exercise of discretion may be appropriate in protracted litigation provided that witnesses are not excluded on the basis of mere numbers. Moreover, where the proffered testimony is presented to the court in the form of a general summary, the time limits should be sufficiently flexible to accommodate adjustment if it appears during trial that the court's initial assessment was too restrictive.

The limits set by the district court were not absolute. As Judge Grady stated in his order, "[t]hese limits are subject to change if events at the trial satisfy the court that any limit is unduly restrictive. It is my intention to allow each party sufficient time to present its case; I have no interest in speed for the sake of speed." Similarly, at a pretrial hearing the court told the parties that there was "nothing absolutely hard and fast" about the limits. After MCI completed presentation of its case in fifteen and one-half days, the court expressed an unwillingness to permit AT & T to exceed its twenty-six day limit, yet it later tempered this by

---

130. Referring to the list submitted by AT & T, the district court noted:

It is almost an understatement to say that defendants' approach to this case is grandiose. Without intending to pass upon any evidence questions at this time, and recognizing that I asked the parties to be very brief in describing the proposed subject matter of the testimony, it does appear to me that much of defendants' proposed testimony would be cumulative and that some of it would be irrelevant.

MCI Communications Corp. v. AT & T, 85 F.R.D. 28, 30 (N.D.Ill.1979). The record in-

dicates that much of AT & T's proposed testimony would in fact have been repetitive. AT & T's list submitted November 14, 1979, for example, names no fewer than a dozen witnesses selected to present testimony on the installation of interconnection services for MCI, seven more who were to testify on the subject of repair services for MCI, and at least six more who were to testify concerning provision of other services to MCI. AT & T also predicted that it would require between twenty-two and forty-six days to cross-examine MCI's witnesses who, by MCI's estimate, could be directly examined in twenty-six days.

reminding the parties, "I want to make it very clear that nobody is being pushed to do anything that is inconsistent with what he perceives to be the best interest of his client." We cannot say that the district court was prepared to adhere strictly to its preliminary time limits without regard to possible prejudice to either party.

* * * Obviously, there must be specific attention to the substance of the testimony and the complexity of the issues, but it does not follow that several weeks for each side will never suffice. The circumstances of each individual case must be weighed by the trial judge, who is in the best position to determine how long it may reasonably take to try the case. MCI was confident that it could establish liability in twenty-six days, and in fact finished eleven days ahead of schedule. We recognize, as did the district court, that presentation of a competent defense may require more time than presentation of a plaintiff's case-in-chief. In light of the substance of AT & T's proffered testimony, however, and the district court's considered view that an efficient, yet effective, presentation of AT & T's defense would take no longer than the time MCI used to present its case, we conclude that the district court did not manifestly abuse its discretion in limiting the time for AT & T's case-in-chief.

Notes and Questions

1. Some commentators urge that "[a]ll jury trials should have time limits less than the time now required." Kirst, Finding a Role for the Civil Jury in Modern Litigation, 64 Judicature 333, 337 (1986). Certainly that would make many jurors happy, particularly in complex cases. A study of complex trials by the American Bar Association, for example, found that "[m]any jurors felt that the lawyers were permitted to introduce unnecessary and apparently irrelevant evidence" and concluded that "limiting the amount of the evidence—the number of witnesses and the number and size (pages) of exhibits—received at trial significantly promotes jury comprehension." See Jury Comprehension in Complex Cases 27–28 (Report of Special Committee of the ABA Section of Litigation, Dec. 1989). Rule 16(c)(15) invites consideration during case management of "an order establishing a reasonable limit on the time allowed for presenting evidence."

2. Lawyers would seem to have a strong incentive to limit the amount of evidence they present. Should judges pressure them to do so? Consider the explanation of the judge in United States v. Reaves, 636 F.Supp. 1575, 1576–79 (E.D.Ky.1986):

> It would seem that early in the career of every trial lawyer, he or she has lost a case by leaving something out, and thereupon resolved never again to omit even the most inconsequential item of possible evidence from any future trial. Thereafter, in an excess of caution the attorney tends to overtry his case by presenting vast quantities of cumulative or marginally relevant evidence.

* * *

Courts cannot rely on the attorneys to object to needless consumption of time by adversaries. Usually, an attorney is willing to suffer through the presentation of his opponent, however redundant, if only he can have equal time.

3. Besides improving comprehension and avoiding boredom, are there benefits to avoiding cumulative evidence? Some research indicates that repetition may mislead the finder of fact by providing the "illusion of validity": "Redundant information makes certain facts *seem* intuitively more probable, but in actuality it does not increase their likelihood." Saks & Kidd, Human Information Processing and Adjudication: Trial by Heuristics, 15 Law & Soc'y Rev. 123, 136–37 (1980).

4. How are attorneys likely to react to court-imposed limitations on the amount of evidence they can present? One judge concluded, with regard to limitations on the amount of time each side would be allowed during trial, that "[t]here is little doubt that * * * the inventive minds of counsel will develop time-directed tactics of gamesmanship, such as diabolically short conclusory directs, giving the adversary the practical option of leaving the witness untouched, or spending a long time bringing out the basis for his conclusions so as to try to undermine them." Leval, From the Bench, 12 Litigation 7, 8 (Fall 1985).

5. How is the court to know in advance of trial whether too much evidence will be offered? Where the problem exists, how is the court to select proper limitations? Were these problems properly solved in MCI v. AT & T?

In Flaminio v. Honda Motor Co., 733 F.2d 463, 473 (7th Cir.1984), the trial court announced that only 33 hours would be allocated for trial, 18 for plaintiffs and 15 for defendants. The appellate court found this directive objectionable:

> [W]e disapprove of the practice of placing rigid hour limits on a trial. The effect is to engender an unhealthy preoccupation with the clock, evidenced in this case by the extended discussion between counsel and the district judge at the outset of the trial over the precise method of time-keeping—a method that made the computation of time almost as complicated as in a professional football game.

In Sims v. ANR Freight System, Inc., 77 F.3d 846 (5th Cir.1996), the appellate court found that the district judge pushed too hard to expedite the trial by requiring the parties to enter stipulated facts, and by actively managing the trial to expedite the presentation of the case. Although all parties agreed the trial should take five to seven days, the judge insisted it be completed in one day and imposed very stringent time limits in service to that goal. The appellate court found that this effort was "too much of a good thing":

> A trial is a proceeding designed to be a search for the truth. * * * Essential to the endeavor is an opportunity for the parties through their lawyers to present information in a manner that is comprehensible to a judge or jury. In this respect, the role played by lawyers in a trial is paramount. When the manner of the presentation of information to a jury is judicially restricted to the extent that the information becomes incomprehensible, then the essence of the trial itself has been destroyed.

Id. at 849. The court nevertheless did not reverse because it found the evidence "overwhelming" in favor of the verdict. Compare General Signal

Corp. v. MCI Telecommunications Corp., 66 F.3d 1500 (9th Cir.1995) (upholding judge's imposition of time limitations on trial) with Sparshott v. Feld Entertainment, Inc., 311 F.3d 425 (D.C.Cir.2002) (ordering new trial on counterclaim because defendant was allowed much less time than plaintiff).

6. To what extent does the prospective duration of trial justify judicial pressure for use of alternatives to in-court testimony and other innovative time-saving techniques?

D. BIFURCATION AND TRIFURCATION

SYMBOLIC CONTROL, INC. v. INTERNATIONAL BUSINESS MACHINES CORP.

United States Court of Appeals, Ninth Circuit, 1980.
643 F.2d 1339.

Before BROWNING and KENNEDY, CIRCUIT JUDGES, and DUMBAULD, DISTRICT JUDGE.

KENNEDY, CIRCUIT JUDGE.

In this antitrust case Symbolic Control, Inc. (Symbolic) appeals from an order of the district court dismissing its suit against International Business Machines Corporation (IBM). After Symbolic had presented evidence limited to the single issue of causation, the suit was dismissed on the ground that upon the facts and the law the plaintiff had shown no right to relief. Fed.R.Civ.P. 41(b). In granting the motion, the district court found Symbolic had "failed to show 'with reasonable certainty and definitiveness' that overt acts or conduct of IBM were an 'actual' and 'substantial' cause of injury to plaintiff;" or "that defendant's conduct 'materially contributed' to plaintiff's injury."

We think the causation analysis used by the district court, as a result of its bifurcation decision, was erroneous, and we reverse on this ground. We do not reach various other issues raised by Symbolic on this appeal.

[Both IBM and Symbolic Control produced a type of computer software called "automatically programmed tool processor" (APT), which is used to prepare programs that will direct a machine tool to cut a metal part. Between 1967 and 1970 IBM developed a version known as NC 360 for its System/360 computers. It distributed NC 360 free of charge. Symbolic was incorporated in 1969 to market APT/70, a processor that was designed for use on the IBM System/360 computer. After it failed to make a single sale, Symbolic sued IBM, asserting that IBM's policy of giving NC 360 away violated the antitrust laws because it involved predatory pricing for the purpose of monopolizing the software market.]

* * *

The district court denied IBM's motion for summary judgment and ordered a bifurcated trial. The first phase of the trial, by the court's order, was to be directed solely to "the issue as to whether plaintiff's business sustained legally cognizable impact by reason of act[s] of IBM." The court made it clear it was to be assumed, solely for purposes of trial in the first phase, that there was a violation of the antitrust laws.

At the close of Symbolic's evidence, the district court dismissed the suit against IBM, holding that the controlling evidence concerning impact of the alleged violation was testimony by users of IBM's NC 360. These customers were the potential users of APT/70. The court held that evidence of possible consequences of IBM's pricing the program, rather than giving it away, was irrelevant, because such evidence would be speculative and that pricing would not have been possible after IBM placed its various versions of NC 360 in the public domain. Relying on this analysis, the court found there was no impact on Symbolic's business, since user testimony revealed that price was not, to them, a relevant factor in the decision to use one product or the other.

Assuming a violation, without evidence on the issue, in order to confine initial inquiry to the question of causation may not always foreclose an adequate causation analysis, but if the definition of the assumed violation remains amorphous, the causation inquiry can become both abstract and incomplete. That is what occurred here.

The theory of Symbolic's case was that IBM had foreclosed competition in a product line. The court assumed a violation had occurred but found that it did not cause the losses sustained by Symbolic. Yet if the assumed violation consists of IBM's giving away a discrete product line in order to bar a potential entrant from competing with the line, it is difficult to assume anything but adverse competitive effects. Closely related is the question of price. Symbolic attempted to establish that it could compete with IBM if IBM priced at cost. Symbolic therefore sought to establish at what price customers would consider rejecting IBM's program in favor of Symbolic's competitive product. Symbolic's price inquiry was foreclosed by the court, apparently on the tautological theory that only the real market conditions controlled and that no actual sales could have been made by Symbolic in a market where the competing product was given away free.

The court's ruling was based, moreover, on the apparent premise of a demand for IBM's product that was impervious to price considerations. It assumes the very question in issue to argue that a product has been accepted over a competing product because of superior quality if the analysis is made wholly without reference to price. While there may be exceptions to this general principle, none was shown in this case.

The trial court made some findings that are inconsistent with its own premise of an assumed violation. For instance, the trial court seemed tacitly to decide the question of legality when it found that "IBM neither could nor would impose a charge on programs already distributed without restriction and in the public domain." To the extent that this statement means that IBM was legally prevented from charging for continued distribution and maintenance of Version 4 of NC 360, it implicitly but unavoidably is a finding that failing to price these improved versions was not predatory. This is contrary to the assumed violation required by the order confining the initial trial to the question of impact.

The bifurcation procedure in this case was therefore defective in two respects. First, the initial premise of a violation lacked specific content and definition; and second, the trial court ruled inconsistently with the premise in any event. Bifurcation of issues is an important device for trial efficiency, and we do not mean to foreclose its use, but the procedure which is adopted must not bar effective review or produce findings that are illogical or circular. Because those defects existed here, the bifurcation procedure became unwieldy. We cannot assess the accuracy of the court's impact findings in this case without evidence of the price structure that would have prevailed absent the violation. It is difficult, moreover, to analyze price structure without reference to a specifically defined violation, resting in turn on a clear definition of product line and market. Our inquiry here is akin to the search for a particular footprint among many, conducted with only a vague notion of the shoe that made it.

The crux of the trial court's holding is that factors other than IBM's alleged violation were the cause of injury to Symbolic: "Yet all the user testimony basic to the fact of injury (impact) establishes that the customers' reasons for not leasing APT/70 had nothing to do with overt acts of IBM." The district court seems to have relied on the finding that the quality of IBM's product was the sole cause of Symbolic's loss. Where two products are assumed to be relatively similar and thus affected by a demand curve that is elastic within at least part of its range, we cannot agree without more evidence than was presented here that quality was the sole factor in the buyer's decision. We hold that, on this record, IBM has not demonstrated that Symbolic's losses were unrelated to conduct of IBM that was, for purposes of the first phase of trial, assumed to be an antitrust violation.

We do not suggest, on the other hand, that Symbolic has made the requisite showing of impact. After further proceedings, it may be established that Symbolic's losses resulted from factors other than the wrongful conduct by IBM.

* * *

It may well be that the diverse factors enumerated in IBM's brief, such as deficient marketing, managerial weakness, and a misreading of the APT opportunity, were the real causes of Symbolic's problems. IBM is in no position to make these arguments in this court, however, because as a direct result of its rule 41(b) motion to dismiss we have no findings of fact as to these issues in the record before us.

———

STATE OF ALABAMA v. BLUE BIRD BODY CO., 573 F.2d 309 (5th Cir.1978):

FAY, CIRCUIT JUDGE.

This Court has approved bifurcation procedures on several occasions. However, this Court has cautioned that separation of issues is not the usual course that should be followed, and that the issue to be tried must be so distinct and separable from the others that a trial of it alone may be had without injustice. This limitation on the use of bifurcation is a recognition of the fact that inherent in the Seventh Amendment guarantee of a trial by jury is the general right of a litigant to have only one jury pass on a common issue of fact. The Supreme Court recognized this principle in *Gasoline Products Co. v. Champlin Refining Co.,* 283 U.S. 494, 51 S.Ct. 513, 75 L.Ed. 1188 (1931) wherein it held that no Seventh Amendment violation occurs when an appellate court orders a new trial on the issue of damages, but lets stand the original jury's findings on liability. The Court explained, however, that a partial new trial may not be "properly resorted to unless it clearly appears that the issue to be retried is so distinct and separable from the others that a trial of it alone may be had without injustice." Such a rule is dictated for the very practical reason that if separate juries are allowed to pass on issues involving overlapping legal and factual questions the verdicts rendered by each jury could be inconsistent.

In an antitrust action brought under the Clayton Act, it is most important to be aware of the Seventh Amendment limitations on a Rule 42(b) bifurcation. This awareness is important because liability under § 4 necessarily includes proof of injury to business and property. Therefore, bifurcation to separate juries of liability and damages in a § 4 case inevitably introduces the possibility that in the liability phase the first jury might find that there was such injury, while the second jury might on the same evidence of injury in the damage phase, find none.

It is exactly this possibility of disparate findings that prompted this Court to earlier say that "in a private antitrust suit there is no neat dividing line between the issue of liability and damages." And, because of this vague dividing line between liability and damages, this Court has also cautioned that separate trials of liability and damages "must be approached with trepidation," and the use of bifurcation "must be grounded upon a clear understanding between the court and counsel of the issue or issues involved in each phase and what proof will be required to pass from one phase to the next."

Notes and Questions

1. Why did the court in *Symbolic Control* bifurcate the case in the first place? The trial of plaintiff's impact case took seven weeks. Consider the amount of time a full dress trial of all issues would have taken; consider also the plaintiff's prospects for success in light of the summary judgment motion. Could the bifurcation have been structured in such a way as to avoid the problems cited by the appellate court?

(a) The appellate court says that the premise of a violation "lacked specific content and definition." How does one provide such content? Would it not be preferable to dispose of such issues in advance to save the parties and the court the expense and burden of a trial of the full case?

(b) The appellate court also says that the bifurcation procedure was defective because the trial court ruled inconsistently with the premise of a violation. It reasons that the trial court erred in finding that the quality of IBM's product was the sole cause of plaintiff's failure because "we cannot agree without more evidence than was presented here that quality was the sole factor in the buyer's decision." Is that a result of the decision to bifurcate or the trial court's exclusion of evidence that plaintiff could compete with IBM if IBM priced its software at cost?

(c) One reading of the Court of Appeals' opinion is that the district court's principal error was in excluding testimony about the effect on potential customers of a decision by IBM to charge for its software. In large part, this difficulty seems to have resulted from uncertainty about the level of pricing that could be considered "predatory" under the antitrust laws; at various times different courts have articulated differing standards. Assuming that the parties agreed on the standard, however, could they have identified a price below which IBM's sales would be assumed to be predatory for purposes of the trial of the impact issue? What difficulties might the district court have encountered in setting that price?

2.   Would the result have been different if IBM had put on its case with regard to impact and the trial court had decided in its favor, rather than granting a motion to dismiss under Rule 41(b)? The appellate court says that it lacks findings because of the filing of the motion to dismiss. Is that a result of the bifurcation?

3.   As the excerpt from *Blue Bird* suggests, the more common bifurcation is between liability and damages. In personal injury cases, some courts routinely direct separate trials. See, e.g., Hosie v. Chicago & North Western Railway, 282 F.2d 639 (7th Cir.1960) (severance granted pursuant to local rules of court despite objections of both plaintiff and defendant). Does such bifurcation result in significant time savings for the parties? Should the court limit discovery to the issues to be addressed in the first segment until that matter is tried? If not, won't the parties have to complete the same amount of discovery as they would if the case were not bifurcated?

It may be that the principal impact of bifurcation is its effect on the outcome of the case. In routine personal injury cases it has long been reported that the defense wins almost twice as frequently when the liability issues are tried separately. See Schwartz, Severance—A Means of Minimizing the Role of Burden and Expense in Determining the Outcome of Litigation, 20 Vand.L.Rev. 1197 (1967); Weinstein, Routine Bifurcation of Jury Negligence Trials: An Example of the Questionable Use of Rule Making Power, 14 Vand.L.Rev. 831 (1961).

This experience with routine cases has been found also in research on mass tort situations. Bordens & Horowitz, Mass Tort Civil Litigation: The Impact of Procedural Changes on Jury Decisions, 73 Judicature 22 (1989), reports empirical experiments using 66 juries showing that plaintiffs received favorable verdicts significantly more often in unitary trials than in bifurcated trials. On the other hand, the damages awarded to successful plaintiffs in unitary trials were significantly lower than were awarded to successful plaintiffs in bifurcated trials. See *id.* at 25–26.

For an economic analysis of the effects of bifurcation, see Landes, Sequential Versus Unitary Trials: An Economic Analysis, 22 J. Legal Stud. 99 (1993). The article relies heavily on relatively detailed formulae for the following conclusions: "a sequential trial lowers the expected cost of litigation compared to a unitary trial for both the plaintiff and defendant because it holds out the prospect of avoiding litigation on subsequent issues if the defendant wins the current issue or the parties settle the remaining issues after the current one is decided. Consequently, a sequential trial (a) increases the plaintiff's incentive to sue, (b) increases the number of lawsuits, and (c) reduces the likelihood that the parties will settle out of court by narrowing the range of mutually acceptable settlements." Id. at 100–01.

4.   One form of bifurcation that defendants sometimes seek is to avoid inappropriate overlap of issues is to separate compensatory and punitive claims, but their concerns may be unjustified. Greene, Woody & Winter, Compensating Plaintiffs and Punishing Defendants: Is Bifurcation Necessary?, 24 Law & Human Behav. 187 (2000), reports that juries in unitary trials don't seem to misuse evidence such as information about defendant's wealth that is admissible only because punitive damages are combined with compensatory damage claims. In addition, bifurcation correlates with higher punitive damages awards.

5.   Severance of affirmative defenses may be more attractive, particularly if the defense will dispose of the entire case, and, with respect to some defenses it is specifically authorized by Fed.R.Civ.P. 12(d). But even with affirmative defenses substantial difficulties are often likely to arise. For example, where the defense is the statute of limitations the plaintiff may claim that the running of limitations is tolled by defendant's concealment of the claim. Resolution of that issue may require the court to address most of the merits of plaintiff's claim. See Marcus, Fraudulent Concealment in Federal Court: Toward a More Disparate Standard?, 71 Geo.L.J. 829, 910–12 (1983) (concluding that bifurcation of concealment will be useful only when that issue focuses on a relatively isolated event separate from the main claims).

6.   *Blue Bird* also says that bifurcation could raise Seventh Amendment problems when different phases of the case would be presented to different juries because the second jury might not accept the findings of the first one and thereby violate the Reexamination Clause of the Seventh Amendment. In class actions certified as to certain issues pursuant to Rule 23(c)(4), that may occur because even after resolution of an overriding common issue there may be individual issues that require discrete resolutions with regard to different class members.

Recently this concern has surfaced as an additional obstacle to class certification in mass tort cases. See Castano v. American Tobacco Co., *supra* p. 340, in which the Fifth Circuit invoked the Reexamination Clause, reasoning as follows:

> There is a risk that in apportioning fault the second jury could reevaluate the defendant's fault, determine that the defendant was not at fault, and apportion 100% of the fault to the plaintiff. In such a situation, the

second jury would be impermissibly reconsidering the findings of the first jury.

84 F.3d at 751; see also In the Matter of Rhone–Poulenc Rorer Inc., 51 F.3d 1293, 1303 (7th Cir.1995) (raising same concern).

Undoubtedly issues that are not sufficiently free-standing to warrant separate trial should not be the subject of bifurcation. But does that lead to a constitutional prohibition on common issue certification where multiple juries will need to be used for full adjudication of individual claims? Presumably the second jury would be instructed it had to accept the first jury's findings. Wouldn't the same problem exist if liability and damages were separated (as described in note 3 above) and damages were tried to a separate jury that assessed them at zero because it believed defendant should not have been held liable? For an argument that there is no such constitutional obstacle, see Woolley, Mass Tort Litigation and the Seventh Amendment Reexamination Clause, 83 Iowa L. Rev. 499 (1998).

In Robinson v. Metro–North Commuter R.R. Co., 267 F.3d 147 (2d Cir.2001), the court was presented with the argument that partial class certification of an employment discrimination case would violate the Reexamination Clause. It disagreed. "Trying a bifurcated claim before separate juries does not run afoul of the Seventh Amendment, but a 'given [factual] issue may not be tried by successive juries.' " Id. at 169 n. 13; accord, Mullen v. Treasure Chest Casino, LLC, 186 F.3d 620, 629–30 (5th Cir.1999). The solution lies in carefully defining the roles of the two juries and crafting the verdict form for the second one to show what has been decided already. See also In re Dow Corning, Inc., 211 B.R. 545 (Bkrtcy, E.D.Mich.1997) (describing a method for handling trial of personal injury claims by recipients of silicone gel implants to guard against the risk that "the second jury can run roughshod over the findings of the first"); compare Bacon v. Honda of America Mfg., Inc., 205 F.R.D. 466 (S.D. Ohio 2001) (bifurcation not allowed in employment discrimination suit to permit class certification because the second jury would be required to re-weigh evidence and issues regarding liability); see generally Gensler, Bifurcation Unbound, 75 Wash. U.L. Rev. 705 (2000) (arguing that separate trials should be employed whenever they would facilitate the handling of cases).

IN RE BENDECTIN LITIGATION

United States Court of Appeals, Sixth Circuit, 1988.
857 F.2d 290.

Before ENGEL, CHIEF JUDGE, and JONES and NELSON, CIRCUIT JUDGES.

ENGEL, CHIEF JUDGE.

[This appeal grew out of consolidated actions for personal injuries allegedly caused by Bendectin, an anti-nausea drug manufactured by defendant Merrell Dow Pharmaceuticals. Owing to removal and transfer by the Judicial Panel on Multidistrict Litigation, the district court eventually had over 800 such cases pending before it, involving over 1100 plaintiffs. To facilitate the handling of these cases, the court initially bifurcated between liability and damages, deciding to apply Ohio law to decide the question of liability. It contemplated that if liability were established the cases would be returned to the originating districts for damage trials. Any plaintiff who so desired could withdraw, but remaining in the case signified acceptance of Ohio law.

Thereafter, the court decided to "trifurcate" the case by subdividing the liability issue into two parts—causation and liability. If plaintiffs prevailed on causation questions, the jury would proceed to decide other liability questions. Fearing undue prejudice to the defendant, the trial court also excluded from the courtroom all visibly deformed plaintiffs and all plaintiffs under the age of ten. The case was then tried for 22 days, after which the jury answered the following question in the negative: "Have the plaintiffs established by a preponderance of the evidence that ingestion of Bendectin at therapeutic doses during the period of fetal organogenesis is a proximate cause of human birth defects?" Judgment was entered for defendant.

On appeal, plaintiffs objected to the trifurcation order. Although it found this order the "most troubling" aspect of the case, the court of appeals affirmed, emphasizing the trial court's discretion in the area.

First, plaintiffs argued that the issues raised were not separable enough because they relied on theories that shifted the burden of proof as to causation to defendants upon a showing of other liability factors. The court disagreed, finding that under Ohio law it would not suffice to show that the drug was a "substantial contributing factor" in bringing about their injuries. It also rejected plaintiffs' "increased risk" theory of liability, under which they could prevail by showing only that the drug caused them an increased risk of injury. Finally, it held that plaintiffs could not rely on alternate liability, based on Sindell v. Abbott Laboratories, 26 Cal.3d 588, 163 Cal.Rptr. 132 (1980), *supra* p. 44 n. 4, because plaintiffs had sued only one defendant, and the doctrine does not apply in a one-defendant case.]

Plaintiffs also argue that the decision to trifurcate the trial was an abuse of discretion because the ruling unfairly prejudiced presentation of their case in a variety of ways. * * *

Plaintiffs next challenge the decision to trifurcate on the proximate causation question because the issue trifurcated was the one which a lay jury would be least qualified to understand, evaluate, and decide. The district judge offered to try the case before a blue ribbon jury, but the plaintiffs rejected the idea. This was, of course, their right. In any event we conclude that if the issues were indeed difficult, their resolution was not rendered more difficult due to trifurcation. If anything, the narrowing of the range of inquiry through trifurcation substantially improved the manageability of the presentation of proofs by both sides and enhanced the jury's ability to comprehend the causation issue.

Plaintiffs' primary argument against trifurcation as unfairly prejudicial is that trying the question alone prejudiced plaintiffs by creating a sterile trial atmosphere. In [In re] Beverly Hills [Fire Litigation, 695 F.2d 207 (6th Cir.1982), an action arising out of a fire in a night club], we addressed similar concerns that trifurcation could possibly prevent the plaintiffs from exercising their right to present to the jury the full atmosphere of their cause of action, including the reality of the injury:

> A strong argument can, it is true, be made against the bifurcation of a trial limited to the issue of causation. There is a danger that bifurcation may deprive plaintiffs of their legitimate right to place before the jury the circumstances and atmosphere of the entire cause of action which they have brought into the court, replacing it with a sterile or laboratory atmosphere in which causation is parted from the reality of injury. In a litigation of lesser complexity, such considerations might well have prompted the trial judge to reject such a procedure. Here, however, it is only necessary for us to observe that the occurrence of the fire itself, a major disaster in Kentucky history by all standards, was generally known to the jurors from the outset. Further, the proofs themselves, although limited, were nonetheless fully adequate to apprise the jury of the general circumstances of the tragedy and the environment in which the fire arose. As a result, we hold that the trial judge did not abuse his discretion in severing the issue of causation here.

Judge Rubin considered this language when he denied the plaintiffs' motion for a new trial. On appeal, plaintiffs also rely heavily on the same language. Sterility is not necessarily the inevitable consequence in a trifurcated trial merely because the jury may not hear the full evidence of defendant's alleged wrongdoing. It more properly refers to the potential danger that the jury may decide the causation question without appreciating the scope of the injury that defendant supposedly caused and without the realization that their duties involve the resolution of an important, lively and human controversy. It is with respect to this latter concern that the plaintiffs urge that they were unfairly prejudiced by the trifurcation. The record reveals that the district judge consciously worked to avoid the potential for unfair prejudice. For example, he instructed the jury:

> Let me suggest to you that what you are about to do may be one of the most important things you will ever do in your entire life. This is a significant case. It involves a lot of people. It involves not only the plaintiffs who are individuals, it involves people, scientists, people who have done experiments, people who are employees of the defendant company. The totality of this case involves people and while you will hear technical evidence, I do point out to you that at all times, you should keep in mind that on both sides, there are people involved.

The court was not alone in efforts to avoid the dangers of sterility. In his final argument, plaintiffs' attorney Eaton told the jury that the trial was not an academic exercise, and that the case involved many real people who sought justice, and who would, as children, be affected by the jury's verdict well into the next century.

Finally, plaintiffs argue that Judge Rubin failed to consider the caveats of Rule 42(b) in his trifurcation decision, and instead justified trifurcation only upon unsubstantiated claims of judicial efficiency, thus unduly prejudicing plaintiffs' case without good reason. We believe, however, that the district judge carefully made the necessary inquiry. In his final order the trial judge noted that Bendectin litigation could "substantially immobiliz[e] the entire Federal Judiciary. There have been only four cases involving Bendectin which have been individually tried. They required an average of 38 trial days." Judge Rubin calculated that if all 1100 cases were tried at that average length on an individual basis, they would be able to keep 182 judges occupied for one year. Contrary to the plaintiffs' claims that Judge Rubin never considered the language of Rule 42(b), he did correctly require plaintiffs to prove that defendant's drug caused their injury, and would not allow plaintiffs to buttress a weak causation case with a strong negligence case. Thus, in line with the language of Rule 42(b), the trial judge considered the causation question to be a separate issue.

In reviewing the district court's decision to trifurcate we further note Rule 42 which "giv[es] the court virtually unlimited freedom to try the issues in whatever way trial convenience requires." C. Wright, A. Miller & F. Elliott, [Federal Practice and Procedure], § 2387 at 278. Thus, a court may try an issue separately if "in the exercise of reasonable discretion [it] thinks that course would save trial time or effort or make the trial of other issues unnecessary." In this case, the district judge considered the time savings in trying this case in this fashion, and surmised that if the plaintiffs won on this issue, another eight weeks of trial would be necessary to resolve the other questions.

* * * Plainly, Judge Rubin had a massive case management problem to resolve, and chose to do so by trying the case on a separate issue that would be dispositive.

* * *

We hold that since the initial trial on the proximate causation issue was a separate issue, promoted efficiency, and did not unduly prejudice plaintiffs, trifurcating this case on the separate issue of proximate cause was proper. We need not decide whether this was the best or even the only good method of trying this case. We need only determine whether, under all the circumstances before him, the trial judge's decision to trifurcate was an abuse of discretion.

* * *

[Plaintiffs also challenged the judge's exclusion from the courtroom of all visibly deformed plaintiffs and those below the age of ten. The judge provided such plaintiffs a separate room in the courthouse from which they could observe the trial by closed-circuit television. Plaintiffs argued that this interfered with communication with counsel and excluded a "humanistic aspect of this litigation."

The appellate court noted that in Helminski v. Ayerst Laboratories, 766 F.2d 208 (6th Cir.1985), it had insisted that "a plaintiff with a solely physical abnormality may not be excluded involuntarily, absent disruptive behavior, even when the abnormality is due allegedly to the defendant's wrongful conduct." *Id.* at 217. Nevertheless, this case was decided after Judge Rubin set out his rules governing trial. In addition, it noted that given the numbers of plaintiffs involved, some rules on allocation of courtroom space were essential.]

[C]oncerned that the presence of dozens or even hundreds of deformed plaintiffs in his courtroom might unfairly deter the jury from deciding the issue at hand in accordance with the evidence, Judge Rubin instead allowed the plaintiffs who were interested to view the trial on closed-circuit television and to assist counsel through communicative devices if they were so willing and able. This, in our view, was a reasonable way to balance the rights of the plaintiffs and the defendants in the absence of hindsight.

NATHANIEL R. JONES, CIRCUIT JUDGE, concurring in part and dissenting in part.

I write separately today for two reasons. First, I write to point out my disagreement with the majority on the exclusion, by the district court, of certain plaintiffs from the courtroom during the twenty-two day jury trial on causation. Secondly, I write to express a few of my concerns regarding the district court's trifurcation order.

* * *

Although I have no problem with the approved trifurcation order in this court's [In re] Beverly Hills [Fire Litigation, 695 F.2d 207 (6th Cir.1982)] decision, I do become hesitant when that decision is applied, seemingly without reservation, to a case, such as this one, which is complex in nature. Because I find several distinctions between this case and *Beverly Hills,* I am reluctant to apply such reasoning wholesale. Thus, I find that if *Beverly Hills* is narrowly construed, several problems become apparent with the majority opinion.

First, all of the victims in the *Beverly Hills* litigation were affected by the same event, a disastrous and tragic fire. Thus, the issue of causation could, quite competently, be tried separately from the issues of liability and damages with only a small chance that the plaintiffs would be prejudiced. This was simply because all plaintiffs were affected in the same manner by a unique, single event. Individual facts about the individual plaintiffs would therefore have had little significance in regard to the question of causation.

The *Bendectin* litigation, however, is quite different. Over eight hundred plaintiffs, whose mothers took the drug at different times and places and under different circumstances, are involved. As such, a single, unique event such as a fire is replaced by over eight hundred distinct events that, in all likelihood, affected the individual plaintiffs in different ways. Although each distinct event involved the ingesting of the same drug, it is hard to believe that *all* eight hundred plus claims can be tied neatly into one package and satisfactorily resolved by the answering of one question, *i.e.,* did Bendectin cause the relevant birth defects? In tying all these claims together, an argument could certainly be made as to prejudice. That is, by not allowing plaintiffs to present evidence as to how they were *individually* affected by the drug [the court's order] could have resulted in prejudice to them in their attempt to establish the required elements of their case. Indeed, although I concur with the majority's *end* result, I disagree with the language used in reaching that conclusion. The majority opinion refers to the fact that the plaintiffs were not "unduly" prejudiced by the court's trifurcation order. I do not agree that this is the burden plaintiffs must meet to establish an abuse of discretion by the lower court with regard to a trifurcation order. Rather, my suggestion is that *any* prejudice to a plaintiff in the litigation of his or her case should be enough to hold that the lower court has abused its discretion. I do not agree with the majority that absent a showing of unduly or excessive prejudice, the court's order should be upheld. Indeed, this court should define the amount of prejudice that must be demonstrated to establish that a trifurcation order was an abuse of discretion. Such a discussion in this case, however, is without difficulty. Plaintiffs here simply failed to meet their burden to demonstrate *any* prejudice. That is, plaintiffs lost their case because they failed to establish any link between their birth defects and the drug Bendectin, not because of any prejudice to them resulting from the trifurcation order.

In conclusion, trifurcation orders present fundamental problems of fairness simply because the typical procedure in litigation does not involve the splitting up of a case, element by element, and trying each point to the jury separately. Rather, the plaintiff's entire case is presented to the jury at once, thereby preventing the isolation of issues in a sterile atmosphere. Simply because a litigant shares his complaint with eight hundred other claimants is not a reason to deprive him of the day in court he would have enjoyed had he been the sole plaintiff. However, as the majority points out, a trifurcation order is authorized and *necessitated* at some point so as to allow a district court to manage and control the complexities and massive size of a case. The duty of this court, however, is to prevent such a case-management tool from becoming a penalty to injured plaintiffs seeking relief via the legal system.

[Judge Jones concluded that the district court could not constitutionally exclude certain plaintiffs from the trial without holding a hearing and making findings. He argued that Helminski v. Ayerst Laboratories, 766 F.2d 208 (6th Cir.1985), should have been applied to this case even though it was decided after the trial court had established rules for the conduct of the trial.]

Notes and Questions

1. Was *Bendectin* a better case for severing issues for separate trial than *Symbolic Control*, *supra* p. 762? For a very thorough examination of the entire course of Bendectin litigation, including the consolidated trial, see M.

Green, Bendectin and Birth Defects (1996); see also Marcus, Reexamining the Bendectin Litigation Story, 83 Iowa L. Rev. 231 (1997).

2. Without severance, could a consolidated case like *Bendectin* ever be tried in a consolidated manner? If not, how does one answer Judge Jones' argument that the court is denying plaintiffs their day in court because they share a complaint with many others? Would severance be used in a suit by a single plaintiff as well?

3. Would a class action have been feasible in *Bendectin*? Did common issues predominate? Could a class have been certified as to certain issues under Rule 23(c)(4)? If not, will courts be tempted to use Rule 42 to accomplish by one device essentially the same result that is not possible under Rule 23? Professor Green observed that even though it was not formally certified as one, the Bendectin multidistrict litigation "much more resembled a class action than a consolidated proceeding." M. Green, *supra* note 1, at 239. Compare In the Matter of Rhone–Poulenc Rorer Inc., 51 F.3d 1293 (7th Cir.1995) (disapproving certification of class action limited to certain issues on ground issues overlapped, and observing that although single-issue certification is permitted, "the district court must carve at the joint.")

4. Note the court's concern with the complexity of the issues. Was that due to the complexity of each case individually, or to the combination of so many cases in a single proceeding?

5. The majority evinces concern about the risk of a "sterile trial." Are these risks present because of the complexity of the issues presented by plaintiffs' individual claims, or due to the combination of cases in a single proceeding? Did the trial court really solve these problems?

Consider the following criticism of the handling of the Bendectin cases:

> The plaintiffs' argument that trifurcation had transformed an ordinary tort suit into a sterile and laboratory inquiry into causation was rejected on grounds that appear utterly implausible. The Sixth Circuit stated that this concern was adequately allayed by the trial judge's instruction to the jury that "[t]his is a significant case. It involves a lot of people" and by the closing argument of plaintiffs' counsel that the trial was "not an academic exercise" and "involved many real people who sought justice." The suggestion that such remarks are an adequate substitute for the presence and testimony of the injured plaintiff and a full presentation of all of the alleged misconduct is incredible on its face. This Bendectin jury was deprived of the evidence most tort juries would routinely hear regarding the totality of circumstances surrounding the plaintiff's injury in a manner likely to affect their deliberations in a substantial way.

Trangsrud, Mass Trials in Mass Tort Cases: A Dissent, 1989 U.Ill.L.Rev. 69, 81.

Regarding the effect bifurcation might have on jury deliberations, note that some empirical research indicates that in complex criminal trials jurors need the entire fabric of the evidence to come to a decision. See Pennington & Hastie, Evidence Evaluation in Complex Decision Making, 51 J. of Personality and Soc. Psy. 242–58 (1986). Researchers investigating mass tort civil cases reported apparent differences between unitary and bifurcated trials:

> [U]nitary trial juries do tend to use some version of the Pennington and Hastie story model to decide the issues. They utilize all the trial evidence while deciding each individual trial issue. Indeed, the initial analysis of the deliberations indicates that unitary trial juries often do not decide liability or causation until they hear evidence concerning damages.
>
> Juries in separated trials appear to employ other, perhaps less sophisticated, heuristics to decide the issues. These latter juries tend to use more extreme heuristics: corporate-capitalist versus the little guy; good guy versus bad guy rhetoric dominates these deliberations. The bifurcation of general causation in the separated trial condition produces greater disbelief about causation yielding fewer verdicts for the plaintiffs. It may be that only more extreme pro-plaintiff juries who appeal to the good-guy-bad guy rhetoric remain in the separated trial condition to vote for the plaintiffs.

Bordens & Horowitz, Mass Tort Civil Litigation: The Impact of Procedural Changes on Jury Decisions, 73 Judicature 22, 27 (1989).

But perhaps there is something to be said in favor of a sterile laboratory atmosphere if it focuses the jury on the pertinent evidence without distraction. Consider Professor Trangsrud's further argument (Trangsrud, *supra* at 82):

> If the Bendectin claims had been tried separately, it is possible that the defendant would have consistently prevailed. It is also possible, however, that juries presented with the entire case against the manufacturer of this drug would have awarded discounted damages to the plaintiffs before them, mindful of the serious character of the plaintiffs' injuries and the inconclusive evidence that the injuries were caused by the defendant's drug. Such an outcome would seem at odds with our current law of causation, but might anticipate reform of that law in the future. Perhaps the law is moving to allow a discounted recovery when a defendant's product increases the risk of disease or injury beyond natural levels, but strict causation cannot be proved due to the passage of time or the imperfect nature of our science.

If the law insists on proof of causation, does this argument actually provide a reason for preferring separate disposition of general causation? According to at least some observers, there never was any substantial medical support for the proposition that Bendectin caused the kinds of injuries for which compensation was sought. Thus, a scientist lamented in print that "the Bendectin cases go on, in spite of what appears to be better evidence for safety than is available for any other substance, including tap water." Scialli, Bendectin, Science, and the Law, 3 Reproductive Toxicology 157, 157 (1989); see Sanders, The Bendectin Litigation, A Case Study in the Life–Cycle of Mass Torts, 43 Hast.L.J. 301, 347 (1992) ("The scientific community seems to have reached something close to a consensus regarding the drug. While no study can remove all residual uncertainty regarding Bendectin's safety, if the drug is a teratogen, it is a relatively mild one."). In 2000, it was reported that a Canadian company proposed marketing Bendectin again as an antinausea drug for pregnant women, albeit under a different name. See Kolata, Controversial Drug Makes Comeback, N.Y. Times, Sept. 26, 2000.

6. Although the judge's decision to proceed first with the issue of general causation was opposed by the plaintiffs, it should be noted that it held risks for defendant Merrell. "Merrell had a much stronger case on the question whether Bendectin caused a given child's birth defects than on whether Bendectin was capable of causing birth defects." Green, *supra* note 1, at 194. The trial occurred before much of the scientific evidence mentioned in note 5 had been developed and, until Merrell's third witness provided what the judge thought was "[t]he most telling piece of evidence I have ever seen in 23 years on the Federal bench," the judge thought the plaintiffs would win. Id. at 229–31.

7. Will anything be gained by bifurcation if plaintiffs win the first phase of the trial? "Mass trials on the issue of 'general' causation create substantial savings only when plaintiffs lose." Trangsrud, *supra* note 5, at 79. Could a plaintiff victory in such a trial improve the chances for settlement?

8. *Phased trials*: The idea of trying class actions in phases has commended itself to courts in some instances. For example, in Jenkins v. Raymark Indus., *supra* p. 331, the court proposed to proceed by phases in resolving the issues raised at trial. The attractiveness of such a plan is that once certain issues are decided, the parties may be more inclined to settle, making further phases unnecessary. But issues that may require individualized proof relating to each class members (such as specific causation, damages, and certain affirmative defenses like statute of limitations) will have to be tried in a later phase that may not be susceptible to common proof in a unitary trial. If individual trials eventually prove necessary, there is a question whether any efficiency has been obtained by certifying a class action for the issues addressed in the common trial. In Castano v. American Tobacco Co., *supra* p. 340, the appellate court doubted that trial of the common issues would lead to the effective termination of the litigation because significant issues still had to be resolved individually. But see Watson v. Shell Oil Co., 979 F.2d 1014 (5th Cir.1992) (approving a "phase one" trial of common issues regarding liability in suit growing out of explosion at refinery, to be followed by three more phases).

9. One of the few "medical monitoring" class actions that were filed in various state courts after *Castano*, *supra* p. 340, that actually went to trial was Scott v. American Tobacco Co., 725 So.2d 10 (La.App.1998). The Louisiana Supreme Court had upheld class certification of an action on behalf of Louisiana smokers against the major tobacco companies alleging design and manipulation of nicotine content to create addiction. The trial court ordered a Phase I trial of all common issues of liability, including fault and causation, as well as classwide defenses. The Phase I jury found liability establishing the class' right to medical monitoring, but determined that the specific monitoring tests had not yet gained sufficient support from the medical community. Therefore, the court entered an order requiring defendants to undertake a program designed to encourage cessation of smoking, but not, "at this point," medical monitoring. Scott v. American Tobacco Co.,

per curiam order, Nov. 3, 2003 (Docket No. 2003–C–1872, La.Ct.App.4th Cir.). A Phase II trial was ordered to determine all items of damage common to the class and the basis for assessment of those items of damage, but since the relief sought was equitable, the trial would be before the court. Phase II would particularly focus on the creation of a fund to carry out the cessation relief.

E.   TRIAL BY STATISTICS

Many important decisions, particularly about groups of people, are based on statistical analyses. In this book, we have often seen litigations involving large numbers of people; statistical methods could be an effective way of dealing with their claims.

Courts confronting large numbers of similar claims sometimes have attempted to use statistical means to deal with the complications resulting from the number of claimants. In the Eastern District of Texas, Judge Robert Parker had more than 3,000 asbestos personal injury cases, and ordered them consolidated for a trial contemplated to involve three phases. Phase I, as was also contemplated in Jenkins v. Raymark Industries, Inc., *supra* p. 331, would decide common defenses and a ratio for punitive damages. Phase II, before the same jury, would decide total or "omnibus" liability to the claimants as a class. Phase III would then involve distributing any awarded damages to claimants.

In In re Fibreboard Corp., 893 F.2d 706 (5th Cir.1990), the court ruled that Phase II was improper and granted a writ of mandate against proceeding in that manner. The plan for that phase was to offer evidence on 30 "illustrative plaintiffs." On the basis of that evidence and other evidence, including expert testimony, the jury would decide the percentage of plaintiffs exposed to each defendant's products, and the percentage of claims barred by various affirmative defenses such as statutes of limitation and adequate warnings. The jury would also determine actual damages as a lump sum for each disease category.

The appellate court held that this trial technique was impermissible. Judge Higginbotham cautioned that "traditional ways of proceeding reflect far more than habit. They reflect the very culture of the jury trial and the case and controversy requirement of Article III." He added: "The inescapable fact is that the individual claims of 2,990 persons will not be presented. Rather, the claim of a unit of 2,990 persons will be presented. Given the unevenness of the individual claims, this Phase II process inevitably restates the dimensions of tort liability." This restatement violated the *Erie* doctrine because "Texas has made its policy choices in its substantive tort rules against the backdrop of a trial." Although the nature of a trial can be modified, "[t]here is a point, however, where cumulative changes in procedure work a change in the very character of a trial."

Judge Higginbotham voiced particular uneasiness about plaintiffs' proposed use of statistics to permit inferences about class members in *In re Fibreboard*:

[W]e are left with a profound disquiet. First, the *assumption* of plaintiffs' argument is that its proof of omnibus damages is in fact achievable; that statistical measures of representativeness and commonality will be sufficient for the jury to make informed judgments concerning damages. We are pointed to our experience in the trial of Title VII cases and securities cases involving use of fraud on the market concepts and mathematical constructs for examples of workable trials of large numbers of claims. We find little comfort in such cases. It is true that there is considerable judicial experience with such techniques, but it is also true we have remained cautious in their use. Indeed, as the district court stated in one massive Title VII case relying on math models:

> [I]t has to judicial eyes a surrealistic cast, mirroring the techniques used in its trial. Excursions into the new and sometimes arcane corners of different disciplines is a familiar task of American trial lawyers and its generalist judges. But more is afoot here, and this court is uncomfortable with its implications. This concern has grown with the realization that the esoterics of econometrics and statistics which both parties have required this court to judge have a centripetal dynamic of their own. They push from the outside roles of tools for "judicial" decisions toward the core of decision making itself. Stated more concretely: the precision-like mesh of numbers tends to make fits of social problems when I intuitively doubt such fits. I remain wary of the siren call of the numerical display ... [Vuyanich v. Republic Nat. Bank of Dallas, 505 F.Supp. 224, 394 (N.D.Tex. 1980) (Higginbotham, J.).]

On remand, Judge Parker substituted a different technique also depending on statistical proof and probability analysis, and proceeded to try the case. Cimino v. Raymark Industries, Inc., 751 F.Supp. 649 (E.D.Tex.1990). In Phase I, samples of claimants from the five asbestos disease categories were drawn by random means, and the claims of these 160 individual claimants were tried to a jury, along with the claims of the nine class representatives. Phase II was designed to resolve the issue of exposure to defendants' products on a class-wide worksite-by-worksite basis, and ended with a stipulation among the parties about what the jury would have found (preserving, however, the defendant's opportunity to object to the use of this trial technique). Then Phase III addressed affirmative defenses that might apply to claimants, and the court determined the appropriate award for the class members in each of the five disease categories by averaging the awards given during Phase I to the sample claimants in that category, with suitable discounting for affirmative defenses. This approach would avoid the need to have individual damage trials for each of the 3,000 class members.

Defendants challenged Judge Parker's use of what he called a "Statistics 101" analysis, and the judge rejected the challenge based on testimony of a statistics professor on the "goodness-of-fit" between the sample cases tried in Phase I and the rest of the claimants in each disease category. He invoked various other uses of statistical evidence in trials in support of this trial method. For example, in civil rights cases statistical analysis had been used to show unequal treatment of racial minorities. In tort cases, life-expectancy or mortality tables are often used in determining damages. In *Cimino*, indeed, defendants had themselves used such techniques when they presented a statistical analysis of a telephone survey in support a motion for a change of venue. Similarly, both sides relied on medical evidence containing many statistical surveys and analyses.

The court of appeals rejected Judge Parker's revised trial method after the trial. Cimino v. Raymark Industries, Inc., 151 F.3d 297 (5th Cir.1998). It pointed out that plaintiffs' statistical expert did not independently validate the variables he used to support his conclusion about "goodness of fit," but accepted information reported by plaintiffs' lawyers. More fundamentally, it emphasized that Phase II provided no occasion for individual examination of claimants' circumstances to make a determination regarding causation, something required by Texas law and the Seventh Amendment. Accordingly, even as to the 169 representative claimants whose cases were tried in Phase I, there was no proper judgment based on a finding of causation in Phase II. Regarding the "extrapolation cases," those of the other claimants whose judgments were to be based on averaging the verdicts for the 160 sample cases, the decision would be even more flawed. "The only juries that spoke to actual damages, the phase I and III juries, received evidence only on the damages to the particular plaintiffs before them, were called on to determine *only*, and *only* determined, each of those some one hundred seventy particular plaintiffs' actual damages and were not called on to determine and did not determine or purport to determine, the damages of any other plaintiffs or group of plaintiffs."

The use of statistical inference was upheld in Hilao v. Estate of Marcos, 103 F.3d 767 (9th Cir.1996). This was a class action seeking recovery for some 10,000 citizens of the Philippines who were tortured or killed, or who disappeared, during the time Ferdinand Marcos was president of that country. The court first held a trial on liability, which led to a jury verdict in favor of 22 plaintiffs. Based on that verdict, the court invited class members to file claim forms under oath, and appointed a special master to gather information on damages. After removing about 5% of the claims as facially invalid, the district court had 137 randomly selected for further inquiry based on testimony of a statistical expert that the rate of validity of claims among these 137 would, to a 95% statistical probability, correspond to the rate of validity in the whole pool of approximately 9,500 claims.

The special master then went to the Philippines and took the depositions of the 137 claimants and their witnesses and, on the basis of this expedition, filed a report concluding that six of the claims (4.37%) were not valid and recommending damage awards for the remaining class members. A jury trial on compensatory damages was then held including testimony from the statistical expert and recorded testimony from the 137 claimants and their witnesses, along with testimony from the special master about his recommendations. Then the jury returned a verdict largely (but not entirely) following the special master's recommendations. Eventually, a judgment for the remainder of the class was entered on the basis of the decisions about the 137 claims, with a reduction for invalid claims.

On appeal, the estate challenged only the method by which the district court determined the validity of the claims of other class members. Stressing "the extraordinarily unusual nature of this case," the court of appeals rejected the estate's due process objection to the procedure employed. In part, this decision was premised on the conclusion that the estate's only valid objection would be to having to pay invalid claims. "The statistical method used by the district court obviously presents a somewhat greater risk of error in comparison to an adversarial adjudication of each claim, since the former method requires a probabilistic *prediction* (albeit an extremely accurate one) of how many of the total claims are invalid." Although there was a somewhat heightened risk of error, plaintiffs' interest in use of this method was enormous since proceeding claim-by-claim would "pose insurmountable practical hurdles." A dissenting judge objected that "[i]f due process in the form of a real prove-up of causation and damages cannot be accomplished because the class is too big or to do so would take too long, then (as the Estate contends) the class is unmanageable and should not have been certified in the first place."

Thus, the possibility of using statistical trial methods in mass tort and related litigation remains uncertain. The Fifth Circuit's rejection in *Cimino* was couched in terms of its reading of requirements for individualized treatment in Texas tort law, and the Ninth Circuit's decision in *Hilao* may have been limited to the extraordinary circumstances presented.

Notes and Questions

1. Consider the following arguments about why statistical methods might produce more accurate decisions:

> Every verdict is itself merely a sample from the large population of potential verdicts. That "population of verdicts" consists of all the awards that would result from trying the same case repeatedly for an infinite number of times. We can remind ourselves that the exact same case could have been tried repeatedly in different contexts: before the same jury; before different juries; or by different lawyers using exactly the same facts. Or, the case could have been tried using different permutations of the same facts or different facts and arguments that could have been assembled out of the same basic case. Clearly, any given trial of a case is but a single instance from among thousands of possible trials of that same basic case. It makes more sense, then, to think of the "true" award as the average of the population of possible awards. The fact that we normally obtain only one award from one trial of each case

obscures the population of possible awards from which that one was drawn.

* * *

Imagine a case were tried 100 times. Then the verdicts are arrayed on a frequency distribution. * * *. It should be apparent that any single verdict is just one from among those. Many of the possible single verdicts constitute over-or under-compensation compared to the mean of that distribution, and that mean is the best estimate of the "true" award. Thus, to find the true award for a case, we would need to re-try each case numerous times and take the mean of the resulting awards. By taking just the one award that results from a single trial we are accepting the likelihood of some error. With traditional individualized cases the legal process always accepts this error, and it always has.

In turn, any array of damage awards conceals the underlying variation due to the measurement error associated with each of the individual awards * * *. A distribution of damage awards really consists of a set of mini-distributions reflecting the error in measurement around some "true" award for each case. The "correct" award can be made visible by certain procedural devices, such as repeated trials of the same case, or aggregation.

Try another thought experiment. Suppose that in an aggregation of cases, every one of 1000 were identical, and from those, 100 were drawn at random for trial. By trying these 100 cases and taking the average award, the court will have done the equivalent of our first thought experiment and will have far more accurately measured the correct damages than is usually done in individualized cases. By granting the mean award to each of the 100 cases, the court awards a more nearly correct amount than if each case received the award assigned by its jury. By awarding that same amount to each of the remaining 900 plaintiffs, the court also does better, in terms of accuracy of award, than it would if it conducted 900 individualized trials.

Saks & Blanck, Justice Improved: The Unrecognized Benefits of Sampling and Aggregation in the Trial of Mass Torts, 44 Stan.L.Rev. 815, 833–35 (1992). But wouldn't this analysis depend on a very high comparability in the claims of all claimants; to the extent they are not nearly identical, is it fair to say that this method would be better than an individual trial? For an argument that Saks and Blanck underestimate the additional risk of error resulting from statistical sampling, see Bone, Statistical Adjudication: Rights, Justice and Utility in a World of Process Scarcity, 46 Vand. L. Rev. 561 (1993). Prof. Bone carefully dissects the use of sampling from a variety of perspectives, including a process-based analysis and a rights-based view as well as in terms of efficiency.

2. Even proponents of using sampling worry about improper use of the technique. For example, Judge Parker, who employed a sampling technique in *Cimino*, was appointed to the court of appeals and presented with similar issues in In re Chevron U.S.A., Inc., 109 F.3d 1016 (5th Cir.1997). Plaintiffs were some 3,000 people who lived in an area where Chevron allegedly once operated a crude oil storage waste pit, and they sought to recover for

personal injuries and property damages due to alleged contamination of the area. The district court ordered that plaintiffs and defendants each designate 15 plaintiffs for a bellwether group of 30 claimants in a "unitary trial" that Chevron claimed would determine its liability (or at least produce verdicts that could be used in settlement discussions). Chevron submitted the affidavit of the same statistics expert who supported the trial method in *Cimino*, asserting that the plan in this case was flawed because the 30 plaintiffs thus selected were "not representative," arguing that a "stratified selection process" should be used to select the representatives if a bellwether trial were to be attempted. The district court refused to change its order, and Chevron sought a writ of mandamus.

Speaking through Judge Parker, the Fifth Circuit granted a writ of mandamus precluding any use of the "bellwether trials" with regard to the claims of other plaintiffs because the 30 selected plaintiffs were not representative, and the plan would rely on "a trial of fifteen of the 'best' and fifteen of the 'worst' cases in the universe of cases involved in the litigation." Judge Parker explained:

> The selected thirty cases included in the district court's "unitary trial" are not cases calculated to represent the group of 3,000 claimants. Thus, the results that would be obtained from a trial of these thirty (30) cases lack the requisite level of representativeness so that the results could permit a court to draw sufficiently reliable inferences about the whole that could, in turn, form the basis for a judgment affecting cases other than the selected thirty. While this particular sample of thirty cases is lacking in representativeness, statistical sampling with an appropriate level of representativeness has been utilized and approved.
> * * *
> We, therefore, hold that before a trial court may utilize results from a bellwether trial for a purpose that extends beyond the individual cases tried, it must, prior to any extrapolation, find that the cases tried are representative of the larger group of cases or claims from which they are selected. Typically, such a finding must be based on competent, scientific, statistical evidence that identifies the variables involved and that provides a sample of sufficient size so as to permit a finding that there is a sufficient level of confidence that the results obtained reflect results that would be obtained from trials of the whole. It is such findings that provide the foundation for any inferences that may be drawn from the trial of sample cases. Without a sufficient level of confidence in the sample results, no inferences may be drawn from such results that would form the basis for applying such results to cases or claims that have not been actually tried.

Judge Jones concurred specially. In her view, the entire sampling idea was dubious:

> [T]here is a fine line between deriving results from trials based on statistical sampling and pure legislation. Judges must be sensitive to stay within our proper bounds of adjudicating individual disputes. We are not authorized by the Constitution or statutes to legislate solutions to cases in pursuit of efficiency and expeditiousness. Essential to due process for litigants, including both the plaintiffs and Chevron in this

non-class action context, is their right to the opportunity for an individual assessment of liability and damages in each case. Nowhere did the district court explain how it was authorized to make the results of this bellwether trial unitary for any purposes concerning the 2,970 other plaintiffs' cases pending before him. In sum, I simply do not share Judge Parker's confidence that bellwether trials can be used to resolve mass tort controversies.

3. By the time Judge Parker held his trial in *Cimino* many other asbestos cases had gone to trial. Could these trial results have been used to generate a statistical database for remedies? Compare Amchem Products, Inc. v. Windsor, *supra* p. 373 (settlement based on such a matrix). After A.H. Robins Co. filed its bankruptcy petition, such a method was employed to develop an aggregate valuation figure for some 300,000 claims that were submitted in the bankruptcy proceeding. Using detailed medical data and other information on a sampling of the 9,500 Dalkon Shield cases that had been resolved (mostly by settlement) prior to the bankruptcy filing, and on some 8,000 randomly selected claims from among the new filings, experts were able to generate estimates of the likely aggregate liability for the 300,000 new claimants. See R. Sobol, Bending the Law 171–97 (1991) (detailing the Dalkon Shield estimation process); Feinberg, The Dalkon Shield Claimant's Trust, 53 Law & Contemp. Probs. 79, 102 (Autumn 1990). Could a similar method be used to establish individual settlements or awards for new claimants? See id. at 97 (suggesting that claims scheme could base compensation amounts on "historical compensation data [that] can be compiled and analyzed to reveal the effect of various factors on recovery in past claims arising out of the same mass tort").

4. In Watson v. Shell Oil Co., 979 F.2d 1014 (5th Cir.1992), a class action on behalf of over 18,000 claimants for damages resulting from a massive oil refinery explosion, a somewhat similar technique was upheld. Regarding punitive damages, the district court established a two-step trial process. In the first stage a jury would determine whether defendants were liable for punitive damages. If liability were found, stage two would involve 20 fully-tried sample plaintiff cases. Based on findings in those 20 cases, the jury would establish the ratio of punitive damages to compensatory damages for the remaining claimants. Then a different jury would resolve issues unique to each plaintiff's compensatory damages claims, which would be tried in waves of five. The court upheld the trial method "because the Phase 2 jury is to make a determination about punitive damages in a mass-disaster context, rather than compensatory damages in products liability litigation." Id. at 1019. The court emphasized that punitive damages turn mainly on the culpability of defendant's conduct, which is common to all plaintiffs, and that there would be no effort to extrapolate compensatory damage amounts.

5. In *In re Fibreboard*, Judge Higginbotham spoke of the "culture of the jury trial." Plaintiffs may have an important stake in that culture. Thus, Professor Trangsrud has argued that "[u]nderlying our tradition of individual claim autonomy in substantial tort cases is the natural law notion that this is an important personal right of the individual. While much less celebrated than other natural rights, such as the right to practice one's own religion or to think and speak freely, the right to control personally the suit whereby a badly injured person seeks redress from the alleged tortfeasor has

long been valued both here and in England." Trangsrud, Mass Trials in Mass Tort Cases: A Dissent, 1989 U.Ill.L.Rev. 69, 74.

At least in some situations, deviation from the traditional trial format may deprive claimants of opportunities they deem significant. Some Dalkon Shield claimants, for example, reacted adversely to the effort to assign values to their claims through the bankruptcy process. Many claimants evidently wanted Robins to apologize for the harms suffered by victims. As one observer reported, "[t]he victims ask the judicial system to stage a morality play wherein the victims can tell their tragic stories, and the judge (like a modern Greek chorus) can certify the truth." R. Bacigal, The Limits of Litigation—The Dalkon Shield Controversy 125–26 (1990). Under the press of mass litigation, do similar concerns of asbestos claimants lose force?

How realistic are these natural law aspirations? Most cases result in settlements worked out by lawyers, and plaintiffs often feel they have little influence on the resolution of their cases. In asbestos litigation in particular, lawyers often settle cases by the bunch rather than treating each as individual. D. Hensler, W. Felstiner, M. Selvin & P. Ebener, Asbestos in the Courts: The Challenge of Mass Toxic Torts 89–97 (1985). Thus, if the goal is to permit the litigants a sense of participation it is not so clear that the traditional way of handling tort litigation protects these interests of plaintiffs:

> Ironically, formal aggregative procedures may provide more opportunities for litigants to participate in a hearing of their case than traditional tort approaches to routine or mass cases. In the Agent Orange litigation, Judge Weinstein held fairness hearings in various cities around the country where veterans appeared to present their views of the settlement. Although it may not have satisfied their desire for vindication, at least a forum was provided for some of the Agent Orange litigants to be heard. Under the Ohio asbestos litigation plan, plaintiffs participated in evaluation conferences, an opportunity * * * they "appeared to appreciate." The Manville and Dalkon Shield litigation trusts provide for claimant hearings.

Hensler, Resolving Mass Toxic Torts: Myths and Realities, 1989 U.Ill.L.Rev. 89, 99–100. Do these features of some mass tort cases provide an important opportunity or window dressing?

6. Professors Walker and Monahan urge that the right way to approach sampling data as evidence in mass tort and similar cases is to scrutinize it in exactly the same way expert evidence is handled under Daubert v. Merrell Dow Pharmaceuticals, 509 U.S. 579, 113 S.Ct. 2786, 125 L.Ed.2d 469 (1993). See Walker & Monahan, Sampling Liability, 85 Va. L.Rev. 329 (1999); Walker & Monahan, Sampling Damages, 83 Iowa L.Rev. 545 (1998). They argue that "[a]mong the principles of complex litigation, the survey method appears novel and controversial, but among the principles of scientific evidence, the survey method is commonplace and universally accepted." 83 Iowa L.Rev. at 561. They criticize the cases discussed in this section on the ground that they "incorporate cautious tentative measures that fail to realize the full potential of statistical sampling to solve many of the problems posed by throngs of claimants." Id. at 546. Nonetheless, Professors Walker and Monahan warn that, at least with regard to determin-

ing liability, "the method of proof [should] be determined by the cost of collecting information. Individualized information should be used where it is practical—i.e., cost effective—to obtain. If individual information is not practical to obtain, however, sampling should be sued so that a judgment can be reached efficiently and expeditiously." Would Professors Saks and Blanck (*supra* note 1) similarly limit its use?

Chapter VIII

PRECLUSIVE EFFECTS OF JUDGMENTS IN COMPLEX LITIGATION

Claim preclusion (or res judicata) and issue preclusion (or collateral estoppel) are central to the disposition of complex litigation. They reflect the policy that once there has been a valid and final judgment, courts should not be required to adjudicate, nor parties to answer for, successive suits arising out of the same transaction or raising issues which have actually been litigated and necessarily determined. Finality and repose are the most significant policies underlying preclusion, but in the context of complex litigation, efficiency and judicial economy are also important objectives. For example, the expansion of joinder, which has played an important role in the growth of complex litigation, will promote judicial economy only if complemented by sufficiently definite preclusion standards so that the parties can know what, in fact, has been settled and who, in fact, is bound by a judgment.

Resolving the claims of many parties in one suit or precluding an entire class and its opponents from further litigation is an economical result which can be achieved through the combined effect of liberal joinder and preclusion. But there are genuine concerns that preclusion doctrines may become too attractive to judges worried about overcrowded dockets and that broad application may sacrifice fairness for finality. Thus a number of considerations must be weighed in each case to determine whether preclusion is appropriate—including whether, in the first suit, notice was adequate, whether there was full and fair opportunity to litigate, and whether the interests of persons sought to be precluded were sufficiently similar to those of the original parties. These sorts of themes, and the interplay of the policies underlying the preclusion doctrines, will be explored in the following pages.

A. CLAIM PRECLUSION (RES JUDICATA)

Claim preclusion (combining the concepts of *merger* and *bar*) requires that the first suit: 1) involved *the same cause of action* as is sued upon in the second suit, 2) ended in a final judgment *on the merits,* and 3) was between the *same parties.*

The *"same cause of action"* requirement has undergone considerable change in recent years. Many jurisdictions now follow the "transactional" test, described in the Restatement (Second) of Judgments, § 24, as extinguishing "all rights of the plaintiff to remedies against the defendant with respect to all or any part of the transaction, or series of connected transactions, out of which the action arose." What constitutes a "transaction" is "to be determined pragmatically, giving weight to such considerations as whether the facts are related in time, space, origin, or motivation, whether they form a convenient trial unit, and whether their treatment as a unit conforms to the parties' expectations or business understanding or usage."

Similarly, the *"on the merits"* requirement has undergone change and no longer can be read as meaning that the merits were actually addressed and decided. Federal Rule of Civil Procedure 41(b) exemplifies the watering down of the "on the merits" requirement in providing that "unless the court in its order for dismissal otherwise specifies, a dismissal under this subdivision and any dismissal not provided for in this rule, other than a dismissal for lack of jurisdiction, or improper venue, or for failure to join a party under Rule 19, operates as an adjudication upon the merits." See Rinehart v. Locke, 454 F.2d 313 (7th Cir.1971) (dismissal under Rule 12(b)(6) for failure to make allegations sufficient to state a claim was "on the merits," barring a later suit based on the same events).

The *"same parties"* requirement raises special problems in the context of complex litigation. Only parties or their privies are bound by res judicata. "Privity" is essentially a legal conclusion that, in fact, a nonparty has a sufficient relationship to a party that it should be bound by the judgment as is the party. Privity may be based on the fact that a party acted on behalf of the nonparty in the first action (as, for example, when a party appears as the representative of a class, or as trustee or guardian representing a beneficiary or ward, or as executor or administrator of an estate). It may also be based on a legal relationship between a party and nonparty that makes it fair to bind the nonparty by the judgment (as with successors in interest, stockholders *vis-à-vis* an earlier suit by their corporation, and third-party beneficiaries *vis-à-vis* an earlier suit by the promisee). The materials in the following sections will explore some of the "same party" problems which arise in complex litigation.

1. PERSONS OR ENTITIES BOUND BY PRIOR JUDGMENT

Complex cases usually do not raise unique considerations concerning the application of the "same cause of action" and "on the merits" requirements of claim preclusion. The "same parties" requirement, however, can be enormously complicated in the context of complex litigation. Complex cases often involve parties acting in some form of representational capacity, as through a trustee or other fiduciary, through an organization acting on behalf of its members, through a governmental body, or through the paradigm of representational litigation, the class action. Some of the problems involved in determining which persons or entities will be bound by a judgment will be considered here.

TYUS v. SCHOEMEHL

United States Court of Appeals, Eighth Circuit, 1996.
93 F.3d 449, cert. denied, 520 U.S. 1166, 117 S.Ct. 1427, 137 L.Ed.2d 536 (1997).

Before BOWMAN, CIRCUIT JUDGE, HENLEY, SENIOR CIRCUIT JUDGE, and MAGILL, CIRCUIT JUDGE.

MAGILL, CIRCUIT JUDGE.

At issue in this § 2 Voting Rights Act case is whether issue preclusion bars certain plaintiffs-appellants from bringing a second suit challenging the St. Louis aldermanic district boundaries, which are drawn based on the 1990 federal decennial census. Although these appellants were not parties to the original lawsuit challenging the aldermanic boundaries, they were "virtually represented" by those plaintiffs to the Aldermen–AAVR suit, and therefore issue preclusion does apply. The district court held that claim preclusion, rather than issue preclusion, applies, so we affirm on alternate grounds.

I.

The city of St. Louis is governed by a Board of Aldermen consisting of twenty-eight aldermen elected from twenty-eight single-member wards. In 1991, St. Louis began to redraw the aldermanic boundaries in accordance with the 1990 census. Although the census revealed that African–Americans comprised a majority in thirteen of the twenty-eight wards, and were a plurality in one additional ward, the majority of aldermen voted to adopt an aldermanic map that provided for sixteen wards in which whites have a voting age majority and twelve wards in which African–Americans have a voting age majority.

A. AAVR Lawsuit

On January 16, 1992, a group of African–Americans filed the AAVR lawsuit, challenging the validity of the new ward boundaries. Among the named plaintiffs were five African-American St. Louis aldermen—Freeman Bosley, Sr., Sharon Tyus, Bertha Mitchell, Claude Taylor, and Irving Clay, Jr. (the Aldermen plaintiffs)—and the African American Voting Rights Legal Defense Fund. Initially, several different counsel represented the plaintiffs. Eventually, these attorneys were replaced with attorney Judson Miner.

In this suit, plaintiffs contended that (1) the boundary lines were drawn in such a way as to fragment concentrations of black population, diluting black voting strength in violation of § 2 of the Voting Rights

Act, 42 U.S.C.A. § 1973 (West 1994 & Supp.1996), and the First, Thirteenth, Fourteenth, and Fifteenth Amendments to the United States Constitution; (2) the boundary lines were drawn in such a way as to pack concentrations of black population into specific wards, diluting overall black voting strength in violation of the above provisions; and (3) the ward boundaries violate the Fourteenth Amendment, because they have populations with a variance in excess of ten percent.

On February 19, 1992, defendants in the Aldermen–AAVR suit (collectively, the City) moved for summary judgment, contending that the map had been drawn in such a way as to provide substantial proportionality. Four affidavits supporting this claim, including a statistical analysis performed by * * * the city's expert, were attached. On April 27, 1992, counsel for plaintiffs opposed this motion with an affidavit from expert witness Dr. Charlene Jones. The affidavit discussed the appropriate means of measuring proportional representation and other issues surrounding both the dilution claim and the Fourteenth Amendment claim.

Meanwhile, a dispute over trial strategy had arisen between the Aldermen plaintiffs and original counsel. On April 24, 1992, the Aldermen plaintiffs hired their current attorney, Judson Miner. On May 5, the Aldermen plaintiffs moved to voluntarily withdraw from the Aldermen–AAVR suit and have their claims dismissed without prejudice.

After having sought leave to withdraw from the Alderman–AAVR suit, the Alderman plaintiffs learned that the original counsel had responded to the City's summary judgment motion with only the Jones affidavit. On May 26, 1992, dissatisfied with this submission, the Alderman plaintiffs sought leave to file out of time a twelve-page memorandum of law and two supporting affidavits in an attempt to bolster the Jones affidavit. This motion, made more than three months after the City's summary judgment motion, was denied by the district court without explanation.

B. *Miller Lawsuit*

On April 27, 1992, with the City's summary judgment motion pending in the Aldermen–AAVR suit, the Aldermen plaintiffs filed a second lawsuit against the City challenging the St. Louis map. In this suit, the plaintiffs raised the same claims as those raised in the Aldermen–AAVR suit. * * * At this time, attorney Miner represented the plaintiffs in both suits. The Aldermen plaintiffs were joined in the Miller suit by Sterling Miller, Clarence Woodruff, and Paula Carter (an African–American Missouri state representative).

C. *Subsequent Orders in the Two Suits*

On June 17, 1992, the district court in the Aldermen–AAVR suit granted the City's motion for summary judgment. * * *

On June 20, the City [moved to dismiss], contending now that, given the grant of summary judgment to the City in the Aldermen–AAVR suit, the *Miller* suit was barred by res judicata and stare decisis.

* * *

The district court converted the City's June 20 motion to dismiss the Miller suit into a summary judgment motion, and on March 2, 1993, the court granted this motion on claim preclusion grounds. The court first noted that the Aldermen plaintiffs, who were never allowed to withdraw from the Aldermen–AAVR suit, were clearly barred from raising their claims by claim preclusion. Further, although plaintiffs Miller, Woodruff, and Carter were not parties to the Aldermen–AAVR suit, they were nevertheless in privity with the plaintiffs in the Aldermen–AAVR suit under a theory of "virtual representation." According to the district court, these plaintiffs had been adequately represented by the plaintiffs in the Aldermen–AAVR suit and thus were bound by the ruling in that suit. * * *

II.

A.

Both suits raise identical dilution claims. Each contends the map boundaries violate § 2 of the Voting Rights Act by fragmenting black voters, thereby diluting black voting strength. Each also contends that the dilution of black voting strength violates the Fourteenth and Fifteenth Amendments. At issue, then, is whether the Miller suit is barred by issue preclusion[5] because the claims raised in that suit were litigated and necessarily decided by the Aldermen–AAVR suit. We hold that it is.[6]

Under issue preclusion, once a court has decided an issue of fact or law necessary to its judgment, "the determination is conclusive in a subsequent action between the parties, whether on the same or a different claim." Restatement (Second) of Judgments § 27 (1982). Issue

---

5. Regarding the interplay between issue preclusion and claim preclusion, the Supreme Court has noted:

> The preclusive effects of former adjudication are discussed in varying and, at times, seemingly conflicting terminology, attributable to the evolution of preclusion concepts over the years. These effects are referred to collectively by most commentators as the doctrine of "res judicata." Res judicata is often analyzed further to consist of two preclusion concepts: "issue preclusion" and "claim preclusion." Issue preclusion refers to the effect of a judgment in foreclosing relitigation of a matter that has been litigated and decided. Claim preclusion refers to the effect of a judgment in foreclosing litigation of a matter that never has been litigated, be-

cause of a determination that it should have been advanced in an earlier suit. Claim preclusion therefore encompasses the law of merger and bar.

Migra v. Warren City Sch. Dist. Bd. of Educ., 465 U.S. 75, 77 n. 1, 104 S.Ct. 892, 894 n. 1, 79 L.Ed.2d 56 (1984).

6. Although the district court applied claim preclusion when granting the City's motion for summary judgment, we believe that issue preclusion is the appropriate preclusion doctrine in this case. We nevertheless may affirm the district court, for "we may affirm the district court's grant of summary judgment on any ground supported by record." White v. Moulder, 30 F.3d 80, 82 (8th Cir.1994), cert. denied, 513 U.S. 1084, 115 S.Ct. 738, 130 L.Ed.2d 641 (1995).

preclusion will also bar relitigation of an issue by one who, although not a party to the original suit, is in privity with a party to that suit.

In addition to the requirement that the party in the second suit sought to be precluded was a party, or in privity with a party, to the original lawsuit, see id., there are four other prerequisites to the application of issue preclusion: (1) the issue sought to be precluded must be the same as that involved in a prior action; (2) the issue must have been actually litigated in the prior action; (3) the issue must have been determined by a valid and final judgment; and (4) the determination must have been essential to the prior judgment. The parties do not contest that the last four requirements for preclusion are met in this case. The sole issue, therefore, is whether the Miller plaintiffs are in privity with the Aldermen plaintiffs, so that the Miller plaintiffs should be bound by the result in the Aldermen–AAVR suit.

B.

Preclusion is rooted in concerns of judicial economy. * * * Additionally, the preclusion doctrines protect defendants, by relieving them of "the expense and vexation attending multiple lawsuits." United States v. Gurley, 43 F.3d 1188, 1197 (8th Cir.1994) (quoting Montana [v. United States,] 440 U.S. at 153, 99 S.Ct. at 973), cert. denied, 516 U.S. 817, 116 S.Ct. 73, 133 L.Ed.2d 33 (1995).

However, due process concerns are present when the party sought to be precluded was not an actual party in the first lawsuit. Because preclusion based on privity is an exception to the "deep-rooted historic tradition that everyone should have his own day in court," Richards v. Jefferson County, Ala., 517 U.S. 793, 798, 116 S.Ct. 1761, 1766, 135 L.Ed.2d 76 (1996), courts must ensure that the relationship between the party to the original suit and the party sought to be precluded in the later suit is sufficiently close to justify preclusion. Thus, "the due process clauses prevent preclusion when the relationship between the party and non-party becomes too attenuated." Southwest Airlines Co. v. Texas Int'l Airlines, 546 F.2d 84, 95 (5th Cir.), cert. denied, 434 U.S. 832, 98 S.Ct. 117, 54 L.Ed.2d 93 (1977).

There are three generally recognized categories of nonparties who will be considered in privity with a party to the prior action and who will be bound by a prior adjudication: (1) a nonparty who controls the original action; (2) a successor-in-interest to a prior party; and (3) a nonparty whose interests were adequately represented by a party to the original action. This case focuses on the third category.

Preclusion based on adequate representation, otherwise known as "virtual representation," was given its clearest statement in Aerojet–General Corp. v. Askew, 511 F.2d 710 (5th Cir.), cert. denied, 423 U.S. 908, 96 S.Ct. 210, 46 L.Ed.2d 137 (1975). In that case, the court noted that "[u]nder the federal law of res judicata, a person may be bound by a judgment even though not a party if one of the parties to the suit is so closely aligned with his interests as to be his virtual representative."

Although this principle is generally accepted, courts are sharply divided on how to implement this strand of issue preclusion.

Some courts permit a wide use of virtual representation, inquiring whether there exists a substantial relationship between the party and nonparty, such that the party adequately represented the interests of the nonparty. Because of the fact-intensive nature of these inquiries, there is no clear test that can be employed to determine if virtual representation is appropriate. It is evident, however, that because virtual representation rests on the notion that it is fair to deprive a nonparty of his day in court, "virtual representation has a pronounced equitable dimension." A nonparty will be barred from bringing his claim only when "the balance of the relevant equities tips in favor of preclusion."

Other courts would permit a nonparty to be bound by a prior judgment under a theory of virtual representation only in very limited, technical situations. For example, in Pollard v. Cockrell, 578 F.2d 1002 (5th Cir.1978), the court noted that "[v]irtual representation demands the existence of an express or implied legal relationship in which parties to the first suit are accountable to non-parties who file a subsequent suit raising identical issues." Id. at 1008. Examples of such a relationship would be " 'estate beneficiaries bound by administrators, presidents and sole stockholders by their companies, parent corporations by their subsidiaries, and a trust beneficiary by the trustee.' " Pollard, 578 F.2d at 1008–09 (quoting Southwest Airlines Co., 546 F.2d at 97). Under this view, virtual representation is little more than the doctrine of preclusion based on representation that has historically been accepted by courts.

We agree with those courts that give wider use to virtual representation. This liberal use better accommodates the competing considerations of judicial economy and due process. Although we are cognizant of the concerns underlying the Pollard decision—that broad use of this doctrine will completely eviscerate the notion that a party is entitled to his day in court—we believe that these concerns are better addressed through a careful application of the doctrine to the facts in a given case than by artificially limiting the scope of the doctrine.

This conclusion is not altered by the recent Supreme Court decision in Richards. In Richards, the Court permitted a group of taxpayers to challenge a municipal tax as an unconstitutional deprivation of property, even though an earlier group of taxpayers had already litigated this issue and lost. The Court began by reaffirming the general rule that " 'one is not bound by a judgment in personam in a litigation in which he is not designated as a party....' " Richards, 517 U.S. at 798, 116 S.Ct. at 1765–66 (quoting Hansberry v. Lee, 311 U.S. 32, 40, 61 S.Ct. 115, 117, 85 L.Ed. 22 (1940)). Because the two sets of plaintiffs were "mere 'strangers' to one another," the Court concluded that the plaintiffs to the earlier suit did not provide "representation sufficient to make up for the fact that [the second set of plaintiffs] neither participated in, nor had the opportunity to participate in, the [earlier] action."

However, the Court did note one important exception to the general rule: a party to the second case will be bound by the result of an earlier case to which it was not a party "when it can be said that there is 'privity' between a party to the second case and a party who is bound by an earlier judgment." Although the Court provided some examples of what could constitute privity, it did not offer a general definition of that term. Rather, the Court acknowledged that "the term 'privity' is now used to describe various relationships between litigants that would not have come within the traditional definition of that term."

Virtual representation falls squarely within this exception. A court will apply virtual representation only when it finds the existence of some special relationship between the parties justifying preclusion. In essence, this is a finding that the two parties are in privity. When, as in *Richards*, the two parties are strangers to each other, then virtual representation would not be appropriate. However, where there is a special relationship between the parties, determined after analyzing the factors listed below, then the parties are in privity, and *Richards* is simply inapposite.

C.

Due to the equitable and fact-intensive nature of virtual representation, there is no clear test for determining the applicability of the doctrine. There are, however, several guiding principles. First, identity of interests between the two parties is necessary, though not alone sufficient. Other factors to be considered "include a close relationship between the prior and present parties; participation in the prior litigation; apparent acquiescence; and whether the present party deliberately maneuvered to avoid the effects of the first action." Petit v. City of Chicago, 766 F.Supp. 607, 612 (N.D.Ill.1991).

Another factor to consider is adequacy of representation, which is best viewed in terms of incentive to litigate. That is, one party "adequately represents" the interests of another when the interests of the two parties are very closely aligned and the first party had a strong incentive to protect the interests of the second party.

Finally, the nature of the issue raised—whether a public law issue or private law issue—is important. Although virtual representation may be used in the private law context, its use is particularly appropriate for public law issues. As the Supreme Court recently noted, when a case challenges a "public action that has only an indirect impact on [a party's] interests," *Richards*, 517 U.S. at 803, 116 S.Ct. at 1768, due process concerns are lessened. In this situation, courts have "wide latitude to establish procedures ... to limit the number of judicial proceedings...."

Further, we note that in public law cases, the number of plaintiffs with standing is potentially limitless. If parties were allowed to continually raise issues already decided, public law claims "would assume immortality." Concerns of judicial economy and cost to defendants, while present in every suit, are particularly important in this context. There is another important consideration: in the public law context, if the plaintiff wins, by definition everyone benefits. Holding preclusion inapplicable in this context would encourage fence-sitting, because nonparties would benefit if the plaintiffs were successful but would not be penalized if the plaintiffs lost.

D.

We conclude that issue preclusion based on virtual representation is appropriate in this case. In reaching this conclusion, we are persuaded by the reasoning of *Petit, supra*. In *Petit*, the city of Chicago, in response to a suit brought by the United States Department of Justice alleging discrimination in hiring and promoting blacks, Hispanics, and women within the Chicago Police Department, developed a new sergeant's exam, consisting of a written test, oral examination, and performance evaluation. Many white applicants for sergeant sought to intervene in the continuing suit, alleging that the city manipulated the test scores in favor of minority applicants. Intervention was permitted, and subsequently many of the intervenors' claims were dismissed with prejudice.

Having failed to obtain redress, many of the intervenors, along with additional white police officers, filed the action in *Petit*, raising the same claims previously dismissed. The court held that res judicata barred all claims, including those of plaintiffs who had not intervened in the earlier suit.

In applying the virtual representation doctrine, the court relied on several factors. The court first mentioned that the claims raised in the two suits were identical, and that the same counsel argued both cases. More significantly, the court took notice of the tactical maneuvering taking place:

> The intervenors cannot avoid an express federal court order that dismissed their claims with prejudice by adding the non-intervenors and refiling this claim. A finding of privity comports with the policy behind res judicata. If the intervenors succeeded originally, all of the white police officers would have benefitted—even the non-intervenors. On the other hand, if the intervenors lost, which they did, the non-intervenors cannot obtain a second determination by bringing this separate action. Such an action would encourage "fence-sitting" and discourage the principles and policies the doctrine of res judicata was designed to promote.

Given the close alignment of interests between the first suit intervenors and nonintervenors, and the tactical maneuvering taking place, the district court held that the nonintervenors had already taken their bite at the litigative apple.

The facts in the present case are similar to those in *Petit*. First, both the Aldermen–AAVR suit and the *Miller* suit raise similar claims, and there was an overlap in plaintiffs between the two suits. Further, attorney Miner was plaintiffs' counsel in the *Miller* suit, and he was substituted as counsel in the Aldermen–AAVR suit on April 24, 1992, well before the City's summary judgment motion was granted. These factors suggest, at least partly, that a close relationship exists between the prior and present parties.

We further note that plaintiff Carter, potential plaintiffs Clay Jr. and Jones, and all of the Aldermen plaintiffs were elected African–American officials. They all shared the same concern: the dilution of the African–American vote in St. Louis. This organizational commonality suggests a special commonality of interests.

More importantly, as in *Petit*, there is tactical maneuvering taking place in *Miller*. In an effort to circumvent trial strategy disagreements, the Aldermen plaintiffs filed the *Miller* suit, simply adding new plaintiffs. This second lawsuit directly contravenes the policies supporting the preclusion doctrines. A victory by the Aldermen plaintiffs in the Aldermen–AAVR suit would have directly benefited the Miller plaintiffs. On the other hand, without virtual representation, a loss by the Aldermen plaintiffs would cause no harm to the Miller plaintiffs. In such a situation, there is no incentive to intervene. Quite the contrary: holding preclusion inapplicable assures that a party would not intervene, for it would allow various members of a coordinated group to bring separate lawsuits in the hope that one member of the group would eventually be successful, benefiting the entire group. This entails a significant cost to the judicial system and "discourage[s] the principles and policies the doctrine of res judicata was designed to promote."

Finally, that the *Miller* case raises an issue of public law is another factor in favor of preclusion. The Miller plaintiffs do not allege that they have been denied the individual right to vote. Rather, they allege that the strength of the black vote in general has been diluted. Because the plaintiffs do not allege that they "have a different private right not shared in common with the public," the plaintiffs raise an issue of public law, and thus the due process concerns attendant with a broad application of preclusion are lessened. Further, given the public nature of this case, if we held preclusion inapplicable, this case could "assume immortality," and fence-sitting would be encouraged.

The Miller plaintiffs contend that preclusion is inappropriate because the Aldermen plaintiffs did not adequately represent their interests at the first trial. They note that counsel in the Aldermen–AAVR suit failed to file a formal motion in opposition to the summary judgment motion. Plaintiffs argue that absent an effective and diligent prosecution of the case at the first trial, virtual representation is inapplicable. We disagree.

As noted above, adequate representation is best viewed in terms of incentive to litigate. The Aldermen plaintiffs had every incentive and opportunity to fully litigate the claims raised in the Aldermen–AAVR suit. No more is required.

Given the factors counseling in favor of preclusion, we determine that the Aldermen plaintiffs adequately represented the interests of the Miller plaintiffs, and thus the two sets of plaintiffs are in privity. The

Miller plaintiffs have vicariously had their day in court and their "one bite at the apple." As such, they are precluded from litigating those issues that were decided by the Aldermen–AAVR suit.[8]

HENLEY, SENIOR CIRCUIT JUDGE, concurring in the result.

The panel's opinion is very well written and seems to make the best of the arguments in favor of finding preclusion here. And, on balance, I agree with the panel's result: that the present case is barred by the previous litigation. Nevertheless, the case is a close one and I am uncomfortable with some of the panel's language. Accordingly, this brief statement of my reasons for concurring only in the result is tendered.

In general, I have some concern about how far we should go in extending preclusive effect to cases of so-called "virtual representation." As the panel points out, due process considerations provide an outer limit on the scope of preclusion. It is one thing to hold that a party in privity under principles of contract or property law should be bound by the results of prior litigation. It is quite another matter, however, to say that strangers to the prior litigation should be bound solely because they would raise the same issue or favor the same legal position.

More specifically, in this case, I believe it is a close question whether our result is fully consistent with the language and spirit of the Supreme Court's decision this term in *Richards*. In *Richards*, the Court held that a suit by persons employed in Jefferson County challenging the constitutionality of an occupation tax was not barred by principles of res judicata even though a prior suit (by the City of Birmingham and several individual taxpayers) had upheld the constitutionality of the same tax. The Court said that the taxpayers in the second suit could not be bound by the decision on the merits in the first suit, because they received neither "notice of, nor sufficient representation in" the prior litigation.

The panel opinion does not directly address the issue of "notice" here and concludes that all that is necessary to satisfy the "sufficient representation" prong of *Richards* is that the plaintiffs in the first suit had the "incentive" to raise the same issues the parties in the second suit would raise. However, the Supreme Court's opinion appears to require something more than just incentive: "a prior proceeding, to have binding effect on absent parties, would at least have to be 'so devised and applied as to insure ... that the litigation is so conducted as to insure the *full and fair consideration* of the common issue.'" Richards, 517 U.S. at 800–01, 116 S.Ct. at 1767, quoting Hansberry v. Lee, 311 U.S. 32, 43, 61 S.Ct. 115, 118, 85 L.Ed. 22 (1940) (emphasis added).

---

8. The Miller plaintiffs contend that preclusion is inapplicable in this case given the changes in voting rights jurisprudence occasioned by Shaw v. Reno, 509 U.S. 630, 113 S.Ct. 2816, 125 L.Ed.2d 511 (1993), and Miller v. Johnson, 515 U.S. 900, 115 S.Ct. 2475, 132 L.Ed.2d 762 (1995), both decided after the filing of the complaint in the Aldermen–AAVR suit.

Although some courts have declined to apply preclusion principles given an intervening change in voting rights law, see, e.g., Parnell v. Rapides Parish Sch. Bd., 563 F.2d 180, 185 (5th Cir.1977), cert. denied, 438 U.S. 915, 98 S.Ct. 3144, 57 L.Ed.2d 1160 (1978), in this case there was no intervening legal change, as argued by the Miller plaintiffs. * * *

Despite these misgivings about the proposition of "virtual representation" preclusion in general and some of the language of the panel's opinion, I believe that on the facts here, the requirements of "notice" and "sufficient representation" were satisfied. In particular, the plaintiffs in the second suit clearly were on notice of the first litigation, because some of them had also been plaintiffs in the prior suit. Moreover, the same counsel represented plaintiffs in both actions. I believe that this identity of counsel and (at least some of the) plaintiffs also suggests that the "sufficient representation" requirement of due process was met. In addition, as the panel opinion points out, it appears that the principal reason for filing the second suit was to evade the judgment in the first suit.

It is noted, however, that the first suit was not filed as a class action, that the litigation was disposed of on motion for summary judgment, and that plaintiffs there filed only one affidavit and no brief opposing summary judgment. On these facts, it is not at all clear to me that under *Richards* a new plaintiff or group of plaintiffs—not on notice that their rights would be litigated in the first suit nor adequately represented there—would be barred from challenging the St. Louis districting plan even though there was a judgment on the merits in the first suit.

For the reasons stated, I concur in the result.

Notes and Questions

1. In the AAVR suit, the court of appeals initially affirmed the district court's grant of summary judgment in a brief memorandum by the same panel that decided the appeal in *Tyus*. After the Supreme Court vacated that decision and directed reconsideration in light of an intervening ruling of the Court, the panel reexamined the issues. African American Voting Rights Legal Defense Fund v. Villa, 54 F.3d 1345 (8th Cir.1995), cert. denied, 516 U.S. 1113, 116 S.Ct. 913, 133 L.Ed.2d 844 (1996).

The court first considered the argument that the district judge should have allowed the filing of the affidavits and memorandum that were offered belatedly. A local rule called for filing of opposing affidavits within 20 days of service of a summary judgment motion. Plaintiffs did obtain an extension until April 27, but the materials in question were not submitted until a month after that, and the appellate court held that the district judge had not committed an abuse of discretion in refusing to consider the later-filed materials. Under Fed.R.Civ.P. 60(b), permission to file late could be granted for excusable neglect. The objectors had explained their delay as follows:

> Due to fundamental differences with counsel, we dismissed our attorneys and advised them of our decision to withdraw from this case so that we could join as plaintiffs in another voting rights case challenging the same St. Louis Ward map brought by another attorney whose strategies we agree with.

The court concluded that this amounted to "disagreements concerning strategy," and that "tactical decisions do not amount to affirmative showings of excusable neglect under Rule 60(b)." It therefore limited itself to considering whether the Jones affidavit created a genuine issue of material fact.

The Jones affidavit urged that the defendants' showing was improper because it focused on voting age population rather than total population in computing black representation. Finding that voting age population was a permissible standard for determining proportionality, the court held that the City's showings demonstrated that proportionality existed under the 1991 plan, and that it had also existed under the preceding 1971 and 1981 plans. Under these circumstances, "the twenty-year history of proportionality is of sufficient duration to be considered as 'sustained,'" and the summary judgment was properly entered.

2. The *Tyus* opinion notes that some courts "permit a nonparty to be bound by a prior judgment under a theory of virtual representation only in very limited, technical situations." It cites Pollard v. Cockrell, 578 F.2d 1002 (5th Cir.1978), as requiring "an express or implied legal relationship in which parties to the first suit are accountable to non-parties who file a subsequent suit raising identical issues." In *Pollard*, certain massage parlors challenged in state court the constitutionality of ordinances regulating them and lost. Then other massage parlors, represented by the same attorneys, raised the same challenges in federal court. The federal court refused to bind the plaintiffs because there was no showing of any other relationship between the two groups of plaintiffs.

Richards v. Jefferson County, 517 U.S. 793, 116 S.Ct. 1761, 135 L.Ed.2d 76 (1996), involved a second suit by a group of taxpayers who had the same objectives as a first group of taxpayers which had already litigated a challenge to a municipal tax. The Court found them insufficiently related for "privity." *Tyus* distinguishes *Richards* as a case where "the two groups are strangers to each other." But there was some interaction between the groups, and they shared a common purpose. Does the stronger relationship between the groups in *Tyus* explain the different result?

In South Central Bell Tel. Co. v. Alabama, 526 U.S. 160, 119 S.Ct. 1180, 143 L.Ed.2d 258 (1999), the Court reaffirmed its earlier approach in *Richards*. Even though the later litigants were represented by the same lawyer, it found that there was "no special relationship between the earlier and later plaintiffs." Because the later plaintiffs were "strangers" to the earlier plaintiffs, they could not be bound by the earlier judgment.

3. Under what circumstances can strangers be deemed to have a sufficiently close identity of interests for privity? In Benson and Ford, Inc. v. Wanda Petroleum Co., 833 F.2d 1172 (5th Cir.1987), one company sued defendants alleging antitrust violations and lost. Then another unrelated company sued defendants alleging the same violations. The plaintiff in the second suit had the same lawyer as the plaintiff in the first suit and had testified in the trial of the first suit. The court refused to bind the second plaintiff by the judgment because of the lack of a relationship that permitted it to control the conduct of the first litigation.

Even a family relationship may not be enough for some courts to justify finding virtual representation even though the claims and counsel are the same. See Freeman v. Lester Coggins Trucking, 771 F.2d 860, 864 (5th Cir.1985) (father who had previously lost suit based upon his own injuries was not barred from relitigating issues in later suit on behalf of child premised on its distinct injuries arising from the same accident). However, if the family member's claims are derivative from the first plaintiff's claims, some courts have followed the rule in § 48(2) of the Restatement (Second) of Judgments (1982), that "[w]hen a person with a family relationship to one suffering personal injury has a claim for loss to himself resulting from the injury, the determination of issues in an action by the injured person to recover for his injuries is preclusive against the family member, unless the judgment was based on a defense that is unavailable against the family member in the second action." See Terrell v. DeConna, 877 F.2d 1267 (5th Cir.1989).

4. Although *Tyus* favored a "liberal use" of virtual representation, Tice v. American Airlines, Inc., 162 F.3d 966 (7th Cir.1998), represents a less favorable view, calling it "a catchy phrase coined to describe a perfectly sensible result," which "takes on a life of its own, and before too long, starts being applied to situations far removed from its intended and proper context." The court in *Tice* commented that the concept had its origin in probate proceedings, in which "it is often necessary to establish a procedure that will bind persons unknown, unascertained, or not yet born," allowing courts to find an identity of interests between the representatives who participated in the litigation and other individuals whose interests were clearly aligned with those of the litigants. "The Wright treatise observes that '[a]ll of the cases that in fact preclude relitigation by a nonparty have involved several factors in addition to apparently adequate litigation by a party holding parallel interests.' " Id. at 971, quoting 18 C. Wright, A. Miller & E. Cooper, Federal Practice & Procedure § 4457 (1998 Supp.) at 420. The court in *Tyce* noted that "in properly certified class actions, parties who have adequate notice and (at a minimum) an opportunity to opt out of an earlier case may, if their interests are sufficiently aligned with one of the earlier parties, be bound by the results of that litigation. See, e.g., Hansberry v. Lee [*supra* p. 285] and Phillips Petroleum Co. v. Shutts, [*supra* p. 412] * * * Unless there is a properly certified class action, handled with the procedural safeguards both state and federal rules afford, normal privity analysis must govern whether nonparties to an earlier case can be bound to the result. There would be little point in having Rule 23 if courts could ignore its careful structure and create *de facto* class actions at will."

Tice found that twelve pilots who challenged an American Airlines policy of not permitting pilots over 60 to act as flight officers were not bound by a judgment in an earlier suit brought by 22 American pilots as a group action authorized by the Age Discrimination in Employment Act, 29 U.S.C.A. § 626(b) (incorporating 29 U.S.C. § 216(b) of the Fair Labor Standards Act). The judgment determined that American's up-or-out policy qualified as a bona fide occupational qualification for purposes of the ADEA. "The *Tice* plaintiffs did not and could not have taken part in any of the earlier challenges to American's policy, nor did they acquiesce to being represented indirectly by those plaintiffs. Aside from the fact that both groups of pilots were employed by American, there is no evidence of any relationship between the [two groups of] plaintiffs." The court also cited *Tyus* for the proposition that "the doctrine is more appropriate in public law cases," noting that rights of older persons under the ADEA are personal and not group based, and that there was no evidence of manipulative litigation practices here.

5. The concurring opinion by Judge Henley found that "notice" and "sufficient representation" were satisfied in *Tyus* but opined that, in the absence of a class action in the first suit, new plaintiffs not on notice in the first suit would not be barred. What level of notice should be required to bind them?

6. An important area for the application of virtual representation arises when a governmental body or public authority sues first, and a citizen or other entity then files a second suit relying on the same law or legal rights asserted by the public authority in the first suit. The question is whether the citizen or entity is deemed to have a sufficiently distinct pecuniary interest so that it should not be considered to have been represented by the public authority.

Southwest Airlines Co. v. Texas International Airlines, 546 F.2d 84 (5th Cir.,), cert. denied, 434 U.S. 832, 98 S.Ct. 117, 54 L.Ed.2d 93 (1977), cited in *Tyus*, provides an example. The cities of Dallas and Fort Worth sued Southwest Airlines for a declaratory judgment that Southwest had to stop commercial air service from an airport that was being phased out in favor of a new airport. The federal district court entered a judgment that Southwest could not be excluded from using the old airport. Other competing airlines, which were using the new airport, then filed suit in state court to deny Southwest access to the old airport based on denial of the claim asserted by the cities in the first suit. The district court enjoined that litigation, and the appellate court affirmed.

Although the appellate court found that the competing airlines had a greater pecuniary interest in the success of the new airport than did the general public, it found that they were bound by the first judgment due to virtual representation. It observed that all those who provided goods and services at the new airport and all investors, developers, hotels, restaurants, and other retail interests in the vicinity could also have a pecuniary interest distinct from that of the general public. "To allow relitigation by all of these parties," it said, "would surely defeat the res judicata policies identified above." It also found that the competing airlines had no "legal interest" apart from that which the city sought to enforce in the first suit. Would it have made a difference if the competing airlines had not requested the same remedy that was denied the city?

7. Do public officials have inherent authority to bind others, or at least other public entities? Consider Nash County Board of Education v. Biltmore Co., 640 F.2d 484 (4th Cir.1981), cert. denied, 454 U.S. 878, 102 S.Ct. 359, 70 L.Ed.2d 188 (1981), in which the state attorney general sued nine dairy companies in state court for violation of the state antitrust law, purportedly acting on behalf of all public school systems in the state. After the state-court action was resolved by a consent decree, one of the school boards filed suit in federal court under the federal antitrust act. The district court dismissed the case on grounds of res judicata, and the court of appeals affirmed. Did the attorney general have authority to represent the school board? The Fourth Circuit held that, under the state antitrust statute and as

a matter of state common law, "an attorney general, in the absence of some restriction on his powers by statute or constitution, has complete authority as the representative of the State or any of its political subdivisions." Should he be required to give notice of the suit to the subdivisions? In the absence of notice, should the subdivisions be bound? Does the attorney general's authority divest the subdivisions of authority to sue on their own behalf? Could the dairies have resisted the first suit on the ground that the attorney general was exceeding his authority? These questions are not addressed in the *Nash County* opinion.

Can the attorney general of the state also act on behalf of the citizens of the state and thereby bind them by the judgment in his suit? In some cases, attorneys general have purported to sue on behalf of their citizens as parens patriae. E.g., Hawaii v. Standard Oil Co., 405 U.S. 251, 92 S.Ct. 885, 31 L.Ed.2d 184 (1972); *cf.* Hart–Scott–Rodino Antitrust Improvements Act of 1976, codified as 15 U.S.C.A. § 15c. Is this action consistent with due process?

8. Sometimes governmental action may extinguish pre-existing rights of citizens to litigate a violation of regulatory norms. Thus, in United States EPA v. City of Green Forest, 921 F.2d 1394 (8th Cir.1990), citizens sued a town for violating the Clean Water Act. That Act allows citizens to sue if governmental officials responsible for enforcement of the environmental laws do not pursue violators. After the citizens sued, the EPA filed its own action. The private plaintiffs tried to intervene in that action when a consent decree was proposed in order to argue for more stringent provisions, but the district court denied intervention. The appellate court held that this denial of intervention was error, but that it was harmless because the private plaintiffs were nevertheless allowed to file objections to the consent decree during the public comment period. The court approved the decree.

Having approved the consent decree, the district court dismissed the private citizens' claims against the town under the Clean Water Act on the ground they were precluded by entry of the consent decree. Emphasizing the "preeminent role that government actions must play in the CWA enforcement scheme," id. at 1403, the appellate court affirmed. This followed because the citizen role, as private attorney general, was intended merely as supplemental to the primary right of the public enforcement agencies, as evidenced by the provision in the statute that citizen suits would not be allowed if governmental agencies had already initiated their own actions.

9. While the matter is not altogether clear, courts usually hold that the preclusive effect of a judgment is determined by the law of the court that rendered the judgment. See, e.g., Federal Deposit Insurance Corp. v. Eckhardt, 691 F.2d 245 (6th Cir.1982); Degnan, Federalized Res Judicata, 85 Yale L.J. 733, 741 (1976); compare Burbank, Interjurisdictional Preclusion, Full Faith and Credit and Federal Common Law: A General Approach, 71 Cornell L.Rev. 733 (1986). Thus, federal law governs whether a prior federal-court judgment is res judicata.

When the court that issued the prior judgment and the court where the judgment is sought to be enforced are not both federal courts or both courts of the same state, full faith and credit considerations come into play. Art. IV, § 1 of the Constitution provides that "Full Faith and Credit shall be given in each State to the public Acts, Records, and judicial Proceedings of every other State." 28 U.S.C.A. § 1738, first adopted in 1790, states that "[t]he records and judicial proceedings of any court" of "any State, Territory, or Possession of the United States" shall have "the same full faith and credit in every court within the United States and its Territories and Possessions as they have by law or usage in the courts of such state, Territory or Possession from which they are taken." Thus both state courts and federal courts (federal courts are covered by the term "court within the United States") must give a state-court judgment the same preclusive effect as would the courts of the state where it was rendered. Similarly, it has been held that state courts must accord full faith and credit to the judgments of federal courts. Stoll v. Gottlieb, 305 U.S. 165, 59 S.Ct. 134, 83 L.Ed. 104 (1938).

Difficult full faith and credit issues have arisen as to the preclusive effect that a federal court must give to a prior state-court judgment in a federal civil rights suit. In Allen v. McCurry, 449 U.S. 90, 101 S.Ct. 411, 66 L.Ed.2d 308 (1980), plaintiff had been convicted in a state criminal court following the state-court judge's refusal to suppress evidence as resulting from an unconstitutional search and seizure. He then brought a § 1983 civil rights suit in federal court against the arresting officers. The Court applied collateral estoppel [see *infra* p. 848 for discussion of the principles of collateral estoppel] to the finding of the state court, rendered after plaintiff had a "full and fair opportunity" to litigate the issue, that plaintiff had not been subjected to an unconstitutional search and seizure. It found that nothing in the language or legislative history of § 1983 shows a congressional intent to deny the binding effect required to be given to a prior state judgment by § 1738. Kremer v. Chemical Construction Corp., 456 U.S. 461, 102 S.Ct. 1883, 72 L.Ed.2d 262 (1982), similarly accorded collateral estoppel effect in a Title VII employment discrimination action to findings in a prior state-court proceeding upholding an administrative determination that plaintiff had not been the victim of discrimination. Migra v. Warren City School District Board of Education, 465 U.S. 75, 104 S.Ct. 892, 79 L.Ed.2d 56 (1984), found no reason to make a distinction between the issue preclusive and claim preclusive effects of state-court judgments. Thus it held that the plaintiff's § 1983 suit for violation of her constitutional rights stemming from her discharge for activities involving school desegregation was precluded by her prior suit in state court for breach of contract and other state-law claims even though the federal civil rights issues had never been raised in state court. Compare the situation where the federal court has exclusive jurisdiction of the federal claim, discussed in connection with the next case.

10. Bone, Rethinking the "Day in Court" Ideal and Nonparty Preclusion, 67 N.Y.U. L. Rev. 193 (1992), challenges the widely-shared assumption that Anglo–American law has always assured litigants their own day in court and, on that basis, urges consideration of broader possibilities of binding nonparties.

2. THE EFFECT OF JUDGMENTS IN CLASS ACTIONS

MATSUSHITA ELEC. INDUS. CO. v. EPSTEIN

Supreme Court of the United States, 1996.
516 U.S. 367, 116 S.Ct. 873, 134 L.Ed.2d 6.

JUSTICE THOMAS delivered the opinion of the Court.

This case presents the question whether a federal court may withhold full faith and credit from a state-court judgment approving a class-action settlement simply because the settlement releases claims within the exclusive jurisdiction of the federal courts. The answer is no. Absent a partial repeal of the Full Faith and Credit Act, 28 U.S.C. § 1738, by another federal statute, a federal court must give the judgment the same effect that it would have in the courts of the State in which it was rendered.

I

In 1990, petitioner Matsushita Electric Industrial Co. made a tender offer for the common stock of MCA, Inc., a Delaware corporation. The tender offer not only resulted in Matsushita's acquisition of MCA, but also precipitated two lawsuits on behalf of the holders of MCA's common stock. First, a class action was filed in the Delaware Court of Chancery against MCA and its directors for breach of fiduciary duty in failing to maximize shareholder value. The complaint was later amended to state additional claims against MCA's directors for, inter alia, waste of corporate assets by exposing MCA to liability under the federal securities laws. In addition, Matsushita was added as a defendant and was accused of conspiring with MCA's directors to violate Delaware law. The Delaware suit was based purely on state-law claims.

While the state class action was pending, the instant suit was filed in Federal District Court in California. The complaint named Matsushita as a defendant and alleged that Matsushita's tender offer violated Securities Exchange Commission (SEC) Rules 10b–3 and 14d–10. These Rules were created by the SEC pursuant to the 1968 Williams Act Amendments to the Securities Exchange Act of 1934 (Exchange Act), 15 U.S.C. § 78a et seq. Section 27 of the Exchange Act confers exclusive jurisdiction upon the federal courts for suits brought to enforce the Act or rules and regulations promulgated thereunder. See 15 U.S.C. § 78aa. The District Court declined to certify the class, entered summary judgment for Matsushita, and dismissed the case. The plaintiffs appealed to the Court of Appeals for the Ninth Circuit.

After the federal plaintiffs filed their notice of appeal but before the Ninth Circuit handed down a decision, the parties to the Delaware suit negotiated a settlement. In exchange for a global release of all claims arising out of the Matsushita–MCA acquisition, the defendants would deposit $2 million into a settlement fund to be distributed pro rata to the members of the class. As required by Delaware Chancery Rule 23, which is modeled on Federal Rule of Civil Procedure 23, the Chancery Court certified the class for purposes of settlement and approved a notice of the proposed settlement. The notice informed the class members of their right to request exclusion from the settlement class and to appear and present argument at a scheduled hearing to determine the fairness of the settlement. In particular, the notice stated that "[b]y filing a valid Request for Exclusion, a member of the Settlement Class will not be precluded by the Settlement from individually seeking to pursue the claims alleged in the ... California Federal Actions, ... or any other claim relating to the events at issue in the Delaware Actions." Two such notices were mailed to the class members and the notice was also published in the national edition of the Wall Street Journal. The Chancery Court then held a hearing. After argument from several objectors, the Court found the class representation adequate and the settlement fair.

The order and final judgment of the Chancery Court incorporated the terms of the settlement agreement, providing:

> "All claims, rights and causes of action (state or federal, including but not limited to claims arising under the federal securities law, any rules or regulations promulgated thereunder, or otherwise), whether known or unknown that are, could have been or might in the future be asserted by any of the plaintiffs or any member of the Settlement Class (*other than those who have validly requested exclusion therefrom*), ... in connection with or that arise now or hereafter out of the Merger Agreement, the Tender Offer, the Distribution Agreement, the Capital Contribution Agreement, the employee compensation arrangements, the Tender Agreements, the Initial Proposed Settlement, this Settlement ... and *including without limitation the claims asserted in the California Federal Actions* ... are hereby compromised, settled, released and discharged with prejudice by virtue of the proceedings herein and this Order and Final Judgment."

The judgment also stated that the notice met all the requirements of due process. The Delaware Supreme Court affirmed.

Respondents were members of both the state and federal plaintiff classes. Following issuance of the notice of proposed settlement of the Delaware litigation, respondents neither opted out of the settlement class nor appeared at the hearing to contest the settlement or the representation of the class. On appeal in the Ninth Circuit, petitioner Matsushita invoked the Delaware judgment as a bar to further prosecution of that action under the Full Faith and Credit Act, 28 U.S.C. § 1738.

The Ninth Circuit rejected petitioner's argument, ruling that § 1738 did not apply. Epstein v. MCA, Inc., 50 F.3d 644, 661–666 (1995). Instead, the Court of Appeals fashioned a test under which the preclusive force of a state court settlement judgment is limited to those claims that "could ... have been extinguished by the issue preclusive effect of an adjudication of the state claims." The lower courts have taken varying approaches to determining the preclusive effect of a state court judgment, entered in a class or derivative action, that provides for the release of exclusively federal claims. We granted certiorari to clarify this important area of federal law.

II

The Full Faith and Credit Act mandates that the "judicial proceedings" of any State "shall have the same full faith and credit in every court within the United States . . . as they have by law or usage in the courts of such State . . . from which they are taken." 28 U.S.C. § 1738. The Act thus directs all courts to treat a state court judgment with the same respect that it would receive in the courts of the rendering state. Federal courts may not "employ their own rules . . . in determining the effect of state judgments," but must "accept the rules chosen by the State from which the judgment is taken." Kremer v. Chemical Constr. Corp., 456 U.S. 461, 481–482, 102 S.Ct. 1883, 1898, 72 L.Ed.2d 262 (1982). Because the Court of Appeals failed to follow the dictates of the Act, we reverse.

A

The state court judgment in this case differs in two respects from the judgments that we have previously considered in our cases under the Full Faith and Credit Act. As respondents and the Court of Appeals stressed, the judgment was the product of a class action and incorporated a settlement agreement releasing claims within the exclusive jurisdiction of the federal courts. Though respondents urge "the irrelevance of section 1738 to this litigation," we do not think that either of these features exempts the judgment from the operation of § 1738.

That the judgment at issue is the result of a class action, rather than a suit brought by an individual, does not undermine the initial applicability of § 1738. The judgment of a state court in a class action is plainly the product of a "judicial proceeding" within the meaning of § 1738. Therefore, a judgment entered in a class action, like any other judgment entered in a state judicial proceeding, is presumptively entitled to full faith and credit under the express terms of the Act.

Further, § 1738 is not irrelevant simply because the judgment in question might work to bar the litigation of exclusively federal claims. Our decision in Marrese v. American Academy of Orthopaedic Surgeons, 470 U.S. 373, 105 S.Ct. 1327, 84 L.Ed.2d 274 (1985), made clear that where § 1738 is raised as a defense in a subsequent suit, the fact that an allegedly precluded "claim is within the exclusive jurisdiction of the federal courts *does not necessarily make § 1738 inapplicable.*" Id., at 380, 105 S.Ct., at 1332 (emphasis added). In so holding, we relied primarily on Kremer v. Chemical Constr. Corp., supra, which held, without deciding whether Title VII claims are exclusively federal, that state court proceedings may be issue preclusive in Title VII suits in federal court. *Kremer*, we said, "implies that absent an exception to

§ 1738, state law determines at least the ... preclusive effect of a prior state judgment in a subsequent action involving a claim within the exclusive jurisdiction of the federal courts." *Marrese*, 470 U.S., at 381, 105 S.Ct., at 1332. Accordingly, we decided that "a state court judgment may in some circumstances have preclusive effect in a subsequent action within the exclusive jurisdiction of the federal courts." Id., at 380, 105 S.Ct., at 1332.

In *Marrese*, we discussed Nash County Board of Education v. Biltmore Co., 640 F.2d 484 (C.A.4), cert. denied, 454 U.S. 878, 102 S.Ct. 359, 70 L.Ed.2d 188 (1981) [*supra* p. 800 n. 7], a case that concerned a state court settlement judgment. In *Nash*, the question was whether the judgment, which approved the settlement of state antitrust claims, prevented the litigation of exclusively federal antitrust claims. We suggested that the approach outlined in *Marrese* would also apply in cases like *Nash* that involve judgments upon settlement: that is, § 1738 would control at the outset. In accord with these precedents, we conclude that § 1738 is generally applicable in cases in which the state court judgment at issue incorporates a class action settlement releasing claims solely within the jurisdiction of the federal courts.

B

Marrese provides the analytical framework for deciding whether the Delaware court's judgment precludes this exclusively federal action. When faced with a state court judgment relating to an exclusively federal claim, a federal court must first look to the law of the rendering State to ascertain the effect of the judgment. If state law indicates that the particular claim or issue would be barred from litigation in a court of that state, then the federal court must next decide whether, "as an exception to § 1738," it "should refuse to give preclusive effect to [the] state court judgment."

1

We observed in *Marrese* that the inquiry into state law would not always yield a direct answer. Usually, "a state court will not have occasion to address the specific question whether a state judgment has issue or claim preclusive effect in a later action that can be brought only in federal court." Where a judicially approved settlement is under consideration, a federal court may consequently find guidance from general state law on the preclusive force of settlement judgments. Here, in addition to providing rules regarding the preclusive force of class-action settlement judgments in subsequent suits in state court, the Delaware courts have also spoken to the particular effect of such judgments in federal court.

Delaware has traditionally treated the impact of settlement judgments on subsequent litigation in state court as a question of claim preclusion. Early cases suggested that Delaware courts would not afford claim preclusive effect to a settlement releasing claims that could not have been presented in the trial court. See Ezzes v. Ackerman, 234 A.2d

444, 445–446 (Del.1967) ("[A] judgment entered either after trial on the merits or upon an approved settlement is res judicata and bars subsequent suit on the same claim.... [T]he defense of res judicata ... is available if the pleadings framing the issues in the first action would have permitted the raising of the issue sought to be raised in the second action, and if the facts were known or could have been known to the plaintiff in the second action at the time of the first action"). As the Court of Chancery has perceived, however, "the *Ezzes* inquiry [was] modified in regard to class actions" by the Delaware Supreme Court's decision in Nottingham Partners v. Dana, 564 A.2d 1089 (1989).

In *Nottingham*, a class action, the Delaware Supreme Court approved a settlement that released claims then pending in federal court. In approving that settlement, the *Nottingham* Court appears to have eliminated the *Ezzes* requirement that the claims could have been raised in the suit that produced the settlement, at least with respect to class actions:

> "[I]n order to achieve a comprehensive settlement that would prevent relitigation of settled questions at the core of a class action, a court may permit the release of a claim based on the identical factual predicate as that underlying the claims in the settled class action even though the claim was not presented and might not have been presentable in the class action."

These cases indicate that even if, as here, a claim could not have been raised in the court that rendered the settlement judgment in a class action, a Delaware court would still find that the judgment bars subsequent pursuit of the claim.

The Delaware Supreme Court has further manifested its understanding that when the Court of Chancery approves a global release of claims, its settlement judgment should preclude on-going or future federal court litigation of any released claims. In *Nottingham*, the Court stated that "[t]he validity of executing a general release in conjunction with the termination of litigation has long been recognized by the Delaware courts. More specifically, the Court of Chancery has a history of approving settlements that have implicitly or explicitly included a general release, which would also release federal claims." Though the Delaware Supreme Court correctly recognized in *Nottingham* that it lacked actual authority to order the dismissal of any case pending in federal court, it asserted that state-court approval of the settlement would have the collateral effect of preventing class members from prosecuting their claims in federal court. Perhaps the clearest statement of the Delaware Chancery Court's view on this matter was articulated in the suit preceding this one: "When a state court settlement of a class action releases all claims which arise out of the challenged transaction and is determined to be fair and to have met all due process requirements, the class members are bound by the release or the doctrine of issue preclusion. Class members cannot subsequently relitigate the claims barred by the settlement in a federal court." In re MCA, Inc.

Shareholders Litigation, 598 A.2d 687, 691 (1991).[4] We are aware of no Delaware case that suggests otherwise.

Given these statements of Delaware law, we think that a Delaware court would afford preclusive effect to the settlement judgment in this case, notwithstanding the fact that respondents could not have pressed their Exchange Act claims in the Court of Chancery. The claims are clearly within the scope of the release in the judgment, since the judgment specifically refers to this lawsuit. As required by Delaware Court of Chancery Rule 23, the Court of Chancery found, and the Delaware Supreme Court affirmed, that the settlement was "fair, reasonable and adequate and in the best interests of the ... Settlement class" and that notice to the class was "in full compliance with ... the requirements of due process." The Court of Chancery "further determined that the plaintiffs[,] ... as representatives of the Settlement Class, have fairly and adequately protected the interests of the Settlement Class." In re MCA, Inc. Shareholders Litigation, supra. Cf. Phillips Petroleum Co., supra, at 812, 105 S.Ct., at 2974 (due process requires "that the named plaintiff at all times adequately represent the interests of the absent class members").[5] Under Delaware Rule 23, as under Federal Rule of Civil Procedure 23, "[a]ll members of the class, whether of a plaintiff or a defendant class, are bound by the judgment entered in the action unless, in a Rule 23(b)(3) action, they make a timely election for exclusion." Respondents do not deny that, as shareholders of MCA's common stock, they were part of the plaintiff class and that they never opted out; they are bound, then, by the judgment.[6]

2

Because it appears that the settlement judgment would be res judicata under Delaware law, we proceed to the second step of the

---

4. In fact, the Chancery Court rejected the first settlement, which contained no opt-out provision, as unfair to the class precisely because it believed that the settlement would preclude the class from pursuing their exclusively federal claims in federal court. See In re MCA Inc. Shareholders Litigation, 598 A.2d 687, 692 (1991) ("[I]f this Court provides for the release of all the claims arising out of the challenged transaction, the claims which the Objectors have asserted in the federal suit will likely be forever barred").

5. Apart from any discussion of Delaware law, respondents contend that the settlement proceedings did not satisfy due process because the class was inadequately represented. Respondents make this claim in spite of the Chancery Court's express ruling, following argument on the issue, that the class representatives fairly and adequately protected the interests of the class. Cf. Prezant v. De Angelis, 636 A.2d 915, 923 (Del.1994) ("[The] constitutional requirement [of adequacy of representation] is embodied in [Delaware] Rule 23(a)(4), which requires that the named plaintiff 'fairly and adequately protect the interests of the class' "). We need not address the due process claim, however, because it is outside the scope of the question presented in this Court. * * *

6. Respondents argue that their failure to opt out of the settlement class does not constitute consent to the terms of the settlement under traditional contract principles. Again, the issue raised by respondents—whether the settlement could bar this suit as a matter of contract law, as distinguished from § 1738 law—is outside the scope of the question on which we granted certiorari. We note, however, that if a State chooses to approach the preclusive effect of a judgment embodying the terms of a settlement agreement as a question of pure contract law, a federal court must adhere to that approach under § 1738.

Marrese analysis and ask whether § 27 of the Exchange Act, which confers exclusive jurisdiction upon the federal courts for suits arising under the Act, partially repealed § 1738. Section 27 contains no express language regarding its relationship with § 1738 or the preclusive effect of related state court proceedings. Thus, any modification of § 1738 by § 27 must be implied. In deciding whether § 27 impliedly created an exception to § 1738, the "general question is whether the concerns underlying a particular grant of exclusive jurisdiction justify a finding of an implied partial repeal of § 1738." *Marrese*, 470 U.S., at 386, 105 S.Ct., at 1334. "Resolution of this question will depend on the particular federal statute as well as the nature of the claim or issue involved in the subsequent federal action.... [T]he primary consideration must be the intent of Congress."

[The Court noted that it had rarely found an implied repeal, and that such a conclusion would only be warranted where two federal statutes were in "irreconcilable conflict." It found no intent by Congress to afford plaintiffs more than one day in court to challenge the legality of a securities transaction, or to prevent litigants who have asserted claims within the jurisdiction of a state court to release Exchange Act claims as part of a judicially-approved settlement. Although the state court had to assess the federal claims to determine the adequacy of the settlement, it had not thereby "trespassed upon the exclusive territory of the federal courts" because "such assessment does not amount to a judgment on the merits of the claims." It also noted that "state court proceedings may, in various ways, subsequently affect the litigation of exclusively federal claims without running afoul of the federal jurisdictional grant in question. In Becher v. Contoure Laboratories, Inc., 279 U.S. 388, 49 S.Ct. 356, 73 L.Ed. 752 (1929), we held that state court findings of fact were issue preclusive in federal patent suits. We did so with full recognition 'the logical conclusion from the establishing of [the state law] claim is that Becher's patent is void.' "]

* * *

In the end, §§ 27 and 1738 "do not pose an either-or proposition." They can be reconciled by reading § 1738 to mandate full faith and credit of state court judgments incorporating global settlements, provided the rendering court had jurisdiction over the underlying suit itself, and by reading § 27 to prohibit state courts from exercising jurisdiction over suits arising under the Exchange Act. Congress' intent to provide an exclusive federal forum for adjudication of suits to enforce the Exchange Act is clear enough. But we can find no suggestion in § 27 that Congress meant to override the "principles of comity and repose embodied in § 1738" by allowing plaintiffs with Exchange Act claims to release those claims in state court and then litigate them in federal court. We conclude that the Delaware courts would give the settlement judgment preclusive effect in a subsequent proceeding and, further, that § 27 did not effect a partial repeal of § 1738.

C

The Court of Appeals did not engage in any analysis of Delaware law pursuant to § 1738. Rather, the Court of Appeals declined to apply § 1738 on the ground that where the rendering forum lacked jurisdiction over the subject matter or the parties, full faith and credit is not required. The Court of Appeals decided that the subject-matter jurisdiction exception to full faith and credit applies to this case because the Delaware court acted outside the bounds of its own jurisdiction in approving the settlement, since the settlement released exclusively federal claims.

As explained above, the state court in this case clearly possessed jurisdiction over the subject matter of the underlying suit and over the defendants. Only if this were not so—for instance, if the complaint alleged violations of the Exchange Act and the Delaware court rendered a judgment on the merits of those claims—would the exception to § 1738 for lack of subject-matter jurisdiction apply. Where, as here, the rendering court in fact had subject-matter jurisdiction, the subject-matter jurisdiction exception to full faith and credit is simply inapposite. In such a case, the relevance of a federal statute that provides for exclusive federal jurisdiction is not to the state court's possession of jurisdiction per se, but to the existence of a partial repeal of § 1738.

* * *

The judgment of the Court of Appeals is reversed and remanded for proceedings consistent with this opinion.

[Statement of JUSTICE STEVENS, concurring in part and dissenting in part, omitted.]

JUSTICE GINSBURG, with whom JUSTICE STEVENS joins, and with whom JUSTICE SOUTER joins as to Part II–B, concurring in part and dissenting in part.

I join the Court's judgment to the extent that it remands the case to the Ninth Circuit. I agree that a remand is in order because the Court of Appeals did not attend to this Court's reading of 28 U.S.C. § 1738 in a controlling decision. But I would not endeavor, as the Court does, to speak the first word on the content of Delaware preclusion law. Instead, I would follow our standard practice of remitting that issue for decision, in the first instance, by the lower federal courts.

I write separately to emphasize a point key to the application of § 1738: A state-court judgment generally is not entitled to full faith and credit unless it satisfies the requirements of the Fourteenth Amendment's Due Process Clause. In the class action setting, adequate representation is among the due process ingredients that must be supplied if the judgment is to bind absent class members. See Phillips Petroleum Co. v. Shutts, 472 U.S. 797, 808, 812, 105 S.Ct. 2965, 2972, 2974, 86 L.Ed.2d 628 (1985); Prezant v. De Angelis, 636 A.2d 915, 923–924 (Del.1994).

Suitors in this action (called the "Epstein plaintiffs" in this opinion), respondents here, argued before the Ninth Circuit, and again before this Court, that they cannot be bound by the Delaware settlement because they were not adequately represented by the Delaware class representatives. They contend that the Delaware representatives' willingness to release federal securities claims within the exclusive jurisdiction of the federal courts for a meager return to the class members, but a solid fee to the Delaware class attorneys, disserved the interests of the class, particularly, the absentees. The inadequacy of representation was apparent, the Epstein plaintiffs maintained, for at the time of the settlement, the federal claims were sub judice in the proper forum for those claims—the federal judiciary. Although the Ninth Circuit decided the case without reaching the due process check on the full faith and credit obligation, that inquiry remains open for consideration on remand. See [majority opinion] n. 5 (due process "w[as] not the basis for the decision below," so the Court "need not address [it]").

I

Matsushita's acquisition of MCA prompted litigation in state and federal courts. A brief account of that litigation will facilitate comprehension of the Epstein plaintiffs' position. On September 26, 1990, in response to reports in the financial press that Matsushita was negotiating to buy MCA, a suit was filed in the Court of Chancery of Delaware, a purported class action on behalf of the stockholders of MCA. Naming MCA and its directors (but not Matsushita) as defendants, the complaint invoked state law only. It alleged that MCA's directors had failed to carry out a market check to maximize shareholder value upon a change in corporate control, a check required by Revlon, Inc. v. MacAndrews & Forbes Holdings, Inc., 506 A.2d 173, 182 (Del.1985). For this alleged breach of fiduciary duty, the complaint sought, inter alia, an injunction against Matsushita's proposed acquisition of MCA.

Matsushita announced its tender offer on November 26, 1990. It offered holders of MCA common stock $71 per share, if they tendered their shares before December 29, 1990. The owners of 91% of MCA's common stock tendered their shares and, on January 3, 1991, for a price of $6.1 billion, Matsushita acquired MCA.

On December 3, 1990, a few days after the required SEC filings disclosed the terms of the tender offer, several MCA shareholders filed suit in the United States District Court for the Central District of California. Based solely on federal law, their complaints alleged that Matsushita, first named defendant, violated SEC Rules 14d–10, 17 CFR § 240.14d–10 (1994), and 10b–13, 17 CFR § 240.10b–13 (1994), by offering preferential treatment in the tender offer to MCA principals Lew Wasserman and Sidney Sheinberg. As stated in the complaint, the public tender offer included a special tax-driven stock swap arrangement for Wasserman, then MCA's chairman and chief executive officer, and a $21 million bonus for Sheinberg, then MCA's chief operating officer and owner of 1,170,000 shares of MCA common stock. These arrangements allegedly violated, inter alia, the SEC's "all-holder best-price" rule (Rule 14d–10), which requires bidders to treat all shareholders on equal terms. The claims of federal securities law violations fell within the exclusive jurisdiction of the federal court. The Epstein plaintiffs also sought class certification to represent all MCA shareholders at the time of the tender offer.

Two days later, counsel in the Delaware action advised MCA's counsel that the Delaware plaintiffs intended to amend their complaint to include additional claims against MCA and its directors and to add Matsushita as a defendant. The additional claims alleged that MCA wasted corporate assets by increasing the corporation's exposure to liability for violation of Rules 10b–13 and 14d–10, that MCA failed to make full disclosure of the benefits MCA insiders would receive from the takeover, and that directors Wasserman and Sheinberg breached their fiduciary duties by negotiating preferential deals with Matsushita. Matsushita, the amended complaint alleged, had conspired with and aided and abetted MCA directors in violation of Delaware law.

Within days, the Delaware parties agreed to a settlement and, on December 17, 1990, submitted their proposal to the Delaware Vice Chancellor. The agreement provided for a modification of a "poison pill" in the corporate charter of an MCA subsidiary, and for a fees payment of $1 million to the class counsel. The settlement agreement required the release of all claims, state and federal, arising out of the tender offer.

The Vice Chancellor rejected the settlement agreement on April 22, 1991, for two reasons: the absence of any monetary benefit to the class members; and the potential value of the federal claims that the agreement proposed to release. The "generous payment" of $1 million in counsel fees, the Vice Chancellor observed, "confer[red] no benefit on the members of the Class." In re MCA, Inc. Shareholders Litigation, 598 A.2d 687, 695 (Del.Ch.1991). And the value of the revised poison pill to the class, the Vice Chancellor said, was "illusionary[,] ... apparently ... proposed merely to justify a settlement which offers no real monetary benefit to the Class." The Vice Chancellor described the state-law claims as "at best, extremely weak and, therefore, [of] little or no value." "[T]he only claims which have any substantial merit," he said, "are the claims ... in the California federal suit that were not asserted in this Delaware action." After the rejection of the settlement, the Delaware lawsuit lay dormant for more than a year.

The federal litigation proceeded. In various rulings, the District Court denied the federal plaintiffs' motion for partial summary judgment, denied the Epstein plaintiffs' motion for class certification, and granted Matsushita's motion for summary judgment dismissing the claims. On April 15, 1992, the District Court entered its final judgment, which the Epstein plaintiffs appealed to the Ninth Circuit.

On October 22, 1992, after the federal plaintiffs had filed their notice of appeal, the Delaware parties reached a second settlement agreement. Matsushita agreed to create a $2 million settlement fund that would afford shareholders 2 to 3 cents per share before payment of fees and costs. The Delaware class counsel requested $691,000 in fees. In return for this relief, the Delaware plaintiffs agreed to release "all claims, rights and causes of action (state or federal, including but not limited to claims arising under the federal securities laws, and any rules or regulations promulgated thereunder, or otherwise) . . . in connection with or that arise now or hereafter out of the [tender offer] . . . including without limitation the claims asserted in the California Federal Actions. . . ." Unlike the first settlement proposal, the second agreement included an opt-out provision.

This time the Vice Chancellor approved the settlement. He stated "it is in the best interests of the class to settle this litigation and the terms of the settlement are fair and reasonable—although the value of the benefit to the class is meager." He found the class members' recovery of 2 to 3 cents per share "adequate (if only barely so) to support the proposed settlement." The federal claims, he reasoned, having been dismissed by the District Court, "now have minimal economic value." And he gave weight to the presence in the second settlement agreement of an opt-out provision.

Addressing the objectors' contention that the proposed settlement was "collusive," the Vice Chancellor recalled that "the settling parties ha[d] previously proposed a patently inadequate settlement," and he agreed that "suspicions abound." Nevertheless, he noted, the "[o]bjectors have offered no evidence of any collusion," so he declined to reject the settlement on that ground. Reducing the counsel fees from the requested $691,000 to $250,000, the Vice Chancellor offered this observation: "[T]he defendants' willingness to create the settlement fund seems likely to have been motivated as much by their concern as to their potential liability under the federal claims as by their concern for liability under the state law claims which this Court characterized as 'extremely weak.'" In a brief order, the Delaware Supreme Court affirmed "on the basis of and for the reasons assigned by the Court of Chancery. . . ."

* * *

II

A

Section 1738's full faith and credit instruction, as the Court indicates, requires the forum asked to recognize a judgment first to determine the preclusive effect the judgment would have in the rendering court. Because the Ninth Circuit did not evaluate the preclusive effect of the Delaware judgment through the lens of that State's preclusion law, I would remand for that determination.[4]

---

4. In its endeavor to forecast Delaware preclusion law, the Court appears to have blended the "identical factual predicate" test applied by the Delaware Supreme Court in Nottingham Partners v. Dana, 564 A.2d 1089, 1106–1107 (1989), with the broader "same transaction" test advanced by Matsushita.

B

Every State's law on the preclusiveness of judgments is pervasively affected by the supreme law of the land. To be valid in the rendition forum, and entitled to recognition nationally, a state court's judgment must measure up to the requirements of the Fourteenth Amendment's Due Process Clause.

In Phillips Petroleum Co. v. Shutts, this Court listed minimal procedural due process requirements a class action money judgment must meet if it is to bind absentees; those requirements include notice, an opportunity to be heard, a right to opt out, and adequate representation. 472 U.S., at 812, 105 S.Ct., at 2974. "[T]he Due Process Clause of course requires that the named plaintiff at all times adequately represent the interests of the absent class members." Ibid. (citing Hansberry v. Lee, 311 U.S. 32, 42–43, 45, 61 S.Ct. 115, 118–119, 120, 85 L.Ed. 22 (1940)). As the *Shutts* Court's phrase "at all times" indicates, the class representative's duty to represent absent class members adequately is a continuing one. See also Gonzales v. Cassidy, 474 F.2d 67, 75 (C.A.5 1973) (representative's failure to pursue an appeal rendered initially adequate class representation inadequate, so that judgment did not bind the class).

Although emphasizing the constitutional significance of the adequate representation requirement, this Court has recognized the first line responsibility of the states themselves for assuring that the constitutional essentials are met. See Hansberry, 311 U.S., at 42, 61 S.Ct., at 118. Final judgments, however, remain vulnerable to collateral attack for failure to satisfy the adequate representation requirement. A court conducting an action cannot predetermine the res judicata effect of the judgment; that effect can be tested only in a subsequent action.

In Delaware, the constitutional due process requirement of adequate representation is embodied in Delaware Court of Chancery's Rule 23, a class action rule modeled on its federal counterpart. Delaware requires, as a prerequisite to class certification, that the named plaintiffs "fairly and adequately protect the interests of the class." Del. Ch. Rule 23(a)(4). In *Prezant*, the Delaware Supreme Court considered whether adequate class representation was "a sine qua non for approval of a class action settlement," and concluded that it was. The state high court overturned a judgment and remanded a settlement because the Court of Chancery had failed to make an explicit finding of adequate representation.

The Delaware Supreme Court underscored that due process demands more than notice and an opportunity to opt-out; adequate representation, too, that court emphasized, is an essential ingredient. Notice, the Delaware Supreme Court reasoned, cannot substitute for the thorough examination and informed negotiation an adequate representative would pursue. The court also recognized that opt-out rights "are infrequently utilized and usually economically impracticable."

The Vice Chancellor's evaluation of the merits of the settlement could not bridge the gap, the Delaware Supreme Court said, because an inadequate representative "taint[s]" the entire settlement process. Id., at 925.[6] * * *

In the instant case, the Epstein plaintiffs challenge the preclusive effect of the Delaware settlement, arguing that the Vice Chancellor never in fact made the constitutionally required determination of adequate representation.[7] They contend that the state court left unresolved key questions: notably, did the class representatives share substantial common interests with the absent class members, and did counsel in Delaware vigorously press the interests of the class in negotiating the settlement.[8] In particular, the Epstein plaintiffs question whether the Delaware class representatives—who filed the state lawsuit on September 26, 1990, two months before the November 26 tender offer announcement—actually tendered shares in December, thereby enabling them to litigate a Rule 14d–10 claim in federal court. They also suggest that the Delaware representatives undervalued the federal claims—claims they could only settle, but never litigate, in a Delaware court. Finally, the Epstein plaintiffs contend that the Vice Chancellor improperly shifted the burden of proof;[9] he rejected the Delaware objectors' charges of "collusion" for want of evidence while acknowledging that "suspicions [of collusion] abound."[10]

Mindful that this is a court of final review and not first view, I do not address the merits of the Epstein plaintiffs' contentions, or Matsushita's counterargument that the issue of adequate representation was resolved by full and fair litigation in the Delaware Court of Chancery.[11] These arguments remain open for airing on remand. I stress, however, the centrality of the procedural due process protection of adequate

---

6. In both *Prezant* and the instant case, a temporary settlement class device was used, telescoping the inquiry of adequate representation into the examination of the fairness of the settlement. According to the Delaware Supreme Court, however, this near simultaneity does not relieve the representative of her duty to demonstrate, nor the court of its duty to determine, the adequacy of representation. *Prezant*, 636 A.2d, at 923. * * *

7. The Vice Chancellor did not have the benefit of the Delaware Supreme Court's clear statement in *Prezant*, decided one year after this settlement was approved. In *Prezant*, however, the Delaware Supreme Court largely reiterated and applied what this Court had stated almost a decade earlier in Phillips Petroleum Co. v. Shutts, 472 U.S. 797, 808, 812, 105 S.Ct. 2965, 2972, 2974, 86 L.Ed.2d 628 (1985).

8. The order approving the class for settlement purposes, the Epstein plaintiffs urge, contains no discussion of the adequacy of the representatives, and the order and final judgment approving the settlement contains only boilerplate language referring to the adequacy of representation. The Delaware Supreme Court approved the Court of Chancery's judgment in a one paragraph order.

9. Delaware law appears to place the burden of proof on the class representatives.

10. In this regard, it is noteworthy that Matsushita did not move to dismiss the Delaware action after the Vice Chancellor, in rejecting the first proposed settlement, surveyed the state-law claims and found them insubstantial. See In re MCA, Inc. Shareholders Litigation, 598 A.2d, at 694 (Vice Chancellor described "the asserted state law claims" as "at best, extremely weak" and of "little or no value").

11. Counsel for Matsushita acknowledged that relief from a judgment may be sought in Delaware pursuant to that State's counterpart to Federal Rule of Civil Procedure 60(b).

representation in class action lawsuits, emphatically including those resolved by settlement.

Notes and Questions

1. Should different claim preclusion principles apply to class actions? The Supreme Court unanimously ruled in *Matsushita* that the fact an earlier case was a class action has no bearing on the interpretation of § 1738. Because the preclusion principles therefore came from state law, the Court was not directly addressing the question whether they should be different in class actions. An issue to be kept in mind throughout this section is whether preclusion principles ought to be modified in class actions.

2. Should the fact that the judgment was reached by settlement rather than litigation matter? In the Ninth Circuit, Matsushita argued that, independent of preclusion principles, the plaintiffs who did not opt out should be bound by contract principles because the class executed a release. The Ninth Circuit ruled that "[t]his attempt to equate class settlements with the settlement of traditional litigation by individual parties falls short [because] the settlement of a class action is fundamentally different from the settlement of traditional litigation." The court found this to be true because the claims to be released belong to class members, who have not consented to do so, and because a judgment in a class action must be approved by the judge, who cannot delegate authority to review the settlement provisions to the class representatives. See 50 F.3d at 666–67. Do these arguments retain validity after the Supreme Court's decision? See In re Prudential Ins. Co. of America Sales Practice Litig., 261 F.3d 355, 366 (3d Cir.2001) ("a judgment pursuant to a class settlement can bar later claims based on the allegations underlying the claims in the settled class action").

3. Should state-court class-action settlements be handled differently when claims within exclusive federal jurisdiction are included? Professors Kahan and Silberman argue that such class-action settlements present peculiar problems, compared with others, because (a) the class attorney has reduced bargaining power, being unable to prosecute the federal claim on the merits, (b) the defendant has increased ability to shop for a receptive plaintiffs lawyer, in that federal-court cases are likely to be combined before a single judge, and (c) the state court is likely to have reduced information to assess the merits of the federal claims being released. Kahan & Silberman, Matsushita and Beyond: The Role of State Courts in Class Actions Involving Exclusive Federal Claims, 1996 Sup.Ct. Rev. 219, 235–46. They therefore recommend a series of additional protective measures that a state court should employ before approving such a settlement judgment, proposing that these might be adopted by statute, court rule or judicial decision. See id. at 251–62.

4. On remand, a divided panel of the Ninth Circuit initially held that the Delaware judgment did not preclude pursuit of the federal securities claims. Epstein v. MCA, Inc., 126 F.3d 1235 (9th Cir.1997). The majority concluded that the question of adequate representation remained open for its review despite the Supreme Court's ruling. It decided that Delaware would not preclude litigation about the adequacy of representation because that question had not been actually litigated in the settlement approval process

even though other class members had objected about collusion and one had asserted that the Delaware attorneys "did not provide adequate representation." Even had the question been fully litigated and decided, the majority added, due process precluded binding the Epstein plaintiffs by the litigation activities of "random, volunteer objectors" and "uncertified objectors." Finally, it rejected the argument that the Epstein plaintiffs could constitutionally be foreclosed because they had notice and an opportunity to object during the settlement approval process. It read Phillips Petroleum Co. v. Shutts, *supra* p. 412, as holding that due process precluded requiring absent class members to take any action to protect their interests.

The judge who wrote that decision then retired, a rehearing was granted, and the judge who had concurred in reversal changed his views. In Epstein v. MCA, Inc., 179 F.3d 641 (9th Cir.1999) (which came to be known as *Epstein III*), the earlier opinion was withdrawn and preclusion applied by a divided court. The opinion was written by the judge who had dissented before. He explained that the issue of due process limitations on the preclusive effect of the Delaware judgment was not open for review, despite the Court's observations in its footnote 5, because it was "logically necessary to the Court's holding" to find that due process was not violated. This conclusion turned on the fact that the Delaware courts have ruled that preclusion is only allowed if due process is observed, so the full faith and credit question would not come up unless due process (as a requirement of Delaware law) was satisfied. He also suggested that concluding otherwise would make the Supreme Court's decision an advisory opinion. Finally, he rejected the argument that Phillips Petroleum Co. v. Shutts barred preclusion, because that decision only requires certain procedural protections in the class action itself (id. at 648):

> Simply put, the absent class members' due process right to adequate representation is protected not by collateral review, but by the certifying court initially, and thereafter by appeal within the state system and by direct review in the United States Supreme Court.

> * * * Due process requires that an absent class member's rights to adequate representation be protected by the adoption of the appropriate procedures by the certifying court and by the courts that review its determinations: due process does not require collateral second-guessing of those determinations and that review.

A dissenter argued that the Delaware Chancery Court's decision (rendered before the Delaware Supreme Court decision in Prezant v. De Angelis, which requires findings on adequacy of representation) does not resolve that question in a way sufficient under Delaware law, and that giving binding effect to such a determination on the facts of this case would violate due process for the reasons stated in the initial decision on remand.

On these issues, consider the arguments of Professors Kahan and Silberman:

> When class members have an opportunity to object to the settlement and to opt out of it, there is little reason to allow a party who refuses to avail itself of these opportunities to attack the settlement collaterally. In effect, a collateral attack in these circumstances is a post-settlement opt-out that undermines the ability to settle a class action altogether. * * *

To grant state courts authority to enter global settlements releasing exclusive federal claims but subjecting such settlements to collateral review is the worst of all worlds. If the process by which state court findings about the adequacy of representation and fairness of the settlement is so imperfect that collateral attack is always possible, the better result would be to prohibit states from approving such global settlements in the first place.

Kahan & Silberman, *supra*, 1996 Sup. Ct. Rev. at 269; 271; cf. Grimes v. Vitalink Communications Corp., 17 F.3d 1553 (3d Cir.1994) (precluding class member who pursued objections in Delaware courts from relitigating them in federal court, but leaving open whether one who did not object in state court could do so in federal court); Nottingham Partners v. Trans–Lux Corp. 925 F.2d 29 (1st Cir.1991) (same). Compare Woolley, The Availability of Collateral Attack for Inadequate Representation in Class Suits, 79 Tex. L.Rev. 383 (2000) (arguing that there must be a constitutional right to litigate adequacy of representation in a later proceeding).

5. Would matters be different had the judgment entered in Delaware resulted from full-fledged litigation? Note that the Court points out that issue-preclusive effects can bind a federal court even as to claims within exclusive federal jurisdiction. Could claim-preclusive effects also be asserted? In Marrese v. American Academy of Orthopaedic Surgeons, 470 U.S. 373, 105 S.Ct. 1327, 84 L.Ed.2d 274 (1985), plaintiffs initially sued in an Illinois state court when denied membership in the defendant organization, claiming violation of their right to associate under state law. After that suit was dismissed for failure to state a claim, they sued in federal court, asserting federal antitrust claims, which are within exclusive federal court jurisdiction. The Seventh Circuit held that these claims should be barred because plaintiffs had a choice between state and federal court and chose to sue in state court. The Supreme Court reversed because the Seventh Circuit had not determined the preclusive effect of the judgment under Illinois preclusion law, noting that usually state preclusion law does not reach claims outside the state court's jurisdiction. If it did, should federal courts be required to preclude federal claims?

6. Some class members opted out of the class. Can they continue to pursue claims based on Delaware state law? In In re TransOcean Tender Offer Securities Litigation, 427 F.Supp. 1211 (N.D.Ill.1977), both state and federal litigation arose out of a tender offer, and in both cases plaintiffs asserted claims under Delaware law. After the Delaware Supreme Court ruled that the state-court class had no valid claim under state law, the defendants argued that this decision bound the federal class plaintiffs who had opted out of the state-court class action. Defendants argued that, under Erie Railroad v. Tompkins, 304 U.S. 64, 58 S.Ct. 817, 82 L.Ed. 1188 (1938), the claims of the opt-outs were barred. The court rejected this argument on the ground that it would violate the due process rights of the opt-outs.

Should a similar insulation from the effects of the class litigation apply to the opt-outs if the class is successful? In Premier Elec. Const. Co. v. National Elec. Contractors Ass'n, Inc., 814 F.2d 358 (7th Cir.1987), the court adopted a "categorical rule" against offensive collateral estoppel in favor of class members who opt out. It acknowledged that the erosion of the mutuality requirement also reduced concern with one-way intervention, which was a major focus of the 1966 amendments to Rule 23. But the rule still requires class members to decide whether to exclude themselves from the binding effect of the case and the court concluded that allowing opt-outs to benefit after removing themselves from the class would undo the work of the 1966 amendments. Moreover, allowing collateral estoppel would promote opting out. See also Becherer v. Merrill Lynch, Pierce, Fenner & Smith, 193 F.3d 415, 433 (6th Cir.1999) ("Because a plaintiff who opts out of a class action could easily have joined it, that plaintiff will generally not be permitted to invoke collateral estoppel.").

STEPHENSON v. DOW CHEMICAL CO.

United States Court of Appeals, Second Circuit, 2001.
273 F.3d 249, aff'd, 539 U.S. 111, 123 S.Ct. 2161, 156 L.Ed.2d 106 (2003).

Before: CARDAMONE and F.I. PARKER, Circuit Judges, and SPATT, District Judge.

PARKER, Circuit Judge.

This appeal requires us to determine the effect of the Supreme Court's landmark class action decisions in Amchem Products, Inc. v. Windsor, 521 U.S. 591, 117 S.Ct. 2231, 138 L.Ed.2d 689 (1997) [supra p. 373], and Ortiz v. Fibreboard Corp., 527 U.S. 815, 119 S.Ct. 2295, 144 L.Ed.2d 715 (1999) [supra p. 302], on a previously settled class action concerning exposure to Agent Orange during the Vietnam War.

* * *

I. BACKGROUND

* * *

The first Agent Orange litigation began in the late 1970s, when individual veterans and their families filed class action suits in the Northern District of Illinois and Southern and Eastern Districts of New York, alleging that exposure to Agent Orange caused them injury. In re "Agent Orange" Prod. Liab. Litig., 635 F.2d 987, 988 (2d Cir.1980) ("Agent Orange I"). By order of the MDL Panel, these actions were transferred to the Eastern District of New York and consolidated for pretrial purposes. Id. Plaintiffs asserted claims of negligent manufacture, strict liability, breach of warranty, intentional tort and nuisance. In re "Agent Orange" Prod. Liab. Litig., 597 F.Supp. 740, 750 (E.D.N.Y.1984) ("Agent Orange III"); aff'd 818 F.2d 145 (2d Cir.1987).

In 1983, the district court certified the following class under Federal Rule of Civil Procedure 23(b)(3):

> those persons who were in the United States, New Zealand or Australian Armed Forces at any time from 1961 to 1972 who were injured while in or near Vietnam by exposure to Agent Orange or other phenoxy herbicides, including those composed in whole or in part of 2, 4, 5–trichlorophenoxyacetic acid or containing some

amount of 2, 3, 7, 8–tetrachlorodibenzo-p-dioxin. The class also includes spouses, parents, and children of the veterans born before January 1, 1984, directly or derivatively injured as a result of the exposure.

* * * The court also ordered notice by mail, print media, radio and television to be provided to class members, providing in part that persons who wished to opt out must do so by May 1, 1984.

Trial of the class claims was to begin on May 7, 1984. On the eve of trial, the parties reached a settlement. The settlement provided that defendants would pay $180 million into a settlement fund, $10 million of which would indemnify defendants against future state court actions alleging the same claims. The settlement provided that "[t]he Class specifically includes persons who have not yet manifested injury." Additionally, the settlement specifically stated that the district court would "retain jurisdiction over the Fund pending its final disposition."

The district court held fairness hearings throughout the country, and approved the settlement as fair, reasonable and adequate. The court rejected the motion to certify a subclass of those class members who objected to terms of the settlement. The court concluded that "[n]o purpose would have been served by appointing counsel for a subclass of disappointed claimants except to increase expenses to the class and delay proceedings."

Seventy-five percent of the $180 million was to be distributed directly " 'to exposed veterans who suffer from long-term total disabilities and to the surviving spouses or children of exposed veterans who have died.' " "A claimant would qualify for compensation by establishing exposure to Agent Orange and death or disability not 'predominately' caused by trauma...." Payments were to be made for ten years, beginning January 1, 1985 and ending December 31, 1994:

> No payment will be made for death or disability occurring after December 31, 1994. Payment will be made for compensable deaths occurring both before and after January 1, 1985. Payments will be made for compensable disability to the extent that the period of disability falls within the ten years of the program's operation.

"Most of the remaining [25%] of the settlement fund established the Agent Orange Class Assistance Program, ... which made grants to agencies serving Vietnam veterans and their families." Explaining the creation of this kind of fund, Judge Weinstein stated that it was "[t]he most practicable and equitable method of distributing benefits to" those claimants who did not meet eligibility criteria for cash payments.

We affirmed class certification, settlement approval and much of the distribution plan. We rejected challenges to class certification, concluding that "class certification was justified under Rule 23(b)(3) due to the centrality of the military contractor defense." We specifically rejected an attack based on adequacy of representation, again based on the military contractor defense which, we reasoned, "would have precluded recovery by all plaintiffs, irrespective of the strengths, weaknesses, or idiosyncrasies of their claims." We additionally concluded that the notice scheme devised by Judge Weinstein was the "best notice practicable" under Federal Rule of Civil Procedure 23(c)(2). Finally, we affirmed the settlement as fair, reasonable and adequate, given the serious weaknesses of the plaintiffs' claims.

In 1989 and 1990, two purported class actions, Ivy v. Diamond Shamrock Chemicals Co. and Hartman v. Diamond Shamrock Chemicals Co., were filed in Texas state courts. These suits, on behalf of Vietnam veterans exposed to Agent Orange,[3] sought compensatory and punitive damages against the same companies as in the settled suit. The plaintiffs alleged that their injuries manifested only after the May 7, 1984 settlement. Additionally, the *Ivy/Hartman* plaintiffs expressly disclaimed any reliance on federal law, asserting only state law claims. Nonetheless, the defendants removed the actions to federal court on the grounds that these claims had already been asserted and litigated in federal court. The MDL Panel transferred the actions to Judge Weinstein in the Eastern District of New York.

* * *

[Plaintiffs argued] that it was unfair to bind them to the settlement when their injuries were not manifested until after the settlement had been reached. The district court rejected this argument, based on the following reasoning:

> All of the courts which considered the Agent Orange Settlement were fully cognizant of the conflict arguments now hypothesized by the plaintiffs and took steps to minimize the problem in the way they arranged for long-term administration of the Settlement Fund.
>
> In many cases the conflict between the interests of present and future claimants is more imagined than real. In the instant case, for example, the injustice wrought upon the plaintiffs is nonexistent. *These plaintiffs, like all class members who suffer death or disability before the end of 1994, are eligible for compensation from the Agent Orange Payment Fund.* The relevant latency periods and the age of the veterans ensure that almost all valid claims will be revealed before that time.
>
> Even when it is proper and necessary for the courts to be solicitous of the interests of future claimants, the courts cannot ignore the interests of presently injured plaintiffs as well as defendants in achieving a settlement. Class action settlements simply will not occur if the parties cannot set definitive limits on defendants' liability. Making settlement of Rule 23 suits too difficult will work

---

3. Two plaintiffs in the *Ivy* litigation alleged injuries stemming from Agent Orange exposure while acting in a civilian capacity, and thus were not members of the class bound by the 1984 settlement. Their claims were severed from the claims of the other plaintiffs.

harms upon plaintiffs, defendants, the courts, and the general public.

The district court therefore dismissed the *Ivy/Hartman* litigation.

We affirmed the district court's dismissal. *Ivy/Hartman II*, 996 F.2d 1425, 1439 [(2d Cir.1993)] We agreed with the district court's assertion of federal jurisdiction under the All Writs Act. * * *

We then addressed plaintiffs' argument that they were not members of the prior class, because they were not "injured" as the term was used in the class definition. We concluded that, for the purposes of the Agent Orange litigation, "injury occurs when a deleterious substance enters a person's body, even though its adverse effects are not immediately apparent." We emphasized that the plaintiffs in the original suit had sought to include such "at-risk" plaintiffs, over defendants' objections, and that we had already affirmed the inclusion of these plaintiffs in the class. See id.

We likewise rejected plaintiffs' argument that their due process rights were violated because they were denied adequate representation and adequate notice in the prior action. We reasoned that "providing individual notice and opt-out rights to persons who are unaware of an injury would probably do little good." We concluded that the plaintiffs were adequately represented in the prior action, and that a subclass of future claimants was unnecessary " 'because of the way [the settlement] was structured to cover future claimants.' "

Shortly before our decision in *Ivy/Hartman II*, the $10 million set aside for indemnification from state court Agent Orange judgments was transferred to the Class Assistance Program, because the district court deemed such a fund unnecessary. The distribution activities had begun in 1988, and concluded in June 1997. During the ten year period of the settlement, $196.5 million was distributed as cash payments to approximately 52,000 class members. The program paid approximately $52 million to "after-manifested" claimants, whose deaths or disabilities occurred after May 7, 1984. Approximately $71.3 million of the fund was distributed through the Class Assistance Program.

[In August, 1998, Joe Isaacson sued the chemical manufacturers who produced Agent Orange in New Jersey state court. Isaacson had served in Vietnam in 1968–69 in the Air Force, working on planes that sprayed Agent Orange. In 1996, he was diagnosed with non-Hodkins Lymphoma, and in his suit he alleged state-law claims that defendants were liable for his condition. In February, 1999, Daniel Stephenson sued the same defendants in federal court in Louisiana. He had served in Vietnam from 1965 to 1970 as a helicopter pilot, and was in regular contact with Agent Orange during that time. In February, 1998, he was diagnosed with multiple myeloma, a bone marrow cancer.

Defendants removed Isaacson's suit to federal court, and the federal court denied his motion to remand. The MDL Panel transferred both

Stephenson's and Isaacson's suits to Judge Weinstein, who consolidated them.]

Defendants moved to dismiss under Federal Rule of Civil Procedure 12(b)(6), asserting that plaintiffs' claims were barred by the 1984 class action settlement and subsequent final judgment. Judge Weinstein granted this motion from the bench following argument, rejecting plaintiffs' argument that they were inadequately represented and concluding that plaintiffs' suit was an impermissible collateral attack on the prior settlement.

Because we disagree with this conclusion, based on the Supreme Court's holdings in *Amchem* and *Ortiz*, we must vacate the district court's dismissal and remand for further proceedings.

II. DISCUSSION

"We review a dismissal under Rule 12(b)(6) de novo, accepting all factual allegations in the complaint as true and drawing all reasonable inferences in the plaintiffs' favor."

A. *Removal Jurisdiction*

[The court held that Issacson's case was properly removed under the All Writs Act, 28 U.S.C. § 1651, because "maintenance of these actions in state court necessarily requires interpretation of the scope of the Agent Orange Settlement and could have the potential to disturb the judgment underlying that settlement." In Syngenta Crop Protection, Inc. v. Henson, 537 U.S. 28, 123 S.Ct. 366 (2002), the Supreme Court held that the All Writs Act does not provide authority for removal.]

B. *Collateral Attack*

The parties devote much energy to debating the permissibility of a collateral attack in this case. Plaintiffs assert that, since the Supreme Court's decision in Hansberry v. Lee, 311 U.S. 32, 61 S.Ct. 115, 85 L.Ed. 22 (1940) [*supra* p. 285], courts have allowed collateral attacks on class action judgments based upon due process concerns. Defendants strenuously disagree and contend that to allow plaintiffs' suit to go forward, in the face of the 1984 global settlement, would "violate defendants' right to due process of law." Defendants likewise strenuously argue that the district court's injunction against future litigation prevents these appellants from maintaining their actions. While it is true that "[a]n injunction must be obeyed until modified or dissolved, and its unconstitutionality is no defense to disobedience," defendants' injunction-based argument misses the point. The injunction was part and parcel of the judgment that plaintiffs contend failed to afford them adequate representation. If plaintiffs' inadequate representation allegations prevail, as we so conclude, the judgment, which includes the injunction on which defendants rely, is not binding as to these plaintiffs.

Defendants contend that Supreme Court precedent permits a collateral attack on a class action judgment "only where there has been no prior determination of absent class members' due process rights." According to defendants, because the "due process rights of absent class members have been extensively litigated in the Agent Orange litigation," these plaintiffs cannot now attack those prior determinations. We reject defendants' arguments and conclude that plaintiffs' collateral attack, which seeks only to prevent the prior settlement from operating as res judicata to their claims, is permissible.

First, even if, as defendants contend, collateral attack is only permitted where there has been no prior determination of the absent class members' rights, plaintiffs' collateral attack is allowed. It is true that, on direct appeal and in the *Ivy/Hartman* litigation, we previously concluded that there was adequate representation of all class members in the original Agent Orange settlement. However, neither this Court nor the district court has addressed specifically the adequacy of representation for those members of the class whose injuries manifested after depletion of the settlements funds. See *Ivy/Hartman II*, 996 F.2d at 1436 (creating a subclass of future claimants was unnecessary because the settlement covered such claimants); *Ivy/Hartman I*, 781 F.Supp. at 919 ("These plaintiffs, like all class members *who suffer death or disability before the end of 1994*, are eligible for compensation from the Agent Orange Payment Fund." (emphasis added.)) Therefore, even accepting defendants' argument, plaintiffs' suit can go forward because there has been no prior adequacy of representation determination with respect to individuals whose claims arise after the depletion of the settlement fund.[6]

Second, the propriety of a collateral attack such as this is amply supported by precedent. In Hansberry v. Lee, 311 U.S. 32, 61 S.Ct. 115, 85 L.Ed. 22 (1940), the Supreme Court entertained a collateral attack on an Illinois state court class action judgment that purported to bind the plaintiffs. The Court held that class action judgments can only bind absent class members where "the interests of those not joined are of the same class as the interests of those who are, and where it is considered that the latter fairly represent the former in the prosecution of the litigation." Additionally, we have previously stated that a "[j]udgment in

6. Defendants rely heavily on a recent Ninth Circuit decision, Epstein v. MCA, Inc., 179 F.3d 641 (9th Cir.1999), in support of their limited collateral review theory. *Epstein* held that a collateral attack is available only "to consider whether the procedures in the prior litigation afforded the party against whom the earlier judgment is asserted a 'full and fair opportunity' to litigate the claim or issue." According to the Ninth Circuit,

Due process requires that an absent class member's right to adequate representation be protected by the adoption of the

appropriate procedures by the certifying court and by the courts that review its determinations; due process does not require collateral second-guessing of those determinations and that review.

Here, neither the district court nor this Court has determined the adequacy of representation with respect to these plaintiffs whose injuries did not arise until after the settlement expired. Without adopting the Ninth Circuit's decision in *Epstein*, we conclude that plaintiffs' collateral attack is proper even under its standard.

a class action is not secure from collateral attack unless the absentees were adequately and vigorously represented."

Allowing plaintiffs' suit would be consistent with many other circuit decisions recognizing the ability of later plaintiffs to attack the adequacy of representation in an earlier class action. For example, the Fifth Circuit holds:

> To answer the question whether the class representative adequately represented the class so that the judgment in the class suit will bind the absent members of the class requires a two-pronged inquiry: (1) Did the trial court in the first suit correctly determine, initially, that the representative would adequately represent the class? and (2) Does it appear, after the termination of the suit, that the class representative adequately protected the interest of the class? The first question involves us in a collateral review of the ... [trial] court's determination to permit the suit to proceed as a class action with [the named plaintiff] as the representative, while the second involves a review of the class representative's conduct of the entire suit—an inquiry which is not required to be made by the trial court but which is appropriate in a collateral attack on the judgment....

Gonzales v. Cassidy, 474 F.2d 67, 72 (5th Cir.1973).

Defendants' citation to Federated Department Stores, Inc. v. Moitie, 452 U.S. 394, 101 S.Ct. 2424, 69 L.Ed.2d 103 (1981), is unavailing. According to that case, a "judgment merely voidable because based upon an erroneous view of the law is not open to collateral attack, but can be corrected only by a direct review and not by bringing another action upon the same cause [of action]." Id. at 398, 101 S.Ct. 2424 (alteration in original). Defendants' reliance on this case misperceives plaintiffs' argument. Plaintiffs do not attack the merits or finality of the settlement itself, but instead argue that they were not proper parties to that judgment. If plaintiffs were not proper parties to that judgment, as we conclude below, res judicata cannot defeat their claims. Further, such collateral review would not, as defendants maintain, violate defendants' due process rights by exposing them to double liability. Exposure to liability here is not duplicative if plaintiffs were never proper parties to the prior judgment in the first place.

We therefore hold that a collateral attack to contest the application of res judicata is available. We turn next to the merits of this attack.

C. Due Process Considerations and Res Judicata

The doctrine of res judicata dictates that "a final judgment on the merits of an action precludes the parties or their privies from relitigating issues that were or could have been raised in that action." Res judicata ordinarily applies "if the earlier decision was (1) a final judgment on the merits, (2) by a court of competent jurisdiction, (3) in a case involving the same parties or their privies, and (4) involving the same cause of action."

Plaintiffs' argument focuses on element number three in the res judicata analysis: whether they are parties bound by the settlement. Plaintiffs rely primarily on the United States Supreme Court's decisions in Amchem Products, Inc. v. Windsor, 521 U.S. 591, 117 S.Ct. 2231, 138 L.Ed.2d 689 (1997), and Ortiz v. Fibreboard Corp., 527 U.S. 815, 119 S.Ct. 2295, 144 L.Ed.2d 715 (1999).

In *Amchem*, the Supreme Court confronted, on direct appeal, a challenge to class certification for settlement purposes in an asbestos litigation. The class defined in the complaint included both individuals who were presently injured as well as individuals who had only been exposed to asbestos. The Supreme Court held that this "sprawling" class was improperly certified under Federal Rules of Civil Procedure 23(a) and (b). Specifically, the Court held that Rule 23(a)(4)'s requirement that the named parties " 'will fairly and adequately protect the interests of the class' " had not been satisfied. The Court reasoned that

> named parties with diverse medical conditions sought to act on behalf of a single giant class rather than on behalf of discrete subclasses. In significant respects, the interests of those within the single class are not aligned. Most saliently, for the currently injured, the critical goal is generous immediate payments. That goal tugs against the interest of exposure-only plaintiffs in ensuring an ample, inflation-protected fund for the future.

Amchem also implied, but did not decide, that the notice provided to exposure-only class members was likewise inadequate. The Court stated that, because many exposure-only individuals, may not be aware of their exposure or realize the ramifications of exposure, "those without current afflictions may not have the information or foresight needed to decide, intelligently, whether to stay in or opt out."

In *Ortiz*, the Supreme Court again addressed a settlement-only class action in the asbestos litigation context. *Ortiz*, however, involved a settlement-only limited fund class under Rule 23(b)(1)(B). The Supreme Court ultimately held that the class could not be maintained under Rule 23(b)(1)(B), because "the limit of the fund was determined by treating the settlement agreement as dispositive, an error magnified" by conflicted counsel. In so holding, *Ortiz* noted that "it is obvious after *Amchem* that a class divided between holders of present and future claims (some of the latter involving no physical injury and attributable to claimants not yet born) requires division into homogeneous subclasses under Rule 23(c)(4)(B), with separate representation to eliminate conflicting interests of counsel."

Res judicata generally applies to bind absent class members except where to do so would violate due process. Due process requires adequate representation "at all times" throughout the litigation, notice "reasonably calculated . . . to apprise interested parties of the pendency of the action," and an opportunity to opt out. Shutts, 472 U.S. at 811–12, 105 S.Ct. 2965.

Both Stephenson and Isaacson fall within the class definition of the prior litigation: they served in the United States military, stationed in Vietnam, between 1961 and 1972, and were allegedly injured by exposure to Agent Orange. However, they both learned of their allegedly Agent Orange-related injuries only after the 1984 settlement fund had expired in 1994. Because the prior litigation purported to settle all future claims, but only provided for recovery for those whose death or disability was discovered prior to 1994, the conflict between Stephenson and Isaacson and the class representatives becomes apparent. No provision was made for post–1994 claimants, and the settlement fund was permitted to terminate in 1994. *Amchem* and *Ortiz* suggest that Stephenson and Isaacson were not adequately represented in the prior Agent Orange litigation.[8] Those cases indicate that a class which purports to represent both present and future claimants may encounter internal conflicts.

Defendants contend that there was, in fact, no conflict because all class members' claims were equally meritless and would have been defeated by the "military contractor" defense. This argument misses the mark. At this stage, we are only addressing whether plaintiffs' claims should be barred by res judicata. We are therefore concerned only with whether they were afforded due process in the earlier litigation. Part of the due process inquiry (and part of the Rule 23(a) class certification requirements) involves assessing adequacy of representation and intra-class conflicts. The ultimate merits of the claims have no bearing on whether the class previously certified adequately represented these plaintiffs.

Because these plaintiffs were inadequately represented in the prior litigation, they were not proper parties and cannot be bound by the settlement. We therefore must vacate the district court's dismissal and remand for further proceedings. We, of course, express no opinion as to the ultimate merits of plaintiffs' claims.

Notes and Questions

1. The Supreme Court granted certiorari in *Stephenson*, but ultimately issued a per curiam decision. Regarding the Isaacson plaintiffs, it vacated the Second Circuit's decision on the ground that the case should never have been removed because it had held that the All Writs Act does not allow such removal in Syngenta Crop Protection, Inc. v. Henson, 537 U.S. 28, 123 S.Ct. 366, 154 L.Ed.2d 368 (2002). Regarding Stephenson's suit, the judgment of the Second Circuit was affirmed by an equally divided court, Justice Stevens not participating. Counsel for plaintiffs characterized this result as a "fabulous total victory" because it did not vacate the Second Circuit's decision regarding Stephenson's suit, but counsel for Dow pointed out that the

---

8. We also note that plaintiffs likely received inadequate notice. [Phillips Petroleum v.] Shutts [*supra* p. 412] provides that adequate notice is necessary to bind absent class members. As described earlier, *Amchem* indicates that effective notice could likely not ever be given to exposure-only class members. Because we have already concluded that these plaintiffs were inadequately represented, and thus were not proper parties to the prior litigation, we need not definitively decide whether notice was adequate.

Supreme Court's decision had no precedential value. See Mauro, High Court Affirms 2nd Circuit in Agent Orange Case, S.F. Recorder, June 10, 2003, at 3.

2. As the final outcome of the Issacson suit points up, the preclusive effects of federal class action judgments may be raised in state court. How should the New Jersey state court decide defendants' res judicata arguments after remand from federal court?

3. The Full Faith and Credit Clause, involved in *Matsushita, supra* p. 803, would not apply to a federal court judgment. Should a federal class action judgment be given preclusive effects? See Fed. R. Civ. P. 23(c)(3). For example, in Canady v. Allstate Ins. Co., 282 F.3d 1005 (8th Cir.2002), in a federal class action alleging that defendant insurers had engaged in redlining in violation of federal civil rights and fair housing acts, the court denied class certification on the ground that plaintiffs lacked standing to sue unrelated insurers in the absence of allegations that they conspired together. Recall La Mar v. H & B Novelty & Loan Co., *supra* p. 278. After the district court dismissed, plaintiffs filed the same class action in state court, asserting state-law claims based on essentially the same allegations. The defendants successfully removed using the All Writs Act (presumably no longer permitted under *Syngenta, supra* note 1), and the district court dismissed on federal preclusion grounds. The appellate court affirmed because "the issues pursued in state court are essentially identical to the issues presented in the original federal litigation." Accordingly, plaintiffs "may not file what is essentially the same action, albeit under different legal theories, in state court merely to obtain a more favorable result than the one already obtained in their first choice of forum." It found that the federal court decision "finally adjudicate[d] the issue of standing under these specific allegations."

4. As an alternative to relying on state courts to give effect to res judicata, federal courts that enter class action judgments can enjoin subsequent litigation filed by class members that is covered by the preclusive effect of the judgment if they retain jurisdiction over the action for purposes of enforcing their decrees. See In the Matter of VMS Securities Litig., 103 F.3d 1317, 1324 (7th Cir.1996) ("in the context of complex class action litigation, a federal district court may appropriately use the All Writs Act to * * * enjoin the prosecution of subsequent state court claims in order to enforce its ongoing orders against relitigation and to guard the integrity of its prior rulings over which it had expressly retained jurisdiction"); compare Grimes v. Vitalink Communications Corp., 17 F.3d 1553 (3d Cir.1994) (questioning whether failure to opt out would suffice to provide personal jurisdiction for such an injunction, at least if entered by a state court).

5. Does *Stephenson* allow collateral attacks so liberally that the finality of class action judgments is threatened? Is its decision consistent with *Epstein III (supra* p. 816 n. 4)? Did the Ninth Circuit misunderstand the Supreme Court's ruling when it held on remand in that case that preclusion applied? See the quotation from the opinion on remand in footnote 6 in *Stephenson.*

In Hospitality Management Associates, Inc. v. Shell Oil Co., 356 S.C. 644, 591 S.E.2d 611 (2004), the court upheld summary judgment that accorded full faith and credit to two nationwide class action settlements in other state courts despite the assertion of opt-out class members that they were entitled to attack the judgments collaterally. Noting the inconclusive Supreme Court handling of *Stephenson*, the court commented:

> [I]t remains an open, and hotly litigated, question as to whether limited collateral review is required on the *Shutts* due process requirements in a class action case (see *Epstein III*), or whether a broader, merits-oriented collateral review is permitted (see *Stephenson*). In addition to the conflict in the federal circuits as exemplified by *Epstein III* and *Stephenson*, there is also disagreement amongst the state courts and legal scholars.

In our opinion, there are important policy considerations favoring both limited and broad collateral review. Certainly, in the specialized context of class action litigation, the significant interest in efficiency and finality favor limited review. If the due process issues are fully and fairly litigated and necessarily decided by the rendering court, then the strong interest in finality militates in favor of an extremely limited collateral review. Without limited review, a nationwide class action could be vulnerable to collateral actions in the 49 other states in which it was not litigated initially. It would seem to be a waste of judicial resources to require reviewing courts to conduct an extensive substantive review when one has already been undertaken in a sister state. As the Ohio court stated in Fine v. America Online: "To allow substantive collateral attacks would be counterintuitive to [the] procedural relief that a class-action suit is intended to afford our judicial system nationwide." 743 N.E.2d at 421–22.

On the other hand, there is a fundamental interest in not allowing constitutionally infirm judgments to be enforced. It would be troublesome to enforce a class action settlement against parties over whom the rendering court did not have personal jurisdiction. We note, however, that the view espoused in *Epstein III* envisions that direct appellate review of a class action is the appropriate vehicle to correct whatever errors may have been made at the trial court level.

We hold that in a case such as this one, only a limited collateral review is appropriate. It would run counter to the class action goals of efficiency and finality to allow successive reviews of issues that were, in fact, fully and fairly litigated in the rendering court. Moreover, second-guessing the fully litigated decisions of our sister courts would violated the spirit of full faith and credit.

Therefore, we concur with the Ninth Circuit's view [in *Epstein III*] and find due process requires that an absent class member's rights are protected by the adoption and utilization of appropriate procedures by the certifying court; thereafter, the merits of the certifying court's determinations are subject to direct appellate review. As for collateral review, however, due process does not afford any second guessing of those determinations. *Epstein III*. Instead, what this limited review entails is "an examination of *procedural* due process and nothing more." Fine v. America Online, 743 N.E.2d at 421. More specifically, we must determine: (1) whether there were safeguards in place to guarantee sufficient notice and adequate representation; and (2) whether such safeguards were, in fact applied.

The court then proceeded to examine the notice given (an extensive multimedia campaign which the court found to be constitutionally sufficient) and the adequacy of representation. On that score, it found that the courts, in contrast to *Amchem*, had procedures in place to ensure adequate representation and that they were implemented throughout the litigations. It therefore found that full faith and credit should be accorded the two class action settlement judgments.

6.   If there is no adversary litigation about the fairness of the settlement, under *Epstein III* is there any limit to collateral review of the fairness of the settlement or the adequacy of representation? Recall the materials on judicial review of proposed class action settlements, *supra* pp. 509–40. Should the absence of objections reassure the court in the collateral proceeding about the fairness of the settlement? If there is an objection, should the second court treat it as sufficient to preclude collateral attack only if it is vigorous and if there is appellate review of objections that were not accepted?

7.   In *Stephenson,* the court says that the original class action provided inadequate representation for those whose injuries manifested themselves after 1994. What solution could there be to such a problem? What should the original class action have provided to overcome this difficulty? Compare the way in which the settlement regimes in *Amchem* and *Ortiz* addressed the question of future claims. Keep in mind that, at the time the class-action settlement was arranged, no class member would know whether he would become sick before 1994, and some might consider the coverage for another decade a reasonable protection. With that in mind, consider the analysis in Nagareda, Administering Adequacy in Class Representation, 82 Texas L. Rev. 287, 322 (2003):

> The ten-year term for cash benefits under the Agent Orange class settlement appears far from arbitrary, however, when one considers that any veteran would have had an exceedingly weak scientific case on the causation element, at least as of 1984, and that the ten-year term for cash benefits extended to more than two decades after the last alleged exposure of class members.

8.   The court in *Stephenson* also says in footnote 8 that notice may have been inadequate in the original Agent Orange litigation with regard to these plaintiffs. But it had earlier held that notice in that suit was adequate in the *Ivy/Hartman* litigation (996 F.2d at 1435):

> In the instant case, society's interest in the efficient and fair resolution of large-scale litigation outweighs the gains from individual notice and opt-out rights, whose benefits here are conjectural at best. As appellants correctly note, providing individual notice and opt-out rights to persons who are unaware of an injury would probably do little good.

Why should the *Stephenson* plaintiffs be treated differently for purposes of notice?

COOPER v. FEDERAL RESERVE
BANK OF RICHMOND

Supreme Court of the United States, 1984.
467 U.S. 867, 104 S.Ct. 2794, 81 L.Ed.2d 718.

JUSTICE STEVENS delivered the opinion of the Court.

The question to be decided is whether a judgment in a class action determining that an employer did not engage in a general pattern or practice of racial discrimination against the certified class of employees precludes a class member from maintaining a subsequent civil action alleging an individual claim of racial discrimination against the employer.

I

On March 22, 1977, the Equal Employment Opportunity Commission commenced a civil action against respondent, the Federal Reserve Bank of Richmond. Respondent operates a branch in Charlotte, N.C. (the Bank), where during the years 1974–1978 it employed about 350–450 employees in several departments. The EEOC complaint alleged that the Bank was violating § 703(a) of Title VII of the Civil Rights Act of 1964 by engaging in "policies and practices" that included "failing and refusing to promote *blacks* because of race."

Six months after the EEOC filed its complaint, four individual employees were allowed to intervene as plaintiffs. In their "complaint in intervention," these plaintiffs alleged that the Bank's employment practices violated 42 U.S.C. § 1981, as well as Title VII; that each of them was the victim of employment discrimination based on race; and that they could adequately represent a class of black employees against whom the Bank had discriminated because of their race. In due course, the District Court entered an order conditionally certifying the following class pursuant to Federal Rules of Civil Procedure 23(b)(2) and (3):

> "All black persons who have been employed by the defendant at its Charlotte Branch Office at any time since January 3, 1974 [6 months prior to the first charge filed by the intervenors with EEOC], who have been discriminated against in promotion, wages, job assignments and terms and conditions of employment because of their race."[3]

After certifying the class, the District Court ordered that notice be published in the Charlotte newspapers and mailed to each individual member of the class. The notice described the status of the litigation, and plainly stated that members of the class "will be bound by the judgment or other determination" if they did not exclude themselves by sending a written notice to the clerk. Among the recipients of the notice

---

3. Certification was also sought for a class of female employees, but the District Court concluded that the evidence did not warrant the certification of a class with respect to the claims of sex discrimination.

were Phyllis Baxter and five other individuals employed by the Bank. It is undisputed that these individuals—the Baxter petitioners—are members of the class represented by the intervening plaintiffs and that they made no attempt to exclude themselves from the class.

At the trial the intervening plaintiffs, as well as the Baxter petitioners, testified. The District Court found that the Bank had engaged in a pattern and practice of discrimination from 1974 through 1978 by failing to afford black employees opportunities for advancement and assignment equal to opportunities afforded white employees in pay grades 4 and 5. Except as so specified, however, the District Court found that "there does not appear to be a pattern and practice of discrimination pervasive enough for the court to order relief." With respect to the claims of the four intervening plaintiffs, the court found that the Bank had discriminated against Cooper and Russell, but not against Moore and Hannah. Finally, the court somewhat cryptically stated that although it had an opinion about "the entitlement to relief of some of the class members who testified at trial," it would defer decision of such matters to a further proceeding.

Thereafter, on March 24, 1981, the Baxter petitioners moved to intervene, alleging that each had been denied a promotion for discriminatory reasons. With respect to Emma Ruffin, the court denied the motion because she was a member of the class for which relief had been ordered and therefore her rights would be protected in the Stage II proceedings to be held on the question of relief. With respect to the other five Baxter petitioners, the court also denied the motion, but for a different reason. It held that because all of them were employed in jobs above the grade 5 category, they were not entitled to any benefit from the court's ruling with respect to discrimination in grades 4 and 5. The District Court stated: "The court has found no proof of any classwide discrimination above grade 5 and, therefore, they are not entitled to participate in any Stage II proceedings in this case." The court added that it could "see no reason why, if any of the would-be intervenors are actively interested in pursuing their claims, they cannot file a Section 1981 suit next week...."

A few days later the Baxter petitioners filed a separate action against the Bank alleging that each of them had been denied a promotion because of their race in violation of 42 U.S.C. § 1981. The Bank moved to dismiss the complaint on the ground that each of them was a member of the class that had been certified in the *Cooper* litigation, that each was employed in a grade other than 4 or 5, and that they were bound by the determination that there was no proof of any classwide discrimination above grade 5. The District Court denied the motion to dismiss, but certified its order for interlocutory appeal under 28 U.S.C. § 1292(b). The Bank's interlocutory appeal from the order was then consolidated with the Bank's pending appeal in the Cooper litigation.

The United States Court of Appeals for the Fourth Circuit reversed the District Court's judgment on the merits in the *Cooper* litigation, concluding that (1) there was insufficient evidence to establish a pattern or practice of racial discrimination in grades 4 and 5, and (2) two of the intervening plaintiffs had not been discriminated against on account of race. The court further held that under the doctrine of res judicata, the judgment in the Cooper class action precluded the Baxter petitioners from maintaining their individual race discrimination claims against the Bank. The court thus reversed the order denying the Bank's motion to dismiss in the Baxter action, and remanded for dismissal of the Baxter complaint. We granted certiorari to review that judgment and we now reverse.

II

Claims of two types were adjudicated in the Cooper litigation. First, the individual claims of each of the four intervening plaintiffs have been finally decided in the Bank's favor.[7] Those individual decisions do not, of course, foreclose any other individual claims. Second, the class claim that the Bank followed "policies and practices" of discriminating against its employees has also been decided.[8] It is that decision on which the Court of Appeals based its res judicata analysis.

There is of course no dispute that under elementary principles of prior adjudication a judgment in a properly entertained class action is binding on class members in any subsequent litigation. See, *e.g., Supreme Tribe of Ben–Hur v. Cauble,* 255 U.S. 356, 41 S.Ct. 338, 65 L.Ed. 673 (1921). Basic principles of res judicata (merger and bar or claim preclusion) and collateral estoppel (issue preclusion) apply. A judgment in favor of the plaintiff class extinguishes their claim, which merges into the judgment granting relief. A judgment in favor of the defendant extinguishes the claim, barring a subsequent action on that claim. A judgment in favor of either side is conclusive in a subsequent action between them on any issue actually litigated and determined, if its determination was essential to that judgment.

III

A plaintiff bringing a civil action for a violation of § 703(a) of Title VII of the Civil Rights Act of 1964, 78 Stat. 255, 42 U.S.C. § 2000e–2(a), has the initial burden of establishing a prima facie case that his employer discriminated against him on account of his race, color, religion, sex, or national origin. A plaintiff meets this initial burden by offering evidence adequate to create an inference that he was denied an employment opportunity on the basis of a discriminatory criterion enumerated in Title VII.

7. Two of those claims were rejected by the District Court and two by the Court of Appeals; all four of those determinations are now equally final.

8. The District Court rejected all of the class claims except that pertaining to grades 4 and 5; the claim on behalf of that subclass was rejected by the Court of Appeals. Again, that distinction between subclasses is no longer significant for the entire class claim has now been decided.

A plaintiff alleging one instance of discrimination establishes a prima facie case justifying an inference of individual racial discrimination by showing that he (1) belongs to a racial minority, (2) applied and was qualified for a vacant position the employer was attempting to fill, (3) was rejected for the position, and (4) after his rejection, the position remained open and the employer continued to seek applicants of the plaintiff's qualifications. *McDonnell Douglas Corp. v. Green*, 411 U.S. 792, 802, 93 S.Ct. 1817, 1824, 36 L.Ed.2d 668 (1973). Once these facts are established, the employer must produce "evidence that the plaintiff was rejected, or someone else was preferred, for a legitimate, non-discriminatory reason." *Texas Dept. of Community Affairs v. Burdine*, 450 U.S. 248, 254, 101 S.Ct. 1089, 1094, 67 L.Ed.2d 207 (1981). At that point, the presumption of discrimination "drops from the case," and the District Court is in a position to decide the ultimate question in such a suit: whether the particular employment decision at issue was made on the basis of race. *United States Postal Service Board of Governors v. Aikens*, 460 U.S. 711, 715, 103 S.Ct. 1478, 1482, 75 L.Ed.2d 403 (1983); *Texas Dept. of Community Affairs v. Burdine*, 450 U.S., at 253, 101 S.Ct., at 1093. The ultimate burden of persuading the trier of fact that the defendant intentionally discriminated against the plaintiff regarding the particular employment decision "remains at all times with the plaintiff," and in the final analysis the trier of fact "must decide which party's explanation of the employer's motivation it believes." *United States Postal Service Board of Governors v. Aikens*, 460 U.S., at 716, 103 S.Ct., at 1482.

In *Franks v. Bowman Transportation Co.*, 424 U.S. 747, 96 S.Ct. 1251, 47 L.Ed.2d 444 (1976), the plaintiff, on behalf of himself and all others similarly situated, alleged that the employer had engaged in a pervasive pattern of racial discrimination in various company policies, including the hiring, transfer, and discharge of employees. In that class action we held that demonstrating the existence of a discriminatory pattern or practice established a presumption that the individual class members had been discriminated against on account of race. Proving isolated or sporadic discriminatory acts by the employer is insufficient to establish a prima facie case of a pattern or practice of discrimination; rather it must be established by a preponderance of the evidence "that racial discrimination was the company's standard operating procedure— the regular rather than the unusual practice." *Teamsters v. United States*, 431 U.S. 324, 336, 97 S.Ct. 1843, 1855, 52 L.Ed.2d 396 (1977). While a finding of a pattern or practice of discrimination itself justifies an award of prospective relief to the class, additional proceedings are ordinarily required to determine the scope of individual relief for the members of the class.

The crucial difference between an individual's claim of discrimination and a class action alleging a general pattern or practice of discrimination is manifest. The inquiry regarding an individual's claim is the reason for a particular employment decision, while "at the liability stage of a pattern-or-practice trial the focus often will not be on individual hiring decisions, but on a pattern of discriminatory decision-making." [*Teamsters, supra,* 431 U.S. at 360 n. 46, 97 S.Ct. at 1867 n. 46, 52 L.Ed.2d at 431 n. 46.]

This distinction was critical to our holding in *General Telephone Co. of Southwest v. Falcon,* 457 U.S. 147, 102 S.Ct. 2364, 72 L.Ed.2d 740 (1982) [*supra* p. 267], that an individual employee's claim that he was denied a promotion on racial grounds did not necessarily make him an adequate representative of a class composed of persons who had allegedly been refused employment for discriminatory reasons. We explained:

> "Conceptually, there is a wide gap between (a) an individual's claim that he has been denied a promotion on discriminatory grounds, and his otherwise unsupported allegation that the company has a policy of discrimination, and (b) the existence of a class of persons who have suffered the same injury as that individual, such that the individual's claim and the class claims will share common questions of law or fact and that the individual's claim will be typical of the class claims. For respondent to bridge that gap, he must prove much more than the validity of his own claim. Even though evidence that he was passed over for promotion when several less deserving whites were advanced may support the conclusion that respondent was denied the promotion because of his national origin, such evidence would not necessarily justify the additional inferences (1) that this discriminatory treatment is typical of petitioner's promotion practices, (2) that petitioner's promotion practices are motivated by a policy of ethnic discrimination that pervades petitioner's Irving division, or (3) that this policy of ethnic discrimination is reflected in petitioner's other employment practices, such as hiring, in the same way it is manifested in the promotion practices."

After analyzing the particulars of the plaintiff's claim in that case, we pointed out that if "one allegation of specific discriminatory treatment were sufficient to support an across-the-board attack, every Title VII case would be a potential companywide class action." We further observed:

> "In this regard it is noteworthy that Title VII prohibits discriminatory employment *practices,* not an abstract policy of discrimination. The mere fact that an aggrieved private plaintiff is a member of an identifiable class of persons of the same race or national origin is insufficient to establish his standing to litigate on their behalf all possible claims of discrimination against a common employer."

Falcon thus holds that the existence of a valid individual claim does not necessarily warrant the conclusion that the individual plaintiff may successfully maintain a class action. It is equally clear that a class plaintiff's attempt to prove the existence of a companywide policy, or even a consistent practice within a given department, may fail even though discrimination against one or two individuals has been proved. The facts of this case illustrate the point.

The District Court found that two of the intervening plaintiffs, Cooper and Russell, had both established that they were the victims of racial discrimination but, as the Court of Appeals noted, they were employed in grades higher than grade 5 and therefore their testimony provided no support for the conclusion that there was a practice of discrimination in grades 4 and 5. Given the burden of establishing a prima facie case of a pattern or practice of discrimination, it was entirely consistent for the District Court simultaneously to conclude that Cooper and Russell had valid individual claims even though it had expressly found no proof of any classwide discrimination above grade 5. It could not be more plain that the rejection of a claim of classwide discrimination does not warrant the conclusion that no member of the class could have a valid individual claim. "A racially balanced work force cannot immunize an employer from liability for specific acts of discrimination." *Furnco Construction Corp. v. Waters,* 438 U.S., at 579, 98 S.Ct., at 2950–2951.

The analysis of the merits of the Cooper litigation by the Court of Appeals is entirely consistent with this conclusion. In essence, the Court of Appeals held that the statistical evidence, buttressed by expert testimony and anecdotal evidence by three individual employees in grades 4 and 5, was not sufficient to support the finding of a pattern of bankwide discrimination within those grades. It is true that the Court of Appeals was unpersuaded by the anecdotal evidence; it is equally clear, however, that it did not regard two or three instances of discrimination as sufficient to establish a general policy.[11] It quite properly recognized that a "court must be wary of a claim that the true color of a forest is better revealed by reptiles hidden in the weeds than by the foliage of countless freestanding trees." *NAACP v. Claiborne Hardware Co.,* 458 U.S. 886,

---

11. It wrote:

"The claim here is a pattern or practice of intentional discrimination against an entire group by treating it less favorably because of race. That is the typical disparate treatment case. This case should accordingly be properly treated as such. However, the result reached by us would not be substantially different whether the class action be considered as a disparate impact or a disparate treatment case."

"This case accordingly presents quite a contrast with *Teamsters* where the 'oral testimony of class members' demonstrated 40 cases of specific instances of discrimination in support of the statistical evidence offered by plaintiffs or with that in our own case of *Chisholm v. United States Postal Service,* 665 F.2d 482, 495 (4th Cir.1981), where there were 20 'class members' testifying of individual discrimination. Here all we have is the testimony of but two class members testifying of individual discrimination in promotion out of either pay grade 4 or pay grade 5

on which a finding of discriminatory practices can be rested. This is even less of a presentation of oral testimony in support of a pattern of discrimination than that found wanting in *Ste. Marie v. Eastern R. Ass'n.,* 650 F.2d 395, 405–06 (2d Cir. 1981), where the Court declared that the small number of incidents of discrimination in promotion over a period of years in that case 'would be insufficient to support the inference of a routine or regular practice of discrimination ... ,' or, in *Goff v. Continental Oil Co.,* 678 F.2d 593, 597 (5th Cir.1982), where the Court held that 'even if all three witnesses' accounts of racial discrimination were true, this evidence would not have been enough to prove a pattern or practice of company-wide discrimination by Conoco.' It follows that these two incidents of failure to promote Ruffin or Harrison, even if regarded as discriminatory, (which we assume only *arguendo*), would not support the District Court's finding of a pattern of class discrimination in promotions out of grades 4 and 5."

934, 102 S.Ct. 3409, 3437, 73 L.Ed.2d 1215 (1982). Conversely, a piece of fruit may well be bruised without being rotten to the core.

The Court of Appeals was correct in generally concluding that the Baxter petitioners, as members of the class represented by the intervening plaintiffs in the Cooper litigation, are bound by the adverse judgment in that case. The court erred, however, in the preclusive effect it attached to that prior adjudication. That judgment (1) bars the class members from bringing another class action against the Bank alleging a pattern or practice of discrimination for the relevant time period and (2) precludes the class members in any other litigation with the Bank from relitigating the question whether the Bank engaged in a pattern and practice of discrimination against black employees during the relevant time period. The judgment is not, however, dispositive of the individual claims the Baxter petitioners have alleged in their separate action. Assuming they establish a prima facie case of discrimination under *McDonnell Douglas,* the Bank will be required to articulate a legitimate reason for each of the challenged decisions, and if it meets that burden, the ultimate questions regarding motivation in their individual cases will be resolved by the District Court. Moreover, the prior adjudication may well prove beneficial to the Bank in the Baxter action: the determination in the Cooper action that the Bank had not engaged in a general pattern or practice of discrimination would be relevant on the issue of pretext. See *McDonnell Douglas,* 411 U.S., at 804–805, 93 S.Ct., at 1825–1826.

The Bank argues that permitting the Baxter petitioners to bring separate actions would frustrate the purposes of Rule 23. We think the converse is true. The class-action device was intended to establish a procedure for the adjudication of common questions of law or fact. If the Bank's theory were adopted, it would be tantamount to requiring that every member of the class be permitted to intervene to litigate the merits of his individual claim.

It is also suggested that the District Court had a duty to decide the merits of the individual claims of class members, at least insofar as the individual claimants became witnesses in the joint proceeding and subjected their individual employment histories to scrutiny at trial. Unless these claims are decided in the main proceeding, the Bank argues that the duplicative litigation that Rule 23 was designed to avoid will be encouraged, and that defendants will be subjected to the risks of liability without the offsetting benefit of a favorable termination of exposure through a final judgment.

This argument fails to differentiate between what the District Court might have done and what it actually did. The District Court did actually adjudicate the individual claims of Cooper and the other intervening plaintiffs, as well as the class claims, but it pointedly refused to decide the individual claims of the Baxter petitioners. Whether the issues framed by the named parties before the court should be expanded to encompass the individual claims of additional class members is a matter of judicial administration that should be decided in the first instance by the District Court. Nothing in Rule 23 requires as a matter of law that the District Court make a finding with respect to each and every matter on which there is testimony in the class action. Indeed, Rule 23 is carefully drafted to provide a mechanism for the expeditious decision of *common* questions. Its purposes might well be defeated by an attempt to decide a host of individual claims before any common question relating to liability has been resolved adversely to the defendant. We do not find the District Court's denial of the Baxter petitioners' motion for leave to intervene in the Cooper litigation, or its decision not to make findings regarding the Baxter petitioners' testimony in the Cooper litigation, to be inconsistent with Rule 23.

Notes and Questions

1. Is *Cooper* based on Title VII or Rule 23? Could a securities fraud class action involve only the "class claims" of purchasers or sellers of the securities, leaving them to assert their "individual claims" separately? Is *Cooper* a specialized rule of claim preclusion for employment discrimination actions?

2. In *Cooper,* did the class members really stand to lose anything by not opting out?

3. Read together, do *Cooper* and *Falcon* (*supra* p. 267) suggest that a class action should never be certified in a discrimination suit when anecdotal evidence is to be presented?

4. Is *Cooper* based on res judicata or collateral estoppel? The Court states that the judgment not only precludes assertion of another class action relating to the period in question, but also precludes relitigation of the question whether the bank engaged in a pattern and practice of discrimination during the period in question. Is that a "claim" that was adjudicated? Does that adjudication place limitations on the type of evidence that plaintiffs may introduce in support of their individual claims?

5. If 500 present and former employees had opted out in *Cooper,* could they file a new class action alleging a pattern and practice of discrimination by the Bank? What relief would be proper if the class were successful?

6. In *Cooper* the class representatives submitted their individual claims during the trial of the class claims. Were they required to do so? If they had gone to trial using only statistical evidence and lost, could they later have sued on the basis of anecdotal evidence of their personal experiences?

7. The evidentiary standards for individual and class action employment discrimination suits can be easier to describe than to apply. In Burney v. Rheem Mfg. Co., 196 F.R.D. 659 (M.D.Ala.2000), an individual suing for discrimination countered defendant's summary judgment motion with statistical evidence. Defendant asserted that plaintiff could not establish a prima facie case of individual discrimination using statistics alone. The court reasoned as follows (id. at 667–68):

> It is clear that in a class action lawsuit alleging discrimination, "statistics alone may be enough to create a prima facie case of classwide discrimination." Carmichael v. Birmingham Saw Works, 738 F.2d 1126, 1131 (11th Cir.1984). It is also clear that a plaintiff may establish a

prima facie case of disparate impact by identifying a specific employment practice that allegedly has a disproportionate impact and then "offering statistical evidence sufficient to show that the practice in question has resulted in prohibited discrimination." Further, in an individual disparate treatment case, statistics may be relevant to establish that an employer's articulated reason for an employment is pretextual.

The role of statistical evidence in establishing a prima facie case of discrimination in an individual disparate treatment case, however, is not as clear. In Carmichael v. Birmingham Saw Works, 738 F.2d 1126 (11th Cir.1984), the court said:

> If they are strong enough, statistics alone may be enough to create a prima facie case of classwide discrimination. And there is no doubt that statistics alone can be relevant and important in an individual case. But statistics alone cannot make a case of individual disparate treatment. * * * Unless the individual plaintiff can point to some specific instance of discrimination, there is no wrong for the court to remedy. * * * For the plaintiff to establish economic injury, he must necessarily show that in fact he was the victim of an identifiable act of discrimination.

8. In Frank v. United Airlines, Inc., 216 F.3d 845 (9th Cir.2000), the court limited the preclusive effect of an earlier class action in ways that point up intrinsic problems with (b)(2) class actions and might impede settlement of such cases in the future. The earlier case challenged United's height and weight limitations for flight attendants because they allowed men to be heavier than women of the same age and height. The case was certified as a (b)(2) class action on behalf of any present or future United flight attendants, and resulted in a district court judgment in 1979 that the United policy was not facially invalid, but that it had been applied in a discriminatory fashion. The district judge added that "[n]othing in the court's decision or order is intended to pass upon the validity of any other weight standard for male or female flight attendants that United might adopt in the future." Both sides appealed, and they settled while the appeal was pending. Plaintiffs agreed to abandon their appeal from the finding that the existing weight policy was not facially discriminatory in return for United's agreement to alter the weight charts slightly by increasing the weight limits. United also agreed to abandon its appeal of the judge's finding of discrimination in application of the policy.

In the 1990s, different flight attendants filed suit alleging that United had discriminated under the policy adopted pursuant to the 1979 settlement. The district court held that plaintiffs were foreclosed from claiming that the standards were discriminatory on their face from the 1979 ruling that United's then-applicable standards were not discriminatory. The court of appeals reversed, citing several reasons that point up difficulties with (b)(2) class settlements.

First, the court broadly asserted that preclusion could not apply because the claims asserted in the current case relate to the period after 1979, and that "[a] claim arising after the date of an earlier judgment is not barred, even if it arises out of a continuing course of conduct." Applying this concept to (b)(2) class actions would seem to undermine the value of any decree regarding the legality or illegality of a given course of conduct.

Second, the court pointed out that the current claims arise from a different weight policy, noting that the district court acknowledged that its ruling was not applicable to unknown future policies. But this changed policy was part of the settlement of the earlier action and represented, from plaintiffs' perspective, an improvement on the one found facially valid in 1979. If there would be preclusion for the former policy, but not for the relaxed one, defendants faced with (b)(2) decrees might feel they cannot alter policies even to the advantage of those who challenged them.

Third, the court noted that monetary claims were presented in the current case, and concluded that the absence of a right to opt out in the earlier case made preclusion unavailable. This raises a very real problem, and one that has presented difficulties due to the 1991 Civil Rights Act's recharacterization of monetary relief in some Title VII cases as damages. It may be that no (b)(2) class action with the possibility of some sort of "damages" relief would ever be able to close the door on future litigation. If so, settlement might seem much less attractive to defendants. Plaintiff classes sometimes trade off "damages" claims and injunctive relief claims (in Martin v. Wilks, *supra* p. 86, plaintiffs were reportedly were more interested in a strong affirmative action injunctive decree and were willing to trade off the possibility of damages for it), but that sort of trade-off is no longer possible under the court's rationale.

9. What bearing should *Cooper* have on settlement of an employment discrimination class action? Could that include the "individual" as well as the "class" claims? Recall Parker v. Anderson, *supra* p. 511, in which the court allowed the dissident class representatives to opt out of the settlement. Would other class members be free to proceed separately on their "individual" claims notwithstanding the settlement?

10. If the individual claims are not affected by disposition of the class action, should the pendency of the class action toll the running of limitations against the individual claims?

11. For an alternative view of res judicata in a class action, consider King v. South Central Bell Tel. & Tel. Co., 790 F.2d 524 (6th Cir.1986). The class action there was brought by the Communication Workers of America (CWA) against South Central Bell on behalf of a class of women denied the opportunity to return to their old jobs after taking pregnancy leave. In 1976 the trial court certified a class pursuant to Rule 23(b)(2) without notice to members of the class. King, an employee of defendant, became pregnant in 1976 and asked permission to take leave to give birth (even using vacation time) to preserve her seniority. Bell refused, and although King was ready to go back to work less than a month after she took maternity leave she was not rehired for two weeks thereafter, and then for a job that paid $45 per week less. Despite King's request, the CWA did not pursue a grievance for her. She filed a charge of sex discrimination with the EEOC and eventually received a right-to-sue letter.

Meanwhile, the class action had settled, and King submitted a claim for the two-week delay in her return but explicitly reserved her claim for about $13,000 in lost wages thereafter due to the reduction in pay she suffered. The class action court approved the settlement, noting that there were some objections to it. King then filed her own suit against Bell, and also sued CWA for acquiescing in Bell's discriminatory policies. The district court granted both defendants summary judgment on grounds of res judicata, and the appellate court affirmed. It reasoned that "King could not opt out because the action did not include that privilege. The most she could do was object to the decree and she did." It also rejected her claims of inadequate representation by the union (which she was suing): "Although representation in this case may be somewhat wanting, the fact that the court received and was aware of King's objections compensates for this fact. Moreover, * * * King had retained her own counsel and there was ample time to challenge the class action settlement by appeal. She chose to attack the settlement collaterally and should not now complain of any inadequacy in representation." Id. at 530. Hence, even the claims against the union were precluded: "general policy principles of res judicata dictate that all claims relating to Bell's maternity leave policies and practices, including any claim she may have against [the union], were resolved by the class action settlement." Id. at 531. Judge Merritt dissented, arguing that the Fifth Circuit's approach to "hybrid" class actions (see *Woolen, supra* p. 448, ftn. 1) violates the due process rights of absent class members who have claims for substantial monetary relief. On this point, consider Justice Ginsburg's arguments in Matsushita Electric Indus. Co. v. Epstein, *supra* p. 810.

GOFF v. MENKE

United States Court of Appeals, Eighth Circuit, 1982.
672 F.2d 702.

Before LAY, CHIEF JUDGE, STEPHENSON, CIRCUIT JUDGE, and GIBSON, DISTRICT JUDGE.

LAY, CHIEF JUDGE.

The security director at the Iowa State Penitentiary, Jim Menke, appeals from the order of the district court, the Honorable Donald E. O'Brien presiding, granting relief to George Goff, an inmate at the penitentiary. Because Goff is a member of a class whose suit was both filed prior to his individual action and involves the issue raised in this action, we vacate and remand his claim for equitable relief to the district court with instructions to dismiss this claim without prejudice and to instruct Goff to pursue any further equitable relief through the class representative in the pending class action.

As a result of misconduct, Goff was, at the time he filed his complaint, in administrative segregation. On October 17, 1980, plaintiff filed a pro se complaint in federal court alleging denial of sufficient exercise in violation of a preliminary injunction issued in *Gavin v. Ray,* No. 78–62–2 (S.D.Iowa May 1, 1978) (order granting preliminary injunction), and denial of his fourteenth, eighth, and first amendment rights. In his complaint, Goff requested (1) that defendant be ordered to immediately stop suspending prisoners' right to exercise; (2) that plaintiff be given $1,000 from each defendant; (3) that plaintiff be removed from "the hole" and placed back in the general population; and (4) that he receive $10,000 in punitive damages "and whatever else the court deems proper." Trial was held on February 6, 1981. Goff appeared pro se with the "legal assistance" of a fellow inmate. The district court granted equitable relief, but denied money damages.

In addressing the issue of equitable relief, the district court stated that it "was appropriate in this case to fashion a remedy which would run to the benefit of all inmates similarly situated to plaintiff without actually certifying a class action." In evaluating Goff's claim, Judge O'Brien both interpreted the *Gavin* order and directly evaluated the eighth amendment issue. *Gavin* involves conditions of confinement and procedures affecting prisoners in administrative and disciplinary segregation at the Iowa State Penitentiary. In *Gavin*, a class of inmates in administrative or disciplinary segregation was certified on July 23, 1980. In granting the preliminary injunction in *Gavin*, Judge William C. Hanson ordered:

> Defendants shall ensure that plaintiffs and others who may be confined in either an administrative or disciplinary status for a period of thirty consecutive days or more are each afforded an opportunity for a total of one hour of exercise each week, except weekly exercise need not be afforded to an inmate who is serving a punishment of 10 days solitary confinement or less.

Judge O'Brien found that prison officials initially interpreted this order as not requiring any exercise until a prisoner had been in administrative or disciplinary segregation for 30 consecutive days. He held that the order required exercise beginning the first week of segregation.

Judge O'Brien then found that the prison had revised its original policy and, at the time of trial, permitted security unit inmates two one-hour exercise periods per week. He held that this policy "is constitutionally adequate for those inmates placed in such status for a period of thirty days or less." But the court also held that "[f]or inmates in restricted status for a longer period, the weekly exercise period should be increased."

Although plaintiff's complaint did not directly raise the issue, Judge O'Brien next addressed the issue of exercise clothing. He found that prisoners were not provided with clothing suitable for outdoor exercise during the winter. Judge O'Brien held that the prison had violated an order of Judge Harold D. Vietor in a class action entitled *Lenz v. Baughman*, No. 79–81–2 (S.D.Iowa June 20, 1980). Judge Vietor ordered prison officials to provide the prisoner plaintiffs with "adequate exercise clothing in winter." Judge O'Brien granted certain specified relief for inmates in security status.

The State urges that the district court erred in granting class-wide relief or any relief when the issues had already been preliminarily resolved and were pending final resolution in a class action to which plaintiff, as a class member, was a party. We must agree.

In deference to the district court, we think the State erred in its original position statement. The State did not move for consolidation of this case with *Gavin*. Furthermore, the State informed the trial court that the issues presented in this case were not related to the issues in *Gavin*. We disagree. For reasons of law as well as judicial economy Goff's case should have been transferred to the trial judge who entered the preliminary relief in the *Gavin* case and, to the extent that injunctive relief was sought, Goff should have been required to proceed through the class representative or through intervention. He could have pursued his individual damage claim in the same court.

Two of the primary purposes underlying Fed.R.Civ.P. 23 are avoidance of both duplicative litigation and inconsistent standards. Both of these policies are undermined when two suits challenging the same prison conditions are allowed to proceed.

After rendition of a final judgment, a class member is ordinarily bound by the result of a class action. This court has on several occasions refused to allow prisoners to relitigate issues decided in prior class actions. If a class member cannot relitigate issues raised in a class action after it has been resolved, a class member should not be able to prosecute a separate equitable action once his or her class has been certified. If class members seek individual money damages, the district court can dispose of those claims on an individual basis. However, in order to avoid duplicative actions as well as inconsistent interpretations of the same decree, wherever possible the individual claims should be processed by the same court which renders the equitable relief.

Judge O'Brien could have dismissed plaintiff's complaint without prejudice and instructed plaintiff to seek the cooperation of the class representative in *Gavin* or to intervene in the *Gavin* action. He might also have held the damage action in abeyance pending resolution of *Gavin*. Additionally, he might have treated Goff's pro se complaint as an attempt to initiate contempt proceedings and transferred it to the *Gavin* docket.

We find that it was an abuse of the district court's equitable power to use plaintiff's complaint—which essentially requested damages and sought to enforce the requirements of the *Gavin* preliminary injunction—to establish class-wide standards governing exercise and exercise clothing. We vacate the equitable relief granted below and remand this claim to the district court with instructions that it should be dismissed without prejudice.

The State informs this court that there are several standing injunctive orders and numerous federal actions separately pending which challenge various conditions at the Iowa State Penitentiary. We view this situation as inefficient; it presents a risk of inconsistent adjudications, and confuses and exhausts prison officials, inmates, and judicial officers. Particularly after the recent riot at the prison and the resulting suspension of normal procedures, we believe it is important to resolve these issues expeditiously and in a manner which will provide clear guidance to prison officials and inmates.

We thus request the Chief Judge of the District Court for the Southern District of Iowa, the Honorable William C. Stuart, to afford both the State and the respective counsel in all pending actions an opportunity to be heard in relation to consolidation of all pending actions which seek injunctive relief relating to constitutional standards governing the conditions of confinement at the Iowa prison. *See Finney v. Mabry,* 458 F.Supp. 720 (E.D.Ark.1978) (consolidated class actions concerning Arkansas prisons); Fed.R.Civ.P. 42(a).[2] The State has submitted to this court some suggestions as to consolidation of the various pending cases which will be forwarded to Judge Stuart. This court does not make direction as to consolidation; that decision belongs more appropriately within the studied discretion of Chief Judge Stuart. We do suggest, however, that efforts to consolidate all claims relating to conditions of confinement in a single class suit would bring about more efficient handling of prisoner complaints, obviate inconsistent decrees, and provide a better overview of the interrelated subject areas relating to conditions within the penitentiary.

Notes and Questions

1. One of the recurring issues in institutional reform litigation concerns how to deal with individual suits by class members, whether on issues raised in the class action or not, and whether for similar relief or different relief from that sought in the class action. Antisuit injunctions against prosecution or filing of individual suits by class members could help to reduce this problem, but in an on-going and fluid institutional setting it is impossible to avoid new claims by class members entirely. This poses a preclusion problem when new claims are filed after a final order is issued in the class action. In *Goff,* that point had not been reached, but the course of action by the appellate court was clearly taken in recognition of the preclusive values at stake.

2. In *Goff,* Judge O'Brien was confronted with an individual class member's claim for injunctive and damage relief which was related to issues dealt with in a preliminary injunction previously issued in the *Gavin* class action and in a final order previously issued in another class action, Lenz v. Baughman. Why was he not entitled to interpret and apply those orders and to grant appropriate relief if he found they had been violated? Why should the preliminary injunction in *Gavin* essentially be accorded preclusive effect? What is the significance of the Eighth Circuit's comment that Judge O'Brien's order had established "class-wide standards"? Is the ultimate justification for the circuit court's ruling simply a matter of efficiency? Is it efficient for all cases, even those arising in another district, to have to go to the class-action court?

3. What type of class actions were the earlier suits in *Goff?* Recall that there is a debate about whether a court can grant classwide injunctive relief without certifying a class under Rule 23(b)(2). See *supra* p. 327 n. 3. Would that be the proper designation? In *Goff* the court mentions the risk of

---

2. District court judges have wide discretion to stay class actions to avoid duplicitous litigation.

inconsistent adjudications. Should prison condition suits therefore be certified under Rule 23(b)(1)(A)? See *supra* pp. 298-302. In either event, doesn't the problem presented in *Goff* show why in some instances class action treatment should be regarded as mandatory? Indeed, *Goff* in effect devises a way to make it mandatory on the class members.

4.   The Fifth Circuit, in supervising the mammoth *Ruiz* class action that ordered major restructuring of the Texas prison system, adopted procedures for consideration of individual claims similar to those in *Goff.* In Johnson v. McKaskle, 727 F.2d 498 (5th Cir.1984), it ordered that all suits filed by class-action prisoners that "assert legal or equitable claims directly related to or dependent upon rights adjudicated and incorporated in the *Ruiz* injunctive decree" be filed in the class-action court. That court could then:

> choose to (a) retain and adjudicate the equitable rights asserted so that their adjudication will be consistent with the injunctive decree and the ongoing administration of that order, (b) retain and adjudicate the legal rights asserted if they are based on the terms of the injunctive decree and should be decided as part of any claims for equitable relief that the court adjudicates, (c) issue a show cause order for criminal or civil contempt and, if appropriate, impose punishment or award compensatory damages or other civil relief, or (d) return the action to the court from which it was transferred if it determines that its decree is not implicated and an independent adjudication in the separate § 1983 proceeding is more appropriate.

A year later, in Green v. McKaskle, 770 F.2d 445 (5th Cir.1985), the Fifth Circuit directed that thereafter prisoner suits should be filed in the court of proper venue (usually where the prisoner is incarcerated or where the incident complained of occurred), apparently because the class-action court had been overwhelmed with cases. The *Green* court also ruled that *equitable claims* by class members "which are comparable to those claims litigated and under ongoing review and supervision of the court in the *Ruiz* class action should not be maintainable as individual causes of action." Id. at 446. It said that class members had the following remedies as to such equitable claims: (1) go "to the class attorney, or the court's special master, to urge consideration of motions to the *Ruiz* court for additional equitable relief or sanctions against any party violating its injunctions," (2) seek to intervene in the class action (almost universally denied), and (3) "object to the binding effect of a class action judgment on the ground that they are not or were not adequately represented in the class action." Id. at 446–47. The court later adopted this approach en banc, reasoning that "[t]o allow individual suits would interfere with the orderly administration of the class action and risk inconsistent adjudications. Individual members of the class and other prisoners may assert any equitable or declaratory claims they have, but they must do so by urging further action through the class representative and attorney, including contempt proceedings, or by intervention in the class action." How realistic is this regime for prisoner plaintiffs?

The court was also unwilling to accord class members who filed individual damage suits any preclusive effect as to the *Ruiz* class action's conclusions of law or remedial decrees. It found that the *Ruiz* class action did not create "rights, privileges, or immunities secured by the Constitution and laws" and therefore could not serve as the basis for an action under 42 U.S.C.A. § 1983 by individual prisoners claiming violation of the decree. Green v. McKaskle, 788 F.2d 1116 (5th Cir.1986). It reasoned that "many of the details of the injunctive relief are negotiated and settled by the parties" and that "they may arrive at agreed stipulations that are extremely detailed which can and do go far beyond constitutional requirements." The court was concerned that "[i]f individual prisoners can seek damages for violations of every detail of a remedial decree, compliance would be deterred by the hopelessness of defendants' position" and there would be "serious problems regarding the ability to give notice to potential defendants preparing themselves conscientiously for the shelter of qualified immunity."

5. Should federal courts be similarly protective of the remedial regime imposed by a state court? Consider Harris v. Pernsley, 755 F.2d 338 (3d Cir.1985), cert. denied, 474 U.S. 965, 106 S.Ct. 331, 88 L.Ed.2d 314 (1985). Plaintiffs in that case were incarcerated in a city prison that was operating under a state court decree regarding prison conditions. In federal court, they challenged many of the same conditions involved in the state suit and sought damages, which the plaintiffs in the state court case had not. The district court dismissed, but the court of appeals reversed, insisting that the federal court had to proceed with the case because it was within federal jurisdiction. Dissenting from denial of certiorari, Chief Justice Burger mourned that "[r]espondents essentially ask the federal courts to duplicate the on-going State court regulation of the Philadelphia prison system."

6. Suits for damages by inmates who were class members of a class action for injunctive relief create considerable problems. Bogard v. Cook, 586 F.2d 399 (5th Cir.1978), provides an example. A federal court certified a class of inmates at the Mississippi State Penitentiary challenging the constitutionality of prison conditions and directed that notice be given to each inmate. Bogard was not one of the 380 who opted out, and he testified at the class trial which resulted in a sweeping declaratory and injunctive order. He later filed suit for equitable relief and damages based on the practice of imposing summary punishments and allowing random gun fire (which was raised in the class action suit) and on his being stabbed two months after the class action record was closed, but several months before the judgment was rendered. The Fifth Circuit refused to bar his suit under res judicata, stating:

> The defendants * * * argue that Bogard should have had the record reopened and had his damage claim litigated as part of the class action. To impose such an obligation on Bogard would in effect impose a three-month statute of limitations on Bogard's stabbing claim. It would forever bar relief to a prisoner because he did not have a class action suit that had been essentially concluded for two months reopened during the time he was recovering from a vicious physical assault that left him a paraplegic. Res judicata does not require such a result and reason forbids it.

> The summary punishments and the shooting that Bogard complains of did occur in time to be litigated in *Gates,* however, and testimony concerning those incidents was introduced at the *Gates* trial. However, we conclude that inmates at Parchman [the prison] could not have

surmised from the class action notice sent them in *Gates* that they were required to seek monetary relief in that suit or opt out. Furthermore, we have no way of knowing that *Gates* would have been manageable as a class action if individual damage relief had been requested.

Principles of res judicata are not ironclad. This court has frequently stated that res judicata will not be applied when it contravenes an important public policy. At the very least, Bogard's claims are of sufficient gravity to require that they not be extinguished by his class status in *Gates* unless it can reasonably be assumed that Bogard should have been aware of the possibility that they could have been presented in that suit.

While the notice received by Bogard and the other class inmates at Parchman clearly apprised them of their rights in a suit seeking equitable reform of the Parchman prison, it was insufficient to alert prisoners to the possibility that they could seek individual money damages for personal wrongs. The relief sought was described in one sentence: "Plaintiff inmates ask the Court to order prison officials to correct all of the conditions alleged above." The quoted portion of the section "Your Rights in the Lawsuit" told them that additional complaints about prison conditions or personal treatment could be presented. The defendants listed in the notice—the Governor, the Penitentiary Board, and the Superintendent—were named as defendants because of their power to amend the practices at the prison. *Gates* was never framed or presented as a suit for monetary relief and nothing in the notice sent to the inmates gave any indication that such relief was possible. It would be a harsh and improper application of res judicata to hold, on the basis of the notice sent out in *Gates,* that prisoners forfeited their rights to personal redress for lack of knowledge that federal law (not followed by the State of Mississippi) required that injunctive and monetary relief be sought in one action.

The Fifth Circuit's lenient view of res judicata in *Bogard* contrasts with much stricter applications of preclusion in prisoner suits today. What would a Mississippi Penitentiary inmate's rights to sue for damages be under the rules laid down for the *Ruiz* class action (*supra* note 4)?

7. A final possibility is presented by Diaz v. Sheppard, 85 F.3d 1502 (11th Cir.1996). Plaintiff there had been a member of a federal court prison conditions class action concerning health care and exercise conditions in the Florida prison system. Defendant was class counsel in the federal class action. Based on a study by doctors and other experts, a settlement was confected containing specific exercise periods. When notice of the settlement was given, plaintiff wrote to defendant "begging" him not to agree to the plan because it did not afford sufficient outdoor exercise, but defendant did not press to increase outdoor exercise and a final judgment was entered in the class action.

Plaintiff then sued defendant for legal malpractice in a Florida state court, arguing that defendant had ignored case law requiring at least one hour per day of out-of-cell exercise. Defendant removed the case to federal court, arguing that the malpractice claim was essentially a belated effort to object to the settlement. The district court dismissed on the ground that class counsel owes no duty to individual class members, but the appellate court held that there was no removal jurisdiction because plaintiff was only seeking money damages (not to change the decree) and a malpractice claim did not arise under federal law just because the suit in which the alleged malpractice occurred was in federal court and based on federal law. It directed that the case be remanded to state court for further proceedings. A dissenter argued that "whether a class member may sue class counsel for malpractice arising out of a federal court-approved settlement is a federal question."

B. ISSUE PRECLUSION IN COMPLEX LITIGATION

Issue preclusion (or collateral estoppel) is critical to resolving complex litigation with finality. It can be material to such questions as joinder, class action devices, and administrative techniques.

Issue preclusion applies if (1) the issue was actually litigated, that is, contested by the parties and submitted for determination by the court, (2) the issue was "actually and necessarily determined by a court of competent jurisdiction," Montana v. United States, 440 U.S. 147, 153, 99 S.Ct. 970, 973, 59 L.Ed.2d 210 (1979), and (3) preclusion in the second trial will not work an unfairness.

1. PERSONS OR ENTITIES BOUND

Persons bound by issue preclusion are parties and their privies. At one time "mutuality" was generally required, and a nonparty who was not bound by a judgment could not assert it as preclusive against one who was bound by it. The mutuality doctrine has been eroded over the years, and was finally rejected for federal courts as to defensive, and, in certain circumstances, as to offensive use of collateral estoppel. See Blonder–Tongue Laboratories, Inc. v. University of Illinois Foundation, 402 U.S. 313, 91 S.Ct. 1434, 28 L.Ed.2d 788 (1971) (defensive use); Parklane Hosiery Co. v. Shore, 439 U.S. 322, 99 S.Ct. 645, 58 L.Ed.2d 552 (1979) (offensive use).

IN RE NISSAN MOTOR CORP. ANTITRUST LITIGATION

United States District Court, Southern District of Florida, 1979.
471 F.Supp. 754.

ATKINS, CHIEF JUDGE.

In July, 1972, P.D.Q. of Miami filed a private class action antitrust suit against Nissan Motor Corporation before this Court on behalf of all non-dealer Datsun purchasers across the country. The suit alleged a nationwide conspiracy between Nissan–U.S.A. and Nissan–Japan to fix prices in violation of § 4 of the Clayton Act, 15 U.S.C. § 15. Once this suit was filed, several others were filed throughout the United States. The cases were transferred by the Judicial Panel on Multidistrict Litigation to this Court for consolidated pretrial proceedings.

P.D.Q. was certified as a class representative by this Court, and thereafter this Court entered judgment on a jury verdict that no nation-wide conspiracy had existed. The Court of Appeals affirmed, but remanded the case for modification of the order awarding costs. Certiorari was denied by the Supreme Court this year.

Defendant Nissan Motors has moved for summary judgment on plaintiffs' customer and territorial allegations and plaintiffs' conspiracy allegations. Plaintiffs have concurrently moved for an *in limine* ruling that this Court's entry of judgment against P.D.Q. has no collateral estoppel effect on the pending statewide actions. These three motions involve an analysis of the proper application of the collateral estoppel doctrine in the case at bar. This Court holds that collateral estoppel may not be invoked on due process grounds and, therefore, the motions by Nissan Motors are denied.

I.

A fundamental principle of due process is that collateral estoppel may not be asserted against one who was not a party in the previous action. * * *

The abrogation of the mutuality doctrine has not affected the validity of that principle. In Blonder–Tongue Laboratories, Inc. v. University of Illinois Foundation, 402 U.S. 313, 91 S.Ct. 1434, 28 L.Ed.2d 788 (1971), the Supreme Court stated:

> "Some litigants—those who never appeared in a prior action—may not be collaterally estopped without litigating the issue. They have never had a chance to present their evidence and arguments on the claim. Due process prohibits estopping them despite one or more existing adjudications on the identical issue which stands directly against their position."

Earlier this year, in Parklane Hosiery Co., Inc. v. Shore, 439 U.S. 322, 99 S.Ct. 645, 58 L.Ed.2d 552 (1979), the Court reaffirmed this position, "[i]t is a violation of due process for a judgment to be binding on a litigant who is not a party or privy and therefore has never had an opportunity to be heard." This Court fully embraced this position in its recent opinion in In re Yarn Processing Patent Validity Litigation, MDL 82 (1979), 472 F.Supp. 174, wherein it was stated:

> "To allow this would enable these nonparticipants to reap the benefits of a favorable determination while escaping the binding effect of an unfavorable determination, because should Lex Tex prevail on the merits, due process considerations would preclude it from asserting collateral estoppel against these defendants in the subsequent action."

Nissan Motors asserts these due process requirements would not be violated in the application of collateral estoppel in the present action. It argues that the P.D.Q. plaintiffs were essentially in privity with remaining class plaintiffs in MDL 120. More specifically, it is alleged that (1) the complaints in the remaining actions are identical with P.D.Q.; (2) the plaintiffs' counsel closely coordinated and shared responsibility in the consolidated pretrial proceedings, including discovery and pretrial hearings; (3) joint motions were filed evincing common legal analysis, theories, and strategies; (4) the pretrial submissions show no material distinctions among any of the plaintiffs; (5) plaintiffs controlled the trial through joint pretrial submissions, which were conducted by a party with identical interests; (6) there was no deficiency in the proceedings or additional evidence of genuine substance to offer at any future trial; and (7) the precise legal issue central to all the plaintiffs' case[s] was decided adversely against them in the *P.D.Q.* trial. * * *

II.

When the issue of class certification was originally raised in the *P.D.Q.* case, this Court was faced with the question of whether a nationwide class would be appropriate. The Court stated that in view of the plaintiffs' reluctance to advance more than a few thousand dollars to finance the action, a nationwide class would be infeasible. The Court ordered the class to be limited to purchasers in New York County, New York, and Dade County, Florida. In a subsequent order on May 28, 1976, the Court indicated that the class actions would be remanded to their original transferor forums for trial. * * *

Throughout the entire length of these proceedings, the Court's rulings have indicated the necessity that the *P.D.Q.* case and the remainder of the actions be tried separately. The defendant, Nissan Motors, now raises the issue of whether under the circumstances, those non-participating plaintiffs may be bound by the *P.D.Q.* litigation because they, in effect, "controlled" the litigation through the P.D.Q. plaintiffs.

None of the cases cited by the defendant lead the Court to that conclusion. In Montana v. United States, 440 U.S. 147, 99 S.Ct. 970, 59 L.Ed.2d 210 (1979), a contractor brought suit in state court contending that the gross receipt tax unconstitutionally discriminated against the Government and companies with which it dealt. Soon after that, the Government filed suit in the United States District Court of Montana. In holding that collateral estoppel should be applied in that case, the Supreme Court stated: "[t]hese interests are similarly implicated when non-parties assume control over the litigation in which they have a direct financial or proprietary interest, and then seek to redetermine issues previously resolved." The Court then listed the factors it found as evincing Government "control" of the litigation. The Government had stipulated that it:

(1) required the first lawsuit to be filed;

(2) reviewed and approved the complaint;

(3) paid the attorney's fees and costs;

(4) directed the appeal from the state district court to the Montana Supreme Court;

(5) appeared and submitted an amicus brief in that court;

(6) directed the filing of a Notice of Appeal to the Supreme Court of the United States; and

(7) effectuated the abandonment of that appeal.

In light of those circumstances, the Supreme Court concluded that "although not a party, the United States plainly had a sufficient 'laboring oar' in the conduct of the state-court litigation to actuate principles of estoppel."

In Southwest Airlines Co. v. Texas International Airlines Inc., 546 F.2d 84 (5th Cir.), cert. denied, 434 U.S. 832, 98 S.Ct. 117, 54 L.Ed.2d 93 (1977), the Fifth Circuit held that due process would not be violated by binding Civil Aeronautics Board carriers to a prior judgment, even though they were not parties to the action, since their interests were sufficiently represented by the *public* authorities that promulgated the ordinance and had the primary responsibility of enforcing it. * * *

Nor does Cauefield v. Fidelity and Casualty Co. of New York, 378 F.2d 876 (5th Cir.1967), have any bearing on this case. *Cauefield* involved the use of the doctrine of "judicial estoppel" from Louisiana law. That case involved plaintiffs who actively participated in the first trial, represented by the same counsel, with evidence and testimony admittedly identical with the state court proceeding. The Court of Appeals concluded that due to the "unusual facts" of that case "absolutely nothing would be gained were appellants permitted to pursue their action...."

The present case differs drastically from the cases cited by the defendant. There has been no showing of any degree of "control" approaching that exhibited in *Montana*. Few, if any, of the "unusual facts" present in *Cauefield* are present here. Nor do we have a case similar to *Southwest Airlines Co.*, where a public authority that promulgated an ordinance and who had the primary responsibility of enforcing it was a party in the first action. Here we have private litigants in both cases.

The Court rejects Nissan Motors' argument that a likeness in complaint, closely coordinated pretrial responsibilities and joint motions and strategies are sufficient to enforce collateral estoppel against parties not represented in an action.[5] This Court has already held that P.D.Q.

---

5. The Court notes that some of the identical factors were present in the *Southwest Airlines Co.* case. The Court found that the CAB carriers had closely followed the *Southwest* litigation and were present at various hearings. It also noted that the airlines submitted amicus briefs, that there was no deficiency in counsel's performance, and that "relitigation would constitute a blatant disregard for the decision of this Court and for the judgment of the federal district court in *Southwest* I. It would damage the public's interest in the most efficient allocation of resources in both the state and federal systems of justice."

The Court in *Southwest* found none of these factors in and of itself was determinative. Rather, it looked at any number of

did not adequately represent the other class plaintiffs. The mere fact the cases were transferred under § 1407 does not have the effect of merging "the suits into a single cause, or change the rights of the parties, or make those who are parties to one suit parties in another." In re Equity Funding Corp. of America Securities Litigation, 416 F.Supp. 161, 176 (C.D.Cal.1976), quoting Johnson v. Manhattan Railway, 289 U.S. 479, 496–97, 53 S.Ct. 721, 77 L.Ed. 1331 (1933). The relevance of that statement to this cause is apparent from the procedural history outlined above. This Court has consistently found these cases inappropriate for consolidation with the *P.D.Q.* action. By adopting a contrary position at this late date, it cannot be fairly said "that the procedure adopted fairly ensures the protection of the interests of absent parties who are to be bound by it." Hansberry v. Lee, 311 U.S. 32, 42, 61 S.Ct. 115, 118, 85 L.Ed. 22 (1940). Nor is it relevant that joint statements were filed by counsel that evinced a common strategy or purpose. It is in the interest of judicial economy that the Court ordered joint submissions, a procedure it follows in other multidistrict cases and which is specifically sanctioned by *The Manual for Complex Litigation. See, e.g.,* §§ 1.93 and 4.53. In § 1.93 at page 86 it is stated that "counsel should be urged to meet and voluntarily provide for joint presentation of common contentions of law and fact and to eliminate repetitive or unnecessary objections, motions, briefs, arguments, depositions and written interrogatories." Plaintiffs also convincingly point out in their memorandum that much of this pretrial material was not introduced by P.D.Q. counsel, and that their strategy at trial would be different than that of P.D.Q.'s counsel. In light of these many factors, this Court cannot confidently state that absolutely nothing further could be gained if the plaintiffs are permitted to pursue their separate actions.

A case almost directly on point is Humphreys v. Tann, 487 F.2d 666 (6th Cir.1973), cert. denied, 416 U.S. 956, 94 S.Ct. 1970, 40 L.Ed.2d 307 (1974). *Humphreys* involved an airline crash between Transworld Airlines and an aircraft owned by Tann. Several wrongful death actions were filed against both. The Panel transferred a number of the cases to the Southern District of Ohio for consolidated pretrial proceedings. The transferee court indicated it would try only one case and remand the others. The trial resulted in acquittal for Tann and liability for Transworld.

Tann then filed a motion for summary judgment before the District Court which was granted; the Sixth Circuit reversed citing *Blonder–Tongue.* The Court made the following statement of direct relevance to this case:

> "We share the concern of the district court for the crowded dockets of federal courts and proper utilization of judicial time. However, we do not believe that these considerations can overcome the due

factors "that could tip the scales toward finding a violation of due process" before concluding that no violation existed. The Court in the present case finds the scales balanced differently.

process objection which was raised by the appellant as his first response to appellee's motion for summary judgment and which he has relied upon continuously."

Nissan Motors attempts to distinguish *Humphreys* on factual grounds. It notes that different legal theories were being pursued, that the non-party plaintiff was not a participant in a critical pretrial conference, that different issues were presented to the jury as would have been in the subsequent cases, and that none of the parties expected to be bound by the testimony in the first case. Although many of these factors alleged by Nissan as present in this case are disputed by the plaintiffs,[6] such an analysis misses the mark.

> "Due process of law in each particular case means such an exertion of the powers of government as the settled maxims of law permit and sanction, and under such safeguards for the protection of individual rights as those maxims prescribe for the class of cases to which this one in question belongs." Chicago, Burlington & Quincy Railroad Co. v. Chicago, 166 U.S. 226, 240, 17 S.Ct. 581, 586, 41 L.Ed. 979 (1896).

See also Hansberry v. Lee, 311 U.S. 32, 40–44, 61 S.Ct. 115, 85 L.Ed. 22 (1940).

The rationale of *Humphreys* is not limited solely to the facts of that case. The test in the Fifth Circuit for a violation of due process is still a "weighing test" that balances the factors in any one case. As *Humphreys* and the cases previously reviewed indicate, the balance is struck for the application of collateral estoppel against one not present in the previous action only under the most extraordinary circumstances. The history and circumstances of this case do not allow the conception of "privity" to be stretched far enough to allow its application in light of the restrictions of due process.

Notes and Questions

1. Would the result be different if the court's decision not to certify a nationwide class had been based on some ground other than inadequacy of representation? If the refusal to certify had been on numerosity grounds, for example, would there be any due process objection to binding nonparty plaintiffs so long as the initial plaintiff's representation was in fact adequate?

2. Does Hansberry v. Lee (*supra* p. 285 require privity, as a matter of due process, in order to bind nonparties? For an argument that it does not, see George, Sweet Uses of Adversity: Parklane Hosiery and the Collateral Class Action, 32 Stan.L.Rev. 655 (1980).

3. *Nissan* points out the potentially one-sided application of collateral estoppel after the demise of mutuality in federal courts under *Parklane* (see also *Friends for All Children, infra* p. 857). Different plaintiffs can file

---

6. The plaintiffs argue that at no time did they agree this would be a "test case." They also assert that P.D.Q. did not intro- duce at the trial much of the evidence and testimony that they will.

identical complaints against the same defendant and coordinate their trial strategies without risk of collateral estoppel effects from defense judgments in other cases. On the other hand, the common defendant may be collaterally estopped as to all the separate plaintiffs on the basis of a single plaintiff's verdict. Could this result make it more attractive to plaintiffs not to seek class certification or to severely limit their classes to geographical areas, relying instead on a "keep separate and conquer" strategy? Should this possibility, in turn, encourage a court to define a wider class or to impose an involuntary class upon plaintiffs?

HARDY v. JOHNS–MANVILLE SALES CORP.

United States Court of Appeals, Fifth Circuit, 1982.
681 F.2d 334.

Before GEE and JOHNSON, CIRCUIT JUDGES, and VAN PELT, DISTRICT JUDGE.

GEE, CIRCUIT JUDGE.

[In a number of suits by victims of asbestos-related diseases against various producers of asbestos, the trial court entered an omnibus collateral estoppel order finding that certain issues had been determined in plaintiffs' favor by the judgment against six manufacturers in Borel v. Fibreboard Paper Products Corp., 493 F.2d 1076 (5th Cir.1973), cert. denied, 419 U.S. 869, 95 S.Ct. 127, 42 L.Ed.2d 107 (1974). *Borel* has been called "the bellwether asbestos case." Willging, Asbestos Case Management: Pretrial and Trial Procedures 9 (1985). On appeal, those defendant manufacturers of asbestos who were not parties in *Borel* argued that they could not be estopped by it because they were not parties to the earlier action.]

The omnibus order under review here does not distinguish between defendants who were parties to *Borel* and those who were not; it purports to estop all defendants because all purportedly share an "identity of interests" sufficient to constitute privity. The trial court's action stretches "privity" beyond meaningful limits. While we acknowledge the manipulability of the notion of "privity," this has not prevented courts from establishing guidelines on the permissibility of binding nonparties through res judicata or collateral estoppel. Without such guidelines, the due process guarantee of a full and fair opportunity to litigate disappears. Thus, we noted in Southwest Airlines Co. v. Texas International Airlines, 546 F.2d 84, 95 (5th Cir.1977):

> Federal courts have deemed several types of relationships "sufficiently close" to justify preclusion. First, a nonparty who has succeeded to a party's interest in property is bound by any prior judgments against that party.... Second, a nonparty who controlled the original suit will be bound by the resulting judgment.... Third, federal courts will bind a nonparty whose interests were represented adequately by a party in the original suit.

The rationale for these exceptions—all derived from *Restatement (Second) of Judgments* §§ 30, 31, 34, 39–41 (1982)—is obviously that in these instances the nonparty has in effect had his day in court. In this case, the exceptions elaborated in *Southwest Airlines* and in the *Restatement* are inapplicable. First, the *Borel* litigation did not involve any property interests. Second, none of the non-*Borel* defendants have succeeded to any property interest held by the *Borel* defendants. Finally, the plaintiffs did not show that any non-*Borel* defendant had any control whatever over the *Borel* litigation. "To have control of litigation requires that a person have effective choice as to the legal theories and proofs to be advanced in behalf of the party to the action. He must also have control over the opportunity to obtain review." *Restatement (Second) of Judgments* § 39, comment c (1982). In, for example, Sea–Land Services v. Gaudet, 414 U.S. 573, 94 S.Ct. 806, 39 L.Ed.2d 9 (1974), the Supreme Court held that a nonparty may be collaterally estopped from relitigating issues necessarily decided in a suit by a party who acted as a fiduciary responsible for the beneficial interests of the nonparties. Even in this context, however, the Court placed the exception within strict confines: "In such cases, 'the beneficiaries are bound by the judgment with respect to the interest which was the subject of the fiduciary relationship....'" Many of our circuit's cases evince a similar concern with keeping the nonparties' exceptions to res judicata and collateral estoppel within strict confines. See, e.g., Southwest Airlines Co. v. Texas International Airlines.

The fact that all the non-*Borel* defendants, like the *Borel* defendants, are engaged in the manufacture of asbestos-containing products does not evince privity among the parties. The plaintiffs did not demonstrate that any of the non-*Borel* defendants participated in any capacity in the *Borel* litigation—whether directly or even through a trade representative—or were even part of a trustee-beneficiary relationship with any *Borel* defendant. On the contrary, several of the defendants indicate on appeal that they were not even aware of the *Borel* litigation until those proceedings were over and that they were not even members of industry or trade associations composed of asbestos product manufacturers.

Plaintiffs can draw little support from the doctrine of "virtual representation" of cases such as *Aerojet–General Corp. v. Askew,* in which we stated that "[u]nder the federal law of res judicata, a person may be bound by a judgment even though not a party if one of the parties to the suit is so closely aligned with his interests as to be his virtual representative" and that "the question whether a party's interests in a case are virtually representative of the interests of a nonparty is one of fact for the trial court." 511 F.2d at 719. In that case we approved a district court's determination that the interests of two government entities were so closely aligned that a prior judgment against one entity bound the other. The proposition that governments may represent private interests in litigation, thereby precluding relitigation, while uncertain at the margin, appears to be an unexceptional special instance of the examples noted in *Restatement (Second) of Judgments* § 41(1) (1982). The facts here permit no inference of virtual representation of interest. As we explained in Pollard v. Cockrell, 578 F.2d 1002, 1008–09 (5th Cir.1978):

> Virtual representation demands the existence of an express or implied legal relationship in which parties to the first suit are accountable to nonparties who file a subsequent suit raising identical issues.... In the instant case ... the [first] plaintiffs were in no sense legally accountable to the [second] plaintiffs; they shared only an abstract interest in enjoining enforcement of the ordinance. The [first] plaintiffs sued in their individual capacities and not as representatives of a judicially certified class. Representation by the same attorneys cannot furnish the requisite alignment of interest....

Thus, in *Pollard* we rejected the contention that one group of massage parlor owners were bound by a judgment in a prior lawsuit brought by another group. Virtual representation was rejected despite nearly identical pleadings filed by the groups and representation by common attorneys. The court's omnibus order here amounts to collateral estoppel based on similar legal positions—a proposition that has been properly rejected by at least one other district court that considered the identical issue. We agree with the Texas Supreme Court that "privity is not established by the mere fact that persons may happen to be interested in the same question or in proving the same state of facts," Benson v. Wanda Petroleum Co., 468 S.W.2d 361, 363 (Tex.1971), and hold that the trial court's actions here transgress the bounds of due process.

Our conclusion likewise pertains to those defendants who, while originally parties to the *Borel* litigation, settled before trial. The plaintiffs here did not show that any of these defendants settled out of the *Borel* litigation after the entire trial had run its course and only the judicial act of signing a final known adverse judgment remained. Such action would suggest settlement precisely to avoid offensive collateral estoppel and, in an appropriate case, might preclude relitigation. All the indications here are, however, that the defendants in question settled out of the case early because of, for example, lack of product identification. Like the non-*Borel* defendants, these defendants have likewise been deprived of their day in court by the trial court's omnibus order.

[The portion of *Hardy* discussing the question whether any issues were actually decided in *Borel* appears *infra* p. 864.]

Notes and Questions

1. Is there any indication that the defendants in *Borel* did an inadequate job defending with respect to the issues addressed by the district court's order? If not, what is the due process objection to binding the remaining defendants by the result?

2. In *Hardy,* the plaintiffs relied on a market share theory of liability because the identity of the manufacturer whose product caused the injury

was unknown. Should that matter to the decision whether to bind nonparty producers?

3.   The court exempts from the effects of *Borel* even those defendants who were sued in that case but settled before trial. Would it matter if these defendants settled for large sums? If the court's reasoning is that it was clear these defendants had no liability in *Borel,* does that mean that plaintiff's lawyers used the litigation as a device to extort settlements from innocent defendants? See also Efforts to Blunt Estoppel By Vacating Judgments, *infra* p. 881.

4.   If collateral estoppel is available against the six defendants who were parties to *Borel,* would those who were not parties to *Borel* be entitled to severance for trial because the jury would be prejudiced by learning of the preclusive effect of the *Borel* verdict? See Bertrand v. Johns–Manville Sales Corp., 529 F.Supp. 539, 545 (D.Minn.1982) ("Bifurcating the trial between those few defendants present in *Borel* * * * and those not present would require more time and effort than applying collateral estoppel would save.") Is it fair to leave these six producers of asbestos in a position in which some plaintiffs may decide to pursue them and to disregard the other producers? To the extent that the plaintiffs rely on a market share liability approach, does that theory prevent severing off the claims against the six *Borel* defendants?

2.   WHICH ISSUES WERE ACTUALLY DETERMINED?

FRIENDS FOR ALL CHILDREN
v. LOCKHEED AIRCRAFT

United States District Court, District of Columbia, 1980.
497 F.Supp. 313.

OBERDORFER, DISTRICT JUDGE.

I.

Plaintiff James Reynolds has moved for a ruling *in limine* to prevent defendant Lockheed or third-party defendant the United States from relitigating certain issues assertedly decided in plaintiff's favor in the prior cases of *Schneider v. Lockheed,* No. 76 0544–1 and *Marchetti v. Lockheed,* No. 76 0544–3. Defendant Lockheed opposes plaintiff's motion; Lockheed maintains that the circumstances of these cases are not appropriate for the application of offensive collateral estoppel. For the reasons set forth herein, plaintiff's motion will be granted. Additionally, the Court has treated this motion, which has been fully briefed by both parties, as a motion for partial summary judgment in the cases of the remaining infant survivors. On the basis of the partial summary judgment, which the Court grants by accompanying Order, a ruling reflecting the substance of plaintiff's motion *in limine* will be incorporated into the comprehensive pretrial order governing the trial of all the remaining claims against Lockheed by the infant survivors.

Trial of plaintiff Reynolds' claims against Lockheed will involve a consideration only of the amount of damages, if any, to which he is entitled as a result of the crash of a Lockheed-built C5 A near Saigon on April 4, 1975. By stipulation of September 14, 1979, filed December 6, 1979, Lockheed agreed not to contest its liability to plaintiff Reynolds and all other infant survivors for injuries proximately caused or aggravated by the crash. Trial of the initial three cases thus involved determination first of whether the plaintiffs now suffer from any injury, disease, defect or disability; and, if so, whether those injuries were the result of the crash. A substantial proportion of the testimony and argument was devoted to the question of whether the forces and conditions associated with the crash were sufficient to cause injury to an infant passenger in the plane's troop compartment. All this testimony was necessarily general, since the precise location or circumstances of each individual infant in the troop compartment is unknown. A single jury, sitting in all three cases, rendered a verdict of $500,000 for plaintiff Schneider and $1,000,000 for plaintiff Marchetti. After a partial settlement of $30,000 occasioned the withdrawal of one of plaintiff Zimmerly's claims, the jury returned a verdict for defendant Lockheed. By order of July 15, 1980, the verdict in *Zimmerly v. Lockheed* was set aside and a new trial ordered for reasons fully explained in a memorandum filed July 22, 1980. By Orders of July 8, 1980, the Court denied Lockheed's motions for a new trial or, in the alternative, for judgment n.o.v. in *Schneider v. Lockheed* and *Marchetti v. Lockheed.*

II.

Plaintiff's motion seeks to prevent Lockheed from retrying in *Reynolds* (and subsequent cases) the questions of whether the explosive decompression at 24,000 feet altitude, hypoxia, impact of the C5 A with the ground at 310 miles an hour, and psychological trauma, alone *or* in combination, were sufficient to (a) proximately cause minimal brain dysfunction (MBD) or (b) proximately aggravate a pre-existing injury, defect, or disease of an infant passenger. In support of this motion, plaintiff relies upon the verdict in *Schneider v. Lockheed,* in which the jury found that each of these forces aggravated a pre-existing condition, and the verdict in *Marchetti v. Lockheed,* in which the jury found that these same forces proximately caused injury to plaintiff. In each case, the jury rendered a special verdict * * * in which it expressly found that the enumerated forces, alone and in combination, proximately caused (in *Marchetti*) and aggravated (in *Schneider*) injuries to plaintiff.

Granting plaintiff's motion would not prevent Lockheed from attempting to argue that the plaintiff has no medical manifestations of injury or that any such manifestations were caused by events unrelated to the crash. Rather, the motion seeks to preclude Lockheed from asserting as it has in the first three trials that the forces associated with the crash were insufficient to cause injury to an infant passenger aboard the C5 A.

[The court determined that a federal court sitting in a diversity case must look to the law of the state (here D.C.) in which it sits for the principles of collateral estoppel. The D.C. Court of Appeals had abrogated the requirement of mutuality, although not reaching the question of offensive use of collateral estoppel. The court determined that D.C. would follow *Parklane Hosiery Co. v. Shore* regarding offensive use.]

* * *

III.

Assuming that offensive collateral estoppel is available as a matter of law, its application to particular cases is a matter within the discretion of the trial court. *See Parklane Hosiery Co. v. Shore,* 99 S.Ct. at 651. None of the circumstances that [*Parklane* indicated] might militate against the use of offensive collateral estoppel are present here.

First, plaintiff Reynolds (and all other surviving infant plaintiffs) could not have joined the prior actions, the results of which they now seek to employ. Suffice it to say that defendant Lockheed has consistently opposed any consolidation of the damage claims of the infant survivors, and cannot be heard to complain because plaintiff failed to join the earlier actions. Accordingly, the use of collateral estoppel in these actions will not undermine judicial efficiency by encouraging plaintiffs not to join similar claims against a common defendant.

Second, there is no unfairness in employing collateral estoppel against Lockheed. All the claims of the infant survivors were filed simultaneously and have proceeded through the pretrial stages in concert. All plaintiffs (as well as defendant Lockheed) have retained the same counsel throughout, and the Court has appointed a single guardian *ad litem* for all. Plaintiffs shared the identical physical experiences; each is alleged to be the victim of the identical forces and conditions. In the two jury trials relied upon to effect the estoppel, the circumstances of the flight were thoroughly developed. The key witnesses, including the flight crew, nurses, and adult passengers, have testified at length. Medical testimony was elicited from articulate experts who had examined a number of the infant passengers, made written reports, been heavily deposed, and testified extensively on direct and cross examination. There can, accordingly, be no suggestion that Lockheed did not contest the *Marchetti* and *Schneider* cases vigorously because it was unaware of the possibility of further damage claims by other plaintiffs. Indeed, the *Schneider* and *Marchetti* cases were early identified as "bellwether" cases, and the possibility of giving the verdicts in these cases collateral effect has been discussed for many months. Lockheed has had a full, fair, and complete opportunity to present its proof on the issues on which plaintiff now seeks to foreclose and narrow further litigation.

Third, the decisions upon which the plaintiffs rely are not inconsistent with any other decisions. Although the jury found for the defendant in *Zimmerly v. Lockheed,* that verdict was the product of confusion and error. It has been set aside. Moreover, a defendant's verdict in *Zimmerly,* even if it were allowed to stand, would not be inconsistent with the conclusion reached here. The jury in *Zimmerly* found that the plaintiff did not suffer from any disease, defect, disability or injury that was caused or aggravated by the crash. This conclusion may well reflect a finding by the jury that plaintiff Zimmerly suffers no injury, disease, defect, or disability from any cause, although the crash might well have caused such injuries. In view of the clarity of the jury's findings on the special verdicts in the *Schneider* and *Marchetti* cases, and the peculiar circumstances that require a new trial for plaintiff Zimmerly, it is unnecessary to speculate further.

Finally, there are no procedural opportunities available to Lockheed in *Reynolds* (or subsequent proceedings) that were unavailable to it in the *Schneider* and *Marchetti* cases. All the remaining cases will be tried in this District Court, subject not only to identical rules of procedure, but also identical rulings on the admissibility of evidence and instructions to the jury. Lockheed cannot possibly be said to have suffered from the circumstances of the first trials in any way that would make it unfair to give the verdicts in these cases future effect.

The Court concludes that the circumstances in the present case are precisely those calling for use of estoppel. The use of a special verdict form removes any relevant doubt about the nature or substance of the jury's findings. And the pendency of as many as 147 other damage claims, all arising out of the same occurrence and all sharing claims that common forces caused common or similar injuries, calls for the use of principles that would limit costly and repetitive litigation. *Parklane Hosiery Co. v. Shore,* 99 S.Ct. at 649; *Blonder–Tongue Labs. v. University of Illinois Foundation,* 402 U.S. 313, 91 S.Ct. 1434, 28 L.Ed.2d 788 (1971). It is possible, of course, that if the potential effect of the forces were relitigated in each subsequent case, Lockheed might conceivably prevail on one or more occasion. But this prospect does not justify expenditure of judicial time and effort that the use of collateral estoppel would avoid. As the Supreme Court stated in *Blonder–Tongue Labs:*

> Permitting repeated litigation of the same issue as long as the supply of unrelated defendants holds out reflects either the aura of the gaming table or "a lack of discipline and of disinterestedness on the part of the lower courts, hardly a worthy or wise basis for fashioning rules of procedure."

The defendant is entitled only to a full and fair opportunity to litigate its claim; Lockheed has plainly had that chance. Nor is this a case where a court decision precludes a jury trial. Here jury verdicts *created* the estoppel against reiterated jury trials of issues already resolved by juries.

The arguments relied upon by Lockheed to oppose the use of estoppel are not persuasive. Defendant cites *McDonnell–Douglas Corp. v. United States District Court,* 523 F.2d 1083 (9th Cir.1975), for the proposition that tort claims of this type are inappropriate for "class action" treatment. *McDonnell Douglas,* however, does not purport to address the question of collateral estoppel. The holding relied upon [by] the defendants relates only to the construction of Rule 23, Fed.R.Civ.P., and is inapposite the issues presented here. Nor is Lockheed correct that collateral estoppel may not be used for issues relating to "damages" in tort. Throughout the first three trials, Lockheed has asserted the general principle that the forces associated with the crash were insufficient to cause injury to an infant. Although each individual plaintiff is clearly unique, and may suffer or claim different injuries from the crash, the question of whether the crash could cause MBD or similar injuries is plainly common to all the cases. The proof of causation introduced by both parties was directed not toward plaintiffs Marchetti and Schneider individually, but rather toward the susceptibility of infants sharing their basic characteristics to the conditions of the crash. The principle of collateral estoppel applies to "issues," not "causes of action," and its applicability is determined by examining the "single, certain and material point[s] arising out of the allegations and contentions of the parties." The issues identified by plaintiff meet this test.

Accordingly, for the purpose of the trial of *Reynolds v. Lockheed,* and in the comprehensive pretrial order governing the trials of all remaining claims of surviving infants, the parties shall adhere to the following principle:

> Neither Lockheed nor the Third–Party Defendant shall attempt to relitigate, re-offer evidence, or re-argue, in the presence of the jury, whether there was insufficient hypoxia, force, psychological trauma, or explosive decompression in the troop compartment of the C5 A as to proximately cause neurological dysfunction (MBD) or proximately aggravate preexisting injury, disease, defect or disability.

IV.

Plainly, the narrowing of issues to be tried will have an effect on the quantity, nature, and order of proof to be presented. Evidence that was admissible to demonstrate the forces connected with the crash, and thus that the crash was the proximate cause of plaintiffs' injuries, will not necessarily be relevant or admissible in the forthcoming trials. *See* Rule 401, Fed.R.Evid. These limitations will affect both parties.

To assist the parties in framing the issues for trial, the comprehensive pretrial order will incorporate a scenario for trial that, unless otherwise ordered by the ultimate trial court, will limit both the issues and the evidence consistent with the Court's finding. Subject to review by the trial judge, trial of the remaining cases could then follow a procedure substantially as follows:

> 1. The jury would be read a stipulation of facts incorporated into the pretrial order that will explain in detail the circumstances of the C5 A crash. The parties may add to this statement pertinent detail, such as a verbal description of the manner in which plaintiffs were seated in the troop compartment, that is relevant to the nature or degree of injuries that plaintiffs may now suffer.

> 2. The trial court would supplement these statements with a preliminary instruction that (a) the Defendant Lockheed Aircraft Corporation has agreed not to contest its liability for injuries resulting from the crash; and (b) the crash and the forces associated with

it were sufficient to cause any brain injury, such as MBD, that plaintiff demonstrates that he now suffers.

3. Plaintiff's case in chief would be limited to evidence showing (a) that plaintiff now suffers or has suffered from brain injury or other physiological injury; and (b) the amount needed to compensate plaintiff for the effects of such injury. Such evidence would be limited to such testimony as the reports of expert medical witnesses who examined plaintiff, school teachers, and expert economic or other testimony showing the amount required to compensate for or treat such disability. Evidence relating to the circumstances of the crash, including graphic testimony and visual descriptions of the crash and its aftermath, would be excluded.[2]

4. Defendants, in their case in chief, could respond with evidence either that (a) plaintiff does not suffer from any injury, or that such injury does not require the compensation demanded by plaintiffs; and/or (b) some or all of plaintiff's present medical condition is the result of causes other than the crash.

5. If defendant elects to attempt to prove that plaintiff's injuries were the result of an alternative cause, it may not introduce evidence tending to show that the crash was not sufficient to cause the injuries alleged, or adduce expert testimony based on that premise.

6. Additionally, if defendant elects to prove the existence of an alternative cause, plaintiff may, in rebuttal, introduce evidence— documentary, oral, or demonstrative—to prove that the forces associated with the crash were sufficiently severe that the crash was, more likely than not, the sole or substantial cause of plaintiff's injuries. This rebuttal evidence will be limited to items received in the trials heretofore concluded, unless otherwise ordered by the ultimate trial court.

7. Defendant should elect, at the time of the final pretrial conference, whether it will attempt to prove the existence of an alternative cause of plaintiff's injuries. This election, which would not take place until all discovery is complete, would permit plaintiff to secure, if necessary, the presence of rebuttal witnesses who would otherwise not be required.

The premise of this scenario is that the issue preclusion makes redundant and cumulative many items of evidence and aspects of testimony which were admissible before the verdicts which effected the

---

2. Plaintiff would, of course, be permitted to show that plaintiff suffered some other injury in the crash, such as a traumatic injury apparent at the time. However, proof of causation would not necessarily permit plaintiff to introduce evidence relating to all the circumstances of the crash. Particularly where the nexus between the crash and an alleged injury which was readily observable on examination shortly after the crash is apparent, such as, for example, where a plaintiff contends he suffered a broken bone or contusions, little or no evidence relating to the circumstances of the crash would be appropriate beyond the stipulation of facts and the opening statement. See Rule 403, Fed.R.Evid.

preclusion. It is no longer necessary to prove what is now precluded. The scenario would thus serve several purposes. First, it may materially shorten the length of time required for each trial, and the substantial expenses attendant thereto. Second, where defendants elect not to prove the existence of an alternative cause, it will obviate the need for dramatic cumulative evidence about the circumstances of the crash that may have powerful emotional as well as probative effect. This evidence would otherwise be admissible. *See* Rule 403, Fed.R.Evid.

The scenario would strike a fair balance between the interests of the parties in a fair and efficient trial, protect the plaintiff against the trouble and expense of proving facts already established by jury verdict, and protect defendant against the inflammatory effect on a jury of photographs and word pictures now redundant to an understanding of the issues.

Notes and Questions

1. Although this case illustrates the potential for saving time by using collateral estoppel, it also illustrates the difficulties of implementing it. Must the court always adopt such a detailed pretrial protocol in order to give effect to collateral estoppel?

After plaintiffs won at trial, the court of appeals found that detailed protocol improper in Schneider v. Lockheed Aircraft Corp., 658 F.2d 835 (D.C. Cir.1981), cert. denied, 455 U.S. 994, 102 S.Ct. 1622, 71 L.Ed.2d 855 (1982). It stressed that the order went against the "very heart of the collateral estoppel doctrine [which] is the requirement that the issue to be precluded must be substantially the same as the issue previously litigated." Although it conceded that many of the criteria that determine substantial identify of issues were present, the court held that the differences in personal characteristics and symptoms of the various plaintiffs outweighed these similarities in making a causation determination. It found that the court's initial collateral estoppel ruling, determining only that it had been established that the circumstances of the accident were sufficient to cause MBD, would only have estopped Lockheed from trying to prove that nobody could have suffered any form of MBD as a result of the accident. But the pretrial order went too far beyond that by deeming the crash sufficient to cause every form of MBD in every plaintiff. "Lockheed was thereby denied its day in court on an issue which was not adjudicated in any previous proceeding: whether the crash could have caused the particular injuries claimed by Zimmerly." Id. at 852. Thus, the court directed a retrial, but it cautioned that "we do not suggest that appropriate collateral estoppel orders cannot be framed in these or other cases." Id. at 853.

2. Assuming the appellate court would allow a different collateral estoppel order, is it critical to this case that a single crash is involved? Will it be possible to say that the foreclosed issue is critical to all the other cases? If so, does the fact that various plaintiffs were in different locations in the plane matter? If not, should collateral estoppel carry over into litigation involving other crashes of Lockheed planes?

3. The court stresses that all claims were filed simultaneously, that they proceeded in concert with all plaintiffs represented by the same lawyer, and that a single guardian *ad litem* was appointed for all plaintiffs. If Lockheed had won the first three cases, should these factors have led the court to apply collateral estoppel in its favor against the other plaintiffs? Even if it did not apply collateral estoppel, would the guardian pursue the other cases to trial in the face of three losses?

4. Professor Ratliff has attacked the way in which *Parklane* grants nonparties an option to take advantage of earlier litigation results, finding the grounds for denying preclusive effect inadequate in operation. He argued that "[t]he *Parklane* protection against wait-and-see plaintiffs is inadequate because of the difficulty of giving notice to unknown optionholders and because there is no workable way to determine which optionholders, having received notice, have legitimate reasons for ignoring it and staying out of the case." Ratliff, Offensive Collateral Estoppel and the Option Effect, 67 Texas L.Rev. 63, 82 (1988). He noted that, of some forty-odd cases specifically citing *Parklane*'s "could easily have joined" language, only five used that standard to disqualify attempts by plaintiffs to take strategic advantage of the option effect. Id. at 86. Consider his example to support his position (id. at 83):

> To illustrate the problem, let us return to Professor Currie's hypothetical train wreck [see *infra* p. 871 n. 13]. Suppose that it occurs in Kansas and that of the fifty potential plaintiffs, nine reside in states other than Kansas. The first case goes to trial in a Kansas state court. Must all plaintiffs, including nonresidents, join in the Kansas case or lose the benefits of collateral estoppel? What if a plaintiff does not intervene because (1) his home state's law is more favorable and more likely to be applied in his home forum, which is also more convenient; (2) his attorney would have to hand over control of his case to a designated lead counsel in Kansas; or (3) the other plaintiffs, prospective coparties, are not believable or have marginal cases? What if some plaintiffs have no notice of the case? What if the procedural rules of Kansas will not permit such an intervention? Finally, from the defendant's standpoint, why should any of this make any difference? The option effect comes into play whatever the plaintiff's motivation. Which should be determinative on the question of fairness: the optionholder's state of mind or the effect of the option on his adversary? If we conclude that the optionholder's motivation is irrelevant, then we are forced to agree with Currie that the option effect, however created, is unfair.

Keep these points in mind as you read the next case.

HARDY v. JOHNS–MANVILLE SALES CORP.

United States Court of Appeals, Fifth Circuit, 1982.
681 F.2d 334.

Before GEE and JOHNSON, CIRCUIT JUDGES, and VAN PELT, DISTRICT JUDGE.

GEE, CIRCUIT JUDGE.

This appeal* arises out of a diversity action brought by various plaintiffs—insulators, pipefitters, carpenters, and other factory workers—against various manufacturers, sellers, and distributors of asbestos-containing products. The plaintiffs, alleging exposure to the products and consequent disease, assert various causes of action, including negligence, breach of implied warranty, and strict liability. The pleadings in each of the cases are substantially the same. No plaintiff names a particular defendant on a case-by-case basis but, instead, includes several—often as many as twenty asbestos manufacturers—in his individual complaint. The rationale offered for this unusual pleading practice is that, given the long latent period of the diseases in question, it is impossible for plaintiffs to isolate the precise exposure period or to identify the particular manufacturer's product responsible. * * * The trial court held that Texas courts, faced with the impossibility of identifying a precise causative agent in these asbestos cases, would adopt a form of *Sindell* liability [see *supra* p. 44 n. 4], described as a "hybrid, drawing from concepts of alternative and/or concurrent liability and the law of products liability to form a type of absolute liability." The trial court ruled that "discovery on percentage share of a relevant market may lead to admissible evidence in the trials of some, and perhaps all, of these cases" and therefore granted leave to consolidate them for discovery purposes. This ruling is not on appeal here.

Defendants' interlocutory appeal under 28 U.S.C. § 1292(b) is directed instead at the district court's amended omnibus order dated March 13, 1981, which applies collateral estoppel to this mass tort. The omnibus order is, in effect, a partial summary judgment for plaintiffs based on nonmutual offensive collateral estoppel and judicial notice derived from this court's opinion in *Borel v. Fibreboard Paper Products Corp.,* 493 F.2d 1076 (5th Cir.1973), cert. denied, 419 U.S. 869, 95 S.Ct. 127, 42 L.Ed.2d 107 (1974) (henceforth *Borel*). *Borel* was a diversity lawsuit in which manufacturers of insulation products containing asbestos were held strictly liable to an insulation worker who developed asbestosis and mesothelioma and ultimately died. The trial court construed *Borel* as establishing as a matter of law and/or of fact that: (1) insulation products containing asbestos as a generic ingredient are "unavoidably unsafe products," (2) asbestos is a competent producing cause of mesothelioma and asbestosis, (3) no warnings were issued by any asbestos insulation manufacturers prior to 1964, and (4) the "warning standard" was not met by the *Borel* defendants in the period from 1964 through 1969. Insofar as the trial court based its omnibus order on the res judicata effect of *Borel,* this aspect of the order is no longer valid. *Migues v. Fibreboard Corp.*, 662 F.2d 1182 (5th Cir.1981). The sole issue on appeal is the validity of the order on grounds of collateral estoppel or judicial notice.

---

* For a discussion of the binding effect of *Borel* on those manufacturers who were not parties there, see *supra* p. 854. This portion of the case deals with the effect on those who were defendants in *Borel*.—Eds.

In *Flatt v. Johns Manville Sales Corp.*, 488 F.Supp. 836 (E.D.Tex. 1980), the same court outlined the elements of proof for plaintiffs in asbestos-related cases. There the court stated that the plaintiff must prove by a preponderance of the evidence that

    1. Defendants manufactured, marketed, sold, distributed, or placed in the stream of commerce products containing asbestos.

    2. Products containing asbestos are unreasonably dangerous.

    3. Asbestos dust is a competent producing cause of mesothelioma.

    4. Decedent was exposed to defendant's products.

    5. The exposure was sufficient to be a producing cause of mesothelioma.

    6. Decedent contracted mesothelioma.

    7. Plaintiffs suffered damages.

The parties agree that the effect of the trial court's collateral estoppel order in this case is to foreclose elements 2 and 3 above. Under the terms of the omnibus order, both parties are precluded from presenting evidence on the "state of the art"—evidence that, under Texas law of strict liability, is considered by a jury along with other evidence in order to determine whether as of a given time warning should have been given of the dangers associated with a product placed in the stream of commerce. Under the terms of the order, the plaintiffs need not prove that the defendants either knew or should have known of the dangerous propensities of their products and therefore should have warned consumers of these dangers, defendants being precluded from showing otherwise. On appeal, the defendants contend that the order violates their rights to due process and to trial by jury. Because we conclude that the trial court abused its discretion in applying collateral estoppel and judicial notice, we reverse.

* * *

In ascertaining the precise preclusive effect of a prior judgment on a particular issue, we have often referred to the requirements set out, *inter alia*, in *International Association of Machinists & Aerospace Workers v. Nix*, 512 F.2d 125, 132 (5th Cir.1975), and cases cited therein. The party asserting the estoppel must show that: (1) the issue to be concluded is identical to that involved in the prior action; (2) in the prior action the issue was "actually litigated"; and (3) the determination made of the issue in the prior action must have been necessary and essential to the resulting judgment.

> If it appears that a judgment may have been based on more than one of several distinctive matters in litigation and there is no indication which issue it was based on or which issue was fully litigated, such judgment will not preclude, under the doctrine of collateral estoppel, relitigation of any of the issues.

Federal Procedure, Lawyers Ed. § 51.218 at 151 (1981) (citations omitted).

Appellants argue that *Borel* did not necessarily decide that asbestos-containing insulation products were unreasonably dangerous because of failure to warn. According to appellants, the general *Borel* verdict, based on general instructions and special interrogatories, permitted the jury to ground strict liability on the bases of failures to test, of unsafeness for intended use, of failures to inspect, or of unsafeness of the product. Strict liability on the basis of failure to warn, although argued to the jury by trial counsel for the plaintiff in *Borel,* was, in the view of the appellants, never formally presented in the jury instructions and therefore was not essential to the *Borel* jury verdict.

Appellants' view has some plausibility. The special interrogatories answered by the *Borel* jury were general and not specifically directed to failure to warn.[8] at length in our review of the *Borel* judgment, the jury was instructed in terms of "breach of warranty." Although the jury was accurately instructed as to "strict liability in tort" as defined in section 402A of the *Restatement (Second) of Torts,* that phrase was never specifically mentioned in the jury's interrogatories. It is also true that the general instructions to the *Borel* jury on the plaintiff's causes of action did not charge on failure to warn, except in connection with negligence. Yet appellants' argument in its broadest form must ultimately fail. We concluded in *Borel:*

> The jury found that the unreasonably dangerous condition of the defendants' product was the proximate cause of Borel's injury. This necessarily included a finding that, had adequate warnings been provided, Borel would have chosen to avoid the danger.

As the appellants at times concede in their briefs, "if *Borel* stands for any rule at all, it is that defendants have a duty to warn the users of their products of the long-term dangers attendant upon its use, including the danger of an occupational disease." Indeed, the first sentence in our

---

8. SPECIAL INTERROGATORY NO. 1: Do you find from a preponderance of the evidence that any of the Defendants listed below was negligent in any of the respects contended by Plaintiff, which negligence was a proximate cause of the injuries and death of the deceased? Answer "Yes" or "No" opposite the named defendant. [The jury answered "No" as to Pittsburgh and Armstrong and "Yes" as to the other four defendants.]

SPECIAL INTERROGATORY NO. 2: [This interrogatory submitted the question whether any of the six defendants were guilty of an act or acts of gross negligence, and the jury found that no defendant was guilty of gross negligence.]

SPECIAL INTERROGATORY NO. 3: Do you find from a preponderance of the evidence that the deceased was guilty of contributory negligence and that such negligence was a proximate cause of the injuries and death of the deceased? [The jury answered "Yes".]

SPECIAL INTERROGATORY NO. 4: Do you find from a preponderance of the evidence that the warranties as contended for by the Plaintiff were violated by any of the Defendants listed below, which breach of warranty was a proximate cause of the injuries and death of the deceased? [The jury answered "Yes" as to each defendant.]

SPECIAL INTERROGATORY NO. 5: What amount of money, if paid now in cash, would fairly and reasonably compensate the Plaintiff, Freida Borel, for the damages she sustained by virtue of the death of her husband?

ANSWER: Actual damages $68,000. Damages for gross negligence "None."

Borel opinion states that that case involved "the scope of an asbestos manufacturer's duty to warn industrial insulation workers of dangers associated with the use of asbestos." Our conclusion in *Borel* was grounded in that trial court's jury instructions concerning proximate cause and defective product. * * * Close reading of these instructions convinced our panel in *Borel* that a failure to warn was necessarily implicit in the jury's verdict. While the parties invite us to reconsider our holding in *Borel* that failure to warn grounded the jury's strict liability finding in that case, we cannot, even if we were so inclined, displace a prior decision of this court absent reconsideration en banc. Further, there is authority for the proposition that once an appellate court has disposed of a case on the basis of one of several alternative issues that may have grounded a trial court's judgment, the issue decided on appeal is conclusively established for purposes of issue preclusion. Nonetheless, we must ultimately conclude that the judgment in *Borel* cannot estop even the *Borel* defendants in this case for three interrelated reasons.

First, after review of the issues decided in *Borel,* we conclude that *Borel,* while conclusive as to the general matter of a duty to warn on the part of manufacturers of asbestos-containing insulation products, is ultimately ambiguous as to certain key issues. As the authors of the *Restatement (Second) of Judgments* § 29, comment g (1982), have noted, collateral estoppel is inappropriate where the prior judgment is ambivalent:

> The circumstances attending the determination of an issue in the first action may indicate that it could reasonably have been resolved otherwise if those circumstances were absent. Resolution of the issue in question may have entailed reference to such matters as the intention, knowledge, or comparative responsibility of the parties in relation to each other.... In these and similar situations, taking the prior determination at face value for purposes of the second action would extend the effects of imperfections in the adjudicative process beyond the limits of the first adjudication, within which they are accepted only because of the practical necessity of achieving finality.

The *Borel* jury decided that Borel, an industrial insulation worker who was exposed to fibers from his employer's insulation products over a 33-year period (from 1936 to 1969), was entitled to have been given fair warning that asbestos dust may lead to asbestosis, mesothelioma, and other cancers. The jury dismissed the argument that the danger was obvious and regarded as conclusive the fact that Borel testified that he did not know that inhaling asbestos dust could cause serious injuries until his doctor so advised him in 1969. The jury necessarily found "that, had adequate warnings been provided, Borel would have chosen to avoid the danger." In *Borel,* the evidence was that the industry as a whole issued no warnings at all concerning its insulation products prior to 1964, that Johns–Manville placed a warnings label on packages of its products in 1964, and that Fibreboard and Rubberoid placed warnings on their products in 1966.

Given these facts, it is impossible to determine what the *Borel* jury decided about *when* a duty to warn attached. Did the jury find the defendants liable because their warnings after 1966, when they acknowledged that they knew the dangers of asbestosis, were insufficiently explicit as to the grave risks involved? If so, as appellants here point out, the jury may have accepted the state of the art arguments provided by the defendants in *Borel,—i.e.,* that the defendants were not aware of the danger of asbestosis until the 1960's. Even under this view, there is a second ambiguity: was strict liability grounded on the fact that the warnings issued, while otherwise sufficient, never reached the insulator in the field? If so, perhaps the warnings, while insufficient as to insulation workers like Borel, were sufficient to alert workers further down the production line who may have seen the warnings—such as the carpenters and pipefitters in this case. Alternatively, even if the *Borel* jury decided that failure to warn before 1966 grounded strict liability, did the duty attach in the 1930's when the "hazard of asbestosis as a pneumoconiotic dust was universally accepted," or in 1965, when documentary evidence was presented of the hazard of asbestos insulation products to the installers of these products?

As we noted in *Borel,* strict liability because of failure to warn is based on a determination of the manufacturer's reasonable knowledge:

> [I]n cases such as the instant case, the manufacturer is held to the knowledge and skill of an expert. This is relevant in determining (1) whether the manufacturer knew or should have known the danger, and (2) whether the manufacturer was negligent in failing to communicate this superior knowledge to the user or consumer of its product.... The manufacturer's status as expert means that at a minimum he must keep abreast of scientific knowledge, discoveries, and advances and is presumed to know what is imparted thereby.

Thus, the trial judge in *Borel* instructed the jury that the danger "must have been reasonably foreseen by the manufacturer." As both this instruction and the ambiguities in the *Borel* verdict demonstrate, a determination that a particular product is so unreasonably hazardous as to require a warning of its dangers is not an absolute. Such a determination is necessarily relative to the scientific knowledge generally known or available to the manufacturer at the time the product in question was sold or otherwise placed in the stream of commerce.

Not all the plaintiffs in this case were exposed to asbestos-containing insulation products over the same 30–year period as plaintiff Borel. Not all plaintiffs here are insulation workers isolated from the warnings issued by some of the defendants in 1964 and 1966. Some of the products may be different from those involved in *Borel.* Our opinion in *Borel,* "limited to determining whether there [was] a conflict in substantial evidence sufficient to create a jury question," did not resolve that as a matter of fact all manufacturers of asbestos-containing insulation products had a duty to warn as of 1936, and all failed to warn adequately after 1964. Although we determined that the jury must have found a violation of the manufacturers' duty to warn, we held only that the jury could have grounded strict liability on the absence of a warning prior to 1964 or "could have concluded that the [post–1964 and post–1966] 'cautions' were not warnings in the sense that they adequately communicated to Borel and other insulation workers knowledge of the dangers to which they were exposed so as to give them a choice of working or not working with a dangerous product." As we have already had occasion to point out in *Migues v. Fibreboard Corp.,* 662 F.2d at 1188–89, our opinion in *Borel* merely approved of the various ways the jury could have come to a conclusion concerning strict liability for failure to warn. We did not say that any of the specific alternatives that the jury had before it were necessary or essential to its verdict.

> The *only* determination made by this court in *Borel* was that, based upon the evidence in that case, the jury's findings could not be said to be incorrect as a matter of law. But this Court certainly did not decide that every jury presented with the same facts would be compelled to reach the conclusion reached by the *Borel* jury: that asbestos was unreasonably dangerous. Such a holding would have been not only unnecessary, it would also have been unwarranted.

> In *Borel,* this Court said: "the jury was *entitled* to find that the danger to Borel and other insulation workers from inhaling asbestos dust was foreseeable to the defendants at the time the products causing Borel's injuries were sold".... This Court did not say that, as a matter of law, the danger of asbestos inhalation was so hidden from every asbestos worker in every situation as to create a duty to warn on the part of all asbestos manufacturers. On rehearing, this Court held that although some asbestos products used by plaintiff Borel contained warnings, there was sufficient evidence that the warnings were inadequate to inform workers of the actual dangers posed by asbestos inhalation to justify submission of that issue to the jury. This Court did not state that every jury would be required, as a matter of law, to find such warnings inadequate.

> In sum, this Court held in *Borel* only that the *Borel* jury, on the evidence presented to it, could have found that asbestos products unaccompanied by adequate warnings were unreasonably dangerous. The proposition that all juries presented with similar evidence regarding asbestos products would be compelled to find those products unreasonably dangerous was not presented in *Borel,* and therefore, this Court did not reach it. Since *stare decisis* is accorded only those issues necessarily decided by a court in reaching its result, the District Court erred in overreading the holding of our opinion in *Borel.*

[*Migues v. Fibreboard Corp.,* 662 F.2d 1182, 1188–89.] Like *stare decisis,* collateral estoppel applies only to issues of fact or law necessarily decided by a prior court. Since we cannot say that *Borel* necessarily decided, as a matter of fact, that all manufacturers of asbestos-containing insulation products knew or should have known of the dangers of their particular products at all relevant times, we cannot justify the trial court's collaterally estopping the defendants from presenting evidence as to the state of the art.

Even if we are wrong as to the ambiguities of the *Borel* judgment, there is a second, equally important, reason to deny collateral estoppel effect to it: the presence of inconsistent verdicts. In *Parklane Hosiery v. Shore,* 439 U.S. at 330–31, 99 S.Ct. at 651, the Court noted that collateral estoppel is improper and "unfair" to a defendant "if the judgment relied upon as a basis for the estoppel is itself inconsistent with one or more previous judgments in favor of the defendant."[13] Not only does issue preclusion in such cases appear arbitrary to a defendant who has had favorable judgments on the same issue, it also undermines the premise that different juries reach equally valid verdicts. One jury's determination should not, merely because it comes later in time, bind another jury's determination of an issue over which there are equally reasonable resolutions of doubt.

The trial court was aware of the problem and referred to *Flatt v. Johns Manville Sales Corp.,* 486 F.Supp. at 841, a prior opinion by the same court. In *Flatt* the court admitted that Johns–Manville had "successfully defended several asbestos lawsuits in the recent past" but stated that "lawsuits in which Johns–Manville has prevailed have been decided on the basis that there was insufficient exposure to asbestos dust, or alternatively, the plaintiff, or decedent, did not contract asbestosis or mesothelioma." Given the information made available to us in this appeal, we must conclude that the trial court in *Flatt* and in the proceeding below was inadequately informed about the nature of former asbestos litigation. On appeal, the parties inform us that there have been approximately 70 similar asbestos cases thus far tried around the country. Approximately half of these seem to have been decided in favor of the defendants. A court able to say that the approximately 35 suits decided in favor of asbestos manufacturers were all decided on the basis of insufficient exposure on the part of the plaintiff or failure to demonstrate an asbestos-related disease would be clairvoyant. Indeed, the appellants inform us of several products liability cases in which the state of the art question was fully litigated, yet the asbestos manufacturers were found not liable. Although it is usually not possible to say with certainty what these juries based their verdicts on, in at least some of the cases the verdict for the defendant was not based on failure to prove exposure or failure to show an asbestos-related disease. In *Starnes v. Johns–Manville Corp.,* No. 2075–122 (E.D.Tenn.1977), one of the cases cited in *Flatt v. Johns Manville Sales Corp., supra,* the court's charge to

---

13. The injustice of applying collateral estoppel in cases involving mass torts is especially obvious. Thus, in *Parklane* the Court cited Prof. Currie's "familiar example": "A railroad collision injures 50 passengers all of whom bring separate actions against the railroad. After the railroad wins the first 25 suits, a plaintiff wins in suit 26. Professor Currie argues that offensive use of collateral estoppel should not be applied so as to allow plaintiffs 27 through 50 automatically to recover." 439 U.S. at 331 n. 14, 99 S.Ct. at 651 n. 14, *citing* Currie, *Mutuality of Estoppel: Limits of the Bernhard Doctrine,* 9 Stan.L.Rev. 281, 304 (1957).

the jury stated that it was "undisputed that as a result of inhaling materials containing asbestos, Mr. Starnes contracted the disease known as asbestosis." The verdict for the defendant in *Starnes* must mean, inter alia, that the jury found the insulation products involved in that case not unreasonably dangerous. This court takes judicial notice of these inconsistent or ambiguous verdicts pursuant to Fed.R.Evid. 201(d). We conclude that the court erred in arbitrarily choosing one of these verdicts, that in *Borel,* as the bellwether.

Finally, we conclude that even if the *Borel* verdict had been unambiguous and the sole verdict issued on point, application of collateral estoppel would still be unfair with regard to the *Borel* defendants because it is very doubtful that these defendants could have foreseen that their $68,000 liability to plaintiff Borel would foreshadow multimillion dollar asbestos liability. As noted in *Parklane,* it would be unfair to apply collateral estoppel "if a defendant in the first action is sued for small or nominal damages [since] he may have little incentive to defend vigorously, particularly if future lawsuits are not foreseeable." 439 U.S. at 330, 99 S.Ct. at 651. While in absolute terms a judgment for $68,000 hardly appears nominal, the Supreme Court's citation of *Berner v. British Commonwealth Pacific Airlines,* 346 F.2d 532 (2d Cir.1965), cert. denied, 382 U.S. 983, 86 S.Ct. 559, 15 L.Ed.2d 472 (1966) (application of collateral estoppel denied where defendant did not appeal an adverse judgment awarding damages of $35,000 and defendant was later sued for over $7 million), suggests that the matter is relative. The reason the district court here applied collateral estoppel is precisely because early cases like *Borel* have opened the floodgates to an enormous, unprecedented volume of asbestos litigation. According to a recent estimate, there are over 3,000 asbestos plaintiffs in the Eastern District of Texas alone and between 7,500 and 10,000 asbestos cases pending in United States District Courts around the country. The omnibus order here involves 58 pending cases, and the many plaintiffs involved in this case are *each* seeking $2.5 million in damages. Such a staggering potential liability could not have been foreseen by the *Borel* defendants.

The trial court's application of issue preclusion to the "fact" that asbestos is in all cases a competent producing cause of mesothelioma and asbestosis involves similar problems. *Borel* dealt with the disease-causing aspects of asbestos dust generated by insulation materials. That case did not determine as a matter of fact that because airborne asbestos dust and fibers from thermal insulation materials are hazardous, all products containing asbestos—in whatever quantity or however encapsulated— are hazardous. The injustice in precluding the "fact" that the generic ingredient asbestos invariably and in every use or mode causes cancer is clearest in the case of appellant Garlock. Garlock points out that its products, unlike the loosely woven thermal insulation materials in *Borel* that, when merely handled, emitted large quantities of airborne asbestos dust and fibers, are linoleum-type products in which the asbestos is encapsulated in a rubber-like coating. According to Garlock, its gasket products do not release significant amounts of dust or fibers into the air and have never been demonstrated to be dangerous in installation, use, or removal. Certainly, defendants ought to be free, even after *Borel,* to present evidence of the scientific knowledge *associated with their particular product* without being prejudiced by a conclusive presumption that asbestos in all forms causes cancer. The court regarded collateral estoppel in this context as precluding merely the "can it" question rather than the "did it" question. The problem is that the "can it" and "did it" questions cannot in this instance be so easily segregated, and a determination that asbestos generally is hazardous threatens to undermine a defendant's possibly legitimate defense that its product was not scientifically known to be hazardous, now or at relevant times in the past. If the trial court's application of issue preclusion on the generic danger of asbestos is not meant to burden a defendant's ability to present such evidence, then we fail to see the intended usefulness of the court's action.

* * *

Like the court in *Migues,* we too sympathize with the district court's efforts to streamline the enormous asbestos caseload it faces. None of what we say here is meant to cast doubt on any possible alternative ways to avoid reinventing the asbestos liability wheel. We reiterate the *Migues* court's invitation to district courts to attempt innovative methods for trying these cases. We hold today only that courts cannot read *Borel* to stand for the proposition that, as matters of fact, asbestos products are unreasonably dangerous or that asbestos as a generic element is in all products a competent producing cause of cancer. To do otherwise would be to elevate judicial expedience over considerations of justice and fair play.

Notes and Questions

1. Consider the following report on the actual course of deliberations in *Borel v. Fibreboard:*

> The twelve members of the jury had been evenly split when they took their first vote, and had subsequently divided eleven to one in favor of the plaintiff. The lone holdout was a man who felt deeply that workers were lucky to have jobs and that no company which provided them should be judged too harshly for its actions, whatever they might be. Finally, after the other jurors had tried vainly to get him to change his mind, a face-saving deal was struck in which, in return for their finding Borel guilty of contributory negligence, he agreed to find that four of the defendants were negligent, and all six of them liable to Borel under the doctrine of strict liability.

P. Brodeur, Outrageous Misconduct 64 (1985). Does this information make you more or less comfortable about according the result in *Borel* collateral estoppel effect?

2. Would the use of more detailed "special verdicts" or "general verdicts accompanied by answer to interrogatories" (Fed.R.Civ.P. 49) have removed the uncertainty as to what the jury found in *Borel*? These devices

are rarely used in federal courts, although the *Borel* court did use special interrogatories, perhaps in part because the attorneys were familiar with special verdict practice which is used in Texas. Could interrogatories have been framed with sufficient precision to determine whether each manufacturer of asbestos-containing insulation products knew or should have known of the dangers of their particular products at all relevant times?

3. Putting aside the parsing of the instructions in *Borel,* are the reasons adopted by the court in *Hardy* for refusing to apply collateral estoppel persuasive? The court suggests that the verdict in *Borel* should not be accorded collateral estoppel effect because the evidence there was not compelling, seemingly invoking a standard similar to the directed verdict standard. Is that standard appropriate in the collateral estoppel context?

4. The *Hardy* court, relying on the *Parklane* warning that "allowing offensive collateral estoppel may also be unfair to a defendant if the judgment relied upon as a basis for the estoppel is itself inconsistent with one or more previous judgments in favor of the defendant," noted that of 70 asbestos cases tried around the county, half had been decided in favor of the defendants. It observed that a court able to say that the 35 suits decided in favor of defendants were all based on insufficient exposure or lack of asbestos-related disease would have to be "clairvoyant." Couldn't it have been ascertained whether any of those cases were actually decided on the issue of the dangerousness of asbestos rather than on issues peculiar to the particular plaintiff? Is the court saying that if there are a number of defendant's verdicts, it will assume a conflict on the specific issues upon which the collateral estoppel is sought and that any such assumed conflicting verdict will prevent the application of collateral estoppel as to an earlier plaintiff's verdict? Doesn't this simply reverse Professor Currie's example of abusive use of offensive collateral estoppel (see footnote 13 in *Hardy*) since now the assumption of a contrary defendant's verdict will deny collateral estoppel effect to all plaintiffs?

5. To what extent should differences in individual plaintiffs defeat the use of offensive collateral estoppel in drug and other mass injury cases? In Vincent v. Thompson, 50 A.D.2d 211, 377 N.Y.S.2d 118 (1975), Parke, Davis & Co. was able to prevent collateral estoppel effect being given to a prior adverse judgment against it on the same product, quadrigen. It argued that differences in the plaintiffs' ages, reactions, and residual injuries made the findings in the first case inapplicable in the second.

6. Is it realistic to say that because Mr. Borel only recovered $68,000, the defendants did not have reason to foresee that a loss in *Borel* would foreshadow multimillion dollar asbestos liability? Borel sought much larger damages in his complaint, there was a long trial with many expert witnesses on both sides, and the case was appealed to the Supreme Court. Can it really be said that this fits the description in *Parklane* of unfairness that "if a defendant in the first action is sued for small or nominal damages, he may have little incentive to defend vigorously, particularly if future suits are not foreseeable"? Is it relevant to the question of the defendants' expectations that extensive medical literature had existed since the 1930's on the dangers of asbestos? See *Borel,* 493 F.2d at 1083–85.

7. The *Hardy* court's cautious approach to collateral estoppel in the products liability context reflects a widespread uneasiness about the impact in such cases of the abandonment of mutuality. For an examination of some of the problems encountered in liberal use of collateral estoppel in such cases, see Schroeder, Relitigation of Common Issues: The Failure of Nonparty Preclusion and an Alternative Proposal, 67 Iowa L.Rev. 880, 928–39 (1982). Will this uneasiness lead to restrictive decisions about what was decided in earlier litigation?

8. Uneasiness about expansive use of collateral estoppel may cause a court to make a more exacting examination of an earlier decision than a reviewing court would do on appeal from the same decision. For example, in Jack Faucett Associates, Inc. v. American Telephone & Telegraph Co., 744 F.2d 118 (D.C.Cir.1984), cert. denied, 469 U.S. 1196, 105 S.Ct. 980, 83 L.Ed.2d 982 (1985), the District of Columbia Circuit refused to accord collateral estoppel effect to a jury verdict that the Second Circuit had affirmed in Litton Systems, Inc. v. American Telephone & Telegraph Co., 700 F.2d 785 (2d Cir.1983), cert. denied, 464 U.S. 1073, 104 S.Ct. 984, 79 L.Ed.2d 220 (1984). Noting that offensive collateral estoppel is "fraught with drumhead potential," the District of Columbia Circuit pointed out that the decision in *Litton Systems* was premised on a stipulation that was not applicable in *Jack Faucett,* and cited interlocutory rulings in a government suit against AT & T that appeared inconsistent with the *Litton Systems* decision. Its principal basis for refusing to apply collateral estoppel, however, was the exclusion in *Litton Systems* of evidence of a state regulatory decision favorable to AT & T. The Second Circuit had held that it was error to exclude this evidence, but had upheld the verdict anyway because the error was not prejudicial. The District of Columbia Circuit found that "we cannot conclude that this evidence . . . could not lead to a different conclusion in a new trial," and that application of collateral estoppel would therefore be unfair. It reasoned that this decision was not inconsistent with the Second Circuit's affirmance of the $90 million verdict against AT & T in *Litton Systems:*

> The *Litton* court was reviewing a jury trial that already had transpired and that had produced a lengthy and complex record. Armed with this documentation, the Second Circuit could review the record and conclude that the omission of a single state regulatory decision did not constitute prejudicial error—did not affect AT & T's substantial rights in the context of that case. In contrast, our inquiry into the fairness of offensive estoppel is not limited narrowly to a review of a specific record and a specific jury. We must consider whether it is possible that the several state regulatory decisions that AT & T has identified could lead a jury in a new trial to reach a different result. Because that possibility cannot be ruled out, offensive estoppel was improvidently granted.

> More important, the premise underlying the argument that the Second Circuit's "harmless error" conclusion binds our decision today is that the standard for "reversible error" and the standard for "errors precluding offensive estoppel" must be the same. This we decline to hold. Indeed, we have noted approvingly, albeit in dicta, another court's conclusion that "newly discovered evidence, *even if insufficient to justify setting aside a judgment,* may warrant refusal to give the judgment

preclusive effect in other actions." Similarly, the Restatement (Second) of Judgments bolsters our conclusion that the same standards are not applicable when deciding whether to overturn a jury's verdict and when deciding whether a trial court properly applied offensive estoppel:

> It is unnecessary that the party seeking to avoid preclusion show, as he must in seeking to set aside a judgment, that the evidence could not have been discovered with due diligence; *the question is not whether a prior determination should be set aside but whether it should be treated as conclusive for further purposes.*

Restatement (Second) of Judgments § 29 comment j, at 297 (emphasis added).

Could the District of Columbia Circuit have concluded that the exclusion of the evidence in *Litton Systems* justified denial of collateral estoppel even if the Second Circuit had held that the exclusion of the evidence was not error?

9. *Hardy* was an attempt to use offensive collateral estoppel against new defendants. There have also been attempts to use it against new plaintiffs. The manufacturer of Bendectin obtained a finding of no general causation in In re Bendectin Litigation, *supra* p. 768. When it was sued by a new plaintiff in a Massachusetts federal court, it claimed he was estopped by the prior finding. The plaintiff had been in a class action that preceded the Ohio trial but had opted out. In Lynch v. Merrell–National Labs., 646 F.Supp. 856 (D.Mass.1986), aff'd, 830 F.2d 1190 (1st Cir.1987), the court refused to apply collateral estoppel, but on the limited ground that a representation had been made to the opt-out plaintiffs that they would not be bound by the results in the Ohio federal court. "But for this it seems that the First Circuit, in the name of judicial economy, might have granted estoppel, especially where the plaintiff had been involved in some way with the prior litigation or could have elected to participate." P. Rhiengold, Mass Tort Litigation § 9.7 (1996). Shouldn't the ground have been that plaintiff would be denied due process if barred by the outcome of a prior trial in which it did not participate? Compare In re Bendectin Products Liability Litig., 732 F.Supp. 744 (E.D.Mich.1990).

10. Courts in which offensive collateral estoppel is sought may be confronted with conflicting prior judgments. In Setter v. A.H. Robins Co., 748 F.2d 1328 (5th Cir.1984), 21 cases against the defendant for liability for the Dalkon Shield had gone to judgment. The defendant had won 12, lost 8, and one resulted in a hung jury. The court found this string of inconsistent decisions sufficient to justify denial of preclusion, but also found that the favorable jury verdict relied upon by the plaintiff was ambiguous, and that a claim for punitive damages would require trial of most or all of the evidence bearing on liability and thus no efficiency would be achieved. Similarly, Grill v. United States, 516 F.Supp. 15 (S.D.N.Y.1981), denied preemptive effect to a judgment in another suit holding that the United States had not fulfilled its statutory duty to warn persons of risks associated with the Swine Flu vaccine.

11. What is the preclusive effect of a judgment in a trial conducted within a Multidistrict Litigation (MDL) consolidation? In re Air Crash Disaster at Stapleton International Airport, 720 F.Supp. 1505 (D.Colo.1989), rev'd on other grounds, 964 F.2d 1059 (10th Cir.1992), involved an earlier

trial in which defendants obtained a favorable verdict on liability against certain plaintiffs. The other plaintiffs in the MDL proceeding were precluded from relitigating the issue, even though they did not participate in the trial. Estoppel was not applied, however, to cases outside the MDL.

12. *Postscript:* In *Hardy,* after the decision reprinted above, the trial court consolidated five individual suits and tried the five cases jointly, with the trial limited to three issues: (1) whether each plaintiff had an asbestos-related disease; (2) whether each plaintiff had been exposed to the products of the various defendants; and (3) the amount of damages each plaintiff was entitled to receive if the jury answered the first questions affirmatively. The jury returned verdicts in favor of all plaintiffs ranging from $436,000 to $713,000, but the court of appeals reversed because plaintiffs had been allowed to introduce in evidence an appellate brief filed in another case by one of the defendants. Hardy v. Johns–Manville Sales Corp., 851 F.2d 742 (5th Cir.1988).

FRALEY v. AMERICAN CYANAMID CO.

United States District Court, District of Colorado, 1983.
570 F.Supp. 497.

KANE, DISTRICT JUDGE.

In this products liability case plaintiff Monika Fraley seeks summary judgment on collateral estoppel grounds. Fraley contracted Type II poliomyelitis sometime in 1971, shortly after her daughter had been vaccinated with Orimune polio vaccine on July 13 and July 24, 1971. The vaccine was manufactured by Lederle Laboratories, a division of American Cyanamid Company. The parties have stipulated that Fraley contracted poliomyelitis as a result of contact with her child.

By this motion Fraley seeks collaterally to estop Lederle from litigating the issue of the adequacy of the warning it gave regarding the risk of use of Orimune polio vaccine. The basis for Fraley's motion is a jury determination in an earlier diversity case that the warnings Lederle provided in its package inserts and in the Physician's Desk Book were inadequate. *Givens v. Lederle Laboratories,* No. 73–59 Civ. T–K (M.D.Fla.1975), app. decision at 556 F.2d 1341 (5th Cir.1977).

The *Givens* plaintiff, a woman in her mid-twenties, contracted polio from an infant daughter who had recently received the Orimune vaccine. A jury returned a verdict of $250,000 in damages. In response to a special interrogatory, the *Givens* jury ruled that the warning regarding Orimune was inadequate. In response to Fraley's third request for admissions, Lederle has admitted that:

1. The *Givens* Orimune warning was identical to the Orimune warning in this case;

2. The adequacy of the Orimune warnings was actually litigated and essential to the final judgment in *Givens;* and

3. No court has ever entered a final judgment which included a finding that the Orimune warnings, either as a package insert or as a portion of the Physician's Desk Reference, was legally adequate.

From these admissions, Fraley argues that Lederle cannot relitigate the adequacy of the Orimune warnings in this case.

[The court held that the federal law of collateral estoppel applied because *Givens* was tried in federal court.]

* * *

As I noted above, Lederle argues that even if federal law of collateral estoppel applies, the issues in the instant action are different than those in the Florida action. In *Givens,* the plaintiff took her daughter to her pediatrician on November 7, 1971. Nine days after the second administration of the polio vaccine, Sherry Givens developed polio.

On appeal Lederle argued, *inter alia* that "the trial court should have granted a directed verdict in its favor because the warning was not inadequate and the failure to warn, if any, was not a proximate cause of Mrs. Givens' disease." Lederle admits that the warning in *Givens* is identical to the warning in this case. It argues that "the issue presented to the court in *Givens* was the adequacy of the warning *to the consumer,* . . . [while the issue to be determined here] . . . is the adequacy of the warning *to the medical profession . . . .*"

I disagree. As the Fifth Circuit noted in *Givens,* "[p]laintiffs' case hinges upon the warning." I understand *Givens* to say that the adequacy of the warning to the consumer and the adequacy of the warning to the doctor were before it. The critical language in *Givens* is as follows:

> When a private doctor administers a drug by prescription . . . it is defective only if the manufacturer does not warn the doctor about any hazard known. There is solid evidence that the vaccine was administered here in a manner more like that at a small county health clinic . . . than by prescription.

* * *

If so, then Lederle is responsible for taking definite steps to get the warning directly to the consumer.

Even if we were to assume the opposite, *i.e.,* that the administration here was really like that of a prescription drug, there was still enough evidence to sustain the jury verdict.

Lederle argues that this last sentence is *dictum* and that the adequacy of the warning to the *Givens'* doctor was not at issue. If anything is *dictum* in the opinion, it is the first two paragraphs pertaining to the warnings to the consumer. There is simply not a syllable of language to suggest that *Givens* was tried on any theory but an inadequate warning to the doctor. On appeal in *Givens,* Lederle argued that there was " 'no evidence whatsoever' showing that *the warning given to the doctor did not adequately* state the risk." (emphasis added). The opinion goes on to detail the options open to Givens had she known about the risks involved. It then says: "*[t]he failure to impress upon the private physician* the real risk involved in using a live virus thus became a cause of Mrs. Givens' paralytic disease." (emphasis added). Accordingly, I am satisfied that the issue decided in *Givens* is identical to the issue before me in this action.

* * *

Under some circumstances, the application of collateral estoppel is unfair to a defendant. One such circumstance arises when the earlier judgment is inconsistent with other judgments in favor of the defendant. "Allowing offensive collateral estoppel may also be unfair to a defendant if the judgment relied upon as a basis for the estoppel is itself inconsistent with one or more previous judgments in favor of the defendant." *Parklane Hosiery Co. v. Shore*, 439 U.S. 322, 330, 99 S.Ct. 645, 651, 58 L.Ed.2d 552 (1979).

The inconsistent judgment Lederle relies upon is *Dunn v. Lederle Laboratories*, 328 N.W.2d 576 (Mich.App.1982), where the plaintiff contracted polio after her infant child was administered polio vaccine. A jury verdict was affirmed on appeal, in part, on the basis that even if Lederle's warnings were inadequate, any failure to warn was not the proximate cause of the plaintiff's injuries.

As far as I am concerned there was a jury verdict in Lederle's favor, but not on the adequacy of the vaccine warning. As such, this situation is distinguishable from *Tretter v. Johns–Manville Corp.*, 88 F.R.D. 329, 333 (E.D.Mo.1980), where all of the earlier judgments relied upon by the parties were limited to a finding that asbestos was unreasonably dangerous.

Dunn is also not inconsistent with *Givens* because the warnings at issue there were materially different than those presented in the Florida action. The *Givens* warning was as follows:

> Fortunately, such occurrences are rare, and it could not be definitely established that any such case was due to the vaccine strain and was not coincidental with infection due to naturally-occurring poliomyelitis or other enteroviruses. This matter of 'vaccine-associated' illness is receiving careful attention and surveillance. Various authorities, on the basis of present information and careful analysis, estimate the risk if it exists to be no more than one case of 'vaccine-associated' paralytic disease for every 3,000,000 or more doses of live, oral, polio virus vaccine distributed.

In *Dunn*, the warning read:

> Fortunately, such occurrences are rare, but considering the epidemiological evidence developed with respect to the total group of 'vaccine-related' cases it is believed by some that at least some of the cases were caused by the vaccine. The estimated risk of vaccine-induced paralytic disease occurring in vaccinees or those in close contact with vaccinees is extremely low. A total of approximately 30 of such cases were reported for the six year period covering 1963 to 1970 during which time about 147,000,000 doses of the vaccine were distributed nationally. Even though this risk is low it should always be a source of consideration.

The *Givens* warning suggests that any vaccine-associated illnesses may have been due to naturally occurring poliomyelitis. The *Dunn* warning does not. It acknowledges that the risk of contracting polio from a vaccine is low, but "should always be a source of consideration." The *Givens* warning suggests that there may be no risk from the vaccine—"if it exists." In my judgment, the differences are sufficient enough that the danger of inconsistent verdicts is nonexistent. The issues in *Dunn* were different than those in *Givens* or this case.

* * *

IT IS HEREBY ORDERED that the plaintiff's motion for partial summary judgment is granted.

Notes and Questions

1. Is there a qualitative difference in attitude between the court in Hardy v. Johns–Manville Sales Corp., *supra* p. 864, and the court in *Fraley?* Is the adequacy of the warning issue involved in *Fraley* a type of issue better suited to estoppel than the issues involved in *Hardy?* Is the court correct in deciding that the finding in *Dunn* that the warnings were adequate was not inconsistent with the decision in *Givens?*

2. Would more information about the actual decision of the jury in *Givens* bear on the propriety of according it collateral estoppel effect? Would it matter if that decision was a compromise? In Milks v. Eli Lilly & Co., 97 F.R.D. 467 (S.D.N.Y.1983), defendant in a DES suit anticipated a collateral estoppel argument based on an earlier state-court verdict against it in another DES suit. It therefore sought to take the depositions of the state-court jurors to show the verdict was a compromise. The state court enjoined defendant from communicating with the jurors and ruled that the verdict was not a compromise after a federal court had refused defendant's request to enjoin the state court's injunction. Putting aside the issue of conflicts between the federal and state courts, how useful would any such depositions be in evaluating the question of whether to accord the verdict collateral estoppel effect? See also Note, Public Disclosures of Jury Deliberations, 96 Harv.L.Rev. 886 (1983).

3. What maneuvers are available to defendants to ward off collateral estoppel before the fact? One method is to arrange for a case that is favorable on the merits to go to trial first. The desire to position a "good" case first may lead to substantial jockeying by plaintiffs' and defendants' counsel. For an example of such maneuvering, see Mekdeci v. Merrell National Laboratories, 711 F.2d 1510 (11th Cir.1983). In addition, defendants may wish to select for the first trial a case that can easily be distinguished from other cases because of its unusual features. Then, if the first case is lost, they may seek to select a very different case for the second trial in hopes that the first loss will not be held to support collateral estoppel and that the second jury will find for defendants, thereby creating a seeming conflict in results that will frustrate further use of collateral estoppel. Of course, defendants' arguments against collateral estoppel in the second case may tend to undermine their later arguments that there is a conflict in results if they win the second case. To what extent should the courts try to

control such maneuvering? Should evidence of such maneuvering affect a court's willingness to accord collateral estoppel effect to an earlier judgment?

EFFORTS TO BLUNT ESTOPPEL BY VACATING JUDGMENTS

If the collateral estoppel effect of a jury verdict cannot be undermined by deposition testimony from the jurors, can that potential effect be undone by the parties to the first litigation? In some cases, after a decision against defendant on liability, the parties have agreed to settle contingent on dismissal and vacation of the findings involved. Should the courts honor these agreements to further the settlement process or disregard them to avoid the burden of relitigation? In Chemetron Corp. v. Business Funds, Inc., 682 F.2d 1149, 1187–92 (5th Cir.1982), the court held that such a strategy was ineffective because the findings of liability were sufficiently final for collateral estoppel purposes even though judgment had not been entered when the earlier case was dismissed pursuant to the settlement. Recall *Hardy, supra* at p. 856 (discussing settlement to avoid collateral estoppel).

Vacation of judgments to avoid collateral estoppel effects plagues the courts. In Nestle Co. v. Chester's Market, Inc., 756 F.2d 280 (2d Cir.1985), Nestle claimed that defendants had violated its trademark "Toll House," as used in connection with cookies. The trial court granted defendants a partial summary judgment, holding that the trademark was invalid. The parties then reached a settlement contingent on vacation of the summary judgment. Nestle admitted this provision of the settlement agreement was designed to insulate it against collateral estoppel effect. The trial court, citing the public interest in adjudicating the validity of trademarks, refused to vacate the judgment.

The appellate court reversed, holding that the trial court's refusal to vacate the summary judgment was an abuse of discretion. It felt that the trial court's concern about finality of judgments was "misplaced in the circumstances of the present case. * * * [H]ere we are faced with a settlement that will bring pending litigation to an end. Because the policies favoring finality of judgments are intended to conserve judicial and private resources, the denial of the motion for vacatur is counterproductive because it will lead to more rather than less litigation." Id. at 282. The court emphasized the interest of the defendants in terminating their litigation expenditures even if that meant that others would be denied the benefit of collateral estoppel: "We see no justification to force these defendants, who wish only to settle the present litigation, to act as unwilling private attorneys general and to bear the various costs and risks of litigation." Id. at 284. Would it matter if defendants profited from their willingness to consent to vacation of the judgment?

Contrast Wilson v. American Motors Corp., 759 F.2d 1568 (11th Cir.1985). Plaintiff there sought access to the transcript of an earlier suit involving the same type of vehicle that caused the injuries giving rise to the present suit. The earlier case had settled, following the jury's response to special interrogatories, on condition that the record of the trial be sealed. The appellate court treated the matter as turning on the public right of access to judicial records, and reversed a trial court refusal to unseal the records. The court did not specifically address the question of collateral estoppel effect, but seemed sympathetic to allowing it despite the settlement agreement (id. at 1571–72 n. 4):

> We feel certain that many parties to lawsuits would be willing to bargain (with the adverse party and the court) for the sealing of records after listening to or observing damaging testimony and evidence. Such suppression of public records cannot be authorized. The situation here is further aggravated by the attempted suppression of a jury verdict because it might adversely affect American Motors in other judicial proceedings. Such action is contrary to the most basic principles of American jurisprudence.

In Manufacturers Hanover Trust Co. v. Yanakas, 11 F.3d 381 (2d Cir.1993), the court refused to extend Nestle Co. v. Chester's Market, Inc., *supra*, to a situation in which the court of appeals' opinion had been filed but mandate had not issued. The court noted that vacating the district court judgment while an appeal was pending (and so reversal was possible) was different from undoing the appellate disposition, and that allowing such a practice would come close to issuing advisory opinions.

In U.S. Bancorp Mortgage Co. v. Bonner Mall Partnership, 513 U.S. 18, 115 S.Ct. 386, 130 L.Ed.2d 233 (1994), the Court refused a request, in a case in which it had granted certiorari, to vacate a lower court decision because the case had been settled. It held that an appellate court has the power so to vacate, but that the power should not be utilized where the mootness results from action of the party seeking to vacate the lower court's judgment, as when a case is settled. The customary route to challenge a lower court decision is to appeal, and the court saw no reason to allow a party instead to employ vacatur "as a refined form of collateral attack." Id. at 27, 115 S.Ct. at 392. It also rejected the argument that allowing vacatur would promote settlements, and said that a similar unwillingness to vacate should be employed by the courts of appeals regarding judgments of district courts. The Court did acknowledge, however, that "exceptional circumstances" might exist to justify vacatur, and that an appellate court could remand for consideration of vacatur pursuant to Rule 60(b).

In Allen–Bradley Co. v. Kollmorgen Corp., 199 F.R.D. 316 (E.D.Wis. 2001), plaintiff sought a declaration of noninfringement of certain of defendant's patents and the court entered an order construing the claims in the patents after a *Markman* hearing. The parties then reached an agreement conditioned on the court vacating its order. Meanwhile, defendant had sued another company in another district for infringement of these same patents, and the defendants in that case sought to intervene in this case, pointing out that they already had a motion for summary judgment on file that relied on this court's decision as a basis for issue preclusion. The court ruled that the interest in the collateral estoppel effect of its earlier decision was too insubstantial to support intervention of right. It also refused to vacate the earlier order, however, due to the extensive judicial investment in the *Markman* hearing. The value of settlement did not, in the judge's view, outweigh the value of leaving the construction of the claims in place.

Chapter IX

ALTERNATIVES TO LITIGATION

It should come as no surprise that many potential litigants view the prospect of litigation with alarm. Since the late 1970s, increasing attention has focused on alternatives to traditional in-court litigation. The subject has become popular enough to develop a widely-recognized acronym—ADR, for alternate dispute resolution—and it is covered in the curriculum of most law schools. It is therefore appropriate to conclude our examination of the judicial system's handling of complex disputes with a review of the alternatives.

Delay and expense are the two consequences of a traditional court trial most often cited as reasons for turning to alternate dispute resolution. Some of the alternatives have been around a long time. For example, mediation and conciliation programs have been tried for decades in various jurisdictions, and contemporary arbitration procedures date back to the 1920s. The search for cheaper and speedier ADR techniques, however, has taken a quantum leap since the mid–1970s as court overcrowding, docket delays, and spiraling costs of litigation have become impressed upon the public consciousness. In many jurisdictions, neighborhood mediation centers, formalized procedures for conciliation, and economical litigation projects with simplified court procedures have been adopted for the disposition of non-complex cases.

Complex cases, however, may not be as readily amenable to resolution by such techniques. Complicated commercial disputes, mass disaster or product liability claims, antitrust and security fraud cases, and civil rights class actions might well benefit from mediation and conciliation attempts. But the very complexity of such cases often demands a more sophisticated approach than the simplified and informal procedures used in, for example, neighborhood or family law dispute resolution. Before parties can be expected to reach a settlement in many complex cases, there will have to be sufficient investigation and exchange of information, focusing of issues, and recourse to the opinions of experts to ensure that the parties are not negotiating from a posture of ignorance. The question then arises whether ADR procedures can be devised to streamline and speed up these activities so that meaningful negotiation or summary decision-making is appropriate. Although some simplification

883

of procedures may be desirable for resolving complex disputes short of trial, a degree of formality is often necessary if earlier and less expensive resolution is to be achieved. This chapter will explore some of the principal techniques now being used for ADR that might be suitable for complex cases.

A. EXTRA–JUDICIAL MECHANISMS

Perhaps the oldest and best-known of ADR mechanisms are extra-judicial, that is, they operate outside the court system. Unlike judicial mechanisms (which will be discussed in the next section), they are essentially an alternative to the public judicial system rather than an adjunct or aid to resolution within the judicial framework.

1. ARBITRATION

The reference of a dispute to an impartial person for final, binding determination has a long history in commercial affairs. In medieval England, courts referred mercantile cases to merchant arbitrators and juries. One of the purposes of the creation of Chambers of Commerce in the American colonial period was to arbitrate disputes among their members. Mentschikoff, Commercial Arbitration, 61 Colum.L.Rev. 846, 854–55 (1961). New York, in 1920, became the first state to pass a modern arbitration statute providing for judicial enforcement of arbitration agreements. However, common law precedents in many states were hostile to arbitration, refusing to order parties to comply with arbitration agreements and to enforce arbitration awards.

The Federal Arbitration Act, passed in 1925, had the principal objective of providing authority in federal courts for the enforcement of arbitration agreements. With such a limited focus, it does not address a large number of the issues that now arise concerning the administration of arbitration in a very different legal environment. Over the years, there have been a number of proposals to amend the FAA, which seem to have failed because of lack of agreement on changes and the feeling that the case-law gloss on the FAA provides adequate guidance. Every state has an arbitration act, many of them modeled on the Uniform Arbitration Act proposed by the National Conference of the Commissioners on Uniform State Laws in 1955. After years of study, a Revised Uniform Arbitration Act was proposed in 2000 (RUAA). It seeks to "incorporate the holdings of the vast majority of state courts and the law that has developed under the [Federal Arbitration Act]." RUAA, § 69c. It also adds new procedural rights, including the possibility of expanded discovery and judicial review which, its opponents argue, would unduly "judicialize" arbitrations and undermine their finality. It has elicited lively debates on a number of issues. See, e.g., Cole, The Revised Uniform Arbitration Act: Is It the Wrong Cure?, 8 No. 4 Disp. Resol. Mag. 10 (2002). By early–2004, it had been adopted in eight states (Hawaii, Nevada, New Jersey, New Mexico, North Carolina, North Dakota, Oregon, and Utah) and was being considered in a large number of other states. Uniform Law Commissioners, The Nat'l Conference of Commissioners on Uniform State Laws, Uniform Arbitration Act (2000), www.nccusl.org/nccusl/unifomract_factsheets/uniformacts-fs-aa-asp.

Scope of the Federal Arbitration Act

The Federal Arbitration Act (FAA) is the principal authority for enforcing arbitration clauses in the U.S. It applies to contracts "evidencing a transaction involving commerce," which has been broadly interpreted as focusing on whether the parties contemplated substantial interstate activity at the time the agreement was made. Prima Paint Corp. v. Flood & Conklin Manufacturing Co., 388 U.S. 395, 87 S.Ct. 1801, 18 L.Ed.2d 1270 (1967), found that a dispute over an agreement to consult locally involved interstate commerce because it was part of a sale of a paint business that was conducted in several states. The term "interstate commerce" has generally been given the expansive interpretation applicable to the "commerce clause." See Wickard v. Filburn, 317 U.S. 111, 63 S.Ct. 82, 87 L.Ed. 122 (1942) (a marketing quota as to a farmer whose wheat was only sold locally involved interstate commerce because it was designed to control the price of wheat, the total nationwide supply of which was affected by his production). An exception in the act for "contracts of employment of seamen, railroad employees, or any other class of workers engaged in foreign or interstate commerce" (§ 1) was held to be limited to seamen and railroad types of employment. Circuit City Stores, Inc. v. Adams, 532 U.S. 105, 121 S.Ct. 1302, 149 L.Ed.2d 234 (2001).

Section 4 of the Federal Arbitration Act provides that a federal court should order compliance with an arbitration agreement if it is "satisfied that the making of the agreement for arbitration or the failure to comply therewith is not in issue." In *Prima Paint, supra,* plaintiff sued to rescind the consulting agreement on grounds of fraud in the inducement of the contract and opposed a stay pending arbitration on the basis of the fraud. The Supreme Court held that the alleged fraud would bar arbitration only if it went to the making of the agreement to arbitrate itself and not merely to other terms of the contract (this has been referred to as the "separability" doctrine). Since plaintiff only claimed fraud with respect to other aspects of the agreement, the Court reasoned, the arbitration provision should be enforced, with the question of rescission of the contract for fraud to be decided by the arbitrator. Even claims that the entire agreement had been cancelled are for the arbitrator, not the court. See Wilson Wear, Inc. v. United Merchants and Manufacturers, Inc., 713 F.2d 324 (7th Cir.1983).

Preemption of Contrary State Rules

Over the years, a number of states have not shared the federal enthusiasm for arbitration and have refused to enforce arbitration clauses under various circumstances. In the last several decades, however, the Supreme Court has applied a strict preemption doctrine to such state attempts to limit arbitration. In Southland Corp. v. Keating, 465 U.S. 1, 104 S.Ct. 852, 79 L.Ed.2d 1 (1984), a class of franchisees sued the franchisor Southland in a California state court, and Southland then petitioned to compel arbitration under an arbitration clause in the franchise contracts. The California Supreme Court held that the California Franchise Investment Law prohibited any condition in a franchise contract requiring arbitration and affirmed denial of Southland's petition to compel arbitration. The Court held that the California statute violated the Supremacy Clause. It found that § 2 of the FAA (which makes arbitration agreements valid and enforceable) "declared a national policy favoring arbitration and withdrew the power of the states to require a judicial forum for the resolution of claims which the contracting parties agreed to resolve by arbitration." Federal policy required that arbitration agreements should be placed "upon the same footing as other contracts."

Later cases confirmed this limitation on state power. See Perry v. Thomas, 482 U.S. 483, 107 S.Ct. 2520, 96 L.Ed.2d 426 (1987) (state statute barring arbitration of employee claims for payment of wages); Securities Industry Ass'n v. Connolly, 883 F.2d 1114 (1st Cir.1989) (state regulations barring securities firms from requiring customers to sign a pre-dispute arbitration agreement); Saturn Distribution Corp. v. Williams, 905 F.2d 719 (4th Cir.1990) (state statute barring non-negotiable arbitration provisions in contracts between automobile manufacturers and dealers); Allied–Bruce Terminix Cos., Inc. v. Dobson, 513 U.S. 265, 115 S.Ct. 834, 130 L.Ed.2d 753 (1995) (state statute invalidating pre-dispute arbitration agreements).

There are, however, limits to preemption under the FAA. In Volt Information Sciences, Inc. v. Board of Trustees of the Leland Stanford Junior University, 489 U.S. 468, 109 S.Ct. 1248, 103 L.Ed.2d 488 (1989), a construction contract between the parties contained an arbitration clause as well as a choice of law clause that said "[t]his contract shall be governed by the law of the place where the Project is located." The California Arbitration Act permitted courts to stay arbitration pending resolution of related litigation between a party to the arbitration agreement and third parties not bound by it where there is a possibility of conflicting rulings on a common issue. The contractor demanded arbitration, while Stanford filed suit in a California court, also joining two other contractors as to whom there was no arbitration agreement. The Supreme Court found no preemption of the California Act by the FAA. It stated that the FAA only required courts to enforce privately—negotiated agreements to arbitrate in accordance with their terms, and here the parties, by adopting the choice-of-law clause, incorporated the California law that would stay arbitration into their agreement.

Demise of the Doctrine of Federal Statutory Exceptions

For many years, it was assumed that arbitration of claims arising under certain federal statutes could not be compelled because of the complexity of the claims and the public interest in enforcement of federal laws. In Wilko v. Swan, 346 U.S. 427, 74 S.Ct. 182, 98 L.Ed. 168 (1953), the Supreme Court held that a customer of a brokerage firm could litigate a misrepresentation claim against the firm under the Securities Act of 1933, despite an arbitration clause. This doctrine was extended in American Safety Equipment Corp. v. J.P. Maguire & Co., 391 F.2d 821 (2d Cir.1968), to federal antitrust suits which were "of a character inappropriate for enforcement by arbitration." However, in Mitsubishi Motors Corp. v. Soler Chrysler–Plymouth, Inc., 473 U.S. 614, 105 S.Ct. 3346, 87 L.Ed.2d 444 (1985), the Supreme Court held that an arbitration clause could be enforced with respect to antitrust claims. Although the case involved "international commerce," the court's reasoning seemed to apply in the domestic context as well. Following *Mitsubishi,* the Supreme Court reversed earlier precedents by holding there is no bar to arbitration of claims under the Securities Act of 1933, the Securities Exchange Act of 1934, and the Racketeer Influenced and Corrupt Organizations Act (RICO). Shearson/American Express, Inc. v. McMahon, 482 U.S. 220, 107 S.Ct. 2332, 96 L.Ed.2d 185 (1987); Rodriguez de Quijas v. Shearson/American Express, Inc., 490 U.S. 477, 109 S.Ct. 1917, 104 L.Ed.2d 526 (1989).

In *McMahon,* the Court held that Wilko v. Swan, 346 U.S. 427, 74 S.Ct. 182, 98 L.Ed. 168 (1953), did not forbid compelled arbitration of claims under section 10(b) of the 1934 Securities Exchange Act. The majority read *Wilko* as holding that arbitration was inappropriate there because it was inadequate to enforce the statutory rights created under the 1933 Securities Act. "[T]he reasons given in *Wilko* reflect a general suspicion of the desirability of arbitration and the competence of arbitral tribunals" which the Court found "difficult to reconcile" with its more recent emphasis on a federal policy favoring arbitration. Beyond that, the Court concluded the arbitration in the securities industry has improved significantly since 1953, when *Wilko* was decided, since the SEC now oversees industry arbitration procedures. Justice Blackmun, in dissent, argued that the decision essentially overruled *Wilko.*

The Court finally explicitly overruled *Wilko* in *Rodriguez,* noting that *Wilko*'s "suspicion of arbitration as a method of weakening the protections afforded in the substantive law * * * has fallen far out of step with our current strong endorsement of the federal statutes favoring this method of resolving disputes." The Court also found that it would be "undesirable for the decisions in *Wilko* and *McMahon* to continue to exist side by side" because this juxtaposition prevented "harmonious construction" of the Securities Act and the Securities Exchange Act and prompted lawyers to try to frame their cases under one statute or the other because of the treatment of the arbitration question.

Gilmer v. Interstate/Johnson Lane Corp., 500 U.S. 20, 111 S.Ct. 1647, 114 L.Ed.2d 26 (1991), involved an age discrimination claim brought under the federal Age Discrimination in Employment Act of 1967 (ADEA). The plaintiff was employed by the defendant stock brokerage company as a manager of financial services, and his employment contract contained an arbitration clause. In upholding a duty to arbitrate, the Court rejected the argument that arbitration was inconsistent with the ADEA, would undermine the administrative role of the Equal Employment Opportunity Commission in enforcing the act, or would deprive claimants of a judicial forum said to be intended by the ADEA. It distinguished Alexander v. Gardner–Denver Co., 415 U.S. 36, 94 S.Ct. 1011, 39 L.Ed.2d 147 (1974), which held that a discharged employee whose grievance was arbitrated pursuant to an arbitration clause was not precluded from bringing a Title VII employment discrimination suit on the same matter. It found that the arbitration in *Gardner-Denver* arose out of a collective-bargaining agreement (with the claimant represented by a union in the arbitration), and not "individual statutory rights" as in this case. Just how broadly *Gilmer* is to be interpreted is still to be seen, but it suggests that arbitration clauses may preclude a right to sue in many situations in the employment area.

Reactions to *Gilmer* have involved attempts to make arbitration a process more amenable to plaintiff's rights and to expand due process rights. California enacted legislation requiring arbitrators to disclose the results of their prior arbitrations. The American Arbitration Association (AAA) in California undertook a pilot project in employment cases that allows reasonable discovery and gives the arbitrator authority to award a claimant whatever relief the substantive law permits. ADR Backlash: Critics Say Compulsory Arbitration Does Not Work Justice, Litigation News (ABA Section on Litigation), March 1995, p. l, c. 5. After two years of study, the AAA also issued a "due process protocol" in 1997 stating that it would not take cases of mandatory arbitration that deprive employees of rights they would have in court. This resulted from a threat to boycott the AAA by the 2,300–member National Employment Lawyers' Association in response to increased numbers of employment contracts that require arbitration and rule out such rights as discovery and punitive damages. See Adams, Arbitration's Waterloo: Bowing to Plaintiffs on Mandatory Contracts, Calif. Law., Oct. 1997, at 22.

Meanwhile the lower courts have generally applied *Gilmer* broadly. Arbitration clauses have been upheld as to claims of individual brokers alleging other forms of discrimination than the Age Discrimination in Employment Act, Mago v. Shearson Lehman Hutton, Inc., 956 F.2d 932 (9th Cir.1992), including wrongful discharge and sexual harassment claims. See Matthews v. Rollins Hudig Hall Co., 72 F.3d 50 (7th Cir.1995); Metz v. Merrill Lynch, Pierce, Fenner & Smith, 39 F.3d 1482 (10th Cir.1994). *Gilmer* has also been applied to employees other than those of stock brokerage companies, see, e.g., Golenia v. Bob Baker Toyota, 915 F.Supp. 201 (S.D.Cal.1996).

A number of cases have upheld arbitration clauses as to Title VII claims where the contract does not arise from a collective bargaining agreement. Bender v. A.G. Edwards & Sons, Inc., 971 F.2d 698 (11th Cir.1992); Alford v. Dean Witter Reynolds Inc., 939 F.2d 229 (5th Cir.1991). When requirements to arbitrate employee complaints are contained in a collective bargaining agreement, it is arguable, as noted in *Gilmer*, that "the tension between collective representation and individual statutory rights" and a possible "disparity in interests between a union and employee" make judicial protection of individual rights particularly important. 500 U.S. at 35, 111 S.Ct. at 1657. But see Austin v. Owens–Brockway Glass Container, Inc., 78 F.3d 875 (4th Cir.1996) ("There is no reason to distinguish between a union bargaining away the right to strike and union bargaining for the right to arbitrate."); Dickerson v. United Parcel Service Inc., 1996 WL 806696 (N.D.Tex.1996) (arbitration compelled pursuant to arbitration clause in collective bargaining agreement with employee's union).

FAA Preemption of State Law Limitations on Arbitration

State limitations on arbitration have not fared well under the Supreme Court's preemption doctrine. In Allied–Bruce Terminix Cos. v. Dobson, 513 U.S. 265, 115 S.Ct. 834, 130 L.Ed.2d 753 (1995), the Supreme Court upheld the enforceability of a predispute arbitration agreement governed by Alabama law, even though an Alabama statute provided that arbitration agreements are unenforceable. This is consistent with the "national policy favoring arbitration" reflected in the Federal Arbitration Act, which "withdrew the power of the states to require a judicial forum for the resolution of claims which the contracting parties agreed to resolve by arbitration." Southland Corp. v. Keating, *supra*. "The basic purpose of the FAA," the Court said in *Allied-Bruce*, "is to overcome courts' refusals to enforce agreements to arbitrate." 513 U.S. at 270, 115 S.Ct. at 838 (citing *Volt Information Sciences, supra*).

The Court's expansive view of preemption was continued in Doctor's Associates, Inc. v. Casarotto, 517 U.S. 681, 116 S.Ct. 1652, 134 L.Ed.2d 902 (1996). The plaintiffs claimed they were induced to invest in a Subway franchise in Great Falls, Montana, by the promise that they would have an opportunity to invest in a preferable location in that city when it was available. They filed suit in a state court in Great Falls, but the defendant moved to compel arbitration, pursuant to an arbitration clause in the franchise agreement, in Bridgeport, Connecticut where it had its home office. Montana law made agreements to arbitrate unenforceable unless a notice to that effect was typed in underlined capital letters on the first page of the contract (which was not done here). The Supreme Court found that the Montana law singled out arbitration for special burdens and therefore was preempted by the Federal Arbitration Act. Professors Carrington and Haagen commented: "By clothing an otherwise unlawful forum selection in the garb of an arbitration clause, Subway successfully evaded Montana's effort to protect weaker parties from precisely this form or predation by stronger ones." Carrington & Haagen, Contract and Jurisdiction, 1996 S.Ct. Rev. 331, 388. Professor Stempel has also criticized the Court's preemption decisions: "[I]n its drive to usher in the new era and reduce the court monopoly on dispute resolution, the Court's decisions have exhibited a disturbing intellectual expediency, an insensitivity to serious problems of consent and fairness, and preference for departing from its general proarbitration thrust in the service of what appear to be litigants less deserving of a respite from the arbitration juggernaut." Stempel, Jurisprudential Inconsistency and the Felt Necessities of the Time: The Supreme Court's Functional and

Formal Arbitration Jurisprudence, Florida State U. Lawyer 33, 34 (1997).

Court Review and "Arbitrability"

In First Options of Chicago, Inc. v. Kaplan, 514 U.S. 938, 115 S.Ct. 1920, 131 L.Ed.2d 985 (1995), the Supreme Court, in a unanimous opinion by Justice Breyer, revisited and clarified the standards for determining "arbitrability," that is, whether the parties agreed to arbitrate the dispute. It also addressed the standards for determining whether the arbitrator(s) or court decides this issue. First Options sought to enforce an arbitration clause in a "workout" option agreement which Kaplan resisted on the ground he had not personally signed the agreement. The arbitration was convened, and the arbitrators ruled against Kaplan, and the district court confirmed the award. The Supreme Court agreed that the courts must "independently decide whether an arbitration panel has jurisdiction over the merits of any particular dispute." Id. at 941. It further determined that in deciding arbitrability, state contract law will be applied to determine whether the parties objectively revealed their intent to arbitrate. If there is an arbitration clause, silence or ambiguity works in favor of arbitration. But if consent to the clause is contested (as here where the plaintiffs did not personally sign the agreement), the parties must be found to have clearly agreed to arbitration, a question for the arbitrator but subject to court review. Professors Carrington and Haagen comment that "[t]he unanimity of the Court in First Options may indicate that the period of its intoxication with arbitration may be coming to an end." Carrington & Haagen, supra p. 396.

The Supreme Court has continued to seek a workable formula for allocating functions between courts and arbitrators under the issue of "arbitrability." Howsam v. Dean Witter Reynolds, Inc., 537 U.S. 79, 123 S.Ct. 588, 154 L.Ed.2d 491 (2002) involved a claim by a customer against her investment firm for misrepresenting the virtues of investments it sold her. The firm sued in federal court to declare that the dispute was "ineligible for arbitration" because it arose more than 6 years before, in violation of a time-limit requirement contained in the rules of the National Association of Securities Dealers (NASD), which rules were agreed to in the arbitration clause in the contract. Justice Breyer's opinion quoted First Options, supra at 961, that "the 'question of arbitrability' is 'an issue for judicial determination unless the parties clearly and unmistakably provide otherwise.'" However, he observed that the phrase "question of arbitrability" was intended only to apply "in the kind of narrow circumstance where contracting parties would likely have expected a court to have decided the gateway matter, where they are not likely to have thought that they had agreed that an arbitrator would do so, and, consequently, where reference of the gateway dispute to the court avoids the risk of forcing parties to arbitrate a matter that they may well not have agreed to arbitrate."

The Howsam opinion noted the kinds of "gateway disputes" that have been held to be for a court: whether the arbitration contract bound parties who did not sign the agreement; whether an arbitration agreement survived a corporate merger and bound the resulting corporation; whether an arbitration clause in a concededly binding contract applies to a particular type of controversy; and whether a labor-management layoff controversy falls within the arbitration clause of a collective-bargaining agreement. However, "procedural" gateway questions are generally for the arbitrator: whether the first two steps of a grievance procedure were completed; allegations of waiver, delay, or like defenses to arbitrability; and whether a condition precedent to arbitrability has been fulfilled. It found "the [NASD] time limit rule closely resembles the gateway questions that this Court has found not to be 'questions of arbitrability'" and therefore to be decided by the arbitrator. This kind of analysis is continued in the 2003 decision in Green Tree Financial Corp. v. Bazzle, see infra p. 914.

Punitive Damages in Arbitration

For several years, there has been uncertainty as to whether punitive damages can be recovered in arbitration proceedings. Most brokerage account agreements provide that they are governed by New York law, which only allows punitive damages to be awarded by courts, not arbitrators. Garrity v. Lyle Stuart, Inc., 40 N.Y.2d 354, 386 N.Y.S.2d 831, 353 N.E.2d 793 (1976). In Mastrobuono v. Shearson Lehman Hutton, Inc., 514 U.S. 52, 115 S.Ct. 1212, 131 L.Ed.2d 76 (1995), the Supreme Court held that the N.Y. choice of law provision in the brokerage contract was insufficient to evince a mutual agreement by the parties to exclude punitive damages and thus arbitrators could award them. See also Kennedy, Matthews, Landis, Healy & Pecora, Inc. v. Young, 524 N.W.2d 752 (Minn.App.1994) (arbitrators may award punitive damages under "common law principles"). The question arises whether, had the brokerage agreement expressly excluded punitive damages (the standard form which was used in Mastrobuono adopted N.Y. law but did not expressly exclude punitive damages), the result might have been different. See Volt Information Sciences, Inc. v. Board of Trustees of Leland Stanford Univ., supra, recognizing a federal policy "to ensure the enforceability, according to its terms, of private agreements to arbitrate."

The Arbitration Process

The advantages often claimed for arbitration include speed, economy, expertise of the decision-maker, privacy, greater informality, convenience of time and place settings, and finality without recourse to appeal. The arbitration process begins with parties voluntarily entering into an arbitration agreement, often as part of a contract, whereby all disputes will be resolved according to stipulated procedures. Although there are agreements providing for only advisory arbitration rulings, classical arbitration calls for a binding result. A number of private organizations have established rules for arbitration. Some of those most often stipulated to by parties are rules of the American Arbitration Association, International Chamber of Commerce, Inter–American Commercial Arbitration Commission, and United Nations Commission on International Trade Law. Within certain industries, organizations offer arbitration services, such as the dispute resolution program of the Insurance Arbitration Forum, Inc., Council of Better Business Bureaus National Program of Consumer Arbitration, and National Association of Securities Dealers and N.Y. Stock Exchange Uniform Arbitration Code.

Most arbitration agreements authorize either party to demand arbitration, thereby setting in motion an agreed-upon dispute-resolution procedure. For a customary set of procedures, consider the normal approach outlined by the American Arbitration Association: First, the Association sends both parties a list of possible arbitrators selected from its panel of arbitrators as technically qualified to handle the dispute. The parties are then allowed to reject unacceptable arbitrators and to number the remaining names by order of preference. Using this information, the Association tries to select a mutually acceptable arbitrator (or arbitrators if the agreement calls for more than one) and, if that is not possible, it selects the arbitrator itself. The Association then arranges a convenient time for the hearing. At the hearing the arbitrator receives all relevant evidence without applying strict rules of evidence. Both parties are entitled to be represented by counsel, and they are urged to present their cases in an orderly and logical manner. American Arbitration Association, A Commercial Arbitration Guide For Business People (2002).

After the hearing, the arbitrator renders a final decision within 30 days. The arbitrator has no further authority after making the decision unless both parties petition to reopen the proceeding, thereby submitting once again to the arbitrator's authority. An arbitral decision is not subject to attack in court on the ground that it was legally erroneous. The FAA, § 9, provides that if the parties have so agreed, a judgment may be entered upon the award. Under § 10, the decision may be set aside by a court only for such things as partiality or corruption of the arbitrator, misconduct of the arbitrator, or action in excess of her power.

Court Injunctive Relief Concerning Arbitration

The arbitration process is usually begun with a written "demand for arbitration" (or "notice of intention to arbitrate"). One of the parties, however, may ignore the demand and bring suit in court. The other party (usually the defendant) may then apply for a *stay of the judicial proceedings* in favor of arbitration. FAA § 3; Uniform Arbitration Act § 2(d). The FAA provides that such an application is to be heard as a motion and that, "upon being satisfied" that the issue involved in the suit is arbitrable under a valid agreement, the court must order the stay. FAA § 6.

Sometimes a party simply ignores the demand for arbitration altogether and refuses to participate. In this situation the party seeking arbitration may ask a court "for an *order directing that such arbitration proceed* in the manner provided for" in the parties' agreement. FAA § 4; Uniform Arbitration Act § 2(a). Both the FAA and the Uniform Arbitration Act provide that if there is a question as to existence of a valid arbitration agreement, the court shall determine that issue "summarily" before ordering arbitration.

The respondent who claims that there is no valid agreement to arbitrate may not wish to participate in an arbitration, but he will not want to lose any rights by unilaterally staying out, either. He has the option of seeking a judicial *stay of the arbitration.* This is expressly made possible by the Uniform Arbitration Act, which provides that the issue as to whether a valid agreement exists "shall be forthwith and summarily tried," § 2(b). Federal courts have asserted the same power under the FAA. See Flink v. Carlson, 856 F.2d 44 (8th Cir.1988).

a. Invalidation of Arbitration Clauses under State Contract Law

Arbitration clauses are now commonplace in contracts with respect to the construction industry, employment, and labor relations. They are increasingly found in commercial contracts and almost always appear in contracts between parties or corporations who come from different countries, as neither side is willing to submit to the courts of the other. The great expansion of arbitration since the early 1990s, however, has come in consumer contracts, such as finance, banking, credit cards, communications services, and health care, with the arbitration clause usually in forms or small print that is not negotiated. Arbitration clauses in adhesion contracts are subjected to close scrutiny. For example, in Prudential Ins. Co. v. Lai, 42 F.3d 1299 (9th Cir.1994), the Ninth Circuit held that employees cannot be bound by an agreement to arbitrate employment discrimination claims unless they "knowingly agreed" to arbitrate them.

The whole range of contract defenses may be grounds for invalidating arbitration clauses, such as misrepresentation, mistake, or coercion, but unconscionability has become a principal ground for invalidation. In Armendariz v. Foundation Health Psychcare Services, Inc., 24 Cal.4th 83, 99 Cal.Rptr.2d 745, 6 P.3d 669 (2000), a suit for wrongful termination under a California fair employment act, the California Supreme Court formulated four minimum requirements for upholding an arbitration clause attacked as unconscionable:

(1) Must allow all remedies that would be available in court—A number of courts have held that an arbitration agreement may not prohibit such remedies as punitive damages and attorney's fees. The arbitration clause in *Armendariz* limiting the remedy to a sum equal to the wages the employee would have earned from discharge up to the date of an arbitration award was found defective.

(2) Must provide for adequate discovery—The court recognized that arbitration need not provide the full range of discovery available in court. However, it interpreted the provisions contained in the California

Arbitration Act as at least entitling them to "discovery sufficient to adequately arbitrate their statutory claim, including access to essential documents and witnesses, as determined by the arbitrator(s) and subject to limited judicial review." Thus it found no grounds for denying arbitration due to lack of discovery.

(3) Must require a written arbitration award and judicial review— The court held that an arbitrator "must issue a written arbitration decision that will reveal, however briefly, the essential findings and conclusions on which the award is based." It found that the arbitration clause here did not preclude written findings and that a challenge based on inadequate judicial review would be premature.

(4) Must not require the claimant to pay arbitration costs—The California Code provides that each party will pay his pro rata share of the expenses and fees of an arbitration. The court noted that "we are unaware of any situation in American jurisprudence in which a beneficiary of a federal statute has been required to pay for the services of the judge assigned to hear her or his case." Although recognizing that parties in court may be required to pay filing fees and other administrative expenses, the court held that the "arbitration process cannot generally require the employee to bear any type of expense that the employee would not be required to bear if he or she were free to bring the action in court."

The *Armendariz* kind of factors have been applied by many courts to render arbitration clauses unconstitutional. See. e.g., Alexander v. Anthony Int'l, L.P., 341 F.3d 256 (3d Cir.2003) (arbitration clause in employment agreement found unconscionable for being too heavily weighted in favor of employer). In State of West Virginia v. Berger, 211 W.Va. 549, 567 S.E.2d 265 (2002), the West Virginia Supreme Court held that a prohibition on punitive damages and class action relief was unconscionable and unenforceable. It rejected the argument that the Federal Arbitration Act preempted state courts from invalidating arbitration clauses as to such matters as remedies, holding that the FAA "does not bar a state court that is examining exculpatory provisions in a contract of adhesion that if applied would prohibit or substantially limit a person from enforcing and vindicating rights and protections * * * that are afforded by or arise under state law that exists for the benefit and protection of the public from considering whether the provisions are unconscionable."

Morrison v. Circuit City Stores, Inc., 317 F.3d 646 (6th Cir.2003), is typical of the growing body of precedents holding arbitration clauses unenforceable, in this case due to a cost-splitting provision and limitations on certain remedies. It held that "a cost-splitting provision should be held unenforceable whenever it would have the 'chilling effect' of deterring a substantial number of potential litigants from seeking to vindicate their statutory rights." A limitation of remedies to injunctive relief, including reinstatement, one year of back pay and lost fringe benefits, two years of front pay if reinstatement is not possible, compensatory damages, and punitive damages up to $5,000. was also found to be unenforceable as limiting the remedies available under Title VII of the civil rights act.

Limitations on remedies such as punitive damages may not result in invalidation of an arbitration clause if such limitations can be construed otherwise. PacifiCare Health Systems, Inc. v. Book, 538 U.S. 401, 123 S.Ct. 1531, 155 L.Ed.2d 578 (2003), involved suit by doctors claiming violation of the Racketeer Influenced and Corrupt Organizations Act (RICO) by health-care organizations in failing to make certain reimbursements. The plaintiffs opposed a motion to compel arbitration on the ground that language in the arbitration clause that ''punitive damages shall not be awarded'' meant they could not obtain ''meaningful relief'' under the RICO statute which authorizes treble damages. Justice Scalia's opinion noted that the RICO treble-damage provision has been found to be remedial, rather than punitive, in nature and that there was uncertainty in the parties' intent as to what was intended by prohibiting ''punitive damages.'' The opinion relied heavily on Vimar Seguros y Reaseguros, S.A. v. M/V Sky Reefer, 515 U.S. 528, 115 S.Ct. 2322, 132 L.Ed.2d 462 (1995), which refused to invalidate an arbitration clause as failing to apply the terms of the Carriage of Goods by Sea Act (COGSA) because, at this interlocutory stage, it was not established that the arbitrators would not apply COGSA as opposed to Japanese law. Since we do not know how the arbitrator will construe the remedial limitations, Justice Scalia wrote, the questions whether they render the parties' agreements unenforceable and whether it is for courts or arbitrators to decide enforceability in the first instance are unusually abstract. Citing *Howsam,* supra at 890, the Court held that ''the proper course is to compel arbitration.''

b.   *Arbitrable and Non-arbitrable Claims in the Same Suit*

In multi-party suits, a contractual right to arbitration may be in effect as to some, but not all of the parties. A common scenario, for example, arises in the construction industry when the Owner of a project enters into separate contracts with the General Partner (who is responsible for construction) and with the Architect (who acts as the Owner's representative in designing and overseeing the project). The Owner may make a claim against the Contractor for alleged defects in construction, and the Contractor may answer that any defects are attributable to the Architect's failings in specifying materials or in inspecting the work. Should the Contractor's defense be upheld, the Owner may wish to assert a claim against the Architect for negligence. See Litton Bionetics, Inc. v. Glen Construction Co., Inc., 292 Md. 34, 437 A.2d 208 (1981). Alternatively, the Contractor may make a claim against the Owner, asserting that it was unable to comply with the plans and specifications for the project because they called for the use of materials that were unobtainable, causing delay and economic loss. Should the Contractor's claim be upheld, the Owner will claim for indemnification from the Architect. See Consolidated Pacific Engineering, Inc. v. Greater Anchorage Area Borough, 563 P.2d 252 (Alaska 1977); Cable Belt Conveyors, Inc. v. Alumina Partners of Jamaica, 717 F.Supp. 1021 (S.D.N.Y.1989).

In cases like these, the party "in the middle"-the Owner in this scenario-has an obvious interest in a single proceeding to resolve the interrelated disputes. If the Owner must first assert a claim against the Contractor, and only later seek to hold the Architect liable, it is faced with duplication of time and expense inherent in preparing and presenting the same case in two different forums. Even more important, there is the real possibility of inconsistent results in the two forums. In a first proceeding, the Owner may be unable to overcome the Contractor's defense based on deficiencies in the project specifications. In a later proceeding, however, it may be found that the defect was caused by poor workmanship rather than by the Architect's negligence in preparing the plans, leaving the Owner "holding the bag" alone.

Since arbitration is exclusively contractual, a party who has never agreed to arbitrate a dispute cannot be forced into the process. Therefore, if the agreement between the Owner and Contractor contains an arbitration clause, but the agreement between the Owner and Architect does not, the Architect cannot be required to arbitrate, and there may be no way to insure that all the claims are heard at the same time in a single proceeding. As a result the Owner would be in a better position if it were not a party to any arbitration agreement at all. In litigation, a court with jurisdiction over all the interested parties can bring them all into the action. In a lawsuit against the Contractor, the Owner would be able to join a claim "in the alternative" against the Architect (see Fed.R.Civ.P. 20(a)); if it is a defendant, the Owner could "implead" the Architect as a "third-party defendant" (see Fed.R.Civ.P. 14(a)); and if there are pending separate "actions involving a common question of law or fact," a court "may order a joint hearing or trial of any or all of the matters in issue in the actions" or may "order all the actions consolidated." (Fed.R.Civ.P. 42(a)).

A key decision regarding the presence of arbitrable and nonarbitrable claims in the same case is Moses H. Cone Memorial Hospital v. Mercury Construction Corp., 460 U.S. 1, 103 S.Ct. 927, 74 L.Ed.2d 765 (1983). The hospital had contracted with Mercury Construction to build an addition, designating an architect to supervise and resolve any disputes. If either party objected to the architect's resolution it could demand arbitration. Mercury demanded payment for certain additional costs, but, while engaging in negotiations, the hospital rejected the claims and filed suit in state court against Mercury and the architect. It sought a declaration that it owed Mercury nothing, and that to the extent that it was liable to Mercury, it was entitled to indemnity from the architect. It maintained that Mercury had waived its right to arbitration and obtained an ex parte injunction prohibiting arbitration. Rather than litigate the arbitration issue in state court, Mercury filed an action in federal district court to compel arbitration of its claims against the hospital. The district court stayed the federal suit pending resolution of the hospital's state-court suit.

The Supreme Court found the stay order improper, rejecting *Colorado River* abstention (see *supra* pp. 184–89) because the state court had not assumed jurisdiction over a res and there was no reason to conclude that the federal forum was any less convenient. The Court said that Congress' clear intent in the FAA was "to move the parties to an arbitrable dispute out of court and into arbitration as quickly and easily as possible." Why couldn't the state court accomplish this as successfully as the federal court by first making a ruling on arbitrability? State courts do have concurrent jurisdiction with federal courts to enforce the FAA. However, the Court expressed the concern that even assuming that "the state court would have granted prompt relief to Mercury under the Act, there still would have been an inevitable delay as a result of the District Court's stay."

The Court also expressed doubts about the obligation of state courts to compel arbitration under § 4 of the FAA (as opposed to granting stays of litigation under § 3). Actually, the language of both sections appears to apply only to federal court proceedings (although it is quite possible that the drafters, in 1925, did not foresee that the FAA would be interpreted to require state courts, as well as federal courts, to apply it). Since the *Moses Cone* decision, the Supreme Court has not chosen to clear up the question of the applicability of §§ 3 and 4 in state-court proceedings. In Volt Information Sciences, Inc. v. Board of Trustees of Leland Stanford Jr. University, 489 U.S. 468, 109 S.Ct. 1248, 103 L.Ed.2d 488 (1989), it indicated that the argument that the two sections did not apply was "not without some merit" and, in a footnote, stated that it had reserved the question in Southland Corp. v. Keating, 465 U.S. 1, 104 S.Ct. 852, 79 L.Ed.2d 1 (1984). See 489 U.S. at 477, 109 S.Ct. at 1254.

The Court went on in *Moses Cone* to find "no force here" to the danger of piecemeal litigation. "It is true," it said, "that if Mercury obtains an arbitration order for its dispute, the Hospital will be forced to resolve these related disputes [with Mercury and the architect] in different forums." But "that misfortune," it explained, was "not the result of any choice between the federal and state courts, [since] it occurs because the relevant federal law requires piecemeal resolution when necessary to give effect to an arbitration agreement."

The effect of *Moses Cone* arguably makes piecemeal litigation more likely. *Without a stay*, both federal and state suits would have proceeded simultaneously. If either court then ordered arbitration, the arbitrable claim between the hospital and Mercury would have gone to arbitration, while the claim against the architect would have remained in the state court, thus necessitating piecemeal disposition. *With a stay*, on the other hand, all further proceedings would have been in the state court. If the state court refused to order arbitration, the case would have proceeded as a unitary case there. If, however, the state court ordered arbitration, it would have to sever the claims and retain the non-arbitrable one, thus necessitating piecemeal disposition. Given these possibilities, it is arguable that a federal-court stay actually would have been more effective in avoiding piecemeal disposition at least if the state court would have ordered arbitration.

Although *Moses Cone* was willing to countenance bifurcation and piecemeal resolution of the dispute in order to enforce an arbitration agreement that only applied to some of the parties, the "doctrine of intertwining" would have cut the other way. The doctrine provided that when arbitrable and nonarbitrable claims arose out of the same transaction, and were sufficiently "intertwined" factually and legally, a federal district court could, in its discretion, deny arbitration as to the arbitrable claims and try all the claims together in federal court. See Belke v. Merrill Lynch, Pierce, Fenner & Smith, 693 F.2d 1023 (11th Cir.1982); Miley v. Oppenheimer & Co., 637 F.2d 318 (5th Cir.1981).

However, in Dean Witter Reynolds Inc. v. Byrd, 470 U.S. 213, 105 S.Ct. 1238, 84 L.Ed.2d 158 (1985), the Court rejected that doctrine, holding that the Federal Arbitration Act divests the district courts of discretion in cases containing both arbitrable and nonarbitrable claims and requires them to compel arbitration of arbitrable claims. The Court stated: "The preeminent concern of Congress in passing the Act was to enforce private agreements into which parties had entered, and that concern requires that we rigorously enforce agreements to arbitrate, even if the result is 'piecemeal' litigation, at least absent a countervailing policy manifested in another federal statute." In response to the suggestion that the findings in the arbitration might be asserted as collateral estoppel in the federal proceeding, the Court noted that the preclusive effect of arbitration findings was uncertain: "[I]n framing preclusion rules in this context, courts shall take into account the federal interests warranting protection. As a result, there is no reason to require that district courts decline to compel arbitration, or manipulate the ordering of the resulting bifurcated proceedings, simply to avoid an infringement of federal interests."

Where there is a severance of arbitrable from nonarbitrable claims, it is generally held that the trial court has the discretion to stay proceedings on the nonarbitrable claims pending resolution of the arbitration. *Cruz v. PacifiCare Health Systems*, 30 Cal.4th 303, 133 Cal. Rptr.2d 58, 66 P.3d 1157 (2003). "A stay is appropriate where '[i]n the absence * * * of a stay, the continuation of the proceedings in the trial court disrupts the arbitration proceedings and can render them ineffective'" *Coast Plaza Doctors Hospital v. Blue Cross of California*, 83 Cal.App.4th 677, 693, 99 Cal.Rptr.2d 809 (2000).

Collateral Estoppel Effect of Arbitration Decision

The ever-increasing use of arbitration makes it important to determine whether collateral estoppel effect will be given to arbitrators' decisions. 28 U.S.C.A. § 1738 (which obliges federal courts to give the same preclusive effect to a state-court judgment as would the court of the state rendering the judgment) does not apply to arbitration awards because they are not "judicial proceedings." Therefore any preclusion rules applicable to arbitration must be fashioned by the federal courts.

The Supreme Court has refused to accord preclusive effect to arbitration awards where it found the cause of action was intended to be judicially enforceable. See Alexander v. Gardner–Denver Co., 415 U.S. 36, 94 S.Ct. 1011, 39 L.Ed.2d 147 (1974) (Title VII employment discrimination suit); Barrentine v. Arkansas–Best Freight System, Inc., 450 U.S. 728, 101 S.Ct. 1437, 67 L.Ed.2d 641 (1981) (suit under minimum wage provisions of the Fair Labor Standards Act); McDonald v. City of West Branch, Michigan, 466 U.S. 284, 104 S.Ct. 1799, 80 L.Ed.2d 302 (1984) (a § 1983 civil rights action by a discharged police officer). The Court has also noted that an arbitrator's expertise "pertains primarily to the law of the shop, not the law of the land" and that "arbitral fact finding is generally not equivalent to judicial fact finding." *McDonald, supra,* 466 U.S. at 290–91, 104 S.Ct. at 1803.

A further question is whether an earlier arbitration award should be given preclusive effect in a later arbitration. In Gonce v. Veterans Administration, 872 F.2d 995 (Fed.Cir.1989), the cases of certain co-workers discharged for alleged abuse of patients reached arbitration first, and the arbitrators found their grievances arbitrable. Other workers argued in their subsequent arbitrations that collateral estoppel effect must be given to the earlier arbitral awards on that point. In Kroeger v. United States Postal Service, 865 F.2d 235 (Fed.Cir.1988), the Federal Circuit had accorded collateral estoppel effect to labor arbitration decisions where the issue was identical. The court refused to follow that case in *Gonce,* finding that the actions taken against the workers were based on separate instances of misconduct and that since there were no transcripts of the proceedings, it was impossible to tell whether mitigating circumstances distinguished the cases. It commented that, pursuant to Supreme Court precedents, the preclusive effect to be given to prior arbitration awards is "for individual resolution, absent a provision in the governing contract that requires earlier awards to bind subsequent arbitrators." Id. at 997.

c. *Consolidation of Arbitration Proceedings*

Sometimes multi-party disputes will involve arbitration clauses in separate contracts involving different groupings of parties. Take, for example, the hypothetical used in the last subsection concerning separate contracts between the Owner and Contractor, and between the Owner and Architect, and assume that both contained arbitration clauses. The Owner might find it advantageous to try to have the two arbitration proceedings "consolidated" in order to avoid piecemeal arbitration.

**MURRAY, RAU & SHERMAN, MATERIALS
ON DISPUTE RESOLUTION**

National Institute for Dispute Resolution, pp. IV–85–95 (1991).

The right to consolidate arbitrations is unclear. The long-standing policy of the American Arbitration Association is that it will not consolidate separate arbitration proceedings unless all the parties consent, or unless all the arbitration agreements explicitly provide for consolidation. The AAA has little incentive to force consolidation upon unwilling parties, and may, in fact, fear that doing so will affect the enforceability of the resulting award. So parties in the Owner's position must often resort to seeking a court order for the consolidation of the separate arbitrations. If a court is willing to order consolidated arbitration, the AAA is "off the hook" and will then administer the consolidated arbitrations.

The willingness of courts to order consolidated arbitration without the consent of all the parties varies greatly. Some courts would find the absence of "privity" between the Architect and Contractor a barrier to ordering a consolidated arbitration. To do so, it is suggested, would be to "rewrite" the contract between the parties. Pueblo of Laguna v. Cillessen & Son, Inc., 101 N.M. 341, 682 P.2d 197 (1984); Louisiana Stadium & Exposition District v. Huber, Hunt & Nichols, Inc., 349 So.2d 491 (La.App.1977). It may even be suggested that where the agreement provides for arbitration under AAA auspices, the parties presumably contracted on the understanding that in accordance with AAA practice, consolidation would not be ordered without their consent. Consolidated Pacific Engineering, Inc. v. Greater Anchorage Area Borough, 563 P.2d 252 (Alaska 1977). A number of recent federal cases decided under the FAA are to the same effect. E.g., Baesler v. Continental Grain Co., 900 F.2d 1193 (8th Cir.1990) (FAA requires courts to "enforce arbitration agreements as they are written"; "absent a provision in an arbitration agreement authorizing consolidation, a district court is without power to consolidate arbitration proceedings"); Protective Life Insurance Corp. v. Lincoln National Life Insurance Corp., 873 F.2d 281 (11th Cir.1989); Del E. Webb Construction v. Richardson Hospital Authority, 823 F.2d 145 (5th Cir.1987); Weyerhaeuser Co. v. Western Seas Shipping Co., 743 F.2d 635 (9th Cir.1984).

Despite the cases mentioned above, some see a "trend of judicial decisions" towards consolidation of arbitration proceedings. Cf. Stipanowich, Arbitration and the Multiparty Dispute: The Search for Workable Solutions, 72 Iowa L.Rev. 473 (1987). A number of courts have ordered consolidation of related arbitrations, even over the objection of one of the parties—at least where the arbitration agreement did not expressly forbid this. Courts that do so assert that this is "an incident of the jurisdiction statutorily conferred on a court generally to enforce arbitration agreements," and necessary in the "interests of efficiency, economy, and avoidance of circuity." See, e.g., Hoover Group Inc. v. Probala & Associates, 710 F.Supp. 677 (N.D.Ohio 1989); Compania Espanola de Petroleos, S.A. v. Nereus Shipping, S.A., 527 F.2d 966 (2d Cir.1975); Litton Bionetics, Inc. v. Glen Construction Co., Inc., 292 Md. 34, 437 A.2d 208 (1981); cf. New England Energy Inc. v. Keystone Shipping Co., 855 F.2d 1 (1st Cir.1988) (applying Massachusetts statute providing for consolidation).

Even if in theory a court has the power to order that related arbitrations be consolidated, problems may still remain concerning just how this consolidated arbitration is to be administered. The arbitration agreement between the Owner and Contractor may differ in important respects from that between the Owner and Architect: The two agreements may specify different locations for the arbitrations; they may call for administration by two different institutions; or they may provide that they are to be governed by the substantive law of two different jurisdictions. Presented with such difficulties, courts tend to refuse to consolidate the arbitrations. See Seguro de Servicio de Salud de Puerto Rico v. McAuto Systems Group, Inc., 878 F.2d 5 (1st Cir.1989) (consolidation "would obviously force [one of the parties] to forego the arbitration locale mandated by their contracts").

One recurrent problem is how the arbitrators in a consolidated arbitration should be selected. Assume that both the Owner/Contractor and the Owner/Architect agreements call for a "tripartite" arbitration panel (in which each party selects one arbitrator, with the third "neutral" arbitrator selected by the other two). A court might instead order that the consolidated arbitration is to be heard by one or three neutrals selected in a different manner. However, this would deprive each party of the invaluable "right" to select "his own" arbitrator. See Atlas Plastering, Inc. v. Superior Court, County of Alameda, 72 Cal.App.3d 63, 140 Cal.Rptr. 59 (1977). Some courts have straightforwardly proceeded to restructure the arbitration panel—for example, by ordering a five-member panel, one member being named by each of the parties and those selected choosing two neutrals in order to insure an odd number. See Compania Espanola de Petroleos, S.A. v. Nereus Shipping, S.A., 527 F.2d 966 (2d Cir.1975) (consolidated arbitration among Shipowner, Charterer, and Guarantor of Charterer's obligations). However, such a large panel is likely to be unwieldy, expensive, and time-consuming; in addition, there exists the possibility of "sweetheart" relationships in which two of the parties join forces and dominate the panel to the prejudice of the third party.

The standard form Owner/Contractor construction agreement prepared by the American Institute of Architects (and endorsed by the Associated General Contractors) provides:

4.5.5. No arbitration arising out of or relating to the Contract Documents shall include, by consolidation or joinder or in any other manner, the Architect, the Architect's employees or consultants, except by written consent containing specific reference to the Agreement and signed by the Architect, Owner, Contractor and any other person or entity sought to be joined. No arbitration shall include, by consolidation or joinder or in any other manner, parties other than the Owner, Contractor, a separate contractor [with whom the Owner has entered into a separate agreement related to the project] and other persons substantially involved in a common question of fact or law whose presence is required if complete relief is to be accorded in arbitration.

AIA Document A201, General Conditions of the Contract for Construction.

This widely-used form does seem to envisage and permit consolidation of arbitrations among owners, contractors, and subcontractors. However, it is clearly intended to bar consolidation of arbitrations involving the Architect. A similar provision barring consolidation appears in the standard-form construction contract prepared and jointly adopted by the National Society of Professional Engineers and the American Consulting Engineers Council.

One explanation for this resistance to consolidation is that by increasing the number of parties, the number of issues, and the number of lawyers, consolidation may well complicate and lengthen the arbitration proceedings. More importantly, the Architect may fear that the unique legal and contractual issues bearing on his own liability may be lost or muddled in a proceeding where claims against him are joined with other claims involving different standards of liability. See *Sweet on Construction Industry Contracts* 441–45 (1987).

A number of state statutes explicitly authorize courts to order the consolidation of related arbitrations. See Cal.Code Civ.Pro. § 1281.3; Mass.Gen.Laws 251 § 2A (consolidation permitted even if contrary to the parties' agreement). There is no such provision in the FAA.

Notes and Questions

1. Is the problem of who gets to choose the arbitrator and present the case an insurmountable barrier to a consolidated arbitration? What procedures might be adopted, and where would they have to be provided for (i.e., the arbitration agreement, the rules of the administering agency, or elsewhere)?

2. The great problem with consolidating arbitrations in the owner-contractor-architect example is that arbitration is a matter of contract, and non-parties cannot be forced into arbitration. But particularly in consumer cases, all the parties are bound by the same contract and arbitration clause. Why should identical claims by consumers against the same company—for example, that they have been subjected to the same unauthorized charge on their monthly statements—not be properly handled by a consolidated arbitration? What would be the company's objection? If a large number of claimants seek consolidation, would a class action be the more appropriate remedy?

d. *Classwide Arbitration*

BLUE CROSS OF CALIFORNIA ET AL. v. THE SUPERIOR COURT OF LOS ANGELES COUNTY

Court of Appeal, Second District, Division 5, California, 1998.
67 Cal.App.4th 42, 78 Cal.Rptr.2d 779.

TURNER, Presiding Justice.

This original writ proceeding presents a question of first impression: whether a California court can, as authorized by state law, order classwide arbitration in a case that falls under the Federal Arbitration Act (the act). (9 U.S.C.A. § 1 et seq.). Stated differently, the issue is whether the act preempts California decisional authority authorizing classwide arbitration. The United States Supreme Court has never reached the question whether the act precludes classwide arbitration under state law. We conclude application of the California classwide arbitration rule is not preempted by the act. Accordingly, we deny the writ petition.

Two named plaintiffs, Elizabeth Farquhar, and Laurie Winett, brought this class action, against Blue Cross of California and Wellpoint Health Networks, Inc. (collectively, Blue Cross). They alleged Blue Cross had "engaged in a widespread practice of selling and administering health plans which violate laws concerning pre-existing condition exclusions, waiting period exclusions, waivered condition exclusions, and temporary exclusions." Blue Cross answered the complaint alleging, in part, that plaintiffs were required by contract to resolve their claims through binding arbitration.

The arbitration provision in Blue Cross's "Personal Prudent Buyer Classic and Basic Hospital Plan for Families and Individuals" stated: "Any dispute between you and Blue Cross of California and/or its affiliates must be resolved by binding arbitration, if the amount in dispute exceeds the jurisdictional limit of the Small Claims Court. Any such dispute will be resolved not by law or resort to court process, except as California law provides for judicial review of arbitration proceedings. Under this coverage, both you and Blue Cross of California and its affiliates are giving up the right to have any dispute decided in a court of law before a jury." [It made no reference to classwide arbitration.]

Blue Cross filed a petition in the trial court to compel arbitration of the individual plaintiffs' claims and to stay the litigation. The trial court ordered in part: "The Motion to Stay Judicial Proceedings is denied as to the class claims alleged in the Complaint. Discovery shall continue as to the class claims for purposes of a possible class certification motion and, ... if a class is certified, the class claims will be referred to class-wide arbitration...."

Blue Cross then filed the present petition for a writ of mandate, prohibition, or other appropriate relief. * * *

A. Ripeness

[The court found that the case involved concrete issues—"may discovery proceed on whether there should be class certification with the potential that plaintiffs will later be joined in classwide arbitration."]

B. The Federal Arbitration Act

The parties agree that the underlying health insurance contracts evidence transactions involving commerce and therefore the arbitration provisions fall within the purview of the act. It provides in section 2 that a written arbitration provision in a contract "evidencing a transaction involving commerce * * * shall be valid, irrevocable, and enforceable, save upon such grounds as exist at law or in equity for the revocation of any contract." Section 4 of the act provides for a petition to compel arbitration in "any United States district court" and for the issuance of an order "directing the parties to proceed to arbitration in accordance with the terms of the agreement." * * * The purpose of the act "was to reverse the longstanding judicial hostility to arbitration agreements that had existed at English common law and had been adopted by American courts" * * * It intended courts to "enforce [arbitration] agreements into which parties had entered," and to "place such agreements" upon the same footing as other contracts, (*Allied–Bruce Terminix Cos. v. Dobson, supra,* 513 U.S. at pp. 270–271, 115 S.Ct. 834.). * * * *

C. The Act's Preemption of State Law

The act is predicated on Congress's authority to enact substantive rules under the Commerce laws. The act "creates a body of federal substantive law" requiring that arbitration agreements be honored. (*Southland Corp. v. Keating, supra,* 465 U.S. at pp. 12 & 15, fn. 9, 104 S.Ct. 852). That federal substantive law is applicable in both state and federal courts.

However, the scope of federal preemption under the act is not complete. The United States Supreme Court has held: "The [act] contains no express pre-emptive provision, nor does it reflect a congressional intent to occupy the entire field of arbitration." (*Volt Info. Sciences v. Leland Stanford Jr. U.* (1989) 489 U.S. 468, 477, 109 S.Ct. 1248, 103 L.Ed.2d 488.) Rather, state law is preempted to the extent it stands as an obstacle to contractual arbitration.* * *

The United States Supreme Court has further delineated the preemptive scope of the act in a series of decisions. Section 2 of the act places arbitration agreements on an equal footing with contracts generally. (*Allied-Bruce Terminix Cos. v. Dobson, supra,* 513 U.S. at pp. 270–271, 115 S.Ct. 834) In view of that purpose, the Supreme Court has held: "Thus, generally applicable contract defenses, such as fraud, duress or unconscionability, may be applied to invalidate arbitration agreements without contravening § 2." (*Doctor's Associates, Inc. v. Casarotto, supra,* 517 U.S. at p. 687, 116 S.Ct. 1652.). However, a state law that invalidates the express terms of an arbitration agreement is preempted by the act. * * *

D. California Decisional Authority Authorizes Classwide Arbitration

Under California decisional authority, classwide arbitration is permissible. (We adopt the term "classwide" arbitration as used by the California Supreme Court in *Keating,* rather than the equally descriptive phrases "class arbitration" or "class action arbitration.") In *Keating v. Superior Court, supra,* 31 Cal.3d at pages 608–614, 183 Cal.Rptr. 360, 645 P.2d 1192, the California Supreme Court considered whether a trial court could order classwide arbitration under adhesive but enforceable franchise contracts. The court first noted the "importance of the class action device for vindicating rights asserted by large groups of persons." The court then reasoned: "If the right to a classwide proceedings could be automatically eliminated in relationships governed by adhesion contracts through the inclusion of a provision for arbitration, the potential for undercutting these class action principles, and for chilling the effective protection of interests common to a group, would be substantial." The Supreme Court rejected the option of requiring each individual franchisee to arbitrate its claims as "resulting in needless duplication and the potential for inconsistent awards." The Supreme Court identified a different problem which justified the use of classwide arbitration as follows: "It is common knowledge that arbitration clauses frequently appear in standardized contracts of adhesion. A primary consideration which has led courts to uphold such clauses, despite the adhesive nature of the contract, is the belief that arbitration is not oppressive and does not defeat the reasonable expectations of the parties. If, however, an arbitration clause may be used to insulate the drafter of an adhesive contract from any form of class proceeding, effectively foreclosing many individual claims, it may well be oppressive and may defeat the expectations of the nondrafting party. One possible solution to this dilemma would be to hold that arbitration agreements contained in contracts of adhesion may not operate to stay properly maintainable class actions."

The California Supreme Court then turned to the question whether consolidation of the arbitration proceedings should be allowed. The court cited federal authority for consolidation of arbitration proceedings by reliance on rule 42(a) of the Federal Rules of Civil Procedure. It concluded that by analogy, rule 23 of the Federal Rules of Civil Procedure, the class action provision, would provide a basis for ordering classwide arbitrations in federal court. The California Supreme Court further noted that other state courts had allowed consolidation of arbitration proceedings even in the absence of statutory authority. Further, in California, consolidated arbitration was authorized by section 1281.3 of the Code of Civil Procedure. The court observed that Code of Civil Procedure section 1281.3 authorized consolidated arbitration even when the arbitration agreements involved provide for different procedures or methods of selecting arbitrators; the statute provides for court resolution of any such conflicts. In *Keating,* the Supreme Court described the potential situation confronting parties in consolidated arbitrations as follows: "Each contract may provide a different procedure for arbitration, or a different method of selecting the arbitrator. Federal courts have held that a court 'can mold the method of selection and the number of arbitrators to implement the consolidated proceedings.' Similarly, Code of Civil Procedure section 1281.3 provides that consolidated arbitration proceedings may be ordered inter alia, where 'one party is a party to a separate arbitration agreement or proceeding with a third party,' and that if the agreements do not mesh in their description of procedure, a court has authority to appoint an arbitrator, and to 'resolve [conflicts among the agreements] and determine the rights and duties of the various parties to achieve substantial justice under all the circumstances.' Thus, a party may be forced into a coordinated arbitration proceeding in a dispute with a party with whom he has no agreement, before an arbitrator he had no voice in selecting and by a procedure he did not agree to." The *Keating* court then contrasted the situation in a classwide arbitration as follows: "In these respects, an order for classwide arbitration in an adhesion context would call for considerably less intrusion upon the contractual aspects of the relationship. The members of a class subject to classwide arbitration would all be parties to an agreement with the party against whom their claim is asserted; each of those agreements would contain substantially the same arbitration provision; and if any of the members of the class were dissatisfied with the class representative, or with the choice of arbitrator, or for any other reason would prefer to arbitrate on their own, they would be free to opt out and do so. Moreover, the interests of justice that would be served by ordering classwide arbitration are likely to be even more substantial in some cases than the interests that are thought to justify consolidation."

The California Supreme Court concluded that "a court is not without authority" to order classwide arbitration. It held that a trial court may, in its discretion, and upon consideration of specified factors, order arbitration on a classwide basis. The California Supreme Court explained the factors to be considered as follows: "Classwide arbitration . . . must be evaluated, not in relation to some ideal but in relation to its alternatives. If the alternative in a case of this sort is to force hundreds of individual franchisees each to litigate its cause with Southland in a separate arbitral forum, then the prospect of classwide arbitration, for all its difficulties, may offer a better, more efficient, and fairer solution. Where that is so, and gross unfairness would result from the denial of opportunity to proceed on a classwide basis, then an order structuring arbitration on that basis would be justified. Whether such an order would be justified in a case of this sort is a question appropriately left to the discretion of the trial court. In making that determination, the trial court would be called upon to consider, not only the factors normally relevant to class certification, but the special characteristics of arbitration as well, including the impact upon an arbitration proceeding of whatever court supervision might be required, and the availability of consolidation as an alternative means of assuring fairness." The court recognized that classwide arbitration would require a greater degree of judicial involvement than is normally associated with arbitration. Evaluated in relation to the alternatives, however, the Supreme Court concluded that "classwide arbitration, for all its difficulties, may offer a better, more efficient, and fairer solution."

The California Supreme Court remanded *Keating* to the trial court for a determination "as to whether the interests of justice require that the order to arbitrate be conditioned upon Southland's acceptance of classwide arbitration." * * * Although *Keating* involved arbitration agreements within the purview of the act, the defendant did not contend, nor did the California Supreme Court decide, whether classwide arbitration was preempted by federal law. Upon review of *Keating,* the United States Supreme Court noted that the question whether classwide arbitration was contrary to the act was neither raised nor decided in the California Supreme Court. Hence, the United States Supreme Court held, it was without jurisdiction to resolve the question as a matter of federal law. * * *

E.   Lower Federal Court Decisions

In construing and applying the act, we are bound to follow opinions of the United States Supreme Court. * * * As noted above, however, the United States Supreme Court has never reached the question whether the act precludes classwide arbitration under state law. Further, we are not bound by lower federal court decisions construing the act.

Blue Cross argues we should adopt a United States Court of Appeals decision which barred classwide arbitration in the federal district courts absent an express agreement to arbitrate class claims. The United States Court of Appeals for the Seventh Circuit has held "that absent a provision in the parties' arbitration agreement providing for class treatment of disputes, a *[United States] district court* has no authority *[under federal law]* to certify classwide arbitration." (*Champ v. Siegel Trading Co., Inc., 55 F.3d 269 (7th Cir.1995).* The *Champ* court reasoned as follows: under section 4 of the act, a federal district court is required to enforce arbitration agreements " 'in accordance with the terms of the agreement.' 9 U.S.C. § 4;" there was nothing in the written arbitration agreements expressly providing for classwide arbitration; the act is silent on the issue of classwide arbitration; several other circuit courts had held that absent an express provision in the parties' arbitration agreement, section 4 of the act barred a district court judge or magistrate from applying the FRCP to *consolidate* arbitrations; and "[f]or a federal court to read [a classwide arbitration] term into the parties' agreement would 'disrupt [ ] the negotiated risk/benefit allocation and direct [ ] [the parties] to proceed with a different sort of arbitration.' " The *Champ* decision adopted the reasoning of other circuit Courts of Appeal with respect to consolidation of arbitrations—that absent an agreement to the contrary, section 4 of the act precludes a federal district judge or magistrate from ordering consolidation in the arbitration setting.

In *Champ* it was argued that federal class action rules applied to an arbitration subject to the act. Rule 23 of the Federal Rules of Civil Procedure authorized class actions. Rule 81(a)(3) of the Federal Rules of Civil Procedure provided that the civil rules applied to proceeding under the act "only to the extent that matters of procedure are not provided for in those statutes." Hence, it was contended that classwide arbitration could be ordered. The Seventh Circuit panel rejected that argument as follows: "First of all, Rule 81(a)(3) says that the Federal Rules fill in only those procedural gaps left open by the [act.]" But as explained above, section 4 of [the act] requires that we enforce an arbitration agreement according to its terms. Such terms conceivably could consist of consolidated or even class arbitration. The parties here did not include in their agreement an express term providing for class arbitration. Thus, one could say that through the proper application of 9 U.S.C. § 4 the [act] has already provided the type of procedure to be followed in this case, namely, non-class-action arbitration. But more to the point, we still could not accept the intervenors' assertions because by its language Rule 81(a)(3) only applies to *judicial* proceedings under the [act.] ... [N]othing in the language of Rule 81(a)(3) purports to apply the Federal Rules of Procedure to the actual proceedings on the merits before the arbitrators, which are normally regulated by the American Arbitration Association's Commercial Arbitration Rules. As the Fourth Circuit has explained it: "[a]n arbitration hearing is not a court of law. When contracting parties stipulate that disputes will be submitted to arbitration, they relinquish the right to certain procedural niceties which are normally associated with a formal trial." One of those "procedural niceties" is the possibility of pursuing a class action under Rule 23. Therefore, absent an express provision in the parties' arbitration agreement providing for class arbitration, Rule 81(a)(3) does not provide a district court with the authority to reform the parties' agreement and order the arbitration panel to hear these claims on a class basis pursuant to Rule 23.

In contrast to *Champ*, the United States Court of Appeals, First Circuit has held a district court *does* have the power to order *consolidated* arbitration where the agreement is silent as to consolidation, but *state law* specifically provides for such procedure. In *New England Energy Inc. v. Keystone Shipping Co.* (1st Cir.1988) 855 F.2d 1, 3, the First Circuit held there was "no compulsion of law or policy barring a district court from issuing [an order consolidating two arbitrations], at least when the agreement between the parties is silent and the pertinent state law specifically provides for such." That court reasoned: the act does not preempt all state law on arbitration, "only laws that would override the parties' choice to arbitrate rather than litigate in court, in direct conflict with the Act's primary purpose of ensuring the enforcement of privately negotiated arbitration agreements"; the particular state statute at issue, the Massachusetts arbitration consolidation provision, did not directly conflict with the act which says nothing about consolidation; and ordering consolidation, where the parties' contracts were silent on the subject, would not conflict with section four of the act, requiring that courts enforce arbitration agreements according to their terms; and this was because such an order would be in accordance with, rather than contradicting, the contractual terms. On the last point, the court stated as follows: "Appellee's argument . . . is not that the Act directly contradicts the Massachusetts statute, but that the state law is superseded in this case because the parties' contracts do not provide for consolidation, and an order to consolidate would therefore conflict with the requirement in section four of the federal Act that courts enforce arbitration agreements according to their terms. We disagree that ordering consolidation pursuant to a state statute when the contract is silent on the subject improperly modifies the agreement struck by the parties in violation of section four." We believe, as appellants argue, that an order not contradicting the contractual terms regarding arbitration is "in accordance with [those] terms. . . . Simply put, arbitration is still arbitration even if it is consolidated arbitration." * * *

We decline to apply the Seventh Circuit decision in *Champ* to this case. As discussed below, we conclude section 4 of the act does not preclude application of the California classwide arbitration rule. Further, we believe the First Circuit *New England Energy* decision is both analogous to our facts and better reasoned. We conclude that when the arbitration agreement between the parties is silent as to classwide arbitration and state law specifically authorizes it in appropriate cases, an order compelling classwide arbitration neither contradicts the contractual terms nor contravenes the policy behind the act.

F. Section 4 of the Act Does Not Preclude Application of the California Classwide Arbitration Rule

As discussed above, the reasoning of the federal circuit court decisions on classwide and consolidated arbitrations turns on section 4 of the act. Significantly, the United States Supreme Court has repeatedly indicated that sections 3 and 4 of the act *do not apply in state courts.* In *Southland Corp. v. Keating, supra,* 465 U.S. at page 16, footnote 10, 104 S.Ct. 852, the court stated: "In holding that the Arbitration Act preempts a state law that withdraws the power to enforce arbitration agreements, we do not hold that §§ 3 and 4 of the Arbitration Act apply to proceedings in state courts. Section 4, for example, provides that the Federal Rules of Civil Procedure apply in proceedings to compel arbitration. The Federal Rules do not apply in such state court proceedings." In *Volt Info. Sciences v. Leland Stanford Jr. U., supra,* 489 U.S. at pages 476–477, 109 S.Ct. 1248, the United States Supreme Court described an argument that sections 3 and 4 of the act were not applicable in state courts as "not without some merit," but unnecessary to reach in that case. Significantly, however, the opinion contains the following discussion: "While we have held that the [act's] 'substantive' provisions—§§ 1 and 2—are applicable in state as well as federal court, we have never held that §§ 3 and 4, which by their terms appear to apply only to proceedings in federal court, see 9 U.S.C. § 3 (referring to proceedings 'brought in any of the courts of the United States'); § 4 (referring to 'any United States district court'), are nonetheless applicable in state court. See *Southland Corp. v. Keating, supra,* at 16, n. 10, 104 S.Ct. 852 (expressly reserving the question whether §§ 3 and 4 of the Arbitration Act apply to proceedings in state courts'); see also *id.,* at 29, 104 S.Ct. 852 (O'Connor dissenting) (§§ 3 and 4 of the [act] apply only in federal court)." (*Volt Info. Sciences v. Leland Stanford Jr. U., supra,* 489 U.S. at p. 477, fn. 6, 109 S.Ct. 1248.) Further, we have reviewed the legislative history of the act and have not found anything therein that would support a conclusion Congress intended section 4 of the act to apply to the states.

Moreover, in *Rosenthal v. Great Western Financial Securities Corp.* (1996) 14 Cal.4th 394, 405–410, 58 Cal.Rptr.2d 875, 926 P.2d 1061, the California Supreme Court held the federal provision for a jury trial as to the existence of an arbitration agreement contained in section 4 of the act did not operate in California courts. Our Supreme Court examined the language of section 4 of the act. It held section 4 of the act "does not explicitly govern the procedures to be used in state courts." Section 4 of the act "contemplates a petition in 'United States district court,' and provides that certain steps are to be taken 'in the manner provided by the Federal Rules of Civil Procedure.'" The *Rosenthal* court further considered principles of federal preemption. It concluded that "a state procedural statute or rule that frustrated the effectuation of section 2's central policy would, where the federal law applied, be preempted by the [act];" however, a state procedure that serves to further, rather than defeat, " 'full and uniform effectuation of the federal law's objectives'— to ensure that arbitration agreements are enforced according to their terms—is to be followed in California, rather than section 4 of the act."
* * *

The United States Supreme Court's decision in *Volt Info. Sciences v. Leland Stanford Jr. U., supra,* 489 U.S. at pages 470 and 476, 109 S.Ct. 1248, indirectly supports our resolution of the present case. At issue in *Volt* was California Code of Civil Procedure section 1281.2, subdivision (c), which allows a court to stay arbitration pending resolution of related litigation. The contract at issue in *Volt* contained a choice of law provision which stated, " '[T]he Contract shall be governed by the law of the place where the Project is located.' " This state's Court of Appeal had interpreted the choice of law provision as an agreement to apply the state rules governing the conduct of arbitration. The United States Supreme Court found no basis for interfering with the state court's interpretation. The court held "that application of the California statute is not pre-empted by the [act] in a case where the parties have agreed that their arbitration agreement will be governed by the law of California." Of particular relevance to the present case, the court stated: "There is no federal policy favoring arbitration under a certain set of procedural rules; the federal policy is simply to ensure the enforceability, according to their terms, of private agreements to arbitrate." Further, the United States Supreme Court held: "[The act] itself contains no provision designed to deal with the special practical problems that arise in multiparty contractual disputes when some or all of the contracts at issue include agreements to arbitrate. California has taken the lead in fashioning a legislative response to this problem, by giving courts authority to consolidate or stay arbitration proceedings in these situations in order to minimize the potential for contradictory judgments." We find persuasive the United States Supreme Court's discussion in *Volt* of the preemptive effect of the act as to state procedural rules.

We conclude that section 4 does not bar state courts from ordering classwide arbitration. Therefore, it does not operate to preclude classwide arbitration under California decisional authority. Further, the California rule allowing classwide arbitration, like the statute at issue in *Rosenthal,* can further rather than defeat the act's goal of enforcing agreements to arbitrate. Therefore, California's rule permitting classwide arbitration is not preempted by section 4.

Blue Cross contends it is federal substantive law, which this court is bound to follow, that no classwide arbitration can be compelled unless the parties have expressly agreed to such procedure. We disagree. First, as discussed above, we conclude section 4 of the act does not apply in state courts to bar in all cases classwide arbitration. Second, even if it did apply, the United States Supreme Court has never held that the language of section 4 of the act providing for the issuance of a district court order "directing the parties to proceed to arbitration *in accordance with the terms of the agreement"* (9 U.S.C. § 4), means that no classwide arbitration can occur unless the parties have expressly so provided. The legislative history of the act and the decisions of the United States Supreme Court make clear that the act's preemptive scope is limited. Its purpose was to abolish anti-arbitration laws and to make agreements to arbitrate specifically enforceable. Consistent with that purpose, we believe the language "in accordance with the terms of the agreement" (9 U.S.C. § 4) means in accordance with the agreement to arbitrate. Third, under federal law, as articulated in *Champ* and the cases on which the Seventh Circuit relied, there is no authority for classwide arbitration. Under those circumstances, the *Champ* court refused to read such authority into the parties' arbitration agreement. Here, on the other hand, state law authorizes classwide arbitration. In the absence of an express agreement *not* to proceed to arbitration on a classwide basis, ordering the parties to arbitrate class claims as authorized by state law does not conflict with their contractual arrangement.

Blue Cross also contends that an order compelling classwide arbitration in this case would interfere with the parties' intentions; it asserts it bargained for individual arbitration conducted according to the rules of the American Arbitration Association (AAA), not this "hybrid" classwide arbitration requiring judicial intervention. This argument is premature. The only issue before this court is whether the *Keating* rule is preempted by the act. No order has been entered certifying a class. No order has been entered requiring classwide arbitration. Whether classwide arbitration is appropriate in this matter is a question left to the trial court's discretion upon consideration of a variety of factors. Moreover, under *Keating,* an arbitration agreement that is silent as to classwide arbitration is amenable to such procedure. Further, there has been no showing that an order compelling classwide arbitration would conflict with the agreement to proceed under AAA rules. Classwide arbitration has been held allowable in cases involving contracts to arbitrate under AAA rules, although no issue was raised as to any conflict. And even if a conflict exists between the AAA rules and classwide arbitration, the trial court may resolve the conflict. (Cf.Code Civ. Proc., § 1281.3). It is unlikely the AAA would refuse to abide by a court order for classwide arbitration. (See *Bock v. Drexel Burnham Lambert Inc.* (N.Y.Sup.Ct.1989) 143 Misc.2d 542, 541 N.Y.S.2d 172, 174) [Apparently, the AAA recognizes that consolidation may be the subject of a court order]. As discussed above, we conclude the trial court is not barred from issuing an order directing classwide arbitration when the agreement between the parties is silent and state decisional authority specifically provides for such arbitration. That the parties agreed to arbitration under AAA rules does not prevent a court from ordering arbitration on a classwide basis.

G. Conclusion

Congress's purpose in enacting the act was simple—to abolish archaic law under which courts refused to enforce arbitration agreements, and to make voluntary agreements to arbitrate disputes specifically enforceable. To that end, the act created federal substantive law requiring that arbitration agreements be enforced. That federal substantive law applies in both state and federal courts. However, Congress did not intend to occupy the entire field of arbitration. Rather, the act preempts state law only to the extent it stands as an obstacle to the enforcement of contractual agreements to arbitrate. As explained in *Southland Corp. v. Keating, supra,* 465 U.S. at page 10, 104 S.Ct. 852, "Congress ... withdrew the power of the states to require a judicial forum for the resolution of claims which the contracting parties agreed to resolve by arbitration." California decisional authority authorizing classwide arbitration *in appropriate cases:* is not preempted by the act; does not directly conflict with the act, which is silent as to classwide arbitration; does not stand as an obstacle to contractual arbitration; does not conflict with the act's purpose; does not require a judicial forum for resolving claims that the parties have agreed to arbitrate; and does not otherwise divert a case from arbitration. It does not invalidate the arbitration agreement or condition its enforceability on compliance with special rules not applicable to contracts generally. It will not produce different outcomes on the merits based solely on whether the claim is asserted in state or federal court. The *Keating* rule can facilitate the enforcement of arbitration agreements by making classwide arbitration available in appropriate cases. It can promote the expeditious resolution of cases by arbitration. In short, the federal decisional authority relied on by Blue Cross did not prevent the respondent court from permitting discovery as to whether to allow classwide arbitration and later potentially include plaintiffs to be part of the class.

ARMSTRONG and GODOY PEREZ, JJ., concur.

Notes and Questions

1. Whether California law authorizes classwide arbitration and, if so, whether the FAA preempts that procedure continues to be hotly debated. The California Supreme Court has granted review in Discover Bank v. Superior Court of Los Angeles County, 129 Cal.Rptr.2d 393 (Ct.App. 2d Dist., Div. 1 2003), review granted and opinion superseded by 65 P.3d 1285 (Cal.2003), which found that the FAA preempts any otherwise applicable California judicial law that class action waivers are substantively unconscionable and unenforceable. However, the arbitration clause involved in *Discover Bank* contained an express waiver of the right to seek a class action, which the court said distinguished it from *Blue Cross*. The court viewed the issue of classwide treatment as substantive, not procedural, therefore requiring the California courts to conform to the FAA:

> [I]t would defeat the purpose of the FAA, which was enacted primarily to ensure that arbitration agreements are enforced according to their terms, to strike the class action waiver from the agreement.... "Arbitration under the Act is a matter of consent, not coercion, and parties are generally free to structure their arbitration agreements as they see fit. Just as they may limit by contract the issues which they will arbitrate ..., so too may they specify by contract the rules under which that arbitration will be conducted." [*Volt*, at 479].... In this case, the prejudice to Discover Bank that would be caused by altering the parties' agreement is clear. As classwide arbitration in California vastly increases the scope of potential liability and damages that a defendant will face without the ability to seek judicial review of the merits of the arbitrator's decision, we conclude the decision to strike a classwide arbitration ban from a valid agreement alters substantive, and not just procedural, rights of both parties.

2. Would *Blue Cross* have reached a different opinion if the arbitration clause had denied classwide arbitration? A number of courts have found such a ban is unconscionable. See Szetela v. Discover Bank, 97 Cal.App.4th 1094, 118 Cal.Rptr.2d 862 (2002), cert. denied, 537 U.S. 1226, 123 S.Ct. 1258, 154 L.Ed.2d 1087 (2003) (class action waiver is substantively unconscionable, granting motion to certify a class in arbitration); Ting v. AT & T, 319 F.3d 1126 (9th Cir.2003); Powertel, Inc. v. Bexley, 743 So.2d 570 (Fla. Dist. Ct. App. 1st Dist. 1999); Dickler v. Shearson Lehman Hutton, Inc., 408 Pa.Super. 286, 596 A.2d 860 (1991). Federal courts have, consistent with Champ, held that unless an arbitration clause specifically provided for classwide arbitration, a court had no authority to certify class arbitration, and arbitration should proceed on an individual basis. Other courts have also found a waiver of class arbitration to be enforceable. See Zawikowski v. Beneficial Nat. Bank, 1999 WL 35304, at *1 (N.D. Ill. 1999) ("nothing prevents the Plaintiffs from contracting away their right to a class action").

GREEN TREE FINANCIAL CORP. v. BAZZLE

Supreme Court of the United States, 2003.
539 U.S. 444, 123 S.Ct. 2402, 156 L.Ed.2d 414.

Justice BREYER announced the judgment of the Court and delivered an opinion, in which Justice SCALIA, Justice SOUTER, and Justice GINSBURG join.

This case concerns contracts between a commercial lender and its customers, each of which contains a clause providing for arbitration of all contract-related disputes. The Supreme Court of South Carolina held (1) that the arbitration clauses are silent as to whether arbitration might take the form of class arbitration, and (2) that, in that circumstance, South Carolina law interprets the contracts as permitting class arbitration. 351 S.C. 244, 569 S.E.2d 349 (2002). We granted certiorari to determine whether this holding is consistent with the Federal Arbitration Act, 9 U.S.C. § 1 *et seq.*

We are faced at the outset with a problem concerning the contracts' silence. Are the contracts in fact silent, or do they forbid class arbitration as petitioner Green Tree Financial Corp. contends? Given the South Carolina Supreme Court's holding, it is important to resolve that question. But we cannot do so, not simply because it is a matter of state law, but also because it is a matter for the arbitrator to decide. Because the record suggests that the parties have not yet received an arbitrator's decision on that question of contract interpretation, we vacate the judgment of the South Carolina Supreme Court and remand the case so that this question may be resolved in arbitration.

I

In 1995, respondents Lynn and Burt Bazzle secured a home improvement loan from petitioner Green Tree. The Bazzles and Green Tree entered into a contract, governed by South Carolina law, which included the following arbitration clause:

> "ARBITRATION—All disputes, claims, or controversies arising from or relating to this contract or the relationships which result from this contract ... *shall be resolved by binding arbitration by one arbitrator selected by us with consent of you.* This arbitration contract is made pursuant to a transaction in interstate commerce, and shall be governed by the Federal Arbitration Act at 9 U.S.C. section 1.... THE PARTIES VOLUNTARILY AND KNOWINGLY WAIVE ANY RIGHT THEY HAVE TO A JURY TRIAL, EITHER PURSUANT TO ARBITRATION UNDER THIS CLAUSE OR PURSUANT TO COURT ACTION BY U.S. (AS PROVIDED HEREIN) ... The parties agree and understand that the arbitrator shall have all powers provided by the law and the contract. These powers shall include all legal and equitable remedies, including, but not limited to, money damages, declaratory relief, and injunctive relief." App. 34 (emphasis added, capitalization in original).

Respondents Daniel Lackey and George and Florine Buggs entered into loan contracts and security agreements for the purchase of mobile homes with Green Tree. These agreements contained arbitration clauses that were, in all relevant respects, identical to the Bazzles' arbitration clause.

At the time of the loan transactions, Green Tree apparently failed to provide these customers with a legally required form that would have told them that they had a right to name their own lawyers and insurance agents and would have provided space for them to write in those names. See S.C.Code Ann. § 37–10–102 (West 2002). The two sets of customers before us now as respondents each filed separate actions in South Carolina state courts, complaining that this failure violated South Carolina law and seeking damages.

In April 1997, the Bazzles asked the court to certify their claims as a class action. Green Tree sought to stay the court proceedings and compel arbitration. On January 5, 1998, the court both (1) certified a class action and (2) entered an order compelling arbitration. Green Tree then selected an arbitrator with the Bazzles' consent. And the arbitrator, administering the proceeding as a class arbitration, eventually awarded the class $10,935,000 in statutory damages, along with attorney's fees. The trial court confirmed the award, and Green Tree appealed to the South Carolina Court of Appeals claiming, among other things, that class arbitration was legally impermissible.

Lackey and the Buggses had earlier begun a similar court proceeding in which they, too, sought class certification. Green Tree moved to compel arbitration. The trial court initially denied the motion, finding the arbitration agreement unenforceable, but Green Tree pursued an interlocutory appeal and the State Court of Appeals reversed. *Lackey v. Green Tree Financial Corp.,* 330 S.C. 388, 498 S.E.2d 898 (1998). The parties then chose an arbitrator, indeed the same arbitrator who was subsequently selected to arbitrate the Bazzles' dispute.

In December 1998, the arbitrator certified a class in arbitration. The arbitrator proceeded to hear the matter, ultimately ruled in favor of the class, and awarded the class $9,200,000 in statutory damages in addition to attorney's fees. The trial court confirmed the award. Green Tree appealed to the South Carolina Court of Appeals claiming, among other things, that class arbitration was legally impermissible.

The South Carolina Supreme Court withdrew both cases from the Court of Appeals, assumed jurisdiction, and consolidated the proceedings. That court then held that the contracts were silent in respect to class arbitration, that they consequently authorized class arbitration, and that arbitration had properly taken that form. We granted certiorari to consider whether that holding is consistent with the Federal Arbitration Act.

II

The South Carolina Supreme Court's determination that the contracts are silent in respect to class arbitration raises a preliminary question. Green Tree argued there, as it argues here, that the contracts are not silent—that they forbid class arbitration. And we must deal with that argument at the outset, for if it is right, then the South Carolina court's holding is flawed on its own terms; that court neither said nor implied that it would have authorized class arbitration had the parties' arbitration agreement forbidden it.

Whether Green Tree is right about the contracts themselves presents a disputed issue of contract interpretation. The Chief Justice believes that Green Tree is right; indeed, that Green Tree is so clearly right that we should ignore the fact that state law, not federal law, normally governs such matters, see *post,* at 2408 (Stevens, J., concurring in judgment and dissenting in part), and reverse the South Carolina Supreme Court outright, see *post,* at 2410–2411 (Rehnquist, C.J., dissenting). The Chief Justice points out that the contracts say that disputes "shall be resolved . . . by one arbitrator selected by us [Green Tree] with consent of you [Green Tree's customer]." And it finds that class arbitration is clearly inconsistent with this requirement. After all, class arbitration involves an arbitration, not simply between Green Tree and a *named customer,* but also between Green Tree and *other* (represented) customers, all taking place before the arbitrator chosen to arbitrate the initial, *named customer's* dispute.

We do not believe, however, that the contracts' language is as clear as the Chief Justice believes. The class arbitrator *was* "selected by" Green Tree "with consent of" Green Tree's customers, the named plaintiffs. And insofar as the other class members agreed to proceed in class arbitration, they consented as well.

Of course, Green Tree did *not* independently select *this* arbitrator to arbitrate its disputes with the *other* class members. But whether the contracts contain this additional requirement is a question that the literal terms of the contracts do not decide. The contracts simply say (I) "selected by us [Green Tree]." And that is literally what occurred. The contracts do not say (II) "selected by us [Green Tree] to arbitrate this dispute and no other (even identical) dispute with another customer." The question whether (I) in fact implicitly means (II) is the question at issue: Do the contracts forbid class arbitration? Given the broad authority the contracts elsewhere bestow upon the arbitrator (the contracts grant to the arbitrator "all powers," including certain equitable powers "provided by the law and the contract"), the answer to this question is not completely obvious.

At the same time, we cannot automatically accept the South Carolina Supreme Court's resolution of this contract-interpretation question. Under the terms of the parties' contracts, the question—whether the agreement forbids class arbitration—is for the arbitrator to decide. The parties agreed to submit to the arbitrator *"[a]ll* disputes, claims, or controversies arising from or relating to this contract or the relationships which result from this contract." And the dispute about what the arbitration contract in each case means (*i.e.,* whether it forbids the use of class arbitration procedures) is a dispute "relating to this contract" and the resulting "relationships." Hence the parties seem to have agreed that an arbitrator, not a judge, would answer the relevant question. See *First Options of Chicago, Inc. v. Kaplan,* 514 U.S. 938, 943, 115 S.Ct. 1920, 131 L.Ed.2d 985 (1995) (arbitration is a "matter of contract"). And if there is doubt about that matter—about the " 'scope of arbitrable issues' "—we should resolve that doubt " 'in favor of arbitration.' " *Mitsubishi Motors Corp. v. Soler Chrysler–Plymouth, Inc.,* 473 U.S. 614, 626, 105 S.Ct. 3346, 87 L.Ed.2d 444 (1985).

In certain limited circumstances, courts assume that the parties intended courts, not arbitrators, to decide a particular arbitration-related matter (in the absence of "clea[r] and unmistakabl[e]" evidence to the contrary). *AT & T Technologies, Inc. v. Communications Workers,* 475 U.S. 643, 649, 106 S.Ct. 1415, 89 L.Ed.2d 648 (1986). These limited instances typically involve matters of a kind that "contracting parties would likely have expected a court" to decide. *Howsam v. Dean Witter Reynolds, Inc.,* 537 U.S. 79, 83, 123 S.Ct. 588, 154 L.Ed.2d 491 (2002). They include certain gateway matters, such as whether the parties have a valid arbitration agreement at all or whether a concededly binding arbitration clause applies to a certain type of controversy. See generally *Howsam, supra.* See also *John Wiley & Sons, Inc. v. Livingston,* 376 U.S. 543, 546–547, 84 S.Ct. 909, 11 L.Ed.2d 898 (1964) (whether an arbitration agreement survives a corporate merger); *AT & T, supra,* at 651–652, 106 S.Ct. 1415 (whether a labor-management layoff controversy falls within the scope of an arbitration clause).

The question here—whether the contracts forbid class arbitration—does not fall into this narrow exception. It concerns neither the validity of the arbitration clause nor its applicability to the underlying dispute between the parties. Unlike *First Options,* the question is not whether the parties wanted a judge or an arbitrator to decide *whether they agreed to arbitrate a matter.* Rather the relevant question here is what *kind of arbitration proceeding* the parties agreed to. That question does not concern a state statute or judicial procedures, cf. *Volt Information Sciences, Inc. v. Board of Trustees of Leland Stanford Junior Univ.,* 489 U.S. 468, 474–476, 109 S.Ct. 1248, 103 L.Ed.2d 488 (1989). It concerns contract interpretation and arbitration procedures. Arbitrators are well situated to answer that question. Given these considerations, along with the arbitration contracts' sweeping language concerning the scope of the questions committed to arbitration, this matter of contract interpretation should be for the arbitrator, not the courts, to decide. Cf. *Howsam, supra,* at 83, 123 S.Ct. 588 (finding for roughly similar reasons that the arbitrator should determine a certain procedural "gateway matter").

III

With respect to this underlying question—whether the arbitration contracts forbid class arbitration—the parties have not yet obtained the arbitration decision that their contracts foresee. As far as concerns the *Bazzle* plaintiffs, the South Carolina Supreme Court wrote that the "trial court" issued "an order granting class certification" and the arbitrator subsequently "administered" class arbitration proceedings "without further involvement of the trial court." Green Tree adds that "the class arbitration was imposed on the parties and the arbitrator by the South Carolina trial court." Respondents now deny that this was so, but we can find no convincing record support for that denial.

As far as concerns the *Lackey* plaintiffs, what happened in arbitration is less clear. On the one hand, the *Lackey* arbitrator (the same individual who later arbitrated the *Bazzle* dispute) wrote: "*I* determined that a class action should proceed in arbitration based upon *my* careful review of the broadly drafted arbitration clause prepared by Green Tree." And respondents suggested at oral argument that the arbitrator's decision was independently made.

On the other hand, the *Lackey* arbitrator decided this question after the South Carolina trial court had determined that the identical contract in the *Bazzle* case authorized class arbitration procedures. And there is no question that the arbitrator was aware of the *Bazzle* decision, since the *Lackey* plaintiffs had argued to the arbitrator that it should impose class arbitration procedures in part because the state trial court in *Bazzle* had done so. In the court proceedings below (where Green Tree took the opposite position), the *Lackey* plaintiffs maintained that "to the extent" the arbitrator decided that the contracts permitted class procedures (in the *Lackey* case or the *Bazzle* case), "it was a reaffirmation and/or adoption of [the *Bazzle* c]ourt's prior determination."

On balance, there is at least a strong likelihood in *Lackey* as well as in *Bazzle* that the arbitrator's decision reflected a court's interpretation of the contracts rather than an arbitrator's interpretation. That being so, we remand the case so that the arbitrator may decide the question of contract interpretation—thereby enforcing the parties' arbitration agreements according to their terms. 9 U.S.C. § 2; *Volt, supra,* at 478–479, 109 S.Ct. 1248.

The judgment of the South Carolina Supreme Court is vacated, and the case is remanded for further proceedings.

Justice STEVENS, concurring in the judgment and dissenting in part.

The parties agreed that South Carolina law would govern their arbitration agreement. The Supreme Court of South Carolina has held as a matter of state law that class-action arbitrations are permissible if not prohibited by the applicable arbitration agreement, and that the agreement between these parties is silent on the issue. There is nothing in the Federal Arbitration Act that precludes either of these determinations by the Supreme Court of South Carolina. See *Volt Information Sciences, Inc. v. Board of Trustees of Leland Stanford Junior Univ.,* 489 U.S. 468, 475–476, 109 S.Ct. 1248, 103 L.Ed.2d 488 (1989).

Arguably the interpretation of the parties? agreement should have been made in the first instance by the arbitrator, rather than the court.

See *Howsam v. Dean Witter Reynolds, Inc.*, 537 U.S. 79, 123 S.Ct. 588, 154 L.Ed.2d 491 (2002). Because the decision to conduct a class-action arbitration was correct as a matter of law, and because petitioner has merely challenged the merits of that decision without claiming that it was made by the wrong decisionmaker, there is no need to remand the case to correct that possible error.

Accordingly, I would simply affirm the judgment of the Supreme Court of South Carolina. Were I to adhere to my preferred disposition of the case, however, there would be no controlling judgment of the Court. In order to avoid that outcome, and because Justice Breyer's opinion expresses a view of the case close to my own, I concur in the judgment.

Chief Justice Rehnquist, with whom Justice O'Connor and Justice Kennedy join, dissenting.

The parties entered into a contract with an arbitration clause that is governed by the Federal Arbitration Act (FAA), 9 U.S.C. § 1 *et seq.* The Supreme Court of South Carolina held that arbitration under the contract could proceed as a class action even though the contract does not by its terms permit class-action arbitration. The plurality now vacates that judgment and remands the case for the arbitrator to make this determination. I would reverse because this determination is one for the courts, not for the arbitrator, and the holding of the Supreme Court of South Carolina contravenes the terms of the contract and is therefore pre-empted by the FAA.

The agreement to arbitrate involved here, like many such agreements, is terse. Its operative language is contained in one sentence:

"All disputes, claims, or controversies arising from or relating to this contract or the relationships which result from this contract ... shall be resolved by binding arbitration by one arbitrator selected by us with consent of you."

The decision of the arbitrator on matters agreed to be submitted to him is given considerable deference by the courts. The Supreme Court of South Carolina relied on this principle in deciding that the arbitrator in this case did not abuse his discretion in allowing a class action. But the decision of *what* to submit to the arbitrator is a matter of contractual agreement by the parties, and the interpretation of that contract is for the court, not for the arbitrator. As we stated in *First Options*:

"Given the principle that a party can be forced to arbitrate only those issues it specifically has agreed to submit to arbitration, one can understand why courts might hesitate to interpret silence or ambiguity on the 'who should decide arbitrability' point as giving the arbitrators that power, for doing so might too often force unwilling parties to arbitrate a matter they reasonably would have thought a judge, not an arbitrator would decide."

Just as fundamental to the agreement of the parties as *what* is submitted to the arbitrator is to *whom* it is submitted. Those are the two provisions in the sentence quoted above, and it is difficult to say that one is more important than the other. I have no hesitation in saying that the choice of arbitrator is as important a component of the agreement to arbitrate as is the choice of what is to be submitted to him.

Thus, this case is controlled by *First Options,* and not by our more recent decision in *Howsam.* There, the agreement provided that any dispute "shall be determined by arbitration before any self-regulatory organization or exchange of which Dean Witter is a member." Howsam chose the National Association of Securities Dealers (NASD), and agreed to that organization's "Uniform Submission Agreement" which provided that the arbitration would be governed by NASD's "Code of Arbitration Procedure." That code, in turn, contained a limitation. This Court held that it was for the arbitrator to interpret that limitation provision:

> " '[P]rocedural questions which grow out of the dispute and bear on its final disposition' are presumptively not for the judge, but for an arbitrator, to decide. John Wiley [& Sons, Inc. v. Livingston, 376 U.S. 543, 557, 84 S.Ct. 909, 11 L.Ed.2d 898 (1964)] (holding that an arbitrator should decide whether the first two steps of a grievance procedure were completed, where these steps are prerequisites to arbitration). So, too, the presumption is that the arbitrator should decide 'allegation[s] of waiver, delay, or a like defense to arbitrability.' "

I think that the parties' agreement as to how the arbitrator should be selected is much more akin to the agreement as to what shall be arbitrated, a question for the courts under *First Options,* than it is to "allegations of waiver, delay, or like defenses to arbitrability," which are questions for the arbitrator under *Howsam.*

"States may regulate contracts, including arbitration clauses, under general contract law principles." "[T]he interpretation of private contracts is ordinarily a question of state law, which this Court does not sit to review." But "state law may nonetheless be pre-empted to the extent that it actually conflicts with federal law—that is, to the extent that it 'stands as an obstacle to the accomplishment and execution of the full purposes and objectives of Congress.' "

The parties do not dispute that this contract falls within the coverage of the FAA. The "central purpose" of the FAA is "to ensure that private agreements to arbitrate are enforced according to their terms." In other words Congress sought simply to "place such agreements on the same footing as other contracts." This aim "requires that we rigorously enforce agreements to arbitrate," in order to "give effect to the contractual rights and expectations of the parties."

Under the FAA, "parties are generally free to structure their arbitration agreements as they see fit." Here, the parties saw fit to agree that any disputes arising out of the contracts "shall be resolved by binding arbitration by one arbitrator selected by us with consent of you." Each contract expressly defines "us" as petitioner, and "you" as the respondent or respondents named in that specific contract. (" 'We' and 'us' means the Seller *above,* its successors and assigns"; " 'You' and 'your' means each Buyer *above* and guarantor, jointly and severally." (emphasis added)). The contract also specifies that it governs all "disputes . . . arising from . . . *this* contract or the relationships which result from *this* contract." (emphasis added). These provisions, which the plurality simply ignores, make quite clear that petitioner must select, and each buyer must agree to, a particular arbitrator for disputes between petitioner and that specific buyer.

While the observation of the Supreme Court of South Carolina that the agreement of the parties was silent as to the availability of class-wide arbitration is literally true, the imposition of class-wide arbitration contravenes the just-quoted provision about the selection of an arbitrator. To be sure, the arbitrator that administered the proceedings was "selected by [petitioner] with consent of" the Bazzles, Lackey, and the Buggses. But petitioner had the contractual right to choose an arbitrator for each dispute with the other 3,734 individual class members, and this right was denied when the same arbitrator was foisted upon petitioner to resolve those claims as well. Petitioner may well have chosen different arbitrators for some or all of these other disputes; indeed, it would have been reasonable for petitioner to do so, in order to avoid concentrating all of the risk of substantial damages awards in the hands of a single arbitrator. As petitioner correctly concedes, the FAA does not prohibit parties from choosing to proceed on a class-wide basis. Here, however, the parties simply did not so choose.

"Arbitration under the Act is a matter of consent, not coercion." Here, the Supreme Court of South Carolina imposed a regime that was contrary to the express agreement of the parties as to how the arbitrator would be chosen. It did not enforce the "agreemen[t] to arbitrate . . . according to [its] terms." I would therefore reverse the judgment of the Supreme Court of South Carolina.

Justice THOMAS, dissenting.

I continue to believe that the Federal Arbitration Act (FAA), 9 U.S.C. § 1 *et seq.,* does not apply to proceedings in state courts. *Allied-Bruce Terminix Cos. v. Dobson,* 513 U.S. 265, 285–297, 115 S.Ct. 834, 130 L.Ed.2d 753 (1995) (Thomas, J., dissenting). See also *Doctor's Associates, Inc. v. Casarotto,* 517 U.S. 681, 689, 116 S.Ct. 1652, 134 L.Ed.2d 902 (1996) (Thomas, J., dissenting). For that reason, the FAA cannot be a ground for pre-empting a state court's interpretation of a private arbitration agreement. Accordingly, I would leave undisturbed the judgment of the Supreme Court of South Carolina.

Notes and Questions

1. The Supreme Court in *Bazzle* avoided issuing a long-awaited ruling on whether provisions in an arbitration clause forbidding a class action are unconscionable. Instead, the Court ruled that it is for the arbitrator, and not the court, to determine whether an arbitration may proceed as a class action when the arbitration agreement is silent on the issue. If, as expected, many

companies rewrite their arbitration clauses to expressly forbid class actions, are these likely to be upheld?

2. Following the decision in *Bazzle*, the American Arbitration Association announced that it "is not currently accepting for administration demands for class arbitration where the underlying agreement prohibits class claims, consolidation, or joinder, unless an order of a court directs the parties to the underlying dispute to present their dispute to an arbitrator or to the Association." The AAA also issued "Supplementary Rules for Class Arbitrations" (Oct. 8, 2003). See http://www.adr.org/index.

3. Are arbitrators more likely than judges to grant classwide arbitration? Are they competent to make that decision? What assistance can (or should) they obtain from a court? Can individual arbitrators perform all the necessary acts for certifying and administering class actions, or should it be done through rules of administering institutions like AAA, or through legislation (amending the FAA and state arbitration statutes) or otherwise?

4. How should a classwide arbitration class action proceed? Which aspects of judicial procedure—such as discovery, giving reasons for rulings and decisions, and judicial review on the merits—should be incorporated? Should courts make the initial decision whether to certify a class and leave the rest to the arbitrator? Or should courts provide ongoing assistance or supervision as to such matters as compelling discovery and witnesses, ruling on privileges, etc.?

5. Consider Note, Classwide Arbitration and 10B–5 Claims in the Wake of *Shearson/American Express, Inc. v. McMahon,* 74 Cornell L.Rev. 380, 401–05 (1989):

> Court approval of the classwide arbitration device requires constructing a model for how such proceedings should evolve. Arbitrating as a class will necessitate some degree of judicial intervention at the outset to allow courts to monitor the certification process. Once the class is certified, the class representative will appear before the arbitration panel as the champion of her class. Classwide arbitration, however, may sacrifice due process protections if court involvement in the proceedings decreases or ceases upon certification.

> Three options should be considered with respect to court involvement in classwide arbitration proceedings. First, the certifying court could decide interlocutory appeals on questions of the adequacy of class proceedings in arbitration. One of the judiciary's due process responsibilities is to "undertake a stringent and continuing examination of the adequacy of representation by the named class representatives at all stages of the litigation." Such appeals would surely delay the arbitration process and detract from its efficiency and economy. However, the advantages to plaintiffs of bringing 10b–5 claims as class actions remain.

> The second option may prove more protective of arbitration's efficiency. Once the court certifies the class, the arbitration can proceed without any appeals as to the adequacy of the class. Thus no judicial involvement during the arbitration will occur. To the extent that absent class members are concerned about the failure to meet any of the Rule

23(a) requirements, they can appeal these issues to the certifying court at the conclusion of the arbitration.

If a court finds, for example, that the class representative did not adequately represent the class, it can nullify the arbitration ruling as against the class. The ruling will stand with respect to the class representative, but not with respect to other plaintiffs' claims. Because the class representative would likely have arbitrated her claim individually had she not championed the class, the arbitration proceeding will have been worthwhile even if it is adjudged ineffective as against the entire class. The class members whom the court subsequently removes from the arbitration may then proceed individually or establish a new class. This model avoids court intervention during the actual arbitration, but sanctions such involvement before and after the proceedings.

The third option is arguably the most efficient method for the hybrid arbitration. This model would allow the arbitrators alone to oversee the certification process. Such a model might allay the skepticism of arbitration purists who insist that court involvement and arbitration are mutually exclusive. It is not viable, however, if courts adequately are to protect plaintiffs' interests; due process issues connected with class action aspects of classwide arbitration are simply too important to be relegated to arbitrators. While the panelists in a 10b–5 arbitration may be experts in securities regulation, they are not experts in the constitutional concerns attached to class certification. As a result, they cannot ensure the fairness of the proceedings to all absent class members.

Moreover, the FAA does not require arbitrators to give reasons or create records for their findings. Therefore, the courts' traditional outsider status in arbitration notwithstanding, court involvement must exist in the classwide arbitration setting in order to attain the optimum balance between efficiency for the parties and courts, and procedural due process for the plaintiffs.

The second option—arbitration without court involvement during the actual proceedings, but with class certification hearings at the filing of the action and a freer appeals process at the close of the arbitration—presents the most effective means of protecting all interests involved. Conceivably, intermittent appeals during the course of a classwide arbitration (the first model described above) may be too inapposite to arbitration policy to gain judicial and/or congressional approval. On the other hand, the second option supports the current arbitration process, and argues only for class action rights on both ends of arbitration proceedings. This option retains the integrity of arbitration and class action proceedings. Thus, courts will be more likely to approve the hybrid device if this model is adopted.

e. *Innovative Techniques in Arbitration*

Arbitration proceedings, pursuant to such rules as the AAA's, have followed a fairly consistent pattern for the last fifty years. The arbitrator acts much like a judge, passively listening to the evidence and argument as presented by the parties and rendering a decision, often at some later time after further study and reflection. Despite the absence of formal rules of evidence and greater informality than in courts, there has not generally been much deviation from this model.

Complex cases now coming to arbitration pose a challenge to arbitrators as they do to courts, and they have begun to result in some innovative techniques that remind us of innovative judicial management of litigation (see Chapter VI). Consider the following discussion taken from an interview concerning Professor Mnookin's service as a co-arbitrator in a $400 million dispute between IBM and Fujitsu:

MNOOKIN, BEYOND LITIGATION

23 Stanford Lawyer 5 (Spring/Summer 1989).

[The dispute] centered on IBM's claims that Fujitsu had copied IBM mainframe operating system software which was delivered to customers without copyright notice attached. Since 1978, however, IBM has registered a copyright for new releases of its system software.

In October of 1982, IBM first confronted Fujitsu with allegations that various Fujitsu programs violated IBM's intellectual property rights. In 1983, after months of negotiations, the parties entered into agreements that attempted to resolve their differences. But uncertainties about the scope of copyright protection, and ambiguities and inadequacies in the agreements, soon led to new disputes.

The 1983 agreements required arbitration of unresolved disputes. In late 1985, when IBM filed a demand for arbitration, there were literally scores of disputes involving hundreds of programs.

In the 1970s, Fujitsu elected to develop IBM-compatible mainframe computer systems, including compatible operating system software products. At the time of Fujitsu's initial decision, IBM did not claim copyright protection for its operating system software.

Both sides felt deeply aggrieved about what had happened in the past. But I think that often business people engaged in a conflict come to a point where they very much want to solve the problem. Then it can be extremely helpful if, as was true here, neutral third parties can facilitate that process, and if the lawyers representing the parties can help figure out what the problem is and how to resolve it.

IBM accused Fujitsu of wrongfully copying its software in violation of copyright laws and the 1983 agreements. On the other hand, Fujitsu accused IBM of failing to live up to provisions in the 1983 agreements for exchanging certain "external" interface information that Fujitsu believed would allow it to maintain compatibility with IBM systems.

Both companies had vital interests at stake: for IBM, the protection of billions of dollars of investment in the development of its operating systems programs; for Fujitsu, the ability to remain in the IBM-compatible operating systems software business.

There was no doubt that both companies had the resources to spend years fighting about individual computer programs. We [the two arbitrators] soon realized, however, that conventional adjudicatory hearings in which the parties would attempt to resolve their differences, program by program, through a common-law process would *not* be an efficient way to get at the core issues.

The task, as we saw it, was to provide ground rules for the future. Two fundamental questions emerged: First, to what extent could Fujitsu use information from future IBM programs to develop and maintain compatible operating system software, and for what price? And second—given Fujitsu's past use of copyrighted IBM programming material—to what extent could Fujitsu use compatible programs it had already developed as a base for its own future software development? [P]erhaps most gratifying [to me] was the opportunity to help design a process for making reasonable determinations about a complicated and evolving technology.

We did things very differently from the ordinary litigation setting. We hired our own tutor—a Carnegie–Mellon professor of computer science—to give us a four-day seminar. We invited each of the parties to send a lawyer to the tutorial. A videotape was also made, so the parties could see what information we were being fed.

We later had a number of "educational sessions" in which experts from each side were given several hours to make presentations. We'd ask questions, and receive informal instruction. There was no formal cross-examination, but the other side's experts were allowed to ask clarifying questions. They could also correct or supplement what had been said in their own later presentation.

In short, we placed much of our basic technical education outside the traditional adversarial process.

Procedural flexibility can be valuable. In this case, the parties gave the arbitration panel considerable discretion to design the process. We were able to choose different dispute settlement techniques for different problems or issues. Broadly speaking, we acted as mediators in developing the framework for the resolution, and as arbitrators in implementing that framework. In addition, we presided over meetings of responsible executives of both parties using a mini-trial format. We also held independent fact-finding meetings with customers. And we resolved some claims with "final offer" arbitration—the technique used in major league baseball to establish disputed salaries for ball players. It was a dynamic process.

Ongoing jurisdiction for the neutrals, which provides for continuity over time, is also very important. The parties in this case had an extended history of disputes. Having in place a framework for resolving future disputes helped build their confidence in particular decisions along the way.

There were two key elements to our resolution. The principal one involves the creation of a Secured Facility regime. This regime both protects IBM's intellectual property and gives Fujitsu the right to extract and use carefully specified interface information from IBM programs released during the next eight years. There are elaborate safeguards to ensure that Fujitsu uses only this specified IBM information in its software development. And, Fujitsu is required to compensate IBM fully and adequately for this access. Under our Order, Fujitsu will pay IBM between $26 million and $51 million for access to programs released in 1989. Payments for each of the subsequent years will be determined later.

The second element involves a "paid-up" license. We created the license so that Fujitsu can freely use, with immunity, its own existing software as a base for future development. Our Order issued on November 29, 1989 required Fujitsu to pay IBM $396 million for this paid-up license.

When our Order was announced in November, each company made a public statement expressing its satisfaction. I have every reason to believe that they both meant it.

We think our resolution respects and protects the vital interests of both parties. On the one hand, Fujitsu is assured that it will receive the specific interface information that provides it with a reasonable opportunity, through its independent development efforts, to maintain IBM compatibility.

IBM, on the other hand, is assured that Fujitsu is using only the specified information and that IBM will be compensated for this use— that its enormous investment in system software is being protected and respected.

And don't forget the consumer. The resolution protects the customer's investment in application programs and promotes competition.

The Secured Facility regime permits a few Fujitsu software engineers, under strict safeguards, to examine a great deal of IBM programming material. But they are permitted to extract only a limited subset of that information, as defined in "Instructions" we have issued. All the extracted information must be documented on survey sheets, which are closely reviewed for compliance. Only then may Fujitsu use the information with immunity in its independent software development.

The arrangement in effect creates a wall between the Fujitsu employees exposed to sensitive IBM information inside the Secured Facility, and those Fujitsu programmers involved in software development. The Fujitsu employees with Secured Facility access have career path restrictions: they are barred for a year thereafter from working on the development of any similar Fujitsu software.

There are other safeguards in place as well, and the arbitration panel has broad remedial authority. Finally, both companies are fully committed to the regime.

2. MINI–TRIALS

The mini-trial is not strictly speaking a trial at all, but a process that combines elements of adjudication with other processes such as negotiation and mediation. It refers to a proceeding, usually presided over by a neutral advisor, in which each side presents its case in shortened form to the Chief Executive Officers (or persons with ultimate authority over the matter and power to settle) of the parties as a prelude to settlement negotiations between them. The term is sometimes incorrectly used to refer to any form of shortened or summarized trial (rather than using the more specific titles, such as "summary jury trial" or "court-annexed arbitration"). The "mini-trial" was created for disputes involving corporate parties and has been primarily conducted by private organizations and governmental entities.

Often litigated matters result from business arrangements that have failed in some way, and the corporate managers therefore shy away from them. Whether or not the corporate manager who oversees the litigation was personally responsible for the matter that is in litigation, he is unlikely to advance his career through continued association with that unhappy episode. Hence the tendency to leave the matter to the lawyers; if the case turns out unsuccessfully, the result can be blamed on them. Throughout the litigation the lawyers are likely to have to combat this tendency in order to force the client to take some responsibility for the conduct of the case. By shifting the responsibility for the outcome back to the client, advocates of the mini-trial argue, it can perform an important function. The process also directly involves the decision-makers who have settlement authority in the settlement process.

When mini-trial treatment is proposed, the parties may be expected to work out an agreement providing for specific procedures. For an example, see E. Green, The CPR Legal Program Mini–Trial Handbooks in Corporate Dispute Management 111–14 (1981), which not only lays out ground rules on presentations, but also includes a schedule calling for trial within six weeks, and only two weeks for discovery. The mini-trial itself is projected to last 2 1/2 days: plaintiff's case-in-chief on the first afternoon, defendant's rebuttal and plaintiff's response on the following morning, defendant's case-in-chief on the second afternoon, and plaintiff's rebuttal and defendant's response on the second morning. Question and answer sessions for the neutral advisor are interspersed throughout, and the third afternoon is reserved for negotiations without the advisor. If a settlement is not reached, the advisor may be summoned back to participate in negotiations.

Advantages of the mini-trial include flexibility for the parties to select their own time table, location, rules and procedures, and neutral advisor; the benefit of directing presentations to the decision-making officials; and the salutary role of a respected neutral advisor in going beyond the power of a judge to ask questions and provide reality-testing. Disadvantages include the cost in contrast to litigation where court services are paid by the public; the absence of the sometimes beneficial aura of a court; the closing of disputes to the public and the press; and possible undesirable effects on the regular judiciary when judges may leave for more lucrative fees in private cases and wealthy litigants can judge-shop while others cannot.

GREEN, GROWTH OF THE MINI–TRIAL
9 Litigation No. 1 at 12, 17–18 (Fall 1982).

A newspaper headline writer coined the term "mini-trial," but the mini-trial is not really a trial at all-mini, midi, or maxi. The mini-trial is a carefully structured and refined method that enables the principals in a dispute to settle the merits. In its most familiar form, the mini-trial blends selected characteristics of the adjudicative process with arbitration, mediation, and negotiation.

The typical mini-trial contains only one of the two features of a trial: after a short period of pretrial preparation, the lawyers (and their experts, if desired) make informal, abbreviated, and confidential presentations of each side's best case. The mini-trial drops the second main feature of a trial: no third party pronounces judgment. The most distinctive characteristic of the mini-trial is that the lawyers present their cases not to a judge, an arbitrator, a jury, or any other third party with the power to make a binding decision, but rather to the principals themselves.

In the classic mini-trial with corporations involved, the principals are business executives with settlement authority. The lawyers design their presentations to give the parties a clear and balanced conception of the strengths and weaknesses of the positions on both sides. In other words, the principals receive a crash course on the subject of the dispute conducted in an informal setting but through the adversary process. The purpose of the presentation phase is to exchange information. The principals enter confidential settlement negotiations immediately afterwards.

In the classic format, mini-trials have been presided over by a jointly selected "neutral adviser." The adviser moderates the proceedings, poses questions, and highlights crucial facts and issues. But during the presentation phase, he does not preside like a judge, an arbitrator, or even a mediator. If the principals do not reach settlement quickly after the information exchange, they may ask the neutral adviser to give a nonbinding opinion about how a judge or a jury would decide the case and why. With these views in hand, the parties then resume direct negotiations.

The mini-trial is not arbitration, a close relation with which it is often confused. Unlike the mini-trial, arbitration is characterized by a final, binding result (often a compromise) announced by a third party after formal and complete presentation by trial lawyers for each side, with little or no participation by the clients.

Selection of the neutral adviser is easier than selection of an arbitrator because his opinion is not binding. This reduces the pressure on the parties. When they select an arbitrator, they think they must find one who will be predisposed to their point of view, or at least not lean to the other side. For a mini-trial to work, however, both parties must respect the neutral adviser. The parties should select the best and most respected neutral they can find. There is no point in maneuvering for advantage. It is interesting how quickly parties with this perspective (rather than the adjudicative point-of-view) identify qualified people to serve as the neutral adviser.

* * *

If the mini-trial offers so many advantages over traditional litigation and settlement, why not write a mini-trial clause into contracts? Some have done so in international joint ventures as well as in the coal grievance program.

But are such clauses enforceable? Since the mini-trial is so new, there is no authority on point. Opinions differ. Some lawyers believe a mini-trial clause would not be specifically enforceable. Settlement of a dispute is voluntary, so the failure of one party to perform an agreed mini-trial does not damage the other party except to the extent of any expenses incurred in preparation for mini-trial. In fact, if the breaching party has decided not to settle, its anticipatory breach will save the other party the time and expenses of a futile process.

On the other hand, it may be possible to specifically enforce a mini-trial clause by setting forth the procedures to be followed at the mini-trial in detail. That would make the court's job of supervising performance far easier. And a step-by-step process of negotiation may not prove to be futile.

There is a persuasive argument that mini-trial clauses should be enforceable. In California, a mini-trial obligation appears to be the type of obligation that is specifically enforceable. *See* Cal.Civil Code §§ 3384, 3390. Furthermore, the closest relative to the mini-trial is arbitration. Neither the California Arbitration Statute (Code of Civil Procedure § 1280 *et seq.*) nor the Federal Arbitration Act (9 U.S.C.A. § 1) defines the term "arbitration." Both the federal and state laws provide for specific enforceability of arbitration provisions. *See* Cal.Code Civ.Proc. § 1281; 9 U.S.C.A. § 2. The courts might enforce mini-trial clauses, given the liberal view toward enforceability of arbitration clauses and the general judicial attitude to clearing calendars.

Note and Questions

1. Given the possibility of molding arbitration to suit the parties' desires, why is there any impetus toward the mini-trial approach? The principal advantage of the mini-trial has been said to be to return responsibility for the outcome to the corporate managers. The suggestion is that the lawyers usurp the power as part of the litigation process; due to their familiarity with the litigation system and their immersion in the case there

is no doubt that the lawyers tend to receive a great deal of responsibility for litigated matters. There is a sense, however, in which this process is encouraged by the corporate managers themselves. Often litigated matters result from business arrangements that have failed in some way, and the businessmen therefore shy away from them. Whether or not the corporate manager who oversees the litigation was personally responsible for the matter that is in litigation, he is unlikely to advance his career through continued association with that unhappy episode. Hence the tendency to leave the matter to the lawyers; if the case turns out unsuccessfully, the result can be blamed on them. Throughout the litigation the lawyers are likely to have to combat this tendency in order to force the client to take some responsibility for the conduct of the case. By shifting the responsibility for the outcome back to the client, the mini-trial performs an important function.

2. Does the mini-trial really offer hope of serving as a dispute resolution device that could replace traditional litigation in complex cases? It reflects corporate unwillingness to make this process binding and thereby to surrender the right to resort to the courts for ultimate satisfaction if the parties cannot agree. What changes in procedure would be necessary to persuade them to agree to be bound? Paradoxically, the resulting procedure would probably look a great deal like our existing litigation process.

3. RENT–A–JUDGE PROGRAMS

Frustration with the court system—and especially with its delay and inconvenience in terms of place and time settings—has led to agreements between parties to hold a private trial before a person hired by them, often a retired judge. In what have come to be known as "rent-a-judge trials," procedures are agreed to by the parties—often using some court procedures and tailor-making other procedures to the needs of the particular case.

In a number of states, statutes have been passed authorizing and laying down standards for "rent-a-judge trials." The best known is California's, which allows the parties to petition the court for an order or reference to a referee selected and paid by the parties, thereby bypassing the litigation system. West's Ann.Cal.Code Civ.Proc. §§ 638–645. Only the petition and any judgment are made public, thus assuring the parties confidentiality, but the court's process may be used to compel attendance of witnesses and jurors. The parties select a referee and agree on procedures for the case. The referee files a report with the trial court which has the same effect as findings of a trial court, and upon which judgment may be entered. See also Texas Civ.Prac. & Rem.Code Ann., § 151.001 et seq. (Vernon 1987) (providing procedures for trial by "special judges").

Advantages of rent-a-judge trials include the ability of parties to select their own time and place for trial without being at the mercy of the court calendar; the greater flexibility of private judges as to time schedules and recesses; the ability of the parties to agree on the person who will serve as judge; the possibility of tailoring the rules and procedures that will be followed to the case; and the confidentiality that would not be possible in a trial.

Notes and Questions

1. Consider the following policy questions concerning the propriety of "rent-a-judge programs" in Hall, *Opening Statement,* 9 Litigation 1, 59 (Winter 1983):

> 1. Should litigants with sufficient funds be able to buy their way to the head of the line to obtain a prompt judgment, while poorer parties must wait through months and years of judicial proceedings?

> 2. Will the possibility of judge shopping available to parties with funds to rent-a-judge favor the wealthy litigants unfairly?

> 3. Will the rent-a-judge procedure have undesirable effects on the regular judiciary, such as encouraging retirements into this more lucrative profession?

> 4. Will there be any undesirable effects on the independence of the retired judges who sell their time, such as prolonging proceedings to raise their fees or showing bias in favor of the party most likely to refer the next case?

> 5. Should we be concerned about secret trials that are closed to the public and the press?

Do these objections also apply to complex litigation, which often involves wealthy parties on both sides? See also Note, The California Rent-a-Judge Experiment: Constitutional and Policy Considerations of Pay-As-You-Go Courts, 94 Harv.L.Rev. 1592 (1981).

2. Rent-a-judge programs have also been criticized as violating due process, equal protection, and the First Amendment. See Gnaizda, Secret Justice for the Privileged Few, 66 Judicature 6 (1982). As we have seen, however, states are often required to enforce agreements to arbitrate. Is it consistent to suggest that states may not create or assist through the judicial process a privately-financed alternative to in-court litigation?

3. A number of for-profit organizations provide the services of former judges for private-judging and other ADR processes such as arbitration and mediation. The largest is the Judicial Arbitration & Mediation Services, Inc. (JAMS). Others that provide the services of judges, as well as attorneys and law professors, include Judicate, Inc., Endispute, and United States Arbitration & Mediation, Inc. See Varchaver, Dispute Resolution, The American Lawyer 60 (April 1992).

4. INDUSTRY–WIDE CLAIMS SETTLEMENT THROUGH A SUBSCRIBER FACILITY: THE ASBESTOS CLAIMS AGREEMENT

Another approach to alternative dispute resolution has emerged from the litigation involving exposure to asbestos. Claims arising out of exposure to asbestos have created perhaps the largest single source of litigation in history. In an effort to find a better way to resolve asbestos claims than litigation offered, representatives of manufacturers and their insurance companies began meeting in 1983 with leading claimants' attorneys. The result was an agreement creating the Asbestos Claims Facility to administer and arrange for the evaluation and possible settlement of all asbestos-related claims against the subscriber companies. The work of the Facility, its ultimate demise, and the creation of a new Center for Claims Resolution are described in an article by Lawrence Fitzpatrick, the President of the Center.

FITZPATRICK, THE CENTER FOR CLAIMS RESOLUTION

53 Law & Contemp.Probs. 13–23 (Autumn 1990).

On June 19, 1985, thirty-two producers of asbestos or asbestos containing products ("producers") and sixteen insurers ("insurers") signed an agreement concerning mass resolution of asbestos-related claims. This Agreement is known as the Wellington Agreement because of the role played by Harry Wellington, then-Dean of the Yale University Law School, as a facilitator in the negotiations between the producers and the insurers. The Wellington Agreement resolved dozens of actual and potential lawsuits between the producers and their insurers over insurance coverage for asbestos losses. The agreement also established a nonprofit organization, the Asbestos Claims Facility ("the Facility"), to administer and arrange for the evaluation, settlement, payment, or defense of all asbestos-related personal injury claims against subscribing producers and insurers.

The Facility began handling claims for its members in September 1985. During the initial stages of operation, it operated through employees borrowed from its members. The Facility began hiring permanent staff during the spring of 1986 and was fully staffed and operational by August 1986.

Despite serious structural problems, the Facility achieved several significant accomplishments in its three years of existence. First, it dramatically increased the number of asbestos claims resolved. As best can be determined from historical records, Facility members resolved approximately 6,000 claims in the ten-plus years of asbestos litigation that preceded the creation of the Facility. In its three years of operation, the Facility disposed of more than 18,500 asbestos claims. While some criticized the Facility for not settling claims fast enough and far enough in advance of trial, the Facility clearly increased the disposition rate of asbestos claims by a substantial margin.

The Facility also implemented programs to deal with asbestos claimants who show signs of exposure to asbestos, but who do not show signs of impairment as a result of that exposure. Prior to the inception of the Facility, such claimants often were forced to file lawsuits to avoid being barred by statutes of limitations, and they ultimately ended their lawsuits by compromising their claims for relatively nominal amounts. Claimants who subsequently developed serious asbestos-related illness often found themselves precluded from additional compensation because of their prior settlements. The Facility instituted "Green Card" and "Pleural Registry" programs for such claimants. Under these programs, the Facility waived the limitation periods and placed the claims on inactive status. If a claimant subsequently became impaired from asbestos exposure, the claimant could seek full compensation for the injury. In its three years of existence, the Facility recorded over 5,500 such dispositions. During the first half of 1988, the number of such cases placed on inactive status exceeded the number of cash settlements.

The Facility also reduced the transactional costs associated with the processing of asbestos claims. Before the Facility was created, approximately 1,100 law firms represented asbestos defendants nationwide. Upon inception, the Facility reduced this number to sixty-three and later reduced the number to fifty-five. While quantifying the exact amount of savings attributable to the Facility is difficult because the volume of the asbestos problem significantly increased after the Facility was created, the Facility clearly saved its members substantial sums in defense costs by limiting the number of law firms in the overall defense effort. The Wellington Agreement prohibited cross-claims and third-party complaints among Facility members, thus saving additional transaction costs.

Finally, from the perspective of its members, the Facility materially improved the trial results in those cases that were tried to a verdict. Before the Facility was created, the defendants prevailed in approximately 28 percent of the cases that went to verdict. In the remaining cases, the plaintiffs' average award was approximately $600,000. With the creation of the Facility and centralization of the defense of its members in one law firm per jurisdiction, the Facility defendants prevailed in approximately 65 percent of the cases that proceeded to verdict, and the average adverse verdict was approximately $330,000.

Since its inception, however, the Facility was plagued by three serious structural problems that eventually led to its dissolution. [These included disputes over calculation of each company's share of the settlements; the one-company-one-vote rule of governance that "allowed members with small shares to combine and out-vote members with larger shares;" and differences in claims-handling philosophies and whether to litigate claims perceived to be meritless. A number of the producer members withdrew, and a majority of the remaining members voted to dissolve it effective October 3, 1988.]

Contemporaneously with the dissolution of the Facility, twenty-one companies announced the creation of the Center for Claims Resolution. While the twenty-one founders of the new claims-handling organization are all former members of the Facility, the Center is neither a continuation of nor successor to the Facility. It is independently funded and operated. Unlike the Facility, insurance companies are not members of the Center. However, virtually all insurers that were formerly members of the Facility and whose policyholders joined the Center have signed an agreement to support the Center's operational costs.

In an effort to eliminate the major structural problems that had plagued the Facility, the Center differs from the Facility in several respects. First, the Center has a much more flexible sharing formula for liability payments and expenses, which determines producer shares across four different time periods and a dozen occupational categories. * * *

Second, in response to the governance problem, the Center weights members' votes according to each member's share of liability and expenses. Unlike the Facility, the Center thus strikes a balance between the right of each member to have a vote and the substantial disparity in the financial participation of its members.

Finally, all members of the Center have agreed to a claims-handling philosophy providing for the early resolution of meritorious asbestos claims. According to this philosophy, the Center will attempt to settle all meritorious claims on the Trial List significantly before the scheduled trial date. A substantial portion of the Center's estimated annual indemnity payments also will be used to resolve non-Trial List asbestos claims that further the goals of the Center and reduce the backlog of asbestos claims pending against its members.

The Center is focusing on the following goals and objectives for the asbestos claims of its members: (1) early resolution of meritorious asbestos claims; (2) resistance and, if necessary, litigation of nonmeritorious asbestos claims; (3) establishment and maintenance of credibility with the judiciary, claimants, members of the plaintiffs' bar, and the public; (4) development of appropriate short-term and long-term strategic plans to fulfill the mission of the Center while maintaining the flexibility to respond to changing circumstances; (5) reduction of allocated legal expenses through internalization of functions currently performed by outside counsel, while maintaining quality representation; (6) reduction of unallocated operating expenses through increased efficiency and productivity within the Center; and (7) attraction, development, and retention of high quality professional and support staff.

To achieve these goals and objectives, the Center will take various actions. As mentioned above, the Center will dispose of all appropriate asbestos claims on the Trial List in a timely and cost-effective manner, and of non-Trial List asbestos claims that further the goals of the Center and reduce the backlog of asbestos claims pending against its members. The Center also will resolve asbestos claims at a level that accurately reflects the exposures of the Center's members, and will continue and expand non-cash disposition programs, such as Pleural Registries and Green Cards. The filing of nonmeritorious asbestos claims will be resisted, and more creative and innovative methods to dispose of asbestos claims will be developed. Finally, to meet its goals and objectives, the Center will develop training programs for Claims Division personnel.

The Center also will dramatically reduce its aggregate defense expenses by (1) internalizing numerous claims-handling functions, currently performed by outside counsel, that can be more efficiently and cost-effectively performed by the Center's staff; (2) achieving the early disposition of all meritorious claims on the Trial List; and (3) participating initially in counsel-sharing arrangements with various non-members.

To deal effectively with the asbestos problem over time, the Center also will devote resources to achieving long-term goals. Among the long-term goals to be addressed by the Center are:

1. *Processing of claims, not lawsuits.* The Center will institute programs to resolve asbestos claims that have not yet been filed as lawsuits. The Center's staff will receive claims directly from claimants, and will conduct an investigation and secure an appropriate independent medical examination whenever necessary. At the close of the investigation, an evaluation and negotiation period will commence. The claim will be settled for a fair value or denied as nonmeritorious. Alternative dispute resolution mechanisms will be utilized for those claims with a genuine dispute as to value.

2. *Independent medical examinations.* The Center will consider the development of a network of independent physicians to perform medical examinations of claimants. These physicians would examine the patient, provide evaluations based on a standard protocol, and submit reports in a predetermined format. Members of the network would not be used as trial experts, thereby enhancing their credibility with, and acceptability to, the plaintiffs' bar. The Center has received a preliminary study of the feasibility of establishing such a network of examining physicians with various specialties.

3. *New uses of Green Cards.* The Center will attempt to expand the Green Card deferral programs that were successfully used by the Facility. For example, the Center may offer a Green Card with a promise to investigate and to attempt to negotiate a resolution of a claim within a specified period upon manifestation of an asbestos-related disease.

4. *Encouragement of limited releases.* With the expansion of the Green Card program, the Center will consider encouraging the use of limited releases. For example, in cases not involving malignancies, the claimant would be offered a limited release and would be encouraged to settle for a reduced dollar amount. Should a malignancy subsequently develop, the claimant would then be allowed to present another claim.

5. *Improved relationships with unions.* With the other long-term programs proposed by the Center, including the program of independent examinations, the Center will develop an effective program for dealing with the unions representing potential claimants. Such a program would explain the Center's various programs and detail its claims-handling philosophy.

6. *Branch legal offices in target regions.* On an as-needed basis, the Center will consider establishing small branch legal offices in target regions to handle routine litigation functions. The development of these branch offices would greatly reduce allocated defense expenses in high-volume areas, while not sacrificing quality legal representation.

7. *Improved communication with the judiciary, press, and plaintiffs' bar.* The Center will develop a program of affirmative, rather than reactive or defensive, public relations. In so doing, it is contemplated that the Center will initiate periodic meetings with judges and with plaintiffs' counsel to solicit their input about its programs.

8. *Cancer insurance or life insurance programs.* The Center will consider the implementation of a program that would provide life insurance as a means of disposing of claims. Such insurance could be triggered to pay proceeds upon confirmation or diagnosis of a malignancy. The Center would need to find an insurance company willing to provide a product resembling group-life insurance. In exchange for the policy, the Center would pay a premium for each nonmalignancy case that is settled.

* * *

The Center does not settle asbestos claims pursuant to a predetermined schedule of benefits. The Center staff analyzes each asbestos claim individually and makes what it considers to be a fair offer on behalf of its members. In analyzing asbestos claims, the Center staff considers several factors, including the severity of the disease, the degree to which Center members contributed to the disease process relative to contributions by nonmembers, and legal trends in the jurisdiction where the claim has been filed.

The Center's analysis of each claim on an individual basis does not preclude it from settling asbestos claims in blocks or groups. The vast majority of the claims settled to date have been disposed of in group fashion after the Center staff reviewed each claim individually. Given the scope of the asbestos problem, the Center sees no practical alternative to this approach.

Although the Center readily accepts claims filed by unrepresented claimants, more than 99 percent of the claims currently being handled by the Center involve claimants represented by counsel. Since the Center membership nearly always represents only a relatively small percentage of the total causation in any given claim, and since the claimant probably will have to proceed in the tort system against recalcitrant nonmembers who refuse to settle, the Center does not anticipate this situation changing in the foreseeable future.

The Center staff typically negotiates settlements directly with counsel for the claimants. In a few jurisdictions, however, outside attorneys negotiate for the Center. The relationship between the Center staff and the asbestos plaintiffs' bar can be fairly characterized as "friendly adversaries." Compared to history and to the current positions of most non-Center producers, the Center staff has engaged in unprecedented dialogue with the attorneys representing asbestos claimants.

During the first four months of its existence, the Center made several positive strides. First, it disposed of more than 12,300 claims. By way of comparison, as noted above, there were approximately 6,000 total dispositions in the ten-plus years of asbestos litigation before the Facility was created, and the Facility disposed of approximately 18,500 claims in its three years of existence.

Second, the Center has resolved the 12,300 claims at average values that compare very favorably with the historical shares of its members in settlements, both before and during the existence of the Facility.

Third, the Center has decreased the backlog of asbestos claims pending against its members. Approximately 61,000 claims were pending against Center members when the Center commenced operation in October 1988. By January 31, 1989, the Center had reduced that number to 57,000, despite an increase in new filings during the period. Of the 57,000 pending claims, approximately 8,000 (14 percent) were from nontraditional occupations, which the Center did not intend to settle in the same manner as traditional claims. Furthermore, approximately 36,000 of the pending claims (63 percent) represented claims filed from 1987 through 1989. Thus, the Center made substantial progress in settling the older, more meritorious claims against its members.

Fourth, the Center has managed to limit the number and amount of adverse trial verdicts against its members. As best the Center can determine, there have been adverse verdicts against non-Center producers in excess of $240 million since the breakup of the Facility. The Center, in contrast, has been forced to go to verdict only a handful of times during the last four months and has generally prevailed at trial or received relatively small adverse verdicts.

Fifth, the Center also has limited its members' defense costs. Most producers who chose not to join the Center have at least informally admitted that their defense costs have roughly doubled since the demise of the Facility. The Center has held defense costs constant for its members and is implementing plans to reduce defense costs substantially in the future.

Finally, the Center has avoided the recent judicial trend to certify class actions or mass consolidations. Although several judges have recently certified such actions, none has yet been certified against any Center members.

Notes and Questions

1. The Asbestos Claims Facility provided one example of an administrative alternative to litigation accomplished by agreement between plaintiffs and certain asbestos companies. Bankruptcy courts have also utilized trust and claim facility mechanisms where companies have filed for reorganization

under Chapter 11. See the discussion of the first major claimant trust resulting from the Johns–Manville bankruptcy, including the court's handling of a payment crisis caused by too rapid payments to claimants with less serious conditions, *supra* pp. 213–14. See also the discussion of the Dalkon Shield claimant fund, which avoided some of the problems seen in the Manville bankruptcy, *supra* pp. 215–16.

2.   The proposed settlement of claims against Dow Corning for injuries allegedly caused by silicone breast implants contemplated an elaborate trust mechanism, with schedules of payments according to different degrees of injury and alternative dispute procedures. See *supra* p. 216. The problem was that there were many more claimants than had been expected, and the payouts had to be reduced. The result was a large number of opt-outs that undermined the settlement and precipitated Dow Corning's filing for Chapter 11 protection.

B. JUDICIAL MECHANISMS

One of the more creative developments in judicial administration has been the creation of mechanisms for getting parties to submit to a non-binding "trial run" in hopes that it will lead to settlement. Trial runs may also serve as a framework for focusing the issues, narrowing and weeding out evidence, and structuring the final trial. Encouraging settlement, long a task performed by judges, inevitably involves some sort of summary evaluation of the relative merits of the cases which is conveyed to the parties to encourage them to move towards a settlement. A more formalized, court-administered "trial run" has the advantage of reducing the capacity of a judge to be arbitrary or biased in his assessments and thus unfairly to pressure parties into settlement. It may also ensure more certainty by giving the parties a better idea of how the evidence is likely to be received at trial.

There are many possible objections to trial runs—even if they are non-binding. If parties are required to engage in a trial run too early in the litigation process—as when discovery is still incomplete or issues not yet fully focused—it may result in unfair pressures to settle when parties still lack a full appreciation of their cases. And even if only invoked just before trial, a trial run substitutes a truncated presentation of evidence for the normal trial with live witness testimony which we have come to believe is an important part of American judicial due process. The discussions of the various techniques which follow will help to evaluate both the merits and demerits of these experimental attempts.

The Civil Justice Reform Act of 1990, 104 Stat 5089, required each federal district court to create a broadly based commission to recommend procedures to deal with cost and delay in litigation, and specifically to consider the use of ADR. The Act also called for a report on the experience resulting from a study of ten pilot district court programs. In 1996, a five-year-long study conducted by the Rand Institute for Civil Justice concluded that many CJRA-inspired reforms had done little to reduce cost or delay. Mediation and mandatory arbitration, for example, yielded no significant decrease in litigation costs, resolution time or attorney satisfaction. A few reforms, however, were found to show promise. Perhaps the most encouraging finding was that a combination of techniques could reduce the time to case disposition by as much as 30 percent. The combination consisted of setting trial dates early, having litigants at settlement conferences or available by phone, reducing discovery time, and having judges manage cases soon after filing. See J. Kakalik, et al., An Evaluation of Mediation and Early Neutral Evaluation Under the Civil Justice Reform Act (1997); J. Kakalik, et al., An Evaluation of Judicial Case Management Under the Civil Justice Reform Act (1997).

A statement issued by the CRP Institute for Dispute Resolution stated that the Rand ADR findings must be understood in the specific context of the six ADR programs studied (four of the ten pilot programs did not include ADR). It maintained that the four mediation programs and two neutral evaluation programs examined were not representative of the 51 mediation and 14 neutral evaluation programs now operating in the federal district courts. In addition, the programs studied were new and examined early, either before or as program refinements were underway. In several of the courts studied, substantial revisions to the ADR programs were made after the Rand data were collected. After reviewing these issues in its Final Report on the CJRA Experience, the U.S. Judicial Conference supported continued use of ADR, but not a nationwide requirement for specific programs. See Judicial Conference, Civil Justice Reform Act: Final Report, 175 F.R.D. 62, 99–102 (1997).

1. SUMMARY JURY TRIALS

The summary jury trial is an abbreviated proceeding in which the lawyers are given an opportunity to summarize their cases before a jury empanelled by the court. A judge or magistrate presides, but evidentiary and procedural rules are not applied with the strictness that would be true in a real trial. A number of courts have experimented with such trials, and require resort to a summary jury trial before going to trial in certain classes of cases.

U.S. District Judge Thomas Lambros, of the Northern District of Ohio, inaugurated the use of summary jury trials in 1981. See Lambros, The Summary Jury Trial and Other Alternative Methods of Dispute Resolution, 103 F.R.D. 461 (1984); Lambros, Summary Jury Trial—An Alternative Method of Resolving Disputes, 69 Judicature 286 (1986). His model of a summary jury trial allows each attorney one hour to describe his party's position to a six-person jury, after which the judge or magistrate delivers a brief statement to the jury of the applicable law. The jury is then encouraged to return a consensus verdict, but may instead return a special verdict anonymously listing each juror's findings on liability and damages. In complex cases the jury may be asked to make rulings on separate issues. After the jury returns, counsel meet with the judge to discuss the verdict and establish a timetable for settlement negotiations. See M. Jacoubovitch & C. Moore, Summary

Jury Trials in the Northern District of Ohio (Federal Judicial Center 1982).

A summary jury trial is usually scheduled only after completion of discovery. Lambros, *supra,* 103 F.R.D. at 470 ("the case must substantially be in a posture for trial" and "discovery must be complete and there must be no motions pending"). Counsel generally use summaries of evidence from depositions and other discovery, and time constraints severely limit the possibility of live witness testimony. Compare Lambros, *supra,* at 471 ("No testimony is taken from sworn witnesses. Counsel simply summarize the anticipated testimony of trial witnesses and are free to present exhibits to the jury.") with Model Stipulated Order for Conditional Summary Trial, U.S.Dist.Ct., D.Mass., issued by Judge Robert Keeton (counsel may present evidence in narrative form, question and answer form, or argument on the facts and law).

Although held in a courtroom, the summary jury trial is usually closed to the public. In Cincinnati Gas & Elec. Co. v. General Elec. Co., 117 F.R.D. 597 (S.D.Ohio 1987), aff'd, 854 F.2d 900 (6th Cir.1988), the district court denied newspapers access to a summary jury trial. The newspapers argued that trials are public events, but the judge rejected the analogy (117 F.R.D. at 601):

> Because the purpose of the summary jury trial is settlement by means of giving the parties insights into the strengths and weaknesses of their case, the proceedings are markedly different. * * * As a matter of necessity, not all of the evidence that would be presented at trial will be covered by the summary proceeding. No live testimony and, thus, no testing of credibility or cross-examination of witnesses, is permitted. Moreover, given the flexibility of this procedure, the summary jury trial in the case deals with only selected issues; others, that will be tried on the merits if this case goes to trial, are simply omitted from the procedure for the sake of simplicity and to focus on those issues that appear to be central to any meaningful settlement discussions in this case.* * * We readily agree that we attempt to have the proceeding mimic trial procedures to the degree possible, but this effort does not detract from the stated goal of settlement; to the contrary, the realism of the procedure is key to successful functioning.

The appellate court affirmed, concluding that "at every turn the summary jury trial is designed to facilitate pretrial settlement of the litigation, much like a settlement conference." 854 F.2d at 904. It rejected the argument that public access would have "community therapeutic value because of the importance of the nuclear power and utility rate issues raised," concluding that public access would be detrimental to facilitating settlement. Id. Judge Edwards dissented in part, stating that since the summary jury trial resembles "both settlement negotiations and a bench trial," the record could not be sealed after settlement. Id. at 905.

Notes and Questions

1.   It appears that summary jury trial procedures have resulted in settlement in a large proportion of cases by creating a greater incentive to settle than do other pre-trial procedures. See Lambros, The Judge's Role in Fostering Voluntary Settlements, 29 Vill. L. Rev. 1363, 1377 (1984) (claiming 90% success rate); Note, Summary Jury Trials and Mock Trials, 24 Tort & Ins. L.J. 563 (1989).

2.   Can a complex case be presented adequately to a jury in half a day? If so, why must trials go on so long? Does the summary jury trial process unfairly disadvantage the party with the burden of proof by severely restricting trial time and exposure to the jury? Can a summarized presentation provide an accurate "trial run?" Compare Posner, The Summary Jury Trial and Other Methods of Alternate Dispute Resolution: Some Cautionary Observations, 53 U.Chi.L.Rev. 366 (1986), and Brunet, Questioning the Quality of Alternative Dispute Resolution, 62 Tulane L.Rev. 1 (1987) (questioning the value of summarized presentations and ability to judge credibility), with Sherman, Reshaping the Lawyer's Skills for Court–Supervised ADR, 51 Tex.Bar J. 47 (1988) (effective summarization can utilize deposition cross-examination and accurately convey the heart of a case).

3.   Unlike a number of the extra-judicial ADR procedures which are voluntary but binding, the summary trial may be mandatory but is not binding. Does the fact that it is not binding really remove any concern as to its impact on due process?

4.   Two provisions in the Federal Rules of Civil Procedure can be used to authorize summary trial procedures. Under amended Rule 16(c)(7), a pretrial conference can be used to provide the parties a "trial run" assessment of their cases and to encourage them to agree to an ADR method. Judge Robert E. Keeton of the District of Massachusetts has invited the principal decision-makers on each side to a pretrial conference at which the issues and strengths of their respective cases are considered. On the basis of this information, the parties are urged to consider settlement or an ADR method.

5.   Another method for disposition of cases without a full trial on all issues is the use of binding "test case" trials on certain issues. This can be accomplished by separate trials under Rule 42(b) or by agreement between the parties to try certain issues separately. See discussion of bifurcation in Chapter VII *supra* at pp. 836–51. This method can be effective in complex litigation. For example, in SCM Corp. v. Xerox Corp., 463 F.Supp. 983 (D.Conn.1978), SCM charged that Xerox had monopolized the plain copier industry by obtaining a large number of patents to block competitors from entering the market. SCM contended that Xerox only used a small percentage of its patents commercially while Xerox claimed a much larger percentage was used. At the suggestion of Judge Jon O. Newman of the District of Connecticut, each party chose two of the 77 disputed patents which it believed would illustrate its position most strongly. A jury trial limited to the four representative patents took less than two days. Based on the jury's findings for Xerox, the rest of the case was disposed of without further trial.

6.   Two federal circuit courts have found that requiring parties to participate in a non-binding summary jury trial is beyond the power of a

court. In re NLO, Inc., 5 F.3d 154 (6th Cir.1993); Strandell v. Jackson County, 838 F.2d 884 (7th Cir.1987). A number of lower courts have upheld mandatory participation. E.g., McKay v. Ashland Oil, Inc., 120 F.R.D. 43 (E.D.Ky.1988); Arabian American Oil Co. v. Scarfone, 119 F.R.D. 448 (M.D.Fla.1988). Twitty v. Minnesota Mining and Manufacturing Co., 16 Pa. D. & C. 4th 458 (C.P. of Philadelphia County 1993), joined those cases stating that "conducting a summary jury trial using jurors ... does not constitute an obstruction of justice, the misuse of a jury, or the deprivation of [plaintiff's] right to a jury trial."

7. The Tort Claimants Committee (TCC) in the Dow Corning bankruptcy proposed a summary jury trial process to provide data to aid the court in estimating the value of nondisease breast implant claims. See In re Dow Corning Corp., 211 B.R. 545 (Bkrtcy, E.D.Mich. 1997). The process, which was not adopted by the court, called for six different summary jury trials designed to produce 384 jury verdicts within a 60–day period, and was to be implemented as follows (id. at 558–60):

    A. Selection of Cases—Four plaintiffs would be selected for each summary trial. Potential plaintiffs would be selected from cases filed and pending against the Debtor at the time the bankruptcy petition was filed. To select the plaintiffs, the TCC and the Debtor would both submit a list of five claimants. Each side would strike three claimants from the other's list. The remaining four claimants—two from each list—would comprise the plaintiffs for one summary jury trial. This process would be repeated five more times until sufficient plaintiffs for six summary jury trials have been selected. The summary jury trial process would consist of a total of 24 plaintiffs.

    B. Expedition of Pretrial Discovery—Within ten days of the selection of the plaintiffs, each party would be required to file a "Summary Estimation Jury Trial Disclosure Form," which would contain certain predetermined information about each of the selected plaintiffs. Pretrial discovery would begin immediately upon receipt of the disclosure form and would last no longer than 30 days. Certain limitations would be placed on the scope of discovery. For instance, plaintiff depositions could not exceed two hours, fact witness depositions could not exceed three hours, and expert witness depositions could not exceed four hours. Disputes concerning witness availability or the location of depositions would be resolved by this Court. Evidentiary disputes would be resolved by the District Court.

    C. Pretrial Conference and Rulings—Upon the close of discovery, parties would have five days to exchange lists of witnesses and exhibits. After this exchange, parties would have an additional five days to file all evidentiary related motions and objections with the District Court. Seven days after the filing of motions and objections, the District Court (or a magistrate judge designated by the District Court) would conduct a pretrial conference at which time the District Court would rule on all evidentiary matters. Three days after the pretrial conference, parties would exchange final exhibit and witness lists.

    D. Summary Estimation Jury Trials—As soon as practicable after completion of all pretrial matters, the summary jury trials would be conducted before the district judge (or a magistrate judge designated by the District Court). Each summary jury trial would consist of "opening statements, direct and cross examination, the presentation of . . . visual exhibits, and final arguments." Each side would have a total of four hours, including time spent on both direct and cross-examination, to present its case. Each summary jury trial would be videotaped for future presentation to a jury.

    E. Venue Selection—Four different venues would be selected for presentation of the videotaped summary jury trials. The TCC and the Debtor would be jointly responsible for venue selection as well as the scheduling of the time and location of each summary jury trial. Cities and states where large numbers of breast implant cases are pending against the Debtor would be appropriate venue choices.

    F. Presiding Judicial Officers—Retired federal and state court judges would be selected to preside over jury selection in the chosen venues. The presiding judicial officers would also be responsible for performing any duties necessary to preserve proper judicial decorum and procedure during presentation of the videotaped summary jury trials to the various juries.

    G. Selection of Jury Pools and Juries—For each venue, the TCC and the Debtor would jointly select a random jury pool. Actual jury selection would be implemented through an expedited voir dire process. Juries would consist of eight persons and two juries would be impaneled for each presentation of a videotaped summary jury trial.

    H. Presentation of Videotaped Summary Jury Trials—The six videotaped summary jury trials would each be presented twice in the four chosen venues.

    I. Rendering of Verdicts—Each jury would deliberate on the evidence and render a verdict. A liability verdict could only be returned by agreement of at least seven of the eight jurors. A damage verdict could only be returned by agreement of at least six of the eight jurors. The protocol would result in 16 verdicts for each of the 24 plaintiffs for a total of 384 verdicts on nondisease breast implant claims.

    J. Summary Jury Verdicts and Purposes of Estimation—Data obtained through the summary jury trials would be used by the Court to assist in estimating the total value of all nondisease breast implant claims.

2. COURT–ANNEXED ARBITRATION

    Court-annexed arbitration has been adopted by local rule in a number of federal district courts. See B. Meierhofer, Court–Annexed Arbitration in Ten District Courts (1989). It is a judicial technique for providing the parties and attorneys an opportunity to present a summary of their cases to a lawyer (or lawyers) and obtain a non-binding decision and gives them informal feedback. Unlike the summary jury trial, court-annexed arbitration is generally expected to take place early in the litigation, without an opportunity for full discovery.

Court-annexed arbitration uses informal proceedings. Typically, counsel, their clients, and the arbitrator or arbitrators (under a number of federal district court programs there are three attorney arbitrators) sit around a table, and counsel make their presentation sitting down. Here, too, live witnesses are either not permitted or discouraged. Since parties must be present, and panel members sometimes address questions directly to them, the rules of evidence are relaxed. See, e.g., Rule 300–9(f)(3) (U.S. Dist Ct., W.D.Tex.): "In receiving evidence, the arbitrators shall be guided by the Federal Rules of Evidence, but they shall not thereby be precluded from receiving evidence which they consider to be relevant and trustworthy and which is not privileged."

One of the principal advantages of court-annexed arbitration over the summary jury trial is that it functions without a judge and thus frees up judicial time. It is also less expensive since, under most current programs, the arbitrators are lawyers who serve with only nominal compensation. The form of presentation in both summary jury trials and court-annexed arbitration is through summarizations of evidence in a relatively short proceeding, usually under half-a-day. As in summary jury trials, confidentiality of the proceedings and arbitral awards are guaranteed by court-annexed arbitration rules. This is easier to achieve in court-annexed arbitration since the proceeding is not held in a court room, and thus the issue of a public hearing is not raised.

The limitation of court-annexed arbitration in some courts to $50,000 or $100,000 claims has prevented it from being used in many complex cases. Is there any reason to so restrict its use? Is it more objectionable to force parties to submit to it where the stakes are high than where they are low? Is there less likelihood of acceptance of the arbitration decision in high dollar amount cases?

A variant from court-annexed arbitration is the moderated settlement conference which has been particularly used in state courts in Texas. See Texas ADR Handbook 119–34 (2003 ed.). Like court-annexed arbitration, the moderated settlement conference involves presenting a summarized case to lawyers who serve as moderators in an informal setting and a non-binding recommendation. Testimony by live witnesses is discouraged by the short amount of time. The setting is informal, consistent with the term "conference." Counsel, clients, and moderators sit around a table. Although the discussion is structured with each side allocated certain time periods, the moderators may permit discussion or questions between counsel and parties and may themselves pose questions to the participants. O'Brien & Kovach, Moderated Settlement Conference, 51 Tex.B.J. 38 (1988).

3. EARLY NEUTRAL EVALUATION (ENE)

The Early Neutral Evaluation (ENE) program was first created by the U.S. District Court, Northern District of California. See Brazil, Kahn, Newman & Gold, Early Neutral Evaluation: An Experimental Effort to Expedite Dispute Resolution, 69 Judicature 279 (1986). It has now been adopted in other federal courts. Under it, a neutral—a respected lawyer with expertise in the subject matter of the case—meets with parties and their lawyers for two hours early in the progress of the litigation and gives them a frank assessment of their cases.

"Typically, one of the clients begins a narrative presentation of the case, without being led by the lawyer. After both sides have presented, the evaluator asks questions. The evaluator tries to help the parties to identify common ground, and to convert this to stipulations or informal agreements. The effort during the process is to isolate the areas of disagreement most central to the case." Lawyers Get Tips on Using Early Neutral Evaluation, 4 ADR Rep. 124 (April 12, 1990). After the discussion, the evaluator leaves the room and writes up her evaluation of the value of the case and two or three key analytical points. If the plaintiff wins, the evaluator ascribes a range of damages.

Before giving the parties her evaluation, the evaluator asks if they wish to discuss settlement before they see the evaluation. Some 25% of cases settle at this point. Id. at 125. If they opt not to discuss settlement, the evaluator explains her evaluation. She then "outlines a case development plan, identifying key areas of disagreement and suggesting ways to posture the case and to conduct discovery as efficiently as possible. The evaluator is required to do case planning. The parties are required to listen, but not to agree. They may decide to come back for a follow-up settlement conference." Id.

Could ENE be useful in a complex case?

4. COURT–ANNEXED MEDIATION

Courts are increasingly annexing mediation by ordering parties to engage in mediation as a prerequisite to going to trial. Since mediation is an inherently unstructured process, courts rarely prescribe procedures for such mediations. Often courts provide a list of qualified mediators, or of dispute resolution and other institutional providers of mediation services, to the parties and let them select a mediator and carry out the mediation without further court involvement. Some courts have mediators or conciliators attached to the court who conduct court-ordered mediations.

Settlement week mediations are a specialized form of court-annexed mediation. Typically courts establish a particular week for mediation settlements. See, e.g., Texas Civ.Prac. & Rem.Code Ann. § 155.001 et seq. (providing that every county with a population of at least 150,000 shall designate settlement weeks to "facilitate the voluntary settlement of civil and family law cases.") Any party to a pending suit may place the case on the "settlement week docket," and the other party or parties are then required to participate in a mediation scheduled that week. Settlement week mediators are often volunteer attorneys.

Orders assigning cases to settlement week typically require the participation of persons on both sides with full authority to settle. Some programs also require the parties to have consulted in advance as to the possibility of settlement. A recurring issue in many settlement week programs is whether and to what extent a court will impose sanctions on attorneys or parties for unsatisfactory compliance with the order to mediate. Courts have generally found no difficulty in imposing sanctions for failure to appear, as determination of this fact would not require recourse to confidential information as to what went on in the mediation. Sanctions for attending without authority to settle or for not providing opposing counsel or the mediator with required documents or information prior to the mediation can also generally be resolved without a need for breaching confidentiality. However, sanctions for an attorney's being unprepared or for not participating in good faith could require breaching confidentiality, and courts have been hesitant to consider sanctions in such situations.

5. EMERGING PATTERNS OF ADR USE IN FEDERAL COURTS

A study of the use of ADR devices in federal courts indicated that, after years of experimentation with processes designed to 'reality test 'or provide an less-expensive "trial run" that will encourage settlement, mediation is the most popular form of ADR:

> Mediation has emerged as the primary ADR process in the federal district courts. In marked contrast to five years ago when only a few courts had court-based programs for mediation, over half of the ninety-four districts now offer—and, in several instances, require—mediation. Most mediation offered in the federal courts is administered wholly by the courts; only a few districts provide mediation through referral to bar groups or private ADR provider organizations.

> Arbitration is the second most frequently authorized ADR program, but falls well short of mediation in the number of courts that have implemented it.... Use of early neutral evaluation (ENE) has increased from two courts five years ago, but still is used in only fourteen courts.... Settlement week and case valuation, the last two forms of court-wide ADR programs, are found in even fewer courts.... Just over half the courts report authorization or use of the summary jury trial.... A complete picture of each court's approach to settlement attests to the continuing viability of judicial settlement efforts and the expanding role of magistrate judges in settlement.... [M]any courts—at least a third—have designated magistrate judges as the court's primary settlement officers.

Plapinger & Stienstra, ADR and Settlement in the Federal District Courts: A Sourcebook for Judges and Lawyers, in Alternative Dispute Resolution: The Litigators' Handbook 406–408 (ABA Section of Litigation 2000).

Index

References are to Pages

ABSTENTION
See Duplicative or Related Litigation (this index)

ADMINISTRATIVE PROCEEDINGS
Equitable abstention under Younger v. Harris, 181–182

AFFIRMATIVE DEFENSES
Severance, 767

AGE DISCRIMINATION CLAIMS
Permissive joinder of plaintiffs, 33

AGENT ORANGE
Rule 23(b)(3) action, 339–340
Settlement review, 537–538

AGGREGATION DEBATE
Generally, 9–15
Combined or individual treatment, 18–19
Consistency of result, 11–13
Economy and efficiency, 10–11
Fairness, 14–15
Individual issues, effect on ability to raise, 15
Litigant autonomy, 13–14
Policies disfavoring aggregation, 13–15
Policies favoring aggregation, 10–12
Sherman, "Aggregate Disposition of Related Cases: The Policy Issues," 10–15
Strategic advantages, effect on, 14–15

ALL WRITS ACT
Generally, 199–209
See Duplicative or Related Litigation (this index)

ALTERNATIVES TO LITIGATION
Generally, 883–946
Related topics:
Arbitration
ADR, emerging patterns in federal courts, 946
Court-annexed
Arbitration, 943–944
Mediation, 945–946
Early neutral evaluation, 944–945
Industry-wide claims settlement through subscriber facility, 931–938
Judicial mechanisms, 938–946
Mini-trials, 927–930

ALTERNATIVES TO LITIGATION—Cont'd
Moderated settlement conference, 944
Rent-a-judge programs, 930–931
Summary jury trials, 939–943
Test case trial on certain issues, 939–943

ANCILLARY JURISDICTION
Compulsory party joinder, 58

ANTI–INJUNCTION ACT
Related topics:
Duplicative or Related Litigation
Relitigation exception, 404–405

ANTITRUST
Class actions, 264–265

APPEAL AND REVIEW
Related topics:
Class Actions
Intervenors' appeal rights, 71

APPRENTICESHIP PROGRAMS
Compulsory party joinder, 45 et seq.

ARBITRATION
Generally, 884–926
Arbitrability, 890–891
Arbitrable and non-arbitrable claims in same suit, 895–899
Classwide arbitration, 903–923
Collateral estoppel effect of decision, 898–899
Consolidation of proceedings
Generally, 899–902
Murray et al, "Materials on Dispute Resolution," 899–902
Cost-splitting provision, 894
Court review, 890–891
Court-annexed, 943–944
Federal Arbitration Act
Generally, 884
Preemption of state law limitations on arbitration, 885
Scope of, 885
Federal statutory exceptions, demise of doctrine, 886–889
Injunctive relief, 892–893
Innovative techniques, 923–926
Mnookin, "Beyond Litigation," 924–926
Preemption

ARBITRATION—Cont'd
Preemption—Cont'd
Contrary state rules, 885–886
FAA preemption of state law limitations, 889
Process and procedure, 891–892
Punitive damages, 891
State contract law, invalidation of arbitration clauses under, 893–895
Unconscionability, 893–894

ASBESTOS LITIGATION
Claims Facility, 931–938
Consolidation and class action, invoking in tandem, 126
Ethical issues and lawyers' conduct, 230
Fitzpatrick, "The Center for Claims Resolution," 932–937
Johns–Manville bankruptcy, 213–214
Limited fund class actions, 318
Multidistrict litigation procedures, 159–160
Proof of causation, 37–38
Settlement of claims, 388

ATTORNEYS
Related topics:
Attorneys' Fees Awards
Class Actions
Judicial selection of counsel
Generally, 664–680
Auctioning the position, 677
Class actions, 668
Disqualification of counsel, 680
Expanding the "empowered plaintiff" model, 678–679
Lead counsel responsibilities, 666–667
Non-lead counsel, limiting actions of, 667–668
Public entities as parties, 679
Securities fraud, 678

ATTORNEYS' FEES AWARDS
Generally, 680–716
Allocation among attorneys, 716
Amount to be awarded, 684–716
Authority to award fees, 681–684
Benchmark, 714–715
Billing rate, 698–699
Blending percentage and hourly approaches, 716
Common fund doctrine
Generally, 681–682
Percentage method, 712 et seq.
Consideration at outset, 676, 702
Contingency factor, 701
Correlation between class recovery and fees, 716
Hours worked, 697–698
Lead counsel, 682–684
Lodestar
Challenge to, 703–716
Effect on interests of plaintiffs, 714
Emergence of, 686–703
Measuring success, 700
Multipliers, 699–701

ATTORNEYS' FEES AWARDS—Cont'd
Percentage method in common fund cases, 712 et seq.
Private attorney general theory, 684
Quality of work, 699–701
Settlement, worth of, 715
Waste prevention, 701–702

AUDITORS
Access to privileged information, 612

BAD FAITH
Document preservation, 568
Sanctions for bad faith conduct by litigants or lawyers, 653

BANKRUPTCY
Related topics:
Dow Corning Bankruptcy
Duplicative or Related Litigation
Limited fund mass tort class actions, 317

BIAS
Recusal based on judge's involvement in litigation, 727–729

BREAST IMPLANTS
See Dow Corning Bankruptcy (this index)

CASE MANAGEMENT
Generally, 626–643
Related topics:
Masters
Sanctions
Trial
Accountability, 632–633
Adversary system, preservation of, 633
Cost effectiveness, 634
Cutoff dates, 639
Historical background, 626–628
Impartiality, 629–630, 631–632
Peckham, "A Judicial Response to the Cost of Litigation: Case Management, Two–State Discovery Planning and Alternative Dispute Resolution," 631–634
RAND Corporation study, 635
Resnick, "Managerial Judges," 628–630
Scheduling, 638–639
Settlement
Judge's role, 642–643
Mandatory discussions, 641
Master, appointment of, 663
Multiparty cases, 643
Promotion of, 639–641
Sanctions for not settling, 641
Summary judgment, tendency toward, 636–637
Trial Court Delay Reduction Act, 639
Work product, invasion of, 637–638

CAUSATION
Product liability litigation, 37–38, 44–45
Severance, 775–776

CERCLA
Intervention of potentially responsible parties, 83

CHOICE OF LAW
Related topics:
    Class Actions
Permissive joinder, 43–44

CIRCUIT CONFLICTS
Multidistrict litigation, 163–164

CIVIL JUSTICE REFORM ACT, 628

CIVIL PROCEDURE
Related topics:
    Discovery
    Federal Rules of Civil Procedure (this index)
    Intervention
    Joinder
Impact of procedure on substance, 20–21
Modeling procedures on complex cases, 21–22

CIVIL RIGHTS
Exhaustion of administrative remedies and equitable abstention, 182
Permissive joinder in title VII and section 1981 cases, 32
Preclusive effect of state court judgment in federal civil rights suit, 802

CLAIM PRECLUSION
Generally, 786–848
Attorney general acting on behalf of citizens, 801
Choice of law, 801
Class action judgments, effect of
    Generally, 803–848
    Antisuit injunctions, 844
    Claims within exclusive federal jurisdiction, 816
    Federal class actions, 828
    Individual claims, 840–841, 844 et seq.
    Notice, adequacy of, 830
    Opt out class members, 818–819, 829
    Overlapping actions, 404
    Prisoner suits, 845 et seq.
    Representation, adequacy of, 830
    Settlements, 816, 830, 839–840
Full faith and credit considerations, 802, 828
Governmental action extinguishing pre-existing rights, 801
Nonparties and virtual representation, 798 et seq.
On the merits requirement, 787
Persons or entities bound by prior judgment, 787–803
Privity requirement, 787, 798
Public entities, 800–801
Requirements, 786–787
Same cause of action requirement, 787
Same parties requirement, 787
Virtual representation, 798 et seq.

CLASS ACTIONS
1966 amendments to Rule 23, 219 et seq.
    Generally, 218–540
Related topics:
    Attorneys' Fees Awards
    Claim Preclusion
Adequacy of representation, 289
Antitrust price-fixing suits, 264–265
Appeal and review
    Class certification decisions, timing of appeal, 370–371
    Objectors to settlement, 519
Arbitration, classwide, 903–923
Certification of class
    Differences in state law, 435
    Subclasses, below
    Timing of decision, 368–370
Choice of law. Jurisdiction and choice of law, below
Class Action Fairness Act of 2004, 401–402, 538–539
Commonality
    Generally, 245–267
    Antitrust price-fixing suits, 264–265
    Certification for some issues, 266
    Consumer class actions, 263–264
    Experts, use of, 265–266
    Individualized defenses, 257
    Predominance issues, 266
    Securities fraud, 254 et seq.
    Subclassing, 256
    Telephone charges, 264
Communications with unnamed members of class, 470–481
Conditional certification, 369
Conflicts of interest
    Among class members, 296
    Settlements, conflicts between counsel and class members, 229
Consolidation, differences with, 126
Conspiracy allegations, 284
Consumer class actions, 263–264
Counsel
    Auctioning the position, 677
    Interim class counsel, 668
    Judicial selection. See Attorneys (this index)
    Lawyer as prime beneficiary, 227 et seq.
    Lead counsel, 668
    Securities fraud, 678
    Settlement conflicts between counsel and class members, 229
Credit card interest charges, 282 et seq.
Cy pres possibility, 411
Decertification and modification of class definition
    Generally, 497–509
    Continuing power to modify, 509
    Dissent within class, 240–241
    Expansion of class
        After merits determination, 508
        As part of settlement, 508
Declaratory relief
    Numerosity requirement, 244–245
Defendant class actions
    Generally, 359–368

CLASS ACTIONS—Cont'd
Defendant class actions—Cont'd
    Certification under Rule 23(b)(1), 367–368
    Numerosity requirement, 243
    Tolling of statute, 469
    Trade association as class representative, 366
Defenses, individualized, 257
Definition of class
    Generally, 231–241
    Effect of class remedy sought, 240
    Members who cannot be identified at present, 239
    Members who cannot be identified by name, 238–239
    Modification. Decertification and modification of class definition, above
    Narrowing definition to address commonality problems, 240
Discovery, 479–481
Economic unfeasibility to sue individually, 243–244
Employment discrimination cases, typicality and commonality problems, 275 et seq.
Ethical considerations
    Generally, 223–230
    Incentives for class representatives, 229–230
    Lawyer as prime beneficiary, 227 et seq.
    Settlement and conflicts of interest, 229
    Solicitation of class representatives, 227–228
Expansion of class. Decertification and modification of class definition, above
Experts, use of, 265–266
Federal jurisdiction, expansion of, 402
Fluid recovery, 408–410
Historical background, 6–7, 218 et seq.
Hybrid class actions, 219
Incentives for class representatives, 229–230
Injunctive relief
    Nationwide certification in various state courts, 438–439
    Numerosity requirement, 244–245
    Rule 23(b)(2) classes, 326 et seq.
Intervention
    Generally, 448–460
    Benefits unique to class actions, 456
    Inadequacy of representation, 456
    Limitation of actions, 460
Joinder, impracticability of, 243
Judgments, effect of. See Claim Preclusion (this index)
Jurisdiction and choice of law
    Generally, 412–440
    Choice of law options, 436 et seq.
    Consent to jurisdiction by failure to opt out, 425–427
    Differences in state law, 435
    Diversity standards, 402
    Enjoining putative class members, 438

CLASS ACTIONS—Cont'd
Jurisdiction and choice of law—Cont'd
    Most significant relationship test, 438
    Personal jurisdiction, 425–427
    Subject matter jurisdiction limitations on state-law class actions
        Generally, 425–427
        Complete diversity, 427–428
        Jurisdictional amount, 428–429
Limitation of actions. Statutes of limitation, below
Manageability, 335–336, 353–354
Medical monitoring, 301, 329–330
Modification of class. Decertification and modification of class definition, above
Mootness
    Generally, 481–497
    Personal stake analysis, 496
    Relation back rule, 494
    Release executed by original plaintiff, 497
    Settlement, 497
    Subclasses, 495
Multi-state class actions, 353 et seq.
Named plaintiffs. Representativeness, below
Nationwide class actions, 353 et seq.
Notice
    Prejudgment notice to class members, below
    Settlement, notice to class members, 510–511
Numerosity
    Generally, 241–245
    Defendant class actions, 243
    Degree of certainty required, 244
    Economic unfeasibility to sue individually, 243–244
    Impracticability of joinder, 243
    Link between numerosity and merits, 245
    When injunctive or declaratory relief sought, 244–245
Opting out
    Generally, 448–460
    Categorical rule against allowing opt-outs for collateral estoppel purposes, 459
    Consent to jurisdiction by failure to opt out, 426
    Curtailing activities of opt-outs, 459–460
    Differences between (b)(2) and (b)(3) cases, 458–459
    Due process, 457
    Employment discrimination actions, 456–457
    Failure to opt out as waiver of objection to discovery, 480
    Hybrid actions, 456
    Intervention by opting out class members, 84
    Notice to class members, 444
    Recapturing actions via consolidation, 459
    Running of statute of limitations, 468

CLASS ACTIONS—Cont'd
Overlapping actions
Generally, 391–405
All Writs Act, 208–209
Anti–Injunction Act, 404–405
Class Action Fairness Act of 2004, 401–402
Dueling orders, 402–403
Federal jurisdiction, expansion of, 402
Injunctive relief, 403–404
Multidistrict litigation procedures, 152–153
Plaintiff counsel who file additional class actions, 401
Preclusive effect of final judgment, 404
State/federal overlap, 401
Personal jurisdiction, 425–427
Precertification
Communications. Unnamed class members, below
Settlement, 510
Prejudgment notice to class members
Generally, 440–448
Advantages to class members, 444
Best notice practicable, 444–445
Cost of identifying class members, 448
Defendant's regular mailings to class, inclusion in, 448
Drafting notice, 446–447
Due process, 445
E-mail, use of, 444
Monitoring action, 444
Opting-out, 444
Proof of claim form, 447
Use of easily understood language, 446
Prerequisites
Generally, 230–298
Adequate definition of class, 231–241
Commonality, 245–267
Numerosity, 241–245
Representativeness, 285–298
Typicality, 267–285
Public accommodation discrimination, typicality and commonality problems, 278
Putative class members, rights of after denial of certification, 467–468
RAND Institute study, 7–9
Remedies
Generally, 405–412
Classwide formula, 408–410
Fluid recovery, 408–410
Injunctive relief, above
Surplus, return to defendant, 412
Removal to federal court, 23
Representativeness
Generally, 285–298
Ability to finance litigation, 297
Adequacy of representation, 289
Conflicts of interest, 296
Due process analysis, 289
Identification with counsel, 297
Professional plaintiffs, 296
Securities fraud, 293–294

CLASS ACTIONS—Cont'd
Representativeness—Cont'd
Strategy differences, 287
Understanding of case, 294–295
Representatives
Incentives, 229–230
Solicitation of, 227–228
Rule 23(b)(2) classes
Generally, 318–330
Employment discrimination actions, 326–327
Injunctive relief only, 327–328
Medical monitoring, 329–330
Monetary relief combined with injunctive or declaratory relief, 326 et seq.
Rule 23(b)(3) classes
Generally, 330–358
Agent Orange litigation, 339–340
Mass torts, 336 et seq.
Maturity of related litigation, 357
Multi-state class actions, 353 et seq.
Opting out, 456
Phased trials, 337
Reliance, issue of, 356
Settlement pressure, 357
Stricter standards, 353 et seq.
Tobacco actions, 358
Trial plan, 337–338
Rule 23(b)(1)(A)—"incompatible standards" actions
Generally, 298–302
Defendant classes, 299–300
Medical monitoring program, 301
Money damages, 299–300
Shareholder suit to compel declaration of dividend, 298
Taxpayer suits to invalidate municipal action, 298
Rule 23(b)(1)(B)—"limited fund" actions
Generally, 302–318
Bankruptcy, 317
Caps on amount recoverable, 316
Mass torts, 314 et seq.
Multiple defendants, 316
Punitive damages, 316
Securities fraud
Generally, 254 et seq.
Conflicts among class members, 256
Misrepresentations, 255
Professional plaintiffs, 296
Reliance issue, 255
Representativeness, 293–294
Settlements
Generally, 372–391
Appeal by objectors, 519
Back-end opt-out rights, 390
Claims procedures, 539–540
Class Action Fairness Act, 538–539
Confidential communications, disclosure of, 519
Conflicts of interest
Generally, 514–515

CLASS ACTIONS—Cont'd
Settlements—Cont'd
Conflicts of interest—Cont'd
Between counsel and class members, 229
Distributing settlement funds, 539–540
Duties of class counsel, 515
Eligibility to recover, criteria, 540
Expansion of class as part of settlement, 508
Factors for reviewing proposals, 533
Future class members, 389–390
Individual settlement with class representative, 510
Judicial control
Generally, 509–540
Appeal by objectors, 519
Claims procedures, 539–540
Conflicts of interest, 514–515
Distributing funds, 539–540
Duties of class counsel, 515
Factors for reviewing proposals, 533
Individual settlement with class representative, 510
Nonmonetary relief, 535–536
Notice to class members, 510–511
Objectors, 516 et seq.
Pre-certification settlement, 510
Roles of class representatives and class counsel, 515
State law differences, 535
Two-tiered process, 510
Withdrawing objection, 518
Mootness, 497
Nonmonetary relief, 535–536
Notice to class members, 510–511
Objectors, 516 et seq.
Pre-certification settlement, 510
Pressure to settle, 357
Proposed amendment of Rule 23, 388
Reverse auctions, 533–534
Roles of class representatives and class counsel, 515
Rule 23(b)(3) actions, 357
State law differences, 535
Tentative or temporary settlement classes, 372
Withdrawing objection, 518
Spurious class actions, 219
Standing of unnamed class members, 283
Statutes of limitation
Generally, 460–470
Absent class members, 460 et seq.
Class status denied, 461, 466–467
Complaints asserting generalized grievances, 466
Denial of certification for undue delay, 466
One-way intervention, 460
Opting out class members, 468
Putative class members, rights of, 467–468
Tolling of statute
Generally, 461 et seq.

CLASS ACTIONS—Cont'd
Statutes of limitation—Cont'd
Tolling of statute—Cont'd
Defendant class actions, 469
Subclasses
Generally, 256
Mootness, 495
Subject matter jurisdiction. Jurisdiction and choice of law, above
Superiority, 332–334
Surplus damages, return to defendant, 412
Telephone charges, 264
Timing of appeals from class certification decisions, 370–371
Timing of class certification decisions, 368–370
Tobacco actions, 358
Trade association as class representative, 366
Typicality
Generally, 267–285
Commonality distinguished, 275
Conspiracy allegations, 284
Credit card interest charges, 282 et seq.
Employment discrimination cases, 275 et seq.
Public accommodation discrimination, 275 et seq.
Unnamed class members
Communications with
Generally, 470–481
Class opponents, communications from, 477
Counsel's duty to communicate, 476
Judicial control over content, 478
Judicial intervention, 475–476
Nonparties, communications from, 478–479
Objecting plaintiff lawyers, communications from, 477
Post-certification, 477–478
Discovery from, 479–481
Standing, 283

COLLATERAL ATTACK, 86–102, 794

COLLATERAL ESTOPPEL
See Issue Preclusion (this index)

COMMON FUND DOCTRINE
See Attorneys' Fees Awards (this index)

COMPULSORY JOINDER
See Joinder in Unitary Federal Forum (this index)

COMPUTERS
See Discovery (this index)

CONFIDENTIALITY
See Discovery (this index)

CONFLICTS OF INTEREST
See Class Actions (this index)

CONSOLIDATION
Related topics:
Duplicative or Related Litigation

CONSOLIDATION—Cont'd
Arbitration proceedings, 899–902

CONSTITUTIONAL LAW
Related topics:
  Due Process
Eleventh Amendment and compulsory party joinder of state governmental entities, 61–62
First Amendment and disclosing information obtained through discovery, 579

CONSUMER ACTIONS
Class actions, 263–264
Fluid recovery, 409

CONTEMPT
Case management sanctions, 649–651

COUNSEL
See Attorneys (this index)
See Class Actions (this index)

COUNTERCLAIMS
Injunction against bringing compulsory counterclaim in subsequent federal action, 198–199

CREDIT CARDS
Interest charges, 282 et seq.

CRIMINAL CONTEMPT
Case management sanctions, 649–651

CY PRES
Remedies in class actions, 411

DALKON SHIELD LITIGATION
Generally, 5–6
A.J. Robins bankruptcy, 5–6
Issue preclusion, 876
Limited fund, 315

DAMAGES
Related topics:
  Punitive Damages
Incompatible standards actions (Rule 23(b)(1)(A)), 299–300

DANGEROUS PRODUCTS OR SUBSTANCES
See Product Liability Litigation (this index)

DECLARATORY JUDGMENT
Stay of federal suit in interests of "wise judicial administration," 189–190

DELAY
Class certification, denial for undue delay, 466
Trial Court Delay Reduction Act, 639

DEPOSITIONS
See Discovery (this index)

DISASTERS
Rheingold, "The MER/29 Story—An Instance of Successful Mass Disaster Litigation," 123–128

DISCOVERY
Generally, 541–625
Class actions, 479–481
Collaborative handling in related litigation, 545–546, 592–593
Common interest exception to waiver doctrine, 610–611
Confidentiality and protective orders
  Generally, 571–594
  First Amendment concerns, 579
  Improper disclosure of covered material, 594
  Information sharing among plaintiff lawyers, 592–593
  Public access approach to discovery, 591
  Public trial right and discovery, 581–582
  Publicizing lawsuit, 581
  Trade secrets, protection of, 593
  Umbrella protective order, 572, 580
Consolidation order, limitation to pretrial discovery, 125
Document preservation
  Generally, 561–571
  Adverse inference in absence of bad faith, 569–570
  Bad faith, 568
  Destruction when no litigation pending, 567–568
  Failure to produce as tantamount to destruction, 568
  Heightened obligation after litigation underway, 569
  Orders, 570–571
  Retention policies, 566 et seq.
  Scope of preservation duty, 569
E-discovery
  Generally, 546–561
  Backup tapes, restoration of, 556–557
  Cost-bearing, 556 et seq.
  E-mail messages on backup tapes, 559, 568
  Home computers, 560–561
  Information management systems, 559–560
  Master, designation of, 662–663
  Retention of electronic materials, 567
Ex parte oral communications with witnesses, 617
Expert witnesses, 618
Fabrication of testimony, 617
Failure to produce as tantamount to destruction, 568
Inadequate specification of grounds for withholding, 605
Inadvertent production of privileged information, 603 et seq.
Litigation support systems, 543 et seq.
Master, appointment of, 662–663

DISCOVERY—Cont'd
Oral communications with witnesses, ex parte, 617
Overview of large case discovery, 542–546
Preserving privilege protection
    Generally, 594–625
    Advice of counsel as element of claim or defense, 624
    Affirmative use as evidence, 623–624
    Auditors demanding access to information, 612
    Common interest exception to waiver doctrine, 610–611
    Fabrication of testimony, 617
    Inadequate specification of grounds for withholding, 605
    Inadvertent production, 603 et seq.
    Oral communications with witnesses, ex parte, 617
    Refreshing testimony (Rule 612), 616–618
    Selective disclosure, 623
    State of mind, use of privileged material to prove, 623
    Waiver by agreement, 605–606
    Witness as retained expert, 618
    Witness preparation, 617
Privilege. Preserving privilege protection, above
Protective orders. Confidentiality and protective orders, above
Sunshine in Litigation Act, 591
Waiver of privilege. Preserving privilege protection, above

DISCRIMINATION CLAIMS
Related topics:
    Employment Discrimination
Compulsory party joinder, 52
Permissive joinder of plaintiffs, 33

DISMISSAL FOR FORUM NONCONVENIENS
See Duplicative or Related Litigation (this index)

DISPUTE RESOLUTION
Related topics:
    Alternatives to Litigation
As goal of civil litigation, 17–18

DISQUALIFICATION
Related topics:
    Judges
Counsel, 680
Master, 663

DIVERSITY JURISDICTION
Broad minimal standard, 402
Compulsory party joinder, 57–58

DOCUMENTS
Related topics:
    Discovery

DOCUMENTS—Cont'd
Retention policies, 566 et seq.

DOW CORNING BANKRUPTCY
    Generally, 215–217
Proposed summary jury trials, 942

DUE PROCESS
Class actions, representativeness, 289
Opting out, 457
Prejudgment notice to class members, 445
Recusal, 726

DUPLICATIVE OR RELATED LITIGATION
    Generally, 103–217
Abstention
    Equitable abstention under Younger v. Harris
        Generally, 171–184
        Administrative proceedings, applicability to, 181
        All pending state civil proceedings, applicability to, 181–182
        Exhaustion of administrative remedies, 182
        Pendency of state proceeding, 182
        Rooker–Feldman doctrine, 183–184
        Waiver by state, 183
    Traditional abstention
        Generally, 156–171
        Adequacy of state court remedy, 170–171
        Reservation of federal claims for de novo determination, 169
        Stay with retention of jurisdiction, 168–169
        Time of the essence, 170
All Writs Act as authority for federal orders relating to state court suits
    Generally, 199–209
    Class actions, overlapping, 208–209
    In aid of jurisdiction exception to Anti–Injunction Act, 206
    Removal, All Writs Act as authority for, 207–208
Anti–Injunction Act. Federal injunction against prosecution of state proceedings, below
Bankruptcy proceedings
    Generally, 209–217
    A.J. Robins bankruptcy (Dalkon Shield), 214–215
    Dow Corning bankruptcy (breast implants), 215–217
    Estimation of claims, 211
    Johns–Manville bankruptcy (asbestos), 211–213
    Jury trial, right to, 211–213
    Proof of claims, 210–211
Consolidation. Pretrial consolidation, below
Dismissal for forum nonconveniens
    Generally, 132–142
    Delays in courts of other country, 141–142

DUPLICATIVE OR RELATED LITIGATION
—Cont'd
Dismissal for forum nonconveniens—Cont'd
Events occurring in other countries,
140–141
Interest analysis, 141
Related suits, existence of, 142
Dual state-federal proceedings
Generally, 164–209
Abstention, above
All Writs Act, above
Federal injunction against prosecution
of state proceedings (Anti–Injunc-
tion Act), below
Stay of federal suit in interests of "wise
judicial administration," below
Equitable abstention. Abstention, above
Federal injunction against prosecution of
state proceedings (Anti–Injunction
Act)
Generally, 190–199
Compulsory counterclaims, 198–199
Elimination of discretion to issue injunc-
tion, 196
Protecting or effectuating federal judg-
ment, exception for, 197–198
Tender offers, 197
Injunctions
Federal injunction against prosecution
of state proceedings (Anti–Injunc-
tion Act), above
Stay orders or injunctions, below
More convenient forum, transfer to
Generally, 128–132
Delay in making motion, 130–131
Dismissal for forum nonconveniens,
above
Venue, proper or improper, 131
Where it might have been brought re-
quirement, 130
Multidistrict litigation procedures, transfer
under
Generally, 142–164
Circuit conflicts, 163–164
Hansel, "An Interview with Chairman
of the Judicial Panel on Multidis-
trict Litigation," 143–145
Law of the case, 162–163
Overlapping class actions, 152–153
Preclusive effect of judgment, 876–877
Pretrial proceedings, transferee judge's
authority, 158 et seq.
Remand for trial, 160
Self-transfer, 160–161
State court cases, 153–154
Stipulation to proceed to trial in trans-
feree district, 161
Weigel, "The Judicial Panel on Multidis-
trict Litigation, Transferor Courts
and Transferee Courts," 154–156
Multiple proceedings in federal court
Generally, 104–164
Dismissal for forum nonconveniens,
above

DUPLICATIVE OR RELATED LITIGATION
—Cont'd
Multiple proceedings in federal court
—Cont'd
More convenient forum, transfer to,
above
Multidistrict litigation procedures, above
Pretrial consolidation, below
Stay orders or injunctions, below
Pretrial consolidation
Generally, 115–128
Class action, differences with, 126
Discovery, limitation to, 125
Free enterprise model of unofficial coor-
dination, 126
Jurisdictional issues, 127–128
Rheingold, "The MER/29 Story—An In-
stance of Successful Mass Disas-
ter Litigation," 123–128
Stay of federal suit in interests of "wise
judicial administration"
Generally, 184–190
Balancing of factors approach, 187
Declaratory judgment action, 189–190
Forum shopping, 187
Interaction of Younger doctrine and Col-
orado River abstention, 188
Stay orders or injunctions re suits in other
federal courts
Generally, 104–115
Consolidation of application for prelimi-
nary injunction and hearing on
merits, 108
First filed standard, 114–115
Likelihood of success on the merits, 114
Transfer motion, 108

EARLY NEUTRAL EVALUATION
Generally, 944–945

E–DISCOVERY
See Discovery (this index)

ELEVENTH AMENDMENT
Compulsory party joinder of state governmental entities, 61–62

E–MAIL
Discovery of messages on backup tapes,
559, 568
Prejudgment notice to class members, 444

EMPLOYMENT DISCRIMINATION CASES
Compulsory party joinder, 52
Confidentiality agreements with employees,
476
Consequences of failure to join, 99 et seq.
Decertification of class, 507
Evidentiary standards, 838–839
Opting out, 456–457
Rule 23(b)(2) classes, 326–327
Typicality and commonality problems, 275
et seq.

ENVIRONMENTAL ENFORCEMENT SUITS
Intervention, 83

EQUITABLE ABSTENTION
See Duplicative or Related Litigation

EVIDENCE
Documentary material, computer imaging, 755
Limiting amount of evidence and duration of trial, 758–762

EXHAUSTION OF ADMINISTRATIVE REMEDIES
Equitable abstention under Younger v. Harris, 182

EXPERTS
Class actions, use of experts, 265–266
Discovery of privileged information, 618

FEDERAL RULES OF CIVIL PROCEDURE
Related topics:
    Case Management
    Class Actions
    Discovery
    Duplicative or Related Litigation
    Joinder in Unitary Federal Forum
Historical background, 2 et seq.

FEDERALISM
    Generally, 22–23
Abstention, 169–170
Masters, use of to enforce decree against state institution, 662

FIRST AMENDMENT
Disclosing information obtained through discovery, 579

FOREIGN COUNTRIES
Events occurring in, dismissal for forum nonconveniens, 140–141

FORUM NON CONVENIENS
Related topics:
    Duplicative or Related Litigation

FORUM SHOPPING
Stay of federal suit in interests of "wise judicial administration," 187

FULL FAITH AND CREDIT
Claim preclusion, 802, 828

GUARDIAN AD LITEM
Appointment of and issue preclusion, 864

HOUSING DISCRIMINATION
Compulsory party joinder, 52

INDISPENSABLE PARTIES
Determination of indispensability, 56–57

INJUNCTIVE RELIEF
Related topics:
    Class Actions
    Duplicative or Related Litigation

INJUNCTIVE RELIEF—Cont'd
Arbitration, 892–893
Compulsory counterclaim in subsequent federal action, injunction against, 198–199
Institutional reform litigation, antisuit injunctions, 844
Overlapping actions, 403–404

INNOVATION
Broad vs. specific rules, 19–20
Combined or individual treatment, 18–19
Dispute resolution as goal, 17–18
Evaluating innovation in litigation, 15–23
Federalism concerns, 22–23
Judicial involvement and management, 15–17
Modeling procedures on complex cases, 21–22
Procedure, impact on substance, 20–21

INSTRUCTIONS TO JURY
Preliminary instructions, 745

INTERVENTION
    Generally, 62–85
Related topics:
    Class Actions
Appeal rights of intervenor, 71
Brunet, "A Study in the Allocation of Scarce Resources: The Efficiency of Federal Intervention Criteria," 28–31, 63–64
CERCLA, intervention of potentially responsible parties, 83
Environmental enforcement suits, 83
Inadequate representation requirement, 72, 456
Justiciability constraints, 71
Limited purpose intervention, 71, 85
Opting out class members, 84
Prejudice to existing parties, 85
Significantly protectable interest requirement, 67–69
Standing, 69 et seq.
Timeliness of application, 84–85

ISSUE PRECLUSION
    Generally, 848–882
Arbitration decision, 898–899
Compromise jury verdicts, 880
Guardian ad litem, appointment of, 864
Inadequacy of representation, 853
Multidistrict litigation, 876–877
Offensive collateral estoppel
        Generally, 874 et seq.
        By persons opting out of class action, 459
One-sided application, 853–854
Persons or entities bound
        Generally, 848–857
        Inadequacy of representation, 853
        One-sided application, 853–854
        Privity, 853
Pretrial protocol, 863

ISSUE PRECLUSION—Cont'd
Privity, 853
Products liability cases, 875
Special verdicts or interrogatories, use of, 873–874
Vacation of judgment, efforts to blunt estoppel, 881–882
Which issues actually determined
Generally, 857–882
Compromise jury verdicts, 880
Guardian ad litem, appointment of, 864
Multidistrict litigation, 876–877
Offensive collateral estoppel, 874 et seq.
Pretrial protocol, 863
Products liability cases, 875
Special verdicts or interrogatories, use of, 873–874
Vacation of judgment, efforts to blunt estoppel, 881–882

JOINDER IN UNITARY FEDERAL FORUM
Generally, 24–102
Related topics:
Intervention
Compulsory party joinder
Generally, 45–62
Absent persons, proceeding without, 54 et seq.
Ancillary jurisdiction, 58
Apprenticeship programs, 45 et sq.
As a practical matter standard, 52–53
Criteria for adding nonparties, 49
Discrimination cases, 52
Diversity jurisdiction, 57–58
Indispensability determination, 56–57
Pendent jurisdiction, 58–59
Rules 19 and 20, 53 et seq.
State governmental entities, joinder problems involving, 60–62
Supplemental jurisdiction under section 1367, 59–60
Consequences of failure to join
Generally, 86–102
Permissive joinder
Generally, 24–45
Brunet, "A Study in the Allocation of Scarce Resources: The Efficiency of Federal Intervention Criteria," 28–31
Causation, proof of, 37–38, 44–45
Choice of law issues, 43–44
Discrimination claims, 33
Product liability cases, 33–34
Same transaction or occurrence test, 34, 39
Title VII and section 1981 claims, 32

JUDGES
Related topics:
Case Management
Chayes, "The Role of the Judge in Public Law Litigation," 3–5
Counsel, selection of. See Attorneys (this index)

JUDGES—Cont'd
Involvement and management, 15–17
Magistrate judges, 663–664
Recusal
Generally, 717–730
Bias based on judge's involvement in litigation, 727–729
Due process, 726
Educational seminars, attendance at, 729–730
Financial interest, 726–727
Reporters, contact with, 729
Statutory provisions, 726–727
Rent-a-judge programs, 930–931
Settlement review. See Class Actions (this index)

JUDGMENT
Related topics:
Claim Preclusion
Vacating judgment to blunt collateral estoppel effects, 881–882

JUDICIAL SURROGATES
Generally, 653–664
Related topics:
Masters
Monitors, 660–661

JURISDICTION
Related topics:
Class Actions
Diversity jurisdiction, broad minimal standard, 402
Pretrial consolidation, jurisdictional issues, 127–128
Supplemental jurisdiction for joinder of additional parties, 57–60

JURY INSTRUCTIONS
Preliminary instructions, 745

JURY TRIAL
Bankruptcy proceedings, 211–213
Contempt, 651
Empowerment of jury. See Trial (this index)
Striking jury demands. See Trial (this index)
Summary jury trials, 939–943
Test case trial on certain issues, 941

LAW OF THE CASE
Multidistrict litigation procedures, transfer upon, 162–163

LEAD COUNSEL
See Case Management (this index)

LIMITATION OF ACTIONS
See Class Actions (this index)

LODESTAR
See Attorneys' Fees Awards (this index)

MAGISTRATE JUDGES
Generally, 663–664

MASS EXPOSURE CASES
Public law adjudication model, 45

MASS TORTS
Bellwether trials, 127, 782
Consolidated trials, 126–127
Limitation of actions, 465
Limited fund actions (Rule 23(b)(1)(B)), 314
    et seq.
Obligations of class counsel, 227
Rheingold, "The MER/29 Story—An In-
    stance of Successful Mass Disaster
    Litigation," 123–128
Rule 23(b)(3) class actions
    Generally, 336 et seq.
    Stricter standards, 353 et seq.
Sampling, 781 et seq.

MASTERS
Generally, 653–664
Related topics:
    Case Management
Decree implementation, 661–662
Discovery   and   pretrial   management,
    662–663
Disqualification, 663
Settlement promotion, 663
Trial, assignment to master, 663

MEDIA
Protective orders, 579 et seq.

MEDIATION
Court-annexed mediation, 945–946

MEDICAL MONITORING, 329–330

METAMORPHOSIS OF LITIGATION
Generally, 2–9
Related topics:
    Aggregation Debate
    Class Actions
Chayes, "The Role of the Judge in Public
    Law Litigation," 3–5
Evaluating innovation in litigation, 15–23
Technology, effect of, 6

MINI–TRIALS
Generally, 927–930
Green,   "Growth   of   the   Mini–Trial,"
    928–929

MONITORS
Generally, 660–661

MOOTNESS
See Class Actions (this index)

MORE CONVENIENT FORUM
See Duplicative or Related Litigation (this
    index)

MOTIONS IN LIMINE
Generally, 736

MULTIDISTRICT LITIGATION
See Duplicative or Related Litigation (this
    index)

MULTIPLE PROCEEDINGS
See Duplicative or Related Litigation (this
    index)

NOTICE
See Class Actions (this index)

OPTING OUT
See Class Actions (this index)

PARTIES
See Intervention (this index)
See Joinder in Unitary Federal Forum (this
    index)

PENDENT JURISDICTION
Compulsory party joinder, 58–59

PERMISSIVE JOINDER
See Joinder in Unitary Federal Forum (this
    index)

PRECLUSION
Generally, 786–882
See Claim Preclusion (this Index)
See Issue Preclusion (this Index)

PREEMPTION
See Arbitration (this index)

PRETRIAL CONSOLIDATION
See Duplicative or Related Litigation (this
    index)

PRETRIAL STATEMENTS
Generally, 734–735
Related topics:
    Trial

PRICE–FIXING
Class actions, 264–265

PRISON SYSTEM
Restructuring, 845–846

PRIVACY
Discovery of material on home computers,
    560–561

PRIVATE ATTORNEY GENERAL
Attorneys' fees awards, 684

**PRIVATE   SECURITIES   LITIGATION   RE-
FORM ACT**
Generally, 222, 678
Commonality in class actions, 254
District court authority, 293
Expanding "empowered plaintiff" model,
    294
Figurehead plaintiffs, 293

PRIVILEGED INFORMATION
See Discovery (this index)

PRODUCT LIABILITY LITIGATION
Causation, proof of, 37–38, 44–45
Choice of law, 43–44
Issue preclusion, 875

PRODUCT LIABILITY LITIGATION—Cont'd
Permissive joinder of plaintiffs, 33–34

PROTECTIVE ORDERS
See Discovery (this index)

PUBLIC ACCOMMODATIONS
Discrimination claims, typicality and commonality problems, 278

PUBLIC LAW
Chayes, "The Role of the Judge in Public Law Litigation," 3–5
Mass exposure cases, public law adjudication model, 45

PUBLIC TRIAL
Discovery and right to public trial, 581–582

PUBLICITY
Protective orders, 581

PUNITIVE DAMAGES
Arbitration, 891
Limited fund actions (Rule 23(b)(1)(B)), 316
Two-step trial process, 783

RECUSAL
See Judges (this index)

RELATED LITIGATION
See Duplicative or Related Litigation (this index)

REMAND FOR TRIAL
Multidistrict litigation procedures, 160

REMEDIES
See Class Actions (this index)

REMOVAL
All Writs Act as authority for, 207–208
Class actions, removal to federal court, 23

RENT–A–JUDGE PROGRAMS
Generally, 930–931

RES JUDICATA
See Claim Preclusion (this index)

SAMPLING
Mass torts, 781 et seq.

SANCTIONS
Generally, 644–653
Related topics:
    Case Management
Contempt, 649–651
Failure to settle, 641
Inherent authority for bad faith conduct, 653
Merits sanctions, 652–653

SECTION 1981 CLAIMS
Permissive joinder of plaintiffs, 32

SECURITIES FRAUD
See Class Actions (this index)

SECURITIES FRAUD—Cont'd
Private Securities Litigation Reform Act, 222, 254, 678

SETTLEMENT
Related topics:
    Case Management
    Class Actions
Industry-wide claims settlement through subscriber facility, 931–938
Moderated settlement conference, 944
Statistical sampling, 783

SEVERANCE
Generally, 767 et seq.
Causation, 775–776

SOVEREIGN IMMUNITY
Compulsory party joinder of state governmental entities, 60–62

SPECIAL MASTERS
See Masters (this index)

SPECIAL VERDICTS
Use for issue preclusion purposes, 873–874

STANDING
Intervenors, 69 et seq.

STATE GOVERNMENTAL ENTITIES
Joinder problems involving, 60–62

STATISTICS
Disparate treatment case, role of statistical evidence, 839
Trial by statistics, 777–785

STATUTES OF LIMITATION
See Class Actions (this index)

STAY ORDERS
Related topics:
    Duplicative or Related Litigation
Abstention with retention of jurisdiction pending exhaustion of state remedies, 168–169

STIPULATIONS
Judicial management, 736
Multidistrict litigation, stipulation to proceed to trial in transferee district, 161

SUPPLEMENTAL JURISDICTION
See Jurisdiction (this Index)

SUMMARY JUDGMENT
Case management and, 636–637
Historical background, 15–16

SUNSHINE IN LITIGATION ACT
Generally, 591

TECHNOLOGY
Related topics:
    Innovation
    Trial
Effect of, 6
Juror competence, 741–743

TELEPHONE COMPANIES
Class actions against, 264

TENDER OFFERS
Federal injunction against prosecution of state proceedings (Anti–Injunction Act), 197

TITLE VII CLAIMS
Related topics:
    Employment Discrimination Cases
Consequences of failure to join, 99–100
Permissive joinder of plaintiffs, 32

TOBACCO LITIGATION
Class actions, 358
Proof of causation, 37–38

TRADE SECRETS
Protective orders, 593

TRANSFER OF PROCEEDINGS
Duplicative or related litigation, 108
Multidistrict litigation. See Duplicative or Related Litigation (this index)

TRIAL
Generally, 731–785
Alternatives to in-court testimony
    Generally, 755–758
    Declarations, 755–756
    Deposition summaries and video presentations, 756
    Written narrative statements, 756
Bifurcation and trifurcation, 762–777
Discovery and right to public trial, 581–582
Evidence, limiting amount and duration of trial, 758–762
Improved trial methods
    Generally, 743–762
    Alternatives to in-court testimony above
    Bifurcation and trifurcation, 762–777
    Jury empowerment, below
    Limiting amount of evidence and duration of trial, 758–762
    Schwarzer, "Reforming Jury Trials," 743–745
Judicial management
    Generally, 734–737
    Final pretrial conference, 734–735
    Motions in limine, 736
    Pretrial order, 737
    Pretrial statement, 735–737
    Stipulations, 736
Jury demands, striking
    Generally, 737–743
    Complexity exception to Seventh Amendment, 738 et seq.
    Juror competence, 741–743
Jury empowerment
    Generally, 745–748
    Discussion of evidence, 746
    Instructions, 745–746
    Interim argument by counsel, 746

TRIAL—Cont'd
Jury empowerment—Cont'd
    Notebooks, 746
    Note-taking, 746
    Questioning witnesses, 746
Limiting amount of evidence and duration of trial, 758–762
Mass tort consolidated trials, 126–127
Master, assignment of, 663
Mini-trials, 927–930
Modification of traditional format, 732
Motions in limine, 736
Multidistrict litigation
    Remand for trial, 160
    Stipulation to proceed to trial in transferee district, 161
Open-ended format, 733
Phased trials, 776
Pretrial order, 737
Pretrial statement, 735–737
Severance, 767 et seq.
Statistics, trial by, 777–785
Technology, use of
    Generally, 748–755
    Buxton & Glover, "Managing a Big Case Down to Size," 748–750
    Computer imaging for documentary material, 755
    McCrystal & Maschari, "Will Electronic Technology Take the Witness Stand?," 750–751
    Parker, "Streamlining Complex Cases," 750
    Video conference, testimony via, 752–753
    Videotaped trials, 751–752
Trifurcation, 762–777
Video conference, testimony via, 752–753
Videotaped trials, 751–753

TRIAL COURT DELAY REDUCTION ACT
Generally, 639

UNCONSCIONABILITY
Arbitration agreements, 893–894

UNION APPRENTICESHIP PROGRAMS
Compulsory party joinder, 45 et seq.

VACATION OF JUDGMENT
Blunting collateral estoppel effects, 881–882

VENUE
Forum non conveniens and venue, 131

WAIVER
Related topics:
    Discovery
Equitable abstention under Younger v. Harris, waiver by state, 183

WORK PRODUCT
Case management and, 637–638
Litigation support system, discovery of, 544